Encyclopedia
of
STRESS

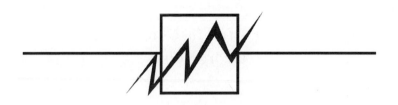

Volume 1 A–D

Editorial Board

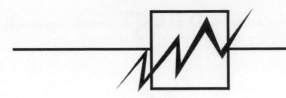

Encyclopedia
of
STRESS

Volume 1   A–D

Editor-in-Chief

GEORGE FINK
Vice President for Research
Pharmos Corporation
Rehovot, Israel
Formerly Director, MRC Brain Metabolism Unit
Edinburgh, Scotland, UK

ACADEMIC PRESS
A Harcourt Science and Technology Company

San Diego   San Francisco   New York   Boston   London   Sydney   Toronto

This book is printed on acid-free paper.

Academic Press
A Harcourt Science and Technology Company
525 B Street, Suite 1900, San Diego, California 92101-4495, USA
http://www.academicpress.com

Academic Press
Harcourt Place, 32 Jamestown Road, London NW1 7BY, UK
http://www.hbuk.co.uk/ap/

Library of Congress Catalog Card Number: 99-62774

International Standard Book Number: 0-12-226735-4 (set)
International Standard Book Number: 0-12-226736-2 volume 1
International Standard Book Number: 0-12-226737-0 volume 2
International Standard Book Number: 0-12-226738-9 volume 3

PRINTED IN THE UNITED STATES OF AMERICA
00 01 02 03 04 05 MM 9 8 7 6 5 4 3 2 1

For Ann Elizabeth

Contents

B

D

Contents of Other Volumes

I

VOLUME 3

N

O

† Deceased.

P

[†] Deceased.

R

S

T

U

V

W

Contents by Subject Area

HUMAN COGNITION
AND EMOTION

PSYCHOLOGICAL THERAPY

Preface

"Stress" remains one of the most frequently used but ill-defined words in the English language. Stress is a phenomenon that has quite different meanings for the politician, social scientist, physician, nurse, psychotherapist, physiologist, molecular biologist, and perhaps you and me. This diversity of meanings was one impetus for creating the *Encyclopedia of Stress*, the aim being to derive a definition of stress from a variety of expert descriptions. The second impetus was the obvious need for an up-to-date compendium on one of the most important social, medical, and psychological phenomena of our age. We were fortunate in attracting stars for our Editorial Board and a set of most distinguished contributors for the 400 or so entries—indeed, the list of contributors is a Who's Who in stress research.

We anticipate that the diversity of our readers will equal the diversity of the topics covered. They will find that the coverage of the Encyclopedia extends well beyond the general adaptation theory of Hans (Janos) Selye and the fight-or-flight response of Walter Cannon. Nevertheless, the general principles annunciated by these two great pioneers in the field still underpin our understanding of the biology of the stress phenomenon. That is, stress is a real or perceived challenge, either endogenous or exogenous, that perturbs body equilibrium or "homeostasis." The stressor may range from overcrowding, traffic congestion, violence, bereavement, redundancy, or unemployment to physical, chemical, biological, or psychological insults. Whether the person can adapt to or cope with the stress will depend on the nature and severity of the stressor and the person's physical and mental state, which in turn depends on genetic, experiential, social, and environmental factors. These issues are discussed in depth in the Encyclopedia, as are the mechanisms of coping and the impact of stress on health and predisposition to diseases such as cancer, infection, rheumatoid arthritis, heart disease, high blood pressure, and mental disorder.

Aggression remains a hallmark of human behavior, even as we move into the third millennium, and so the Encyclopedia covers several topical areas that have only recently been analyzed systematically. These include war and specific wars, posttraumatic stress disorder (PTSD; formerly thought of vaguely as "shell shock"), rape, torture, marital discord and spousal abuse, and the Holocaust. In tackling these topics we accept that our entries may not include all the nuances that are necessary for a full understanding of what these phenomena are all about and described so graphically and sensitively in Tolstoy's *War and Peace* or Pat Barker's monumental *Regeneration* trilogy on the horrific psychological traumas of the First World War. Nevertheless, an important start has been made in that we now accept that PTSD is not just a lack of "bottle" (courage or "guts"), but rather a syndrome that needs to be and can be understood within the framework of medicine and psychology.

Biologically, the stress response reflects a set of integrated cascades in the nervous, endocrine, and immune defense systems. As in most areas of biology, molecular genetics has made a significant difference in the precision with which we now understand the physiopathological processes of the stress response. And so the adage formerly applied to diabetes mellitus may now apply equally to stress: "Understand stress and you will understand medicine."

In summary, we hope that this first *Encyclopedia of Stress* will indeed define the phenomenon and at the same time provide a valuable source of information on a phenomenon that affects us all. In setting out on this adventure we were aware that there is nothing new under the sun and that stress has been around since the first biological particles, bacteria, or even viruses competed for the same mechanisms of replication. There is a tendency for each generation to imagine that stress and its untoward effects are uniquely harsh for them, but it is not this misconception that underlies this work. Rather, the stress of "stress" itself—the massive accumulation of knowledge—made it seem propitious to bring the information together in a systematic manner that allows ready access to all who need or wish to understand the phenomenon.

The idea of producing this Encyclopedia was conceived at an Academic Press reception in San Diego held in conjunction with the annual meeting of the Society for Neuroscience in 1996. I am deeply indebted to Erika Conner for enabling conversion of the idea to a concept and then a project and to Jennifer Wrenn, Christopher Morris, and Carolan Gladden, all of Academic Press, for their enthusiasm, encouragement, and herculean efforts that converted the concept into a reality. For giving generously of their intellect, expertise, sound advice, and unstinting work, I am greatly indebted to my friends and colleagues on the Editorial Board, who made the project such a satisfying experience. To all our contributors go our profound thanks for taking time out from wall-to-wall schedules to produce their entries, which together have made this Encyclopedia.

George Fink
August 1999

Guide to the Encyclopedia

The *Encyclopedia of Stress* is a complete source of information on the phenomenon of stress, contained within the covers of a single unified work. It consists of three volumes and includes 394 separate articles on the entire scope of this subject, including not only the physiological, biochemical, and genetic aspects of stress, but also the relationship of stress to human health and human cognition and emotion.

Each article in this Encyclopedia provides a brief, but complete overview of the selected topic to inform a broad spectrum of readers, from research professionals to students to the interested general public. In order that you, the reader, will derive the greatest possible benefit from your use of the *Encyclopedia of Stress*, we have provided this Guide.

ORGANIZATION

The *Encyclopedia of Stress* is organized to provide maximum ease of use for its readers. All of the articles are arranged in a single alphabetical sequence by title. Articles whose titles begin with the letters A to D are in Volume 1, articles with titles from E to M are in Volume 2, and articles from N to Z are in Volume 3.

Volume 3 also includes a complete subject index for the entire work and an alphabetical list of the contributors to the Encyclopedia.

So that information can be located more quickly, article titles generally begin with the specific noun or noun phrase indicating the topic, with any general descriptive terms following. For example, "Korean Conflict, Stress Effects of" is the article title rather than "Stress Effects of the Korean Conflict" and "Cir- cadian Rhythms, Genetics of" is the title rather than "Genetics of Circadian Rhythms."

TABLE OF CONTENTS

A complete table of contents for the *Encyclopedia of Stress* appears at the front of each volume. This list of article titles represents topics that have been carefully selected by the Editor-in-Chief, George Fink, and the Associate Editors.

The Encyclopedia provides coverage of 14 specific subject areas within the overall field of stress. For example, the Encyclopedia includes 88 different articles dealing with human cognition and emotion. (See p. xxiii for a table of contents by subject area.) The list of subject areas covered is as follows:

Animal Studies
Disasters
Diurnal Rhythms
Drugs (Effects)
Drugs (Treatment)
General Concepts
Human Cognition and Emotion
Human Physical Illness
Human Psychopathology
Immunology and Inflammation
Laboratory Studies and Tests
Other Therapies
Physiological, Biochemical, and
  Genetic Aspects
Psychological Therapy

ARTICLE FORMAT

Articles in the *Encyclopedia of Stress* are arranged in a standard format, as follows:

- Title of article
- Author's name and affiliation
- Outline
- Glossary
- Defining statement
- Body of the article
- Cross-references
- Bibliography

OUTLINE

Entries in the Encyclopedia begin with a topical outline. This outline highlights important subtopics that will be discussed within the article. For example, the article "Cushing's Syndrome, Medical Aspects" includes subtopics such as "Epidemiology,""Etiology," "Clinical Picture," "Laboratory Findings," and "Treatment."

The outline is intended as an overview and thus it lists only the major headings of the article. In addition, second-level and third-level headings will be found within the article.

GLOSSARY

The Glossary section contains terms that are important to an understanding of the article and that might be unfamiliar to the reader. Each term is defined in the context of the article in which it is used. The Encyclopedia has approximately 2000 glossary entries. For example, the article "Cholesterol and Lipoproteins" includes this glossary term:

cholesterol A fat-soluble particle in the body used to form cholic acid in the liver and for the formation of cell membranes.

DEFINING STATEMENT

The text of each article in the Encyclopedia begins with an introductory paragraph that defines the topic under discussion and summarizes the content of the article. For example, the entry "Dexamethasone Suppression Test (DST)" begins with the following statement:

In the Dexamethasone Suppression Test (DST), the potent, synthetic adrenal steroid hormone dexamethasone is used to test the "drive" of the hypothalamic-pituitary-adrenal cortical (HPA) axis. Dexamethasone acts primarily at the pituitary gland to suppress the secretion of ACTH, which, in turn, suppresses the secretion of hormones from the adrenal cortex. . . .

CROSS-REFERENCES

Virtually all articles in the Encyclopedia have cross-references directing the reader to other articles. These cross-references appear at the conclusion of the article text. They indicate articles that can be consulted for further information on the same topic or for other information on a related topic. For example, the article "Dexamethasone Suppression Test (DST)" contains references to the articles "Adrenal Cortex," "Adrenocorticotropic Hormone (ACTH)," "Corticotropin Releasing Factor (CRF)," "Cushing's Syndrome," and "Hypothalamo–Pituitary–Adrenal Axis."

BIBLIOGRAPHY

The Bibliography section appears as the last element in an article. The reference sources listed there are the author's recommendations of the most appropriate materials for further reading on the given topic. The Bibliography entries are for the benefit of the reader and thus they do not represent a complete listing of all the materials consulted by the author in preparing the article.

COMPANION WORKS

Encyclopedia of Stress is one of a continuing series of multivolume reference works in the life sciences published by Academic Press. (Please see the Website **www.academicpress.com/reference/** for more information.) Other such titles include the *Encyclopedia of Human Biology, Encyclopedia of Reproduction, Encyclopedia of Microbiology, Encyclopedia of Cancer, Encyclopedia of Immunology,* and *Encyclopedia of Virology.*

Acute Stress Disorder and Posttraumatic Stress Disorder

Rachel Yehuda and Cheryl M. Wong

Mt. Sinai School of Medicine and Bronx Veterans Affairs

GLOSSARY

acute stress disorder A mental condition that can occur following exposure to extreme stress or trauma but by definition does not last longer than 1 month [i.e., after 1 month, if the symptoms persist, it is appropriate to consider the diagnosis of posttraumatic stress disorder (PTSD)].

avoidant symptoms Experiences that represent measures taken by the individual to avoid feeling, thinking, or coming into contact with reminders of the trauma; these experiences can also include having difficulty recalling important events of the trauma, avoiding people and places associated with the trauma, and generally feelings of emotional numbness, detachment from others, and feeling like there is no future.

depersonalization An alteration in the perception or experience of the self so that one feels detached from, and, as if one is an outside observer of, ones' mental processes or body (e.g., feeling like one is in a dream).

derealization An alteration in the perception or experience of the external world so that it seems strange or unreal (e.g., people may seem unfamiliar or mechanical).

dissociation A disruption in the usually integrated functions of consciousness, memory, identity, or perception of the environment. The disturbance may be sudden or gradual, transient, or chronic.

dysphoria An unpleasant mood such as sadness, anxiety, or irritability.

flashback A recurrence of a memory, feeling, or perceptual experience from the past.

hyperarousal symptoms Experiences that involve more physical reactions to trauma, including difficulty with sleep and concentration, irritability, and anger, needing to be on guard overly much, and having an exaggerated startle response to unexpected noises.

intrusive symptoms Experiences in which trauma survivors "relive" the trauma or become distressed by reminders of the trauma. These include unwanted thoughts and images, nightmares and bad dreams, extreme distress when exposed to a trigger or reminder, and a physiological response to triggers, including palpitations, sweating, and shortness of breath.

posttraumatic stress disorder A mental condition that can occur following exposure to extreme stress or trauma and lasts for 1 month or longer. Acute PTSD lasts from 1 to 3 months according to current formulations in the DSM-IV. Chronic PTSD lasts 3 or more months according to current formulations in the DSM-IV. In delayed onset PTSD, the onset of symptoms begins 6 or more months after the traumatic event(s) according to current formulations in the DSM-IV.

stressor In this context, it is a life event or life change that is so challenging as to potentially be associated with the onset, occurrence, or exacerbation of a psychological symptom or a mental disorder.

traumatic event (according to DSM-IV) An experience that involves death or serious injury or another threat to one's physical integrity. A person does not need to actually experience the physical injury to be "traumatized"—just the knowledge that a person could have been severely injured or had a serious threat of injury and the feelings that accompany this realization are enough to produce a posttraumatic reaction.

B oth acute stress disorder (ASD) and posttraumatic stress disorder (PTSD) are conditions that can occur in people who have been exposed to a traumatic life event. Traumatic events are thought to occur in at least 50% of the population. A traumatic event is defined in the "American Psychiatric Association's Diagnostic and Statistical Manual for Mental Disorders," 4th ed. (DSM-IV) as an experience in which a person underwent, witnessed, or was confronted with "an event that involved actual or threatened death or serious injury, or a threat to the physical integrity of self or others" and a subjective response of "intense fear, helplessness, or horror." The definition of trauma is purposely identical for both ASD and PTSD because what differentiates the two conditions is the point in time following the event at which the symptoms are experienced. Not all people who have experienced trauma will develop ASD and/or PTSD. ASD defines the immediate response to trauma for up to 4 weeks posttrauma, whereas PTSD encompasses a more chronic response to trauma beginning 1 month after the trauma and lasting at least 1 month after that. Recent estimates suggest that as much as 14% of persons in the United States will develop these conditions at some point during their lives. Given the chronic nature of PTSD and the extreme disability that can be associated with this condition, this statistic is alarming and points to PTSD as a major public health problem.

I. INTRODUCTION

Posttraumatic stress disorder was originally defined in 1980 to describe long-lasting symptoms that occur in response to trauma. The diagnosis revived psychiatry's long-standing interest in how stress can result in behavioral and biological changes that ultimately lead to disorder. At the time the formal diagnosis of PTSD was being conceptualized, the field was focused heavily on describing the psychological consequences of combat Vietnam veterans and others who had chronic symptoms following exposure to events that had occurred years and even decades earlier. It was widely assumed that the symptoms that persisted in these survivors were extensions of those that were present in the earlier aftermath of a traumatic event. Indeed, some data from recently traumatized burn victims supported the idea that symptoms such as intrusive thoughts were present in the early aftermath of a trauma. However, at the time the diagnosis was established, there were no longitudinal data—either retrospective or prospective—that formally established the relationship between acute vs chronic posttraumatic symptoms.

Chronic PTSD was not initially conceptualized as being qualitatively different from what might have been observable in trauma survivors in the acute aftermath of the trauma. Rather, chronic PTSD suggested a failure of restitution of the stress response. The implicit assumption behind the diagnosis was that most trauma survivors initially developed symptoms as a direct result from exposure to the event.

As the awareness of the longterm effects of trauma became more widespread, investigators began to explore the reaction of trauma survivors in the immediate aftermath of the event. Studies of the acutely traumatized revealed that survivors do experience symptoms in the immediate aftermath. Clinicians felt it important to provide mental health interventions as early as possible so as to perhaps prevent the development of more chronic conditions. ASD first appeared as a diagnosis in the DSM-IV in 1994 in order to provide a diagnosis for people before they were eligible to receive the diagnosis of PTSD (i.e., having symptoms for less than 1 month's duration). Thus, ASD arose in part out of the need for justification for acute intervention. However, as described later, the syndrome of ASD has features that are not directly associated with the more chronic response of PTSD.

One of the important findings to be generated from research in the last two decades is that PTSD does not occur in everyone exposed to trauma, nor is PTSD the only possible response to trauma. Prospective longitudinal studies have now demonstrated that mood and other anxiety disorders can also occur following a traumatic event, and these may be present even in the absence of PTSD. The question of why some people develop PTSD and others do not has not been fully resolved and is the subject of current investigation in the field. However, insofar as this condition no longer serves to characterize a universal stress response, it has been important to redefine the nature of traumatic stress responses and determine the risk factors for developing these conditions. It has also been important to consider the relationship between acute and chronic stress response.

II. RELATIONSHIP BETWEEN ACUTE STRESS DISORDER (ASD) AND POSTTRAUMATIC STRESS DISORDER (PTSD)

Figure 1 shows a time continuum that describes the onsets of ASD and acute, chronic, and delayed PTSD. In ASD, symptoms must last for at least 2 days up to 4 weeks. In PTSD, the symptoms last for a period of at least a month following the traumatic event(s) and can be either acute (symptom duration of 3 months or less) or chronic (symptom duration of more than 3 months). The onset of PTSD can be delayed for months and even years.

Proponents of ASD hoped the diagnosis would help survivors mobilize acute intervention, thereby preventing more chronic disability. The idea of an

acute stress disorder was initially considered to be superfluous with the diagnosis of adjustment disorder, which was defined in 1980 to describe early symptoms after any stressful event. The proponents of ASD, however, were interested in emphasizing that, unlike adjustment disorders that were expected to resolve even without treatment, ASD was expected to develop into PTSD. Furthermore, ASD focused on a different set of symptoms that were precursors of PTSD such as dissociation.

Indeed, the symptom of dissociation is a prominent difference between ASD and adjustment disorder. Interestingly, dissociation per se is not a symptom of PTSD. However, there is much support for the idea that if people dissociate at the time of trauma, they are at an increased risk to develop PTSD (Table I).

Most studies examining the relationship between dissociation at the time of a trauma and development of PTSD have been retrospective, in some studies, assessing the dissociation 25 years after the traumatic experiences. This means that assessment of dissociation is based largely on subjective recollections of victims. However, in studies that have been prospective, peritraumatic dissociation was still found to be one of the best predictors of PTSD 6 months and 1 year following the trauma in a group of mixed civilian trauma. Posttraumatic depression was also a good predictor for the occurrence of PTSD at 1 year. This would perhaps support the idea of including

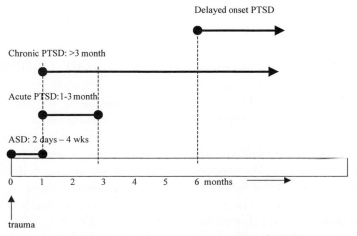

FIGURE 1 Time line comparing ASD and PTSD

TABLE I

Comparison in Symptoms among Adjustment Disorder, ASD, and PTSD

Adjustment disorder	ASD	PTSD
With anxiety	Intrusive reexperiencing	Intrusive reexperiencing
With depression	Avoidance	Avoidance
With mixed anxiety and depression	Hyperarousal	Hyperarousal
With disturbance of conduct		
With mixed disturbance of emotions and conduct	Dissociation	
	Subjective sense of numbing, detachment, or absence of emotional responsiveness	
	A reduction in awareness of his or her surroundings (e.g., "being in a daze")	
	Derealization	
	Depersonalization	
	Dissociative amnesia (i.e., inability to recall an important aspect of the trauma)	

dissociation as a criterion for ASD given its predictive property for the future development of PTSD.

ASD and PTSD are both characterized by the development of intrusive, avoidant, and hyperarousal symptomatology following a traumatic event. These three symptom clusters represent different expressions of the response to trauma.

Intrusive symptoms describe experiences in which the survivor "relives" the event in their mind. After a traumatic event, it is common for the survivor to have thoughts of the event appear in one's mind and to think about the event despite not wanting to. Frightening thoughts or nightmares about the event are also common, and the person may feel very distressed. Sometimes a survivor may even have physical symptoms such as heart palpitations, sweating, and an increased breathing rate in response to being reminded of the event.

In addition to experiencing one or more of the just-mentioned intrusive symptoms, the survivor may make one or more attempts to avoid being reminded of the traumatic experience. The individual may go out of her way to avoid being in situations that remind her of the event. The individual may forget details about the traumatic event. The survivor may also experience a more generalized feeling of wanting to shut out the world, which is manifested by a feeling of emotional numbness and an inability to connect with others.

Finally, the trauma survivor may experience a range of more physiological symptoms, such as an inability to sleep, inability to concentrate, and anger and irritability. The individual may constantly feel alert and on guard, scanning the environment for signs of danger. The survivor may be very sensitive to noises and have an exaggerated startle response to unexpected or loud sounds. These symptoms are called hyperarousal symptoms.

The conceptualization of ASD remains in evolution at the writing of this volume. The salient question is whether ASD is really a "disorder" that indicates a deviation from a normative response to stress. To the extent that ASD is a good predictor of PTSD, it may be that this syndrome captures elements of a maladaptive response.

III. EPIDEMIOLOGY

In considering the prevalence rates of ASD and PTSD, the main observation is that neither are inevitable responses to stress.

The range of prevalence rates of ASD for various types of trauma, including traumatic brain injury (TBI), disasters, and shootings, ranges from 7.2 to 33%, which interestingly are about the same as those for PTSD (see later).

The range of prevalence rates of PTSD in trauma

survivors in DSM-IV is 3–58%. This great variation is thought to reflect mostly a difference in the type and quality of the trauma experienced. However, it may also reflect study methodology (i.e., whether people were evaluated in person or on the phone; whether they were selected randomly or from a convenience sample, and/or whether the study was conducted in the immediate aftermath of the trauma or years later). Studies have found that there were differences in the rates of PTSD depending on the type of trauma experienced. For example, 65% of men and 45.9% of women with PTSD reported rape as their most upsetting trauma. Other types of trauma associated with high probabilities of PTSD development include combat exposure (38.8%), childhood neglect (23.9%) and childhood physical abuse (22.3%) in men, and sexual molestation (26.5%), physical attack (21.3%), being threatened by a weapon (32.6%), and childhood physical abuse (48.5%) in women.

In the aggregate, PTSD is estimated to occur on average in 25% of individuals who have been exposed to traumatic events with rates considerably higher for life-threatening events than for those with lower impact. Lifetime prevalence of exposure to at least one traumatic event was also found to range from 40 to 55% in various studies. In the National Comorbidity Survey (NCS), it was found that about 8% of the population were exposed to four or more types of trauma, some of which involved multiple occurrences. The lifetime prevalence of PTSD has consistently been demonstrated to be twice as high in women as in men.

IV. RISK FACTORS FOR ASD AND PTSD

Risk factors can be divided into two broad categories: those pertinent to the traumatic event (e.g., severity or type of trauma) and those relevant to individuals who experience the event (e.g., gender, prior experiences, personality characteristics). Although some risk factors for PTSD appear to be related to prior experiences, data have also emerged implicating biological and possibly genetic risk factors for PTSD.

Risk factors for the development of ASD include female gender, high depression scores in the immediate aftermath of the event, an avoidant coping style, and the severity of the traumatic event. These are similar to the risk factors that have been associated with the development of chronic PTSD. However, it should be noted that this has not been an area of extensive study.

Risk factors for PTSD also include female gender, posttraumatic depression, an avoidant coping style, and the severity of trauma. However, additional risk factors have also been noted, such as a history of stress, abuse, or trauma, a history of behavioral or psychological problems, preexisting psychiatric disorders, a family history of psychopathology, genetic factors, subsequent exposure to reactivating environmental factors, initial psychological reaction to trauma such as emotional numbing, early separation, preexisting anxiety and depressive disorders, and depression at the time of trauma. Parental PTSD has also been found to be a risk factor for the development of PTSD.

V. COMORBID DISORDERS

PTSD rarely occurs in the absence of other conditions. Approximately 50–90% of individuals with chronic PTSD have a psychiatric comorbidity. This reinforces the idea that PTSD is not distributed randomly throughout the population, but rather that there are subgroups of people that are more vulnerable to the development of PTSD and other psychiatric disorders. This also raises the question of whether PTSD develops as a separate disorder from other psychiatric comorbidities seen in association from it or whether people who have these constellations of disorders are more likely to get PTSD.

Common comorbidities in PTSD patients include major depressive disorder, alcoholism, drug abuse, personality disorders, anxiety disorders such as panic disorder, and generalized anxiety disorder and dissociative disorder.

Symptoms of depression are observed frequently in trauma survivors with PTSD. A significant correlation between early PTSD symptoms and the occurrence of depression seems to predict the chronicity of PTSD. The sequence in which PTSD and major depressive disorder (MDD) occurs following trauma is of particular interest. Some studies proposed that depression is "secondary" to PTSD because its onset followed that of PTSD. In the NCA, patients with comorbid PTSD and MDD reported that the onset of the mood disorder followed that of PTSD in 78.4% of the sample. Vietnam veterans also reported that the onset of their phobias, MDD, and panic disorder followed that of the PTSD. Retrospective studies were flawed in that patients may not recall accurately which symptom came first after being symptomatic for decades. In contrast, Israeli combat veterans reported a simultaneous onset of PTSD and MDD in 65% of the sample, with 16% reported having the MDD precede the PTSD.

In a groundbreaking prospective, longitudinal study, it was demonstrated that the presence of depression in the early aftermath of a trauma was associated with the subsequent development of PTSD. These data contradict the notion that comorbid conditions in PTSD reflect secondary consequences of the PTSD symptoms and suggest instead that other psychiatric symptoms influence the presence of PTSD symptoms. Indeed, a history of previous psychiatric symptoms is a predictor of PTSD, but posttraumatic symptoms may also be strong predictors.

VI. BIOLOGICAL FINDINGS IN ASD AND PTSD

One of the most provocative observations in both ASD and PTSD that has emerged is that the biological findings do not conform to classic patterns of biological stress responses that have been described in animal and human models of the stress response. This is particularly true in the area of neuroendocrinology of PTSD. The distinctness in the biology of PTSD and stress further supports the idea that PTSD represents a circumscribed and specific response to a traumatic event that may be different from a normative response in which the reaction does not reach a certain magnitude or, if it does, becomes attenuated quickly.

There have been only a few studies of the biology of ASD; however, the biological alterations in ASD seem to resemble those in PTSD. First and foremost, there has been a demonstration of the enhanced negative feedback inhibition of the hypothalamic–pituitary–adrenal (HPA) axis, similar to findings in PTSD (see later). At 2 weeks posttrauma, rape victims who subsequently recovered from ASD at 3 months showed a "normal" response to dexamethasone administration, whereas rape victims who failed to recover from ASD at 3 months showed a hypersuppression of cortisol on the dexamethasone suppression test (DST).

In another study, women with a prior history of rape or assault had significantly lower cortisol levels in the immediate aftermath of rape compared to those who did not. A past history of rape or assault is generally considered to be a potent predictor for the development of PTSD. In a study of motor vehicle accident victims, a lower cortisol response in the immediate aftermath of the trauma was associated with the presence of PTSD at 6 months, whereas higher cortisol levels at the time of the trauma were associated with the development of depression at 6 months. These data indicate that it might be possible to identify "high-risk" ASD patients through biological means.

In PTSD, there have been far more studies that have yielded fairly consistent results. The studies demonstrate a different profile of HPA alterations in PTSD compared to that in other psychiatric disorders such as major depression. In the aggregate, these studies have demonstrated a hypersensitization of the HPA axis to stress that is manifested by a decreased cortisol release and an increased negative feedback inhibition. Hypersecretion of the corticotropin-releasing hormone (CRH) has also been described in PTSD, as has blunting of the adrenocorticotropic hormone (ACTH) response to CRH. Other studies have demonstrated lower 24-h urinary cortisol excretion levels in PTSD patients compared to other psychiatric groups and normal controls. PTSD subjects have also been shown to have lower plasma cortisol levels in the morning and at several time points throughout the circadian cycle and to have a greater circadian signal-to-noise ratio compared to normal controls.

In addition, studies support the notion that the enhanced negative feedback regulation of cortisol is an important feature of PTSD. PTSD subjects have an increased number of lymphocyte glucocorticoid receptors (which are needed for cortisol to exert its effects) compared to psychiatric and nonpsychiatric control groups and show an enhanced suppression of cortisol in response to dexamethasone. This response is distinctly different from that found in depression and other psychiatric disorders.

There have been numerous other systems studies in PTSD such as the sympathetic nervous system, the serotonergic system, and the immune system. Psychophysiological, neuroanatomical, cognitive, and behavioral alterations have also been noted; however, it is beyond the scope of this volume to encompass and discuss all these findings.

VII. TREATMENT OF ASD AND PTSD

There are several types of specialized treatments that have been developed in recent years to address the specific needs of trauma survivors who suffer from both ASD and PTSD. These treatments include cognitive behavioral therapy, psychotherapy, group therapy, and medication therapy. Chronic PTSD appears to be more resistant to treatment than acute PTSD. It is usually necessary to employ a combination of therapies in the treatment for PTSD, but the success rate of specialized trauma-focused treatment is quite encouraging.

VIII. SUMMARY

ASD and PTSD represent responses that can occur following exposure to traumatic events. To date, it is useful to conceptualize ASD and PTSD as two distinct conditions that are very much related. ASD often but not always leads to a development of PTSD. ASD and PTSD seem to share similar symptoms, prevalence, risk factors, and neurobiological alterations. ASD appears to be easier to treat than chronic PTSD, which suggests that it is probably useful to

treat traumatic stress symptoms earlier rather than later in the course of adaptation to trauma.

Acknowledgments

This work was supported by NIMH R-02 MH 49555 (RY), Merit Review Funding (RY), and APA/PMRTP 5T32-MH-19126-09/10 (CMW), and VA-Research Career Development award (CMW).

See Also the Following Articles

Avoidance; Brain Trauma; Depersonalization; Dissociation; Posttraumatic Stress Disorder, Delayed; Posttraumatic Stress Disorder in Children; Posttraumatic Stress Disorder, Neurobiology of

Bibliography

Andreasen, N. C. (1980). Posttraumatic stress disorder. *In* "Comprehensive Textbook of Psychiatry" J. I. Kaplan, A. M. Freedman, and B. J. Saddock, (Eds.), 3rd ed., Vol. 2, pp. 1517–1525. Williams & Wilkins, Baltimore.

Breslau, N., Davis, G. C., Andreski, P., Peterson, E. L., and Schultz, L. R. (1997). Sex differences in posttraumatic stress disorder. *Arch. Gen. Psychiatry* **54**, 1044–1048.

Foa, E. B. (Ed.) (1993). "Posttraumatic Stress Disorder: DSM-IV and Beyond." American Psychiatric Press, Washington, DC.

Friedman, M. J., Charney, D. S., and Deutch, A. Y. (Eds.) (1995). "Neurobiological and Clinical Consequences of Stress: From Normal Adaptation to Post-traumatic Stress Disorder." Lippincott-Raven, Hagerstown, MD.

Kessler, R. C., Sonnega, A., Bromet, E., and Nelson, C. B. (1995). Posttraumatic stress disorder in the National Comorbidity Survey. *Arch. Gen. Psychiatry* **52**, 1048–1060.

Shalev, A. Y., Freeman, S., Peri, T., Brandes, D., Shahar, T., Orr, S. P., and Pitman, R. I. K. (1998). Prospective study of posttraumatic stress disorder and depression following trauma. *Am. J. Psychiat.* **155**, 630–637.

Yehuda, R. (Ed.) (1998). "Psychological Trauma." American Psychiatric Press, Washington, DC.

Yehuda, R. (Ed.) (1999). "Risk Factors for Posttraumatic Stress Disorder." Progress in Psychiatry Series, American Psychiatric Press, Washington, DC.

Yehuda, R., and McFarlane, A. C. (Eds.) (1997). Psychobiology of posttraumatic stress disorder. Ann. N.Y. Acad. Sci.

Acute Stress Response: Experimental

Karel Pacak

*National Institute of Neurological Disorders and Stroke and
National Institute of Child Health and Human Development,
National Institutes of Health*

Richard McCarty

University of Virginia

I. Overview of Acute Stress Responses
II. Stress-Responsive Neuroendocrine Systems
III. Types of Acute Stressors
IV. Summary and Conclusions

GLOSSARY

footshock A laboratory stressor that involves placing a laboratory rat or mouse into a chamber with a floor of metal rods spaced equally apart. Scrambled electric current of known intensity is passed through the metal rods and this results in a mildly painful stimulus to the animal's footpads. This has been a favored stressor in many laboratories because the intensity, duration, and frequency of the footshocks are under the control of the experimenter.

hemorrhage An acute decrease in blood volume. In laboratory studies, hemorrhage has been employed as a physiological stressor and blood is often withdrawn via an arterial or venous catheter.

hypoglycemia A reduction in blood glucose levels. This physiological change has been employed as a stressor in laboratory studies and insulin is often administered to effect a reduction in blood glucose.

immobilization Often employed as a laboratory stressor, immobilization involves restricting the movement of a laboratory animal (typically a rat or mouse) by taping its limbs to padded metal mounts affixed to a frame. A variation on this approach includes restraint, where an animal's movement is restricted by placing it into a plexiglas cylinder.

neuroendocrine signature The concept that exposure to a given stressor elicits a pattern of neuroendocrine responses that is specific to that stressor.

I. OVERVIEW OF ACUTE STRESS RESPONSES

Humans and animals respond to exposure to a particular stressor by mobilizing a host of neural, neuroendocrine, endocrine, and metabolic systems. Each stressor produces a specific neurochemical "signature," with quantitatively if not qualitatively distinct central and peripheral mechanisms involved. These neurochemical changes occur not in isolation but rather in concert with physiological, behavioral, and even experiential changes. In evolutionary terms, natural selection has favored this pattern of coordinated stress responses by enhancing the survival and propagation of genes. This pattern of stress responsiveness is referred to by Goldstein as "primitive specificity." These and other findings are included in the description of acute stress responses that follows.

A stressor may be viewed as a stimulus that disrupts homeostasis. Stressors may be divided into several groups based upon their character, duration, and intensity. Regarding duration, stressors may be characterized as acute (single, intermittent, and time-limited exposure versus continuous exposure) or chronic (intermittent and prolonged exposure versus continuous exposure).

Physical stressors include cold, heat, intense radiation, noise, vibration, and many others. Chemical stressors include ether, all poisons, and insulin. Pain stress may be elicited by many different chemical and physical agents. Psychological stressors profoundly affect emotional processes and may result in behavioral changes such as anxiety, fear, or frustration. Social stressors include an animal's placement into the territory of a dominant animal and in humans unemployment and marital separation among others. Many stressors used in animal research, however, are mixed and act in concert, such as handling, immobilization, anticipation of a painful stimulus, and hemorrhage with hypotension.

In terms of duration, stressors may be divided into two main categories: acute versus chronic stressors.

It should be noted that many stressors differ in their intensity. The adaptive responses that are elicited in response to an acute stressor include the physiological and behavioral processes that are essential to reestablish homeostatic balance. During an acute stress response, physiological processes are important to redirect energy utilization among various organs and selectively inhibit or stimulate various organ systems or their components to mobilize energy reserves and to be prepared for exposure to additional, unpredictable challenges. Thus, upon exposure to metabolic stressors, certain tissues tend to reduce their consumption of energy while others, especially those that are important for locomotor activity, receive sufficient nutrients to function properly. The central nervous system also has priority during metabolic stress responses and preferentially receives a sufficient amount of nutrients from the circulation. The increased supply of energy to "crucial" organs is achieved preferentially by release of catecholamines and glucocorticoids that in general increase gluconeogenesis and glycogenolysis, inhibit glucose uptake, and enhance proteolysis and lipolysis. The immune system is another essential component of these physiologically adaptive stress responses.

Behavioral adaptation is viewed as a facilitation of adaptive and an inhibition of nonadaptive central and peripheral neural pathways that enable an organism to cope successfully with stressful situations. These behavioral responses include altered cognitive and sensory thresholds, increased alertness, selective memory enhancement, suppression of feeding and reproductive behaviors, and stress-induced analgesia. If physiological or behavioral responses fail to reestablish homeostasis or are excessive and abnormal, diseases of adaptation may be more likely to occur in susceptible individuals. This is apparent upon exposure to chronic or repeated stressors but may happen as well during acute stress reactions in a situation where the intensity of the stressor is abnormally high. Both physiological and behavioral responses are affected by activation of the primary stress effector systems, including the sympathetic nervous system (norepinephrine release), the adrenomedullary system (epinephrine release), the hypothalamic-pituitary-adrenocortical system [adreno-

corticotrophic hormone (ACTH) and glucocorticoid release], the parasympathetic nervous system (acetylcholine release), and the renin-angiotensin system (renin release from juxtaglomerular cells in the kidney). Several other systems contribute to a reestablishment of homeostasis, including the hypothalamic-pituitary-thyroid axis (e.g., responsive to cold and heat), the hypothalamic-pituitary-gonadal axis (temporary decrease in reproductive function to shift energy to other more important organ systems), release of growth hormone, and changes in immune function. All of these systems act directly by altering the release or the biological effects of many mediators of acute stress responses (e.g., neurotransmitters, hormones, cytokines, etc.) or they act indirectly by altering levels of monitored variables, with consequent reflexive adjustments determined by internal homeostats.

II. STRESS-RESPONSIVE NEUROENDOCRINE SYSTEMS

Included below are some examples of ways in which the major stress-responsive physiological systems are altered following exposure to acute stressors.

A. Hypothalamic-Pituitary-Adrenocortical Axis

The hypothalamic-pituitary-adrenocortical axis is one of the main effector systems that is activated in animals upon exposure to an acute stressor. Generally via several feedback mechanisms at different levels, glucocorticoids released from the adrenal cortex regulate their own synthesis and secretion by actions within the adrenal gland (inhibition of glucocorticoid synthesis), the anterior pituitary (inhibition of corticotrophs), and the hypothalamus [inhibition of corticotropin-releasing hormone (CRH) synthesis and secretion] as well as higher brain centers (e.g., hippocampus). Glucocorticoids readily penetrate the blood–brain barrier and suppress acute stress-induced increases in central neural levels of norepinephrine. Norepinephrine is thought to be the most potent stimulator of CRH neurons within the hypothalamic paraventricular nucleus. Thus, central noradrenergic neurons that terminate in the paraventricular nucleus and synapse on CRH neurons are generally believed to be the site of another negative feedback mechanism by which glucocorticoids attenuate neuroendocrine responses to acute stressors.

During an acute stress response, ACTH and glucocorticoids vary depending on the type and intensity of the stressful stimulus. Exposure of animals to cold stress evokes a very modest increase in plasma ACTH, exposure of animals to hemorrhage or hypoglycemia evokes ACTH responses that reflect the intensity of the stimulus, pain elicits moderate ACTH responses, and immobilization for 120 min evokes the greatest increase in plasma levels of ACTH. The correlation between norepinephrine release in the hypothalamic paraventricular nucleus and plasma ACTH responses may demonstrate the participation of paraventricular norepinephrine in stress-induced activation of the hypothalamic-pituitary-adrenocortical axis (Fig. 1). Although a strong correlation is found between norepinephrine responses in the paraventricular nucleus and plasma ACTH responses during exposure to different stressors, such correlations may not reflect causal interrelationships. During exposure to metabolic stressors such as hypoglycemia or hemorrhage, increments in plasma ACTH are much higher than those of norepinephrine in the paraventricular nucleus, suggesting that some other paraventricular neurotransmitter or extraparaventricular neuromediators participate in the regulation of the hypothalamic-pituitary-adrenocortical axis following exposure to these stressors. Exposure to pain elicited marked norepinephrine responses in the paraventricular nucleus and moderate plasma ACTH responses, suggesting that paraventricular norepinephrine is responsible for the activation of the hypothalamic-pituitary-adrenocortical axis upon exposure to pain stress. During immobilization stress, the relationship between paraventricular norepinephrine and plasma ACTH was intermediate, suggesting that both paraventricular norepinephrine and other paraventricular and extraparaventricular neuromediators participate in the regulation of the hypothalamic-pituitary-adrenocortical axis during immobilization stress. Cold stress elicited only mini-

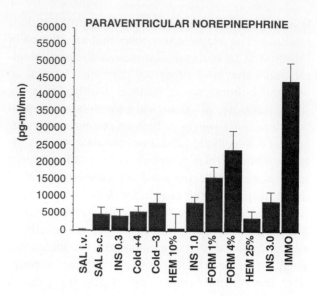

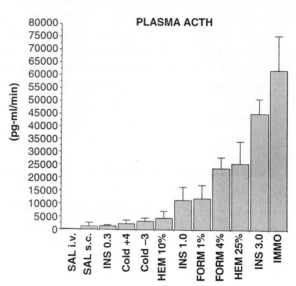

FIGURE 1　Area under curve measures for microdialysate levels of norepinephrine in the hypothalamic paraventricular nucleus and plasma levels of ACTH from animals exposed to a variety of stressors.

mal paraventricular norepinephrine and plasma ACTH responses, suggesting that other neuroendocrine axes (e.g., thyroid axis) participate in the regulation of homeostasis during acute exposure to cold.

Acute activation of the hypothalamic-pituitary-adrenocortical axis is attended by elevations of plasma glucocorticoids that exert many metabolic effects to mobilize energy necessary for survival of the organism and restoration of homeostasis. Regulatory metabolic effects include gluconeogenesis, glycogenolysis, lipolysis, inhibition of lipogenesis, and proteolysis. Other regulatory effects include anti-inflammatory, anti-allergic, and behavioral effects. Permissive effects of glucocorticoids are important for other hormones or factors to function properly (e.g., catecholamine-induced vascular resistance and cardiac performance are decreased in cases of adrenal insufficiency). Generally, permissive effects of glucocorticoids are responsible for maintenance of a basal or resting state, while regulatory effects are seen when glucocorticoids reach abnormally high concentrations such as when an animal is exposed to an acute and extremely intense stressor

B. Hypothalamic-Pituitary-Gonadal Axis

Exposure of animals and humans to acute stress is associated with small and often short-lived increases in plasma luteinizing hormone and androgens. In humans, acute stress-induced increases in androgens appear to be caused by an alteration in plasma volume and a decrease in androgen metabolic clearance rather than from a net increase in androgen release. The mechanisms by which luteinizing hormone is increased under stress conditions are not clear but one possibility is that high levels of ACTH may stimulate gonadotropin hormone-releasing hormone neurons in the hypothalamus. Stress-induced responses are also dependent upon estrogen levels. Thus, in female animals during proestrous or in gonadectomized animals there is no increase in luteinizing hormone upon exposure to acute stress, but instead a rapid decrease in circulating luteinizing hormone may be observed. Norepinephrine and serotonin as well as interleukin-1 also participate in the regulation of the hypothalamic-pituitary-gonadal axis during acute stress and most likely exert inhibitory effects on gonadotropin-releasing hormone neurons or luteinizing hormone. Follicle-stimulating hormone may follow the same stress response pattern as luteinizing hormone, but often the changes are very small or do not occur at all. The presence of circulating estradiol may provide some protection against the adverse and inhibitory effects of acute stress on the gonadal axis.

In contrast, upon exposure to chronic stress, there are decreases in reproductive function to conserve and redirect energy for other organ systems that are vital for immediate survival. Such inhibition occurs at all levels, including the hypothalamus (inhibition of gonadotropin hormone-releasing hormone secretion), the anterior pituitary (inhibition of luteinizing hormone release), and the gonads (reduced sex hormone secretion). Stress-induced activation of the hypothalamic-pituitary-adrenocortical axis is one of the main factors contributing to this inhibition of gonadal function since corticotropin-releasing hormone and glucocorticoids are known to inhibit gonadotropin hormone-releasing hormone. In addition, glucocorticoids exert inhibitory effects at the level of the anterior pituitary and the gonads.

Sex differences in stress-induced regulation and in responses of primary stress effector systems exist and the presence of circulating estrogen and androgen has been implicated in these differences. It is postulated that estrogens and androgens are responsible for sex hormone-dependent brain organization that reflects differences in responsiveness to stress. For example, estrogen effects on corticotropin-releasing hormone expression may be related to greater stress-induced hypothalamic-pituitary-adrenocortical responses and for a higher incidence of depression, anxiety, and other disorders in human females exposed to stress. In experimental animals, these sex differences are eliminated following surgical removal of the gonads.

C. Hypothalamic-Pituitary-Growth Axis

It is well documented that acute exposure to various stressors (e.g., hypoglycemia, exercise, hemorrhage, pain) increases secretion of growth hormone from the pituitary gland. In contrast, other stressors such as cold, handling, hypertonic saline, and electric shock produce marked decreases in plasma growth hormone levels. Acute administration of glucocorticoids also increases growth hormone concentrations in plasma. Thus, it appears that acute stress responses that are associated with elevations in plasma glucocorticoid levels may increase plasma growth hormone levels through stimulation of the growth hormone gene via glucocorticoid-responsive elements in its promoter region.

In contrast, chronic stress (a state of chronically elevated circulating levels of glucocorticoids) inhibits growth hormone release from the anterior pituitary gland and increases resistance of peripheral tissues to the actions of insulin-like growth factors (e.g., IGF-1). Such inhibition may occur via corticotropin-releasing hormone-induced increases in somatostatin secretion. Thus, dwarfism that occurs in an environment of severe and chronic psychosocial deprivation may reflect a chronically inhibited growth axis.

Little is known about the neural pathways that are involved in stress-induced activation or inhibition of growth hormone secretion. Some evidence suggests that growth hormone responses correlate with changes in catecholamine content in several hypothalamic nuclei, including the paraventricular, dorsomedial, and arcuate nuclei, but more detailed and sophisticated studies are needed to clarify the involvement of catecholamines and other neurotransmitters or neuromodulators in stress-induced growth hormone axis regulation.

D. Hypothalamic-Pituitary-Thyroid Axis

In contrast to mildly stressful situations, high-intensity stress-induced activation of the hypothalamic-pituitary-adrenocortical axis is associated with inhibition of the thyroid axis. This inhibitory action is reflected by a decrease in release/production of hypothalamic thyrotropin-releasing hormone, decreased production/secretion of thyroid-stimulating hormone, and by inhibition of conversion of thyroxine to the more biological active triiodothyronine in peripheral tissues. The exception to this pattern is exposure to acute cold stress, forced swimming, or noise stress where profound thyroid axis activation occurs. This is not surprising since during cold exposure, an organism needs to generate significant amounts of energy to maintain body temperature and thyroid hormones are known to increase heat production and therefore core temperature. Upon exposure to cold stress, there is increased secretion of hypothalamic thyrotropin-releasing hormone, which leads to increases in release of thyroxine within 15–20 min and triiodothyronine within 1–2 h. The

mechanism by which cold-induced activation of thyrotropin-releasing hormone occurs is not fully understood, although catecholamines are thought to participate in this process. It is well known that in a hypothyroid state, plasma catecholamines are elevated and during a hyperthyroid state plasma catecholamines are either unchanged or decreased. In thyroidectomized rats, larger increments in plasma epinephrine and norepinephrine occur during cold exposure, suggesting compensatory activation of catecholamine secretion as a result of the loss of the thyroid gland. The organism is faced with difficulty in maintaining body temperature when the hypothalamic-pituitary-thyroid axis is unable to enhance thermogenesis.

The reason that the thyroid axis is inhibited upon exposure to other stressors is unknown but one possible explanation is that an organism conserves energy necessary for survival and restoration of homeostasis. Corticotropin-releasing hormone, somatostatin, and cytokines (e.g., IL-1 and IL-6) most likely contribute to acute stress-induced inhibition of the thyroid axis.

E. Prolactin

Prolactin is another anterior pituitary hormone that is increased during exposure of animals to various stressors such as exercise, hypoglycemia, hemorrhage, immobilization, and pain stress. Other situations associated with elevated plasma prolactin levels are nipple stimulation during lactation, chest wall lesions (herpes, incisions), and the acute stress of blood withdrawal. The mechanisms by which acute stressors increase prolactin secretion remain unknown. The physiological consequences of prolactin hypersecretion during stress are not clear, although it is hypothesized that prolactin enhances immune function.

F. Immune System

The immune system is an important component of acute stress responses although interactions between immune system components and other stress effector systems are very complex and still poorly understood. Upon exposure to various acute stressors, inflammatory cytokines such as tumor necrosis factor and interleukin (IL)-1 and -6 are increased. These substances participate in the maintenance of immunologic homeostasis as well as in regulation of the hypothalamic-pituitary-adrenocortical axis. Interleukin-6 appears to be a very potent stimulator of the hypothalamic-pituitary-adrenocortical axis that most likely occurs via activation of paraventricular CRH neurons. Neuronal pathways participating in interleukin-induced CRH activation are still not well characterized. Stress-induced elevated plasma glucocorticoid levels in turn have profound inhibitory effects on various immune functions. For example, production of cytokines, mediators of inflammation, leukocyte function and traffic, cell-mediated immunity, and suppressor T-cell function are all decreased by stress-induced elevations in glucocorticoid levels.

Immunosuppressive and anti-inflammatory effects of glucocorticoids are essential to prevent harmful infections or unwanted exaggerated immune reactions so as to increase chances for survival. This is well-documented from studies where Lewis rats that are characterized by hyporesponsiveness of the hypothalamic-pituitary-adrenocortical axis (deficient CRH neurons?) have increased susceptibility to inflammatory diseases upon exposure to a variety of stressful stimuli.

G. Autonomic Nervous System

The sympathoneuronal and adrenomedullary systems are two major stress effector systems. Numerous recent studies have demonstrated differential responses of these two effector systems during exposure to various stressors. In several recent studies, an attempt was made to measure simultaneously release of norepinephrine in the hypothalamic paraventricular nucleus (the most important area in the regulation of the hypothalamic-pituitary-adrenocortical axis and the site where noradrenergic neurons synapse on CRH neurons) using *in vivo* microdialysis and plasma levels of catecholamines and ACTH. These multiple neuroendocrine measures provided an answer to whether stressor-specific noradrenergic activation of the hypothalamic-pituitary-adrenocortical axis and stressor-specific responses of sympathoadrenal and adrenomedullary systems occur. During exposure to any of several stressors, there was a significant correlation between plasma levels of

ACTH and paraventricular microdialysate levels of norepinephrine. Although for all stressors levels of norepinephrine in the paraventricular nucleus correlated significantly with plasma ACTH levels, detailed examination of these variables showed differences and not necessarily causal interrelationships. During exposure to metabolic stressors, such as hypoglycemia and hemorrhage, increments of plasma ACTH were much larger than those of norepinephrine in the paraventricular nucleus, suggesting that ACTH release can occur by pathways other than activation of noradrenergic neurons terminating in the paraventricular nucleus. Other intra- or extra-paraventricular nonadrenergic neurons are most likely responsible for stimulating ACTH release during these stressors. In response to pain stress, relatively small ACTH responses were associated with large increases in paraventricular norepinephrine release, suggesting that norepinephrine in this brain region could be a stimulator of CRH neurons. The slope of the relationship between paraventricular norepinephrine release and plasma ACTH responses was intermediate during immobilization stress, suggesting that both noradrenergic and nonadrenergic neurons participate in the regulation of the hypothalamic-pituitary-adrenocortical axis in response to the combined psychological and physical stress of immobilization.

These and other findings can be applied to a new concept of stressor-specific neurocircuits in brain and neuroendocrine signatures that are related to specific stressors. The recognition and description of stressor-specific neurocircuits, including mapping of neurotransmitters participating in these neurocircuits, may lead to the development of new therapies for stress-related disorders.

III. TYPES OF ACUTE STRESSORS

Included below are descriptions of the responses to some of the acute stressors that have been employed frequently in laboratory animal studies of stressful stimulation. In the majority of these studies, the focus of attention was directed at the sympathetic-adrenal medullary system or the hypothalamic-pituitary-adrenocortical system. In the former, measures of

TABLE I

Selected Behavioral and Physiological Adaptations Designed to Restore Homeostasis during Acute Exposure to Stressful Stimulation

Behavioral adaptation	Physiological adaptation
Increased arousal and alertness	Oxygen redirection to CNS and stress-activated tissues
Euphoria or dysphoria	Nutrients redirected to CNS and stress-activated tissues
Suppression of appetite or feeding behavior	Increased blood pressure and heart rate
Suppression of reproductive behavior	Increased respiratory rate
	Increased gluconeogenesis, glycogenolysis, and lipolysis
	Detoxification of endogenous or exogenous toxic products
	Inhibition of reproductive system
	Inhibition of colonic motility

plasma levels of norepinephrine and epinephrine were reported and in the latter plasma levels of ACTH and/or corticosterone were made.

A. Hypoglycemia

Hypoglycemia is characterized by a fall in plasma glucose levels under various conditions, including starvation, hepatic dysfunction, administration of insulin, pancreatic B cell tumor, alcohol use, and adrenal insufficiency. Acute decreases in blood glucose levels are associated with increases in circulating levels of epinephrine, ACTH, and cortisol, with little if any concurrent sympathoneuronal system activation as indicated by circulating norepinephrine levels. The selective adrenomedullary activation during hypoglycemia constitutes key evidence for the differential regulation of stress effector systems. Hypoglycemia is characterized by many symptoms associated with neuroglycopenia, including tremulousness, sweating, hunger, palpitations, anxiety, psychotic behavior, seizures, and coma.

The central neuronal circuitry responsible for the elicitation of hunger and eating in response to hypoglycemia remains poorly understood. Stimulation of catechololamine release by insulin-induced hypoglycemia is thought to involve both neurogenic and nonneurogenic mechanisms. Neurogenic mecha-

nisms participate in the initial acute phase (the first 30 min after insulin administration) in which plasma epinephrine levels increase but plasma norepinephrine levels remain unchanged. Glucose-sensitive receptors in the hypothalamus and preganglionic cholinergic nerves that innervate the adrenal medulla are involved in this phase when an absolute fall in plasma glucose levels rather than actual hypoglycemia is an important mechanism to trigger catecholamine responses. Nonneurogenic mechanisms participate in the second phase (30–50 min after insulin administration) and produce increases in both plasma epinephrine and norepinephrine. These responses are independent of a functionally intact nerve supply to the adrenal medulla and can be reversed by glucose administration, suggesting that hypoglycemia is the mechanism that triggers catecholamine responses. However, it should be mentioned that several other studies have not found a biphasic pattern of hypoglycemia-induced catecholamine responses, which may be explained by differing experimental conditions, including the severity of hypoglycemia.

B. Hemorrhage

Depending upon whether hypotensive or nonhypotensive hemorrhage occurs, various physiological responses are elicited, including activation of the hypothalamic-pituitary-adrenocortical axis, increased vasopressin release, and elevated plasma catecholamine levels. Similar to hypoglycemia, hemorrhage elicits relatively small increases in paraventricular levels of norepinephrine. Activation of all of these systems is an important counterregulatory mechanism to maintain homeostasis.

In clinical studies, acute hypotensive hemorrhage is an extremely dangerous situation since it may lead to shock. Acute hemorrhagic shock is characterized by an activation of all of the main stress effector systems. Clinical symptoms of the former include low energy level, fatigue, a feeling of being cold, dizziness, and sleepiness; clinical signs of the latter include cool or mottled extremities, increased heart rate, low blood pressure, pallor, and altered mental status, ranging from restlessness and agitation to coma. Restoration of blood volume is a high priority, although fluid replacement that is too rapid may be harmful since it may shut down the level of activity of the sympathoadrenal system in the critical period when survival depends on the activity of these stress effector systems.

C. Hypoxia

Asphyxiation produces the biochemical triad of hypoxemia, hypercarbia, and acute respiratory acidosis. Chemoreceptors, located especially in the carotid bodies adjacent to the carotid sinuses, respond to decreased arterial oxygen concentrations, increased arterial carbon dioxide concentrations, and decreased arterial blood pH. Chemosensitive cells near the ventral surface of the medulla respond to these same stimuli. Acute exposure to hypoxemia and hypercarbic acidosis is associated with increased or unchanged plasma levels of norepinephrine and epinephrine and with increased sympathetic nerve traffic as measured by microneurography. Findings of unchanged plasma norepinephrine levels during acute hypoxemia may be explained by increased norepinephrine clearance. The activation of sympathoneuronal and adrenomedullary systems is associated with increases in heart rate, respiration, and vasoconstriction. Sympathectomy decreases and adrenalectomy eliminates increases in heart rate and cardiac output that result from severe hypoxia.

Acute mountain sickness caused by sudden exposure to hypoxia is a frequent cause of morbidity and mortality in people who travel to high altitudes. It is estimated that 30 million people are at risk for altitude-related diseases in the western United States every year. Approximately 20% of tourists who travel to ski resorts in Colorado experience acute mountain sickness. Symptoms of acute mountain sickness include headache, nausea, anorexia, insomnia, cough, difficulties in physical activity, mental changes, seizures, hallucinations, and, finally, in severe cases, coma. All of these symptoms may occur suddenly after a few hours in a high-altitude environment and require immediate medical attention.

D. Pain

Following exposure of laboratory animals to acute pain induced by formalin administration, only small increments in plasma ACTH levels occur despite large increments in plasma norepinephrine and epinephrine levels. Brainstem centers are the recipients of ascending pathways carrying nociceptive information and are perhaps the most important brain areas in pain mechanisms. Glutamate, aspartate, substance P, and calcitonin gene-related peptide are neurotransmitters that participate in acute pain responses. It is known that behavioral analgesia or inhibition of spinal neurons that respond to painful stimuli may be eliminated by electric stimulation or opiate microinjection into several brainstem regions.

E. Cold

Cold exposure has been employed as a stressful stimulus in laboratory studies. Several experimental approaches have been taken in these studies. In one such approach, animals are placed in their home cages in a cold environment maintained at a constant temperature and remain there for varying periods of time. Typically the stress session can extend from several hours to multiple days. Alternatively, animals are immersed in water at a given temperature for less than an hour. Exposure to a cold environment at or below 0°C results in dramatic increases in plasma norepinephrine but only modest increases in plasma levels of epinephrine and ACTH. In contrast, placement of laboratory rats in cold water (20–25°C) for as little as 15 min is attended by substantial increases in plasma levels of epinephrine and norepinephrine. The increases in plasma levels of both catecholamines in response to cold swim stress are negatively correlated with water temperature over the range of 20–34°C, with the highest levels of plasma catecholamines at the lowest water temperatures. Indeed, plasma levels of epinephrine during swim stress at 18–20°C are among the highest ever measured for a laboratory stressor.

F. Footshock

Footshock has been especially valuable as a stressor in studies of neural and endocrine responsiveness. Footshock allows investigators exquisite control over the frequency, intensity, and duration of the stressful stimulus. In addition, footshock is often employed as an aversive stimulus in studies of learning and memory, allowing for studies that link physiological and behavioral responses. Footshock stress activates the sympathetic-adrenal medullary and hypothalamic-pituitary-adrenocortical systems, especially at moderate to high intensity footshock levels (1–2 mA).

G. Immobilization

For more than 30 years, Kvetnansky and his colleagues have employed immobilization as a consistent feature of their studies on physiological adaptations to stress. Immobilization is a potent stressor and includes physical as well as psychological dimensions. Typically, laboratory rats are fixed to a holder by taping their limbs to padded metal mounts. The stress sessions usually last from 30 to 120 min and may be repeated each day for up to 1 month to assess responses to acute versus repeated stress. A single session of immobilization results in extremely high levels of circulating norepinephrine, epinephrine, ACTH, and corticosterone when compared to other laboratory stressors. Levels of norepinephrine, epinephrine, and ACTH usually peak within the first 30 min of immobilization and then decrease to a stable but highly elevated level for the remainder of the stress session. In contrast, plasma levels of corticosterone peak later in the stress session and remain high for the remainder of the period of immobilization.

IV. SUMMARY AND CONCLUSIONS

Since its inception, the field of stress research has lacked a strong theoretical foundation upon which investigators could formulate questions, design experiments, and interpret their findings and the work of others. From the beginning of his career, Hans Selye offered a definition of stress that was all encompassing and he advanced a view that exposure to any stressor results in a consistent pattern of physiological responses. Although these concepts are no longer at the forefront of stress research, they have left an indelible imprint.

In the absence of a strong theoretical foundation, much of the effort in the field of stress research has been linked to the development of techniques for measuring biologically active molecules or visualizing substances within various tissues, especially neural tissue. The nature of the stressor in a given study was for a time almost an afterthought. Thus, many laboratories developed their own unique stressors and focused much of their creative energies on assay methodologies. Without a set of consistent stress paradigms, comparisons of research results across laboratories were difficult.

In this overview of acute stress responses, we have provided a brief background on the major stress-responsive neuroendocrine systems. Then we examined the pattern of neuroendocrine responses across some of the commonly used laboratory stressors. After distilling the results of thousands of studies of neuroendocrine activation during acute stress, the case for specificity of physiological responses to different stressors is overwhelming. These neuroendocrine signatures allow an animal to respond to a given stressor with an optimal recruitment of physiological responses to meet the immediate demands of the situation. It is important to keep in mind that most acute stress paradigms present the subject with a great deal of uncertainty and loss of control. The subject has never experienced the stressor before and has no knowledge of how long the stressor will persist, if escape is possible, if stressor intensity will remain constant, and so on. These psychological variables affect central neural circuits that coordinate neural and endocrine activation and must be considered in interpreting the findings of a given acute stress experiment.

See Also the Following Articles

Animal Models for Human Stress; Homeostasis; Hypoglycemia

Bibliography

Buckingham, J. C., Cowell, A.-M., Gillies, G. E., Herbison, A. E., and Stell, J. H. (1997). The neuroendocrine system: Anatomy, physiology and responses to stress. *In* "Stress, Stress Hormones and the Immune System" (J. C. Buckingham, G. E. Gillies, A.-M. Cowell (Eds.), pp. 9–47. Wiley, New York.

Chrousos, G. P. (1998). Stressors, stress, and neuroendocrine integration of the adaptive response. *Ann. N. Y. Acad. Sci.* **851**, 311–335.

Goldstein, D. S. (1995). "Stress, Catecholamines, and Cardiovascular Disease." Oxford Univ. Press, New York.

Johnson, E. O., Kamilaris, T. C., Chrousos, G. P., and Gold, P. W. (1992). Mechanisms of stress: A dynamic overview of hormonal and behavioral homeostasis. *Neurosci. Biobehav. Rev.* **16**, 115–130.

McCarty, R., and Gold, P. E. (1996). Catecholamines, stress and disease: A psychobiological perspective. *Psychosom. Med.* **58**, 590–597.

Pacak, K., Palkovits, M., Kopin, I. J., and Goldstein, D. S. (1995). Stress-induced norepinephrine release in the hypothalamic paraventricular nucleus and pituitary-adrenocortical and sympathoadrenal activity: *In vivo* microdialysis studies. *Front. Neuroendocrinol.* **16**, 89–150.

Pacak, K., Palkovits, M., Kvetnansky, R., Yadid, G., Kopin, I. J., and Goldstein, D. S. (1995). Effects of various stressors on *in vivo* norepinephrine release in the hypothalamic paraventricular nucleus and on the pituitary-adrenocortical axis. *Ann. N. Y. Acad. Sci.* **771**, 115–130.

Rivier, C., and Rivest, S. (1991). Effect of stress on the activity of the hypothalamic-pituitary-gonadal axis: Peripheral and central mechanisms. *Biol. Reprod.* **45**, 523–532.

Acute Trauma Response

William C. Chiu and Michael P. Lilly

University of Maryland School of Medicine

I. Neuroendocrine Response to Injury
II. Immune Response to Injury
III. Metabolic Response to Injury
IV. Interactions of the Biologic Responses
V. Therapy and Modification of Responses

GLOSSARY

apoptosis Programmed cell death; deletion of cells by fragmentation into membrane-bound particles that are phagocytosed by other cells.

cytokine A protein that acts as an intercellular mediator in the generation of an immune response.

glucocorticoid A steroid compound that influences intermediary metabolism and exerts an anti-inflammatory effect.

reflex A reaction in response to a stimulus applied to the periphery and transmitted through nervous centers in the brain or spinal cord.

sodium pump sodium–potassium adenosine triphosphatase An enzyme responsible for maintaining the sodium and potassium electrical gradient between intracellular and interstitial compartments.

T he acute trauma response encompasses a complex interplay of multiple host homeostatic processes as a consequence of injury. Although the overall response to trauma is conceptualized most easily by considering the individual components of the neuroendocrine, metabolic, and immune systems, it is important to recognize that many molecular, cellular, humoral, and physiologic mechanisms and cascades develop interactively. The ultimate ability of the injured patient to recover from the insult depends on the dynamic relationship between this host response and timely medical or surgical intervention (Fig. 1).

I. NEUROENDOCRINE RESPONSE TO INJURY

The classic neuroendocrine reflex is composed of afferent stimuli, central nervous system integration and modulation, and efferent output. Following traumatic injury, multiple discrete chemical and physiologic perturbations are detected by specific

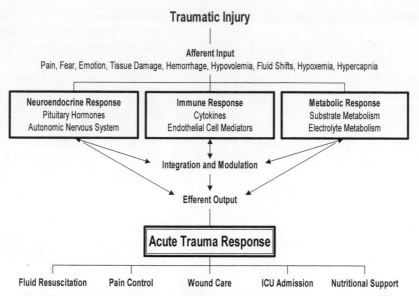

FIGURE 1 Schematic diagram depicting interactions of the neuroendocrine, immune, and metabolic systems after traumatic injury. Processing and integration of multiple stimuli, and modulation through the interactions of various mediators, form the overall biologic response. Modification of this response by therapeutic interventions facilitates achieving and maintaining homeostasis.

sensors. After local transduction of stimuli, these signals are transmitted to the central nervous system via specific neural pathways and are directed to highly specialized cellular nuclei for processing and integration with other signals. The resultant efferent output is the secretion of various hormonal substances by individual organ systems. Modulation of the intensity and pattern of release of these hormones is affected by short reflex arcs and long regulatory feedback loops, whether stimulatory or inhibitory.

A. Afferent Input

After a severe injury, tissue destruction and hemorrhage appear to be two of the most important early alterations. From the site of injury, peripheral sensory receptors of primary nociceptive afferent neurons detect mechanical deformation and thermal changes. Damaged cells release chemicals, such as histamine, potassium, serotonin, thrombin, and others, which also provide nociceptive input. The cell bodies of these neurons reside in the dorsal root ganglia and transmit signals to the spinal dorsal horn, where secondary neurons and collateral pathways project to tertiary neurons in the brain stem and thalamus.

Hypovolemia is the most common cause of circulatory shock after injury. Significant blood loss leads to a decrease in effective circulating volume and blood pressure. Tissue injury and fluid sequestration may contribute to hypovolemia. These changes are sensed by pressure-sensitive baroreceptors in the aorta and carotid arteries and by volume-sensitive stretch receptors in the atria and vena cava. Fibers from these primary neurons ascend in the vagus nerve to the nucleus of the solitary tract. Secondary neurons project to the medullary reticular formation and cardiovascular pressor and depressor areas of the brain stem.

Many other alterations, including fear and anxiety or changes in oxygen concentration, temperature, and energy substrates, provide afferent input to the neuroendocrine system. The perception of danger, or threat of injury, stimulates the central limbic system with fiber projections to the hypothalamus. Optic, olfactory, or auditory information may provide substantial signals. Injuries that affect airway, breathing, or circulation may result in hypoxia, hypercarbia, or acidosis. Chemoreceptors located in the carotid and aortic bodies, and in the central nervous system, detect decreases in the plasma concentration of oxygen and increases in the concentration of carbon dioxide or hydrogen ions. Fibers from these neurons project to both cardiovascular and respiratory centers of the medulla. Hemorrhage and exposure after trauma leading to hypothermia and core temperature changes are sensed in the hypothalamic preoptic area.

B. Integration and Modulation

Multiple signals from different pathways are modulated at several levels. The primary input depends on the nature, intensity, and duration of the stimulus. Sequential or repetitive stimulation, as well as the status and responsiveness of the receptor, influence the response. The sensory signal arrives at the medullary center for integration with other ascending signals, interneurons, and descending inhibitory inputs. The various signals from nociceptors, baroreceptors, chemoreceptors, somatosensory afferents, and limbic system project from brain stem nuclei to converge at the hypothalamus.

C. Efferent Output

1. Pituitary Regulation

There are two main components to the efferent limb of the neuroendocrine response: hormones under hypothalamic–pituitary axis control and hormones under autonomic nervous system control. The hypothalamic–pituitary–adrenal (HPA) axis has been studied extensively and represents a model neuroendocrine response system to stress. Although corticotropin-releasing hormone (CRH), adrenocorticotropic hormone (ACTH), and cortisol are secreted sequentially, the fine control of the system is achieved through neural integration, feedback loop regulation, and intermediary substances. Multiple inputs are integrated at the hypothalamic paraventricular nucleus (PVN) to generate the efferent arc.

CRH is the primary stimulant of the synthesis and secretion of ACTH by corticotrophs in the anterior pituitary gland. ACTH is released as a cleavage prod-uct of proopiomelanocortin and subsequently acts to stimulate the synthesis and release of glucocorticoids from the adrenal cortex.

Cortisol is the primary glucocorticoid in the response to stress and has widespread effects on host metabolism. Among its many metabolic actions are potentiation of glucagon and epinephrine leading to hyperglycemia, stimulation of gluconeogenesis in the liver, stimulation of amino acid release in skeletal muscle leading to proteolysis, and an increase in lipolysis and fatty acid release. Cortisol is also essential in the compensatory hyperosmolar response necessary to achieve complete blood volume restitution. The magnitude of injury influences the intensity of the CRH–ACTH–cortisol response. Along with the elevation in plasma cortisol levels, the normal diurnal variation is lost. In pure hypovolemia, plasma cortisol levels normalize rapidly when blood volume has been restored. Persistently elevated cortisol suggests ongoing stimulation from tissue hypoxia or supervening infection and is associated with reduced survival.

Hypothalamic thyrotropin-releasing hormone (TRH) stimulates the release of thyroid-stimulating hormone (TSH) from the anterior pituitary. TSH is responsible for the release of primarily thyroxine (T_4) from the thyroid gland, which is converted to triiodothyronine (T_3) peripherally. Thyroid hormones also have multiple metabolic effects, the most important of which are increases in oxygen consumption and heat production. After injury, peripheral conversion of T_4 to T_3 is impaired and there is no compensatory rise in TSH release.

The role of endogenous opioids after injury and hemorrhage is an area undergoing active investigation. The opioids, including endorphins and enkephalins, are secreted by cells in the central nervous system, intestinal wall, and adrenal medulla. They act upon various receptors to produce different effects. In the central nervous system, opioid peptides act as neurotransmitters to attenuate pain by inhibiting nociception. The excess release of endogenous opioid peptides has been linked to the cardiovascular collapse of shock. One suggested mechanism for opioid-induced hypotension after acute hemorrhage is a decrease in sympathetic outflow, mediated by serotoninergic pathways. After hemorrhagic or septic shock, administration of the opiate receptor antagonist naloxone has been shown to improve cardiovascular function, systemic blood pressure, and survival time.

Growth hormone (GH), gonadotropins, and prolactin are other anterior pituitary hormones involved in the neuroendocrine response. GH promotes protein synthesis and is elevated following injury. Gonadotropin-releasing hormone stimulates the release of follicle-stimulating hormone and luteinizing hormone, both of which are suppressed after injury. Although the hypothalamus exerts tonic suppression of pituitary prolactin release, elevated levels have been reported after injury in adults.

Arginine vasopressin (AVP), or antidiuretic hormone, is synthesized in the hypothalamus and is transported to the posterior pituitary gland for storage. The secretion of AVP is increased immediately after injury. Stimuli for AVP release include increased plasma osmolality and changes in effective circulating volume. Actions of AVP include reabsorption of free water in the renal distal tubules and collecting ducts, peripheral and splanchnic vasoconstriction, and hepatic glycogenolysis and gluconeogenesis.

2. Autonomic Regulation

Catecholamines are essential components of the physiologic response to injury. Norepinephrine is released primarily from the axon terminals of postganglionic neurons with subsequent overflow into plasma. The rate of norepinephrine release correlates with the intensity of sympathetic nervous system activity. Epinephrine is secreted directly into the circulation from stimulation of the adrenal medulla. Like other hormones, catecholamines exert both hemodynamic and metabolic actions, including enhanced cardiovascular function, vasoconstriction, hepatic glycogenolysis and gluconeogenesis, and peripheral lipolysis.

The renin–angiotensin–aldosterone system serves to maintain intravascular volume. Renin catalyzes the conversion of angiotensinogen to angiotensin I within the kidney, which in turn is converted into angiotensin II in the pulmonary circulation. Angiotensin II and ACTH are stimuli for the secretion of aldosterone from the adrenal cortex. The predominant action of aldosterone is enhancement of the Na^+/K^+-ATPase enzyme in the renal distal convoluted tubules and collecting ducts to increase the reabsorption of sodium and the elimination of potassium.

Insulin and glucagon play opposing roles in the maintenance of substrate homeostasis. Insulin is the primary anabolic hormone and promotes the storage of carbohydrate, protein, and lipid. After injury, sympathetic nervous system activity inhibits insulin secretion from pancreatic β islet cells and cortisol inhibits glucose uptake with the net result of hyperglycemia and catabolism. Glucagon is synthesized in pancreatic α islet cells and increases protein and lipid catabolism by increasing hepatic glycogenolysis and gluconeogenesis.

II. IMMUNE RESPONSE TO INJURY

Immune cells and inflammatory mediators activated by tissue injury are important components in the response to trauma. Among the substances released by activated inflammatory cells are cytokines, endothelial cell factors, and eicosanoids. The actions of these varied mediators in hemorrhage, sepsis, and injury are the subject of intense investigation.

A. Cytokines

Cytokines are a class of small proteins produced by the full range of inflammatory cells. They are active at low concentrations and may have paracrine, autocrine, or endocrine effects. Cytokines regulate the production of immune cells and other cytokines by either potentiating or attenuating the inflammatory response.

Manifestations of cytokine response include fever and alterations in cardiovascular and respiratory function. Excessive cytokine release has been implicated in the ongoing inflammation and injury associated with sepsis and multiple organ failure. The number of cytokines involved is too numerous to list in this brief review, but the best characterized include the interleukins, tumor necrosis factor α (TNF-α), the interferons, and granulocyte–macrophage-colony stimulating factor (GM-CSF).

After injury, TNF-α, or cachectin, is one of the

earliest cytokines released by monocytes, macrophages, T cells, and endothelial cells. TNF-α has been shown to act synergistically with interleukin-1 (IL-1) to induce hypotension, tissue injury, and death in animals. Its metabolic effects include proteolysis in skeletal muscle and hepatic gluconeogenesis.

The interleukins are a family of cytokines also derived from monocytes, macrophages, T cells, and endothelial cells. The best characterized of these cytokines in trauma is IL-1. The two species IL-1α and IL-1β have differential actions, but IL-1β is believed to be more biologically relevant. Among its many systemic effects are mediating fever by stimulating the synthesis of E series prostaglandins in the thermoregulatory center of the hypothalamus, promoting synthesis of hepatic acute-phase proteins, and promoting skeletal muscle proteolysis.

Interferon-γ is a glycoprotein released by stimulated helper T cells. It activates circulating and tissue macrophages to release TNF-α and other interleukins. GM-CSF is a growth factor cytokine that plays a prominent role in wound healing after injury. It augments the maturation of functional leukocytes and delays the apoptosis of immune cells.

B. Endothelial Cell Mediators

Endothelial cell-derived substances have predominantly local actions of vasomotor regulation and modulation of coagulation, but may have additional systemic effects on cardiovascular and neuroendocrine systems, as well as cytokine stimulation. Nitric oxide (NO) was formerly known as endothelium-derived relaxing factor. It has been shown that a basal release of NO induces a tonic state of arteriolar vasodilatation. Cellular injury, endotoxin, and hypoxia stimulate an increased release of NO, and its effects are primarily exacerbation of the vasodilatory state. Conversely, endothelins exert potent vasoconstrictor properties. Endothelin-1 is the most biologically active member of this family and is estimated to have 10 times more vasoconstrictor potency than angiotensin II. Increased serum levels of endothelin-1 correlate with the severity of injury. The platelet-activating factor stimulates the production of thromboxane (TxA2) and promotes platelet aggregation.

Its actions include increasing vascular permeability by altering the shape of endothelial cells.

C. Eicosanoids

The eicosanoids are phospholipid mediators derived from arachidonic acid through the action of phospholipase A and include prostaglandins, thromboxanes, and leukotrienes. Actions of prostaglandins and prostacyclin include increased vascular permeability, leukocyte migration, and vasodilation. TxA2 is synthesized in platelets, acts as a potent vasoconstrictor, and promotes platelet aggregation. The leukotrienes mediate anaphylaxis by promoting capillary leakage, bronchoconstriction, and vasoconstriction.

III. METABOLIC RESPONSE TO INJURY

A. Substrate Metabolism

Altered substrate metabolism after injury is often compared and contrasted with that during fasting. The adaptive responses to fasting of decreased substrate utilization and decreased metabolic rate are modified by the stress responses to pain, tissue damage, hemorrhage, and inflammation. The early phase is characterized by generalized catabolism, protein wasting, negative nitrogen balance, and hyperglycemia. Fever, increased myocardial work, and early wound healing all increase energy expenditure and metabolic rate. After existing hepatic glycogen stores are depleted, lipids become the primary source of fuel. Lipolysis is enhanced by catecholamines, cortisol, and glucagon. Hyperglycemia results from increased hepatic glycogenolysis and gluconeogenesis, mediated by cortisol and catecholamines, from inhibition of insulin-mediated glucose uptake and in the periphery.

The increased urinary excretion of nitrogen reflects net proteolysis. The severity of injury correlates with the degree of total body protein turnover. Following trauma, the major source of amino acids is skeletal muscle, the primary carriers of nitrogen being alanine and glutamine. Although the total amino acid concentration is unchanged, changes in alanine and glutamine synthesis and release depend on the extent of overall injury and oxygen consumption.

B. Electrolyte Metabolism

Decreased effective circulating volume is exacerbated by tissue damage and obligatory sequestration of fluid into extravascular compartments. After trauma, not only is there interstitial accumulation of fluid from the capillary leak of injured and inflamed tissue, but there is also mobilization of salt and water into the intracellular compartment. Previous studies have shown that the cellular membrane sodium–potassium adenosine triphosphatase (Na^+,K^+-ATPase), or sodium pump, is impaired in shock leading to muscle cell membrane depolarization. An influx of sodium and chloride ions, followed by water, results in cell swelling, further depletion of extracellular volume, and may lead to irreversible shock.

The renal conservation of salt and water may also be affected by increased glomerular filtration fraction, increased proximal reabsorption of sodium, and increased blood flow to juxtamedullary nephrons through aldosterone and glucocorticoid effects. Increased levels of AVP contribute to water retention and may manifest as oliguria. In the presence of hypovolemia or hypotension, there is an increased risk of acute tubular necrosis. Adequate resuscitation with balanced salt solutions helps maintain the medullary osmolar gradient and tubular fluid flow.

IV. INTERACTIONS OF THE BIOLOGIC RESPONSES

Although the effects of individual hormonal and immune substances have been well characterized, their interrelationships in the overall biologic response have yet to be well elucidated. Multiple stimuli certainly interact and converge in the central nervous system. This concept is supported by studies demonstrating potentiated responses of ACTH to hemorrhage after a simultaneous or repetitive application of subthreshold stimuli.

One focus of interest has been the interactions of immune mediators with the HPA system. Im-

paired host wound healing and decreased resistance to infection in some critically injured patients have popularized the concept of injury-induced immunosuppression. Although it is known that pharmacologic doses of corticosteroids produce immunosuppression, it is unclear whether the physiologic increase in endogenous cortisol directly causes immunosuppression. Instead, the immune dysfunction after injury may also be mediated by the stimulation of the autonomic nervous system or other hormones.

Evidence shows that IL-1 may activate the HPA axis by a central action on the hypothalamus. IL-1 increases the release of CRH from isolated rat hypothalamus and other studies have shown that IL-1-stimulated ACTH release is associated with a decreased CRH content in the median eminence. Other investigators have reported increased levels of circulating ACTH and corticosterone in rats after an intravenous injection of IL-1.

It is still unclear whether IL-1 has a direct or an indirect effect on the HPA axis. There is some evidence that these actions of IL-1 may be mediated by prostaglandins. Microinjections of the prostaglandin antagonist into the preoptic area block the ACTH response to intravenous IL-1β. In addition, the effect of IL-1β on ACTH release may not be a result of changes in CRH. Reports have suggested that IL-1β stimulates norepinephrine and dopamine release in the hypothalamus and that the ACTH response to IL-1 injection in the median eminence can be blocked by adrenergic antagonists. Similarly, TNF-α has also been shown to increase levels of circulating ACTH. Like IL-1, this stimulatory effect may also be related to activation of the HPA system through a prostaglandin-mediated increase in CRH release.

Studies have documented the immunosuppressive effects of androgens, citing differences between male and female immune function. Androgen-deficient mice have enhanced IL-2 and interferon-γ production by peripheral T cells. In addition, it has been shown that castrated male mice subjected to soft tissue trauma and hemorrhage had elevated plasma corticosterone levels and splenocyte proliferation compared to sham animals.

The local production of various hormones from immune cells may lead to paracrine effects. Lymphocytes have been shown to produce ACTH, a TSH-like peptide, and a GH-like peptide, among others. Immune cells also possess various hormone receptors. Receptors for CRH, TRH, growth hormone-releasing hormone, ACTH, and opioids have been found on leukocytes. These findings certainly point to a communication between immune and neuroendocrine systems. Considerably more research is needed to understand these complex interactions further.

V. THERAPY AND MODIFICATION OF RESPONSES

A. Fluid Resuscitation

Initial management after severe injury involves the control of hemorrhage, administration of intravenous isotonic crystalloid fluids, and blood transfusion, if needed, which immediately improves the effective circulating volume. The replenishment of intravascular volume results in an increase in capillary hydrostatic pressure, reversing the flux of water out of the interstitial compartment. Reflex sympathetic vasoconstriction and catecholamine release are diminished as increased blood pressure is sensed by baroreceptors. The result is improved capillary perfusion and organ function and the prevention of the adverse consequences of tissue ischemia and cellular hypoxia.

B. Pain Management

The administration of narcotic analgesics provides pain control, reduces sympathetic nervous system activity, reduces the release of endogenous opioids, and decreases cortical and limbic inputs. Studies have shown that the preoperative administration of morphine diminishes the usual rise in plasma ACTH, cortisol, GH, and glucose. Furthermore, studies have shown that denervation of the wound or regional anesthesia ablates afferent signals and suppresses adrenal stimulation.

C. Local Wound Care

Tissue damage incites the local release of cytokines, immune complexes, and complement split products from phagocytes and lymphocytes. An exaggerated local inflammatory response from the wound may amplify and cause adverse systemic effects. Therefore, early removal of debris and debridement of devitalized tissues will attenuate this inflammation. Stabilization of fractured limbs prevents repetitive soft tissue trauma and fasciotomy relieves compartment syndrome to improve tissue perfusion.

D. Intensive Care Unit Admission

One of the goals of resuscitation is to restore and maintain optimal perfusion and prevent tissue ischemia. Vasomotor changes, myocardial dysfunction, shock, hypothermia, and respiratory insufficiency all contribute to the difficulty of gauging the adequacy of therapy without intensive care unit (ICU) admission. In an ICU environment, all physiologic functions may be monitored closely for evidence of deterioration and to assess the response to therapy. A pulmonary artery catheter allows the monitoring of cardiac filling pressures and cardiac output. Systemic oxygen delivery and consumption estimates can be derived from these measurements to facilitate resuscitation.

E. Nutritional Support

Most victims of mild injuries easily withstand the increased metabolic demand and limited catabolism without nutritional supplementation. Those with severe injuries require replenishment of nutritional substrates to avoid excessive energy depletion and protein wasting. Nutritional formulas are provided by either the enteral or the parenteral route. The beneficial effects of enteral nutrition include the maintenance of gut mucosal barrier function and the enhanced production of trophic gut hormones.

Although glutamine is the most abundant amino acid in the body, its concentration in plasma and tissues is depleted after injury. Studies have shown that glutamine-enriched nutrition can improve muscle protein synthesis and improve nitrogen balance. Arginine, a nonessential amino acid, has been shown to augment macrophage and natural killer cell activity. In critical illness, supplemental arginine improves nitrogen retention and wound healing. The majority of experimental data on these immune-enhancing formulas is still too inconclusive to justify their use.

F. Summary

The acute trauma response consists of multiple biologic components reacting to various signals from local wounded tissue and systemic alterations. In severe injury, the exaggerated and unchecked release of mediators results in detrimental systemic effects and may lead to multiple organ failure. In addition to host endogenous modulation of these mediators, timely therapeutic interventions may modify local inflammation, neuroendocrine signals, and systemic alterations. Recovery from trauma ultimately depends on the coordination of the neuroendocrine, immune, and metabolic systems toward restoring homeostasis and survival. Future research in this area may elucidate new therapeutic options for the critically injured trauma patient.

Acknowledgment

This article was supported in part by National Institutes of Health Grant K08 DK02181–Clinical Investigator Award (M.P. Lilly).

See Also the Following Articles

Apoptosis; Catecholamines; Cytokines; Immune Response; Immune Suppression

Bibliography

Chaudry, I. H., Ayala, A., Ertel, W., and Stephan, R. N. (1990). Hemorrhage and resuscitation: Immunological aspects. *Am. J. Physiol.* 259 (*Regul. Integrative Comp. Physiol.* 28), R663–R678.

Faist, E., Schinkel, C., and Zimmer, S. (1996). Update on the mechanisms of immune suppression of injury and immune modulation. *World J. Surg.* 20, 454–459.

Gann, D. S., and Foster, A. H. (1994). Endocrine and metabolic responses to injury. *In* "Principles of Surgery" (S. I. Schwartz, G. T. Shires, and F. C. Spencer, Eds.), 6th ed. McGraw-Hill, New York.

Gann, D. S., and Lilly, M. P. (1984). The endocrine response to injury. *In* "Progress in Critical Care Medicine" (W. H. Massion, series Ed.), Vol. 1. Karger, Basel.

Gann, D. S., and Wright, P. A. (1995). Shock: The final common pathway? *Adv. Trauma Crit. Care* 10, 43–59.

Guirao, X., and Lowry, S. F. (1996). Biologic control of injury and inflammation: Much more than too little or too late. *World J. Surg.* 20, 437–446.

Koretz, R. L. (1995). Nutritional supplementation in the ICU: How critical is nutrition for the critically ill? *Am. J. Respir. Crit. Care Med.* 151, 570–573.

Lilly, M. P., and Gann, D. S. (1990). The neuroendocrine response to injury. *In* "Blunt Multiple Trauma: Comprehensive Pathophysiology and Care" (J. R. Border, M. Allgöwer, S. T. Hansen, Jr., and T. P. Rüedi, Eds.). Dekker, New York.

Lilly, M. P., and Gann, D. S. (1992). The hypothalamic-pituitary-adrenal-immune axis: A critical assessment. *Arch. Surg.* 127, 1463–1474.

Lin, E., Lowry, S. F., and Calvano, S. E. (1999). The systemic response to injury. *In* "Principles of Surgery" (S. I. Schwartz, G. T. Shires, and F. C. Spencer, Eds.). 7th ed. McGraw-Hill, New York.

Madden, K. S., Sanders, V. M., and Felten, D. L. (1995). Catecholamine influences and sympathetic neural modulation of immune responsiveness. *Annu. Rev. Pharmacol. Toxicol.* 35, 417–448.

McEwen, B. S. (1998). Protective and damaging effects of stress mediators. *N. Engl. J. Med.* 338, 171–179.

Monk, D. N., Plank, L. D., Franch-Arcas, G., Finn, P. J., Streat, S. J., and Hill, G. L. (1996). Sequential changes in the metabolic response in critically injured patients during the first 25 days after blunt trauma. *Ann. Surg.* 223, 395–405.

Schadt J. C. (1989). Sympathetic and hemodynamic adjustments to hemorrhage: A possible role for endogenous opioid peptides. *Resuscitation* 18, 219–228.

Schlag, G., and Redl, H. (1996). Mediators of injury and inflammation. *World J. Surg.* 20, 406–410.

Addison's Disease

see Adrenal Insufficiency

Adenylyl Cyclases and Stress Response

Ferenc A. Antoni

MRC Brain Metabolism Unit, Edinburgh, Scotland

I. Properties of Adenylyl Cyclase
II. Adenylyl Cyclase in Stress

GLOSSARY

heterotrimeric G proteins A group of proteins that consist of three subunits (α, β, γ) and couple cell surface receptors to their effector enzymes. Upon activation of cell surface receptors by their ligands, heterotrimeric G proteins dissociate into the α-subunit and the $\beta\gamma$-complex, both of which regulate the activity of effector enzymes such as adenylyl cyclase in the cell membrane.

protein kinases Enzymes that tag proteins with phosphoryl residues derived from ATP. The activity of protein kinases may be regulated by a variety of intracellular messengers, protein–protein interactions, or phosphorylation by other protein kinases.

second messengers These are generated by extracellular stimuli arriving at the cell surface and transduce the extracellular signal toward the interior of the cell.

$\mathbf{A}$ denylyl cyclases (EC 4.6.1.1) are enzymes that generate the second messenger adenosine-3,'5'-monophosphate (cAMP) from ATP.

I. PROPERTIES OF ADENYLYL CYCLASE

Signaling through cAMP is fundamentally important in the central nervous system. Genetic and phar-macological studies have revealed that alterations of both the synthetic (adenylyl cyclase) and the catabolic (cyclic nucleotide phosphodiesterase; PDE) limbs of the cAMP cascade may cause profound disruption of learning and memory. Further work has implicated cAMP signaling in the development of opiate dependence, alcoholism, disorders of mood and affect, and neuronal death.

There are currently nine isotypes of adenylyl cyclase known in mammals. These are differentially controlled by heterotrimeric G proteins, Ca^{2+}, and protein phosphorylation (Fig. 1). In turn, heterotrimeric G proteins are regulated by G-protein-coupled cell surface receptors. Several isotypes of adenylyl cyclase are expressed in the brain and show unique topographical distribution. Colocalization of adenylyl cyclases with distinct functional properties within the same cell seems highly plausible. This raises the possibility of the formation of cellular domains, e.g., neuronal growth cones, where cAMP-dependent signaling has distinct functional characteristics than in other parts of the cell such as the cell body. Further, the formation of subplasmalemmal microdomains with different types of adenylyl cyclases and PDEs also seems possible.

Some adenylyl cyclases such as adenylyl cyclase types I and VIII are stimulated by intracellular Ca^{2+} and calmodulin. These enzymes are prominently expressed in the cerebral cortex and are important for learning and memory. Type I adenylyl cyclase shows synergistic stimulation by Ca^{2+}/calmodulin and G_s-

26   *Adenylyl Cyclases and Stress Response*

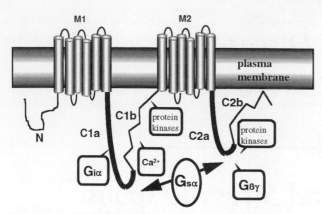

FIGURE 1 Schematic representation of mammalian adenylyl cyclases and their control. N, N-terminal cytoplasmic loop; M1 and M2, intramembrane domains; C1a, C2a, homologous catalytic domains (thick line), C1b, C2b, nonhomologous regulatory domains (thin lines). Approximate sites of isotype-specific modulation reported for various cyclases to date are indicated in boxes along the polypeptide chain. The C1a and C2a domains must come into physical contact to form the catalytic core. This is facilitated by $G_{s\alpha}$, which binds to the C2a domain. Most adenylyl cyclases are inhibited by $G_{i\alpha}$, which binds to a site on the C1a domain.

coupled receptors. Therefore, this enzyme may function as a coincidence detector for the activation of ionotropic glutamate receptors and G_s-coupled receptors for a wide range of neuroeffectors. Another type of adenylyl cyclase, isotype II, is synergistically stimulated by $G_{s\alpha}$ and $G_{\beta\gamma}$ or by $G_{s\alpha}$ and protein kinase C-dependent phosphorylation. These properties suggest that the type II enzyme is a coincidence detector for neurotransmitter receptors coupled to G_s and $G_{i/o}$ or G_s and G_q. These pairings are remarkable as they suggest that the direction as well as the magnitude of the effects of neurotransmitters on cAMP synthesis are dependent on the context of the stimulus applied. A third group of adenylyl cyclases is inhibited by Ca^{2+} ions. These enzymes are likely to participate in signaling circuits where periodic surges of cAMP levels alternate with increases of intracellular Ca^{2+}, i.e., intracellular oscillations. Typically in neuroendocrine cells, cAMP produces depolarization of the membrane potential and rise of intracellular Ca^{2+}. The rise in intracellular Ca^{2+} triggers various effector mechanisms, e.g., secretion or gene expression, and also provides negative feedback to

the adenylyl cyclase system to limit the rise of cAMP levels. Depending on the kinetics of cAMP synthesis and degradation the cell may repolarize and return to the unstimulated state or enter a phase of oscillatory behavior.

II. ADENYLYL CYCLASE IN STRESS

Stressful stimuli increase the level of cAMP in the neocortex and the adenohypophysis. In the cerebral cortex this is thought to be the consequence of the activation of adenylyl cyclase through G_s-coupled receptors such as β_1-adrenergic and corticotropin releasing factor type 1 and type 2 receptors. In the anterior pituitary gland, cAMP is the major intracellular messenger activated by corticotropin releasing factor. Here, the adenylyl cyclase system operates as a coincidence detector for activation by $G_{s\alpha}$-and protein kinase C-dependent phosphorylation.

Adrenal corticosteroid hormones interfere with the regulation of the cAMP pathway both in the short and in the long term. Examples of long-term influence include control of the levels of adenylyl cyclase in neocortex and hippocampus. In these tissues Ca^{2+}/calmodulin-stimulated adenylyl cyclase activity is reduced by adrenalectomy and repeated stress. By contrast, the level of type II adenylyl cyclase mRNA was increased by repeated stress in the hippocampus. Regarding short-term effects, in pituitary corticotrophs Ca^{2+}-mediated feedback inhibition of cAMP accumulation is essential for the early glucocorticoid feedback inhibition of ACTH release stimulated by corticotropin releasing factor.

In peripheral tissues, cAMP is also a major intracellular mediator of the stress response in the adrenal cortex, the liver, and fat tissue. The levels of cAMP-degrading PDEs are increased by glucocorticoids in adipose tissue; effects on adenylyl cyclase expression have not been studied so far.

Bibliography

Antoni, F. A. (1996). Calcium checks cyclic AMP—Mechanism of corticosteroid feedback in adenohypophysial corticotrophs. *J. Neuroendocrinol,* 8, 659–672.

Antoni, F. A. (1997). Calcium regulation of adenylyl cyclase—Relevance for endocrine control. *Trends Endocrinol-Metab* 8, 7–13.

Cooper, D. M. F., Karpen, J. W., Fagan, J. W., and Mons, N. E. (1998). Ca^{2+}-sensitive adenylyl cyclases. *Adv. Sec. Mess. Phosphoprot. Res.* 32, 23–52.

Gannon, M. N., Akompong, T., Billingsley, M. L., and McEwen, B. S. (1994). Adrenalectomy-induced alterations of calmodulin-dependent hippocampal adenylate cyclase activity: Role of guanine nucleotide-binding proteins. *Endocrinology* 134, 853–857.

Jurevicius, J., and Fischmeister, R. (1996). cAMP compartmentation is responsible for a focal activation of cardiac Ca^{2+} channels by β-adrenergic agonists. *Proc. Natl. Acad. Sci. USA* 93, 295–299.

Mons, N., and Cooper, D. M. F. (1995). Adenylate cyclases—critical foci in neuronal signaling. *Trends Neurosci.* 18, 536–542.

Orth, D. N., and Kovacs, W. J. (1998). The adrenal cortex. In "*Williams Textbook of Endocrinology*" (J. D. Wilson, D. W. Foster, H. M. Kronenberg, and P. R. Larsen, Eds.) pp. 517–664. Saunders, Philadelphia.

Sunahara, R. K., Dessauer, C. W., and Gilman, A. G. (1996). Complexity and diversity of mammalian adenylyl cyclases. *Ann. Rev. Biochem.* 36, 461–480.

Villacres, E. C., Wong, S. T., Chavkin, C., and Storm, D. R. (1998). Type I adenylyl cyclase mutant mice have impaired mossy fiber long-term potentiation. *J. Neurosci.* 18, 3186–3194.

Wolfgang, D., Chen, I., and Wand, G. S. (1994). Effects of restraint stress on components of adenylyl cyclase signal transduction in the rat hippocampus. *Neuropsychopharmacology* 11, 187–193.

Adjustment Disorders

Mihai Dascalu and Dragan Svrakic

Washington University School of Medicine, St. Louis

I. Definition
II. Epidemiology
III. Etiology
IV. Diagnosis
V. Course and Prognosis
VI. Treatment
VII. Conclusions

DSM-IV Diagnostic and Statistical Manual of Mental disorders is the latest and most up-to-date classification of mental disorders. It was published in 1994.

TCI (Temperament and Character Inventory) A self-report questionnaire that allows diagnosis of personality disorders using a quantitative rating of seven factors, four dimensions of temperament (harm avoidance, novelty seeking, reward dependence, and persistence) and three dimensions of character (self-directedness, cooperativeness, and self-trancendence).

GLOSSARY

bereavement Loss through death.

bereavement process The umbrella term for bereavement reactions over time.

bereavement reactions Psychological, physiological, or behavioral responses to bereavement.

crisis A self-limited response to hazardous events and experienced as a painful state. It can last from a few hours to weeks.

The adjustment disorders are abnormal reactions that occur in response to stressful life events. These reactions are clinically significant, but do not meet criteria for other psychiatric disorders and occur within 3 months of the initial presence of the stressor and last 6 months or less after the stressor ends or is resolved. Adjustment disorder is one of the most often used psychiatric diagnoses. It is somewhat unique because it is one of the few psychiatric conditions linked to an etiological event, is one of the least stigmatizing psychiatric diagnosis, and compared to the major psychiatric illnesses it is, by definition, time limited.

I. DEFINITION

Adjustment disorder is characterized in DSM-IV by the development of emotional or behavioral symptoms in response to one or more identifiable psychosocial stressors. The symptoms are considered clinically significant because they either impair the individual's functioning or are subjectively perceived to cause distress in excess of what would be expected from exposure to the stressor(s). These symptoms neither fulfill criteria for an Axis I diagnosis nor represent the exacerbation of a preexisting Axis I or Axis II disorder. They are not caused by normal bereavement. The symptoms occur within 3 months of the onset of a stressor and in response to it and do not last longer than 6 months after the end of the stressor or its consequences. The nature and severity of the stressors is not specified in DSM-IV. They include interpersonal, occupational, or medical problems. The stress may be single or multiple, such as loss of job associated with divorce and physical illness. The stress may happen once or it may be chronic, lasting more than 6 months (such as living in poverty), or recurrent (such as seasonal business difficulties). It can affect only one person or many (as in a flood or an earthquake). Whatever the nature of the stressor the person is overwhelmed by it. The individuals may experience anxiety, depression or behavioral symptoms (e.g., erratic actions) or various combinations. If the symptoms progress to meet criteria for another Axis I disorder (e.g., major depression), a diagnosis of adjustment disorder can no longer be used.

Historically a diagnosis similar to adjustment disorder first appeared in DSM- II. Transient situational disorder was understood in a developmental context and its subtypes were defined accordingly; for example, "adjustment reaction" of childhood, adolescence,

or adulthood. It required an unusually severe stress. The term adjustment disorder first appeared in DSM-III. A link to severe and unusual stress was no longer required, and the subtypes were recategorized according to their symptomatic presentation. In DSM-II and DSM-III the duration of adjustment disorder was not specified. In DSM-III-R, the duration of the illness was restricted to 6 months after the cessation of the stressor, and the subtype adjustment disorder with physical complaints was added.

II. EPIDEMIOLOGY

The adjustment disorders are considered to be very common. One epidemiological study conducted in children and adolescents found a prevalence rate of 7.6%. Precise data are not available for adults because the structured interviews used in general population do not include adjustment disorder. Several studies of the prevalence of adjustment disorders were done in clinical samples including patients admitted in the hospital for medical or surgical problems. The reported rates were between 5 and 13% in adults and up to 42% in children and adolescents. In a recent study of 1039 consecutive referrals to consultation–liaison psychiatry services, a diagnosis of adjustment disorder was made in 125 patients (12.0%). It was the sole diagnosis in 81 patients (7.8%) and in 44 (4.2%) it was diagnosed comorbidly with other Axis I and II diagnoses, most frequently with personality disorders and organic mental disorders. It had been considered as a rule-out diagnosis in a further 110 patients (10.6%).

Several studies found that this disorder is more common in women (sex ratio, 2:1).

III. ETIOLOGY

Adjustment disorder is caused by one or more stressors. There is a significant individual variation in response to stress so the severity of the stressors is not always predictive of the development of the illness.

A. Individual Factors

It is not clear why there is so much individual variation in the development of psychopathology in persons who experience similar stressors and also why when a reaction occurs the symptoms are so variable. Psychoanalytic researchers have highlighted the importance of development of adequate defense mechanisms as a child. Those who were able to develop mature defense mechanisms seem to be less vulnerable to and recover more quickly from the stressor. In this context, the roles of the mother and the rearing environment in a person's capability to respond adequately to stress are critical.

More recently, it has been shown that immature defense mechanisms correlate highly with poor character development as defined by the TCI (Temperament and Character Inventory). Poor character development is considered to be the common feature for the whole group of personality disorders as defined by DSM-IV. This implies that people who have a personality disorder are at a high risk for developing abnormal reaction to stress and then adjustment disorder. Conform to the definition both disorders can be diagnosed in the same time.

Several studies showed that children and adolescents are at a higher risk of developing an adjustment disorder than adults and that the illness is more frequent in females than in males.

B. Other Factors

The stressor severity is a complex function of multiple factors; for example, degree, quantity, duration, reversibility, environment, and timing. The severity of the stressors is not always predictive of the occurrence and severity of adjustment disorder, but without a doubt, serious and/or chronic stressors are more likely to cause an adjustment reaction. It is not clear if all persons are likely to develop symptoms if stress levels are increased enough. The nosological and phenomenological distinction between crisis and stress is critical for the understanding of individual variability in response to stress.

IV. DIAGNOSIS

A. Diagnostic Clues

The chief complaint may be a "nervous breakdown," inability to manage problems of life, or anxiety or depression associated with a specific stressor; the patient's history reveals normal functioning before the onset of the stressor; and the patient's mental status examination shows symptoms of anxiety, depression, or disturbed conduct.

B. Clinical Features

Several studies reported that between 50 and 87% of patients present with depressed mood. Other common symptoms encountered in more than 25 % of the patients include insomnia, other vegetative symptoms (e.g., palpitations), behavioral problems, social withdrawal, and suicidal ideation or gesture.

The development of depressive symptoms alone is less characteristic of children and adolescents. Two recent studies found that among children and adolescents with adjustment disorder, the majority presented with mixed emotional or mixed emotional and behavioral syndromes. In one study, 77% of adolescents but only 25% of adults had behavioral symptoms (disturbance of conduct).

Studies of adjustment disorder that used structured diagnostic instruments have reported a high level of comorbidity. In a mixed group of children, adolescents, and adults, approximately 70% of patients with adjustment disorder had at least one additional Axis I diagnosis.

Several studies have reported a significant association of adjustment disorder with suicidal behavior in adolescents and young adults. A couple of studies done in patients hospitalized after a suicidal gesture showed that more than 50% of the patients met criteria for adjustment disorder with depressed mood. Three retrospective studies of suicide completers below age 30 found that between 9 and 19% of the cases met criteria for adjustment disorder. This data suggest the seriousness of the illness in a subset of persons.

C. Subtypes of Adjustment Disorder

The adjustment disorders are classified according to the predominant clinical symptoms. Six subtypes are identified and coded in DSM-IV. Three define discrete symptomatic presentations (depressed mood, anxious mood, disturbance of conduct) and two describe mixed clinical presentations (mixed disturbance of anxiety and depressed mood, mixed disturbance of emotions and conduct). The final subtype, adjustment disorder unspecified, is a residual category for presentations not accurately described by one of the other subtypes. One additional subtype, adjustment disorder with suicidal behavior, was proposed for inclusion in DSM-IV. It was ultimately rejected because of concerns that it would discourage a more systematic assessment of symptoms in patients presenting with suicidal behavior.

1. Adjustment Disorder with Depressed Mood: The predominant manifestations are depressed mood, tearfulness, and hopelessness. This type must be distinguished from major depressive disorder and uncomplicated bereavement.

2. Adjustment Disorder with Anxiety. Symptoms of anxiety—such as palpitations, jitteriness, and agitation—are present in adjustment disorder with anxiety, which must be differentiated from anxiety disorders. The patient is usually nervous, fearful, and worried.

3. Adjustment Disorder with Mixed Anxiety and Depressed Mood: Patients exhibit features of both anxiety and depression that do not meet the criteria for an already established anxiety disorder or depressive disorder.

4. Adjustment Disorder with Disturbance of Conduct: The predominant manifestation involves conduct in which the rights of others are violated or age-appropriate societal norms and rules are disregarded. Examples of behavior in this category are truancy, vandalism, reckless driving, and fighting. The category must be differentiated from conduct disorder and antisocial personality disorder.

5. Adjustment Disorder with Mixed Disturbance of Emotions and Conduct: The combination of disturbance of emotions (anxiety and/or depression) and conduct sometimes occurs.

6. Adjustment Disorder Unspecified: Adjustment disorder unspecified is a residual category for atypical maladaptive reactions to stress. Examples include inappropriate responses to the diagnosis of physical illness, such as massive denial and severe noncompliance with treatment and social withdrawal without significant depressed or anxious mood.

Adjustment disorders are also classified according to the clinical course. They are acute if the symptoms last less than 6 months and chronic if the symptoms last longer than 6 months.

D. Differential Diagnosis

Adjustment disorders must be differentiated from a normal reaction to stress or from other psychiatric disorders that occur following a stress.

1. In acute stress disorder and posttraumatic stress disorder, the stress needs to be severe and it is more clearly specified. The stressors are psychologically traumatizing events outside the range of normal human experience so they are expected to produce the syndromes in the average human being. Both acute stress disorder and posttraumatic stress disorder are characterized by a specific constellation of affective and autonomic symptoms, which is not encountered in adjustment disorders.

2. In normal bereavement, despite difficulties in social and occupational functioning, the person's impairment remains within the expectable bounds of a reaction to a loss of a loved one.

3. Others disorders include major depressive disorder, brief psychotic disorder, generalized anxiety disorder, somatization disorder, conduct disorder, drug abuse, academic problem, occupational problem, or identity problem.

4. If the criteria for any of the above disorders are met, that diagnosis should be used instead of adjustment disorder, even if a stressor was present.

V. COURSE AND PROGNOSIS

A. Course

Adjustment disorder begins shortly after a significant stressor. By definition, the symptoms have to commence within the first 3 months after the onset of the stressor. Usually they start in the first couple of weeks. In most cases when the stressor ceases the symptoms remit quickly.

B. Prognosis

By definition, adjustment disorder is not an enduring diagnosis. The symptoms either resolve or progress to a more serious illness. In most cases, the prognosis is favorable with appropriate treatment, and most patients return to their previous level of functioning within 3 months. It appears that children and adolescents have a poor prognosis. Several studies, which surveyed adolescents up to 10 years after a diagnosis of adjustment disorder, found that only 44 to 60% of the original sample were well at follow-up. Some of the patients developed major mental disorders, such as schizophrenia, bipolar disorder, major depressive disorder, or substance-related disorders. It is not clear whether the poor outcome is due to adjustment disorder itself or to the frequent existence of comorbidity. At least one study that matched two groups for comorbidity (one with adjustment disorder and the other one without) found that adjustment disorder added no additional risk for poor outcome.

VI. TREATMENT

Little is known about the proper treatment of adjustment disorder. There are few, if any, treatment studies in patients with adjustment disorder, and systematic clinical trials are necessary because adjustment disorder is one of the most common psychiatric diagnoses. The typical pharmacological intervention is always symptomatic. When given, medication is aimed to alleviate a specific symptom, but should always be in addition to psychosocial strategies.

A. Stressors

Whenever possible the etiologic stressors should be removed or ameliorated. Interventions designed to minimize the impact of the stressors on daily functioning should be considered.

B. Psychotherapy

This remains the treatment of choice for adjustment disorder. It can help the patient adapt to the stressor if it is not reversible or time limited. It can also serve a preventive role if the stressor does remit.

1. Crisis intervention is a brief type of therapy that may be useful to decrease stress and facilitate the development of external support. It is designed to resolve the situation quickly by supportive techniques, suggestions, reassurance, and environmental manipulation. The frequency and length of encounters with the therapist is tailored to the patients needs, and sometimes even short-term hospitalization might be warranted.

2. Individual psychotherapy offers the patient the opportunity to understand the personal meaning of the stressor and to develop coping skills.

3. Group psychotherapy can be remarkably useful for patients who experienced similar stresses; for example, a group of renal dialysis patients.

4. Family therapy can sometimes help in some patients, especially those with adjustment disorder with disturbance of conduct who may have difficulties with the school, authorities, or the law.

C. Pharmacotherapy

This may be useful in some patients when prescribed for brief periods. Depending of the subtype of adjustment disorder, an antianxiety agent or an antidepressant may help. Some patients with severe symptoms may also benefit from short course psychostimulant or antipsychotic medication. There are no studies regarding the use of specific medical agents in adjustment disorder. Few, if any, patients can be adequately treated by medication alone, and psychotherapy should be added to the treatment.

VII. CONCLUSIONS

Adjustment disorders are an important and prevalent cause of personal discomfort, absenteeism, addiction, and suicide. This diagnosis should not be used to avoid stigmatization of a patient. Short psychotherapy is the treatment of choice, but pharmacotherapy is often used as an acute way to stabilize the patient and to prevent potentially disruptive behavior.

See Also the Following Articles

ADOLESCENCE; ANXIETY; BEREAVEMENT; CHILDHOOD STRESS

Bibliography

Cloninger, C. R., and Svrakic, D. M. (in press). Personality disorders. *In* "Comprehensive Textbook of Psychiatry" (H. I. Kaplan and B. J. Sadock, eds.), 7th ed.

Kaplan, H. I., Sadock, B. J., and Grebb, J. A. (1994). "Synopsis of Psychiatry", 7th ed. Williams & Wilkins, Baltimore.

Morrison, J. (1995). "DSM-IV Made Easy". Guilford, New York.

Newcorn, J. H., Strain, J. (1995). "Adjustment Disorders". *In* "Comprehensive Textbook of Psychiatry" (H. I. Kaplan and B. J. Sadock, eds.), Williams & Wilkins, Baltimore.

Popkin, M. K., Callies, A. L., Colon, E. A., and Stiebel, V. (1990). Adjustment disorders in medically ill inpatients referred for consultation in a university hospital. *Psychosomatics* **31** (4),410–414.

Snyder, S., Strain, J. J., and Wolf, D. (1990). Differentiating major depression from adjustment disorder with depressed mood in the medical setting. *Gen. Hosp. Psychiatr.* **12** (3), 159–165

Strain, J. J., Smith, G. C., Hammer, J. S. McKenzie, D. P., Blumenfield, M., Muskin, P., Newstadt, G., Wallack, J., Wilner, A., Schleifer, S. S. (1998). Adjustment disorder: A multisite study of its utilization and interventions in the consultation-liaison psychiatry setting. *Gen. Hosp. Psychiatr.* **20**(3), 139–149.

Adolescence

Gary N. Swanson

Allegheny General Hospital, Pittsburgh

I. Introduction
II. Normal Adolescence
III. Common Stressors
IV. Unusual Stressors

GLOSSARY

adolescence A stage of life from puberty to adulthood usually thought of as occurring between the ages of 12 and 19. It is characterized by marked physical, psychological, and social change. The developmental task of adolescence is the change from dependence to independence

identity A central aspect of the healthy personality, consisting of an inner awareness of continuity of self and an ability to identify with others, share in their goals, and participate in society.

puberty A normal growth process that begins in early adolescence, lasts 2–4 years, and leads to sexual and physical maturity.

resiliency The ability to overcome or adapt to stress by maintaining developmental progress and adequate social and academic functioning.

I. INTRODUCTION

Adolesence has been characterized as a challenging stage of life, defined by the psychological task of identity formation. Adolescents develop better coping skills as they mature both as a consequence of their cognitive and emotional development and because of the changes they experience. Teenagers generally respond successfully to many common stressors, such as puberty, school demands, family changes, and peer relations. Unusual stressors may lead to some difficulties, especially in those who are more vulnerable.

Traumatic stressors, although not universally harmful, often impinge on the emotional well being of teenagers and may leave lasting scars. An adolescent's ability to cope with stressors depends on a number of factors, including family support, cognitive development, previous experiences, and their own unique temperament.

II. NORMAL ADOLESCENCE

The discrete stage of adolescence has been recognized for only a short period of time. It seems to have come about in Western society as a consequence of the Industrial Revolution, when social changes necessitated the prolongation of childhood. Children, who had previously been able to enter the adult world at an early age, did not have the skills or abilities to perform adult work. Child labor laws were passed, and public schools were established. Families were also better able to financially provide for children for a longer period of time. The transition from childhood to adulthood lengthened, encompassing most of the second decade of life. Indeed, many teenagers nowadays maintain their dependency on their parents during college, thereby extending this transition even further. Puberty is often identified as the starting point of adolescence, although this can normally start as early as 9 or 10. The end-point has been less well defined, as there are differences in the legal age of adulthood (18–21), and the criteria of independence, the completion of school, starting a new family, and getting a job are even more variable.

Adolescence is often thought of as a period of rebellion, marked by conflicts with parents as a child grows to be an adult. Anna Freud, G. Stanley Hall, and others characterized this stage of life as a time of "storm and stress." Psychoanalysts believed that it was an indication of pathology if these stormy relations did not occur. Erik Erikson believed that the psychological task of this stage of life is the development of identity. Specifically, he thought that the adolescent would commit to a core set of values and assume a sex role and career plan. Failure to complete this task would result in "identity diffusion," leading to further difficulties in adulthood. Adolescence was the period of an identity crisis, which led to considerable emotional turmoil.

However, Offer and associates have shown that the vast majority (~80%) of adolescents do not experience significant emotional distress. Instead, these teenagers manage the transition to adulthood smoothly, without experiencing a severe identity crisis. They have a positive self-image and are not afraid of the physical changes associated with puberty. They do not report significant conflicts with their parents and have positive feelings toward their families. They are confident, optimistic about the future, and are willing to work hard in order to reach a goal.

However, a significant minority (~20%) of teenagers reports difficulties in these areas. They report that they feel emotionally empty and overwhelmed by life's problems. They feel much less able to control the world around them. These adolescents also report that they are much less able to talk with their parents about their problems. They appear to be more vulnerable to stressors and may exhibit more behavioral and emotional problems as a result. It seems that the stereotype of the moody, confused, and rebellious teenager is more applicable to this smaller group than to most adolescents.

Considerable cognitive development occurs during adolescence. Early adolescents become very self-conscious, which leads to a tendency to be more egocentric. They tend to believe that the thoughts and feelings that they have are unique. Furthermore, they do not seem to recognize that their peers are going through the same situation. In time, older teenagers become better able to empathize, to think abstractly, and to be introspective. They are able to consider possibilities and to imagine other realities. This leads them to become more philosophical, and to question the rules and realities of their lives in an attempt to gain a clearer understanding of the world. These cognitive abilities lead them to question their identity and to see themselves as individuals with some control over who and what they will be.

These changes become manifest in the adolescents' social environment. In particular, the family becomes less influential, while peer groups become more so.

Adolescents begin to establish and exercise independence from parental controls. They learn to negotiate, although some conflicts arise. They spend more time with their friends than they did in childhood. They often imitate influential peers and adults. They "try on different hats" to see what they might look like in order to establish an identity of their own. However, although they may dress like their friends or listen to music that their parents abhor, they often retain similar values and beliefs as their parents.

Adolescents tend to get better at coping with stress as they get older. They learn skills over time, utilizing their individual temperament and modeling parental coping strategies. Early in adolescence, teens tend to reactive defensively, denying problems and thinking wishfully. They misinterpret situations, making misattributions to others and overlooking information that would help them to see things more clearly. They also tend to either under- or overestimate both potential risks and their ability to handle them.

They may vent their frustration or anxiety in open emotional outbursts or they may withdraw and try to keep their feelings hidden. They seek solace and support from others, but do not readily ask for or listen to advice. As they develop, they become better able to appraise problems themselves. They try to change the stressful situation and to negotiate solutions. They learn that communication skills, the art of compromise, and assertiveness are more effective responses than are emotional outbursts or withdrawal. They learn how much of their feelings they need to reveal and become more adept at managing their emotions. They also become better at reading social cues and reacting appropriately. They think about ways to deal with problems and discuss potential solutions with others. Successful responses to stress lead to more success, although at times they may revert to previous, less effective strategies, usually in an impulsive fashion. Most adolescents develop the skills necessary to cope with stress effectively, although some do not.

III. COMMON STRESSORS

Adolescents face a variety of challenges as a normal part of their lives. These include the physical and sexual changes associated with puberty; the demands of school; the desire to initiate and maintain friendships, both platonic and romantic; the need to start working and to make a career choice; and the gradual development of independence from the family. All of these changes can be stressful, but most teenagers report that they do not feel overwhelmed or unable to deal with them. Regardless of gender, socioeconomic status, or race, teens identify their most important concerns as career, school performance, and college plans. Many worry about violence, theft, and work. Some report concerns about peer conflicts and parental expectations. Teens are least worried about drugs and alcohol. Boys are more concerned about sexuality and extracurricular activities, while girls are more concerned about their appearance.

A. Puberty

Puberty, as the starting point for adolescence, is often thought of as very stressful. The physical changes are obvious, as is increased sexual interest. Parents and teachers often attribute all behavioral changes to "raging hormones," but the fact is that there are other social, and psychological factors that must be considered as well. Nevertheless, there is a biological effect of puberty on cognitive, social, and emotional development as well. In particular, the timing of puberty can be stressful and does seem to have an impact on academic and psychosocial functioning. Boys appear to benefit academically and socially if they reach puberty early, although they often end up having a shorter stature than their later-developing peers. Early in adolescence, girls seem to have a better body image and are more popular if they develop early. However, as a group, they do not seem to do as well academically. Furthermore, by the time adolescence ends, later developing girls have a better body image than girls who reached puberty earlier do.

This may be related to the fact that girls with a later onset of puberty are more slender, which more closely fits with current cultural standards of attractiveness. More importantly, girls who reach puberty later have had a longer time to anticipate and adapt to these changes and as a result seem better able to cognitively process and cope with pubertal changes when they do occur. Finally, puberty may be most stressful when it is very early or very late, as this leads the adolescent to be markedly different from other peers. This information coincides with Offer's reports that most adolescents are comfortable with, and not distressed by, the changes of puberty, as most adolescents will enter puberty at about the same time as their peers and experience it as a normative process.

B. Peer Relationships

Peer relationships take on much more importance during adolescence. Teenagers expand their social relationships, looking to increase their connections with others. Girls in general seem to develop a capacity for intimacy sooner than boys do. Most teenagers believe they can make friends easily and that they can tell their friends intimate details about themselves. Early adolescents are very interested in being popular and want to fit in with a popular same-sex peer group. There is a degree of stress associated with this, especially if a young teenager wants to belong to a group, yet does not. Most are able to find a group, however, and do not find establishing friendships difficult. These peer groups are often very supportive and discourage deviant behavior.

In middle adolescence, boys and girls begin to mix. Romance and dating become extremely important. Once again, teenagers report some stress during this phase, as they grapple with the new social skills required to establish romantic relationships. However, most report that they believe they are interesting to members of the opposite sex and believe that they are capable of finding a romantic partner.

Dating usually begins between the ages of 12 and 16. Adolescents may face some peer pressure to date and may be dropped from a particular group if they do not do so. Similarly, they may feel pressure to engage in a similar level of sexual activity as their peers. The pressure to conform to a perceived peer norm, which is in conflict with cultural, religious, family, or individual values, seems to be the most stressful aspect of romantic relationships. There are many similarities between adult and adolescent love relationships.

However, adolescent relationships are notably more transient, with strong feelings that do not usually lead to enduring intimacy or self-disclosure. Cognitive development as adolescence progresses helps teenagers to better cope with relationship changes. Gay adolescents are especially vulnerable to stress, due to feelings of isolation from peers and family and to difficulty integrating homosexuality into their identity.

Parents of teenagers frequently describe family life as stressful, due to the ongoing development of adolescent independence. This reflects a change in family roles, which parents may perceive as more difficult than adolescents do. Early adolescence is marked by considerable variation in roles, as the adolescent vacillates between asserting independence and maintaining dependency. There is some anxiety associated with becoming independent, felt by both parent and child. As they become older, most teenagers are confident about their ability to make decisions and try to demonstrate this to their parents. However, although they are in the process of individuating, they do not sever their emotional attachments to their parents, nor do they become free of their parents' influences. Adolescents appear to be less distressed when parents utilize an authoritative parenting style which encourages and supports independence. Parents provide limits and controls with explanations, while allowing the adolescent to express their views. Nevertheless, tensions are still present as negotiations proceed and opposing needs are balanced.

C. Race and Culture

Racial and cultural issues pose interesting challenges, particularly for the adolescent. A child forms both gender and ethnic identities around the ages of 3–5. Children become familiar with cultural differences and history long before puberty begins. However, it is in adolescence that teenagers make a conscious commitment to be a member of their culture. They will generally embrace the values of their culture, which may not be the same as the dominant culture. This may lead to stress, especially if they have frequent interactions with peers of other cultures. They also can understand the abstract concepts of racism and inequality. They may be more likely to experience these as they leave their family and have more contact with peers and adults from other walks of life. Nonwhite adolescents are twice as likely as their white peers to be funneled into the juvenile justice system rather than the mental health system when they have a problem with the law. They are also more likely to identify their main stressors as environmental ones (such as living in a dangerous neighborhood) rather than more personal ones. Most teens come to terms with their ethnic identity and with negative stereotypes and prejudices. They are able to accept themselves and their place within both society and their own ethnic culture. Those that do not do so have more difficulty with self-image and psychological adjustment. Adolescents who immigrate to a new country face additional stress, as they become more dependent on their families at a time when they are trying to develop independence. If they do push to be more independent, they may be more likely to join an inappropriate peer group.

D. Academics and School

School situations and academic demands are yet other common stressors that teenagers confront. The transition to middle school and the transition to high school are both major life events. Most teenagers report a combination of eagerness and apprehension as they move up to a bigger school with more challenging assignments, more complicated schedules, and more competent upperclassmen. Middle schools represent a challenge as they are more impersonal and may require independence than early adolescents are capable of. Most middle school students have not mastered the social skills needed for this setting, although they may learn them quickly if provided with opportunities to succeed in small groups.

High schools offer more extracurricular activities, which provide opportunities to join in new peer groups, but the many choices may be overwhelming and confusing, and some adolescents may end up feeling excluded. Grades become more meaningful, especially for those planning on college. Parental expectations, SAT scores, and college applications create tension, as does the search for a job after graduation.

E. Work

Most teenagers express a desire to work and feel satisfaction in a job well done. Earning money helps older adolescents become more independent and enables them to practice some of the skills they will need as adults. However, trying to balance a part-time job with school demands, sports, and social activities is often difficult. Adolescents who work are less invested in school, spending less time on homework and missing classes more often than peers who do not work. They usually work in low-paying jobs and have little authority or opportunity to advance. Those who work the most hours tend to have the lowest grades. However, part-time work has also been associated with better self-esteem and a sense of responsibility in adolescents. Teenagers cope with the stress of work best if they can balance the time they work with their other priorities. Working raises other issues, as adolescents may be overwhelmed with the choices they have.

Establishing a life goal is a daunting task for adolescents. Many are reluctant to commit to a specific career path, as this means eliminating other possibilities. This lack of commitment may be interpreted as a lack of motivation by parents, leading to conflicts. Adolescents also have many misconceptions and cognitive distortions about themselves and the careers they are considering. Accurate information and a frank discussion of their strengths and weaknesses are important. The support of a mentoring adult is often very helpful, as is providing the perspective that any choice is not etched in stone. This issue is also one that tends to extend adolescence most often, as it is commonly the last one resolved.

IV. UNUSUAL STRESSORS

Some teenagers face more unusual challenges. These can include family problems, such as mental or physical illness; drug or alcohol abuse; parental separation or divorce; social problems, such as poverty and violence; and individual problems, such as pregnancy, serious illness, and school failure. In some instances, teens may experience traumas such as abuse or the death of a loved one. Adolescents with adequate cognitive abilities, emotional development, and supportive families seem better able to cope with these problems successfully. Teenagers who have experienced multiple stressors, have a previous history of psychopathology, or have little parental support are much more vulnerable.

A. Parent with Medical/Psychiatric Illness

Adolescents who are raised in homes where a parent has a serious medical or psychiatric illness have the ability to understand the illness better than younger children and may have more questions as a result. They are also more likely to exhibit anger and acting out behaviors. This may occur because of the conflict involved between the family's needs for help from the adolescent and the adolescent's needs to become more independent. Younger children may be more likely to avoid discussion of the parent's illness and to experience intrusive thoughts and feelings, while adolescents are more likely to exhibit symptoms of anxiety and depression. This is particularly true of teenage girls whose mothers have cancer. Parental coping skills play a part in how adolescents respond to parental illness. Parents who are less anxious and depressed have a positive effect on their children. There are some important differences to be considered when a family member has a severe mental illness as opposed to a physical illness. Parents with mental illness are much less likely to be in treatment, which means that professional education and advice are much less forthcoming. There is considerable stigma associated with mental illnesses (although some physical illnesses carry a stigma, such as HIV infection). Adolescents may therefore be much less likely to seek peer or adult support as a result. Teenagers are at a higher risk for depression and other mood disorders when their parents have a chronic mental illness, but studies have not been able to separate genetic influences from psychosocial effects on children and adolescents. Finally, parental conflicts, divorce, and inconsistent parenting practices often are present in families where a parent has a severe mental illness. These multiple risk factors compound the stress on an adolescent, more so than in families where a parent has a severe physical illness. Adolescents who cope best when parents have a serious medical or psychiatric illness share several characteristics. They tend to be actively involved in school, church, work, and other outside activities. They have a close relationship with a supportive adult. They also understand that they are not responsible for their parents' illness. Their families are more cohesive, flexible, and are able to maintain family rituals. Finally, their families effectively communicate information and feelings about the parental illness and are able to make plans for the future.

B. Parental Alcohol Abuse

The effects of parental alcohol abuse have also been studied, although more attention has been paid to younger children in alcoholic families. Adolescents raised in alcoholic families have been found to have a higher risk of conduct disorder, substance abuse, sexual acting-out, physical and sexual abuse, and academic problems. They also have more difficulties in their peer relationships and are more likely to have romantic relationships with adolescents with substance abuse problems themselves. Some adolescents may take on a more adult role within the family in an attempt to maintain family functioning, while others may disengage. Boys seem to have a higher risk of problems than girls do. Teenagers who cope effectively with parental alcoholism tend to have healthy and supportive relationships with adults outside of the family. Families that are able to maintain family rituals (such as holiday celebrations, family dinners, and church attendance, for example) have teenagers that are more resilient in the face of parental substance abuse.

Adolescents with an easy temperament, at least average intelligence, and an internal locus of control are also more resilient. Not all teenagers from alcoholic homes require treatment, although parents with alcoholism should be referred for treatment. However, it is not clear what effect, if any, parental recovery has on adolescents who are already exhibiting problems. Alateen, a self-help program for adolescents from alcoholic families, has been effective in providing information and improving mood and self-esteem for teenagers. Group, individual, and family therapy have been helpful. All interventions should provide education regarding the adolescent's increased risk of substance abuse in an attempt at prevention.

C. Parental Marital Conflict and Divorce

Parental conflict and divorce is a fairly common, but nonetheless major, stressor in today's culture. Most research on separation and divorce has focused on younger children. Studies with adolescents suggest that they too may have difficulty adjusting to this stressor. In addition, children who experience divorce may not manifest problems until adolescence. It is important to remember that most children and adolescents do adapt to divorce and are able to function effectively as adults. Younger adolescents whose parents divorce are more likely to be noncompliant and aggressive and to have problems with substance abuse than are adolescents in nondivorced families. Gender differences have been reported. Adolescent girls from divorced families have had more problems with self-esteem and promiscuity, while adolescent boys have a higher incidence of substance abuse. Both boys and girls have lower academic achievement, but teenage boys are also likely to drop out of school if their parents have divorced and they are living with their mother. Girls are at a greater risk of dropping out if they live with their remarried mother and stepfather. These findings appear to hold even when factors such as race and socioeconomic status are controlled for. Conflict between divorced mothers and their adolescent daughters is common, possibly connected to the teenage girls' tendency to increased sexual acting out. Adolescent boys have a higher risk of disengaging from their family and to engage in delinquent behavior with peers. This may be related to the absence and lack of influence of the noncustodial father, which is all too common in divorce. Many factors mediate adolescents' responses to divorce. An authoritative custodial parent seems to be the most important factor, as the parent is able to provide the understanding and support needed while maintaining an authority position in the family. Generally, teenagers are better able to cognitively process and understand the reasons for parental divorce than younger children are. However, those who have limited insight, poor problem solving skills, and a history of temperamental difficulty are more vulnerable to experiencing problems with the divorce. The degree of conflict between parents and the amount of contact with each parent are also important. Depression and delinquency have been connected to prolonged parental conflict.

D. Poverty and Violence

Sociocultural stressors such as poverty and violence have long been recognized as stressful for children and adolescents. However, it is very difficult to disentangle the specific effects these stressors have from each other as well as from other associated risk factors, such as parenting styles and other environmental stressors. Approximately 20% of American children live in poverty—the highest rate for any Western industrialized country. Black children are twice as likely to experience poverty as white children are. Length of time spent in poverty varies, although around 90% of poor children spend less than 5 years in poverty. Contrary to popular belief, poverty is more common in rural rather than urban areas.

Adolescents who experience poverty have a higher rate of delinquency, depression, and poor self-image. They may also incorporate the idea of poverty into their identity rather than to see it as a temporary external condition. Again, parental responses and styles have a marked effect on adolescent coping strategies. Families living in poverty are more likely to utilize inconsistent, punitive, and authoritarian parenting styles, which leads to increased stress and conflict. In contrast, poor but supportive parents, who have a positive outlook on the future, have less distressed teenagers. Teenagers are also able to recognize when they live in less desirable neighborhoods and are well aware of the risks of violence. Living with this chronic stress is difficult and can have a marked effect on their outlook on the future. They may be more fatalistic and experience more Posttraumatic Stress Disorder (PTSD) symptoms as a result of their exposure to violence. Anecdotes abound, both describing those who have problems and those who have been resilient. However, at this time there are no systematic studies that have assessed these issues.

E. Pregnancy

Some teens face significant individual stressors, such as pregnancy, serious illness, or school failure. These teens already tend to be at a higher risk for other stressors, as outlined above. However, considerable study has been given to these issues. Teenage girls who get pregnant are less prepared than their adult counterparts to raise children. They know less about infants and are more distressed by the pregnancy. 40 percent choose abortion, while 45% choose to keep their child. The other 15% either miscarry or choose adoption. Teenage mothers are less responsive to the needs of their babies than are adults. However, longitudinal studies have shown that a majority of teenage mothers complete high school and hold regular employment thereafter. Most support themselves and their children, although they are on welfare at times. They do not end up having more children than peers who have children later. Most importantly, the majority seems to cope effectively over the long run.

Teenage girls who ultimately choose abortion, on the other hand, report considerable psychological distress during the time of pregnancy. This seems to fade somewhat after the abortion. However, studies of women who have undergone abortion indicate that most negative reactions and distress occur in those who are young, unmarried, previously nulliparous, and who delay the procedure until the second trimester. Adolescents are much more likely to fit into this profile and so appear to be at a higher risk for psychological sequelae as a result of the abortion. The debate about the psychological effects of abortion is unresolved, as this particular group remains difficult to study due to the many other stressors that they face.

F. Serious Illness

It is estimated that 5–10% of teenagers face a serious illness during adolescence. Adolescents who suffer from serious illnesses struggle with a variety of issues. Early adolescents tend to try to deny the existence of their illness, using avoidant coping strategies. These problems are more likely to occur in families where there is little cohesiveness. This often leads to treatment noncompliance and more problems with the illness itself. Conversely, chronic or serious illnesses may impair normal adolescent development.

This seems to be due to the fact that the illness and treatment requirements make the adolescent more dependent on his parents. They in turn may be more unwilling to let the teenager be more independent. Adolescents may also incorporate their illness into their identity. In some situations, such as diabetes, these may be unavoidable due to the nature of the illness. For those who have cancer, however, this may be more problematic. Adolescents with a history of cancer are not more likely to be depressed, but they are more likely to have somatic complaints and preoccupations and to be distrusting of their bodies. They also tend to have greater difficulties in romantic relationships. Misattributions and misunderstandings about their illness and its prognosis should be addressed when present. Parents and adolescents often need much more education and support than they receive. Efforts should be made to help adolescents understand both their illness and treatment, and information should be made readily available to them. This should occur in a stepwise fashion, allowing teenagers some time to adjust to changes and react to them emotionally and intellectually.

G. Dropping Out of School

Approximately 10–15% of adolescents drop out of school. Often, they have parents or siblings who have done the same. Parental attitudes about education have a great impact on academic performance, even in adolescence. Adolescents whose home lives are already distressed or whose fathers are absent are much more likely to drop out. Those who have already failed a class or who have been held back a grade are at greater risk as well. Many are working, and many have children. Teenagers find dropping out is very stressful and would recommend against it. Job opportunities are limited and they are often unable to function independently. Successful prevention requires strong cooperation between parents and schools, providing the support and guidance necessary to vulnerable teens.

H. Trauma

Trauma often leads to emotional and behavioral changes. Most studies on trauma have looked at younger children, children and adolescents together, or at adolescents who were traumatized as children. However, adolescents can be abused physically, sexually, emotionally, or in combination. Due in part to their increasing independence and to their cognitive and emotional development, adolescents are less likely than are children to be abused by family members. However, they are more likely to be the victims of rape, assault, or robbery than younger children or adults. Catastrophic life events also may occur, including the death of a parent, sibling or peer due to illness, accident, or violence. Teenagers who have been abused may come to attention for incidents that have just recently occurred and been disclosed or may have occurred many years earlier. The length of time since the occurrence of abuse or trauma does not mitigate the severity of symptoms or the need for treatment. It is also not clear if abuse or trauma at an earlier or later age leads to more problems. Adolescents are less likely to be abused than are young children. However, many adolescent victims of abuse have been abused as children. Therefore, teenagers who present with physical or sexual abuse may have a lengthy history of abuse and may have more difficulty as a result.

1. Abuse

Teenagers who have been sexually abused are less likely to show unusual sexual behaviors or preoccupations than are young children. Abused teens also are more likely than children to disclose purposefully, usually out of anger toward the perpetrator. Adolescents are also more likely to have their reports substantiated. However, because they are older, victimized adolescents may be blamed, just as women who are victims of domestic violence are often blamed for not seeking help or leaving an abusive situation. In addition, adolescents who are physically abused may be seen as provoking a parent, thereby "earning" physical discipline. This is particularly true

in teenagers who have a history of physical aggression, threats, delinquent behavior, noncompliance, and/or defiance. The juvenile justice system is more likely to be involved in these situations and may be less cognizant of the possibility of abuse than either mental health or child protective services.

When evaluating adolescents who have been abused, it is important to be sensitive and to allow them some control over what, when and how much they disclose. Teenagers will often want to avoid talking about the issue and to minimize the effects it has had on them. Recognition and support for their attempts to cope with the abuse should be provided, in keeping with their psychological development, especially their need to be independent and successful. In addition, it may be helpful to separate the problem from their identity as a person. Chaffin *et al.* suggest a statement such as, "I've talked with a lot of people your age who have been through sexual abuse about the effects it has had on them. Everyone's different, but I want to find out if some of the things that have bothered some other people have bothered you. I'd also like to find out what sorts of things you have done that seem to help the most." It is also important to understand the adolescent's attributions about the abuse. As adolescents are more independent and society holds them more responsible for their actions, they may be more likely to blame themselves.

Furthermore, teens may want to maintain the idea that they have control over what happens to them, in keeping with their developmental stage. At the same time, adolescents will often fear disclosure to their peers, perhaps believing that they will be stigmatized or that their peers will hold them responsible.

Nevertheless, having the support and understanding of a peer is often very helpful. In assessing an adolescent who has been abused, it is important to obtain a complete history as well as to address possible PTSD symptoms. In addition, any problems with aggression, impulsivity, social skills, attention span, academic performance, depression, anxiety, substance abuse, and delinquency should be explored. Abused adolescents are also at a higher risk for eating disorders, sleep problems, and self-injurious behavior.

Treatment interventions should be individualized, but may include sexual education, information about PTSD symptoms and abuse, and, perhaps most importantly, an attempt to work out with the adolescent an explanation as to why the abuse happened. Group and individual therapies have both been utilized with success. Treatment interventions should address both the needs of parents and the adolescent. Social skills, problem-solving, and cognitive treatments have been effective with adolescents, but family interventions in particular seem to help maintain progress over the long term. Court-mandated treatment helps to keep abusive parents in treatment.

2. Death

Adolescents rarely experience the death of a parent, sibling, or of a close friend. Furthermore, studies of children who have lost a parent usually group younger children with adolescents. As a result, unique characteristics of adolescent bereavement are difficult to identify. Adolescents are able to conceptualize death abstractly. This allows them to consider religious and philosophical issues and may lead to more uncertainty than in younger children. Adolescents who have never experienced a death have a difficult time adjusting to this change. Adolescents who have experienced the death of a parent are at a higher risk for delinquency, anxiety and depressive symptoms, somatic complaints, and PTSD symptoms.

Teenage boys who lose a father are at a higher risk for behavioral and emotional problems as are early adolescents. Sudden deaths are clearly more difficult to cope with than deaths that occur after a protracted illness, as adolescents have a chance to prepare emotionally and intellectually for the event. However, a strong and supportive surviving parent can offer some protection. Once again, teens that can confide in an another adult (such as a relative, teacher, or neighbor) seem to cope better, as they are able to talk about their dead parent openly. It is important to remember that subsequent events, such as graduation, making a sports team, dating, or getting a job, may reopen grief feelings and should be considered as additional stressors. Nevertheless, the majority of adolescents appear to cope effectively with the death of a parent. The death of a peer is also a rare event. Studies in this area have been limited and have primarily focused on peers who commit suicide. In these instances, adolescents have exhibited depressive symptoms, but have not had an increase in suicide attempts.

See Also the Following Articles

Alcohol and Stress, Social and Psychological Aspects; Childhood Stress; Divorce, Children of; Economic Factors and Stress; Familial Patterns of Stress; School Stress and School Refusal Behavior

Bibliography

Chaffin, M. *et al.* (1996). Treating Abused Adolescents. In "The APSAC Handbook on Child Maltreatment" (J. Briere *et al.*, eds.). Sage, Thousand Oaks, CA.

Cobb, N. (1995). "Adolescence—Continuity, Conformity and Change," 2nd ed., Mayfield, Mountain View, CA.

Eth, S., Pynoos, R. (1985). "Developmental perspectives on psychic trauma in childhood." In "Trauma and Its Wake" (C. Figley, Ed.). Brunner/Mazel, New York.

Haggerty, R., *et al.* (1996), "Stress, Risk and Resilience in Children and Adolescents." Cambridge Univ. Press, Cambridge, England.

Lewis, M. (1997). "Child and Adolescent Psychiatry—A Comprehensive Textbook." Williams & Wilkins, Baltimore.

Noshpitz, J. *et al.* (1997). "Handbook of Child and Adolescent Psychiatry," Vol. 3 and 4. Wiley, New York.

Offer, D. *et al.*, (1990). "Normality and Adolescence. In "The Psychiatric Clinics of North America: Adolescence: Psychopathology, Normality and Creativity" (A. Rothenburg, Ed.). W. B. Saunders, Philadelphia, PA.

Youngblade, L., and Belsky, J.(1990). "Social and emotional consequences of child maltreatment." In "Children at Risk." (R. Ammerman and M. Hersen, eds.). Plenum, New York.

Adrenal Cortex

G. P. Vinson

*St. Bartholomew's and Royal London
School of Medicine and Dentistry, Queen
Mary and Westfield College*

B. J. Whitehouse

King's College

J. P. Hinson

*St. Bartholomew's and Royal London
School of Medicine and Dentistry, Queen
Mary and Westfield College*

GLOSSARY

aldosterone The principal mineralocorticoid secreted by the adrenal cortex.

angiotensin II An octapeptide that provides the major hormonal support of the growth and function of the zona glomerulosa of the adrenal cortex and of aldosterone secretion.

cortex The outer, steroid-forming part of the adrenal gland.

corticosteroids The collective name for the steroid hormones (glucocorticoid and mineralocorticoid) that are secreted by the adrenal cortex.

corticosteroid binding globulin (CBG) The carrier protein to which cortisol binds in the circulation.

corticotrophin (corticotropin, adrenocorticotropic hormone, ACTH) The pituitary hormone that largely controls growth and activity of the adrenal cortex, particularly the zona fasciculata and cortisol secretion.

cortisol The principal glucocorticoid secreted by the adrenal cortex.

cytochrome-P450 A family of enzymes associated with the synthesis of steroid hormones that utilize molecular oxygen to form hydroxyl groups on the steroid molecule.

dehydroepiandrosterone (DHEA, or DHA) By amount the major androgen-like hormone secreted by the adrenal cortex.

DHEAS DHA-sulfate.

glucocorticoids Steroid hormones (especially cortisol) from the zona fasciculata of the adrenal cortex that affect carbohydrate metabolism.

medulla The inner, catecholamine (adrenaline)-secreting core of the adrenal gland.

mineralocorticoids Steroid hormones (especially aldosterone) from the zona glomerulosa of the adrenal cortex that affect mineral (especially sodium/potassium) homeostasis.

renin-angiotensin system (RAS) The blood-borne complement of enzymes and substrates that gives rise to angiotensin II.

zona fasciculata The middle part of the adrenal cortex, secreting glucocorticoids, especially cortisol.

zona glomerulosa The outer, mineralocorticoid (especially aldosterone)-secreting part of the adrenal cortex.

zona reticularis The inner part of the adrenal cortex, secreting both glucocorticoids and androgens, but also containing apoptotic (dying) cells.

The adrenal cortex is the outer part of the adrenal gland, which consists of three types of cell arranged in zones called the zona glomerulosa, the zona fasciculata, and the zona reticularis. The cortex is responsible for secreting steroid hormones of the type classified generally as corticosteroids. These are C_{21} steroids which belong to two classes based on their biological activity. Mineralocorticoids are those whose primary action is to regulate sodium and potassium homeostasis. By far the most important is aldosterone, which is produced by the zona glomerulosa, and its secretion is regulated by a number of factors including angiotensin II. The glucocorticoids, of which the most important in humans is cortisol (hydrocortisone), are produced by the fasciculata/reticularis zones. They play a vital protective role in stress through wide-ranging actions on the cardiovascular, nervous, inflammatory, and immune systems and protein and carbohydrate metabolism. Secretion of cortisol is regulated by corticotropin (ACTH), secreted by the anterior pituitary gland. Other steroids are also formed, including dehydroepiandrosterone (DHEA) and androstenedione.

I. STRUCTURE OF THE ADRENAL CORTEX

The adrenals are paired glands lying close to the anterior part of the kidney. Their combined wet weight is about 0.01–0.02% of the total body-weight, and thus they weigh about 8 g in the adult human in both males and females.

A. Morphology

The gland has two main parts, the medulla at the center and the cortex surrounding it. These two parts have different developmental origins; the medulla forms part of the sympathetic nervous system, whereas the cortex, like the gonads, has a distinct embryological origin in the germinal ridge. The medulla and cortex also have different functions, though both are associated with the response to stress. Their functional differences lie both in the nature of the hormones they produce—catecholamines such as adrenaline and noradrenaline from the medulla and steroids from the cortex—and the ways in which these secretions are controlled—by neural stimulation in the case of the medulla, but by other hormones circulating in the blood in the case of the cortex.

Histologically, the cells of the adrenal cortex are arranged as three major layers, or zones, organized as concentric shells. The cells of the different zones are generally distinguished by their shape and size and by their ultrastructure as well as by their arrangement and position within the gland. The three zones are called the *zona glomerulosa,* the *zona fasciculata,* and the *zona reticularis.* Broadly, the zona glomerulosa lies just below the connective tissue capsule and consists of whorl-like arrangements of cells. Cells of the zona fasciculata are arranged as a series of cords running centripetally, which extend to the less clearly organized network of cells of the zona reticularis (see Figs. 1 and 2).

Other zones are recognized in different species, although these are usually smaller and may be transient. In humans, the most prominent of these is the fetal cortex (see below). The cells of the cortex are renewed from a region just below the glomerulosa; this may be the role of the cells of the zona intermedia, which has been described as a small band of cells in some species. The cells migrate centripetally over a period of time, and as they do so, they acquire the functional and morphological characteristics of the cells of the zones that they pass through.

FIGURE 1   General structure of the mammalian cortex showing the positions of the zona glomerulosa (zg), zona fasciculata (zf), and zona reticularis (zr) and their relationship to the capsule (c), nerve cells (n), arteriolar supply (a), medullary arteries (ma), sinuses (s), medulla (m), and isolated islets (i) of chromaffin (medullary) cells lying in the inner cortex. Drawing by Bridget Landon. Figure reproduced (with permission) from G. P. Vinson, J. P. Hinson, and I. E. Toth. (1994). The neuroendocrinology of the adrenal cortex. *J. Neuroendocr.* **6,** pp. 235–246, Blackwells, Oxford.

In humans, the zona glomerulosa seldom occupies more than 5% of the total cortical volume and its cells are gathered into more or less isolated islets. The cells are relatively small and round, with a high nuclear-to-cytoplasmic ratio. Ultrastructurally, the mitochondria of zona glomerulosa cells are characterized by their lamelliform or shelf-like cristae. The smooth endoplasmic reticulum is sparse: ribosomes and polysomes are visible throughout the cytoplasm.

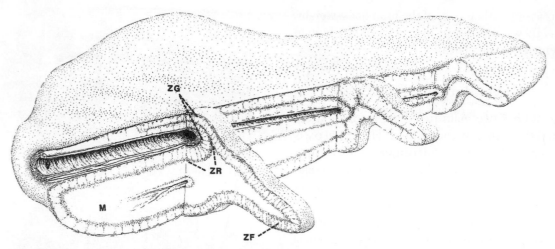

FIGURE 2 General structure of the human adrenal gland. Arrangement of adrenal cortex in the region of the cortical cuff. Notice the folding results in a doubling of the cortical thickness and the juxtaposition here of the inner zona glomerulosa and the central vein in cortical cuff region. C = cortex; M = medulla; ZG = zona glomerulosa; ZF = zona fasciculata; ZR = zona reticularis; V = central vein. Drawing by B. Landon. Figure reproduced with permission from "The Adrenal Gland" (V. H. T. James, Ed.), Raven Press, 1992.

The zona fasciculata cells are larger, with abundant cytoplasm, and the mitochondria contain tubulovesicular cristae, although these may vary between the outer and inner parts of the zone. In conventional stains, these cells are lighter in appearance than zona reticularis cells and hence have been termed *clear cells* as opposed to the *compact cells* of the zona reticularis, which stain more deeply.

The zona reticularis occupies one-third of the cortex, and its cells are intermediate in size between those of the zona glomerulosa and zona fasciculata. The mitochondria of zona reticularis cells are elongated with tubulovesicular cristae; microbodies (lipofuchsin granules) and lipid droplets also occur.

In humans the adrenal is prominent in fetal life, when it reaches a maximum of about 0.3% of body weight. This declines slightly in the third trimester and precipitously in the neonate. The large size of the gland is attributable to the presence of an additional zone—the fetal zone—which lies between the definitive cortex and the medulla. The cells of the fetal zone are larger than those of other zones and stain only palely in conventional histology. In the fetus, the cells of the definitive cortex contain lamelliform cristae (like the zona glomerulosa of the adult gland),

whereas the mitochondria of the fetal zone cells are tubulovesicular. Studies on the origin and ultimate fate of the cells of the fetal zone are inconclusive. Some have held that the fetal zone cells arise from a second discrete proliferation, although this has been contested, and they may arise, like the reticularis, from the outer zones. Similarly, there are two explanations for its disappearance after birth; one that the zone involutes, the other that it is transformed into elements of the definitive cortex.

B. Circulation and Innervation

The intraglandular circulatory system deserves some attention, particularly because of its responses during stimulation. The adrenal is one of the most highly vascularized organs within the body, and detailed studies have shown that virtually every cell borders the thin and attenuated endothelial cells which line the vascular space (see Fig. 1). The general pattern in mammals is as follows: a variable number of arteries supply the gland which divide in the capsular or subcapsular region to form an arteriolar plexus. Two types of vessels arise from this plexus; first, there are the thinly walled capillaries, frequently called sinuses, which run centripetally through the cortex. These are the most abundant of the cortical vessels and may be assumed to supply all of the cortical cells. Second, there are the much more sparsely distributed medullary arteries, with thicker walls, which run through the cortex to supply the medulla directly. It is likely that blood from the cortical sinuses and the medullary arteries mixes in the medulla, and, on the basis of the relative abundance of the vessels, it is reasonable to assume that the medulla receives most of its supply from the sinuses. Accordingly the cortex exerts an endocrine control over the medulla, and, in particular, glucocorticoids (see below) are required for the development in the medulla of a key enzyme required for the synthesis of adrenaline. It is in the medulla that the sinuses are drained into the single common vein for the whole gland (see Fig. 1). In the human gland there are also arteriovenous loops in which blood is apparently carried from the subcapsular arterioles in vessels which sweep down through the zona glomerulosa and the zona fasciculata, then loop back to the exterior of the gland to sites close to their origins. Also, as the vein leaves the gland, a portion of the cortex is introverted from the exterior to surround the vessel as the "cortical cuff" (Fig. 2).

Most early studies reported that nerve fibers which entered the gland passed straight to the medulla without branching and with no evidence of nerve endings. In fact much evidence now shows that nerve fibers reach the cortex, arising partly from the medulla, but also partly through direct innervation. In general, neural arborization is most dense in the capsular and subcapsular regions and nerves may contact both adrenocortical cells and blood vessels. Both catecholaminergic and peptidergic fibers have been identified.

II. HORMONES OF THE ADRENAL CORTEX

The hormones of the adrenal cortex are steroids: compounds that contain the *perhydrocyclopentanophenanthrene* structure consisting of four linked rings, three of six carbon atoms and one of five. There are four major groups of these compounds, classified according to the number of carbon atoms they contain.

1. C_{27} compounds. These are the sterols, including cholesterol.
2. C_{21} steroids. These include progesterone, the hormone of pregnancy and of female cyclic reproductive function, as well as the compounds produced more or less exclusively by the adrenal cortex. The adrenal C_{21} steroids, collectively termed corticosteroids, are of two major types according to their activities, the mineralocorticoids and the glucocorticoids. The activity of the mineralocorticoids is primarily concerned with the regulation of sodium and potassium homeostasis. The most potent mineralocorticoid in all mammals is aldosterone, although other corticosteroids possess some mineralocorticoid activity. The glucocorticoids were originally defined on the basis of their actions on carbohydrate metabolism but are known to have a wide variety of functions (see below). In humans and many other species (including canine, ovine, bovine) cortisol (hydrocortisone) is the most prominent secreted glucocorticoid, and smaller amounts of cortisone and corticosterone are also produced. In the rat and some other rodents (and in many nonmammalian vertebrates), adrenal 17α-hydroxylase activity (see below) is weak, and corticosterone is the major secreted adrenocortical product.
3. C_{19} steroids. These include the androgens, which support male structure and reproductive function. Of these, testosterone is the most potent but is normally produced in only small amounts by the adrenal. However, androstenedione, dehydroepiandrosterone (DHEA), and its sulfate (DHEAS) are prominent adrenal secretory products which may be converted to testosterone peripherally.
4. C_{18} steroids. These include the estrogens, female sex hormones, which are not usually secreted by the adrenal. However, androstenedione and DHEA(S) from the adrenal may be converted to estrogens elsewhere and this is the major source of circulating estrogen in postmenopausal women. In the fetus, DHEAS from the fetal adrenal is converted first to 16α-hydroxy-DHEAS and then to estriol sulfate by placental enzymes.

The circulating concentrations of the major adrenal steroids are shown in Table I.

A. Biosynthesis of the Corticosteroids

Although their biological activities may be very different (see below), the close structural similarities of the corticosteroids reflect their biosynthetic relationship. Several groups of enzymes are involved in their synthesis within the adrenal cortex, and these are summarized in Fig. 3 and in Table II.

Steroid hormones are formed from cholesterol. Cholesterol may be formed *de novo* from acetate in the adrenal or it may be imported into the gland from circulating low-density lipoprotein (LDL) through a process of receptor-mediated endocytosis. Cholesterol is stored as esters in the lipid droplets within the adrenocortical cell.

The rate-limiting step in these sequences is thought to be (1) the delivery of cholesterol to the inner mitochondrial membrane and CYP11A. Current evidence suggests that this is primarily facilitated by a specific protein, designated the steroidogenic acute regulatory, or StAR, protein. (2) Much evidence suggests that a second "late pathway" rate-limiting step lies between 18-hydroxydeoxycorticosterone or corticosterone and aldosterone.

TABLE I
Examples of Plasma Concentrations of Adrenal Hormones in Normal Subjects[a]

Steroid	Concentration
Aldosterone (pmol liter^{-1})	100–400
Androstenedione (nmol liter^{-1})	
Adults	2–13
Children	<2
Cortisol (nmol liter^{-1})	
07.00–09.00 h	280–720
21.00–24.00 h	60–340
Dehydroepiandrosterone sulfate (μmol liter^{-1})	
Adults	2–11
Children	<2

[a] Values may show considerable variation as all adrenal steroids show a diurnal rhythm, and steroid secretion may also be affected by age, nutritional status, and stage of the menstrual cycle.

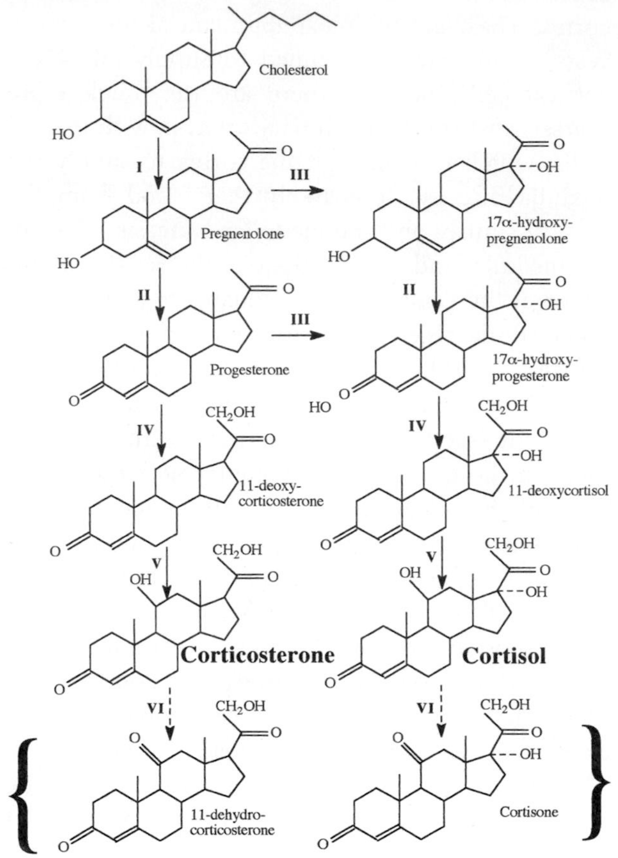

FIGURE 3   Pathways for biosynthesis of (a) glucocorticoids, (b) aldosterone, and (c) androgens and estrogens. The formation of aldosterone from 11-deoxycorticosterone is catalyzed by a single enzyme, CYP11B2 (aldosterone synthase). This may include the formation of other intermediates, corticosterone and/or 18-hydroxydeoxycorticosterone, that are not shown. Cortisol and, to a lesser extent, corticosterone are the major end-products of the glucocorticoid pathway, though cortisone and 11-dehydrocorticosterone (which are biologically inactive) may also be secreted. All of the dehydrogenase-catalyzed reactions may be reversible, however, i.e., cortisol may be formed from cortisone and androstenedione from testosterone.

However, since CYP11B2 (aldosterone synthase) can catalyze all of the steps between deoxycorticosterone and aldosterone, this could only be achieved by the regulation of the supply of the alternative precursors.

Inborn errors of steroid metabolism exist which may result from congenital defects in the enzymes involved in steroid biosynthesis. A feature of all of

b

c

FIGURE 3   *continued*

TABLE II

Enzymes Involved in Steroid Biosynthesis

Number[a]	Type	Systematic designation	Other names	Activity
I	Cytochrome-P450	CYP11A	P-450$_{SCC}$	Cholesterol side-chain cleavage
II	Dehydrogenase	3β-Hydroxysteroid-dehydrogenase, iso-merase		Conversion pregnenolone to progesterone
III	Cytochrome-P450	CYP17	P450$_{17\alpha}$, 17-hydroxylase, 17-lyase	Hydroxylation at C-17, 20 lyase (side-chain cleavage)
IV	Cytochrome-P450	CYP21	P450$_{21}$, 21-hydroxylase	Hydroxylation at C-21
V	Cytochrome-P450	CYP11B1	P450$_{11\beta/18}$, 11β-hydroxylase	Hydroxylation at C-11 (and C-18)
VI	Dehydrogenase	11β-hydroxysteroid-dehydrogenase		Conversion cortisol to cortisone
VII	Cytochrome-P450	CYP11B2	Aldosterone synthase	Conversion 11-deoxycorticosterone to al-dosterone (and 18-hydroxycortico-sterone)
VIII	Dehydrogenase	17-Hydroxysteroid dehydrogenase		Conversion androstenedione to testoster-one, estrone to estradiol and reverse
IX	Cytochrome-P450	CYP18	Aromatase	Conversion C-19 steroids (e.g., testoster-one, DHA) to estrogens

[a] See Fig. 3.

these is that the end-product of biosynthesis (for example, cortisol) is produced in inappropriately low amounts. Accompanying this may be the excessive production of the steroid intermediate that immediately precedes the enzyme block. For example, 21-hydroxylase deficiency, the most common form, results in excessive secretion of 17α-hydroxyprogesterone (cf. Fig. 3). This has little intrinsic biological activity, though it can be converted to androgens, resulting in virilization and hirsutism. Another defect, of 11β-hydroxylase, may result in the secretion of large amounts of 11-deoxycorticosterone, which can have profound mineralocorticoid effects, with excessive sodium retention resulting in hypertension. The lack of cortisol in these patients results in enhanced secretion of ACTH, leading both to the excessive secretion of steroid intermediates and also to the growth (hyperplasia) of the gland—hence the general term *congenital adrenal hyperplasia* or CAH. These fortunately rare conditions can usually be treated by administration of cortisol.

Knowledge of the mechanisms for corticosteroid biosynthesis have led to the development of numerous and more or less specific inhibitors of adrenal steroidogenesis. These are listed in Table III.

B. Transport and Metabolism of Corticosteroids

Under normal conditions around 90% of the circulating cortisol is bound to a specific plasma binding protein, called corticosteroid binding globulin (CBG). There is no comparable plasma binding pro-

tein for aldosterone, which may be loosely bound to plasma albumin. It is generally thought that only the unbound steroid fraction is biologically active. This view has, however, been questioned, but the conditions required for bioactivity of the bound fraction remain unclear.

The liver is the major site for corticosteroid metabolism, and in humans metabolites are generally excreted in the urine rather than by the biliary/fecal route, which predominates in some other species. The main reactions involved are reduction of ring A, hydroxylation, and conjugation as sulfates or glucuronides.

III. CONTROL OF ADRENOCORTICAL SECRETION

A. Control of Cortisol Secretion

Cortisol (together with cortisone and corticosterone) is produced exclusively by the zona fasciculata and the zona reticularis of the adrenal cortex. Its secretion is almost entirely related to the degree of stimulation by circulating adrenocorticotropic hormone (ACTH), which is secreted by the anterior pituitary gland. In the absence of ACTH (e.g., after removal of the pituitary, or hypophysectomy), glucocorticoid levels in the blood fall to about 5% of normal values within 2 h, and this fall may be reversed by administration of ACTH. Under normal conditions, cortisol secretion has a clear diurnal rhythm, paralleling the pattern of ACTH secretion, with an early morning peak and an evening nadir. However, the secretion of ACTH is itself stimulated by all forms of stress, whatever the time of day.

Physiologically, the acute actions of ACTH are as follows: (1) to increase secretion of corticosteroids and (2) to increase blood flow through the gland. Chronically as well as maintaining elevated glucocorticoid levels, ACTH also brings about increased gland weight, which is attributable both to increases in adrenocortical cell number and size and to increased blood content of the gland. Adrenocorticotrophic hormone is also required to maintain steroid synthetic enzymes which decline after a few days in the hypophysectomized animal. Morphologically, the ef-

TABLE III
Inhibitors of Steroidogenesis in the Adrenal Cortex

Drug	Principle enzymic site of action (cf. Table II)
Aminoglutethimide	CYP11A, cholesterol side-chain cleavage
Metyrapone	CYP11B1, 11β-hydroxylase
Etomidate	CYP11B1, 11β-hydroxylase
Trilostane	3β-hydroxysteroid-dehydrogenase/isomerase
Ketoconazole	CYP17, 17α-hydroxylase

fects of hypophysectomy on adrenal weight are attributable to the degeneration of the zona fasciculata and zona reticularis, while the zona glomerulosa is comparatively unaffected. In the inner zones, cell numbers decline markedly (through *apoptosis*), and the remaining cells are shrunken because of major decreases in mitochondrial volume and smooth endoplasmic reticulum.

B. Control of Glomerulosa Function and Aldosterone Secretion

Physiologically, the most important stimuli for aldosterone secretion are altered electrolyte and fluid status (particularly sodium loss) or extracellular fluid volume reduction by hemorrhage, the use of diuretics, and postural changes: aldosterone levels are increased by upright posture. Restriction of dietary sodium intake causes hypertrophy of the zona glomerulosa and elevation of aldosterone secretion, with no concomitant effect on glucocorticoids.

The action of sodium depletion and other physiological stimulation of the zona glomerulosa is attributable to the actions of several stimulants which may act in concert. The renin–angiotensin system is especially important. This mechanism, which becomes more active when sodium intake is decreased (or sodium loss increased) or when blood volume decreases, has as its end-product the formation of a peptide hormone, called angiotensin II, which acts on zona glomerulosa cells to stimulate the secretion of aldosterone. Administered chronically, it can also reproduce the morphological changes in the zona glomerulosa which are associated with sodium depletion.

Other stimulants of aldosterone secretion include ACTH (though only transitorily) and potassium ions, whereas the atrial natriuretic peptides (ANP) cause a decrease in circulating aldosterone concentrations.

There are numerous other factors that stimulate aldosterone secretion and zona glomerulosa function under experimental conditions, although the physiological importance of their actions remains to be clarified. These include serotonin, catecholamines, acetylcholine, vasoactive intestinal peptide, vasopressin, oxytocin, other neuropeptides, and prostaglandin E. Other inhibitors include somatostatin and dopamine.

C. Control of Adrenal Androgen Secretion

Adrenal androgen secretion [androstenedione and DHEA(S)] rises throughout childhood, paralleling the increase in adrenal size, and peaks just before the onset of puberty in a period that has been termed adrenarche. Secretion of these hormones remains high until 40–50 years of age, when they begin to decline (the *adrenopause*). The mechanism for regulation of adrenal androgen secretion is not completely clear, and although ACTH is a potent stimulant, the secretion of cortisol and the adrenal androgens may be dissociated under some conditions, during adrenarche, for example, when adrenal androgen secretion rises while cortisol is unchanged.

IV. ACTIONS OF CORTICOSTEROIDS

Early in the study of adrenal physiology it was discovered that this gland is essential for life because of the actions of the adrenocortical hormonal products, not those of the medulla. Among the effects of loss of adrenocortical hormones are depletion of sodium ions from the body, decreased blood volume, hypotension, increased plasma potassium levels, muscular weakness, reduced cardiac contractility, and depletion of liver and muscle glycogen together with a generally impaired capacity to respond to physical stress. It was from these beginnings that it became clear that two types of corticosteroid activity were involved. Table IV shows the relative glucocor-

TABLE IV
Relative Glucocorticoid and Mineralocorticoid Activity of Corticosteroids

Steroid	Mineralocorticoid activity	Glucocorticoid activity
Aldosterone	1	0.15
Cortisol	0.001	1
Deoxycorticosterone	0.03	0.02
Corticosterone	0.004	0.4

ticoid and mineralocorticoid activity *in vivo* of some common steroids, and it can be seen that, in practice, few corticosteroids are completely specific in their effects. Thus cortisol, which normally shows about 1/1000th the mineralocorticoid activity of aldosterone *in vivo,* may have appreciable effects on electrolyte metabolism when plasma levels are elevated as in Cushing's syndrome.

Although the hormones were first classified on the basis of their physiological actions, they may also be differentiated on the basis of their binding affinity for tissue receptors. There are two main types of receptor: type I, originally detected in the kidney, was considered to be the mineralocorticoid receptor, and the more widely distributed type II receptor was thought to be responsible for glucocorticoid actions. More recently, with the cloning and characterization of the receptors, an unexpected finding has been that the recombinant mineralocorticoid (type I) receptor does not show the expected steroid specificity *in vitro* since it binds aldosterone and cortisol with equal affinity. As the levels of glucocorticoids in plasma may be up to 1000 times higher than those of aldosterone (Table I), this raises the problem of how a specific mineralocorticoid effect can be exerted in the intact animal. Currently, it is believed that the presence of 11β-hydroxysteroid dehydrogenase (cf. Table II) in mineralocorticoid target tissues explains this paradox. This enzyme converts glucocorticoids to their 11-keto derivatives (cortisone and 11-dehydrocorticosterone), which do not bind effectively to the receptor. In this way the receptor is protected, and cortisol and corticosterone do not cause sodium retention at normal physiological levels.

A. Mineralocorticoid Actions

The main actions of hormones which bind to type I (mineralocorticoid) receptors are to increase the reabsorption of sodium in the kidney and at other secretory epithelial sites, thus reducing the sodium content of urine, sweat, saliva, and so on. Effectively, sodium ions are exchanged for hydrogen and potassium ions, leading to decreased sodium and increased potassium excretion and increased urine acidity. With prolonged mineralocorticoid treatment, extracellular fluid volume expansion occurs, but after a few days the kidney escapes from the mineralocorticoid effect on sodium but not potassium excretion, and thus a major effect of prolonged mineralocorticoid exposure is that body potassium levels are reduced. Hypertension (high blood pressure) is a well-known consequence of excess corticosteroid secretion and is seen in conditions with elevated aldosterone secretion such as Conn's syndrome as well as in conditions of elevated cortisol secretion such as Cushing's syndrome. The mechanisms by which steroids increase blood pressure is not fully understood.

B. Glucocorticoid Actions

The effects of glucocorticoid receptor activation are varied and complex. Almost all tissues of the body have been found to contain type II receptors and a very large number of systems and processes are affected by these steroids. They are essential for the maintenance of cardiovascular and metabolic homeostasis, particularly during physically stressful conditions. In addition, they play a role in modulating inflammatory and immune responses and affect central nervous system function. In the perinatal period, glucocorticoids are particularly important in controlling lung development and maturation, which may present particular problems in premature infants who have not been sufficiently exposed to glucocorticoid.

The major metabolic effects of glucocorticoids are the stimulation of protein catabolism and hepatic glycogen synthesis. The actions essentially oppose those of insulin and are most evident in the unfed state. General inhibition of protein synthesis may be partly responsible for the inhibition of growth caused by corticosteroid administration to young subjects.

In general, glucorticoids exert powerful suppressive effects on the immune and inflammatory systems, and synthetic glucocorticoids are widely used to control the symptoms of many inflammatory and autoimmune diseases. These effects seem to be produced through the ability of the hormones and drugs to inhibit the production and actions of the cytokines that mediate the responses. Paradoxically, however, it has recently been recognized that endogenous corticosteroids may also augment some aspects of the immune response.

Corticosteroids can freely cross the blood–brain barrier and exert complex effects on behavior. Approximately 70% of patients with Cushings syndrome are reported to be depressed; in contrast, treatment with exogenous glucocorticoid is commonly associated with improved mental state.

C. Stress

The relationship between increased adrenocortical activity and stresses of many different types has been known since the 1930s, and levels of cortisol in plasma are frequently measured as an index of stress. However, the mechanisms through which glucocorticoids confer resistance to stress is still debated. There is general agreement that the actions of glucocorticoids in the cardiovascular system which increase vascular reactivity and improve cardiac performance are beneficial under acutely stressful conditions. However, in the past it was often considered that the suppressive effects of glucocorticoids on the inflammatory and immune systems could not be rationalized in the context of protection against stress. More recently it has been suggested that glucocorticoids, by virtue of their ability to suppress the response to infection and injury, may protect against the overreaction of these systems and the risk of excessive vasodilatation, edema, and other damaging effects. The corollary of this is that an inadequate adrenocortical response to stress may be harmful in that defence reactions will proceed unchecked. This may be true of some patients; for example, in active rheumatoid arthritis or, possibly, in chronic fatigue syndrome. In some senses, glucocorticoids appear to regulate defence mechanisms in two opposing ways. In their "permissive" mode (at levels found in the normal diurnal cycle) the hormones act to prime the body for normal activity, whereas the suppressive effects (at levels found during severe stress) prevent overreaction.

Chronic excess of glucocorticoids also has deleterious effects on the organism. This is most obvious in Cushings syndrome, the symptoms of which include depression, hypertension and cardiovascular disease, osteoporosis, immunosuppression, visceral obesity, insulin resistance, and metabolic abnormalities. It has also been argued that more subtle forms of exposure to increased levels of corticosteroids such as might be experienced in chronic psychosocial stress could increase susceptibility to infection and tumors and be associated with severe depression and aging-related memory impairment.

See Also the Following Articles

ADRENAL MEDULLA; ADRENOCORTICOTROPIC HORMONE (ACTH); ALDOSTERONE; ANDROGEN ACTION; ANGIOTENSIN; CORTICOSTEROIDS AND STRESS; CUSHING'S SYNDROME

Bibliography

Barnes, P. J., and Adcock, I. (1993). Anti-inflammatory actions of steroid: Molecular mechanisms. *Trends Physiol. Sci.* **14**, 438–441.

Belloni, A. S., Mazzochi, G., Mantero, F., and Nussdorfer, G. (1987). The human adrenal cortex—Ultrastructure and base-line morphometric data. *J. Submicrosp. Cytol.* **19**, 657–658.

Bravo, E. L. (1986). Aldosterone and other adrenal steroids. *In* "Handbook of Hypertension: Pathophysiology of Hypertension-Regulatory Mechanisms" (A. Zanchetti and R. C. Tarzi, Eds.), Vol. 8, pp. 603–625. Elsevier, Amsterdam.

Chrousos, G. P. (1995). The hypothalmic-pituitary-adrenal axis and immune-mediated inflammation. *N. Engl. J. Med.* **332**(20), 1351–1362.

Chrousos, G. P., and Gold, P. W. (1998). A healthy body in a healthy mind and vice versa—The damaging power of uncontrollable stress. *J. Clin. Endocrinol. Metab.* **83**, 1842–1845.

Clark, B. J., and Stocco, D. M. (1996). StAR—A tissue specific acute mediator of steroidogenesis. *Trends Endocr. Metab.* **7**, 227–233.

Flower, R. J., and Rothwell, N. J. (1994). Lipocortin-1: Cellular mechanisms and clinical relevance. *Trends Physiol. Sci.* **15**, 71–76.

Funder, J. (1990). Target tissue specificity of mineralocorticoids. *Trends Endocrinol. Metab.* **1**, 145–148.

Gaillard, R. C., and Al-Damluji, S. (1987). Stress and the pituitary–adrenal axis. *Bailliers Clin. Endocrinol. Metab.* **1**(2), 319–354.

McEwen, B. S. (1998). Protective and damaging effects of stress mediators. *N. Engl. J. Med.* **338**(3), 171–179.

Miller, W. L., and Tyrell, J. B. (1994). The adrenal cortex. *In* "Endocrinology and Metabolism" (P. Felig, J. D. Baxter, and L. A. Frohman, Eds.), 3rd ed. McGraw–Hill, New York.

Munck, A., and Naray-Fejes-Toth, A. (1992). The ups and downs of glucocorticoid physiology. Permissive and suppressive effects revisited. *Mol. Cell. Endocrinol.* 90, C1–C4.

Munck, A., Guyre, A. P., and Holbrook, N. J. (1984). Physiological functions of glucocorticoids in stress and their relation to pharmacological actions. *Endocr. Rev.* 5, 24–44.

Nestler, J. E. (1997). Dehydroepiandrosterone: Fountain of youth or snake oil? *The Endocrinologist* 7, 423–428.

Neville, A. M., and O'Hare, M. J. (1982). "The Human Adrenal Cortex." Springer-Verlag, Berlin.

Quinn, S. J., and Williams, G. H. (1988). Regulation of aldosterone secretion. *Ann. Rev. Physiol.* 50, 409–426.

Stewart, P. M., and Edwards, C. R. W. (1990). Specificity of the mineralocorticoid receptor: Crucial role of 11β-hydroxysteroid dehydrogenase. *Trends Endocrinol. Metab.* 1, 225–230.

Vallotton, M. (1987). The renin-angiotensin system. *Trends Physiol. Sci.* 8, 64–74.

Vinson, G. P., Whitehouse, B. J., and Hinson, J. P. (1992). "The Adrenal Cortex." Prentice–Hall, Englewood Cliffs, NJ.

Yates, F. E., Marsh, D. J., and Maran, J. W. (1980). The adrenal cortex. *In* "Medical Physiology" (V. B. Mountcastle, Ed.), pp. 1558–1560. Mosby, St Louis.

Adrenaline

Tessa M. Pollard

University of Durham, United Kingdom

GLOSSARY

adrenal glands Endocrine glands situated above the kidneys, composed of two distinct parts, the adrenal medulla, which secretes adrenaline and noradrenaline, and the adrenal cortex, which secretes corticosteroids.

adrenergic receptors Mediate the action of adrenaline. There are two types, named α- and β-receptors.

atherogenic Encouraging the process of atherosclerosis, which is a change in the lining of the arteries consisting of an accumulation of lipids, complex carbohydrates, blood and blood products, fibrous tissue, and calcium deposits.

catecholamines A group of hormones, including adrenaline, noradrenaline, and dopamine, which are synthesized from the amino acid tyrosine.

job strain A construct used by Karasek to describe work which makes heavy demands but offers little decision latitude for the worker.

sympathetic tone The basal rate of activity of the sympathetic nervous system.

$\mathbf{A}$drenaline, also known as epinephrine, is the main catecholamine produced by the adrenal medulla. Its secretion into the adrenal vein is under the control of sympathetic nerves and is the most important indirect pathway of sympathetic activation. Adrenaline plays a major role in the body's physiological response to stress and affects most systems of the body. The axis as a whole is referred to here as the sympathetic adrenal medullary (SAM) axis.

I. THE EFFECTS OF ADRENALINE

Adrenaline has many of the same actions on the body as direct sympathetic stimulation, but the effects last considerably longer. Once in the bloodstream adrenaline stimulates α- and β-adrenergic receptors. Through stimulation of cardiac muscle β-receptors it causes an increased heart rate, force of contraction, and cardiac output. Its actions on vascular smooth muscle adrenergic receptors cause the shunting of blood away from the skin, mucosa, and kidneys to the coronary arteries, skeletal muscle, and brain. Adrenaline also enhances blood platelet adhesiveness and reduces clotting time. It promotes the role of glucagon in converting glycogen to glucose, leading to an increased secretion of glucose into the bloodstream and production of glucose in the liver. Experimental studies have shown a highly significant increase in glucose levels during infusion of adrenaline. In addition, lipolytic activity in adipose tissues is stimulated, with a resultant increase in levels of plasma free fatty acids, providing another source of energy. There is also an increase in plasma cholesterol levels, including both low-density and high-density fractions, but this effect may be at least partially explained by a reduction in plasma volume (McCann *et al.* 1995, *Psychosom. Med.* 57, 165–176). Oxygen supply is improved, both as a function of vascular changes and bronchodilation. As a result the body is prepared for immediate physical and mental activity and the response is often referred to as the "fight or flight" reaction. This emergency function of the adrenal medulla was first identified by Cannon in 1914. At least over a few hours of secretion there appears to be no regulatory mechanism to counteract the effects of adrenaline; that is, these effects are sustained for as long as secretion of the hormone is maintained.

It is thought that repeated adrenaline secretion, or chronically raised levels of adrenaline, are likely to increase risk of cardiovascular disease, partly by changing sympathetic tone and partly by inducing changes which accelerate the process of atherosclerosis. Infusion of adrenaline leads to a sustained rise in blood pressure and repeated elevation of blood pressure may eventually lead to hypertension via enhanced sympathetic tone and damage to the blood vessels. Despite the fact that acute increases in lipid concentrations can probably be explained by changes in plasma volume, it is likely that chronic elevation of adrenaline levels may lead to longer term elevation of lipid levels. The free fatty acids whose release is stimulated by adrenaline are used by the liver for the synthesis of very low-density lipoproteins, which then become modified to low-density lipoproteins, which are strongly implicated in the atherogenic process. Adrenaline may have a direct role to play in myocardial infarction or cerebrovascular accident through its effects on platelets and clotting time and by the precipitation of cardiac arrhythmias.

Adrenaline can alter a number of aspects of immune function and may well mediate some of the apparent effects of stress on susceptibility to infectious disease and cancers. Studies show that individuals who show large increases in adrenaline in response to laboratory stressors also show the largest immune changes. Furthermore, adrenergic blockers have been demonstrated to prevent stress-induced increases in natural killer cell number and activity. Adrenaline is thought to act on the immune system by altering lymphocyte migration from lymphoid organs such as the spleen.

II. MEASURING ADRENALINE LEVELS

It is possible to determine adrenaline levels in plasma or urine. The main methods used are high-performance liquid chromatography and radioenzymatic assay. The former uses high pressure to separate catecholamines and this is usually followed by electrochemical detection. The latter relies on radioactive labeling—a radioactive substrate is added together with an enzyme and the amount of radioactive metabolite formed is measured. Both techniques have been validated and are known to be reliable, but neither is cheap. Recently it has been shown that platelets take up adrenaline in proportion to plasma concentrations and may, therefore, provide an alternative medium for the assessment of SAM activation.

Levels of hormone in plasma and urine reflect neuroendocrine activity over different time periods and it is important to use the appropriate medium. The SAM axis responds to stimuli within a few seconds of their impact and plasma adrenaline has a half-life of 1 to 2 min, so that levels of hormone in plasma reflect the SAM activity of only the preceding minute or so. Thus assessment of plasma adrenaline levels is only generally useful for laboratory studies of acute stressors, when an indwelling venous catheter can be used (since venipuncture itself is known to cause an increase in adrenaline levels). Samples must be spun and frozen very shortly after collection.

Levels of excreted free adrenaline or its metabolites can be measured in urine and have been shown to provide an accurate measure of circulating levels. Hormone assayed in urine usually represents a pooling of levels over a period of hours. This is true partly because hormone measured in urine is an integration of the hormone excreted into the urine produced by the body since the previous urination and partly because excreted hormone reflects hormone secreted some time before. Information on the time lag between secretion and excretion is sparse, although some laboratory studies have produced results which indicate that urinary adrenaline excretion rate reflects plasma adrenaline levels within an hour. When samples are collected over a few hours it is important to make some correction for variation in the amount of urine produced during that time. It is also possible to collect all the urine produced in a given 24-h period in order to look at the overall level produced during a day. However, it is not always easy for subjects to comply with the demands of 24-h collection and some checking for completeness of the sample is often needed by assessing either total volume or creatinine clearance. Again, degradation and oxidation is a problem and an antioxidant such as sodium metabisulfite is usually added to urine samples collected for the purpose of catecholamine determination.

III. PSYCHOSOCIAL DETERMINANTS OF ADRENALINE VARIATION

Researchers interested in understanding psychosocial determinants of adrenaline variation have investigated changes in hormone levels within individuals as well as differences between individuals. In general, the former approach has been more successful. As we have seen, adrenaline levels respond quickly to changing circumstances and a lot of information can be gained from examination of changes in hormone levels over time. Comparisons between individuals usually focus on longer term measures, such as 24-h urinary excretion rates, and thus only make use of averaged information for each subject. Data on within-individual variability is lost, and it is known that adrenaline excretion rates vary as much or more within individuals as they do between them. Furthermore, absolute levels of hormone are influenced by a large number of factors other than stress or the psychosocial environment, so that it is much more useful if each person can be used as his or her own control.

The main findings of studies examining the reasons for variation in adrenaline levels are summarized below, looking first at laboratory studies and then at those which have been conducted in people going about their normal lives.

A. Laboratory Studies of the Determinants of Adrenaline Secretion

The largest body of research on adrenaline responses in humans has been undertaken in laboratories. In general, the focus of these studies has been measuring the adrenaline response to situations and stimuli which are assumed to be stressful. Mason reviewed the early work in an important article which appeared in 1968 (Mason 1968, *Psychosom. Med.* **30**, 631–653). He described situations in which adrenaline levels had been shown to rise in humans. These included watching engaging movies, taking examinations, and performing set tasks such as intelligence tests or mental arithmetic (see Fig. 1). He concluded from these findings that adrenaline can rise in emotionally arousing situations which are pleasant as well as in those which are unpleasant. Since the 1960s other workers have reported results which can be interpreted in the same way. As a result of these findings Frankenhaeuser put forward a model in which the SAM axis was considered to be activated in response to mental or physical effort, regardless of emotional content. These studies provided some indication that adrenaline responses in women are less marked than those in men.

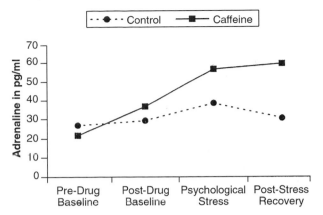

FIGURE 1 The effects of caffeine consumption on the plasma adrenaline response to a stressor in men. Caffeine (3.5 mg/kg) was given to 25 young men who were then asked to perform a mental arithmetic test. The control data were collected when the same men completed the same procedure after consumption of a placebo. The adrenaline response to the stressor was significantly greater after caffeine. (Data from Lane *et al.* 1990, *Psychosom. Med.* **52**, 320–336.)

B. Adrenaline Variation in Real Life

1. Influences of Habitual Health-Related Behaviors

Adrenaline levels respond to a number of features of human behavior, not just the experience of psychosocial stress. Those that have received most attention and are probably most important are the intake of caffeine, nicotine, alcohol, and engaging in exercise. All have been shown to stimulate adrenaline secretion. Caffeine also appears to potentiate adrenaline responses to stress (Fig. 1). In laboratory studies it is possible either to eliminate these influences or to control them. Researchers hoping to isolate the effects of psychosocial stressors outside the controlled laboratory environment have a more difficult task. They have sometimes approached the problem by asking subjects to avoid these influences. However, such an approach can bring problems of its own, perhaps, for example, inducing stress in smokers asked to abstain from cigarettes. Thus others have asked subjects to keep detailed records of their behavior and have included this information in subsequent analyses.

2. Adrenaline Variation across Societies

Biological anthropologists have approached the issue of cross-cultural variation in adrenaline levels and have tried to relate the observed variation to differences in lifestyle. Such cross-sectional data suffer from the problems described above, but some of the findings are nevertheless suggestive. In general people living in more urbanized environments appear to excrete higher levels of urinary adrenaline than those engaged in traditional subsistence farming work, despite the lower levels of physical activity characteristic of urbanites. For example, a comparison of urinary adrenaline excretion rates in young Western Samoan men living in villages or the capital, Apia, showed that men living in the city, whether nonmanual workers, students, or laborers, excreted higher levels of urinary adrenaline than villagers on average (James *et al.* 1985, *Hum Biol.* **57**, 635–647). Similarly Tokelauans living on Fakaofo had higher levels of urinary adrenaline than residents of Nukunonu, a nearby island less influenced by the wage economy. Still higher levels were excreted by Tokelauan migrants to New Zealand living in the urban center of Wellington (Jenner *et al.* 1987, *Hum. Biol.* **59**, 165–172). In both these studies the results were explained largely with respect to working behavior, with the suggestion that engagement in paid work, as opposed to traditional subsistence work, was more stressful.

3. Adrenaline Variation in Everyday Working Life

In addition to their laboratory work Frankenhaeuser and her team also pioneered investigations of the ways in which work-related stress might affect adrenaline levels. Two main kinds of comparisons have been made. The first contrasts hormone levels in people at work and at leisure, usually using a within-subject design, and the other compares the effects of different types of work on hormone variation. The comparison of work and leisure addresses the question of whether nonmanual work *per se* causes an increase in adrenaline secretion. It is then relevant to ask what particular aspects of work are associated with elevated adrenaline levels.

There is good evidence that adrenaline levels are higher in men at work than in the same men at leisure. In a particularly large study researchers in Oxford also found that in a diverse sample of British men, who provided urine samples on a normal working day and on Sunday, a rest day, urinary adrenaline levels were higher on the working day. Women who gave samples as part of the same study also showed significantly raised adrenaline levels on work days. However, there is some suggestion that the effect is not as consistent in women and in another study conducted in the same area it was found that while men's urinary adrenaline levels were raised on working days, those for women were not, despite the fact that men and women reported experiencing very similar levels of demand (Fig. 2).

Taken together, the results of a series of studies can be interpreted to show that workload and time pressure are the key features leading to elevated adrenaline levels at work. For example, increased urinary adrenaline levels in Swedish bus drivers in heavy traffic have been attributed to greater perceived time pressure created by the demands of remaining on schedule. Elevated adrenaline levels have also been seen in sawmill workers operating under time pressure and in people working on conveyer belts.

Efforts have been made to relate variation in adrenaline levels at work to the model of job strain proposed by Karasek and widely tested and applied in studies of workplace stress. Karasek and Theorell proposed that endocrine mechanisms explain the apparent link between job strain and ill health, particularly cardiovascular disease. They have proposed that adrenaline is secreted at higher levels in those experiencing job strain due to a heavy workload and lack of decision latitude. However, Karasek acknowledges that adrenaline can also rise with increased workload, whether decision latitude is high or low. There is, then, a general consensus that adrenaline levels are most strongly related to arousal or effort, as in Frankenhaeuser's original model.

4. Chronic Stress

The impact of chronically stressful life circumstances on general circulating levels of adrenaline has been investigated to a limited extent. For the most part such studies can only be conducted on a

A

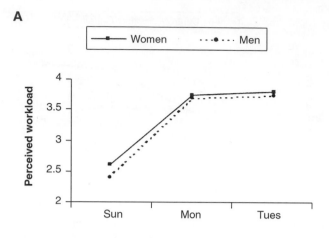

B

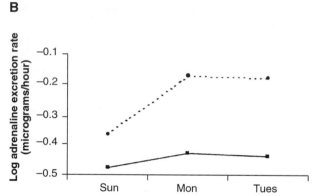

FIGURE 2 The change in workload and urinary adrenaline excretion rate from a rest day (Sunday) to working days. Data were collected from 53 women and 51 men in a variety of occupations. (A) Workload measured using a self-report questionnaire and (B) urinary adrenaline levels, assessed in 2-h afternoon samples corrected for changes in urine flow rate. The increase in demand from the rest day to working days was significant in both men and women but the increase in adrenaline level was only significant in men. (Data from Pollard *et al.* 1996, *Ann. Behav. Med.* **18**, 229–237.)

between-individual basis and suffer from the limitations imposed by that approach.

There has been little consensus from studies on the effects of the death of a spouse or of caring for a spouse with Alzheimer's disease. However, intriguing recent evidence suggests that people who have experienced chronic life stress of this kind may show increased SAM reactivity to a laboratory stressor (Pike *et al.* 1997, *Psychosom. Med.* **59**, 447–457).

IV. INDIVIDUAL DIFFERENCES IN SAM REACTIVITY

Not all people show the same SAM responsivity to stressors and it has been proposed that more reactive individuals are at greater risk of cardiovascular disease.

A. Sex Differences

Most early studies of the effects of stress on adrenaline in humans were conducted only with male subjects. When researchers began to include women they found that their responses to stressors were not always the same as men's, as noted above. It is thought probable that the high circulating levels of estrogen seen in premenopausal women modify the way in which adrenaline is secreted in response to stress. Evidence for such an effect comes from comparisons of post and premenopausal women and from studies of women given exogenous estrogen as, for example, in hormone replacement therapy for postmenopausal women. There has been less success in identifying a change in adrenaline reactivity at different phases of the menstrual cycle, perhaps because the differences in estrogen levels are not as marked. There is little evidence to support an alternative explanation for increased adrenaline responses in men—that they find exposure to stressors more stressful.

B. Personality

Researchers investigating the hypothesized link between Type A behavior and coronary heart disease have suggested that the mechanism by which such a link is most likely to operate is through increased reactivity of cardiovascular and neuroendocrine systems in people exhibiting Type A behavior. Some studies have provided evidence that Type A subjects, compared to Type B subjects, show larger acute increases in adrenaline levels when confronted by stressors in laboratories. However, others have not found such an effect and in a meta-analysis of studies to that date Harbin (Harbin 1989, *Psychophysiology* 26, 110–119) showed that while there was good evidence of greater heart rate and systolic blood pressure responses in Type A individuals, particularly men, no differences between Type A and Type B individuals were apparent in adrenaline responses. At least one investigation of the possibility of greater reactivity in those demonstrating negative affectivity or neuroticism has also failed to demonstrate an association.

V. CONCLUSION

Adrenaline has widespread and important effects on the body and these effects have clear-cut implications for cardiovascular disease. It is the hormone most consistently shown to respond to stress both in laboratory studies and in people going about their everyday lives. However, it also responds to experiences not usually considered stressful since it rises with mental arousal or effort, whether of a negative or a positive connotation. Furthermore, the adrenaline response may not be consistent across all individuals, in particular premenopausal women do not appear to be as reactive as men or postmenopausal women. Thus adrenaline can certainly be considered a stress hormone, but it is not simply an objective marker of stress.

See Also the Following Articles

Adrenal Cortex; Adrenal Medulla; Beta-Adrenergic Blockers; Cardiovascular System and Stress; Catecholamines; Immune Suppression; Workplace Stress

Bibliography

Balick, L. R., and Herd, J. A. (1987). Assessment of physiological indices related to cardiovascular disease as influenced by job stress. *J. Org. Behav. Manag.* 8, 103–115.

Baum, A., and Grunberg, N. (1995). Measurement of stress hormones. *In* "Measuring Stress: A Guide for Health and Social Scientists" (S. Cohen, R. C. Kessler, and L. U. Gordon, Eds.), Oxford Univ. Press, New York.

Dimsdale, J. E., and Ziegler, M. G. (1991). What do plasma and urinary measures of catecholamines tell us about human response to stressors? *Circulation* 83, II36–II42.

Frankenhaeuser, M. (1989). A biopsychosocial approach to work life issues. *Int. J. Health Serv.* 19, 747–758.

James, G. D., and Brown, D. E. (1997). The biological stress response and lifestyle: Catecholamines and blood pressure. *Annu. Rev. Anthropol.* **26**, 313–335.

Landsberg, L., and Young, J. B. (1985). Catecholamines and the adrenal medulla. *In* "Textbook of Endocrinology" (J. D. Wilson and D. W. Foster, Eds.). W.B. Saunders, Philadelphia.

McKinnon, W., Baum, A., and Morokoff, P. (1988). Neuroendocrine measures of stress. *In* "Social Psychophysiology Theory and Emotion: Theory and Clinical Applications" (H. Wagner, Ed.). Wiley, Chichester.

Panter-Brick, C., and Pollard, T. M. (1999). Work and hormonal variation in subsistence and industrial contexts. *In* "Hormones, Health and Behavior: A Socio-Ecological and Lifespan Perspective" (C. Panter-Brick and C. M. Worthman, Eds.). Cambridge Univ. Press, Cambridge, UK.

Polefrone, J. M., and Manuck, S. B. (1987). Gender differences in cardiovascular and neuroendocrine response to stressors. *In* "Gender and Stress" (R. C. Barnett, L. Biener, and G. K. Baruch, Eds.). Free Press, New York.

Pollard, T. M. (1997). Physiological consequences of everyday psychosocial stress. *Colleg. Antropolog.* **21**, 17–28.

Stoney, C., Davis, M., and Matthews, K. A. (1987). Sex differences in physiological responses to stress and in coronary heart disease. *Psychophysiology* **24**, 127–131.

Ziegler, M. G. (1989). Catecholamine measurement in behavioral research. *In* "Handbook of Research Methods in Cardiovascular Behavioral Medicine" (N. Schneiderman, S. M. Weiss, and P. G. Kaufman, Eds.). Plenum, New York.

Adrenal Insufficiency

H. S. Willenberg, S. R. Bornstein, and G. P. Chrousos

National Institute of Child and Health Development

I. Definition and Etiology of Adrenal Insufficiency
II. Clinical Presentation and Diagnosis
III. Treatment
IV. Additional Aspects and Implications for Stress

GLOSSARY

adrenal crisis Acute manifestation of adrenal insufficiency with symptoms including hypotension, hypovolemic shock, fever, and hypoglycemia. This condition is a medical emergency.

adrenal insufficiency A condition characterized by hypocortisolism. See also *primary adrenal insufficiency, secondary adrenal insufficiency,* and *tertiary adrenal insufficiency.*

AIDS Acquired Immunodeficiency Syndrome.

Cushing's disease State of chronic hypercortisolism due to increased secretion of corticotropin from pituitary adenomas. See also *Cushing's syndrome.*

Cushing's syndrome State of chronic hypercortisolism in general with typical clinical features. See also *Cushing's disease.*

Primary adrenal insufficiency State of hypocortisolism due to a pathologic process that involves the adrenal glands in the first place. See also *secondary adrenal insufficiency* and *tertiary adrenal insufficiency.*

Secondary adrenal insufficiency State of hypocortisolism due to a diminished capacity of the pituitary gland to secrete corticotropin. See also *primary adrenal insufficiency* and *tertiary adrenal insufficiency.*

Sheehan's syndrome Pathologic condition caused by intrapituitary postpartum hemorrhage.

Tertiary adrenal insufficiency State of hypocortisolism due to a pathologic process that involves the hypothalamus in the first place. See also *primary adrenal insufficiency* and *secondary adrenal insufficiency.*

I. DEFINITION AND ETIOLOGY OF ADRENAL INSUFFICIENCY

Adrenal insufficiency is caused by a disease process located in the adrenal glands (primary), the pituitary (secondary), or the hypothalamus (tertiary) (Table I). Regardless of the etiology, it is characterized by hypocortisolism and/or hypoaldosteronism. Depending on the lesion that causes adrenal hypofunction, isolated or combined impairment of adrenal hormone secretion may ensue. Usually, secondary adrenal insufficiency is limited to glucocorticoid deficiency.

One-and-a-half centuries ago, **Thomas Addison** was the first to describe **primary adrenal insufficiency**. Therefore, all primary forms of this condition are also termed Addison's disease. Since clinical symptoms usually do not occur until more than 90% of the adrenal cortex is destroyed, both organs have to be affected.

Autoimmune destruction of the adrenal glands is the most common cause of primary adrenal insufficiency in the industrialized world, accounting for about 70% of the cases. In autoimmune disease there is destruction of the entire adrenal cortex, typically leaving small glands. Patients with this condition are prone to develop other disorders of autoimmune origin, for example, celiac disease, autoimmune thyroid disease, vitiligo, and alopecia. In the course of a polyglandular autoimmune endocrinopathy hypothyroidism, hypoparathyroidism, type I diabetes mellitus, pernicious anemia, and hypogonadism may manifest.

The destruction of the adrenal cortex can also be the consequence of chronic infectious diseases, such as tuberculosis, AIDS, toxoplasmosis and histoplasmosis. Postprimary tuberculosis still accounts for about 20% of the cases in the industrialized world. This condition is usually complicated by the involvement of other organ systems. Of the fungal infections that are also known to cause adrenocortical dysfunc-

TABLE I
Etiology of Adrenal Insufficiency

Primary adrenal insufficiency	*Secondary and tertiary adrenal insufficiency*
I. Autoimmune (idiopathic) disease	I. Glucocorticoid-induced adrenal suppression
II. Expansive disease	1. Following glucocorticoid therapy
1. Infection	2. Following surgical correction of hypercortisolism
(tuberculosis, fungi)	II. Expansive disease
3. Hemorrhage	1. Primary or secondary hypothalamic/pituitary tumors
(sepsis, anticoagulants, trauma)	2. Infection (tuberculosis)
4. Secondary tumor (metastasis)	3. Inflammation (autoimmune, sarcoidosis)
III. Congenital-hereditary diseases	III. Iatrogenic hypopituitarism
1. Congenital adrenal hyperplasia	1. Following neurosurgery
2. Congenital adrenal hypoplasia	2. Following hypothalamic/pituitary radiation
3. Congenital unresponsiveness to ACTH	IV. Other
4. Adrenoleukodystrophy	1. Postpartum hemorrhage
5. Adrenomyeloneuropathy	(Sheehan's syndrome)
IV. Drugs	2. Trauma
1. Inhibitors of steroidogenesis	3. Apoplexy
2. Adrenolytic agents	
3. Glucocorticoid antagonists	
Isolated hypoaldosteronism	Adrenomedullary insufficiency or dysfunction
1. Hyporeninism	1. Tuberculosis
2. Diabetes, AIDS	2. Infiltration by tumors
3. Congenital-inherited biosynthetic defect	3. Diabetes
4. Protracted heparin treatment	4. Congenital-inherited dysautonomia

tion, histoplasmosis is the most common. Other causes of primary adrenal insufficiency have a rather low prevalence.

Tests of adrenocortical reserve are frequently impaired in chronic systemic diseases, including sarcoidosis, amyloidosis, and AIDS. Bilateral metastatic infiltration or intraadrenal hemorrhage due to sepsis (*meningococcus*) or anticoagulation are rare. Hereditary or congenital adrenal dysfunction is particularly important in the pediatric patient population and includes enzyme deficiencies of adrenal steroidogenesis, isolated glucocorticoid deficiency and triple A syndrome, congenital adrenal hypoplasia, and the demyelinating X-linked lipid metabolism disorders—adrenoleukodystrophy and adrenomyeloneuropathy.

Iatrogenic forms of primary adrenal insufficiency include bilateral adrenalectomy; treatment with glucocorticoid receptor antagonists, such as RU486 (mifepristone); adrenolytic agents, such as mitotane and suramin, and drugs that inhibit steroidogenesis, such as aminoglutethemide, metyrapone, ketoconazole, and trilostane.

Secondary adrenal insufficiency due to a diminished secretion of corticotropin is frequent. Iatrogenic suppression of the hypothalamic-pituitary adrenal axis or "adrenal suppression" in the course of glucocorticoid treatment and subsequent discontinuation is the most common cause. Also, adrenal suppression is observed in patients with endogenous Cushing syndrome after correction of the hypercortisolism by curative surgery. Other iatrogenic causes of secondary adrenal insufficiency include hypopituitarism following surgical intervention for pituitary and hypothalamic tumors and radiation. Space-occupying lesions in the hypothalamic–pituitary area may result in hypopituitarism, such as craniopharyngiomas, metastatic infiltration, and vascular lesions. In addition, trauma, Sheehan's syndrome (intrapituitary postpartum hemorrhage), and apoplexy are also possible causes of impaired pituitary–adrenocortical function.

Tertiary adrenal insufficiency is an uncommon form of adrenal insufficiency. Main causes include hemorrhage due to trauma, space-occupying lesions, and ischemia in the hypothalamus. In addition, the hypothalamus is also a site for the endocrine feedback regulation by glucocorticoids and, therefore, involved in iatrogenic adrenal insufficiency as described above.

Some disease states of unknown pathophysiology, such as posttraumatic stress disorder, chronic fatigue syndrome, and fibromyalgia, may also be associated with dysfunction of the hypothalamic-pituitary-adrenal axis, characterized by mild hypocortisolism. Guidelines for the diagnosis and therapy of these controversially discussed conditions are under development. Psychologic care, introduction into self-help groups, and symptomatic treatment are current therapeutic approaches.

II. CLINICAL PRESENTATION AND DIAGNOSIS

The main clinical manifestations of adrenal insufficiency are caused by hypocortisolism and hypoaldosteronism. All forms of adrenal insufficiency may present as an **acute adrenal crisis** or as chronic state with exacerbations.

Acute symptoms include anorexia and/or vomiting, somnolence, orthostatic or persistent hypotension, hypovolemic shock, fever, and hypoglycemia. Adrenal crisis is a medical emergency.

Patients with **chronic adrenal insufficiency** may present with weakness, failure to thrive (children), weight loss, anorexia, fatigue, nausea and vomiting, orthostatic hypotension and dizziness, and abdominal pain. In primary adrenal insufficiency, lack of negative pituitary and hypothalamic feedback by glucocorticoids causes increased secretion of ACTH, which has melanocyte-stimulating activity causing hyperpigmentation (creases of palms, buccal mucosa, breast areolas and nipples, and scars). In congenital adrenal hyperplasia, hyperandrogenism (virilization of girls, premature puberty of boys) is observed. In combined glucocorticoid and mineralocorticoid deficiency, relative hypovolemia leads to compensatory secretion of antidiuretic hormone with resulting hyponatremia, while the lack of aldosterone leads to salt loss and retention of potassium and proton ions.

An adrenal crisis can be diagnosed on the basis of

a single cortisol measurement at the time of crisis. Low serum sodium concentrations in combination with hyperkalemia and elevated plasma renin activity levels strongly suggest primary adrenal insufficiency, while elevated serum potassium levels are not typical for secondary forms of hypocortisolism. Hypoglycemia may occur in children, women, and very thin men. Lymphocytosis with eosinophilia, azotemia, high serum-calcium levels, and metabolic acidosis may be present. Routine laboratory parameters may demonstrate no abnormalities in early adrenal hypofunction. Specific study methods to ensure and further differentiate diagnosis of adrenal insufficiency should not delay therapeutic intervention during an adrenal crisis.

Adrenal stimulation tests provide evidence of a dysfunction of the hypothalamic-pituitary-adrenal axis. Among them the rapid (30–60 min) corticotropin test is useful for the diagnosis of adrenal insufficiency, while the corticotropin-releasing hormone test and the long 48-h ACTH stimulation tests are useful for the differentiation of primary and secondary adrenal insufficiency (Table II). While basal cortisol production may be normal, impaired increase in steroid output may be present and difficult to diagnose. Therefore, these tests, particularly the rapid ACTH test, are valuable tools in establishing the diagnosis of adrenal hypofunction in cases of decreased adrenal reserve and in monitoring recovery of the hypothalamic-pituitary-adrenal axis after discontinuation of glucocorticoid therapy or correction of hypercortisolism.

In several countries, screening for congenital adrenal hyperplasia has been shown to decrease the risk of early death and to be cost-effective in health programs.

III. TREATMENT

The therapeutic goal is an optimal replacement of glucocorticoids and, if necessary, mineralocorticoids. In addition, there is need of an additional glucocoticoid substitution therapy in certain stress-related circumstances. Therefore, all patients with this condition and their close relatives and friends need careful education about the management of their disease and should be given a special pass.

Usually, patients do very well with oral glucocorticoids. The treatment of choice is hydrocortisone ($10–15$ mg/m^2/day). To simulate the circadian rhythm of glucocorticoid secretion split doses are given, two-thirds in the morning, one-third in the afternoon (Table III). Before minor surgery or dental extraction or during periods of intercurrent illness, steroid dosage has to be doubled or even tripled. During severe stress (such as car accidents, sepsis, or major surgery) an individual with intact adrenals normally increases his or her cortisol secretion about fivefold. Therefore, during such situations, replacement doses higher than 200 mg per day are not required in patients with adrenal insufficiency. Following an operation, provided that there are no com-

TABLE II
Differentiation Between Primary, Secondary, and Tertiary Adrenal Insufficiency

Adrenal insufficiency	Primary	Secondary	Tertiary
Plasma ACTH, baseline	Elevated	Low/normal	Low/normal
Plasma ACTH after ovine CRH	Elevated		Delayed Response
Plasma cortisol, baseline during crisis	<18 μg/dl	<18 μg/dl	<18 μg/dl
Plasma cortisol after ACTH (60 min)	<20 μg/dl	<20 μg/dl	<20 μg/dl
Plasma cortisol after oCRH	No elevation	No elevation	No elevation
Urinary free cortisol or 17-hydroxysteroids after 48h ACTH infusion	No elevation	Two- to threefold elevation	Two- to threefold elevation
Plasma aldosterone, baseline	Decreased	Normal	Normal
Plasma renin activity, supine and upright	Elevated	Normal	Normal

TABLE III

Example for Glucocorticoid Replacement Therapy

Glucocorticoid	Morning	Noon	Late afternoon
Hydrocortisone[a]	15 mg	10 mg	5 mg
Cortisone acetate	25 mg	—	12.5 mg
Prednisone	5 mg	—	—

[a] Hydrocortisone is recommended.

plications, the hydrocortisone doses should be returned to the normal replacement regimen within a few days. Parenteral administration may be required. Though cortisol and cortisone have mineralocorticoid effects, doses of 30 mg per day cover only about 50% of the daily needs. Therefore, 0.05 to 0.1 mg of fludrocortisone, a synthetic mineralocorticoid, are given to Addisonian patients. Furthermore, these patients should be put on a sodium-enriched diet because they are frequently not able to conserve this electrolyte despite replacement therapy.

In some cases of secondary and tertiary adrenal insufficiency, treatment with corticotropin may be more effective than glucocorticoid therapy, such as in dermatomyositis and multiple sclerosis. In fact, administration of corticotropin leads to secretion of adrenal androgens, glucocorticoids, and mineralocorticoids and generally prevents the adrenal glands from hypotrophy but not the hypothalamic–pituitary unit from suppression. Oral glucocorticoid replacement is generally sufficient and easier to adjust to the individual requirements in the great majority of the patients.

In **acute adrenocortical insufficiency**, therapy should be initiated immediately after saving blood for determination of cortisol and corticotropin levels. Hypovolemic shock requires rapid replacement of sodium and water deficits. This is accomplished by intravenous infusion of 5% glucose in normal saline solutions lacking potassium. Cortisol should be administered, starting with a bolus of 100 mg. Adrenal crisis is often precipitated by acute stress. Therefore, appropriate increase in glucocorticoid replacement serves to restore glucocorticoid function.

After successful treatment and improvement of the patient's condition, glucocorticoids can be administered orally again and the doses can be lowered to maintenance levels.

IV. Additional Aspects and Implications for Stress

Glucocorticoids not only participate in endocrine feedback loops with corticotropin and corticotropin-releasing hormone at the levels of the pituitary gland and the hypothalamus, respectively, but also in feedback loops with other peptides derived from the immune system. Of those mediators, interleukin-6 is a key interface between the immune system and the hypothalamic-pituitary adrenal axis. This cytokine is found to be elevated in patients with hypocortisolism and believed to play a role in the "steroid withdrawal syndrome."

Glucocorticoids are associated with a switch in production of Th1 to Th2 cytokines. Absence of glucocorticoids leads to an enhanced Th1 profile, promoting autoimmune and allergic phenomena, including autoimmune thyroid disease, rheumatoid arthritis, and asthma.

Adrenal insufficiency is a state of hypocortisolism and, thus, a state of decreased effectiveness of the adaptive response. Profound dysregulation of the hypothalamic-pituitary adrenal axis with loss of drive (secondary and tertiary forms) or loss of feedback (primary forms) makes a balanced homeostasis impossible. Therefore, frequently, manifestations of adrenal insufficiency are observed under stressful conditions, such as inapparent infection, physical challenge, and surgery. Once the diagnosis of adrenal insufficiency is established, careful diagnosis, and causal therapy of a possible underlying disease are also pivotal.

When Brown-Secard and Thomas Addison recognized that the adrenal glands were organs necessary for life he did not have knowledge of Hans Selye's concept of stress. Adrenal dysfunction practically means disintegration of the powerful stress system, which is necessary for maintenance of homeostasis. Cases of adrenal insufficiency document the importance of such a system. Its dysfunction may result in severe life-threatening states.

See Also the Following Articles

Adrenal Cortex; Autoimmunity; Cushing's Disease

Bibliography

Bornstein, S. R. (1996). The Adrenal Functional Unit. Georg Thieme-Verlag, Stuttgart.

Chrousos, G. P. (1998). Stressors, stress, and neuroendocrine integration of the adaptive response: 1997 Hans Selye Memorial Lecture. *Ann. N.Y. Acad. Sci.* **851,** 311–335.

Papanicolaou, D. A. (1997). Cytokines and adrenal insufficiency. *Curr. Opin. Endocrinol. Diabetes* **4,** 194–198.

Stratakis, C. A., and Chrousos, G. P. (1998). Adrenal diseases. *In* "Principles of Molecular Medicine" (J. L. Jameson, Ed.). Humana Press, Totowa, NJ.

Tsigos, C., Kamilaris, T., Chrousos, G. P. (1996). Adrenal Diseases. In Moore W. T., Eastman R., Eds., "Diagnostic Endocrinology," 2nd edition. B. C. Decker Inc., Toronto, p. 123–156.

Adrenal Medulla

Richard Kvetňanský
Slovak Academy of Sciences, Slovak Republic

Richard McCarty
University of Virginia

I. Biosynthesis and Release of Adrenal Medullary Catecholamines
II. Stress Effects on the Biosynthetic Capacity of the Adrenal Medulla
III. Factors Influencing the Transcription of Adrenal mRNAs During Stress
IV. Summary and Conclusions

GLOSSARY

adrenal medulla The inner portion of the adrenal gland that is part of the sympathetic–adrenal medullary system. The adrenal medulla receives neural input from sympathetic preganglionic fibers arising from the intermediolateral cell column of the thoracic and lumbar regions of the spinal cord. The adrenal medulla is known primarily for its ability to synthesize and secrete the stress hormone, epinephrine.

chromaffin cell Cell type that makes up the bulk of the adrenal medulla. So named because of the capacity of these cells to take up and stain with chromium salts. In most mammalian species, there are two types of chromaffin cells—those that synthesize, store, and secrete norepinephrine and those that synthesize, store, and secrete epinephrine. These cells also synthesize, store and secrete a range of biologically active peptides.

dopamine-β-hydroxylase An enzyme contained within vesicles that catalyzes the conversion of dopamine to norepinephrine.

neuropeptide Y A 36 amino acid peptide found in cell bodies and nerve terminals of the central and peripheral nervous systems. This peptide is also localized within chromaffin cells of the adrenal medulla as well as other nonneuronal cells. This peptide has important effects on the cardiovascular system and is also a smooth muscle cell mitogen.

phenylethanolamine N-methyltransferase An enzyme localized within epinephrine-containing chromaffin cells of the adrenal medulla, adrenergic neurons of the central nervous system and some other peripheral tissues. This enzyme catalyzes the conversion of norepinephrine to epinephrine.

tyrosine hydroxylase An enzyme localized to catecholamine synthesizing cells that catalyzes the conversion of tyrosine to dihydroxyphenylalanine (DOPA). The hydroxylation of tyrosine is the rate-limiting step in catecholamine biosynthesis.

The adrenal medulla played a pivotal role in studies of the physiology of stress for most of the twentieth century. As the nineteenth century came to a close, the pharmacologist John Jacob Abel of Johns Hopkins University identified epinephrine (EPI) as the endogenous substance from the adrenal gland with pronounced effects on the cardiovascular system. Soon thereafter, he described the synthesis of EPI in the laboratory. The physiologist Walter Branford Cannon of Harvard University conducted a series of seminal experiments on the importance of adrenal medullary secretion of epinephrine during various types of stressful stimulation in animals and humans. Based upon his studies, Cannon introduced the terms "homeostasis" and "fight-or-flight" to the scientific literature and these terms remain in use to the present.

The adrenal medulla of many mammalian species, including rats and humans, has norepinephrine (NE)-containing and EPI-containing secretory cells. These two types of adrenal chromaffin cells are innervated by sympathetic preganglionic fibers of the splanchnic nerve. Secretion of catecholamines from adrenal medullary chromaffin cells is controlled in part by these sympathetic preganglionic nerve fibers and the secreted catecholamines are carried from the site of exocytotic release by blood that drains from the adrenal medulla and into the adrenal vein. NE and EPI are then carried throughout the body (with the exception of those portions of the central nervous system where the blood–brain barrier is intact) and exert effects on most of the major organ systems of the body.

I. BIOSYNTHESIS AND RELEASE OF ADRENAL MEDULLARY CATECHOLAMINES

The catecholamine biosynthetic pathway is summarized in Table 1. Catecholamines are synthesized from the amino acid precursor tyrosine. There are two primary sources of tyrosine, from the diet and from hydroxylation of the amino acid, phenylalanine, in the liver. Upon entry into an adrenal chromaffin

TABLE I
Overview of the Biosynthetic Pathway of Catecholamines in the Adrenal Medulla

Epinephrine (EPI)
   ↑   Phenylethanolamine-N-methyltransferase (PNMT)
Norepinephrine (NE)
   ↑   Dopamine-β-hydroxylase (DBH)
Dopamine (DA)
   ↑   Aromatic amino acid decarboxylase (AADC)
Dihydroxyphenylalanine (DOPA)
   ↑   Tyrosine Hydroxylase (TH)
Tyrosine (TYR)

cell, tyrosine is converted to dihydroxyphenylalanine (DOPA) by the soluble cytoplasmic enzyme, tyrosine hydroxylase (TH). TH activity is regulated in part by concentrations of Fe^{++}, O_2, Mg^{++}, adenosine triphosphate (ATP) and the co-factor, tetrahydrobiopterin. Under most conditions, TH is the rate-limiting step in catecholamine biosynthesis. DOPA is converted into dopamine (DA) by aromatic amino acid decarboxylase (AADC). AADC activity depends on levels of its co-factor, pyridoxal phosphate. Dopamine is taken up into storage vesicles and converted into NE by dopamine-β-hydroxylase (DBH), an enzyme found in soluble and membrane-bound forms within storage vesicles. DBH activity is influenced by levels of copper, ascorbic acid and O_2. NE is then converted into EPI by the soluble cytoplasmic enzyme, phenylethanolamine N-methyltransferase (PNMT).

Separate populations of adrenal chromaffin cells contain NE and EPI as the final products of catecholamine biosynthesis. The latter are distinguished from the former by the presence of PNMT. Under resting conditions, low levels of EPI but very little NE are released into blood from the adrenal medulla. During some types of stressful stimulation, however, significant amounts of NE may be released from the adrenal medulla and may comprise up to 35% of the total circulating NE. The remaining 65% of NE is released from sympathetic nerve terminals and enters blood from the site of release at the neuroeffector junction.

NE and EPI are stored in chromaffin granules that are formed from the Golgi apparatus and enclosed by a single membrane. The chromaffin granules contain water, various proteins, ATP and lipid in addition to either NE or EPI. The most prominent proteins include the chromagranins. Release of catecholamines from adrenal chromaffin cells is via exocytosis.

Until the mid-1980s, the view of the adrenal medullary system was relatively simplistic. Acetylcholine was released from sympathetic preganglionic nerve terminals and bound to nicotinic cholinergic receptors on the adrenal chromaffin cells. The interaction of acetylcholine with its nicotinic receptor led to a depolarization of the chromaffin cell membrane, resulting in an increase in membrane permeability to sodium. Increased intracellular sodium initiated a series of events that led to an increase in the influx of calcium. Amine storage vesicles fused with the chromaffin cell membrane and released their contents of EPI or NE via exocytosis. Although it was known in the mid-1980s that chromagranins, ATP and a fraction of the soluable DBH were released during exocytosis, the focus of attention was on EPI and its biological effects.

Since the mid-1980s, a wealth of new information has accumulated and the adrenal medulla can no longer be viewed as a tissue that is under the exclusive control of acetylcholine and is concerned primarily with the synthesis, storage, and secretion of catecholamines (refer to Table 2). Indeed, more than16 biologically active substances have been localized to adrenal chromaffin cells and a number of them have been shown to be released following depolarization of the chromaffin cell membrane. In addition, various biologically active neuropeptides are co-localized with acetylcholine within sympathetic preganglionic nerve terminals. Several of these neuropeptides, including substance P and others, appear to act as neuromodulators of cholinergic transmission. Finally, chromaffin cells have a range of membrane-bound receptors for various biologically active molecules that are released from preganglionic nerve terminals or are delivered to chromaffin cells

via the circulation. These substances may also interact in complex ways to regulate secretory patterns of adrenal chromaffin cells. Each chromaffin cell may also have its own secretory phenotype based upon the complement of peptide and classical neurotransmitter receptors contained on its outer cell membrane.

In some instances, peptides released from adrenal chromaffin cells may exert negative feedback effects on continued chromaffin cell secretory activity by stimulating chromaffin cell receptors. This type of intramedullary feedback loop introduces a new layer of complexity to the regulation of adrenal medullary secretion.

II. STRESS EFFECTS ON THE BIOSYNTHETIC CAPACITY OF THE ADRENAL MEDULLA

A. Plasma EPI and Stress

Many different approaches have been taken to assess the functional status of the adrenal medulla. Beginning in the 1950s, fluorometric assays of cate-

TABLE II

A Partial Listing of Neuropeptides Contained within Adrenal Medullary Chromaffin Cells and within Preganglionic Nerve Terminals and Medullary Ganglion Cells. A Partial Listing of Neurotransmitter and Neuropeptide Receptors Found on Adrenal Medullary Chromaffin Cells Is also Included

Chromaffin cell peptides	Nerve terminal peptides	Receptors
Calcitonin gene-related peptide	Calcitonin gene-related peptide	Nicotinic
Enkephalin	Enkephalin	Muscarinic
Galanin	Galanin	Substance P
Adrenomedullin	Acetylcholine	Bradykinin
Vasopressin	Substance P	Vasopressin
Guanylin	Dynorphin	Neurotensin
CRH	Cholecystokinin	Angiotensin II
ACTH	Vasoactive Intestinal Polypeptide	Atrial natriuretic factor
Cerebellin	Pituitary adenylate cyclase activating peptide (PACAP)	Cholesystokinin
Neuropeptide Y		Neurokinins
Renin		Endothelins
Chromogranins A, B, and C		
Secretogranins		
Synaptophysin		
ATP		
Interleukin-1		

cholamines were employed to study the effects of stress on whole gland content of epinephrine and norepinephrine. In addition, fluorometric assays allowed for quantification of urinary excretion rates of catecholamines in laboratory animals and in humans. The earliest studies of plasma levels of catecholamines also made use of fluorometric assays. However, studies of plasma catecholamines in laboratory animals and in humans were greatly facilitated by the introduction of highly sensitive radioenzymatic thin-layer chromatographic techniques in the 1970s and high pressure liquid chromatography with electrochemical detection (HPLC-EC) beginning in the 1980s.

Studies of plasma levels of EPI have revealed a number of facets of adrenal medullary regulation. The adrenal medulla is for all intents and purposes the sole source of circulating EPI in all mammalian species that have been studied, including humans. In all such studies, the subjects must be surgically prepared with indwelling arterial or venous catheters to reduce to the greatest extent possible any stress associated with blood collection. Basal plasma levels of EPI in laboratory rats and in humans are often less than 50 pg/ml. Plasma EPI levels increase rapidly in response to even minor stressors and there is a monotonic relationship between the intensity of a stressor and the increment above baseline in plasma levels of EPI.

Prior stress history exerts a profound effect on the secretory response of the adrenal medulla to subsequent exposure to a stressor. For example, if a laboratory rat is exposed to the same stressor each day for several weeks, the adrenal medullary response to the next exposure to that same stressor is reduced significantly compared to first time stressed controls. In contrast, if these same chronically stressed animals are instead exposed to a novel stressor, the adrenal medullary response is significantly greater compared to a first time stressed control group. The former pattern has been referred to as habituation and the latter response has been referred to as sensitization. The mechanisms explaining these effects are not fully understood. However, it has been assumed that splanchnic stimulation of the adrenal medulla is reduced during the development of habituation and is enhanced during a sensitizing experience.

An important research question since the late 1960s has been the processes by which the adrenal medulla responds to acute versus chronic intermittent exposure to stressful stimulation. This research question has been subject to ongoing refinement as new and more sensitive neurochemical and molecular biological techniques have become available. Most of the studies in this field of inquiry have been focused on regulatory processes affecting catecholamine biosynthesis and release. As noted above, however, the adrenal medulla secretes a complex array of biologically active peptides, but many fewer studies have examined how biosynthesis and release of these neuropeptides are affected by chronic intermittent stress and exposure to novel stressors.

Exposure to a single episode of immobilization stress for up to 2 h is attended by a significant decrease of 15–20% in the total adrenal medullary content of EPI. An animal or human experiencing this sustained exposure to an acute stressor does not know when the stressor will be terminated, and once terminated, if and when the stressor will begin again. In the face of this uncertainty, how does the adrenal medulla meet the immediate needs of replenishing supplies of EPI in adrenal chromaffin cells and what, if any, provisions are made for an uncertain future?

Given that the synthesis of EPI within the adrenal medulla involves a complex interplay of several different enzymes, studies have focused on three key enzymes—TH, DBH, and PNMT. The most extensive literature is available for TH because of its role as the rate-limiting step in catecholamine biosynthesis; however, the other two enzymes have also received considerable attention. The discussion to follow will focus in large part on the effects of acute versus repeated immobilization stress in laboratory rats because there is an extensive literature relating to this stressor and the studies have been performed in a systematic fashion.

B. Effects of Acute Immobilization Stress on Adrenal Catecholamine Synthesizing Enzymes

Following a single 2-h period of immobilization stress, there are profound changes in mRNA levels of adrenal biosynthetic enzymes but very little change in enzyme activity. Compared to values in unstressed controls, TH mRNA levels increase by approximately 300%, DBH mRNA levels increase by approximately 100%, and PNMT mRNA levels increase by approximately 200%. In contrast, TH, DBH, and PNMT enzyme activities do not change significantly following a single 2-h period of immobilization stress. Note here the dissociation between levels of message for the catecholamine biosynthetic enzymes versus actual levels of enzyme activity. Note, too, that increases in DBH mRNA levels are just as likely not to be increased significantly following a single episode of immobilization stress.

These changes in mRNA levels for adrenal catecholamine synthesizing enzymes following a single period of immobilization stress are transient. Twenty-four hours following a single 2-h period of immobilization stress, mRNA levels for TH, DBH and PNMT return toward baseline levels and are no longer significantly different from unstressed control levels (Table 3).

C. Effects of Repeated Immobilization Stress on Adrenal Catecholamine Synthesizing Enzymes

The adrenal response to repeated immobilization stress is summarized in Table 4. Compared to unstressed control rats, rats exposed to immobilization stress for 2 h per day for 6 consecutive days have significant elevations in adrenal medullary mRNA levels of TH, DBH, and PNMT. In addition, TH, DBH, and PNMT enzyme activities are increased significantly and each of these changes persists for at least

TABLE III

Adrenal mRNA Levels (in Arbitrary Units) of TH, DBH, and PNMT under Basal Conditions and Immediately and 24 h Following a Single 2-h Period of Immobilization Stress (IMMO)

Enzyme	Baseline	Post-IMMO	24-h post-IMMO
TH	1.00 ± 0.21	$7.50 \pm 0.50**$	1.60 ± 0.25
DBH	1.00 ± 0.10	$1.88 \pm 0.49*$	1.42 ± 0.50
PNMT	1.00 ± 0.32	$3.00 \pm 0.33**$	1.52 ± 0.20

Values are means $\pm$ SEM.
* $P < 0.05$; ** $P < 0.01$ compared to unstressed controls.

TABLE IV

Adrenal mRNA Levels and Activities (Expressed as Percent of Unstressed Controls) of TH, DBH, and PNMT under Basal Conditions and Immediately Following 6 Daily 2-h Periods of Immobilization Stress (6 × IMMO)

Enzyme	Baseline	mRNA levels 6 × IMMO	Enzyme activity 6 × IMMO
TH	100 ± 25	$375 \pm 20^{\wedge\wedge}$	$320 \pm 25**$
DBH	100 ± 15	$385 \pm 40**$	$255 \pm 25**$
PNMT	100 ± 10	$330 \pm 25**$	$160 \pm 10*$

Values are means $\pm$ SEM.
* $P < 0.05$; ** $P < 0.01$ compared to unstressed controls.

24 h. A similar pattern of results has been obtained following as few as two consecutive daily bouts of immobilization stress.

These findings reveal that the adrenal medulla exhibits a transient increase in TH, DBH, and PNMT transcriptional activities following a single 2-h period of immobilization stress. However, these increases in transcriptional activities are not accompanied by increases in enzyme activities. If animals are exposed daily to immobilization stress for 2–6 days, increases in TH, DBH, and PNMT transcriptional activities, as well as levels of enzyme activity, are enhanced and these increases are maintained for at least 24 h. Thus, the adrenal medulla of repeatedly stressed animals exhibits a significant and long-lasting enhancement of catecholamine biosynthetic capacity. However, as noted above, these increases in catecholamine biosynthetic capacity develop as the adrenal medulla habituates to repeated immobilization stress and actually releases significantly less EPI with each repeated daily exposure to stress. The increase in catecholamine biosynthetic capacity is unmasked when a repeatedly stressed animal is exposed to a novel stressor and EPI release from the adrenal medulla is amplified over and above that of a first-time stressed control.

The pattern of transcriptional activation and translational control of catecholamine synthesizing enzymes differs in other models of stress. For example, in animals continuously exposed to a cold environment, TH mRNA levels increased by approximately 3-fold above baseline within 3–6 h after the start of cold exposure and remained elevated throughout.

Levels of TH protein peaked after 3 days of continuous cold exposure and TH activity peaked after 6–7 days of continuous cold exposure. Other stressors such as insulin-induced hypoglycemia, administration of 2-deoxyglucose, and hypoxia have been shown to effect increases in TH mRNA, TH protein levels, and TH activity in the adrenal medulla.

Finally, it is important to note that stress-induced increases in catecholamine biosynthetic enzymes also occur in tissues other than the adrenal medulla. For example, such changes have been described in various sympathetic ganglia, within several hypothalamic nuclei, and in noradrenergic cell bodies of the nucleus locus ceruleus.

III. FACTORS INFLUENCING TRANSCRIPTION OF ADRENAL mRNAS DURING STRESS

A. The Splanchnic Nerve

The chromaffin cells of the adrenal medulla are innervated by terminals arising from the splanchnic nerve. It has been hypothesized that splanchnic input is critical for the enhanced transcription of genes for TH, DBH, PNMT and various neuropeptides during stressful stimulation. Kvetnansky, Sabban, and their colleagues have tested this hypothesis by examining the effects of adrenal denervation on transcriptional activation of TH, PNMT, and neuropeptide Y (NPY) by various stressors.

In their first experiment, the right adrenal gland was sham-operated and the left adrenal gland was denervated in a group of laboratory rats. These animals were then immobilized for 2 h and were sacrificed 3 h later. Adrenal RNA was isolated and analyzed by Northern blot. The results indicated that the immobilization-induced increases in mRNAs for PNMT and TH were not dependent upon an intact splanchnic nerve. In contrast, splanchnectomy abolished the stress-induced increase in neuropeptide Y mRNA (refer to Table 5). In other experiments, it has been shown that an intact splanchnic nerve is required for the increase in enzyme activites for TH and PNMT following immobilization stress. Taken together, these results demonstrate that the splanch-

TABLE V

Influence of the Splanchnic Nerve on Transcriptional Activation of TH, PNMT, and NPY under Basal Conditions and 3 h Following a Single 2-h Period of Immobilization Stress (IMMO). Values are Expressed as a Percent of the Sham-Operated Right Adrenal Gland

Treatment	TH mRNA	PNMT mRNA	NPY mRNA
Sham	100 ± 33	100 ± 17	100 ± 29
Sham + IMMO	479 ± 76**	863 ± 82**	259 ± 35*
Denervated	100 ± 21	110 ± 21	88 ± 35
Denervated + IMMO	426 ± 72**	776 ± 132**	79 ± 14

Values are means ± SEM.

* $P < 0.05$, ** $P < 0.01$ compared to the appropriate sham or denervated control group.

(Reproduced from Sabban, *et al.* 1996.)

nic nerve does play a critical role in the immobilization-stress-induced increase in NPY mRNA and in the increase in TH and PNMT enzyme activities. However, other as yet unidentified factors are responsible for the immobilization-stress-induced increases in TH mRNA. It should be noted that glucocorticoids are an important regulator of PNMT gene expression.

In another set of experiments, Kvetnansky, Sabban, and their co-workers examined the role of splanchnic input on increases in TH mRNA following three different stressors—cold exposure, insulin-induced hypoglycemia, and immobilization (refer to Table 6). With chronic cold exposure and with insulin-induced hypoglycemia, TH mRNA was increased several-fold above basal levels in the intact adrenal but this increase was completely abolished in the denervated adrenal. In contrast, with immobilization stress there was a significant increase in TH mRNA levels in both the intact and the denervated adrenals. Additional experiments have demonstrated that the immobilization-induced increase in TH mRNA levels is also not dependent upon the pituitary gland. The factors that regulate the increase in TH mRNA in immobilized animals are as yet unknown.

B. Modulation of Transcription

A detailed discussion of the transcription factors and promotors involved in stress-induced increases in mRNAs for TH, DBH, and PNMT as well as various

TABLE VI

Influence of the Splanchnic Nerve on Transcriptional Activation of TH under Basal Conditions and after Exposure to the Following Stressors: Cold Stress for 5 Days at 5°C, Insulin-Induced Hypoglycemia (5 h after Administration of 5.0 I.U./Kg), or a Single 2-h Period of Immobilization Stress (IMMO) with Sacrifice 3 h later. Values are Expressed in Arbitrary Units

Treatment	Cold stress	Insulin	IMMO
Sham Control	100 ± 5	100 ± 23	100 ± 30
Sham + Stress	302 ± 36**	375 ± 68**	478 ± 77**
Denervated Control	106 ± 12	101 ± 34	100 ± 19
Denervated + Stress	104 ± 13	112 ± 37	425 ± 70**

Values are means $\pm$ SEM.

** $P < 0.01$ compared to the appropriate sham or denervated control group.

(Adapted from Kvetnanský and Sabban, 1998.)

neuropeptides is beyond the scope of this chapter. However, it has been shown that the genes coding for the catecholamine biosynthetic enzymes contain several regulatory genomic elements. These include the CRE, GRE, AP1, AP2, POU/Oct, and SP1 sites. The signaling molecules that may influence the transcription rates of the genes for TH, DBH, and PNMT include P-CREB, JNK, c-fos, Egr-1, and others. These and other promoters and signaling molecules interact in a complex fashion to regulate mRNA levels for the various adrenal medullary biosynthetic enzymes and neuropeptides under basal conditions and during exposure to stress.

IV. SUMMARY AND CONCLUSIONS

The adrenal medulla and the concept of stress are inextricably intertwined. The adrenal medulla may function in concert with the sympathetic nervous system or it may function somewhat independently in meeting the homeostatic demands presented by a variety of stressful stimuli. Although epinephrine secretion has been the primary focus of physiological studies of the adrenal medulla, it is now apparent that the adrenal medulla secretes a complex array of neuropeptides that exerts effects within the adrenal medulla and throughout the body. The adrenal medulla is innervated by preganglionic sympathetic nerve terminals that release acetylcholine and various co-localized peptides, including substance P.

A major focus of studies beginning in the early 1970s concerned the ways in which the adrenal medulla responds to acute versus repeated exposure to stress. With the advent of sensitive and specific assay techniques, it has been shown that a complex cascade of biosynthetic changes occurs within the adrenal medulla as animals adapt to stressful stimuli.

Finally, an important lesson that has been learned relates to the stressor-specific pattern of molecular responses of the adrenal medulla. Although many stressors result in increases in mRNA levels for TH and other biosynthetic enzymes, these changes may be dependent upon an intact splanchnic nerve or may depend on an as yet undescribed mechanism that is independent of the splanchnic nerve.

In spite of thousands of experiments on the adrenal medulla and stress, there are many important questions that await answers. What mechanism explains the reduced secretion of EPI from the adrenal medulla of animals exposed to chronic intermittent stress and the enhanced secretion of EPI following exposure of chronically stressed animals to a novel stressor? What factors regulate the increased levels of mRNAs for TH, DBH, and PNMT following exposure to various stressors? What roles are played by the various neuropeptides that are released from splanchnic nerve terminals and from adrenal medullary chromaffin cells, and how do these substances interact with EPI? These and other questions are being addressed by many research groups throughout the world. As answers become available, our knowledge of the physiological and molecular aspects of stress will be enhanced.

See Also the Following Articles

Adrenaline; Adrenal Cortex; Catecholamines; Dopamine

Bibliography

Goldstein, D. S. (1995). *Stress, Catecholamines and Cardiovascular Disease.* New York: Oxford University Press.

Johnson, E. O., Kamilaris, T. C., Chrousos, G. P., and Gold, P. W. (1992). Mechanisms of stress: A dynamic overview of hormonal and behavioral homeostasis. *Neuroscience and Biobehavioral Reviews* 16: 115–130.

Kvetňanský, R., and Sabban, E. L. (1993). Stress-induced changes in tyrosine hydroxylase and other catecholamine biosynthetic enzymes. *In* M. Naoi and S. H. Parvez (Eds.), *Tyrosine Hydroxylase: From Discovery to Cloning*, pp. 253–281. Utrecht, The Netherlands: VSP Press.

Kvetňanský, R., and Sabban, E. L. (1998). Stress and molecular biology of neurotransmitter-related enzymes. *In* P. Csermely (Eds.), *Stress of Life: From Molecules to Man, Annals of the New York Academy of Sciences,* Volume 851, pp. 342–356. New York: New York Academy of Sciences.

McCarty, R., and Gold, P. E. (1996). Catecholamines, stress and disease: A psychobiological perspective. *Psychosomatic Medicine* 58, 590–597.

McCarty, R., and Stone, E. A. (1984). Chronic stress and regulation of the sympathetic nervous system. *In* E. Usdin, R. Kvetňanský and J. Axelrod (Eds.), *Stress: The Role of Catecholamines and Other Neurotransmitters,* pp. 563–576. New York: Gordon and Breach.

Sabban, E. L., Nankova, B., Hiremagalur, B., Orrin, S., Rusnak, M., Viskupic, E., and Kvetňanský R. (1996). Molecular mechanisms in immobilization stress elicited rise in expression of genes for adrenal catecholamine biosynthetic enzymes, neuropeptide Y and proenkephalin. *In* R. McCarty, G. Aguilera, E. L. Sabban and R. Kvetnansky (Eds.), *Stress: Molecular Genetic and Neurobiological Advances,* pp. 611–628. New York: Gordon and Breach.

Stone, E. A., and McCarty, R. (1983). Adaptation to stress: Tyrosine hydroxylase activity and catecholamine release. *Neuroscience and Biobehavioral Reviews* 7: 29–34.

Tank, A. W., Augonis, C. A., Best, J. A., Chen, Y., Nagamoto, K., Piech, K. M., and Sterling, C. R. (1996). Regulation of tyrosine hydroxylase gene expression by multiple receptor-mediated pathways during stress or nicotine treatment. *In* R. McCarty, G. Aguilera, E. L. Sabban and R. Kvetňanský (Eds.), *Stress: Molecular Genetic and Neurobiological Advances,* pp. 647–662. New York: Gordon and Breach.

Wong, D. L., Ebert, S. N., and Morita, K. (1996). Glucocorticoid control of phenylethanolamine N-methyltransferase gene expression: Implications for stress and disorders of the stress axis. *In* R. McCarty, G. Aguilera, E. L. Sabban and R. Kvetňanský (Eds.), *Stress: Molecular Genetic and Neurobiological Advances,* pp. 677–693. New York: Gordon and Breach.

Adrenergic Blockers

see Beta-Adrenergic Blockers

Adrenocortical Function

see Corticosteroids and Stress

Adrenocorticotropic Hormone (ACTH)

Michael E. Rhodes

Allegheny University of the Health Sciences, Pittsburgh

GLOSSARY

adrenal androgens Hormones produced by the adrenal cortex that have weak male sex hormonelike effects.

adrenal cortex The outer layer of the adrenal glands, which secrete several steroid hormones, including glucocorticoids, mineralocorticoids, and adrenal androgens. The adrenals lie just above the kidneys.

amygdala Group of nerve cells in the temporal lobes of the brain that stimulates the secretion of corticotropin releasing hormone and, in turn, the rest of the hypothalamic-pituitary-adrenal cortical axis.

catecholamine Any of a group of amines derived from catechol that have important physiological effects as neurotransmitters and hormones. Examples of catecholamines include epinephrine (adrenaline), norepinephrine (noradrenaline), and dopamine.

circadian rhythms (diurnal rhythms) A daily rhythmic activity cycle, based on 24-h intervals, that is exhibited in the physiological functions, including hormone secretions, of many organisms.

corticotropin releasing hormone (CRH) A hormone produced by neuroendocrine cells of the hypothalamus that is transported down the pituitary stalk to the anterior pituitary gland, where it stimulates the secretion of corticotropin.

cortisol (hydrocortisone) The principal glucocorticoid produced by the adrenal cortex in man. Under normal circumstances, cortisol feeds back to the pituitary gland, hypothalamus, and other brain areas to reduce the secretion of CRH and ACTH, thereby reducing the secretion of cortisol and other adrenal cortical hormones.

Cushing's syndrome A clinical condition resulting from chronic elevation of circulating glucocorticoids. Clinical signs and symptoms of Cushing's syndrome include obesity of the face and trunk, weakness and atrophy of limb muscles, increased blood pressure, imbalance of glucose metabolism, and psychological changes.

glucocorticoids Hormones produced by the adrenal cortex that increase glucose production in the liver, inhibit glucose metabolism by body tissues, and promote lipid breakdown in fat tissue. The principal glucocorticoid in man is cortisol (hydrocortisone). When administered in high, therapeutic doses, glucocorticoids suppress immunological function, reduce inflammation, and decrease connective tissue and new bone formation.

hippocampus Group of nerve cells in the temporal lobes of the brain that inhibits the secretion of corticotropin releasing hormone and, in turn, the rest of the hypothalamic-pituitary adrenal cortical axis.

hormone A chemical substance formed in one organ or part of the body and carried in the blood to another organ or part of the body. Hormones can alter the functional activity, and sometimes the structure, of just one organ or of various numbers of them.

hypothalamic-pituitary-adrenal cortical (HPA) axis A hormone axis consisting of cells in the hypothalamus of the brain that secrete corticotropin releasing hormone (CRH) and vasopressin (AVP), which stimulate the secretion of corticotropin (ACTH) from the anterior pituitary gland into the bloodstream. In turn, ACTH stimulates the adrenal cortex to secrete glucocorticoids, mineralocorticoids, and adrenal androgens into the bloodstream.

hypothalamus Area at the base of the brain that controls vital body processes including the production of hormones that stimulate and inhibit the secretion of anterior pituitary hormones.

mineralocorticoids Hormones produced by the adrenal cortex that reduce the excretion of sodium and enhance the excretion of potassium and hydrogen ions by the kidney. The principal mineralocorticoid in man is aldosterone.

pituitary A gland, connected to the base of the brain by the pituitary stalk, that secretes several hormones into the bloodstream that stimulate the adrenal cortex, the thyroid gland, the gonads (testes and ovaries), and other tissues of the body.

vasopressin (AVP; antidiuretic hormone: ADH) A hormone produced by cells in the hypothalamus that is transported down the pituitary stalk to (1) the anterior pituitary gland, where, along with CRH, it stimulates the secretion of corticotropin and (2) the posterior pituitary gland, where it is carried by the bloodstream to the kidneys, where it reduces the excretion of water.

C orticotropin (adrenocorticotropic hormone; ACTH) is a 39-amino-acid peptide hormone produced by cells of the anterior pituitary gland and carried by the peripheral circulation to its effector organ, the adrenal cortex, where it stimulates the synthesis and secretion of glucocorticoids, mineralocorticoids, and adrenal androgens. Adrenocorticotropic hormone is secreted in response to corticotropin releasing hormone (CRH) from the hypothalamus. The actions of CRH are augmented not only by another hypothalamic hormone, arginine vasopressin (AVP), but also by several other stimulatory and inhibitory factors, including catecholamines and immune factors.

I. INTRODUCTION

Advances in the measurement of ACTH and its related peptides have elucidated their extensive distribution in the body outside the pituitary gland, with differential processing in different tissues. Adrenocorticotropic hormone and other peptides, including β-endorphin, a peptide known for its analgesic and euphoric effects in the brain, are produced in the pituitary from the chemical breakdown of a large precursor protein, proopiomelanocortin. Evidence from light-microscopic studies has suggested that in the anterior pituitary ACTH is secreted by basophils. With the electron microscope ACTH-producing cells appear irregularly shaped and full of secretory granules. Radioimmunoassay of plasma ACTH is now the method of choice for evaluating ACTH secretion, although glucocorticoid concentrations in the blood are also measured as an index of ACTH secretion.

The complete structure of ACTH is known and the hormone has been synthesized. The entire molecule is not needed for biological activity. The first 16 amino acids beginning with the N-terminal amino acid are all that is required for minimal biological activity. Progressive increases in activity occur as the length of the chain increases until full biological

activity is present with a polypeptide over 22 amino acids long. Adrenocorticotropic hormone, measuring 39 amino acids long, has a circulating half-life of 7–15 min.

II. CONTROL OF SECRETION

The regulation of ACTH secretion primarily involves the stimulatory effect of the hypothalamic hormones, CRH and AVP, and the inhibitory effect of glucocorticoids. The participation of other regulators in addition to CRH and AVP, modulating ACTH secretion in the absence of or during stress, cannot be discounted (Fig. 1). A number of other factors, such as angiotensin II, catecholamines, and immune factors, have been shown to stimulate ACTH secretion.

Areas of the brain, including the amygdala, hippo-

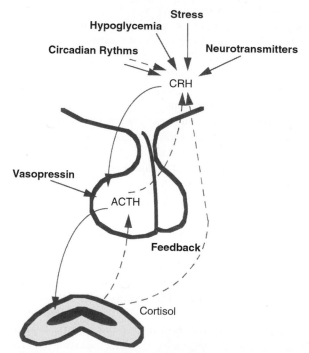

FIGURE 1 Factors influencing the ACTH secretion from the anterior pituitary. Vasopressin and cortisol feedback directly modulate ACTH secretion, while other factors such as stressors, circadian rhythms, cortisol feedback, and neurotransmitters modulate its release by influencing the secretion of the CRH from the hypothalamus. Dashed lines represent negative feedback or inhibition; solid lines respresent stimulation.

campus, and hypothalamus, stimulate and inhibit the HPA axis to different degrees depending on the time of day, season of the year, and physical and environmental stressors. The HPA axis has a normal circadian (24-h) rhythm: the secretion of CRH, ACTH, and adrenal hormones is greatest at 7–8 A.M., an hour or so after awakening, and lowest in early morning between 2 and 3 A.M.. The difference in blood concentrations of ACTH and adrenal glucocorticoids such as cortisol is about fourfold between the valley and the peak several hours later.

The HPA axis is very stress responsive. Both physical and psychological stressors can cause increased activity of this hormone axis. In particular, novel stressors (stressors that are new experiences) cause HPA axis activation; with a person's repeated encountering of the stressor, there is less and less HPA axis response. This is particularly true of demanding tasks, which initially provoke an HPA axis response, but not after the person achieves mastery of the task through training and experience. Public speaking in front of a new audience can be a stressful experience to the novice but causes little or no stress, and therefore no activation of the HPA axis, in the experienced speaker.

Increased ACTH secretion is also observed in pregnancy and at differents periods during the menstrual cycle because of the effects of estrogen in the circulation. Pathological (abnormal) function of the HPA axis can occur from several causes. These include repeated, uncontrollable environmental stressors, functional psychiatric illnesses such as major depression and schizophrenia, and disorders of the HPA axis itself, such as hormone-secreting tumors of the pituitary gland and adrenal cortex. Major depression is the best-studied psychiatric illness in this regard; 30–50% of major depressives have mildly to moderately increased HPA axis activity, consisting of increased blood concentrations of ACTH and cortisol at all times of the day and night, with preservation of the circadian rhythm of these hormones.

III. NEGATIVE FEEDBACK MECHANISMS

The mechanisms regulating ACTH secretion during stress are multifactorial, with the stimulatory effect of the hypothalamus, mainly from CRH and AVP, and the inhibitory influence of glucocorticoids. The HPA axis is regulated by two primary processes. One is "closed-loop" negative feedback of cortisol to hormone receptors in the hippocampus, hypothalamus, and pituitary gland. There are three types of "closed-loop" negative feedback systems. In the long-loop system, glucocorticoids exert a negative feedback on the anterior pituitary, hypothalamus, and hippocampus. With the short-loop system, ACTH itself feeds back on the hypothalamus, exerting negative feedback. With the ultrashort-loop system, the releasing hormone (CRH) acts directly on the hypothalamus to control its own secretion. All of these systems act to suppress the secretion of CRH, ACTH, and cortisol itself (Fig. 2). The second primary pro-

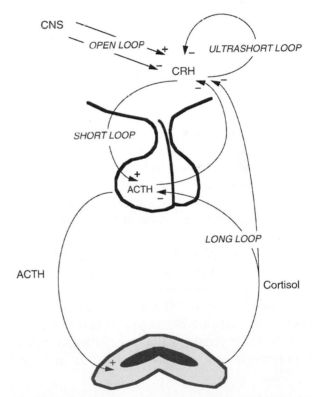

FIGURE 2 Examples of endocrine feedback mechanisms responsible for regulation of the HPA axis. The closed-loop negative-feedback system is comprised of the long, short, and ultrashort loops. The open-loop system includes both stimulatory and inhibitory inputs from the CNS that drive the HPA axis independent from closed-loop systems. (+) Positive-feedback or stimulation; (−) negative-feedback or inhibition.

cess of ACTH regulation is "open-loop" driving of the HPA axis by the central nervous system (CNS).

There are two main types of Cushing's syndrome, ACTH dependent and ACTH independent. Adrenocorticotropic hormone-dependent Cushing's syndrome results from increased pituitary secretion of ACTH, usually from a pituitary tumor (Cushing's disease), inappropriate ACTH secretion by nonpituitary tumors, often in the lungs, and inappropriate CRH secretion by nonhypothalamic tumors, in turn stimulating excessive pituitary ACTH secretion. These conditions, all involving excess ACTH production, cause enlargement of the adrenal glands and excessive cortisol secretion from continuous stimulation.

Adrenocorticotropic hormone-independent Cushing's syndrome is caused by primary tumors or abnormalities of the adrenal cortex itself, resulting in excessive cortisol secretion and suppression of ACTH production by the pituitary. Prolonged administration of glucocorticoids for the treatment of certain illnesses also may cause ACTH-independent Cushing's syndrome.

The excessive pituitary production of ACTH and adrenal production of cortisol in Cushing's disease are only partially suppressible by low-dose dexamethasone, a synthetic and potent glucocorticoid, but more suppressible by higher doses. In contrast, patients with nonpituitary sources of ACTH production rarely show suppression of ACTH and cortisol by dexamethasone.

Adrenocorticotropic hormone is released from the anterior pituitary in response to various stimuli and its release is sustained or inhibited by intricate feedback systems, with ACTH at the heart of this dynamic homeostatic network of "loops." As part of the HPA axis, ACTH is considered one of the major "stress" hormones. It is now apparent that AVP and CRH cooperate as the major factors involved in the control of ACTH release.

See Also the Following Articles

Adrenal Cortex; Cushing's Syndrome; Glucocorticoid Negative Feedback; HPA Axis

Bibliography

Aguilera, G. (1994). Regulation of pituitary ACTH secretion during chronic stress. *Front. Neuroendocrinol.* **15**, 321–350.

McCann, S. M. (1982). The role of brain peptides in the control of anterior pituitary hormone secretion. *In* "Neuroendocrine Perspectives" (E. E. Muller and R. M. Macleod, Eds.), Vol. 1, pp. 1–22. Elsevier Biomedical Press, Amsterdam.

Orth, D. N., Kovacs, W. J., and DeBold, C. R. (1992). The adrenal cortex. *In* "Williams Textbook of Endocrinology" (J. D. Wilson and D. W. Foster, Eds.), 8th ed., pp. 489–619. W. B. Saunders, Philadelphia.

Porterfield, S. P. (1997). Posterior pituitary gland. *In* "Endocrine Physiology," pp. 47–56. Mosby, St. Louis.

Reichlin, S. (1992). Neuroendocrinology. *In* "Williams Textbook of Endocrinology" (J. D. Wilson and D. W. Foster, Eds.), 8th ed., pp. 135–219. W. B. Saunders, Philadelphia.

Rubin, R. T. (1994). Neuroendocrine aspects of stress in major depression. *In* "Stress in Psychiatric Disorders" (R. P. Libenman and J. Yager, Eds.), pp. 37–52. Springer-Verlag, New York.

Schimmer, B. P., and Parker, K. L. (1996). Adrenocorticotropic hormone: Adrenocortical steroids and their synthetic analogs: Inhibitors of the synthesis and actions of steroid hormones. *In* "Goodman & Gilman's The Pharmacological Basis of Therapeutics" (J. G. Hardman and L. E. Limbird, Eds.), 9th ed., pp. 1459–1485. McGraw–Hill, New York.

Thorner, M. O., Vance, M. L., Horvath, E., and Kovacs, K. (1992). The anterior pituitary. *In* "William's Textbook of Endocrinology" (J. D. Wilson and D. W. Foster, Eds.), 8th ed., pp. 221–222. W. B. Saunders, Philadelphia.

Adrenogenital Syndrome

Shaun A. McGrath and Pierre-Marc G. Bouloux

Royal Free Hospital, London

GLOSSARY

allele One of two or more copies of a particular gene located on a chromosome.

androgens Group of sex steroids that stimulate the development of male sex organs and male secondary sexual characteristics.

azoospermia The complete absence of sperm from the seminal fluid.

compound heterozygote A pair of alleles that are both mutated with abnormalities distinct from each other.

euneuchoid Phenotypic appearance resulting from prepubertal hypogonadism and characterized by disproportionately long lower segment length as compared with the upper segment.

homozygote Where both members of a pair of genes are identical.

hyperplasia Increase in size and number of normal cells in an organ or tissue.

hypogonadism Condition which results from failure of sex steroid production.

phenotype The expression of characteristics of a person determined by his/her genes and influenced by environmental factors.

virilization Clinical consequences of excessive androgen production in females characterized by temporal balding, a male body form, muscle bulk, deepening of the voice, enlargement of the clitorus, and hirsutism.

Adrenogenital syndrome represents a spectrum of inherited enzymatic disorders of cortisol biosynthesis, more commonly referred to as Congenital Adrenal Hyperplasia (CAH). In each, cortisol production is decreased leading to a feedback increase of pituitary ACTH (corticotropin) secretion causing adrenal hyperplasia and overproduction of either cortisol precursors or androgen excess. The incidence of the classic disorder is between 1 in 5,000 to 20,000 live births in most populations.

I. CLASSIFICATION OF ADRENOGENITAL SYNDROME

Congenital Adrenal Hyperplasia (CAH) can be classified according to the specific type of enzyme deficiency leading to decreased cortisol production or more commonly, however, by the time and mode of onset of the clinical features. "Classic" CAH refers to the more severe form of enzyme deficiency with a prenatal, neonatal, or early childhood presentation. "Nonclassic" CAH represents a milder variant of the disorder, associated with less severe enzyme deficiency and later, even sometimes adulthood, presentation. Congenital Adrenal Hyperplasia can also be classified as salt-wasting or non-salt-wasting, virilizing, or feminizing (see Table I).

II. MOLECULAR GENETICS AND BIOCHEMICAL ABNORMALITIES IN ADRENOGENITAL SYNDROME

The family of disorders resulting in CAH are caused by deficient activity (either reduction in the amount of enzyme or impaired enzymatic function) in one of the five steps involved in cortisol biosynthesis (Fig. 1). 21-Hydroxylase (21-OHase) deficiency is the most frequent form. This enzyme converts progesterone to deoxycorticosterone and 17-hydroxyprogesterone (17-OHP) to 11-deoxycortisol in the endoplasmic reticulum. Less commonly,

TABLE I

Classification and Presentation of Congenital Adrenal Hyperplasia at Diagnosis[a]

Deficiency	Salt-losing	Virilization	Feminization (undervirulization)	Precocious puberty	Delayed puberty	Hypertension	Infertility, menstrual disturbance, hirsutism, and acne
21-OH (>90%)	Yes (not in late onset nonclassic cases)	Yes (severity varies)	No	Yes (possible presenting complaint)	No	No	Yes
11β-OH (~5%)	No (almost all cases)	Yes (severity varies)	No	Yes	No	Yes (most cases)	Yes
3β-HSD	Yes	No (mild or none at birth)	Yes (in males with classic cases)	Yes	No	No	Yes
17α-OH	No	No	Yes	No	Yes	Yes	No
StAR	Yes	No	Yes	No	Yes	No	No

[a] Abbreviations: 21-OH, 21-hydroxylase; 11β-OH, 11β-hydroxylase; 3β-HSD, 3β-hydroxysteroid dehydrogenase; 17α-OH, 17α-hydroxylase; StAR, steroidogenic acute regulatory protein.

deficient activity of 11β-hydroxylase (11β-OH) in the mitochondria or 3β-hydroxysteroid dehydrogenase (3β-HSD) and 17α-hydroxylase (17α-OH) in the ER can result in adrenogenital syndrome. Last, the steroidogenic acute regulatory protein is essential for transporting cholesterol to the mitochondria for steroid biosynthesis in the adrenal and gonad, and an abnormality in the gene encoding this protein leads to the very rare but devastating congenital lipoid adrenal hyperplasia.

Figure 2 illustrates the mechanism whereby deficient 21-OH enzyme activity leads to a decreased cortisol production and an increased adrenal androgen production by shunting of precursors through alternative steroidogenic pathways. The biochemical abnormalities resulting from enzyme blockade can be deduced by examining the site of the block (Fig. 1).

The genes encoding the various enzymes whose abnormalities are responsible for CAH have been identified and cloned. There is considerable hetero-

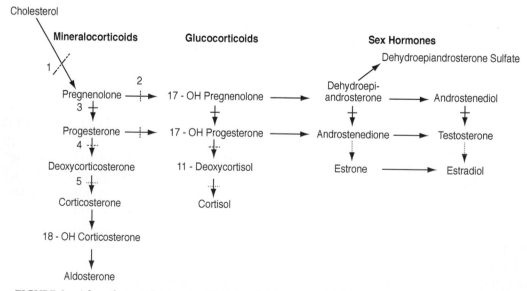

FIGURE 1   Adrenal steroidogenesis. (1) StAR; (2) 17α-OH; (3) 3β-HSD; (4) 21-OH; (5) 11β-OH.

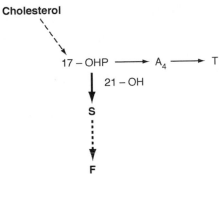

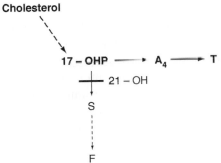

FIGURE 2 Biochemical consequences of enzyme blockade. 21-Hydroxylase deficiency leads to shunting of cortisol precursors to increase adrenal androgen production. Abbreviations; 17-OHP, 17-hydroxyprogesterone; A_4, androstenedione; T, testosterone; S, 11-deoxycortisol; F, cortisol.

geneity of mutations within the gene and although CAH is considered a homozygous recessive disorder, many patients with 21-OH deficiency are compound heterozygotes, explaining the phenotypic variability of the disorder. Although mild, late-onset forms of 21-OH deficiency have genetic correlates; there has been no genetic proof that a similar situation exists for 3β-HSD deficiency despite the cases diagnosed on clinical and biochemical grounds during the past decade.

III. CLINICAL FEATURES OF ADRENOGENITAL SYNDROME

The clinical spectrum of mild to severe forms of CAH reflects the degree of deficiency in cortisol and aldosterone (or both) and also the excess or deficient production of androgens. This, in turn, is determined by the particular genetic abnormality (see Table I).

A. Classic CAH

1. Abnormal Genitalia

Abnormalities in all five steps of cortisol synthesis can present with abnormal genitalia. In the female, virilization of the external genitalia by adrenal androgens *in utero* leads to phallic enlargement, labial fusion, and formation of a urogenital sinus, so-called "female pseudohermaphroditism." Severe cases can be mistakenly diagnosed as hypospadias with "undescended" testes and incorrect gender assignment at birth can result. Males with deficient androgen production can be mistaken as females ("male pseudohermaphrodites") but, more commonly, affected males have normal sexual development.

2. Salt-Wasting Crisis

Salt-wasting crisis may occur in all types of CAH except 11β-OH and 17α-OH deficiency. Most commonly an affected male infant 2–3 weeks old presents with failure to thrive followed by an acute illness consisting of diarrhea, vomiting, dehydration, and circulatory collapse. Plasma electrolytes typically show hyperkalemia, hyponatremia, and metabolic acidosis. Sodium conservation improves with age in some patients, although it is unclear why this should occur.

3. Virilization and Precocious Puberty

In females, clitoral enlargement in early childhood may occur due to overproduction of adrenal androgens. In males the penis may enlarge but the testes remain small. In both, public hair growth may occur early and excess linear growth with concomitant epiphyseal closure may eventuate. Circulating androgens may prematurely activate the hypothalamic-pituitary-gonadal axis and the child may have true precocious puberty. Short stature due to premature epiphyseal closure invariably occurs unless the condition is treated early.

4. Delayed Puberty

This is a rare manifestation of CAH and can occur in poorly controlled 21-OH deficiency with suppression of gonadotrophins by excess adrenal androgens or by failure of sex steroid production in the very rare 17α-OH deficiency.

5. Primary Amenorrhoea

This uncommon presentation may occur in less severe variants of 17α-OH deficiency or 3β-HSD deficiency where phenotypic females with euneuchoid appearance and poorly developed secondary sexual characteristics (breast development and pubic hair) fail to menstruate due to deficient production of ovarian estrogen.

B. Nonclassic CAH

Nonclassic forms of CAH have their onset of symptoms in late childhood or in adulthood.

1. Precocious Puberty

Less severe forms of CAH with no evidence of salt-wasting can present for the first time in later childhood. Accelerated linear growth and bone age can result in reduced ultimate adult height unless the correct diagnosis is made and treatment given.

2. Hypertension

In those types of CAH where excess mineralocorticoids are produced, hypertension may result which may become apparent only in later life.

3. Acne and Hirsutism in the Female

Nonclassical types of CAH with excess androgen production can be indistinguishable from those women with polycystic ovaries, which are frequently present on ultrasound. Approximately 1–3% of hyperandrogenism in adult females is due to "late-onset" CAH.

4. Infertility and Menstrual Disorders

Fertility can be impaired in both males and females with CAH. In females this is due to excess progestagens and androgens suppressing the normal cyclicity of the hypothalamic-pituitary-gonadal axis and in males azoospermia may be reversed with glucocorticoid replacement.

C. Diagnostic Investigations

Once the clinical suspicion is raised, the diagnosis of CAH can be made by measuring the level of steroid precursors in the basal state (see Table II) or after ACTH stimulation (see Fig. 3). 17-Hydroxyprogesterone can also be measured in saliva and examining the urinary steroid profile for abnormal concentrations or ratios of metabolic products of the various steroids can be diagnostic (see Table II). The adrenal glands can be imaged by ultrasound, CT scan, or MRI and may show evidence of bilateral hyperplasia in contrast to the focal lesion which may be seen with an adrenal tumor. Prenatal diagnosis can be made by measurement of 17-OHP or androstenedione in amniotic fluid. HLA typing and linkage analysis of cultured fetal cells from chorionic villus sampling in the first trimester or amniocentesis later in gestation can reliably predict genotype for 21-OH deficiency. Polymerase chain reaction on DNA extracted from uncultured or cultured fetal cells can be employed to screen for abnormalities in the 21B gene responsible for 21-OHase deficiency.

IV. TREATMENT OF ADRENOGENITAL SYNDROME

The aims of treatment are to correct cortisol and mineralocorticoid deficiency and to suppress adrenal androgen production thereby preventing virilization. If successful, this should allow normal maturation, growth, development, and fertility in adult life. The subject should be monitored for the potential adverse effects of overtreatment with glucocorticoids.

The daily dose of glucocorticoid therapy should correspond to the normal adrenal production rate of approximately 7 mg/m^2/day usually given in split dosage. The decision on dosage schedule and preparation of replacement glucocorticoid is still controversial. Larger dosing at night with longer acting, more potent glucocorticoids like dexamethasone decreases the exaggerated morning ACTH (and also adrenal androgen) peak of the circadian rhythm but theoretically can suppress nocturnal growth hormone release. Dosage of glucocorticoid should be increased two- to threefold in the event of a febrile

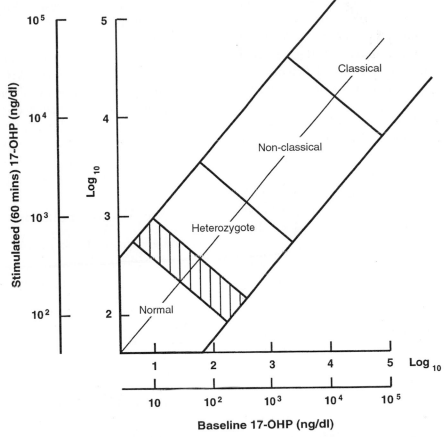

FIGURE 3 Nomogram for genotyping 21-OH deficiency based on baseline plasma 17-OHP and values obtained following stimulation with 250 mcg ACTH (Synacthen). Note there is considerable overlap between the normal unaffected individual and the heterozygote. (Figure for M. C. Young and I. A. Hughes with permission).

TABLE II
Basal Biochemical Profile in Congenital Adrenal Hyperplasia[a]

	Serum							Urine		
Deficiency	17-OHP	A_4	DHEA-S	T	S	P	PRA	17KS	Pregnantriol	THS
21-OH	↑ ↑	↑	−, ↑	↑	−, ↓	−	−, ↑ ↑	↑ ↑	↑ ↑	↓
11β-OH	−, ↑	↑	↑	↑	↑ ↑	−	−, ↓ ↓	↑ ↑	↑	↑ ↑
3β-HSD	−, ↑	−, ↑	↑	↓	−, ↓	↓	↑	↑ ↑	−, ↓	−, ↓
17α-OH	↓	↓	↓	↓	↓	↑	↑	↓	↓	↓
StAR	↓	↓	↓	↓	↓	↓	↑	↓	↓	↓

[a] Abbreviations: 21-OH, 21-hydroxylase; 11β-OH, 11β-hydroxylase; 3β-HSD, 3β-hydroxysteroid dehydrogenase; 17α-OH, 17α-hydroxylase; StAR, steroidogenic acute regulatory protein.

illness and for more severe stresses higher doses or even parenteral therapy may be required. Longterm, the adjustment of the dose of glucocorticoid depends on clinical assessment combined with the results of monitoring in the cases of 21-OHase deficiency, 17-OHP, adrenal androgens, and/or urinary 17-ketosteroid production.

Mineralocorticoid replacement therapy with 9α-fludrocortisone should be used in all those patients with salt-wasting forms of CAH. The use of mineralocorticoid therapy in nonclassic late-onset variants of the disorder with raised plasma renin activity, which reflects salt loss, often allows reduction in the dosage of glucocorticoid and subsequently less risk of iatrogenic side-effects.

Prenatal treatment of affected females *in utero* with dexamethasone to prevent virilization of the fetus has been used with varying success. To be effective, treatment must be started at less than 10 weeks (preferably 5–7 weeks) gestation and continued until delivery in affected females but discontinued in males and those unaffected females. Mendelian inheritance dictates that treatment will be continued until parturition in only 1:8 fetuses. Maternal side-effects such as weight gain, hypertension, diabetes, and edema are common but fortunately more severe side-effects are rare.

The timing of corrective surgery and correct gender assignment is a highly controversial issue and the subject of much debate. In severe forms of 21-OHase and 11β-OHase deficiency, virilization may be so severe that genotypic females may need to be raised as males and ovariectomy will be required and prostheses inserted into the scrotum at puberty. There is evidence that exposure to androgens *in utero* can alter gender and sexual identity in affected females in whom there is an above-average increase in tomboyish behavior and lesbianism. These sequelae expatiate on the need for early and adequate treatment of the condition.

Glucocorticoids are not used for replacement in the treatment of nonclassic CAH but to suppress adrenal hyperandrogenism by inhibiting the morning ACTH peak by delivery of small doses of dexamethasone (e.g., 0.5 mg) or prednisone (e.g., 5 mg) at night. In the nonclassic and classic variants an antiandrogen can be used in combination with glucocorticoids to treat symptoms of hyperandrogenism.

See Also the Following Articles

Adrenocorticotropic Hormone (ACTH); Androgen Action

Bibliography

Azziz, R., Dewailly, D., and Owerbach, D. (1994). Clinical review 56: Nonclassical adrenal hyperplasia: Current concepts: *J. Clin. Endocrinol. Metab.* **78**, 810–815.

Cutler, G. B., Jr., and Laue, L. (1990). Congenital adrenal hyperplasia due to 21-hydroxylase deficiency. *N. Engl. J. Med.* **323**, 1806–1813.

Merke, D. P., and Cutler, G. B., Jr. (1997). New approaches to the treatment of congenital adrenal hyperplasia. *J. Am. Med. Assoc.* **277**, 1073–1076.

Pang, S. (1997). Congenital adrenal hyperplasia. *Endocrinol. Metab. Clin. North Am.* **26**, 853–891.

Seckl, J. R., and Miller, W. L. (1997). How safe is long-term prenatal glucocorticoid treatment? *J. Am. Med. Assoc.* **277**, 1077–1079.

White, P. C., and New, M. I. (1992). Genetic basis of endocrine disease 2: Congenital adrenal hyperplasia due to 21-hydroxylase deficiency. *J. Clin. Endocrinol. Metab.* **74**, 6–11.

Young, M. C., and Hughes, I. A. (1998). Congenital adrenal hyperplasia. *In* "Clinical Endocrinology" (A. Grossman, Ed.), 2nd ed., pp. 450–473. Blackwell, London, UK.

Adrenomedullin
see Vasoactive Peptides

Aerobics, in Stress Reduction

Eco J. C. de Geus

Vrije Universiteit, Amsterdam, The Netherlands

GLOSSARY

aerobic exercise Prolonged dynamic muscular work energized by the oxidation of food (fat, carbohydrates, and protein).

endogenous opioids A class of neuromodulators that can reduce pain and induce a positive (euphoric) mood.

insulin resistance Inability of tissue to respond to insulin take-up of additional glucose. Insulin resistance is associated with increased risk for cardiovascular disease.

monoamines A class of neurotransmitters that are known to influence mood. Antidepressive medication is based on boosting the action of two monoamines (norepinephrine and serotonin) in the central nervous system.

stress reactivity The bodily response to the perception of threat or challenge. There is increased activity of the sympathetic nervous system that becomes manifest as increases in levels of heart rate, blood pressure, and levels of stress hormones.

I. SITES OF INTERACTION BETWEEN STRESS AND AEROBIC EXERCISE

This article reviews the evidence that regular aerobic exercise counters the detrimental effects of psychological stress. The hypothesized psychological, psychophysiological, and physiological effects of exercise are summarized in Fig. 1. In order to protect against psychological stress and stress-related disease, exercise is hypothesized to have all of the following effects: (1) to improve psychological coping with stress, (2) to reduce physiological reactivity to stress, and (3) to counteract the disregulatory effects of stress-reactivity on disease risk factors.

II. PSYCHOLOGICAL COPING WITH STRESS

Most of the research on the beneficial psychological effects of regular aerobic exercise has concentrated on improvements in well-being, often defined as the absence of negative affect, or on improved self-esteem and self-efficacy. Reducing negative affect, e.g., anxiety, hostility, or depression, decreases the chance that an event will be perceived as stressful (primary appraisal). Increasing feelings of self-efficacy increase the chance that coping skills are perceived to be adequate to deal with a stressful situation (secondary appraisal). Well-being and self-esteem further modify interpersonal behavior such that less conflict is generated and they favor adaptive problem-oriented coping and social support-seeking over detrimental coping strategies like denial and social isolation. Thus, exercise-induced improvements in psychological coping with stress may decrease the number of situations that are perceived to be stressful. This decreases the frequency and duration of physiological stress reactions mediated by the autonomic nervous system, which is important, because such stress reactivity, when often repeated, is thought to give rise to physiological disregulation and ultimately to disease (see Fig. 1).

Regular exercisers have consistently been found to show the "iceberg-profile": they have higher vigor (the peak of the iceberg) and lower levels of anxiety, tension, apprehension, depression, and fatigue in comparison to nonexercisers. They are also found to

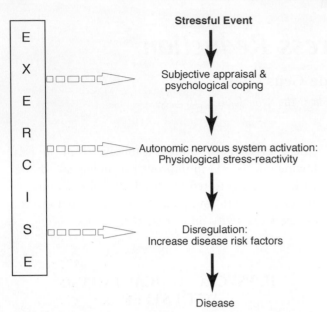

Stressful Event

↓

Subjective appraisal &
psychological coping

↓

Autonomic nervous system activation:
Physiological stress-reactivity

↓

Disregulation:
Increase disease risk factors

↓

Disease

FIGURE 1 Hypothesized influences of aerobic exercise on the psychological and physiological effects of stressful events.

have better self-esteem and self-efficacy and to score better on tests of coping skills. However, coexistence of a healthy mind and a healthy body does not prove that the healthy mind is a consequence of the healthy body (such causality was never suggested by Juvenal, the Roman satirist who originated the adage of *mens sana in corpore sano*—he just prayed for both). The beneficial psychological make-up of exercisers in cross-sectional studies may be based on common underlying influences on both exercise behavior and psychological distress. These may be of a genetic origin or they may reflect environmental influences like low socioeconomic status and poor social support networks that affect both exercise behavior and psychological well-being. Most importantly, the association may reflect a reversed causality, namely that emotionally well-adjusted, agreeable, and self-confident individuals are simply more attracted to sports and exercise or that only such persons have the necessary energy and self-discipline to maintain an exercise regime. In short, the favorable psychological profile of exercisers may reflect self-selection.

To prove that exercise can be used as a prophylaxis against stress and stress-induced disease longitudinal training studies are needed. Such training studies must be carefully designed. Subjective expectations,

distraction, social attention/interaction, and trainer enthusiasm must be separated from the effects of aerobic exercise per se. Therefore, the effectiveness of aerobic training must be compared to a placebo treatment, which may consist of stress-management training, meditation, muscle relaxation, or a nonaerobic exercise program that aims to increase strength or flexibility rather than aerobic fitness. The subjects must not be allowed to choose between these treatments, but randomly assigned to either aerobic training or control treatment to prevent self-selection of subjects with a specific psychological make-up or a relatively high aerobic endowment into the training group.

To date, a relatively small number of studies with such well-controlled experimental designs exist. In fact, the number of studies with solid primary data appear to be about a quarter of the number of reviews published on this theme. Several of the well-designed longitudinal studies have reported improved mood or reductions in coping behavior, depression, and anxiety after a program of aerobic exercise training in comparison to control manipulations. Unfortunately, many others have failed to replicate these training effects, and most of the studies reporting beneficial psychological effects of exercise have used extreme populations, such as highly anxious or delinquent subjects. Even in "normals," the training-induced changes in anxiety, depression, or self-esteem—when found—were generally largest in the subjects with the least favorable psychological profile before the start of the training. Without denying the potential of exercise as a therapy in subsets of subjects, most of the many reviews on this topic express cautious optimism about the use of exercise for stress prevention in the population at large.

III. PSYCHOPHYSIOLOGICAL STRESS REACTIVITY

The various training-induced adaptations in the organization of the autonomic nervous system and its target organs, e.g., dominance of the parasympathetic over the sympathetic nervous system, greater sensitivity for hormonal cues (β-adrenergic receptors, insulin-sensitivity), and better vascularization of muscle tissue, may all critically influence the pattern and the intensity of physiological responses to stress, even if psychological coping with stress is unchanged. Although peak reactivity may not be influenced or even larger in exercisers, habituation during stress and recovery after stress may be faster, analogous to their physiological adaptation to bouts of exercise. An extensive set of studies has compared stress reactivity of well-trained exercisers with that of untrained nonexercisers. In about half of these studies reduced stress reactivity and/or enhanced recovery was found in exercisers. The reverse was found only twice. Although these studies support the idea of lower stress reactivity in exercisers, they were mostly cross-sectional in nature. Consequently, self-selection factors and differences in endowment for fitness and/or psychological make-up may explain the differences in reactivity rather than exercise behavior. Again, training studies can yield more meaningful answers.

Figure 2 provides an example of a typical design of a study to assess exercise training effects on physiological stress reactivity (de Geus *et al.* 1993, *Psychosom. Med.,* **55,** 347–363). In this study, four groups of adult males were submitted to an aerobic training program consisting of two to three sessions weekly over periods of either 4 or 8 months. Control subjects were put on a waiting list for 4 months or remained untrained entirely. Part of the trained subjects were detrained; after an initial 4-month training program, they had to abstain from intensive exercise for 4 months. The effectiveness of aerobic training was measured by the peak oxygen consumption during a supramaximal exercise test, expressed as milliliters of oxygen consumed per kilogram of body weight (VO_2-max). The VO_2-max is generally

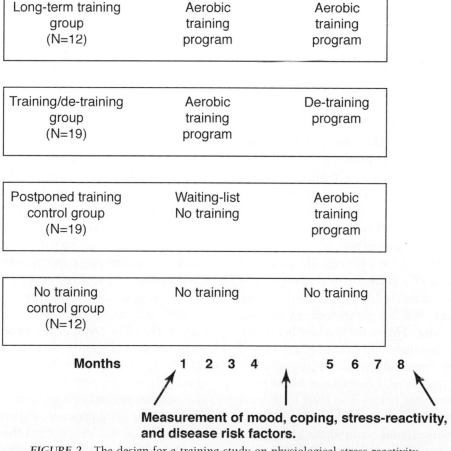

FIGURE 2 The design for a training study on physiological stress reactivity.

held to be the best indicator of aerobic fitness and is highly correlated to actual endurance performance (e.g., Cooper test or shuttle-run). The average improvement in VO_2-max amounted to 14% after 4 months and 16% after 8 months, which is the gain usually attained in long-term and intensive training programs. In spite of improved fitness, this study found no evidence of an effect of aerobic exercise training on an extensive set of physiological responses that included heart rate and blood pressure, stress hormones, indices of cardiac sympathetic and parasympathetic drive, and of peripheral vascular versus cardiac output responding. Stress reactivity tended to decrease over repeated measurements, but the decreases in reactivity were *not* affected by aerobic training or ensuing detraining. These results correspond fully with those of 18 other studies showing that aerobic training does not systematically reduce reactivity to stress or enhance recovery afterwards.

IV. ACUTE EFFECTS OF EXERCISE

Taking the meager experimental support from well-designed training studies, how can we explain the commonly held belief in the stress-alleviating effect of exercise and the fact that most exercisers are motivated by reasons of stress reduction and psychological well-being? The source of this belief may be largely found in the *acute* psychological effects of exercise. In the training studies described above, psychological and psychophysiological testing was preferably done when subjects had not been exercising for a few days. This was done to prevent confounding the results due to possible acute effects of exercise. Studies that have specifically addressed these acute exercise effects have provided strong evidence of improved mood; reduced feelings of tension, anxiety and anger; and increased feelings of vigor directly after exercise. This acute "feeling better" effect of exercise is paralleled by various physiological effects. Although heart rate generally remains elevated above the base level, postexercise blood pressure is seen to decrease below base level for several hours. Neuromuscular activity and peripheral pulse volume are decreased, and brain alpha activity, an indicator of a relaxed but alert mental state, is in-

creased. Most importantly, there is evidence of reduced heart rate and blood pressure responses to stress in the hours directly after exercise.

Among the hypothesized mechanisms for the acute psychological and physiological effects of exercise, those related to the endogenous opioids have been most often cited. An endogenous opioid, β-endorphin, has been held responsible for the euphoric (after-)effects of running that have been ominously termed the "runner's high" and for a benign endorphin-mediated "exercise addiction." However, elevations in peripheral β-endorphin (a typical distress hormone often co-released with ACTH) are seen only during strenuous exercise, not during mild to moderate exercise. More importantly, β-endorphin levels are associated with negative, i.e., expectation of future pain and exhaustion, rather than positive mood, even during exercise. Finally, the opiate antagonist naloxone does not prevent the exercise-induced elevation in the pain threshold or in mood improvement, suggesting that these are largely independent of endorphin action. Since monoaminergic systems in the brain are involved in the pathogenesis of depression and anxiety, a more plausible explanation for exercise-induced mood effects may reside in its effect on central monoamines. Animal models suggest that exercising increases noradrenaline and dopamine metabolism in the brain and that it also increases brain serotonin content. It shares these effects with antidepressives like MAO inhibitors and serotonin-reuptake blockers. Beneficial effects on monoaminergic neurotransmission may also explain why improved mood after training programs is most often found in groups of highly anxious or depressed subjects. An improvement in monaminergic neurotransmission may be effective only if it is severely compromised, as is the case in anxiety and depression.

Whatever its physiological and psychological causes, the tight contingency between exercise and mood improvement directly afterward would form a solid basis for the popular belief that exercise relieves stress. Exercising may be an excellent short-term coping strategy that helps an individual unwind more rapidly from daily pressures experienced in school, on the job, or at home, even if the effects on mood are short lasting. Likewise, the accumulation of episodes of blunted cardiovascular responsiveness may reduce the health risks of stress, even if reductions in stress reactivity are confined to stressors encountered in postexercise periods.

For exercisers, exercising may become a major coping strategy up to a point where stopping exercise could lead to loss of well-being and self-esteem. In fact, most of the popular ideas on the psychological benefits of exercise may stem from exercisers themselves. It must be noted, however, that in most Western countries only 10 to 15% of the population is engaged in exercise with high enough intensity (>70% maximal heart rate), duration (minimally 20 min), and frequency (three times a week) to maintain aerobic fitness level. About 60% has irregular exercise habits or performs mild exercise only, e.g., regular walking or bicycling. The remaining 25% is nearly completely sedentary, and this figure appears to be rather resistant against campaigning to increase physical activity. A major future research question is whether exercise of lesser frequency and intensity can be effective for psychological well-being. A sec-ond question is why exercisers exercise and why nonexercisers do not.

V. EXERCISE AND STRESS: OPPOSING EFFECTS ON DISEASE RISK FACTORS

A final interaction between stress and exercise can be found at the level of disease risk factors, where exercise may systematically oppose the physiological impact of repeated stress reactivity. Evidence for such an interaction comes from the field of cardiovascular disease study. Chronic stress is thought to negatively influence a set of atherogenic factors like high LDL cholesterol ("bad"), low HDL-cholesterol ("good"), high triglycerides, high insulin, high heart rate and blood pressure, and a disturbed balance in the coagulation and fibrinolysis of the blood. This cluster of risk factors is not random but is the multifaceted symptom of a basic abnormality called "insulin resistance syndrome," rooted in obesity and inefficiency

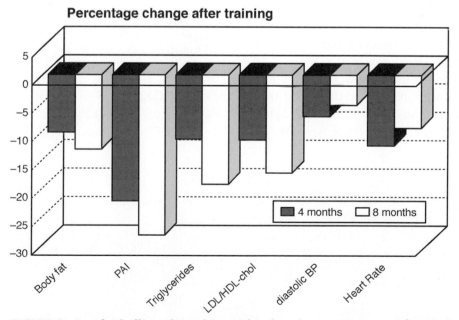

FIGURE 3 Beneficial effects of 4 and 8 months of aerobic exercising on a cluster of risk factors suspected to be affected by psychophysiological stress reactivity: percentage body fat; plasminogen activator inhibitor (PAI) activity, a risk indicator for disturbances in the coagulation/fibrinolysis balance; triglycerides; ratio of LDL ("bad") over HDL ("good") cholesterol; diastolic blood pressure; and heart rate.

of the (muscular) tissue to take up glucose. These risk factors affect the integrity of the arterial walls in synergy, such that stress-induced increases in levels in one of these parameters increase the pathogenic effects of all of the others.

A few hours of exercise a week is known to be able to counter *all* these detrimental effects. Although no effects on stress reactivity (task–baseline) are found, virtually all training studies show a decrease in absolute levels of heart rate and diastolic blood pressure during baseline and stress conditions. This effect is completely revesed after detraining, which strongly argues for a causal effect of exercise. Ambulatory studies have confirmed that the significant decrease in heart rate and blood pressure remains intact in naturalistic situations. In addition, regular exercise reduces the LDL/HDL cholesterol ratio and triglyceride levels and increases fibrinolytic potential of the blood and does so most likely through "preventive maintenance" of muscular insulin sensitivity. Figure 3 shows some of the simultaneous beneficial effects on various risk factors using data from the 4- and 8-month training programs described in Fig. 2.

In conclusion, aerobic exercise should be seen as an excellent way to compensate or prevent stress-related deterioration of cardiovascular health, *even if* the psychological make-up or the acute bodily reactivity to stress are unchanged after months of training. These health benefits suffice to strongly encourage the promotion of aerobic fitness programs to compensate the aversive effects of daily stress.

See Also the Following Articles

EXERCISE; INSULIN RESISTANCE; RELAXATION TECHNIQUES

Bibliography

Bouchard, C., Shepard, R. J. and Stephens, T. (1994). "Physical Activity, Fitness and Health." Human Kinetics, Champaign, IL.

Dishman, R. K. (1997). Brain monoamines, exercise, and behavioral stress: Animal models. *Med. Sci. Sports Exerc.* 29(1), 63–74.

Gauvin, L., Rejeski, W. J., and Norris, J. L. (1996). A naturalistic study of the impact of acute physical activity on feeling states and affect in women. *Health Psychol.* 15(5), 391–397.

Gauvin, L., and Spence, J. C. (1996). Physical activity and psychological well-being: Knowledge base, current issues, and caveats. *Nutr. Rev.* 54(4), S53–S65.

de Geus, E. J. C., van Doornen, L. J. P., and Orlebeke, J. F. (1993). Effects of aerobic fitness and regular exercise on psychological make-up and physiological stress-reactivity. *Psychosom. Med.* 55, 347–363.

Moore, K. A., and Blumenthal, J. A. (1998). Exercise training as an alternative treatment for depression among older adults. *Altern. Ther. Health and Med.* 4(1), 48–56.

Shepard, R. J. (1994). "Physical Fitness and Health." Human Kinetics, Champaign, IL.

Sonstroem, R. J., and Morgan, W. P. (1989). Exercise and self-esteem: Rationale and model. *Med. Sci. Sports Exerc.* 21(3), 329–337.

Yeung, R. R. (1996). The acute effects of exercise on mood state. *J. Psychosom. Res.* 40(2), 123–141.

Affective Disorders

Dean Frederick MacKinnon

Johns Hopkins University School of Medicine

GLOSSARY

affect Objective manifestations of emotional state, including facial expression, demeanor, neurovegetative functioning, and behavior, but also verbal statements reflecting mood, self attitude, and vital sense.

disease A clinical syndrome with characteristic signs and symptoms, related to dysfunction in a bodily organ, caused at least in part by biological forces.

mood Sustained subjective emotional state.

neurovegetative functioning Motivated behavior essential to biological functioning, including sleep, appetite, and libido.

psychosis Severe symptoms of mental illness involving dysfunction in rational thought and reality testing, including hallucinations and delusions.

self-attitude Feelings of personal worth, ranging from grandiosity to self-loathing.

vital sense Feelings of physical well-being, including energy, clarity, and speed of thought, sense of illness, or invulnerability.

Affective disorders are psychiatric syndromes characterized by significant disturbances of mood, the sense of self-worth, and the feelings and functions of physical well-being. Affective disorders can lead to occupational and interpersonal impairment and often (perhaps not often enough) the pursuit of treatment. Suicide is an all-too-common outcome of a severe affective disorder. Mood swings routinely wreck marriages and careers. The clinical features, management, and biology of mania and major depression are described elsewhere in this volume, therefore this article is concerned mainly with the concept of affective disorders as diseases like and in some ways unlike other episodic medical diseases, such as asthma and congestive heart failure. With pulmonary and cardiac disorders, as with affective disorders, episodes of illness may be triggered by environmental stress, but it is not correct to say they are caused by stress.

I. THE SUBJECTIVE EXPERIENCE OF AFFECTIVE DISORDERS

On being diagnosed with an affective disorder, many patients are surprised to hear their psychiatrist attribute their distress to a "chemical imbalance" in the brain. The clinician may go on to explain that affective disorders are believed to be medical disorders, akin to asthma or congestive heart failure, where the potential for an episode of illness is always present, but manifests intermittently. Some patients are relieved to hear this, especially when told of the successful record of biological treatment. Other patients tend to doubt the medical model and find it more natural to understand their illness as the result of stressful circumstances. The immediate certainty felt by many affectively ill patients that their disease is not primarily a dysfunction of the brain separates the affective disorders from other medical disorders. Few medical patients think breathlessness is the normal result of breathing dust or that ankle swelling is the normal result of eating too many salty potato chips. But a depressed mood, sleepless nights, lack of appetite, feelings of worthlessness, and wishes for death often seem to a depressed patient to follow inevitably an unwanted change in life. The elated mood in mania seems to the inexperienced patient to be the natural consequence of possessing superhuman energy and confidence.

Patients with repeated episodes of mania and depression eventually come to see the disease as primary rather than as the secondary result of life circumstances, as this composite case history illustrates:

> Professor M is a 50-year-old scientist admitted for worsening depression and suicidal thoughts. The family history was notable for the father's erratic marital and occupational decisions and diagnoses of depression and eating disorder in a sister. Childhood was otherwise relatively untraumatic and education highly successful. Professor M has had primarily homosexual relationships, with some heterosexual interludes as well, and has never been married. There is no history of substance abuse, and no major medical problems. Depressive episodes began in the early 30s, after the death of a step-parent, with worsening sadness, insomnia, low energy, loss of interest in usual activities, inability to function at work, and suicidal fantasies. The episode resolved with counseling over the course of a year. Subsequent episodes were associated always with losses, often with the end of a relationship. The first hospitalization occurred in the mid 40s, when the patient experienced a desire for suicide, along with other symptoms of depression, after learning a partner had been unfaithful. In addition to the depressive episodes, which are often notable for agitation and suicidal ideation, there have been some hypomanic episodes as well, with increased energy, creative drive, spending, traveling, and sexual disinhibition (including several heterosexual encounters). Upon admission the patient appeared tired, slightly disheveled, with a low mood and suicidal plan but insufficient energy to follow through with it. The patient reported the dawning awareness that this episode of depression seemed not to have been set off by a loss, either real or perceived, and that it now seemed more plausible that the affective disorder was a primary problem, not just a symptom of emotional injury.

The question remains whether this patient's other episodes were indeed caused by losses, as the patient always believed, or were triggered by them, *or whether the losses were in some cases caused by the affective disorder*. Was the patient's emotional state so inconstant that romantic partners found the relationship intolerable? Did a drop in energy and motivation result in a weakened research grant application, the rejection of which heralded a suicidal episode? Did the patient feel elated because of a vacation in the tropics or did the motivation to travel stem from a markedly heightened capacity for excitement, pleasure, and financial largesse? The general question—does stress cause affective instability or

does affective instability cause stress—cannot be answered definitively by asking the patient. The patient's perspective may be skewed by the presence of an episode of affective disorder. There is a fundamental difference between an affective disorder and a disorder of the visceral organs: in the latter case the intact mind, seated in the brain, receives unambiguous information from another organ about a disease process; e.g., pain, shortness of breath, weakness. With affective disorders, the major symptoms are *in the mind*. An ill mind does not see itself clearly.

II. AFFECTIVE DISORDERS AS CLINICAL SYNDROMES

Affective disorders are diagnosed clinically. The only way a clinician can know a patient has an affective disorder is to elicit historical information from the patient and those who have observed the patient. The clinician is more certain of the diagnosis upon hearing the patient's own description of troubling mental phenomena and personally observing signs (e.g., emaciation, lethargy, agitation, rapid speech, etc.) consistent with the clinical syndrome. There are no laboratory tests to reveal affective disorder.

The clinical syndrome of all affective disorders is persistent and pervasive disturbances in mood, self-attitude, vital sense, and neurovegetative functioning. In depression, the varieties of mood disturbance include not just melancholia or sadness, but apathy, anxiety, and irritability. The mood of a manic patient may be elated, but also irritable to the point of belligerence, or expansive without a sense of euphoria, or merely "driven": energized, but restless and uncomfortable.

Self-attitude, the feeling of personal worth, is insidiously disturbed in affective disorders. The disturbance in self-valuation often impedes treatment. Depressed patients may delay treatment because the suffering they experience seems somehow warranted or deserved; ultimately suicide may be desired because the patient feels such a burden on others. Manic patients may feel smarter than the doctor and others and may feel misunderstood or insulted by the suggestion they may be ill.

Affectively ill patients have a disturbance in the sense of physical well-being, or vital sense. In depressed patients, physical well-being is lacking; patients feel tired, weak, slow, inept; cognition is halting or uncertain. Manic patients tend to feel energized, quick, powerful, and righteous. Neurovegetative functioning, the body's internal regulation of activity and metabolism, is typically disturbed in both syndromes. Depressed patients may have insomnia or may sleep to excess without feeling rested. Manic patients may feel little to no need to sleep and may arise rested after a few hours and carry on in this manner to the marvel (or annoyance) of others. Appetites tend to diminish with depression (though some will overeat or binge); in mania the drive for food is less often disturbed, but the drives for sex, acquisition, and excitement are enhanced.

III. VARIETIES OF AFFECTIVE DISORDER

There are many ways to slice affective disorders. The most salient clinical distinction is between manic-depressive and melancholic (depressive) disorders. Modern nosology refers to these disorders as bipolar disorder and major depressive disorder. In the Diagnostic and Statistical Manual (DSM-IV) bipolar disorder and major depressive disorder are considered, along with minor variants (cyclothymia, dysthymia) under the rubric "mood disorder" rather than "affective disorder." The two terms are not completely interchangeable. The term affective disorder is preferred here because the manic and depressive disorders are disorders of much more than mood and cannot be defined simply in terms of mood.

In bipolar disorders, the primary problem appears to be faulty regulation of moods, leading to instability and, in the extreme forms, severe manic and depressive episodes. The depressive disorders seem to involve an extremely low set point for the mood. To use an automotive analogy, a bipolar disorder is akin to a problem with the cruise control in which the speed ranges from 20 m.p.h. above to 20 m.p.h. below the desired cruising speed, leading to erratic driving. In depression, it is as if the car were stuck in neutral or grinding away in first gear.

The affective disorders are classified according to

severity and chronicity. Figure 1 illustrates the spectrum of affective disorders, ranging from mild, transient normal mood fluctuations to severe rapid cycling bipolar disorder type I.

A German psychiatrist of the late 19th/early 20th century, Emil Kraepelin, in observing hundreds of patients, noted however that some patients had episodes that did not fit neatly into the categories of mania and depression. These patients seemed to experience a mixture of manic and depressive symptoms. These episodes were termed "mixed states." To explain mixed states, Kraepelin considered separately the components of emotion, intellect, and volition and observed that these components do not necessarily cycle in synchrony (Fig. 2). A patient in a typical manic state will have elevations of emotion, intellect (i.e., racing thoughts), and volition (i.e., heightened energy). The typical melancholic depression manifests with a nadir in all three components. In contrast, a patient in a dysphoric mania may have a low mood, combined with rapid cognition and volition. Such a patient will appear irritable, argumentative, restless, and feel highly uncomfortable. In practice, the mixed state is seen as a high-risk state for suicide. Another (somewhat rare) form of mixed state is a manic stupor, in which the patient will have a euphoric mood and racing thoughts but otherwise appear inert, as if paralyzed by excitement. In an agitated depression the patient has low mood and the congruent mental sluggishness, manifest often as ruminations on a single, depressive theme, but at the same time the patient's energy is increased; the patient may pace the floor incessantly. It is worth considering that the apparent independence of these three components of cyclical affective disorders in some patients indicates the involvement of three independent biological systems (with, perhaps, a primary biological disturbance in a system related to all three).

IV. HISTORY OF THE CONCEPT OF AFFECTIVE DISORDERS

Descriptions of melancholia and mania date back to Hippocrates, and many medical writers throughout history were able to describe the manic de-

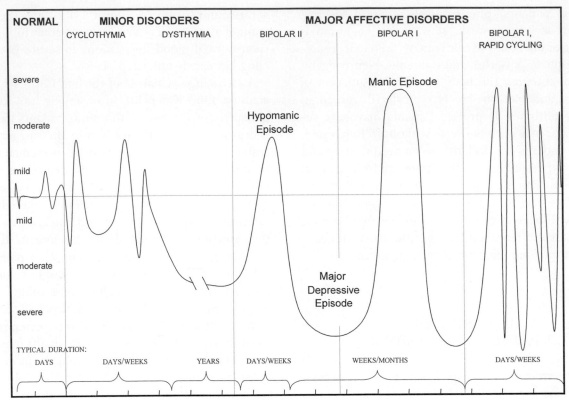

FIGURE 1   Affective disorder diagnoses as a function of the frequency and amplitude of mood variability. Note that normal mood changes may be frequent but are mild and transient, while the more severe mood swings tend to last weeks, months, and, in the case of dysthymia, years.

pressive syndrome in a way familiar to modern psychiatrists. Until the 19th century the prevailing explanations for affective disorders relied on the humoral theory. Abnormal balances of bodily fluids like black bile (the roots for the term "melancholia") or yellow bile (an excess of which was associated with the choleric, or irritable, temperament) were felt to be the cause of affective imbalance.

By the 19th century, ideas about the organic basis of disease had become more sophisticated, and observations of psychopathology were made systematically with the view that affective disorders had their basis in an as-yet-unknown disease of the brain. An exemplar of this trend was, again, Emil Kraepelin, who delineated the patterns of symptoms and course in the institutionalized severely mentally ill under his care. Kraepelin noted a general difference in the course and affective symptomatology between two groups of patients: those having remitting/relapsing forms of psychosis marked by prominent signs of

affective disturbance, and those having chronic psychosis with affective flattening. Kraepelin called the remitting/relapsing disorder manic depressive insanity and the chronic psychotic conditions "paranoia" (including dementia praecox, now better known as schizophrenia).

Psychiatric epidemiologists have established that affective disorders are found not only in the severely, institutionalized mentally ill, but are fairly common in the general population. About 1 in 100 individuals in population surveys meets diagnostic criteria for bipolar disorder and 5–10% have a major depressive episode at some time in life. Most patients with affective disorders do not develop psychosis or require hospitalization; a rather large percentage never enter treatment.

Historical accounts of the obviously manic and melancholic are not too hard to find; it is harder to account for the large number of those who, it is supposed, experienced milder forms of mania and

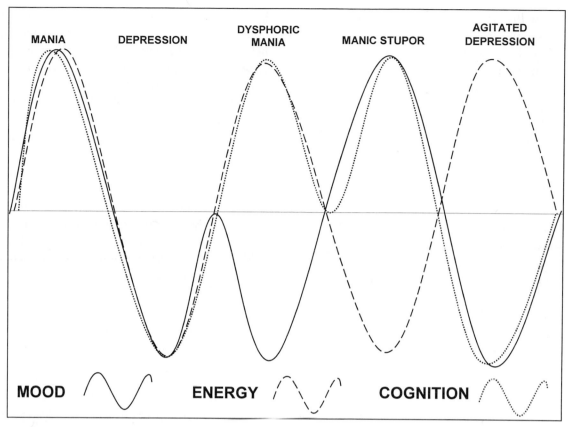

FIGURE 2 Kraepelin's schema of mixed affective states. The coexistence of a morose mood (low mood) with physical restlessness or agitation (high energy) and racing thoughts (high cognition) produces a dysphoric, or "mixed" mania.

depression but understood these experiences in non-medical terms. Traces of these individuals perhaps are found in the annals of art, literature, politics, business, philosophy, exploration, science, and religion, where the experience of mild depression in a receptive mind may engender enduring insights about the fragility of existence or tenderness to the suffering of others. Mild manic states may have contributed to expansive works of art or to ambitious, risky endeavors. Affectively colored cultural contributions are not necessarily pathological, though the experience of the passionate, creative, or daring historical figure might resemble in detail the experience of a typical patient with an affective disorder. It is just as possible that the availability of antidepressants and lithium in times past might have robbed the world of some works of genius as it is possible that the geniuses themselves might have been spared much suffering and contributed even more had treatment been available.

V. AFFECTIVE DISORDERS AS DISEASES

Efforts to link affective disorders to external circumstances have yielded distinctions between mourning and melancholia (Freud) and reactive versus endogenous depression. But if it is unclear whether stress causes depression or vice versa, then a simpler, assumption-free explanatory model is required if we are to understand the dejection that results from, say, a romantic setback, versus the prolonged sadness that accompanies the grieving process, versus an affective disorder. Unlike emotional reactions, affective disorders are clinical syndromes with stereotypical patterns of sign, symptoms, course, and treatment response. Unlike grieving, affective disorders are associated in some cases with known brain disease. Affective disorders are best understood as medical diseases.

Like other medical diseases, affective disorders are not limited by culture, intelligence, education, socioeconomic status, or experience. Nor do the symptoms of affective disorder vary much across cultures. A manic individual in England may have delusions of being a member of the Royal Family, while an American may feel he has been elected President, and a Nigerian may develop a scheme to unite all of Africa under his leadership. Each of these people has the same form of symptom, a grandiose delusion. A depressed golfer in Scotland may avoid the links, a depressed grandmother in Manila might avoid her beloved grandchildren; each demonstrates the same symptom: anhedonia (i.e., the absence of pleasure).

The typical symptoms of affective disorder cluster over a similar course and respond to the same biological treatments anywhere in the world. Affective disorders, moreover, may arise from known medical causes. Huntington's disease, a genetic disorder of progressive dementia and abnormal movement, carries a high risk for manic-depressive disorder. Some patients develop their first depression after a stroke (particularly a stroke in the left frontal part of the brain). Certain blood pressure medicines cause a clear depressive syndrome; knowledge of the pharmacology of such drugs spawned research into medications to reverse the depressive syndrome. Cortisol-like drugs (e.g., prednisone) commonly induce manic symptoms in people with no history of affective disorder. If such known changes to the anatomy and biochemistry of the brain can trigger the characteristic signs and symptoms of affective disorder, then it seems reasonable to conclude that the commonly observed affective disorders arise from biological mechanisms as yet unknown, but knowable.

In contrast, clinical problems related to mood alone are strongly culture bound, generally have few if any symptoms other than a bad mood, and cannot be mimicked by drugs or other medical diseases. Such symptoms as a shy person's fear and avoidance of public pronouncement or the crushing despair felt by a hot-tempered lover spurned may provide an opportunity to learn and grow (perhaps with the help of psychotherapy); otherwise these feelings may arise again when a similar situation arises. Mood reactions of this sort are best viewed primarily as an unpleasant or unmanageably intense mood change reflecting a temperamental vulnerability stretched to the limit. Grief, on the other hand, has a syndromal quality to it, with characteristic sensations: the "welling up" feeling, the false recognition of the departed in a crowd. Uncomplicated grief is not a disease, of course, but a normal part of human experience; thus it is best viewed as a highly individualized experience rich with personal meaning. In real clinical situations, it is not always simple to tell grieving from moping from depression, but it is essential to try.

VI. BEHAVIOR AND PERSONALITY IN AFFECTIVE DISORDER

Affective disorders are diseases, but disease is not all that troubles a patient with an affective disorder. Affective disorders often drive self-destructive and self-defeating behavior. There is an extremely high rate of suicide among patients with severe affective disorder—perhaps as many as 1 in 6 die by their own hand. A much larger number attempt suicide. When the suicidal behavior does not result in death, it nevertheless leads to strained relationships with those the patient intended to leave behind.

Suicidal behavior thus contributes to broken homes, but there are other behaviors associated with mania and depression that undermine marriages and careers. In depression, a patient may become surly; may withdraw to bed, avoiding family, friends, and work; may seek solace in alcohol or drugs. Manic patients may spend, drive, and love recklessly; may flout the law and social mores; and often abuse alcohol and drugs.

It is important to note that such behaviors are not essential to affective disorders. Many people who attempt suicide, avoid work, spend recklessly, or drink heavily lack the signs and symptoms of affective disorders. Many patients with affective disorders (perhaps most) manage, somehow, to constrain their behavior. Patients who change their behavior in the midst of an episode of affective disorder may benefit from gentle confrontation and counseling about the consequences of their behavior. Some therapists think of the self-defeating and self-deprecating thoughts and attitudes that arise during depression as behaviors amenable to confrontation and redirection; this approach is the basis of cognitive therapy.

Greater symptom severity may drive one patient's behavior to go awry while a less afflicted patient remains relatively steady, but personality and life circumstances also contribute. Some affectively ill patients prone to dysfunctional behavior may have personality disorders at baseline. Personality disorder diagnoses are used by psychiatrists to describe problematic, enduring patterns of temperament and behavior. These disorders may themselves be defined by their affective components, e.g., the "labile" affect of the borderline patient or the "constricted" affect of the schizotypal patient. Thus it may be hard to tell if a patient who seems to meet diagnostic criteria for a personality disorder may really have an affective disorder. Patients in a manic state often display labile affect (and other "borderline" or "narcissistic" traits), and depressed patients often appear odd and constricted. Thus, the wise diagnostician waits to assign a personality disorder diagnosis to an affectively ill patient until after the affective syndrome clears up and the patient can be observed in the well state.

The circumstances of a patient's life prior to the onset of an affective disorder also influence the degree of behavioral dysfunction that results. A libertine when stable is more likely than a saint to engage in reckless acts, if only because the means to such acts are more familiar. An academically and economically marginal college student knocked out of school by depression may have a harder time getting back on track than a middle-class mid-career middle-manager in a solid marriage. Patients and families are wisely counseled not to make major changes in career, family, or housing in the midst of an episode of mania or depression. The fewer the changes, the less the risk of serious impairment and the easier the rehabilitation once the episode clears.

VII. AFFECTIVE VERSUS OTHER PSYCHIATRIC DISORDERS

Comparison of affective disorders to other psychiatric diseases helps illuminate the affective disorder syndrome. While affectively ill patients may demonstrate cognitive dysfunction (poor attention and concentration in depression, disorganization and distractibility in mania), mania and depression are not a cognitive disorder, like dementia, since the cognitive difficulties tend to clear up with treatment of the affective illness. Indeed, it is a most gratifying clinical experience to see an elderly person, apparently in a deep dementia, regain awareness of the world after being treated for depression. In contrast to a psychotic disorder like schizophrenia, psychotic symptoms in a patient with an affective disorder tend only to occur when the patient is in the grip of severe mania or depression. In practice, however, the boundaries of affective and psychotic disorders are not always well defined. Some believe schizophrenia and bipolar disorder have the same cause, with "schizoaffective" disorder as an intermediate type. Consistent evidence from family studies demonstrates, however, that schizophrenia and bipolar disorder tend to "breed true," i.e., the risk for bipolar disorder in the relative of a patient with schizophrenia is not appreciably elevated over the risk for someone in the population in general. Anxiety disorders, too, may be related to affective disorders; indeed there is epidemiologic evidence to believe that is the case. Panic disorder and obsessive-compulsive disorder, for example, are seen frequently in patients with affective disorder. Anxiety disorders share some of the characteristic symptoms of affective disorders: disturbances of mood and physical well-being, but miss the typical affective disturbances in self-worth, sleep, and appetite.

In summary, affective disorders are fairly common and often severe medical diseases afflicting the mood, self-attitude, vital sense, and bodily functions of sleep, appetite, and libido. Some patients exhibit marked changes in behavior while others maintain the appearance of normality despite their symptoms. Although a patient with an affective disorder (and loved ones and caregivers) will often search for a meaningful explanation for the symptoms, the source of the problem is likely to be in the functioning of the brain. Stress may trigger the onset of an affective disorder in a vulnerable individual; affective disorders certainly cause stress. Patients with affective disorders require not only biological treatment of the disease, but also management of self-destructive behavior and rehabilitation once the episode clears.

See Also the Following Articles

ASTHMA; DEPRESSION AND MANIC-DEPRESSIVE ILLNESS; DEPRESSION MODELS; HEART DISEASE/ATTACK; NEGATIVE AFFECT; SUICIDE, BIOLOGY OF; SUICIDE, PSYCHOLOGY OF

Bibliography

Goodwin, F. K., and Jamison, K. R. (1990). "Manic Depressive Illness." Oxford Univ. Press, New York.

Jamison, K. R. (1993). "Touched with Fire: Manic-Depressive Illness and the Artistic Temeperament." Free Press, New York.

Jamison, K. R. (1995). "An Unquiet Mind." Vintage Books, New York.

Kraepelin, E. (1990). "Manic Depressive Insanity and Paranoia" (reprint edition). Ayer, Salem, NH.

McHugh, P. R., and Slavney, P. R. (1998). "The Perspectives of Psychiatry" (2nd ed.) Johns Hopkins Univ. Press, Baltimore, MD.

Mondimore, F. M. (1999). "Bipolar Disorder: A Guide for Patients and Families." Johns Hopkins Univ. Press, Baltimore, MD.

Robins, L. N., and Regier, D. A. (1991). "Psychiatric Disorders in America: The Epidemiologic Catchment Area Study." Free Press, New York.

Sims, A. (1988). "Symptoms in the Mind: An Introduction to Descriptive Psychopathology." Balliere Tyndall, Philadelphia, PA.

Stryon, W. (1992). "Darkness Visible." Vintage Books, New York.

African-Americans, Stress in

see Blacks, Stress in

Aggression

Emil F. Coccaro

University of Chicago

GLOSSARY

antisocial behavior Behavior in which the rights of others are violated. This includes behavior that provide grounds for arrest, deceitfulness, failure to honor obligations, lack of remorse, and irritability and aggressiveness against person and property (e.g., vandalism).

criminal behavior Behavior in which a crime is committed, usually behavior that is identified by the criminal justice system.

delinquent behavior Usually refers to the kind of "antisocial" behavior seen in children and adolescents and includes aggression and other dysfunctional behaviors (e.g., school truancy).

epidemiologic survey A study in which a representative sample of a population of individuals is studied to estimate the number of individuals from that general population that have a certain condition or diagnosis.

genetic studies Studies designed to estimate if a condition or disorder has an underlying genetic component. These include (1) family studies, which can show that a condition runs in families or no (2) twin studies, which can show if a condition is more likely to occur in identical as opposed to fraternal twins and therefore must have a genetic component; and (3) adoption studies, which can show the separate and interactive contributions of environmental and genetic factors.

heritability estimate A mathematical estimate of the magnitude of the importance of genetic factors in a condition or disorder.

neurochemistry Aspect of biological functioning related to chemicals which transmit signals from one nerve to another.

problem solving The ability to find solutions to everyday types of problems.

psychosocial Potential influences on behavior (or on conditions/disorders) that are not apparently due to genetic or biological factors.

serotonin norepinephrine, and dopamine Widely distributed neurochemicals in the brain which are involved in mediating a variety of brain and behavioral functions.

transgenerational A general term which refers to an observation noted from generation to generation (e.g., grandparents to parents to offspring).

violent behavior Behavior in which physical aggression in some form is present. Violent behavior is a nonspecific term.

I. TYPES OF AGGRESSION

Aggression can be defined as an intentional act committed by an individual which has the potential to result in the physical or emotional harm of a person or of an object. While aggression is typically thought of as constituting a physical assault, acts of aggression also include verbal outbursts in which the individual's voice is used to convey anger in an "uncontrolled" manner. Broadly speaking, aggression can be subdivided into two types: impulsive aggression and premeditated or nonimpulsive aggression. Aggression is referred to as impulsive when the aggressive act is unplanned or in response to an aversive stimulus, generally uncontrolled, and committed without the expectation of a achieving a tangible objective. By contrast, premeditated aggression is controlled, involves planning, and is associated with an expectation of reaching a specific goal such as, for example, intimidation of the victim. While acts of impulsive aggression can sometimes be criminal in nature, premeditated aggression is more likely to occur in the context of other criminal behavior. Because impulsive, rather than premeditated, aggression appears to be associated with specific biological and pharmacological response characteristics, this article generally focuses on impulsive aggression.

II. EPIDEMIOLOGY OF AGGRESSION

Despite the clinical importance of impulsive aggression, there is very little epidemiologic data regarding impulsive aggressive behavior specifically. Existing epidemiologic data exclusively refer to homicide and physical assault; i.e., aggression in general. Currently, the age-adjusted rate for homicide in the United States, based on vital statistics records, is 0.01%. Epidemiologic survey data find that approximately 25% of all males report a history of some physical fighting since 18 years of age; a rate that is twice as high as is found in adult females. Accordingly, approximately 10–15% of the general population report that they have engaged in physical fighting as an adult. This proportion translates into at least 25.0–37.5 million individuals in the United States alone. While we cannot know what proportion of homicides or physical assault were impulsive in nature, it is likely that a substantial proportion represent impulsive aggressive acts.

III. GENETICS OF AGGRESSION

Data from twin, adoption, and family studies support the hypothesis that aggression is under significant, if variable, genetic influence. The differences seen in these results is due, most likely, to the fact that different studies examined "aggression" in different ways using differing assessment measures. Specifically, "aggression" has been examined in these types of studies by using categories which more or less reflect aggression (such as "delinquent behavior," "antisocial behavior," "criminal behavior," and "violent behavior") in populations with psychiatric diagnoses or by using scales which more or less reflect the severity of aggression in the general population or in university students. In clinical populations, genetic influences appear to underlie both delinquent behavior and antisocial behavior. In general popula-

tions, heritability estimates for measures of aggression range from substantial in children to moderately substantial in adults (44-72%) to apparently nonexistent in adolescents. Most noteworthy is the observation that the aggression measures with the greatest heritability estimates reflect anger and hostility and/or anger, impulsiveness, and irritability. These are the type of behavioral traits which appear to be associated with impulsive aggressive behaviors and which in turn have been shown to be strongly correlated with biological factors and with psychopharmacological response to treatment with antiaggressive agents (see later).

IV. PSYCHOSOCIAL ASPECTS OF AGGRESSION

The most important psychosocial factors involved in the development of aggression appear to be low socioeconomic status (SES), ineffective parenting style, physical punishment in childhood, and exposure of aggression in and outside the family. Factors involved in maintaining aggression appear to be poor development of problem-solving skills, a bias to attribute hostile intent to others, and a deficiency in appropriately detecting environmental and social cues.

A. Low SES and Parenting Style

Low socioeconomic status has been linked to the development of aggression in numerous studies. However, it is likely that low SES exerts its effect on aggression through more relevant behavioral factors such as being raised in a criminally violent family and exposure to gang activity and violence. The stress associated with poverty is associated with negative parental interactions and, consequently, parental irritability, a factor which was associated with aggressiveness in children. More specifically, marital problems in low-SES families has been linked to aggression in children. In addition, an association between lack of maternal responsiveness (and poor child rearing) in low-SES homes and aggressiveness has also been reported, a finding consistent with earlier reports showing that nonnurturing parents tend to have aggressive children. A critical predictor in this regard appears to be lack of favorable warmth toward the children. This latter factor appears to be associated with an impairment in effective parenting so that children in these families do not fully internalize "right from wrong."

B. Exposure to Violence

Exposure to violence both inside and outside the home has also been linked to aggression. Physical punishment and child abuse has also been associated with the development of aggression in children. In transgenerational studies, parents who behaved aggressively toward their children had aggressive children who, in turn, raised similarly aggressive children. Harsh discipline and child abuse (regardless of SES status) appears to specifically predict the development of impulsive, but not nonimpulsive, aggressive behavior in children. Witnessing aggression has also been associated with the development and instigation of aggression and it is likely that the presence of aggressive environmental cues may increase the immediate risk of aggression in susceptible individuals.

C. Deficiency in Problem Solving

A deficiency in problem-solving skills has been noted to be involved in the maintenance of aggression in impulsive aggressive children in particular. Impulsive aggressive children tend to have interpersonal problems and often get rejected by their peers. While aggressivity may appear to be a prime reason for peer rejection, cognitive factors may also play a role in this regard. Specifically, aggressive children tend to attribute hostile intent to others with whom they are interacting. It *is* important to note that the attribution of hostile intent to others may act as the provocation for an aggressive encounter. This hostile attribution is specific to their own interactions; these children do not attribute hostile intentions to other children. The tendency of aggressive children to attribute hostile intent to others may be related to the observation that aggressive children, specifically impulsive aggressive children, have difficulty "reading" relevant social cues. For example, impulsive, but not

nonimpulsive, aggressive children have been found to incorrectly label a visual cue (i.e., a "sad" face is identified as reflecting another emotion).

It is important to recognize, however, that these various psychosocial factors demonstrate a variable association with aggressive behavior. Like genetic factors, psychosocial factors can only predict aggressiveness as a probabilistic function of who may become aggressive given the presence of other factors. Clues to the understanding of this finding may be found in examining the role of biology in aggressive behavior.

V. BIOLOGY OF AGGRESSION

Among the constitutional/developmental biological factors possibly involved in aggression, the most studied factors relate to brain neurochemistry, specifically monoamines such as serotonin and other centrally acting neurotransmitters.

A. Serotonin (5-HT)

Evidence of a role of brain serotonin (5-HT) in human aggression is especially strong. In fact, the inverse relationship between impulsive aggressive behavior is the most consistent of all findings in biological psychiatry. Various measures reflecting brain 5-HT function have been shown to correlate inversely with life history, self-report questionnaire, and laboratory measures of aggression. Most notable is the replicated observation that evidence of reduced central 5-HT is present in impulsive, but not premeditated, aggressive subjects. This indicates that impulsive aggressive behavior can be distinguished biologically from nonimpulsive aggression and, accordingly, is a valid subtype of human aggressive behavior. An inverse relationship between 5-HT and aggression is reported in most, though not all, studies. However, where studies are at variance with this basic finding issues related to sample populations probably account for the differences in reported findings.

B. Catecholamines and Vasopressin

While there are less data available to support the role of non-5-HT brain systems and modulators in human impulsive aggression, there are limited data suggesting a facilitory role for catecholamines (i.e., dopamine, norepinephrine) and vasopressin in impulsive aggressive behavior. The relationship of catecholamines and vasopressin to aggression and serotonin, specifically, is noteworthy. In the case of the catecholamines, the typically inverse relationship between aggression and 5-HT may not be seen when catecholamine system function is reduced. Accordingly, correlations between measures of 5-HT and aggression are generally absent in depressed subjects, who typically demonstrate diminished norepinephrine system function. In the case of central vasopressin and aggression, 5-HT appears to be inversely related to both central vasopressin and to aggression in both animal and human subjects. In human subjects, the relationship between central vasopressin and aggression is present even after its relationship with 5-HT is accounted for. In animal studies, both central vasopressin activity and aggression can be suppressed by treatment with SSRI agents.

C. Testosterone and Cholesterol

In addition to non-5-HT central neurotransmitters, at least two peripheral substances appear to have a relationship with aggression. Based on data from both animal and human studies, testosterone appears to have a facilitory relationship with aggression testosterone. The relationship between testosterone to aggression and 5-HT is less clear although chronic testosterone exposure appears to downregulate central 5-HT receptors in some studies. Another peripheral, though centrally active, substance which appears to influence aggressive behavior is cholesterol. Over the past decade data from a variety of studies suggest that a reduction in circulating levels of cholesterol may be associated with an increase in aggressive behavior in both human and animal subjects. While a link to 5-HT has not been conclusively demonstrated in human subjects, studies in nonhuman primates clearly demonstrate that the reduction in circulating cholesterol levels is associated with a re-duction in measures which reflect central 5-HT function.

D. Localization of Biological Abnormalities

Reductions in CSF levels of neurotransmitter metabolites (e.g., 5-HIAA) suggest a central location to alterations in biological systems. However, CSF metabolites cannot reflect abnormalities in specific locations. Abnormalities in hormonal responses to pharmacological challenge agents do suggest an abnormality in the hypothalamus (a part of the limbic system involved in the regulation of emotion and behavior) of impulsive aggressive individuals. Recent brain-imaging studies are now reporting data suggesting hypofunction of parts of the prefrontal cortex and relative hyperfunction of deeper subcortical structures. For example, FDG-PET scan data demonstrate lower metabolic rates bilaterally in the lateral and medial areas of the prefrontal cortex of impulsive, but not premeditated, murderers compared with normal control. In contrast, metabolic rates of subcortical structures (e.g., hippocampus, amygdala, thalamus, and midbrain) in the right hemisphere were found to be elevated in both impulsive and premeditated murderers compared with normal controls. Since prefrontal structures are thought to regulate inhibition and subcortical structures are thought to regulate arousal, these data suggest that impulsive aggressive individuals have, compared to normal controls, less prefrontal inhibition in the context of greater subcortical emotional drive. Premeditated aggressive individuals, by contrast, have normal prefrontal inhibition but greater subcortical emotional drive. These data, in addition to the neurotransmitter-specific data discussed earlier, suggest that aggression in impulsive aggressive individuals could be treated by strategies which increase prefrontal inhibitory mechanisms and reduce subcortical facilitory mechanisms.

VI. PSYCHOPHARMACOLOGY OF AGGRESSION

As might be expected from the results of the biological study of aggression, several psychopharmacologic agents appear to have anti- or proaggressive effects. Classes of agents shown to have "antiaggressive" effects in double-blind, placebo-controlled trials include mood stabilizers (e.g., lithium), 5-HT uptake inhibitors (e.g., fluoxetine), anticonvulsants (e.g., diphenylhydantoin, carbamazepine, and depakote), and NE β-blockers (e.g., propanolol and nadolol). Classes of agents which may have "proaggressive" effects include tricyclic antidepressants (e.g., amitriptyline), benzodiazapines (e.g., alprazolam), and stimulant and hallucinatory drugs of abuse (e.g., amphetamines, cocaine, and phencyclidine). The most notable findings from the relatively small literature of the double-blind, placebo-controlled clinical trials of "antiaggressive" agents is that their antiaggressive efficacy is limited to the impulsive aggressive, and not the nonimpulsive aggressive, individual. This indicates that psychopharmacology at this time may have little to offer society in the management of criminally motivated aggression. It remains to be seen, however, what the effect of treatment might be with agents which possibly dampen the function of deeper subcortical structures. A second potentially important finding is emerging evidence of a differential psychopharmacology in this area so that some subjects may respond to some agents but not others. In our recent studies with fluoxetine, we have noted an inverse relationship between pretreatment 5-HT function and antiaggressive response to fluoxetine. Moreover, most fluoxetine nonresponders appeared to respond to treatment with divalproate. Given the differential biology of impulsive aggression, it is likely that multiple strategies may be effective in impulsive aggressive individuals depending on their own individual neurobiological substrate.

See Also the Following Articles

ANGER; ANTISOCIAL BEHAVIOR; FAMILIAL PATTERNS OF STRESS; HOSTILITY; IMPULSE CONTROL; PROBLEM-SOLVING SKILLS TRAINING; VIOLENCE

Bibliography

Barratt, E. S., Stanford, M. S., Felthous, A. R., and Kent, T. A. (1997). The effects of phenytoin on impulsive and premeditated aggression: A controlled study. *J. Clin. Psychopharmacol.* 17, 341–349.

Coccaro, E. F. (1998). Central neurotransmitter function in human aggression. *In* "Neurobiology and Clinical Views on Aggression and Impulsivity," (M. Maes and E. Coccaro, eds.), pp. 143–168. Wiley, New York.

Coccaro, E. F., and Kavoussi, R. J. (1997). Fluoxetine and impulsive aggressive behavior in personality disordered subjects. *Arch. Gen. Psychiat.* 54, 1081–1088.

Coccaro, E. F., Siever, L. J., Klar, H. M., Maurer, G., Cochrane, K., Mohs, R. C., and Davis, K. L. (1989). Serotonergic studies in affective and personality disorder: Correlates with suicidal and impulsive aggressive behavior. *Arch. Gen. Psychiat.* 46, 587–599.

Cowdry, R. W., and Gardner, D. L. (1988). Pharmacotherapy of borderline personality disorder: Alprazolam, carbamazepine, trifluoroperazine, and tranylcypromine. *Arch. Gen. Psychiat.* 45, 111–119.

Dodge, K. A., Lochman, J. E., Harnish, J. D., and Bates, J. E. (1997). Reactive and proactive aggression in school children and psychiatrically impaired chronically assaultive youth. *J. Abnorm. Psychology.* 106, 37–51.

Huesmann, L. R., Leonard, E., Lefkowitz, M., and Walder, L. (1984). Stability of aggression over time and generations. *Dev. Psychopathol.* 20, 1120–1134.

Linnoila, M., Virkkunen, M., Scheinin, M., Nuutila, A., Rimon, R., and Goodwin, F. K. (1989). Low cerebrospinal fluid 5-hydroxyindoleacetic acid concentration differentiates impulsive from nonimpulsive violent behavior. *Life Sci.* 33, 2609–2614.

Miles, C. G. (1997). Genetic and environmental architecture of human aggression. *J. Pers. Soc. Psychol.* 72, 207–217.

Raine, A., Meloy, J. R., Bihrle, S., Stoddard, J., LaCasse, L., and Buchsbaum, M. S. (1998). Reduced prefrontal and increased subcortical brain functioning assessed using positron emission tomography in predatory and affective murderers. *Behav. Sci. Law* 16, 319–332.

Virkkunen, M., Rawlings, R., Tokola, R., Poland, R. E., Guidotti, A., Nemeroff, C., Bissette, G., Kalogeras, K., Karonen, S. L., and Linnoila, M. (1994). CSF biochemistries, glucose metabolism, and diurnal activity rhythms in alcoholic, violent offenders, fire setters, and healthy volunteers. *Arch. Gen. Psychiat.* 51, 20–27.

Aggressive Behavior

J. M. Koolhaas

University of Groningen, The Netherlands

GLOSSARY

aggressive behavior A set of social behaviors closely associated in time with overt fighting.

defensive aggression A set of behaviors performed in defense to an attack by a conspecific or a potential predator.

dominant The member of a social group that is the winner of the social interactions with all other group members.

offensive aggression A set of aggressive behaviors performed against a conspecific aimed to protect resources.

subordinate Those members of a social group who lose in interactions with the dominant and never challenge the dominant.

violence A form of aggressive behavior which has lost its original biological function and which may cause serious damage to the opponent.

Aggressive behavior is a highly functional form of social behavior that can be observed in almost all vertebrate animal species. Several forms of aggressive behavior can be distinguished. Offensive aggression has its most common function in the establishment and maintenance of the structure of a social group. Defensive aggression has an important function in the self-protection against attacks from others. The differential physiological basis of the two forms of aggressive behavior is the most important factor underlying the incidence of stress pathology in social groups.

I. AGGRESSIVE BEHAVIOR: FORM AND FUNCTION

The existence of different kinds of aggression has long been recognized mainly on the basis of animal research. Two of these, namely instrumental and irritable aggression, are particularly relevant to bridging the gap between human and animal aggressive behavior. Instrumental aggression is a form of aggressive behavior which is instrumentally used to obtain desiderata, while irritable aggression is performed in reaction to aversive (social) events. This distinction seems to be analogous to the distinction between offense and defense made on the basis of animal experiments. Offensive behavior is displayed by a dominant resident against an unfamiliar male conspecific intruder of the home territory. Defensive behavior is performed by an animal which is attacked by either a dominant male or a predator. The offense–defense distinction plays a prominent role in understanding the biology and physiology of animal aggression.

Besides this distinction in offense and defense, other forms of aggressive behavior can be distinguished as well, such as infanticide, predator aggression, and maternal aggression, which can be observed in females in the late stages of pregnancy and in the early phases of nursing. This article concentrates on intraspecific aggressive behavior in males.

Aggressive behavior has a wide variety of functions depending on the type of aggression. It may serve to protect the home range and its recourses against intruders and to maintain the social hierarchy of a group; it may function as defense against predators or attacking conspecifics; and it can be used instrumentally to obtain desiderata. Overt aggressive behavior like fighting is usually preceded by an extensive repertoire of introductory threatening behaviors which may be highly ritualized in some species. Aggressive behavior always involves at least two participants and the interaction usually ends with flight or submission of one of the competitors. Although aggressive behavior is highly functional, it is potentially harmful. Therefore, throughout the animal kingdom, strong reconciliation and appeasement mechanisms have developed to keep aggression in control and to prevent its adverse consequences. Much of the scientific and public interest in aggression, however, is motivated by the violent, hostile, and presumably less adaptive forms of aggression observed in everyday human life and clinically across a wide spectrum of psychiatric and neurologic disorders. The relationship between the functional and the maladaptive extremes of the aggression spectrum is still far from clear and forms a major obstacle in the integration of animal research with data on human aggression. For the sake of clarity, the violent aspects of aggression are not discussed.

II. PHYSIOLOGY OF AGGRESSIVE BEHAVIOR

Aggressive behavior or the threat of aggression is accompanied by strong neuroendocrine and autonomic stress responses in the two participants of the social interaction. However, the magnitude and the nature of this response depends on the outcome of the aggressive interaction, i.e., winning or losing. Because the formation and maintenance of social hierarchies is one of the most important functions of aggressive behavior, much of the stress of everyday life has its origin in this social structure. The relationship between aggression and stress obviously relates to the physiology of aggression. Therefore, the most important physiological mechanisms underlying aggressive behavior are briefly summarized. A complicating factor is the fact that various forms of aggressive behavior have a different physiological basis. Moreover, the causal physiological mechanisms cannot always be distinguished from the physiological consequences of the aggressive interaction. These consequences are in turn dependent on the outcome of the aggressive interaction, i.e., victory or defeat.

A. Neuroendocrine Factors

Traditionally, high levels of offensive aggressive behavior have been linked to high levels of plasma testosterone. However, the direct causal relationship between testosterone and the expression of offensive behavior is still discussed. It seems that various kinds of aggressive behavior may be differentially dependent upon testosterone, while experiential factors strongly interfere with the degree in which aggression depends on plasma testosterone levels. Winning experience seems to result in a temporary increase in plasma testosterone levels, whereas losing results in a long-lasting decrease. At the level of the brain, testosterone is metabolized into estrogen and dihydrotestosterone. Evidence in rodents suggests the existence of separate estrogen-dependent and androgen-dependent neuronal mechanisms of offense.

Due to the high emotional character of aggression and the high amount of physical activity, it is usually accompanied by a high activation of the pituitary adrenocortical system and the sympathetic adrenomedulary system. However, the reactivity of these neuroendocrine systems appears to differ as an important trait characteristic between highly aggressive and nonaggressive individuals. Aggressive males are characterized by a high reactivity of the sympathetic nervous system and the adrenal medulla, while nonaggressive males show a higher reactivity of the pituitary of the adrenocortical axis and the parasympathetic branch of the autonomic nervous system.

B. Genetic Factors

The role of genetic factors in aggression has long been recognized. Bidirectional genetic selection in rodents usually leads to highly significant differences in aggressive behavior within three or four generations. Extensive studies in human twins confirm a considerable genetic contribution to the individual level of aggression and violence. The initial studies in humans focused on the XYY syndrome in relation to criminal violence. Because there are no animal models of the XYY syndrome, several studies in mice addressed the question to what extent biological variation in aggressive behavior might be due to genetic variation at the Y chromosome. It appeared that the pairing region of the XY chromosomes includes the steroid sulfatase gene, which might be responsible for at least some of the individual variation in aggression. Behavioral analyses of the rapidly increasing number of genetically manipulated mouse strains show the involvement of at least 11 other genes involved in elevated levels of aggression. Most of these genes code for important aspects of the neurobiology of aggression such as serotonergic and monoaminergic neurotransmission and gonadal steroid receptors and metabolism. However, due to the involvement of these neurobiological systems in a wide variety of other behaviors, the behavioral abnormalities in these mice are not restricted to aggression per se. Although molecular genetic studies on aggression in humans are relatively scarce, the first reports show genetic heterogeneity or mutations in some of these genes such as the gene coding for monoamine oxidase A. However, psychophysiological analyses of MAO-deficient families show a wider neurospsychiatric syndrome.

C. Central Nervous System Organization

There is a large body of literature on the central nervous system organization of aggressive behavior in animals. However, the specific involvement of various limbic and midbrain structures depends on the kind of aggressive behavior in question. Offensive behavior involves specific hypothalamic, premamillary, and preoptic areas; the medial nucleus of the amygdala; and the prefrontal cortex. Defensive aggression involves the medial hypothalamus, the septal area, and the periaqueductal gray. Evidence suggests that the neuronal systems involved in these two types of aggressive behavior are remarkably similar across species and may be homologous to those in humans. In the human literature much attention has been paid to the so-called dyscontrol syndrome, or episodic rage, which is probably attributed to seizure activity in certain brain areas. Also in chronic neuropsychiatric patients some aspects of violence seem to be due to a history of seizures or frontal cerebral lesions.

The most consistent findings of central nervous system functioning in aggressive behavior, however, involve serotonin (5-HT). Low concentrations of 5-hydroxyindoleacetic acid, a metabolite of serotonin, in the cerebrospinal fluid have been consistently found as a trait characteristic in highly violent, aggressive, or suicidal patients. These findings are supported by many animal studies showing the anti-aggressive effects of selective 5-HT1a or 5-HT1b receptor agonists. Several other neurotransmitters including noradrenaline, dopamine, and GABA are shown to be involved in the control of animal aggressive behavior as well, but their role in human aggression is far from clear so far.

Recent MRI and PET scan studies in humans with a history of violence and antisocial behavior show a reduced bloodflow and glucose utilization in temporal and prefrontal cortical regions.

III. AGGRESSIVE BEHAVIOR AND STRESS

An aggressive interaction elicits a strong stress response in both the winner and the loser of the interaction. Evidence shows that winning and losing (or offense and defense) elicit a differential stress response both in terms of the magnitude of responses and of the neuroendocrine stress systems involved. Because winning and losing of social interactions form the basis of the social structure in groups of animals, this differential response might underlie the relationship between the position in the social structure and the vulnerability for stress pathology.

A. Winner

Relatively few studies consider the physiological changes during aggressive behavior in the victor of the social interaction. However, the available literature clearly shows that winning elicits a moderate activation of the hypothalamic-pituitary-adrenal (HPA) axis and of the sympathetic adrenomedulary system. Both human and animal studies also show an activation of the pituitary gonadal axis in males. More chronically, dominant males in a social group may suffer from sympathetic nervous system-mediated forms of stress pathology. For example, dominant males have a higher incidence of cardiovascular abnormalities such as arteriosclerosis and hypertension, in particular, in unstable social groups.

B. Loser

Most social stress studies concentrate on defense, i.e., the loser of a social interaction, or the subordinate males in a social structure. A comparison of the stress response elicited by various stress procedures reveals that social defeat can be considered as one of the most severe stressors. Not only the corticosterone response, but also the response of adrenaline and noradrenaline are by far the largest during social defeat stress. Recent evidence shows that stressors show not only quantitative differences, but may also differ qualitatively in the pattern of activated physiological systems. For example, a comparison of the electrocardiovascular response to restraint stress and social defeat reveals that the two types of stressors differ strongly in the balance of activation of the two branches of the autonomic nervous system. Social defeat seems to activate exclusively the sympathetic branch, whereas during restraint stress the parasympathetic nervous system shows a considerable activation as well. This differential autonomic balance may explain the high incidence of electrocardiovascular abnormalities observed during social defeat. Social defeat by a male conspecific induces not only strong acute increases in plasma catecholamines, corticosterone, heart rate, blood pressure, body temperature, prolactin, and testosterone, but also increases in a variety of central nervous system neurotransmitters including serotonin, noradrenalin, dopamine, and endorphins. There is a general tendency to extrapolate these acute effects observed during and shortly after a defeat to a lasting pathology when the stressor is present chronically, for example, in the subordinate males in a social group. Indeed chronic subordination stress has been reported to induce a downregulation of serotonergic and noradrenergic neurotransmission, lower plasma testosterone levels, and increased activation of the HPA axis. Most of these changes are consistent with the idea that in a variety of animal species subordinates develop depressionlike symptoms. The subordinate position is also related to an increased sensitivity to addictive substances and immunosuppression, resulting in an enhanced vulnerability for infectious disease. Recent evidence shows also that a single social defeat can induce changes in physiology and behavior that can last from days to several weeks. In fact, most of the behavioral and physiological changes observed after chronic subordination stress can also be observed weeks after a single social defeat.

IV. AGGRESSIVE BEHAVIOR AND COPING

An important concept in aggression research which relates to stress concerns the relationship between aggression and coping. A number of studies in a variety of species show a strong positive correlation between the individual level of offensiveness and the tendency to actively cope with any kind of environmental stressor. Aggressive males have a general tendency to deal actively with different kinds of environmental challenges. The antipode of this active, problem-focused coping is a reactive or emotion-focused coping style. This is expressed as the absence of aggressive behavior in a social situation and passivity in other challenging environmental conditions. These coping styles, as observed in several animal species, are also characterized by differential neuroendocrine and neurobiological profiles. They can be considered as important trait characteristics determining the individual adaptive capacity.

Personality factors or trait characteristics have long been recognized to play a role in human stress psychophysiology as well. For example, the distinction between proactive and reactive coping styles in relation to individual levels of aggression is also made in human beings. The different coping styles as found in animal studies seem to be analogous to the distinction in the human type A and type B personalities used in cardiovascular psychophysiology. The type A personality is described as aggressive, hostile, and competitive and is physiologically characterized by a high sympathetic reactivity. Although the A–B typology has been seriously questioned in the literature, factors related to aggression such as anger and hostility have been repeatedly shown to play a role in the individual capacity of human beings to cope with environmental challenges.

See Also the Following Articles

BEHAVIOR, OVERVIEW; COPING, STRESS AND; DEFENSIVE BEHAVIORS; FIGHT-OR-FLIGHT RESPONSE; SEROTONIN; VIOLENCE

Bibliography

Benus, R. F., Bohus, B., Koolhaas, J. M., and van Oortmerssen, G. A. (1991). Heritable variation in aggression as a reflection of individual coping strategies. *Experientia* 47, 1008–1019.

De Waal, F. (1996). "Good Natured: The Origins of Right and Wrong in Humans and Other Animals." Harvard Univ. Press, Cambridge, MA.

Folkow, B., Schmidt, T., and Unvas-Moberg, K. (Eds.) (1997). Stress, health and the social environment. *Acta Physiol. Scand.* 161 (Suppl. 640), 1997.

Kaplan, J. R., and Manuck, S. B. (1990). Monkeys, aggression, and the pathobiology of atherosclerosis. *Aggr. Behav.* 24, 323–334.

Martinez, M., Calco-Torrent, A., and Pico-Alfonso, M. A. (1998). Social defeat and subordination as models of social stress in laboratory rodents: A review. *Aggr. Behav.* 24, 241–256.

Maxon, S. C. (1998). Homologous genes, aggression and animal models. *Dev. Neuropsychol.* 14, 143–156.

Sapolsky, R. M. (1994). "Why zebra's don't get ulcers: a guide to stress, stress-related diseases, and coping." W.H. Freeman, New York.

Stoff, D. M., and Cairns, B. (Eds.) (1996). "Aggression and Violence: Genetic, Neurobiological, and Biosocial Perspectives." Erlbaum, Mahwah, NJ.

Aging and Psychological Stress

Brenda W. J. H. Penninx and Dorly J. H. Deeg

Vrije Universiteit, The Netherlands

I. Aging
II. Psychological Stress: Prevalence of Depression and Anxiety in Old Age
III. Determinants of Psychological Stress in Old Age
IV. Consequences of Psychological Stress in Old Age

GLOSSARY

generalized anxiety disorder Chronic, persistent, and excessive feelings of anxiety and worry.

major depressive disorder Depressed mood or loss of interest in activities in combination with three or more additional symptoms such as loss of appetite, sleep disturbance, fatigue, feelings of worthlessness, thoughts about death, or concentration problems.

minor depression Clinically relevant depressed mood not fulfilling the diagnostic severity criteria for major depressive disorder.

obsessive-compulsive disorder Repetitive thoughts, images, or impulses that are experienced as intrusive or repetitive behaviors that are performed in response to an obsession or certain rules.

panic disorder Recurring sudden episodes of intense apprehension, palpitations, shortness of breath, and chest pain.

phobia Fear and avoidance out of proportion to the danger.

P opulation aging is a worldwide phenomenon. For the human individual, aging is accompanied by several changes that may cause psychological stress. This chapter describes the extent of psychological stress experienced in old age as indicated by the level of depressive and anxiety symptomatology. Determinants as well as consequences of psychological stress in old age are described, and the role of aging is clarified. Figure 1 shows the conceptual model for the effect of aging on psychological stress that is used throughout this chapter.

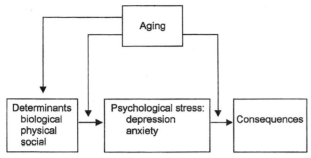

FIGURE 1 Conceptual model of the effect of aging on psychological stress.

I. AGING

In the Western world, the oldest of the old, persons ages 85 years and older, comprise the fastest growing segment of the aged. This is due to a decreasing trend in the number of children born as well as to dramatic changes in mortality leading to increased life expectancy. Life expectancy has consistently been higher for women than for men. Consequently, the elderly population is composed of more women than men.

Aging has profound consequences for the individual. For the most part, individual aging is associated with many adverse changes in human anatomy and physiology. Consequences of these changes are, for instance, losses in the sense of balance and movement, poorer hearing and vision, slower reactions and weaker muscles. For a large part of adult life, people are normally provided with "biological" reserves. In later life, these reserves are reduced, which can cause a weakening of one or another biological function essential to life. Consequently, conditions such as heart disease, cancer, respiratory infection, and kidney failure may arise. The biological age-related changes and the consequent development of degenerative and chronic conditions have a large impact on the physical functioning of older persons. The number of older persons with difficulties in mobility and activities of daily living increases dramatically with increasing age.

In addition to the impact on biological and physical areas, other aspects of life are affected as well. Individual aging is accompanied by a series of social transitions, some entered into voluntarily, some imposed by circumstances. In general, aging tends to be associated with relationship losses, either because of retirement, widowhood, or death of age-peers such as siblings or friends. Increasing age also brings changes in relationship needs, for example, as the result of increasing impairment. Older adults may become more dependent on others when they lose the ability to fulfill certain social or instrumental tasks themselves. The existing balance in their relationships may be disrupted, introducing strain and discomfort.

Most of the age-related changes, biological, physical, or social, can be expected to constitute losses rather than gains. Several of these changes are potentially stressful to older persons. Chronic conditions, for instance, can introduce pain, disability, despair, and fear for treatment and pending death. Widowhood, the need for instrumental support, and the loss of personal relationships might cause feelings of loneliness, dependency, and helplessness. When adjustment to these burdening circumstances is inadequate, an older person might experience substantial psychological stress. In the next section, the prevalence of psychological stress in old age is described, indicated by two prevalent psychopathological disorders: depression and anxiety.

II. PSYCHOLOGICAL STRESS: PREVALENCE OF DEPRESSION AND ANXIETY IN OLD AGE

A. Depression

The most prevalent psychopathological disorder in old age is depression. Prevalence rates of depression vary considerably depending on the sample studied and methods used. Studies in clinical settings generally find much higher prevalences of depression than studies in community settings. Depression can be assessed using either diagnostic criteria or symptom checklists. Diagnostic criteria are described in the Diagnostic and Statistical Manual of Mental Disorders (DSM) published by the American Psychiatric Association and are used throughout the world. According to these criteria, a major depressive disorder requires significant depressed mood and loss of interest in activities in combination with three or four additional symptoms (loss of appetite, sleep disturbance, fatigue, feelings of worthlessness, etc.). These symptoms are not to be physiologically caused by a general medical condition and must extend for at least a 2-week period.

Symptom checklists ask for presence, intensity, or frequency of a series of symptoms during the preceding 1 or 2 weeks in order to measure the extent of depressive symptomatology. Some examples of commonly used symptom checklists are the Center for Epidemiologic Studies-Depression Scale, the Geriatric Depression Scale, and the Zung Depression Scale. These instruments are well-validated and have been proven to be valid and reliable instruments in older populations. It is possible to score relatively high on a symptom checklist without meeting diagnostic criteria for major depressive disorder. In fact, depressive symptom checklists identify for the largest part persons with a significant high level of depressive symptoms who not fulfill the diagnostic severity threshold of major depressive disorder. This condition is often referred to as "depressed mood" or "minor depression."

Major depressive disorder is relatively rare among older community-dwelling persons, affecting only about 1 to 2% of the community-dwelling population. Major depressive disorder appears to be less prevalent among older adults than among middle-aged adults. Table I shows the prevalence rates of major depressive disorder in a community-based ran-dom sample of older men and women aged 55 years and older who participated in the Longitudinal Aging Study Amsterdam in the Netherlands. This table shows that among older persons, the prevalence of major depressive disorder shows a slightly declining trend with increasing age. At all ages, older women generally show a higher rate of major depressive disorder than men.

When using a depressive symptom checklist it becomes obvious that a much higher proportion of the population suffer from significant symptoms of depression. Prevalences of minor depression in older community-based populations range from 12 to 20%. Data from several community studies converge in suggesting that there is a curvilinear relationship between age and depression scores over the entire adult life span, with the highest scores among younger adults and those over age 75. Table I illustrates the positive association between a significant level of depressive symptoms and age in older participants of the Longitudinal Aging Study Amsterdam. In line with findings for major depressive disorders, women generally show higher rates of significant depressive symptoms than men. The elevation in scores among the very old has been shown not to be an artifact of greater endorsement of somatic symptoms. In sum, the prevalence of minor depression increases across old age, whereas the prevalence of clinical major depression by and large does not.

TABLE I

Prevalence Rates (in Percentages) for Depression in Older Men and Women in Different Age Groups[a]

Disorder	Age		
	55–65 years	65–75 years	75–85 years
Major depressive disorder[b]			
Men	1.2	0.9	0.5
Women	3.4	3.7	2.2
Significant depressive symptoms[c]			
Men	8.5	8.0	13.7
Women	9.5	14.0	21.1

[a] Data are from the Longitudinal Aging Study Amsterdam.
[b] Based on diagnostic DSM criteria using the Diagnostic Interview Schedule.
[c] Indicated by a score on the Center for Epidemiologic Studies Depression Scale of 16 or more.

TABLE II

Prevalence Rates (in Percentages) for Anxiety Disorders in Older Men
and Women in Different Age Groups[a]

Disorder	Age		
	55–65 years	*65–75 years*	*75–85 years*
Panic disorder[b]			
Men	0.3	0.0	0.3
Women	1.4	3.0	2.0
Obsessive compulsive disorder[b]			
Men	0.0	0.0	0.0
Women	0.3	2.7	0.8
Phobic disorder[b]			
Men	1.2	0.6	2.3
Women	4.2	4.4	4.9
Generalized anxiety disorder[b]			
Men	2.8	10.3	5.4
Women	5.2	12.6	8.5

[a] Data are from the Longitudinal Aging Study Amsterdam.
[b] Based on diagnostic DSM criteria using the Diagnotic Interview Schedule.

B. Anxiety

A variety of anxiety disorders are described in the DSM, including (1) panic disorder, which refers to recurring sudden episodes of intense apprehension, palpitations, shortness of breath, and chest pain; (2) phobias, which are fears and avoidance out of proportion to the danger; (3) obsessive-compulsive disorder, consisting of repetitive thoughts, images, or impulses experienced as intrusive or of repetitive behaviors that are performed according to certain rules or in a stereotyped fashion; and (4) generalized anxiety disorder, entailing chronic, persistent, and excessive anxiety and worry.

The prevalence of anxiety disorders tends to decline over the life time. Nevertheless, anxiety disorders are still common in older adults. Table II reports the prevalence rates of various anxiety disorders in the Longitudinal Aging Study Amsterdam. In this older population, anxiety disorders are more common among women than men, but are not associated with age. Generalized anxiety disorders are more common than panic disorders and phobic disorders. Obsessive-compulsive disorder was the least prevalent.

Comorbidity of anxiety disorders is not uncommon in older age. In the Dutch study, about 10% of the older persons with an anxiety diagnosis suffered from two or more anxiety disorders. Also, anxiety and depression frequently cooccur at any age. Thirty-six percent of the older persons with a major depressive disorder had one or more anxiety disorders. Vice versa, 13% of those with an anxiety disorder had a major depressive disorder.

III. DETERMINANTS OF PSYCHOLOGICAL STRESS IN OLD AGE

This section gives a brief overview of the determinants of depression and anxiety in old age (see Fig. 1). Major depressive disorder and minor depression in older age have distinct underlying etiologies. Major depressive disorder is more strongly associated with longstanding vulnerability factors such as personality and heredity than minor depression. A large proportion of older persons with a major depressive disorder have had depressive episodes during earlier phases of their lives. Consequently, a personal history of depressive disorder is one of the strongest risk factors for a major depressive disorder in old age. Other hereditary and personality characteristics, such as a family history of depressive disorder or neuroticism, have also been found to be predictive. Also, anxiety disorders in late life often are associated with long-standing vulnerability factors such as personality and heredity. Thus, both major depressive disorders and anxiety disorders in old age most often represent recurring episodes of early-onset depressive disorders.

Furthermore, some acquired biological vulnerabilities may predispose an older individual for psychopathological disorders. Age-related physiological and brain structure changes have been suggested as plausible risk factors for late-onset depression because of parallels between these changes and pathological changes observed in depression, such as dysregulation of the monoamine system, increased monoamine oxidase activity, deficits in norepinephrine functioning, downregulation of serotonin receptors, and deep white- and gray-matter disease. Age-related decreases in noradrenergic function provide one plausible biological mechanism that increases the predisposition toward late-onset anxiety.

Whereas biological vulnerability seems to increase with age, in terms of psychological predisposition older adults may be less vulnerable than younger adults. Stressful life events have shown inconsistent relationships to depression in old age. The relationship between life events and depression may actually be less strong in older than in younger adults. Older individuals have had the opportunity to learn how to cope with stressful circumstances and how to adjust their expectations so as to have fewer feelings of failure. On the basis of age and experience, older persons have developed more effective skills with which to manage stressful life events and to reduce emotional distress. Specific stressors, such as loss of partner or other intimates, are more normative in old age and usual in that part of the life cycle than in younger age and therefore less disruptive. Although their impact might be smaller than in younger age, social circumstances have still been found to be predictive for depressive as well as anxiety symptomatology. The absence of a partner, less social relationships, and negative life-events are associated with more feelings of depression and anxiety in old age. Also, depression and anxiety are more common in older persons with unfavorable socioeconomic circumstances, such as low income or education.

The importance of physical health for the presence of psychological stress is undisputed. Especially for minor depression, physical illnesses are consistently shown to be included among the strongest risk factors. Several explanations can be given. First, depression can occur as an outcome of certain somatic illnesses or medication, reflecting a biologically mediated process. For example, the structural and neurochemical changes involved in stroke and parkinsonism can lead to depression. Second, physical illness can act as a stressor and has several psychosocial consequences. For example, loss of function, role and independence, negative body image and sense of identity, pain, and promoted sense of helplessness can be a reaction of being ill and consequently cause increased feelings of depression or anxiety. Finally, it should be mentioned that physical illnesses and depression or anxiety may exhibit similar symptoms, causing artificially raised correlations. For example, silent myocardial infarctions can produce anxietylike symptoms.

Minor depression has been associated with various different chronic diseases, such as lung disease, arthritis, cancer, stroke, and myocardial infarction. There is some evidence for disparity in depressive symptoms across different chronic diseases. Feelings of depression and anxiety appear to be most frequently experienced by older patients with osteoarthritis, rheumatoid arthritis, and stroke as opposed to patients with heart disease, diabetes, and lung disease. Physical disability may play an explanatory role in this disparity across diseases. Arthritis and stroke are, in general, accompanied by physical limitations. The extent of physical disability is an important factor in the development of psychological stress. People with acquired physical disabilities inevitably encounter additional losses, such as the loss of function, role, and body image and may experience a greater dependency on others and a more negative view of themselves, their future, and their world, leading to more feelings of depression. Several studies among older persons have shown that symptoms of depression and anxiety are better predicted by problems with activities of daily living than by number of chronic conditions.

Section II showed that anxiety and major depressive disorders are not more prevalent in old age than in youth. By contrast, minor depression shows an increasing trend with increasing age. Nevertheless, the risk factor profile for minor depression over the lifespan is rather stable in terms of the domains represented. Risk factors in younger persons have also been found in old age (e.g., physical health problems, negative life events, lack of social support). However, the importance of risk factors relative to each other may vary across the life span, since the distribution of these risk factors is related to age. For instance, the oldest-old report more social isolation and impoverishment and have more physical health problems and disability. These relative increases in risk factors, especially in physical health problems, have been found to completely explain the increased prevalence of depression in the oldest-old. Thus, what seems to be an association between age and depressive symptoms is in fact the result of other risk factors. Age per se is not a risk factor for minor depression when other factors are taken into account.

In sum, major depressive disorders and anxiety disorders are strongly associated with long-standing vulnerability factors such as personality and heredity. Minor depression is more often a reaction to the stressors encountered in later life such as worsened health status, economic stress, and the changing social context.

IV. CONSEQUENCES OF PSYCHOLOGICAL STRESS IN OLD AGE

The presence of psychological stress in old age has several adverse health consequences. These consequences have mainly been studied for depression. Since there has been a striking lack of attention to the health consequences of late-life anxiety, this section mainly focuses on the adverse health outcomes of depression.

Independent of disease severity, depressed older persons are two to three times more likely to die during 2- to 10-year follow-up periods than nonde-

pressed older persons. These increased mortality risks have been found for older persons with major depressive disorders as well as for those with minor depression. Consistent associations with depression have also been found for less extreme indicators of physical health decline. For instance, depression increases the risk for subsequent onset of physical disabilities in mobility or in activities of daily living. The risk for subsequent disability appears to be similar or even greater than the risks in persons with chronic medical diseases. Researchers have further detailed the evidence for health decline associated with depression by documenting increased risk of developing hypertension, stroke, and cardiovascular heart disease among older depressed persons. In addition, cardiovascular patients who are depressed have poorer prognoses than nondepressed patients. There is evidence that high levels of depressive symptoms in myocardial infarction patients predict an increased future risk for recurrent myocardial infarction and mortality.

It is unclear whether the effect of major depressive disorders or depressive symptoms on the physical health decline is different in young and old persons. For mortality, a few studies described that the association between depression and mortality is weaker among older persons, but other studies did not find a difference between young and old persons. For other health outcomes, the possible differentiating effect of age in the association between depression and decline in health status is hardly examined.

How can the adverse health consequences of depression in older persons be explained? First, psychological stressors have physiological accompaniments, including altered autonomic balance and increased hypothalamic-pituitary-adrenal axis function, both of which are biologically plausible contributors to pathogenesis. When anger or depression is induced in laboratory studies, persons exhibit larger sympathetic nervous system-mediated cardiovascular responses. Psychological stress appeared to elevate resting heart rate and blood pressure, decrease heart rate variability, and increase ventricular arrhythmias and myocardial ischemia. In addition, depressed persons have been shown to exhibit hypersecretion of the adrenal steroid cortisol, adrenal hypertrophy, and an increased cortisol response to adrenocorticotrophic hormone. Depressed and anxious persons show increased sympathetic nervous system activation during everyday life, as documented by larger increases in daytime urinary epinephrine excretion and downregulation of lymphocyte β-adrenergic receptors. There is also evidence that parasympathetic nervous system function is reduced in both anxious and depressed persons. These direct physiologic processes may explain why depressed older persons are more vulnerable to subsequent health deterioration or to the onset of some conditions.

Second, increased behavioral risk profiles in depressed persons may explain their higher risk for adverse health consequences. Behavioral risk factors appear to cluster in the same individuals. Increased smoking and alcohol consumption are well-documented in depression. Depressed persons not only smoke more often, they are found to be less likely to quit smoking and might inhale more deeply and smoke more of the cigarette than nondepressed smokers. Also greater 24-h caloric intake and a cholesterol/HDL ratio have been found. Depressed persons engage less in physical activities such as walking, gardening, and vigorous exercise activities such as sports.

Third, related somatic symptoms of depression such as fatigue or sleeplessness may worsen older persons' health status. This explanation is in line with findings that vital exhaustion (which has shared common characteristics with depression such as listlessness, loss of energy, irritability, and sleep problems) increases the risk of developing cardiovascular disease. Another mechanism linking depression to subsequent health deterioration may be via psychological mechanisms. Depressed mood may impede recovery processes by discouraging persons from obtaining adequate medical attention and rehabilitation and following treatment regimens.

In sum, depression has several adverse health consequences ranging from increased risks of mortality, decline in physical function and onset of cardiovascular disease. Subsequent health deterioration can be due to physiological changes induced by depression, the unhealthier behavioral risk profile of depressed older persons, the somatic accompaniments of depression, or the decreased motivation of depressed older persons for self-care.

This chapter described that, although the prevalence of major depressive disorder in old age is rather low, anxiety disorders and significant depressive feelings (minor depression) are common in old age. The prevalence of minor depression increases across older age. Major depressive disorders and anxiety disorders are strongly associated with long-standing vulnerability factors such as personality and heredity, whereas minor depression is more often a reaction to the stressors encountered in later life such as worsened health status, economic stress, and the changing social context. Several adverse health consequences of depression have been described ranging from mortality, declined physical function, and cardiovascular disease.

Unfortunately, appropriate care is often not provided for psychopathological problems in older persons. This is partly due to the poor recognition of these problems by physicians. Significant feelings of anxiety or depression in older persons more often go unrecognized and untreated than in younger persons. Older persons are more likely to attribute depressive and anxiety symptoms to physical problems and, therefore, tend to present their problems as somatic complaints, rather than as a psychological problem. Furthermore, older persons' fear of stigmatization may cause underreporting, and bias of clinicians (ageism or age-related prejudice) causes underrecognition of psychopathological disorders in late life.

Depression and anxiety are potentially modifiable conditions. Consequently, recognition, prevention, and treatment are important points of intervention. Although more appropriate care for psychopathological disorders, consisting of increased counseling and use of medications, appeared to be effective in improving older persons' health and well-being, few formal clinical trials have been conducted. Such experimental studies are necessary to examine in more detail whether and how early recognition and treatment of depression and anxiety are able to prevent a downward spiral in the health status of older persons.

See Also the Following Articles

AGING AND STRESS; ALZHEIMER'S DISEASE; ANXIETY; CAREGIVERS, STRESS AND; DEPRESSION MODELS; IMMUNE SYSTEM, AGING

Bibliography

American Psychiatric Association (1994). "Diagnostic and Statistical Manual of Mental Disorders," 4th ed. American Psychiatric Press, Washington, DC.

Birren, J. E., Sloane, R. B., and Cohen, G. D. (1992). "Handbook of Mental Health and Aging," 2nd ed. Academic Press, San Diego, CA.

Fielding, R. (1991). Depression and acute myocardial infarction: A review and reinterpretation. *Soc. Sci. Med.* **32**, 1017–1027.

Flint, A. J. (1994). Epidemiology and comorbidity of anxiety disorders in the elderly. *Am. J. Psychiatr.* **151**, 640–649.

Gatz, M., Kasl-Godley, J. E., and Karel, M. J. (1996). Aging and mental disorders. *In* "Handbook of the Psychology of Aging" (J. E. Birren and W. Schaie, Eds.), pp. 365–382. Academic Press, San Diego, CA.

Gurland, B. J. (1983). "The Mind and Mood of Aging." Haworth, New York.

Salzman, C., and Leibowitz, B. D. (1991). "Anxiety in the Elderly: Treatment and Research." Springer-Verlag, New York.

Schneider, L. S., Reynolds, C. F., Lebowitz, B. D., and Friedhoff, A. J. (1994). "Diagnosis and Treatment of Late Life Depression." American Psychiatric Press, Washington, DC.

Aging and Stress, Biology of

Michael A. Horan

University of Manchester Medical School

Roger N. Barton and Gordon J. Lithgow

University of Manchester

I. Aging and Cellular Stress Resistance
II. Stress Responses in Intact Organisms

GLOSSARY

biological aging Aging is very difficult to define. For biologists, it often refers to the progressive changes that occur during adult life, many of which are deleterious. Aging rate cannot be measured in individuals. For populations, aging rate is estimated by the slope of the line relating the logarithm of mortality rate to age (Gompertz acceleration parameter). It can also be expressed by the mortality rate doubling time (MRDT): about 8 years for humans and 3 months for laboratory mice. However, in extreme old age in many species, this relationship breaks down. MRDT is closely related to maximum lifespan.

epistasis Expression of one gene wipes out the phenotypic effects of another.

population aging This term refers to time-related changes in the age-structure of populations. Thus, owing to a combination of increased life expectancy and reduced birth rates, the relative and absolute numbers of old people present in many human populations has greatly increased.

psychological aging For psychologists, aging refers to the changes in behavior and mental processes that arise as individuals progress through life.

senescence Sometimes used synonymously with aging. Sometimes it refers only to those changes that are deleterious. Cellular senescence refers to a phenotype of those cells that are usually capable of mitosis but, after a number of cycles of cell division, have lost the ability to replicate but are not dead (Hayflick limit).

Aging *in vivo* is often related to damage done to molecules, cells, and organs by a variety of toxic factors, either produced endogenously or derived from the environment. For our purposes, potentially (or actually) harmful conditions are considered as stressors and the psychological and biological reactions thereto as the *stress response*. In the discussion that follows, we try to address two important issues concerning the relationships between stress and aging: (1) Do stressors affect the rate of aging and, (2) Does aging affect responses to stressors?

I. AGING AND CELLULAR STRESS RESISTANCE

Stressors for cells include the nonenzymatic glycation of proteins and DNA, as well as oxidative damage to diverse molecules that could be caused by free radicals generated mainly as a by-product of metabolism, by solar radiation, by a variety of stressors that elicit the heat shock response, and by numerous other toxic factors from the environment. Normal function, and even survival, is dependent on the ability of cells to (1) sustain homoeostasis by being able to adapt to and/or resist stressors, and (2) repair or replace damaged molecules and organelles.

A. Oxidative Stress

Oxygen radicals are reactive molecular species produced by one-electron reduction of oxygen. It is estimated that about 4% of oxygen consumed by mitochondria is converted to the reactive oxygen species (ROS) hydrogen peroxide and superoxide during oxidative phosphorylation. These ROS can be converted by a number of distinct processes to highly reactive hydroxyl radicals which can damage proteins, lipids, and DNA. Not surprisingly, organisms have important defences against oxidative stress including the small molecules uric acid, glutathione, ascorbic acid, and vitamin E. Oxidative stress induces the synthesis of several antioxidant enzymes including superoxide dismutase (SOD), catalase and glutathione peroxidase. These enzymes protect cells and tissues against oxidative damage by converting ROS to nonreactive species.

What is the importance of defenses against oxidative damage during aging? The continued effectiveness of inducible responses to environmental damage are certainly thought to be major factors in resistance to diseases, and even the rate of aging. Indeed, it has been proposed that a capacity for increased lifespan is latent within most (if not all) species and might be uncovered by treatments that enhance cellular stress resistance. This is based on the observation that all known laboratory-based strategies that extend organism lifespan, whether by genetic intervention or environmental manipulation, are associated with an increased ability to respond to environmental stressors and decreased susceptibility to stress-induced damage.

B. Systemic Stress Responses and Aging

One of the most exciting concepts relating stress and aging is that the rate of aging is governed by the rate of accumulation of macromolecular damage and, therefore, that processes determining this rate also define lifespan. Damage accumulates when repair or degradation of damaged molecules cannot keep pace with the rate of damage, which itself is determined by the production of damaging agents (e.g., ROS) and their subsequent detoxification (e.g., by antioxidant enzymes). This idea is well developed in the "free radical" theory of aging and its subsequent modifications. The modern oxygen radical theory states that the decline in function and increasing mortality rate associated with aging are due to ROS production and their subsequent reaction with cellular components causing irreparable damage. Despite considerable interest in this theory, there is virtually no evidence that it explains the natural aging rate. However, we are now developing a more general picture of how cellular stress resistance and aging rates might be related, mainly from studies of model genetic systems (*Saccharomyces cerevisiae*, *Caenorhabditis elegans*, and *Drosophila melanogaster*).

C. Fungal Systems and Aging

Saccharomyces cerevisiae divides by asymmetric budding, leaving a mother cell and a smaller daughter cell. The mother cell exhibits limited division potential and consequently, a limited lifespan. At the end of the yeast lifespan, the cell becomes granulated and dies. Yeast provide excellent systems for the dissection of complex biological problems, and aging is no exception. Many genes are now known to influence yeast lifespan. The first mutations isolated that conferred an increased lifespan came from a genetic screen for mutations that also conferred stress resistance, in this case to starvation. These mutations clustered in four genes, *UTH1, UTH3, UTH4* and *SIR4*.

An important biomarker of aging, observed in species as diverse as primates and nematodes is the accumulation of damaged mitochondrial DNA (mtDNA). It is thought that the cause of these altered forms is oxygen radical damage. The filamentous fungi *Podospora anserina* and *Neurospora crassa* have provided interesting information on at least one form of aging-related mtDNA mutation. In *Podospora*, aging is associated with the release of a circular DNA molecule (αsenDNA) from the cytochrome oxidase subunit I gene (COI) in the mitochondrial genome. Mutations in the nuclear genes *gr* (*greisea*) or *i viv* result in the repression of the production of this αsenDNA. Combinations of these mutations result in indefinite lifespans. The *gr* gene has been cloned and encodes a protein homologous to the ACE1 transcription factor, known to regulate the superoxide dismutase (*SOD1*), and metallothionein (*CUP1*) genes in budding yeast. Therefore, the alterations in stress-associated transcription factors cause dramatic alterations in the rate of accumulation of aging-associated damage, which correlates with lifespan.

D. *Caenorhabditis Elegans*

This is a small (1.2 mm) soil-dwelling roundworm. It has a three-day life cycle with four larval stages (L1–L4) before the final moult to the adult form. Most worms are hermaphrodites (XX), though males (X0) do exist at a ratio of about 1:500. The hermaphrodites reproduce by self-fertilization and live for about 20 days. This organism has proved to be very useful in aging research as single gene mutations have arisen that both extend lifespan (*age* mutations) and increase resistance to environmental stressors.

Age mutations can bring about up to 3-fold increases in lifespan attributable to a smaller acceleration of mortality rate with advancing age. Further, the mutations also induce increased resistance to several stressors: heat, UV radiation, oxidation, and heavy metals. Many, but not all, mutations that enhance resistance to such stressors are associated with increased lifespan, which suggests a direct relationship between longevity and stress-resistance.

The epistasis analysis of *age* mutations has established two genetic pathways that determine lifespan. The cloning of genes in the first pathway,

age-1, *daf-2*, and *daf-16* has shown that an insulin-like signaling pathway governs both aging and responses to stressors in this species. The *age-1* gene encodes a homologue of the mammalian phosphatidyl inositol-3-kinase catalytic subunit (PI3K). The *daf-2* gene encodes a protein, which is 35% identical to human insulin receptor and 34% identical to the insulin-like growth factor 1 receptor (IGF-1R). The *daf-16* gene is a Fork head transcription factor.

With the free radical theory in mind, worms carrying either *age-1* (*hx546*) or *daf-2* (*e1370*) have been assessed for antioxidant enzyme activities, Cu/Zn SOD and catalase. The net effect of these two enzymes is to prevent the production of the highly reactive hydroxyl radical, which is thought to be responsible for age-associated damage to proteins, lipids, and nucleic acids. The activities of both of these enzymes are elevated in *age-1* and *daf-2* mutant worms in mid- and late-life. This is consistent with the idea that *age* mutations result in resistance to intrinsic oxidative stressors. Worms mutant in *age-1* are certainly resistant to extrinsic oxidative stress as measured by survival during exposure to hydrogen peroxide (H_2O_2) and the O_2^- generator, paraquat. These results suggest that the insulin signaling pathway negatively regulates antioxidant enzyme activity and that extended lifespan results from enhanced antioxidant defenses. This strongly suggests that over expression of antioxidant enzymes is sufficient to confer extended lifespan.

Oxidative stress is also thought to be one mechanism by which insulin action may be impaired. For example, it has been shown that whole-body glucose uptake (reflecting metabolic clearance rate, MCR) during a euglycaemic glucose clamp declines with age in humans. On the basis of parallel increases in plasma superoxide production, red-cell membrane microviscosity and oxidation state of glutathione, it was postulated that insulin action is impaired by free-radical production. However, any such hypothesis based purely on correlation studies must be regarded as very tentative.

E. *Drosophila Melanogaster*

This insect has been widely used in both stress and aging studies. Transgenic *Drosophila* lines containing additional copies of the Cu/Zn SOD and catalase genes have been generated and most lines that have elevated antioxidant-enzyme levels are also long-lived. This demonstrates the importance of these two enzymes in determining lifespan. More recent experiments suggest that the expression of MnSOD in neurons alone is sufficient to extend lifespan.

The transgenic *Drosophila* experimental system has also been used to test the role of molecular chaperones in determining aging rates. In these experiments, it was shown that additional copies of HSP-70 could reduce age-specific mortality rates in *Drosophila*. Just how HSP-70 retards aging is unknown but these findings are consistent with other experiments in both *C. elegans* and *Drosophila* in which animals given a mild thermal stress and allowed to recover go on to develop acquired thermotolerance, and exhibit extended lifespan. In these later experiments, HSPs are induced and may be the principal cause of slowed aging.

Drosophila has also been utilized for studying the effects of multiple genes on stress responses and aging. Selection has been undertaken for *Drosophila* lines that differ in their levels of stress tolerance and at least one laboratory has demonstrated that selection for stress-resistance produces lines with increased longevity. In addition, some long-lived *Drosophila* lines, selected for late reproduction, are stress resistant.

F. The Heat Shock Response

The most extensively studied response to acute stressors is the expression of heat shock proteins (HSP). HSPs are the products of a family of highly conserved genes, found from bacteria to mammalian cells, that are rapidly transcribed and translated in cells and tissues exposed to a variety of stressors. Recent studies have provided evidence that in the intact animal, even a behavioral or psychological stress can elicit the response. HSP genes are regulated by heat shock transcription factors (HSF), which are themselves sensitive to a variety of stressors. The HSPs facilitate the disassembly and disposal of damaged proteins and the folding, transport, and insertion of newly synthesized proteins into cellular or-

ganelles. Thus, they facilitate the removal of damaged structures as well as their replacement.

There is very good evidence that expression of HSP genes is sufficient to increase resistance to thermal stress (thermotolerance) in many circumstances. Across different species, distinct HSP families are important in thermal tolerance. HSP-104 is responsible for tolerance to several environmental stressors in the yeast *Saccharomyces cerevisiae*, and inducible HSP-70 confers thermoltolerance in *Drosophila* embryos and in a range of cultured mammalian cells. The addition of antibodies to HSP-70 compromises survival after thermal stress in fibroblasts.

G. Stress Proteins and Aging in Mammals

There is good evidence that stress proteins (e.g., HSPs, antioxidants) directly influence aging. It is also likely that the converse is true: aging seems to influence the extent to which stress proteins are synthesized in response to a variety of stressors. The expression of HSP-70 has been studied in inbred strains of animals at different ages and also in cells cultured to senescence. These studies show that there is a striking reduction in the magnitude of the induced response with both age and senescence.

Considerable specificity has been observed for responses to different stressors. For example, the physical restraint of an animal induces HSP-70 expression selectively in the adrenal cortex and in the media of blood vessels. These responses are dependent on the activation of the hypothalamic–pituitary–adrenal (HPA) axis and the sympathetic nervous system, respectively (see later). Old rats show a reduced HSP-70 response at both sites. Other work has shown a reduced HSP-70 response in the myocardium of old rats and that this is associated with reduced protection from ischemia in the Langendorff isolated heart model. Interestingly, an HSP response may be selective for the nature of the stressor. For example, the hepatic HSP-70 response of old rats to passive heat stress is attenuated whereas that to exertional heat stress is not.

HSPs are also important in the cellular actions of glucocorticoids, the archetypical stress hormones: we deal with how aging modifies glucocorticoid responses to stressors a little later. High-affinity intracellular binding of glucocorticoids (like estrogens and gestagens) requires their receptors to be present as a heteromeric complex containing a HSP-90 dimer; other proteins such as HSP-70, p59/HSP-56 and p23 may also be present, although HSP-70 appears to be involved in the assembly of the complex rather than a component of it. This complex also serves to prevent the receptor from homodimerization and binding to chromatin, and possibly to inhibit its degradation.

II. STRESS RESPONSES IN INTACT ORGANISMS

There is a diverse literature from which information can be gleaned on how complex body systems respond when an organism is subjected to stressful stimuli, but we have chosen to concentrate mainly on those aspects to which we have contributed directly. Experimental studies show that old rats and mice are dramatically more sensitive than the young to the lethal effects of bacterial lipopolysaccharide (endotoxin). Similarly, old, multiply injured humans experience a very high death rate from injuries of a severity that would cause only sporadic deaths in the young.

A. Laboratory Studies

It has long been known that old age is a risk factor for developing "malignant systemic inflammation" during infections and after tissue injury (systemic inflammatory response syndrome; SIRS). However, there have been few systematic studies and consequently little information on aging and the inflammatory response, though there have been a number of *in vitro* studies on neutrophil function.

Methodological problems obscure firm conclusions but the majority of *in vitro* studies have reported impaired neutrophil responses to a variety of stimuli. In contrast, other *in vivo* studies suggest that inflammation may be exaggerated or dysregulated. We have shown old rats to be dramatically sensitive to the lethal effects of endotoxins and that this was associated with early and marked neutrophil infiltration of the lungs and liver. Similarly, in a model of pneumonia in mice, the old animals had much more marked inflammatory infiltrates. Our studies of experimental, human, cutaneous wound healing have also shown greater and prolonged neutrophil infiltration in the old, together with lesser and delayed macrophage infiltration.

Although the endocrine and metabolic consequences of physical injury or experimental infections have not been studied in the context of aging, the responses to the lesser stress of physical restraint have. This study reported a delayed return to baseline corticosterone concentrations in the old rats. It was hypothesized that, as glucocorticoids are toxic to hippocampal neurons and the hippocampus exerts a tonic restraint on activation of the HPA axis, repeated stressful episodes promote hippocampal cell loss, reduce tonic restraint, and predispose to exaggerated HPA axis activation in the old animals.

B. Endocrine and Metabolic Responses

A characteristic pattern of change in hormone secretion and the flux of metabolites is seen in a stressed animal. Typically the sympathoadrenal and HPA systems are stimulated, together with secretion of glucagon and the pituitary hormones growth hormone (GH), prolactin and vasopressin. In contrast, there is suppression of adrenal androgen production, and complex changes take place in the hypothalamic–pituitary–gonadal and hypothalamic–pituitary–thyroid axes that lead to lower concentrations of at least some of their end hormones. As regards metabolites, glycogen and fat are broken down so that the concentrations of glucose, lactate, nonesterified fatty acids (NEFA), glycerol, and ketone bodies increase in the plasma.

Persistence of stressful stimuli cause net protein breakdown in muscle, while in the liver the synthesis of a set of plasma proteins known as the acute-phase reactants (APR) is induced.

Any effects of stressors will be superimposed on a background of "normal" age related changes. In brief, there is little change in plasma ACTH or cortisol during aging in humans. The concentration of noradrenaline, which is derived from sympathetic nerve terminals as well as the adrenal medulla, tends to rise whereas that of adrenaline does not. There is decreased secretion of GH, which takes place mainly at night, but probably not of prolactin or glucagon. Aging is accompanied by a decline in the turnover rate of glucose and a small increase in its concentration, reflecting insulin resistance. There is a tendency for the concentrations of fat metabolites also to increase, but the changes in their turnover rates are more controversial. Protein turnover decreases as would be expected from the decline in lean body mass with age.

1. Responses to Hypoglycemia

The effect of aging on the endocrine responses to hypoglycemia has been of considerable interest because of the possibility of hypoglycemic episodes in treated elderly diabetics. Earlier studies, using a standard insulin tolerance test (0.1 U/kg), mostly showed no difference between old and young people, although there are sporadic findings of decreased cortisol, GH, glucagon and adrenaline responses, and an exaggerated rise in noradrenaline in the elderly.

More controlled experiments with infusion of insulin have confirmed this lack of consistent change in endocrine responses to hypoglycemia, but have shown a tendency for fewer signs of sympathoadrenal activation (e.g., increased heart rate) in the elderly which is not always reflected in diminished responses of plasma catecholamines. There is no unanimity over their sensitivity to the symptoms of neuroglycopenia.

2. Responses to Psychological Stress

A variety of procedures have been used to study the effect of age on responses to psychological stress in the laboratory, nearly all of which have shown reduced heart rate responses in the old. A number of authors have measured catecholamines, finding a tendency for the noradrenaline, but not the adrenaline, response to increase with age as well as an increase in baseline values. There have been few studies of HPA responses to psychological stress in the elderly and these demonstrate no failure to activate the system.

In only one study of the effects of *chronic* stress do different age groups appear to have been compared directly. Urinary free cortisol excretion has been measured in subjects aged 47–78 whose spouses had life-threatening illnesses. There was a correlation with age only in those who were identified as suffering from severe depressive illness. Others have studied elderly people caring for spouses with Alzheimer-type dementia and compared them with spouses not needing to provide care; the care-giving spouses were classified as "high"- and "low"-stress. Plasma noradrenaline was higher in the high-stress group than the others; there were no differences in plasma adrenaline, or cortisol, or in the sensitivity or receptor density of lymphocyte β-adrenergic receptors. Although younger subjects were not studied, the results were contrasted with the β-adrenergic down-regulation observed in young men experiencing the chronic stress of homelessness. A further study reported a tendency for higher insulin but not glucose concentrations in those caring for demented spouses.

3. Response to Trauma

a. The General Response

The acute rises in cortisol and noradrenaline after elective surgery tend to be exaggerated in old people, while the opposite is seen for pituitary hormones. During the first few hours after moderate to major surgery plasma cortisol in elderly patients was either similar to, or significantly higher than, its value in younger ones. There was no difference in plasma ACTH, while the GH response was lower in the elderly. However, in men aged 43–77 yr undergoing colectomy there was no correlation between plasma cortisol and age. Cortisol and ACTH concentrations also tended to be higher in old than in young patients after cholecystectomy. After a minor procedure (inguinal herniorrhaphy), too, plasma cortisol was higher in the elderly, while there was no difference in the response of noradrenaline, adrenaline or aldosterone.

Over the next few days after injury, plasma cortisol, and perhaps noradrenaline, tends to decline to normal levels more slowly in the elderly than in the young. After moderate to major surgery, cortisol continues to be higher in the old; no corresponding change in ACTH is detectable. There is also no difference in plasma GH over this period. The rate of 17-ketogenic steroid excretion (a crude index of cortisol production rate) was raised for a longer period after surgery in older patients, even though the absolute values were not different between young and old. In apparently the only study of the effect of aging responses very soon after accidental injury, we have found no difference in plasma cortisol between patients aged 17–40, 41–65, and 66–92 yr with a wide range of injury severities.

b. HPA Axis Activation after Hip Fracture

We have studied hip-fracture patients who are often frail and in poor health. Cortisol concentrations remain elevated two weeks later (unlike younger people with similar severity injuries). The same was true of the cortisol concentrations after taking dexamethasone overnight (suggesting impaired feedback inhibition by cortisol). These differences persisted when further measurements were made eight weeks after the injury. Such a prolonged period of raised cortisol concentrations could have deleterious systemic effects.

Most reported cortisol concentrations have been measured in the morning and comparisons would be invalidated if there were changes in its nychthemeral rhythm. Reliable indices of HPA function can be based on urinary measurements made over a 24-h period. We have found that hip-fracture patients had a higher cortisol production rate and urinary free cortisol excretion rate than healthy elderly women. The latter index, which is particularly useful as it usually reflects the integrated concentration of free, biologically active cortisol in plasma, rose on average about three-fold. Cortisol production rate rose proportionately less because the metabolic clearance rate of cortisol was lower in the injured patients so that only a modest rise in production rate was necessary to account for the observed increases in plasma cortisol concentration and free cortisol excretion.

A puzzling aspect of our studies is that hip-fracture patients did not show an increase in plasma ACTH. In fact, when concentrations were measured at the end of a 2-h baseline period leading up to injection of corticotrophin-releasing factor (CRF), decreased values were seen compared with the healthy elderly. The total areas under the cortisol- and ACTH-time curves after giving CRF reflected this disparity, that for cortisol being greater and that for ACTH smaller in the patients, although the incremental areas were both decreased. The correlation between cortisol and ACTH seen in the control subjects was completely lost in the hip-fracture patients, and their apparent sensitization to ACTH was not reflected in the slope of the dose-response curve. Combined with a lack of change in the response to small doses of exogenous ACTH[1-24], this suggests the presence of a stimulus acting independently of ACTH. However, it is very difficult to know what such a stimulus might be.

4. Myocardial Infarction

There have been two comparisons of responses to acute myocardial infarction in elderly and younger patients. One study found no difference in plasma cortisol or ACTH, measured over a period of 12 days after the event, between patients aged 65–81 and 33–55 yr; there was also no difference in the response to a standard ACTH stimulation test on the 12th day. The other study reported similar peak CRP levels in patients aged <60 and >70 yr. This study is valuable because it appears to be the only attempt to compare acute-phase protein concentrations between age groups after a standard insult, although it is well known that an acute-phase response occurs in old patients. Comparability is important to establish because CRP levels have been used to distinguish the effects of aging from those of underlying inflammatory disease.

See Also the Following Articles

Aging and Psychological Stress; Heat Shock Response, Overview; Hypoglycemia; Immune System, Aging

Bibliography

Horan, M. A., Little, R. A. (1998). *Injury in the aging.* Cambridge: Cambridge University Press.

Johnson, T. E., Lithgow, G. J., Murakami, S. (1996). Hypothesis: Interventions that increase the response to stress offer the potential for effective life prolongation and increased health. *J. Gerontol.* 51:B392–395.

Lithgow, G. J. (1996). Invertebrate gerontology: The *age* mutations of *Caenorhabditis elegans, Bioessays* 18: 809–815.

Ricklefs, R. E., Finch, C. E. (1995). *Aging: A natural history.* New York: Scientific American Library.

Agoraphobia

see Panic Disorder and Agoraphobia

AIDS

Michael H. Antoni and Dean G. Cruess
University of Miami

I. Stress and AIDS
II. Stress, Immunity, and Health in HIV Infection
III. Stress Management for HIV-Infected Individuals

GLOSSARY

antibody A molecule produced by B lymphocytes in response to an antigen, which has the particular property of combining specifically with the antigen which induces its formation.

antigen A molecule that induces the formation of an antibody.

cytokine A generic term for soluble molecules that mediate interactions between cells of the immune system.

cytotoxicity The ability to kill cells.

interleukins A class of molecules involved in signaling between cells of the immune system.

lymphocytes A class of immune cells, central to all adaptive immune responses, that specifically recognize individual pathogens, whether they are inside host cells or outside in the tissue fluids or blood. Lymphocytes fall into two basic categories: T lymphocytes (T cells) or B lymphocytes (B cells).

pathogen An organism which causes disease.

phagocytosis The process by which cells engulf material and enclose it within a vacuole in the cytoplasm.

proliferation The clonal expansion of lymphocytes resulting from mitogen or antigen challenge.

T-helper/inducer (CD4) cells A functional subclass of T cells which can help to generate cytotoxic T cells and cooperate with B cells in the production of antibodies.

AIDS (Acquired Immune Deficiency Syndrome) is a global disease of epic proportions which overwhelmingly affects young people rendering them unable to defend against common pathogens. Human Immunodeficiency Virus (HIV), the causative agent of this syndrome, is a retrovirus that works by systematically disarming multiple components of the immune system leaving the infected person susceptible to many of the lethal infections and cancers that encompass AIDS.

I. STRESS AND AIDS

AIDS is the leading cause of death among men and women ages 15–44 in this country. HIV infection can be viewed as a chronic disease whose clinical course is dependent, in part, upon an infected individual's ability to maintain optimal cell-mediated immunologic control over extant and encountered pathogens. There is mounting evidence linking psychosocial stressors with HIV infection and AIDS. Many psychosocial and behavioral phenomena, including stressful events, stress responses, and distress states, have been associated with impairments in the immune system, which could potentially exacerbate the immunologic abnormalities and health consequences observed among HIV-infected individuals. Such associations may be mediated, in part, by stress-related alterations in neuroendocrine functioning

118

(e.g., adrenal hormone regulation) on the one hand or health behaviors (e.g., substance use, self-care) on the other. Specific immunologic components important in contributing to the course of HIV infection have also been shown to be associated with stressors and distress states.

A. How HIV Infection Affects Immune System Functioning

1. T-Helper/Inducer Lymphocyte Distribution

HIV binds with the CD4 receptor, which is most prevalent on a type of T lymphocyte called a T helper/inducer or CD4 cell. As the infection progresses, there are decrements in CD4 cell counts and impairments in the ability of T lymphocytes to respond to antigenic challenge, opening the door to a wide range of "opportunistic" infections and cancers. HIV epidemiological and clinical immunology research indicates that precipitous drops in CD4 cell counts, particularly when they fall below 200 cells/mm^3, are highly predictive of the onset of physical symptoms and general clinical decline. Since CD4 cells are depleted in the advancing stages of HIV infection, increases in functional aspects of lymphocytes might be important in predicting those HIV-infected individuals (with low CD4 counts) who develop opportunistic infections quickly. Some of these functions include the ability to kill tumors and viruses, a process called "cytotoxicity."

2. Cytotoxic Functions

One type of "psychologically sensitive" immune function believed to offer "primary" protection from replicating HIV, as well as surveillance over other pathogens, is cytotoxicity. High-impact psychosocial stressors such as bereavement, which is quite prevalent among HIV-infected individuals and those who are at risk, appear to be associated with decreases in a specific type of cytotoxicity called natural killer cell cytotoxicity (NKCC). Impairments in NKCC may be especially important during HIV infection, since CD4 cells are depleted both quantitatively and qualitatively. Natural killer cells may compensate to some degree for HIV-induced CD4 cell deficiencies. While other cells such as CD8+ lymphocytes may also perform key cytotoxic functions in HIV+ persons, less is known about their associations with psychosocial factors.

3. Herpesvirus Infections

Some immune measures may reflect the potential contribution of reputed cofactors of HIV disease progression, including rising antibody titers to herpesviruses such as Epstein–Barr virus (EBV), reflecting viral reactivation. Herpesvirus reactivation may "transactivate" HIV-infected cells contributing to increases in HIV viral load. HIV-infected individuals who experience elevated life stressors, distress, depression, an inability to cope with these stressors, and/or a sense of social isolation may be at greater risk for reactivation of specific herpesviruses. Both NKCC and T-cell-mediated cytotoxic functions are generally responsible for keeping these viruses in check. Conversely, stress-associated impairments in cytotoxicity may facilitate herpesvirus reactivation in HIV-infected individuals with subsequent HIV replication and progression to AIDS.

4. Cytokine Dysregulation

Maintaining adequate cytotoxic capabilities may depend on retaining T-helper cell-type-1 (TH1) predominance and production of cytokines or "immunohormones" such as interleukin-2 (IL-2) and IL-12. However, a "shift" to TH2 predominance and the production of cytokines such as IL-4 and IL-10 occurs in HIV infection. T-Helper cell-type 1 cells stimulate both specific (T-cell-associated) and nonspecific (NK-cell-associated) cytotoxicity by producing IL-2 and γ-interferon (γ-IFN). Interleukin-12, a recently discovered cytokine produced by monocytes, may also be important because of its ability to stimulate NK cells and T cells to release γ-IFN. In addition to affecting cytotoxicity, stressors and distress states have been associated with decrements in other key immune system functions, such as phagocytosis and lymphocyte proliferation, which may also be important in HIV infection.

B. Stress, Psychoneuroimmunology, and HIV Infection

The field of psychoneuroimmunology (PNI) examines how stressors, stress responses and distress states relate to the immune system by way of neural and endocrine processes. One's perception of the nature of a stressor and/or the availability of a coping response to that stressor accompany a series of physiological events leading to specific autonomic, neuroendocrine, and neuropeptide changes. While neuroendocrine and nervous system mediators of stressor-associated changes in immune system functioning have been identified in humans, most work has occurred outside the HIV arena.

1. Endocrine–Immune Interactions

Many different neurotransmitters, neurohormones, and neuropeptides within the central nervous system (CNS) have been studied as potential mediators of stressor-induced immunomodulation. Two well-delineated "stress response pathways," the hypothalamic-pituitary-adrenal (HPA) axis and the sympathoadrenomedullary (SAM) system, have received the most attention. Elevations in glucocorticoids, a product of the HPA axis, enhance HIV replication, are immunosuppressive, and also accompany affective disorder and stressful experiences. Once glucocorticoids such as cortisol bind to intracytoplasmic receptors on immune cells, the complex travels to the nucleus and binds to DNA sequences that control glucocorticoid-regulated transcription genes for cytokine synthesis. Elevated levels of cortisol are associated with impaired immune system functioning and accompanying decreases in TH1-like cytokine production. Current PNI research examines how distress or depression-associated cortisol elevations impact immune function (e.g., NKCC) in HIV-infected individuals and how these changes might relate to disease progression by way of impaired surveillance of latent pathogens such as the herpesviruses.

Elevations in peripheral catecholamines, such as norepinephrine (NE), a product of SAM activation, also depress immune functioning via β-adrenergic receptors on lymphocytes. Sympathetic noradrenergic fibers innervate both the vasculature and parenchymal regions of lymphocytes and associated cells in several lymphoid organs, where NE terminals are generally directed into T-lymphocyte zones. Alterations in electrical activity and NE metabolism in the hypothalamus occur following injection of antigen or cytotokine products of T lymphocytes stimulated *in vitro*, suggesting bidirectional communication between the nervous and immune systems.

Lymphocytes are known to have receptors for many neurohormones including serotonin and cholinergic and β-adrenergic agonists, with most evidence for receptors involving β-adrenergic sites. Administration of β-adrenergic agonists has been associated with decreases in mouse and human NKCC and decreased T-lymphocyte proliferation, and these effects appear to be mediated by increases in intracellular cyclic AMP (cAMP). Patients treated with glucocorticoids show increased β-adrenergic responsiveness due to an increased receptor number and enhanced receptor–adenyl cyclase coupling, evidencing a synergy between SAM and HPA axis-generated stress hormones. *In vivo* human studies involving infusion of adrenergic agents have also shown a decrease in leukocyte number and decreased lymphocyte proliferative response to mitogens following epinephrine administration. These immunomodulatory effects are also most likely mediated by cyclic nucleotide action. In addition, agents that increase lymphocyte cAMP (e.g., isoproterenol, prostaglandin E) can impair lymphocyte proliferation and cytoxicity, whereas agents that increase lymphocyte cGMP levels (e.g., carbamylcholine) enhance lymphocyte proliferative and cytotoxic abilities.

Stress hormones may have profound effects on monocyte/macrophage cell lines and related cytokines (e.g., IL-1). Such effects could have implications for "upstream" activities such as antigen processing and presentation to CD4 cells. In addition to catecholamines and corticosteroids, pituitary and adrenal peptide stress hormones, such as metenkephalin, β-endorphin, and substance P, have been shown to stimulate T-cell cytotoxicity, NKCC, and γ-interferon production as well as macrophage functioning.

2. Stress, Endocrine Regulation, and HIV Infection

The regulation of adrenal hormones may have direct relevance for the pathogenesis of HIV infection.

One study found that the ability of HIV to infect normal human lymphocytes was enhanced by supplementing the cell culture medium with corticosteroids. Viral susceptibility may be related to the efficacy of lymphocyte or NK cytotoxic abilities, which may be compromised by glucocorticoid secretions during stress. Recent work suggests that HIV-infected persons have HPA axis abnormalities, which may increase with the progression of disease, favoring a shift from TH1-like to TH2-like cytokine production. HIV-infected persons display elevated resting levels of cortisol, which are associated with lower CD4 cell counts and decreased NKCC. Cortisol specifically promotes decreased production of TH1-like cytokines such as interleukin-2 (IL-2) while promoting increased production of TH2-like cytokines such as IL-4 and IL-10. Since cortisol can induce programmed cell death in mature lymphocytes, the HPA axis may also play a role in the progression of HIV infection by facilitating the destruction of viable cells.

Through repeated exposure to multiple stressors, HIV-infected persons may become particularly vigilant, physically tense, and sympathetically activated for extended periods of time. Those undergoing chronic sympathetic nervous system arousal with subsequent release of NE from sympathetic nerve terminals may experience health decrements, since these endocrines may down-regulate the proliferation of naive (uncommitted) T lymphocytes. These cells are already significantly depleted in HIV infection, even after successful antiretroviral treatment. Diminished naive T-lymphocyte proliferation may render HIV-infected persons less able to respond to novel pathogens, opening the door to opportunistic infections. In sum, the literature supports the notion that elevated levels of cortisol and catecholamines are associated with impaired immune system functioning. Distress or depression-associated neuroendocrine changes impact immune function (e.g., NKCC) in HIV-infected individuals and such functional changes might relate directly to HIV disease progression by way of impaired surveillance of latent and novel pathogens, which, once reactivated, can stimulate HIV proliferation.

II. STRESS, IMMUNITY, AND HEALTH IN HIV INFECTION

HIV-infected persons encounter a large number of major stressors, which, based on the way they perceive them, may result in different emotional responses. These affective responses may relate to altered levels of certain neuroendocrine substances (e.g., cortisol and catecholamines) that have been shown to have depressive effects on lymphocytes. These stress responses may also be accompanied by behaviors (e.g., substance use, unprotected sex, and poor medication adherence) that could have negative implications for the health of HIV-infected persons. We now summarize the evidence relating depression and health behaviors to immune function and the evidence relating immune alterations to stress-intervening variables (stressor appraisals, coping responses, and social supports) that may influence physical health status.

A. Depression and Immunity in HIV Infection

Depression and depressed affect are associated with immunosuppression in healthy individuals. Among HIV-infected persons, some studies have found that depressive state was unrelated to changes in CD4 counts or HIV-related symptoms over 6- and 12-month periods, respectively. Other studies examining immunologic and health changes over longer periods found interesting but conflicting results. One found that gay men scoring above the criterion for depression showed a faster rate of decline in CD4 cell counts over a 66-month follow-up period compared to those scoring below this value. This association was strongest in men who were at the earliest stages of disease. In a separate cohort showing more progressed disease at the time of the depression evaluation, these findings were not evident.

Another study showed that chronically depressed affect (sustained severe depressed mood over a 2-year period) predicted declines in CD4 counts among HIV+ gay men without AIDS as compared to a group of nonchronically depressed men matched on age and CD4 levels. Subsequent work, incorporating more sophisticated statistical procedures and time-dependent covariates (including medication regimen), showed that depression, in combination with elevated stressful life events, does in fact predict a faster rate of disease progression in HIV+ men over a 5-year period. Depressed affect may be associated with an accelerated decline in CD4 counts and a faster rate of clinical disease progression among HIV-infected men. This association appears stronger when the potential confounding somatic effects of the disease are controlled by either sampling (excluding progressed subjects), questionnaire refinement (excluding somatically based depression items from the test battery), or statistical controls. Beyond studying the influence of depressive symptoms it is also important to consider the role of anxiety-related symptoms (e.g., tension, rumination) in the quality of life, immune status, and physical health of HIV-infected individuals.

B. Health Behaviors and Immunity in HIV Infection

Drug and alcohol use is associated with a wide variety of immunologic effects that may have direct health implications for HIV-infected individuals. Alcohol use is related to decreased lymphocyte number and proliferative responses. Alcoholism and related liver disease is associated with impaired NKCC and decreased NK cell numbers. Evidence suggests that alcohol abuse may amplify the suppressive effects of depression on NKCC. The use of substances ranging from injected drugs to cigarettes has been associated with faster disease progression in HIV-infected people. Thus, it is plausible that substance abuse may contribute to a decline in immunologic status and possibly faster disease progression.

Little is known about the direct immunomodulatory effects of different forms of sexual behaviors, but it is plausible that repeated exposure to novel strains of HIV and other sexually transmitted pathogens [e.g., herpes simplex virus (HSV) and human papillomavirus (HPV)] may contribute directly to the development of opportunistic infections (e.g., systemic HSV-2 infections) and cancers (e.g., HPV-associated cervical and anal intraepithelial neoplasias). In addition, exposure to these pathogens may indirectly contribute to accelerated disease course by promoting HIV replication.

Maintaining positive health behaviors such as adequate sleep, nutrition, exercise, and, perhaps most importantly, adherence to prescribed medications are a central part of managing HIV infection. Triple combination antiretroviral therapy with protease inhibitors offer some hope that viral replication can be slowed more efficiently and with a lower likelihood of resistance or undue side-effects than prior antiretroviral regimens. Failure to adhere to the rigid and demanding medication regimens can substantially increase the risk of developing drug-resistant strains of the virus. The resulting treatment philosophy, now more than ever, views HIV infection as a chronic disease in which patient management is critical. Incomplete adherence cannot only compromise the effects of the particular protease inhibitor being used, but can also reduce the efficacy of other related compounds to which cross-resistance has developed. The key is consistent adherence to a demanding medication schedule in the context of an already stressful daily existence. Since depressed affect, substance use, risky sexual behaviors, and poor adherence to HIV medications may all contribute to adverse health outcomes among HIV-infected individuals, it is also important to understand the factors that intervene on these phenomena.

C. Intervening Variables

The mounting stress of HIV infection may cause infected persons to appraise their world as uncontrollable, resulting in an inability to deal with additional challenges and a greater likelihood of depression, substance use, risky sexual behaviors, and poor self-care. This sequence is more likely among those with inadequate coping skills and sustained social support losses. Several psychosocial factors, such as perceived loss of control, maladaptive coping strategies and social isolation have been related to impaired immune functioning in a wide variety of healthy populations. These processes (and intervention-associated changes in these processes) may be associated with immunologic alterations in HIV-infected people. Recently, studies have demonstrated a possible link between these psychosocial processes and the physical course of the infection.

1. Perceived Loss of Control

Various stressors, especially those viewed as uncontrollable, have been associated with decrements in immune function in healthy people. Some of these are particularly prevalent among HIV-infected people attempting to cope with their illness and include bereavement, the stress of being a caregiver for a loved one with a terminal disease, and divorce or break-up. There is less conclusive evidence linking stressors with immune and health changes among HIV-infected individuals. Some studies find no association between life events and CD4 counts or HIV-related symptoms, while others find that elevated life events are predictive of increases in HIV-related symptoms. Other studies have reported decrements in immune function surrounding a specific and common stressor for HIV-infected gay men—death of a partner to AIDS. Focusing on a stressor such as partner loss, which is universally perceived as uncontrollable, may be the key to ascertaining psychoneuroimmunology (PNI) associations among HIV+ persons. The PNI literature on stressor effects in animals and humans has emphasized that uncontrollable stressors have stronger immunomodulatory effects than controllable stressors, and this may be due to the different neuroendocrine cascades occurring during each of these types of stressor transactions.

2. Coping Strategies

Coping strategies, such as active coping, active confrontation, "fighting spirit", and denial, have been related to changes in physical health during HIV-infection. The use of active coping was associated with decreased symptom development in HIV-infected gay men. A "fighting spirit" coping strategy also predicted less symptom development, while denial coping predicted a greater number of HIV-related symptoms over a 12-month period. Other coping strategies such as avoidance and denial have also been associated with declines in immune function in HIV+ men. During the stressful period of HIV antibody testing, greater avoidance of distressing AIDS-related thoughts predicts greater anxiety, depression, and confusion as well as lower lymphocyte proliferative responses and NKCC after notification of positive serostatus. Increases in the use of denial during the postnotification period also predict a faster progression to AIDS over a 2-year follow-up. Gay men with AIDS who used a strategy called "realistic acceptance" showed a shorter survival time than those not endorsing this strategy. Realistic acceptance appears to reflect excessive rumination and focus on HIV-related matters, almost to the exclusion of many other facets of life. It may be that while denial is maladaptive and predictive of poorer health outcomes, obsessing and ruminating about the disease may also have negative health ramifications. Newer work has produced evidence that greater use of "distraction" as a coping strategy predicts a slower subsequent course of disease over a 7-year follow-up. Distraction here reflects an effort to focus on living and pursuing activities that are meaningful rather than denying the existence of the infection or refusing to focus on it excessively. This sort of balance between acceptance and non rumination has also been identified as a common trait of those who are long-term survivors of HIV infection and AIDS.

3. Social Isolation

HIV-infected people face a variety of stressors and challenges that they must continually negotiate in an effort to deal with the potentially overwhelming psychological and physical health consequences of their illness. Stigmatization, alienation from friends and family, increased reliance on medical personnel, social disconnectedness, and gradual deterioration of physical health status and immune functioning may leave these individuals feeling socially isolated. Social resources have been found to buffer the negative physical and psychological effects of major life-threatening events. Low social support availability predicts a faster decline in CD4 counts over a 5-year period among HIV-infected men with hemophilia. Larger social network size and greater informational support provided by that network predicts greater survival time in HIV-infected men, but only among those with AIDS. Greater perceived social support also predicts a slower progression of disease in initially asymptomatic HIV+ gay men over a 5-year period. It remains to be demonstrated whether actively intervening to increase the quality of HIV-infected people's social support influences their long-term psychological adjustment, immune functioning, physical health status, and subsequent disease progression.

To summarize, HIV infection is a chronic disease often associated with severe psychosocial and physical stressors, which can potentially overwhelm those infected in a number of domains. The stressors that encompass HIV and AIDS impact the way in which those infected appraise day-to-day situations, choose coping strategies, acquire support, and deal emotionally with stressful events in their lives, which in turn can alter stress hormones as well as influence their ability to engage in healthy behaviors. These processes can then lead to alterations in immune system functioning, which may have repercussions for the development of symptoms and increased HIV viral load. Figure 1 displays the interconnectedness of these multiple factors in HIV disease.

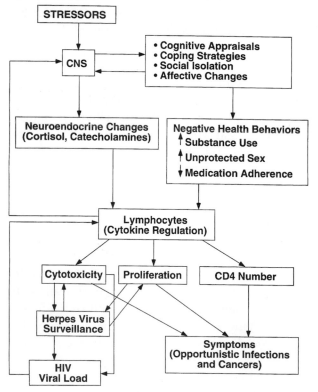

FIGURE 1 Model relating stressors, psychosocial factors, neuroendocrine changes, health behaviors, immune status, and disease in HIV infection. CNS, central nervous system; CD4, T-helper lymphocytes; HIV, human immunodeficiency virus.

III. STRESS MANAGEMENT FOR HIV-INFECTED INDIVIDUALS

Stressors, stress responses, coping strategies, and social resources are related to psychological adjustment, immune system function, and the physical course of HIV infection. Stress-management interventions that modify how individuals process and deal with stressors help to reduce distress and facilitate adjustment and buffer the impact of stressors on the immune system. Some of these gains appear to be brought about by the ability of these interventions to modify stressor appraisals, improve coping strategies, and enhance social support in HIV-infected persons. Psychosocial interventions that provide information, skills, and support to infected persons can help normalize neuroendocrine levels and can also facilitate the adoption and maintenance of positive health behaviors, including better adherence to demanding antiretroviral medication protocols. Since interventions may also decrease denial and depressed affect, they may, in turn, decrease negative health behaviors (e.g., substance use and risky sex) that are associated with immune system decrements. The improvements in immune function that have been associated with these psychosocial interventions raises the interesting question of whether stress management can help reconstitute the immune system once antiretroviral agents have contained HIV. Although we are now learning much about how stressors and stress management interventions influence HIV disease in gay men, far less is known about other HIV-infected populations that are growing in numbers (e.g., poor minority women, injection drug users). Understanding the mechanisms through which stressful experiences and stress management interventions contribute to quality of life and the physical course of HIV infection may help the growing populations of infected persons who are attempting to manage this chronic disease.

See Also the Following Articles

Autoimmunity; Avoidance; Herpesviruses; Immune Suppression

Bibliography

Ader, R., Felton, D., and Cohen, N. (1991). "Psychoneuroimmunology" 2nd ed. Academic Press, New York.

Antoni, M. H., Esterling, B., Lutgendorf, S., Fletcher, M. A., and Schneiderman, N. (1995). Psychosocial stressors, herpesvirus reactivation and HIV-1 infection. *In* "AIDS and Oncology: Perspectives in Behavioral Medicine" (M. Stein and A. Baum, Eds.), Erlbaum, Hillsdale, NJ.

Antoni, M. H., Schneiderman, N., Fletcher, M. A., Goldstein, D., Ironson, G., and LaPerriere, A. (1990). Psychoneuroimmunology and HIV-1. *J. Consult. Clin. Psychol.* **58**, 38–49.

Chrousos, G. (1995). The hypothalamic pituitary adrenal axis and immune mediated inflammation. *N. Engl. J. Med.* **332**, 1351–1362.

Glaser, R., and Kiecolt-Glaser, J. (1994). "Handbook of Human Stress and Immunity." Academic Press, New York.

Glaser, R., and Kiecolt-Glaser, J. (1987). Stress-associated depression in cellular immunity: Implications for acquired immune deficiency syndrome (AIDS). *Brain Behav. Immun.* **1**, 107–112.

Herbert, T., and Cohen, S. (1993). Stress and immunity in humans: A meta-analytic review. *Psychosom. Med.* **55**, 472–486.

Ironson, G., Solomon, G., Cruess, D., Barroso, J., and Stivers, M. (1995). Psychosocial factors related to long-term survival with HIV/AIDS. *Clin. Psychol. Psychother.* **2**, 249–266.

Kiecolt-Glaser, J., and Glaser, R. (1995). Psychoneuroimmunology and health consequences: Data and shared mechanisms. *Psychosom. Med.* **57**, 269–274.

Maier, S. F., Watkins, L. R., and Fleshner, M. (1994). Psychoneuroimmunology: The interface between behavior, brain, and immunity. *Am. Psychol.* **49**, 1004–1017.

McCabe, P. M., and Schneiderman, N. (1985). Psychophysiologic reactions to stress. *In* "Behavioral Medicine: The Biopsychosocial Approach" (N. Schneiderman and J. T. Tapp, Eds.), pp. 99–131. Erlbaum, Hillsdale, NJ.

McEwen, B. (1998). Protective and damaging effects of stress mediators. *N. Engl. J. Med.* **338**, 171–179.

Pantaleo, G., Graziosi, C., and Fauci, A. S. (1993). The immunopathogenesis of human immunodeficiency virus infection. *N. Engl. J. Med.* **328**, 327–335.

Roitt, I., Brostoff, J., and Male, D. (1993). *Immunology,* 3rd ed. Mosby, London.

Airplane Crashes

see Lockerbie Air Crash

Alarm Phase and General Adaptation Syndrome

Richard McCarty

University of Virginia

Karel Pacak

National Institute of Neurological Disorders and Stroke
National Institute of Child Health and Human Development
National Institutes of Health

GLOSSARY

dishabituation Facilitation of a habituated stress response following exposure to an intense or a novel stressor.

general adaptation syndrome As proposed by Selye, the general adaptation syndrome (GAS) reflected the physiological changes experienced by animals, including humans, during prolonged stress and consisted of three distinct phases. These included the alarm phase, the resistance phase, and the exhaustion phase.

habituation A decrease in the amplitude of the stress response after repeated daily exposure to the same stressor.

sensitization Enhancement of a nonhabituated stress response by a stressor of high intensity.

I. HANS SELYE AND THE GENERAL ADAPTATION SYNDROME

Hans Selye deserves much of the credit for popularizing the concept of stress in the scientific and medical literature of the 20th century. Much of the credit also goes to him for the confusion that has resulted in issues relating to the definition of stress and the conceptualization of how stress plays a role in disease etiology. From the beginning of his career, Selye emphasized a medical model in advancing his views on stress. In his landmark paper published in *Nature* in 1936, Selye first advanced his notion of stress as a "non-specific response of the body to any demand placed upon it." He was unwavering in promoting this hallmark feature of his definition of stress until his death in the early 1980s.

Selye also advanced the notion of the stress response unfolding in specific stages that comprised the general adaptation syndrome (GAS) (Table I). Upon exposure of an animal or human to a given stressor, there would be a rapid onset alarm phase. The alarm phase was thought to consist of two distinct phases: shock and countershock. The disruptive effects of the stressor would be expressed in a dramatic alteration in homeostatic processes, including regulatory processes affecting blood pressure, circulating levels of glucose, electrolyte balance, distribution of blood flow, and membrane permeability. These shock-related responses to the stressor would be counteracted in part by the countershock responses of the adrenal cortex, through the release of corticosteroids, and the adrenal medulla, through the release of epinephrine.

If the stressful stimulus persisted over a prolonged period of time, the second stage of the GAS, the resistance phase, would develop. During the resistance phase, the organism would achieve a state of increased adaptation to the untoward effects of the stressor but would be more susceptible to the deleterious effects of other homeostatic challenges. In this phase of the GAS, Selye argued that the adrenal cortex played a key role through a balanced release of syntoxic and catatoxic steroid hormones. Syntoxic glucocorticoid hormones inhibited inflammatory responses while catatoxic hormones promoted in-

TABLE I

Stages of the General Adaptation Syndrome

Stage 1: **Alarm phase**
  Shock
  Countershock
Stage 2: **Resistance phase**
  Syntoxic hormones (anti-inflammatory)
  Catatoxic hormones (proinflammatory)
Stage 3: **Exhaustion phase**
  Depletion of adaptation energy
  Increase in ulceration of the gastrointestinal tract
  Increased susceptibility to infectious agents
  Typically ends in death

flammatory responses to pathogens. Selye was never able to isolate and identify catatoxic adrenal hormones.

At some undefined point, if the stressful stimulus continued and perhaps increased in intensity, the organism would enter the third and final stage of the GAS, the phase of exhaustion. Selye suggested that the onset of this third stage was triggered by depletion of adaptation energy stores. This depletion of adaptation energy was attended by enhanced activity of the hypothalamic-pituitary-adrenocortical axis and the onset of pathophysiological changes in the immune system and gastrointestinal tract, resulting ultimately in death of the organism. Two critical features of stress for many years, gastrointestinal ulcers and increased susceptibility to infectious agents, are reflected in the changes that were thought to accompany the phase of exhaustion. As for adaptation energy, Selye was never able to measure it, only to infer its depletion when the organism died from lack of it.

II. SHORTCOMINGS OF THE GENERAL ADAPTATION SYNDROME

Not surprisingly, several aspects of Selye's conception of stress and the specific features of the GAS have been the subject of criticism over the years. It is safe to say that Selye's attempts to popularize the concept of stress as it relates to physical and mental health were extremely successful. In contrast, his conceptualization of stress and the details of the GAS have not stood the test of time. We address a few of these issues below.

Selye's definition of stress has been a major source of concern for investigators in this field for many years. His emphasis on the nonspecificity of the stress response has been especially troubling and some have argued that his writings on this subject were contradictory. For example, although Selye emphasized the nonspecificity of the stress response across many different types and intensities of stressors, he did allow room for individual differences in the stress response. Indeed, he was forced to do this to explain the fact that there were many different pathophysiological changes associated with stress. If the stress response was indeed invariant between individuals, there should be only one type of stress-related disorder. However, he addressed this problem by positing that "conditioning factors" acted to accentuate or inhibit particular components of the stress response, leading to individual differences in expression of the deleterious effects of stress. These conditioning factors could be related to genetic, maturational, or environmental influences. Still, he argued that once the effects of these conditioning factors were stripped away, a constellation of nonspecific responses would remain. Few if any investigators support this suggestion today.

Selye's work also placed the adrenal cortex at the center of the stress universe. Indeed, an elevation in secretion of steroid hormones from the adrenal cortex became for some a necessary condition for stress to occur. Beginning with the work of John Mason and his colleagues in the 1960s, the centrality of adrenal steroids in the stress response was supplanted by an emphasis on participation of multiple neural and neuroendocrine pathways in the stress response, with no single system assuming a position of preeminence.

III. PRIOR STRESS HISTORY AFFECTS FUTURE STRESS RESPONSES

Work from our laboratory has focused on one area of Selye's GAS that received little attention. Specifically, we looked at the effects of prior stress history on the pattern of responses to subsequent exposure to a stressor. In this work, we focused our attention on sympathetic-adrenal medullary responses to stress and we measured plasma levels of norepinephrine (NE) and epinephrine (EPI) in laboratory rats. Plasma levels of NE and EPI have been shown to provide an accurate assessment of the activity of the sympathetic nerves and the adrenal medulla, respectively. For all of these studies, rats were surgically prepared with indwelling tail artery catheters that permitted remote sampling of blood.

Three types of nonassociative learning have been studied within a framework of quantifying hormonal responses to stressful stimulation: (1) habituation, a decrease in the amplitude of the stress response after repeated exposure to the same stressor; (2) sensitization, enhancement of a nonhabituated stress response by an intense stressor: and (3) dishabituation; facilitation of a habituated stress response following exposure to an intense/novel stressor.

A. Habituation

Chronic intermittent exposure of laboratory rats to a stressor of low or moderate intensity leads to a significant reduction in plasma levels of NE and EPI compared to control animals exposed to the same stressor for the first time. Several different stressors have been evaluated, including forced swimming, restraint, immobilization, footshock, and exercise. It is important to note that these chronic intermittent stress paradigms provide animals with a high degree of predictability regarding such parameters as type of stressor, stressor intensity, duration of each stress session, and the time of onset of the stressor each day. When provided with this information after several stress sessions, animals are able to activate stress-responsive hormonal systems to the minimum extent necessary to maintain cardiovascular and metabolic homeostasis during each subsequent exposure to the same stressor. This progressive dampening of plasma catecholamine responses to a familiar and highly predictable stressor provides for a significant conservation of energy expenditure.

B. Sensitization

When animals are exposed to a high-intensity stressor there are recurring disruptions in cardiovascular and metabolic processes. One such stressor that has been studied is immersion of laboratory rats in water maintained at 18 or 24°C for 15 min per day for 27 consecutive days. When compared to controls exposed to cold swim stress for the first time, animals exposed to chronic intermittent swim stress had significantly greater elevations in plasma levels of NE and EPI. This sensitized response of the sympathetic-adrenal medullary system to chronic intermittent cold swim stress is dependent upon stressor intensity. Chronic intermittent swim stress in water maintained at higher temperatures (30°C) results in habituated responses.

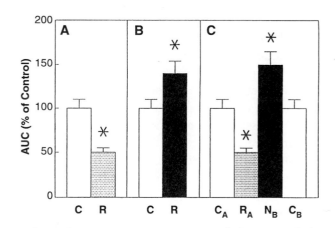

FIGURE 1   Nonassociative properties of plasma catecholamine responses [area under curve (AUC) expressed as a percentage of control] in rats exposed to chronic intermittent stress. (A) Habituation of plasma catecholamine responses of repeatedly stressed (R) rats to a mild stressor compared to first-time stressed controls (C). (B) Sensitization of plasma catecholamine responses of repeatedly stressed (R) rats to an intense stressor compared to first-time stressed controls (C). (C) Dishabituation of plasma catecholamine responses of rats repeatedly exposed to stressor A (R_A) when presented with a novel stressor B (N_B). The plasma catecholamine responses of the respective controls (C_A and C_B) are presented for comparison. Note that in the same group of animals, the response to a familiar stressor (R_A) may be diminished, whereas the response to a novel stressor (N_B) may be enhanced.

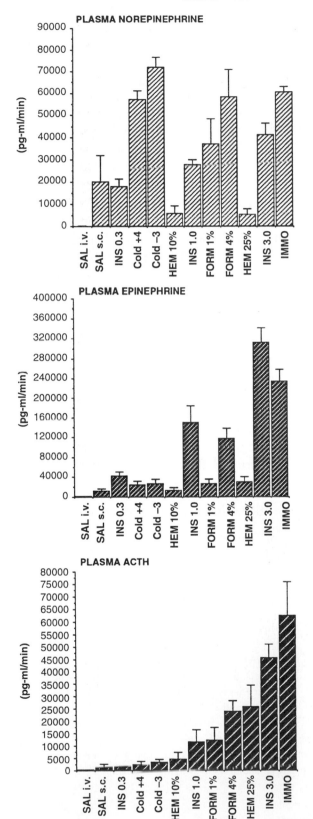

C. Dishabituation

Dishabituation involves an enhancement of the physiological response to a novel stressor in animals exposed repeatedly or continuously to an unrelated stressor. For example, if laboratory rats are exposed to a brief period of footshock stress each day for several weeks, the plasma catecholamine response to footshock gradually decreases over time compared to the response of a naïve control. However, if these same rats are exposed to a novel stressor (e.g., restraint stress), their plasma catecholamine response is amplified compared to the response of naïve controls to restraint stress. Data from our laboratory and the work of others suggest that exposing chronically stressed animals to an unfamiliar stressor presents a much greater challenge to behavioral and physiological homeostasis than presentation of the same stressor to a naive control. In this instance, departure from the expected appears to be the critical variable in eliciting an enhanced physiological response to stress. Chronically stressed animals live in a moderately stressful but highly predictable environment. The experimenter arrives at approximately the same time each day, the stress session begins at approximately the same time each day, the intensity of the stressor and the duration of the stress session are held constant, and most of the day is free from disturbance. Against this backdrop of consistency, a novel stressor represents an abrupt and at times a dramatic departure from the consistency of the past (Fig. 1).

FIGURE 2 Responses of plasma levels of ACTH, epinephrine (EPI), and norepinephrine (NE) during exposure to various stressors in conscious rats. Each bar represents the mean value for the net areas under the curve (AUCs) for that stressor, where the net AUC for each animal was calculated from the baseline AUC subtracted from the total AUC. Stressors included saline injection either intravenously or subcutaneously (SAL iv or SAL sc), insulin (0.3 or 3.0 IU/kg), cold exposure (4° or −3°C), hemorrhage (10 or 25% of total estimated blood volume), formalin injection (1 or 4% solution), and immobilization (IMMO).

IV. THE DEATH KNELL OF NONSPECIFICITY

Although the issue of nonspecificity of stress responses had been discussed by a host of investigators, no study had attempted to compared neuroendocrine response profiles across a range of different stressors. Recently, such a study was conducted and the measures of the stress response included plasma levels of ACTH, corticosterone, NE, and EPI as well as microdialysate levels of NE within the hypothalamic paraventricular nucleus (PVN). The PVN contains cell bodies of neurons that release corticotropin releasing hormone (CRH) into the pituitary portal system and NE-containing nerve terminals within this nucleus provide a potent stimulatory signal for release of CRH. The acute stressors that were employed in this study included the following: hemorrhage (10 or 25% of estimated blood volume), intravenous insulin (0.1, 1.0, or 3.0 IU/kg), subcutaneous administration of formaldehyde (1 or 4% solution), exposure to a cold environment for 180 min (4°C or −3°C), and immobilization for 120 min.

The results of this study indicated that the neuroendocrine signatures varied dramatically across stressors (Fig. 2). In addition, for those stressors that varied in intensity (hemorrhage, insulin, formaldehyde, and cold exposure), some increments in a given neuroendocrine response were greater from one intensity to the next compared to another neuroendocrine response. For example, the ACTH response to a 25% hemorrhage exceeded by five times the plasma ACTH response to a 10% hemorrhage. In contrast, the plasma EPI response to a 25% hemorrhage exceeded by only two times the plasma EPI response to a 10% hemorrhage. Similarly, the plasma ACTH response to a 4% formaldehyde solution was two times that of the response to a 1% solution. However, the plasma EPI response to a 4% formaldehyde solution was four times greater than the response to a 1% solution.

These two categories of findings (e.g., unique neuroendocrine signatures combined with the absence of proportionate increases across all neuroendocrine responses with increases in stressor intensity) are in striking contrast to the predictions associated with Selye's doctrine of nonspecificity. The results of this study are consistent with a primitive form of specificity whereby each stressor provokes a neuroendocrine response pattern that allows, within some limits, for maximal homeostatic balance to be maintained.

V. SUMMARY AND CONCLUSIONS

It has been more than 65 years since Selye published his often-cited paper in the journal *Nature*. The interdisciplinary field of stress research has matured to a significant degree since that time and thousands of papers on this topic have appeared in the scientific literature. Many of Selye's original concepts of stress have not stood the test of time as improved analytical techniques and new discoveries in neuroanatomy, neuroendocrinology, and molecular biology have occurred at a remarkable pace. However, it is important to recognize that Selye did establish a connection between stress and disease that continues to occupy basic and clinical researchers in their laboratories and clinics throughout the world.

See Also the Following Articles

Adrenal Cortex; Adrenal Medulla; Disease, Stress Induced; Selye, Hans

Bibliography

Chrousos, G. P., and Gold, P. W. (1992). The concept of stress and stress system disorders. *J. Am. Med. Assoc.* **267**, 1244–1252.

Goldstein, D. S. (1995). "Stress, Catecholamines, and Cardiovascular Disease." Oxford Univ. Press, New York.

McCarty, R., and Gold, P. E. (1996). Catecholamines, stress and disease: A psychobiological perspective. *Psychosom. Med.* **58**, 590–597.

McEwen, B. S. (1998). Protective and damaging effects of stress mediators. *N. Engl. J. Med.* **338**, 171–179.

Alcohol, Alcoholism, and Stress: A Psychobiological Perspective

Anna N. Taylor and Michelle L. Pilati

UCLA School of Medicine and Greater Los Angeles Veterans Administration Health Care System

GLOSSARY

alcohol abuse The use of alcohol in a manner harmful to the individual and/or others, such as contributing to the failure to fulfill familial or work obligations, but not a severe enough problem to meet criteria for alcohol dependence. The DSM-IV makes a distinction between substance abuse and dependence; once criteria for dependence have been met a diagnosis of substance abuse is not possible.

alcohol dependence The DSM-IV criteria include a failure to control alcohol use despite repeated attempts, continued use despite the knowledge of adverse consequences, and, in general, compulsive use of alcohol. Alcohol dependence may or may not be accompanied by physiological dependence.

alcoholism Although there is no formally accepted definition of alcoholism, the criteria for alcohol dependence are most frequently used by researchers studying phenomena related to excessive alcohol use.

endorphin compensation hypothesis A hypothesis that proposes that the use of alcohol following stress is an attempt to compensate for a decrease in the levels of β-endorphin resulting from the termination of the stressor.

stress-response dampening model A model that proposes that alcohol use is reinforced by its ability to ameliorate responses to stress.

tension reduction hypothesis A hypothesis proposing that alcohol use is motivated by the ability of alcohol to decrease tension or stress.

The effects of alcohol on the body and brain are as diverse as the effects of stress. Even more complex is the relationship between alcohol, alcoholism, and stress. At the physiological level, both acute and chronic alcohol exposure alter responsiveness to a variety of stressors. Even more complicated, and less understood, is the role of psychosocial stress in the etiology of alcoholism. There is a body of literature attesting to the role of stress and the inability to cope effectively with environmental challenges in the development and maintenance of all substance addictions. Furthermore, there is growing evidence for inherited changes in responses to alcohol, specifically alcohol's ability to ameliorate responses to stressors, that may confer a susceptibility to alcohol abuse. Our understanding of the relationship between alcohol and stress is based on numerous and diverse lines of research employing both animals and humans as subjects.

I. ALCOHOL AND THE STRESS RESPONSE

A. Alcohol and the Neuroendocrine Response to Stress

Acute alcohol administration has a stimulatory action on the hypothalamo-pituitary-adrenal (HPA) axis and related brain systems in humans and rodents, i.e., the brain and pituitary β-endorphin (β-EP) systems and the sympathetic nervous system. These alcohol-induced neuroendocrine effects are characterized by dose-dependent elevations in plasma corticosteroids, ACTH, β-EP, and catecholamines (reviewed in Pohorecky, 1990, *Alcohol Alcohol.* **25**, 263–276; Pohorecky, 1991, *Alcohol Clin. Exp. Res.* **15**, 438–459). Ethanol activation of the HPA axis was shown to be abolished by hypophysectomy or treatment with corticotropin releasing factor

(CRF) antiserum in rodents, suggesting that it is primarily modulated by ACTH secretion and that CRF is an essential intermediate in the stimulation of ACTH by ethanol. Acute ethanol exposure generally activates the HPA axis when blood alcohol concentrations (BACs) exceed intoxicating levels of 100 mg/dl, although HPA activation can also occur at lower BACs. In contrast, the ethanol-induced HPA response of some individuals may be either unaffected or blunted. The contribution of environmental and genetic factors to this variability is discussed below.

Chronic exposure to ethanol has a more variable effect on the HPA axis and the β-EP system, ranging from stimulation to either response attenuation or tolerance. For example, a small percentage of alcoholic individuals ($<5\%$) develop clinical features of hypercortisolism or Cushing's syndrome. However, animal studies suggest that chronic ethanol exposure can result in tolerance to the stimulatory effect of ethanol on CRF release in vitro (Redei *et al.*, 1988, *Endocrinology* **123**, 2736–2743) and can impair the ability of the HPA axis to respond to stress (Dave *et al.*, 1986, *Endocrinology* **118**, 280–288). Indeed, alcoholic men have been reported to show blunted ACTH and cortisol responses to CRF and ACTH challenges as well as other signs of HPA axis dysfunction, i.e., impaired feedback regulation (Wand and Dobs, 1991, *J. Clin. Endocrinol. Metab.* **72**, 1290–1295).

B. Alcohol and Cardiovascular Responses to Stress

Although alcohol ingestion, like stress, is known to elevate heart rate, evidence indicates that the tachycardia produced by stress can be decreased by alcohol ingestion (reviewed in Pohorecky, 1991, *Alcohol* **7**, 537–546). Indeed, heart rate, as a psychophysiological measure of the stress response, has provided evidence for the general assumption that alcohol is often used as a means of relief from the physical and psychological effects of stress. However, human research designed to assess the "stress-response dampening" model of alcohol use (Sher and Walitzer, 1996, *J. Abnorm. Psychol.* **95**, 159–167) has had mixed results (Sayette, 1993, *Alcohol Clin. Exp. Res.* **17**, 802–809). There is some indication that

contradictions in experimental findings may be due to varying alcohol doses, differences in the subjects employed, and differences in the timing of the stress exposure and the alcohol presentation. Making the issue even more complex is the evidence indicating that altered responses to alcohol may have a genetic basis, possibly even conferring susceptibility to alcohol abuse on those with a family history of such substance abuse problems (discussed below). While studies failing to see a stress-response dampening effect of alcohol have often employed rather low doses, providing a logical explanation for differing results, it has also been established that alcohol increases baseline levels of physiological arousal (Stewart, 1996, *Psychol. Bull.* **120**, 83–112). Thus, when looking at the effects of alcohol on the response to a given stressor and calculating change from baseline, results will differ depending on whether the baseline used is a pre- or postethanol measurement.

II. EFFECTS OF STRESS ON ALCOHOL CONSUMPTION

A. Stress and Alcohol Use

Animal studies indicate that stress increases alcohol consumption when the stress, whether physical or social, is chronic, unavoidable, and uncontrollable (reviewed in Pohorecky, 1990, *Alcohol Alcohol.* **25**, 263–276). Evidence from human and animal studies indicates that alcohol has profound anxiolytic effects. In rodents, tolerance to the anxiolytic effects of low or moderate doses of ethanol was shown to develop rapidly and, as such, may explain the augmented consumption of alcohol required to maintain its tension-reducing effects. Additionally, adverse experiences early in life, such as maternal separation, have been found to be associated with excessive alcohol consumption in monkeys (Higley *et al.*, 1991, *Proc. Natl. Acad. Sci. USA* **88**, 7261–7265) as well as in humans (Cloninger, 1987, *Science* **236**, 410–416). Furthermore, prenatal factors, such as maternal stress and drug or alcohol consumption during pregnancy, can alter alcohol-induced physiological and behavioral stress responses in adulthood (Taylor *et al.*, 1988, *Adv. Exp. Med. Biol.* **245**, 311–317).

As noted above, it is a common assumption that alcohol is often used as a means of coping with stress—the Tension Reduction Hypothesis has been in existence for 5 decades (reviewed in Pohorecky, 1990, *Alcohol Alcohol.* **25**, 263–276). Basically, the Tension Reduction Hypothesis argues that alcohol is consumed to alleviate tension or stress. In more recent times, however, with the observation that alcohol may or may not dampen physiological responses to stress, new theories have evolved. One that is consistent with many observations and the effectiveness of new pharmacological treatments for alcoholism is the Endorphin Compensation Hypothesis (Volpicelli *et al.*, 1987, *Br. J. Addict.* **82**, 381–392). This hypothesis proposes that alcohol is consumed following termination of stress as the presence of stress increases levels of β-EP. Alcohol is sought for its ability to increase β-EP levels and compensate for the deficit that results when the stress has been removed. Consistent with this hypothesis is the use of naltrexone, an opiate antagonist, in the treatment of alcoholism.

B. Trauma and Alcohol Use

Despite the controversy as to whether alcohol is used to minimize the impact of stress or to compensate for some poststress condition, there is an abundance of correlational data linking increases in alcohol use with exposure to or the experience of traumatic or uncontrollable stressful events. For example, studies have demonstrated that there is an increase in social indices of alcohol use (such as arrests for driving while intoxicated) following disasters (Stewart, 1996, *Psychol. Bull.* **120**, 83–112).

Not only are changes in a population's alcohol consumption associated with traumatic events that affect a community, e.g., natural disasters, but a high percentage of those seeking treatment for alcoholism are survivors of abuse and/or suffering from posttraumatic stress disorder or other anxiety disorders. Although it may be difficult to determine a direct relationship between victimization and alcohol misuse, attempts to define whether alcohol abuse preceded, coincided with, or followed trauma have consistently found that trauma did, in fact, precede alcohol mis-

use. Furthermore, trauma severity is positively correlated with alcohol consumption and the severity of alcohol-related problems (Stewart, 1996, *Psychol. Bull.* **120**, 83–112).

As with much of the alcohol literature, gender differences with respect to the role of trauma in the development of alcohol dependence exist. While women seeking treatment for a substance problem are more likely than men to have been abused, stressful life events have been shown to be more associated with the alcohol use of men than women (Frone *et al.*, 1994, *Psychol. Addict. Behav.* **8**, 59–69). There is reason to believe that, whereas stress plays a role in the etiology of all drug dependence, the drug selected by men is more likely to be alcohol. Thus, there appears to be a gender difference in the drug of choice for the individual struggling with the aftermath or presence of stressful life conditions.

C. Alcoholism, Stress, and Relapse

Stressful life events have long been thought to play a role in the return to alcohol use following cessation of problematic drinking behavior. The role of stress in relapse has received much attention, with more recent reviews concluding that less severe psychosocial stress may not increase the likelihood of relapse, while severe acute stressors and chronic stressors perceived as highly threatening may contribute to an increased risk of relapse. In considering the role of stress in relapse, however, the capabilities of the individual must be considered (Brown *et al.*, 1995, *J. Stud. Alcohol.* **56**, 538–545). The impact of even severe stress and whether this leads to relapse is mediated by both protective and risk factors that render the individual more or less likely to return to problematic alcohol use. Risk factors that may increase the likelihood of relapse to substance abuse include the persisting physiological symptoms of abstinence, e.g., HPA axis dysfunction, characterized by a blunted ACTH response to challenge with CRF [Wilkins *et al.*, 1992, *Recent Developments in Alcoholism*, M. Galanter, (Ed.), pp. 57–71, Plenum, New York].

The role of stress has been the focus of many alcoholism treatments. Most notably, the relapse prevention model introduced by Marlatt and George (1984, *Br. J. Addict.* **79**, 261–273) proposes that the goal of treatment for addictive behaviors must be to develop means of coping with stressful situations. In order to change addictive patterns, situations that are "high risk" for relapse need to be identified and methods for coping with such situations developed. According to the model, cessation of addictive behavioral patterns can be achieved through the mastery of handling such high-risk situations. The relapse prevention model has been the focus of much research, although empirical support for its effectiveness is difficult to obtain. Despite research suggesting that relapse does occur in situations identified as being "high risk," the subjective nature of such retrospective reports calls any definitive conclusions into question.

III. MODIFIERS OF THE STRESS–ALCOHOL INTERACTION

A. Genetics

It is well known that various murine and rodent strains differ in their sensitivities to alcohol. In the past 2 decades, with the application of selective breeding techniques, rodent models of alcoholism have been derived with high and low oral alcohol preference. Such animal models are particularly useful in the identification of genetic traits associated with the physiological and behavioral bases of alcohol drinking. For example, results indicate that the β-EP system of alcohol-preferring rats is hyperresponsive to alcohol (see Froelich in NIAAA, Monograph No. 23). Thus, activation of the endogenous opioid system may either enhance the reinforcing effects of low-dose alcohol or attenuate the aversive effects of high-dose alcohol and thereby affect alcohol consumption.

The genetic basis for susceptibility to alcohol abuse and dependence has long been accepted and numerous studies have been conducted to determine how those with a family history of alcoholism (family history positive, FHP) might differ from those without such an "inherited risk" (family history negative, FHN). There is increasing support that altered neuro-endocrine responses to alcohol in the sons of alcoholic men provide a posssible basis for the genetic component in the development of alcoholism. For example, nonalcoholic male offspring of alcoholic fathers (known to be at three- or fourfold higher risk for alcoholism than sons of nonalcoholics), in comparison to the sons of nonalcoholics, demonstrate lower cortisol responses to alcohol (Schuckit, 1998, *J. Stud. Alcohol* **59**, 485–494), an impaired ACTH response to CRF (Waltman *et al.*, 1994, *Alcohol Clin. Exp. Res.* **18**, 826–830), increased alcohol-induced plasma β-EP levels (Gianoulakis *et al.*, 1996, *Arch. Gen. Psychiat.* **53**, 250–257), and an enhanced ACTH response to the opioid receptor antagonist naloxone (Wand *et al.*, 1999, *J. Clin. Endocrinol. Metab.* **84**, 64–68). Taken together, these findings indicate that FHP men have altered hypothalamic CRF neuronal activity. Although it is not clear how these alterations may contribute to the development of abusive patterns of alcohol use, these studies suggest that the CRF-mediated response of the HPA axis or the β-BE systems to alcohol may serve as a marker to distinguish individuals at risk for alcoholism. Interestingly, these markers do not effectively distinguish FHP women, supporting the notion that there are gender differences in the role of genetic factors in the etiology of alcoholism.

B. Expectancy

Adding an additional level of complexity to the determination of the effects of alcohol on the human stress response is the vast literature demonstrating that expectancies have a significant impact on the response to alcohol ingestion. It may be that many reported differences in the literature are created by the influence of cognition on reactivity to alcohol and are due to the timing of stress presentation with respect to alcohol use. Sayette (1993) has investigated the effects of such timing and proposes that intoxication prior to stress exposure may alter the cognitive reaction to the stimulus and, as a result, the response to the stressful stimulus may be minimized. Thus, it may be that alcohol does not dampen the stress response per se, but rather that alcohol alters the appraisal of the stressful stimulus and the physiological response is then reduced.

IV. CONCLUSION

It appears clear that there is a relationship between alcohol and stress, although the nature of this association is complex and not easily described. A brief look at the relevant literature demonstrates that the interaction of alcohol and stress varies with characteristics of the subject studied, the environment, the alcohol dose, the nature of the stressor imposed, and the timing of the exposure to alcohol and the stressor. Thus, stress, alcohol, and alcoholism are interrelated, but the nature of this relationship is highly variable.

See Also the Following Articles

ALCOHOL AND STRESS, SOCIAL AND PSYCHOLOGICAL ASPECTS; BETA-ENDORPHIN; DRUG USE AND ABUSE; ETHANOL AND ENDOGENOUS OPIOIDS

Bibliography

Brown, S. A., Vik, P. W., Patterson, T. L., Grant, I., and Schuckit, M. A. (1985). Stress, vulnerability, and adult alcohol relapse. *J. Stud. Alcohol* **56**, 538–545.

Cloninger, C. R. (1987). Neurogenetic adaptive mechanisms in alcoholism. *Science* **236**, 410–416.

Dave, J. R., Eiden, L. E., Karanian, J. W., and Eskay, R. L. (1986). Ethanol exposure decreases pituitary corticotropin-releasing factor binding, adenylate cyclase activity, proopiomelanocortin biosynthesis and plasma beta-endorphin levels in the rat. *Endocrinology* **118**, 280–288.

Froelich, J. C. (1993). Interactions between alcohol and the endogenous opioid system. *In* S. Zakhari (Ed.), "Alcohol and the Endocrine System" (pp. 21–36). NIAAA Research Monograph 23.

Frone, M. R., Cooper, M. L., and Russell, M. (1994). Stressful life events, gender, and substance use: An application of tobit regression. *Psychol. Addict. Behav.* **8**, 59–69.

Gianoulakis, C., Krishnan, B., and Thavundayil, J. (1996). Enhanced sensitivity of pituitary β-endorphin to ethanol in subjects at high risk of alcoholism. *Arch. Gen. Psychiat.* **53**, 250–257.

Higley, J. D., Hasert, M. F., Suomi, B. J., and Linnoila, M. (1991). Nonhuman primate model of alcohol abuse: Effects of early experience, personality, and stress on alcohol consumption. *Proc. Natl. Acad. Sci. USA* **88**, 7261–7265.

Hunt, W. A. and Zakhari, S. (Eds.) (1995). "Stress, Gender, and Alcohol-Seeking Behavior." NIAAA Research Monograph No. 29, NIH Publ. No. 95–3893.

Marlatt, G. A., and George, F. R. (1984). Relapse prevention: Introduction and overview of the model. *Br. J. Addict.* **79**, 261–273.

National Institutes of Health (1997). "Alcohol and Health." Ninth Special Report to the U.S. Congress, DHSS, NIH, NIAAA, NIH Publ. No. 97–4017.

Pohorecky, L. A. (1990). Interaction of ethanol and stress: Research with experimental animals—An update. *Alcohol Alcohol.* **25**, 263–276.

Pohorecky, L. A. (1990). Interaction of alcohol and stress at the cardiovascular level. *Alcohol* **7**, 537–546.

Pohorecky, L. A. (1991). Stress and alcohol interaction: An update of human research. *Alcohol Clin. Exp. Res.* **15**, 438–459.

Redei, E., Branch, B. J., Gholami, S., Lin, E. Y. R., and Taylor, A. N. (1988). Effect of ethanol on CRF release *in vitro*. *Endocrinology* **123**, 2736–2743.

Sayette, M. A. (1993). Heart rate as an index of stress response in alcohol administration research: A critical review. *Alcohol Clin. Exp. Res.* **17**, 802–809.

Schuckit, M. (1998). Biological, psychological and environmental predictors of the alcoholism risk: A longitudinal study. *J. Stud. Alcohol* **59**, 485–494.

Sher, K. J., and Walitzer, K. S. (1986). Individual differences in the stress-reponse-dampening effect of alcohol: A dose-response study. *J. Abnorm. Psychol.* **95**, 159–167.

Stewart, S. H. (1996). Alcohol abuse in individuals exposed to trauma: A critical review. *Psychol. Bull.* **120**, 83–112.

Taylor, A. N., Branch, B. J., Van Zuylen, J. E., and Redei, E. (1988). Maternal alcohol consumption and stress responsiveness in offspring. *In* G. P. Chrousos, D. L. Loriaux, and P. W. Gold (Eds.), "Advances in Experimental Medical Biology: Mechanisms of Physical and Emotional Stress" (Vol. 245, pp. 311–317). Plenum, New York.

Volpicelli, J. R., Tiven, J., and Kimmel, S. C. (1987). Uncontrollable events and alcohol drinking. *Br. J. Addict.* **82**, 381–392.

Waltman, C., McCaul, M. E., and Wand, G. S. (1994). Adrenocorticotropin responses following administration of ethanol and ovine corticotropin-releasing hormone in the sons of alcoholics and control subjects. *Alcohol Clin. Exp. Res.* **18**, 826–830.

Wand, G. S., and Dobs, A. S. (1991). Alterations in the hypothalamic-pituitary-adrenal axis in actively drinking alcoholics. *J. Clin. Endocrinol. Metab.* **72**, 1290–1295.

Wand, G. S., Mangold, D., and Mahmood, M. (1999). Adrenocorticotropin responses to naloxone in sons of alcohol-dependent men. *J. Clin. Endocrinol. Metab.* **84,** 64–68.

Wilkins, J. N., Gorelick, D. A., Nademanee, K., Taylor, A. N., and Herzberg, D. S. (1992). Hypothalmic-pituitary function during alcohol or cocaine exposure and withdrawal. *In* M.

Galanter (Ed.), "Recent Developments in Alcoholism" (pp. 57–71). Plenum, New York.

Zakhari, S. (Ed.) (1993). "Alcohol and the Endocrine System," NIAAA Research Monograph No. 23, NIH Publ. No. 93–3533.

Alcohol and Stress: Social and Psychological Aspects

Michael A. Sayette

University of Pittsburgh

GLOSSARY

anxiolytic Anxiety or stress reducing.
stress The perception of an event as aversive, in that it concerns harm, loss, or threat.
stressor An event that elicits stress.

I. INTRODUCTION

Nearly everyone, from clinicians and researchers to social and problem drinkers, believes that drinking alcohol can reduce stress. Moreover, this effect of alcohol has been suggested as a reason why people begin and maintain their drinking, despite its abuse potential. These two propositions—that alcohol reduces stress and that people drink in order to obtain this stress-reducing effect—were initially formalized by Conger in the mid-1950s in what has become known as the tension reduction hypothesis. Although the term "tension" has been replaced over the years by terms such as "stress" or "anxiety," Con-

ger's two basic propositions continue to generate a tremendous amount of investigation. Research includes both field studies and laboratory experimentation and has involved both human and animal subjects.

II. EFFECTS OF ALCOHOL ON STRESS

Historically, the term "stress" has been variously used to describe the stimuli or events that produce a state of anxiety or apprehension as well as to describe the complex physiological response to an aversive stimulus. Because people respond to the same stimuli in different ways, however, it has been suggested that stress be defined as the appraisal, or interpretation, of an event as signaling harm, loss, or threat. This approach, adopted here, recognizes that an event may be construed as stressful by one individual, but benign by another. The perception of stress is posited to activate a multidimensional response that may involve a wide range of biological responses (e.g., psychophysiological, neurochemical), behaviors (e.g., escape or avoidance behavior), and, in the case of humans, subjective awareness of distressed affect. Not surprisingly, studies of the relationship between alcohol and stress have varied dramatically in terms of both the stressors that are used and stress responses that are measured. Such variability likely has contributed to the complex pattern of findings that characterize this research area.

A. Animal Studies

Conger's original formulation was based on studies using animals, including rats and cats. It therefore is not surprising that extensive animal research (most often using rodents) has been conducted testing the alcohol–stress relationship. Typical stressors include a novel environment, food and water deprivation, experimental conflict in which conflicting motives and responses are activated, and noxious stimuli [e.g., electric shock administration, exposure to (aversive) bright environments, and placing an intruder into a resident's cage]. These studies tend to show alcohol producing an anxiolytic effect, though the relationships are complex.

Data supporting an anxiolytic effect of alcohol appear strongest in studies using experimental conflict paradigms. These studies begin by training an animal to run down an alley to obtain food reward. Next a shock is administered to punish this approach behavior. The level of conflict is inferred by the suppression of the approach to the food. Typically alcohol ingestion, through its fear-reduction properties, facilitates the approach behavior.

Whether alcohol reduces stress in animals may depend in part on how stress responding is assessed and the dose of alcohol administered. Pohorecky, who has long chronicled progress in this area, concludes that moderate doses of alcohol have modified both anxiety-related behaviors (such as aggression and conflict) and stress-induced neurochemical changes. These latter responses are present in both the brain and in plasma. The former include levels or turnover of noradrenaline, serotonin, β-endorphins, and GABA, while the latter includes catecholamines, corticosterone, testosterone, nonestrified fatty acids, and amino acids. Moderate doses of alcohol consumption also appear to alter stress-induced changes in the functional activity of the hypothalamo-pituitary-adrencortical axis. These findings suggest neurobiological mechanisms underlying potential

anxiolytic effects of moderate (but not high) doses of alcohol.

B. Human Studies

The effects of alcohol consumption on human stress have proven to be far more complex than originally thought. While some would argue that the effects are sufficiently unreliable that the notion of alcohol reducing stress should be rejected altogether, most still would conclude that alcohol can reduce stress. The challenge has been to understand the conditions under which alcohol's anxiolytic effects should be most apparent and the possible mechanisms underlying this effect.

A number of factors have been examined that may affect alcohol's effects on stress. These include *individual difference* factors and *situational* factors.

1. Individual Difference Factors

Individual difference factors include gender, personality traits, drinking history, and a family history of alcoholism. Until recently, the vast majority of studies in this area included only male participants. Despite early reports to the contrary, the consensus drawn from the largest studies that have included both genders is that alcohol's effects on stress seem to be comparable for men and women. These studies have assessed stress using psychophysiological (e.g., heart rate) and self-report measures, and it is possible that other types of measures of emotional response might reveal gender differences. Even when women appeared more responsive than men to a stressor in sober conditions, this gender difference was not altered by alcohol. There is some evidence, however, to suggest that men and women differ in their beliefs about how alcohol consumption affects them. It therefore is possible that at low doses of alcohol, men and women may experience different effects, due to nonpharmacological effects of drinking experiences.

Individuals characterized by personality traits such as sensation seeking or impulsivity have been found to be at increased risk for developing alcohol-related problems. Some have suggested that these individuals may derive enhanced anxiolytic effects from alcohol consumption. Presumably, this would increase the reinforcement value of drinking. Though the studies have not been uniform in their conclusions, there is some support for this hypothesis.

Another individual difference factor that has been studied is drinking history. Specifically, some investigations have found that heavier drinkers, due to their development of tolerance, require greater quantities of alcohol than lighter drinkers to obtain the anxiolytic effects of alcohol. These findings converge with the aforementioned animal data to emphasize the importance of dose in determining the effects of the alcohol–stress relationship. It may be that alcohol's anxiolytic effects are restricted to a relatively narrow range of doses.

In contrast to studies that have subjected participants to a single dose of alcohol during one session, there have been studies that permit evaluation of drinkers over extended time periods. During the mid-1960s through the mid-1970s, a number of experiments examined the effects of alcohol use on stress among alcoholic participants. While these studies often were limited by small sample sizes, they were impressive for their intensive monitoring of participants for weeks at a time. The methodologically strongest studies of this group indicate an association between alcohol consumption and improved emotional states among these alcoholic participants.

The presence of a family history of alcoholism represents an established risk factor for alcoholism. Several experiments have examined young adults with such a family history. Though at this point in their lives these individuals are not problem drinkers, some of these studies have found that offspring of alcoholic fathers nevertheless experience an increased anxiolytic effect of alcohol. These offspring may be more responsive to a wide range of stimuli while sober and therefore may be especially sensitive to the sedating effects of alcohol. More research is being conducted on this matter, as it is possible that some of these findings may be due to family history differences other than alcohol's effects on stress.

2. Situational Factors

Situational factors have been proposed that may influence alcohol's effects on stress. Alcohol is more likely to reduce stress if it is consumed in the presence of pleasantly distracting activity (e.g., drinking

at a party or while watching television) than if consumed without distraction. A second factor that has been suggested to moderate alcohol's affects on stress is the temporal relationship between drinking and the stressor administration. When alcohol is consumed following a stressor (e.g., after a bad day at work) it may be less effective in reducing stress than if intoxication precedes the stress (e.g., drinking just prior to attending a party). While this latter prediction has been supported by laboratory studies, it remains to be seen if such a pattern also holds in the natural environment.

C. Mechanisms

Investigators have proposed a number of mechanisms underlying alcohol's putative anxiolytic effect. These include the view that stress reduction is mediated by a direct pharmacologic influence on the nervous system as well as the notion that stress reduction is mediated by alcohol's effects on information processing. Both perspectives recognize that alcohol's anxiolytic effects are potentially reinforcing and can contribute to alcohol use.

Among those who argue that alcohol's anxiolytic effect results from a direct effect of alcohol on the nervous system, there has been debate over whether stress reduction is centrally or peripherally mediated. Support for peripheral mediation comes from research showing alcohol to increase peripheral vasoconstriction while dampening heart rate during a stressor administration. Such work suggests that stress reduction could be restricted to those cardiovascular functions mediated primarily by β-adrenergic action. Other studies have not supported the view that alcohol's anxiolytic effects are primarily a function of β-adrenergic blocking action. Data from a variety of sources instead seem to favor the role of central nervous system functioning in mediating alcohol's putative anxiolytic effect. More research is needed to better establish the pharmacologic mechanism for stress reduction.

In contrast to theories positing a direct effect of alcohol on stress response systems are models that view an anxiolytic effect to be a result of alcohol's pharmacologic effects on information processing. These models propose that, at moderate and heavy doses, alcohol will impair cognitive processing. This cognitive impairment may or may not alleviate stress, depending on one's circumstances. There are several different models that relate to this indirect explanation. One suggests that alcohol's narrowing of perception to immediate cues and reduction of cognitive abstracting capacity restrict attention to the most salient, immediate aspects of experience. Given this assumption, the concurrent activity in which an intoxicated person engages helps to determine alcohol's effects. Intoxication in the presence of concurrent distraction is predicted to attenuate stress responding, whereas, without a neutral or pleasantly distracting activity, intoxication is not predicted to prove anxiolytic.

Other approaches suggest that alcohol serves to disrupt the appraisal or encoding of new information. Depending on the situation, this cognitive impairment may be anxiolytic. For example, alcohol may be more likely to reduce stress if intoxication precedes the stressor than if it follows a stressor; as in the latter case, the stressful information would already be encoded prior to drinking. It has also been suggested that alcohol may be particularly effective in disrupting the encoding of information in terms of its self-relevance. The inhibition of encoding processes presumably leads to a reduction in performance-based self-evaluation—which in situations where such evaluation is unpleasant, may reduce stress responses, thus increasing the probability of drinking.

III. EFFECTS OF STRESS ON ALCOHOL CONSUMPTION

A. Animal Studies

Animal studies of the effects of stress on drinking behavior have used three types of stressors: shock, restraint, and psychological stressors such as isolation and dominance, sleep deprivation, and early weaning and handling. Alcohol ingestion has been measured during the stressor administration, on the day of the stressor, or on the days following the stressor.

Studies using laboratory animals have found that both physical and psychological stressors are associated with an increased tendency to develop a pattern of drug or alcohol use. One explanation for this relationship is that stress increases the reinforcement properties of drugs, perhaps by increasing glucocorticoid secretion, which in turn may enhance the drug-induced release of dopamine.

Across a number of studies, it appears that the probability of alcohol ingestion is especially enhanced following the termination of a stressor. This may be accounted for in part by the ability of alcohol ingestion to replenish endogenous opiate levels that may become depleted during periods of stress. Studies also suggest that a number of factors may affect the relationship between stress and drinking in animals. Individual differences in preference for alcohol may affect the stress–alcohol interaction, with stress particularly likely to increase subsequent drinking among animals that have a low initial preference for alcohol. Another difference that has been observed concerns neonatal experience, with rats that were weaned earlier being associated with increased alcohol consumption. So too have genetic factors been implicated as moderators of the effects of stress on alcohol ingestion, with various strains of mice ingesting different amounts of alcohol following stress.

B. Human Studies

In the 1940s, cross-cultural studies led to the proposal that societies that experienced the most stress were also the societies with the highest per capita levels of drinking. To examine whether stress precipitates alcohol consumption in humans, both survey and experimental studies have been conducted.

A number of retrospective studies have examined the relationship between stress and drinking. These studies indicate a modest increase in drinking (as well as a modest increase in heavy drinking) following stress. This effect may be influenced by a host of individual difference factors, including ethnicity, gender, and age.

Prospective studies have accumulated that assess both drinking and stress over specified time periods. These studies generally reveal a tendency for stress levels to correlate with drinking levels. Further, in many instances, individuals appear to drink in order to cope with stress.

In addition to survey research, experiments have been designed to test the causal relationship between stress and drinking. Often these studies first expose participants to some form of stressor (e.g., threat of shock, a stressful social interaction, false performance feedback). Next, their alcohol intake is assessed while they participate in what is ostensibly a wine or beer taste-rating task. The critical dependent measure, unbeknownst to participants, is the quantity of alcohol consumed. Data from these tasks have been inconclusive. Indeed, some studies have found clear effects, such that individuals who were stressed consumed more alcohol than their nonstressed counterparts. Other studies have failed to observe this pattern, and in some cases the reverse has been found, with stress leading to a reduction in drinking. As previously noted with respect to animal research, it may be that drinking is especially likely to increase after the stressor has terminated. Another issue that may obfuscate these findings with human participants is the varied approaches to inducing stress. In some cases, for example, it is unclear just how effective the stressors were. In summary, while laboratory studies have been equivocal, findings from survey research suggest that increases in stress are associated with increased alcohol consumption.

See Also the Following Articles

ALCOHOL, ALCOHOLISM, AND STRESS: A PSYCHOBIOLOGICAL PERSPECTIVE; ANXIOLYTICS; BETA-ADRENERGIC BLOCKERS

Bibliography

Cappell, H., and Greeley, J. (1987). Alcohol and tension reduction: An update on research and theory. *In* "Psychological Theories of Drinking and Alcoholism" (H. Blane and K. Leonard, Eds.), pp. 15–54. Guilford Press, New York.

Conger, J. (1956). Reinforcement theory and the dynamics of alcoholism. *Quart. J. Studies Alcohol* 17, 296–305.

Cooper, M. L., Russell, M., Skinner, J. B., Frone, M. R., and Mudar, P. (1992). Stress and alcohol use: Moderating effects of gender, coping, and alcohol expectancies. *J. Abnorm. Psychol.* 101, 139–152.

Hull, J. G. (1987). Self-awareness model. *In* "Psychological Theories of Drinking and Alcoholism" (H. Blane and K. Leonard, Eds.), pp. 272–304. Guilford Press, New York.

Langenbucher, J. W., and Nathan, P. E. (1990). Alcohol, affect, and the tension reduction hypothesis: The re-analysis of some crucial early data. *In* "Why People Drink: The Parameters of Alcohol as a Reinforcer" (M. A. Cox, Ed.), pp. 151–168. Gardner, New York.

Piazza, P. V., and Le Moal, M. (1998). The role of stress in drug self-administration. *Trends Pharmacol. Sci.* 19, 67–74.

Pohorecky, L. A. (1990). Interaction of ethanol and stress: Research with experimental animals—An update. *Alcohol Alcoholism* 25, 263–276.

Pohorecky, L. A. (1991). Stress and alcohol interaction: An update of human research. *Alcoholism Clin. Exp. Res.* 15, 438–459.

Sayette, M. A. (1993). An appraisal–disruption model of alcohol's effects on stress responses in social drinkers. *Psychol. Bull.* 114, 459–476.

Sher, K. (1987), Stress response dampening. *In* "Psychological Theories of Drinking and Alcoholism" (H. Blane and K. Leonard, Eds.), pp. 227–271. Guilford Press, New York.

Sher, K. (1991). "Children of Alcoholics: A Critical Appraisal." Univ. of Chicago Press: Chicago.

Steele, C. M., and Josephs, R. A. (1990). Alcohol myopia: Its prized and dangerous effects. *Am. Psychol.* 45, 921–933.

Volpicelli, J. R. (1987). Uncontrollable events and alcohol drinking. *Br. J. Addict.* 82, 381–392.

Aldosterone

John W. Funder

Baker Medical Research Institute, Melbourne, Australia

GLOSSARY

aldosterone The classic salt-retaining steroid hormone secreted from the zona glomerulosa of the adrenal cortex.

aldosterone synthase/CYP11B2 The enzyme abundantly expressed in adrenal zona glomerulosa and demonstrated by PCR and biosynthesis studies in heart, blood vessels, and brain which, by a sequential three-step process, converts the methyl ($-CH_3$) group at carbon 18 to an aldehyde ($-CHO$) group.

apparent mineralocorticoid excess (AME) An autosomal recessive syndrome of inactivating mutations in the gene coding for 11β-hydroxysteroid dehydrogenase type 2, producing juvenile hypertension, marked salt retention reflecting inappropriate cortisol occupancy of epithelial mineralocorticoid receptors, and premature death.

carbenoxolone The hemisuccinate of glcyrrhetinic acid, previously used as a treatment for peptic ulcer.

glycyrrhetinic acid The active principle of licorice, which can block 11β-hydroxysteroid dehydrogenase, leading to sodium retention and blood pressure elevation.

11β-hydroxysteroid dehydrogenase type 2 The enzyme expressed at very high abundance (3–4 million copies per cell) in epithelial aldosterone target cells which converts cortisol and corticosterone (which have affinity for mineralocorticoid receptors similar to that of aldosterone) to the nonactive metabolites cortisone and 11-dehydrocorticost-

erone, thus allowing aldosterone to access the relatively nonselective mineralocorticoid receptors.

mineralocorticoid receptors The intracellular receptors via which aldosterone acts in epithelial tissues to promote unidirectional transepithelial sodium transport and in nonepithelial tissues to elevate blood pressure and produce cardiac hypertrophy and cardiac fibrosis.

Aldosterone is classically the salt-retaining hormone secreted from the zona glomerulosa of the adrenal cortex and acting via mineralocorticoid receptors in epithelial target tissues to promote unidirectional transepithelial sodium transport. Mineralocorticoid receptors (MR) have a similar, high affinity for aldosterone and the physiological glucocorticoids (cortisol and corticosterone). In epithelia MR can selectively bind aldosterone, as the physiological glucocorticoids are much more highly bound in plasma and are metabolized by the enzyme 11β-hydroxysteroid dehydrogenase. Recently, additional complexity has been introduced into the pathophysiology of aldosterone at the level of both extra-adrenal synthesis and nongenomic actions. Aldosterone is a stress hormone in terms of reproductive and environmental stressors rather than the physical and psychological stressors which elevate adrenocorticotropic hormone and glucocorticoid section.

I. BACKGROUND

Classically, aldosterone is the physiological mineralocorticoid hormone uniquely secreted from the zona glomerulosa of the adrenal cortex and acting via intracellular mineralocorticoid receptors in epithelial target tissues to promote unidirectional transepithelial sodium transport. While this remains the case, over the past decade there has been mounting evidence for additional complexity in terms of aldosterone secretion and action. This ranges from extra-adrenal aldosterone synthesis to major pathophysiological actions via nonepithelial mineralocorticoid receptors to rapid, nongenomic actions via a range of receptor mechanisms. There remain major residual areas of ignorance; only in March 1999 was the first aldosterone-induced protein identified, a serine-threonine kinase (sgk) which directly or indirectly activates epithelial sodium channels; the mechanism of sgk action, and potential roles for other aldosterone-induced proteins in both epithelial and nonepithelial tissue, remain to be established.

II. ALDOSTERONE SECRETION: ADRENAL AND EXTRA-ADRENAL

Aldosterone was isolated in 1953. It was initially called "electrocortin," reflecting its effects on electrolyte transport, but given the definitive name of aldosterone in recognition of its unique aldehyde ($-CHO$) group at carbon 19, in contrast with the methyl group in other steroids. Formation of this aldehyde group, which is crucial for the ability of aldosterone to access mineralocorticoid receptors in epithelia (*vide infra*) is achieved by a three-step process catalyzed by the enzyme aldosterone synthase (CYP 11B2), expression of which in the adrenal cortex is confined to the outermost cell layer, the zona glomerulosa. By polymerase-chain reaction (PCR) techniques aldosterone synthase expression has recently been described in blood vessels, heart, and brain, with unequivocal demonstration of enzyme activity in the two former tissues. While such extra-adrenal synthesis does not appear to contribute to circulating hormone levels, the extent to which it supports local tissue effects of aldosterone *in vivo* remains to be determined.

III. REGULATION OF ALDOSTERONE SECRETION

In vivo aldosterone secretion from the zona glomerulosa is predominantly and independently regulated by angiotensin II and plasma potassium concentra-tions. Adrenocorticotropic hormone (ACTH) can also raise aldosterone secretion, but unlike the other two secretagogs its action is not sustained. While a myriad of other possible modulators of aldosterone secretion have been reported, including endothelin, nitric oxide, and uncharacterized factors from the pituitary and adipose tissue, the relative importance of such inputs to pathophysiological control *in vivo* has not been established. Both experimentally and clinically, changes in angiotensin II and/or plasma potassium appear sufficient to explain changes in aldosterone secretion rates from nonneoplastic adrenals.

IV. MINERALOCORTICOID RECEPTORS: CLONING

Classical mineralocorticoid receptors binding aldosterone with high affinity and blocked by the antagonist spironolactone have been studied since the mid-1970s, with the human MR cloned and expressed by the late 1980s. The human MR comprises 984 amino acids and, like other members of the steroid/thyroid/retinoid/orphan (STRO) receptor superfamily, has a domain structure which includes a ligand-binding domain (LBD) and a DNA-binding domain. (DBD). Like other members of the STRO receptor superfamily, MR act by regulating gene expression; sgk expression in A6 cells is actinomycin-inhibitable, and aldosterone-induced sodium transport is both actinomycin- and puromycin-inhibitable in toad bladder models of mineralocorticoid action. Mineralocorticoid receptors are part of a subfamily, with the receptors for glucocorticoids, progestins, and androgens sharing $\geq 50\%$ amino acid identity in the LBD and $\geq 90\%$ in the DBD.

V. MINERALOCORTICOID RECEPTORS: CHARACTERIZATION

The initial MR cloning and expression studies also highlighted two questions in terms of aldosterone action, questions which had been previously addressed by studies on MR in tissue extracts. First, when mRNA from a variety of rat tissues was probed with MR cDNA, the highest levels of MR expression were found in hippocampus rather than classic epithelial aldosterone target tissues. Second, when the affinity of various steroids was determined by their ability to compete for [³H]aldosterone binding to expressed human mineralocorticoid receptors, cortisol was shown to have high affinity for MR, equivalent to that of aldosterone, and corticosterone (the physiological glucocorticoid in rat and mouse) to have slightly higher affinity. There are thus at least two operational questions, of which the first is the physiological role(s) of MR in nonepithelial tissues, such as hippocampus (and other brain areas and heart, for example). The second is how aldosterone occupies MR, in epithelia or in nonepithelial tissues, in the face of at least equivalent receptor affinity and the much higher circulating levels of the physiological glucocorticoids.

VI. ALDOSTERONE SPECIFICITY-CONFERRING MECHANISMS: TRANSCORTIN, 11β-HYDROXYSTEROID DEHYDROGENASE TYPE 2

Differential plasma binding of steroids has long been recognized as one factor favoring aldosterone occupancy of MR. The physiological glucocorticoids cortisol and corticosterone circulate at least 95% protein bound, predominantly to the specific globulin transcortin but also to albumin; aldosterone has negligible affinity for transcortin and is only ~50% albumin bound in plasma, giving it an order of magnitude advantage in terms of plasma free to total concentrations. Second, the enzyme 11β-hydroxysteroid dehydrogenase (11β-HSD) type 2 is abundantly expressed in epithelial aldosterone target tissues. 11β-Hydroxysteroid dehydrogenase has a very low K_m (high affinity) for cortisol and corticosterone, acting essentially unidirectionally to convert them to cortisone and 11-dehydrocorticosterone. These 11-keto congeners have very low affinity for MR, and when they do occupy MR act as antagonists. Aldosterone, in contrast, is not so metabolized; its 11β-OH group cyclizes in solution with the unique and very active

aldehyde group at C18, forming an 11,18-hemiacetal and rendering aldosterone not a substrate for 11β-HSD2.

VII. APPARENT MINERALOCORTICOID EXCESS

The crucial role of 11β-HSD2 in conferring aldosterone specificity in otherwise nonselective epithelial MR is underlined by the clinical syndrome of apparent mineralocorticoid excess (AME). In this rare, autosomal recessive disorder patients present with very high blood pressure and marked sodium retention, despite low plasma levels of renin and aldosterone. The syndrome can be diagnosed by an abnormally high ratio of urinary free cortisol to cortisone, reflecting loss-of-function mutation of the sequence coding for 11β-HSD2. Under such circumstances the mutant enzyme shows poor or absent ability to convert cortisol to cortisone; the abnormally high renal cortisol inappropriately occupies MR, leading to uncontrolled sodium retention and hypertension. A milder version of the syndrome can be produced by licorice abuse, as the active principle of licorice (glycyrrhetinic acid) blocks 11β-HSD2 activity, as does the erstwhile antipeptic ulcer drug carbenoxolone, the hemisuccinate of glycyrrhetinic acid.

VIII. EXTRAEPITHELIAL ACTIONS OF ALDOSTERONE

The physiological roles of extraepithelial MR and the extraepithelial effects of aldosterone have similarly been in part elucidated. Hippocampal MR appear involved in integration of baseline circadian ACTH secretion and that in response to stress; given the high reflection coefficient of aldosterone at the blood–brain barrier it appears improbable that these receptors, unprotected by 11β-HSD2, are ever occupied by aldosterone. Other brain MR, in contrast, are clearly occupied at least to some extent by aldosterone, despite being similarly unprotected. There is ample experimental evidence that aldosterone occupancy of MR in the anteroventral 3rd ventricle

(AV3V) region (which is outside the blood–brain barrier) is necessary for mineralocorticoid–salt hypertension: intracerebroventricular infusion of MR antagonists abolishes the elevation of blood pressure following peripheral infusion of aldosterone to rats or feeding a high-salt diet to salt-sensitive strains of rats.

IX. ALDOSTERONE, CARDIAC HYPERTROPHY, AND CARDIAC FIBROSIS

Aldosterone occupancy of cardiac MR has similarly been shown in a variety of experimental models to produce cardiac hypertrophy and fibrosis. These effects are independent of hemodynamic changes, as clamping blood pressure by the concomitant infusion of intracerebroventricular MR antagonist does not alter the effects of peripherally infused aldosterone on cardiac hypertrophy and fibrosis. They are also crucially dependent on an aldosterone–salt imbalance; infusion of the same dose of aldosterone to rats fed a low-salt diet is not followed by increases in blood pressure or in cardiac hypertrophy and cardiac fibrosis. Cardiac MR, like those in the CNS, are unprotected by 11β-HSD2; like the AV3V effects of aldosterone on blood pressure, the cardiac effects seem to require only a minority of MR to be occupied by active mineralocorticoid to produce a response. Importantly, and in contrast with epithelia, occupancy of extraepithelial MR by glucocorticoids does not mimic the effect of aldosterone. Also in contrast with the epithelial effects of aldosterone via MR, which have a time course of hours, the extraepithelial effects of aldosterone take days/weeks to be manifest: increases in collagen type I and type III mRNA in the heart are not seen until the 3rd week of continuous aldosterone infusion and plateau levels of blood pressure elevation until 4–6 weeks. The mechanisms underlying these epithelial/extraepithelial differences in the action of aldosterone via identical MR are not understood, but presumably reflect at least in part tissue-specific differences in coactivators, corepressors, and response elements involved.

X. ALDOSTERONE: A STRESS HORMONE?

Aldosterone is a stress hormone depending on the definition of stress. Psychological or physical stressors which raise ACTH and adrenal catecholamine output do not lead to major or sustained elevations in aldosterone levels; stressors in terms of fluid and electrolyte balance (e.g., diarrhea, florid sweating, pregnancy, and lactation on a low-sodium diet) raise aldosterone to act in a tight feedback loop to retain sodium and water. Our renin-angiotensin-aldosterone system appears to have evolved in a context of sodium deficiency, often more of a issue for herbivores than for omnivores, and we have much less well-developed mechanisms for suppressing aldosterone secretion than for elevating it. On contemporary salt intakes our inability to lower aldosterone secretion commensurately may thus in a counterintuitive sense be in itself a stressor for the organism, which requires 2–5% of the normal modern salt intake except in response to the stress of reproduction, gastrointestinal infection, or environmental extremes. The evolutionary craving for salt, and its routine addition to a range of foodstuffs, may thus constitute a stress in terms of the cardiovascular system, most noticeably hypertension but with increasing evidence for direct, salt-requiring effects of aldosterone on the heart. The recent RALES trials, in which adding low dose spironolactone to conventional ACE inhibitor/loop diuretic/digitalis therapy for heart failure substantially lowered mortality, would also seem to constitute evidence for aldosterone operating as a stress hormone in this sense.

See Also the Following Articles

Adrenal Cortex; Adrenocorticotropic Hormone (ACTH)

Bibliography

Brilla, C. G., and Weber, K. T. (1992). Mineralocorticoid excess, dietary sodium, and myocardial fibrosis. *J. Lab. Clin. Med.* **120**, 893–901.

Curnow, K. M. (1998). Steroidogenesis, enzyme deficiencies and the pathogenesis of human hypertension. *Curr. Op. Endocrinol. Diab.* **5**, 223–228.

Funder, J. W. (1977). Glucocorticoid and mineralocorticoid receptors: Biology and clinical relevance. *Ann. Rev. Med.* **48**, 231–240.

Robert, V., Heymes, C., Silvestre, J. S., Sabri, A., Swynghedauw, B., and Delcayre, C. (1999). Angiotensin AT1 receptor subtype as a cardiac target of aldosterone: role in aldosterone-salt-induced fibrosis. *Hypertension* **33**, 981–986.

White, P. C., Curnow, K. M., and Pascoe, L. (1994). Disorders of steroid 11 beta-hydroxylase isozymes. *Endocr. Rev.* **15**, 421–438.

Allostasis and Allostatic Load

Bruce S. McEwen

Rockefeller University

GLOSSARY

allostasis The ability to achieve stability, or homeostasis, through change, as defined by Sterling and Eyer, is critical to survival of an organism by promoting adaptation, or the reestablishment of homeostasis, to an environmental challenge. Through allostasis, the autonomic nervous system, the hypothalamic–pituitary–adrenal (HPA) axis, and cardiovascular, metabolic, and immune systems protect the body by responding to internal and external challenges. Allostasis is achieved by the actions of mediators, such as catecholamines and glucocorticoids. Allostatic load is the price of this accommodation and constitutes a wear and tear on the body from the chronic overactivity or underactivity of allostatic systems.

allostatic load The excessive level, over weeks, months, and years, of mediators of allostasis, resulting either from too much release of these mediators or from the inefficient operation of the allostatic systems that produce the mediators and fail to shut off their release when not needed.

In contrast to homeostatic systems, such as blood oxygen, blood pH, and body temperature, which must be maintained within a narrow range, allostatic (adaptive) systems have much broader boundaries of operation. Allostatic systems enable an organism to respond to its physical state (e.g., awake, asleep, supine, standing, exercising) and to cope with noise, crowding, isolation, hunger, extremes of temperature, physical danger, psychosocial stress, and microbial or parasitic infections. For example, blood pressure rises when we get up in the morning and fluctuates with exercise and other demands of the waking period; these fluctuations make it possible for the individual to function in response to a changing social and physical environment.

I. TURNING ON AND TURNING OFF ALLOSTASIS

Whether exposed to danger, an infection, a crowded and noisy neighborhood, or having to give a speech in public, the body responds to challenge by turning on an allostatic response, thus initiating a complex pathway for adaptation and coping, and then shutting off this response when the challenge has passed. The primary allostatic responses involve the sympathetic nervous system and hypothalamo-pituitary–adrenal (HPA) axis. "Turning on" these systems leads to release of catecholamines from sympathetic nerves and the adrenal medulla and the secretion of adrenocorticotrophic hormone (ACTH) from the anterior pituitary gland, which stimulates the release of glucocorticoids from the adrenal cortex.

"Turning off" these responses leads to a return to baseline concentrations of cortisol and catecholamines, and this normally happens when the danger is past, the infection contained, the living environment is improved, or the talk has been given. As long as the allostatic response is limited to the period of challenge, protection via adaptation predominates over adverse consequences. However, over weeks, months, or even years, exposure to elevated levels of stress hormones can result in allostatic load, with resultant pathophysiological consequences.

II. TYPES OF ALLOSTATIC LOAD

Four situations can lead to allostatic load, resulting in overexposure to stress hormones over time. The first is frequent stress, e.g., blood pressure surges can trigger myocardial infarction in susceptible persons, and experiments in primates have shown that repeated blood pressure elevations over weeks and months accelerates atherosclerosis, which increases the risk of myocardial infarction. Thus, the frequency of stressful events determines the degree of this type of allostatic load, leading to increased exposure to hormones and other allostatic mediators.

A second type of allostatic load is the failure to habituate to repeated challenges, such as the case in some individuals' cortisol response during a repeated public speaking challenge (Kirschbaum, C., Prussner, J. C., Stone, A. A., Federenko, I., Gaab, J., Lintz, D., Schommer, N., and Hellhammer, D. H. 1995. *Psychosom. Med.* 57, 468–474).

The third type of allostatic load is caused by an inability to shut off allostatic responses. This pertains to the termination of stress and also to the decline of these same hormones during the natural diurnal cycle. With respect to the stress response, blood pressure in some persons fails to recover after acute mental arithmetic stress, and hypertension accelerates atherosclerosis. Intense athletic training also induces allostatic load in the form of elevated sympathetic and HPA activity, which results in reduced body weight and amenorrhea and the often-related condition of anorexia nervosa. Regarding the diurnal cycle,

women with a history of depressive illness have decreased bone mineral density because the allostatic load of chronic, moderately elevated glucocorticoid levels that are associated with depression cause chronic, reduced levels of osteocalcin (Michelson, D., Stratakis, C., Hill, L., Reynolds, J., Galliven, E., Chrousos, G., and Gold, P. 1996. *N. Engl. J. Med.* 335, 1176–1181).

The fourth type of allostatic load is caused by inadequate allostatic responses that trigger compensatory increases in other allostatic systems. When one system does not respond adequately to a stressful stimulus, the activity of other systems is increased because the underactive system is not providing the usual counterregulation. For example, if adrenal steroid secretion does not increase appropriately in response to stress, secretion of inflammatory cytokines (which are counterregulated by adrenal steroids) increases. In Lewis rats, the failure to mount an adequate HPA response results in increased vulnerability to autoimmune and inflammatory disturbances; thus an infection or wound that causes an inflammation will lead to an increased inflammatory response.

In another model, rats that become subordinate in a psychosocial living situation called the "visible burrow system" have a stress-induced state of HPA hyporesponsiveness (Albeck, D. S., McKittrick, C. R., Blanchard, D. C., Blanchard, R. J., Nikulina, J., McEwen, B. S., and Sakai, R. R. 1997. *J. Neurosci.* 17, 4895–4903). In these rats, the HPA response to experimenter-applied stressors is very limited and hypothalamic corticotropin-releasing factor messenger RNA levels are abnormally low. Although specific health consequences are not yet known, these stress nonresponsive rats are believed to be the most likely to die over longer times in the visible burrow. Human counterparts of the state of HPA hyporesponsiveness include individuals with fibromyalgia and chronic fatigue syndrome (Jefferies, W.M. 1994, *Med. Hypoth.* 42, 183–189).

III. ROLE OF BEHAVIOR IN ALLOSTATIC LOAD

Anticipation and worry can also contribute to allostatic load. Anticipation is involved in the reflex that prevents us from blacking out when we get out of bed in the morning and is also a component of worry, anxiety, and cognitive preparation for a threat. Anticipatory anxiety can drive the output of mediators such as ACTH, cortisol, and adrenalin; thus prolonged anxiety and anticipation are likely to result in allostatic load. For example, salivary cortisol levels increase within 30 min after waking in individuals who are under considerable psychological stress due to work or family matters. Moreover, intrusive memories from a traumatic event (e.g., as in posttraumatic stress disorder) can produce a form of chronic stress and can drive physiological responses.

Allostasis and allostatic load are also affected by health-damaging or health-promoting behaviors such as smoking, drinking, choice of diet, and amount of exercise. These behaviors are integral to the overall notion of allostasis—how individuals cope with a challenge—and also contribute to allostatic load by known pathways (e.g., a rich diet accelerates atherosclerosis and progression to noninsulin-dependent diabetes by increasing cortisol, leading to fat deposition and insulin resistance; smoking elevates blood pressure and atherogenesis; exercise protects against cardiovascular disease).

IV. EXAMPLES OF ALLOSTATIC LOAD

A. Cardiovascular and Metabolic Systems

In infrahuman primates, the incidence of atherosclerosis is increased among the dominant males of unstable social hierarchies and in socially subordinate females (Manuck, S. B., Kaplan, J. R., Adams, M. R., and Clarkson, T. B. 1988. *Health Psychol.* 7, 113–124). In humans, low job control predicts an increased risk for coronary heart disease (Bosma, H., M. G., Marmot, H., Hemingway, A. C., Nicholson, Brunner, E., and Stansfield, S. A. 1997. *Br. Med. J.* 314, 558–565), and job strain (high psychological demands and low control) results in elevated ambulatory blood pressure at home and increased left ventricular mass index (Schnall, P. L., Schwartz, J. E., Landsbergis, P. A., Warren, K., and Pickering, T. G.

1992. *Hypertension* 19, 488–494), as well as increased progression of atherosclerosis (Everson, S. A., Lynch, J. W., Chesney, M. A., Kaplan, G. A., Goldberg, D. E., Shade, S. B., Cohen, R. D., Salonen, R., and Salonen, J. T. 1997. *Br. Med. J.* 314, 553–558).

Quantifying allostatic load, a major challenge, has been attempted with measures of metabolic and cardiovascular pathophysiology. In one study, 10 measures of activity of allostatic systems were assessed in aging subjects in 1988 and aging in 1991 (Seeman, T. E., Singer, B. H., Rowe, J. W., Horwitz, R. I., and McEwen, B. S. 1997. *Arch. Intern. Med.* 157, 2259–2268). Allostatic load was scored by determining the number of measures for which an individual was in the most extreme quartile, e.g., highest in systolic blood pressure, overnight urinary cortisol, catecholamines, waist/hip ratio (WHR), glycosylated hemoglobin, the ratio of HDL to total cholesterol, or the lowest quartile in dehydroepiandrosterone (DHEA) sulfate or HDL cholesterol. For baseline data in 1988, subjects with higher levels of physical and mental functioning had lower allostatic load scores; these individuals also had less prevalent cardiovascular disease, hypertension, and diabetes. Moreover, among this higher functioning group, those with higher baseline allostatic load scores were more likely to experience incident cardiovascular disease between 1988 and 1991 and were significantly more likely to show a decline in cognitive and physical functioning.

B. The Brain

Repeated stress has consequences for brain function, especially for the hippocampus, which has high concentrations of adrenal steroid receptors. The hippocampus participates in episodic and declarative memory and is particularly important for the memory of "context," the time and place of events that have a strong emotional bias, and glucocorticoids are involved in consolidation of contextual fear conditioning. Impairment of hippocampal function decreases the reliability and accuracy of context memories, which may cause an individual to miss important information and get into a more stressful situation. The hippocampus is also a regulator of the stress response and acts to inhibit shutoff of the HPA stress response (Herman, J. P., and Cullinan, W. E. 1997. *Trends Neurosci* **20**, 78–84).

The mechanism for stress-induced hippocampal dysfunction and memory impairment is twofold. First, acute stress elevates adrenal steroids, which suppresses the mechanisms in the hippocampus and temporal lobe that subserve short-term memory. Stress can impair memory acutely, but fortunately these effects are reversible and relatively short lived. Second, repeated stress causes an atrophy of dendrites of pyramidal neurons in the CA3 region of the hippocampus through a mechanism involving both glucocorticoids and excitatory amino acid neurotransmitters released during and in the aftermath of stress. This atrophy is reversible if the stress is short lived, but stress lasting many months or years can kill hippocampal neurons. Stress-related disorders such as recurrent depressive illness, posttraumatic stress disorder, and Cushing's syndrome are associated with atrophy of the human hippocampus as measured by magnetic resonance imaging. It is not yet clear to what extent this atrophy is reversible or permanent.

Failure to turn off the HPA axis and sympathetic activity efficiently after stress is a feature of age-related functional decline in experimental animals and humans. Stress-induced cortisol and catecholamine secretion returns to baseline more slowly in some aging animals that show other signs of accelerated aging at the same time. One other sign of age-related impairment in rats is that the hippocampus fails to turn off the release of excitatory amino acids after stress, which may accelerate progressive structural damage and functional impairment. Long-term stress also accelerates the appearance of several biological markers of aging in rats, including the excitability of CA1 pyramidal neurons by a calcium-dependent mechanism and loss of hippocampal pyramidal neurons. An important factor may be the enhancement by glucocorticoids of calcium currents in hippocampus in view of the key role of calcium ions in destructive as well as plastic processes in hippocampal neurons.

One speculation is that allostatic load over a lifetime may cause a loss of resilience in which allostatic systems wear out or become exhausted, leading to either a failure to shut off or a failure to respond. A vulnerable link in HPA regulation and cognition is the hippocampal region of the brain; according to the "glucocorticoid cascade hypothesis," wear and tear on this brain region leads to disregulation of the HPA axis as well as cognitive impairment. Supporting evidence comes from the finding that some, but not all, aging rats have impairments of both episodic, declarative, and spatial memory and HPA axis hyperactivity, both of which can be traced to hippocampal damage. Data in humans showing hippocampal atrophy and cognitive impairment accompanying progressive elevations of cortisol levels over 4 years suggest that similar events may occur in our own species (Lupien, S. J., DeLeon, M. J., De Santi, S., Convit, A., Tarshish, C., Nair, N. P. V., Thakur, M., McEwen, B. S., Hauger, R. L., and Meaney, M. J. 1998. *Nature Neurosci.* **61**, 69–73).

Early stress and neonatal handling influence the course of aging and age-related cognitive impairment in animals (Meaney, M., Aitken, D., Berkel, H., Bhatnager, S., and Sapolsky, R. 1988. *Science* **239**, 766–768). Early experiences are believed to set the level of responsiveness of the HPA axis and autonomic nervous system. These systems overreact in animals subject to early unpredictable stress and underreact in animals exposed to the neonatal handling procedure. In the former condition, brain aging is accelerated, whereas in the latter, brain aging is reduced.

C. The Immune System

The immune system responds to pathogens or other antigens with its own form of allostasis that may include an acute-phase response as well as the formation of an immunological "memory." At the same time, the immune system reacts to other allostatic systems such as the HPA axis and the autonomic nervous system; these systems tend to contain acute-phase responses and dampen cellular immunity. However, not all of the effects are suppressive. Acute stress causes lymphocytes and macrophages to redistribute throughout the body and to "marginate" on blood vessel walls and within certain compartments such as the skin, lymph nodes, and bone marrow. This "trafficking" is mediated in part by adrenal steroids. If an immune challenge is not encountered, and the hormonal stress signal ceases, immune cells return to the bloodstream. However, when a challenge occurs, as is the case in delayed-type hypersensitivity, acute stress enhances the traffic of immune cells to the site of acute challenge. The immune-enhancing effects of acute stress last for a number of days and depend on adrenal steroid secretion. Thus, acute stress has the effect of calling immune cells "to their battle stations" and this form of allostasis enhances responses for which there is an established immunologic "memory."

When allostatic load is increased by repeated stress, the outcome is completely different; the delayed hypersensitivity response is inhibited substantially rather than enhanced (Dhabhar, F. S., and McEwen, B. S. 1998. *Brain. Behav. Immun.* **11**, 236–306). The result of such suppression of cellular immunity resulting from chronic stress includes consequences such as increased severity of the common cold, accompanied by increased cold virus antibody titers (Cohen, S., Tyrrell, D. A. J., and Smith, A. P. 1991. *N. Engl. J. Med.* **325**, 606–612).

V. IMPLICATIONS OF ALLOSTATIC LOAD IN HUMAN SOCIETY

The gradients of health across the range of socioeconomic status relate to a complex array of risk factors that are differentially distributed in human society. A study of elderly people who had a lifetime of sustained economic hardship pointed to a more rapid decline of physical and mental functioning (Lynch, J. W., Kaplan, G. A., and Shema, S. J. 1997. *N. Engl. J. Med.* **337**, 1889–1895).

Undoubtedly the best example is the Whitehall studies of the British Civil Service, in which stepwise gradients of mortality and morbidity were found across all six grades of the British Civil Service (Marmot, M. G., Davey Smith, G., Stansfeld, S., Patel, C., North, F., Head, J., White, I., Brunner, E., and Feeney, A. 1991. *Lancet* **337**, 1387–1393). Hypertension was a sensitive index of job stress, particularly in factory workers, in other workers with repetitive jobs and time pressures, and in workers whose jobs were unstable due to departmental privatization (M. G. Marmot, personal communication). Plasma fibrinogen, which predicts increased risk of death

from coronary heart disease (CHD), is elevated in men in lower British Civil Service grades. In less stable societies, conflict and social instability have been found to accelerate pathophysiological processes and increase morbidity and mortality. For example, cardiovascular disease is a major contributor to the almost 40% increase in the death rate among Russian males in the social collapse following the fall of Communism (Bobak, M., and Marmot, M. 1996. *Br. Med. J.* **312**, 421–425). Blood pressure surges and sustained elevations are linked to accelerated atherosclerosis as well as increased risk for myocardial infarction.

Another stress-linked change is abdominal obesity, measured as increased waist/hip ratio. WHR is increased at the lower end of the socioeconomic status gradient in Swedish males (Larsson, B., Seidell, J., Svardsudd, K., Welin, L., Tibblin, G., Wilhelmesen, L., and Bjorntorp, P. 1989. *Appetite* **13**, 37–44) and is also increased with decreasing civil service grade in the Whitehall studies (Brunner, E. J., Marmot, M. G., Hanchahal, K., Shipley, M. J., Stansfield, S. A., Juneja, M., and Alberty, K. G. M. M. 1997, *Diabetologia* **40**, 1341–1349.) Immune system function is also a likely target of psychosocial stress, increasing vulnerability to infections such as the common cold, as noted earlier.

See Also the Following Articles

HIPPOCAMPUS, CORTICOSTEROID EFFECTS ON; HOMEOSTASIS; HYPERTENSION; WAIST-HIP RATIO

Bibliography

Adler, N. E., Boyce, T., Chesney, M. A., Cohen, S., Folkman, S., Kahn, R. L., and Syme, L. S. (1994). Socioeconomic status and health: The challenge of the gradient. *Am. Psychol.* **49**, 15–24.

Landfield, P. W., and Eldridge, J. C. (1994). Evolving aspects of the glucocorticoid hypothesis of brain aging: Hormonal modulation of neuronal calcium homeostasis. *Neurobiol. Aging* **15**, 579–588.

McEwen, B. S. (1992). Re-examination of the glucocorticoid cascade hypothesis of stress and aging. *In* "Progress in Brain Research" (D. Swaab, M. Hoffman, R. Mirmiran, F. Ravid, and F. van Leeuwen, eds.) pp. 365–383. Elsevier, Amsterdam.

McEwen, B. S., DeLeon, M. J., Lupien, S. J., and Meaney, M. J. (1999). Corticosteroids, the aging brain and cognition. *Trends Endocrinol. Metab.* 10, 92–96.

McEwen, B. S., and Stellar, E. (1993). Stress and the individual: Mechanisms leading to disease. *Arch. Intern. Med.* 153, 2093–2101 (1993).

McEwen, B. S. (1998). Protective and damaging effects of stress mediators. *N. Engl. J. Med.* 338, 171–179.

McEwen, B. S., and Sapolsky, R. M. (1995). Stress and cognitive function. *Curr. Opin. Neurobiol.* 5, 205–216.

McEwen, B. S., Biron, C. A., Brunson, K. W., Bulloch, K., Chambers, W. H., Dhabhar, F. S., Goldfarb, R. H., Kitson, R. P., Miller, A. H., Spencer, R. L., and Weiss, J. M. (1997). Neural-endocrine-immune interactions: The role of adrenocorticoids as modulators of immune function in health and disease. *Brain. Res. Rev.* 23, 79–133.

Meaney, M. J., Tannenbaum, B., Francis, D., Bhatnagar, S., Shanks, N., Viau, V., O'Donnell, D., and Plotsky, P. M. (1994). Early environmental programming hypothalamic-pituitary-adrenal responses to stress. *Sem. Neurosci.* 6, 247–259.

Sapolsky, R. M. (1996). Why stress is bad for your brain. *Science* 273, 749–750.

Sapolsky, R., Krey, L., and McEwen, B. S. (1986). The neuroendocrinology of stress and aging: The glucocorticoid cascade hypothesis. *Endocr. Rev.* 7, 284–301.

Schulkin, J., McEwen, B. S., and Gold, P. W. (1994). Allostasis, amygdala, and anticipatory angst. *Neurosci. Biobehav. Rev.* 18, 385–396.

Seeman, T. E., and Robbins, R. J. (1994). Aging and hypothalamic-pituitary-adrenal response to challenge in humans. *Endocr. Rev.* 15, 233–260.

Sterling, P., and Eyer, J. (1988). Allostasis: A new paradigm to explain arousal pathology. *In* "Handbook of Life Stress, Cognition and Health" (S. Fisher and J. Reason, eds.), pp. 629–649. Wiley, New York.

Alternative Therapies

Christine Maguth Nezu, Arthur M. Nezu, Kim P. Baron, and Elizabeth Roessler

MCP Hahnemann University

GLOSSARY

alternative therapy Many different diagnostic systems and therapies that differ from and, in some cases, oppose conventional Western medicine practice.

aromatherapy A branch of herbal medicine which specifically utilizes plants' essential oils to promote health and treat illness.

ayurveda A traditional Indian system of medicine that addresses the balance of mind, body, and spirit.

chiropractic A Western systems alternative therapy approach to health concerned with the relationship of the spinal column and the musculoskeletal structures of the body to the nervous system.

conventional medicine The treatment available in modern systems of Western health care.

herbal medicine A system of medicine based upon the healing properties of medicinal plants (leaf, flower, seed, root, or extract) for the promotion and maintenance of health and the treatment of physical, physiological, and spiritual concomitants of disease.

homeopathy A method of treating disease in which minute doses of a medicinal substance are used to treat a wide range of medical conditions. These same substances, at undiluted doses, would produce the very same symptoms of the disease in a healthy person that the diluted agent is actually attempting to cure in the patient.

mind/body therapies Systematic psychological and self-help experiences designed to impact upon psychological, emotional, behavioral, and physical functioning.

osteopathy A system of healing which emphasizes the role of the musculoskeletal system in health and illness.

prana A term used in Ayurvedic medicine to represent life-force energy.

qi A term used in traditional Chinese medicine that refers to the vital motivating energy of the body/mind.

systems approaches Therapies associated with a complete and coherent theory of human functioning and proposed mode of therapeutic action.

tactile therapies Therapies that encompass a wide range of treatments and include soft tissue and/or energy mobilization techniques which are performed by a trained clinician on an individual.

traditional Chinese medicine (TCM) A complete system of medicine that has been practiced in China for 2000 years.

I. STRESS AND STRESS-RELATED SYMPTOMS

The concepts of stress, stress-related disorders, and stress-related symptoms are widely accepted as transactional processes involving the individual and the environment. The multifactorial phenomena of stress-related symptoms is always a function of some combination of psychosocial, predisposing, triggering, and buffering risk factors interacting with genetic predispositions. Even within individuals themselves, the concept of stress is transactional, often involving nervous, endocrine, and immune systems. The dynamic and transactional aspects of stress-related medical disorders differ from other medical problems, such as acute infectious diseases, physical trauma, and needed surgical procedures. Such acute problems have been successfully approached and treated through conventional Western medicine. However, it is not surprising that conventional medicine has been less successful in meeting the challenge of developing effective ways to help people manage stress-related symptoms or healing stress-related disorders. Because such problems are complex, multifaceted, and probably best approached through multiple avenues or paths, the choice of alternative approaches or therapies that can complement conventional medical treatment may be particularly important to the treatment of stress-related problems.

II. ALTERNATIVE THERAPIES

Alternative and complementary medicine is a holistic approach to health care, originating from various historic philosophies and cultural contexts, which aims to treat the body, the mind, and the spirit. The symptoms of illness are perceived as the outward signs of an imbalance between the physical, mental, and emotional aspects of functioning as well as the vitality, or spirit, of the patient.

From a holistic perspective, stress is viewed as an imbalance, where the demands of the situation have exceeded the current resources and homeostasis is interrupted. The stressful situation can be environmental (e.g., toxins, external social pressures, lack of financial resources), internal (e.g., high expectations, perfectionism, poor diet, excessive use of medications or substances such as alcohol, anger, guilt, immune disruption, qi imbalance, cell mutations), or behavioral (e.g. exhaustion, chronic sedentary lifestyle, addictive behaviors).

A. Problems of Categorization

It is difficult to determine which therapeutic strategies to include under the "alternative" rubric. For example, psychological strategies such as relaxation may be considered conventional treatment for specific mental health problems such as fears or phobias, but "alternative" when employed as a strategy to improve cardiovascular functioning. Moreover, the categories of alternative and complementary approaches are becoming less clear as more is learned regarding the etiopathogenesis of chronic, stress-related illnesses and the boundaries of thoughts, emotions, behavior, and actual physical functioning are less easily distinguished. Finally, alternative therapies that are now making the frontier for problems formerly in the domain of conventional medicine in the Western countries have often been accepted as conventional approaches in other cultures and health systems for some time.

III. OVERVIEW OF ALTERNATIVE THERAPY APPROACHES

This brief overview offers a glimpse of the various alternative approaches to treatment of stress-related symptoms. Although alternative approaches to stress-related disorders that are very diverse are presented, they share in common a more holistic perspective toward the deleterious effects of stress, the resulting impact of stress on overall health, and the ways to manage or alleviate this impact. The overview is drawn from descriptive, historic, and empirical literature sources.

A. Herbal Medicine

Herbal medicines associated with stress-related symptoms include Ginkgo biloba, hypericum perforatum (St. John's wort), ginseng, and kava as well as aromatherapy, frequently considered a branch of herbal medicine.

1. Ginkgo Biloba

Ginkgo biloba is derived from the maidenhair tree and has primarily been studied for its effect on the brain, but has also been shown in studies to reduce the negative effects of experimentally induced stress on rats. Moreover, an extract of the herb demonstrated superior stress-reducing effects over antidepressants and over placebo in rats. There are a few studies reporting efficacy of ginkgo biloba with humans. However, one study conducted by Cohen and Bartlik found ginkgo biloba to improve sexual dysfunction induced by stress in both men and women participants. While the mechanism of action remains unclear, there is some evidence for a mechanism of action similar to how many antidepressant drugs work.

2. Hypericum Perforatum

Extracts of Hypericum perforatum, popularly known as St. John's wort, have been widely used in Germany for the treatment of depression. There are numerous studies indicating that certain extracts produce comparable effects to popular antidepressants such as tricyclics, although side-effects such as gastrointestinal irritation, tiredness, and restlessness have been reported. In a meta-analysis of 37 randomized trials evaluating the effects of hypericin versus placebo or antidepressants, this report supports the efficacy of St. Johns wort for comparably reducing depressive symptomalogy, while producing fewer and less severe side-effects than common antidepressants.

3. Kava

Kava, which means "bitter" in Polynesian languages, is derived from a black pepper plant in the South Pacific called *Piper methysticum*. Explorers' journals have historically documented the effects of kava for centuries: when consumed, it produces a numbing effect on the tongue, results in feelings of tranquility and relaxation, and contains genitourinary antiseptic qualities. However, too much kava can cause adverse dermatological effects and negative interaction with some medications. The psychopharmacological knowledge of kava remains unclear. A recent randomized, placebo-controlled study of 101 outpatients with various anxiety disorders according to the DSM-III-R criteria found kava to be superior to placebo by reducing anxiety and causing fewer side-effects after 12 weeks and continuing throughout the 25-week study. In sum, the authors showed short-term and long-term positive anxiolytic effects of kava and good tolerance. However, the lack of English studies and the few German controlled trials with humans warrant further investigation.

4. Ginseng

Ginseng, a popular herb in traditional Chinese medicine, is primarily utilized for its effects on anxiety, concentration, and physical stress. Dua and colleagues found that rats administered *Panax ginseng* crude extract showed significantly fewer ulcerogenic indices in response to an experimental stress (e.g., swimming stress; immobilization stress) as compared to the saline-treated control.

In a double-blind placebo-controlled study, Sotaniemi and colleagues evaluated the efficacy of ginseng on the psychological and physiological effects in people with non-insulin-dependent diabetes mellitus. Participants who received ginseng showed improved mood, vigor, well-being, and psychomotor performance.

Several studies indicate the mechanisms through which ginseng works. Some studies show the pain-blocking effects of ginseng on stress-induced mice, while others suggest ginseng may enhance nitric oxide synthesis, promote cytokine induction, or enhance natural killer cell activity in healthy subjects and in patients with chronic fatigue syndrome and with acquired immunologic syndrome.

5. Aromatherapy

When aromatherapy is conducted, essential oils may be inhaled; ingested; applied through massage; and/or given as a suppository, topical ointment, in baths, or as a compress. Clinically, aromatherapy has been used for stress-related problems such as depression, infections, insomnia, hypertension, and arrhythmias. Although well-conducted clinical trials on the efficacy of aromatherapy are limited and the mechanisms of action unclear, some studies do exist suggesting aromatherapy may play a role in stress reduction. Two controlled clinical trials investigated the efficacy of aromatherapy on 100 cardiac surgery patients and on postcardiotomy patients. The former study found that aromatherapy foot massage decreased anxiety among 100 postcardiac surgery patients as compared with the control group, and Buckle found that one hybrid of lavender massage reduced anxiety in postbypass patients over another hybrid of lavender massage. Other studies have promoted the use of aromatherapy massage for palliative care patients, suggesting that the intervention may reduce physical symptoms, improve quality of life, and decrease anxiety.

The mechanism of action, however, is still unknown. Animal studies have shown that fragrances both suppress the immune system and block the suppression of the immune system. Theoretically, it has been suggested that the active constituents are absorbed into the bloodstream through the skin or the olfactory system, long known to be connected with the brain's limbic system. This system is associated with emotions and is also important in monitoring heart rate, blood pressure, respiratory rate, and stress.

B. Homeopathy

Homeopathy, founded in the late 18th century by Dr. Samuel Hahnemann, is based on the philosophy that "like cures like" and "potency increases as dilution increases." Such a philosophy is completely opposite to allopathy, which targets disease with the use of agents that produce effects different than those of the disease treated. To date, there are significantly more descriptive studies in the literature than there are clinical trials. In a review of clinical trials in homeopathy for a wide range of disorders, Kleijnen and colleagues found that of 105 controlled clinical trials, 81 showed positive effects from homeopathy and 24 trials showed no positive effects as compared to placebo.

C. Diet and Nutrition

Healthy lifestyle, including proper diet, nutrition, and exercise, is now recognized as a means of preventing illness and promoting healing of stress-related disorders. Several lifestyle diets which have gained popularity since the late 1980s include (a) the Atkins Low Carbohydrate Diet, which aims to increase ketosis (burning of stored fat); (b) the Gerson Diet, aimed to increase levels of potassium and decrease levels of sodium through the consumption of natural foods; and (c) the Ornish Diet. Ornish's Lifestyle Health Trial, a randomized, placebo-controlled trial of outpatients with coronary artery disease, found that lifestyle changes (vegetarian diet, stress management, exercise, twice-weekly discussion groups) reduced significant cardiovascular problems, such as coronary arteriosclerosis, whereas the control group under the usual prescription of a 30% fat diet, remained the same or even deteriorated.

In addition to overall dietary changes, other specific treatments which have been recently studied include the use of fish oil, garlic, and marijuana. For instance, fish oil has been found to improve stress-related problems involving the circulatory, neuroendocrine, and immune systems. Both garlic and marijuana have been proposed as having immunological benefits, but further studies are needed.

D. Systems Approaches to Healing

There are several alternative healing traditions considered to be a more systems approach to health and illness. These approaches employ a combination of alternative strategies within an overall theoretical context. Western systems, such as osteopathy and chiropractic medicine, view illness as a product of misalignments of the musculoskeletal system and the spine, respectively. Alternatively, Eastern approaches, such as Ayurveda and traditional Chinese medicine (TCM), view illness as an internal imbalance or disruption in energy flow. The Eastern philosophies aim to heal the mind, body, and spirit and view these as interconnected.

This section describes the philosophies behind each of the systems. Although some of these forms of medicine have been practiced for thousands of years, structured research reports are limited. One reason for the dearth of literature is that Western and Eastern systems work from very different scientific paradigms. There are many variables in Eastern medicine, such as Qi, which are difficult to operationalize and research in Western science. Therefore, much of the literature includes descriptive studies.

1. Western Systems

a. Osteopathy Osteopathy, founded by Andrew Taylor Still, posits that the body, in normal structural relationship with adequate nutrition, is capable of maintaining its own defenses against pathologic conditions. Structural difficulties in the body can cause numerous problems such as emotional problems, breathing problems, heart problems, arthritis, headaches, and digestive problems depending on which area in the musculoskeletal system is restricted or under stress. Assessment includes an evaluation of the patient's posture, gait, motion symmetry and soft tissue, and treatment encompasses various types of manual manipulation such as mobilization and articulation. In treating the whole person, rather than the disease state, a doctor of osteopathy (D.O.) will often prescribe a variety of additional treatments such as education, breathing techniques, relaxation techniques such as stretching methods, and postural correction to reduce the tension to the effected areas of the body.

Research to date focuses on the philosophy of osteopathic medicine and manipulation techniques and less on treatment outcome. Most of the clinical outcome studies that do exist have focused on back pain.

b. Chiropractic Chiropractic, derived from the Greek word meaning "done by hands" and founded by Daniel David Palmer, is based upon the premise that vertebral subluxation (a spinal misalignment causing abnormal nerve transmission) significantly contributes to illness. As such, injury or stress may impede on the balance of the central nervous system,

the autonomic nervous system, and the peripheral nervous system that is required to maintain health. It is underscored, for instance, that subluxations impede on communication within the central nervous system, between the brain and various organs, thereby causing pain. Treatment includes realigning the spine in order to restore nerve function. Whereas osteopaths provide manual therapy to a variety of areas in the body, chiropractors focus specifically on the spinal maladjustments.

Similar to osteopathy, much of the clinical work and research conducted to date focuses on stress-related neuromuskuloskeletal problems such as back pain, neck pain, and headache, with more recent research also investigating visceral disorders such as hypertension, asthma, and dysmennorhea. Treatment involves adjusting the spine through stretching and gentle touch, allowing the nerves to once again send out proper signals.

Several comprehensive reviews exist on clinical outcome studies in spinal manipulation. Although methodological problems exist, several studies have found manipulation therapy to be more effective than placebo treatment for a variety of medical problems.

2. Eastern Systems

a. Ayurveda According to the teachings of Ayurveda, which means "the science of life and longevity" in Sanskrit, each human has a predominant dosha, or body type. These include vata (meaning wind and controls movement), pitta (meaning bile and controls metabolism), and kapha (meaning phlegm and controls structure). The three doshas, which are present in all our cells, organs, and tissues, are composed of one or more of the five elements in our universe: earth, air, fire, water, and space. The Ayurvedic doctor treats the individual rather than the disease and assesses the individual's body type in order to determine proper or contraindicated treatment. A balanced dosha results in a healthy individual whereas doshas in disequilibrium, resulting from internal or external stressors, cause disease. Treatment aims to restore the balance of the doshas or to maintain the proper balance of the life-force, or prana. In order to return balance, rechanelling energies may include a variety of methods such as medication, exercise, diet, herbs, aromatherapy, oil massages, yoga, and medicated enemas.

Research on Ayurvedic medicine is limited mostly because Western science finds it difficult to measure prana. Ayurvedic herbal formulations are recommended for specific medical disorders but there are difficult obstacles to studying the effects of ayurvedic prescriptions. This is due to both the individualized nature of assessment and treatment as well as the interaction of specific meditative techniques that are prescribed in synergy with these preparations.

b. Traditional Chinese Medicine Similar to Ayurvedic Medicine, traditional Chinese medicine considers and treats the individual rather than the disease and searches for imbalances and disharmony in the body. Also like Ayurveda, the TCM physician may prescribe a variety of therapies such as herbs, exercise, massage, acupuncture, and Qigong. According to TCM, all living beings, humans, animals, and plants contain Qi. The flow of Qi, through hundreds of pathways called meridians, helps to sustain us. Proper flow of Qi maintains health, whereas blockage of meridians leads to illness. The primary goal of techniques such as acupuncture, in which needles are inserted into specific meridian points, is to readjust the body's Qi so that the body may heal itself. Qigong meditation and exercise are also based upon this principle.

Research in TCM is also difficult because of the nature of treating illness in an individualistic manner. However, there are many studies from other countries, as well as the United States, that indicate the positive effects of TCM on immune functioning and potential for treatment of stress-related medical disorders.

E. Mind/Body Therapy Approaches

Many of the mind/body approaches are drawn from psychological and behavioral science and are covered in other areas of this text. When employed to reduce psychological distress or prevent stress-related symptoms, these therapies are considered mainstream. However, when used for stress-related medical disorders or chronic illness, these same strategies are considered alternative because they have not been traditionally employed for medical treatment of physical problems in Western medicine. Their use in stress management, however, has been scientifically documented.

Biofeedback involves a practitioner and patient working together using various forms of technological feedback (e.g. heart rate, galvanic skin response, temperature) to monitor nervous system and emotional responsivity. It helps people to become more aware of their physical and emotional response and recognize how their body responds to stressful experiences.

Cognitive behavioral psychotherapy incorporates both cognitive and behavioral psychotherapeutic techniques. Cognitive therapy techniques teach patients to interrupt troublesome thoughts and replace them with more realistic, positive thoughts. Behavioral strategies are aimed at teaching important psychological and behavioral skills such as assertiveness training and communication training. Cognitive behavioral interventions combine both of these treatment strategies along with skills in identifying and managing troublesome emotions. Strategies include social problem solving therapy, anger management, and relapse prevention of addictive problems.

Guided-imagery and visualization techniques involve picturing a tranquil personal state or the internal workings of one's own body. These therapies have been shown to decrease anxiety and reduce the incidence of stress-related disorders, such as headaches and pain. Meditation, relaxation, and hypnosis have been used to encourage overall healing and well-being as well as for focused interventions regarding various stress-related disorders. Many of these strategies have been associated with the experience of a calm mental state that refreshes the mind and body.

Relaxation techniques have been well tested scientifically as a means by which to help patients bring the relaxation response under voluntary control. These include autogenic training, progressive muscle relaxation and systematic desensitization.

Many mind/body strategies have been demonstrated to be effective through randomized and controlled studies for a wide range of stress-related psychiatric and medical disorders. These include depression, anxiety, digestive disorders, skin disorders, fatigue, tension and migraine headaches, high blood pressue, and insomnia. Specific strategies are discussed in detail in other sections.

F. Tactile Therapies

Tactile treatments employ soft tissue mobilization, manipulation of muscles, and ridding other restrictions in an effort to decrease constraints due to stress and its resulting pain. In comparison to alternate stress techniques, massage has been demonstrated to exceed relaxation strategies in several studies. Another technique, trigger point release, is based upon the premise that stress-induced metabolic wastes accumulate in palpable areas of the muscles or "knots." Applying sustained pressure to these areas can release the muscle spasm, resulting in decreased tension. Rolfing, a philosophy based on the deleterious impact of gravity and stress on the body, attempts to physically "rid" myofascial restrictions caused by tensional forces. The goal is to release tension and pain, enhancing the body's functional efficiency and energy.

Energy mobilization refers to unrestricting the flow of energy believed to be blocked by stress or other dysfunction. Several different therapies are based on this concept. For example, in Therapeutic Touch (TT), the clinician facilitates the smooth and steady movement of energy. This technique, often not involving direct contact, but rather placement of the practitioner's hands directly above the patient, has been shown to decrease anxiety, pain, and other stress-related ailments. Reiki, meaning "universal life energy," also attempts to restore energy flow. In contrast to TT which "readjusts" the patient's own energy, in Reiki, the energy source is outside the patient's body. The clinician transfers his or her energy to help revive the patient's energy flow. Polarity therapy is composed of energy mobilization based on positive and negative magnetic fields as well as diet, exercise, and counseling. The goal of this intervention is to use the magnetic force created by the clinician's body to release the restricted energy flow due to stress.

Meridian point therapy, a TCM technique, involves applying specific pressure to precise areas of the body in an effort to facilitate the smooth flow of energy, thus decreasing stress and pain. Acupressure, similar to acupuncture, targets meridians with manual pressure rather than needles. Practice traditions support the use of acupressure over acupuncture for stress-related dysfunction. Shiatsu, incorporating acupressure, gentle stretching, and joint manipulation, is also often successful at treating psychological stress and related problems, such as pain, sexual and digestive conditions, and overall poor health. Finally, in magnetic therapy, magnets are applied to either meridians or directly to painful areas with the expectancy that this will stimulate healing at specific areas.

G. Movement Therapies

Physical activity can decrease stress. Research supports the concept that aerobic exercise is related to decreased psychosocial stress. In a literature review of a decade of research, exercise was consistently shown to improve mood, psychological well-being, and self-esteem. Techniques included in the movement therapy category are aerobic exercise, T'ai Chi Ch'uan, Yoga, and the Alexander and Feldenkrais techniques.

Specific types of exercise appear to better reduce stress. High-intensity aerobic exercise (i.e., higher elevations of heart rate) has consistently provided better stress relief than lower intensity aerobic activity, and aerobic activity appears to attenuate stress better than anaerobic activity, such as weight lifting.

T'ai Chi Ch'uan (often referred to as Tai Chi) is a form of Chinese martial arts gaining popularity in non-Eastern cultures for its promotion of relaxation. Tai Chi has a physical component comprised of slow, fluid movements (with energy expenditure equated to walking about 3.7 miles/h) as well as a cognitive/ meditative element. One or both elements may be responsible for stress relief.

Yoga involves "centering" oneself through physical stretches and psychological focusing and awareness. Of the many types of yoga, Hatha yoga, comprised of stretching and distinct breathing techniques, is specifically designed to release physical and psychological stress. Studies show yoga results in increased relaxation when compared to simulated yoga and no intervention, and the use of yoga has been promoted regarding its stress reduction benefits for patients with coronary artery disease.

Other specific movement therapies have been proposed to help decrease deleterious effects of stress. For example, the Alexander technique is aimed at improving balanced posture, breathing, and fluidity of movement as well as increasing insight to and control over the effects of stress on the body and mind. Correspondingly, the Feldenkrais technique addresses psychological and physical disorders by ridding restrictions believed to be caused by, often unrealized, inappropriate use of the body. Techniques include slow, fluid movements to relearn proper ways to move the body and result in feelings of relaxation and groundedness.

H. Expressive Therapies

Dance therapy has its roots in both physical movement and psychology with the presumption that stress and negative feelings impair physical functioning. The goals of dance therapy include decreasing physical and psychological tension through expressive movement. The result involves stress relief, pain reduction, increased circulation and respiration, decreased negative psychological components such as depression and fear, and amelioration of positive thoughts and feelings. Increased sense of control and feeling of well-being can also ensue.

Writing, as a means of expression, has demonstrated powerful effects on the physical and psychological consequences of stress. In addition to decreased reported levels of distress, individuals writing about a stressful event have demonstrated improvements in immune functioning and have needed fewer physician visits. One proposed underlying mechanism of action is that writing facilitates the organization of thoughts and feelings, enhancing one's understanding of the event. This enables the body to stop protecting itself from the stressor and reestablish homeostasis.

Other expressive therapies that have been advocated for their stress-reducing effects include music therapy and art therapy. Music therapy has been shown to produce physiologic relaxation effects. Art therapy is viewed by its proponents as an important means of emotional expression.

IV. COMMON THEMES OF ALTERNATIVE THERAPIES FOR STRESS

There are common themes and concepts that emerge in any overview of alternative therapies. First, no one treatment emerges as the most advantageous in combating stress-related symptoms or even specific medical disorders. In fact, powerful interventions have been shown to incorporate several alternative strategies simultaneously. Second, a consistent theme throughout many of these approaches is one of a holistic approach that underscores the importance of individualized intervention, taking into account the preferences and beliefs of the patient. Finally, many alternative strategies view health as a state of harmony and energy balance, wherein the physical, emotional, mental, and spiritual aspects of energy are interrelated.

See Also the Following Articles

COMPLEMENTARY MEDICINE IN NORTH AMERICA; DIET AND STRESS; EXERCISE; HOMEOSTASIS; RELAXATION TECHNIQUES

Bibliography

Altenberg, H. E. (1992). "A Meeting of East and West: Holistic Medicine." Japan, New York.

D'Zurilla, T. J., and Nezu, A. M. (1989). Clinical stress management. In "Clinical Decision Making in Behavior Therapy: A Problem Solving Perspective" (A. M. Nezu and C. M. Nezu, Eds.), pp. 371–400. Research Press, Champaign, IL.

Linde, K., Ramirez, G., Mulrow, C., Pauls, A., Weidenhammer, W., and Melchart, D. (1996). St. John's wort for depression—An overview and meta-analysis of randomized clinical trials. *Br. Med. J.* **313**, 253–258.

Micozzi, M. S. (1996). "Fundamentals of Complementary and Alternative Medicine." Churchill-Livingstone, New York.

Muller, W. E., Rolli, M., and Hafner, U. (1997). Effects of hypericum extract (LI 160) in biochemical models of antidepressant activity. *Pharmacopsychiatry,* **30**(Suppl.), 102–107.

Ornish, D. (1990). "Dr. Dean Ornish's Program for Reversing Heart Disease." Ballantine Books, New York.

Pennebaker, J. W., Kiecolt-Glaser, J. K., and Glaser, R. (1988). Disclosure of traumas and immune function: Health implications for psychotherapy. *J. Consult. Clin. Psychol.* **56**, 239–245.

Plante, T. G., and Rodin, J. (1990). Physical fitness and enhanced psychological health. *Curr. Psychol. Res. Rev.* 9(1), 3–24.

Porsolt, R. D., Martin, P., Lenegre, A., Fromage, S., and Drieu, K. (1990). Effects of an extract of ginkgo biloba (EGb 761) on learned helplessness and other models of stress in rodents. *Pharmacol. Biochem. Behav.* 36, 963–971.

Rapin, J. R., Lamproglou, I., Drieu, K., and Defeudis, F. V.

(1994). Demonstration of the anti-stress activity of an extract of ginkgo biloba (EGb 761) using a discrimination learning task. *Gen. Pharmacol.* 25(5), 1009–1016.

Schanberg, S., and Kuhn, C. (1996). Massage therapy reduces anxiety and enhances EEG patterns of alertness and math computations. *Int. J. Neurosci.* 86, 197–205.

Vollaire, M. (1998). NIH Consensus Conference confirms acupuncture's efficacy. *Alt. Ther.* 4, 21–30.

Altitude, Effects of

see Pressures, Effects of Extreme High and Low and Stress

Alzheimer's Disease

Kristine Yaffe, Casey Helmkamp, and Bruce Miller

University of California San Francisco and George Washington School of Medicine

I. Alzheimer's Disease
II. Stress and Cognition
III. Conclusion

GLOSSARY

allostatic load A conceptual model of cumulative exposure to stress as measured by the additive effect of stress on the autonomic nervous system, the hypothalamic–pituitary–adrenal axis, and the cardiovascular, metabolic, and immune systems.

Alzheimer's disease The most common type of dementia characterized by progressive worsening of memory and other cognitive functions due to a neurodegenerative disorder of the brain.

cognition The ability to manipulate new pieces of information.

dementia A syndrome of acquired intellectual impairment characterized by persistent deficits in memory and at least one of the following areas of mental activity: language, visuospatial skills, personality or emotional state, and cognition (abstraction, mathematics, judgement), which is of significant severity to impair functioning.

hippocampus Part of the brain located in the medical temporal region that is involved in memory and cognition.

risk factors Precursors or statistical predictors of subsequent clinical events.

I. ALZHEIMER'S DISEASE

Scientific knowledge regarding the etiology, diagnosis, treatment, and prevention of Alzheimer's disease (AD) continues to expand. Regarding etiology, it is widely accepted that AD has strong genetic risk factors, and these genetic factors are under active investigation in animal and human research. However, despite many decades of research into nongenetic risk factors for AD, there is little consensus regarding the relative contribution of environmental factors to AD, including stress. Despite tantalizing hints from animal research suggesting that brain injury can be induced by both acute and chronic stress, the relationship between degenerative brain disease and stress has not been studied in a systematic fashion.

The clinical features of AD create inherent difficulties in determining the connection between environment and disease. In particular, proving a causal relationship between AD and stress requires linking events that may begin early in life to an illness that does not emerge until middle or even late life. Furthermore, retrospective attempts to determine who did, and who did not, suffer from stress are fraught with error, particularly because there are no definitive biological or sociological markers for stress in humans. The prospective studies that may be required to determine the relationship between stress and AD have not yet been performed. Therefore, simple formulas relating stress and AD are lacking. Finally, even though animal models of stress show pathology in brain regions affected in AD, the pathology between the two differs, raising the question of the relevance of these animal models to AD.

Despite these caveats, there is an expanding literature to suggest a relationship between stress and brain disease in animals. Furthermore, the brain regions that are vulnerable to stress in animals are the same areas that exhibit the earliest pathological changes in AD. Others lines of research demonstrate alterations in a variety of stress-related hormones in the setting of AD, although whether this is a cause or an effect of AD will be discussed later. Finally, studies have demonstrated that AD puts substantial stresses on the family structure, particularly the primary caregiver, and that these stresses can manifest in clinical disease.

This article describes the clinical, imaging, and neuropathological features of AD and defines the known environmental and genetic risk factors for this condition. The effects of stress on learning are also described and evidences for alterations in stress hormones in the setting of AD are described. The known stresses that the disease places on the patient and the family unit are outlined. Finally, future questions and srategies for determining a relationship between AD and stress are suggested.

A. Clinical Overview

AD is a degenerative brain disorder marked in the early stages by deficits in memory, language, visuospatial skills, cognition, and personality. A "definite" diagnosis of AD requires progressive deficits in memory and cognition that interfere with day-to-day functioning and a histopathological confirmation of AD by biopsy or autopsy. In previous decades, misdiagnosis rates for this condition during life were high, reaching over 50%. However, research has helped to better define the clinical features of AD and, in some centers, in cases that come to autopsy the clinical diagnosis is confirmed in over 90%.

AD affects approximately four million Americans and the prevalence increases dramatically with age, doubling every 5 years after the age of 60. Prevalence is estimated at 6% over the age of 65, 20% over the age of 80, and 45% over the age of 95. About 13% of the United States population is 65 or older, and the "very old," individuals at greatest risk for this condition, are the most rapidly growing portion of the population. Annual health care expenses and lost wages associated with AD are estimated at 80 to 100 billion dollars. Clearly, AD is a major health problem that is likely to increase in magnitude in the coming decades.

There is a typical clinical pattern of progression in AD with higher cortical functions lost first followed by deterioration in motor and sensory skills. However, individual patients may differ greatly in their clinical patterns, age of onset, and disease progression. Usually, amnesia, or the loss of the ability to learn new information, is the first sign of AD, with misplaced keys, difficulty with remembering names, and missed appointments as common early symptoms. The hippocampus, a brain region known to show vulnerability to stress, is necessary for the learning of new information, and this area is affected in the first stages of AD. Hippocampal dysfunction leads to severe problems with episodic memory, and this deficit is profoundly disabling to the patient. In addition to hippocampal involvement, diminished brain acetylcholine contributes to the amnestic defect in AD.

Language decline follows a characteristic pattern, beginning with diminished list generation ("How many animals can you list in 1 min?"); word-finding trouble, or anomia, often follows this. A fluent aphasia ensues associated with diminished language comprehension. This aphasia syndrome develops secondary to pathology in the posterior left parietal and temporal regions. Eventually patients may become mute as the disease spreads anteriorly and subcortically.

Visuospatial deficits are evident early in the clinical presentation, and such abilities as navigation, cooking, or manipulation of mechanical objects are impaired. Drawing is usually abnormal and many patients lose the ability to perform organized motor movements, which is called apraxia. Pathology in the right parietal lobe is linked to visuospatial deficits, whereas damage to the left parietal lobe is responsible for apraxia. The relationship between these visuospatial deficits in AD and the spatial learning problems found in animals with hippocampal damage due to stress warrants further investigation.

The typical time course from diagnosis to death is 7 to 11 years. Factors that determine the site of initial pathology and clinical progression are unknown. Whether physiological stresses influence clinical course is also unknown but certainly deserves study.

B. Brain Imaging in Alzheimer's Disease

Structural imaging techniques such as computerized axial tomography (CT) and magnetic resonance imaging (MRI) demonstrate generalized cerebral atrophy with AD. However, general cerebral atrophy is seen in healthy aging adults and in patients with non-AD dementia. Therefore it is difficult to use atrophy as a diagnostic marker. MRI is preferable to CT because it has better spatial resolution, particularly in the temporal regions that are vulnerable in AD. Quantitative analysis with MRI (or CT) separates most, but not all, healthy elderly from those with AD. The most robust structural markers for AD are

measures of medial temporal lobe structures such as the parahippocampal gyrus and hippocampus. The combination of hippocampal atrophy measured by MRI and neuronal loss measured by magnetic resonance spectroscopy may become the best way to differentiate normal aging from AD.

Positron emission tomography (PET) and single photon emission computed tomography (SPECT) typically show decreased perfusion in the temporal-parietal cortex and hippocampus. These areas are where plaques, tangles, and neuronal loss are the most concentrated. These various imaging techniques are helpful in diagnosing AD, although based on clinical features alone, diagnosis can usually be made.

C. Neuropathology of Alzheimer's Disease

The key neuropathologic features of AD are amyloid plaques, neurofibrillary tangles, and neuronal and synaptic loss. The center of the amyloid plaque is derived from the amyloid precursor protein found on chromosome 21. A 42 amino acid protein cleaved from the amyloid precursor protein forms β-pleated sheets that are plentiful in presynaptic neuoronal regions. Surrounding the amyloid is a gliotic reaction with inflammatory markers. Some suggest that the inflammatory response to the amyloid is toxic to neurons. However, in cell and animal models the amyloid by itself is neurotoxic. The hippocampus and posterior temporal-parietal cortex have the greatest plaque density. Amyloid plaques are found in healthy aging adults, but in a less concentrated way compared to patients with AD. The other key feature of AD is the neurofibrillary tangle that forms within the neuron. The neurofibrillary tangle contains abnormally phosphorylated tau. Tau helps hold microtubules together and represents a key component of the cellular cytoskeleton. Neurofibrillary tangles are rare in healthy aging adults, but are also seen in patients with non-AD dementias. Neurochemically, AD patients show multiple neurotransmitter deficits, which include significant losses of acetylcholine, somatostatin, and serotonin, and variable losses of dopamine. The nucleus basalis of Meynert in the basal forebrain is a major source of acetylcholine and shows a marked cellular loss. These neurotransmitter losses contribute to the clinical syndrome associated with AD. Cholinergic deficiency leads to deficits in memory, attention, and behavior, all of which can be improved with treatment.

D. Risk Factors of Alzheimer's Disease

1. Genetics

Family history is a major risk factor for developing AD. Presenile AD is often inherited in an autosomal dominant fashion. More than 40% of presenile familial cases are associated with mutations in the presenilin gene, which is found on chromosome 14. Other much rarer causes for presenile AD are mutations in the amyloid precursor protein gene on chromosome 21 or the presenilin 2 gene on chromosome 1. These mutations both account for approximately 1% of all such cases.

There are also susceptibility genes associated with AD. The (E) epsilon apolipoproteins are coded on chromosome 19. Heterozygosity for the E4 allele increases the risk for AD by at least 2-fold, whereas E4 homozygosity increases the risk 10- to 20-fold.

Most cases of AD associated with E4 are late onset, and 90% of those who live to the age of 90 with E4 will get AD. Another *possible* susceptibility gene is the α_2-macroglobulin mutation present in 30% of the population. Although studies are preliminary, it appears to be as important a susceptibility gene as E4 and increases the risks for developing both early and late onset disease. The mechanism for E4 and α_2-macroglobulin-associated AD is unknown, although both proteins interact with amyloid and probably aid with the clearance of amyloid at the cellular level. Whether stress can mediate the genetic risk factors described has not been evaluated systematically.

2. Nongenetic Risk Factors

Aging, previous head injury, small head size, depression, and low education are all thought to increase the chance of developing AD. Estrogens stimulate neuronal sprouting in the hippocampus, and decreased estrogen after menopause may increase the risk of AD. Antioxidants such as ascorbic acid and

α-tocopherol may reduce the risk of AD and other dementias. Furthermore, some studies have suggested that taking nonsteroidal anti-inflammatory drugs may lower the risk of developing the disease, presumably via the reduction of inflammation associated with AD pathology. The interaction between stress and these nongenetic factors remains unknown.

What some of the environmental risk factors have in common is that they may diminish neuronal concentrations and lead to a decreased cognitive reserve. Individuals with a greater cognitive reserve may be able to sustain more brain "insults" before manifesting symptoms of dementia than those with less cognitive reserve. Both genetic and nongenetic factors determine cognitive reserve. Genetic determinants of synaptic density can influence brain size and weight, neuronal efficiency, and native intellectual ability. Nongenetic factors influencing cognitive reserve include education, age, and a history of head trauma. The cognitive reserve hypothesis predicts that individuals with more reserve can sustain more cerebral pathology and damage than individuals with less capacity. This hypothesis has been observed empirically in AD. Lower baseline cognitive function is associated with a greater risk of developing AD, independent of education. Greater cognitive function is linked to larger brain size, faster nerve conduction, and increased synaptic concentration, all of which may prevent or defer the onset of AD. Stress has been indicated as a possible risk factor for AD. Stress, through the mechanisms outlined later, could lower cognitive reserve.

II. STRESS AND COGNITION

A. Rodent Models

In rodent models of stress, high physiologic concentrations of glucocorticoids are toxic to hippocampal neurons and lead to neuronal death in this critical brain region. The hippocampus is particularly rich in corticosteroid receptors. Some studies suggest that in elderly animals, stress alone leads to elevations of glucocorticoids, which in turn leads to hippocampal degeneration. Additionally, a variety of ischemic and excitotoxic experiments that induce neuronal stress have been used to implicate glucocorticoids in hippocampal death.

Transient global ischemia will selectively reduce CA1 pyramidal neurons. These neurons are among the first to demonstrate pathology in AD. Blocking glucocorticoids attenuates the loss of these cells significantly. Seizure-induced damage to hippocampal neurons in CA3 (spared in the first stages of AD) and in CA1 is also diminished by blocking glucocorticoids. One potential mechanism for both of these models may be the accumulation of reactive oxygen species, stimulated by glucocorticoids.

Furthermore, the hippocampus plays a role in negative feedback inhibition of glucocorticoid secretion so that hippocampal damage has a forward cascade effect in which higher plasma glucocorticoid concentration caused by hippocampal loss produces an increased plasma glucocorticoid concentration. This, in turn, facilitates even more neuronal loss. In these rodent models, cumulative exposure to high glucocorticoid levels throughout life disrupts electrophysiological function and leads to the death and atrophy of rodent hippocampal neurons. The consequences of this neuronal death are severe cognitive deficits in learning and memory.

Supporting the clinical relevance of this model is the finding that basal plasma corticosterone levels among aged rats correlate significantly with hippocampal degeneration and with spatial learning deficits. Adrenalectomy in midlife that is followed by low-level cortisol replacement slows hippocampal degeneration and cognitive decline in rats, suggesting that elevated glucocorticoid levels contribute directly to the development of the cognitive impairment. Other methods that reduce rat brain exposure to high concentrations of glucocorticoids also reduce hippocampal cell loss in aging rats.

B. Stress and Aging in Humans

Allostatic load is a conceptual model of cumulative exposure to stress. It is the additive effect of stress on the autonomic nervous system, the hypothalamic–pituitary–adrenal (HPA) axis, and the cardiovascular, metabolic, and immune systems. Allostatic load may be associated with an increased risk of a variety of diseases. Activation of the most common allostatic response (HPA axis) releases catecholamines from nerves and the adrenal medulla, leading to the secretion of corticotropin from the pituitary, which in turn mediates the release of cortisol from the adrenal cortex. Inactivation returns the system to basal levels. If inactivation is hindered, there is overexposure to stress hormones, leading to pathophysiologic consequences, with one of them possibly being impaired hippocampal-dependent cognition. A higher allostatic load is associated with poorer cognitive and physical functioning and with an increased risk of decline in cognitive and physical functioning.

In humans, the hippocampus is implicated in the regulation of glucocorticoid activity as well. It modulates the stress response and acts to inhibit the response of the HPA axis to stress; lesions to the hippocampus are associated with increased basal glucocorticoid levels. Normal aging is associated with reductions in hippocampal volume.

In nondemented adults, several lines of evidence suggest that elevated cortisol levels, both acute and chronic, are associated with cognitive impairments. When healthy adults are exposed to varying doses of dexamethasone, they demonstrate worsening in immediate and delayed paragraph recall. Healthy adults who have been exposed to brief psychosocial laboratory stress and then exhibit a high cortisol response demonstrate poorer memory performance than those that do not have a high cortisol response. Similarly, when subjects who are given cortisol are tested for procedural and declarative memory and spatial thinking, they have poorer performance in the declarative memory and spatial thinking tasks than those who receive placebo. In a longitudinal study of healthy elders, those with increasing cortisol levels and high basal cortisol levels performed worse on tasks measuring explicit memory and selective attention than those with decreasing cortisol levels or increasing cortisol levels with moderate basal cortisol levels. Furthermore, subjects with significant prolonged cortisol elevations have demonstrated reduced hippocampal volume and deficits in hippocampus-dependent memory tasks compared to subjects with normal cortisol. There is an inverse relationship between failure of negative feedback inhibition of cortisol secretion in the elderly and cognitive performance. All of these findings support the idea that exposure to elevated levels of cortisol compromises hippocampal integrity and impairs hippocampus-dependent cognitive tasks. It is still not resolved whether elevated cortisol is related causally to cognitive decline in normal aging or whether the hippocampal-related cognitive deficits are a marker of reduced hippocampal function, including regulation of the HPA axis, with subsequent elevations in cortisol.

C. Stress and Alzheimer's Disease

Cortisol elevation and associated hippocampal-dependent cognitive impairments have been implicated in such diseases as Cushing's syndrome and AD. In Cushing's syndrome, which causes prolonged cortisol elevation, hippocampal volume correlates negatively with plasma cortisol levels and positively with scores on verbal memory tests. The extent of cortisol hypersecretion correlates with the extent of hippocampal atrophy, which in turn correlates with the extent of hippocampal-dependent cognitive impairment.

Many studies have reported an increase in serum cortisol levels in AD. Hypercortisolemia and reduced feedback inhibition of cortisol secretion have been found frequently in AD. In one study of dementia patients, there was a positive relationship between 24-hour cortisol levels, severity of cognitive decline, and hippocampal atrophy in AD and in multi-infarct dementia. However, other studies have failed to report elevated cortisol levels in AD. Some investigators have not found differences in serum cortisol concentration, corticosteroid-binding globulin, or free plasma cortisol in AD patients compared to age-matched normal controls. Furthermore, basal cortisol levels have not been reported to increase with age, duration of illness, or age of onset in a group of patients with AD. This argues against changes in neuroendocrine function as a major contributor to AD.

It may be that the hypercortisolemia associated with AD is related to the clinical progression of the disease. Again, whether this is a causal relationship or an epiphenomenon of AD is still not clear.

A proposed mechanism for the hypercortisolemia sometimes observed in AD is increased hypothalamic corticotropin-releasing hormone (CRH). However, CRH may be increased in normal elderly controls as well as in patients with AD. Despite the lack of a clear mechanism and despite conclusive evidence supporting a casual relationship, it does seem that the HPA access is not functioning properly in AD.

Evidence indicates that families and caregivers of patients with AD experience substantial stress. More psychological distress (higher burden, depression, hassles, and lower uplifts) is reported in spouse caregivers of patients with AD as compared to spouses of nondemented controls. These spouses also had higher glucose levels, suggesting an association between physiological stress and psychological stress. These increased stressors can lead to clinical disease in the caregiver. The result of aiding dementia patients in the activities of daily living has been associated with an increased risk of the caregiver developing a serious illness. Caregiver "overload" can explain the reported decline in the physical health of caregivers. In light of this reported decline in caregiver health, it is important that caregivers have a network of social support to help ease the stress of caring for a patient with AD. In fact, caregiver health has been shown to improve with attention to stress, coping mechanisms, and greater social support.

III. CONCLUSION

In summary, rodent models show that elevated cortisol levels cause hippocampal neuronal death. Studies of nondemented humans support an association between elevated levels of cortisol, both acute and chronic, and decreased hippocampal-dependent memory. Because the hippocampus is one of the most affected areas of the brain in AD, it seems logical that increased cortisol, due to stress, could cause hippocampal damage and increase the risk of developing AD. However, this causal relationship has not been proven clearly. In AD, hypercortisolemia has been demonstrated frequently, but it is unclear whether it is a causal relationship or due to decreased cortisol regulation associated with the hippocampal atrophy that is a fundamental part of the disease. To resolve this issue, prospective studies in elderly at risk for AD are needed.

See Also the Following Articles

Aging and Psychological Stress; Aging and Stress; Elder Abuse; Memory Impairment

Bibliography

Cummings, J. L., Vinters, H. V., Cole, G. M., and Khachaturian, Z. S. (1998). Alzheimer's disease: Etiologies, pathophysiology, cognitive reserve, and treatment opportunities. _Neurology_ 51(Suppl. 1), S2–S17.

Lawlor, B. A., Mohs, R. C., Losonczy, M., Ryan, T. M., _et al._ (1994). Hypercortisolism and brain ventricular size in normal aging and Alzheimer's disease. _Am. J. Geriatr. Psychiat._ 2, 251–252.

Lupien, S. J., Lecours, A. R., Lussier, I., _et al._ (1994). Basal cortisol levels and cognitive deficits in human aging. _J. Neurosci._ 14, 2893–2903.

Lupien, S. J., and McEwen, B. S. (1997). The acute effects of corticosteroids on cognition: Integration of animal and human model studies. _Brain Res. Rev._ 24, 1–27.

McEwen, B. S., (1998). Protective and damaging effects of stress mediators. _N. Eng. J. Med._ 338, 171–179.

McEwen, B. S., and Magarinos, A. M. (1997). Stress effects on morphology and function of the hippocampus. _Ann. N.Y. Acad. Sci._ 821, 271–284.

Newcomer, J. W., Craft, S., Hershey, T., Askins, K., and Bardgett, M. E. (1994). Glucocorticoid-induced impairment in declarative memory performance in adult humans. _J. Neurosci._ 14, 2047–2053.

O'Brien, J. T., Schweitzer, I., Ames, D., Tuckwell, V., and Mastwyck, M. (1994). HPA axis function in depression and dementia: A review. _Biol. Psychiat._ 36, 389–394.

Sapolsky, R. M. (1996). Why stress is bad for your brain. _Science_ 273, 749–750.

Sapolsky, R. M., Krey, L. C., and McEwen, B. S. (1986). The neuroendocrinology of stress and aging: The glucocorticoid cascade hypothesis. _Endocr. Rev._ 7, 284–301.

Seeman, T. E., Singer, B. H., Rowe, J. W., Horwitz, R. I., and McEwen, B. S. (1997). Price of adaptation-allostatic load and its health consequences: MacArthur studies of successful aging. _Arch. Intern. Med._ 157, 2259–2268.

Weiner, M. F., Vobach, S., Olsson, K., Svetlik, D., and Risser, R. C. (1997). Cortisol secretion and Alzheimer's disease progression. _Biol. Psychiat._ 42, 1030–1038.

Ambulatory Blood Pressure Monitoring

Thomas G. Pickering

New York Presbyterian Hospital

  I. Technique
 II. Advantages of Ambulatory Blood Pressure Monitoring
III. White Coat Hypertension
 IV. The Influence of Personality and Mood
  V. Effects of Acute Stress
 VI. Effects of Chronic Stress

GLOSSARY

ambulatory blood pressure monitoring (ABPM) A technique for measuring blood pressure over prolonged periods of time (typically 24 h) in free-living subjects. Most devices measure the blood pressure from a cuff placed on the upper arm inflated at regular intervals (usually every 15–20 min) by the monitor, which is a battery-operated device a little bigger than a Walkman radio.

dippers and nondippers Blood pressure normally decreases by at least 10% during the night in comparison with the average daytime level. The difference between the average daytime and nighttime blood pressure has been used to classify people as dippers (>10% difference) or nondippers (<10% difference).

white coat effect The increase of blood pressure associated with the physician's office setting, usually expressed as the difference between the clinic and average daytime pressures.

white coat hypertension Hypertension defined by a persistently elevated clinic or office blood pressure together with a normal blood pressure at other times (usually measured with ABPM).

Ambulatory Blood Pressure Monitoring is a technique for measuring blood pressure over prolonged periods of time (typically 24 h) in free-living subjects. The monitors are fully automatic and battery operated, and readings are taken every 15–30 min, stored in the memory, and downloaded at the end of the recording period. The blood pressure can be related to acute stressors occurring during the recording period (in relation with the subjects' diary entries) or with chronic stress.

I. TECHNIQUE

Ambulatory Blood Pressure Monitoring is performed using small fully automatic battery-operated monitors which weigh less than one pound and can be worn on a belt while subjects go about their normal daily activities. The monitor typically contains a pump which inflates the blood pressure cuff at preset intervals, a pressure detection system (usually operating by the oscillometric method), and a memory chip for storing the readings. The cuff is usually placed on the nondominant arm above the elbow and is connected to the monitor by a thin tube. Subjects are asked to keep their arm still and by their side while a reading is taken. The monitors do not work reliably during vigorous activity (e.g., exercise) or in environments where there is a lot of noise or vibration. Subjects may be asked to keep a diary describing their activity, mood, and location at the time of each reading. Blood pressure during sleep can also be recorded. At the end of 24 h the subject returns and the readings are downloaded into a computer for analysis. Several types of monitor are available, but not all have been validated for accuracy according to standard protocols.

II. ADVANTAGES OF AMBULATORY BLOOD PRESSURE MONITORING

Ambulatory Blood Pressure Monitoring has revolutionized the study of the relationships between stress and blood pressure. Previously, reliance was made on blood pressure measured either in an office or in a laboratory setting. In the former case, a very limited number of readings is usually made, and the blood pressure that is recorded may represent the effects of the white coat effect rather than the effects of everyday stress. And while reactivity testing in the laboratory permits multiple measurements to be made during exposure to standardized stressors, the situation is artificial, and generalizability to blood pressure measured in real life is very poor. Ambulatory Blood Pressure Monitoring can give three different types of information relating to blood pressure: the average level; short term changes; and the diurnal rhythm. Normally the blood pressure falls by about 10% during the night, but in about 25% of people the changes are smaller than this—the so-called nondipping pattern. There is now substantial evidence that the average level of blood pressure as measured by ABPM gives a better predictor of cardiovascular risk than conventional clinic measurements. In addition, nondippers have been reported to be at higher risk than dippers. The pathological significance of short-term blood pressure variability is unclear, although it is hypothesized that increased variability may be an independent risk factor.

III. WHITE COAT HYPERTENSION

One of the important phenomena identified by ABPM is white coat hypertension, which occurs in about 20% of patients with mild hypertension. Such patients usually have less target organ damage than patients with the same level of clinic pressure but whose pressure remains high outside the clinic, and they also appear to be at lower risk of cardiovascular morbidity. The origins of white coat hypertension are unexplained, but it is usually attributed to the stress associated with an encounter with a physician. It has been suggested that the phenomenon may be a conditioned response.

IV. THE INFLUENCE OF PERSONALITY AND MOOD

Ambulatory Blood Pressure Monitoring can be used to measure blood pressure during normal daily activities, including work. By having subjects keep a diary of their activities and emotions it is possible to correlate behavioral factors and blood pressure. Thus, while anger is the mood that is associated with the greatest increase of blood pressure, blood pressure also increases when subjects report that they are happy as compared to having a neutral mood. There are also reports of associations between negative moods and ambulatory blood pressure. The analysis of such interactions requires that there is statistical control for other influences such as posture, location, and activity. A number of reports have found that subjects who score high on hostility report more negative moods and have higher blood pressures in association with them than subjects who are less hostile. Hostile subjects also have higher nocturnal blood pressure and show a more rapid increase on waking.

V. EFFECTS OF ACUTE STRESS

Blood pressure is typically highest during the hours of work, which may be the result of both physical and mental activity being greater than at home. In men, blood pressure usually falls when they get home in the evening, but in women it may not do so, particularly if they have small children. The effects of commonly occurring activities on blood pressure are shown in Table I. A study of men working in machine shops found a significant correlation between the frequency of somatic complaints such as palpitations, fatigue, and dizziness and ambulatory systolic pressure. Paramedics show 10 mmHg higher blood pressures when they are in an ambulance and 7 mmHg elevations at the scene of an accident than during nonworkday activities.

VI. EFFECTS OF CHRONIC STRESS

Occupational stress has been investigated in several studies. In a study of 50 normotensive working

TABLE I

Average Changes of Blood Pressure Associated with Fifteen Commonly Occurring Activities

Activity	Systolic (mmHg)	Diastolic (mmHg)
Meetings	+20.2	+15.0
Work	+16.0	+13.0
Transportation	+14.0	+9.2
Walking	+12.0	+5.5
Dressing	+11.5	+9.7
Chores	+10.7	+6.7
Telephone	+9.5	+7.2
Eating	+8.8	+9.6
Talking	+6.7	+6.7
Desk Work	+5.9	+5.3
Reading	+1.9	+2.2
Business (at home)	+1.6	+3.2
Television	+0.3	+1.1
Relaxing	0	0
Sleeping	−10.0	7.6

women doing technical and clerical jobs, who also kept diaries describing their activities, emotions, and perceptions of stress, it was found that the average pressures were 116/78 mmHg at work, 113/74 mmHg at home, and 102/63 mmHg during sleep. The most powerful behavioral predictor of systolic pressure was the perception that one's job is stressful, which was associated with higher pressures in all three situations—at work, at home, and during sleep. The perception that there was more stress at work than at home on the day of the study was associated with higher systolic pressures at work, but not at home or during sleep. Potential sources of domestic stress were also related to blood pressure. Being married was associated with higher work diastolic pressures, while having children was associated with higher systolic and diastolic pressures both at work and at home. Women who reported higher levels of stress at home than at work also had relatively higher diastolic pressures at home than at work. Thus, single women whose main source of stress was at work showed a pattern similar to the one seen in men, while married women with children, whose level of stress may be higher at home, did not show the typical decrease of blood pressure when they returned home.

Young physicians, when on call for the emergency room, show an elevation of ambulatory blood pressure in comparison to a weekend day, which exceeded 10 mmHg for systolic pressure in 40% of cases. Blood pressure while asleep was not affected, however. In this case the acute work stress raised the blood pressure during the exposure to stress, but to what extent this was due to mental as to opposed to physical activity is not clear. A very different picture is obtained with more chronic stress: subjects whose jobs are characterized as high-strain (defined by a combination of high demands and low control) have elevated ambulatory blood pressures in comparison with subjects in less stressful jobs, not only during the hours of work, but, more surprisingly, while they are at home and asleep. That this is a causal relationship is suggested by the finding that over a 3 year period those who remain in high-strain jobs show a persistent elevation of blood pressure, and those whose jobs become less stressful show a decrease of pressure. These results provide the strongest evidence to date that exposure to chronic stress can elevate the blood pressure throughout the 24-h period. Interestingly, there appears to be no relation between blood pressure and job strain in women, despite the fact that women are more likely than men to be in high-strain jobs. This might be because women react to different types of stress than men: another study found that lack of social support predicted ambulatory blood pressure in women, while hostility was a better predictor in men.

See Also the Following Articles

Allostasis and Allostatic Load; Hypertension

Bibliography

Goldstein, I. B., Jamner, L. D., Shapiro, D. (1992). Ambulatory blood pressure and heart rate in healthy male paramedics during a workday and a nonworkday. *Health Psychol.* 11, 48–54.

James, G. D., Moucha, O. P., and Pickering, T. G. (1991). The normal hourly variation of blood pressure in women: Average patterns and the effect of work stress. *J. Hum. Hypertens.* 5, 505–509.

Linden, W., Chambers, L., Maurice, J., Lenz, J. W. (1993). Sex differences in social support, self-deception, hostility, and ambulatory cardiovascular activity. *Health Psychol.* 12, 376–380.

Pickering, T. G. (1994). Psychosocial stress and hypertension B: Clinical and experimental evidence. *In* "Textbook of Hypertension" (J. D. Swales, Ed.), pp. 640–654. Blackwell Scientific, London.

Pickering, T. G., Devereux, R. B., James, G. D., Gerin, W., Landsbergis, P., Schnall, P. L., and Schwartz, J. E., (1996). Environmental influences on blood pressure and the role of job strain. *J. Hypertens.* 14(Suppl. 5), S179–S186.

Pickering, T. G., James, G. D., Boddie, C., Harshfield, G. A., Blank, S., and Laragh, J. H. (1988). How common is white coat hypertension? *J. Am. Med. Assoc.* 259(2), 225–228.

Schnall, P. L., Schwartz, J. E., Lansbergis, P. A., Warren, K., and Pickering, T. G. (1999). A longitudinal study of job strain and ambulatory blood pressure: Results from a three-year follow-up. *Psychosom. Med.* 60, 697–706.

Verdecchia, P., Porcellati, C., Schillaci, G., Borgioni, C., Ciucci, A., Battistelli, M., Guerrieri, M., Gatteschi, C., Zampi, I., Santucci, A., Santucci, C., and Reboldi, G. (1994). Ambulatory blood pressure: An independent predictor of prognosis in essential hypertension. *Hypertension* 24, 793–801.

Amenorrhea

Bruce R. Carr

University of Texas Southwestern Medical Center at Dallas

GLOSSARY

hypergonadotropic hypogonadism A condition characterized by elevated gonadotropins due to ovarian failure and diminished ovarian hormone secretion.

hypogonadotropic hypogonadism A condition characterized by low gonadotropins due to alterations of the central nervous system-hypothalamic-pituitary axis associated with diminished ovarian hormone secretion.

polycystic ovarian syndrome A disease characterized by menstrual disturbances, obesity, hyperandrogenism, and polycystic ovaries.

primary amenorrhea A condition characterized by absence of menstruation by age 16 in a phenotypic female.

secondary amenorrhea A condition characterized by cessation of menstruation for 3 to 6 months in a female who has previously menstruated.

I. CLASSIFICATION OF AMENORRHEA

There are a number of causes of amenorrhea and some are related to stress. The usual definition of amenorrhea is the cessation of menstrual flow. Women who fail to menstruate by age 16 are often defined as having primary amenorrhea and women who have previously been menstruating and now exhibit at least 3 months of amenorrhea are known as having secondary amenorrhea. In this evaluation women who present with delayed puberty also have amenorrhea and should not be considered as a separate entity. Women who present with sexual ambiguity since birth or significant virilization may also present with amenorrhea, but these should be evaluated as separate disorders. Utilizing this approach, the diagnosis and treatment is somewhat simplified. It should be pointed out that classifications consisting of primary and secondary amenorrhea are not utilized because they do not describe the pathophysiology. The classification chosen is presented in Table I. The largest category is chronic anovulation, which includes women who have the ability to ovulate but do not and is subcategorized into those women who are producing estrogen (eugonadotropism) and those who are not producing estrogen (hypogonadotropic hypogonadism). A second category is ovarian failure (hypergonadotropic-hypogonadism) in which the germ cells are usually absent and the third category are abnormalities and defects in development of the female reproductive tract.

A. Chronic Anovulation

The major cause of amenorrhea is chronic anovulation. In this disorder women have ovaries and follicles but for various reasons do not ovulate normally but with appropriate therapy can ovulate and later conceive. In women with chronic anovulation, their ovaries do not secrete estrogen and progesterone in the normal cyclic pattern. Those women who exhibit bleeding after receiving an oral or intramuscular progestin challenge are producing estrogen and fall into the category of chronic anovulation with estrogen present. On the other hand, those women who fail to exhibit a menstrual bleed after a progestin challenge have levels of estrogen and are categorized as chronic anovulation with estrogen absent.

1. Chronic Anovulation with Estrogen Present

Women with chronic anovulation who experience withdrawal menstrual bleeding following a progestin challenge and exhibit normal follicle-stimulating hormone (FSH) levels are said to be in a state of

TABLE I
Classification of Amenorrhea (Not Including Disorders of Congenital Sexual Ambiguity)[a]

I. Anatomic defects (outflow tract)
   A. Labial agglutination/fusion
   B. Imperforate hymen
   C. Transverse vaginal septum
   D. Cervical agenesis—isolated
   E. Cervical stenosis—iatrogenic
   F. Vaginal agenesis—isolated
   G. Müllerian agenesis (Mayer-Rokitansky-Kuster-Hauser syndrome)
   H. Complete androgen resistance (testicular feminization)
   I. Endometrial hypoplasia or aplasia—congenital
   J. Asherman syndrome (uterine synechiae)

II. Ovarian failure (hypergonadotropic hypogonadism)
   A. Gonadal agenesis
   B. Gonadal dysgenesis
      1. Abnormal karyotype
         a. Turner syndrome 45,X
         b. Mosaicism
      2. Normal karyotype
         a. Pure gonadal dysgenesis
            i. 46,XX
            ii. 46,XY (Swyer syndrome)
   C. Ovarian enzymatic deficiency
      1. 17α-Hydroxylase deficiency
      2. 17,20-Lyase deficiency
   D. Premature ovarian failure
      1. Idiopathic—premature aging
      2. Injury
         a. Mumps oophoritis
         b. Radiation
         c. Chemotherapy
      3. Resistant ovary (Savage syndrome)
      4. Autoimmune disease
      5. Galactosemia

III. Chronic anovulation with estrogen present (eugonadotropism)
   A. PCOS
   B. Adrenal disease
      1. Cushing's syndrome
      2. Adult-onset adrenal hyperplasia
   C. Thyroid disease
      1. Hypothyroidism
      2. Hyperthyroidism
   D. Ovarian tumors
      1. Granulosa-theca cell tumors
      2. Brenner tumors
      3. Cystic teratomas
      4. Mucinous/serous cystadenomas
      5. Krukenberg tumors

IV. Chronic anovulation with estrogen absent (hypogonadotropic hypogonadism)
   A. Hypothalamic
      1. Tumors
         a. Craniopharyngioma
         b. Germinoma
         c. Hamartoma
         d. Hand-Schüller-Christian disease
         e. Teratoma
         f. Endodermal sinus tumors
         g. Metastatic carcinoma
      2. Infection and other disorders
         a. Tuberculosis
         b. Syphilis
         c. Encephalitis/meningitis
         d. Sarcoidosis
         e. Kallmann syndrome
         f. Idiopathic hypogonadotropic hypogonadism
         g. Chronic debilitating disease
      3. Functional
         a. Stress
         b. Weight loss/diet
         c. Malnutrition
         d. Psychological
            Eating disorders (anorexia nervosa, bulimia)
         e. Exercise
   B. Pituitary
      1. Tumors
         a. Prolactinomas
         b. Other hormone-secreting pituitary tumors (ACTH, thyrotropin-stimulating hormone, growth hormone)
         c. Nonfunctional tumors (craniopharyngioma)
         d. Metastatic carcinoma
      2. Space-occupying lesions
         a. Empty sella
         b. Arterial aneurysm
      3. Necrosis
         a. Sheehan syndrome
         b. Panhypopituitarism
      4. Inflammatory/infiltrative
         a. Sarcoidosis
         b. Hemochromatosis

[a] Used with permission from Carr, B. R. (1992). Disorders of the ovary and female reproductive tract. In "Williams Textbook of Endocrinology" (Wilson and Foster, Eds.), pp. 733–798. W. B. Saunders, Philadelphia.

chronic estrous due to acyclic production of estrogen. The ovarian follicles of women with this disorder do not secrete estrogen but instead secrete androgens such as androstenedione, which is converted in peripheral tissues by extraglandular aromatase into the weaker estrogen estrone. This condition may be due to problems primarily in the ovary or in the hypothalamic-pituitary-gonadal feedback loops. The consequence is that these women fail to ovulate and produce estrogen and do not experience cyclic withdrawal bleeding. The primary cause of chronic anovulation with estrogen present is polycystic ovarian syndrome (PCOS). Polycystic ovarian syndrome is a complex disorder (probably inherited and may be related to insulin resistance) characterized by the development of hirsutism or androgen excess, obesity, and menstrual disturbances including amenorrhea, oligomenorrhea, or dysfunctional uterine bleeding at the time of expected puberty. The clinical picture varies and laboratory tests may be helpful but are only supportive in confirming the diagnosis. In the majority, but not in all women with PCOS, plasma luteinizing hormone (LH) levels are elevated at the same time the plasma FSH levels are normal or low. Some have suggested that a ratio of LH to FSH of greater than 2 to 3 may be a useful laboratory distinction; however, the evaluation of a single sample of gonadotropins may lead to the wrong diagnosis and only 80% of women may exhibit this finding. In addition, the majority of women with PCOS have moderately elevated serum androgen levels. An ultrasound demonstrating multiple superficial small follicles surrounding the surface of the ovary in a ring-like pattern associated with increased stromal density in a woman with amenorrhea appears to be the best test to confirm the diagnosis. However, as stated previously, the diagnosis of PCOS syndrome is not based on pathological changes in the ovaries or plasma hormone abnormalities but is primarily based on the clinical evidence of chronic anovulation with varying degrees of androgen excess and menstrual disturbances. The etiology of this disorder is multifactorial and is not yet clearly understood. Chronic anovulation with estrogen present, obesity, hirsutism, and even polycystic ovaries can be seen in a variety of other endocrine disorders in addition to PCOS (see Table I). These women may present with

Cushing's syndrome, hyperthyroidism, hypothyroidism, and/or late adult-onset adrenal hyperplasia due to 21-hydroxylase or 11β-hydroxylase deficiency. Rarely, patients with chronic anovulation with estrogen present can present with ovarian tumors such as a Brenner tumor or cystic teratomas and even ovarian cancers where the ovary and/or tumor secrete increased amounts of androstenedione which aromatize in extraglandular sites to estrogen. As a result, such patients may present with a pattern similar to that of a woman with polycystic ovarian syndrome which resolves at the time of the removal of the tumor or the treatment of the primary disorder.

2. Chronic Anovulation with Estrogen Absent

Women with chronic anovulation with estrogen absent due to low or absent estrogen production fail to experience withdrawal bleeding or only experience vaginal spotting following a progestin challenge. Usually the FSH level is either in the normal or low range. This is an important point since evaluating just the FSH level alone (if within the normal range, for example, 4 to 8 IU/ml) does not confirm the cause of amenorrhea. Chronic anovulation with estrogen absent is a result of hypogonadotropic hypogonadism, which is secondary to organic or functional disorders of the central nervous system-hypothalamic-pituitary axis. It may be clinically helpful but not always practical to subdivide these into hypothalamic or pituitary causes (see Table I). Hypothalamic tumors or other destructive disorders of the hypothalamus are relatively rare causes of amenorrhea and require radiographic evaluation such as a computerized axial tomography (CAT scan) or magnetic resonance (MR) imaging. In women with tumors, headaches and other neurological symptoms or signs are often present. The most common cause of chronic anovulation with estrogen absent is a functional disorder of the hypothalamus or central nervous system in the presence of a normal MR or CAT scan. In these cases the cause of chronic anovulation is due to one of exclusion. A history of stress or a stressful event can often be obtained. These events include loss of a loved one, entering a stressful work environment, or going off to college. In these cases, the stress reduces hypothalamic secretion of gonadotropin-releasing hormone (GnRH), leading to reduced gonadotropin secretion followed by reduced ovarian estrogen secretion and amenorrhea results. This can happen even in women with normal body weight. Other causes related to stress and emotional disorders include weight loss and dieting, which are particularly common in young teenage girls. The most severe from of weight loss-induced amenorrhea is in anorexia nervosa, characterized by distorted attitudes toward eating and weight, self-induced vomiting, extreme emaciation, and distorted body images. Women who excessively exercise, particularly in such activities as marathon running, ballet dancing, or more recently, working out in the gym with weights and using steroids to reduce their percentage of body fat, may develop amenorrhea. Amenorrhea is more likely to develop in women with a previous history of abnormalities in menstruation prior to the onset of excessive exercise or weight loss. It is known that women who develop amenorrhea associated with stress, exercise, or dieting exhibit alterations in the menstrual cycle which can be associated with normal cyclic bleeding early in the onset of increased exercise, weight loss, or dieting. Later, as the disorder progresses problems in the production of progesterone during the luteal phase occur followed by anovulatory cycles associated with oligomenorrhea and, finally, amenorrhea develops. In some of these women a withdrawal bleed after progestin challenge may occur in the anovulatory phase with some estrogen being produced, but in most women, the failure to exhibit a withdrawal bleed following a progestin challenge suggests that the disease is more severe. If untreated it may lead to problems of estrogen deficiency such as osteoporosis. Following a reduction of stress or exercise and increased weight gain, we may see reversal from amenorrhea to ovulatory menstrual cycles requiring no further treatment. Other chronic debilitating diseases such as AIDS, malabsorption, or cancer may result in hypogonadotropic hypogonadism. A relatively rare cause of hypothalamic amenorrhea in women is due to Kallmann's syndrome, which has been shown to be associated with defects in olfactory bulb development. It is known that GnRH neurons develop in this same rostral part of the brain as the olfactory bulbs. Thus, women with Kallmann's syndrome exhibit not only

low gonadotropins and amenorrhea but also lack of the sense of smell or anosmia. As stated previously, the diagnosis of functional disorders of the CNS-hypothalamic-pituitary axis resulting in amenorrhea may be suggested by the patient's history but usually requires some form of imaging using MR or CAT scan.

Disorders of the pituitary include not only tumors but Sheehan's syndrome or postpartum necrosis of the pituitary due to hemorrhage, spontaneous necrosis of the pituitary, congenital absence of the pituitary, empty sella, or inflammatory or infiltrative disorders (see Table I). However, the most common cause of amenorrhea associated with the pituitary are those disorders associated with increased prolactin secretion. These women present with amenorrhea plus galactorrhea associated with an increased prolactin level. In women with amenorrhea and elevated prolactin levels, imaging of the pituitary is required and a thyroid stimulating hormone level (TSH) is obtained as well. Hyperprolactinemia and galactorrhea may be associated with taking antidepressant drugs or with recent breastfeeding. The majority of women with hyperprolactinemia do not exhibit demonstrable pituitary tumors. Thus, it has often been questioned at what level of serum prolactin should head imaging begin. Some have suggested prolactin levels exceeding 50 μg/l. Women with prolactin levels greater than 50 μg/l have about a 20% chance of presenting with a pituitary tumor, whereas those who have 100 μg/l have a 50% risk, and those with over 200 μg/l have an approximately 90 to 100% chance of harboring a prolactin secreting tumor.

B. Ovarian Failure

Ovarian failure in women or gonadal failure in men is associated with increased gonadotropins and hence the term hypergonadotropic hypogonadism is often used. The development of amenorrhea and hypoestrogenism associated with elevated gonadotropins prior to the age of 40 defines ovarian failure. However, it should be pointed out that cessation of ovarian function due to loss of germ cells and follicles in the ovary can occur at any age, even *in utero*, such as in gonadal dysgenesis or ovarian agenesis. When ovarian failure occurs prior to puberty the presentation is that of a phenotypic female with primary amenorrhea and lack of secondary sexual development. When it occurs after pubertal development, the presentation is secondary amenorrhea with the primary complaint being hot flashes. As is true for disorders of chronic anovulation, ovarian failure can result from several causes (see Table I). These include gonadal agenesis or dysgenesis. Gonadal dysgenesis can be associated with normal or abnormal karyotypes. Women harboring Y chromosome material have an increased risk of gonadal tumors and the gonads should be removed. Rare causes of ovarian failure include 17α-hydroxylase deficiency, resistant ovary syndrome, autoimmune disorders associated with galactosemia, and iatrogenic causes due to chemotherapy or radiation therapy. The diagnosis of ovarian failure should be suspected in all cases of primary amenorrhea and sexual infantilism and in women with secondary amenorrhea who develop hot flashes and other signs of estrogen deficiency. As stated earlier, this is confirmed by documenting an increased FSH at the menopausal range (i.e., > 30–40 IU/liter).

C. Female Reproductive Tract Defects

Defects of the female reproductive tract can result in amenorrhea by obstruction or absence of endometrial tissue. Some of these may be developmental and some may be due to iatrogenic causes. Women with anatomical defects have normal ovaries, ovarian function, and develop secondary sexual characteristics. Ovulation can be proven by changes in the basal body temperature or by elevated serum progesterone levels in the luteal phase. These women also have a normal female 46,XX karyotype. The logical approach to the evaluation and classification of anatomic defects is to start from the lowest entry at the opening of the reproductive tract and move upward. Thus, anatomic causes include labial agglutination or labial fusion and imperforate hymen. If the obstruction is farther up into the vagina it is known as a transverse vaginal septum. Rarely a complete absence of the cervix may be suspected. Women with all these conditions often present with increasing abdominal pain which results in accumulation of blood behind the obstruction. In such instances the pain is cyclic and predictable in nature and associated with the onset of menstruation. If the diagnosis is delayed, endometriosis, adhesions, and infertility may result. Two additional disorders are not associated with obstruction and pain but result from lack of development of the uterus and vagina. These include Müllerian agenesis or dysgenesis associated with a 46,XX karyotype and testicular feminization or complete androgen resistance in which there is a testis and a 46,XY karyotype. However, this diagnosis is easily confirmed by the observation of the absence of pubic and axillary hair due to the androgen resistance. Individuals with testicular feminization should have their testes removed to prevent tumor development following completion of breast development which occurs at ages 12–14. In rare instances a woman may have both absence of the uterus and lack of female secondary sexual characteristics. In such individuals a karyotype should be obtained. Those individuals with a 46,XY karyotype have androgen deficiency most commonly due to 17α-hydroxylase, testicular regression, or gonadal dysgenesis. Those with the 46,XX karyotype will have Müllerian agenesis plus another disorder such as ovarian failure and/or hypogonadotropic hypogonadism.

In addition, reproductive tract defects may be due to iatrogenic causes such as scarring and stenosis of the cervix following dilatation and curettage, conization, laser, or loop electrosurgical excision procedure (LEEP) procedures to treat cervical dysplasia. Destruction of the endometrium following a vigorous curettage after postpartum hemorrhage or therapeutic abortion or subsequent to infection associated with a missed abortion results in scar tissue or uterine synechiae (Asherman's syndrome). The diagnosis of this defect is rare in the absence of a previous surgical procedure or pregnancy. The diagnosis of female reproductive tract defects is established by history and physical examination. The presence of a labial agglutination, fusion, imperforate hymen, and transverse vaginal septum are easily recognized. An ultrasound can be obtained to confirm the location of the blockage and presence or absence of the uterus. To evaluate and confirm diagnosis of Asherman's syndrome, a hysteroscopic procedure or occasionally hysterosalpingography may be indicated. Occasionally a laparoscopy may be required to confirm the final diagnosis of the reproductive tract anomaly.

II. CLINICAL EVALUATION OF AMENORRHEA

Evaluation of amenorrhea should begin with a thorough history and physical examination. If a woman presents with primary amenorrhea and absence of secondary sexual characteristics, this may suggest a primary gonadal problem or ovarian failure. In contrast, women who present with previous regular menstrual periods but develop amenorrhea following a dilatation and curettage for hemorrhage suggests the diagnosis of uterine adhesions. The evaluation of amenorrhea requires knowledge of the classification as described previously (Table I). A flow chart to aid in evaluating women with amenorrhea is presented in Fig. 1. This evaluation includes women with a female phenotype but excludes women with disorders of virilization or sexual ambiguity. The laboratory tests required include a pregnancy test, FSH, prolactin, and TSH. We find it helpful to evaluate the estrogen status

based on the progestin withdrawal test as discussed in the classification section. This is helpful prior to determining therapy for infertility as well. Evaluation of the estrogen status includes two parts: (1) the examination of the patient, looking for signs of previous estrogen secretion such as breast development and current estrogen secretion, which includes the presence of a well-rugated, moist vagina with abundant clear stretchable cervical mucus known as spinnbarkeit. The estrogen status can be confirmed by a progestin challenge using medroxyprogesterone acetate (5 to 10 mg one or twice daily for 5 days) or progesterone in oil (100 to 200 mg) administered intramuscularly, particularly when patient compliance is an issue. It should be pointed out that Depo-Provera should not be utilized since this in fact causes amenorrhea. The one exception to this overall evaluation is a women that is known on physical examination to have an absent uterus and in this case it is more prudent and cost effective to perform a few tests to confirm

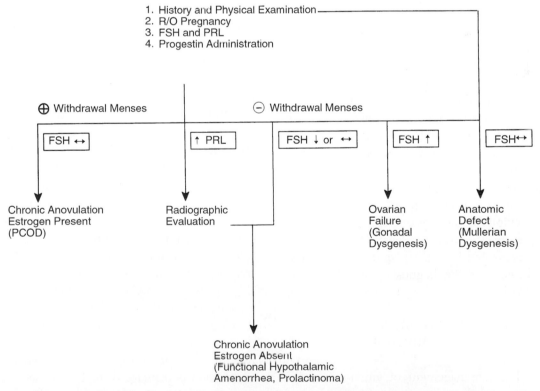

FIGURE 1 Suggested flow chart to aid in the evaluation of women with amenorrhea. Used with permission from Carr B. R. (1994). "Current Evaluation and Treatment of Amenorrhea: Guidelines for Practice," pp. 1–11. American Society for Reproductive Medicine, Birmingham, AL.

the diagnosis than to differentiate Müllerian agenesis from complete testicular feminization syndrome. Following the initial visit the patient returns and the physician evaluates the level of FSH, prolactin, and response to progestin challenge. If the FSH is elevated, the evaluation is directed to ovarian failure or hypergonadotropic hypogonadism. If the FSH, however, is low or normal, then the evaluation of the progestin challenge test is utilized to differentiate the two categories of chronic anovulation. Finally, if the serum prolactin is elevated, a TSH should be measured and the pituitary further evaluated by either an MR or CAT scan.

The majority of women with significant elevations of prolactin do not respond to a progestin challenge and thus are included in the category of chronic anovulation with estrogen absent. Such women should experience withdrawal bleeding following a cycle of estrogen plus progestin but this test and results are somewhat confusing since a high percentage of women would not bleed after one cycle of therapy. Evaluation of the outflow tract or reproductive tract is made on physical examination and if needed by hysterosalpingography, ultrasound, or hysteroscopy. During the physical examination if the patient exhibits a vagina, a patent cervix, which can be confirmed by uterine sounding, as well as a uterus without a history of pregnancy or operative procedure, a disorder of the female reproductive tract is unlikely. After disorders of the reproductive tract are ruled out, a normal or low FSH indicates a disorder of the hypothalamus or pituitary. Most of these women have functional disorders of the hypothalamus, although lesions of the hypothalamus and pituitary may be present. The use of an MR or CAT scan, as discussed previously, depends on the history, clinical presentation, and the prolactin level. Overall the algorithm as presented in Fig. 1 is quite useful in the majority of cases and the diagnosis is simplified and easily obtained.

III. MANAGEMENT OF AMENORRHEA

In general the management of amenorrhea depends on the cause but also on the current desires of the patient.

A. Chronic Anovulation

The treatment of women with chronic anovulation can be subdivided to match the classification of those who are making estrogen and those who are not. In women who are producing estrogen but are not ovulating, the treatment depends on the desires of the patient. If the patient is obese, weight loss should be encouraged and this may in fact improve the overall clinical situation, including insulin resistance, if present, and hypercholesterolemia. If the woman is not hirsute and does not desire pregnancy, monthly withdrawal menses should be induced by either progesterone therapy or, more simply, with oral contraceptive pills, which reduces the risk of hemorrhage, i.e., dysfunctional uterine bleeding and endometrial neoplasia. On the other hand, if the woman is hirsute but does not desire pregnancy excess male hormone production can be suppressed through oral contraceptive pills and/or antiandrogens. Oral contraceptives pills are also indicated if there are disorders in menstruation, i.e., dysfunctional uterine bleeding. Finally, if pregnancy is desired, then ovulation can be induced with either clomiphene citrate or gonadotropins or occasionally laparoscopic ovarian wedge resection.

In those women who are not making estrogen with chronic anovulation the treatment needs to be directed at eliminating the primary cause such as weight loss, exercise, or stress. Treatment in women with amenorrhea and low estrogen should be aggressive since delayed treatment can lead to reduced bone mass development and early osteoporosis. In women with elevated prolactin levels but in the absence of prolactin secreting tumors, cyclic estrogen–progestin therapy or, more commonly, oral contraceptive pills can be prescribed. Oral contraceptive pills and HRT therapy not only prevent bone loss but also maintain secondary sexual characteristics. If pregnancy is desired it is important that body weight and nutritional requirements for the potential developing fetus be returned to normal prior to induction of ovulation. But if the amenorrhea persists, in spite of reduction in stress and increase in body weight and percentage of body fat, then gonadotropins or pulsatile GnRH therapy is often successful in inducing ovulation and pregnancy. In those women who present with pituitary tumors that secrete prolactin, the treatment of choice is pharmacological, utilizing dopamine agonists such as bromocriptine.

B. Ovarian Failure

Most cases of gonadal or ovarian failure are permanent and patients should be started on hormone replacement therapy, particularly estrogen, as soon as possible. Again, estrogen maintains secondary characteristics and prevents premature osteoporosis and coronary heart disease. If the diagnosis of gonadal failure is made in a woman prior to breast development such as in Turner's syndrome, a regimen of low-dose estrogen gradually increased over a period of time may be important in producing normal breast development. Growth hormone may also be used prior to estrogen therapy in achieving greater height if indicated. In women with gonadal dysgenesis, as mentioned, estrogen treatment begins with low-dose, i.e., conjugated, estrogens (0.3 mg) for 3 to 6 months, slowly increasing the dosage from 0.625 to 1.25 mg over a year to augment breast development. It is necessary to initiate progestin therapy after approximately 1 year of estrogen therapy to induce withdrawal bleeding to prevent endometrial hyperplasia. However, if progestin is started prior to the initiation of breast development, then breast development may be abnormal. Women with disorders such as 17α-hydroxylase deficiency should be treated with glucocorticoids as well as with hormone therapy. Women with autoimmune ovarian failure have been treated with a variety of medicines but none appear to be successful, so hormone replacement therapy appears appropriate. Occasionally repositioning of the ovary or oophoropexy may be helpful prior to women receiving radiation therapy. In addition, it has been hypothesized but not proven that pretreatment with LHRH analogs or oral contraceptive pills prior to chemotherapy may be successful in maintaining ovarian function.

Women with amenorrhea due to ovarian failure are rarely able to conceive on their own. In some cases, ovarian follicular depletion may not be complete and spontaneous ovulation and a rare pregnancy may occur. The current treatment for infertility due to ovarian failure is to utilize donor oocytes obtained from normal ovulatory women that are retrieved followed by *in vitro* fertilization in which the sperm of the patient's husband is used to fertilize the donor eggs. The fertilized embryo is then transferred to the patient, who has been appropriately treated with exogenous estrogen and progesterone synchronized to mimic the normal ovulatory cycle.

C. Female Reproductive Tract Disorders

The primary treatment of outflow tract disorders is surgical, i.e., the incision of labial fusion, imperforate hymen, and vaginal septum, which leads to the return of regular menstrual periods and fertility. With respect to specific disorders, chronic labial adhesions in children can be treated with intermittent estrogen cream; however, a functional vagina in women with Müllerian agenesis or testicular feminization is more difficult to achieve. First, an attempt at nonsurgical dilation of a blind-ending vaginal pouch or perineal dimple is indicated. If this fails a reconstruction of the vagina utilizing skin grafts is performed. Disorders of cervical obstruction can be treated by dilation of the cervix and pregnancy can be achieved by intrauterine insemination. If the cervix is absent, however, the treatment usually requires a hysterectomy since retained blood behind the obstruction can cause significant pain and infection. Uterine scarring or Asherman's syndrome is best treated by direct hysteroscopic resection of the adhesions.

See Also the Following Articles

Eating Disorders; Estrogen; Menopause and Stress; Premenstrual Syndrome (PMS)

Bibliography

Abraham, S. F., Beumont, P. J. V., Fraser, I. S. *et al.* (1982). Body weight, exercise and menstrual status among ballet dancers in training. *Br. J. Obstet. Gynaecol* **89**, 607.

Blackwell, R. E., Boot, L. R., Goldenberg, R. L., and Younger, J. B. (1979). Assessment of pituitary function in patients with serum prolactin levels greater than 100 ng/mL. *Fertil. Steril.* **32**, 177–182.

Carr, B. R. (1994). "Current Evaluation and Treatment of

Amenorrhea: Guidelines for Practice", pp. 1–11. The American Society for Reproductive Medicine, Birmingham, AL.

Rock, J. A., Zacur, H. A., Dlugi, A. M. *et al.* (1982). Pregnancy success following corrections of imperforate hymen and complete transverse vaginal septum. *Obstet. Gynecol.* 59, 448.

Shangold, M. M., and Levine, H. S. (1982). The effect of marathon training upon menstrual function. *Am. J. Obstet. Gynecol.* 143, 862.

Speroff, L., Glass, R. H., and Kase, N. G. (1994). "Clinical Gynecologic Endocrinology and Infertility", 5th ed., pp. 401–483. Williams & Wilkins, Baltimore, MD.

Stein, I. F., and Leventhal, M. L. (1935). Amenorrhea associated with bilateral polycystic ovaries. *Am. J. Obstet. Gynecol.* 29, 181.

Turner, H. H. (1938). A syndrome of infantilism, congenital webbed neck, and cubitus valgus. *Endocrinology* 23, 66.

Warren, M. P., and Vande Wiele, R. L. (1973). Clinical and metabolic features of anorexia nervosa. *J. Obstet. Gynecol.* 117, 435.

Amnesia

Jon S. Simons and Kim S. Graham

MRC Cognition and Brain Sciences Unit, Cambridge, United Kingdom

GLOSSARY

episodic memory Store of personally experienced events from the past, including details not only of the content of the episode but also of its context—when and where it occurred.

hippocampal complex Structures located in the medial temporal lobe of the human brain (e.g., the hippocampus, subiculum, parahippocampal gyrus, and entorhinal cortex); implicated in the learning and temporary storage of recent memories.

semantic memory Our general knowledge about the world, such as information about words and their meanings, facts, concepts, objects, and people; typically retrieved without recollection of where and when the information was initially acquired.

temporal lobe/neocortex The area of the brain considered the permanent store of our episodic and semantic memories.

T he term *amnesia* refers to a partial or total loss of memory and can be due to organic brain damage and/or some forms of psychological stress. The loss of memory can affect events or experiences occurring either subsequent to the onset of the disorder (anterograde amnesia) or those that took place prior to its appearance (retrograde amnesia). Furthermore, while amnesia most often occurs for personal autobiographical events (episodic memory), some patients also show a loss of semantic memory, our factual knowledge about the world.

I. ORGANIC AMNESIA

The most well-studied case of organic amnesia in the literature is that of HM, who became amnesic in his mid-20s after an operation to relieve symptoms of severe epilepsy. The operation on HM involved surgery to the hippocampal complex and parts of the temporal lobe in both brain hemispheres. Although HM's epilepsy improved following surgery, he became profoundly amnesic, unable to remember events just after they had happened (anterograde amnesia) or those that had occurred up to a few years prior to his operation (retrograde amnesia). There are now over 50 reported patients who, like

HM, have exhibited an impairment to new learning after damage to the hippocampal complex. It is thought, therefore, that this region in the human brain is critically involved in the acquisition of new episodic and semantic memories.

As well as being unable to remember events from moment to moment, HM's memory impairment extended back in time for a number of years prior to his surgery. This pattern of memory loss, in which memories from the distant past (e.g., childhood, early adulthood, etc.) are remembered better than more recently experienced events (e.g., from the day, week, or year before), is a phenomenon that has fascinated memory researchers for over 100 years. The fact that memory loss can be so dramatically affected by the age of the memory suggests that the system that is critical for the acquisition of human memories, the hippocampal complex, is not necessarily involved in the permanent storage of all our episodic and semantic memories. It has been suggested that other areas of the brain, such as the temporal lobes, are the location for our enduring stores of human memory. Support for this hypothesis comes from patients who show the opposite pattern of memory impairment to HM and other patients with damage to the hippocampal complex: better recall of recent memories compared to those from childhood, early adulthood, and so on. Crucially, these patients typically present with selective damage to the temporal neocortex with sparing of structures in the medial temporal lobe. Current theories of human memory propose, therefore, that the hippocampal complex and the temporal neocortex play distinct, but complementary, roles in the acquisition and storage of human memory.

II. STRESS-RELATED AND TRANSIENT AMNESIC STATES

Compared to instances of organic amnesia, patients with stress-related impairments to memory are rare. One of the main types of nonorganic memory loss is called psychogenic or dissociative amnesia. The memory impairment is characterized by a loss of one's identity and of personal autobiographical memories from the past (retrograde amnesia). It is commonly transient in nature and patients often show a full recovery after the appropriate treatment or therapy. The cause and nature of the amnesia varies from case to case, but in many circumstances the memory loss can be linked to a precipitating stressor in the person's life (e.g., financial and health worries, accidents, violence, natural disasters, etc.). For example, studies of soldiers following World War II suggested that up to 5% had no memory of the traumatic combat events they had just experienced.

Although one of the diagnostic criteria for psychogenic amnesia is that there is no evidence of structural brain damage, the increasing use of sophisticated neuroimaging techniques that measure levels of blood flow in the brain suggests that there can be altered brain function in some cases, although the reasons for this are currently unclear. For example, it has been shown that a patient with a persistent psychogenic amnesia for the whole of his past life processed his autobiographical memories in the same way that control subjects processed nonpersonal memories. This study suggests that some patients with psychogenic amnesia may treat previously personally salient episodic memories in a neutral, "semantic" way as if they no longer belong to them in order to escape the emotional associations of the traumatic episode(s) that triggered the amnesia.

The important link between stress and memory can be further revealed in a syndrome called Transient Global Amnesia (TGA). Although not termed a psychogenic amnesia (patients are rarely confused about their own identity), the disorder is characterized by abrupt confusion and a complete anterograde amnesia, which eventually shrinks after some hours (typically 4–6). While there are known risk factors for TGA, such as a history of epilepsy or migraine, in as many as 30% of cases attacks can be directly linked to precipitating stresses, such as strenuous exertion, pain, immersion in water, and emotional events. Recent neuroimaging studies have revealed physiological changes (low blood flow) in the hippocampal complex during an attack. Extreme stress may result in memory impairment because the hippocampal complex is part of a complicated network in the human brain that mediates fear-related behavior and stress responses as well as aspects of memory function. Highly stressful situations may overstimulate the hippocampus and related structures leading to decreased blood flow in this region of the brain and subsequent memory loss.

See Also the Following Articles

DISSOCIATION; MEMORY AND STRESS; MEMORY IMPAIRMENT

Bibliography

Baddeley, A. D., Wilson, B. A., and Watts, F. N. (1995). "Handbook of Memory Disorders." Wiley, New York.

Cohen, N. J., and Eichenbaum, H. B. (1993). "Memory, Amnesia, and the Hippocampal System." MIT Press, Cambridge, MA.

Parkin, A. J. (1998). "Case Studies in the Neuropsychology of Memory." Psychology Press, Hove, East Sussex, UK.

Squire, L. R. (1987). "Memory and Brain." Oxford Univ. Press, Oxford, UK.

Amygdala

Michael S. Fanselow and Greg D. Gale

University of California, Los Angeles

I. Introduction
II. Multiple Sources of Input: Afferents to Amygdala
III. Variegated Outputs: Efferents from Amygdala
IV. Conclusions and Functions

GLOSSARY

long-term potentiation (LTP) A relatively long-lasting form of synaptic plasticity that has been proposed as a mechanism that mediates some forms of learning and memory

Pavlovian fear conditioning A training procedure in which an aversive event is paired with neutral stimuli, resulting in a variety of behavioral and autonomic conditioned responses. Typically used to assess learning and memory in animals.

I. INTRODUCTION

The amygdala, an almond-shaped cluster of interconnected nuclei in the medial temporal lobe, may be the neural structure most intimately tied to emotion. It has long been known that damage to the amygdala produces a profound disturbance in emotional behavior. The linkage is particularly compelling in the case of negative emotions such as fear. In both human and nonhuman animals, fear-related behavior, which is typically analyzed with Pavlovian fear conditioning, depends on the amygdala. Humans with bilateral amygdala damage have difficulty recognizing negative emotions in the facial expressions of others and as a result may make inappropriate social advances. Rats with lesions of the amygdala lose their fear of cats. Additionally, the ability for emotion to influence declarative memory storage may be mediated by the amygdala. The amygdala is well situated for a role in stress and emotion. Features of the environment, initially processed by several different brain regions, converge on the amygdala. Much of this information relates to external and internal stress. Plasticity within certain nuclei of the amygdala allows this structure to connect these stressors with environmental features that predict stress. The amygdala also has efferent projections to many of the structures that cope with stress. Therefore, it may act as a feedfoward device that generates behavior in anticipation of stress. We first review the major afferents to the amygdala that bring it this environmental information. Then we turn to the efferents that project to the brain regions that generate behavioral responses to stress. We conclude with a description of the processing that goes on within the amygdala that enables this feedforward regulation of stress.

II. MULTIPLE SOURCES OF INPUT: AFFERENTS TO AMYGDALA

A. Nucleus Tractus Solitarius

The nucleus tractus solitarius (NTS) projects to the amygdala's central nucleus (CcA), both directly and indirectly, via the parabrachial nucleus. A large body of evidence implicates the NTS in stress-related responses. It receives first-order projections from several cranial nerves including the vagus. These inputs primarily reflect the contribution of visceral sensory information but also convey general somatic input. In addition, ascending pain-related fibers originating from the spinal cord terminate in the NTS. Thus, the NTS can provide the amygdala with visceral sensory, somatosensory, and pain-related information.

B. Thalamus

The amygdala receives a wide range of sensory information via monosynaptic projections from the thalamus. Considerable functional importance has been attributed to projections from the posterior thalamus to the amygdala. Those arising from the medial geniculate provide the lateral nucleus with auditory information. Pain information represented in the posterior intralaminar nucleus of the thalamus also projects to several amygdaloid nuclei. Stimulation of these posterior thalamic projections to the lateral nucleus can support Pavlovian fear conditioning to an auditory cue. Parts of the ventroposterior medial thalamic nucleus that primarily receives visceral and gustatory information projects to the amygdala. These projections may support the amygdala's role in avoidance of novel flavors. In summary, the thalamus is a significant and direct source of information about the internal and external milieu for the amygdala.

C. Periaqueductal Gray

The midbrain periaqueductal gray (PAG) is a key structure for integrated defensive behavior. While much of the emphasis has been on descending projections from the amygdala to PAG (see later) these projections are largely reciprocal. There are strong projections from PAG to amygdala, particularly the central nucleus. In certain situations lesions of the dorsolateral PAG will enhance conditioned fear responses that depend on the amygdala. This has led to the suggestion that the ascending projections from the dorsolateral PAG may exert an inhibitory influence on the amygdala.

D. Cortex

There is a massive exchange of information between the amygdala and cortex. Along with the sensory projections from the thalamus, the amygdala receives both modality-specific and multimodal neocortical projections. Unimodal projections coding aspects of visual, auditory, and somatosensory information project primarily to the amygdala lateral nucleus and the basolateral nucleus (BLA). Importantly these projections tend not to originate from primary sensory cortex. Rather, unimodal sensory information originates from secondary sensory regions. For example, auditory projections arise from Te2 and Te3 and visual information arrives through perirhinal cortex. The insular cortex, which receives monosynaptic projections from primary somatosensory cortex, sends substantial projections to both the basolateral and lateral nuclei. It has been suggested that these projections provide the amygdala with nociceptive information that can support fear conditioning. Thus, in terms of cortical information, the amygdala predominately receives highly processed sensory representations that likely play important roles in the coordination of appropriate behavioral responses.

The hippocampal formation projects to the amygdala via sparse projections from the entorhinal cortex, CA1, and subiculum. Fibers from the entorhinal cortex and subiculum pass through the ventral angular bundle and electrical stimulation of this tract results in a monosynaptic response in the BLA. These projections seem to play an important role in providing contextual or place information for amygdala-dependent behaviors as lesions of this tract produce deficits in contextual fear conditioning. At least as far as simple emotion-related behaviors, the thalamoamygdala and corticoamygdala circuits appear to have some redundant function and act compensatorially because damage in both pathways appears necessary to eliminate amygdala-dependent behaviors. It is possible that the cortical pathways may allow amygdala-dependent stress responses to be more finely contoured to the specifics of environmental stimulation, but such an analysis has not been performed.

E. Summary

The amygdala receives information from a wide range of sources and a diverse array of neural pathways. Most of this sensory information has been highly processed before it arrives at the amygdala. This suggests that the amygdala may provide an information-integrating function in the regulation of stress.

III. VARIEGATED OUTPUTS: EFFERENTS FROM AMYGDALA

In addition to providing reciprocal projections to many of the sensory regions from which it recieves input, the amygdala also sends efferent projections to regions responsible for behavioral, autonomic, and endocrine responses to stress. This anatomical relationship allows amygdala activty to influence the unconditional response to stress and also provides substrates by which stimuli predictive of impending stressors can produce anticipatory behavioral adjustments.

A. Hypothalamus

Physical stressors produce a variety of neuroendocrine responses including increases in plasma adrenocorticotropin (ACTH), corticosterone, norepinephrine, and epinephrine. Control of these responses are mediated in part by a direct action of the hypothalamic paraventricular nucleus (PVN) on pituitary secretion. The PVN has been shown to re-

ceive direct projections from the central nucleus, providing a pathway by which amygdala activity can contribute to endocrine stress responses. A variety of studies have demonstrated a role for the amygdala in the expression of neuroendocrine responses to stress. Lesions of the amygdala attenuate the elevation of plasma epinephrine, norepinephrine, and corticosterone normally observed following footshock and similarly attenuate the elevation of plasma ACTH produced by immobilization stress but do not completely block these responses. Additionally, electrical stimulation of the amygdala alters corticosterone levels. These findings imply an amygdala contribution to the expression of neuroendocrine responses. However, given that amygdala lesions do not completely block or alter baseline hormone levels it is possible that the amygdala-lesion-induced attenuation of hormone responses reflects disruption of feedforward amygdala-dependent conditional responses rather than an amygdala control of unconditional endocrine responses.

Lesions of both the central nucleus of the amygdala and the lateral hypothalamus block the increase in arterial blood pressure caused by a conditional fear stimulus, leading to the suggestion that projections from the amygdala to the lateral hypothalamus mediate this response. Importantly, the hypertension to the shock unconditional response remains intact following hypothalamic lesions. Thus the lateral hypothalamus seems to mediate conditional but not unconditional sympathetic autonomic arousal to fear stimuli.

B. Periaqueductal Gray

The central nucleus of the amygdala projects heavily to the caudal half of the midbrain periaqueductal gray. These projections initially innervate more dorsal regions of the PAG, areas that serve active or circastrike defensive behaviors and autonomic arousal. Stimulation of the medial and central amygdala inhibits the behaviors that are generated by stimulation of these dorsal regions of the PAG.

As one moves caudally in the PAG, the central nucleus projections gradually rotate to innervate the ventral portions of PAG. These ventral PAG areas are essential for conditional fear-related defenses such as freezing. This area is also critical for the opioid analgesia that accompanies fear. Consistent with this pattern, cells in the caudal ventral PAG express fos following fear conditioning. However, this part of the PAG is not critical for the autonomic responses to conditional fear stimuli. The amygdala, predominantly through projections emanating from the central nucleus, exerts control over species-specific defensive behaviors organized by the periaqueductal gray.

C. Brain Stem

The central nucleus amygdala sends projections throughout the brain stem. One function of these projections is to provide control over autonomic function. For example, stimulation of the rabbit's central nucleus causes a heart rate deceleration mediated by monosynaptic projections to the dorsal motor nucleus of the vagus. This response mimics the bradycardia rabbits show to conditional fear stimuli that also depends on the central nucleus. While amygdala lesions block the bradycardiac conditioned response to the stimulus paired with electric shock, it is important to note that these lesions do not affect baseline heart rate or the unconditional heart rate response to the conditional stimulus in rabbits. Thus projections from the central nucleus of the amygdala to brain stem autonomic nuclei may mediate parasympathetically controlled conditional responses.

Amygdala stimulation enhances reflexes organized in the brain stem such as eyeblink and startle. There are monosynaptic projections from the central nucleus to the nucleus reticularis pontis caudalis, which is the part of the brain stem acoustic startle circuit that is modulated by conditional fear stimuli. Although lesions of the amygdala block the ability for fear stimuli to modulate these reflexes, it is important to note that the reflex itself is left intact.

Thus, projections from the amygdala's central nucleus to several brain stem regions allow for widespread modulation of autonomic function and reflexive behaviors.

D. Cortex

In addition to receiving substantial cortical projections recent work suggests that the amygdala is in a position to exert widespread influence over cortical

activity. The CeA sends substantial ascending projections to the cholinergic basal forebrain, which in turn projects diffusely to virtually all cortical regions. Basal forebrain stimulation has been shown to reliably produce desynchronization of cortical EEG as does CeA stimulation. Recently it has been shown that basal forebrain stimulation can support associative changes in receptive field properties of auditory cortical neurons. Based on these findings it has been suggested that cholinergic modulation of cortical activity, mediated by amygdala projections to the basal forebrain, is critical for the induction of the stimulus-specific changes in cortical receptive fields observed during Pavlovian fear conditioning. In addition to modulating cortical dynamics, the amygdala also exerts a strong influence over hippocampal activity. Lesions of the BLA attenuate the induction of LTP in the dentate gyrus while BLA stimulation significantly facilitates LTP induction. Thus, the amygdala plays a critical role in the induction of cortical- and hippocampal-dependent processes thought to underlie learning and memory.

To summarize, the central nucleus, which receives input from most of the amygdalar nuclei, projects to regions responsible for autonomic, hormonal, and behavioral responses. The amygdala is in a position to muster the full arsenal of the body's responses to stress.

IV. CONCLUSIONS AND FUNCTIONS

The amygdala receives a plethora of sensory input from both the environment and the body. Much of this input relates to stressful and threatening events. However, the amygdala also receives both simple and highly processed sensory information that can serve a signaling function. This suggests that the amygdala may integrate these sources of information. An early suggestion was that the amygdala recognizes signals for events with emotional significance. This is perhaps most clear in fear conditioning where cues that predict an event come to produce a number of fear related responses. These behaviors are lost at least in rats, rabbits, and humans without an amygdala. There is long-term potentiation of amygdala responses to stimulation of its thalamic, hippocampal, and cortical afferents. Cells in the lateral nucleus receive both nociceptive somatosensory information and auditory information and exposure to fear conditioning itself can potentiate the responses of these cells. In this manner, stimuli that predict stress can come to activate the amygdala, even if they are not stressful in their own right. Thus, neural plasticity within the amygdala provides the ability for this structure to anticipate stress through learning processes such as Pavlovian conditioning. Consistent with such a view, the amygdala is essential for the acquisition of Pavlovian fear conditioning. In turn, the amygdala projects to most of the brain areas responsible for rapid coping with impending danger. The amygdala may also allow organisms to better cope with future stress by modulating cortical, hippocampal, and striatal circuits involved in declarative memory and motor learning. Through such anticipatory mechanisms the amygdala provides for the adaptive feedforward regulation of stress.

See Also the Following Articles

BRAIN AND BRAIN REGIONS; DEFENSIVE BEHAVIORS; EMOTIONS: STRUCTURE AND ADAPTIVE FUNCTION; FEAR

Bibliography

Aggleton, J. P. (1992). "The Amygdala: Neurobiological Aspects of Emotion, Memory, and Mental Dysfunction." Wiley–Liss, New York.

Bechara, A., Tranel, D., Damasio, H., and Adolphs, R. (1995). Double dissociation of conditioning and declarative knowledge relative to the amygdala and hippocampus in humans. *Science* 269, 1115–1118.

Cahill, L., and McGaugh, J. L. (1998). Mechanisms of emotional arousal and lasting declarative memory. *Trends Neurosci.* 21, 294–299.

Fanselow, M. S. (1994). Neural organization of the defensive behavior system responsible for fear. *Psychonom. Bull. Rev.* 1, 429–438.

Fanselow, M. S., and LeDoux, J. E. (1999). Why we think plasticity underlying Pavlovian fear conditioning occurs in the basolateral amygdala. *Neuron* 23(2), 229–232.

Fendt, M., and Fanselow, M. S. (1999). The neuroanatomical and neurochemical basis of conditioned fear. *Neurosci. Biobehav. Rev.* 23, 743–760.

Kapp, B. S., Frysinger, R. C., Gallagher, M., and Haselton, J. R. (1979). Amygdala central nucleus lesions: Effect on heart rate conditioning in the rabbit. *Physiol. Behav.* 23(6), 1109–1117.

LeDoux, J. E. (1996). "The Emotional Brain: The Mysterious Underpinnings of Emotional Life." Simon & Schuster, New York.

LeDoux, J. E., Iwata, J., Cicchetti, P., and Reis, D. J. (1988). Different projections of the central amygdaloid nucleus mediate autonomic and behavioral correlates of conditioned fear. *J. Neurosci.* 8(7), 2517–2529.

Maren, S., and Fanselow, M. S. (1995). Synaptic plasticity in the basolateral amygdala induced by hippocampal formation stimulation *in vivo*. *J. Neurosci.* 15(11), 7548–7564.

Maren, S., and Fanselow, M. S. (1996). The amygdala and fear conditioning: Has the nut been cracked? *Neuron* 16, 237–240.

Rizvi, T. A., Ennis M., Behbehani, M. M., and Shipley, M. T. (1991). Connections between the central nucleus of the amygdala and the midbrain periaqueductal gray: Topography and reciprocity. *J. Comp. Neurol.* 303(1), 121–131.

Roozendaal, B., Koolhaas, J. M., and Bohus, B. (1991). Attenuated cardiovascular, neuroendocrine, and behavioral responses after a single footshock in central amygdaloid lesioned male rats. *Physiol. Behav.* 50(4), 771–775.

Shi, C. J., and Davis, M. (1999). Pain pathways involved in fear conditioning measured with fear-potentiated startle: lesion studies. *J. Neurosci.* 19(1), 420–430.

Androgen Action

Robert J. Handa
Colorado State University

Richard H. Price, Jr.
Loyola University, Chicago

GLOSSARY

concentration gradient A region consisting of a high concentration of a compound adjacent to an area of low concentration of that same compound.

coregulatory protein A protein which interacts with a transcription factor and the transcriptional machinery. Coregulatory proteins have a profound effect on transcription rate, either increasing (coactivator) or decreasing (corepressor) it.

diurnal rhythm A biological rhythm based on the 24-h day.

glucocorticoid A form of steroid hormone which is produced primarily by the adrenal glands and is released following stress.

lipophilic Affinity for fatty substances.

luteinizing hormone (LH) A peptide hormone which is released from the pituitary gland and promotes testosterone synthesis from within the testes.

promoter The regulatory region of a gene. Often promoters are upstream of the protein-encoding regions of a gene.

RNA polymerase holoenzyme The complex of proteins which are directly involved in transcribing a gene.

steroid hormones A class of hormones which are derived from cholesterol.

transcriptional Pertaining to the process of synthesizing RNA from a DNA template.

transcription initiation site The region of a gene to which the RNA polymerase holoenzyme binds to begin transcription.

I. ANDROGENS

Androgens are a class of steroid hormones that circulate at high levels in males. Androgens are also produced in females though at much lower levels. The predominant mode of androgen action is by binding in target tissues to a specific receptor termed the androgen receptor (AR). This receptor can regulate the expression of a set of androgen-responsive genes. The synthesis, transport, and release of androgens to the bloodstream and their actions on target tissues are addressed in this article.

A. Major Forms of Androgens

The term "androgen" is derived from the Greek roots *andro* (man) and *gennan* (to produce). The biological definition of an androgen is any substance which specifically promotes the growth of the male gonads. There are four major forms of circulating androgens. Testosterone (T) is the predominant form in males and is analagous to estrogen in females. Other common forms of androgens are dihydrotestosterone (DHT), androstenedione, dehydroepiandrosterone (DHEA), and its sulfonylated derivative, DHEAS. The most potent androgens are T and DHT, while DHEA/S and androstenedione are weak androgens. Both males and females produce all forms of androgens, though in differing amounts. The majority of androgens produced by males is T, which circulates at 10-fold higher levels than DHT. In females, the predominant forms of circulating androgens are DHEA/S followed by androstenedione and finally T. Overall, androgen levels are roughly 10-fold higher in males than in females. Androgen levels do, however, undergo a moderate daily variation in what is called a diurnal rhythm. In men, highest levels of testosterone are found in the bloodstream during the early morning hours, whereas low levels are found in the blood during the evening. In rodents, a nocturnal species, testosterone levels peak in the first few hours after nightfall. In women, cyclic variations in testosterone have been reported with peak levels occuring during the preovulatory phase of the menstrual cycle.

B. Origins

In males, testosterone is produced largely by Leydig cells in the testes. In females, T is produced by the interstitial and stromal thecal cells in the ovaries. In addition to the gonadally derived testosterone which circulates at high levels in males, a small proportion is synthesized in target tissues from the testosterone precursors androstenedione and DHEA/S, which circulate at low levels in males and only act very weakly on their own. Dihydrotestosterone is synthesized to a limited extent in the gonads; the majority is locally converted from T in many androgen target tissues. Androstenedione and DHEA/S are largely produced by the adrenal cortex. Recent studies have also demonstrated that the brain has the appropriate enzymes to produce androgens *de novo*. The extent to which this synthesis affects physiology remains to be determined. Androgen synthesis and metabolism can occur anywhere the enzymes which catalyze such reactions are present. Though the primary tissues of origin are presented above, precursors and metabolites are produced in many tissues.

C. Synthesis Pathways

The biosynthetic pathway which produces endogenous androgens is common to many steroid hormones and begins with the conversion of cholesterol to pregnenolone in the mitochondria of steroid-synthesizing cells. Cholesterol is composed of 27 carbon atoms, including a 17-carbon sterol backbone with an 8-carbon side chain. The major androgens including testosterone have no side chain and are composed of only 19 carbon atoms.

The enzymes which catalyze the steroid synthesis pathway belong to a family of iron-coordinating proteins called cytochrome P450 enzymes. The steps in the testosterone synthesis pathway are briefly described here and are detailed in Fig. 1. Regulation of testosterone synthesis begins at the level of cholesterol transport from cellular storage sites to the inner mitochondrial membrane by the steroidogenic acute regulatory protein. Once in the mitochondrion, the P450 side-chain cleavage enzyme (P450scc or CYP11A) catalyzes the oxidation and removal of the six carbon atoms which comprise the majority of the side chain on cholesterol. The product, pregnenolone, then diffuses passively out of mitonchondria to the smooth endoplasmic reticulum. Here the actions of the P450c17 (CYP17) enzyme further shorten the side chain, removing all carbons, leaving only a ketone at the C17 position. The final two steps in testosterone biosynthesis are catalyzed by dehydrogenases, which have specificity for the C3- and C17-bound oxygens, respectively. The dehydrogenase which converts the C3 ketone to a hydroxyl group also isomerises the C5 double bond to a C4 double bond.

D. Metabolites of Testosterone

In target tissues, testosterone can be converted by further enzyme catalysis. Aromatase can convert testosterone to estrogen by oxidoreduction of the C3 ketone and removal of the C10 methyl group, which allows aromatization of the A-ring in the sterol backbone. This leads to a product which has very different effects than the parent compound. Testosterone can also be converted by the enzyme 5-α reductase to DHT, which is a more potent androgen than testosterone. The primary site of DHT formation is in peripheral target tissues such as the prostate, liver, and skin. The local metabolism of testosterone to DHT allows the androgenic signal to be amplified in a tissue-specific manner. Androgens are also metabolized to 17-ketosteroids in the liver for urinary excretion.

E. Secretion and Transport

Steroid hormones are lipophilic and thus can easily pass through cell membranes. For this reason, they are secreted along a concentration gradient from synthetic cells to the circulating plasma and do not need to be secreted by a vesicular membrane fusion pathway. Consequently, circulating levels of androgens accurately reflect rates of synthesis. There are, however, circulating plasma-binding proteins known as the steroid hormone-binding globulins (SHBG) which bind to testosterone and related

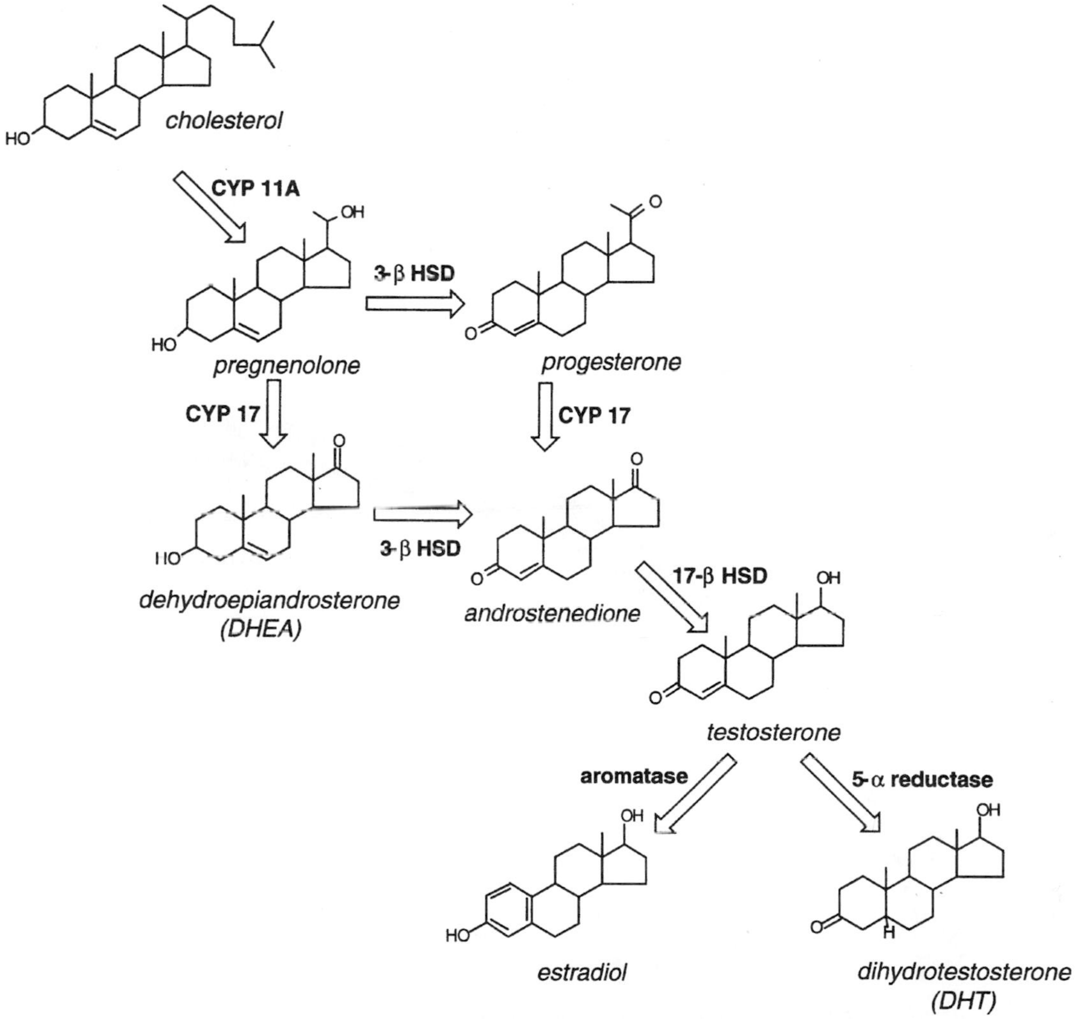

FIGURE 1 Schematic diagram showing the biosynthetic pathway of androgens from cholesterol. Enzymes responsible for catalysis are shown in bold. The names of steroid molecules are designated in italics.

compounds and transport them throughout the organism. Nonspecific interactions with other plasma proteins such as serum albumin also occur. The SHBGs can protect the steroids from degradative enzymes which shorten their half-life and can prevent renal excretion. Once at a target tissue, steroid hormones are able to easily enter cells by diffusing across the plasma membrane. Once in the cell, steroid hormones are bound by intracellular receptors. In the case of androgens such as T and DHT, the specific receptor has been termed the androgen receptor.

II. THE ANDROGEN RECEPTOR

A. Molecular Organization

Androgen receptors are dynamic proteins which are members of a superfamily of nuclear receptor proteins. This superfamily has a common structure composed of functional domains, depicted schematically in Fig. 2A. The domains include a hormone-binding domain near the carboxyl terminus and a DNA-binding domain near the center of the linearized protein. The other domains include a hinge

A

ANDROGEN RECEPTOR

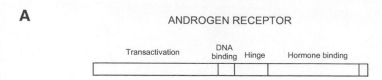

B

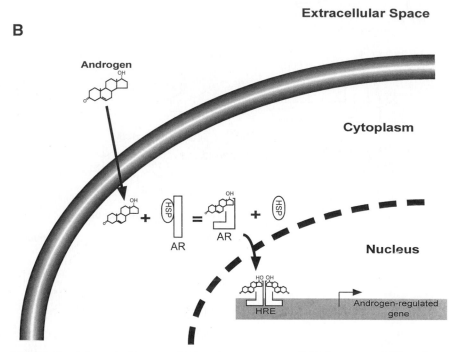

FIGURE 2 Schematic diagram of (A) androgen receptor (AR) domains and (B) pathway for activation of gene transcription. HRE, hormone response element; HSP, heat-shock protein. DNA is depicted as a gray bar in the nucleus; cell membrane is depicted as a broad bar separating the cytoplasm and extracellular space. Dashed line indicates the nuclear membrane.

region to facilitate conformational change and a transactivation domain, which is important for interaction of the steroid receptor with transcriptional machinery. In the absence of hormone, the androgen receptor is maintained in an inactive state by a complex of chaperone proteins called heat-shock proteins.

B. Function

As mentioned, the androgen receptor is a transcription factor and modulates gene expression in a hormone-dependent manner. The control of gene expression by androgen receptors is dependent also on factors such as the appropriate promoter context and the presence of coactivator proteins. The activation pathway of androgen receptors by hormone is depicted in Fig. 2B. When androgen binds to the hormone-binding domain of the androgen receptor, the heat-shock proteins are displaced and the receptor undergoes a conformational change. This change sequesters the ligand-binding domain with hormone attached into a hydrophobic pocket and reveals the DNA-binding domain, which has high affinity for certain DNA sequences called hormone response elements (HRE). Upon activation, other regions are revealed which allow dimerization with other hormone-bound androgen receptors. The activated dimers then are able to bind to the HRE, a palendromic sequence of nucleotides in DNA. These HREs are not present in the promoter region of all genes, only those that are androgen responsive. Examples of such genes are the cytokine interleukin-6 and the androgen receptor itself.

C. Coregulatory Proteins

Once the activated androgen receptor is bound to the HRE, for gene expression to occur it still must communicate on a molecular level with the RNA polymerase holoenzyme, which occupies the transcription initiation site. It is generally accepted that this contact is not direct, but occurs through coregulatory proteins which do not bind to DNA directly but act through protein–protein contacts.

III. PHYSIOLOGICAL ACTIONS OF ANDROGENS

The specific set of genes which is regulated by androgens leads to diverse physiological functions. In general, growth-associated processes are involved, such as those in prostate, hair, skin, muscle, and bone. Typical examples of androgen-dependent functions are those associated with puberty in males. Increasing levels of T during the mid-teen years lead to a deepening of the voice, growth of facial and axillary hair, activation of sebaceous glands, coarsening of the skin, and growth of long bones and muscle. Androgens also regulate spermatogenesis, a process which is initiated as testicular size increases during puberty. Spermatogenesis persists throughout the life of the male but begins to decline as circulating testosterone levels decline.

IV. ANDROGEN-ASSOCIATED PATHOLOGY

As noted above, androgens are involved in many anabolic processes. When these growth processes go awry in the testes or prostate, cancerous pathology can result. One of the most common treatments for prostate cancer is to block androgen receptor function with antagonist drugs.

Some of the developmental defects associated with malfunctioning androgen signaling have led to the discovery of specific androgen functions. The most common syndrome associated with a nonfunctional androgen receptor is called androgen insensitivity syndrome or *tfm* (testicular feminized male). This rare disorder in genetic males results in a phenotypically female individual with breast development, a lack of pubic hair, and formation of feminized genitalia. Another syndrome showing hermaphroditism is a defect in the 5-α reductase gene. Individuals with this defect cannot produce DHT and thus have ambiguous genitalia until puberty, when testosterone levels rise to partially compensate for the DHT deficiency.

V. INTERACTIONS BETWEEN STRESS AND ANDROGENS

Studies using animal models have shown that stress can affect circulating levels of testosterone, and testosterone can influence responses to stress. Observations of baboons in their natural habitat have shown that in response to a stressful stimulus, testosterone levels respond differently depending on the animal's rank in a dominance hierarchy. Dominant males show an increase in testosterone levels following stress while subordinate males' testosterone levels decrease. The reason for this differential response appears to be related to the animal's normal circulating level of glucocorticoids. The subordinate males are in a state of chronic stress based on an elevated basal level of circulating glucocorticoids. In contrast, dominant males have low basal levels of circulating glucocorticoids. In response to an acute stressor, both dominant and subordinate males show rapid increases in circulating glucocorticoid levels and decreases in LH secretion. However, dominant males appear to be less sensitive to the inhibitory effects of glucocorticoids on testosterone production. This differential response of testosterone levels to stressful stimuli promotes the reproductive fitness of the dominant males while reducing that of subordinate males.

VI. SUMMARY

The androgens are best known for their functions in reproduction and anabolic growth, though they have been shown to be important for other physiological functions such as regulating stress responses and neural development. Ongoing research is attempting to more precisely identify the role of androgens in cognitive functioning.

See Also the Following Articles

Aggressive Behavior; Cholesterol and Lipoproteins

Bibliography

Brown, T. R. (1995). Androgen receptor dysfunction in human androgen insensitivity. *Trends Endocrinol. Metab.* **6**, 170–175.

Hiipakka, R. A., and Liao, S. (1998). Molecular mechanism of androgen action. *Trends Endocrinol. Metab.* **9**, 317–324.

Lindzey, J., Kumar, M. V., Grossman, M., Young, C., and Tindall, D. J. (1994). Molecular mechanisms of androgen action. *Vitam. Horm.* **49**, 383–432.

Sapolsky, R. M. (1990). Stress in the wild. *Sci. Am.* **262**, 106–113.

Sapolsky, R. M. (1997). "The Trouble with Testosterone and Other Essays on the Biology of the Human Predicament." Scribner, New York.

Wilson, J. D. (1996). Role of dihydrotestosterone in androgen action. Prostate Suppl. **6**, 88–92.

Anger

Raymond W. Novaco

University of California, Irvine

I. Anger and Stress
II. Experience and Expression of Anger
III. Anger Physiology
IV. Cognition and Anger
V. Anger Dyscontrol and Regulation
VI. Anger Treatment

GLOSSARY

aggression Behavior intended to cause psychological or physical harm to someone or to a surrogate target. The behavior may be verbal or physical, direct or indirect.

anger A negatively toned emotion, subjectively experienced as an aroused state of antagonism toward someone or something perceived to be the source of an aversive event.

anger reactivity Responding to aversive, threatening, or other stressful stimuli with anger reactions characterized by automaticity of engagement, high intensity, and short latency.

cathartic effect The lowering of the probability of aggression as a function of the direct expression of aggression toward an anger instigator. The lowering of arousal associated with such catharsis is more or less immediate and can be reversed by reinstigation.

escalation of provocation Incremental increases in the probability of anger and aggression, occurring as reciprocally heightened antagonism in an interpersonal exchange.

excitation transfer The carryover of undissipated arousal, originating from some prior source, to a new situation having a new source of arousal, which then heightens the probability of aggression toward that new and more proximate source.

hostility An attitudinal disposition of antagonism toward another person or social system. It represents a predisposition to respond with aggression under conditions of perceived threat.

inhibition A restraining influence on anger expression. The restraint may be associated with either external or internal factors.

The relationship of anger to stress is at least threefold: (1) anger is an affective response to survival threats or otherwise stressful circumstances; (2) as a high-arousal state, it constitutes an internal stressor, causing wear and tear on the body when it is recurrently activated, and (3) it can be part of a personality style of coping with the stressors of daily life. Viewing anger in terms of stress, rather than simply as an emotional state, facilitates recognizing that contextual factors contribute to the activation of anger and discerning that chronicity in anger activation is likely to have significant costs to physical and psychological well-being. Stress and trauma have cumulative effects that predispose a person to experience anger. The human stress framework offers advantages for understanding the determinants, manifestations, and consequences of anger as well as the treatment of anger dyscontrol.

I. ANGER AND STRESS

Anger is a negatively toned emotion, subjectively experienced as an aroused state of antagonism toward someone or something perceived to be the source of an aversive event. It is triggered or provoked situationally by events that are perceived to constitute deliberate harm-doing by an instigator toward oneself or toward those to whom one is endeared. Provocations usually take the form of insults, unfair treatments, or intended thwartings. Anger is prototypically experienced as a justified response to some "wrong" that has been done. While anger is situationally triggered by acute, proximal occurrences, it is shaped and facilitated contextually by conditions affecting the cognitive, arousal, and behavioral systems that comprise anger reactions. Anger activation is centrally linked to threat perceptions and survival responding.

As a normal human emotion, anger has considerable adaptive value, although there are sociocultural variations in the acceptability of its expression and the form that such expression takes. In the face of adversity, it can mobilize psychological resources, energize behaviors for corrective action, and facilitate perseverance. Anger serves as a guardian to self-esteem, operates as a means of communicating negative

sentiment, potentiates the ability to redress grievances, and boosts determination to overcome obstacles to our happiness and aspirations. Akin to aggressive behavior, anger has functional value for survival.

Despite having multiple adaptive functions, anger also has maladaptive effects on personal and social well-being. Generally, strong physiological arousal impairs the processing of information and lessens cognitive control of behavior. Because heightened physiological arousal is a core component of anger, people are not cognitively proficient when they become angry. Also, because the activation of anger is accompanied by aggressive impulses, anger can motivate harm toward other people, which in turn can produce undesirable consequences for the angered person, either from direct retaliation, loss of supportive relationships, or social censure. An angry person is not optimally alert, thoughtful, empathic, prudent, or physically healthy. Being a turbulent emotion ubiqitous in everyday life, anger is now known to be substantially associated with cardiovascular disorders.

II. EXPERIENCE AND EXPRESSION OF ANGER

In parallel to these counterpoised functions of anger is the duality of psychosocial images associated with anger experience and anger expression. The emotional state is depicted as eruptive, destructive, unbridled, savage, venomous, burning, and consuming but also as energizing, empowering, justifying, signifying, rectifying, and relieving. The metaphors, on the one hand, connote something pressing for expression and utilization, and, alternatively, they imply something requiring containment and control. This duality in psychosocial imagery reflects conflicting intuitions about anger, its expression, and its consequences that abound in ordinary language and are reflected in both scholarly literature and artistic works from the classical period to contemporary times. This Janus-faced character of anger foils attempts to understand it and to therapeutically intervene with recurrently angry individuals.

The facial and skeletal musculature are strongly affected by anger. The face becomes flushed, and the brow muscles move inward and downward, fixing a hard stare on the target. The nostrils flare, and the jaw tends toward clenching. This is an innate pattern of facial expression that can be observed in toddlers. Tension in the skeletal musculature, including raising of the arms and adopting a squared-off stance, are preparatory actions for attack and defense. The muscle tension provides a sense of strength and self-assurance. An impulse to strike out accompanies this subjective feeling of potency.

When people report anger experiences, they most typically give accounts of things that have "happened to them." For the most part, they describe events physically and temporally proximate to their anger arousal. As a rule, they provide accounts of provocations ascribed to events in the immediate situation of the anger experience. This fosters the illusion that anger has a discrete external cause. The provocation sources are ordinarily identified as the aversive and deliberate behavior of others; thus, anger is portrayed in the telling as being something about which anger is quite fitting. People are very much inclined to attribute the causes of their anger to the personal, stable, and controllable aspects of another person's behavior.

However, the response to the question "What has made you angry?" hinges on self-observational proficiencies and is often based on intuitions. Precisely because getting angry involves a loss in self-monitoring capacity, people are neither good nor objective observers when they are angry. Inspecting any particular episode, the immediate "causes" of the anger are readily identifiable. Far less commonly do people disaggregate their anger experiences into multicausal origins, some of which may be prior, remote events and ambient circumstances rather than acute, proximal events. Anger experiences are embedded or nested within an environmental–temporal context. Disturbances that may not have involved anger at the outset leave residues that are not readily recognized but which operate as a lingering backdrop for focal provocations.

Anger is inherently a disposition to respond aggressively, but aggression is not an automatic consequence of anger because aggressive behavior is regulated by inhibitory control mechanisms, engaged by internal and external cues. In this regard, physical constraints, expectations of punishment or retaliation, empathy, consideration of consequences, and prosocial values operate as regulatory controls on aggression. While the experience of anger creates a readiness to respond with aggression, that disposition may be otherwise directed, suppressed, or reconstituted. Thus, the expression of anger is differentiated from its experience.

One aspect of anger that influences the probability of aggression is its degree of intensity. The higher the level of arousal, the stronger the motivation for aggression and the greater the likelihood that inhibitory controls will be overridden. Strong arousal not only impels action, it impairs cognitive processing of aggression-mitigating information. A person in a state of high anger arousal is perceptually biased toward the confirmation of threat, is less able to attend to threat-discounting elements of the situation, and is not so capable of reappraising provocation cues as benign. Because anger and aggression occur in a dynamic interactional context, the occurrence of aggression will, in turn, influence the level of anger. Thus, anger reactivity can be seen as a mode of responding characterized by automaticity, high intensity, and short latency.

Important forms of the dynamic interrelation of anger and aggression are the escalation of provocation and the "cathartic effect." Escalation involves increases away from equilibrium, whereby succeeding events intensify their own precursors. In the case of anger and aggression, escalation refers to incremental change in their respective probabilities, occurring as reciprocally heightened antagonism in an interpersonal exchange. Anger-elicited aggression may evoke further anger in response, progressively generating justification for retaliation. In contrast, when physical aggression is deployed by an angry person against the anger instigator and there is no retaliation, anger arousal and further aggression are diminished in that situation. This is called the "cathartic effect"—its conditions should not be confused (as they often are) with those involving aggression by nonangry people, vicarious or observed aggression, or aggression not received by the anger instigator. However, the arousal-reducing effect of aggression carried out by angry people against those who have made them angry is reinforcing of aggressive behavior. This means that when anger is reinstated by a new provocation, the likelihood of aggressive behavior is increased. The cathartic expression of anger, whether through destructive aggression or through verbal communication intended to be constructive, can be understood as an organismic action to restore equilibrium.

Alternative to the deliberate expression of anger is suppression, which is largely a product of inhibitory controls. Anger suppression can be functional in promoting interpersonal or social conciliation. For example, when there is a high probability of impending violence, it is prudent to restrain anger expression to diminish the likelihood of triggering a physical assault. Whether in a domestic, occupational, or street context, anger is adaptively muffled when physical retaliation can be expected or when a cool head is needed to solve a problem. In the short term, suppressing even the verbalization of anger may not only be beneficial interpersonally, it may also lead to more regulated physiological reactivity levels. However, recurrent deployment of anger suppression as a stress-coping style will most likely have deleterious effects on cardiovascular health.

III. ANGER PHYSIOLOGY

A defining condition of anger is physiological arousal, the activation of which has evolutionary roots. For our prehistoric ancestors, when a threat to survival or survival resources was detected, it was advantageous to be mobilized to response energetically and to sustain effort. The "fight-or-flight" response refers to this hardwired physiological mechanism that gets instantaneously triggered to engage survival behavior, to focus attention on the survival threat, and to enable the organism to not succumb to pain. Anger is the emotional complement of the organismic preparation for attack, which also entails the orchestration of signals of attack readiness so as to ward off opponents or to coerce compliance.

The arousal of anger is marked by physiological activation in the cardiovascular, endocrine, and limbic systems as well as other autonomic and central nervous system areas and by tension in the skeletal musculature. Autonomic arousal has been identified

as a concomitant of anger in an abundance of laboratory studies and self-report surveys. It is noteworthy that autonomic arousal, especially cardiovascular changes, have been commonly observed in conjunction with anger by scholars from the Classical age (especially Seneca, Aristotle, and Plutarch) to the early behavioral scientists of the 19th and 20th centuries (especially Charles Darwin, William James, G. Stanley Hall, and Walter B. Cannon). Laboratory research has reliably found anger arousal to entail increases in both systolic and diastolic blood pressure and, to a somewhat lesser extent, heart rate. Associated with this cardiovascular activation is facial flushing, which is often reported by people reflecting on their anger experience. Indeed, in terms of psychosocial imagery, there is no better metaphor for anger than hot fluid in a container.

Autonomic arousal is primarily engaged through adrenomedullary and adrenocortical hormonal activity. The secretion by the andrenal medulla of the catecholamines, epinephrine and norepinephrine, and by the andrenal cortex of glucocorticoids provides a sympathetic system effect that mobilizes the body for immediate action (e.g., the release of glucose, stored in the liver and muscles as glycogen). In anger, the catecholamine activation is more strongly norepinephrine than epinephrine (the reverse being the case for fear). The adrenocortical effects, which have longer duration than the adrenomedullary ones, are mediated by secretions of the pituitary gland, which also influences testosterone levels. The pituitary–adrenocortical and pituitary–gonadal systems are thought to affect readiness or potentiation for anger responding.

The central nervous system structure that has been identified in anger activation is the amygdala, the almond-shaped, limbic system component located deep in the temporal lobe. Activation in the corticomedial amygdala is associated with anger and attack priming. The central nervous system neurotransmitter serotonin, which is also present in blood platelets, affects anger potentiation, as low levels of this hormone are associated with irritable mood. Serotonin imbalances are related to deficits in the modulation of emotion.

These various physiological mechanisms thus pertain not only to the intensity of anger arousal but also its duration. Arousal activation eventually decays to baseline levels, but recovery time may be prolonged by exposure to new arousal sources or by rumination. The potency of a provocation may be heightened by the carryover of undissipated excitation from a prior arousal source, which may not have been anger specific (i.e., an otherwise stressful circumstance, such as exposure to bad news, work pressure, or traffic congestion). This "excitation transfer" of arousal residues facilitates anger, augments its intensity, amplifies blood pressure, and raises the probability of aggression. Residual arousal from unresolved anger events can transfer to future conflicts and further intensify anger reactivity to instigating events. In turn, unexpressed anger is associated with exaggerated and more prolonged cardiovascular responses to a variety of stressful stimuli.

In this regard, a stress framework is highly useful. It is unquestionably the case that physiological arousal is activated by exposure to commonly identified stressors, such as noise, crowding, difficult tasks, and high-pressure job environments filled with time demands or exposure to abrasive interactions. Both acute and prolonged exposure to such conditions may induce physiological activation that decays slowly. Therefore, when someone experiences an event that pulls for the cognitive label "anger" and this event occurs concurrent with already elevated arousal, the anger system is then more easily engaged.

IV. COGNITION AND ANGER

Neurophysiological evidence suggests that we have a neural architecture (especially the limbic system) specialized for the processing of emotion and emotion–cognition interactions. The activation of the amygdala, for example, is centrally involved in detecting events as threats. In parallel, higher level cognitive reasoning elaborates this information in what are termed appraisal processes. The perception of threat is conjoined with sympathetic nervous system activation of autonomic arousal components, such as heart rate, blood pressure, and respiration increases that prepare the body for emergency action.

In addition to potentiating action, anger in such states of mobilization has adaptive value as a source of information. To others, it communicates perceived wrongdoing, threat of aggression, or intent of reprisal. Such information exchange prior to aggression can facilitate social and interpersonal negotiations toward conflict resolution. For the self, it serves as information for prioritizing and decision making. The intensity of anger, for example, can help focus and maintain attention on relevant goals and help one estimate progress toward those goals. When pressed to make a decision, anger serves as a summary affective cue that can be processed without need for elaborate analysis.

However, to get angry about something one must pay attention to it. Anger is often the result of selective attention to cues having high provocation value. A principal function of cognitive systems is to guide behavior, and attention itself is guided by integrated cognitive structures, known as schemas, which incorporate rules about environment–behavior relationships. What receives attention is a product of the cognitive network that assigns meaning to events and the complex stimuli that configure them. Expectations guide attentional search for cues relevant to particular needs or goals. Once a repertoire of anger schemas has been developed, events (e.g., being asked a question by someone) and their characteristics (e.g., the *way* the question was asked, *when* it was asked, or *who* asked it) are encoded or interpreted as having meaning in accord with the preexisting schema. Because of their survival function, the threat-sensing aspect of anger schemas carries urgent priority and can preempt other information processing.

Since the writings of the Stoic philosophers of the classical period, anger has been understood to be strongly determined by personal interpretations of events. The concept of appraisal is that of interpretation, judgment, or meaning embedded in the perception of something—not as a cognitive event occurring after that something has happened. The appraisal of provocation is *in* the seeing or hearing. Appraisal, though, is an ongoing process, so various reappraisals of experience will occur and will correspondingly affect whether or not the probability of aggression is lessened, maintained, or intensified. Rumination about provoking circumstances will of course extend or revivify anger reactions. As well, the occurrence of certain thoughts can prime semantically related ideas that are part of an anger schema.

Perceived malevolence is one of the most common forms of anger-inducing appraisal. When another person's behavior is interpreted as intending to be harmful to oneself, anger and aggression schemas are activated. In turn, receiving information about mitigating circumstances (e.g., learning that the person was fatigued and working overtime) can defuse the appraisal of personal attack and promote a benign reappraisal. Perceiving malevolence pulls for anger by involving the important theme of justification, which includes the externalization of blame. When harm or injustice have been done, social norms of retaliation and retribution are engaged. Indeed, one view of anger is that it is a socially constituted syndrome or a transitory social role governed by social rules. Thus, its meaning and function would be determined by the social systems in which it occurs and of which it is an integral part.

Justification is a core theme with regard to the activation of anger and aggression, being rooted in ancient religious texts, such as the Bible and the Koran, as well as in classical mythologies about deities and historical accounts of the behavior of ancient rulers. Correspondingly, anger and physical aggression are often viewed as applying a legitimate punitive response for transgression or as ways of correcting injustice. Frequently, however, an embellished justification serves the exoneration of blame for destructive outcomes of expressed anger.

V. ANGER DYSCONTROL AND REGULATION

Anger is a highly functional human emotion, and it is one to be appreciated as a rich part of cultural life, but the survival value of the aggression-enabling function of anger is an archaic remnant with rare contemporary necessity. The challenges presented by civilized society are predominantly psychological rather than physical, thus attenuating anger's adaptive worth. Effective coping with the demands of modern life requires understanding complex information, problem solving, and prudent action, not energized rapid responding. Even in emergency situations, anger requires regulation. Contrary to intuitions, anger can be detrimental to survival in a physical threat crisis. It is counterproductive for energy conservation in a prolonged fight, for monitoring additional threat elements and hazards, and for effective strategy selection in circumstances where survival threat lingers and/or remains obscure. The regulation of the intensity and duration of anger arousal is pivotal to its merit or utility.

While the physiological components of anger, such as increased bloodflow, may be adaptive for survival in a short-term danger episode, the by-products of recurrent engagement of anger are hazardous in the long term. Unregulated anger commonly has been found to be associated with physical and psychological health impairments. In the realm of physical health, chronic anger has been established as having detrimental effects most centrally on the cardiovascular system, and these are related to mortality. Persons high in generalized hostility who are reactively angry are at considerable risk for coronary heart disease. When such persons are confronted with a stressful demand, they have strong cardiovascular responses in blood pressure, neurohormonal secretions, and cholesterol. A hostile, cynical, and distrusting outlook also necessitates high vigilance for thwarting and malevolence, resulting in prolonged neurohormonal activation conducive to atherosclerosis.

In addition to these pathogenic effects for a personality style that is overly expressive of anger, the coronary system is also impaired by recurrently suppressed anger, long been identified as a causal variable in the etiology of essential hypertension. People who have difficulties expressing anger tend to be at risk for chronically elevated blood pressure, as mediated by high plasma renin activity and norepinephrine. The suppression of anger has been robustly correlated to elevated blood pressure in laboratory studies and to sustained hypertension in field studies. Also, studies using ambulatory recorders of blood pressure have found that persons who are high in hostility and who have a tendency to inhibit the expression of that hostility have greater cardiovascular reactivity to provocation events as well as elevated resting blood pressure.

With regard to psychological well-being, anger occurs in conjunction with a wide range of psychiatrically classified disorders, including a variety of impulse control dysfunctions, mood disorders, personality disorders, and forms of schizophrenia, especially paranoid schizophrenia. As well, the activation of anger has long been recognized as a feature of clinical disorders that result from trauma, such as dissociative disorders, brain-damage syndromes, and, especially, posttraumatic stress disorder. Anger also appears in mental state disturbances produced by general medical conditions, such as dementia, substance abuse disorders, and neurological dysfunctions resulting from perinatal difficulties.

Among hospitalized psychiatric patients in long-term care in both civil commitment and forensic institutions, anger is a salient problem, as identified by both clinical staff and by the patients themselves. Importantly, it is linked to assaultive behavior by psychiatric patients both inside and outside such facilities. Such patients typically have traumatic life histories, replete with experiences of abandonment and rejection as well as economic and psychological impoverishment. For them, anger becomes entrenched as a mode of reactance to stressful or aversive experiences, and it is a significant aspect of their resistance to treatment. Chronically angry people are reluctant to surrender the anger–aggression system that they have found useful to engage, because they discount the costs of its engagement. Psychiatric hospital staff, especially those on acute admissions units and in long-term institutions, have very stressful occupations as a result of the anger episodes of the patients in their care. Posttraumatic stress disorder commonly occurs among staff who have been victims of assault by patients.

VI. ANGER TREATMENT

In the treatment of anger disorders, cognitive-behavioral approaches have been found to be effective with a wide range of clinical populations. These psychotherapeutic approaches incorporate many elements of behavior therapy, such as training in self-monitoring, relaxation, and social skills. Cognitive-behavioral treatments centrally seek to modify cognitive structures and the way in which a person processes information about social situations. They strongly emphasize self-regulation, cognitive flexibility in appraising situations, arousal control, and the learning of prosocial values and scripts. Making extensive use of therapist modeling and client rehearsal, anger proneness is modified by first motivating client engagement and then by restructuring cognitive schemas, increasing capacity to regulate arousal, and facilitating the use of constructive coping behaviors.

One cognitive-behavioral approach to anger treatment that has received significant support for its efficacy is based on model that is called "stress inoculation"(SI). In this treatment approach, anger provocation is simulated by therapeutically paced exposure to anger incidents created in imaginal visualization and in role play. The progressively graduated exposure, directed by the therapist, involves a hierarhy of anger incidents produced by the collaborative work of client and therapist. This graduated, hierarchical exposure, done in conjunction with the teaching of stress coping skills, is the basis for the "inoculation" metaphor.

The SI cognitive-behavioral approach to anger treatment involves the following key components: (1) client education about anger, stress, and aggression; (2) self-monitoring of anger frequency, intensity, and situational triggers; (3) construction of a personal anger provocation hierarchy, created from the self-monitoring data and used for the practice and testing of anger coping skills; (4) arousal reduction techniques of progressive muscle relaxation, breathing-focused relaxation, and guided imagery training; (5) cognitive restructuring by altering attentional focus, modifying appraisals, and using self-instruction; (6) training behavioral coping in communication and respectful assertiveness as modeled and rehearsed with the therapist; and (7) practicing the cognitive, arousal regulatory, and behavioral coping skills while visualizing and role playing progressively more intense anger-arousing scenes from personal hierarchies.

See Also the Following Articles

Aggression; Fight-or-Flight Response; Heart Disease/Attack; Hostility; Relaxation Techniques; Schizophrenia; Violence

Bibliography

Averill, J. R. (1982). "Anger and Aggression: An Essay on Emotion" Springer-Verlag, New York.

Berkowitz, L. (1993). "Aggression: Its Causes, Consequences, and Control." McGraw–Hill, New York.

Chesney, M., and Rosenman, R. H. (1985). "Anger and Hostility in Cardiovascular and Behavioral Disorders." Hemisphere, Washington, DC.

Follette, V. M., Rusek, J. I., and Abueg, F. R. (1998). "Cognitive Behavioral Therapies for Trauma." Guilford, New York.

Friedman, H. (1992). "Hostility, Coping, and Health." American Psychological Association, Washington, DC.

Johnson, E. H., Gentry, W. D., and Julius, S. (1992). "Personality, Elevated Blood Pressure, and Essential Hypertension." Hemisphere, Washington, DC.

Lazarus, R. S. (1991). "Emotion & Adaptation." Oxford Univ. Press, Oxford.

Ortony, A., Clore, G. L., and Collins (1988). "The Cognitive Structure of Emotions." Cambridge Univ. Press, New York.

Potegal, M., and Knutson, J. F. (1994). "The Dynamics of Aggression: Biological and Social Processes in Dyads and Groups." Erlbaum, Hillsdale, NJ.

Siegman, A. W., and Smith, T. W. (Eds.). "Anger, Hostility, and the Heart." Erlbaum, Hillsdale, NJ.

Angiotensin

Ovidiu Baltatu, Michael Bader, and Detlev Ganten

Max-Delbrück-Center for Molecular Medicine, Berlin, Germany

I. Components of the Renin–Angiotensin System
II. Endocrine Plasma Renin–Angiotensin System
III. Paracrine Tissue Renin–Angiotensin System
IV. Renin–Angiotensin System and Stress

GLOSSARY

blood–brain barrier A term for the impermeability of the endothelial cells of cerebral capillaries to components of the blood due inter alia to tight junctions so that endo- and transcytotic transport across the capillary wall occurs in a highly specific and regulated manner.

cardiovascular control Those that control cardiovascular homeostasis by neural and local mechanisms.

cardiovascular homeostasis Maintenance of the cardiovascular parameters, especially blood pressure and blood volume, at levels optimal for blood supply to all organs.

A ngiotensin II is the active peptide product of the renin–angiotensin system (RAS). The RAS is a complex effector system that may exert its biological functions in an endocrine, paracrine, or autocrine manner. It is considered to be one of the main regulators of cardiovascular and fluid-electrolyte homeostasis.

I. COMPONENTS OF THE RENIN–ANGIOTENSIN SYSTEM

A. Angiotensinogen

Angiotensinogen (AOGEN) is the only known precursor molecule to be converted by the renin–angiotensin (RAS) system into active angiotensins. It is a glycoprotein with a molecular weight between 61 and 65 kDa and shows close structural similarities to the serine protease inhibitor family. Originally found to be synthesized in the liver, AOGEN is known to be present in several other organs, especially in glial cells of the brain.

B. Renin

Renin is a very specific aspartyl proteinase whose only known substrate is AOGEN. Renin cleaves the decapeptide angiotensin I (Ang I) from the amino-terminus of mature AOGEN. Renin is produced primarily by the kidney and released into the circulation, but is also produced in other tissues. Renin synthesis is stimulated by the sympathetic nervous system and by loss of volume and sodium.

C. Angiotensin Converting Enzyme

Angiotensin converting enzyme (ACE) is a dipeptidylcarboxypeptidase which cleaves the C-terminal histidine–leucine of Ang I to generate angiotensin II (Ang II). It is found in high concentrations in the lung, kidney, and heart and is distributed throughout the brain. High amounts are detected in areas lacking the blood–brain barrier such as diencephalon, pituitary, and pineal gland. Angiotensin converting enzyme is also able to hydrolyze other substrates, such as bradykinin, opioid peptides, and substance P. Thus, ACE is additionally involved in physiological mechanisms beyond the RAS.

D. Active Angiotensins

The best studied peptide of the system is Ang II, and the functions of the RAS are largely attributed to this active metabolite. Besides Ang II, additional peptides of the RAS have been found to be biologically active, such as Ang III, Ang IV, and Ang II (1–7). In fact, Ang III may be even more potent than Ang II in the brain when acting on a common receptor. Ang II (1–7) can be formed via an ACE-independent mechanism and has the same potency as Ang II in vasopressin release. Studies on Ang IV suggest a biological role for this peptide as well.

There is evidence that proteases other than renin and ACE can produce bioactive angiotensin species. Such proteases include cathepsin G, tonin, tissue plasminogen activator, chymase, and other neutral peptidases.

E. Receptors

The use of highly specific ligands has led to the description and cloning of two main Ang II receptors, namely AT_1 and AT_2. Most of the known "classic" cardiovascular effects of Ang II are attributed to the AT_1 receptor. In contrast to humans, two different subtypes have been found for this receptor in rodents, AT_{1a} and AT_{1b}. While AT_{1a} has been localized in blood vessels, kidney, lung, liver, and specific brain areas which are involved in the control of blood pressure and fluid homeostasis, AT_{1b} receptors were originally described in glandular tissues, such as anterior pituitary and adrenal gland.

II. ENDOCRINE PLASMA RENIN–ANGIOTENSIN SYSTEM

The endocrine RAS is dependent on renin released by the kidney into the blood so that AOGEN is cleaved in the circulation to liberate the inactive decapeptide Ang I. Angiotensin converting enzyme then cleaves Ang I to yield the octapeptide Ang II, the active molecule of the system. Circulating Ang II is one of the most potent vasoconstrictors and acts on specific receptors to elicit the following localized effects: vasoconstriction of the vasculature, sodium and water reabsorption in the kidney, release of aldosterone from the adrenal glands, induction of inotropic and arrythmogenic effects in the heart, and thirst is incited at specific brain areas outside the blood–brain barrier. Figure 1 summarizes the roles of the RAS in cardiovascular and fluid-electrolyte regulation.

III. PARACRINE TISSUE RENIN–ANGIOTENSIN SYSTEM

In addition to the circulating RAS, a local formation and action of Ang II has been observed at the level of various organs. The components of the RAS have been detected in several tissues including heart, vasculature, kidney, adrenal glands, and brain. The local formation and action of Ang II in peripheral organs can therefore occur independent from the circulating RAS. However, RAS components required for angiotensin synthesis, such as renin and AOGEN, can be also taken up from the circulating blood. The latter is only possible for organs accessible to blood proteins, such as kidney, heart, adrenal glands, and brain areas situated outside the blood–brain barrier.

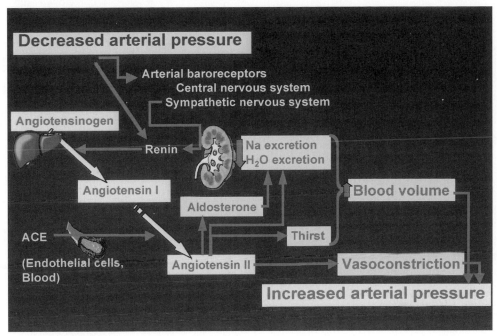

FIGURE 1 The endocrine renin–angiotensin system and cardiovascular regulation.

Nevertheless, there are areas in the brain which are inaccessible to the circulating RAS because of the blood–brain barrier but express functional angiotensin receptors. In these brain regions only locally formed angiotensins can act.

The tissue RASs seem to regulate long-term organ function and may be responsible for pathological structural changes. Figure 2 illustrates the functions of the endocrine and tissue RASs.

IV. RENIN–ANGIOTENSIN SYSTEM AND STRESS

Both physical and emotional stressors induce peripheral and central responses designed to preserve cardiovascular homeostasis. As one of the main regulators of cardiovascular homeostasis, the RAS is stimulated by stressors that lead to a lowering in the blood pressure, such as hemorrhage, loss of blood volume and sodium, or increased activity of the sympathetic nervous system. The RAS manifests synergistic roles, increasing blood pressure and maintaining organ perfusion and electrolyte and volume balance.

The physical and behavioral responses to stress are integrated at the level of the central nervous system including areas known to regulate the homeostasis of the milieu interieur. The AOGEN and the angiotensin receptors are present in areas responsible for the maintenance of homeostasis such as the hypothalamic and brain stem nuclei (Fig. 3) and participate in the stress response.

The sympathetic nervous system, the component of the autonomic nervous system which is essentially involved in the "fight or flight" reaction, is modulated by the RAS not only in the periphery but also in central areas of autonomic control. During the reaction to stress there is an increase in blood levels of renin besides epinephrine. In the central nervous system an interrelationship between the activity of the brain RAS and the sympathetic system and other central autonomic pathways has also been shown.

Various stressor agents activate the hypothalamic–pituitary axis. The secretion of vasopressin and corticotropin releasing hormone (CRF) is increased during stress to induce multiple effects, such as the secretion of corticotropin and consequently cortisol. Angiotensin II together with other neurotransmitters and neuromodulators modulates the activity of the

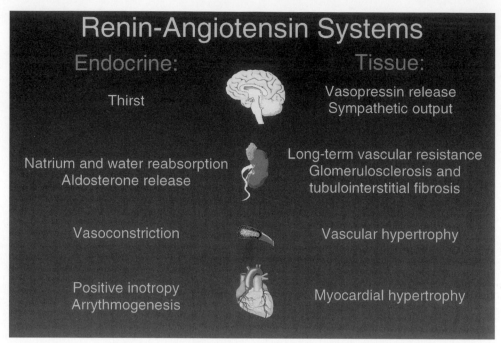

FIGURE 2 Functions of the endocrine and tissular RASs.

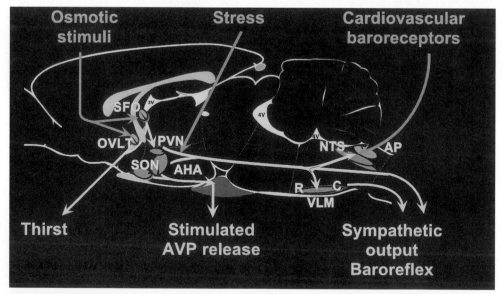

FIGURE 3 Central control of homeostasis by angiotensins. Angiotensinogen and angiotensin receptors are densely expressed in the areas responsible for the control of homeostasis: the areas situated outside the blood–brain barrier and accessible to blood Ang II are SFO, OVLT and AP; areas inside the blood–brain barrier and accessible only to the locally formed Ang II are SON, PVN, NTS and VLM. OVLT: organum vasculosum of lamina terminalis; SFO: subfornical organ; AP: area postrema; SON: supraoptic nucleus; PVN: paraventricular nucleus; AHA: anterior hypothalamic area; VLM: ventrolateral medulla, R: rostral, C: caudal; NTS: nucleus of tractus solitarii.

hypothalamic–pituitary axis and stimulates the release of vasopressin and CRF. In addition, it has been proposed that the brain RAS is involved in behavioral responses, such as cognition, memory and central analgesia.

See Also the Following Article

Bibliography

Ardaillou, R. (1997). Active fragments of angiotensin II: Enzymatic pathways of synthesis and biological effects, *Curr. Opin. Nephrol. Hypertens.* 6, 28–34.

Bunnemann, B., Fuxe, K., and Ganten, D. (1993). The renin–angiotensin system in the brain: An update 1993. *Regul. Pept.* 46, 487–509.

Clauser, E., Curnow, K. M., Davies, E., Conchon, S., Teutsch, B., Vianello, B., Monnot, C., and Corvol, P. (1996). Angiotensin II receptors: Protein and gene structures, expression and potential pathological involvements. *Eur. J. Endocrinol.* 134, 403–411.

Ferrario, C. M., Brosnihan, K. B., DIZ, D. I., Jaiswal, N., Khosla, M. C., Milsted, A., and Tallant, E. A. (1991). Angiotensin-(1-7): a new hormone of the angiotensin system. *Hypertension* 18, 126–133.

Fink, G. D. (1997). Long-term sympatho-excitatory effect of angiotensin II: A mechanism of spontaneous and renovascular hypertension. *Clin. Exp. Pharmacol. Physiol.* 24, 91–95.

Ganong, W. F. (1995). Reproduction and the renin–angiotensin system, *Neurosci. Biobehav. Rev.* 19, 241–250.

Henry, J. P. (1992). Biological basis of the stress response. *Integr. Physiol. Behav. Sci.* 27, 66–83.

Inagami, T. (1995). Recent progress in molecular and cell biological studies of angiotensin receptors. *Curr. Opin. Nephrol. Hypertens.* 4, 47–54.

Lippoldt, A., Paul, M., Fuxe, K., and Ganten, D. (1995). The brain renin–angiotensin system: Molecular mechanisms of cell to cell interactions. *Clin. Exp. Hypertens.* 17, 251–266.

Morgan, L., Pipkin, F. B., and Kalsheker, N. (1996), Angiotensinogen: molecular biology, biochemistry and physiology. *Int. J. Biochem. Cell Biol.* 28, 1211–1222.

Sernia, C., Zeng, T., Kerr, D., and Wyse, B. (1997). Novel perspectives on pituitary and brain angiotensinogen. *Front. Neuroendocrinol.* 18, 174–208.

Stock, P., Liefeldt, L., Paul, M., and Ganten, D. (1995). Local renin–angiotensin systems in cardiovascular tissues. Localization and functional role. *Cardiology* 86 (Suppl 1), 2–8.

Unger, T., Chung, O., Csikos, T., Culman, J., Gallinat, S., Gohlke, P., Hohle, S., Meffert, S., Stoll, M., Stroth, U., and Zhu, Y. Z. (1996). Angiotensin receptors. *J. Hypertens.* 14, S95–S103.

Wright, J. W., and Harding, J. W. (1994). Brain angiotensin receptor subtypes in the control of physiological and behavioral responses. *Neurosci. Biobehav. Rev.* 18, 21–53.

Wright, J. W., Krebs, L. T., Stobb, J. W., and Harding, J. W. (1995). The angiotensin IV system: Functional implications. *Front. Neuroendocrinol.* 16, 23–52.

Zini, S., Fournie, Z. M., Chauvel, E., Roques, B. P., Corvol, P., and Llorens, C. C. (1996). Identification of metabolic pathways of brain angiotensin II and III using specific aminopeptidase inhibitors: predominant role of angiotensin III in the control of vasopressin release. *Proc. Natl. Acad. Sci. USA* 93, 11968–11973.

Animal Models (Nonprimate) for Human Stress

John E. Ottenweller

East Orange Department of Veterans Affairs Medical Center and University of Medicine and Dentistry of New Jersey

I. Human Stress Disorders
II. Stress Responses
III. Animal Models
IV. Summary

GLOSSARY

acute stress Changes in physiology and behavior that occur during and shortly after exposure to a stressor.

chronic stress Changes in physiology and behavior that persist for days or weeks during repeated stressors or after exposure to a stressor or stressors.

Posttraumatic Stress Disorder A psychological disorder that follows exposure to a traumatic event and is characterized by intrusive imagery, sleep disturbances and nightmares, poor concentration and memory, hypervigilance and numbness.

stressor A change in the environment that is sensed by an organism, is aversive or potentially harmful to that organism and elicits acute and/or chronic stress responses.

An organism undergoes a series of physiological changes when exposed to a stressor. In the short term, several brain centers can be activated, including among others the locus coeruleus in the brain stem, the paraventricular nucleus in the hypothalamus, and amygdala and hippocampus in the limbic system. Activation of these centers leads to increased sympathetic nervous system (SNS) activity and elevated hypothalamic-pituitary-adrenocortical axis (HPAA) hormones. These responses are homeostatic mechanisms that allow an individual to cope with a stressor and eventually turn off the stress response through negative feedback. However, if people are exposed to a very severe or prolonged stressor, more persistent changes characteristic of posttraumatic stress disor-der or a general stress reaction can become established. Animal models of stress have been utilized to study these and other facets of acute and chronic stress responses.

I. HUMAN STRESS DISORDERS

Posttraumatic Stress Disorder is the only chronic stress disorder recognized in the *Diagnostic and Statistical Manual of Mental Disorders* published by the American Psychiatric Association, but it is grouped with Anxiety and Panic Disorders, which are characterized by acute stress responses. Stress can also contribute to depressive disorders. In addition, a number of medical conditions result from stress. It is well recognized that stress is linked to cardiovascular disease, particularly hypertension and sudden cardiac death. Stress can also suppress immune function, leading to susceptibility to infections. In some abused children, stress can produce growth hormone deficiency and small stature. Stress and excessive excercise in women can interfere with ovarian cyclicity and fertility. These are only a few examples of the ways stress directly affects health through its actions on diverse systems within the body.

II. STRESS RESPONSES

A. Neuroendocrine and Immune Responses

Stress affects a number of physiological systems whose regulatory mechanisms interact, and corticotropin-releasing hormone (CRH) appears to have an important integrative function. In the brain stem, increased CRH is required for normal sympathetic nervous system activation by stress. In the hypothalamus, CRH increases with stress and its secretion leads to release of adrenocorticotropin by the pituitary gland, which in turn stimulates the adrenal cortex to secrete glucocorticoids. Although its exact function remains unclear, CRH is also present in the limbic system. Thus, CRH appears to have a central role in coordinating the major responses to stress.

The catecholamines, epinephrine, and norepinephrine, also play a critical role in the stress response. Plasma epinephrine comes from the adrenal medulla and is more responsive to psychological stressors, whereas plasma norepinephrine comes largely from the sympathetic nerve terminals and is more responsive to physical stressors. In addition to increasing heart rate and blood pressure during stress, the catecholamines stimulate the breakdown of glycogen and fats to increase the availability of energy for the brain and muscles.

Almost all endocrine systems respond to stress in one way or another. Depending on the duration, intensity, and nature of the stressor, plasma prolactin and vasopressin can be elevated and growth hormone can be suppressed or stimulated. The hypothalamic-pituitary-thyroid and hypothalamic-pituitary-reproductive axes are generally suppressed by stress. In addition, plasma insulin usually decreases and glucagon increases.

These endocrine changes can be related to changes in immune function. Infection activates a number of cytokines that induce fever, stimulate the HPAA, and inhibit the reproductive axes. In addition, the glucocorticoids can inhibit immune function, and a number of the other hormones have immunomodulatory roles. Thus, the interactions between the endocrine and immune systems in response to stress are bidirectional.

B. Psychological Responses

Exposure to stressors can result in posttraumatic stress disorder, and the stress response is a major component of anxiety disorders and phobias. Stress can also significantly impact cognitive function by impairing or enhancing it depending on the stressor and the type of learning or memory being assessed.

In addition to these effects of stress, a number of psychological processes including habituation and sensitization, predictability, controllability, and coping can modify the responses to stressors.

There is a coordinated response to a stressor by most systems in the body that allows an individual to cope with the stressor and restore baseline conditions after the stressor has ended. One of the primary concerns when evaluating animal models of stress is what features of the stress response are important to judge the validity of the models. From the discussion above, it is clear that this will depend on the organ system being studied and the stressors being modeled. For example, many researchers use animal models involving psychological stress because they argue that most human stressors are primarily psychological or have a large psychological component, but common physical stressors in people are often overlooked, including among others disease and infection, exercise, childbirth, surgery, and physical trauma during even minor accidents (broken bones, cuts, strains, and burns). An example of having to consider the organ system being studied is research into the effects of cardiovascular stress which has often used dogs, rabbits, and pigs rather than rodents because the cardiovascular systems of the former are more like those of humans. Thus, there are many valid animal models of human stress directed toward understanding different facets of the stress response.

III. ANIMAL MODELS

The endocrine, immune, and behavioral responses to stressors have been studied most often using rodents in which the neural, endocrine, and immune substrates involved in the stress response have been delineated. However, a lot of applied stress research in animal husbandry is overlooked; the effects of stress on reproduction, weight gain, and health have often been studied in commercially important species. Finally, as noted above, cardiovascular responses to stress have often been studied in rabbits, dogs, and pigs because of subtle differences between people and rodents in cardiovascular regulation.

A. Acute Stress

1. Physical Stressors

Most studies of acute responses to a variety of stressors have been carried out in rodents. Commonly used acute stressors include restraint, shock, swimming, cold, loud noises, novelty, and social conflict. These stressors can be applied for periods as short as 1–2 min or as long as 6–8 h. The acute response to these stressors may be followed during the stressor and for several hours after the stressor has ended. It is clear that most, if not all, of these stressors have substantial short-term effects on behavior, physiology, and immune function. It is commonly thought that the acute stress response is self-limiting because the responding systems are adaptive and negative feedback loops will terminate the responses. Failure to terminate the acute stress response appropriately can lead to persistent changes that are characteristic of a chronic stress state.

Most of these acute stressors are applied in sessions during which the animals must be removed from their home cages, which in itself is a mild stressor. Thus, the stressors also include a novelty component involving removal from the home cage and handling. In order to isolate the effects of a particular stressor, sometimes the stressed animals are compared with controls that have been removed from their cages and put in a novel environment, whereas other times all the animals are handled 1–2 weeks before exposure to the stressor in order to habituate them to handling and novelty.

Restraint stressor protocols are described in another entry in this encyclopedia. Electrical shock as a stressor has been used mostly in rodents and includes both footshock and tailshock. One of the advantages of shock is that stressor intensity can be graded monotonically while duration and other parameters are held constant. With the other stressors listed above, it is more difficult to manipulate and assess stressor intensity and to prevent confounding effects of stressor duration. Footshock is administered in Skinner boxes with electrified grids on the floor, and the animals are freely moving. Tailshock is administered to restrained animals through electrodes attached to the tail. One advantage of footshock is

that animals are freely moving, but this also creates a problem because they can learn to reduce the amount of shock they receive by assuming particular stances on the grid. Tailshock permits one to administer uncontrollable, inescapable shock, to insure the delivery of the same amount of shock to each rat, and to verify the intensity of each shock.

Swim stressors are now used more frequently in rodents because Animal Welfare Committees are increasingly reluctant to approve shock stressors. The rodents are placed in a container of water for 5–30 min with either running water or a weight to prevent floating. Intensity of stress is manipulated by the duration of the swimming and the temperature of the water; the colder the water, the more intense the stressor. Swimming is a compound stressor with an exercise or exertion component and an aversive component involving cold temperatures and being wet. Exposure to cold alone, without swimming, is also used as a stressor. However, when repeated or long-term cold exposure is used, there are physiological adaptations to low temperatures that may be independent of stress responses and confound the interpretation of findings, e.g., the thyroid hormone axis is generally suppressed by stressors, but stimulated by long-term exposure to cold. Finally, loud noises around 120 decibels have been used as stressors, but some species will rapidly adapt during a session of repeated or continuous exposures to this level of sound.

2. Psychological Stressors

There are also acute stressors which are thought to produce more psychological than physical stress, e.g., novelty and a variety of social stressors. Novelty stressors can entail simply moving the home cage to a different room, transferring the animal to a bare cage or a cage with unused bedding, or exposing the animal to unfamiliar objects. These stressors are listed in the order that is generally thought to reflect increasing stressor intensity. Some acute social stressors that have been used include exposure to predators, exposure to conspecifics in species with dominance hierarchies, and exposure to pheromones from more dominant conspecifics. Finally, the division of stressors into physical and psychological is mostly heuristic in that all physical stressors clearly have a major psychological component and psychological stressors often have a physical component, as when some fighting is allowed between conspecifics in social conflict paradigms. Conversely, it has been shown that anticipation of physical stressors, e.g., shock or immobilization, imparts a strong psychological component to these stressors.

3. Nonstressed Controls

In utilizing animal models of stress, it is important to select appropriate control groups. If the stress effect is small or one is studying complex interactions between stress and other factors, it is important to provide the most stress-free environment for control animals. Animals in stress studies are often maintained in large vivariums without an appreciation of the stressfulness of this housing. Loud noises in general and particularly during animal care, handling during cage changes, and other experimenters working in the same room often lead to elevated stress hormones in control rats. In addition, data collection must be as stress-free as possible, e.g., either very rapid or through indwelling catheters to insure basal hormone levels in controls. It may also be important to house nonstressed controls apart from stressed animals because stressed rats may bring back stress-specific odors to their home cages.

4. Acute Stress Responses and Stressor Intensity

The acute stress response is characterized by the changes in the endocrine systems described above. One critical question in experimental models is how to evaluate and compare the stressfulness of different stressors. One possibility is to study responses to a graded series of stressor intensities and determine which stress-responsive systems respond in a monotonic way to increasing stressor intensity. For example, one study has shown that acute prolactin responses to foot shock are a better index of stressfulness than adrenocortical hormones or catecholamines because the responses of the latter are not as well graded, i.e., they tend to be all-or-nothing types of responses.

B. Chronic Stress

1. Chronic Stressors

Commonly used chronic stressors include repeated exposures to the acute stressors listed above, continuous performance tasks, overcrowding, and complex social situations when appropriate for the species. Repeated exposures to the same stressor can lead to habituation, i.e., smaller responses over time and eventually no response to the stressor. Two approaches have been used to prevent this habituation. In the first, different acute stressors are alternated on consecutive days. The second approach uses relatively few exposures to a very intense stressor that prevents habituation and may actually produce sensitization, i.e., larger responses to the stressor over time. Whether habituation or sensitization occurs can be related to the intensity of the stressor, inasmuch as animals will habituate to low-intensity shock stress and sensitize to the same shock stress at higher intensities.

Continuous performance tasks are generally operant tasks that require frequent responses to avoid aversive stimuli or, in a few cases, to obtain positive reinforcement. Frequent motor responses are one aspect of this stressor, but another is the requirement for frequent or continuous attentiveness over days. Increasing the number of animals (three or more) in a cage is stressful, but so also is single housing of social species. Finally, several chronic stress models involve daily changing of cagemates in species with dominance hierarchies, which leads to continual disruption of and need to reestablish the hierarchies. Most recently, a few laboratories have added naturalistic environments to the disruption of dominance hierarchies and social interactions. In these chronic social stressors, rank in the hierarchy usually determines stressfulness with more dominant individuals generally showing less stress.

Finally, there is an extensive literature on two other specific animal stress models, i.e., learned helplessness and fear conditioning. The learned helplessness paradigm was used in the past as a model to understand the physiological underpinnings of depression and to screen compounds for antidepressant activity. In this model, an animal was first exposed to inescapable shock, and then it failed to escape subsequent shock when given the opportunity. Antidepressants will reverse this failure to escape, and so the paradigm was used to screen novel compounds for antidepressant activity. More recently, inescapable stress without the helpless behavior has been used for animal models of depression.

Another model of psychological stress is fear-conditioned behavior. In these models, an animal is stressed in a particular context and later returned to the context without the stressor. Upon reexposure to the context, the animal becomes hyperresponsive, which may be manifested in fear-potentiated startle, freezing behavior, or elevated stress hormones, e.g., glucocorticoids.

2. Chronic Stress Responses

The chronic stress state is characterized by persistent changes in physiology and behavior that last beyond the time when the acute stress response should have dissipated. Posttraumatic stress disorder is such a state whose effects can last for years or decades after the precipitating traumatic stressor. In animals, most persistent stressor effects are followed for days or weeks, although there are neonatal stress regimens whose effects have been reported to last throughout the life of the animal. It remains unclear how physiological systems which constantly adapt to changes in the environment maintain a new set point for a such long time after some stressful situations. For example, the plasma glucocorticoid response to an acute stressor is well understood; a multilevel, negative feedback system returns glucocorticoid levels to baseline 1–3 h after most stressors. However, baseline glucocorticoid levels can remain elevated for 3–5 days after repeated exposure of rats to tailshock. It is unclear whether this is due to persistently increased activity in the stress-mediating areas of the brain leading to increased CRH release or persistent changes within the HPAA itself that are only reversed after several days.

Most animal models of chronic stress are characterized by persistent neuroendocrine, immunological, and behavioral changes. The entire hypothalamic-pituitary-adrenal axis is activated, the thyroid and reproductive axes are suppressed, growth hormone is suppressed, and prolactin is stimulated. Most studies report immune suppression after chronic stress, but there can be enhanced immune function, e.g., chronic stress will exacerbate pathology in experimental allergic encephalomyolitis, an autoimmune animal model for multiple sclerosis. The behavioral changes that are usually seen include hyperarousal indicated by increased startle responses and fear of novelty indicated by decreased exploration in an open field. In addition, chronic stress can inhibit spatial memory in the Morris Water Maze, but it can enhance acquisition of a classically conditioned eye-blink response. Thus, the effects on learning and memory may depend on the kind of stressor and the type of learning being tested.

3. Psychological Modifiers

In addition to these behavioral effects of stressors, a number of psychological variables will affect the stress response. In most studies, the ability or perception of the ability to control the occurrence of stressors produces smaller stress responses. In these studies, one animal has control of stressor presentation and a second is yoked so that it receives the same stressors but without control; yoked animals show larger responses. The ability to perform coping or escape responses during stressors also has a major role in determining stressfulness; animals permitted coping reactions or escape responses show smaller stress responses than those which are not. The predictability of a stressor can also be manipulated so an animal can anticipate an upcoming stressor. In most experiments, unpredictable stressors result in greater responses, but one study of rats exposed to stressors in their home environment showed that predictable stress can lead to increased chronic stress responses.

IV. SUMMARY

This short description of animal models for human stress could not be comprehensive because so many different types of stressors are used, the effects even with the same stressor are often dependent on the particular stress paradigm, and there are important differences among animal species in their responses to particular stressors. Instead, this article illustrated the wide range of stressors that have been used and the diversity of the stress respondents that have been studied. When studying stress, it is important to remember that many, if not all, of the stress-responsive systems are reacting to a stressor even if the experimenter is measuring only one respondent. Finally, animal models of stress have been critical in understanding how the human body responds to stress, what the health consequences of those responses are, and what therapies can be used to treat stress.

See Also the Following Articles

Acute Stress Disorder and Posttraumatic Stress Disorder; Acute Stress Response, Experimental; Posttraumatic Stress Disorder, Neurobiology of; Primate Models, Overview

Bibliography

Cameron, O. G. (1994). "Adrenergic Dysfunction and Pyschobiology." American Psychiatric Press, Washington, DC.

Chrousos, G. P., McCarty, R., Pacak, K., Cizza, G., Sternberg, E., Gold, P. W., and Kvetnansky, R. (1995). Stress, basic mechanisms and clinical implications. *Ann. N.Y. Acad. Sci.* **771.**

Csermely, P. (1998). Stress of life from molecules to man. *Ann. N.Y. Acad. Sci.* **851.**

Fabris, N., Markovic, B. M., Spector, N. H., and Jankovic, B. D. (1994). Neuroimmunomodulation, the state of the art. *Ann. N.Y. Acad. Sci.* **741.**

Goldberger, L., and Breznitz, S. (1982). "Handbook of Stress, Theoretical and Clinical Aspects." MacMillan, New York.

Hernandez, D. E., and Glavin, G. B. (1990). Neurobiology of stress ulcers. *Ann. N.Y. Acad. Sci.* **597.**

Moberg, G. P. (1985). "Animal Stress." American Physiological Society, Bethesda, MD.

Locke, S., Ader, R., Besedovsky, H., Hall, N., Solomon, G., and Strom, T. (1985). "Foundations of Psychneuroimmunology." Aldine, New York.

Schneiderman, N., McCabe, P., and Baum, A. (1992). "Perspectives in Behavioral Medicine, Stress and Disease Processes." Erlbaum, Hillsdale, NJ.

Selye, H. (1980/1983). "Selye's Guide to Stress Research," Vols. 1 and 2. Van Nostrand Reinhold, New York.

Shapiro, A. P. (1996). "Hypertension and Stress, A Unified Concept." Erlbaum, Mahwah, NJ.

Tache, Y., and Rivier, C. (1993). Corticotropin-releasing factor and cytokines: Role in the stress response. *Ann. N.Y. Acad. Sci.* **697.**

Yehuda, R., and McFarlane, A. C. (1997). Psychobiology of posttraumatic stress disorder. *Ann. N.Y. Acad. Sci.* **821.**

Anorexia Nervosa

see Eating Disorders and Stress

Antibody Response

Roger John Booth

University of Auckland, New Zealand

GLOSSARY

antigens Molecular shapes, often on infectious agents or produced during infections, that can be recognized by antibodies and other immune receptors.

antibodies Proteins produced by B lymphocytes with the ability to bind specifically to molecular shapes.

autoantibodies Antibodies able to bind to normal components of the body.

B lymphocytes Cells produced by the bone marrow and exported to secondary lymphoid organs where they are able to respond to antigens by producing antibodies specific to them.

immunoglobulins A synonym for antibodies. Different classes of immunoglobulins function in different ways. IgA is important in secretions, IgG and IgM are important in blood and other internal body fluids, and IgE is important in allergy.

stress proteins A family of molecules produced by cells and organisms under stress. These are sometimes called heat-shock proteins and are highly conserved across many different organisms.

T lymphocytes Cells produced by the thymus and exported to secondary lymphoid organs where they are able to respond to antigens. A subset of T lymphocytes called helper cells (TH) assist B lymphocytes to produce antibodies.

I. WHAT IS AN ANTIBODY RESPONSE?

Antibodies are produced as part of the immune system's behavior toward antigens of foreign material such as infectious agents like bacteria and viruses. They are soluble proteins which have the ability to bind specifically to shapes on particular antigens and to neutralize them or to lead to their inactivation and removal (see Fig. 1).

Antibodies are produced by a class of lymphocytes called B lymphocytes derived from the bone marrow and active in secondary lymphoid organs such as lymph nodes, spleen, tonsils, and other gut-associated lymphoid organs. There are many millions of B lymphocytes in the body but each B lymphocyte has the capacity to make antibodies with only one shape of antigen-binding site. In order to be activated to produce antibodies against a particular antigen, B lymphocytes must interact with antigens through specific cell-surface receptors (see Fig. 2) and usually also require assistance from a class of T lymphocytes (derived from the thymus) called helper T lymphocytes (TH). Some antigens, such as lipopolysaccharide (LPS) cell wall products of some bacteria, can stimulate B lymphocytes to make antibodies without much in the way of T cell help and are called T-independent antigens.

II. STRESS PROTEINS AS ANTIGENS

When cells or microorganisms are subjected to physical stresses such as changes in temperature or the composition of the medium in which they exist, they increase synthesis of "stress" proteins (or "heat-shock" proteins). These stress proteins represent a highly conserved cellular defense mechanism mediated by multiple, distinct gene families which participate in many essential biochemical pathways of protein maturation and function actively during both times of stress and normal cellular homeostasis. They are thought to operate to protect the stressed cells by scavenging abnormal proteins and protecting newly synthesized proteins through a chaperon function.

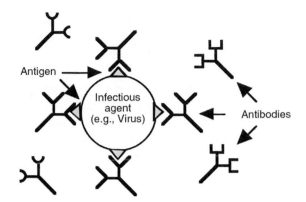

FIGURE 1 Antibodies interacting with specific antigenic shapes through their antigen-binding site.

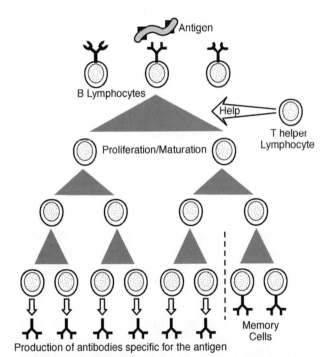

FIGURE 2 The B lymphocytes in secondary lymphoid organs display surface immunoglobulins with antigen-binding specificity of the antibodies they are capable of producing when stimulated. Through these surface immunoglobulin receptors, antigens, select appropriate B lymphocytes from the antigen-sensitive repertoire. Further activation signals come from helper T lymphocytes. The result is the proliferation of activated B lymphocytes and the production of antibody-forming cells and memory cells which are capable of responding more rapidly to antigens in the future.

They are also strongly immunogenic and so play a prominent part in immune responses against microorganisms. For example, several protein antigens involved in antibody and other responses to mycobacteria have been identified as members of highly conserved heat-shock protein families suggesting that immune responses against microorganisms are dominated by responses against the stress protein family. Furthermore, these highly immunogenic microbial stress proteins have very similar structures to stress proteins in human cells. Through this "molecular mimicry," immune cross-reactions between microbial and human stress proteins may be involved in some chronic inflammatory and autoimmune disorders such as rheumatoid arthritis, ankylosing spondylitis, systemic lupus erythematosus, and inflammatory bowel diseases. Liaison between heat-shock proteins and the immune response may therefore be both beneficial to the host as antigenic targets and detrimental to the host as promoters of autoimmunity.

III. STRESS AND ANTIBODY RESPONSE IN ANIMALS

A considerable body of research has investigated the effects of stress on antibody responses in animals and, as summarized in Table I, a variety of factors have been found to be important.

When rats or mice are subjected to the physical stressors such as restraint or exposure to coldness, the effect on antibody responses depends on whether

TABLE I
Factors Affecting the Relationship between Stress and Antibody Responses in Animals

Types of stresses or stressors
Immediate short-term threat versus long-term uncontrollable stress
Social or psychological versus physical stressors
Activation of B lymphocytes versus synthesis of antibodies
Route of immunization
Timing of stressor relative to antigen
Balance of neuroendocrine hormones
Season of the year

the stressor is short or long term. For example, short periods of restraint stress (2 h over 2 consecutive days) enhance the primary antibody response to an injected antigen in mice, while longer periods of restraint (6 h over 4 days) do not. The augmented response occurs in both IgM and IgG antibody classes. The effect is mediated at least in part by hormones from the adrenal cortex and can be blocked by α-adrenoceptor agonist drugs such as phentolamine and potentiated by β-adrenoceptor agonists such as propranolol. The temporal relationship between the stressor and antigen challenge is also important. Antibody responses are markedly suppressed in mice restrained before antigen injection but not significantly affected when the animals are stressed after immunization.

An important group of hormones involved in stress-induced inhibition of antibody (and other) immune responses are the corticosteroids. These are produced by the cortex of the adrenal gland in response to stress-induced signals from the hypothalamus via the pituitary gland. Injection of the hypothalamic hormone corticotropin-releasing factor (CRF) into a rat 20 min before antigen administration diminishes both primary and secondary antibody responses, while CRF infusion 24 h after antigen does not to affect antibody levels, suggesting that CRF (and corticosteroids) affect the initial induction phase of the antibody response. Corticosteroids have a direct inhibitory effect on B lymphocyte activation but also act on T cells to diminish helper activity. Conditions that lead to inhibition of antibody responses against T helper-dependent antigens often lead to enhanced responses against T-independent antigens, and adrenalectomy blocks both these effects by removing the gland that produces corticosteroids.

As well as corticosteroids, two other types of hormonal mediate stress effects on antibody responses. The pituitary hormone prolactin generally facilitates antibody responses and so acts as a balance to corticosteroid inhibitory effects. In addition, the pineal hormone melatonin counteracts many stress responses including antibody inhibition. In doing this, melatonin appears to act on helper T cells to induce the release of opioid peptides with immuno-enhancing properties. Melatonin and opioid effects therefore may come into play to effect immune recovery following corticosteroid-induced immune depression that results from stressful situations.

We cannot, however, consider the effects of stress on antibody responses simply in terms of enhancement or suppression because response kinetics can be different under stressed and nonstressed conditions. For example, in some studies, repeated cycles of physical restraint stress in mice delayed the development of antibodies to a virus infection but did not affect the ultimate magnitude or class of antibodies produced. Such a delay could nevertheless have consequences for the course of an infection and allow prolonged multiplication of an infectious agent leading to the development of illness symptoms. A further factor affecting stress effects on antibody responses is the season of the year during which the stress occurs. In rats, unstressed animals display increased antibody responsiveness in spring–summer and decreased responsiveness in autumn–winter. This annual rhythm is accentuated in stressed animals and might therefore contribute to greater stress-induced susceptibility to infection during the winter months.

Although much animal experimentation has focused on physical stressors, social stress can also affect antibody responses in animals. For example, rats exposed to the odors of other stressed rats exhibit altered antibody responses as if they themselves had been stressed. Also, defeat associated with territorial defense affects a rat's ability to generate antibodies in response to an injected antigen. The more time such rats spend in submissive postures, the lower their antibody levels. Social status in monkeys also affects antibody-related factors. Low social status is associated with less body weight, greater elevated cortisol responses to social reorganizations, and less aggressive behavior. Correspondingly, low-status monkeys have diminished immune responsiveness and a greater probability of being infected by upper respiratory tract viruses. Clearly, a variety of factors mediate effects of stress on antibody production but these effects occur as part of a bidirectional network of interactions between the immune system and the nervous system rather than a one-way, cause–effect process. This means that immune activity or defects in immunity can also influence the way animals behave. As an example, certain inbred strains of mice have a propensity to develop autoimmunity and produce high concentrations of antibodies against some of its own (self-) antigens. In these mice, there is an association between high titers of autoantibodies and emotional behaviors resembling those of stressed animals. Disturbed emotional reactivity in these strains may reflect the effect of autoimmunity on the hypothalamic-pituitary-adrenal axis highlighting the bidirectional nature of the communication pathways between immune and nervous systems.

IV. STRESS AND ANTIBODY RESPONSE IN HUMANS

Investigations into the effects of stress on human antibody responses have tended to focus less on deliberately applied physical stressors (as in the animal experiments) and more on stressful situations in which people find themselves. One particularly fruitful situation for this area has been the study of students undergoing university examinations. For example, when saliva samples from healthy students are compared a week before, 2 weeks after, and during examinations, antibodies normally present in saliva (the IgA class) are lower during the examination period. Moreover, the better a student's social support during the preexam period, the higher his or her salivary IgA during examinations. The stress of examinations is also associated with increased norepinephrine concentrations in saliva, particularly in students most aroused adrenergically by the examination. Antibody titers against Epstein–Barr virus (EBV) also increase during examination periods, indicating poorer immune control of latent virus reactivation. Immunoglobulin A (IgA) is the dominant antibody isotype not only in saliva but on all mucosal surfaces where it acts as a first line of defense against microbial invasion. Because it is relatively noninvasive to measure, salivary IgA has been assessed in a variety of stressful situations aside from examinations. As with the conclusions from animal studies, it seems that some short-term stresses promote antibody production (at least in the saliva) while others, particularly longer-term stresses, depress it. For example, in one study salivary IgA in professional soccer coaches was found to increase transiently during

a match, while in another, nurses who reported more frequent episodes of anxiety had significantly lowered salivary IgA secretion rates. Such effects can be moderated by other factors such as a sense of humor. Mild stress, as measured by the frequency of daily hassles, correlates with diminished salivary IgA concentration, especially in people with low scores on a humor scale.

When salivary IgA is produced in response to challenge with a novel antigen similar results are found. Following oral immunization, adults who report more desirable events on a day-to-day basis have higher concentrations of antigen-specific salivary IgA than when they report more undesirable events. Undesirable events appear to lower antibody level primarily by increasing negative mood, while desirable events increase antibody levels by decreasing negative mood. These effects can be moderated by using coping skills such as deliberate relaxation. Significant increases in salivary IgA concentration occur in healthy volunteers after relaxation even though no change is observed in salivary corticosteroids.

It is not only IgA antibodies that are affected by stress but IgG and IgM antibody classes in the blood as well. For example, in women immunized with a novel antigen, keyhole limpet hemocyanin, those reporting more stressful events in their lives tended to have lower baseline and 3-week postimmunization serum IgG antibody levels. In contrast, women reporting more "good" events tended to have higher IgG levels. Psychological distress scores correlated negatively and psychological well-being scores correlated positively with IgG antibody concentrations.

Similar effects are observed when immunizing people with more clinically relevant antigens such as hepatitis B vaccine. In one study, the antibody response of medical students given a series of three hepatitis B vaccinations around the time of major examinations depended on stress and anxiety levels. Those students who produced antihepatitis B antibodies after the first injection were significantly less stressed and anxious than those who did not. In addition, students who reported greater social support demonstrated higher titers of antibodies against hepatitis B antigens. Other research has found that the effects of stress depend on the dose of hepatitis B vaccine. Using a low-dose vaccine, antibody levels

7 months after the first vaccination were found to be negatively related with a Stress Index score measured at 2 months. In contrast, when a higher vaccine concentration was used, psychological stress was not found to be related to the antibody levels at any time point. Under certain conditions therefore, stress-induced immunomodulation in humans might be dependent on antigen dose.

The context in which a stressful event occurs for a person is important in determining its effect on immune function. Events may be perceived as stressful but if they have additional meaning or significance for the person undergoing them this may qualify their effects. For example, air traffic control is often considered to be a stressful occupation because of the intensity, responsibility, and unpredictability of the workload. Yet when psychophysiological stress reactions were assessed in air traffic controllers before and after each of two working sessions, the working sessions caused a marked increase in the concentration and secretion rate of salivary IgA, in contrast to the expected immunosuppressive effects. Corticosteroid but not salivary IgA levels were correlated with the amount of actual or perceived workload, indicating that positive emotional engagement rather than a negative stress effect may have been responsible for the observed changes.

The importance of context is also apparent from studies of emotional disclosure. When volunteers are asked to write anonymously and confidentially about traumatic events in their lives they generally report the process to be quite upsetting and stressful. However if, through their writing, they create a new relationship with the traumatic events, the effect on immune function appears supportive rather than inhibitory. This is exemplified by a study in which volunteers wrote about emotionally upsetting events every day for 4 days and then were immunized with hepatitis B vaccine. Compared with people in a control group who wrote about mundane topics, participants in the emotional expression group showed significantly higher antibody levels against hepatitis B antigens 4 and 6 months after their initial vaccination. Another study reported significantly lower EBV antibody titers (suggesting better cellular immune control over the latent virus) in people after a "stressful" emotional disclosure intervention.

By contrast, the stress of caring for a relative with progressive dementia such as Alzheimer's disease is a relatively hopeless chronic situation with little prospect of abatement. Following vaccination with an influenza virus vaccine, such caregivers exhibit a poorer anti-influenza antibody response and virus-specific T-cell response compared with the control subjects. Greater impairment in the dementia victim is associated with greater depression and loneliness in caregivers.

V. STRESS, ANTIBODIES, AND HUMAN DISEASE

Extrapolating from the effects of stress on responses to vaccination, we might also expect there to be a relationship between stress and infectious disease in humans. A variety of recent studies show this to be so, particularly in the case of upper respiratory tract infections. Family functioning affects the frequency of influenza B infection, with indices of infection being significantly associated with both family cohesion and adaptability. This raises the possibility that family dysfunction may lead to altered immune responses, which in turn increase susceptibility to infection. A study of a large number of infants, children, adolescents, and young adults in a rural Caribbean village found that abnormal glucocorticoid response profiles, diminished immunity, and frequent illness were associated with unstable family or household conditions. Family relationships and concomitant stress and immunosuppression may therefore be important intermediary links between socioeconomic conditions and child health. In support of this, a study of preschool children observed that a subset of children (labeled as "reactive") sustained higher illness rates under conditions of high family stress but lower rates in low-stress conditions.

Non-family-based stresses are also important in susceptibility to infections as demonstrated by a series of studies from Sheldon Cohen and colleagues in which volunteers were asked to complete questionnaires about perceived stress before being intentionally inoculated intranasally with a cocktail of viruses associated with upper respiratory tract infections. Psychological stress was associated in a dose–

response manner with an increased risk of acute infectious respiratory illness following virus inoculation, and this risk was attributable to increased rates of infection rather than to an increased frequency of symptoms after infection.

Subsequently, Cohen and colleagues repeated the experiment with a new group of volunteers but this time, as well as the perceived stress questionnaire, they asked people to answer questions about their interpersonal and social support systems before they sprayed the virus concoction into their noses. Again they observed a relationship between high levels of perceived stress and increased likelihood of infection, but additionally found the opposite relationship between social support and illness. Those people with more types of social ties were less susceptible to common colds, produced less mucus, were more effective in ciliary clearance of their nasal passages, and shed less virus. The presence of a diverse social network therefore buffers the potentially adverse effects of perceived stress with respect to susceptibility to infection. Further work is still required to determine the role of virus-specific antibody responses in these effects.

Finally, autoimmune illnesses typically involve high titers of antibodies against various normal components of the body, and severity is usually correlated with autoantibody titer. There are reports that stress, depression, anxiety, and anger are associated with symptomatology in patients with various autoimmune illnesses although to date, there has been little work directly linking stress, antibody levels, and illness severity. One study that has done so investigated antinuclear autoantibody titers in women and found a significantly higher incidence in women who had been sexually abused as children. These findings suggest that sexually abused girls may show evidence of an alteration in normal immune homeostatic function.

VI. CONCLUSIONS

We have seen from the animal studies that stress affects antibody responses in different ways depending on the animal, the type and timing of the stressor, and its context. Some, but not all, of the

effects appear to be mediated by the classic "stress" hormones of the hypothalamus-pituitary-adrenal axis. In order to make sense of the relationship between stress and antibody responses in humans, however, we must look beyond a purely biological or physical construction of the immune system and link its characteristics to psychological, social, and cultural processes. With Kevin Ashbridge. I have proposed that the immune system is engaged in the process of self-determination and therefore shares with the neurological and psychological domains the common goal of establishing and maintaining self-identity. From this perspective, the framework in which immune recognition occurs cannot be considered only as the context in which cells, receptors, and antigens operate, but as all the domains of life in which individuals define themselves. As a result, the meaning of events surrounding an antigenic stimulus (e.g., exposure to an infectious agent) are likely to condition the features of any observed antibody response. As discussed above, this is particularly apparent in humans where the effects of stressful events on antibody responses are dependent upon the context of meaning of those events.

See Also the Following Articles

Acute Stress Response, Experimental; Autoimmunity; Cytotoxic Lymphocytes; Immune Response; Immune Suppression; Infection; Lymphocytes; Neuroimmunomodulation

Bibliography

Booth, R. J., and Ashbridge, K. R. (1992). Teleological coherence: exploring the dimensions of the immune system. *Scand. J. Immunol.* 36(6), 751–759.

Booth, R. J., and Ashbridge, K. R. (1993). A fresh look at the relationship between the psyche and immune system: Teleological coherence and harmony of purpose. *Adv. Mind-Body Med.* 9(2), 4–23.

Booth, R. J., Petrie, K. J., *et al.*(1997). Changes in circulating lymphocyte numbers following emotional disclosure: Evidence of buffering? *Stress Med.* 13(1), 23–29.

Booth, R. J. (1998). Stress and the immune system. *In* "Encyclopedia of Immunology" (I. M. Roitt and P. J. Delves, Eds.), pp. 2220–2228. Academic Press, London.

Cohen, S., and Williamson, G. M. (1991). Stress and infectious disease in humans. *Psychol. Bull.* 109, 5–24.

Cohen, S., Tyrrell, D. A., *et al.* (1991). Psychological stress and susceptibility to the common cold. *N. Engl. J. Med.* 325(9), 606–612.

Cohen, S., and Herbert, T. B. (1996). Health psychology—Psychological factors and physical disease from the perspective of human psychoneuroimmunology. *Annu. Rev. Psychol.* 47, 113–142.

Cohen, S., Doyle, W. J., *et al.* (1997). Social ties and susceptibility to the common cold. *J. Am. Med. Assoc.* 277(24), 1940–1944.

Cohen, S., Line, S., *et al.* (1997). Chronic social stress, social status, and susceptibility to upper respiratory infections in nonhuman primates. *Psychosom. Med.* 59(3), 213–221.

Flinn, M. V., and England, B. G. (1997). Social economics of childhood glucocorticoid stress response and health. *Am. J. Physic. Anthropol.* 102(1), 33–53.

Glaser, R., Kiecolt-Glaser, J. K., *et al.* (1992). Stress-induced modulation of the immune response to recombinant hepatitis B vaccine. *Psychosom. Med.* 54(1), 22–29.

Glaser, R., Kiecolt Glaser, J. K., *et al.* (1998). The influence of psychological stress on the immune response to vaccines. *Ann. N.Y. Acad. Sci.* 840, 649–655.

Herbert, T. B., and Cohen, S. (1993). Stress and immunity in humans: A meta-analytic review. *Psychosom. Med.* 55(4), 364–379.

Jabaaij, L., Vanhattum, J., *et al.* (1996). Modulation of immune response to rDNA hepatitis B vaccination by psychological stress. *J. Psychosom. Res.* 41(2), 129–137.

Kaufmann, S. H. (1992). Heat shock proteins in health and disease. *Int. J. Clin. Lab. Res.* 21(3), 221–226.

Khansari, D. N., Murgo, A. J., *et al.* (1990). Effects of stress on the immune system. *Immunol. Today* 11(5), 170–175.

Kiecolt-Glaser, J. K., Glaser, R., *et al.* (1996). Chronic stress alters the immune response to influenza virus vaccine in older adults. *Proc. Nat. Acad. Sci. USA* 93(7), 3043–3047.

Maestroni, G. J., and Conti A. (1991). Anti-stress role of the melatonin immuno-opioid network: Evidence for a physiological mechanism involving T cell-derived, immunoreactive beta-endorphin and MET enkephalin binding to thymic opioid receptors. *Int. J. Neurosci.* 61(3–4), 289–298.

Petrie, K. J., Booth, R. J., *et al.* (1995). Disclosure of trauma and immune response to a hepatitis B vaccination program. *J. Consult. Clin. Psychol.* 63(5), 787–792.

Sheridan, J. F., Dobbs, C., *et al.* (1994). Psychoneuroimmunology: Stress effects on pathogenesis and immunity during infection. *Clin. Microbiol. Rev.* 7(2), 200–212.

Stone, A. A., and Bovbjerg, D. H. (1994). Stress and humoral immunity: A review of the human studies. *Adv. Neuroimmunol.* 4(1), 49–56.

Antidepressant Actions on Glucocorticoid Receptors

Joyce L. W. Yau and Jonathan R. Seckl

University of Edinburgh, Scotland

I. Glucocorticoid Receptors
II. Neuroendocrine Abnormalities in Depressive Disorders
III. Antidepressant Actions
IV. How Antidepressants May Regulate Glucocorticoid Receptors

GLOSSARY

atypical antidepressants Includes compounds that act similarly to tricyclic antidepressants but have a different chemical structure as well as compounds with different pharmacological actions.

dexamethasone suppression test A clinical test to check the sensitivity of the hypothalamic-pituitary-adrenal stress axis. The synthetic steroid dexamethasone is injected and the fall in plasma cortisol levels is measured. Patients with major depression fail to respond with the normal fall in plasma cortisol as seen in control subjects.

glucocorticoid receptors An ≈94-kDa intracellular protein which mediates the effects of glucocorticoid hormones. They are also known as ligand-activated transcription fac-

Encyclopedia of Stress VOLUME 1
Copyright © 2000 by Academic Press. All rights of reproduction in any form reserved.

tors since in the hormone-bound state these receptors specifically bind to and modulate the activity of target gene promoters.

glucocorticoids A major subclass of steroid hormones produced by the zona fasciculata cells of the adrenal cortex which regulate fuel metabolism and mediate part of the stress response as well as aspects of immunosuppression and inflammation and behavioral functions.

monoamine oxidase inhibitor Type of antidepressant drug which inhibits one or both forms of brain MAO, thus increasing the cytosolic stores of noradrenaline, dopamine, and serotonin in nerve terminals.

transcription factors Regulatory agents which are not part of the regulated gene(s). These trans-acting factors regulate gene transcription by binding directly or through an intermediate protein to the gene at a particular DNA sequence, called a cis-regulatory region, usually located in the 5'-flanking promoter region of the gene.

tricyclic antidepressants Drugs that act by inhibiting uptake of noradrenaline and/or 5-HT by monoaminergic nerve terminals, thus acutely facilitating transmission.

Following the termination of the stress response, negative feedback exerted by circulating glucocorticoids (GCs; corticosterone in rats, cortisol in humans) via glucocorticoid receptors (GR) act upon the hypothalamic-pituitary-adrenal (HPA) axis to restore low basal GC levels. In patients with major depression, the HPA axis is hyperactive as indicated by elevated circulating cortisol levels. This has led to the hypothesis that GR expression and/or function in depression may be abnormal. Successful therapy with antidepressant drugs restores HPA axis feedback sensitivity and lowers basal cortisol levels. One important aspect of antidepressant action may be to facilitate GR-mediated feedback inhibition upon the HPA axis, by its actions on GR.

I. GLUCOCORTICOID RECEPTORS

The glucocorticoid receptor is a ligand-activated transcription factor that resides primarily in the cytoplasm as part of a multiprotein complex with heatshock proteins (hsp). This complex maintains unbound GRs in a ligand-accessible but inactive protein conformation. Glucocorticoids are lipophilic substances and readily cross the cell membrane to inter-

act with the intracellular GR. When activated by the binding of glucocorticoids (cortisol, corticosterone), the GR undergoes a conformational change, dissociates from the hsp complex, and translocates to the nucleus, where it binds to specific DNA sequences termed glucocorticoid responsive elements (GRE) in the promoter region of glucocorticoid-responsive genes to influence gene transcription (Fig. 1).

The hormone-activated GR can also act by interacting with other transcription factors in the absence of specific DNA binding. For example, GR inhibits activating protein-1 (AP-1), a transcription factor composed of dimers of Jun and Fos family proteins, and thus represses transcription of AP-1 regulated genes such as collagenase and interleukin-2. Interaction with other transcription factors, such as cAMP response element binding protein (CREB), enhances GR-mediated transcription.

A. Glucocorticoid Feedback Regulation

Two types of adrenal steroid receptor have been described in the brain, a Type 1 receptor, indistinguishable from the peripheral mineralocorticoid receptor (MR), and a Type 2 receptor, indistinguishable from the peripheral GR. Mineralocorticoid receptor has a more restricted localization in brain and is most densely localized in hippocampal and septal neurons. Glucocorticoid receptor, in contrast, is more diffusely distributed and is found particularly in areas within the limbic brain, not only in neurons but also in glia and vascular tissues. The hippocampus plays an important role in learning and memory and is also involved in HPA axis control. Much evidence supports an inhibitory role of the hippocampus which thus suppresses HPA function. For example, lesions to the hippocampus usually lead to hypersecretion of GCs from the adrenals. Mineralocorticoid receptor and GR are particularly highly expressed in the hippocampus as shown using molecular (e.g., *in situ* hybridization; see Fig. 2), ligand binding and immunohistochemical approaches. These two types of receptors bind GCs with differing affinities and act in coordination to regulate HPA axis function with the high-affinity MR controlling basal HPA activity during the nadir of the circadian

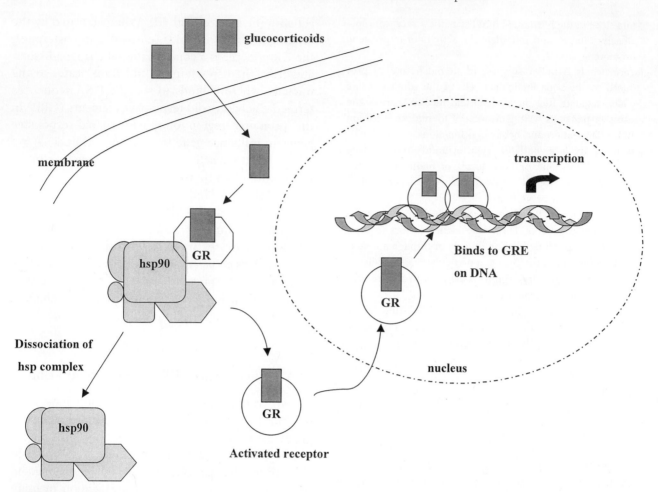

FIGURE 1 Simplified model of activation of glucocorticoid receptors. Glucocorticoids diffuse across the plasma membrane and bind to the glucocorticoid receptor (GR). Hormone binding causes a conformational change which causes dissociation of the GR/heat-shock protein (hsp) complex and nuclear translocation. The activated GR binds as a homo- or heterodimer to glucocorticoid response element sequences (GREs) in the regulatory region of target genes to regulate transcription.

rhythm of GC secretion while the lower affinity GR are involved in the termination of the stress response.

B. Hippocampal MR and GR Density and HPA Activity

Manipulations that increase hippocampal GR, such as neonatal handling, a subtle environmental stress where rat pups are physically removed from their mothers for 15 min daily during the first 2 weeks of life, improves sensitivity to GC negative feedback inhibition. In contrast, manipulations that decrease hippocampal GR density without neuronal damage reduce GC feedback sensitivity and therefore

lead to prolonged exposure to elevated GCs. Thus the density of GR in the hippocampus is of crucial importance to feedback regulation of circulating GC levels. Hippocampal MRs are also important in terms of control of inhibitory tone over the HPA axis. Rat strains with high levels of hippocampal MR expression, such as the Lewis rat, show lower basal and stress-induced HPA activity compared with Wistar rats, from which they are derived. Conversely, aged rats, which generally have reduced hippocampal MR (and GR) expression, show increased basal HPA activity and central administration of endotoxin to rats, which impairs MR function causing chronically elevated basal HPA activity.

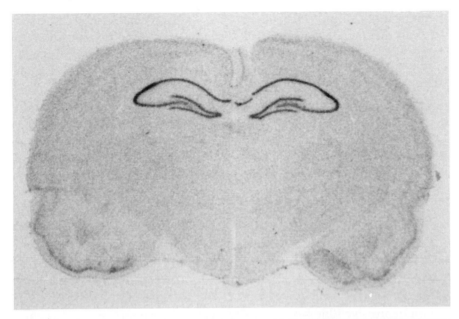

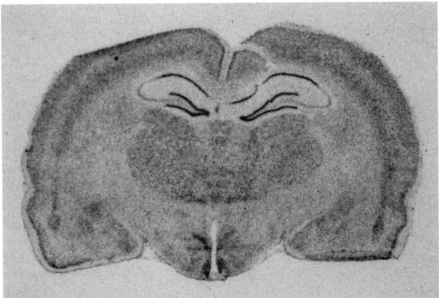

FIGURE 2 *In situ* hybridization localization of type 1 (mineralocorticoid receptor, MR; top) and type 2 (glucocorticoid receptor, GR; bottom) mRNA expression in the rat brain at the level of the dorsal hippocampus. Autoradiographs show MR expression is almost restricted to the hippocampus while GR is more widespread but also highly expressed in the hippocampus.

II. NEUROENDOCRINE ABNORMALITIES IN DEPRESSIVE DISORDERS

Hyperactivity of the HPA axis is frequently found in patients with major depression, who show in-creased concentrations of cortisol in plasma, urine, and cerebrospinal fluid and abnormal 24-h secretory patterns. These patients also fail to respond with the normal fall of plasma cortisol levels following administration of dexamethasone, a synthetic steroid that binds to GR. This forms the basis of the dexamethasone suppression test, one of the most widely studied endocrine tests in the history of psychiatry. A significant percentage (20–50%) of patients with major depression fail to suppress cortisol in response to dexamethasone challenge. This indicates inadequate GC feedback, which could be at any of a number of levels of the HPA axis (Fig. 3).

In response to an intravenous dose of corticotrophin releasing hormone (CRH), patients with depression secrete decreased amounts of ACTH. One possible mechanism to explain the blunted responsiveness to CRH could be pituitary hyporesponsiveness to CRH, itself due to CRH receptor desensitization (a consequence of sustained exposure to high CRH concentrations). Alternatively, another ACTH secretagog may be implicated in HPA activation in depression (such as vasopressin). Finally, increased cortisol in patients with depressive illnesses may be inhibiting ACTH, but perhaps inadequately for the degree of elevation of plasma cortisol. To test this,

recently, a combination of dexamethasone suppression and then CRH stimulation (the dexamethasone/CRH test) has been used in patients with depression. Dexamethasone-pretreated patients show enhanced ACTH and cortisol responses to CRH, in contrast to earlier observations. These findings suggest that in severe depression, hypercortisolemia per se attenuates the ACTH response to CRH and that the equivalent basal state of the HPA axis is in fact activated. The sensitivity (i.e., likelihood to differentiate normal from pathological state) of this DEX/CRH test is ~80%, which exceeds that of the standard dexamethasone suppression test. Thus a limbic-hypothalamic defect resulting in excessive CRH output could explain the increased cortisol secretion in depression (Fig. 3). This concept is supported by studies showing increased CRH levels in cerebrospinal fluid, increased postmortem hypothalamic CRH peptide and mRNA, and a lower than normal number of central CRH receptors among depressed patients.

Since GCs bind to MR and GR in brain sites involved in feedback control of HPA axis activity (i.e., MR and GR in the hippocampus and GR in parvocellular neurons of the hypothalamus, anterior pituitary, and other sites), it has been suggested that depression may be associated with a primary imbalance of MR/GR expression and/or function. Although there is no direct evidence for reduced receptor concentrations in the brains of patients with depression, a decreased concentration of GR in lymphocytes of depressed patients supports this possibility. However, whether GR in lymphocytes and brain are similarly regulated is unclear and perhaps unlikely. Few studies have determined the levels of these receptors in postmortem brain tissue from depressed patients.

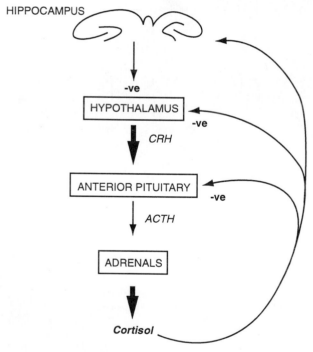

FIGURE 3 Schematic diagram of feedback control of HPA axis in depression. Cortisol suppress the axis by binding to GRs in key feedback sites, hippocampus, paraventricular nucleus (PVN) of the hypothalamus, and pituitary gland. In major depression there is a hyperactive HPA axis with excess CRH and cortisol secretion, likely due to a hippocampal-hypothalamic defect.

III. ANTIDEPRESSANT ACTIONS

Antidepressant drugs have been in use since the 1950s. Although clinically effective, their mechanism of action is still not clearly understood. There are two major classes of antidepressants, monoamine oxidase inhibitors and monoamine reuptake inhibitors; both increase the concentration of biogenic amines [noradrenaline (NA) and/or serotonin (5-HT)] in the synaptic cleft. The ability of antidepressant drugs to facilitate monoaminergic transmission led to the monoamine theory proposed in 1965, which suggests that depression results from functionally deficient monoaminergic transmission in the CNS. However, studies have not consistently shown a lack of biogenic amines or their metabolites in body fluids of depressed patients. There is also a clear discrepancy between the rapid effect of antidepressants in increasing synaptic concentrations of biogenic amines and the time course for the clinical efficacy of antidepressant treatment which takes 2–3 weeks. A common, intracellular adaptation beyond the levels of 5-HT and NA and their receptors could account for the actions of the different types of antidepressants. Successful antidepressant treatment leads to normalization of HPA axis hyperactivity. Therefore one such mechanism of antidepressant action is thought to be through direct modulation of GR and/or MR in tissues involved in HPA feedback regulation.

A. Effects on HPA Function in Humans

Longitudinal studies in which depressed patients who were nonsupressors of dexamethasone were retested weekly suggested that a return to dexamethasone suppressibility of plasma cortisol levels precedes the resolution of depressive psychopathology. Moreover, antidepressants may sometimes reduce CRH levels in human spinal fluid, suggesting that long-term administration of antidepressants may suppress the HPA system and that lowering HPA activity and clinical response are causally related. Finally, antidepressant-resistant depression can be improved with GR synthesis inhibitors such as metyrapone.

B. Effects on HPA Function and Hippocampal Corticosteroid Receptors in Rats

Numerous studies in rats have shown that long-term *in vivo* treatment with a range of tricyclic and nontricyclic antidepressants can enhance GC feedback inhibition (as indicated by decreased basal and/or stress-induced GC secretion) and/or increasing

corticosteroid receptor expression, particularly MRs, in the hippocampus (Table I). An increase in MR and/or GR mRNA or binding in rat hippocampus can be observed irrespective of preferential inhibitory action of the antidepressant on reuptake of monoamines. This effect is dependent on the duration of antidepressant administration and requires weeks rather than days of treatment. For example, administration of the tricyclic antidepressant amitriptyline, or moclobemide, a reversible inhibitor of MAO-A, increased levels of hippocampal MR transiently by 40–70% between 2 and 5 weeks after the start of treatment. This is compariable to the increases in MR mRNA after long-term treatment with antidepressants. The levels of hypothalamic and hippocampal GR were also significantly increased by 20–25% at 5 weeks of treatment. The antidepressant-induced increases in brain GRs may underlie the observed decrease in basal circulating ACTH and corticosterone levels and in some cases decreased adrenal size. Indeed, the time course of antidepressant actions on GRs in the animal studies coincides with their long-term actions on HPA activity and follows closely that of clinical improvement of depression in humans. It is interesting to note that the antidepressant-induced increases in hippocampal MR are more pronounced than GR and that the increases in the receptors are not maintained despite continual antidepressant treatment (Table I). Systemic administration of anti-mineralocorticoids has been found to impair the therapeutic efficacy of antidepressants consistent with an important role for MRs in vulnerability to depression. Mineralocorticoid receptor controls basal HPA activity and, although not directly involved in the termination of the stress response, may influence the effects of GR on feedback control of the HPA axis. It is unclear how the lower plasma corticosterone levels are maintained long after hippocampal GR expression has returned to control levels and are no longer increased following long-term antidepressant treatment.

C. Effects in Transgenic Mice with Reduced GR Levels

Transgenic mice with impaired GR function were created by attenuating mRNA expression with a GR

TABLE I

Antidepressant Drug Effects on Mineralocorticoid and Glucocorticoid Receptor mRNA
Expression and Binding Sites in Rat Hippocampus

Antidepressant class	Drug	Dose/route	Duration	Hippocampal	
				MR	GR
Tricyclic	Amitriptyline (NA = 5-HT uptake)	20 mg/kg/day i.p.	2 weeks	87% incr. (mRNA)	56% incr. (mRNA)
		10 mg/kg/day i.p.	10 weeks	17–28% incr. (mRNA)	No effect
		10 mg/kg/twice s.c. daily	3 weeks	16–29% incr. (mRNA)	24–29% incr. (mRNA)
		4.5 mg/ky/day, p.o.	2–5 weeks	40–74% incr. (binding sites)	0–26% incr. (binding sites)
			7 weeks	18% incr. (binding sites)	No effect
	Imipramine (NA >5-HT uptake)	5 mg/kg/day i.p.	2–6 weeks	0–70% incr. (mRNA)	No effect
	Desipramine (NA uptake)	10 mg/kg/day i.p.	2 weeks	60% incr. (mRNA)	42% incr. (mRNA)
		10 mg/kg/day p.o.	4 weeks	32–36% incr. (mRNA)	No effect
MAO inhibitor	Moclobemide	4.5 mg/kg/day p.o.	2–5 weeks	65–76% incr. (binding sites)	0–10% incr. (binding sites)
			7 weeks	19% incr. (binding sites)	No effect
"Atypical"	Citalopram (5-HT uptake)	20 mg/kg/day	2 weeks	17% incr. (mRNA)	No effect
	Fluoxetine (5-HT uptake)	5 mg/kg/day i.p.	2–6 weeks	0–56% incr. (mRNA)	No effect
	Venlafaxine (5-HT >NA uptake)	10 mg/kg day, p.o.	4 weeks	25% incr. (mRNA)	No effect

Abbreviations: i.p., interperitoneal; s.c., subcutaneous; p.o., oral route; incr., increase.
Note. The relative potency of antidepressant drugs in blocking reuptake of noradrenaline (NA) and serotonin (5-HT) is shown in brackets.

antisense transgene. These animals have numerous characteristics of human depression, including increased HPA activity, resistance to suppression of GCs by dexamethasone, feeding disturbances, and cognitive deficits. Long-term treatment with the antidepressant desipramine increased hypothalamic GR mRNA and binding, reduced HPA axis activity as shown by the partial reversal of enhanced ACTH and corticosterone secretion, and improved cognitive function. These data support the hypothesis that a dysfunctional GR system could be involved in the etiology of depression.

D. Behavioral Effects of Antidepressant Actions via GR

There is now increasing evidence to link elevated cortisol levels in a subgroup of elderly humans to impaired memory associated with the hippocampus. Depression shows similar neuroendocrine abnormalities to those of unsuccessful aging, such as elevated GCs and impaired memory [dexamethasone nonsuppressors show significantly more commission errors in a word-learning paradigm (declarative memory) compared to suppressors]. Chronically elevated GCs increase the vulnerability of the hippocampus to other insults which may lead to structural and even neurotoxic tissue damage. Recent magnetic resonance image studies have shown smaller hippocampal volumes in recurrent major depression and in healthy elderly subjects in whom cortisol levels are rising with age. Successful antidepressant drug therapy in major depression reverses hippocampal atrophy and cognitive impairments. Long-term treatment of middle-aged rats with the antidepressants amitriptyline or desipramine until 2 years old reduced the occurrence of hippocampal-dependent spatial memory impairments and this may, in part, be a consequence of the reduced GC levels. Whether antidepressants can have the same effect in elderly humans with elevated cortisol levels and cognitive impairments has yet to be studied.

IV. HOW ANTIDEPRESSANTS MAY REGULATE GLUCOCORTICOID RECEPTORS

Recent studies have focused on possible underlying mechanisms whereby antidepressant actions can modulate hippocampal GR. There is evidence to suggest that antidepressant effects, perhaps by increasing monoamines in the synaptic cleft, in particular 5-HT (serotonin), starts the cascade of events leading to increased transcription of GR. Serotonin acting via a ketanserin-sensitive cell surface receptor leads to increased second messenger (e.g., cAMP) levels in the cytosol of the cell, which in turn increases tertiary messengers, cAMP-dependent transcription factors in the nucleus, which might bind to the promoter of the GR gene to increase transcription (Fig. 4).

A. Serotonin

Serotonin increases GR mRNA and binding sites directly in hippocampal neurons in culture. This effect involves the second messenger, cAMP, and is blocked by ketanserin (mostly a 5-HT2 receptor antagonist). Thus 5-HT may act via a ketanserin-sensitive cell surface 5-HT receptor to increase GR. Antidepressant drugs may therefore increase hippocampal GR expression *in vivo* via its actions on po-

tentiating monoaminergic (e.g., 5-HT and NA) neurotransmission.

B. Transcription Factors

Chronic antidepressant administration increases the expression of the nuclear transcription factor cAMP response element binding protein (CREB) in the rat hippocampus. Interestingly, temporal cortex CREB concentrations in major depressive disorder patients treated with antidepressants at the time of death were higher than in untreated patients. cAMP response element binding protein could be activated by 5-HT and NA receptors that directly stimulate cAMP production (e.g., $5\text{-}HT_{4,6,7}$ or β-adrenergic receptors) or 5-HT or NA receptors (e.g., $5\text{-}HT_{2A,C}$ and α_1-adrenergic receptors) that lead to stimulation of Ca^{2+}-dependent protein kinases. Upregulation of CREB appears to be a common action of chronic antidepressant treatments and since CREB can upregulate GR gene transcription, this may be one aspect whereby antidepressants facilitate GR-mediated feedback inhibition and thereby reverse GC hypersecretion in depression. Chronic amitriptyline treatment in rats has also been shown to increase the expression of another transcription factor, NGFIA, in the hippocampus. This transcription factor may bind to the GR promoter to increase transcription of GR.

C. Direct Modulation of GR

Treatment of primary cultures of rat brain hypothalamic neurons for 48 h with the antidepressants desipramine and amitriptyline increases GR mRNA despite the lack of monoaminergic terminals in these cultures. A direct effect of antidepressants on GR was also shown when mouse fibroblast LTK⁻ cells or Neuro 2A, treated with desipramine, produced a 50–200% increase in the reporter gene chloramphenicol acetyltransferase (CAT) activity transcribed from a GR gene promoter region. These fibroblast cells do not secrete catecholamines and therefore the desipramine-induced increase in GR gene activity involves a mechanism independent of NA-reuptake inhibition.

Intriguingly, desipramine treatment for 24 h in mouse L929 fibroblast cells induced GR to translocate from the cytoplasm to the nucleus (using GR

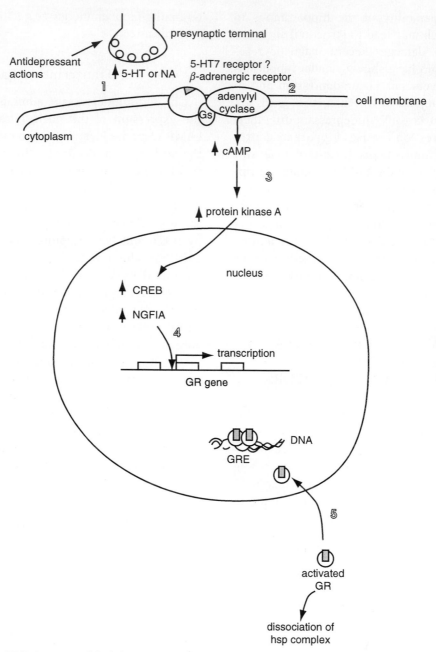

FIGURE 4   Model of the action of chronic antidepressant treatments on GR. Antidepressants increase monoamines (5-HT or NA) in the synaptic cleft (1), which activate cell surface monoamine receptors coupled to the cAMP-protein kinase A cascade (2). This leads to increases in the second messengers cAMP and protein kinase A (3), leading to an increase cAMP-dependent transcription factors in the nucleus (4), which may bind to the GR gene promoter to increase transcription. Alternatively, antidepressants may act directly to increase GR activity/DNA binding by inducing GR translocation from the cytoplasm to the nucleus (5).

immunostaining technique) in the absence of any endogenous or exogenous steroid. Desipramine also potentiates dexamethasone-induced GR translocation and dexamethasone-induced GR-mediated gene transcription. One possible explanation for this steroid-independent modulation of GR could be that desipramine directly acts on one or more hsps and facilitates the dissociation of the receptor from the hsp complex. Whether this occurs *in vivo* is not known but suggests that antidepressants may facilitate GR-mediated feedback inhibition by facilitating GR translocation and function. Thus antidepressants via a variety of mechanisms facilitate GR and MR function and hence reduce HPA overactivity. The importance of the mechanisms of antidepressant and other potential therapeutic effects are the subject of active study.

See Also the Following Articles

Depression and Manic-Depressive Illness; Depression Models; Glucocorticoid Negative Feedback; Glucocorticoids, Overview; HPA Axis

Bibliography

Barden, N. (1996). Modulation of glucocorticoid receptor gene expression by antidepressant drugs. *Pharmacopsychiatry* **29**, 12–22.

Barden, N., Reul, J. M. H. M., and Holsboer, F. (1995). Do antidepressants stabilize mood through actions on the hypothalamic-pituitary-adrenocortical system? *Trends Neurosci.* **18**, 6–11.

De Kloet, E. R., Vreugdenhil, E., Oitzl, M. S., and Joëls, M. (1998). Brain corticosteroid receptor balance in health and disease. *Endocr. Rev.* **19**, 269–301.

Dinan, T. (1994). Glucocorticoids and the genesis of depressive illness: A psychobiological model. *Br. J. Psychiat.* **164**, 356–371.

Holsboer, F., and Barden, N. (1996). Antidepressants and hypothalamic-pituitary-adrenocortical regulation. *Endocr. Rev.* **17**, (1991). 187–205.

Jacobson, L., and Sapolsky, R. (1991). The role of the hippocampus in feedback regulation of the hypothalamic-pituitary-adrenal axis. *Endocr. Rev.* **12**, 118–134.

Reul, J. M. H. M., and de Kloet, E. R. (1985). Two receptor systems for corticosterone in rat brain: Microdissection and differential occupation. *Endocrinology* **117**, 2505–2511.

Reul, J. M. H. M., Stec, I., Söder, M., and Holsboer, F. (1993). Chronic treatment of rats with the antidepressant amitriptyline attenuates the activity of the hypothalamic-pituitary-adrenocortical system. *Endocrinology* **133**, 312–320.

Seckl, J. R., and Fink, G. (1992). Antidepressants increase glucocorticoid and mineralocorticoid receptor mRNA expression in the rat hippocampus *in vivo*. *Neuroendocrinol* **55**, 621–626.

Antihypertensive Drugs
see Beta-Adrenergic Blockers

Antisocial Disorders

Kathleen Pajer

University of Pittsburgh Medical Center

GLOSSARY

antisocial personality disorder A type of personality disorder characterized by features such as frequent violations of social and legal norms, grandiose thoughts, arrogance, manipulative behavior, superficial charm, a lack of attachment to others, little capacity for empathy, and an absence of guilt. Synonyms: **sociopathy, psychopathy, and dyssocial personality.**

conduct disorder A behavior disorder of childhood and adolescence characterized by features such as truancy, stealing, running away, frequent fighting, vandalism, or other illegal activities.

developmental psychopathology A field of study that focuses on the development and longitudinal course of psychiatric disorders across the life cycle.

continuity A term used in developmental psychopathology to refer to behaviors that continue from one stage of life to another, e.g., from adolescence to adulthood.

discontinuity Another term from the field of developmental psychopathology referring to behaviors that do not persist from one life stage to another.

escalation A term used in criminology to describe an increase in the frequency of illegal acts or an increase in the severity of such behavior over time.

desistence A term used by criminologists to describe the cessation of criminal activity in a person who has previously committed illegal acts.

T he term antisocial disorders describes several groups of behaviors, all of which are illegal, irresponsible, or harmful to others. In the field of psychiatry, children and adolescents with antisocial behavior are said to have conduct disorder (CD), and adults who display consistently antisocial behavior are diagnosed with antisocial personality disorder (ASPD). The legal system categorizes children or adolescents who display antisocial behavior by breaking the law as juvenile delinquents; adults are referred to as criminals or adult offenders. Nearly all people who commit illegal acts have either CD or ASPD (depending on their age), but not all people who meet criteria for one of the psychiatric disorders have actually been arrested or incarcerated.

I. DEFINITION

A. Clinical Example

A.W. is a 40-year-old male who was released from prison 6 months ago. This was his second prison term and both had been served for burglary. A.W. was first sent to prison for 3 years when he was 25 years old. He had been working as a security system installer. He would install an alarm system and then return later and rob the house. A.W. proudly says that he robbed more than 800 houses in a 3 year period. After he served his sentence, he was out for a short time and learned how to open safes. He did several large jobs in houses and businesses before getting caught and sent back to prison for 10 years.

A.W. has a history of violence, consisting of fights in bars and on the street with other men, and fighting with his wife and girlfriends. His family believes he may have murdered his first wife and successfully hidden the body, but this has never been proven. A.W. openly admits that he initiates violence because he is "bored" or "irritated." He himself was a childhood victim of severe violence perpetrated by his alcoholic father, who would also attack A.W.'s mother. He reports many beatings with his father's hands and fists, as well as with a belt, board, and electrical cord. He suffered multiple episodes of head trauma. A.W. started fighting peers when he was 12 and hit his father back for the first time when he was 14.

School was not easy for A.W. and he had numerous learning problems. He left school in the 7th grade at the age of 15 and joined the Army, using his dead brother's social security number. Testing in the Army revealed that he was bright and actually was functioning on a 12th grade level, but he got into so many fights that he eventually received a dishonorable discharge.

A.W.'s health is not good. He suffered his first grand mal seizure while in prison 3 years ago. He now has them regularly, despite medication. He has chronic bronchitis and hypertension. He used to drink heavily, but stopped 10 years ago when put back into prison and reports that he will not drink again. He denies any drug use other than early experimentation with marijuana.

There have been several long-term female relationships in A.W.'s life, although he has had multiple brief liaisons. He has seven children, born to three different women. His first wife disappeared after the birth of their second child, and it was widely known that A.W. was angry because he thought she was seeing another man. He has had two other important relationships, and both these women have complained that he was physically abusive. He denies being abusive to his children, but has not been home enough to actually parent them. He reports sadness about that, as four of his children are in foster care.

B. Classification of Antisocial Disorders

The adult syndrome of ASPD was first described by Hervey Cleckley in his famous book *The Mask of Insanity* (1941, Mosby, St. Louis). Cleckley's original characterization of interpersonal, behavioral, and affective deviance has remained the core of subsequent diagnostic criteria. As exemplified by A.W.'s history, people with this disorder are narcissistic, superficially charming, manipulative, often aggressive and short-tempered, have multiple, unstable relationships, lack empathy and guilt, and display irresponsible behavior, often with overt criminality. The Diagnostic and Statistical Manual-IV (DSM-IV)

(American Psychiatric Association Press, 1994) has defined ASPD as a persistent pattern of behavior that does not take into account the rights of others, or seeks to do overt harm to others. Criteria include an inability to maintain a stable relationship or employment, irresponsible behavior such as avoidance of financial obligations or parenting duties, cruel behavior toward animals or humans, and repeated arrests (or illegal activities, even if not caught). The International Classification of Diseases - 10th Edition (ICD-10) (World Health Organization, 1992) has similar criteria for dyssocial personality. Most adults with antisocial personality disorder began to display deviant behavior in childhood or adolescence. Youths with three or more of the following symptoms by age 13 are classified as having conduct disorder in the DSM-IV: stealing with or without confrontation with the victim, running away, acts of cruelty or bullying, fighting, truancy, forcing someone into sexual relations, carrying or using a weapon, vandalism, or arrests.

Psychiatric diagnoses are traditionally made through clinical interviews, interviewer-rated symptom questionnaires, or self-report questionnaires. Each of these methods is more difficult to use with the person who has antisocial personality features. These patients are rarely suffering or complaining of symptoms. In fact, in a brief interaction such as an examination, they may be quite charming and engaging. They are often puzzled as to why a psychiatric evaluation has been requested and usually blame others for their actions. Self-report inventories are problematic because of the high rate of lying in this population. The two most frequently used methods of assessment are highly structured interviews that follow strict diagnostic criteria such as those found in DSM-IV or the Hare Psychopathy Checklist (PCL) (see references). Filling out the PCL requires the use of multiple sources of information, rather than just using a clinical interview.

C. Epidemiology

The estimated prevalence of CD in prepubertal children ranges between 2 and 8% for boys and less than 2% for girls. The gender gap narrows in adolescence and rates increase, with 3–12% of boys meeting criteria for the diagnosis compared to 8–10% of girls. CD is more common in poor urban areas than in suburban or rural neighborhoods, but poverty is a consistent correlate.

ASPD is also much more common in males than in females. From 5 to 15% of the general population may meet criteria for this disorder, but in the prison populations, the estimates range from 20 to 80%.

II. DEVELOPMENT AND COURSE OF ANTISOCIAL BEHAVIOR

In general, most of the studies on the development and course of antisocial disorders have studied males, although more studies are now including antisocial females. The majority of the studies have also used delinquent or criminal populations, so it is often difficult to generalize findings to nonincarcerated populations.

A. Biological Factors

There are several major lines of research into the biological factors that may underlie antisocial behaviors. One hypothesis is that CD or ASPD is caused by a general hypoarousal of the nervous system, producing a lack of response to stimuli that would normally provoke stress, fear, or pain. This lack of response would lead people with antisocial disorders to pursue excessive stimulation, manifested by sensation-seeking and risk-taking behaviors. Furthermore, they would be unable to learn from aversive consequences or punishment because their stress response would not be robust enough. Studies of heart rate, skin conductance, electroencephalogram (EEG) changes, and basal cortisol levels in subjects with antisocial behavior all support a theory of hypoarousal. Some of these characteristics in childhood and adolescence have been reported to predict adult sociopathy. Indicators of hypoarousal also differentiated between sociopathic and nonsociopathic subjects in a group of men whose fathers were all incarcerated, implying that the abnormalities in arousal may have a genetic basis.

A second line of research on putative biological mechanisms for sociopathy stems from neuropsychological and neuroimaging studies. Both types of data indicate that antisocial behavior is associated with abnormalities in the prefrontal and frontotemporal areas of the brain. These areas of the brain are responsible for the "executive functions" of the brain: impulse control, evaluation and integration of new data, and regulation of emotional tone and motivation. Abnormalities in these brain areas could lead to a pattern of sociopathic behavior by reducing the ability to delay gratification, decreasing the ability to learn new behaviors in response to past mistakes, and producing intense emotional states such as rage on an unpredictable basis.

Neurotransmitter function and gonadal hormonal influences on aggressive and impulsive behaviors in subjects with sociopathy have also been investigated. The findings in both domains are somewhat contradictory, but this may be due to methodological differences between studies.

In general, decreased serotonin neurotransmission in the central nervous system appears to be associated with aggression, although some researchers suggest that the link may actually be between low serotonin and impulsivity. Testosterone levels appear to be higher in some groups of violent males, but the relationship seems to be a reflection more of dominance than of pathological aggression.

B. Childhood Risk Factors

Several risk factors present in childhood are associated with adult sociopathy. One of the most consistent findings, whether measured retrospectively or prospectively, is exposure to harsh, inconsistent parental discipline. The severity of the punishments can range from frequent verbal shaming to overt physical abuse, but the key prognostic factor appears to be the unpredictability of the hostile parental behaviors.

Children who have attentional problems with hyperactivity seem to be at particularly high risk of developing antisocial behavior. These studies have reported the same results for boys and girls. If the child also has a low IQ and one antisocial parent, then early sociopathic behavior is quite likely.

C. Developmental Paths

The course or path of childhood and adolescent antisocial behavior varies from person to person, but the continuity between this type of behavior and adult sociopathy is one of the most robust findings in clinical psychiatric research. Children who begin to display antisocial behavior prepubertally appear to be at the highest risk for severe sociopathy and progression to overt adult criminality.

Both childhood and adolescent onset CD may progress through levels of increasing severity and frequency of the behaviors, a process known as escalation. Escalation is associated with an early onset of antisocial behavior, a history of family sociopathy, violence and aggressive behaviors, social marginalization in childhood, school failure, attention deficit and hyperactivity symptoms, and continued association with deviant peers. The behaviors may also simply cease in adolescence or early adulthood (desistence). Desistence is associated with a later onset of sociopathic behavior, an absence of aggression, a strong family structure, and early school and social success. The course of the disorder may also change when a person becomes involved with drugs or alcohol.

The majority of data on developmental paths have come from studies of males. Although less is known about females, a comprehensive review of the existing literature reported that girls with CD also appear to be at an increased risk for adult sociopathy. Additionally, many of these girls develop other psychiatric disorders and have a great deal of difficulty functioning as mothers or employees. Fewer girls progress to overt criminality when compared to boys, but many remain aggressive and destructive toward family members (e.g., their children or spouses).

III. PREVENTION AND TREATMENT

As discussed earlier, antisocial behaviors often begin in childhood or adolescence. Once established, they are very difficult to treat. As a result, researchers in the last two decades have begun to study the effectiveness of prevention and some innovative prevention programs have reported surprisingly good results.

Although the programs differ somewhat, they have one common feature. All of them provide services to the child in every domain of his or her life. The programs often focus on mothers identified to be at risk for producing antisocial children and work to improve maternal physical and psychological health during pregnancy or following delivery. Didactic parenting training, coupled with close supervision by a visiting nurse, has also been helpful. Helping the mothers to establish their own support systems and showing them how to negotiate through the intricacies of the medical, welfare, and mental health systems have also been effective. The second phase of preventive programs is usually to assist the child in learning social skills in preschool and the community and early recognition and treatment of comorbid disorders such as attentional problems. Prevention programs that focus on whole communities of children or teens at risk have also had some success. These interventions usually occur in selected schools and consist of improving self-esteem through academic achievement or increasing prosocial behavior with game-based activities and rewards.

Standard psychiatric or psychological treatments are not very useful with patients who have antisocial disorders. The most effective treatment strategies are multimodal. Interventions that combine individual cognitive behavioral psychotherapy, pharmacotherapy for aggression or hyperactivity, parenting training, school supervision, and anger management skills (often for the entire family) have the highest rates of success.

Once a youth has committed an illegal act and is arrested, or adjudicated delinquent, it is much harder for him or her to receive treatment rather than punishment. Data suggest that employing multimodal treatment programs, in combination with a compensation process, to atone for the offense and psychiatric treatment of comorbid disorders works better than incarceration at promoting desistence.

The same treatment dilemma exists for adults with ASPD. Those who do not engage in criminal behavior rarely present for treatment unless they are in the midst of a crisis such as a divorce. The personality characteristics of these patients make them poor candidates for psychotherapy. They may be noncompliant with any type of long-term treatment because they are only temporarily motivated to reduce the discomfort produced by the crisis. Adults with ASPD who have committed crimes do present for treatment while incarcerated, but this is usually because of comorbid psychiatric disorders such as depression. Pharmacologic treatment of these comorbid problems or specific problematic behaviors such as aggression is possible, but the underlying pattern of sociopathic behavior is rarely altered.

See Also the Following Articles

AGGRESSIVE BEHAVIOR; CHILD ABUSE; CRIME VICTIMS; PSYCHOTIC DISORDERS; SEXUAL ASSAULT; VIOLENCE

Bibliography

Farrington, D. P. 1995. The development of offending and antisocial behavior from childhood: Key findings from the Cambridge study in delinquent development. *J. Child Psychol. Psychiat.* 36, 929–964.

Hare, R. D. 1990. "Manual for the Revised Psychopathy Checklist." Multi-Health Systems, Toronto.

Kazdin, A. E. 1993. Treatment of conduct disorder: Progress and direction in psychotherapy research. *Dev. Psychopathol.* 5, 277–310.

Loeber, R. 1988. Natural histories of conduct problems, delinquency, and associated substance use: Evidence for developmental progressions. *In* "Advances in Clinical Child Psychology" B. B. Lahey, and A. E. Kazdin, (eds.). pp. 73–124. Plenum Press, New York.

Moffitt, T. E. 1993. Adolescent-limited and life-course-persistent antisocial behavior: A developmental taxonomy. *Psychol. Rev.* 674–701.

Pajer, K. A. 1998. What happens to "bad" girls? A review of the adult outcomes of antisocial adolescent females. *Am. J. Psychiat.* 155, 862–870.

Raine, A. 1993. "The Psychopathology of Crime: Criminal Behavior as a Clinical Disorder." Academic Press, San Diego.

Stoff, D. M., Breiling, J., and Maser, J. D., eds. 1997. "Handbook of Antisocial Behavior." Wiley, New York.

Anxiety

Arne Öhman

Karolinska Institutet, Sweden

Anxiety is an aversive emotional state associated with the apprehensive anticipation of more or less likely future dangers. It incorporates somatic symptoms of tension and dysphoric feelings.

I. ANXIETY AND FEAR

Anxiety is closely related to fear. The traditional distinction has been that anxiety, in contrast to fear, lacks an obvious eliciting stimulus. According to the definitions given here, anxiety and fear occupy different temporal locations in relation to threatening events, anxiety typically being anticipatory to, and fear elicited by, threatening stimuli. Furthermore, whereas the threat in anxiety often is imagined, it is typically real in fear. These differences promote different phenomenologies in the two states, with anxiety dominated by an unpleasant feeling of foreboding and fear by an urge to escape. However, the perhaps most fruitful distinction can be derived from the controllability of the threat. Fear is predicated on the hope that the situation can be coped with, i e , that it is controllable. Fear, therefore, is a source of motivation because it supports active attempts to deal with the threat by, for example, escape or avoidance. Anxiety, on the other hand, results when the coping attempt fails, i.e., when the situation is perceived as uncertain or uncontrollable. With few or inefficient means to cope with the threat, the option left is apprehensive anticipation of the more or less likely expected disaster.

This analysis gives anxiety and fear a joint origin in an evolved defense system that has served through eons of time to protect organisms from survival threats. The primary emotional counterpart is fear, which supports adaptive coping with threat. However, depending on restrictions in the controllability of the situation, there is a dynamic interplay between the closely related emotional qualities of fear and anxiety. Because fear is the prototype reflected in anxiety, the two emotional states have many similarities, e.g., in terms of components (aversive feelings, physiological responses, behavior). Thus, the two states may often be hard to distinguish, but this is due to the fact that they are fused in the real world rather than to conceptual obscurity.

Placing anxiety and fear at different regions of a controllability dimension has the added virtue of relating both these states to another related concept dominated by dysphoric feelings, that of depression. Thus, whereas fear is the emotional concomitant in situations of somewhat controllable threat, anxiety takes over when the uncontrollability of the situation undermines active coping attempts. With further and more lasting uncontrollability, coping becomes fruitless, which makes the organism helpless and replaces anxiety with depression. Thus, the conceptual view advanced here is compatible with the emerging notion of negative affect as a pervasive higher-order factor behind both anxiety and mood disorders.

II. DIFFERENT TYPES OF ANXIETY

A. Situational versus Free-Floating Anxiety

There are several more or less interdependent bases for distinguishing between different types of anxiety. The controllability analysis puts anxiety on a continuum between fear and depression. There are other related continua that are often invoked in this context. One is that of situational versus free-floating anxiety. Situational anxiety is bound to a particular stimulus such as in phobic anxiety. Whether anxiety of this type should be called anxiety or fear depends on the controllability of the fear stimuli in the situation. In situationally unfocused or free-floating anxiety, the intensity of the anxiety does not vary with the situation but is always present at a noticeable level.

B. Panic Attacks versus Generalized Anxiety

Free-floating, or as it is often called, generalized anxiety is correlated with worries (e.g., about finances or academic performance). It is often contrasted with panic attacks, which have been claimed to represent a distinct subtype of anxiety. A panic attack is a sudden surge of often overwhelming anxiety dominated by physical symptoms such as shortness of breath, dizziness, palpitations, trembling, sweating, nausea, hot flashes, and chest pain. It may also involve feelings of depersonalization and fears of dying or going crazy. A panic attack may appear spontaneous, coming out of the blue, or be situationally provoked. For example, a social phobic may experience panic when forced to face a threatening social context.

Some people have occasional panic attacks with no or only little residual anxiety between the attacks. However, because a panic attack is such an overwhelmingly aversive experience, the person may start to develop anticipatory anxiety for further attacks. As a result, occasional attacks will now appear against a fluctuating background of anticipatory anxiety, and the distinction between panic and generalized anxiety will be somewhat blurred.

C. Factor-Analytically Derived Varieties of Anxiety

Factor-analytic work on observed and self-reported anxiety symptoms in normals and patients confirms clinical observations in delineating two clusters of anxiety. Thus there is one cluster of "somatic overreactivity" composed of symptoms such as sweating, flushing, and shallow breathing and reports of heart palpitations, intestinal discomforts, and aches and pains. The other cluster may be called "cognitive or psychic anxiety" and is composed of intrusive and unwanted thoughts, worrying, ruminations, restlessness, and feelings of muscle tension.

D. Trait versus State Anxiety

The distinction between panic and generalized anxiety is related to another important distinction. A particular person may suffer from habitually elevated anxiety, never feeling completely free of apprehension and worry. This habitually elevated anxiety is called trait anxiety. Nevertheless, the level of anxiety may still vary somewhat across time and situations. The momentary level of anxiety at a particular point in time, e.g., during a panic attack, on the other hand, is called state anxiety. Even though a person with high trait anxiety tends also to have high state anxiety in most situations, there may be situation in which the state anxiety of a low-trait anxious person is still higher because of stressful circumstances.

E. Clinical versus Normal Anxiety

Anxiety is both a phenomenon of everyday life and an important sign of psychopathology. Thus, there is a need to distinguish between normal and clinical anxiety. In general, clinical anxiety is more intense, recurrent, and persistent than normal anxiety. Furthermore, whereas normal anxiety is proportional to the real danger of the situation, the intensity of clinical anxiety is clearly above what is reasonable, given the objective danger involved. As a result, clinical anxiety tends to paralyze individuals and undermine their coping efforts. Consequently, it results in impeded psychosocial or physiological functioning which may promote contact with treatment facilities.

III. ANXIETY AND COGNITION

To be anxious implies a preoccupation with threat and danger. For example, persons with high anxiety tend specifically to overestimate the likelihood of being befallen by negative events, but they do not differ from persons with low anxiety in judging the likelihood that they will experience positive events. Anxiety and cognition, in fact, are intimately related to each other in a two-way communication in which anxiety determines cognition and cognition determines anxiety.

A. Attentional Bias for Threat

The immobility exhibited by animals that freeze in the face of danger is associated with hypervigilance to the environment. Similarly, there is a large research literature documenting that anxiety is associated with hypervigilance and an attentional bias for threat. For example, when simultaneously exposed to two visual stimuli, one threatening and the other nonthreatening, anxiety patients tend systematically to attend to the threatening stimulus as revealed by shortened reaction times to probe stimuli occurring at the location of the threatening stimulus. Low-anxiety persons, on the other hand, tend to shy away from threat because their reaction times are faster to probes replacing nonthreatening stimuli. This general finding is valid regardless whether the threat is conveyed by pictorial (e.g., angry faces) or word (e.g., "cancer") stimuli. Similarly, if persons high or low in anxiety are asked to name the color in which words are printed (the Stroop paradigm), the color-naming latency is longer for threatening than for nonthreatening words in anxious but not in nonanxious persons. This implies that highly-anxious persons are distracted by attention to the threatening word content.

The attentional bias for threatening stimuli in highly anxious research participants does not require conscious recognition of the stimuli. Several studies have shown that similar results are obtained when the threatening stimuli are presented masked by other stimuli, thus precluding their conscious recognition. For example, using the Stroop color–word paradigm, longer color-naming latencies to threatening words are observed in highly anxious persons, even if the word is shown only for 20 ms and immediately masked by illegible letter fragments of the same color. This finding implies that the attentional bias operates at an automatic, preattentive level of information processing. Thus, outside the conscious awareness of individuals, this attentional bias determines that they will preferentially attend to threatening events in their surroundings. This preference for focusing attention on threat no doubt helps maintain the anxiety.

B. Expectancy and Interpretational Bias

Attentional bias provides a case where anxiety drives cognition. However, it is also abundantly clear that cognition drives anxiety. This is particularly well documented for panic. A compelling argument can be advanced to the effect that catastrophical interpretations provide a necessary condition for the elicitation of panic. According to the dominating model, stress or anxiety results in an autonomic arousal that is perceived by the person. The perception of this bodily change prompts more anxiety and further autonomic arousal in a vicious circle. But it is only when the interpretation of the bodily symptoms becomes catastrophic, e.g., the person feels that they signal serious illness or imminent death, that the full-blown panic attack emerges.

Several lines of evidence support this model. For example, when panic attacks are pharmacologically promoted in panic patients (e.g., through lactate infusion or CO_2 inhalation) panic is unlikely if patients are informed about the expected effects of the manipulation. If they are not informed, or misinformed, on the other hand, panic patients, but not social phobics, are likely to experience panic. Similarly, if panic patients inhaling CO_2 are led to believe that they can manipulate the CO_2 saturation in the inhaled air by a panic button, this induced sense of illusory control protects them from panic attacks and decreases their self-rated anxiety. Conversely, if panic patients are led to believe through false physiological feedback that their heart is racing, they become more anxious and show more psychophysiological arousal than control subjects.

IV. ANXIETY DISORDERS

Disorders of anxiety are common in the population, afflicting about a quarter of adult individuals. One group of the anxiety disorders, phobias, is more closely related to fear than to anxiety as these concepts have been used in this text.

A. Panic Disorder

Recurrent panic attacks have a key position in the diagnosis of anxiety disorders and they are what the diagnostician looks for first. Panic disorder is a condition characterized by recurring and crippling panic, typically associated with distressing worries about future panic attacks. As a result the normal social life of the individual is compromised. Typically panic disorder occur in the context of agoraphobia, when the person starts to avoid situations in which he or she would be left helpless and vulnerable in the event of a panic attack.

B. Generalized Anxiety Disorder

If the anxiety is manifested as uncontrollable and excessive anxiety and worry about events or activities (e.g., finances, school performance), generalized anxiety disorder may be diagnosed. Patients with this disorder worry more or less constantly and their worries are less controllable and more self-driven and ruminative than normal worries. Typically the worry is combined with somatic symptoms or other anxiety symptoms such as restlessness, fatigue, irritability, muscle tension, and concentration and sleep difficulties.

C. Posttraumatic Stress Disorder

Posttraumatic stress disorder has its origin in intense traumas, i.e., situations whose danger and aversiveness are outside the range of usual human experience, such as in natural disasters, war, violent crime, or severe accidents. In this disorder, the traumatic event is persistently reexperienced (e.g., in the form of "flashbacks"), stimuli or events associated with the trauma elicit intense anxiety and are avoided, and the person feels generally numbed with regard to emotions. Common anxiety symptoms experienced by persons suffering from posttraumatic stress disorder include sleep and concentration difficulties, irritability or angry outbursts, hypervigilance, and an exaggerated startle reflex.

D. Obsessive-Compulsive Disorder

Obsessions refer to persistent thoughts, impulses, or images and compulsions refer to repetitive behaviors such as hand washing and checking, or mental activities such as praying or silently repeating words. The essential features of obsessive-compulsive disorder are recurrent, uncontrollable obsessions or compulsions which are performed with the ostensible purpose of reducing anxiety. The obsessions and compulsions are associated with marked distress and they interfere with the normal routines, even though the victim, at least at some point, has recognized that they are excessive or unreasonable.

V. THE NEUROPSYCHOLOGY OF ANXIETY

From the perspective taken here, in which anxiety is seen as closely related to fear, it is a natural assumption that their neural circuitry shows considerable overlap. It is an attractive notion that this circuit is sensitized and hyperreactive in anxiety states. Furthermore, there are novel data suggesting that an area related to the amygdala, the bed nucleus of the stria terminalis, has similar efference to that of the amygdala in controlling different components of fear and anxiety. However, it is more dependent on long-lasting, contextual stimuli for its activation than on the specific, short-lasting conditioned fear stimuli that activate the amygdala. This effect appears to be mediated by an effect of corticotropin releasing hormone in the bed nucleus of the stria terminalis. Thus, this finding opens the possibility of separable but closely related anatomical loci for fear and anxiety. Fear may be primarily dependent on the effects of specific stimuli on the amygdala and anxiety on the effect of contextual stimuli and corticosteroid release in the bed nucleus of the stria terminalis.

This emerging view provides a contrast to the influential notions on the neuropsychology of anxiety formulated by Gray (1982). He argued that a septal–hippocampal circuit provides the neural substrate for the Behavioral Inhibition System (BIS), which is at the heart of anxiety. The BIS is activated by signals of punishment, frustrative nonreward, and novel stimuli or innate fear stimuli. Its output includes narrowing of attention, inhibition of gross motor behavior, increased stimulus analysis, exploration of the environment (e.g., scanning), and the mobilization of hypothalamic circuits for rapid action channeled through the fight/flight system in the central gray of the upper brainstem. According to this view, it is the BIS that accounts for generalized anxiety. Panic and fear, on the other hand, are represented by unconditioned activation of the fight/flight system in the brain stem.

The most conspicuous discrepancy between Gray's model, on the one hand, and the more contemporary models of LeDoux, Davis, and Fanselow, on the other, is the absence of the amygdala in Gray's formulation. This is particularly striking, given the central role of the amygdala in the more novel models. If freezing/immobility is taken as the behavioral marker of anxiety, the neural substrate, according to these models, would be centered on the amygdala but include a link to the ventral periaqueductal gray matter in the midbrain, which controls freezing. And accepting Gray's notion that unconditioned activation of the fight/flight system can serve as a model of panic, panic and unconditioned fear responses would be controlled by pathways bypassing the amygdala directly to activate fight/flight from the dorsal periaqueductal gray. Thus, the neural basis of the different forms of anxiety remains somewhat controversial, particularly with regard to the role of the amygdala in anxiety. However, given the headway made during recent years, there is hope that a more satisfactory model will soon emerge.

See Also the Following Articles

Anxiolytics; Coping Skills; Defensive Behaviors; Fear; Obsessive-Compulsive Disorder; Panic Disorder and Agoraphobia

Bibliography

American Psychiatric Association (1994). "Diagnostic and Statistical manual of mental disorders," 4th ed, pp. 393–444. Author, Washington, DC.

Barlow, D. H. (1988). "Anxiety and Its Disorders." Guilford, New York.

Davis, M., and Lee, Y. L. (1998). Fear and anxiety: Possible roles of the amygdala and bed nucleus of the stria terminalis. *Cognit. Emot.* **12**, 277–305.

Eysenck, M. (1992). "Anxiety: The Cognitive Perspective." Erbaum, Hillsdale, NJ.

Fanselow, M. S. (1994). Neural organization of the defensive behavior system responsible for fear. *Psychonom. Bull. Rev.* **1**, 429–438.

Gray, J. A. (1982). "The Neuropsychology of Anxiety." Oxford Univ. Press, Oxford, UK.

LeDoux, J. E. (1996). "The Emotional Brain." Simon & Schuster, New York.

Mineka, S., and Zinbarg, R. (1996). Conditioning and ethological models of anxiety disorder: Stress-in-dynamic-context anxiety models. *In* "Nebraska Symposium of Motivation: Perspectives on Anxiety, Panic, and Fear" (D. A. Hope, Ed.), Vol. 43, pp. 135–210. Univ. of Nebraska Press, Lincoln, NE.

Öhman, A. (1993). Fear and anxiety as emotional phenomena: Clinical phenomenology, evolutionary perspectives, and information-processing mechanisms. *In* "Handbook of Emotions" (M. Lewis & J. M. Haviland, Eds.), pp. 511–536. Guilford, New York.

Rosen, J. B., and Schulkin, J. (1998). From normal fear to pathological anxiety. *Psychol. Rev.* **105**, 325–350.

Anxiolytics

Malcolm Lader
University of London

I. Antianxiety Drugs
II. Benzodiazepines
III. Other Compounds
IV. Antipsychotic Drugs
V. Antidepressants
VI. Antihistamines
VII. β-Adrenoceptor Antagonists

GLOSSARY

anxiolytic A medicinal substance that allays anxiety.

benzodiazepines A group of drugs used as anxiolytics, hypnotics, muscle relaxants, and anesthetic inducers.

dependence A state of drug usage evidenced by drug-seeking behavior or physical symptoms on withdrawal.

γ-aminobutyric acid An inhibitory neurotransmitter.

An anxiolytic is a medicinal substance that allays anxiety and tension. Barbiturates have been replaced by benzodiazepines, such as diazepam. These drugs potentiate γ-aminobutyric acid (GABA). Their main use is to treat anxiety as a symptom, syndrome, or disorder. Unwanted effects include drowsiness, memory impairment, and dependence. Long-term usage is a controversial topic. Other anxiolytic compounds include buspirone, antipsychotic drugs in low dosage, antidepressants, particularly selective serotonin re-uptake inhibitors and monoamine oxidase inhibitors, antihistamines, and β blockers.

I. ANTIANXIETY DRUGS

A. Definitions

The term "sedative" originally meant that which has the property of allaying, assuaging, or calming.

More recently it has come to imply feelings of drowsiness or torpor, a state originally called "oversedation." In place of sedative, the term "tranquillizer" has been introduced in an attempt to distinguish between the older sedatives and the newer drugs. Another term enjoying some popularity is "anxiolytic," a word of dubious etymology, meaning to dissolve anxiety. The term "antianxiety medication" is preferable.

B. History

The use of anxiety-allaying drugs goes back thousands of years to the discovery that grapejuice and grain mash were fermentable and that alcohol possessed psychotropic properties.

The 19th century saw the introduction of bromides chloral and paraldehyde. The last 19th century sedatives were the barbiturates, with the disadvantages of drowsiness, tolerance to their effects, dangers of overdose, and the likelihood of physical and psychological dependence. Meprobamate is similar. The first benzodiazepine was chlordiazepoxide ("Librium"), but well over 1000 benzodiazepines and related compounds have been synthesized, including diazepam, the most widely used of all.

II. BENZODIAZEPINES

Barbiturates have been largely replaced by benzodiazepines, with one important reason being the safety in overdose of the benzodiazepines as compared to barbiturate toxicity. Nevertheless, misgivings concerning the benzodiazepines have been expressed. Their widespread use and the possibility of dependence even at normal therapeutic doses led to pleas for the restriction of prescribing. However, these drugs are also widely used by many physicians for patients with circulatory disorders, tension headaches, pains in chest and back, and digestive disorders. Many still view these drugs quite favorably.

A. Pharmacokinetics

For the prescriber, two aspects of the pharmacokinetics of benzodiazepine are germane: the speed of onset of action and the duration of action. Thus, given orally, diazepam enters the brain rapidly and exerts a prompt effect in anxiety and panic states.

Metabolic half-lives of the benzodiazepines also vary greatly. Nordiazepam is the major and active metabolite of diazepam with a long half-life, about 60 h. It is also the major metabolite of clorazepate, medazepam, prazepam, ketazolam, and, to a large extent, chlordiazepoxide. In contrast, lorazepam, oxazepam, and temazepam have half-lives averaging 12 h or less. Alprazolam is a triazolobenzodiazepine with a half-life of 9–16 h. Any relationship between plasma benzodiazepine concentrations and clinical anxiolytic response is unestablished.

B. Basic Pharmacology

Benzodiazepines potentiate the inhibitory neurotransmitter, γ-aminobutyric acid.

Benzodiazepines do not act directly on GABA receptors but on their own receptors.

Benzodiazepines can alter the turnover of neurotransmitters such as noradrenaline and 5-hydroxytryptamine. The main sites of action of benzodiazepines are in the spinal cord where muscle relaxant effects are mediated, the brain stem, perhaps accounting for the anticonvulsant properties, the cerebellum (causing ataxia), and the limbic and cortical areas involved in the organization of emotional experience and behavior.

A benzodiazepine antagonist, flumazenil, has been introduced. It binds to benzodiazepine receptors, preventing and reversing the action of the benzodiazepine.

C. Clinical Pharmacology

In normal individuals the depressant effects of single higher doses of the benzodiazepines can be detected readily. At lower doses, however, impairment of psychological functioning is quite difficult to quantify and subjective effects are usually absent. In the clinical context with anxious patients and with repeated doses, impairment of functioning is more difficult to demonstrate.

Benzodiazepines have marked and quite specific effects on memory functions and interfere with episodic memory, i.e., the system concerned with remembering personal experiences. This effect is independent of any sedation or attentional impairment.

D. Clinical Uses

The main use of benzodiazepines is in the management of anxiety and stress-related conditions, especially by family physicians. Often, it is the symptom of anxiety, no matter what its context, which is the main indication. Few differences have been found among the benzodiazepines, although their superiority with respect to placebo has been established.

Benzodiazepines are also effective treatments for panic disorder, preventing the episodes rather than aborting them. Alprazolam can suppress panics but relapse and even rebound may occur when the benzodiazepine is discontinued, even if tapered off.

Other uses for which the short-acting benzodiazepines are appropriate are as adjuncts to relaxation therapy, preoperative medication, and deep sedation for minor operative procedures such as dentistry. In the latter use, the drugs render the patient calm, conscious and cooperative, yet there is often total anterograde amnesia for the operation.

E. Unwanted Effects

The commonest unwanted effects are tiredness, drowsiness, and torpor, so called "oversedation." The effects are dose and time related, being most marked within the first 2 h after large doses. Furthermore, drowsiness is most common during the first week of treatment. Both psychomotor skills, such as driving, and intellectual and cognitive skills are affected.

However, anxiety itself is associated with a decrement in mental functioning. Thus it is a moot point whether it is better for the community to have many of its members driving vehicles while anxious, distractible, and jumpy or sedated by benzodiazepines.

As with most depressant drugs, potentiation of the effects of alcohol can occur.

Paradoxical behavioral responses may occur in patients taking benzodiazepines. Such events include increased aggression and hostility, acute rage reactions, "psychokinetic stimulation," uncharacteristic criminal behavior such as shoplifting, and uncontrollable weeping.

Other unwanted effects include excessive weight gain, skin rash, impairment of sexual function, menstrual irregularities, and, rarely, agranulocytosis. The use of benzodiazepines in pregnancy is unestablished. Benzodiazepines pass readily into the fetus and have been suspected of producing respiratory depression in the neonate. Finally, benzodiazepines are present in the mother's milk and can oversedate the baby.

F. Overdosage

Overdosage with benzodiazepines is extremely common; deaths due to these drugs alone are uncommon. Generally, sleep lasts 24–48 h, but patients are generally rousable.

G. Tolerance and Dependence

Clinically, tolerance has not been studied in any detail. However, escalation of dosage with benzodiazepines is comparatively rare.

Tolerance to clinical effects in patients maintained on moderate doses of benzodiazepines is more controversial. The efficacy of antianxiety compounds in chronically anxious patients taking the drug for 6 months or so is still unestablished. Undoubtedly, many chronically anxious patients are helped by benzodiazepines, but many other patients who suffer from recurrent crises take benzodiazepines chronically rather than in response to each crisis. Dependence is easily demonstrable in those patients who have escalated their doses. The mildest symptoms are anxiety, tension, apprehension, dizziness, insomnia, and anorexia. More severe physical dependence is manifested by withdrawal symptoms of nausea and vomiting, tremor, muscle weakness, and postural hypotension. Occasionally, hyperthermia, muscle twitches, convulsions, and confusional psychoses may occur. Symptoms seen on withdrawal from normal doses of benzodiazepines are listed in Table I. The proportion of patients taking benzodiazepines chronically who experience withdrawal symptoms on discontinuation of medication ranges between 27 and 45%, depending on the criteria used.

TABLE I
Type of Symptom and Its Frequency on Withdrawal from Normal Doses of Benzodiazepines

Symptom	Frequency
Anxiety, tension	++++
Agitation, restlessness	+++
Bodily symptoms of anxiety	++
Irritability	++
Lack of energy	++
Impaired memory and concentration	++
Depersonalization, derealization	+
Sleep disturbance	++++
Tremor, shakiness	+++
Headache	+++
Muscle pains, aches, twitchings	++
Loss of appetite	++
Nausea, dry retching	++
Depression	+
Perspiration	+
Metallic taste, hyperosmia	++++
Blurred vision, sore eyes, photophobia	+++
Incoordination, vertigo	+++
Hyperacusis	++
Paraesthesias	++
Hypersensitivity to touch, pain	++
Paranoid reaction	+

Abuse of benzodiazepines, i.e., the nonmedical use of large doses, often in a polydrug context, is mainly seen with hypnotic compounds.

III. OTHER COMPOUNDS

A. Benzodiazepine Receptor Partial Agonists

Knowledge of benzodiazepine receptor mechanisms has raised the hope that compounds could be developed that are partial agonists and/or selective to some subtypes of receptor. Such compounds would be less efficacious than full agonists but may have better adverse effect profiles and less dependence potential, i.e., superior risk/benefit ratios.

1. Abecarnil

Abecarnil is a β-carboline that has anxiolytic properties in doses of 3–9 mg/day. However, efficacy has been difficult to demonstrate convincingly, although the side effect profile does appear to resemble that of a comparator benzodiazepine.

2. 5-HT$_{1A}$ Partial Agonists

This class of compounds, many of whom are chemically azapirones, has a complex pharmacology. The first one, buspirone, has been available in many countries for several years. These drugs suppress activity in presynaptic serotonergic neurones, diminishing serotonin activity and leading to downregulation of 5-HT$_2$ and perhaps other 5-HT receptors. Buspirone is much less sedative than benzodiazepines, with little propensity to induce psychomotor or cognitive impairment.

In formal clinical trials, buspirone proved equi-effective and equipotent to diazepam. However, patients on buspirone improve more slowly.

Buspirone has fewer and less severe side effects than diazepam. Headache, dizziness, and nausea are the commonest complaints, may be severe, and may necessitate lowering the dosage or discontinuing the drug. Discontinuation is not accompanied by either rebound or withdrawal.

IV. ANTIPSYCHOTIC DRUGS

Phenothiazines such as chlorpromazine and trifluoperazine and a range of other antipsychotic drugs are used by some to treat anxiety. The dosage recommended is quite low, typically less than half the initial antipsychotic dose. Sometimes, even at this dosage, the antipsychotic drug is not well tolerated by the anxious patient because unwanted autonomic effects such as dry mouth and dizziness too closely resemble their own symptoms. Even more disconcerting but uncommon are extrapyramidal symptoms such as restlessness (mild akathisia) and parkinsonism. It is not clear if tardive dyskinesia is a real risk but this possibility should dissuade the practitioner from the indiscriminate use of these drugs as anxiolytics.

V. ANTIDEPRESSANTS

Several of these drugs, such as amitriptyline, doxepin, and mianserin, have useful secondary sedative properties. They are used to treat depressed patients with anxiety or agitation. SSRIs are effective in and licensed for various anxiety disorders and are regarded by many as the treatment of choice in chronic anxiety disorders. The serotonin and norepinephrine reuptake inhibitor, venlafaxine, has been licensed for the treatment of generalized anxiety disorder.

A. Monoamine Oxidase Inhibitors

The efficacy of this group of antidepressants in phobic states is well established, particularly for phenelzine. However, their unwanted effects such as postural hypotension, peripheral edema, and drug and dietary interactions have limited their usefulness. The selective and reversible inhibitor moclobemide has also been shown to have efficacy in phobic disorders, without most of the unwanted effects.

VI. ANTIHISTAMINES

The sedative actions of tricyclic antidepressants and antipsychotics are mediated mainly by secondary central antihistaminic effects. Some antihistamines have been used for decades to treat psychosomatic complaints characterized by anxiety. Such a compound is hydroxyzine, which has been demonstrated to have useful therapeutic properties in generalized anxiety disorder.

VII. β-ADRENOCEPTOR ANTAGONISTS

Anxiety states are accompanied by many different bodily symptoms, some of which are mediated by the sympathetic system. In particular, palpitations, tremor, and gastrointestinal upset are related to the overactivity of β-adrenergic pathways. Consequently, blockade of this activity by means of β-adrenoceptor antagonists may help patients with anxiety, especially those with symptoms listed earlier.

See Also the Following Articles

ANXIETY; PHARMACOLOGICAL TREATMENTS OF STRESS

Bibliography

Curran, H. V. 1991. Benzodiazepines, memory and mood: A review. *Psychopharmacology* 105, 1–8.

Gelenberg, A. J., ed. 1994. Buspirone: Seven-year update. *J. Clin. Psychiat.* 55, 222–229.

Lader, M. 1994. Benzodiazepines: A risk-benefit profile. *CNS Drugs* 1, 377–387.

Layton, M. E., and Dager, S. R. 1994. Optimum treatment of panic disorder. *CNS Drugs* 2, 208–215.

Russell, J., and Lader, M., eds. 1993. "Guidelines for the Prevention and Treatment of Benzodiazepine Dependence." Mental Health Foundation, London.

Apoptosis

Cynthia L. Mann

University of North Carolina at Chapel Hill
National Institute of Environmental Health Sciences,
National Institutes of Health

John A. Cidlowski

National Institute of Environmental. Health Sciences,
National Institutes of Health

GLOSSARY

apoptosis A form of cell death which deletes cells from a population in a deliberate manner without eliciting an immune response.

glucocorticoids Steroid hormones which regulate carbohydrate metabolism and inhibit the inflammatory response.

glucocorticoid receptor An intracellular receptor which binds glucocorticoids and then translocates to the nucleus where it influences gene expression.

caspases A family of cysteine proteases which cleave target molecules and amplify the apoptotic cascade.

Apoptosis is the process which deletes cells from a population in a deliberate manner. Apoptosis derives its name from the Greek word for the "falling off" of leaves from a tree or petals from a flower. The term not only recapitulates the morphology of apoptotic cells but also reflects the delicate balance of life and death that must be maintained within tissues. Many factors can influence tissue homeostasis, including stress. Stress hormones play a fundamental role in the stress response and can disrupt tissue homeostasis by interfering with normal apoptosis in the tissue. The immune system is particularly vulnerable to the actions of stress hormones. Persistent stress, which can result in a sustained increase in steroid hormone levels, causes prolonged immunosuppression in part, via stimulation of lymphocyte apoptosis.

I. APOPTOTIC MORPHOLOGY

Lymphocyte apoptosis can be classified by a set of morphological features. Apoptotic cells and their organelles shrink as a result of water and ions leaving the cell. Chromatin condenses into discrete masses, and as apoptosis proceeds, the nucleus breaks into fragments. Later in apoptosis, the plasma membrane convolutes and blebs. These convolutions pinch off to form apoptotic bodies which are then subjected to phagocytosis. Thus, an acute inflammatory response to the death of the cell is avoided.

II. GLUCOCORTICOID RECEPTOR SIGNALING

The physiological pathways which convey a stress signal are illustrated in Fig. 1. Stress causes neural transmission to the hypothalamus leading to the release of corticotropin releasing hormone (CRH), which, in turn, causes the release of corticotropin from the pituitary. Corticotropin induces the secretion of glucocorticoids from the adrenal cortex. Glucocorticoids induce changes in a number of tissues, including the immune system. Glucocorticoid induced destruction of lymphocytes has been well illustrated in the rat model of thymocyte apoptosis. The rat thymus undergoes a 50% reduction in weight and an 80% reduction in the thymocyte population within 48 h after an intraperitoneal injection of dexamethasone. The glucocorticoid receptor (GR) mediates glucocorticoid-induced apoptosis, an effect which can be blocked by administration of the GR antagonist RU486. Figure 2 illustrates the signaling cascade for glucocorticoid-induced lymphocyte apoptosis. Once GR is bound by glucocorticoids, it translocates from the cytoplasm to the nucleus,

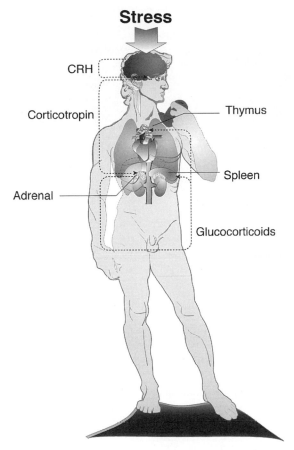

Stress

CRH

Corticotropin

Adrenal

Thymus

Spleen

Glucocorticoids

FIGURE 1 Stress facilitates immunosuppression by stimulating immune cell death. Stress stimulates the release of corticotropin releasing hormone (CRH) from the hypothalamus, which then stimulates the release of corticotropin from the pituitary gland. Corticotropin stimulates the adrenal glands to release glucocorticoids, which then suppress the immune system.

where it then affects the transcription of many different genes. The ability of the GR to translocate and bind to the DNA is essential for glucocorticoid-induced apoptosis, as cells which are deficient in translocation or lack the GR DNA binding domain do not undergo glucocorticoid-induced apoptosis. The translocation of hormone-bound GR to the nucleus initiates a signaling cascade which ultimately results in the death of the cell.

The array of genes which are positively regulated by glucocorticoids is diverse. However, the significance of these genes to the execution of apoptosis is not known. Glucocorticoids also negatively regulate some cell growth genes, including *c-myc*, *c-myb*, and

c-Ki-ras. The role for glucocorticoid-mediated repression or activation of these target genes during apoptosis is not completely understood. However, a paradigm for glucocorticoid-induced cell death can be described whereby the ratio of survival factors to death factors regulated by glucocorticoids determines the fate of the cell. If the survival factors outweigh the death factors, the cell will survive. Conversely, if glucocorticoids diminish the number of survival factors and increase the levels of death factors, the cell will die.

III. DOWNSTREAM SIGNALS

Through mechanisms which are not yet understood, glucocorticoid-mediated changes in gene expression initiate a signaling cascade which culminates in cell death. This signaling cascade includes changes in intracellular calcium concentrations, the activation of a protease cascade, and the activation of nucleases.

Glucocorticoid-induced apoptosis is accompanied by a sustained increase in intracellular calcium levels. This rise can be blocked by RNA and protein synthesis inhibitors. Apoptosis can also be rapidly induced in lymphocytes by thapsigargin, an agent which increases intracellular calcium by stimulating the release of calcium from intracellular stores.

Activation of the caspase protease cascade is central to glucocorticoid-induced apoptosis. Members of the caspase family autoactivate and activate one another to amplify an apoptotic signal, much like the complement cascade. The crescendo of caspase protease activity ultimately activates nucleases and rapidly dismantles cellular macromolecules. Caspases are cysteine proteases which cleave after aspartic acid residues in a context-specific manner. Caspase-3 (YAMA/CPP32/Apopain) is the most prominent member of the family and is a putative effector of apoptosis. Its precursor form, procaspase-3, is a 32-kDa cytosolic protein that must be cleaved to 20 and 11 kDa subunits which then heterodimerize to form the active tetramer. Activation of procaspase-3 to caspase-3 is dependent on the release of cytochrome C and dATP from the mitochondrion. Caspases then dismantle the cell by deregulating pro-

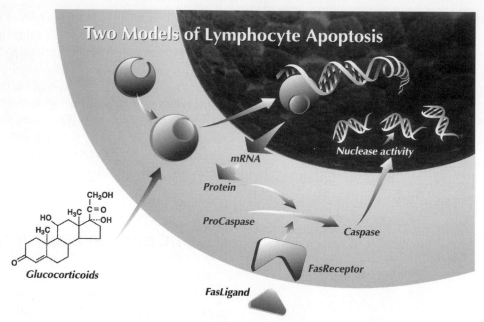

FIGURE 2   A model of glucocorticoid-induced lymphocyte apoptosis. Endogenous glucocorticoids like cortisol act by binding to the glucocorticoid receptor (GR), which then translocates to the nucleus where it influences gene expression. Changes in gene expression alter the profile of proapoptotic genes and antiapoptotic genes within the cell. Eventually, procaspases are activated to caspases, which then amplify and execute the apoptotic signaling cascade. Ultimately, nucleases are activated by the protease cascade and internucleosomal fragmentation of the DNA ensues.

teins, inactivating inhibitors of apoptosis, and cleaving structural molecules such as laminins.

Internucleosomal DNA degradation is a biochemical hallmark of apoptosis and can be observed within as little as 2 h after glucocorticoid treatment. Fragmentation of DNA is a commitment step in apoptosis, as the cell cannot reconstitute its genome once it has been destroyed. Degradation of DNA as well as the concomitant loss of viability can be blocked by nuclease inhibitors such as zinc and aurintricarboxylic acid.

IV. INHIBITORS OF APOPTOSIS

Apoptosis can be inhibited by a number of factors, including mitogenic stimuli. Growth factors such as IL-2 and IL-4 can rescue T cells from glucocorticoid-induced apoptosis. In another study, IL-9 rescued thymic lymphoma cells from glucocorticoid-induced death, but IL-2 did not. Thus, the interplay of cell type with proapoptotic and antiapoptotic stimuli determines the fate of the cell.

The bcl-2 family of proteins modulates the effect of apoptotic stimuli on a cell. Although some members of the family, like BAD, induce apoptosis, others, such as bcl-2 and bcl-X_L, inhibit apoptosis. Both bcl-2 and bcl-X_L control cytochrome C release from the mitochondrion, which activates caspase-3 activity. The relative amounts and phosphorylation status of each bcl-2 family member help determine the outcome of a response to an apoptotic signal. For example, hypophosphorylated BAD will bind bcl-2 and bcl-X_L and induce apoptosis. However, phosphorylated BAD cannot bind and will permit the cell to survive.

V. CONCLUSION

Stress has a profound effect on the immune system. Glucocorticoids are important mediators of the stress response because of their ability to induce cell death in immune cells. As described in this article, the pathways which culminate in glucocorticoid-induced cell death are complex and involve the balance of proapoptotic and antiapoptotic stimuli in the cell. Future research in this area will yield a more thorough understanding of the impact of stress on the immune system.

See Also the Following Articles

Bibliography

Baughman, G., *et al.* (1991). Genes newly identified as regulated by glucocorticoids in murine thyocytes. *Mol. Endocrinol.* 637–644.

Compton, M., and Cidlowski, J. (1986). Rapid *in vivo* effects of glucocorticoids on the integrity of rat lymphocyte genomic deoxyribonucleic acid. *Endocrinology* **118**, 38–45.

Compton, M., Carson, L., and Cidlowski, J. (1987). Glucocorticoid action on the immune system. *J. Steroid Biochem.* **27**, 201–208.

Eastman-Reks, S., and Vedeckis, W. (1986). Glucocorticoid inhibition of *c-myc, c-myb,* and *c-Ki-as* expression in a mouse lymphoma cell line. Cancer *Res.* **46**, 2457–2462.

Fernandes-Alnemri, T., Litwack, G., and Alnemri, E. (1994). CPP32, a novel human apoptotic protein with homology to Caenorhabditis elegans cell death protein Ced-3 and mammalian interleukin-1B-converting enzyme. *J. Biol. Chem.* **269**, 30761.

Liu, X., *et al.,* (1996). Induction of apoptotic program in cell-free extracts: Requirement for dATP and Cytochrome C. *Cell.* **87**, 147–157.

McConkey, D., *et al.* (1989). Glucocorticoids activate a suicide process in thymocytes through an elevation of cytosolic Ca^{2+} concentration. *Arch. Biochem. Biophys.* **269**, 365–370.

Mor, F., and Cohen, I. (1996). IL-2 rescues antigen-specific T cells from radiation or dexamethasone-induced apoptosis. *J. Immunol.* **156**, 515–522.

Nazareth, L., Harbour, D., and Thompson, E. (1991). Mapping the human glucocorticoid receptor for leukemic cell death. *J. Biol. Chem.* **266**, 12976–12980.

Nicholson, D. A., *et al.* (1995). Identification and inhibition of the ICE/Ced-3 protease necessary for mammalian apoptosis. *Nature* **376**, 37.

Renauld, J., *et al.* (1995). Interleukin-9 is a major anti-apoptotic factor for thymic lymphomas. *Blood* **85**(5), 1300–1305.

Shimizu, T., *et al.* (1990). Inhibition of both etoposide-induced DNA fragmentation and activation of poly(ADP-ribose) synthesis by zinc ion. *Biochem. Biophys. Res. Commun.* **169**, 1172–1177.

Thulasi, R., Harbour, D., and Thompson, E. (1993). Suppression of c-myc is a critical step in glucocorticoid-induced human leukemic cell lysis. *J. Biol. Chem.* **268**, 18306–18312.

Voris, B., and Young, D. (1981). Glucocorticoid-induced proteins in rat thymus cells. *J. Biol. Chem.* **256**, 11319–11329.

Yang, J., *et al.* (1997). Prevention of apoptosis by Bcl-2: Release of cytochrome C from mitochondria blocked. *Science,* **275**, 1129–1132.

Zha, J., *et al.* (1996). Serine phosphorylation of death agonist BAD in response to survival factor results in binding to 14-3-3 not Bcl-XL. *Cell* **87**, 619–628.

Arginine Vasopressin (AVP)

see Vasopressin

Arterial Baroreflex

Gianfranco Parati

*IRCCS Istituto Auxologico Italiano,
Milan, Italy*

Marco Di Rienzo

*IRCCS Fondazione Don C. Gnocchi,
Milan, Italy*

Giuseppe Mancia

*University of Milano–Bicocca and
Ospedale S. Gerardo, Monza, Italy*

GLOSSARY

alpha coefficient Commonly employed frequency-domain method for spontaneous baroreflex analysis based on the calculation of the square ratio between the spectral powers of heart interval and systolic blood pressure around 0.1 or 0.3 Hz.

autoregressive moving average (ARMA) techniques Techniques in which the reciprocal relations between blood pressure and heart interval variability are quantified, in a closed-loop fashion, with the help of a mathematical model including both the effects of one parameter on the other one (moving average component) and the effects of previous values of each considered parameter on its present value (autoregressive component).

arterial baroreceptors Mechanoreceptors located within the arterial wall (mainly in the carotid arteries, renal arteries, and aortic arch) sensitive to changes in arterial wall transmural pressure.

arterial baroreflex Reflex loop including arterial baroreceptors (peripheral input sensors), afferent neural pathways, central neural integration, efferent neural pathways, and effector organs (e.g., sinus node at the heart level and arteriolar smooth muscle cells at peripheral vascular level).

frequency-domain methods Methods for spontaneous baroreflex modulation and blood pressure/heart rate variability analysis based on the quantification of blood pressure and heart rate changes as a function of their frequency (i.e., in the frequency domain, by spectral analysis).

sequence technique Commonly employed time-domain method for spontaneous baroreflex analysis, based on the identification of spontaneously occurring beat-by-beat hypertension/bradycardia or hypotension/tachycardia sequences over 4 or more consecutive beats.

spectral analysis Technique for the detailed analysis of any given signal (in our context, BP and HR time series) able to split the raw signal into its different frequency components.

spontaneous baroreflex modulation of the heart Reflex changes in heart rate triggered by spontaneous (i.e., not induced by laboratory stimuli) fluctuations in blood pressure.

time-domain methods Methods for spontaneous baroreflex modulation and blood pressure/heart rate variability analysis based on the quantification of blood pressure and heart rate changes as a function of time (i.e., in the time domain).

The arterial baroreflex represents a mechanism of fundamental importance for blood pressure homeostasis [Mancia, G., and Mark, A. L., 1983, *In* (J. T. Shepherd and F. M. Abboud, Eds.), "Handbook of Physiology: The Cardiovascular System IV" Vol. 3, Part 2, pp. 755–793. American Physiologic Society, Bethesda, MD], and an impairment of its cardiac and vascular influences is believed to play a role in several cardiovascular diseases. Baroreflex abnormalities have been described early in the course of diabetes mellitus and hypertension, contributing in the former case to the occurrence of hypotensive episodes and in the latter to the maintenance of the blood pressure elevation. A baroreflex dysfunction characterizes also patients after a myocardial infarction and carries a worse prognosis. The clinical relevance of a baroreflex dysfunction is supported also by studies showing that interventions which improve baroreflex sensitivity, such as physical training or β-adrenergic receptor blockade, may also beneficially affect the patient's prognosis.

The above findings have led to a great interest for the assessment of baroreflex sensitivity in humans, both in the laboratory and in the clinical setting. This article briefly addresses the role of the arterial baroreflex in cardiovascular physiology, its possible clinical relevance, and the methods most commonly employed for assessing its effectiveness in human cardiovascular regulation, with emphasis on the exciting possibilities offered by modern approaches based on computer analysis of spontaneously occurring blood pressure and heart rate fluctuations.

I. ANATOMY AND PHYSIOLOGY

Intravascular pressure is continuously sensed by stretch receptors, located in the systemic and pulmonary arteries and veins. The two main populations or receptors engaged in this task, and thus known as "baroreceptors," can be found at the carotid sinus and at the aortic arch, respectively (i.e., in two key regions for continuous monitoring of blood pressure and thus of blood supply to vital organs, in particular to the brain). Other "baroreceptor" populations importantly involved in regulating perfusion pressure to vital organs are those located in the walls of cerebral and renal arteries, where they appear to play a major role in the local "autoregulation." Arterial baroreceptors, in combination with the stretch receptors located in the cardiac walls and in the lungs (so-called "cardiopulmonary receptors") play a role also in regulating the secretion of humoral substances involved in blood pressure and volume homeostasis (e.g., renin, vasopressin, catecholamines).

An increase in vascular or cardiac pressure determines an increase in arterial or cardiac transmural pressure, which represents the natural stimulus for stretch receptors located in the vascular or cardiac walls, and thus an increase in firing along their afferent fibers. The opposite occurs for a reduction in cardiac or vascular transmural pressure. The afferent impulses which follow baroreceptor stimulation by a blood pressure rise relay within the nucleus of the solitary tract (NTS) in the brainstem. This is followed by inhibition of brainstem sympathetic centers and stimulation of brainstem parasympathetic centers. This baroreceptor reflex arc forms a negative-feedback loop in which a rise in blood pressure results in the inhibition of central sympathetic outflow to the heart and peripheral circulation, through a sequential action on the intermediolateral cell column; preganglionic neurons; sympathetic ganglia; and, finally, on postganglionic sympathetic nerves

directed to heart, arterioles, veins, and kidneys. The baroreflex negative-feedback loop which responds to a rise in blood pressure also includes an increase in the activity of parasympathetic brain stem centers and in the efferent parasympathetic activity directed to the heart. The final result is a reflex reduction in blood pressure and heart rate, aimed at counteracting the initial increase in blood pressure. A brainstem noradrenergic pathway is also involved in this process, interacting with the NTS to participate in the suppression of sympathetic outflow. This noradrenergic inhibitory pathway is stimulated by centrally acting α-adrenergic agonists, such as clonidine, that may thus potentiate through this mechanism the baroreceptor-mediated vasodepressor response.

In the opposite fashion, a fall in blood pressure is responsible for a reduction in baroreceptor transmural pressure and thus for a reduction in baroreceptor afferent firing. This in turn diminishes central inhibition, resulting in an increase in sympathetic outflow and a reduction in vagal efferent activity and thus in a reflex rise in blood pressure and heart rate aimed at counteracting the initial fall in blood pressure.

The arterial baroreflex loop, including the arterial baroreceptors, their afferent fibers, central integrating neurons, efferent fibers, and peripheral "effector" organs, represents the major regulatory mechanism involved in cardiovascular homeostasis and plays a pivotal role in buffering blood pressure fluctuations and in promoting heart rate variability. Moreover, data is available that its derangement in a number of diseases, characterized by autonomic impairment, may not only contribute to the clinical manifestations of these pathological conditions, but it may also have a prognostic relevance in increasing the risk of cardiovascular events. This makes the accurate assessment of baroreflex function in humans a key methodological issue.

II. METHODS FOR ASSESSING BAROREFLEX FUNCTION

A. Laboratory Methods for Assessing Baroreflex Sensitivity

Several methods are available to assess the arterial baroreflex function in the laboratory. These techniques have been successfully used to clarify its physiological role in cardiovascular modulation, its alterations in disease, and also how this alteration can be modified by treatment. All of them require the application of an external stimulus on the subject under evaluation and offer a "spot" quantification of baroreflex sensitivity obtained in standardized laboratory conditions.

A number of pioneering methods to assess baroreflex sensitivity, including carotid sinus massage, electrical stimulation of carotid sinus nerves, anesthesia of carotid sinus nerves and vagi, and occlusion of common carotid arteries, are now only of historical interest. Other laboratory methods currently employed in this field include (a) the Valsalva maneuver (which, however, also triggers alterations in chemoreceptor and cardiopulmonary receptor activity, thus making heart rate responses poorly specific), (b) head-up tilting and lower body negative pressure application (which are also not specific because cardiopulmonary receptor deactivation, due to a reduction in venous return and central blood volume, and vestibular stimulation, in case of tilting, also contribute to the cardiovascular adjustments), (c) the intravenous bolus injection of a small dose of a pressor or a depressor agent free from any major direct effect on the heart (to increase or reduce systolic blood pressure and reflexly lengthen or shorten, respec-

tively, R-R interval; the slope of the regression line fitting the systolic blood pressure and R-R interval changes is taken as a measure of baroreflex sensitivity), and (d) the use of a neck chamber device (which allows its inner air pressure to be increased or reduced in a graded and long-lasting fashion, thus resulting into graded, long-lasting, and quantifiable reductions and increases in carotid transmural pressure and, as a result, in the input stimulus to carotid baroreceptors). The key advantage of this last method is that it allows not only heart rate but also blood pressure modulation by arterial baroreceptors to be specifically investigated (Fig. 1). This goes with the disadvantage, however, that only carotid baroreceptor function is addressed and that the effect of carotid baroreceptor involvement is counteracted by the aortic baroreflex, which is deactivated during the blood pressure fall induced by carotid baroreceptor stimulation and stimulated during the blood pressure rise induced by the carotid baroreceptor deactivation.

Despite the useful information they provide on arterial baroreflex function in humans, all the above laboratory methods also carry a number of limitations, including the need of external artificial stimulation on the cardiovascular system, the limited reproducibility of the data so obtained, and the inability to characterize the dynamic features of neural cardiovascular reflex modulation in real-life

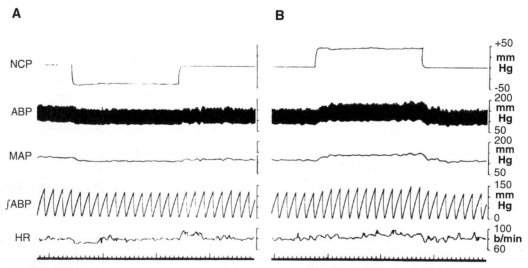

FIGURE 1 Blood pressure and heart rate effects of a 2-minute application of negative (A) and positive pneumatic pressure (B) within a neck chamber device. Abbreviations: NCP, neck chamber pressure; ABP, arterial blood pressure recorded through a catheter in the radial artery; MAP, mean arterial pressure; ∫ABP, BP values integrated every 10 sec; HR, heart rate (from Ludbrook, J., *et al.*, 1977).

conditions. This has stimulated the development of new techniques aimed at overcoming these problems.

B. Modern Techniques for the Analysis of Spontaneous Baroreflex Modulation of Heart Rate

An important step forward in the investigation of the arterial baroreflex in humans is represented by techniques that analyze the sensitivity of spontaneous baroreflex control of heart rate [Parati, G., Omboni, S., Frattola, A., Di Rienzo, M., Zanchetti, A., and Mancia, G., 1992, *In* "Blood Pressure and Heart Rate Variability" (M. Di Rienzo, G. Mancia, G. Parati, A. Pedotti, and A. Zanchetti, Eds.), pp. 123–137. IOS Press, Amsterdam], (i.e., techniques that are based on the analysis of spontaneously occurring blood pressure and heart rate fluctuations). All these techniques do not require any external intervention on the subject under evaluation. Moreover, they can be used not only to assess baroreflex sensitivity in standardized laboratory conditions, but also to investigate the dynamic features of baroreflex modulation of heart rate in daily life (Table I).

A. The Sequence Method

The "sequence" method is based on time-domain computer identification of spontaneously occurring sequences of four or more consecutive beats characterized by either progressive increases in systolic blood pressure (SBP) and reflex lengthening in R-R

TABLE I
Methods for Assessing Spontaneous Baroreflex Function

Sequence technique (sequences of beats with baroreflex-mediated SBP-triggered R-R interval changes); see text.
R-R interval–SBP cross correlation
Modulus of R-R interval–SBP transfer function at 0.1 Hz
Squared ratio of R-R interval/SBP spectral powers at 0.1 and 0.3 Hz (α-coefficient)
R-R interval–SBP impulse and step response by ARMA modeling
Closed-loop R-R interval–SBP transfer function (trivariate ARMA modeling)
Statistical dependence of R-R interval and SBP fluctuations

interval, or by progressive reductions in SBP and reflex shortening in R-R interval (Bertinieri, G., Di Rienzo, M., Cavallazzi, A., Ferrari, A. U., Pedotti, A., and Mancia, G., 1988, *Am. J. Physiol.* **254**, H377–H383; Parati, G., Di Rienzo, M., Bertinieri, G., Pomidossi, G., Casadei, R., Groppelli, A., Pedoti, A., Zanchetti, A., and Mancia, G., 1988, *Hypertension* **12**, 214–222) (Fig. 2). Similarly to what is done for the laboratory method based on the iv bolus injection of vasoactive drugs, with the sequence technique the slope of the regression line between spontaneous systolic blood pressure and heart interval changes is taken as an index of the sensitivity of arterial baroreflex modulation of heart rate (BRS). The experimental demonstration of the specificity of the sequence method (i.e., that R-R interval changes observed in each sequence in response to the spontaneous changes in SBP are actually dependent on the baroreflex) was obtained in conscious cats in which blood pressure and heart rate were continuously recorded for 3–4 h both before and after sino-aortic denervation (SAD). In intact animals thousands of sequences of either the hypertension/bradycardia or the hypotension/tachycardia type were identified, whereas after SAD the number of both sequences became negligible (Fig. 3).

1. Methodological Aspects: Recent Breakthroughs

From a methodological point of view, the sequence method requires beat-to-beat monitoring of SBP coupled with an ECG to obtain a precise assessment of R-R interval–SBP relationships. If computer scanning of the SBP signal is done at sufficiently high sampling frequency (>168 Hz) and if the blood pressure waveform undergoes a parabolic interpolation of its peak, the R-R interval can be indirectly estimated through the blood pressure signal only (by quantifying pulse interval, i.e., the interval between consecutive systolic peaks) with a degree of accuracy comparable to that of R-R interval detection from an ECG tracing. A further simplification of the technical requirements for application of the sequence technique to humans is also possible because continuous SBP recording can now be obtained through noninvasive devices with sufficient accuracy both at rest and in ambulatory conditions (Parati, G., Casadei, R., Groppelli, A., Di Rienzo, M., and Mancia, G., 1989, *Hyper-*

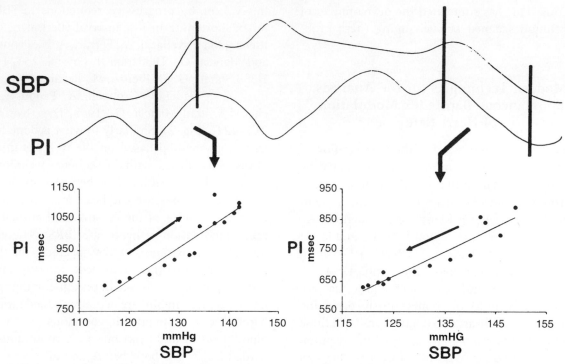

FIGURE 2 Scheme illustrating the method for spontaneous baroreflex analysis based on assessment of hypertension/bradycardia and hypotension/tachycardia sequences. The corresponding regression lines between changes in systolic blood pressure (SBP) and changes in pulse interval (PI) are also shown (from Parati, G., *et al.*, 1992).

tension **13**, 647–655). Use of these devices provides baroreflex sensitivity estimates through the sequence method that are similar both at rest and in ambulatory subjects with those simultaneously obtained by intraarterial recordings.

2. Results of the Sequence Technique in Daily Life

The results provided by the studies where the sequence technique was employed have clearly documented the high degree of variability which physiologically characterizes BRS in different behavioral conditions. The dynamic nature of the baroreflex assessment offered by this technique, as well as by other methods for spontaneous baroreflex analysis, has offered us the unique possibility to monitor both the slow and fast changes in baroreflex function occurring in different behavioral conditions, the most striking ones being those associated with the sleep–wake cycle. The typical patterns of spontaneous baroreflex modulation of heart rate over 24 h which characterize a group of young subjects and a group of

elderly subjects are shown in Fig. 4. Besides the occurrence of a minute-to-minute variability, in young individuals BRS showed a clear-cut modulation between the day and night, displaying its lowest values during the daytime, under daily physical and emotional challenges, and its highest values during night sleep. In elderly subjects, 24-h BRS was not only on average smaller than in young individuals, but it also displayed a loss of the physiological day–night modulation, thus suggesting a multifold age-related impairment of baroreflex heart rate modulation (Parati, G., Frattola, A., Di Rienzo, M., Castiglioni, P., Pedotti, A., and Mancia, G., 1995, *Am. J. Physiol.* **268**, H1606–H1612).

B. The Spectral Technique (Alpha Coefficient)

Assessment of spontaneous baroreflex sensitivity by this technique is based on the identification of regular systolic blood pressure and R-R interval oscillations throughout a recording period and the quantifi-

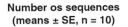

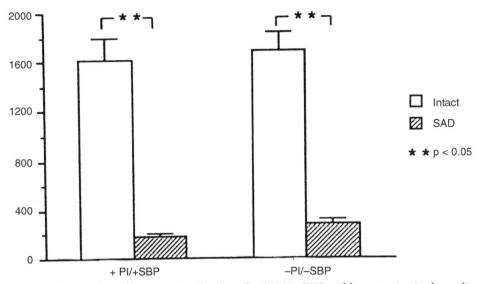

FIGURE 3 Number of hypertension/bradycardia (+PI/+SBP) and hypotension/tachycardia (-PI/-SBP) sequences. Data are shown as average values (±SE) derived from the analysis of 3-h intraarterial recordings for a group of 10 intact cats and for a group of 10 cats in which intraarterial blood pressure was recorded 3 weeks after sino-aortic denervation (SAD). Asterisks refer to the statistical significance of the differences between the intact and the SAD conditions (from Bertinieri, G., *et al.*, 1988, with permission).

cation, by either the Fast Fourier Transform (FFT) or autoregressive modeling, of their spectral powers in the frequency regions around 0.1 Hz [the so-called "low frequency" (LF) region] and 0.3 Hz ["high frequency" (HF) region], where these signals usually display a high coherence (>0.5) (i.e., where the oscillations in R-R interval and systolic blood pressure are linearly related). Baroreflex sensitivity estimates are obtained through the calculation of the squared root of the ratio between heart interval and systolic blood pressure powers, referred to as the "alpha coefficient" in the frequency regions around 0.1 and 0.3 Hz (Fig. 5) (Pagani, M., Somers, V., Furlan, R., *et al.*, 1988, *Hypertension*, **12**, 600–610). The interpretation of data obtained by computing the alpha coefficient is a more complex one, however, as compared to the sequence technique. First, when assessing the squared ratio between the R-R interval and SBP, the phase relationship between these variables is frequently disregarded. Moreover, the SBP–R-R coupling in the HF region largely survives after SAD, which demonstrates the contribution of nonbaroreflex mechanisms to its determination.

Despite the methodological differences between the above time-domain and frequency-domain methods for assessing baroreflex sensitivity, the quantification of the average BRS parameters obtained by use of alpha coefficients, both in the LF and in the HF regions, and that derived from calculation of the R-R interval–systolic blood pressure sequence slope appear to be surprisingly similar. In either case, "spontaneous" BRS estimates so obtained are quantitatively different from (although closely related to) BRS values derived through the application of laboratory techniques. This emphasizes the complementary nature of the information on baroreflex function provided by laboratory and "spontaneous" methods, which focus on different aspects of arterial baroreflex modulation of heart rate.

C. Autoregressive Moving Average (ARMA) Modeling Techniques

The modern approaches to spontaneous baroreflex analysis mentioned above derive BRS esti-

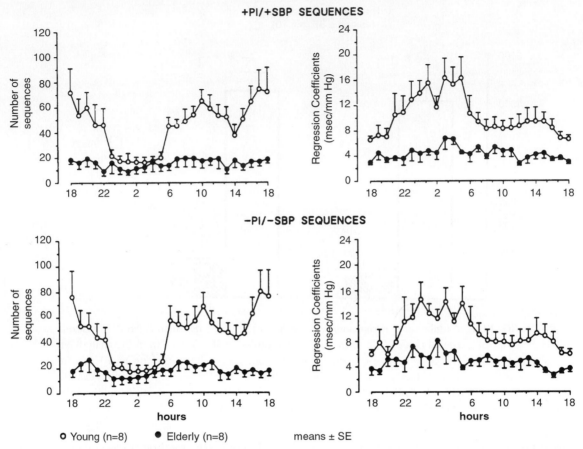

FIGURE 4 Number of hypertension/bradycardia and hypotension/tachycardia sequences (left) and sequence regression coefficients (right). Data are shown as average hourly values (±*SE*) for a group of young and a group of elderly individuals (from Parati, G., *et al.*, 1995, with permission).

mates from the direct quantification of the input–output relationship between SBP and the R-R interval. Other more complex methods have been proposed, however, which evaluate baroreflex function by mathematical modeling of cardiovascular regulatory mechanisms. In this instance, biological signals are used to identify the parameters of a preselected mathematical model of the baroreflex. This is aimed at accounting for the inherent complexity of BP–R-R interval interactions which physiologically occur in a "closed-loop" condition, i.e., in a condition where changes in BP induce reflex changes in R-R interval (BP → R-R feedback), but also where, at the same time, changes in R-R

interval are responsible for changes in BP mediated through changes in cardiac output (R-R → BP feedforward) (Patton, D. J., Triedman, J. K., Perrott, M., Vidian, A. A., and Saul, P., 1996, *Am. J. Physiol.* **270**, **39**, H1240–H1249). As for the sequence and the alpha coefficient methods, the baroreflex sensitivity values obtained by this approach are also significantly lower than those provided by the laboratory methods based on the drug bolus injection technique, in spite of a significant between-method correlation, which can be explained by the fact that ARMA estimates address baroreflex function according to a more complex and comprehensive perspective.

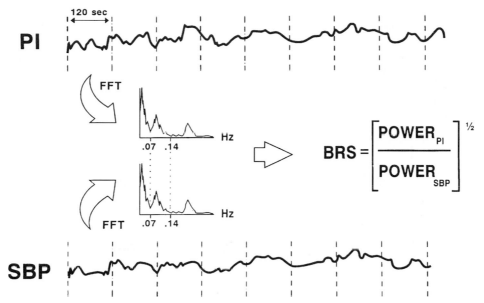

FIGURE 5 Schematic drawing illustrating how baroreflex sensitivity can be assessed in the frequency domain by calculation of the α-coefficient. Abbreviations: BRS, baroreflex sensitivity; SBP, systolic blood pressure; PI: pulse interval; FFT: Fast Fourier Transform (from Parati, G., *et al.*, 1992, with permission).

III. CLINICAL VALUE OF BAROREFLEX SENSITIVITY

A. Spontaneous Baroreflex Sensitivity in Health and Disease

Data obtained by time- and frequency-domain methods for assessing spontaneous baroreflex sensitivity have provided a large body of information on daily baroreflex function in healthy subjects and on its derangement in disease. This information consists in the detailed evidence on the fast and marked changes in baroreflex sensitivity associated with changes in behavioral conditions. It also consists of the description of the day and night reduction in baroreflex sensitivity in hypertensive or aged subjects as compared to normotensive or young individuals. It finally consists of the data on the impairment of baroreflex sensitivity in circumstances such as cigarette smoking (an impairment which escapes recognition when traditional laboratory methods are employed) and on the striking baroreflex dysfunction typical of patients with primary autonomic failure or of patients with obstructive sleep apnea syndrome (Parati, G., Di Rienzo, M., Bonsignore, M. R., Insa-laco, G., Marrone, O., Castiglioni, P., Bonsignore, G., and Mancia, G., 1997, *J. Hypertension* 15, 1621–1626.).

Assessment of spontaneous baroreflex sensitivity has been performed also in diabetic patients with or without clinical and laboratory evidence of autonomic dysfunction, as documented by the classic Ewing tests. The results have shown that both time and frequency domain methods can identify impairments of baroreflex control of heart rate when traditional laboratory tests still yield normal responses, and heart rate variability is only marginally reduced (Fig. 6) (Frattola, A., Parati, G., Gamba, P., Paleari, F., Mauri, G., Di Rienzo, M., Castiglioni, P., and Mancia, G., 1997, *Diabetologia* 40, 1470–1475), emphasizing the superiority of these techniques as compared to traditional laboratory procedures in the early detection of autonomic abnormalities that may carry a higher risk of morbidity and mortality.

B. Prognostic Value of Baroreflex Sensitivity

The possible clinical relevance of a reduced baroreflex sensitivity in coronary artery disease patients

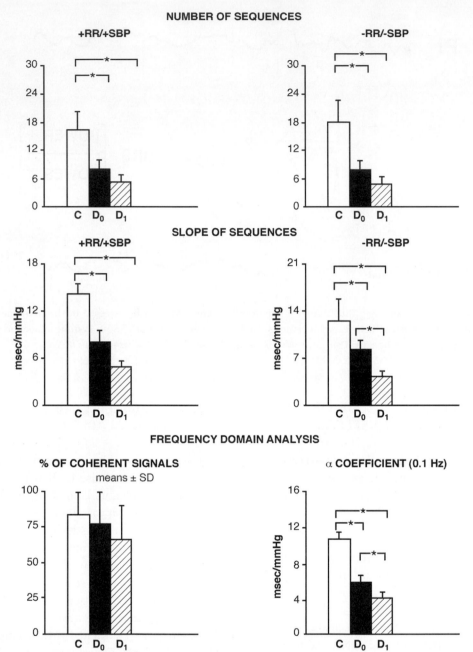

FIGURE 6 Time- and frequency. Domain estimates of the spontaneous sensitivity of the baroreceptor-heart rate reflex in control healthy subjects (C) (m = 24) and in diabetic patients without (D_0) (m = 20) or with (D_1) (m = 32) autonomic dysfunction at classical laboratory tests ($*p < 0.05$) (from Frattola, A. *et al.*, 1997, with permission).

has been suggested by both animal and human studies. The observation that a blunted reflex vagal modulation of the heart may be associated with a higher risk of major arrhythmias has stimulated a number of clinical studies aimed at assessing the possible link between baroreflex sensitivity and patient's prognosis after acute myocardial infarction. Indeed, 2 to 7 days after an acute myocardial infarction baroreflex sensitivity was found markedly depressed by several studies. More consistent evidence on the clinical value of a reduced baroreflex sensitivity has been provided by a recently performed multicenter prospective study aimed at assessing the relative prognostic importance of several markers of neural autonomic cardiac modulation in postmyocardial infarction patients (ATRAMI Trial) (La Rovere, M. T., Bigger, T. J., Marcus, F. I., Mortara, A., and Schwartz, P. J., 1998, *Lancet* **351**, 478–484). The results of this trial indicate that baroreflex sensitivity is significantly related to patients' prognosis, even after accounting for the independent effect of other established prognostic markers such as the degree of heart rate variability and left ventricular function. In fact, baroreflex sensitivity seems to represent a prognostic marker which does not provide redundant information as compared to heart rate variability. This is in line with the report that in patients after acute myocardial infarction subjects with and without a higher frequency of life-threatening cardiac arrhythmias, respectively, displayed a clear difference in baroreflex sensitivity, but not a comparably clear-cut difference in heart rate variability. In spite of the above evidence, the real value of baroreflex sensitivity in the evaluation of patients' prognosis after an acute myocardial infarction cannot yet be regarded as unequivocally clarified, however. Indeed, a clear-cut relationship between impairment of baroreflex sensitivity on one side and the infarct size or the degree of left ventricular dysfunction on the other side was not found in a number of papers. The negative results on the relation between baroreflex sensitivity and patients' prognosis obtained in some studies might also have depended, however, on the rather crude method which was employed to test the effectiveness of baroreceptor-heart rate control in these studies, which consisted in most instances in the evaluation of the reflex bradycardia which follows the increase in blood pressure obtained by one or only a few bolus iv injections of phenilephrine.

The potential importance of baroreflex sensitivity as a clinically relevant marker in cardiac patients has been further supported by a series of studies which showed that pharmacological and nonpharmacological interventions able to reduce sympathetic activity and to increase vagal activity and baroreflex sensitivity may be protective against cardiac mortality and, in particular, sudden cardiac death. Administration of β-adrenoreceptor blocking agents, which modulate cardiac sympathetic stimulation and increase baroreflex sensitivity, was shown to improve morbidity and mortality in myocardial infarction patients even in the case of congestive heart failure. A similar mechanism might explain the beneficial prognostic effect in those patients who use ACE inhibitors and who exercise, interventions which have also been reported to increase baroreflex sensitivity after AMI. Data are available that baroreflex sensitivity may have a prognostic value also in two other pathological conditions, namely congestive heart failure and diabetes mellitus. In heart failure patients, the risk of death was significantly higher in patients with lower baroreflex sensitivity as assessed by a neck chamber device, although the prognostic impact of a low baroreflex sensitivity was no more significant when the influence of an increased sympathetic activity was simultaneously considered. This might depend on the inverse relationship that characterizes sympathetic and parasympathetic cardiovascular modulation, because evidence is available that deterioration of left ventricular function is associated with a decrease in parasympathetic tone. A reduced vagal tone thus may identify not only patients at high risk of sudden death, but also those at high risk of pump failure, both parameters being closely related to prognosis in heart failure. On the other hand, a number of clinical studies have clearly shown the importance of a reduced vagal activity and of a deranged sympathetic activity on the prognosis of patients with diabetes mellitus. Indeed a number of diabetic patients with clinically evident autonomic dysfunction die suddenly and unexpectedly, probably because of cardiac arrhythmias. Moreover, several studies suggest that even subclinical autonomic dysfunction may be predictive of future mortality in patients with diabetes mellitus. In conclusion, even if we do not have yet a clear demonstration that the prognosis of patients with myocardial infarction, heart failure, or diabetes, and the values of baroreflex sensitivity are causally linked to each other, the available evidence is strongly in favor of such a possibility. Further progress in this field is likely to be supported by the recent development of more sensitive and specific methods to assess spontaneous reflex cardiac autonomic modulation.

IV. CONCLUSION

This article has summarized the role of the arterial baroreflex in human cardiovascular physiology and pathophysiology and the pros and cons of different methods for assessing baroreflex sensitivity in humans. Laboratory methods have so far largely contributed to our present knowledge of arterial baroreflex function in humans. Modern techniques for spontaneous baroreflex analysis, however, have more recently provided us with a much deeper insight into the features of daily life baroreflex function as compared to what is offered by traditional laboratory tests. The recent evidence obtained in myocardial infarction patients, in patients with congestive heart failure, and in diabetic patients through even the relatively crude estimates of baroreflex sensitivity offered by laboratory tests has increased the interest in baroreflex analysis in humans. Whether the richer information provided by the new methods for assessing spontaneous baroreflex sensitivity might further improve the prognostic evaluations of such patients, however, needs to be tested by large-scale longitudinal studies.

See Also the Following Articles

Beta-Adrenergic Blockers; Cardiovascular System and Stress; Heart Disease/Attack; Hypertension

Bibliography

Bristow, J. D., Honour, A. J., Pickering, G. W., Sleight, P., and Smyth, H. S. (1969). Diminished baroreflex sensitivity in high blood pressure. *Circulation* 39, 48–54.

Di Rienzo, M., Bertinieri, G., Mancia, G., and Pedotti, A. (1985). A new method for evaluating the baroreflex role by a joint pattern Analysis of pulse interval and systolic blood pressure series. *Med. Biol. Eng. Comput.* 23(Suppl. I), 313–314.

Di Rienzo, M., Parati, G., Mancia, G., Pedotti, A., and Castiglioni, P. (1997). Investigating baroreflex control of circulation using signal processing techniques: New approaches for evaluating the baroreflex function. *IEEE Eng. Med. Biol.* 10, 86–95.

Eckberg, D. L., Cavanaugh, M. S., Mark, A. L., and Abboud, F. M. (1975). A simplified neck suction device for activation of carotid baroreceptors. *J. Lab. Clin. Med.* 85, 167–173.

Hohnloser, S. H., Klingenheben, T., Van de Loo, A., *et al.* (1994). Reflex versus tonic vagal activity as a prognostic parameter in patients with sustained ventricular tachycardia and ventricular fibrillation. *Circulation* 89, 1068–1073.

Hull, S. S., Vanoli, E., Adamson, P. B., Verrier, R. L., Foreman, R. D., and Schwartz, P. J. (1994). Exercise training confers anticipatory protection from sudden death during acute myocardial ischemia. *Circulation* 89, 548–552.

Imholz, B. P. M., Langewouters, G., Van Montfrans, G. A., Parati, G., van Goudoever, J., Wesseling, K. H., and Mancia, G. (1993). Feasibility of ambulatory continuous 24 h finger arterial pressure recording. *Hypertension* 21, 65–73.

Ludbrook, J., Mancia, G., Ferrari, A., and Zanchetti, A. (1977). The variable neck-chamber method for studying the carotid baroreflex in man. *Clin. Sci. Mol. Med.* 53, 165–171.

Mancia, G., Ludbrook, J., Ferrari, A., Gregorini, L., and Zanchetti, A. (1978). Baroreceptor reflexes in human hypertension. *Circ. Res.* 43, 170–177.

Mancia, G., Groppelli, A., Di Rienzo, M., Castiglioni, P., and Parati, G. (1997). Smoking impairs baroreflex sensitivity in humans. *Am. J. Physiol.* 273, H1555–H1560.

Omboni, S., Parati, G., Di Rienzo, M., Wesseling, K. H. Wieling, W., and Mancia, G. (1996). Spectral analysis of blood pressure and heart rate variability in autonomic disorders. *Clin. Autonom. Res.* 6, 171–182.

Omboni, S., Parati, G., Castiglioni, P., Di Rienzo, M., Imholz, B. P., Langewouters, G. J., Wesseling, K. H., and Mancia, G. (1998). Estimation of blood pressure variability from 24 hour ambulatory finger blood pressure. *Hypertension* 32, 52–58.

Osculati, G., Giannattasio, C., Seravalle, G., Valagussa, F., Zanchetti, A., and Mancia, G. (1990). Early alterations of the baroreceptors control of heart rate in patients with acute myocardial infarction. *Circulation* 81, 939–948.

Osterziel, K. J., Hanlein, D., Willenbroock, R., Eichhorn, C.,

Luft, F., and Dietz, R. (1995). Baroreflex sensitivity and cardiovascular mortality in patients with mild to moderate heart failure. *Br. Heart J.* **73**, 517–522.

Parati, G., Pomidossi, G., Ramirez, A. J., Cesana, B., and Mancia, G. (1985). Variability of the haemodynamic responses to laboratory tests employed in assessment of neural cardiovascular regulation in man. *Clin. Sci.* **69**, 533–540.

Parati, G., Saul, J. P., Di Rienzo, M., and Mancia, G. (1995). Spectral analysis of blood pressure and heart rate variability in evaluating cardiovascular regulation: A critical appraisal. *Hypertension* **25**, 1276–1286.

Parati, G., Di Rienzo, M., Castiglioni, P., Villani, A., Tortorici, E., and Mancia, G. (1997). Spontaneous baroreflex sensitivity: from the cardiovascular laboratory to patient's bedside. *In* "Frontiers of Blood Pressure and Heart Rate Analysis" (M. Di Rienzo, G. Mancia, G. Parati, A. Pedotti, and A. Zanchetti, Eds.), pp. 219–240. IOS Press, Amsterdam.

Parlow, J., Viale, J. P., Annat, G., Hughson, R., and Quintin, L. (1995). Spontaneous cardiac baroreflex in humans: Comparison with drugs-induced responses. *Hypertension* **25**, 1058–1068.

Smyth, H. S., Sleight, P., and Pickering, G. W. (1969). Reflex regulation of arterial pressure during sleep in man: A quantitative method of assessing baroreflex sensitivity. *Circ. Res.* **24**, 109–121.

Arthritis

Ronald L. Wilder

National Institute of Arthritis and Musculoskeletal and Skin Diseases, National Institutes of Health

I. Types of Arthritis
II. Rheumatoid Arthritis
III. Does Stress Play a Role in Rheumatoid Arthritis?

GLOSSARY

arthritis A group of disorders characterized by chronic pain and progressive impairment of joints and adjacent soft tissues.

autoimmunity An immune response directed at self tissues that can result in inappropriate tissue injury.

corticosteroids Natural or synthetic steroid hormones with potent anti-inflammatory actions.

cytokines Proteins produced by a variety of cells that mediate intercellular communication or other effector functions such as generation or control of the inflammatory response.

HPA axis An abbreviation for the hypothalamic-pituitary-adrenal axis.

hypothalamus A part of the brain that contains cells that coordinate numerous body functions including the activity of the stress response system.

inflammation A nonspecific response to injury that is intended to neutralize the cause of the injury and to orchestrate repair. It is characterized by heat, pain, redness, and swelling.

immunity A specific response to injury or potential injury that is intended to neutralize the cause or potential threat. Macrophages, lymphocytes, antibodies, and cytokines are important components of the immune response.

lymphocytes A general name for a category of cells that play key roles in mediating an immune response. There are two general types, i.e., B and T lymphocytes. B lymphocytes are primarily involved in producing antibodies. T cells are involved in cellular immune processes and in regulating the activity of other cell types, including B cells.

macrophages A type of cell that plays a key role in inflammatory processes. They engulf foreign materials and secrete an extensive array of biologically active substances such as cytokines.

major histocompatibility complex A group of genes located on human chromosome 6. Their name is derived from their role in triggering rejection of transplanted tissues. They also have major roles in regulating the responsiveness of the immune system.

neuroendocrine–immune loop A theory emphasizing the bidirectional interactions between the brain and the endocrine and immune systems. The immune system stimulates and regulates the activity of the nervous and endocrine systems, and they, in turn, regulate the activity of immune system.

rheumatoid arthritis A specific type of arthritis that is characterized by progressive, symmetrical, destructive inflammation of multiple joints, particularly hands, wrists, and feet.

sympathoadrenal axis A term referring to the adrenal medullary and autonomic sympathetic nervous systems. The major products produced are the catecholamines, epinephrine, and norepinephrine.

synovium A thin, delicate membrane that lines the cavity of joints. Its major function is to secrete substances such as hyaluronic acid that reduce the friction associated with joint movement. Inflammation of the synovium is called synovitis. Synovitis is a major component of multiple types of arthritis.

tumor necrosis factor A cytokine produced by activated macrophages that induces a variety of types of inflammatory injury.

Arthritis is the general term for a large, diverse group of musculoskeletal diseases characterized by chronic pain and progressive impairment of joints and surrounding soft tissues. These illnesses are very common and extremely costly to individuals, families, and society because they seriously impair work ability and decrease individual and household incomes. Affected individuals suffer from inability to conduct basic personal tasks, household tasks, and discretionary activities of living. For example, individuals with arthritis go out less frequently, spend less time with hobbies, and have much more difficulty earning a living or maintaining a household. Moreover, some forms of arthritis result in premature mortality in addition to severe disability.

Arthritis, particularly rheumatoid arthritis, is associated with an increased incidence of psychological distress and depression. Some of this distress is an intrinsic component of the disease process itself. In addition, the lack of independence and the inability to participate in various activities lead to frustration and feelings of helplessness. Not surprisingly, arthritis can strain marriages and family relationships.

I. TYPES OF ARTHRITIS

There are many forms of arthritis. Clinicians generally categorize arthritis into two major groups—monoarticular and polyarticular. Monoarticular disease is pain or swelling in a single joint, whereas polyarticular disease involves multiple joints. Monoarticular arthritis commonly results from joint infection or gout or other types of crystal deposition in the joint. However, any of the diseases that produce multiple joint involvement can also present with a monoarticular pattern of joint involvement. Polyarticular joint disease is categorized into two subgroups: inflammatory and noninflammatory. For example, osteoarthritis is a very common noninflammatory polyarticular disease, whereas rheumatoid arthritis is a common inflammatory polyarticular disease. The inflammatory and noninflammatory joint diseases differ widely in etiology and clinical findings. For example, the diseases may vary in regard to their mode of presentation (acute, subacute, or chronic), age at presentation, pattern of joint involvement, X-ray changes, and associated clinical laboratory abnormalities. More than 30 different forms of polyarticular arthritis have been defined. With regard to stress and arthritis, rheumatoid arthritis has been the focus of most research.

II. RHEUMATOID ARTHRITIS

Rheumatoid arthritis is the most prominent member of the polyarticular forms of inflammatory arthritis. Most patients with rheumatoid arthritis have a symmetric arthritis that involves the small joints of the hands and wrists. The disease may also affect joints of the feet, ankles, knees, hips, elbows, shoulders, neck, and jaw. The lower spine is usually not affected. Prominent symptoms include stiffness upon awakening in the morning, fatigue, and severe joint tenderness and swelling. Later, joint deformity and limitation of motion become prominent. Patients may also develop skin nodules. In severe cases, other parts of the body may be involved, including the eyes, lungs, heart, and nervous system. A hallmark of the disease is an association with an abnormal immunoglobulin called rheumatoid factor, which is present in the serum of about 80% of the patients.

Rheumatoid arthritis is considered a multifactorial autoimmune disease in that no single factor appears to explain its causation or pathogenesis, i.e., multiple factors interact to produce the disease process. The disease is much more common in women than in men. Women outnumber men by about 3 or 4 to 1. The most likely period of onset for women is around menopause. Rheumatoid arthritis is uncommon in men less than age 45, but its incidence approaches that of women in older men. Before menopause, it is common for women to develop rheumatoid arthritis within a year of pregnancy. Interestingly, the period around menopause and after pregnancy is associated with a decreased ability to produce corticosteroids in response to stressful stimuli. Conversely, rheumatoid arthritis rarely develops during a pregnancy, and patients with rheumatoid arthritis frequently improve significantly during a pregnancy. Pregnancy is associated with the production of high levels of the stress hormone cortisol, and many investigators believe that cortisol plays a major role in suppressing the expression of rheumatoid arthritis during pregnancy.

Genetic factors also play a role in determining susceptibility to and the severity of rheumatoid arthritis. The disease clusters in families and is associated with other autoimmune diseases. Current research indicates that multiple genes including genes associated with the major histocompatibility complex on chromosome 6 are involved in regulating susceptibility. The etiology of rheumatoid arthritis is not known with certainty. Many investigators suspect that an infectious agent is involved. Recent evidence supports the possibility that a parvovirus called B19 is involved, but much more investigation is required to confirm or refute this concept. A sustained autoimmune inflammatory process in the joints mediates the destruction of joints in rheumatoid arthritis. The joints are normally lined by a thin delicate membrane called the synovium. In rheumatoid arthritis, the lining layer becomes massively thickened and infiltrated by inflammatory cells including macrophages and lymphocytes. The synovial tissue stromal cells also increase markedly in number. The hallmark of the disease, however, is destructive erosion of bone and cartilage at the margins of the joint where the synovium attaches to bone. This erosive destruction leads to the loss of joint space and deformities of the joint. Current evidence indicates that the destructive process is driven by sustained production of proinflammatory protein mediators called cytokines. Tumor necrosis factor-α, or TNF-α, is considered to be one of the most important cytokines in rheumatoid arthritis. Major investigative efforts are currently directed at neutralizing the effects of TNF-α in the joints. Interestingly, the anti-inflammatory corticosteroids are one of the most potent natural occurring inhibitors of TNF-α production known. High levels of TNF-α production in rheumatoid arthritis has raised questions about the adequacy of corticosteroid production and the integrity of the neuroendocrine–immune stress loop in patients with rheumatoid arthritis.

III. DOES STRESS PLAY A ROLE IN RHEUMATOID ARTHRITIS?

The subjects of corticosteroids and rheumatoid arthritis are historically tightly linked. Cortisone was first isolated from adrenal tissue in the 1930s, but interest in corticosteroids rocketed when Hench and Kendall and colleagues described dramatic anti-inflammatory actions of cortisone in patients with rheumatoid arthritis. Their discovery resulted in a Nobel Prize in 1950. Subsequently, it was realized that long-term high-dose therapy with cortisone resulted in devastating side-effects. This development led to highly polarized views of the role of corticosteroids in RA. These controversies continue today.

Corticosteroids are prime examples of key stress hormones. They serve an essential role in a variety of systemic adaptive responses. We now call these adaptive responses the stress response. This response is necessary to preserve physiologic integrity. Importantly, it is now known that components of the stress response system interconnect extensively with components of the immune and inflammatory response systems. This interaction is bidirectional. Production of inflammatory cytokines such as TNF-α normally triggers the production of cortisol as part of a systemic activation of the stress response and the hypothalamic-pituitary-adrenal and sympathoadrenal axes. Cortisol, in turn, suppresses the production of TNF-α and normally prevents unchecked overproduction of the toxic inflammatory mediator. Thus, the feedback interconnections among the neuroendocrine–immune loop normally function to restrain the inflammatory system.

The importance of this feedback loop is exemplified by the LEW rat. The LEW rat is an inbred strain that has blunted or sluggish activation of the stress system in response to numerous stressors, including TNF-α. Interestingly, these rats are also highly susceptible to inflammatory arthritis resembling rheumatoid arthritis and other forms of autoimmune disease, and these diseases are markedly attenuated if the rats are treated with physiologic dose corticosteroids very early in the course of disease. The origin of the stress system defect in these rats has not been completely defined, but it clearly involves the brain and the hypothalamus. The LEW rat contrasts strikingly with the F344 inbred rat, which has an overactive stress response system and is resistant to arthritis and a variety of other autoimmune diseases.

The observations in the LEW and F344 rats have led to extensive investigations that are still ongoing, investigating the hypothesis that the stress response system is hypoactive in patients with rheumatoid arthritis. Data available to date suggest that the stress system is, in fact, underactive. Whether its underactivity is a primary or acquired pathogenic factor is not known. In any event, most investigators accept the view that stress and abnormalities of the stress system may play a role in rheumatoid arthritis.

See Also the Following Articles

AUTOIMMUNITY; CYTOKINES; IMMUNE SUPPRESSION; MENOPAUSE

Bibliography

Goronzy, J. J., and Weyand, C. M. (1997). Rheumatoid arthritis. *In* "Primer on the Rheumatic Diseases" (J. H. Klippel, Ed.), pp. 155–161. Arthritis Foundation, Atlanta.

Papanicolaou, D. A., Wilder, R. L., Manolagas, S. C., and Chrousos, G. P. (1998). The pathophysiologic roles of interleukin-6 in human disease. *Ann. Intern. Med.* **128**, 127–137.

Sternberg, E. M., Hill, J. M., Chrousos, G. P., Kamilaris, T., Listwak, S. J., Gold, P. W., and Wilder, R. L. (1989). Inflammatory mediator-induced hypothalamic-pituitary-adrenal axis activation is defective in streptococcal cell wall arthritis- susceptible Lewis rats. *Proc. Natl. Acad. Sci. USA* **86**, 2374–2378.

Sternberg, E. M., Young, W. S., Bernardini, R., Calogero, A. E., Chrousos, G. P., Gold, P. W., and Wilder, R. L. (1989). A central nervous system defect in biosynthesis of corticotropin-releasing hormone is associated with susceptibility to streptococcal cell wall-induced arthritis in Lewis rats. *Proc. Natl. Acad. Sci. USA* **86**, 4771–4775.

Wilder, R. L. (1995). Neuroendocrine-immune interactions and autoimmunity. *Ann. Rev. Immunol.* **13**, 307–338.

Wilder, R. L. (1996). Hormones and autoimmunity: Animal models of arthritis. *Baillieres Clin. Rheumatol.* **10**, 259–271.

Wilder, R. L. (1997). Corticosteroids. *In* "Primer on the Rheumatic Diseases" (J. H. Klippel, Ed.), pp. 427–431. Arthritis Foundation, Atlanta.

Wilder, R. L. (1998). Hormones, pregnancy, and autoimmune diseases. *Ann. N.Y. Acad. Sci.* **840**, 45–50.

Asthma

Ad A. Kaptein

University of Leiden, The Netherlands

GLOSSARY

asthma A respiratory disorder characterized by episodes of widespread narrowing of the airways caused by constriction of the bronchial smooth muscles, swelling of the bronchial tissue, increased mucus secretion, infiltration of inflammatory cells, or a combination of these factors.

psychology The study of human behavior.

stress Stress responses are said to arise when demands exceed the personal and social resources that the individual is able to mobilize.

Asthma is derived from a Greek word meaning "panting, attending with sound." Symptoms of this most prevalent respiratory disorder in the world are episodes of shortness of breath, wheezing, coughing, and sputum production. The hallmark of asthma is its reversible nature: asthma patients are free of symptoms most of the time. Asthma attacks are elicited by a range of stimuli, e.g., house dust mite, cat and dog dander, cold air, and emotional stress. Asthma attacks disappear either spontaneously or by medical (pharmacological) management. The prevalence of asthma worldwide ranges from 10 per 1000 to 200 per 1000. This prevalence is rising, the reasons for which are largely not clear. The psychological, social, and economic consequences of asthma must be characterized as impressive. Daily activities and feelings of well-being are negatively affected by asthma attacks. Recent estimates of costs due to the medical care for patients with asthma and work absenteeism are calculated to amount to $1 billion in the U.S. Four issues are discussed, the order of which reflects more or less the historical views on the complex interaction between asthma and stress.

I. STRESS: A CAUSE OF ASTHMA?

During the first decades of the 20th century asthma was considered a disorder which was caused by psychological factors—one of them stress. In psychodynamic or psychoanalytic theories, asthma was looked upon as an example of a somatic dysfunction that "really" was the expression of an underlying, unconscious psychodynamic conflict. As such, asthma was just a symptom that symbolically expressed an anxiety neurosis ("asthma nervosum"). It was proposed that the continuous functional stress arising out of everyday contacts with the environment causes chronic disturbances in the organ systems of the individual. Based on Cannon's work on the autonomic nervous system, disturbances of vegetative functions were considered to arise because either fight-or-flight behavior or dependent help-seeking behavior is blocked. Whenever the overt expression of fight-or-flight behavior is blocked, the resulting sustained excitation of the sympathetic nervous system would lead to disturbances in neuroendocrine systems that ultimately lead to diseases like hypertension or migraine headaches. When, on the other hand, the wish of "being taken care of" is blocked because of internal denial or external circumstances, increased parasympathetic activity mediated by the neuroendocrine system would lead to diseases such as peptic ulcer or asthma.

Empirical studies did not find support for psychodynamic views on patients with asthma. It seems virtually impossible to gather evidence that would support the primacy of psychological or stress factors as the cause of asthma. Furthermore, the patients who were studied by the proponents of psychodynamic theories were referred to them in a last-resort option after regular medical management failed to control the asthmatic symptoms. It is most likely that "psychopathology," as assessed by the clinicians, contributed to inadequate illness behavior in these patients, which resulted in an unsatisfactory medical outcome (see Section III).

Psychodynamic thinking about stress as a major cause of asthma has lost its influence in the research arena. In the clinical arena, however, many asthma patients and mothers of children with asthma in particular still express their feelings of uncertainty and even guilt by asking themselves whether they have caused their asthma by themselves.

II. STRESS: A TRIGGER OF ASTHMA ATTACKS

Asthma patients report a great number of psychological stimuli that in their view cause asthma attacks: emotional excitement, anxiety, worry, sadness, anger, and frustration. In modern health psychology theories, attributions by patients about symptoms and signs are considered relevant as they guide coping behavior (see Sections III and IV). In theories about illness perceptions, attributions about causes of symptoms have been shown to determine outcomes such as return to work. However, in asthma it is virtually impossible to identify objectively which stimulus or stimuli triggers an asthma attack.

Laboratory research has produced some evidence about the effects of stress (emotional arousal) on pulmonary function, dyspnea, and asthma attacks. In these studies asthmatic patients were subjected to stressful stimuli (e.g., mental arithmetic, unpleasant films about autopsies) after which pulmonary function was assessed. Reviews indicate that in some 40% of the asthmatic patients studied, clinically significant decreases in pulmonary function were found, demonstrating that for a proportion of asthma patients stress represents a trigger for asthmatic symptoms.

A recent line of research in the possible association between stress and asthma attacks pertains to psychoneuroimmunological theories. Stress impacts on immune function. Increasingly, inflammation of the airways is considered to be a characteristic feature of asthma. Stress may reduce the ability of organisms to ward off infectious agents, which in turn may increase susceptibility to inflammation and thereby to asthma attacks.

III. STRESS: A DETERMINANT OF ASTHMA SEVERITY?

Physicians, psychologists, and patients cannot help but observe the impressive interindividual variation in the consequences of suffering from asthma, regardless of the objective severity of asthma. Given identical levels of asthma severity, patients vary in number and length of hospital admissions for asthma, severity of prescribed medication, and negative impact on psychological and social well-being ("quality of life").

Various research groups focused on the relation between the stress caused by suffering asthma and the subsequent outcome in asthma patients. This approach pertains to "psychomaintenance," or to how psychological and behavioral factors maintain and increase both perceived severity and medical intractability of the illness once it has already developed. Behavioral scientists in Denver, Colorado studied the psychological responses of patients with asthma to the stress associated with being short of breath. It was found that two stress responses in particular, panic–fear symptomatology and panic–fear personality, predicted several aspects of medical outcome independent of medical severity of asthma: length of hospitalization, severity of medication at discharge, and risk of rehospitalization. In addition to panic–fear as a stress response and panic–fear as a personality trait, attitudes toward asthma have been found to add to the predictive power of psychological factors in the medical outcome of asthma treatment in adults and in children. In health psychology, psychomaintenance is now usually referred to as illness behavior: the affective, behavioral, and cognitive responses of patients toward symptoms and consequences of the illness. The model below (Fig. 1) illustrates how stress and other aspects of illness behavior impact on medical outcome.

illness → *illness behavior* → *medical outcome*
asthma panic-fear, length of hospitaliz-
stress, ation,
attitudes severity of medication
at discharge,
risk of rehospitaliza-
tion

FIGURE 1 A theoretical model of illness behavior.

IV. STRESS REDUCTION: A USEFUL ADJUNCT IN ASTHMA MANAGEMENT?

Given the established relation between illness behavior of patients with asthma and medical outcome, behavioral scientists are now focusing on the effects of stress-management interventions (self-management) on medical and behavioral outcomes. In various meta-analyses, the effectiveness of self-management programs for children and adults with asthma has been described.

A typical self-management program for adults with asthma consists of 8 to 10 2-h small-group sessions where patients are taught various asthma-management competencies. These competencies include preventive medication skills (e.g., taking preventive medications as prescribed), precipitant avoidance skills (e.g., taking appropriate actions related to avoiding or minimizing exposure to identifiable allergic and/or emotional precipitants of symptoms), symptom intervention skills (e.g., making correct decisions regarding the urgency and extent of self-care and medical care needed), communication skills (e.g., establishing an ongoing patient health care provider relationship for clinical care), and health promotion skills (e.g., resolving significant problems or stressful life situations that adversely affect asthma management).

Outcome criteria in self-management programs for patients with asthma usually are frequency, severity and duration of symptoms, degree of limitations in daily activities, use of medication (severity, frequency) and health care facilities (outpatient visits, number and length of hospitalization), and behavioral outcomes (e.g., feelings of anxiety, stigma, and depression and quality of life). The self-management approach is summarized in Figure 2.

illness → *illness behavior* → *medical and*
asthma self-management, *behavioral*
stress-management, *outcome*
asthma management symptoms,
skills hospitalization,
activities
limitations,
anxiety, quality
of life

FIGURE 2 Self-management approach to asthma.

The empirical evidence for the effectiveness of the self-management approach in patients with asthma is, overall, positive.

Current issues in research about stress and asthma pertain to refinements in the self-management programs and to tailoring elements of self-management training to the needs of a particular patient. Teaching patients to correctly perceive symptoms of shortness of breath and to take appropriate corrective action are important issues as are compliance with medication, and cost-effectiveness of self-management programs for patients with asthma.

See Also the Following Articles

FIGHT-OR-FLIGHT RESPONSE; IMMUNE SUPPRESSION

Bibliography

Busse, W. W., Kiecolt-Glaser, J. K., Coe, C., Martin, R. J., Weiss, S. T., and Parker, S. R. (1995). Stress and asthma. *Am. J. Respir. Crit. Care Med.* 151, 249–252.

Cohen, S. (1996). Psychological stress, immunity, and upper respiratory infections. *Curr. Dir. Psychol. Sci.* 5, 86–90.

Creer, T. L., Wigal, J. K., Kotses, H., and Lewis, P. (1990). A critique of 19 self-management programs for childhood asthma. II. Comments regarding the scientific merit of the programs. *Ped. Asthma Allerg. Immunol.* 4, 41–55.

Devine, E. C. (1996). Meta-analysis of the effects of psycho-educational care in adults with asthma. *Res. Nursing Health* 19, 367–376.

Isenberg, S. A., Lehrer, P. M., and Hochron, S. (1992). The effects of suggestion and emotional arousal on pulmonary function in asthma: A review and a hypothesis regarding vagal mediation. *Psychosom. Med.* 54, 192–216.

Kaplein, A. A., and Creer, T. L. (Eds.) (2000). "Respiratory Disorders and Behavioural Science." Harwood, Reading, UK.

Kinsman, R. A., Dirks, J. F., and Jones, N. F. (1982). Psychomaintenance of chronic physical illness. *In* (T. Millon, C. Green, and R. Meagher, Eds.), "Handbook of Clinical Health Psychology" pp. 435–466. Plenum, New York.

Kotses, H., and Harver, A. (Eds.) (1998). "Self-Management of Asthma." Marcel Dekker, New York.

Lehrer, P. (1998). Emotionally triggered asthma: A review of research literature and some hypotheses for self-regulating therapies. *Appl. Psychophysiol. Biofeedback* **23**, 13–41.

Petrie, K. J., and Weinman, J. A. (Eds.) (1997). "Perceptions of Health & Illness." Harwood, Reading, UK.

Steptoe, A. (1984). Psychological aspects of bronchial asthma. *In* (S. Rachman, Ed.), "Contributions to Medical Psychology" Vol. 3, pp. 7–30. Pergamon, New York.

Steptoe, A. (1997). Stress and disease. *In* (A. Baum, S. Newman, J. Weinman, R. West, and C. McManus, Eds.), "Cambridge Handbook of Psychology, Health and Medicine." pp. 174–177. Cambridge Univ. Press, Cambridge, UK.

Wilson, S. R., Scamagas, P., German, D. F., Hughes, G. W., Lulla, S., Coss, S., Chardon, L., Thomas, R. G., Starr-Schneidkraut, N., Stancavage, F. B., and Arsham, G. M. (1993). A controlled trial of two forms of self-management education for adults with asthma. *Am. J. Med.* **94**, 564–576.

Wright, R. J., Rodriguez, M., and Cohen, S. (1998). Review of psychosocial stress and asthma: An integrated biopsychosocial approach. *Thorax* **53**, 1066–1074.

Atherosclerosis

Mark W. Ketterer and Mark Randall

Henry Ford Health Sciences Center, Detroit

I. Natural History
II. Technical Limitations
III. Putative Mechanisms
IV. Epidemiological Data
V. Treatment Data

GLOSSARY

adhesion/aggregation The process by which active platelets connect with vessel walls and each other to form a thrombus.

angina Pain or pressure generally occuring in the chest or abdomen, sometimes radiating to the left arm, and believed to be caused by ischemia of the myocardium. "Equivalent" symptoms may include dyspnea, dizziness, weakness, and palpitations.

angioplasty The introduction of a small balloon via a guidewire to an occluded segment of an artery followed by one or more inflations to reduce the narrowing caused by the blockage (also: percutaneous transluminal coronary angioplast or PTCA).

arrhythmia Disorders of the normal sequencing of muscle contraction of the heart leading to inefficiency or, in some types, cessation of blood flow.

claudication Pain and weakness in the legs when walking caused by atherosclerosis of the arteries feeding the legs.

collagen fibrils The smallest structure of collagen (supportive tissue) formed by assembling molecules.

infarction Cessation of blood flow by thrombus formation and causing tissue death.

ischemia An imblance of oxygen flow/availability and tissue need; usually due to obstruction by atherosclerosis.

perfusion The passage of a substance (e.g., oxygen) into tissues.

risk factors Behaviors or characteristics that have found to be epidemiologically related to the development of a condition.

smooth muscle cells Cells found in the tunica media (middle layer) of arteries which proliferate with injury.

sudden cardiac death Death occuring within 1 h of symptom onset. Almost always attributable to atherosclerotic disease complicated by thrombus formation.

syndrome X The occurrence of anginalike symptoms in the absence of atherosclerotic disease or ischemia.

transient ischemic attack A brief period of dizziness, confusion, or cognitive dysfunction caused by ischemia of the brain.

Atherosclerosis is a chronic illness of the arterial walls with a stuttering course that, when severe enough, results in passive or vasoactive/thrombotic obstruction of blood flow to a localized area of the body, causing tissue damage, dysfunction, or death.

I. NATURAL HISTORY

Atherosclerosis is an occlusive disease of the arterial walls that may occur at multiple sites in the body, but is most malignant when it threatens blood flow to critical organs such as the heart or brain. By itself, atherosclerosis is of no clinical significance. But when atherosclerosis obstructs blood flow either transiently (ischemia) or long enough to kill tissue (infarction), it can cause transient dysfunction or permanent organ damage. From a population standpoint, the most common clinical manifestation of atherosclerosis occurs when the heart is affected (angina, myocardial infarction, and/or sudden cardiac death). Atherosclerosis of major arteries feeding the brain can cause transient ischemic attack, multi-infarct dementia, or large, localized cerebrovascular accidents, while those to the legs can cause intermitant claudication and necrosis/gangrene and those to the kidneys can cause renal dysfunction or failure. While the initiation of atherosclerotic blockages, or "plaques," is believed to occur throughout the lifespan, in at least some individuals initiation can occur as early as infancy in the form of "fatty streaks." By the time a population cohort reaches late adolescence or early adulthood (e.g., young men killed in combat in Korea or Vietnam), about one third of young males display some degree of occlusion on postmortem and a few percent have "clinically significant" lesions (luminal blockages of 50% or greater in one of the major epicardial arteries of the heart). In middle-age, probably most individuals have at least some low-level atherosclerotic disease. But women remain less at risk until menopause when their risk begins to rise, matching males about 12–15 years later. However, even at advanced ages of 80 or greater, some people have coronary arteries entirely free of atherosclerosis. In some individuals, at some sites, the myocardium has the ability to grow collaterol arteries around occluded sites (perhaps provoked by exercise), which then serve as natural bypasses in the event of abrupt closure of the main trunk. Characteristics epidemiologically associated with the development or aggravation of atherosclerosis are referred to as "risk factors." Age (older), sex (male), smoking (more), hypercholesterolemia, family history of early heart disease (early), hypertension, diabetes, and sedentariness are generally accepted risk factors for atherosclerosis.

Initiation of atherosclerosis occurs when the endothelium (a one-cell-thick lining of the arterial wall) is damaged. Multiple mechanisms have been suggested for this event and are not necessarily mutually exclusive. Mechanical strain, chemical insult, and infectious/inflammatory responses are thought to play a role. The cellular repair mechanisms result initially in a fatty streak. Recurrent insult to the site provokes migration of smooth muscle cells and collegen fibrils, resulting in a fibrous plaque. Continued insult and attempted healing can produce an "unstable" plaque with a thin cap covering dead cells and a lipid-rich medium. Rupture of such a plaque, followed by platelet adhesion/aggregation and thus thrombus formation, is thought to be the sequence resulting in 85–90% of all myocardial infarctions. Vasomotor events (widespread constriction or localized spasm of arterial segments) may result in increased myocardial workload and/or superimposed thrombotic events, causing ischemia which may trigger life-threatening arrythmias for other patients.

The biochemical signals provoking each step of this process are still a matter of debate and investigation. But the validation of these theories is always to be found in intervention trials targeting the process but measuring the clinically important outcome. The role of platelet aggregation, for example, found its strongest validation in the powerful effect of antiplatelet substances (e.g., aspirin) in preventing cardiac events.

II. TECHNICAL LIMITATIONS

The ability to study atherosclerosis is limited by the available technology (Pearson & Heiss, 1993). Firm measurement is most accurately obtained by postmortem examination of the arteries. Short of this, coronary angiography in living subjects is considered the "gold standard." But even angiography has limitations: lesions that are low grade or tubular or longitudinal in shape are easily missed by the cardiologist's visual rating of the film; the cost and risk of the procedure means that the ethical justification for studying "normals" is difficult; and one-third of cardiac patients whose first symptom is sudden death or who are entirely asymptomatic will not appear in angiographic samples. Indirect measures include the provocation of ischemia (by physical exertion, sympathomimetic agents, and/or mental stress) and subsequent measurement by electrocardiographic changes or fixed (presumably permanently dead tissue) and reversible (transiently ischemic) myocardial wall-motion changes (measured on echocardiograms or, more commonly, blood-pool-tagged radionuclide imaging) or radionuclide-tagged perfusion defects of the myocardial walls. It should be emphasized that symptoms (dizziness, palpitations, dyspnea, or chest pain/pressure) either at rest or on provocation are only weakly linked with ischemia, even in patients with documented coronary atherosclerosis. In patients with high risk factor loading, chest pain/pressure or dyspnea reliably provoked by exertion and relieved by rest or nitroglycerin may be the only symptom pattern indicative of ischemia. Crushing, substernal chest pain/pressure is considered classic for a myocardial infarction, but only occurs in about 50% of such events.

III. PUTATIVE MECHANISMS

The means by which psychosocial/emotional stress may cause or aggravate atherosclerosis are multiple. First, stress is clearly a factor in diminished smoking cessation/abstinence and noncompliance to pill-taking, dietary restrictions (cholesterol, sugar, or salt), and exercise. Given the relatively new theory of inflammatory mechanisms and the known impact of stress on immune mechanisms, it is possible that stress may impact atherosclerosis by fostering chronic, recurrent episodes of plaque infection by *Chlamydia pneumoniae*. The best studied putative mechanism lies in acute or chronic emotional arousal provoking: peripheral vasoconstriction increasing myocardial workload, vasospasm, and thus endothelial tears or, at later stages, plaque rupture of susceptible lesions. It is clear that about one-half of patients with previously documented coronary atherosclerosis will demonstrate ischemia when mentally stressed (most reliably by verbal confrontations eliciting anger). For the clinician, the question of mechanism may be largely moot since the benefits of diagnosis/treatment would accrue regardless of the mechanism and the quality-of-life benefit alone justifies treatment.

IV. EPIDEMIOLOGICAL DATA

About two dozen studies have attempted to find cross-sectional associations between psychosocial/emotional stress and atherosclerotic severity in angiographic samples. The fatal flaw in these studies is the failure to appreciate that the "controls" (i.e., patients whose results are normal or "subclinical") used in these samples contain physically symptomatic individuals with sufficient risk factor loadings to provoke concern. The occurrence of physical symptoms in the absence of disease implies that most of these patients have high levels of somatized emotional distress (most notably panic disorder or depression and referred to as "Atypical Chest Pain" or "Syndrome X"). Thus the "normals" are not representative of a general or healthy population and are not appropriate as controls in studies intended to address etiology.

Only one study has examined an angiographic sample while obtaining a healthy age-/sex-/SES-matched control group. Ketterer *et al.* recruited 176 males undergoing coronary catheterization with no prior history of revascularization and 56 males who had no history of atherosclerotic disease (at any site). Traditional risk factors and multiple measures of psychosocial/emotional distress were quantified. In univariate analyses, several psychosocial measures (more depression as rated by a spouse or friend, more denial of depression as measured by discrepancies in spouse/friend-minus-patient indices, more unprovoked nocturnal awakening, and lesser frequency of suicidal ideation) were found to be associated with atherosclerotic severity. In univariate analyses, a number of traditional risk factors (fewer years of education, more packyears of smoking, greater obesity) and several cardiovascular medications (digoxin, aspirin, antilipidemics, and ACE inhibitors) were also found to be associated with atherosclerotic severity and one of the psychosocial risk factors.

It is notable that spouse/friend (and *not* self-)-reported depression, less suicidal ideation, and more nocturnal awakening succeed as positive predictors. This pattern of stigmatized symptoms (e.g., suicidal ideation) but *not* unstigmatized (e.g., nocturnal awakening) symptoms and spouse/friend- but *not* self-reported depression succeeding as predictors suggests denial as a major confound in measuring distress in this population. Indeed, marginally stronger as a correlate of severity was "denial" of depression (measured by spouse/friend minus self-reported depression on parallel versions of the same scale). Denial of depression retained significance even after controlling for traditional risk factors and cardiovascular medications. In fact, a dose–response relationship was observed for severity of atherosclerosis and denial of anxiety and anger as well as depression. This pattern of results unavoidably invalidates results obtained only from patient self-report measures of emotional distress since the apparent accuracy of self-report data is not only weakened by denial, but also confounded with atherosclerotic disease severity.

Angiographic study of atherosclerotic progression is limited by the ethical constraint (and costs) against using the procedure in healthy people with no clinical need. One attempt to study atherosclerotic progression exists in a patient population for whom clinical need (i.e., increased symptoms) existed. This report found increased progression in patients with more Type A behavior by Jenkins Activity Survey. Because we do not know the status of the arteries of patients in the original sample who did not undergo repeat angiography, nor do we know whether intertest angioplasty occurred which might affect the second reading, it is doubtful that this study provides much insight.

V. TREATMENT DATA

Ornish attempted an aggressive lifestyle modification program in 28 patients who underwent repeat angiography and 20 controls. Patients in the intervention group displayed modest (5%) regression of some plaques and were less likely to display progression than patients in a randomly assigned, usual care control group. Because the intervention had three prongs (vegetarian diet, daily exercise, and stress management), it is difficult to know whether one prong or another was more, less, or unimportant in the outcome. Ornish has not published data regarding hard clinical outcomes (myocardial infarction or death), although at least one report indicates decreased chest pain. Subsequent studies have found that lipid-lowering agents can also cause this sort of modest regression.

See Also the Following Articles

Cardiovascular System and Stress; Cholesterol and Lipoproteins; Heart Disease/Attack

Bibliography

Cannon, R. O., Camici, P. G., and Epstein, S. E. (1992). Pathophysiological dilemma of "syndrome x." *Circulation* 85(3), 883–892.

Davies, M. J., and Woolf, N. (1993). Atherosclerosis: What is it and why does it occur? *Br. Heart J.* 69(1), 3–11.

Kaplan, J. R., Manuck, S. B., Clarkson, T. B., Lusso, F. L., Taub, D. M., and Miller, E. W. (1983). Social stress and atherosclerosis in normocholesterolemic monkeys. *Science* 220, 733–735.

Ketterer, M. W., Brymer, J., Rhoads, K., Kraft, P., Kenyon, L., Foley, B., Lovallo, W. R., and Voight, C. J. (1996). Emotional distress among males with "syndrome x." *J. Behav. Med.* 19(5), 455–466.

Ketterer, M. W., Kenyon, L., Foley, B. A., Brymer, J., Kraft, P., and Lovallo, W. R. (1996). Denial of depression as an independent correlate of coronary artery disease. *J. Health Psychol.* 1(1), 93–105.

Krantz, D. S., Sanmarco, M. I., Selvester, R. H., and Matthews, K. A. (1979). Psychological correlates of progression of atherosclerosis in men. *Psychosomat. Med.* **41**(6), 467–475.

Mayou R. (1989). Atypical chest pain. *J. Psychosomat. Res.* **33**(4), 393–406.

Ornish, D., Brown, S. E., Scherwitz, L. W., Billings, J. H., Armstrong, W. T., Ports, T. A., McLanahan, S. M., Kirkeeide, R. L., Brand, R. J., and Gould, K. L. (1990). Can lifestyle changes reverse coronary heart disease? *Lancet* **336**(8708), 129–133.

Pearson, T. A. (1984). Coronary arteriography in the study of coronary artery disease. *Epidemiolog. Rev.* **6**, 140–166.

Pearson, T. A., and Heiss, G. (1993). Atherosclerosis: Quantitative imaging, risk factors, prevalence and change. *Circulation* (Suppl.) **87**(3), 1–82.

Pickering, T. G. (1985). Should studies of patients undergoing coronary angiography be used to evaluate the role of behavioral risk factors for coronary heart disease? *J. Behav. Med.* **8**, 203–211.

Ross R. (1999). Atherosclerosis—An inflammatory disease. *N. Engl. J. Med.* **340**(2), 115–126.

Atrial Natriuretic Peptide (ANP)

see Vasoactive Peptides

Attention-Deficit/Hyperactivity Disorder, Stress and

L. Eugene Arnold

Ohio State University

I. Definition and Overview
II. Aggravation, Complication, or Mimicking of ADHD Symptoms by Stress
III. ADHD Symptoms as Stressors
IV. Conclusion

I. DEFINITION AND OVERVIEW

Attention-deficit/hyperactivity disorder (ADHD) is a common disorder of cognition and behavior orig-inating in childhood. According to the American Psychiatric Association's Diagnostic and Statistical Manual of Mental Disorders, 4th edition (DSM-IV), diagnosis requires, in addition to sufficient symptoms, that some of the symptoms must have caused impairment before age 7, some impairment is present in two or more settings, and there must be evidence of significant impairment in social, academic, or occupational functioning.

For the inattentive type, there must be six of the following nine symptoms: (1) often failing to pay attention to details or making careless mistakes, (2) frequent difficulties sustaining attention,

(3) often not seeming to listen, (4) often failing to follow instructions or failing to finish things, (5) frequent difficulty organizing, (6) often avoiding tasks that require sustained mental effort, (7) often losing necessary things, (8) frequent easy distraction, and (9) frequent forgetfulness.

For diagnosis of the hyperactive-impulsive type, six of the following nine symptoms are necessary: (1) frequent fidgeting or squirming, (2) often leaving seat, (3) often running or climbing excessively, (4) frequent difficulty playing quietly, (5) often acting as if driven by motor, (6) often talking excessively, (7) often blurting out answers before questions have been completed, (8) frequent difficulty awaiting turns, and (9) often interrupting or intruding.

For the combined type, the full-blown syndrome, there must be six symptoms from each cluster (Table I).

ADHD itself is not considered a stress disorder. However, it is related to stress in a number of ways. As with most disorders of health, both physical and mental, the symptoms can be aggravated by stress. Many of them can be mimicked by stress. Further, the symptoms of the disorder, especially if untreated, can cause stress both in the individual afflicted and in family members, especially parents, and in teachers, other caretakers, and peers. Later in life, residual symptoms of ADHD can stress spouses or significant others, employers, and co-workers. Finally, adults with residual ADHD can stress their children, whether or not the children also have ADHD. The following description assumes the untreated natural course of the full-blown disorder (combined type).

II. AGGRAVATION, COMPLICATION, OR MIMICKING OF ADHD SYMPTOMS BY STRESS

Individuals with ADHD have a more tenuous functioning capacity than normal. They are more impulsive, less organized, less attentive to detail, less patient, and frustrated more easily. They are also more likely to have additional problems, such as anxiety (about one-third), depression, or learning disorders (20–25%), which further compromise their func-

tional abilities. They often have less adequate verbal memory or other perceptual, associative, or mnemonic ability. Some authorities believe that they are less easily rewarded by ordinary daily activities that normal people find sufficiently rewarding to maintain attention and interest, resulting in a frequent boredom and lack of satisfaction. All this adds up to less coping ability. Consequently, the amount of stress needed to induce stress symptoms is less than for other people. Because stress by itself can induce concentration and memory problems, it can add an extra increment of impairment to the attention and memory problems of ADHD. Similarly, stress-induced anxiety can add to the restlessness of ADHD, and impulse control often deteriorates further with stress.

Children who are suffering stress symptoms may appear to present with ADHD even if they do not have it. The hypervigilance, anxiety, restless sleep, and preoccupied inattention of posttraumatic stress disorder can mimic the distractability, restlessness, and inattentiveness of ADHD. The anxiety, misbehavior, withdrawal, depression, preoccupation, easy frustration, and impaired performance of an adjustment disorder can mimic the inattentiveness, misbehavior, impaired performance, and restlessness of ADHD. The agitation, withdrawal, impaired concentration, and irritability of stress-induced depression can mimic the restlessness, inattentiveness, and impulsiveness of ADHD.

III. ADHD SYMPTOMS AS STRESSORS

Untreated symptoms of ADHD stress the person who has the disorder, their family—parents, siblings, spouse, and children—teachers, employers, and peers.

A. ADHD as a Stressor of the Person Afflicted

Children or adults with ADHD, though of normal or even superior intelligence, find it difficult to achieve at a level commensurate with their ability. They have to try harder to achieve the same results

TABLE I
Diagnostic Criteria for Attention-Deficit/Hyperactivity Disorder

A. Either (1) or (2)

   (1) Six (or more) of the following symptoms of **inattention** have persisted for at least 6 months to a degree that is maladaptive and inconsistent with developmental level

   Inattention

      (a) Often fails to give close attention to details or makes careless mistakes in schoolwork, work, or other activities

      (b) Often has difficulty sustaining attention in tasks or play activities

      (c) Often does not seem to listen when spoken to directly

      (d) Often does not follow through on instructions and fails to finish schoolwork, chores, or duties in the workplace (not due to oppositional behavior or failure to understand instructions)

      (e) Often has difficulty organizing tasks and activities

      (f) Often avoids, dislikes, or is reluctant to engage in tasks that require sustained mental effort (such as schoolwork or homework)

      (g) Often loses things necessary for tasks or activities (e.g., toys, school assignments, pencils, books, or tools)

      (h) Is often easily distracted by extraneous stimuli

      (i) Is often forgetful in daily activities

   (2) Six (or more) of the following symptoms of **hyperactivity/impulsivity** have persisted for at least 6 months to a degree that is maladaptive and inconsistent with developmental level

   Hyperactivity

      (a) Often fidgets with hands or feet or squirms in seat

      (b) Often leaves seat in classroom or in other situations in which remaining seated is expected.

      (c) Often runs about or climbs excessively in situations in which it is inappropriate (in adolescents or adults, may be limited to subjective feelings of restlessness)

      (d) Often has difficulty playing or engaging in leisure activities quietly

      (e) Is often "on the go" or often acts as if "driven by a motor"

      (f) Often talks excessively

   Impulsivity

      (g) Often blurts out answers before questions have been completed

      (h) Often has difficulty awaiting turn

      (i) Often interrupts or intrudes on others (e.g., butts into conversations or games)

B. Some hyperactive-impulsive or inattentive symptoms that caused impairment were present before age 7 years

C. Some impairment from the symptoms is present in two or more settings (e.g., at school or work and at home)

D. There must be clear evidence of clinically significant impairment in social, academic, or occupational functioning

E. Symptoms not not occur exclusively during the course of a pervasive developmental disorder, schizophrenia, or other psychotic disorder and are not better accounted for by another mental disorder (e.g., mood disorder, anxiety disorder, dissociative disorder, or a personality disorder)

Source: Permission granted from the *Diagnostic and Statistical Manual of Mental Disorders, Fourth Edition.* Copyright 1994 American Psychiatric Association.

as peers of the same intelligence. The impulsiveness of the disorder may repeatedly get the child or adult into trouble before they realize what has happened.

For example, a child with inattention may have to struggle for an hour or two to complete the same homework that a peer of normal attentional focus can complete in a half-hour. Even then, he may forget to turn it in on time and thus not get full credit for it. Similarly, inattention can interfere with sports performance, a source of the greatest interest and pride for many children. Inattentively missing the catch of an easy pop fly, making impulsive mistakes, or failing to hear or carry out the coach's instruction, thus incurring the contempt of peers and coach, or being chosen 18th when sides are chosen can all stress one's self-esteem. Even at home, children with

ADHD may find their achievement and behavior compared unfavorably with those of siblings of equal potential. They may be acutely aware of parental (or teacher) disappointment in their performance or behavior and conclude that they are not loved, at least not as much as siblings or classmates. Needing more prompting by teachers (and/or parents) for daily function, they may feel "picked on" and alienated from the usual sources of caregiver support. Thus the developmental tasks of childhood, including acquisition of academic and social skills, basic skills of civilization, work habits, friendships, secure family relations, autonomous functioning, self-control, and self-confidence, are accomplished—if at all—at a more stressful price in the presence of ADHD.

In adolescence and young adulthood, the inattentiveness and impulsiveness of ADHD lead to poorer driving records than those of age mates (two to four times as many accidents). Parents are thus understandably reluctant to sign for a driving permit as early as the adolescent wishes and are reluctant to allow use of the family car once a driver's license is obtained. Given the importance of "wheels" for peer esteem and adolescent and young adult social life, this parental reluctance aggravates any family conflict, further cripples peer relations, and adds further increments of psychological stress. The impulsiveness and disorganization of the disorder also lead to a higher rate of teenage pregnancy in girls with ADHD and probably in girlfriends of boys with ADHD, not to mention greater exposure to venereal disease. After all, precautions (including abstinence) require some reflection, organization, and impulse control. Thus the interaction of ADHD with developmental issues of adolescence compound the ADHD-induced stresses from earlier childhood.

Adults with inattention become bored or frustrated with many job opportunities that others find tolerable or even interesting. They may wallow miserably in a lower-skilled job than their abilities deserve. Conversely, they may have an erratic work history as their dissatisfaction and short attention span lead them to seek relief in job changes or even impulsively quitting without another job lined up. Employer dissatisfaction with poor attention to detail, restlessness, or failure to follow instructions may also lead to short tenures on many jobs. Thus occupation, which

should be one of the supports of self-esteem and satisfaction, may become an additional stressor economically and psychologically in the presence of ADHD. Similar patterns of frustration, boredom, restlessness, and difficulty sustaining commitment may dog social and intimate relationships, with lower rates of successful marriage. Failed love, separation, and divorce are well-documented stressors for anyone.

B. ADHD as a Stressor of Parents and Teachers

The constant activity, easy frustration, irritability, disorganization, tendency to lose things, and difficulty following instructions found in children with ADHD can stress any adult attempting to manage their behavior, structure their activities, or teach them. It is particularly frustrating to teachers when they recognize that the child has the intellectual ability but is not doing the work. Many teachers agonize over the wasted potential or even blame themselves for the child's poor performance. An unsuccessful intelligent pupil is stressful to the teacher's self-image. Erroneous conclusions that the child is lazy or obstinate can poison the teacher–pupil relationship and stress both teacher and child, possibly spilling over into the teacher–parent relationship and stressing all three parties.

Parents are stressed by similar disappointments and child performance difficulties at home, less intense than at school, but more consistent and enduring (every day, every year). Neglected chores, disorganized messiness, impulsive accidents and poor judgment, hectic overactivity and intrusiveness, conflicts with siblings, undone homework, calls from school, poor report cards, and other stresses were not what most parents anticipated at the child's birth. Such disappointments make it hard for parents to love (or at least hard to like) the child, leading to guilt feelings over being a rejecting parent. Criticisms of the child's behavior and the parents' child-rearing practices by well-meaning friends and relatives may add to the parents' feeling of failure. The child's impulsive destructiveness and accident proneness, as well as chronic need for professional services, round out the picture of a "high-maintenance child" who stresses the parents economically, physically, and psychologically.

Research has confirmed the profound impact of the ADHD child's problems on the parents. In a well-controlled study of parent–child interactions, the placebo condition showed the mothers of boys with ADHD to be very directive, commanding, and negative with the child, with little positive interaction; when a dose of stimulant medicine was given to alleviate the child's ADHD symptoms, the same mothers became much friendlier and more respectful of the child, allowed the child more autonomy, and gave many fewer negative messages to the child. This demonstrated that the negative parental attitude often seen toward ADHD children is not part of the parents' personality, but a response to the child's problems. ADHD tends to bring out the worst in those around the afflicted person.

The negativity often spreads into the marital relationship as the frustrated parents disagree about how to handle the child's problems. For example, the father may blame the mother because he can get the child to behave for short times (sometimes by heavy-handed means) and the mother cannot get the child to behave during the much longer intervals she is responsible for. The mother may feel the father's disciplinary approach is abusive. Each may blame the others' genes. One parent may wish the child medicated while the other objects to this. One parent may be enthusiastic about behavior modification but finds the system sabotaged by the other parent's failure to cooperate. In some cases one parent does not even recognize or admit there is a problem, while the other parent struggles with numerous complaints from school. One indicator of the marital stress engendered by a child with ADHD is the higher divorce rates reported for parents of such children. (This may be a partial cause as well as effect: divorce is stressful to children, and stress may nudge a subclinical case over the diagnostic threshold by aggravating otherwise mild symptoms.)

C. ADHD as a Stressor of Peers

Siblings, classmates, or teammates of children with ADHD are often unsung victims of the afflicted child's symptoms. The afflicted child's (proband's) needs for attention, supervision, and services tend to drain parent, teacher, and coach resources from siblings, classmates, and teammates. This relative neglect can sometimes be carried to the point of actual neglect as all efforts of a family are focused on the impaired member. The whole family may have to forego outings that the proband cannot handle or may cater to the proband, either out of pity or out of fear of impulsive tantrums. Older siblings' social life may be impacted by the need to monitor the proband, by embarrassment, or by the proband's intrusiveness. Younger siblings may be steamrollered by the proband's overactivity and inattentive thoughtlessness or actually be endangered by the proband's reckless impulsiveness.

Classmates or teammates may find their education or projects, activities, or games disrupted by the hyperactive child's impulsive intrusiveness, failure to wait a turn, failure to carry out an assigned part of the team's effort, need for excessive attention, failure to finish the activity, impulsive arguing, irritability, or other failure to be a good team player. It should be no surprise that children with ADHD typically fare poorly in peer sociometric ratings. Tragically, the hyperactive child's normal wish for friendships, implemented by clumsy, intrusive, impatient attempts to impose friendships, often only makes the situation worse. Thus, in the presence of ADHD, the normal need for peer relations stresses both the hyperactive child and the available peers.

When ADHD persists into adulthood, the brunt of peer difficulties falls more on the significant other, who may have to endure financial uncertainty as well as a disorganized lifestyle and interpersonal inconsistency and unpredictability. Again, the high rate of failed marriages and other relationships stresses both the direct victim of ADHD and the indirect peer victims. Employers and co-workers also suffer some stress from the ADHD worker's inconsistent performance, restlessness, disruptiveness, failure to listen to or follow instructions, and failure to carry out assigned parts of a project. In some cases the need for the unpleasant task of firing adds to the employer's stress. Even when the ADHD employee quits voluntarily, there is the stress of finding and training a replacement.

D. ADHD as Stressor of the Hyperactive Adult's Children

An important but as yet largely unstudied area is the stress on children of having parents with ADHD. Theoretically, parenting characterized by inattentiveness, inconsistency, impatience, impulsiveness, and disorganization would be stressful for any child. Because ADHD is highly heritable, an adult with ADHD has a good chance of having a child with ADHD. Because ADHD children have a special need for parental support and structure, we might expect that they would be especially vulnerable to the inattentive, unstructured disorganization of an ADHD parent. Conversely, what parenting skills the ADHD parent has will be challenged by the additional stress of a child with ADHD, in a vicious cycle. Thus both parent and child would be stressed by their mutual handicap.

IV. CONCLUSION

Untreated ADHD may be considered a stress generator, with a large ripple effect impacting practically all of society: the 3–5% of the population who have ADHD, their parents, siblings, teachers, classmates, teammates, mates, children, employers, co-workers, and even unknown other drivers. Thus effective programs for preventing, curing, or controlling ADHD symptoms could ameliorate the fabric of stress throughout society.

See Also the Following Articles

Anxiety; Childhood Stress; Impulse Control; Learning and Memory, Effects of Stress on; School Stress and School Refusal Behavior

Bibliography

American Psychiatric Association, 1994. "Diagnostic and Statistical Manual of Mental Disorders," 4th Ed. (DSM-IV). American Psychiatric Press, Washington, DC.

Arnold, L. E., ed. 1978. Parents of hyperactive and aggressive children. *In* Helping Parents Help Their Children. A Handbook for Professionals Who Guide Parents, pp. 192–207. Brunner/Mazel, New York.

Arnold, L. E. 1996. Sex differences in ADHD: Conference summary. *J. Abnormal Child Psychol.* **24**, 555–569.

Arnold, L. E. 1999. Treatment alternatives for attention-deficit/hyperactivity disorder. *In* "Diagnosis and Treatment of ADHD: An Evidence-Based Approach," (P. S. Jensen, and J. Cooper, eds.). American Psychiatric Press, Washington, DC. Also in *J. Attent. Disord.,* in press.

Arnold, L. E., and Jensen, P. S. 1995. Attention-deficit disorders. *In* "Comprehensive Textbook of Psychiatry/VI" (H. I. Kaplan and B. J. Sadock, eds.), pp. 2295–2310. Williams & Wilkins, Baltimore.

Elia, J., Ambrosini, P. J., and Rapoport, J. L. 1999. Drug therapy: Treatment of attention-deficit-hyperactivity disorder. *N. Engl. J. Med.* **340**, 780–788.

Autoimmunity

Bruce S. Rabin

University of Pittsburgh

GLOSSARY

antibody A protein that combines with the antigen that caused the antibody to be produced. Antibodies have "specificity" in that they combine most strongly with the particular antigen that stimulated their production. Antibodies are produced by a type of white blood cell called a B lymphocyte. Each B lymphocyte can only produce a single type of antibody, but the B lymphocyte produces thousands of that particular antibody molecule each second. Antibodies bind to antigens that are located outside of tissue cells.

antigen A substance that activates the immune system to produce a specific response that reacts against the antigen that activated the immune response. An antigen is usually something that is foreign to the body such as an infectious agent.

autoimmunity An immune reaction that is directed against an individual's own tissue. The immune reaction may damage tissue and cause disease.

cytokine One of numerous proteins made by a cell which can influence the activity of other cells. Cytokines bind to cytokine receptors on cells with different receptors binding different cytokines. Lymphocytes and antigen-presenting cells produce cytokines which, depending on the particular cytokine and the cell that it binds to, may either up-regulate or down-regulate the activity of other immune cells. Cytokines are also involved in the regulation of endocrine hormone production and contribute to the modulation of activity of the central nervous system.

lymphocytes White blood cells responsible for the immune response. Different types of lymphocytes originate from a common stem cell in the bone marrow. Lymphocytes that continue their maturation in the bone marrow become B lymphocytes, which function by producing antibody. Lymphocytes that migrate from the bone marrow to the thymus gland for their maturation become T lymphocytes that function in cell mediated immunity, which is antibody independent.

tolerance The specific absence of an immune response to an antigen. This is usually an active process that is related to the deletion of antigen-reactive lymphocytes or a mechanism which suppress the ability of the lymphocytes to respond to antigen. Lymphocytes which have receptors for self-antigen (one's own tissue antigens) are eliminated by the tolerance mechanism(s).

A utoimmune disease occurs when the immune system reacts against ones own (self-) tissue with resultant immune-mediated damage to the tissue. As is described, there is considerable epidemiological data indicating that stress may contribute to the etiology and/or pathogenesis of autoimmune disease. There are autoimmune diseases which result from the total elimination of a tissue. For example, the immune destruction of the insulin-producing cells of the pancreas produces insulin-dependent diabetes. However, most self-tissues present large masses of antigen and their removal presents a formidable task. An autoimmune attack on tissues such as the skin, the central nervous system, muscle, joint spaces, or the liver usually produces a chronic immune response without complete elimination of the tissue. When tissue is chronically attacked by the immune system, the sequela of the chronic production of soluble components of the immune system can present clinical problems in addition to the actual tissue damage. These include pain, lethargy, loss of appetite, and depression, all of which are mediated by the production of cytokines which influence the activity of the brain. Thus, not only does the immune process associated with autoimmune diseases pro-

Encyclopedia of Stress
VOLUME 1

duce tissue damage and the physiologic abnormalities associated with the loss of function of the involved tissue or organ, but there are also behavioral changes. Before discussing the considerable epidemiological evidence linking the onset or the exacerbation of an autoimmune disease with the perception of psychological stress, consideration is directed to how stress may alter the function of the immune system in a manner that could promote the onset of an autoimmune response or the exacerbation of an existing disease.

I. HOW CAN AN AUTOIMMUNE DISEASE BE INITIATED AND HOW CAN STRESS CONTRIBUTE TO THE PROCESS?

A. Failure to Eliminate Autoreactive B Lymphocytes

The B lymphocytes are produced and mature in the bone marrow as part of the normal process of B cell maturation. Some B lymphocytes randomly develop immunoglobulin receptors that are reactive to self-antigens. Thus, they have the capability of releasing antibodies that react with self antigens. To prevent the development of autoimmune diseases, the autoreactive B lymphocytes must be eliminated before they can produce harmful reactions. The process of removal of autoreactive lymphocytes is called "tolerance." Tolerance may be associated with actual death of the lymphocyte or its functional inactivation. The development of tolerance of newly formed autoreactive B lymphocytes must continue throughout life.

If the process of B cell tolerization were highly effective, no individuals would have autoreactive antibodies in their blood. However, nearly all normal individuals can be found to have low levels of antibodies directed to self-antigens. This suggests that the process of tolerization of newly developed B lymphocytes to self-antigens is not entirely effective.

As there is an epidemiological association of autoimmune disease with stress, it is possible that stress interferes with the tolerization of autoreactive B lymphocytes. Whether this is due to a stress-mediated decrease in the amount of circulating self-antigens which must be present in the marrow for B cell tolerance to develop, a decreased accessibility of self-antigens to the developing B lymphocytes in the marrow, a decreased susceptibility to tolerization of the autoreactive B lymphocytes, or other reasons is undetermined. For example, it is possible that stress hormones alter the kinetics of maturation of B lymphocytes so that there is a shorter window of opportunity for B lymphocytes to become tolerant to self-antigens, alter blood flow to the bone marrow so that there is a decreased concentration of self-antigens present, or alter the release of self-antigens from tissue so that the concentration of these antigens is decreased in the blood.

B. Failure to Eliminate Autoreactive T Lymphocytes

The T lymphocytes arise in the bone marrow but mature in the thymus gland. Some of the maturing T lymphocytes have receptors on their surface membrane that will combine with self-antigen. It is in the thymus where the autoreactive T lymphocytes undergo the process of tolerization. Similar to autoreactive B lymphocytes, T cell tolerization may involve cell death or functional inactivation.

If all autoreactive T lymphocytes were eliminated in the thymus, there should be no autoimmune diseases. That autoimmune diseases occur indicates that the process is not totally efficient or that there are ways for T cells to escape from tolerance. If the hormonal response to stress alters mechanisms whereby T cell tolerance occurs, stress may increase the likelihood of an autoimmune disease occurring. It is possible that the hormonal response to stress alters the interactions between the cells that are responsible for the induction of tolerance of T lymphocytes. This may result in increased numbers of autoreactive T cells being present in the peripheral lymphoid tissues.

C. Alteration of Cell Regulation

In the spleen, lymph nodes, and blood, where many immune reactions are initiated, there are a variety of regulatory interactions which occur between cells of the lymphoid system. The mechanism of regulation is likely through the secretion of soluble factors by a particular type of cell that alters the activity of other cells. The hormonal response to stress may alter the function of the regulatory cells which then may predispose to an autoimmune response. Examples included are listed below.

1. Macrophages produce transforming growth factor-β (TGF-β), which inhibits proliferation of T and B lymphocytes. If stress hormones inhibit TGF-β production, activation of autoreactive T or B lymphocytes may be enhanced.

2. The CD4 Th2 lymphocytes produce the cytokines IL-4 and IL-10. These cytokines suppress CD4 Th1 lymphocyte function. Increased Th2 CD4 lymphocyte function, which is associated with a change in the balance between Th1 and Th2 function, has been associated with activation of latent viral infections. Th1 activity is important as it suppresses latent virus activation. An immune reaction against tissue cells expressing viral antigens has been associated with the onset of autoimmune disease. Thus, stressor-induced alteration of the balance of immune function may contribute to the development of autoimmunity through the mechanism of latent virus activation.

3. The CD4 Th1 lymphocytes produce interferon-γ, which suppresses CD4 Th2 lymphocyte function. An increase of Th1 relative to Th2 activity has been associated with tissue damage in autoimmune disease. If the hormonal response to stress suppresses Th2 and increases Th1 CD4 lymphocyte function, an alteration of the course of autoimmune disease may occur.

There is a paucity of basic science studies relating to how an alteration of the balance between the various components of the immune system occurs when different concentrations of stress hormones are present. Such information is required before a determination can be made regarding the biological impact of stressor induced alterations of regulatory immune cell function.

D. Increased Susceptibility to Infection

Often, an acute stress or the experience of chronic stress decreases the function of the immune system. An increased susceptibility to upper respiratory viral infections and the reactivation of latent viral infections are the best documented indications of a biological effect of stressor-induced immune alterations. However, it is likely that resistance to any infectious agent is impaired by stress.

Infectious agents have been associated with the development of autoimmune diseases. Some infectious agents have antigenic sites that are identical to self-antigens. The presence of self and foreign antigenic sites on a single protein molecule frequently results in the breaking of tolerance to the self-antigen. For example, if infected with a bacteria that has an antigenic component on its surface that is identical to an antigen that is present on ones own tissues, tolerance can be broken. The antibody that is produced has the potential of altering the function of tissue or damaging tissue. Rheumatic fever is caused by this immune mechanism.

When a virus infects a tissue, an immune reaction to the virus kills the infected tissue cell. One of the mechanisms of cell killing is related to the release of enzymes from CD8 lymphocytes, neutrophils, and macrophages. The enzymes may degrade (denature) some of the molecules of self-antigen, resulting in a self-molecule that retains an antigenic site characteristic of the self-tissue and, in addition, has some antigenic sites that differ from self. When this molecule is processed by the cells of the immune system tolerance is broken and an immune response to the self-antigenic determinant results.

II. IF STRESS SUPPRESSES IMMUNE FUNCTION, HOW DOES STRESS PREDISPOSE TO THE DEVELOPMENT OF AUTOIMMUNE DISEASE?

A logical concern relates to how stress, which is usually associated with a decrease in the function of the immune system, can be associated with diseases which are thought to be caused by increased immune activity. This can occur through alteration of the regulatory components of the immune system, as described above, or through an increased susceptibility to infectious diseases with a subsequent increased risk of an autoimmune response.

Obviously, the relationship between the effects of stress on altering the function of the immune system and the development of an autoimmune disease is complex. Further complications are related to different patients with the same disease having different etiologies to their disease. Eventually, clarification of the factors that contributed to the development of an autoimmune disease in a particular patient depends on identifying the immune pathway that was responsible for the disease in that patient. That allows a more precise characterization of the role of stress in the pathogenesis of autoimmune disease to be identified.

III. THE RELATIONSHIP OF STRESS TO SPECIFIC AUTOIMMUNE DISEASES

The following presents specific autoimmune diseases that have been shown to have an increased frequency of occurrence or which have an exacerbation at a time of stress. However, there are many unanswered questions in regard to the pathogenesis of autoimmune disease involving onset, remissions, and exacerbations. Many of the studies where stress in a persons life is associated with an autoimmune disease are flawed by the process itself. For example, if an individual who has been diagnosed with an autoimmune disease is asked to recall negative events in their life, that individual may try harder to recall such events or add meaning to events that would seem less important if the individual did not have an autoimmune disease. A person experiencing negative life events may see a physician more frequently just because they are not feeling well emotionally and may be more likely to be diagnosed with a disease at an early stage. It is also possible that early stages of disease that produce metabolic alterations (such as thyroid disease or diabetes) may have behavioral changes due to the altered concentration of endocrine hormones in their blood which increase their likelihood of experiencing negative life events.

A. Psoriasis

Psoriasis is a skin disease that affects approximately 2% of the population. The involved areas of the skin are a pink color with white flaky scales. The skin lesions frequently undergo remissions and relapses. Psoriasis involves the infiltration of the skin with T lymphocytes and the production of disease-causing cytokines by the lymphocytes. An immune response to infectious agents in the skin may stimulate cytokine release. A hypothetical model can be constructed which supports the possibility that stress participates in the course of psoriasis by releasing neuropeptides from nerves which terminate in the skin. The neuropeptides, particularly substance P, may enhance the migration of lymphocytes into the skin which stimulate localized disease-enhancing cytokine release.

There are numerous published studies indicating that stress is associated with the exacerbation of symptoms in patients with psoriasis. A summary of the literature evaluating stress effects on the course of psoriasis supports the role of stress as a modulator of disease activity and suggests that the severity of the stressor may be associated with more severe disease Additional studies have suggested that relaxation procedures which may produce a psychological relaxation (which would have an effect on the immune system if they decreased sympathetic nervous system activation) are capable of ameliorating the clinical appearance of disease in patients with psoriasis. However, there are many factors which make interpretation of the studies difficult. Usually the number of subjects is low and the stage of disease and the actual pathogenesis of the disease in the subjects may vary. Coping skills (including psychosocial support, physical fitness, optimism, sense of humor, and belief systems) which help to buffer the effects of stress on the immune system may vary. Even whether the subject experienced high levels of stress as a youth or the subject's mother experienced high levels of stress during pregnancy may influence an individual's response to stress.

B. Rheumatoid Arthritis (RA)

Rheumatoid arthritis is associated with a large accumulation of lymphocytes in the joint spaces. There is destruction of the joint spaces and considerable pain. Systemic manifestations include tendonitis, pericarditis, vasculitis, and subcutaneous nodules pleuritis. The disease frequently has a relapsing and remitting course.

It is usually assumed that the disease is produced by activation of the immune system to an antigen. As identical twins are often discordant for RA it is likely that there is an environmental (antigen) involved in the disease pathogenesis. However, there has not been identification of specific antigen(s) to which the immune response is directed.

If the disease is a response to an antigen the functional competency of the immune system and its modification by stress hormones could modify the disease course. If stress does alter the course of RA, it may be through dysregulation of the normal relationship of the various lymphocyte subpopulations to each other. Reports of the effect of stress on the clinical course of RA have been variable and do not provide an unambiguous understanding regarding whether stress alters the onset or course of disease.

Another approach to evaluating whether stress influences the course of disease in patients with RA is to evaluate the effect of stress reduction interventions. Psychological interventions have suggested that slight clinical improvement can be achieved in patients with RA. Thus, regardless of the difficulty in defining an immunologic etiology in RA or a definitive understanding of the pathogenesis of the disease, there is suggestive evidence for an interaction between stress and the disease process.

There are extensive studies which indicate that psychological intervention programs can decrease the pain perceived by patients with RA. Whether the pain reduction produces an alteration in the amount of opioid produced, both within the CNS and peripherally, and whether there is a subsequent change in immune system function which ameliorates the disease process has not been determined.

Recently diagnosed subjects with RA have a lower activation of the sympathetic nervous system following a mental challenge stress task than control subjects without RA. Those subjects with the greatest amount of pain had the lowest sympathetic activation. The lack of an intact stress response in RA subjects may indicate that the immune pathogenesis of RA differs from the immune pathogenesis of other autoimmune diseases or that RA is more likely to occur in subjects who have an impaired hormonal response to stress.

An impaired hypothalamic-pituitary-adrenal (HPA) axis hormonal response to stress may allow the immune system to become overactivated, promoting an autoimmune process. Indeed, experimental animals which have an increased susceptibility to the induction of arthritis have been found to have functional differences of their HPA axes (susceptible animals have a decreased production of corticosterone) in comparison to experimental animals which are resistant to the induction of arthritis. An abnormal HPA response to immune and inflammatory stimuli has been reported in patients with RA.

Whether humans with RA have an altered response to stress because of modification of CNS function by cytokines or whether there is an innate difference within the CNS that modifies their response to stress has not been defined. However, subjects with another autoimmune disease, multiple sclerosis, have an intact response to the same psychological stressor that produced a diminished response in subjects with RA.

C. Graves' Thyroid Disease

Graves' hyperthyroidism is associated with weakness, nervousness, weight loss, fatigue, warm and sweaty skin, menstrual irregularities, heat sensitivity, protrusion of the eyes, and an enlarged thyroid gland. The pathogenesis is due to an antibody that binds to a receptor on thyroid epithelial cells that binds thyroid stimulating hormone (TSH). The thyroid stimulating antibody mimics the binding of TSH and stimulates the release of thyroid hormone. However, unlike TSH, which decreases in concentration as the concentration of thyroid hormone increases (reducing the releases of thyroid hormone), there is no inhibition of the physiologic effects of the thyroid stimulating antibody.

There are several studies which found that high levels of stress are more likely to occur in an individual who develops Graves' disease than in individuals who do not develop Graves'. These studies suggest that patients had more negative life events in the months preceding the clinical diagnosis of disease. However, not all studies support an association between prior stress and the onset of Graves'.

It is possible that if thyroid hormones are increased in concentration prior to the clinical diagnosis of disease, behavioral alterations are induced which either contribute to negative life events or the subject's awareness of negative life events. As thyroid hormone measurements are not made in the months preceding the appearance of clinical manifestation of Graves' disease, a possible influence of thyroid hormones on life events cannot be ruled out.

D. Multiple Sclerosis (MS)

Multiple sclerosis produces weakness, visual dysfunction, and paralysis. Multiple sclerosis lesions develop in the brain and the spinal cord where myelin surrounding nerve fibers is destroyed by lymphocytes and macrophages. There is an infiltrate of CD4 and CD8 lymphocytes, macrophages, and plasma cells. Nerve conduction is impaired. Identical twins have approximately a 50% concordance for MS, indicating that both genetic and environmental factors are involved with the disease pathogenesis.

The exact pathogenesis of MS is uncertain, but there is considerable evidence suggesting participation of the immune system. This includes characteristic changes in the immunoglobulin content of spinal fluid, which suggests an immune reaction occurring within the CNS; the mitogenic responsive of lymphocytes from patients with MS to antigens derived from the CNS; the clinical response to immunosuppressive therapy; and the existence of an experimental model that is induced by immunization with myelin basic protein, an antigen found in myelin.

The studies of stress as a contributor to the etiology of MS are not definitive. They suffer from the faults of small sample size, heterogeneity of the extent and pathogenesis of disease, various stress buffering capabilities of subjects, and concomitant clinical depression having an effect on immune system function. Definition of the exact immune mechanism(s) which produce demyelination is also a hindrance, as without knowing which immune mechanisms are responsible for the tissue damage it is impossible to know which pathway is being altered by stress.

An increase of Th1 lymphocyte function would be compatible with an immune change that could increase the risk for the development of MS. Interestingly, cerebrospinal fluid (CSF) of patients with MS contains cytokines which promote CD4 Th1 lymphocyte activity. An indirect indication of predominant Th1 activity in MS patients is the paucity of IgE-mediated disease in MS patients, as Th1-derived cytokines suppress the Th2 cells that promote B lymphocytes to synthesize IgE. Stress has been found to increase the production of cytokines from Th1 lymphocytes while sparing alteration of cytokine production by Th2 lymphocytes.

There have been many studies which have looked at the association of stress with the clinical course of patients with MS. The studies found that MS patients had significantly more life stress prior to the onset of disease or disease exacerbation than did controls. The most common life events which were related to exacerbation were those involving financial or interpersonal concerns.

An interesting observation regarding stress and disease activity in MS was made during the Persian Gulf war. This study reported a decreased rate of exacerbations of MS during the war. This observation indicates that an intense psychological stressor can have a profound effect on suppressing immune system function and decrease disease activity. However, this is a unique situation that does not argue against less intense life-event stressors having an influence on the exacerbation of the clinical course of MS.

Overall, the clinical observations and the possible stressor-induced immune changes suggest that stress can alter the course of MS. Studies of stress intervention are needed to confirm or refute this hypothesis. Care will have to be directed to the clinical homogeneity of the patient population including HLA characteristics, social support and other buffering systems available to the patient, use by the patient of medications, and how strongly the patient believes in the potential effectiveness of the intervention therapy.

E. Insulin-Dependent Diabetes Mellitus (IDDM)

A frequent pathogenesis of IDDM is related to immune-mediated destruction of the insulin-producing β-islet cells. Antibodies to insulin and islet cell antigens are present prior to the clinical onset of disease and may indicate a destructive inflammatory process is occurring. Sensitized T lymphocytes that have a cytotoxic effect on islet cells are also present.

The disease is frequently preceded by a viral infection and may be initiated by an immune response to a virus that specifically infects β-islet cells. Indeed, virus has been isolated from the islets of newly diagnosed diabetic subjects and, when the virus is injected into mice, IDDM has occurred with an associated immune-mediated destruction of the β-islet cells. Active viral infection is suggested because of a rising antibody titer in the patients serum to the isolated virus.

There are several reports associating life-event stressors with the onset of IDDM. Unlike diseases such as rheumatoid arthritis or multiple sclerosis, which have a relapsing and remitting course, IDDM does not remit. Therefore, studies showing an association of stress with alteration of clinical activity are nonexistent, but studies showing an association of stress with disease onset are numerous. Stressor-induced alterations of immune function may contribute to disease onset by (1) suppressing immune function and increasing susceptibility to viral infection and (2) altering the balance of regulatory lymphocyte populations which then allows an autoimmune response to occur.

Early reports linking stressors in an individuals life with an increased susceptibility to the development of IDDM were not rigorously controlled and presented small sample sizes. However, there are studies which suggest that there may be an association between stress and susceptibility to the onset of IDDM. These studies should be considered to be preliminary, as they have not addressed important questions.

Specifically, does stress increase the risk of IDDM onset in all individuals or only those who are HLA-DR3 and/or HLA-DR4 positive? If this association only occurs in HLA-susceptible individuals, should the control group of individuals who do not have high levels of stress be restricted to HLA-DR 3- and/or HLA-DR-4-positive individuals?

The only way to control for genetic differences between subjects is to study identical twins. The concordance for IDDM in identical twins is approximately 50%. Environmental factors are usually designated as explaining the lack of 100% concordance. Environmental factors may include viruses, but may also include stress and the ability of a subject to cope with the stressor. A study conducted in identical twins both concordant and discordant for IDDM where factors such as stress, psychosocial support, physical fitness, belief systems, sense of humor, and being an optimist or a pessimist are considered would make a significant contribution to our understanding of the relationship between stress and susceptibility to autoimmune disease. If identical twins discordant for IDDM experience the same stressors, does the twin who develops IDDM have better coping skills?

Studies which have contributed to the suggestion of an association between stress and the onset of IDDM in children have found that severe emotional stress, usually associated with parental loss, especially occurring early in life, increased the risk for the subsequent development of IDDM.

IV. SUMMATION

Characterization of the potential interrelationship between stress and the development or exacerbation of an autoimmune disease requires knowledge of at least two parameters: (1) What components of the immune system are functionally altered by stress? and (2) How does alteration of the immune system initiate immune-mediated damage to self-tissue? Unfortunately, detailed information regarding each of the two questions is still lacking. However, there is abundant evidence from epidemiological studies that the experience of stress is associated with autoimmune disease onset or exacerbation. Continued studies of stressor-induced immune alteration and the mechanism of onset of autoimmune disease will help to clarify their relationship.

See Also the Following Articles

Bibliography

Anderson, K. O., Bradley, L. A., Young, L. D., McDaniel,
L. K., and Wise, C. M. (1985). Rheumatoid arthritis: Review
of the psychological factors relating to etiology, effects and
treatment. *Psychol. Bull.* 98, 358–387.

Hagglof, B., Blom, L., Dahlquist, G., Lonnberg, G., and Sahlin,
B. (1991). The Swedish childhood diabetes study: Indica-
tions of severe psychological stress as a risk factor for
Type I (insulin-dependent) diabetes mellitus in childhood.
Diabetologia 34, 579–583.

Herbert, T. B., and Cohen, S. (1993). Stress and immunity
in humans: A meta–analytic review. *Psychosoma. Med.*
55, 364–379.

Kung, A. W. C. (1995). Life events, daily stresses and coping
in patients with Graves' disease. *Clin. Endocrinol.* 42,
303–308.

Sternberg, E. M. (1995). Neuroendocrine factors in susceptibility to inflammatory disease: Focus on the hypothalamic–
pituitary–adrenal axis. *Horm. Res.* 43, 159–161.

Wilder, R. L. (1995). Neuroendocrine–immune system interactions and autoimmunity. *Annu. Rev. Immunol.* 13,
307–338.

Autonomic Nervous System

William R. Lovallo and John J. Sollers III

Veterans Affairs Medical Center and University of Oklahoma Health Sciences Center, Oklahoma City

I. Background
II. Autonomic Nervous System Compared to the
    Somatic Motor System
III. Autonomic Nervous System Has Three Branches
IV. Neurons and Neurotransmitters
V. Anatomy of the Autonomic Nervous System
VI. Autonomic Regulation of Specific Organ Systems
VII. Local Regulation of Autonomic Function
VIII. Physical and Psychological Stress
IX. Summary

GLOSSARY

brainstem The portion of the brain connecting the cerebral
hemispheres with the spinal cord, consisting of the pons,
or upper part, and medulla, or lower part.

endocrine Pertaining to the secretory glands of the body
which release hormones that act on distinct glands and
tissues to regulate function.

homeostasis A concept expressing the collective actions of
the autonomic nervous system and endocrine systems to
maintain physiological systems within a balanced range of
optimal values consistent with the maintenance of life.

hypothalamus The collection of nuclei located below the thalamus that act on the endocrine system and the autonomic
nervous system to organize life-sustaining functions such
as feeding, fluid balance, and sexual activity.

limbic system The structures of the cortex and basal ganglia
that are involved with the emotions.

neurotransmitter A chemical substance supporting transmission of a nerve impulse across a synapse or neuroeffector junction.

receptor A complex protein molecule embedded within a
plasma membrane having chemical affinities for a range of
biochemical substances which can change the conformation of the receptor and alter the electrical potential across
the plasma membrane or exert actions within a cell.

In the course of daily life, we have to sustain
ourselves and maintain our health. We must rest or
be active, obtain food and digest it, and, occasionally,

we must cope with an exceptional challenge. At all times, during normal activity and during extreme stress, our brain coordinates the actions of our vital organs and our muscles to ensure our survival. This continual adaptation calls for two-way communication between the brain and the body. The brain has to sense what is happening to the body, and it must help the vital organs regulate themselves. The brain uses two systems to do this, the nervous system and the endocrine system. This article describes one branch of the nervous system, called the *autonomic nervous system* (ANS), which plays a central role in homeostasis and the stress response. We start with a description of the anatomy and physiology of the ANS and end with some general comments on how the ANS works during adaptation to stress.

I. BACKGROUND

The peripheral nervous system has two branches, the *somatic motor system* that controls voluntary movement and the ANS that regulates the internal organs and the eyes. In considering the ANS and its role in the stress response, there are five points to consider: (1) the ANS, along with the endocrine system, coordinates and regulates the vital organs; (2) the ANS is part of a *layered* set of controls over organ function, starting at the local organ and ending with the brain; (3) the ANS is controlled by two brain areas, the *brainstem* and *hypothalamus;* (4) during normal activity, the vital organs regulate themselves with little outside help, but during stress the ANS coordinates their actions; and (5) during *psychological stress,* bodily changes originate in the brain—higher brain centers act on the brainstem and hypothalamus to cause changes in the body via the ANS.

Historically, two critical figures have shaped our current model of the functions of the ANS during stress. Claude Bernard (1813–1878), the French physiologist, argued that living things must respond to changes in their *external and internal environments* to maintain proper cellular and organ function in keeping with physiological requirements. These principles are the basis for our thinking about how our bodies respond to stress. Walter Cannon (1871–1945), a noted American physiologist, termed this

regulatory process "*homeostasis,*" and he showed that homeostasis was served primarily by actions of the ANS along with the endocrine system. Cannon demonstrated that the ANS reacts to emergencies in a pattern of widespread activation that he called the *fight-or-flight response.*

II. AUTONOMIC NERVOUS SYSTEM COMPARED TO THE SOMATIC MOTOR SYSTEM

There are four points of comparison between the somatic motor system and the ANS: (1) the somatic nervous system and the ANS are both *motor systems*—they regulate the activity of muscle fibers or secretory cells; (2) the somatic nervous system provides *voluntary* control over our muscles, while the ANS *automatically* regulates the vital organs and related tissues without voluntary control; (3) somatic nerves always activate contraction of the somatic muscles, while ANS fibers will either *activate or inhibit* the vital organs; and (4) Fig. 1 shows two anatomical differences between the somatic nervous system and the ANS. In the somatic nervous system, a nerve fiber goes directly to a skeletal muscle. The ANS is more complex, with two sets of nerve fibers. *Preganglionic fibers* first travel to a ganglion, a specialized collection of nerve cell bodies. Next, they synapse with *postganglionic* fibers that travel to the target organ.

III. AUTONOMIC NERVOUS SYSTEM HAS THREE BRANCHES

The ANS has three branches: the sympathetic, parasympathetic, and enteric systems. The two major branches, the sympathetic and parasympathetic, are diagrammed in Fig. 2.

A. Sympathetic Branch

Sympathetic preganglionic fibers exit from the middle, thoracic, and lumbar segments of the spinal cord. The sympathetic branch is so named because it operates in *sympathy* with the emotions. In general,

A Somatic motor system

B Autonomic motor system

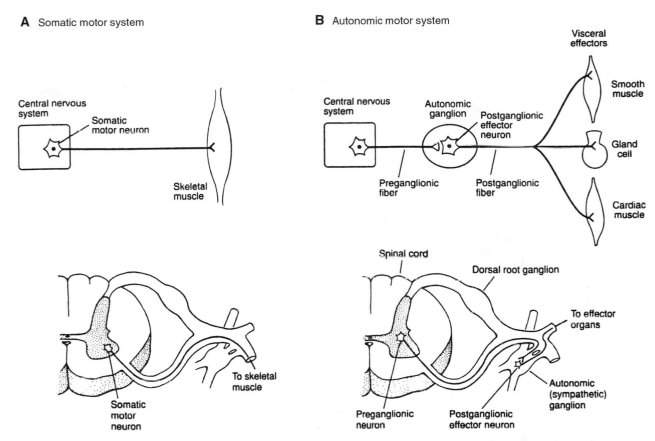

FIGURE 1 Neuronal innervation of somatic muscles and vital organs. (A) Somatic muscle innervation. In the somatic nervous system, motor neurons originate in the motor portions of the cortex. They descend through the spinal cord and travel to skeletal muscle directly to muscle fibers without synapsing with other neurons. (B) Autonomic innervation. In the autonomic nervous system, there are two sets of neurons. Preganglionic neurons originate in the brainstem. They exit from the medulla or descend in the spinal cord and enter an autonomic ganglion. In the ganglia, they synapse with postganglionic neurons, which travel to specific effector organs. There are three types of autonomic effectors: smooth muscle, secretory cells, and cardiac muscle. From Dodd, J., and Role, L. W. (1995). The autonomic nervous system. *In* "*Principles of Neural Science*" (E. R. Kandel, J. H. Schwartz, and J. H. Jessel, Eds.), pp. 762–775. Used with permission.

the sympathetic branch regulates energy-using functions, such as fight or flight, in order to maintain homeostasis in the face of external threats.

B. Parasympathetic Branch

In the parasympathetic branch, preganglionic fibers leave the central nervous system at points above and below the sympathetic fibers, hence the name *para*sympathetic. The upper group exits the medulla by way of the *cranial nerves*. These exit the central nervous system directly from the pons and medulla and serve the head, neck, cardiovascular system, and

gut. The lower group exits the sacral segments of the spinal column. Parasympathetic activity generally serves energy-conserving functions; it regulates energy intake, such as feeding and digestion, and reproductive functions and it is most active during routine activities.

C. Enteric Branch

As the name implies, the enteric system pertains exclusively to the organs of digestion—the pancreas, the gall bladder, and the gastrointestinal tract. Some consider the enteric nervous system to be a branch

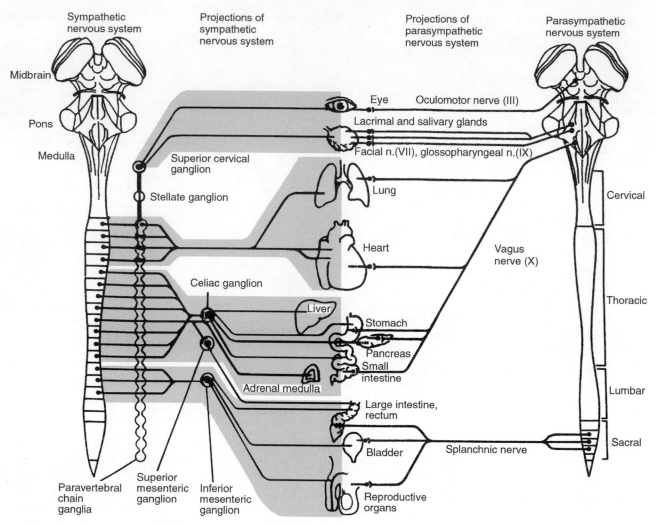

FIGURE 2   Organization of the sympathetic and parasympathetic branches of the autonomic nervous system. The sympathetic nerves exit the spinal cord at the thoracic and lumbar levels. These preganglionic neurons travel to the chain ganglia, and some pass through the chain ganglia to arrive at several other ganglia located in the neck and abdomen. The parasympathetic nervous system sends preganglionic fibers from the brainstem or the sacral level of the spinal cord. Its preganglionic neurons travel to ganglia located near or within the organs it innervates. Most of the autonomically innervated organs receive input from both the sympathetic and parasympathetic branches. The two branches exert opposing effects on the organs they innervate. A small number of organs receive input from only one branch of the autonomic nervous system. From Dodd, J., and Role, L. W. (1995). The autonomic nervous system. *In "Principles of Neural Science"* (E. R. Kandel, J. H. Schwartz, & J. H. Jessel, Eds.), pp. 762–775. Used with permission.

of the ANS, while others view it as part of the digestive system.

IV. NEURONS AND NEUROTRANSMITTERS

There are two points of communication in the ANS. At the ganglion, there is a *synapse* between each preganglionic and each postganglionic neuron. At the target organ, there is a *neuroeffector junction* between the postganglionic neuron and a muscle cell or secretory cell.

At both places, neurons communicate using specialized chemicals called *neurotransmitters*. These substances are released onto specialized receptors that activate either a postganglionic neuron or an effector cell. There are two ANS neurotransmitters, *acetylcholine* and *norepinephrine* (also called noradrenaline).

Preganglionic neurons always use acetylcholine to communicate to their postganglionic neurons. Postganglionic neurons use two neurotransmitters. In the parasympathetic branch, postganglionics secrete acetylcholine at their neuroeffector junctions. In the sympathetic branch, these fibers secrete norepinephrine at their effectors. There are two exceptions in which target organs of the sympathetic branch are activated by acetylcholine: (1) the specialized sweat glands of the palms of the hands and soles of the feet and (2) the medulla of the adrenal gland.

Autonomic ganglia have an important feature. They are not simply relay stations. Instead, they have small neurons that communicate directly between the larger pre- and postganglionic neurons. These small neurons secrete dopamine, which inhibits the ganglionic neurons. As a result, the autonomic ganglia produce the first level of integrative control over the vital organs.

V. ANATOMY OF THE AUTONOMIC NERVOUS SYSTEM

The brainstem contains several autonomic control centers that regulate the actions of the sympathetic and parasympathetic branches. Preganglionic fibers descend from these reflex control centers to their autonomic ganglia, and postganglionic fibers travel to the target organs, with the exceptions noted above.

A. Sympathetic Division

Sympathetic fibers exit from the spinal cord at thoracic levels 1–12 and lumbar levels 1–3. The sympathetic ganglia are located near the spinal cord and far away from the innervated organs. As shown in Fig. 2, there are two sets of sympathetic ganglia. The so-called *chain ganglia* run parallel to the spinal column and are highly interconnected. A second, more distinct group includes the cervical and stellate ganglia, located in the neck, and the celiac, superior and inferior mesenteric, and renal ganglia found in the abdomen.

The arrangement of sympathetic fibers supports the idea that the sympathetic nervous system acts in a unitary way. Sympathetic preganglionic fibers follow four basic patterns of dispersal (see Fig. 2): (1) some preganglionic fibers enter the nearest ganglion and their postganglionic fibers exit at the same level of the ganglionic chain; (2) other preganglionic fibers ascend the sympathetic chain ganglion to synapse in the cervical and stellate ganglia before they send postganglionic fibers to the eye, head, neck, mouth, and upper limbs and heart—the stellate ganglion serves the heart particularly; (3) the blood vessels and skin of the lower body are served by postganglionic fibers that receive input from preganglionic fibers that descend from the lumbar and sacral ganglia; and (4) finally, certain preganglionic fibers pass directly through the chain ganglia without synapsing. They collect to form the three splanchnic nerves. The splanchnic nerves then pass through the diaphragm to enter the abdomen before finally arriving at the celiac, mesenteric, and renal ganglia. The postganglionic fibers of the splanchnic nerves innervate the liver, spleen, stomach, gut, and kidneys.

We have noted above that during stress, the ANS coordinates the actions of the vital organs. The sympathetic nervous system is designed especially to promote such coordinated action: (1) its ganglia are close to the spinal cord and far from their target organs; (2) a single preganglionic fiber may serve postganlionics at several levels of the chain ganglia; (3) a ratio of 1 preganglionic to 10 postganglionic fibers allows for mass coordinated action that is well suited for fight-or-flight responses as well as other systemically integrated challenges to homeostasis; and (4) epinephrine secretions from the adrenal medulla act on uninnervated β-adrenoreceptors throughout the body, further helping to coordinate responses to all types of challenges.

As can be seen in Fig. 2, the sympathetic branch of the ANS serves the eye, salivary glands, lungs, heart, liver, spleen, stomach, gut, kidney, genitalia, and all of the blood vessels with the exception of the cerebral vessels. The specific action of sympathetic input and the receptor type are summarized in Table I for each effector organ.

A notable exception to the organization of the sympathetic nervous system is the innervation of the adrenal gland. In this case, sympathetic preganglionic fibers exit the cord along with the splanchnic

TABLE I

Responses of Effector Organs to Autonomic Nerve Impulses[a]

Effector organs	Sympathetic receptors	Sympathetic impulses and responses	Parasympathetic impulses and responses
Eye			
Radial muscle, iris	α	Contraction (pupil enlargement)[++]	—
Sphincter muscle, iris		—	Contraction (pupil constriction)[+++]
Ciliary muscle	β_2	Relaxation for far vision[+]	Contraction for near vision[+++]
Heart			
SA node	β_1	Increase in heart rate[++]	Decrease in heart rate; vagal arrest[+++]
Atria	β_1	Increase in contractility and conduction velocity[++]	Decrease in contractility, and (usually) increase in conduction velocity[++]
AV node	β_1	Increase in automaticity and conduction velocity[++]	Decrease in conduction velocity; AV block[+++]
Ventricles	β_1	Increase in contractility, conduction velocity, automaticity, and rate of idioventricular pacemakers[+++]	Slight decrease in contractility
Arterioles			
Coronary	α, β_2	Constriction[+]; dilation[++]	Dilation[±]
Skin and mucosa	α	Constriction[+++]	Dilation
Skeletal muscle	α, β_2	Constriction[++]; dilation[++]	Dilation[+]
Cerebral	α	Constriction (slight)	Dilation
Pulmonary	α, β_2	Constriction[+]; dilation	Dilation
Abdominal viscera, renal	α, β_2	Constriction[+++]; dilation[+]	—
Salivary glands	α	Constriction[+++]	Dilation[++]
Veins (systemic)	α, β_2	Constriction[++]; dilation[++]	—
Lung			
Bronchial muscle	β_2	Relaxation[+]	Contraction[++]
Bronchial glands	?	Inhibition (?)	Stimulation[+++]
Stomach			
Motility and tone	α, β_2	Decrease (usually)[+]	Increase[+++]
Sphincters	α	Contraction (usually)[+]	Relaxation (usually)[+]
Secretion		Inhibition (?)	Stimulation[+++]
Intestine			
Motility and tone	α, β_2	Decrease[+]	Increase[+++]
Sphincters	α	Contraction (usually)[+]	Relaxation (usually)[+]
Secretion		Inhibition (?)	Stimulation[++]

continues

nerves and travel directly to the adrenal medulla without synapsing first. The adrenal medulla secretes the important stress hormone epinephrine (adrenaline). The medulla contains specialized secretory cells that are embryologically from the same precursor cells as postganglionic fibers. As they develop, they specialize into secretory endocrine cells that produce epinephrine as an active hormone.

B. Parasympathetic Division

As shown in Fig. 2 and Table I, parasympathetic ganglia are located close to or within the organs they innervate. Preganglionic fibers arise from the brainstem and sacral region of the spinal cord. The eye, face, and mouth are served by cranial nerves III, VII, and IX. The cardiopulmonary and digestive

Continued

Effector organs	Sympathetic receptors	Sympathetic impulses and responses	Parasympathetic impulses and responses
Gallbladder and ducts		Relaxation[+]	Contraction[+]
Kidney	β^2	Renin secretion[++]	—
Urinary bladder			
Detrusor	β	Relaxation (usually)[+]	Contraction[+++]
Trigone and sphincter	α	Contraction[++]	Relaxation[++]
Ureter			
Motility and tone	α	Increase (usually)	Increase (?)
Uterus	α, β_2	Pregnant: contraction (α); nonpregnant: relaxation (β)	Variable
Sex organs, male	α	Ejaculation[+++]	Erection[+++]
Skin			
Pilomotor muscles	α	Contraction[++]	—
Sweat glands	α	Localized secretion[+]	Generalized secretion[+++]
Spleen capsule	α, β_2	Contraction[+++], relaxation[+]	—
Adrenal medulla		—	Secretion of epinephrine and norepinephrine
Liver	α, β_2	Glycogenolysis, gluconeogenesis[+++]	Glycogen synthesis[+]
Pancreas			
Acini	α	Decreased secretion[+]	Secretion[++]
Islets (β cells)	α	Decreased secretion[+++]	—
	β_2	Increased secretion[+]	—
Fat cells	α, β_1	Lipolysis[+++]	—
Salivary glands	α	Potassium and water secretion[+]	Potassium and water secretion[+++]
	β_2	Amylase secretion[+]	—
Lacrimal glands		—	Secretion[+++]
Nasopharyngeal glands		—	Secretion[++]
Pineal gland	β_2	Melatonin synthesis	—

[a] Receptor types refer to receptors of the sympathetic nervous system. There are three types of sympathetic receptors: alpha (α), beta-1 (β_1), and beta-2 (β_2). α-1 Receptors are most sensitive to norepinephrine released from sympathetic nerve terminals. β-1 Receptors are located only at the heart. They are sensitive to norepinephrine released by sympathetic nerve terminals and circulating epinephrine. β_2 Receptors are mostly not innervated by sympathetic nerves. They are primarily sensitive to circulating epinephrine. The parasympathetic nervous system acts exclusively on cholinergic receptors by secretion of acetylcholine, regardless of the organ in question.

[+] Little action.
[+++] Large effect.

systems are served by the vagus nerve (cranial nerve X), while the functions of excretion and control of reproductive organs are served by the splanchnic nerves.

The parasympathetic nervous system is designed to promote highly specific regulation of individual organs: (1) parasympathetic preganglionic fibers are long and travel to specific ganglia linked to specific organs; (2) postganglionic fibers are short and are sometime found entirely within the innervated tissue; and (3) the ratio of pre- to postganglionic fibers is about 1:3 with one preganglionic fiber affecting only a single organ.

VI. AUTONOMIC REGULATION OF SPECIFIC ORGAN SYSTEMS

Figure 2 and Table I summarize the autonomic contribution to the regulation of specific organ systems. In general, the sympathetic and parasympathetic branches of the ANS have opposite effects on the organs they innervate. For most organs, the balance of sympathetic to parasympathetic outflow determines the level of activity. However, it should be remembered that the activity of an organ is only partly determined by the ANS. All organs have their own intrinsic levels of activity and are more or less self-regulating. Therefore, the regulation of an organ always involves interaction between its intrinsic functions and inputs from the ANS. This regulatory interplay is nicely illustrated in the activity of the heart, which is controlled by intrinsic mechanisms, ANS inputs, and hormones.

The heart's intrinsic regulation includes control over the force and rate of its contractions. (1) The heart regulates its contractions using the *Frank–Starling reflex*. The left ventricle contracts more forcefully if it has been filled more completely between beats. This inherent contractile property of cardiac muscle provides significant regulation of the heart's contraction without help from the ANS. (2) The rate at which the heart beats is controlled by two internal cardiac pacemakers known as the atrioventricular and sinoatrial nodes. These pacemakers work in tandem by alternating phases of excitation and quiescence to allow the heart to beat regularly and effectively without ANS control. These intrinsic cardiac mechanisms are entirely adequate to sustain life as long as there are no rapid changes in external demand that would threaten homeostasis.

At times, the heart needs to rapidly change its rate or force of contraction. When we suddenly rise from a chair or need to escape from a predator, the ANS and endocrine system must supply external control to the heart for an adequate response to occur. The ANS controls on the heart are of three types. (1) The parasympathetic branch acts on the heart by way of the vagus nerves to lower the heart's rate and force of contraction. Parasympathetic control of the heart predominates when the person is at rest and even during moderate challenge; as external demands increase, parasympathetic input is reduced, allowing the heart to beat more rapidly and forcefully. (2) The sympathetic nervous system acts on the heart via the cardiac nerves to augment its intrinsic rate and force of contraction. Under most circumstances both branches are active, but the influence of the parasympathetic branch is usually greater. During more major demands, such as moderate levels of

exercise, the parasympathetic outflow is almost absent and the sympathetic influence increases to a maximum. (3) In addition, endocrine input, in the form of circulating epinephrine, can greatly augment the sympathetic contribution to rate and force of contraction. These three influences acting in concert, reduced parasympathetic input, increased sympathetic outflow, and the availability of epinephrine, can result in a sevenfold increase in the volume of blood the heart pumps in each minute.

This example illustrates that the heart has the ability to function normally without outside control. However, the ANS is needed to provide external control to meet rapid external demands and to help each organ operate in concert with others. In most cases circulating hormones such as epinephrine compliment the actions of the ANS. Similar arguments apply to the regulation of other organ systems.

VII. LOCAL REGULATION OF AUTONOMIC FUNCTION

Since ANS controls, especially sympathetic activity, are more or less nonspecific for each organ, there has been considerable interest in local mechanisms that can fine-tune organ activity. The previous section illustrated the interplay of intrinsic and extrinsic regulation of the heart as a means of fine-tuning local control. There is still another level of fine-tuning available to the ANS. In all organs, local ANS regulation is provided by the action of locally released biochemicals that are classified as peptides, neuromodulators, and metabolites. These act by several mechanisms either at the smooth muscle or the autonomic–neuroeffector junction to modify ANS activity or its effectiveness.

An example of the action of local modulators is seen in the regulation of blood vessel contraction. Blood flow into the tissues is regulated by sympathetic activity at local blood vessels. The sympathetic nerves release norepinephrine at the sympathetic neuroeffector junction, causing contraction of networks of smooth muscle cells, increasing constriction of the blood vessel, and reducing blood flow into a local volume of tissue. If this were the only influence, the cardiovascular system could not regulate blood flow according to the needs of local tissues.

For example, the increased sympathetic activation during exercise would inhibit needed blood flow to the exercising muscles.

However, there are overlapping local mechanisms that compensate for the nonspecificity of sympathetic outflow, and two are mentioned here. (1) Metabolites can act locally on smooth muscle cells to regulate their activity. Carbon dioxide produced by tissue metabolism leads to local production of *nitric oxide,* and nitric oxide causes relaxation of vascular smooth muscle cells. This results in relaxation of blood vessels allowing improved blood flow. In this process of *autoregulation,* exercising muscles cause more nitric oxide when they are working harder, leading to greater relaxation in the local resistance vessels and increasing the local blood supply. (2) Neuromodulators can act on the sympathetic nerves themselves to regulate their actions on smooth muscle cells. In the sympathetic nerves, *adenosine diphosphate* is released along with norepinephrine at the adrenergic nerve terminal. Adenosine diphosphate is rapidly metabolized to adenosine. The adenosine then acts locally at adenosine receptors on the sympathetic nerve terminal to decrease the release of norepinephrine. This neuromodulation results in lowered sympathetic stimulation of local smooth muscle cells; the greater the level of sympathetic outflow, the greater the production of adenosine and the greater the modulation of the nerve terminal.

In the case of the blood vessel wall, autoregulation and neuromodulation provide significant control of sympathetic activity, allowing local regulation of blood flow at the tissue level. Each tissue has its own local regulatory mechanisms that permit fine-tuning of the effects of sympathetic activity, which would otherwise be highly nonspecific. Similar processes occur in the parasympathetic nervous system.

VIII. PHYSICAL AND PSYCHOLOGICAL STRESS

Physical and *psychological stress* result from very different causes, but they both influence the actions of the vital organs. First, consider physical challenges to homeostasis and the layered organization of the controls on the vital organs. As noted above, the vital organs have several layers of control. First, there are

local intrinsic controls over each organ. Second, there are ganglionic mechanisms that regulate output of the ANS postganglionic neurons. Third, the brainstem and hypothalamus exert very complex, elaborate reflex regulation of the entire ANS.

This layered scheme helps to illustrate the differences between physical and psychological stress. During constant moderate conditions, organs can regulate their own activity using internal mechanisms and local reflexes. Under changing circumstances, the organs need to work together to maintain homeostasis. So, during mild thirst, the ANS coordinates the kidneys and sweat glands to conserve fluids. This coordination involves both the brainstem and the hypothalamus. During a true stressor, such as exercise, the ANS and endocrine systems provide even greater levels of coordinated action. Parasympathetic activity is largely inhibited. The concerted actions of the sympathetic nervous system become active in an elaborate pattern to support the exercise response. In addition, endocrine activity allows for further coordination across organ systems. Exercise therefore calls on coordination of the pulmonary, cardiovascular, and renal systems, among others, to provide adequate supplies of oxygenated blood to the exercising muscles.

The controls discussed so far involve *physiological challenges* to homeostasis. The signals that cause the ANS to respond are peripheral, starting in sensory pathways and vital organs. *Psychological stress* has a different origin. When we are anxious, anticipating future challenges, or worrying about past failures, our bodies can undergo significant changes in activity. These changes originate in the highest centers in the brain, including the *cortex* and *limbic system.* Therefore, we can see that there is a final layer of control over the ANS, above the hypothalamus and brainstem. These higher systems exert a *top-down* influence on the lower centers to regulate outflow to the ANS. In this manner, psychological stimuli may act as stressors in themselves.

IX. SUMMARY

The brain has two primary means to regulate the vital organs; the ANS and the endocrine system. The ANS innervates all tissues outside of the central nervous system. It acts by regulating the contraction of smooth muscle cells, cardiac muscle cells, and secretory cells. Each organ has intrinsic activity and local controls over its function. During changes in the internal or external environment, the ANS serves to regulate the organs to restore and maintain homeostasis. The ANS itself is controlled by the brainstem and hypothalamus, which have highly evolved and elaborate reflex centers and control networks. However, the highest level of control, above the hypothalamus and brainstem, is provided by the limbic system and cortex. During times of emotional distress, descending influences act via the limbic system to override or significantly alter the activity of the hypothalamus and brainstem. These in turn will change the activity of the ANS to alter the state of the body.

See Also the Following Articles

Homeostasis; Sympathetic Nervous System

Bibliography

Burnstock, G., and Hoyle, C. H. (Eds.) (1992). "*Autonomic Neuroeffector Mechanisms.*" Reading, UK, Harwood.

Dodd, J., and Role, L. W. (1995). The autonomic nervous system. *In* "*Principles of Neural Science*" (E. R. Kandel, J. H. Schwartz, and J. H. Jessel, Eds.), pp. 762–775. New York, Elsevier.

Karczmar, A. G., Koketsu, K., and Nishi, S. (Eds.) (1986). *Autonomic and enteric ganglia. In* "Transmission and Its Pharmacology." Plenum, New York.

Lovallo, W. R. (1997). "*Stress & Health: Biological and Psychological Interactions.*" Thousand Oaks, CA, Sage.

Nilsson, S., and Holmgren, S. (Eds.) (1994). "*Comparative Physiology and Evolution of the Autonomic Nervous System.*" Reading, UK, Harwood.

Autotolerance

Marco E. F. Melo

American Red Cross, Maryland

Kamal D. Moudgil and Eli E. Sercarz

La Jolla Institute for Allergy and Immunology, California

I. Normal Self-Reactivity vs Autoimmune Disease States
II. Genetic, Hormonal, and Environmental Factors in Tolerance/Autoimmunity
III. Heat Shock Proteins: Self-Tolerance and Autoimmunity
IV. Concluding Remarks

GLOSSARY

autotolerance or self-tolerance Ability to accept an antigen in the body without raising a pathogenic inflammatory response.

B-cell determinant or B-cell epitope The portion of an antigenic molecule making contact with a given antibody.

chaperone protein Protein required for proper folding and assembly of another protein.

cryptic T-cell determinant A determinant that is immuno-genic as a peptide but does not trigger an immune response during immunization with the whole protein.

dominant T-cell determinant The most readily processed and presented T-cell determinant.

heat shock proteins Normal proteins synthesized by many organisms, from bacteria to mammals, during stressful situations. They serve as chaperones for other proteins within the cell protecting them from denaturation or other destructive processes.

T-cell determinants Portion of a protein that provides all the residues required for recognition within a major histocompatability complex context by a T-cell receptor.

S tress is a normal part of life and in most situations it can even be considered healthy. Prolonged and unwanted stress, however, can have adverse effects on mental and physical health. The stress response can include changes in the hormonal equilibrium, such as the release of catecholamines and glucocorticoids, or the increase in the expression of heat shock proteins (Hsp). Such reorganization of the biochemical and hormonal state of the body must occur in order to heighten the performance of the organism in the given situation. This article discusses the possible interactions of stress and the immune system and specifically the effects of stress on the acquisition or breakdown of autotolerance.

I. NORMAL SELF-REACTIVITY VS AUTOIMMUNE DISEASE STATES

Immunological tolerance is conventionally defined as the state of nonreactivity of the immune system to a given antigen; however, such a definition does not refer to a state of health or disease. Alternatively, tolerance can also be defined as the ability to accept a foreign antigen without raising a pathogenic inflammatory response; in this case, the presence of antibody and/or cellular response to the antigen could be irrelevant.

The fate of T cells directed against the assemblage of T-cell determinants on a protein antigen on attempted tolerance induction is quite complex. The most readily processed and presented determinants, the dominant ones, negatively select T cells with high and medium avidity for the determinant, inducing clonal deletion. Only T cells with the lowest avidity avoid this selective step. High avidity T cells in the periphery are similarly purged during attempted tolerance induction. It appears that T cells can exhaustively differentiate and die after a productive interlude: this could include an anergic phase. However, during differentiation, medium and lower avidity T cells may become activated in the local lymph nodes. In the thymus, these T cells, which bind weakly to self-major histocompatability complex (MHC) ligands, can be positively selected and develop into the repertoire that recognizes foreign antigens. Those T cells with extremely low avidity for self-antigen will be neglected, both during immunization or tolerization protocols.

Thus, it may be concluded that a very similar hierarchy exists both for immunization and for tolerance induction. Comparable rules affecting determinant dominance and recessiveness exist and there is no distinction between self and foreign determinants in this regard: the most available determinant on the unfolding protein molecule that has the highest affinity for a MHC class II molecule will gain the dominant position in the hierarchy. From the discussion in the previous paragraph, T cells remaining after self-tolerance induction in the thymus (central tolerance) or periphery (peripheral tolerance) should be enriched for receptors of lower avidity for antigen. In fact, there is an extensive literature on potential autoreactive T cells and natural antibodies in healthy individuals. Likewise, at the level of the antigen, those determinants that have not induced tolerance are usually of lower average avidity for a MHC molecule and will therefore tend to induce Th2 rather than Th1 responses.

In certain circumstances, autoreactive cells can play an important physiologic role. One striking example is the physiologic production of autoantibodies against antigens of old red blood cells (RBC) that contain galactosyl residues that normally are hidden in the membrane of young RBC. Such autoantibodies are not harmful and may even help eliminate senescent cells. This is perhaps the clearest example of an autoimmune housekeeping process. Another example are the inflammatory processes that sometimes affect the mammalian central nervous system (CNS). Because of the complex neuronal network, any inflammatory response in the CNS has been professed to be harmful, but Schwartz and colleagues have shown that the innate immune system can facilitate the process of regeneration in the severed spinal cord! Hence, in certain circumstances, both autotolerance and autoreactivity to self may represent physiological states.

Can the immune system differentiate a self-derived antigen from foreign proteins? Probably not, because under physiological conditions, both self and foreign antigens are constantly being processed and presented to T cells. Furthermore, in order to be tolerogenic, an antigen must be potentially immunogenic, and various studies indicate that the requirements for tolerogenicity and immunogenicity are very similar.

In some situations there is a detectable immune response against saprophytic microorganisms or even to self-antigens, but such immune responses have no pathological consequences. In many situations, there is immunological unresponsiveness to both self and "beneficial foreign antigens." Such a state of unresponsiveness can be attributed to different mechanisms: anergy, deletion, suppression, or ignorance. Anergy and deletion are achieved by mechanisms within the cell, whereas suppression is achieved by mechanisms involving other cells. Harris and colleagues have shown that autotolerance could be an active process involving regulatory T suppressor cells. A good example supporting this hypothesis is tolerance to the fifth component of complement (C5), in which autoreactive B cells are held in check by suppressor T cells. Furthermore, dendritic cells have been shown to be the most potent antigen-presenting cell (APC) for inducing and maintaining tolerance against C5 in MHC class II-restricted T cells.

Calkins and co-workers presented evidence that idiotype-specific suppressor T cells may also control the autoimmune response to RBCs in mice of the NZB strain. It is known that CD4$^+$ T cells play an active role in promoting an autoantibody response to RBC in this strain, but that this autoimmune response is downregulated in young mice by syngeneic CD8$^+$ T suppressor cells. Removal of CD8$^+$ cells from spleen cells of young Coombs-negative mice leads to development of an *in vitro* response to mouse RBC. It is postulated that as NZB mice get older, the balance between the activity of CD8$^+$ regulatory cells and B cells producing anti-mouse RBC antibody becomes insufficient to control the autoimmune response.

The main natural ports of entry of antigens in the body are the mucosal surfaces of the gut and lungs. It has been shown that the mucosal introduction of antigen can lead to either tolerance or immunity. Although there are a great number of antigens to which the gut and lungs of a vast population are exposed every day, only a small percentage of people acquire allergic reactions to dust and an even smaller percentage develop allergies to food components. It is very likely that the mucosal-associated immune system possesses immunosuppressive (tolerogenic) mechanisms. In individuals without such regulatory mechanisms, the mucosal surfaces can become a site of constant, ungoverned inflammation, such as that in inflammatory bowel disease. If the luminal content of the gut or of the airways harbors antigens with significant molecular similarity with self-antigens (molecular mimicry), other autoimmune diseases could be triggered. Furthermore, food antigens can affect the microbiota in the gut and such a change can expose the immune system to stress proteins.

Another mechanism by which the self-reactive T-cell repertoire in the periphery is kept silent (without causing inflammatory disease) involves a "programmed cell death machinery" regulated by the expression of two proteins at the surface of the cell, Fas and FasL. In humans and mice with mutant forms of Fas (lpr mice) and FasL (gld mice), severe autoimmune symptoms develop early in life. Individuals with such mutations develop autoimmune arthritis, nephritis, and lymphoproliferative disorders. Interestingly, lymphocytes from mice with such mutations seem to be more resistant to stress (ionizing radiation)-induced apoptosis than normal B6 mice.

Prolonged stress has been demonstrated to increase endogenous opioids. It has been shown that morphine dramatically induces Fas expression in T cells. These cells then have increased susceptibility to undergo apoptosis upon stimulation with cells expressing FasL. Because of endogenous opioid production, stressful events could induce apoptosis mediated by opioid-induced Fas expression.

II. GENETIC, HORMONAL, AND ENVIRONMENTAL FACTORS IN TOLERANCE/AUTOIMMUNITY

Genetically determined and environmental factors, as well as age and the reproductive status of an individual, influence the intensity of both the stress and the immune responses. Some autoimmune diseases are associated weakly, whereas others are associated strongly with products of the major histocompatibility complex, which portrays only one component of genetic susceptibility factors. There is one systemic human disease with a clear mendelian monogenic background: autoimmune polyendocrinopathy-candidiasis-ectodermal dystrophy (APECED). This polyglandular syndrome has an autosomal-recessive pattern that maps to chromosome 21. Its autoimmune phenotype suggests that the affected gene, named autoimmune regulator (AIRE), plays an important role in the control of immune recognition and in peripheral tolerance. Future research on patients with APECED would contribute to further understanding of self-tolerance and to the elucidation of the genetic factors involved in other autoimmune disorders.

Environmental stress also affects regulation of the immune response. Multiple housing appears to be a stressful situation for male mice of certain strains. This apparently mild treatment (mice are generally multiply housed) was administered to male strain C57BL/6 mice in studying the autoimmune response against bromelain-treated autologous mouse erythrocytes (Br-ME). Bromelain treatment exposes surface antigenic determinants on erythrocytes, mimicking the process of aging in RBCs. These RBCs are cleared from the circulation by an autoimmune housekeeping process mediated by autoantibodies. It was observed that male C57BL/6 mice housed one per cage have greatly enhanced B-cell autoimmune reactivity to Br-ME as compared to mice housed in groups of six per cage. Similarly, it was demonstrated that male C57BL/6 mice, housed singly, have enhanced T-cell reactivity to an exogenous antigen, hen lysozyme, as compared to mice housed in groups of six per cage. The decreased T-cell reactivity in the latter group of mice was attributed to poor APC function under the stress of crowding.

The hormonal status of an individual can affect the immune system profoundly. It is well known that the autoimmune activity of rheumatoid arthritis tends to fluctuate following physiological hormonal changes during puberty, pregnancy, menopause, and periods of psychological stress. Furthermore, interactions of hormones with the immune system might explain why certain autoimmune diseases are predominant in one gender. It has been reported extensively that hormonal changes during pregnancy bring about a Th2 state that is protective against Th1 autoimmune diseases such as arthritis and diabetes, whereas allergy and SLE tend to flare during pregnancy. There is a payback, however, in that women suffering from Th1 disease must pass through a heightened flare period during the first trimester following birth. It is likely that this flare could be lessened by treating women with estriol, to continue the type of balance characteristic of pregnancy. It was reported that estriol can ameliorate multiple sclerosis in humans and collagen-induced arthritis in mice. It is possible that other putative Th1-mediated autoimmune diseases that improve during late pregnancy, could also be treated with estriol.

Considering that one-half of the fetal antigenic representation is derived from the father, the fetus is a type of "foreign antigen" in the maternal body, and it is important to understand how the maternal immune system tolerates it. Revealing the immunology of pregnancy would help us understand why some autoimmune diseases improve during pregnancy since the tolerogenic mechanisms involved in maintenance of the fetus might also be involved in modulating autoimmunity. One possible mechanism involves the T cells, which colonize the female reproductive tract, the placenta and endometrial glandular epithelium. A large fraction of these T cells secrete immunoregulatory cytokines during pregnancy. Mouse models have shown that during allogeneic pregnancy the increase in number of intrauterine T cells was more than that in syngeneic pregnancy (Born et al. 1999). Maternal-fetal tolerance might also involve interaction between FasL on the trophoblast and Fas expressed on the mother's T cells (Jiang and Vacchio 1998). This way the fetal tissue expressing FasL would eliminate maternal lymphocytes reactive against fetal/paternal antigens. Four additional possible mechanisms for maternal–fetal tolerance include (1) the lack of MHC class I expression in the placenta; (2) the expression in the placenta of a nonclassical (class Ib) HLA molecule, HLA-G; (3) the ability of the trophoblast to suppress maternal T cells by catabolizing tryptophan; and (4) cytotoxic T lymphocyte-associated protein-4 (CTLA-4), a negative regulator of T-cell activation, may be involved in the maintenance of tolerance at the maternal–fetal interface.

III. HEAT SHOCK PROTEINS: SELF-TOLERANCE AND AUTOIMMUNITY

Stress proteins, including heat shock proteins, are normal proteins that are physiologic constituents of both prokaryotic and eukaryotic cells. The synthesis and expression/display of these proteins is induced by various kinds of stress factors, including physical or metabolic stress. These proteins in turn exert a chaperonic function, protecting other proteins within the cell from undergoing denaturation or other forms of destructive processes under stressful conditions.

Heat shock proteins are highly conserved among various species. Like other self-antigens, self-Hsps would also be processed and presented in a constitutive manner. Two aspects of the biology of Hsps are of importance in understanding the role of these proteins in self-tolerance and immune responsiveness: (a) on the one hand, induction of a given self-Hsp under stress ensures survival of the cell, but on the other hand, upregulated synthesis and expression of self-Hsp might lead to the efficient display of previously poorly displayed (cryptic) determinants within these proteins and (b) due to the highly conserved nature of different homologs of a particular self-Hsp, there is a high probability that T cells induced by one Hsp might cross-react with a related homologous Hsp. This cross-reactive T-cell response could either be involved in the induction of autoimmunity or it might be protective or beneficial against autoimmunity.

On the basis of previous work, we suggest that T cells potentially directed against efficiently processed and presented (dominant) self-determinants within self-Hsps would be rendered tolerant, whereas T cells potentially reactive against relatively poorly processed and presented (cryptic) determinants would escape tolerance induction. The latter subset of T cells can be recruited by previously cryptic determinants on self-Hsps if the display of these determinants is enhanced under conditions of inflammation and/or disease, both of which comprise stressful conditions for the host. In this regard, the induction of Hsps under stress would subserve a useful function for the cell by protecting other cellular proteins, but in this process, there might be an inadvertent induction of autoreactivity. However, the final outcome would depend on the specificity of the T cells elicited against the self-determinants displayed under stress as well as on the cytokines secreted by these T cells.

Infection-related stress also plays a role in breaking tolerance. During the course of chronic active hepatitis there is an overexpression of self 60-kDa heat shock protein (Hsp60). Lohse and collaborators suggested that stress caused by this infection triggers a pathologic autoimmune response to self-Hsp60, which plays a role in the perpetuation of chronic inflammatory liver disease. Similarly, exacerbation of hepatitis during infections might be due to an autoimmune response to Hsp60.

Infections by bacteria and viruses have been implicated in the pathogenesis of many human autoimmune diseases, and again, one group of target antigens of interest in this regard is the Hsps. Infection of the host by the pathogen might lead to induction of a T-cell response to the foreign (pathogen's) Hsp. These T cells can, in turn, be engaged by the cross-reactive determinants within the corresponding self-Hsp of the host. This would be particularly important under conditions of stress, when the synthesis and expression of self-Hsp are likely to be enhanced. Under these circumstances, the situation would be ripe for the induction of autoimmunity. A rather opposite aspect of this foreign self-Hsp cross-reactivity is the beneficial aspect. If a given set of determinants is regulatory in nature, then the foreign Hsp can prime a subset of regulatory T cells. These T cells can, in turn, be engaged by the conserved, cross-reactive determinants within self Hsp, and vice versa.

We have observed that during the course of adjuvant-induced arthritis (AA), Lewis rats raised a T-cell response to many determinants within the 65-kD a mycobacterial heat shock protein (Bhsp65). The determinants to which Lewis rats responded were spread all over the length of Bhsp65. The determinant region 177–191 contains a previously characterized, potentially arthritogenic nonapeptide, (180–188) of Bhsp65. Interestingly, with the progression of disease in Lewis rats, there was a shift in the profile of T-cell responsiveness to Bhsp65; in the late (recovery) phase of AA, there was emergence of T-cell reactivity to five Bhsp65 carboxy-terminal determinants (BCTD) coupled with downregulation of the response to certain amino-terminal determinants. Pretreatment of naive Lewis rats with peptides comprising BCTD afforded significant protection from the subsequent induction of AA. These results, along with the finding that T-cell responses to BCTD were observed early after *Mycobacterium tuberculosis* injection in the Wistar Kyoto (WKY) rats (which have the same MHC class II haplotype as the Lewis rats but are resistant to AA), suggest that T-cell responses to BCTD are involved in natural remission from acute inflammatory arthritis in Lewis rats and presumably also contribute to the AA resistance of WKY rats.

Based on our findings that arthritic Lewis rats in the late phase of AA raised responses to both BCTD and to the corresponding C-terminal determinants of self (rat) Hsp65, we suggest that the observed diversification of response to BCTD might have been triggered *in vivo* by self-Hsp65. Thus, the T-cell response to self-Hsp might play an important regulatory role in natural remission from acute AA. Similarly, van Eden's group has shown that pretreatment of Lewis rats with Bhsp65 peptide 256–270 also protects these rats from AA; the T-cell response directed against this peptide is cross-reactive with the corresponding determinant from rat Hsp65. In this regard, it is noteworthy that a protective role for self-Hsp65 has also been implicated in remission from acute arthritis in patients with chronic juvenile arthritis (JCA). In one study, the peak of T-cell reactivity to self-Hsp65 immediately preceded remission from acute arthritis in patients with JCA.

Van Noort and collaborators have shown that α-crystallin, a small Hsp, is highly expressed around active multiple sclerosis (MS) lesions in human brain. Moreover, when expressed at the levels found in the MS patient's brain, α-crystallin can act as an immunodominant myelin antigen to human T cells isolated from both MS patients and normal volunteers. Because T cells reactive to this small Hsp are present in the peripheral blood of healthy volunteers, the main problem in multiple sclerosis might be antigen presentation rather than the peripheral T-cell repertoire. Supporting this hypothesis, we have shown that stress-producing events can modify the immune response to antigens and that a major mechanism of such alteration involves the ability of APC to present peptides to the T cells.

IV. CONCLUDING REMARKS

Interactions among immune, nervous, and endocrine systems play an important role in coordinating the balance between tolerance and autoimmunity. Under stress, this balance can be temporarily compromised, leading either to immunosuppression or to an autoimmune disease. The mechanisms by which stress can lead to these two different outcomes are not completely understood. However, some of the key physiologic processes influenced by stress include an increased expression of immunogenic determinants due to heightened antigen processing and presentation, induction and expansion of the response to heat shock proteins, and alterations in the hormonal system (e.g., HPA axis activity). The outcome of these events is significantly modulated by genetic and environmental factors.

Acknowledgment

This work was supported in part by Grants 5K08 AI01509 and AI-11183 from the National Institutes of Health.

See Also the Following Articles

AUTOIMMUNITY; CHAPERONE PROTEINS; HEAT SHOCK PROTEINS; HEAT SHOCK RESPONSE; IMMUNE RESPONSE

Bibliography

Anderton, S. M., van der Zee, R., Prakken, B., Noordzij, A., and van Eden, W. (1995). Activation of T cells recognizing self 60-kD heat shock protein can protect against experimental arthritis. *J. Exp. Med.* **181,** 943–952.

Born, W., Cady, C., Jones-Carson, J., Mukasa, A., Lahn, M. and O'Brien, R. (1999). Immunoregulatory functions of T cells. *Adv. Immunol.* **71,** 77–144.

Calkins, C. E., Cochran, S. A., Miller, R. D., and Caulfield, M. J. (1990). Evidence for regulation of the autoimmune anti-erythrocyte response by idiotype-specific suppressor T cells in NZB mice. *Int. Immunol.* **2,** 127–133.

Carosella, E. D., Dausset, J., and Rouas-Freiss, N. (1999). Immunotolerant functions of HLA-G. *Cell. Mol. Life Sci.* **55,** 327–333.

de Graeff-Meeder, E. R., van Eden, W., Rijkers, G. T., Prakken, B. J., Kuis, W., Voorhorst-Ogink, M. M., van der Zee, R., Schuurman, H. J., Helders, P. J., and Zegers, D. J. (1995). Juvenile chronic arthritis: T cell reactivity to human HSP60 in patients with a favorable course of arthritis. *J. Clin. Invest.* **95,** 934–940.

Galili, U., Rachmilewitz, E. A., Peleg, A., and Flechner, I.

(1984). A unique natural human IgG antibody with anti-galactosyl specificity. *J. Exp. Med.* **160**, 1519–1531.

Gammon, G., and Sercarz, E. (1989). How some T cells escape tolerance induction. *Nature* **342**, 183–185.

Grewal, I. S., Heilig, M., Miller, A., and Sercarz, E. E. (1997). Environmental regulation of T-cell function in mice: Group housing of males affects accessory cell function. *Immunology* **90**, 165–168.

Grewal, I. S., Miller, A., and Sercarz, E. E. (1997). The influence of mouse housing density on autoimmune reactivity. *Autoimmunity* **26**, 209–213.

Harris, D. E., Cairns, L., Rosen, F. S., Cairns, L., Rosen, F. S., and Borel, Y. (1982). A natural model of immunologic tolerance: Tolerance to murine C5 is mediated by T cells, and antigen is required to maintain unresponsiveness. *J. Exp. Med.* **156**, 567–584.

Jansson, L., Olsson, T., and Holmdahl, I. R. (1994). Estrogen induces a potent suppression of experimental autoimmune encephalomyelitis and collagen-induced arthritis in mice. *J. Neuroimmunol.* **53**, 203–207.

Jiang, S.-P., and Vacchio, M. S. (1998). Multiple mechanisms of peripheral T cell tolerance to the fetal "allograft." *J. Immunol.* **160**, 3086–3090.

Kaufman, K. A., Bowen, J. A., Tsai, A. F., Bluestone, J. A., Hunt, J. S., and Ober, C. (1999). The CTLA-4 gene is expressed in placental fibroblasts. *Mol. Hum. Reprod.* **5**, 84–87.

Lacroix-Desmazes, S., Kaveri, S. V., Mouthon, L., Ayouba, A., Malanchere, E., Coutinho, A., and Kazatchkine, M. D. (1998). Self-reactive antibodies (natural autoantibodies) in healthy individuals. *J. Immunol. Methods* **216**, 117–137.

Lohse, A. W., Dienes, H. P., Herkel, J., Hermann, E., van Eden, W., and Meyer zum Buschenfelde K. H. (1993). Expression of the 60 kDa heat shock protein in normal and inflamed liver. *J. Hepatol.* **19**, 159–166.

Melo, M. E. F., Gabaglia, C., Moudgil, K., Sercarz, E., and Quinn, A. (1999). The influence of nasal installation on the immune response is strain and dose-dependent. Submitted for publication.

Miller, R. D., and Calkins, C. E. (1988). Active role of T cells in promoting an in vitro autoantibody response to self erythrocytes in NZB mice. *Immunology* **63**, 625–630.

Moudgil, K. D. (1998). Diversification of response to hsp65 during the course of autoimmune arthritis is regulatory rather than pathogenic. *Immunol. Rev.* **164**, 175–184.

Munn, D. H., Zhou, M., Attwood, J. T., Bondarev, I., Conway, S. J., Marshall, B., Brown, C., and Mellor, A. L. (1998). Prevention of allogeneic fetal rejection by tryptophan catabolism. *Science* **281**, 1191–1193.

Peterson, P., Nagamine, K., Scott, H., Heino, M., Kudoh, J., Shimizu, N., Antonarakis, S. E., and Krohn, K. J. (1998). APECED: A monogenic autoimmune disease providing new clues to self-tolerance. *Immunol. Today* **19**, 384–386.

Reap, E. A., Roof, K., Maynor, K., Borrero, M., Booker, J., and Cohen, P. L. (1997). Radiation and stress-induced apoptosis: A role for Fas/Fas ligand interactions. *Proc. Natl. Acad. Sci. USA* **94**, 5750–5755.

Schlesinger, M. J. (1994). How the cell copes with stress and the function of heat shock proteins. *Pediatr. Res.* **36**, 1–6.

Schwartz, M., Moalem, G., Leibowitz-Amit, R., and Cohen, I. R. (1999). Innate and adaptive immune responses can be beneficial for CNS repair. *Trends Neurosci.* **22**, 295–299.

Sercarz, E. E., Lehmann, P. V., Ametani, A., Benichou, G., Miller, A., and Moudgil, K. (1993). Dominance and crypticity of T cell antigenic determinants. *Annu. Rev. Immunol.* **11**, 729–766.

Stockinger, B. (1999). T lymphocyte tolerance: From thymic deletion to peripheral control mechanisms. *Adv. Immunol.* **71**, 229–265.

van Noort, J. M., van Sechel, A. C., Bajramovic, J. J., El Ouagmiri, M., Polman, C. H., Lassmann, H., and Ravid, R. (1995). The small heat-shock protein α-crystallin as candidate autoantigen in multiple sclerosis. *Nature* **375**, 798–801.

Vaz, N., Faria, A. M., Verdolin, B. A., and Carvalho, C. R. (1997). Immaturity, aging and oral tolerance. *Scand. J. Immunol.* **46**, 225–229.

Wood, K. J. (1996). New concepts in tolerance. *Clin. Transplant.* **10**, 93–99.

Yin, D., Mufson, R. A., Wang, R., and Shi, Y. (1999). Fas-mediated cell death promoted by opioids. *Nature* **397**, 218.

Avoidance

Béla Bohus

University of Groningen, Netherlands

GLOSSARY

active avoidance To learn and perform spatial motor patterns in order to avoid deleterious consequences of stressors such as painful foot or tailshock in rodents.

coping An individual's behavioral and physiological response repertoire to master an aversive (stressful) situation.

fear conditioning A procedure that produces a fear state in the absence of the adverse stimulus by coupling a compound stimulus such as light or sound or a context (e.g., an environment) with the adverse stimulus; following a single presentation or few repetitions of the stimulus or context plus the adverse event such as footshock, its behavioral and physiological consequences become conditioned.

inhibitory avoidance To learn and remember to avoid a former stressful experience by inhibiting or not performing an innately preferred behavioral response.

A voidance means literally "to keep away from" (something or somebody). From a psychobiological point of view it refers to brain and behavioral processes which characterize an individual's reaction to a certain environment or the environment's image in the brain. Avoidance is recently mainly mentioned in relation to trauma and posttraumatic stress disorder (PTSD). Avoidance, together with intrusive memory or reexperience and hypervigilance, are the major long-term sequelae of trauma and PTSD. It is maintained that stress, as a psycho-

biological entity, is prominent in the etiology and course of mental disorders like PTSD. From a theoretical point of view, PTSD is often related to the traditional views of fear conditioning. The relation implies that long-term consequences of a single, relatively short-term traumatizing stress event are the result of cognitive process like learning and memory. This further implies that avoidance is not a simple stimulus–response process, but the result of conditioning and appears as a conditioned response with behavioral and other physiological features. From the point of view of physiological stress management, avoidance reflects processes which help an individual cope with his or her environment. Avoidance as a learned process means that an individual predicts the occurrence of the aversive character of the environment. In addition, avoidance as a behavioral response means controlling the environment, thereby minimizing the deleterious consequences of expected stressful events. The notion, however, may also concern human psychopathology, where PTSD patients will avoid situations in which they feel lost and cannot count on outside help. On first glance, avoidance in PTSD patients may be an adaptive response to reduce stress in a particular environment. In time, however, the person may rely too heavily on avoidance and thereby it becomes harmful for the individual. The difference between the physiological and pathological features is based on elements described as "defense versus coping" by Ursin and Olff (1993). It is not the aim here to solve this debate. For pragmatic reasons, therefore, coping and avoidance are viewed here as a positive response outcome expectancy which is the result of a learning process. Accordingly, this article primarily focuses on the conditioned character of behavioral and neuroendocrine stress responses in relation to various forms of avoidance.

I. CONDITIONED BEHAVIORAL AND NEUROENDOCRINE RESPONSE: ACTIVE AVOIDANCE

Learning about the nature of the social and physical environments and remembering their characteristics is a basic adaptive capacity of animals, including humans. This use of learning and memory means that the features of the environment are conditioned. Stress, as the reaction to environmental changes, is an essential component of adaptive alterations and therefore should be conditioned. The complexity of stress responses assumes that both behavioral and neuroendocrine (physiological) components are conditioned and serve a biologically essential survival mechanism. It is therefore surprising that the conditioned character of the stress response is not always widely emphasized. Rather, based on the classic view of the nonspecificity of stress responses, conditioning of physiological responses has been interpreted as a highly specific process from which the "nonspecific" stress component should be eliminated. The characteristics of avoidance, which is an essential form of behavioral reaction in stressful environments, suggest that the classic view of nonspecificity is no longer tenable.

In the animal kingdom, a wide variety of behavioral repertoires are available to deal with stressful environments. It was argued that several components of these behaviors are independent from the environment (i.e., can be described as nonspecific). For example, in rodents, displacement such as grooming, wet-shaking, chewing, teeth chattering, urination, and defecation occur in novel and known stressful environments. Most notably these behavioral elements are independent of the temporal and spatial properties of a certain environment. Other behaviors, most prominently avoidance behavior, are considered specific responses and the result of conditioning. Animals (but also humans) learn the spatial and temporal characters of the environment and their emotional consequences. More importantly, it is also learned that with an appropriate action it is possible to prevent the occurrence of stress. Avoidance behavior leads to avoiding the stressful stimulus, thereby reducing the adverse consequences of stress.

The name of the Russian physiologist Ivan Petrovich Pavlov is inevitably connected to the subject of conditioning. Although his work is primarily known for conditioning with food reward, he also emphasized the conditioning of aversive events, designated as defense conditioning. The classical conditioning procedure as developed for dogs by Pavlov made its entry into the American behavioral sciences in an altered form. This is because mostly rodents such as rats and mice were used as experimental subjects, which prevented the use of classical defense conditioning, a biologically relevant response in dogs, but not in rodents. Instead, spatial paradigms such as the shuttle box avoidance paradigms were developed. In this paradigm a rodent could escape painful electric footshock by shuttling from one (aversive) compartment to the other (safe) one. If the occurrence of shock is preceded by a compound stimulus like the sound of a buzzer or light, the animal can learn to predict the aversive properties of the situation and move from the unsafe environment to the safe one. This paradigm has been designated as active avoidance conditioning, which is effective in behavioral management of stressful situations. The question still remains as to how this situation-specific conditioned behavior contributes to the complexity of the physiological stress responses. A prominent hormonal stress response, namely the rise in plasma corticosterone level as the consequence of the activation of the hypothalamus-pituitary-adrenal cortical system, is a useful marker of the stress level experienced by the individual. If we accept this proposition, then evidence suggests that avoidance behavior reduces the aversive character of the environment. Following the learning phase of active avoidance behavior, which is obviously highly stressful, the plasma corticosterone level decreases in rats and remains low during perfect avoidance. The low plasma corticosterone level is the result of the rats' knowledge that avoidance means safety rather than forgetting about the aversive character of the situation. It was also shown that preventing the rats from making the avoidance response leads to a high rise in plasma corticosterone levels even if no further footshock is delivered. Observations by Jay Weiss were the first to demonstrate that behavioral controllability and predictability of a stressful situation determine the magnitude of the rise of plasma corticosterone levels in the rat. If rats are able to avoid painful tailshock or to predict their occurrence, the plasma hormone levels do not rise as high as in the case of unavoidable or unpredictable tailshock.

II. INHIBITORY OR PASSIVE AVOIDANCE

The past two decades have witnessed the use of other avoidance behavioral techniques in the psychobiology of stress. Passive or inhibitory avoidance paradigms provide a relatively reproducible, more efficient, and less time-consuming way of studying avoidance behavior. In contrast to multiple trials of the active avoidance paradigms, passive avoidance is usually based upon a single learning trial followed by a retention test or tests at different intervals following learning. Another principle difference with the active avoidance paradigm is the use of punishment of innate behaviors to develop avoidance. For example, rodents prefer dark to light or unknown environments. If their innate tendency is punished by use of an aversive stimulus such as footshock, they avoid performing these innate behaviors further. The use of the term "inhibitory avoidance" is more proper because the animals use an active strategy to refrain from performing an innate pattern. Passive kinds of behaviors such as freezing and immobility are not typical in inhibitory avoidance. Rather, the animal displays mostly conflict behaviors (i.e., changing the pattern of approaching and avoiding the space or object of preference). The magnitude of the inhibitory behavior, often expressed in the latency of avoidance, is related to the intensity of the aversive stimulus used during the learning. The inhibitory kind of avoidance behavior can also be induced by punishing the innate preference for sweet taste by inducing illness using toxic substances such as cyclohexamide or lithium chloride or psychoactive substances such as amphetamine, morphine, or apomorphine. A single association between saccharin and the toxic or psychoactive drug induces avoidance of the preferred taste.

In terms of coping, these avoidance paradigms result in effective behavioral stress management. Induction of avoidance behavior is associated with the conditioning of a hormonal response such as the rise of the plasma corticosterone level. The reduction of the hormone level takes, however, much longer than that observed in the active avoidance paradigm. It is unlikely that longer existence of high corticosterone level means less effective stress management. The difference may be rather related to the strength of conditioning or to the absence (inhibitory avoidance) or presence (active avoidance) of feedback on the success of the coping response.

III. FEAR CONDITIONING

The active avoidance paradigm provides us an excellent model of specific and successful behavioral coping with stress and it is used widely for stress research. At the same time, fear conditioning paradigms are used to investigate aversive (emotional) conditioning processes (e.g., LeDoux, 1995). The basis of this procedure is to pair a neutral stimulus of tone or light with a painful electric footshock. Following a few or several repetitions, the tone or light becomes the conditioned stimulus to elicit the fear of the aversive experience even in the absence of footshock. Whereas the behavioral and physiological, in particular, cardiovascular, consequences of fear conditioning are well documented, knowledge of neuroendocrine changes is somewhat limited. The behavioral response is invariably freezing, which is accompanied by high blood pressure and tachycardia. Rises in plasma prolactin, adrenocorticotrophin, and corticosterone have been reported during fear conditioning.

Whereas Pavlovian fear conditioning uses defined cues as conditioned stimuli, mostly in a repetitive fashion, procedures are also adapted where the complexity of the physical or social environment serves as conditioned stimulus. Such procedures are usually referred to as contextual conditioning and consist of pairing a given environment with an aversive event such as inescapable footshock or defeat by a dominant conspecific. Exposure to the same environment without the aversive event results in a conditioned fear response. Behaviorally speaking, the conditioned response is almost invariably freezing. The principal features of the conditioned neuroendocrine responses in the context are marked rises in plasma epinephrine, norepinephrine, corticosterone, prolactin, and renin levels. It was also found that the extent of conditioned fear and the levels of plasma corticosterone in rats are positively correlated in this context.

The most obvious question about fear conditioning is whether freezing is functionally the same coping response as avoidance. Whereas former views often maintained that action means successful coping, evidence now indicates that fight-or-flight and conservation-and-withdrawal are equally effective coping strategies. These two ways of coping, which are also designated as active and passive coping, may be properties of the individuals or of the environment. Individuals may use one or the other coping strategy based on genetic factors or on early or adult experiences. The environment determines the selection of the strategy. Active avoidance paradigms select for the active fight-or-flight strategy, whereas the fear-conditioning paradigms select for passive, conservation-and-withdrawal approaches.

IV. CLOSING COMMENTS

The term avoidance has been discussed here mainly as an adaptive reaction of the individual to environmental challenge. It was also mentioned that avoidance is a typical attribute to the syndromes of PTSD. Classic views maintain that avoidance conditioning is motivated by fear and reinforced by fear reduction. It was mentioned that the different dynamism of plasma corticosterone level reduction during active avoidance behavior may be related to the positive feedback of response performance. Successful avoidance may then reduce fear and lead to reduced

stress hormone levels. Fear is, however, not only involved in PTSD, but also in other anxiety disorders such as phobias, panic states, obsessive-compulsive disorder, and generalized anxiety. As in PTSD, avoidance of situations that are likely to bring on these feelings is an essential requisite of these disorders. The three aspects of avoidance discussed here provide potential animal models to investigate the brain mechanisms and underlying neuroendocrine processes of the various forms of human anxiety disorders. There is, however, no clear evidence that one of the forms of avoidance is an exclusive model of PTSD, panic, phobia, or obsessive-compulsive disorder. Only integrated behavioral, neurobiological, and neuroendocrine studies in humans and animals show promise toward understanding stress-related physiology and pathology.

See Also the Following Articles

Coping, Stress and; Fear

Bibliography

Bohus, B. (1998). Neuroendocrinology of stress: Behavioral and neurobiological considerations. *In* "Methods in Neuroendocrinology" (L. D. Van de Kar, (Ed.), pp. 163–180. CRC Press, Boca Raton, FL.

Dantzer, R. (1993). Coping with stress. *In* "Stress. From Synapse to Syndrome" (S. C. Stanford and P. Salmon, Eds.), pp. 167–189. Academic Press, London.

Kellner, M., and Yehuda, R. (1999). Do panic disorder and posttraumatic stress disorder share a common psychoneuroendocrinology? *Psychoneuroendocrinology* 24, 485–504.

LeDoux, J. (1995). Emotion: Clues from the brain. *Ann. Rev. Psychol.* 46, 209–235.

LeDoux, J. (1996). "The Emotional Brain." Simon & Schuster, New York.

Ursin, H., and Olff, M. (1993). The stress response. *In* "Stress: From Synapse to Syndrome" (S. C. Stanford and P. Salmon, Eds.), pp. 3–22. Academic Press, London.

Weiss, J. M. (1968). Effects of coping responses on stress. *J. Comp. Physiol. Psychol.* 65, 251–260.

Bacterial Infections

see Infection

Baroreceptors

see Arterial Baroflex

Bed Wetting

see Enuresis

Behavior, Overview

Robert Dantzer

Integrative Neurobiology, INSERM, Bordeaux, France

I. Behavioral Responses to Stress
II. Interactions between Behavioral and Physiological Components of the Stress Response
III. Behavioral Sources of Stress

GLOSSARY

appetitive stimulus A stimulus that induces approach and exploratory responses.
aversive stimulus A stimulus that induces avoidance and escape responses.
behavioral sequence A succession of appetitive and consummatory components. The appetitive sequence enables the subject to approach the goal object. Upon reaching the goal, appetitive behavior normally ceases and makes place to consummatory behavior that enables the subject to appropriate its goal.

Behavior is an important component of the stress reaction since it enables the subject to cope with the situation. The type of coping response that is displayed by the subject is important for shaping the physiological response to emotional demands. Conversely, baseline activity of the physiological systems that are involved in the stress response influences the probability of occurrence of the different types of coping response that are available for the subject. In addition to these bidirectional relationships between behavior and physiology, most stressful situations do not occur independent of the subject, but are dependent on the way the subject behaves and perceives psychosocial factors.

I. BEHAVIORAL RESPONSES TO STRESS

The stress response was initially described in the context of catastrophic events such as hemorrhage, surgical injury, burns, septic shock, and intoxications. These events cause a reflexlike response that is nonspecific and depends on the importance of the deviation from homeostasis. However, more common stressors such as psychosocial factors do not act this way. The response depends on the evaluation by the subject of the potential threat these factors represent. Novelty, uncertainty, and the absence or loss of control are important dimensions in this evaluation process. An emotional response occurs if the event is recognized as potentially harmful, and it involves both physiological and behavioral adjustments. Novelty occurs when the situation contains no or very few familiar elements. Subjects exposed to novelty explore the situation in order to identify potential sources of danger that need to be avoided and potentially interesting objects that can be safely approached. When novelty is too intense, fear predominates over exploration, and escape attempts replace investigatory behavior.

Uncertainty refers to the inability to predict what is going to happen when exposed to a threatening situation. In many cases, potentially harmful events do not happen all of a sudden, they are preceded by warning signals that can be used to predict their occurrence via a process of classical (or Pavlovian) conditioning. A tone that occurs before a painful electric shock becomes a fear signal. Inversely, a bell that rings when there is no electric shock is a safety signal. In an uncertain situation, the subject tries to find regularities in the succession of events to which he or she is exposed in the form of fear or safety signals, and this enables him or her to make the situation more predictable. The behavioral response to a fear signal is an anticipatory response that helps the organism to protect itself from the pain or aversiveness of the danger. The response to a safety signal is a decrease in the tension and/or anxiety induced by the possible occurrence of the harmful situation. Response to a fear signal usually consists of moving out of the threatening situation (active avoidance) when the subject is directly in contact with the threatening situation. When the subject is at a close distance from the threat and cannot move away, he usually refrains from getting in contact with the threat (passive avoidance). This response is associated with immobility and freezing.

When the situation is appetitive rather than aversive, events that regularly precede the occurrence of a reward become positive-conditioned stimuli or secondary reinforcers. They induce the development of conditioned behavioral responses that involve approach and other appetitive components of the normal behavioral response to the reward. If a secondary reinforcer is no longer followed by the occurrence of the reward, it induces a state of frustration that is characterized by agitation, aggression, and other displacement activities (see below).

In situations that involve physical contact with conspecifics, behavioral responses to stress form part of the agonistic repertoire. Agonistic behavior refers to the complex of aggression, threat, appeasement, and avoidance behaviors that occurs during encounters between members of the same species. Attack is usually a highly ritualized behavior when it occurs in property-protective fights. The offender attacks its opponent at protected parts of the body such as the neck in rats, whereas the defender tries to protect these targets for bites. When defeated, the defender adopts a submissive posture exposing to the attacker more vulnerable body sites. Submission usually puts an end to the fight.

Confronted with a potentially harmful situation, the subject usually tries to do something in order to avoid the danger. Coping refers to the efforts undertaken to actively resolve the situation. Active and passsive avoidance responses are examples of coping responses. Behavioral manifestations of coping vary according to the situation and the way the threat can be controlled. In laboratory animals, for instance, coping is typically studied by enabling the subjects to escape or avoid painful electric shocks when they emit a specific response such as a lever press, a wheel turn, or a move from one compartment to the other in a two-compartment cage. While animals in the escape/avoidance group are permitted to terminate electric shock or delay their occurrence, animals in another group serve as yoked controls since they receive the same electric shock as the previous animals, but their behavioral response has no effect on the occurrence and duration of electric shocks. As a further control, other animals are placed in the same apparatus as animals of the other two groups, but they are never exposed to electric shocks. Controllability can be studied in human subjects by asking them to press a button, usually to terminate an intense noise. As in the animal experiment, the yoked group has usually no control over the noise.

Helplessness refers to an individual's inability to control the situation when he has the opportunity to do so. This happens after a previous experience of uncontrollable stress and is then referred to as learned helplessness. Learned helplessness has cognitive, motivational, and emotional components.

Coping attempts can be classified according to the method that is employed to confront the situation. Approach coping refers in animals to all ways of dealing directly with the situation, e.g., active avoidance or attack. In human subjects, approach coping can be cognitive (logical analysis and positive reappraisal) or behavioral. In this last case, it includes seeking guidance and support and taking concrete actions to deal directly with the situation or its aftermath. Cognitive avoidance coping comprises intrapsychic processes aimed at denying or minimizing the seriousness of the situation or its consequences as well as accepting the situation as it is. Behavioral avoidance coping includes seeking alternative strategies to directly confronting the problem.

In general, approach coping enables the subject to deal directly with the problem and is therefore characteristic of problem-oriented coping. In cases the problem cannot be directly dealt with, it is often preferable to engage in avoidance coping that focuses mainly on managing the emotions associated with it (emotion-oriented coping). In the case of behavioral avoidance coping, behavioral activities that are normally elicited by the stimuli present in the situation are redirected toward more easily accessible targets. A typical example is the redirected aggression that develops toward a subordinate when an animal in a social group is attacked by the dominant member of the group. Whereas redirected activities belong to the same behavioral repertoire than the thwarted behavioral activity, displacement activities belong to a different behavioral repertoire. This is the case for the aggressive behavior that is targeted toward conspecifics or other objects in the environment in an animal which does not get the food it was expecting. A well-studied form of displacement activity is schedule-induced behavior. Schedule-induced behaviors, also known as adjunctive activities, typically occur when hungry animals are exposed to intermittent food rewards, delivered in very small amounts independent of the animals' behavior. Immediately after animals have eaten the minimum amount they get, they vigorously engage in other activities depending on what is available in the situation. They drink exaggerated amounts of water if a drinking tube is accessible, attack a conspecific when present, or gnaw a piece of wood if available. To qualify as an adjunctive behavior, the behavioral activity must occur as an adjunct to the reinforcement schedule; be not directly involved in, or maintained by, the reinforcement contingency; and be persistent and excessive. Independent of the object toward which they are directed, adjunctive behaviors occur at a maximum rate immediately after the reinforcement and decrease in probability when food deprivation is alleviated.

II. INTERACTIONS BETWEEN BEHAVIORAL AND PHYSIOLOGICAL COMPONENTS OF THE STRESS RESPONSE

Compared to uncertainty and lack of control, predictability and controllability have deactivating effects on the physiological arousal evoked by the stress situation. In social conflict situations, activation of stress hormones is in general more pronounced in subordinate animals which behave defensively or passively than in offensive animals that remain active and become dominant. However, the social role is more important than the social status since dominance is associated with a reduced arousal response only when dominant animals are recognized as such by their peers and do not need to reaffirm their status each time they are challenged by subdominant animals.

Schedule-induced polydipsia is associated with lowered plasma levels of stress hormones. This property is shared by other consummatory activities. The dearousal properties of coping behavior are not always that clear. Coping attempts are associated with increased activation of the sympathetic nervous system and they result in decreased physiological activation only when they have been successful and the threat is over. In addition, repeated occurrence of displacement activities sensitizes the dopaminergic neuronal structures that are involved in appetitive behavior.

The relationship between behavioral and physiological components of the stress responses is not unidirectional from behavior to physiology, but truly bidirectional in the sense that the likelihood of a given behavioral response is dependent on the subject's initial physiology. Individuals with high activity of the sympathetic adrenal–medullary axis are more likely to try to cope in an active way with a threat than individuals with a low activity of the sympathetic adrenal–medullary axis. Inversely, individuals with a relatively higher activity of the hypothalamic-pituitary-adrenal axis are more likely to resign and display helplessness than individuals with a normal or a lower activity of this axis.

III. BEHAVIORAL SOURCES OF STRESS

Psychobiological theories of stress emphasize the previously described bidirectional relationships between the behavioral and physiological components of the stress response. However, they do not account for the powerful influence of the subject's own behavior on the probability of occurrence of the stress situation.

A typical example for understanding this point is represented by the type A behavior pattern (TABP). The TABP is defined as an action–emotion complex that individuals use to confront challenges. The complex involves behavioral dispositions such as aggressiveness, competitiveness, and impatience; specific behaviors such as muscle tenseness, alertness, rapid and emphatic vocal stylistics, and accelerated pace of activities; and emotional responses such as irritation, covert hostility, and above-average potential for anger. Type B individuals are characterized by the relative absence of type A behaviors and confront every challenge with placid nonchalance. Type A individuals have a higher risk of developing coronary heart diseases than type B individuals. The deleterious effects of type A behavior appear to be associated with a higher physiological reactivity to external demands, especially when there are elements of competition. These findings corroborate the above-mentioned influence of behavioral factors on the physiological response to stress. In accordance with the bidirectionality of hormone–behavior relationships, type A behavior does not occur at will. It is determined at least in part by biological factors and autonomic hyperactivity. All of this makes type A behavior a typical psychobiological construct. However, this concept is not sufficient to account for what happens in the real world. Type A individuals actually create their own problems by putting themselves in situations of competition and taking all steps to transform the events they are confronted into challenges that need to be met in a more hostile way than their peers would be inclined to do.

A similar situation occurs in sensation-seeking individuals. There is evidence that individuals with this personality trait display enhanced responses to novelty and danger. The probability for a given individual to be a sensation seeker is determined by innate and experiential factors. However, what is characteristic of sensation seekers is their strong preference for sensation-inducing situations rather than their increased response to such situations. In sum, individuals are not passively exposed to stress, they actually create their own stress by the way they behave and perceive their environment.

See Also the Following Articles

AGGRESSIVE BEHAVIOR; BEHAVIOR THERAPY; DEFENSIVE BEHAVIORS; EVOLUTIONARY ORIGINS AND FUNCTIONS OF THE STRESS RESPONSE; HEALTH BEHAVIOR AND STRESS

Bibliography

Dantzer, R. (1994). "The Psychosomatic Delusion." The Free Press, New York.

Goldberger, L., and Breznitz, S. (Eds) (1993). "Handbook of Stress: Theoretical and Clinical Aspects," 2nd ed. The Free Press, New York.

McFarland, D. J. (Ed.) (1981). "The Oxford Companion to Animal Behaviour." Oxford, UK: Oxford University Press.

Stanford, S. C., and Salmon, P. (Eds) (1993). "Stress, From Synapse to Syndrome." Academic Press, London.

Behavior Therapy

Padmal de Silva

Institute of Psychiatry, University of London

GLOSSARY

behavioral analysis The detailed analysis of a behavior, which is considered essential before treatment is undertaken.

classical conditioning A basic form of learning where a neutral stimulus, which is presented repeatedly with a stimulus that elicits a particular response, eventually begins to elicit that response.

learning theory The body of theory that exists in experimental psychology that attempts to account for how animal and human behavior change takes place.

operant conditioning A basic form of learning where a response is strengthened or weakened by systematically manipulating the consequences of the response, such as providing a reward.

Behavior therapy may be broadly defined as the application of learning theory and other aspects of experimental psychology in the treatment of psychological disorders.

I. INTRODUCTION

The term "behavior therapy" is commonly used to refer to a particular approach to the treatment of psychological disorders. It has several key features. Behavior therapy sees many psychological problems as instances of maladaptive learning or, in some cases, failure to learn. The focus in behavior therapy is the presenting problem itself. It is not assumed that the presenting problem is a manifestation of an underlying primary problem. The aim of behavior therapy is to modify the problem behavior at a behavioral level, using behavioral means. In this endeavour, the principles of learning, and other methods and findings of experimental psychology, are utilized. Specifically, the principles of classical conditioning and those of operant, or instrumental, conditioning are key cornerstones of this approach.

Other features of behavior therapy include the emphasis on the detailed analysis of the problem behavior (in terms of stimuli, responses, consequences, etc.), the key role given to measurement and quantification, and the use of an experimental approach, where treatment follows a hypothesis-testing paradigm. This also includes a strong emphasis on outcome evaluation.

II. HISTORICAL DEVELOPMENT

Historically, behavior therapy developed over a period of time, culminating in its full emergence as a major psychological treatment approach in the 1950s. The basic concept of behavior change via behavioral means is of course very old, and there are examples of this from very early times, including the use of behavioral techniques in early Buddhism two-and-a-half millenia ago in India and in Rome around the beginnings of the Christian era. However, the key developments in the context of modern psychology can be traced to the work of a few key individuals, including John B. Watson, who demonstrated the applicability of learning principles in the understanding of the development of irrational fears. Watson and Rosalie Rayner, in 1920, created new fears in an 11-month-old child named Albert using classical conditioning principles. Four years later, Mary Cover Jones—one of Watson's students—published what might be described as the first formal application of learning principles to the treatment of a problem behavior. A 3-year-old boy, Peter, with a fear of rabbits was treated via the association of the feared stimulus with other positive and pleasant stimuli.

In the 1940s and 1950s much work along these lines was done in South Africa, mainly by Joseph Wolpe. Wolpe, who later emigrated to the United States, undertook serious experimental work—first with animals and then with human subjects—on the modification and elimination of maladaptive responses. His book, "Psychotherapy by Reciprocal Inhibition," published in 1958 by Stanford University Press, is widely regarded as a landmark publication signaling the emergence of behavior therapy as a major therapeutic approach. Wolpe's work was supplemented by further work, both theoretical and empirical, by other leading figures such as Hans Eysenck, Monte Shapiro, Victor Meyer, and others in London and by Stanley Rachman, an associate of Wolpe who emigrated from South Africa to England in the early 1960s and joined Eysenck.

An equally significant contribution to the development of behavior therapy was made by B. F. Skinner, whose book "Science and Human Behavior" (1953, Macmillan, New York) is also regarded as a classic in this field. The work of Skinner and associates concentrated on the use of operant conditioning principles, recognizing the key role of consequences in the maintenance and modification of behavior.

The establishment of *Behaviour Research and Therapy* in 1963 as a journal devoted to the field behavior therapy was another major step in the establishment of behavior therapy.

More recent developments have expanded and widened the scope and basis of behavior therapy. In the early stages, behavior therapy, drawing on the principles of classical conditioning, was used for what were then called "neurotic disorders." The largest group of patients treated in the early days in this way were those with phobias, or irrational and maladaptive fears. In fact, most of the cases described in Wolpe's 1958 book were individuals suffering from phobias. Those with obsessive-compulsive problems, sexual difficulties, and addictions were also treated. Operant conditioning principles were used to help in the management of behavioral problems in children and to modify problem behaviors

in those with pervasive learning disability (mental retardation) and with chronic psychotic illness. These early developments were later supplemented (1) by the ideas of social learning theory, which pointed out that human behavior change takes place not just with direct experience but also through vicarious learning and social transmission and (2) by ideas and techniques of cognitive psychology and cognitive therapy, which showed the importance of cognitions (thoughts, attitudes, beliefs) in determining and/or influencing human behavior. The incorporation of cognitive therapy principles developed by Aaron T. Beck in Philadelphia and others eventually led to what is today referred to by many as "cognitive behavior therapy."

III. TECHNIQUES OF BEHAVIOR THERAPY

Behavior therapy is widely applied today for a range of problems. It is considered to be a major, robust approach to helping people to get over problem behaviors and develop more adaptive ones. Some of the major behavior therapy techniques are described briefly in this section.

A. Exposure Therapy

This is the main approach used for phobias. The principle here is that exposure to the feared—and avoided—stimulus, in therapeutic conditions, leads to a reduction and eventual elimination of fear. This may be done either in real life (*in vivo*) or in imagination or fantasy. The client is exposed in a graded series of steps to the fear stimulus or situation. As an anxiety-countering strategy, deep muscle relaxation may be used. Clients are usually treated individually, but group treatments are also undertaken. In recent years, clients have also been taught to engage in this type of exposure therapy by themselves, i.e., self-managed exposure therapy, after assessment by a qualified therapist and agreement on a plan of treatment.

In contrast to the graded exposure approach, intensive and/or prolonged exposure is also used. In the early days, this was generally known as "flooding." *In vivo* flooding and imaginal flooding are both used. Essentially, the client is exposed to the fear-arousing situation for a prolonged period of time, which is done without a graded, step-by-step approach. Highly anxiety-arousing situations are used from the beginning. A treatment session usually ends when the client's initial high anxiety has subsided to a significant degree.

B. Modeling

In modeling, the client is exposed to other individuals, or models, engaging in the target behaviors in an appropriate, nonanxious manner. Modeling is used in fear reduction. The active participation of the client is a key aspect. Modeling is also used widely in the treatment of those who have difficulties in assertiveness and other social skills. Again, participant modeling, rather than simply observing the models, is needed to achieve the desired changes.

C. Response Prevention

This is a technique that is usually employed in conjunction with exposure. The best known application of this approach is in the treatment of compulsive behaviors in obsessive-compulsive disorder. The client is exposed to situations that arouse anxiety and create an upsurge of the urge to engage in the target compulsive behavior. For example, a client with contamination fears and associated compulsive hand-washing rituals may be exposed to items which he or she believes are contaminating, such as dirty table surfaces or door handles in a public convenience. This exposure leads to high anxiety and to a high urge to engage in a cleansing, hand-washing compulsion. However, as part of the prearranged treatment plan, the client refrains from engaging in this compulsive behavior. The compulsive urge and the anxiety both gradually dissipate with time, and the session is ended when a significant reduction is achieved. Repeated sessions lead to progressively lower anxiety and less strong compulsive urges.

Response prevention following exposure is also used with clients with alcohol problems, drug addiction, and compulsive binge eating, among others.

D. The Use of Reinforcement

Reinforcement is the strengthening of a behavior so that the probability of its occurrence is enhanced. Using reinforcers, or rewards, to strengthen desirable behavior is a major behavior therapy technique. There are two types of reinforcers. A positive reinforcer is something pleasant or welcome that is presented as a consequence of the desired behavior being performed. For example, a child may be given a sweet as a reward each time he puts on his socks by himself. A negative reinforcer is something unpleasant and/or unwelcome that is removed, or avoided, as a consequence of the target behavior being carried out.

It is common in behavior therapy to use social reinforcers as a major means of positive reinforcement of desired behaviors. These include verbal praise, approval, and attention.

E. Token Economies

A token economy is a whole system of reinforcement used for motivating clients. For example, a group of children in a class or a group of chronic schizophrenic patients in a large hospital ward may be helped in this way. Desired target behaviors are immediately reinforced with tokens: plastic chips, stars on a chart, or points. Maladaptive behavior can lead to the loss of tokens. The tokens are exchangeable for real reinforcers; these are called "back up reinforcers" in this context. For example, 10 tokens may be exchanged for a bar of chocolate. A token economy program has a set of detailed and explicit rules and procedures that specify how tokens are to be earned and how they are to be exchanged for back up reinforcers.

F. Aversive Procedures

In the early days of behavior therapy, aversive procedures were commonly used. In aversion therapy, undesirable target behaviors are systematically followed by an aversive consequence, e.g., electric shocks. Clients seeking treatment for deviant sexual interests were, for example, treated with a paradigm where the deviant stimulus (e.g., pictures of fetish object) was accompanied repeatedly by the delivery of a shock. Such aversive procedures are not commonly used today, partly for ethical reasons, but also because these techniques were found to achieve a suppression of the unwanted response rather than its elimination. However, covert aversion (where the unpleasant consequences of an undesirable behavior are presented through powerful imagery) is used with some success. Real physical aversion is still used sometimes to control self-injurious acts in clients with severe problem behaviors.

G. Extinction

The most effective technique for reducing and/or eliminating an undesirable behavior is to eliminate the reinforcement that follows that behavior. If this can be done systematically, then the behavior gets effectively extinguished. For example, a child's frequent tantrums may be reinforced by the parental attention that such behavior elicits, and the withholding of this reinforcement can lead to the extinction of this behavior. However, sometimes the reinforcer maintaining the target behavior cannot be identified. A further difficulty is that implementation of a treatment program such that the problem behavior is not even occasionally reinforced is often difficult in practice.

H. Time Out

Time out (short for "time out from positive reinforcement") is the temporary withdrawal of a client's (usually a child's) access to positive reinforcers immediately following the performance of the target maladaptive behavior. In child behavior problems (e.g., hitting others, disruptive shouting), the child is taken to a bland time out area for a limited period of time, following the undesirable behavior.

IV. PRACTICE OF BEHAVIOR THERAPY

In clinical practice, behavioral techniques are used, sometimes in combination, after a careful analysis of the problem. Such detailed behavioral analysis is a necessary first step before therapy is undertaken.

While simple, uncomplicated clinical problems may need only simple and straightforward therapy programs, many clinical cases in real life present complex problems that may require the imaginative use of several behavioral techniques, concurrently or sequentially. At each step, a careful analysis is made of the outcome of the intervention and, if necessary, the program is revised. This experimental, or hypothesis-testing, approach is a major feature of the behavioral approach in its application.

In many instances, the behavioral techniques may need to be combined with cognitive techniques. It was noted in an earlier section that the term "cognitive behavior therapy" is used by many practitioners for this approach. This approach remains essentially within the broad framework of behavior therapy, but there is emphasis on acknowledging the significance of cognitions. Cognitive techniques are added to the behavioral ones as needed. In the treatment of panic attacks, for example, the behavioral technique of graded exposure to identified panic-provoking situations is combined profitably with helping the client to identify any faulty cognitions (e.g., "My heart is beating fast, this means I may collapse") and providing evidence that these are unfounded.

V. CONCLUSIONS

Behavior therapy has come a long way since its tentative beginnings in the early decades of this century. It is a well-developed, versatile approach to the treatment of a wide range of behavioral problems, and there is much empirical evidence for the efficacy of its various therapeutic techniques. Some of these techniques are also widely used in helping modifying the behavior of nonclinical subjects, e.g., in improving classroom behavior. As an approach to the modification of human behavior, behavior therapy remains well grounded in experimental psychology, especially learning theory. Its emphasis on the careful observation and assessment of problems, defining target behaviors, quantification and measurement, and rigorous outcome evaluation makes it a robust scientific approach.

See Also the Following Articles

Bibliography

Ellis, A. 1997. Extending the goals of behavior therapy and cognitive behavior therapy. *Behav. Ther.* **28**, 333–339.

Eysenck, H. J., and Martin, J., eds. 1987. "Theoretical Foundations of Behavior Therapy." Plenum, New York.

Last, C. G., and Hersen, M., eds. 1994. "Adult Behavior Therapy Casebook." Plenum, New York.

Plaud, J. J., and Eifert, G. H., eds. 1998. "From Behavior Theory to Behavior Therapy." Allyn & Bacon, Boston.

Salkovskis, P. M. 1996. "Trends in Cognitive and Behavioural Therapies." Wiley, Chichester.

Turner, S. M., Calhoun, K. S., and Adams, H. E., eds. 1992. "Handbook of Clinical Behavior Therapy," 2nd Ed. Wiley, New York.

Wolpe, J. 1990. "The Practice of Behavior Therapy," 4th Ed. Pergamon, Elmsford, NY.

Bereavement

Paula J. Clayton

University of Minnesota

I. Depressive Symptoms and Course
II. Physical Symptoms, Substance Use, and Medical Treatment
III. Depressive and Anxiety Disorders
IV. Complicated or Traumatic Bereavement
V. Mortality
VI. Pathologic Outcomes and Predictors of Outcome
VII. Treatment

GLOSSARY

bereavement The state or fact of being bereaved; bereaved, suffering the death of a loved one; the loss of a loved one by death.

disorders So disturb the regular or normal functions of; an abnormal physical or mental condition: ailment.

grief Deep and poignant distress caused by or as if by bereavement; a cause of such suffering.

mourning The act of sorrowing; a person's death [is wearing]; a period of time during which signs of grief are shown.

outcome Something that follows as a result or consequence.

traumatic grief A disordered psychic or behavioral state resulting from mental or emotional stress or physical injury; an agent, force, or mechanism that causes trauma.

Although no one would dispute that the loss by death of someone close is a significant life event, the degree of adversity that the death brings to the individual is variable. Research in the field is just beginning to identify and study the most severely affected. In studying bereavement, most investigators have used entry into widowhood as the model, although response to the death of a child is probably more stressful. This article concentrates on research on *bereavement,* which by definition is a reaction of a person to loss by death. Other terms in the literature that should not be confused with bereavement are *grief,* which is the emotional and psychological reaction to any loss but not limited to death, and *mourning,* which is the social expression of bereavement or grief, frequently formalized by custom or religion.

At this point there have been numerous longitudinal follow-up studies of recently bereaved. The majority deal with the widowed, although there are excellent studies of children who have lost a parent. Despite the fact that the mode of selection, response rate, gender, age group, time since the death to the first interview, comparison groups, and the selection of instruments and outcome measures differ greatly from study to study, the similarities of outcome outweigh the differences. Our own data highlight the major outcomes, although important additional findings have been identified and there are still areas of controversy.

Bereavement is the ideal condition to study the effect of stress on the organism. It is not species specific, so it can be defined identically across species and generations of species. It is a real event, not artificial, imagined, or devised, it is datable, and it occurs in present time so it can be studied immediately, not retrospectively, and even prospectively. Finally, the significance of the event would not be disputed. Before reviewing the morbidity and mortality associated with this clear-cut, easily defined stress, it is important to emphasize that by far the most usual outcome following this experience is numbness for a very brief period, depression for a variable time, and then recovery. Recovery is the return of the individual to a reasonable level of functioning or a change in a positive direction. In some this takes months, in others, up to 2 years or more. This is described eloquently by Lund *et al.* in older adults. Only 10–15% develop chronic depression, with fewer experiencing traumatic grief. In studying the biology of this particular stress, whole populations will have to be studied so that we define the usual, natural outcomes as well as the abnormal responses.

I. DEPRESSIVE SYMPTOMS AND COURSE

In studying relatives reactions to the loss of a significant person, data were collected on three different samples. The first sample [Clayton, P., Demarais, L., Winokur, G. (1968). *Am. J. Psychiat.* **125**, 168–178] was a group of 40 bereaved relatives of people who had died at a general hospital in St. Louis. The second sample [Clayton, P. J., Halikas, J. A., and Maurice, W. L. (1971). *Dis. Nerv. Syst.* **32**, 597–604] was a sample of widows and widowers chosen from the death certificates and seen at 1, 4, and 13 months after the deaths of their spouses. The third sample [Clayton, P. J., and Darvish, H. S. 1979. *In* "Stress and Mental Disorder" (J. E. Barrett, ed.), pp. 121–136, Raven Press. New York] was a consecutive series of young (under 45 years old) widowed also seen

within a month after the death and again at 1 year. The last two samples were matched through the voter registry with married people of the same age and sex who had not had first-degree relatives die and who were also followed prospectively to ascertain their morbidity and mortality. The findings are exemplified in Table I, which displays the depressive symptoms that were endorsed at 1 and 13 months. In the first month, a large majority of the sample experienced depressed mood, anorexia and beginning weight loss, insomnia that was initial, middle, and terminal, marked crying, some fatigue and loss of

TABLE I

Frequency of Depressive Symptoms at 1 and 13 Months[a]

Symptom	1 month %+ (n = 149[b])	13 months %+ (n = 149[b])
Crying	89	33[c]
Sleep disturbance	76	48[c]
Low mood	75	42[c]
Loss of appetite	51	16[c]
Fatigue	44	30[d]
Poor memory	41	23[c]
Loss of interest	40	23[c]
Difficulty concentrating	36	16[c]
Weight loss of 2.25 kg or more	36	20[d]
Feeling guilty	31	12[c]
Restlessness (n = 89)	48	45
Reverse diurnal variation	26	22
Irritability	24	20
Feels someone to blame	22	22
Diurnal variation	17	10
Death wishes	16	12
Feeling hopeless	14	13
Hallucinations	12	9
Suicide thoughts	5	3
Fear of losing mind	3	4
Suicide attempts	0	0
Feeling worthless	6	11
Feels angry about death	13	22[e]
Depressive	42	16[c]

[a] From P. J. Clayton (1982). Bereavement. *In* "Handbook of Affective Disorders" (E. S. Paykel, ed.). Churchill Livingstone, London.
[b] N varies from symptom to symptom, mostly 148.
[c] Significant by McNemar's χ^2, $df = 1$, $p \leq 0.001$.
[d] Significant by McNemar's χ^2, $df = 1$, $p \leq 0.01$.
[e] Significant by McNemar's χ^2, $df = 1$, $p \leq 0.02$.

interest in their surroundings, but not necessarily the people around them, restlessness, and guilt. The guilt that these people expressed was different than the guilt seen in the depressed patient. For the most part it was guilt of omission surrounding either the terminal illness or the death. Irritability was common, but overt anger was uncommon. Suicidal thoughts and ideas were rare. When they did occur they occurred in younger men after the death of a spouse or in men and women after the death of a child. Hallucinations were not uncommon. Many widows and widowers, when asked, admitted that they had felt touched by their dead spouse or had heard his voice, had seen his vision, or had smelled his presence. The misidentification of their dead spouses in a crowd was extremely common.

We matched some of our subjects with well-studied hospitalized depressives [Clayton, P. J., Herjanic, M., Murphy, G. E., and Woodruff, R. A., Jr. (1974). *Can. Psychiat. Assoc. J.* **19**, 309–312] and found, as Freud suggested, symptoms such as feeling hopeless, worthless, a burden, psychomotor retardation, wishing to be dead, and thinking of suicide differentiated the depressed from the bereaved.

By the end of the first year the somatic symptoms of depression had improved remarkably. Low mood (usually associated with specific events or holidays), restlessness, and poor sleep continued. The few psychological symptoms of depression, although rare, resolved less easily. In our studies the symptoms were as frequent in men as in women, in people who had lost a spouse suddenly or after a lingering death, in people who had good or bad marriages, and people who were religious or nonreligious. Young people were more likely to have a severer immediate reaction, but by a year their outcome was similar. There was no relationship between income and outcome.

As Table II shows, when the frequency of depressive symptoms was compared to the community controls, all symptoms were more common among the bereaved. When depressive symptoms reported at 13 months were examined by those with symptoms for the entire year and those who had just developed them, the percentage who had new symptoms was similar to those reported by the controls who had had no deaths. This is shown in Table III. Those who were disturbed early were more likely to be disturbed later. Delayed grief, such as "*delayed*" post-

TABLE II
Frequency of Depressive Symptoms at Any Time in the First Year of Bereavement and in Controls[a]

Symptom	Probands % (n = 149[b])	Control % (n = 131[b])
Crying	90	14[c]
Sleep disturbance	79	35[c]
Low mood	80	18[c]
Loss of appetite	53	4[c]
Fatigue	55	23[c]
Poor memory	50	22[c]
Loss of interest	48	11[c]
Difficulty concentrating	40	13[c]
Weight loss of 2.25 kg or more	47	24[c]
Feeling guilty	38	11[c]
Restlessness	63	27[c]
Irritability	35	21[d]
Diurnal variation	22	14
Death wishes	22	5[c]
Feeling hopeless	19	4[e]
Hallucinations	17	2[e]
Suicidal thoughts	8	1[f]
Fear of losing mind	7	5
Suicide attempts	0	0
Worthlessness	14	15
Depressive syndrome	47	8[e]

[a] From P. J. Clayton (1982). Bereavement. *In* "Handbook of Affective Disorders" (E. S. Paykel, Ed.). Churchill Livingstone, London.
[b] N varies from symptom to symptom.
[c] Significant by χ^2, $df = 1$, $p \leq 0.0001$.
[d] Significant by χ^2, $df = 1$, $p \leq 0.05$.
[e] Significant by χ^2, $df = 1$, $p \leq 0.0005$.
[f] Significant by χ^2, $df = 1$, $p \leq 0.01$.

traumatic stress disorder, may be an interesting ideologic concept but remains unproven. It is also counterintuitive because the usual recognized reaction to a physical or psychological insult is an immediate injury with a gradual resolution, which was also confirmed in another study [Byrne, G. J. A., and Raphael, B. (1994). *Psychol. Med.* **24**].

II. PHYSICAL SYMPTOMS, SUBSTANCE USE, AND MEDICAL TREATMENT

We systematically ask about physical symptoms, usually associated with major depression, in both

TABLE III
Frequency of Depressive Symptoms at 13 Months[a]

Symptom	Those with Symptoms at 1 Month %+	Those with Symptoms at 1 Month n	Those Without Symptoms at 1 Month (New Symptoms) %+	Those Without Symptoms at 1 Month (New Symptoms) n
Crying	36	132	6	16
Sleep disturbance	59	113	11	35
Low mood	49	111	22	37
Loss of appetite	28	76	4	72
Fatigue	45	65	19	83
Poor memory	34	61	15	88
Loss of interest	40	57	12	84
Difficulty concentrating	33	52	6	94
Weight loss of 2.25 kg or more	22	51	17	92
Feeling guilty	25	49	6	97
Restlessness	63	43	28	46
Reverse diurnal variation	39	38	17	109
Irritability	37	35	15	113
Feels someone to blame	63	32	11	111
Diurnal variation	24	25	7	122
Death wishes	33	24	7	124
Feeling hopeless	55	20	6	128
Hallucinations	29	17	6	131
Suicidal thoughts	0	8	3	139
Fear of losing mind	0	5	4	143
Suicide attempts	0	0	0	147
Feeling worthless	56	9	8	139
Feel angry about death	63	19	16	128
Depressive syndrome	27	63	8	86

[a] From P. J. Clayton (1982). Bereavement. *In* "Handbook of Affective Disorders" (E. S. Paykel, Ed.). Churchill Livingstone, London.

TABLE IV
Frequency of Physical Symptoms in 1 Year in Bereaved and Controls[a]

Symptom	Probands %+ (n = 149[b])	Controls %+ (n = 131[b])
Headaches	36	27
Dysmenorrhea	38	20
Other pains	44	18[c]
Urinary frequency	30	23
Constipation	27	24
Dyspnea	27	16[d]
Abdominal pain	26	11[e]
Blurred vision	22	13
Anxiety attacks	15	8
Alcohol use	19	9[d]
Tranquilizers	46	8[f]
Hypnotics	32	2[f]
Physician visits	79	80
Three or more	45	48
Six or more	27	29
Hospitalizations	22	14
General poor health	10	7

[a] From P. J. Clayton (1986). Bereavement and its relation to clinical depression. *In* "New Results in Depression" (Hippius *et al.*, Eds.). Springer-Verlag, Berlin/Heidelberg.
[b] N varies slightly from symptom to symptom.
[c] Significant by χ^2, $df = 1$, $p \leq 0.005$.
[d] Significant by χ^2, $df = 1$, $p \leq 0.05$.
[e] Significant by χ^2, $df = 1$, $p \leq 0.001$.
[f] Significant by χ^2, $df = 1$, $p \leq 0.0001$.

recently widowed and controls. They are depicted in Table IV. In general, physical symptoms were not more frequent in recently bereaved and controls. Nor did they change much over the year. The largest difference was recorded in "other pains," which were mainly in the elderly bereaved and consisted of arthritic-type pains. In our studies there were no more physician visits or hospitalization in the year following the bereavement. This is controversial.

The most striking finding of this research is illustrated in Table IV. After a significant stress, such as bereavement, the use of alcohol, tranquilizers, and hypnotics increased significantly. For the most part

these were not new users but people who had used them before. Cigarette smoking also increased. The morbidity and mortality of bereavement may be related to these changes in behavior. It also highlights how people behave after significant stress.

In a separate study [Frost, N. R., and Clayton, P. J. (1977). *Arch. Gen. Psychiat.* 34, 1172–1175] 249 psychiatric in-patients and similarly matched hospital controls were examined and no significant differences were found between the groups for the loss of a first-degree relative or spouse in the 6 months or 1 year prior to admission to the hospital. In each case only 2% reported such a loss in the 6 months and 3 or 4% in the 7–12 months prior to hospitalization. In psychiatric patients, the major diagnosis was a mood disorder. There were diagnoses of alcoholism in both bereaved psychiatric patients and bereaved hospitalized controls that related to their increased drinking after the death.

III. DEPRESSIVE AND ANXIETY DISORDERS

In our first study of widowhood, 35% of the subjects had a depressive syndrome at 1 month, 25% at 4 months, and 17% at 1 year. Forty-five percent were depressed at some point during the year and 11% were depressed for the entire year. Adding the second younger sample, 42% were depressed at 1 month and 16% met the criteria at 1 year. Forty-seven percent were depressed at some time during the year compared to 8% of controls and again, 11% for the entire year. These findings are remarkably similar to those of studies reported extensively by Zisook and Shuchter. They identified a large sample of widows and widowers from the death certificates and solicited volunteers to be interviewed. The demographics of the final sample were very similar to the first widowed sample reported here. They reported that 24% of their sample were depressed at 2 months, 23% at 7 months, 16% at 13 months, and 14% at 25 months. Seven percent were chronically depressed, very similar to the 8.8% reported by Byrne and Raphael. In all of these studies the best predictor of depression at 13 months was depression at 1 month. In the Zisook and Shuchter studies, a past history of depression also predicted depression at 1 year. In our own studies, because we did not have enough depressives, it was any psychiatric morbidity prior to death that predicted depression at 1 year. The other common correlate of depression at 1 year was poor physical health prior to the death of the spouse. As a result, prior poor physical or mental health predicted poor outcome at 13 months. Although there are methodologic issues in defining both anticipation of a death (e.g., expected versus unexpected) and outcomes (depression, death, remarriage, etc.) [Clayton, P. J., Parilla, R. H., Jr., and Bieri, M. D. (1980). *In* "The Psychosocial Aspects of Cardiovascular Disease: The Patient, the Family and the Staff," pp. 267–275. Columbia Univ. Press, New York], in our data, unexpected deaths produced more severe immediate responses but the differences disappeared

by 13 months. The same was true for Byrne and Raphael. Using the best definitions of unexpected death, a death in a healthy individual that occurred in less than 2 h, Lundin compared such bereaved to those bereaved after longer terminal illnesses and found that morbidity, especially psychiatric morbidity, as measured in physician visits, increased significantly in the sudden death survivors. Even after years later (Lundin, T. 1984. *Br. J. Psychiat.* 145, 424–428) they had higher ratings in a number of grief symptoms.

In more then one study, about 25% of the recently bereaved met criteria for some anxiety disorder immediately following bereavement. More then half, however, had generalized anxiety disorder, which correlated with the severity of the depressive disorder. As Surtees showed without clarifying the nature of the anxiety disorder, the major disorders that affect the recently bereaved are depressive disorder alone or concurrent depression and anxiety. He confirmed that new episodes of any anxiety disorder were rare after bereavement. It may be wisest to conclude that these are anxiety symptoms embedded in a depression disorder. He has shown that the anxiety symptoms abate before the depressive symptoms.

IV. COMPLICATED OR TRAUMATIC BEREAVEMENT

Lindemann probably wrote the first papers on bereavement that dealt with prospective observations of 13 bereaved subjects who were hospitalized at Massachusetts General Hospital after the Coconut Grove fire. He combined these observations with those of his own patients who lost a relative during treatment, with relatives whom he saw of patients who died at the hospital, and of relatives of members of the armed forces. Although he considered his observations to be of normal grief, many of them were probably related to a pathologic response. More recently, investigators have begun to quantify the abnormal response [Prigerson, H. G., Maciejewski, P. K., Reynods, C. F., II, Bierhals, A. J., Newsom, J. T., Fasiczka, A., Frank, E., Doman, J., and Miller, M. (1995). *Psychiat. Res.* 59, 65–79] by developing an inventory of complicated grief that is related to the severity of depressive symptoms, but with distinct symptoms. Building on earlier inventories, such as the Texas grief inventory [Fashingbauer, T. R., Zisook, S., and DeVaul, R. (1987). *In* "Biopsychosocial Aspects of Bereavement" S. Zisook, ed., pp. 109–124. American Psychiatric Press, Washington, DC] and the grief measurement scale [Jacobs, S., Kasl, S. V., Ostfeld, A. M., Berkman, L., Kosten T. R., and Charpentier, P. (1987). *Hosp. J.* **2**, 21–36] they took symptoms such as preoccupation with death, crying, searching and yearning for the deceased, disbelief about the death, being stunned, and not accepting the death and added questions about preoccupation with thoughts of the deceased, anger, distrust, detachment, avoidance, replication of symptoms that the deceased experienced, auditory and visual hallucinations and guilt, loneliness, bitterness, and envy of others who had not lost someone close. Their instrument was shown to be reliable and have criterion validity. Whether it is just defining the most severe depression is not yet clear. Modifying the grief measurement scale in accordance with the symptoms described previously, Prigerson and colleagues looked at a previously ascertained sample who were followed from before the death to until 25 months after the death. They found that if they identified bereaved at 6 months who scored high on their inventory, at 13 months there was a correlation between high scores and a change in smoking and eating, depression, and high systolic blood pressure. At 25 months, these people had an increased risk to develop heart trouble and cancer and more often expressed suicidal ideation as ascertained on a single item. If they tried to separate the sample on traumatic grief at 2 months, they could not predict unfavorable outcomes. Using a similar approach, a scale has been developed to measure core bereavement items [Burnett, P., Middleton, W., Raphael, B., and Martiner, N. (1997). *Psychol. Med.* **27**, 49–57]. This scale also measures images and thoughts around the death, yearning and pining about the death, and some grief symptoms such as sadness, loneliness, longing, tearfulness, and loss of enjoyment. This inventory was developed using parents of deceased children, bereaved spouses, and bereaved adult children who scored high in descending order on the inventory.

However, the questionnaire has not yet been correlated with outcome. Another set of symptoms has been defined for a complicated grief disorder [Horowitz, M. J., Seigel, B., Holen, A., Bonanno, G. A., Milbrath, C., and Stinson, C. H. (1997). *Am. J. Psychiat.* **154**, 904–910].

Some of the symptoms in all of these inventories seem similar to symptoms that occur in posttraumatic stress disorder and it is difficult to justify a new category except that in the bereaved the death was usually not traumatic. Clearly these investigators are defining an important bereavement response that defines survivors with a poorer outcome. For other researchers who are studying human reactions to stress, symptoms such as these should be identified and studied prospectively. The identification of such a syndrome also makes it possible to study, more specifically, various interventions [Zygmont, M., Prigerson, H. G., Houck, P. R., Miller, M. D., Shear, M. K., Jacobs, S., and Reynolds, C. F. III, (1998). *J. Clin. Psychiat.* **59**, 5], which showed that both paroxetine and nortriptyline decrease traumatic grief symptoms significantly.

V. MORTALITY

In more recent years, the method of study (collecting health data on a large core of men and women and following them prospectively to ascertain the point of widowhood and using the Cox hazards regression module to estimate the effect of bereavement on mortality while controlling for the effects of other covariates) should have improved the validity of mortality data greatly. Nevertheless, there still are controversies. Three studies have used these methods. It has been reported [De Leon, C. F. M., Kasl, S. F., and Jacobs, S. (1993). *J. Clin. Epidemiol.* **46**, 519–527] that elderly, young–old (65–74 years), and old–old men (more then 74 years) showed an increased mortality in the first 6 months of widowhood. However, because there was an age difference between future widowed and nonwidowed, when they were age adjusted, the death rate fell to a nonsignificant level. Among young–old women there was also an increased risk of death in the first 6 months that decreased only slightly after the age adjustment, but enough to make it of borderline significance. The authors suggested that the "true risk period" may be even shorter than 6 months. In another study [Schaefer, C., Quesenberry, J. C. P., Jr., and Wi, S. (1995). *Am. J. Epidemiol.* **141**, 1142–1152], it was also reported that mortality following bereavement was elevated significantly in both men and women after adjusting for age, education, and other predictors of mortality. Here, the highest mortality rates occurred 7–12 months following the bereavement. Finally, Ebrahim and co-workers studied men but included never married, divorced, separated, widowed, and married men and found that there was no increase in mortality in men who became widowed during the follow-up time. In this study there were 7735 men aged 40–59 who were interviewed extensively at the first point and followed 5 years later. There were only 24 men who became widowed in that follow-up period, which probably limited the findings. There is also a twin study of mortality after spousal bereavement [Lichtenstein, P., Gatz, M., and Berg, S. (1998). *Psychol. Med.* **28**, 635–643]. Without relating whether the twins were mono- or dizygotic, they found an increased mortality for young–old (under 70 years) men and women during the first year of bereavement. The death hazard diminished the longer the bereaved were followed. They analyzed their data for smoking status, excessive alcohol consumption, education, body mass, cardiovascular disease, respiratory disease, and other chronic illness and found that these did not affect the relative hazard estimates. Other studies show that remarriage, which is much more likely to occur in men, protects men from death either because the healthier remarry or the remarriage in and of itself is protective. The death rates of those who remarry is similar to married men of the same age. Taken as a whole, these studies support that there is probably an increased mortality after bereavement in men and women under 70 in the first year.

From these studies there does not seem to be an increased mortality from any one particular cause, such as cancer or cardiovascular disease. Other studies, however, have shown an increase in suicide after a bereavement, although when looking at smaller samples, most of those who suicided were psychiatrically ill prior to their spouses' deaths.

VI. PATHOLOGIC OUTCOMES AND PREDICTORS OF OUTCOME

Before reviewing the predictors of pathologic outcomes it should be noted that all studies of widowhood, including those on mortality, emphasize that psychological stability predicts a good outcome, although unfortunately no one has measured personality traits or variables prior to entry into widowhood. Good health predicts a better outcome, and not having a sleep difficulty or having low scores on depression ratings in the first month of bereavement also predicts a better outcome.

There are many ways to assess outcome. Loneliness certainly is the most characteristic outcome following bereavement. It persists in many for years. Under psychological morbidity, chronic depression as measured a year after the death and complicated bereavement both lead to significant morbidity. There is also physical morbidity. The mortality noted postbereavement still needs further study.

There are very few definitive predictors of chronic depression. A past history of psychiatric illness, particularly depression, predicts it, poor prior physical health may predict it, and depression at 1 month after the bereavement definitely predicts it. Perhaps the bereavement that follows an instantaneous and totally unexpected death predicts it. Studies will clarify the predictions as data collection improves. All the other variables, gender, young age, perceived lack of social supports, and socioeconomic income, do not predict it. Gender is important to note because major depression is overwhelmingly more common in women than in men but chronic depression after bereavement is not. Stress-related depression affects both genders equally.

VII. TREATMENT

The vast majority of people who experience a loss will recover gradually without any interventions. In those who become chronically depressed or have traumatic grief, an intervention at 6 months after the bereavement is indicated. Clearly interpersonal therapy (ITP) was designed as a therapy that concentrates on loss so it seems a likely psychotherapic tool.

Antidepressants have also been used and shown to be efficacious. A study of treatment of bereavement-related major depressive episodes in later life with nortriptyline, ITP, the combination, or neither [Reynolds, C. F. III., Miller, M. D., Pasternak, R. E., Frank, E., Perel, J. M., Cornes, C., Houck, P. R., Mazumdar, M. S.H., Des, M. A., Kupfer, D. J. (1999). *Am. J. Psychiat.* **156**, 202–208] showed that nortriptyline alone or with IPT improved the depressive disorder significantly. Interpersonal therapy alone was not significantly different than the placebo. The outcomes are notable because very few relapsed when the treatments were stopped and the response rate was relatively high in both nortriptyline treatment groups and the placebo group. Thus it looks like it is a good condition to treat with antidepressant medication. It is also important to remember that should the patient be psychotic or suicidal, ECT is probably indicated.

See Also the Following Articles

ANXIETY; GENDER AND STRESS; GRIEVING; MAJOR DEPRESSIVE DISORDER

Bibliography

Dohrenwend, B. (Ed.) (1998). "Adversity, Stress, and Psychopathology." Oxford Univ. Press.

Ebrahim, S., Wannamethee, G., McCallum, A., Walher, M., and Shaper, A. G. (1995). Marital status, change in marital status, and mortality in middle-aged British men. *Am. J. Epidemiol.* **142**, 834–842.

Frost, .N. R., and Clayton, P. J. (1977). Bereavement and psychiatric hospitalization. *Arch. Gen. Psychiat.* **34**, 1172–1175.

Lindemann, E. (1944). Symptomalogy and management of acute grief. *Am. J. Psychiat.* **101**.

Lundin, T. (1984). Morbidity following sudden and unexpected bereavement. *Br. J. Psychiat.* **144**, 84–88.

Lund, D. A., Caserta, M. S., and Dimond, M. F. (1993). *In* "Handbook of Bereavement" M. S. Stroebe, W. Stroebe, and R. O. Hansson, (Eds.). Cambridge Univ. Press, Cambridge.

Parkes, C. M., and Weiss, R. S. (1983). "Recovery from Bereavement." Basic Books, New York.

Prigerson, H. G., Bierhals, A. J., Kasl, S. V., Reynolds, C. F., III, Shear, K., Day, N., Beery, L. C., Newsom, J. T., and Jacobs, S. (1997). Traumatic grief as a rich factor for mental and physical morbidity. *Am. J. Psychiat.* **154**, 616–623.

Raphael, B. (1983). "The Anatomy of Bereavement." Basic Books, New York.

Surtees, P. G. (1995). In the shadow of adversity: The evolution and resolution of anxiety and depressive disorders. *Br. J. Psychiat.* **166**, 583–594.

Zisook, S. (Ed.) (1987). "Biopsychosocial Aspects of Bereavement." American Psychiatry Press, Washington, DC.

Zisook, S., and Shuchter, S. R. (1991). Depression through the first year after the death of a spouse. *Am. J. Psychiat.* **148**, 1346–1352.

Zisook, S., and Shuchter, S. R. (1993). Major depression associated with widowed. *Am. J. Geriat. Psychiat.* **1**, 316–326.

Zisook, S., and Shuchter, S. R. (1993). Uncomplicated bereavement. *J. Clin. Psychiat.* **54**, 365–372.

Beta-Adrenergic Blockers

Mark B. Hamner and George W. Arana

Medical University of South Carolina and VA Medical Center

GLOSSARY

adrenergic receptors Sites of action of norepinephrine or epinephrine in the central nervous system or in the peripheral sympathetic nervous system.

anxiety Apprehension of danger and dread accompanied by restlessness, tension, tachycardia, and dyspnea unattached to a clearly identifiable stimulus.

autoreceptors Sites on the nerve axon terminal which respond to the neuron's own neurotransmitter.

β-adrenergic antagonist A drug that prevents stimulation of the beta-adrenergic receptors of the nerves of the sympathetic nervous system and therefore decreases the activity of the heart and reduces blood pressure and may have other properties such as reduction of physiologic symptoms of anxiety.

norepinephrine A hormone, closely related to epinephrine and with similar actions, secreted by the medulla of the adrenal and also released as a neurotransmitter by sympathetic nerve endings and by axonal projections from the neurons in the locus ceruleus in the brain.

posttraumatic stress disorder An anxiety disorder developing in persons who have experienced a physically or emotionally traumatic event that is outside the range of normal human experience, such as combat, physical assault, rape, or disasters such as home fires.

stress Any factor that threatens the health of the body or has an adverse effect on its functioning, such as injury, disease, or worry.

I. INTRODUCTION AND DEFINITION

The β-adrenergic receptor antagonists have been used since the late 1950s for the treatment of hypertension, cardiac arrhythmias, angina, thyrotoxicosis, glaucoma, migraine, tremor, and, in psychiatry, anxiety, akathisia, and other syndromes. Development of propranolol, the prototype β-blocker, followed Ahlquist's hypothesis that the effects of catecholamines are mediated by α- and β-adrenergic receptors. β-Receptors are widely distributed in the vasculature and in neurons of the central and peripheral nervous system. The β-receptors are stimulated by norepinephrine. Noradrenergic systems are likely critical in mediating anxiety and stress response. Thus there has long been interest in β-blockers in psychiatry because of their pharmacologic effects in dampening behavioral or physiological responses to noradrenergic stimulation. Agents that have been most frequently studied in various psychiatric disorders include propranolol (Inderal), metoprolol (Lopressor), nadolol (Corgard), acebutolol (Sectral), labetalol (Normodyne Trandate), pindolol (Visken), and atenolol (Tenormin).

II. CHEMISTRY

The β-blockers share structural similarity with dichloroisoproteninol, first synthesized in the 1950s. However, dichloroisoproteninol is a partial agonist, an action which was thought to preclude its use clinically. The first pure antagonist, pronetholol, was associated with thymic tumors in mice. Propranolol, the next compound to be developed, became the prototype β-blocker. The chemical designation, molecular formula, and molecular weight of seven representative β-blockers are shown in Table I. The molecular structures are illustrated in Fig. 1.

III. PHARMACOLOGY

A. Pharmacodynamics

The β-blockers are competitive antagonists of norepinephrine and epinephrine β-adrenergic receptors. Epinephrine and norepinephrine are released as stress hormones from the adrenal medulla. Norepinephrine is also released from neurons in the peripheral sympathetic nervous system. These catecholamines are involved in cardiovascular regulation and stress responses. In the central nervous system (CNS), norepinephrine is produced by neurons in the brainstem tegmentum. The locus ceruleus is the primary noradrenergic nucleus, with widespread projections to the spinal cord, cortex, limbic regions, and cerebellum. Central nervous system noradrenergic systems are involved in emotional regulation, learning and memory, pain perception, control of blood pressure, and the neuroendocrine response to stressful stimuli.

The effects of norepinephrine in the brain are mediated by two classes of receptors: α- and β-receptors. These are further divided into α_1- and α_2- and β_1-, β_2-, and β_3-subtypes. Activation of α_1-receptors produces neuronal excitation partly linked to phosphoinositide activation. α_2-Receptors are inhibitory autoreceptors which decrease norepinephrine release. Consequently, α_2-receptor activation reduces both central and peripheral noradrenergic activity. α_2-Receptors are located in the central nervous system (CNS) on locus ceruleus noradrenergic neurons. Clonidine is an example of an α_2-agonist with antihypertensive properties due to reduction in noradrenergic activity. In contrast, yohimbine, an α_2-receptor antagonist, may release norepinephrine, resulting in

TABLE I
Basic Chemistry of Selected β-Blockers

β-Blocker	Chemical designation	Molecular formula	Molecular weight
Acebutolol	±N-[3-Acetyl-4-[2-hydroxy-3-1[1(methylethyl)amino]propoxy]pheryl]butanamide	$C_{18}H_{28}N_2O_4HCL$	327.9
Atenolol	4-[2'-hydroxy-3'-[(1-methylethyl)amino]propoxy]-	$C_{14}H_{22}N_2O_3$	266.00
Labetalol	5-[1-hydroxy-2-[(1-methyl-3-phenylpropyl)amino]ethyl]salicylamide conochloride	$C_{19}H_{24}N_2O_3$	364.9
Metoprolol	1-(isopropylamino)3-[p-(2-methoxy-ethyl)phenoxyl]-2-propanol (2:1) *dextro-tartrate salt*	$C_{34}H_{56}N_2O_{12}$	684.82
Nadolol	1-(*tert*-butylamino)-3-[(5,6,7,8-tetrahydro-*cis*-6,7-naphthyl)oxy]-2-propanol	$C_{17}H_{27}NO_4$	309.40
Pindolol	1-(indol-4-yloxy)-3-(isopropylamino)-2-propanol	$C_{14}H_{20}N_2O_3$	248.33
Propranolol	1-(isopropylamino)-3-(1-naphthyloxy)-2-propanol hydrochloride	$OCH_2CHOHCH_2$ $NHCH(CH_3)_2$	295.81

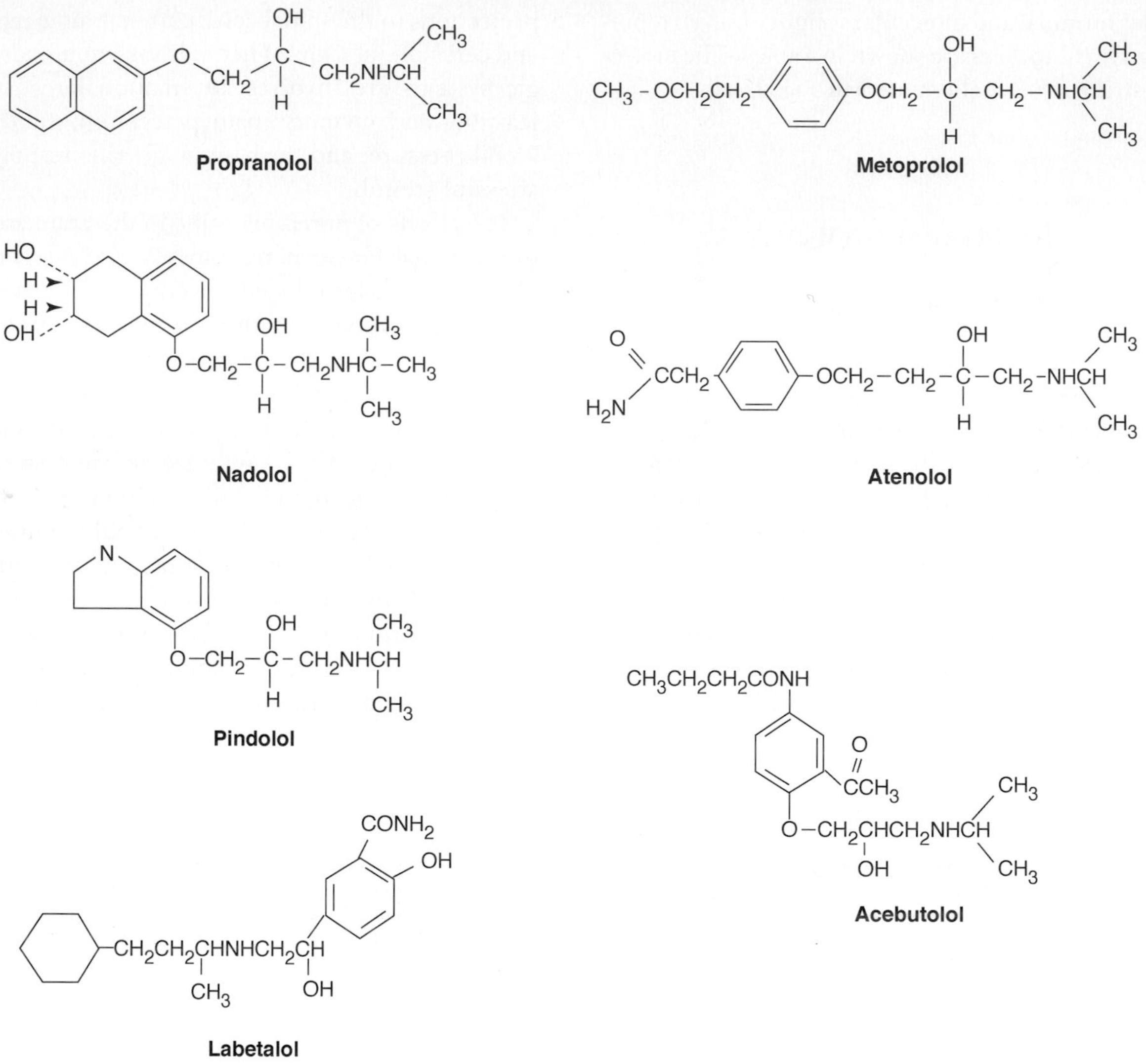

FIGURE 1   Molecular structures of the β-adrenergic receptor antagonists.

anxiety due to central noradrenergic activation and vasoconstriction in the periphery.

β-Receptors are widely distributed in both the CNS and the periphery. β_1-Receptors are localized in the cardiac sinoatrial and atrioventricular nodes and myocardium. β_2-Receptors are located in the pulmonary bronchi, the eye, peripheral vasculature, bladder and uterus, and liver (where they mediate glucose metabolism). β_2- and β_3-receptors are also involved in lipid metabolism.

The numerous β-blockers vary based on their relative pharmacokinetics, pharmacodynamics, and lipid solubility. Examples of these differences include relative β_1- versus β_2-antagonism, intrinsic sympathomimetic properties, α-adrenergic receptor affinity, lipid solubility, direct vasodilator properties, certain pharmacokinetic properties, and effects on other neurotransmitter systems (e.g., serotonergic properties). Lipid solubility is important because entry of drug into the brain is dependent on its ability to cross the blood–brain barrier, which is a highly lipid structure. The pharmacokinetics and pharmacodynamic and lipid solubility properties of the seven representative β-blockers are shown in Table II.

Propranolol is a nonselective β_1- and β_2-antagonist. Atenolol is a relatively selective β_1-antagonist.

t	Relative β-receptor selectivity	α_1-Antagonist properties	Sympathomimetic properties	Direct vasodilator activity	Metabolism	Excretion	Plasma half-life (hours)	Protein binding	Lipid solubility
utolol	$\beta_1 > \beta_2$	–	–	–	Hepatic	Renal 30–40%, nonrenal 50–60%	3–4	26%	Low
lol	$\beta_1 > \beta_2$	–	+	–	Minimal	Renal 50%, nonrenal 50%	6–7	6–16%	Low
talol	$\beta_1 = \beta_2$	+++	–	–	Hepatic	Renal 30–40%, nonrenal 50–60%	6–8	50%	Moderate
prolol	$\beta_1 > \beta_2$	–	–	–	Hepatic	Renal ≤5%, nonrenal ≥95%	3–7	12%	High
lol	$\beta_1 = \beta_2$	–	–	–	Minimal	Renal 65–70%, nonrenal 30–35%	14–24	30%	Low
lol	$\beta_1 > \beta_2$	–	–	–	Hepatic	Renal 35–40%, nonrenal 60–65%	3–4	40%	Moderate
anolol	$\beta_1 = \beta_2$	–	–	–	Hepatic	Renal 90–95%, nonrenal 5–10%	4	90%	High

Table II shows the relative β_1- versus β_2-affinities for the commonly used β-blockers.

B. Pharmacokinetics

Propranolol is almost completely absorbed following oral administration. Nadolol, atenolol, and metoprolol are partially absorbed. Nadolol, in contrast to the other listed agents, has a relatively long plasma half-life which allows once-daily dosing. Propranolol is avidly protein bound (90%) and undergoes extensive hepatic metabolism. In contrast, nadolol and atenolol are not as extensively metabolized and undergo renal excretion.

Nadolol and atenolol are the least lipophilic of the β-blockers and therefore have less penetrance of the blood–brain barrier, yielding more peripheral as opposed to central effects. In contrast, propranolol and metoprolol are more lipophilic and therefore have relatively greater central nervous system effects. Pindolol is of intermediate lipophilicity—this agent has been of recent interest as a possible antidepressant-potentiating drug due to its intrinsic sympathomimetic activity and serotonergic effects. All of the β-blockers are excreted in human milk and therefore should be used with caution in nursing mothers.

IV. ROLE IN STRESS, LEARNING, AND MEMORY

An extensive preclinical and clinical literature suggests that the CNS noradrenergic system is an important mediator in human as well as in animal response to stress. As such, β-blockers are of interest because of their ability to dampen noradrenergic hyperarousal. There is also emerging evidence to suggest that β-blockers may attenuate learned responses or memory subsequent to anxiety-provoking stimuli in both preclinical and human studies. These latter data suggests that β-adrenergic activation may be required for certain memories associated with emotional arousal.

Animal studies suggest that the β-adrenergic system is involved in enhancing memory associated with stress. In humans, administration of propranolol selectively impaired memory for an emotionally laden story but did not impair memory for a matched but emotionally neutral story. This latter observation suggests that emotional memory in humans may be affected by β-blockers. Of great interest for future study would be the utility of these agents in attenuating memories associated with acute stress in emotionally traumatized individuals and whether the long-term sequlae [e.g., posttraumatic stress disorder (PTSD)] could therefore be minimized. Another question for study is whether patients taking β-blockers chronically might have subtle impairment in memory for emotionally significant events.

V. THERAPEUTIC USE IN PSYCHIATRY

A. Anxiety Disorders

An extensive literature suggests that β-blockers may reduce autonomic symptoms in patients with panic disorder, generalized anxiety disorder, social phobia, and posttraumatic stress disorder. They may not be as useful for subjective or cognitive anxiety (e.g., fear, worry, dread, or intrusive memories).

1. Social Phobia

Social phobia may include anxiety in specific social situations [e.g., giving a speech (performance anxiety)] or be generalized to a number of different social situations (generalized social phobia). Social phobia can result in significant occupational as well as social difficulties. β-blockers are helpful in specific performance anxiety when used on an as-needed basis but do not appear helpful for generalized social phobia. In performance anxiety, the β-blockers reduce autonomic symptoms associated with the performance situation (e.g., tremor, tachycardia, and diaphoresis). A test dose of the β-blocker should be administered at home before the individual gives the actual performance to ensure tolerability. Customary dose ranges of β-blockers used in social phobia may be 10 to 40 mg daily for propranolol or 50 to 100 mg daily for atenolol. For specific or discrete performance anxiety, the dose should be given one to two hours before the activity.

Two studies have been consistent with the common clinical impression that β-blockers are not effective for generalized social phobia. A trial of atenolol versus placebo or phenelzine in social phobia showed better efficacy for phenelzine as compared with placebo or atenolol. Atenolol was comparable to placebo. Similarly, a placebo-controlled trial of behavior therapy versus atenolol or placebo in social phobia was consistent with superior efficacy for behavior therapy, with atenolol being comparable to placebo.

2. Posttraumatic Stress Disorder

Posttraumatic stress disorder is a chronic anxiety disorder that may occur after a severe life-threatening stress (e.g., combat or rape). Symptoms include reexperiencing the trauma via intrusive memories, "flashbacks" (sudden acting or feeling as if the trauma was recurring), nightmares, avoidance of reminders of the trauma, and symptoms of increased autonomic arousal (e.g., exaggerated startle, hypervigilance, and insomnia). Posttraumatic stress disorder can result in severe occupational and social impairment. A number of clinical studies have suggested norepi-

nephrine hyperactivity in PTSD. For example, exaggerated norepinephrine or norepinephrine metabolite responses may occur secondary to pharmacological, psychological, or physical stressors.

Despite the evidence for noradrenergic hyperarousal in PTSD, there has been suprisingly little study to date of β-Blockers in the disorder. Two of three clinical reports were promising in suggesting potential efficacy. One report suggested that propranolol may reduce intrusion and arousal symptoms in Vietnam veterans with PTSD. In contrast, propranolol was not efficacious in an open trial in Cambodian refugees with PTSD. Another report in children with PTSD who were victims of physical or sexual abuse suggested that propranolol at a dose of 2.5 mg/kg/day could reduce both reexperiencing and hyperarousal symptoms. Controlled studies are needed in both chronic as well as acutely traumatized populations. The potential role of β-blockers in modifying memory related to acute emotional trauma, as discussed in Section IV, is especially intriguing.

3. Panic Disorder and Generalized Anxiety Disorder

The β-blockers can reduce autonomic symptoms associated with generalized anxiety disorder (GAD) or panic attacks but do not appear effective for cognitive or psychological aspects of anxiety (e.g., worry, fear, or dread). This is likely because β_1 but not β_2 receptors are located in the brain and β_2 blockade does not appear to affect psychological anxiety. The psychological and cognitive symptoms respond better to benzodiazepines, buspirone, or antidepressants. There are also negative reports on the efficacy of β-blockers in panic and anxiety.

Doses of propranolol used in GAD range from 40 to 320 mg per day in two to four divided doses. A preliminary clinical report suggested that a long-acting β-blocker, betaxolol, in doses of 5 to 20 mg daily were effective in GAD patients. Betaxolol, a relatively β_1-selective agent, penetrates the CNS to a much greater extent than other long-half-life agents such as nadolol or atenolol.

B. Aggression and Violence

A number of case reports, clinical series, and controlled studies suggest that β-blockers can reduce aggression associated with chronic psychotic disorders, dementia, and head trauma. Behaviors such as impulsivity, largely attributable to orbitofrontal cortical dysfunction, are most likely to respond to β-blockers. This may reflect the extensive frontocortical noradrenergic afferent projections. Relatively lipophilic agents (e.g., propranolol, metoprolol, or nadolol) have been utilized because of their CNS effects. Doses of propranolol or equivalent β-blocker used in treating violent behaviors range from 40 to 520 mg/day in divided doses. Many of the clinical reports involve violent patients refractory to other medications (e.g., antipsychotics or mood stabilizers). For example, nadolol at a dose of 120 mg per day may be more effective than placebo as an adjunct to antipsychotics in aggressive schizophrenic patients. Elderly patients with dementia and associated aggression or agitation may improve with lower doses of propranolol (10–80 mg/day) than used in younger aggressive patients. An important confound in interpreting the controlled trials of β-blockers in violence is the episodic nature of aggressive behavior. Also, most studies of β-blockers in violence have involved drug combination rather than monotherapy. For patients who have not responded to other psychotropics, a β-Blocker trial may be indicated with close monitoring for adverse effects (e.g., hypotension), especially in light of the high doses for therapeutic effect.

C. Alcohol Withdrawal

Alcohol withdrawal in part involves autonomic instability mediated by significant CNS and peripheral noradrenergic activation. The β-blockers therefore can help reduce certain autonomic symptoms. Unlike the benzodiazepines, β-blockers are not cross-reactive with alcohol, so they are not likely to be effective as a monotherapy for alcohol detoxification. They may be effective as an adjunctive agent to benzodiazepines or other firstline withdrawal agents. A randomized, double-blind trial of atenolol as an adjunct to benzodiazepines found that administration of atenolol based on heart rate parameters improved vital signs and tremor more rapidly than placebo and resulted in less benzodiazepine use and decreased length of hospitalization. Atenolol was ad-

ministered based on the following heart rate parameters: less than 50 beats per min, no drug; 50 to 79, 50 mg once daily; greater than 80, 100 mg daily. Further study is needed of this potential adjunctive use of β-blockers.

D. Treatment of Medication Side Effects

1. Antipsychotic-Induced Akathisia

Akathisia is motor restlessness associated with antipsychotics, in particular the first-generation or traditional agents such as chlorpromazine (Thorazine), fluphenazine (Prolixin), or haloperidol (Haldol). Categorized as an extrapyramidal system side effect (EPS), akathisia can result in substantial noncompliance with antipsychotic medication. Unlike other EPSs such as parkinsonism, akathisia may respond better to β-blockers or benzodiazepines than antiparkinsonism medications such as benztropine (Cogentin). The EPSs in general are thought secondary to blockade of dopamine (D_2) receptors in the nigrostriatal pathway. The D_2 receptor blockade is common to all antipsychotic agents, although the new generation or "atypical" antipsychotics may have reduced akathisia incidence perhaps due to their higher ratio of serotonin-to-dopamine receptor blockade. Akathisia differs somewhat from other EPSs in that the mechanism may involve loss of tonic dopamine inhibition of the locus ceruleus due to D_2 receptor blockade. The resulting increased noradrenergic release from the locus ceruleus results in the subjective anxiety and motor restlessness characteristic of akathisia. This mechanism may explain the enhanced efficacy of β-blockers or benzodiazepines, both of which decrease noradrenergic function (β-blockers via postsynaptic receptor blockade and benzodiazepines via decreased locus ceruleus firing rate) as opposed to antiparkinson agents such as Cogentin or Symmetrel.

For treatment of akathisia, propranolol is given in doses of 10 to 30 mg three times daily (or similar doses of other β-blockers may be considered). β-Blockers may be given alone or in combination with benzodiazepines or antiparkinsonism medications. The new generation or "atypical" antipsychotics have less potential to induce akathisia.

2. *Lithium-Induced Tremor*

The low-amplitude action tremor characteristic of lithium may occur at therapeutic or even subtherapeutic doses. In fact, new-onset or worsening of the tremor (higher amplitude, increased frequency) may be a warning sign for lithium toxicity. A stable tremor at therapeutic doses can cause motor dysfunction (e.g., difficulty writing) and therefore may require treatment to enhance lithium tolerability as well as compliance. Lithium should be given at the lowest effective maintenance dose.

Analogous to their use in benign essential or familial tremor, β-blockers [e.g., propranolol in the daily dose range of 20 to 100 mg (in two or three divided doses)] can be effective. In addition to the patient being maintained on the lowest effective lithium dose, administration of a single nighttime dose of lithium (which may also reduce lithium-associated renal morphologic changes) and reduction of caffeine consumption can help minimize the tremor.

E. Antidepressant Potentiation

Several reports have suggested that the β-blocker pindolol, which increases forebrain neuronal release of serotonin in animals, may potentiate and possibly reduce the latency of response to selective serotonin reuptake inhibitor antidepressants. Pindolol is a lipophilic and relatively nonselective β_1- and β_2-blocker that also has intrinsic sympathomimetic properties. The serotonin augmentation is likely due to its selective serotonin 5-HT1A receptor effects. Whether β-blockers cause or exacerbate depression remains controversial.

VI. THERAPEUTIC USE IN MEDICAL DISORDERS

The β-blockers, originally developed for the treatment of hypertension and angina, had expanded roles in clinical medicine as antiarrhythmics, prevention of cardiovascular mortality after myocardial infarction, treatment of complications of cardiomyopathies, and various other noncardiovascular as well as psychiatric uses (Table III).

A. Hypertension

The β-blockers are effective as a monotherapy or in combination with other antihypertensives. They may reduce morbidity (e.g., left ventricular hypertrophy) and mortality associated with hypertension.

B. Angina Pectoris

The β-blockers are useful as monotherapy or in combination with certain antianginals including nitrates and some calcium channel blockers. The reduction in symptoms, especially in exertional angina, is attributable to decreased cardiac workload due to slower heart rate allowing longer diastolic filling time and improved coronary artery perfusion.

C. Cardiac Arrhythmias

The β-blockers are efficacious in controlling supraventricular tachyarrhythmias and reduction of ventricular arrhythmias. The mechanism includes decreased heart rate by reduced adrenergic stimulation of sinoatrial or atrioventricular node pacemakers and by cardiac membrane stabilization.

TABLE III
Doses of β-Blockers Used in Psychiatry

Generic name	Trade name	Usual starting dose (mg)	Usual maximum dosage (mg)
Acebutolol	Sectral	400 qd	600 bid
Atenolol	Tenormin	50 bid	75–150 bid
Labetalol	Normodyne, Trandate	100 bid	400–800 bid
Metoprolol	Lopressor	50 bid	75–150 bid
Nadolol	Corgard	40 qd	80–240 qd
Pindolol	Visken	5 bid	30 bid
Propranolol	Inderal	10–20 bid or tid	80–140 bid or tid

D. Congestive Heart Failure

The β-blockers may reduce symptoms and improve functional status in congestive heart failure patients (CHF) with careful administration. They may be indicated for patients who continue to be symptomatic with standard therapies. However, β-blockers may also precipitate congestive heart failure. Their use in dilated cardiomyopathy is based on the theory that they may attenuate the adverse effects on cardiac function of excessive adrenergic stimulation secondary to CHF.

E. Other Medical Uses

Additional medical diseases in which the reduction of excessive adrenergic stimulation with β-blockers may be useful include acute dissecting aortic aneurysm, dilation of the aorta associated with Marfan's syndrome (propranolol), pheochromocytoma, glaucoma, hyperthyroidism, tremors, migraine prophylaxis, and portal hypertension. Different β-blockers are used in these various indications depending on their relative pharmacologic effects (e.g., relative β_1- versus β_2-antagonism or degree of vasodilating properties).

VII. SAFETY AND TOLERABILITY

A. Side Effects

The β-blockers are generally well-tolerated. Side effects are listed in Table IV. The more frequent side effects are a consequence of the pharmacodynamic effects (i.e., β_1- and, if applicable, β_2-receptor blockade). These more common side effects include hypotension, dizziness, bradycardia, and sexual dysfunction. The β_1-selective agents have decreased risk of bronchospasm (asthma exacerbation) than those with β_2-effects. Cardiovascular side effects can be minimized by careful dose titration, monitoring pulse and blood pressure, and patient education. Patients with coronary heart disease can have exacerbation of angina pectoris with discontinuation (especially abrupt withdrawal) of β-blockers. There may also be rebound hypertension in patients with a history of hypertension and worsening of congestive

TABLE IV
Side Effects of β-Blockers

Cardiovascular
Hypotension
Bradycardia
Lightheadedness or dizziness
Congestive heart failure
(with predisposing cardiac disease)
Atrioventricular block
Exacerbation of intermittent claudication
Exacerbation of angina pectoris, primarily with abrupt or rapid discontinuation
Raynaud's phenomenon exacerbation
Respiratory
Dyspnea
Asthma (risk decreased with β-1 selective agents)
Metabolic
Hypoglycemia in diabetic patients
Gastrointestinal
Nausea
Diarrhea
Abdominal pain
Genitourinary
Sexual dysfunction (erectile dysfunction)
Urinary hesitancy
Neuropsychiatric
Fatigue
Lassitude
Dysphoria
Insomnia
Vivid nightmares
Depression (possible)
Psychosis (rare)

heart failure. Diabetic patients may have increased glucose dysregulation (especially hypoglycemia) and may have decreased autonomic symptoms of hypoglycemia (i.e., less subjective awareness of "warning" symptoms) due to β-blockade. The β_1-agents overall are safer to use in patients with bronchospasm, peripheral vascular disease, Raynaud's disease, and diabetes. Importantly, topically administered β-blockers (e.g., for glaucoma patients) can have systemic effects. Insomnia and nightmares are associated with sleep architecture changes from most β-blockers although some (e.g., betaxolol) may have fewer adverse sleep effects. Although fatigue or lassitude may occur in some individuals with chronic β-blocker administration clinical depression is probably rare as a causal association. Central nervous system effects may be minimized by using peripheral-acting (less lipophilic) agents.

B. Use in Pregnancy

The β-blockers should be used with caution in pregnant or nursing women and only if the benefit clearly outweighs potential risks. All of the β-blockers are pregnancy category C. Which means there is insufficient data in humans to demonstrate safety in pregnancy or to show definite relationship with defects. Embryotoxicity and neonatal toxicity have been observed in animals given β-blockers. There are no adequate studies in pregnant women. There are reports of intrauterine growth retardation and neonatal toxicity (bradycardia, hypoglycemia, and respiratory depression) in neonates of mothers treated with β-blockers. The safety and efficacy of β-blockers in children is not well established.

C. Drug Interactions

Of primary concern are pharmacodynamic interactions with other antihypertensive agents [e.g., clonidine or reserpine (postural hypotension)], atrioventricular block with other antiarrhythmics (e.g., digoxin or verapamil), or agents that have negative cardiac inotropic effects (e.g., diltiazem). There are several pharmacokinetic interactions: alcohol, cholestyramine, and aluminum hydroxide gels reduce absorption of β-blockers. Phenytoin, rifampin, and phenobarbital and smoking increase hepatic clearance of extensively metabolized β-blockers. Antipyrine, lidocaine, and theophylline have reduced clearance by β-blockers. Cimetidine decreases hepatic metabolism of propranolol and metoprolol.

VIII. SUMMARY

β-blockers have been among the most useful and effective class of compounds used for medical, neurological, and psychiatric conditions. Since their introduction to clinical medicine in the late 1960s, they have been effective in the treatment of cardiovascu-

lar, endocrine, neurological, and various psychiatric illnesses, especially anxiety disorders, drug-induced toxicities (i.e., akathisia and tremor), and, recently, potentiation of antidepressant effect in some treatment-resistant disorders.

The possible use of β-blockers to attenuate or reduce the impact of situational trauma or PTSD needs further exploration. Doctors are learning about the importance of the use of SSRIs to possibly improve the course of affective illness or advance episode frequency. In an analogous fashion, the potential role of β-blockers for prevention and prophylaxis of stress-related disorders needs further study.

See Also the Following Articles

Aggression; Anxiety; Catecholamines; Heart Disease/Attack; Hypertension; Panic Disorder and Agoraphobia

Bibliography

Allan, E. R., Alpert, M., Sison, C. E., Citrome, L., Laury, G., and Berman, I. (1996). Adjunctive nadolol in the treatment of acutely aggressive schizophrenic patients. *J. Clin. Psychiat.* **57**, 455–459.

Arana, G. W., and Santos, A. B. (1995). β-adrenergic receptor antagonists. *In* "Comprehensive Textbook of Psychiatry" (H. I. Kaplan, and B. J. Sadock, Eds.), 6th ed. Williams & Wilkins, Baltimore.

Bright, R. A., and Everitt, D. E. (1992). Beta-blockers and depression: Evidence against an association. *J. Am. Med. Assoc.* **267**, 1783–1787.

Cahill, L., Prins, B., Weber, M., and McGaugh, J. L. (1994). Beta-adrenergic activation and memory for emotional events. *Nature* **371**, 702–704.

Cooper, S. J., Kelly, C. B., McGilloway, S., and Gilliland, A. (1990). Beta 2-adrenoceptor antagonism in anxiety. *Eur. Neuropsychopharmacol.* **1**, 75–77.

Davidson, J. R. T. (1998). Pharmacotherapy of social anxiety disorder. *J. Clin. Psychiat.* **59**(Suppl. 17), 47–51.

Famularo, R., Kinscherff, R., and Fenton, T. (1988). Propranolol treatment for childhood post-traumatic stress disorder, acute type: A pilot study. *Am. J. Dis. Child.* **142**, 1244–1247.

Hamner, M. B., Diamond, B. I., and Hitri, A. (1994). Plasma norepinephrine and MHPG responses to exercise stress in PTSD. *In* "Catecholamine Function in Post-Traumatic Stress Disorder: Emerging Concepts" (M. M. Murburg, Ed.). American Psychiatric Press, Washington, DC.

Kinzie, J. D. (1989). Therapeutic approaches to traumatized Cambodian refugees. *J. Trauma Stress* **2**, 75–91.

Kolb, L. C., Burris, B. C., and Griffiths, S. (1984). Propranolol and clonidine in the treatment of post traumatic stress disorders of war. *In* "Post Traumatic Stress Disorder: Psychological and Biological Sequlae" (B. A. van der Kolk, Ed.). American Psychiatric Press, Washington, DC.

Kraus, M. L., Gottlieb, L. D., Horwitz, R. I., and Anscher, M. (1985). Randomized clinical trial of atenolol in patients with alcohol withdrawal. *N. Engl. J. Med.* **313,** 905.

Liebowitz, M. R., Schneier, F., Campeas, R., *et al.* (1992). Phenelzine vs. Atenolol in social phobia: A placebo-controlled comparison. *Arch. Gen. Psychiat.* **49,** 290–300.

McFall, M. E., Murburg, M. M., Ko, G. N., and Ueith, R. C. (1990). Autonomic response to stress in Vietnam combat veterans with post-traumatic stress disorder. *Biol. Psychiat.* **27,** 1165–1175

Ratey, S. J., Sorgi, P., O'Driscoll, G. A., *et al.* (1992). Nadolol to treat aggression and psychiatric symptomatology in chronic psychiatric inpatients: A double-blind, placebo-controlled study. *J. Clin. Psychiat.* **53,** 41–46.

Southwick, S. M., Krystal, J. H., Morgan, A. C., *et al.* (1993). Abnormal noradrenergic function in posttraumatic stress disorder. *Arch. Gen. Psychiat.* **50,** 266–274.

Tome, M. B., Isaac, M. T., Harte, R., and Holland, C. (1997). Paroxetine and pindolol: A randomized trial of serotonergic autoreceptor blockade in the reduction of antidepressant latency. *Int. Clin. Psychopharmacol.* **12,** 81–89.

Turner, S. M., Beidel, D. C., and Jacob, R. G. (1994). Social phobia: A comparison of behavior therapy and atenolol. *J. Consult. Clin. Psychol.* **62,** 350–358.

Beta-Endorphin

Jardena J. Puder and Sharon L. Wardlaw

Columbia University College of Physicians & Surgeons

I. Structure, Synthesis, and Localization
II. β-Endorphin and Neuroendocrine Responses
III. β-Endorphin and Stress-Induced Analgesia
IV. β-Endorphin and Cardiovascular and Other Responses

GLOSSARY

adrenocorticotropin (ACTH) The pituitary hormone which regulates adrenal corticosteroid synthesis and release. Adrenocorticotropin, like β-endorphin, is derived from pro-opiomelanocortin.

endogenous opioid peptides Peptides with morphinelike actions which are synthesized in the brain and in peripheral tissues.

endorphins A general term which refers to all of the endogenous opioid peptides. β-endorphin refers to a specific peptide.

naloxone A compound which binds to opiate receptors and blocks the effects of morphine and the endogenous opioid peptides.

proopiomelanocortin The larger precursor protein from which β-endorphin is derived.

β- Endorphin is one of the endogenous opioid peptides which is synthesized primarily in the pituitary gland and in the brain. Stress stimulates the release of β-endorphin in both the pituitary and the brain. During times of stress, β-endorphin and the other endogenous opioid peptides have been implicated in analgesia and in neuroendocrine regulation, including the suppression of reproductive function. These peptides also play a role in autonomic regulation, modulation of cardiovascular responses and cerebral blood flow, and in the regulation of behavior and immune function.

I. STRUCTURE, SYNTHESIS, AND LOCALIZATION

β-Endorphin is a 31-amino-acid peptide which is derived from the larger molecular weight precursor protein proopiomelanocortin (POMC). β-Endorphin is one of the three major classes of endogenous opioid peptides. The other two classes are comprised of the enkephalins and the dynorphins, which are derived from separate precursor proteins. Proopiomelanocortin is synthesized independently in the anterior and intermediate lobes of the pituitary gland, in the brain, and in several peripheral tissues including the gastrointestinal tract, reproductive tract, the placenta, and in cells of the immune system. The posttranslational processing of POMC is tissue specific and results in the production of peptides of very different biological activities. In the anterior pituitary, POMC is processed predominantly to ACTH and β-lipotropin (β-LPH) but some β-endorphin is also produced. Adrenocorticotropin is secreted from the pituitary into the peripheral circulation and is critical for the maintenance of adrenocortical function and cortisol secretion. β-Endorphin is also secreted in parallel with ACTH. In the brain, ACTH and β-LPH are further processed to yield α-melanocyte-stimulating hormone and β-endorphin. The regulation of POMC gene expression and peptide release is also tissue specific but under conditions of stress, β-endorphin is released from both the pituitary and the brain. The hypothalamic releasing factor, corticotropin releasing hormone (CRH), which plays a key role in coordinating the organism's response to stress, has been shown to stimulate pituitary and brain β-endorphin. β-Endorphin exerts its effects by binding to specific opioid receptors, particularly the μ- and δ-receptors, which have been recently cloned and localized throughout the brain.

β-Endorphin is released from the anterior pituitary into the peripheral circulation in parallel with ACTH in response to a variety of stresses. Numerous studies have documented parallel increases in peripheral blood levels of ACTH and β-endorphin in response to exercise. This appears to be related to the intensity and duration of the exercise. A number of correlations between β-endorphin levels in blood and central nervous system or cardiovascular responses during stress have been reported. One must be cautious, however, in attributing a causal relationship for circulating β-endorphin in many of these cases because in many instances,

brain β-endorphin may also be stimulated at the same time. In addition, peripherally released β-endorphin does not readily cross the blood–brain barrier. In the brain, β-endorphin is synthesized in only two regions, the arcuate nucleus of the hypothalamus and the nucleus of the solitary tract in the brain stem, but β-endorphin fibers project widely to many regions throughout the brain.

II. β-ENDORPHIN AND NEUROENDOCRINE RESPONSES

Endogenous opioid peptides have multiple effects on pituitary function. Effects on gonadotropin (LH and FSH), prolactin, ACTH, vasopressin, and oxytocin release have all been demonstrated. There is evidence for a specific role for β-endorphin during stress with respect to the regulation of LH and the hypothalamic-pituitary-gonadal (HPG) axis and of ACTH and the hypothalamic-pituitary-adrenal (HPA) axis. Stress is known to impair reproductive function in many species. Stress has been shown to suppress the release of LH from the pituitary with subsequent suppression of ovarian and testicular function. Corticotropin releasing hormone, which is released from the hypothalamus during stress, has been shown to cause a similar suppression of the HPG axis. There is convincing evidence that the suppressive effects of stress and CRH on the HPG axis are mediated by β-endorphin. Thus both CRH and β-endorphin are important in suppressing reproductive function during times of stress. Exogenous and endogenous opioids also have well-documented effects on the HPA axis. There are some differences, however, depending on the dose and duration of treatment and the species studied. In the human, morphine and β-endorphin have been shown to suppress ACTH and cortisol release in normal subjects and to blunt the HPA response to surgical stress. β-Endorphin has been shown to suppress CRH release from the hypothalamus *in vitro* and to suppress CRH release into hypophyseal portal blood *in vivo*. Conversely, opioid antagonism has been reported to stimulate the HPA axis and to enhance the HPA response to stress. Thus β-endorphin may be important in limiting the HPA response under conditions of stress.

III. β-ENDORPHIN AND STRESS-INDUCED ANALGESIA

It has long been known that pain perception is affected by stress. Electrical stimulation of specific brain regions has been shown to induce analgesia that was blocked by treatment with naloxone and other opioid antagonists, implying that this analgesia was mediated by the release of endogenous opioids. Certain forms of stress-induced analgesia are also blocked by naloxone. It is now clear that stress-induced analgesia is mediated by both opioid and nonopioid pathways. There is considerable pharmacological and neuroanatomic evidence to implicate β-endorphin as a mediator of stress-induced analgesia. Recently a genetic approach has been used to generate mice that are unable to synthesize β-endorphin. These transgenic mice do not exhibit the naloxone-reversible analgesia normally seen after a mild swim stress. These studies provide convincing evidence that β-endorphin plays an important role in stress-induced analgesia.

IV. β-ENDORPHIN AND CARDIOVASCULAR AND OTHER RESPONSES

The endogenous opioid peptides are localized to regions within the brain that are important in controlling the autonomic nervous system and cardiovascular responses. β-Endorphin is synthesized in the nucleus of the solitary tract in the medulla, an area important in cardiovascular regulation. The effects of opioids on cardiovascular function are complex and depend on the type of opioid injected, the site of injection, and whether the animal is anesthetized or stressed. Although discrepancies exist, it appears that in general, opioids diminish stress-induced cardiovascular effects. Opioid mech-

anisms appear to facilitate parasympathetic and to inhibit sympathetic nervous system reactivity during stress. Endogenous opioid peptides are also important in regulating cerebral blood flow especially during periods of hypoxia. β-Endorphin, in particular, has been shown to regulate hypothalamic blood flow.

Both stress and opioids have suppressive effects on immune function. Naloxone has also been shown to block stress-induced immune suppression, indicating a role for endogenous opioids in this process. β-Endorphin is produced by cells of the immune system and may have local paracrine effects on immune function. Circulating, pituitary-derived β-endorphin may also affect immune function. Finally, endogenous opioids may affect the psychological as well as the physiological adaptations to stress.

See Also the Following Articles

Adrenocorticotropic Hormone; Gonadotropin Secretion, Effects of Stress on; Pro-opiomelanocortin

Bibliography

Akil, H., Watson, S. J., Young, E., Lewis, M. E., Khachaturian, H., and Walker, M. (1984). Endogenous Opioids: Biology and function. *Ann. Rev. Neurosci.* 7, 223–255.

Benyó, Z., and Wahl, M. (1996). Opiate receptor-mediated mechanism in the regulation of cerebral blood flow. *Cerebrovasc. Brain Metab. Rev.* 8, 326–357.

Castro, M. G., and Morrison, E. (1997). Post-translational processing of proopiomelanocortin in the pituitary and in the brain. *Crit. Rev. Neurobiol.* 11, 35–57.

Ferin, M. (1993). Neuropeptides, the stress response, and the hypothalamo-pituitary-gonadal axis in the female rhesus monkey. *Ann. N. Y. Acad. Sci.* 697, 106–116.

Ferin, M., Van Vugt, D., and Wardlaw, S. L. (1984). The hypothalamic control of the menstrual cycle and the role of endogenous opioid peptides. *Recent Prog. Horm. Res.* 40, 441–485.

Goldfarb, A. H., and Jamurtas, A. Z. (1997). β-Endorphin response to exercise. *Sports Med.* 24, 8–16.

Mansour, A., Fox, C. A., Akil, H., and Watson S. J. (1995).

Opioid-receptor mRNA expression in the rat CNS: Anatomical and functional implications. *Trends Neurosci.* **18,** 22–29.

McCubbin, J. A. (1993). Stress and endogenous opioids: Behavioral and circulatory interactions. *Biol. Psychol.* **35,** 91–122.

Pechnik, R. N. (1993). Effects of opioids on the hypothalamo-pituitary-adrenal axis. *Annu. Rev. Pharmacol. Toxicol.* **32,** 353–382.

Rubinstein, M., Mogil, J. S., Japón, M., Chan, E. C., Allen, R. G., and Low, M. (1996). Absence of opioid stress-induced analgesia in mice lacking β-endorphin by site-directed mutagenesis. *Proc. Natl. Acad. Sci. USA* **93,** 3995–4000.

Blacks, Stress in

Wesley E. Profit
Consulting Psychologist,
Brockton, Massachusetts

Itsuko Mino
Harvard University

Chester M. Pierce
Harvard University

I. The Structure of Stress in Blacks
II. The Dynamics of Stress
III. Practical Considerations
IV. Special Problems

GLOSSARY

blacks People who, by and large, are perceived to have had ancestors brought to the New World as slaves.

discrimination A negating selection and differential comparison not based on merit.

prejudice An injurious and intolerant preconceived judgement.

racism Intentional or unintentional bias directed at individuals or groups based upon notions of the superiority or inferiority of skin color.

stress In minority communities, stress occurs when an individual or group's resources are overextended, even to the point of causing paralysis, apprehension, disintegration, and ineffectiveness from perceived and/or actual duress and assaults from the majority community.

If the phrase "the good life" connotes, at least anecdotally, the idea of a life free from distressful events and, perhaps, one filled with *eu*stressful experiences, then on every measure or index of the elements for such a life, African Americans (Blacks) fall short by comparison to Americans of European ancestry. Blacks make less money, live in poorer housing, attend worse schools, have greater difficulty obtaining access to adequate health care, survive on a poorer diet, and die sooner. Further, Blacks are more likely to suffer from stress-related diseases, such as hypertension and heart disease. Blacks more often engage in self-destructive behaviors such as alcoholism, drug abuse, and unsafe sex. They spend more time in the criminal justice system, serving sentence or on probation or on parole. While having fewer employment opportunities and benefits, they have higher likelihood of losing a job. On the whole, Blacks are more likely to inhabit mundane stressful environments such as ghettoes, penal facilities, and public, as opposed to private, institutions for medical and mental health care. Thus Blacks live closer to the edge of poverty, are more vulnerable to repetitive life minidisasters, and generally have a tougher time making ends meet and keeping their families intact. They serve as the biopsychosocial barometer and prototype for stress in any minority group in the United States. Blacks who live the "good life" are therefore the exception not the rule, the unusual not the average, and the few not the many. For these reasons Blacks as a group have a more stressful existence.

I. THE STRUCTURE OF STRESS IN BLACKS

In the United States Blacks as a group always have been burdened by the stigma of skin color. The notion of the superiority of skin color has ensured this burden in spite of any class attributes the Black may possess such as financial status, educational attainment, or vocational expertise. Forcibly stripped of their own customs, language, religion, and history, slaves were left with little of their own traditions. Yet, of all groups in the country, Blacks were deemed the most unsuitable to be assimilated. It has been only in the most recent times that legal restraints against racial admixture have been relaxed (despite the long history of intermixing, including White masters impregnating Black females in order to produce sons and daughters who became their fathers' slaves). To this day issues around Black–White racial admixture provoke much of the tension Blacks and Whites have in regard to each other. This is the matrix for a good deal of the racial discord which manifests itself in verbalizations about the appropriate speed, amount, and quality of racial integration or assimilation. The intergroup struggle is over "the place" that Blacks should occupy.

A. Who Is Black?

Defining a Black is no small problem in the United States. Due to complicated historical, legal, and social factors, Blacks vary in phenotype from porcelain white to jet black. A Black may be defined in terms of how he or she is perceived—thus many Blacks in the eye of all beholders are "White." Or one is defined by what one claims or perceives oneself to be—thus many ethnic Latinos are Black. Likewise Blacks are defined by whether they accept and/or are accepted for membership in a subgroup—some Cape Verdeans might be labeled Black. Nowadays there are numerous Black immigrant groups which are African American including African Caribbeans, African Europeans, and Africans. Doubtlessly many people who

might be assigned as Blacks by fellow citizens are in fact classified in some other federal category, e.g., a Samoan, who is officially a Pacific Islander.

No matter how defined, a person called Black has a psychological reality that has added common stress. Basically, skin color concerns limit and shape the person's hopes, fears, doubts, and desires. For Blacks these concerns seem ubiquitous, omnipresent, and never-ending. One can never get rid of the skin color badge, which tells the general population that this person may be a proper subject to be guided, controlled, trivialized. Often such a subject is almost automatically assumed to be a person who should show deference and gratitude. Many Blacks believe that generally Whites don't believe that Blacks deserve, desire, or need the same comforts as themselves. Blacks are not expected to have lofty ambitions or unusually creative ideas. These kinds of opinions lead to deleterious stereotypes such as considering the Blacks lazy, violent, sexual, amoral, and so on. Intergroup stress is born from stereotypes which permit and justify discrimination and prejudice. What to do with Blacks has confounded and confused the practice of American democracy (Myrdal, G., 1944, *An American Dilemma,* Harper and Row, New York). Even so there is an unbroken history which chronicles the political and ethical forces which preach incessantly for all disciplines to find ways to help reduce American intergroup stress. The thrust of these studies speaks to the nature of racism.

B. The Nature of Racism

Racism operates to ensure advantage for Whites and disadvantage for Blacks in almost every sphere of life. This advantage has been cataloged in many ways. For instance, in the top 1000 industrial and top 500 service firms, 96% of senior officials are White. For years the statistic has held that Whites need less education to make more money than Blacks. Likewise, college-educated Blacks will earn in a lifetime only about two thirds of what a college-educated White will earn. Health disparities between Blacks and Whites persist (Dressler, W. W., 1993, Health in the African American community: Accounting for health inequalities, *Med. Anthropol. Q.*

7, 325–345). The survival gap between Blacks and Whites actually widened in the 1990s for heart disease, cancer, AIDS, and infant mortality. Since introduction of newer drugs in 1995, Whites have had a 32% decrease in AIDS related deaths. During this same time African Americans experienced only a 13% drop (Center for Disease Control, September 19, 1997, Morbidity and Mortality Weekly Report, 46). It is thought that treatment regimes are not widely available for Blacks. In addition, racism contributes to the paucity of health expertise in the Black community. For instance, White males, 32% of the U.S. population, constitute 67% of the U.S. physician population (Nickens, H. W., and Cohen, J. J., 1996, An affirmative action, *J. Am. Med. Assoc.* **275**, 572–574).

The stress that Blacks as a group suffer in the United States relates to the practice of racism, which results in Blacks being dehumanized by the dominant group in order that Blacks should lack the same civil rights and societal opportunities and benefits presented to Whites. Although individual experiences, assets, and even random chance events influence and modify how an individual Black fares in the United States, all must respond to the pressure of being a member of a group designated as disenfranchised and inferior.

The nature of racism obliges Blacks as individuals and as a group to answer and act upon, regularly, four interrelated ultra questions or ultra dilemmas. How these ultra questions are negotiated constitutes both what causes and what relieves stress for Blacks in the United States.

Here are the questions: In any heteroracial contact in the United States

(1) How does a Black know when, where, and how to resist an oppression versus when, where, and how to accommodate to the oppression?

(2) How does a Black know and differentiate when a White acts and speaks as an individual versus as a member of a domineering, if not hostile, collective?

(3) How does a Black differentiate, where there is some degree of acceptance, between being tolerated versus being welcomed?

(4) Is it possible for both the White oppressor and the Black oppressed to be mentally healthy at the same time?

Resolving these ultra questions, which insist upon being answered and must be resolved, even though they can't or won't be solved, constitutes the everyday task of any Black–White interaction. Due to the nature of racism in the United States, almost always the task is fraught with stress. As an example, the Index of Race Related Stress (IRRS) is a test of encounters with racism, which discriminates Blacks from others (Utsey, S. O., and Ponterotto, J. G., October 1996, Development and validation of the Index of Race Related Stress (IRRS), *J. Counsel. Psychol.* **43**, 490–501). The specific items on that test describe commonplace interactions in which there is intrinsic stress.

II. THE DYNAMICS OF STRESS

Unrelenting and routine messages of being unwanted and different keeps the perception of a threatened, tenuous existence in the minds of Blacks, who labor under huge handicaps of crippling inequities. On the other hand, few Whites, even those who could cite remarkable racial progress, would perceive the fragility and uncertainty that many Blacks face each day. For instance, non-Whites would be aghast at the time and energy mobilized by Blacks around race considerations to interact in and monitor even such a routine encounter as saying "good morning" to a colleague.

A. Perceptual Differences

A major consideration in intergroup stress is how participants obtain and sustain pride. From the Black perspective White pride depends heavily on assurances of White superiority no matter what the issue. Functionally, therefore, the goal for Whites is to be able to impress their will on Blacks. For Blacks, operationally, pride depends on being treated fairly. Functionally, therefore, the goal for Blacks is to protect self-esteem and self-confidence. When unable to impress their will on Blacks, White wrath and frustration is characterized by a sense of perplexity. When unable to garner esteem and confidence, Black wrath and frustration is characterized by a sense of unfairness. Critical in these concerns is that Blacks, unlike Whites, know that they are much more likely to receive quick and harsh sanctions when they are overly aggressive toward the other group.

In negotiating across races Blacks are distressed by perceiving that there has been "too little and too late" from the dominating group. Whites may perceive in the same negotiation that there has been "too much and too soon" for the dominated group. The tension developed in this dynamic expresses racial hostility and counterhostility.

In terms of intergroup stress, Black strategy recognizes the anger and despair from having been exploited and made expendable across American history. Also there is awareness that during this history Blacks have been shabbily betrayed and subjected, hypocritically, to value ideals said to be for everyone but emphatically closed to them, e.g., "all men are created equal." At the same time there is sensitivity about the dread that Whites may have about losing complete control or losing the ability to contain Blacks. This dread, from the Black perspective, includes, improbably, fearsome retaliatory violence from Blacks if conditions alter. It is for these reasons that White–Black interactions may be entered into with stressful elements of mutual distrust, caution, and tentativeness.

B. Continuing Traumatic Stress

The perception by many Blacks that the White collective is unrelenting in devising means to disparage, discourage, and disrespect Blacks keeps them always mobilized against possible assaults. This required constancy of mobilization against possible assault may contribute, in ways as yet understudied, to negative health outcomes for Blacks. Individual Blacks cope with this requirement, at various times and situations, in various ways. These coping methods range from stances of "healthy paranoia" to bland denial. Through American history Black children have been taught at home, in their communities, and in their churches that failure to be vigilant against White capriciousness can result in fatality.

Therefore, it is not unusual in all-Black gatherings for members to focus on what can't be done rather than on what can be done. This is a feature of defensive thinking which has had survival value for Blacks in the United States even as it may have restricted or diluted and delayed useful actions. Defensive thinking results from the many offensive mechanisms Whites use in their interaction with Blacks. Blacks must reply, respond, and accommodate to actions by Whites. These actions are offensive in the sense that they were initiated and controlled by White preferences and also frequently they are offensive in terms of making Blacks feel reduced.

Defensive thinking in intergroup considerations is rapid, not specifically focused (for offenses must be anticipated at all times and places), less precise (for survival depends on rapid adaptation to particular assaults which arise in different ways at different times and places), and less focused (for the defender must be wary of multiple attacks along a wide spectrum of possibilities). Defensive thinking concerns itself therefore with multiple possibilities and the end result of such possibilities. The offender on the other hand may dwell much more on specific possibilities and the process toward achievement of these. The dynamic of defensive and offensive thinking causes, promotes, and sustains intergroup stress. Since usually the consequences of such interaction are more significant for Blacks, they receive a greater burden of stress.

Everyone may agree that offensive mechanisms serve the strategy of curbing and controlling how the defender can move about and use time and space. What may be more contested is the notion that at least in interpersonal relations, the strategy also controls and monopolizes the defender's energy. Few Whites may appreciate the enormous energy requirements that are demanded by Blacks in even casual and cordial social intercourse. This too is an understudied area which may contribute greatly to social and health outcomes in Blacks.

The chief energy demand on Blacks is how to recognize, evaluate, anticipate, and dispose of race-inspired microaggressions. These are automatic, subtle, stunning, seemingly innocuous messages, often nonverbal, which devaluate the Black; e.g., a Black man and White man enter an elevator whereupon the single White female passenger clutches her handbag as she moves as close as possible to the White man. Microaggressions, the major and inescapable expression of racism in the United States, take a cumulative toll on Black individuals. As such they enter into the formation of Black group stress. What may be more important is that these cumulative, minor but incessant put-downs often remain as psychopollutants in the social environment. Their lingering intractability is a major contributor to the continuing traumatic stress suffered by Blacks as individuals and as a group.

III. PRACTICAL CONSIDERATIONS

For Blacks to live with effectiveness, efficiency, and peace with other groups in the United States means a reduction in their stress and despair. It is in the interest of the whole community for the sake of social stability and enhancement that such a reduction occurs.

Blacks, like all groups under stress, need to be prepared for the unknown future and able to act autonomously in the midst of pressure. They must maintain the hope that they can sustain and the faith that they will sustain.

A. Promoting Autonomy

In-group attention and behavior persuades and influences out-group behavior. As an in-group Blacks need more dedicated efforts at promoting autonomy to banish dependency. These efforts are largely educative and can be made through vehicles controlled by the Black subculture. The thrust of the efforts is directed toward increasing confidence, esteem, and dignity with the goal of sustaining hope and faith. Of course, the mainstream culture also must see it in its own interest to participate in and encourage such initiatives.

Given the nature of racism and the dynamics of White–Black stress, Blacks, as has been the case through history, must press their own cause. They welcome and need allies to help them in this effort. Traditionally such allies have seen racial progress as in their own interest as well as ethically correct.

Clear, honest, systematic communication serves as the lubricant for intergroup progress. However, even when there is a modicum of mutual trust and respect the lubricant may fail. Often the failure is because of the baffling issue on each side over who speaks for which segments of the group and with what degree of accuracy and authenticity.

People are stressed when their sources of dependency gratification are threatened or removed. Blacks operate with much less control of dependency sources. To escape from perceived and actual dependency, Blacks with their allies have fought fiercely for political empowerment (Gilliam, F. D., Jr., and Kaufman, K. July 1998, Is there an empowerment life cycle?: Long-term Black empowerment and its influence on voter participation, Urban Aff. Rev. 33, 741–766). The empowerment which has been won was bought at great cost by the alliance chiefly of Black and White activists, idealists, and pragmatists. The important battle sites of American racism have been social and economic actions on behalf of Blacks to gain equal civil rights, equal employment, and housing and educational opportunities. The struggles at these sites will continue if there is to be intergroup harmony.

Forces in the mainstream culture attempt to undercut Black confidence in competing in this struggle. The obligation of Blacks as a group is to emphasize the importance and the potential for success in continuing this struggle. This constitutes using historical awareness as a cultural vehicle to persist, optimistically, even when evidence points out starkly that Blacks are neither wanted nor needed.

B. Historical Awareness

The Black culture's task in historical awareness is to maintain pride that Blacks have survived despite unspeakable obstacles, to increase the repertoire of survival mechanisms, and to indicate avenues of hope. Accomplishing the task means that Blacks and probably all others must be educated in a more dedicated and favorable but true way about Black survival. Such educative efforts would alter the image of Blacks in the eyes of themselves and of others. Just a wider knowledge of Blacks' efforts at resistance, including rebellions and escapes, would be inspirational. A cursory focus on survival methods, used and continued from slavery times, through the emancipation era, Jim Crow times, and the Civil Rights revolution would be instructive. Discussion in formal and informal education settings about the development and pros and cons of such survival mechanisms as crafty concealment (Br'er Rabbit stories), passive aggression (observation of slow-moving slaves on the plantation), constant intelligence gathering (to anticipate and dilute abuse), and modest ambitions (to remain in reasonable good graces with the captor) would illuminate much about the evolution of Black Americans, their stereotypes, and their resiliency and adaptation under stress.

Functionally, the more people, but especially Blacks, know about and preserve the knowledge of everyday Black heroism as well as extraordinary heroism, the easier it will be to accomplish the aims of the task of historical awareness. At the same time such education would provide guidelines and suggestions about how individuals can succeed in extreme situations. For instance, Black youths would understand the paramount necessity of foreknowledge and preparation for the assaults, hostility, and travail that await them. Many Blacks will verbalize astonishing complacency about their treatment in the United States. They express contentment and even satisfaction with the status quo. Despite presentations in the media, the problem of Black America is not that it is too aggressive. The problem may be that Black America, generally, is too passive. As a legacy of slavery many Blacks, in order to survive, overuse and/or use indiscriminately denial of the awfulness of racism.

IV. SPECIAL PROBLEMS

This raises the issue of special problems which are important to Blacks in the quest to attenuate and eliminate racial duress. Many problems could be listed. All have roots and relevance in the task of historical awareness. All address the tensions from perceptual differences between Blacks and Whites as well as between Blacks themselves. These tensions involve the esteem in which Blacks should be held and the quality and quantity of Black expectations

and hopes. Some problems are special because they may demand serious rethinking or shift in focus by Blacks as they interact with Whites. Among such problems are the need for Blacks to dwell more on general contributions to the society, the need for Blacks to be more conscious of leadership–followership dynamics, and the need to be more discriminating in forgiving White transgressions.

Black survival has depended on almost exclusive focus on only Black–White contests. The skill and tenacity by Blacks on Black–White issues has been a huge reason for what has been accomplished in civil rights for themselves and by irradiation for other minority groups, females, the disabled, homosexuals, and so on.

However it has become routine for Blacks and others to consider contributions, notions, and conceptualizations in other areas to be the business of non-Blacks. Even with the burgeoning opportunities of today, Blacks are still considered atypical if not unsuited for positions previously held only by Whites. The Blacks' reluctance to venture beyond the boundaries of race-related activities abbreviates the general society. Sadly, the desire by Whites to make Blacks unable and unwelcomed to venture past rigid traditional boundaries insures that the general society is bereft of the progress that would result if the entire society participated in matters of general concern. There will always be group stress as long as most Blacks and Whites, for instance, still consider it remarkable that Blacks do relatively commonplace things as fly commercial airlines, conduct cancer research, or design bridges. For Blacks to venture out requires special effort by Blacks to prepare its youth for engagement in the world, not merely engagement with Whites for the direct purpose of surviving in the White world. This presupposes a hope that Whites will find it in the interest of the total society to accept and nurture such adventures.

Intimately related to this problem of modest ambition is the problem of suspicion of success. This too is a legacy born perhaps of the need for slaves not to endanger themselves or their fellows by being too distinctive and individualistic. Such a psychology combined with complicated feelings of low esteem, projected doubt, and envy may help account for the problems of Blacks in cooperating and coordinating as followers to an evolving leader. The oft-repeated lament among Blacks about being pulled down if one is on top or forgetting those at the bottom when one is on top needs to be heard and corrected. Since Whites can capitalize on and manipulate this dynamic, intergroup stress continues often unabated by not having to contend with the most effective Black leadership.

To survive in the new world Blacks not only had to use massive denial of their oppression but also had to forgive their oppressors. It can be argued that had they at any point, say in Emancipation times, expressed their rage and hostility fully, they would have been annihilated. The weight of history shows that Blacks, even today, are passive, if not docile, about their victimization. The media, which they don't control, probably overplays their violent nature. In fact most of their violence is inner directed. The overstatement by Whites may be the result of reprisal fears, knowing well that such retaliation might be justified and that many Whites believe that they themselves would never tolerate such degradation. This promotes stress for Whites. Similarly, the general passivity and capacity to excuse imposes a burden of stress on Blacks. This is because despite effective denial, there remains conscious awareness that forgiveness comes at the loss of accountability for righteous shame and anger following great hurt. As in all the listed problems, there is undoubted merit as well as much humaneness in the way Blacks have approached them in the past. Such aspects should be kept. What would aid in stress reduction for Blacks and for Blacks interacting with other groups is to marry such aspects to some system of accountability and responsibility when forgiveness is granted. The system should help curb the possible reduction in self-image that results from foregoing all aggression. In fact such conditions would enhance self-image since those who were forgiven would see the forgivers as strong, assertive, and organized. The authors are non-White. Perhaps the greatest cause for stress among Blacks is the dictum of racism which allows, permits, and insists that Whites know what is best for and what is needed for Blacks. In fact, Whites tell Blacks how it is to be Black. In order not to mimic such a mechanism, the authors have written from the minority perspective, keeping in mind that Whites might be stressed if they are told how to be White. It is recognized that much of what is written will not match the perceptions of many Whites. Perhaps these almost inevitable perceptual clashes hinder racial progress.

Yet, stress reduction for Whites or Blacks means each group must be mindful of doing things that will be helpful to the other. Each group must make more effort to understand the other in order to sustain and further the remarkable racial progress made in the 20th century. Meanwhile, Blacks will continue to wrestle with an ultra dilemma relating to stress resolution which every group in human history has had to ask and answer: Has freedom ever been purchased without the sacrifice of human life?

See Also the Following Articles

Cultural Factors; Economic Status and Stress; Minorities and Stress; Social Status and Stress

Bibliography

Center for Disease Control (1997). Morbidity and Mortality Weekly Report, 46, September 19.

Dressler, W. W. (1993). Health in the African American community: Accounting for health inequalities. *Med. Anthropol. Q.* 7, 325–345.

Gilliam, F. D., Jr., and Kaufman, K. (1998). Is there an empowerment life cycle?: Long-term Black empowerment and its influence on voter participation. *Urban Aff. Rev.* 33, 741–766.

Myrdal, G. (1994). "An American Dilemma." Harper and Row, New York.

Nickens, H. W., and Cohen, J. J. (1996). An affirmative action. *J. Am. Med. Assoc.* 275, 572–754.

Utsey, S. O., and Ponterotto, J. G. (1996). Development and validation of the Index of Race Related Stress (IRRS). *J. Counsel. Psychol.* 43, 490–501.

Blood Pressure

Andrew Sherwood and Robert A. Carels

Duke University Medical Center

GLOSSARY

ambulatory blood pressure Measurements recorded during the course of normal daily activities using a wearable blood pressure monitor.

cardiac output The volume flow rate (in liters per minute) of blood ejected from the left ventricle of the heart into the systemic circulation.

diastolic blood pressure The lowest pressure (in millimeters of mercury) in the arterial system occurring during cardiac diastole.

hemodynamics Assessment of the circulation in terms of blood pressure, cardiac output, and systemic vascular resistance.

hypertension Resting blood pressure which is higher than 140/90 mm Hg.

reactivity A psychophysiological trait expressed as cardiovascular response to one or more psychological stressors.

sympathetic nervous system A division of the autonomic nervous system that is activated in association with psychological stress and is involved in cardiovascular regulation.

systemic vascular resistance The total peripheral resistance of the systemic vasculature (in dynes-seconds per centimenters[5]).

systolic blood pressure The highest pressure (in millimeters of mercury) in the arterial system occurring during cardiac systole.

Blood pressure is one of the most widely recorded physiological functions of the body. It is a measurement of the pulsatile pressure fluctuations in the arterial system that provides the driving force behind blood flow to the tissues. It is one of the body's vital signs, indicating present cardiovascular function as well as risk for future cardiovascular morbidity and mortality.

I. BLOOD PRESSURE MEASUREMENT

When the left ventricle of the heart contracts, a bolus of blood is ejected into the systemic circulation, creating a pulse pressure waveform that propagates through the arterial tree. The peak pressure reached in the arterial system is referred to as systolic pressure, since it occurs in association with cardiac systole, or the heart's contraction phase. Once systolic pressure is reached, pulsatile pressure falls as the heart relaxes during diastole, with the lowest pressure, referred to as diastolic pressure, occurring just prior to the onset of the next systolic phase. Pulse pressure is defined as the difference between systolic and diastolic pressure. Mean arterial pressure refers to the average pressure in the arterial system. All blood pressure measurements are recorded in millimeters of mercury (mm Hg).

Systolic and diastolic pressure are the most commonly measured aspects of arterial blood pressure. The emphasis on these parameters in medicine is partly a reflection of their relative ease of measurement using noninvasive techniques. Although arterial blood pressure varies according to where it is measured in the arterial tree, it is most commonly assessed in the brachial artery, which runs through the upper region of the arm. Two commonly employed measurement techniques, auscultatory and oscillometric, employ an occlusion cuff which contains an inflatable bladder applying pressure through the arm to first interrupt and then progressively restore blood flow through the brachial artery.

With the auscultatory method, a stethoscope, or microphone is positioned over the brachial artery, distal to the occlusion cuff. When the pressure in the occlusion cuff is above systolic pressure, the brachial artery is compressed and no sounds are detected distal to the cuff. When the slowly deflating occlusion cuff drops below the systolic pressure, the compressed artery opens momentarily and the brief episode of turbulent blood flow distal to the cuff is detected as a faint "tapping" sound; the first Phase I Korotkoff sound is used to indicate systolic blood pressure. As the cuff pressure continues to fall, the Korotkoff sounds increase in intensity and quality, followed by a muffling of the sound (Phase IV) and ultimately their disappearance (Phase V). Diastolic pressure is usually defined as Phase V in adults, while in children Phase IV may be a closer approximation. With the auscultatory technique mean arterial pressure cannot be measured directly, but may be estimated as diastolic pressure plus one-third of the pulse pressure.

The oscillometric method also employs the occlusion cuff in a similar manner to that for auscultatory measurement. However, with the oscillometric technique, cuff pressure oscillations coincident with pulsatile pressure variations in the artery form the basis of blood pressure measurement. As the occlusion cuff is deflated, systolic pressure is indicated by a sharp rise in cuff pressure oscillations. The lowest pressure at which the cuff oscillations are at their greatest amplitude identifies mean arterial pressure. Diastolic pressure is recorded as the point at which the cuff pressure oscillations decrease no further in amplitude.

The auscultatory and oscillometric methods are by far the most widely utilized methods for measuring blood pressure. One of their limitations is that because they use a slowly deflating occlusion cuff, blood pressure measurements are limited in frequency to approximately once per minute. Other techniques include direct arterial pressure recording via a pressure transducer on the tip of an intraarterial catheter, a method often employed to monitor vital signs during major surgery. One advantage of this invasive method is that it provides a continuous measurement of blood pressure on a beat-by-beat basis. A number of research-orientated techniques, including cuff-tracking, vascular unloading, arterial tonometry, and pulse transit time provide methods to assess blood pressure beat-by-beat, yet nonivasively, each offering specific strengths and limitations. All of the methods described above have been employed in studies examining the effects of stress on blood pressure.

II. HYPERTENSION

Hypertension is defined as systolic blood pressure of 140 mm Hg or greater and/or diastolic blood pressure of 90 mm Hg or greater. These criteria, based on seated clinic blood pressure measurements, are recognized by the World Health Organization/International Society of Hypertension and the United States Joint National Committee on Prevention, Detection, Evaluation, and Treatment of High Blood Pressure (JNC). Pressures in excess of 140/90 mm Hg are further categorized in terms of severity of hypertension, defined as Stages 1 through 3 (JNC VI). While blood pressures less than 140/90 mm Hg were once considered normal, the JNC now includes the category of "high normal," defined as the pressure range of 130–139/85–89 mm Hg. This relatively new categorization reflects a growing recognition that the clinical criteria for hypertension are somewhat arbitrary and that cardiovascular morbidity associated with high blood pressure is more of a progressive phenomenon than one associated with a specific pressure threshold that engenders a sudden rise in health risk. Only pressures below 120/80 mm Hg are considered optimal. Prevalence of hypertension is related to age, race, and gender. Hypertension incidence is higher in blacks than in whites, particularly in the United States. In young to middle-aged adults, prevalence is much greater in males than females, while incidence increases quite dramatically in women after menopause. Though hypertension is defined by elevation of arterial blood pressure, its clinical significance is derived from morbid events affecting the heart, brain, and kidneys. Complications such as myocardial infarction and stroke are not directly due to elevated pressures, but to the resulting structural changes in the heart and blood vessels. One of the structural consequences of hypertension, hypertrophy of the left ventricle (LVH), is the strongest known predictor, other than advancing age, of cardiovascular morbidity and mortality.

Hypertension is a disease that typically develops over years or decades, and in approximately 90% of cases it is diagnosed as Primary (or Essential) Hypertension, indicating nonspecific etiology. The natural history of hypertension is characterized by not only a progressive increase in blood pressure, but also is accompanied by a progressive rise in systemic vascular resistance (SVR). The structural autoregulation theory of hypertension, originated by Folkow, helps explain why hypertension becomes a disease of elevated SVR. Arterial resistance vessels (arterioles) serve to regulate blood flow in accordance with local tissue demands. Vascular smooth muscle hypertrophy occurs as a physiological adaptation to increased blood pressure, which allows the vessel to maintain its ability to regulate blood flow at higher pressures. However, a consequence of this restructuring of the vessel is that it creates a rise in SVR, which increasingly provides the basis for the hypertension. Thus structural autoregulation is a cascading pathophysiological adaptation. However, the unresolved question is what causes an individual's pressure to initially rise from normotensive levels, allowing the onset of pathophysiological processes. The answer to this question is likely multiple interacting factors, which vary across individuals, as reflected in Page's Mosaic Theory of hypertension. However, there is overwhelming evidence that the sympathetic nervous system is frequently implicated in the early stages of hypertension. In some, though not all instances, this may give rise to a "hyperkinetic circulatory state" in which blood pressure elevations are due to abnormally high cardiac output (CO) levels. It is the potentially pathophysiological effects of the sympathetic nervous system that suggest that stress may be implicated in the etiology of hypertension.

III. STRESS AND BLOOD PRESSURE

A. Psychophysiology of Stress

The impact of emotions and stress on blood pressure was recognized as early as the 17th century, as reflected in William Harvey's studies of the circulation. However, it was not until the 20th century that the psychophysiological mechanisms by which stress influenced blood pressure became better understood. In 1915, Walter Cannon proposed that the sympathetic nervous system served to mobilize the cardiovascular system in preparation for fight or flight by engendering an increase in blood pressure and blood flow to the skeletal muscle vasculature. In the 1940s, the work of Hess identified the "defense response," which was characterized by an integrative behavioral and cardiovascular activation pattern in response to electrical stimulation of the hypothalamus. This early animal research set the groundwork for our conception of the stress response as a psychophysiological phenomenon that primes the body in anticipation of recourse to sudden physical exertion.

In the latter half of the 20th century, human research on the effects of stress on blood pressure has been dominated by what has been termed "cardiovascular reactivity" studies in which a variety of cardiovascular measures are recorded while volunteers are subjected to psychologically challenging tasks in a research laboratory setting. One of the earliest human studies was reported by Brod and colleagues in 1959, describing detailed cardiovascular response patterns observed while participants performed a stressful mental arithmetic task. Responses typically paralleled those of the animal "defense response" with increased blood pressure and circulatory mobilization that occurred in the absence of significant metabolic demands. Essentially the same approach used by Brod has since been utilized extensively and has led to the documentation of responses to a wide variety of "laboratory stressors" including reaction time tasks, Stroop colorword conflict tasks, cold-pressor tasks, simulated public speaking, and a variety of psychomotor tasks. One of the consistently striking observations from these studies is the individual differences in the magnitude of blood pressure responses; while at one extreme some individuals may show essentially no change in BP, others may respond with an increase of 50 mm Hg or more to exactly the same laboratory stressor. There is compelling evidence that these individual differences in blood pressure "reactivity" to stress are relatively robust, exhibiting consistency across a variety of laboratory tasks and showing stability over time.

Blood pressure alone provides a limited picture of the hemodynamic pattern of changes elicited by stress. Hemodynamic studies emphasize the interrelationships among blood pressure, cardiac output (CO), and systemic vascular resistance (SVR). Since BP is the product of CO and SVR, the concurrent measurement of BP and CO permits the derivation of SVR, providing a more complete description of the hemodynamic response. Two very early stress studies conducted in the 1940s used invasive procedures to measure CO and, moreover, considered the measurement procedures themselves as presenting the source of psychological stress. These studies demonstrated how the stress response associated with anxiety was characterized by a mobilization of the cardiovascular system, leading to BP increases due to an increase in CO. The same response pattern to a mental arithmetic task was observed over a decade later by Brod. In this classic study, CO was measured invasively using dye dilution and forearm blood flow was also measured, leading to the demonstration that the increased CO during psychological stress appeared to be distributed to the skeletal muscle vasculature. These studies demonstrated that the fight/flight response, previously observed in animals, could be elicited in humans by psychological stressors.

With the development of noninvasive methods to measure cardiac output unobtrusively, there has been a resurgence in the past 2 decades of laboratory studies of the hemodynamic aspects of the stress response. These studies have consistently illustrated that there are dramatic individual differences in the hemodynamic patterns underlying blood pressure increases during stress. Thus, apparently similar cardiovascular responses to a stressor in terms of blood pressure change may belie very different underlying hemodynamic mechanisms. While some individuals exhibit BP increases during stress due to an increase in CO and a decrease in SVR (fight/flight response), others may vasoconstrict, leading to an increase in BP due entirely to increased SVR. Observations of this kind have led to an extension of descriptive categories in cardiovascular reactivity research from "high" vs "low" or "hot" vs "cold" reactors, referring to the magnitude of blood pressure responses, to "myocardial" and "vascular" reactors, referring to the

predominant hemodynamic mechanism underlying the blood pressure response. The mechanisms and potential health consequences of these individual differences are currently under exploration.

B. Stress and Hypertension

Although acute stress can indisputably raise blood pressure for brief periods into the range defining hypertension, its role in the etiology of sustained hypertension remains controversial.

1. Observational Studies of Stress Reactivity

There is some evidence that risk of hypertension development may be related to stress reactivity. Hypertensive individuals have been found to show greater BP reactivity than normotensives. Individuals with normal BP who have hypertensive parents also typically exhibit greater BP reactivity to laboratory stressors than normotensives with no family history. Whereas studies describing only observations of the magnitude of blood pressure responses have reported inconsistent findings for the effects of race, a number of studies have reported that black men, who are at increased risk for hypertension, appear to exhibit abnormally elevated vascular tone, indexed by SVR, during exposure to a variety of laboratory stressors. Gender differences in reactivity have also been observed, with men exhibiting greater SBP and SVR increases than premenopausal women. These gender differences in SVR response are consistent with those observed for race in that men are more likely to develop hypertension than premenopausal women.

Since hypertension is a disease whose natural history involves progressively increasing BP, which in turn is secondary to progressively increasing SVR, the tendency for individuals at greater risk for developing hypertension to exhibit pronounced stress-induced BP and/or SVR reactivity is provocative. Reactivity studies have also demonstrated that stress can modify renal function, leading to sodium and fluid retention in some individuals, which may heighten and prolong stress-induced BP elevations; altered renal function may be one of the target organ effects of stress that could impact long-term blood regulation. Additionally, several recent studies have reported an association between BP reactivity and left ventricular hypertrophy (LVH), whereby the magnitude of BP response during stress is directly related to LV mass.

2. Prospective Studies of Stress Reactivity

Although correlational evidence of the kind described above is provocative, it is inconclusive since it does not rule out the possibility that associations of stress reactivity to hypertension risk and/or end-organ damage may simply be a manifestation of underlying pathophysiology; the stress response may be a marker rather than a mechanism of disease. Prospective studies should help resolve these cause–effect limitations by focusing on the temporal relationship of the correlated observations. As previously noted, hypertensive individuals are characterized by BP hyperreactivity, but is BP hyperactivity in normotensives associated with the subsequent development of hypertension? Evidence relating to this question comes both from human and animal studies.

a. Animal Studies

In 1969, Forsyth described the effects of prolonged daily exposure to unsignaled shock-avoidance schedules in rhesus monkeys. After several months, three of four animals developed hypertension. However, these findings were not replicated in other species. Beginning in the 1970s, a series of elegant studies were reported by Henry and colleagues on the effects of chronic social conflict in mice. When reared in isolation and subsequently transferred to colonies that made social conflict unavoidable, hypertension developed after several months, suggesting that chronic social stress could be a cause of hypertension. However, subsequent studies in other species were again less definitive. The importance of genetic susceptibility was demonstrated by Lawler's 1980s studies of "borderline hypertensive" rats, which developed hypertension when exposed to prolonged aversive reinforcement contingencies, whereas control animals typically remained normotensive. Other studies have suggested that the development of hypertension in "salt-sensitive" strains of animals of various species is exacerbated by exposure to stressful behavioral paradigms. In summary, the animal studies suggest that stress may play a role in the development of hypertension, but its impact is only likely to be important in the context of a preexisting disposition to develop the disease.

b. Human Studies

There has been much interest in the possibility that individuals characterized by unusually large magnitude blood pressure reactivity may be at increased risk for the development of hypertension. Several studies have generated indirect support for the so-called "stress reactivity hypothesis." In an early study of white males, blood pressure reactivity in response to a hand cold-pressor task was examined as a predictor of the development of hypertension at 20- and 36-year follow-up. The study revealed that subjects in the top quartile of systolic BP reactivity had a greater incidence of hypertension from age 40 onward compared to the less reactive subjects. Other relatively long-term follow-up studies have shown the cold-pressor task to predict the development of elevated blood pressure. One criticism of these studies is that the cold pressor may not be a purely behavioral stressor since it is a painful stimulus for most individuals; although, in common with other laboratory behavioral stress tasks, its cardiovascular effects are mediated primarily by sympathetic nervous system activation.

Blood pressure reactivity to a reaction-time task involving threat of shock was found by Light and colleagues to predict increases in blood pressure 10 to 15 years later. High levels of systolic blood pressure during the reaction time task were associated with higher clinic and ambulatory systolic pressure at follow-up, even after controlling for parental history of hypertension and baseline resting systolic and diastolic blood pressure. Several studies in adolescents and young adults examining reactivity to mental arithmetic as a predictor of hypertension have also found evidence that high blood pressure reactivity and/or delayed recovery of the stress-induced BP response predict the development of hypertension at follow-up 1–5 years later. Other studies have made similar observations based on initial reactivity assessments using video games, Stroop color/word conflict, and mirror trace tasks. The studies reported to date are inconsistent in whether SBP reactivity, DBP reactivity, or both are predictive of hypertension development. This discrepancy may also reflect differences in the population sample being studied as well as differences in the nature of the blood pressure response associated with the specific stressor employed in a given study. It is also of note that the degree to which reactivity has predicted the development of high pressure or hypertension has been generally modest. As suggested by the animal studies, genetic susceptibility (i.e., family history of hypertension) is likely to be an important determinant of hypertension development, but was not considered in all of the reactivity studies. Furthermore, if stress reactivity is viewed as a disease *mechanism,* then the predictive value of high reactivity is likely to be largely moderated by the extent to which repeated acute stress responses occur in the time interval from assessment to follow-up. Assessing the frequency of stress responses over the long-term presents a methodological challenge that has yet to be met in reactivity studies.

3. Psychosocial Factors and Hypertension

Only a few prospective studies have examined the relationship of psychosocial factors to the subsequent development of hypertension. The Framingham Heart Study examined the role of anxiety, anger intensity, and anger suppression in normotensive men. After controlling for biological risk factors, anxiety at baseline remained an independent predictor of hypertension in middle-aged men. The National Health and Nutrition Examination Survey I Epidemiologic Follow-up Study also followed several thousand initially normotensive individuals for 7 to 16 years to test the hypothesis that symptoms of anxiety and depression increased the risk of developing hypertension. High anxiety and depression were independent predictors of incident hypertension ($\geq 160/95$ mm Hg) in white men ages 45 to 64 years and black men ages 25 to 64 years.

4. Studies of Chronic Stress

Studies of environments that may engender chronic states of stress also provide a test of the effects of stress on blood pressure. In a study of individuals residing near Three Mile Island Nuclear Power Plant, blood pressure was found to rise shortly after the 1979 accident in which part of the facility was destroyed. Blood pressure remained elevated for 5 years and was associated with increased sympathetic nervous system activity compared to individuals residing further from the nuclear plant. Studies of prisoners also suggest that living in overcrowded conditions is associated with elevated BP. Occupations considered to be associated with chronic stress include air traffic controllers, who have been found to show a much greater incidence of hypertension than workers in comparable, but less stressful, occupations. A relationship between occupational stress and elevated blood pressure and/or hypertension is supported by other studies, including those utilizing ambulatory BP measurement technology to measure BP in the working environment.

IV. AMBULATORY BLOOD PRESSURE

A. Methodology

Advances in computer and miniaturization technology over the past 20 years have aided the development of wearable ambulatory blood pressure (ABP) monitors. Ambulatory blood pressure monitors are able to capture the normal activities and environmental interactions during the course of an individual's day. Utilizing common BP measurement techniques, ABP monitors permit frequent noninvasive BP recordings based upon auscultatory and/or oscillometric measurement principles. Ambulatory blood pressure monitors are typically programmed to take BP measurements several times per hour, at variable intervals, throughout the workday, evening, and overnight. During waking hours, individuals are ordinarily instructed to follow a normal schedule and immediately following each reading to complete a brief diary indicating factors such as time, posture, activity, location, and current emotional/cognitive state. Factors such as posture and physical activity have been shown to systematically influence blood pressure. Location and emotional state have also been found to affect BP, but the magnitude of their effects varies greatly from individual to individual.

B. White Coat Hypertension

Because morbid events are often associated with hypertension, blood pressure is routinely measured during visits to a physician's office. However, psychological stress associated with visiting a doctor's office can spuriously inflate clinic BPs in some patients. Individuals whose BPs are in the hypertensive range when measured in the clinic, but are normal in other contexts, as indicated by ABP measurements and/or automated home measurements, are classified as "white coat" hypertensives. Although most studies have found no association between psychological factors and "white coat" hypertension, there is some evidence that anxiety may be a related characteristic. Multiple ABP measurements throughout the day are thought to be more representative than clinic measures of the overall load that is placed on the cardiovascular system. Thus, 24-h ABP recordings can provide important supplementation of clinic readings in the accurate diagnosis of hypertension and are more closely correlated with end-organ damage, including left ventricular mass, than clinic BP.

C. ABP and Emotional States

Ambulatory blood pressure monitoring is particularly well suited for capturing acute affective states that occur in response to daily stress. Several studies have indicated that emotions, as indicated by diary ratings of moods, influence ABP levels. Both negative and positive moods have been found to be associated with increased ABP. However, a great deal of individual variability in the reporting of diary-rated moods has been observed, suggesting that certain individuals may be more susceptible to experiencing emotional upset throughout the day. Similarly, the effects of emotions on ABP are more pronounced in some individuals than others. Nonetheless, studies indicate that for diary ratings of negative emotions, including "stress," "frustration," and "tension," greater emotional intensity is accompanied by higher ABP. There is some evidence that psychosocial characteristics that are risk factors for cardiovascular disease, including anxiety, depression, and lack of social support, are associated with greater fluctuations in diary ratings of negative moods; these individuals have also

been found to exhibit a greater impact of emotion on ABP. There is also evidence to suggest that negative emotional dispositions, such as hostility, may have an impact on ABP, but only in certain social contexts.

D. ABP and Location

1. Work

If a 24-h day is divided into work, home, and overnight periods, most people's BP will be highest during work, lower while at home, and lowest during the overnight period. However, these locational effects on BP vary greatly from one individual to the next. This suggests that location per se is not directly associated with BP, but rather location is associated with a variety of behavioral (e.g., activity level, posture) and psychosocial factors (e.g., mood, social support, stress) which under certain circumstances may influence BP. Ambulatory blood pressure studies conducted on individuals across a variety of occupations (e.g., paramedics, physicians, clerical personnel) indicate that perceived or actual occupational stress does, in fact, increase ABP levels. These associations have prompted researchers to examine specific job characteristics that might contribute to elevations in blood pressure across a variety of occupations. One model of job characteristics that contributes to work-related stress is Karasek and Theorell's "job strain" model. Karasek and Theorell maintain that a deleterious combination of high psychological job demands together with low decision latitude at work results in a condition of "job strain." Numerous studies have found that higher levels of job strain are associated with higher BP, particularly in men. There is also evidence that job strain is associated with increased LV mass, which may be a consequence of ABP effects.

2. Home

Behavioral and psychosocial influences on ABP at home are likely to be very different from behavioral and psychosocial influences at work. The home environment may be influenced by factors such as the quality of familial relationships and their ability to provide social support, the level of domestic responsibilities, and the existence of role conflict or dissatisfaction. Although research on the home environment and ABP is sparse, one study that examined BP in working women found that married working women had higher ABP than unmarried working women. These findings suggest that, compared to unmarried working women, the higher ABP levels found in married working women may reflect their greater combined work and home responsibilities, possibly suggesting a total greater workload. Elevated ABP in the home environment may also be associated with home stress, making it more difficult to "unwind," both psychologically and physiologically, after work.

3. Sleep

Sleep BPs may be influenced, at least in part, by events that occur during waking hours. Studies have found that the daily experience of negative moods on blood pressure appears to carry over from daytime waking to nighttime sleep. Individuals that frequently report anger during the day tend to have higher levels of blood pressure, especially during sleep. There has been some speculation that unresolved stressful experiences and negative mood states that occur during the day might contribute to disrupted sleep patterns, a diminished quality of sleep, or somatic tension that influences BP levels. The magnitude of nocturnal decline in BP has been found to relate to LV mass; individuals who show a lesser fall in nighttime BP, sometimes referred to as "nondippers," have been characterized by increased LV mass compared to "dippers." This evidence underscores the importance of studying nighttime BPs and its possibly complex biopsychosocial determinants.

See Also the Following Articles

Hyperreactivity (Cardiovascular); Psychosocial Factors and Stress; Sympathetic Nervous System

Bibliography

Johnson, E. H., Gentry, W. D., and Julius, S. (Eds.) (1992). "Personality, Elevated Blood Pressure and Essential Hypertension." Hemisphere, Washington, D.C.

Manuck, S. B., Kasprowicz, A. L., and Muldoon, M. F. (1990). Behaviorally-evoked cardiovascular reactivity and hypertension: Conceptual issues and potential associations. *Ann. Behav. Med.* **12**, 17–29.

O'Rourke, M. F., Kelly, R., and Avolio, A. (1992). "The Arterial Pulse." Lea & Febiger, Malvern, PA.

Pickering, T. (1997). The effects of occupational stress on blood pressure in men and women. *Acta Physiol. Scand.* **640** (Suppl.), 125–128.

Shapiro, D., Jamner, L. D., Lane, J. D., Light, K. C., Myrtek, M., Sawada, Y., and Steptoe, A. (1996). Blood pressure publication guidelines. *Pychophysiology* **33**, 1–12.

Steptoe, A. (1997). Behavior and blood pressure: Implications for hypertension. In "Handbook of Hypertension: Pathophysiology of Hypertension" (A. Zanchettii and G. Mancia, Eds.) Vol. 17, pp. 674–708. Elsevier, Amsterdam, The Netherlands.

Borderline Personality Disorder

Harold W. Koenigsberg and Larry J. Siever

The Mount Sinai School of Medicine and The Bronx Veterans Affairs Medical Center

GLOSSARY

neurotransmitter One of a number of chemical substances that, when released at the terminal of one neuron and captured by a specialized receptor on the surface of another neuron, transmits a signal from one neuron to another.

personality Enduring patterns of perceiving, relating to, and thinking about the environment and oneself.

personality disorder The disturbance resulting from maladaptive personality traits that cause functional impairment or substantial distress.

I. PHENOMENOLOGY AND EPIDEMIOLOGY OF BORDERLINE PERSONALITY DISORDER

Borderline personality disorder (BPD), a disorder characterized by emotional instability and impulsivity, is one of the more serious personality disorders. It is associated with high levels of distress, significant impairments in social and occupational functioning, and a risk of suicide approaching 10%. As a personality disorder, BPD reflects an enduring and inflexible maladaptation in an individual's characteristic pattern of perceiving, relating to, and thinking about the environment and self. In BPD, the individual is highly reactive to psychosocial events such as losses, separations, and frustrations. The individual with BPD may show intense but shifting extremes of emotion, often involving anger and depression. He or she may engage in impulsively self-destructive acts or may recurrently threaten or attempt suicide. His or her relationships with others are typically intense and unstable, often oscillating between idealization and devaluation of others. By the same token, their own sense of identity is unstable and people with BPD are unsure of their goals, values, or sense of self. They may be terrified of real or imagined abandonment and may frantically attempt to control others to prevent this. Under the stress of losses, frustrations, or intense interpersonal relationships, individuals with BPD may regress, becoming more infantile or experiencing transient lapses in reality testing, which can take the form of hallucinations or delusional ideas. They often experience a sense of boredom and inner emptiness. It is estimated that about 2% of the population meets criteria for BPD. It is more often diagnosed in women and is more common among first-degree relatives of those with the disorder.

II. ROLE OF NEUROBIOLOGY

BPD appears to be the result of converging biological predispositions and early life experience. Two biologically mediated dimensions of personality are particularly prominent in BPD; impulsive-aggression and affective instability. In borderline patients the impulsive-aggression is most often self-directed, but it can also be directed to others. Impulsive-aggression has been shown to be associated with dysregulation in the serotonin neurotransmitter system. Cerebrospinal fluid levels of 5-HIAA, a breakdown product of serotonin, are inversely correlated with the degree of impulsive-aggressive and suicidal behavior in depressed patients and in patients with personality disorders. Borderline patients show a blunted response to the ingestion of fenfluramine, a serotonin-releasing and potentiating agent that triggers release of the hormone prolactin, and the degree of blunting in the prolactin response to fenfluramine correlates with the level of impulsive-aggression manifest in the patient's life history. Similar results were found using other serotonergic challenge agents.

The noradrenergic (norepinephrine) neurotransmitter system is also implicated in aggression in personality disordered patients. Cerebrospinal fluid levels of MHPG, a norepinephrine breakdown product, have been shown to correlate positively with impulsive-aggressive behavior. The responsivity of the noradrenergic system can be assayed by measuring the growth hormone response to clonidine. Growth hormone release in response to clonidine correlates directly with irritability. Because norepinephrine activity is associated with alertness, attention to external stimuli, and extraversion, it may be connected with outward-directed aggression. The interaction between serotonin and noradrenergic systems may determine the nature of aggression in BPD. Low serotonergic activity may predispose to impulsive aggression, which appears to be outward directed when noradrenergic activity is high and inward directed when noradrenergic activity is low. It has been suggested that the activity of another neurotransmitter, arginine vasopressin, may correlate directly with levels of aggression in personality disorders.

Affective instability may be associated with dysregulation of the neurotransmitter, acetylcholine. When borderline patients were given an acetylcholine-potentiating agent, physostigmine, they responded by becoming transiently more dysphoric for several minutes, whereas nonborderline personality disorder patients did not show this reaction. The affective effect of physostigmine was associated with the patients' degree of affective instability, identity confusion, unstable relationships, and feelings of emptiness and boredom, suggesting that these symptoms may all be related to affective instability.

III. ROLE OF LIFE EXPERIENCE

Early life experience also appears to contribute to the development of BPD. Histories of repeated childhood physical or sexual abuse are commonly found among borderline patients, although such abuse experiences are also associated with a variety of other psychiatric disorders as well. Severe physical or emotional neglect may also predispose to BPD. Intense levels of aggressive drive, resulting either from an inborn predisposition or from exceptionally powerful anger-inducing life experiences such as abuse, painful illness, or devastating losses, are also believed to contribute to borderline pathology. Some have suggested that individuals who go on to develop borderline personalities have had impairments in their ability to evoke memories of their caretakers for use in soothing themselves in the absence of the caretaker. Others emphasize the interaction of the affectively unstable child with a caretaking environment in which strong feelings are disavowed and the child is made to feel that his or her feelings are invalid.

IV. PSYCHOLOGICAL STRUCTURES IN THE BORDERLINE PATIENT

Psychoanalytic investigators have postulated that borderline individuals protect themselves from recognizing the consequences of their unacceptable feelings by developing inflexible and maladaptive defense mechanisms, such as splitting. Splitting is a defense in which the individual partitions his or her psychic experience into compartments that keep aggressive feelings away from images of loved and needed others. The partitioning of memory, which is the essence of splitting, may itself be a consequence of the impact of affective instability on emotion state-dependent memory processes. Thus the use of splitting, with its associated anxiety-controlling effects, may derive from a psychobiological vulnerability to affective dysregulation. The extensive use of the splitting defense fragments the individual's internal images of self and others, which produces a confused sense of self and identity and contradictory pictures of others.

V. TREATMENT OF BORDERLINE PERSONALITY DISORDER

Because of their ingrained nature, personality disorders are slow to change, and the impulsiveness and affective instability characteristic of BPD make this disorder often difficult to treat. While no single treatment has been identified as the treatment of choice for BPD, patients have responded well to a number of psychotherapeutic approaches and to medications. The anticonvulsant and mood stabilizer carbamazepine has been shown to reduce hostility and self-destructive behavior in borderline patients. Valproic acid, which has similar uses, also appears to control impulsivity in borderline patients. Borderline patients also show a global positive response to the mood stabilizer lithium carbonate. Monoamine oxidase inhibitors, which affect several neurotransmitter systems, reduce depression, anxiety, hostility, self-destructiveness, and interpersonal sensitivity in BPD. Selective serotonin reuptake inhibitor antidepressants have been shown to diminish hostility in borderline patients and may also reduce impulsive-aggression and depression. Low doses of antipsychotic medications have reduced the transient psychotic symptoms, hostility, impulsiveness, and, in some studies, depression in BPD. At present, it remains an open question whether the beneficial effects of medication last beyond the 6- to 12-week periods examined in most studies. For patients with severe self-destructiveness and those who tend to be more action oriented than introspective, a form of cognitive behavioral therapy, dialectical behavior therapy (DBT), has been shown to diminish self-destructive behavior and reduce the need for inpatient treatment. Psychodynamic psychotherapies, which have helped borderline patients develop an integrated sense of themselves and others and have led to enhanced interpersonal and career functioning, are suitable for patients who can contain dangerous behavior within the structure of an outpatient treatment contract and who are interested in identifying, understanding the origins of, and changing maladaptive interpersonal patterns. For some patients, sequential treatment with medication, DBT, and psychodynamic psychotherapy may be the optimal approach.

See Also the Following Article

MULTIPLE PERSONALITY DISORDER

Bibliography

Coccaro, E. F., Kavoussi, R. J., Hauger, R. L., Coper, T. B., and Ferris, C. F. 1998. Cerebrospinal fluid vasopressin levels correlates with aggression and serotonin function in personality-disordered subjects. *Arch. Gen. Psychiat.* 55, 708–714.

Cowdry, R. W., and Gardner, D. L. 1988. Pharmacotherapy of borderline personality disorder: Alprazolam, carbamazepine, triflupoperazine, and tranylcypromine. *Arch. Gen. Psychiat.* 45, 111–119.

Kernberg, O. F. 1975. "Borderline Conditions and Pathological Narcissism." Aaronson, New York.

Koenigsberg, H. W. 1993. Combining psychotherapy and pharmacotherapy in the treatment of borderline patients. *In* "American Psychiatric Press Review of Psychiatry" (J. M. Oldham, M. B. Riba, A. Tasman, eds.), Vol. 12. American Psychiatric Press, Washington, D.C.

Linehan, M. M. 1993. "Cognitive-Behavioral Treatment of Borderline Personality Disorder." Guilford, New York.

New, A. S., Trestman, R. L., and Siever, L. J. 1995. Borderline personality disorder. *In* "Impulsivity and Aggression" (E. Hollander and D. Stein, eds.). Wiley, New York.

Siever, L., and Trestman, R. L. 1993. The serotonin system and aggressive personality disorder. *Int. Clin. Psychopharm.* 8 (Suppl. 2), 33–39.

Siever, I. J., and Davis, K. L. 1991. A psychobiological perspective on the personality disorders. *Am. J. Psychiat.* 148, 1647–1658.

Steinberg, B. J., Trestman, R., Mitropoulou, V., Serby, M., Silverman, J., Coccaro, E., Weston, S., de Vegvar, M., and Siever, L. J. 1997. Depressive response to physostigmine challenge in borderline personality disorder patients. *Neuropsychopharmacology* 17, 264–273.

Brain and Brain Regions

Alan G. Watts

University of Southern California

GLOSSARY

diencephalon That part of the forebrain containing the thalamus and hypothalamus (including the preoptic area).

immediate-early gene A gene whose product (usually a transcription factor) is rapidly produced as a consequence of receptor activation.

telencephalon That part of the forebrain containing the cortical regions (including the hippocampus), basal ganglia, bed nuclei of the stria terminalis, amygdala, and septal complex.

I. INTRODUCTION—STRESS AND THE BRAIN

A wide variety of stimuli evoke motor events that can be considered stress responses. In simple organisms these are made up of little more than sets of stereotyped reflex responses. If the stressor is sufficiently intense or prolonged these often consist of avoidance responses accompanied by endocrine-mediated alterations in metabolism. However, there is no evidence to suggest that invertebrates can associate emotional affect such as fear or anxiety with particular stressors. Only with the evolution of more complex central nervous systems in general, and the telencephalon in particular, do we begin to see this type of associative processing.

Stress responses in vertebrate species include endocrine secretions (e.g., from steroidogenic tissue in the interrenal/adrenal glands, etc.), autonomic motor events (e.g., piloerection, increased secretion from the chromaffin cell/adrenal medulla system, alterations in cardiovascular tone), and sets of behavioral motor actions (e.g., avoidance responses, changes in defensive behavior, fear-conditioned freezing, etc.) as well as those attendant emotional percepts generally recognized as being the most characteristic human signatures of stress (e.g., fear, anxiety, etc). From a neural systems perspective these examples show that virtually all parts of the central nervous system can be used to varying degrees for processing the information associated with stress. Here we broadly consider which parts of the central nervous system (1) are concerned with processing the sensory information used to generate stress responses; (2) are responsible for mediating the motor aspects of the stress response; and (3) are involved with the integrative mechanisms that control stress responses in the face of influences from, for example, learning and memory mechanisms. To do this we explore concepts that are based on data derived from a number of experimental techniques, including lesions, neuroanatomical tract tracing, and the mapping of immediate early gene expression within the brain and spinal cord.

Many physiological stressors originating in the viscera are addressed by evoking simple reflex responses to annul their potentially damaging consequences. Little complex central processing is required and control is often exerted by classic negative feedback (homeostatic) mechanisms from the action of the target. An example of reactive homeostatic components of the stress response is the sympathetic activation evoked to counter the immediate visceral effects of many stressors. For example, if stress-related hypotension or hypoglycemia are prolonged or of sufficient intensity they are rapidly negated by reactive stress responses that are evolutionarily rather old: sympathetically mediated vasoconstriction and catecholamine secretion by chromaffin cells, respectively.

In contrast, however, most stress responses typically have a more proactive (anticipatory) than a reactive (reflex) character, which involves complex neural processing. With stress activation of the hypothalamo-pituitary-adrenal (HPA) axis for example, although adreno corticotropic hormone (ACTH) and glucocorticoid secretion are obviously triggered by the stressor, they are not motor responses that act to remove the *immediate* consequences of the stress in a manner similar to the reactive sympathetic responses just described. Instead, the actions of stress-induced increases in circulating glucocorticoid (mediated in part by interactions with leptin, insulin, and the thyroid hormones) anticipate the *possibility* that the stressor will lead to a debilitating sequence of events, particularly the catabolic effects of negative energy balance that require the mobilization of energy stores, particularly protein. Understanding the neural complexity required for processing what are effectively anticipatory events provides the framework for explaining why so many neural systems are involved with modulating stress responses.

II. BRAIN REGIONS CONCERNED WITH PROCESSING STRESS-RELATED INFORMATION

A. Sensory Processing

Generally speaking, virtually all extero- and viscero- (intero-) sensory modalities are processed along two types of pathway once they enter the central nervous system (CNS) (Fig. 1). The first (Fig. 1, pathway A) is a relatively direct and rapidly effective route that requires little central integrative processing. These types of reflex pathways result in rapid and simply organized (stereotyped) motor responses. Much of the neural processing for these reflexes occurs in the spinal cord (for the behavioral motor components of stress responses), brainstem (for the autonomic motor aspects of stress responses), and hypothalamus (for the motor output of neuroendocrine stress responses). In the second instance (Fig. 1, pathway B), sensory information is also directed to those areas of the brain that provide the additional and often critical modulatory information about

arousal state and behavioral planning (timing signals, priorities, etc.), so furnishing the animal with the adaptive plasticity for generating stress responses. Brain regions in the telencephalon (cerebral cortex, amygdala, hippocampus, the septal complex) provide pivotal contributions here. They can prioritize stress responses with relation to other behaviors (e.g., placing a higher priority to fleeing a predator than to feeding) and with modulating the organization of stress responses, decreasing or increasing their intensity based on past experience (learning and memory). As a consequence, they are also likely to be involved with generating the detrimental effects of chronic emotional stress. Finally, Fig. 1 shows that the effects of a stress-associated motor event can serve as feedback signals modulating the motor output of the system both by reducing the level of sensory input and motor output (simple negative feedback) as well as by more indirect effects on central integrative processes.

1. Spinal Cord

Neurons in the dorsal horn of the spinal cord are the first recipients of nerve afferents from the skin and viscera that process information related to somatosensory modalities (pressure, temperature, pain). The spinal cord also receives sensory information from muscle spindles related to body position. Dorsal horn neurons are involved with organizing reflexes related to stress responses, but they are not directly involved with generating the more complex motor events usually thought of as stress responses. However, they do project much of this sensory information to the brainstem and thalamus for the higher order processing (using the scheme illustrated in Fig. 1). Ultimately, this can then be associated with the type of contextual information responsible for generating stress responses that are accompanied by fear and anxiety. Clearly, because information related to pain can evoke ACTH release, nociceptive information entering the dorsal horn can affect neuroendocrine motor neurons in the hypothalamic paraventricular nucleus (PVH). However, the pathways responsible for this are not entirely clear.

2. Brainstem

Parts of the brainstem receive first-order sensory information from the cranial nerves related to the

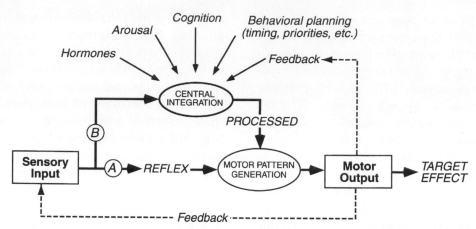

FIGURE 1   Schematic representation of the two paths along which sensory information is processed in the brain. (A) A reflex route that includes little complex processing and allows for rapid stereotyped stress responses; (B) a route that allows sensory information to be integrated with other types of information within the brain to provide for stress responses of greater complexity and flexibility. Feedback processes can control the function of both paths.

visual (oculomotor) and vestibular systems as well as somatosensory (the hypoglossal and trigeminal systems) and gustatory (the glossopharyngeal nerve) information from the oropharynx. In many respects how the brainstem processes these inputs in a stress-related manner is similar to how exterosensory information is processed bidirectionally by the dorsal horn of the spinal cord (Fig. 1). Projections from the parabrachial nucleus are probably important for projecting pain-related information received from the dorsal horn and cranial nerves that ultimately impact those parts of the hypothalamus regulating the adrenal gland.

The brainstem is also critical for processing those sensory modalities originating in the internal environment that can generate stress responses. It receives numerous inputs from sensory receptors in the viscera that in general are conveyed to the nucleus of the solitary tract (NTS) by the vagus nerve. In turn, the NTS initiates visceral reflexes such as the baroreceptor reflex that regulates cardiovascular function within normal set-point homeostasis. However, neural projections from the NTS along with other brainstem regions also project this information to the forebrain (including the PVH) and telencephalon that in turn regulate the HPA axis directly. This explains why many viscerosensory stimuli (e.g., hypoglyce-

mia, hypotension) evoke robust ACTH and glucocorticoid secretion.

3. Thalamus

With the exception of olfactory information (which directly enters the cortex most likely impacting stress-related motor circuits by way of the amygdala and bed nuclei of the stria terminalis), all exterosensory modalities are processed by the thalamus before being projected to the amygdala and cerebral cortex. Consequently, those specific thalamic regions associated with particular sensory modalities have been implicated in processing stress-related sensory information. For example, the medial geniculate region is thought to contribute to the fear-conditioning evoked by pairing an auditory stimulus with footshock.

B. Motor Regions

1. Spinal Cord

The spinal cord contains two sets of motor neurons that are directly related to expressing stress responses. First, α-motor neurons in the ventral horn are clearly the mediators of all behavioral motor system stress responses. And second, the intermediolateral column in the thoracic and upper lumbar spinal cord contains the sympathetic preganglionic neurons that innervate the adrenal medulla and are directly responsible for stimulating adrenaline release during stress. These cholinergic neurons also mediate other components of the sympathetic stress responses and are innervated by a variety of afferents including those from the hypothalamus.

2. Brainstem

Visceral stress responses are also mediated by sets of preganglionic neurons in the brainstem. For example, stress-induced modifications to cardiovascular and other visceral functions are mediated through the dorsal motor nucleus of the vagus.

3. Hypothalamus

The hypothalamus is a critical motor region that can modulate most viscerally directed stress responses. It also contains all the motor neurons used for the neuroendocrine component of the stress response. Foremost among these are the corticotropin-releasing hormone (CRH) neurons in the medial parvicellular part of the PVH. The axons of these neurons terminate on the capillaries of hypophysial vasculature in the median eminence and release CRH and vasopressin (AVP) to stimulate ACTH release from corticotropes in the anterior pituitary. The PVH and supraoptic nucleus also contain magnocellular neurons that release oxytocin and AVP during stress events. As with all other motor responses, these neuroendocrine neurons can be activated in relatively simple reflex manner (for example, by hemodynamic stressors) as well as by inputs from telencephalic regions. In addition, the PVH provides strong projections to sympathetic and parasympathetic preganglionic neurons and is likely a key element in modulating the activity of these systems during stress.

One of the classic functions of the hypothalamus is the generation of motivated behaviors. These include ingestive, reproductive, and defensive behaviors. During the 1940s Hess demonstrated that electrical stimulation of specific regions of the lateral hypothalamus (LHA) would elicit rage or fearful behavior. It is likely that the often inhibitory influences of stress on, for example, feeding and reproductive behaviors are integrated within the hypothalamus with the relevant control networks of these behaviors. The exact

mechanisms used for these interactions are not clear, but again, they very likely involve inputs from the telencephalon.

Finally, it is important to remember that the hypothalamus contains the suprachiasmatic nucleus. In mammals this cell group is the circadian clock. Although the mechanism by which it generates a timing signal is still not known, it is clear that it influences the way stress responses are generated.

Afferents from those brain regions known to regulate the HPA axis and other stress motor functions are organized as two basic projection patterns: those that provide inputs directly to the PVH and those that provide indirect inputs, projecting first to other cell groups which in turn then project to the PVH. Figure 2 shows that direct inputs to the PVH can be divided into four afferent sets that provide the rich source of information for integration by neuroendocrine and preautonomic cell groups.

1. The only direct telencephalic inputs to the PVH come from some of the bed nuclei of the stria terminalis (BST) and the substantia innominata (Fig. 2A).
2. Two groups of direct PVH inputs originate intrahypothalamically (Fig. 2B). First, the PVH is surrounded by local GABAergic neurons that are not organized as a distinct hypothalamic nucleus, but electrophysiological and anatomical data suggest that they form an important group of direct intrahypothalamic inputs (Fig. 2B$_1$). They receive a massive input from the suprachiasmatic nucleus (SCH; see below), from the infralimbic cortex, and from other hypothalamic nuclei such as the ventromedial and ventral premammillary nuclei, which in turn receive massive telencephalic inputs. Second, a well-defined group of projections (Fig. 2B$_2$) originate from the arcuate and dorsomedial nuclei and the preoptic area (in particular the median preoptic and anteroventral periventricular nuclei). These nuclei also receive inputs from the telencephalon, including the BST and lateral septal complex (LS). The overall function of these two groups of direct intrahypothalamic inputs is unclear, but Risold and colleagues (1997) have suggested that some might constitute a set of neuroendocrine pattern generators similar in principle to those in the brainstem and spinal cord that control patterning in the behavioral motor system.

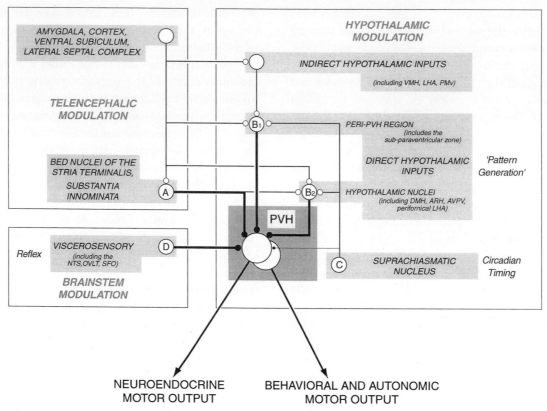

FIGURE 2 Schematic to illustrate the organization of inputs to the paraventricular nucleus of the hypothalamus. This nucleus is a key regulator of neuroendocrine and other autonomic stress responses. However, it receives only a restricted number of direct inputs from the telencephalon, hypothalamus, and brainstem. Many other hypothalamic and telencephalic regions provide information indirectly by way of these more direct inputs. Finally, circadian timing signals from the suprachiasmatic nucleus impact the PVH directly and to a greater extent through other hypothalamic cell nuclei with direct inputs. Abbreviations: ARH, arcuate nucleus; AVPV, anteroventral periventricular nucleus; DMH, dorsomedial necleus; LHA, lateral hypothalamic area; NTS, nucleus of the solitary tract; OVLT, vascular organ of the lamina terminalis; PMv, ventral premammillary nucleus; PVH, paraventricular nucleus of the hypothalamus; SFO, subfornical organ; VMH, ventromedial nucleus of the hypothalamus.

The importance of input sets 1 and 2 to stress responses is that they relay information to the PVH from a host of diencephalic and telencephalic regions (Figs. 2A, 2B₁, and 2B₂). Thus, these areas each receive numerous topographically ordered inputs from the cortex, ventral subiculum (SUBv), amygdala, and the lateral septal complex. Collectively, these inputs are responsible for relaying a great deal of the information critical for controlling stress responses to exterosensory stimuli and under a variety of circumstances that requires complex telencephalic processing.

3. The suprachiasmatic nucleus (SCH) provides the circadian timing signal that regulates all behaviors and has a critical bearing on the expression of stress responses. Although the SCH provides a small direct PVH projection, its major output (Fig. 2C) is to the subparaventricular zone in the peri-PVH region and to the dorsomedial nucleus. Collectively, its efferents to these regions (Figs. 2B1, 2B2, and 2C) are the likely mediators of circadian influence on the PVH-related stress responses.

4. Afferents from a variety of brainstem nuclei project topographically within the PVH and convey

viscerosensory information derived from the vagus and glossopharyngeal nerves (Fig. 2D). These inputs likely serve two functions; to stimulate patterns of ACTH secretion in response to homeostatic challenges that can generally be described as reflex in nature; and to provide the "gain control" signals required for neuroendocrine CRH neuron function in the basal state. Afferents from the vascular organ of the lamina terminalis and the subfornical organ that provide humoral sensory information about blood osmolality and angiotensin II concentrations respectively can also, in terms of function, be included with these direct viscerosensory inputs.

C. Integrative Regions

1. Brainstem

The brainstem contains monoaminergic cell groups that have very wide-ranging connections that in the past have been referred to as the "reticular activating system." Included here are the locus coeruleus, the raphe nuclei, parts of the NTS, and pedunculapontine nuclei. Collectively, they receive sensory inputs from the oropharynx and viscera as well as numerous inputs from the forebrain. They innervate virtually the whole of the neural axis and are thought to regulate behavioral arousal. In some instances (e.g., the locus coeruleus), they are implicated in the stress responses by virtue of their electrophysiological behavior and gene expression. Collectively, however, the precise role of these cell groups in regulating stress responses remains unclear.

2. Hippocampus

It has been known for some time that hippocampal lesions or the severing of hippocampal efferents into the lateral septal complex disrupt ACTH secretion and thus glucocorticoid stress responses. The SUBv is the hippocampal subfield most clearly implicated in this context. SUBv lesions increase CRH and vasopressin gene expression in the neuroendocrine PVH and also elevate plasma ACTH concentrations, suggesting that the SUBv usually provides inhibitory inputs to the PVH. Although specific details about the pathways or the mechanisms involved are not understood, the absence of direct projections from any hippocampal region to the PVH demonstrates that these effects are not mediated directly. The best candidate in this regard is a SUBv-BST-PVH pathway (Fig. 2A). The most studied overall function of the hippocampus is in learning and memory, particularly regarding short-term spatial memory and animal navigation. However, how this type of information relates to the modulation of stress responses is entirely unknown.

3. Septal Complex

The septal complex is a collection of forebrain cell groups that lie directly medial to the lateral ventricles. They are characterized by having bidirectional and topographically organized connections with the hippocampus; the lateral septal complex (LS) receives afferents, and the medial septal complex projects back to the hippocampus. As such the LS is in a position to integrate information from all sensory modalities. By virtue of their efferent connections, those parts of the LS that are most closely associated with regulating endocrine stress responses are located in its rostral (LSr) and ventral (LSv) parts. Although the LSv provides sparse inputs directly into the PVH, it does project strongly to at least two regions that can affect stress responses directly: the peri-PVH region (Fig. 2B$_1$) and those parts of the hypothalamic preoptic area which then project into the PVH (Fig. 2B$_2$). In turn, LSv neurons receive topographically ordered projections from the SUBv. In addition to any effects it might have on the HPA axis, the LS probably plays an important role in the expression of defensive behavior and as such may well affect the ordering of behavioral priorities during stress events. Certainly, patterns of immediate early gene expression suggest that the LS is somehow concerned with modulating defensive behavior during fear conditioning.

4. Amygdala

The amygdala has long been considered critical for regulating stress responses and their learned components that have fear as the emotional percept. However, the precise role of amygdala is still unclear with regard to its specific contribution. The amygdala is traditionally subdivided into lateral, basolateral, medial, central, and cortical regions. However, recent debate has challenged the usefulness of the amygdala as a unitary concept, suggesting that a more viable division is first into cortical (with glutamate as a transmitter) and striatal (with GABA as a transmitter) parts, followed by four functional systems based on the segregation of inputs and outputs. In this scheme, the traditionally defined amygdalar nuclei are included into one of these functional systems. For example, the central nucleus of the amygdala is part of the striatal amygdala and, by virtue of its connections to the BST and parabrachial nucleus, regulates the autonomic aspects of the stress response. Regarding outputs, the hippocampus and BST are important components in the output structure of those amygdalar nuclei most closely associated with stress responses. Although, again, like other parts of the telencephalon, the complex organization of stress responses dictates that all parts of the amygdala are likely involved at some level.

5. Bed Nuclei of the Stria Terminalis

The BST are a set of numerous, often small, and rather poorly differentiated cell groups located immediately rostral and dorsal to the preoptic area of the hypothalamus. Their precise role has proven difficult to define mostly because experiments have targeted large regions that encompass a number of nuclei. However, neuroanatomical evidence suggests that each BST cell group has precise and often distinct connections. As a whole the BST receive topographically organized projections from the amygdala and hippocampus and in turn project to many parts of the hypothalamus. The importance of the BST to stress responses is that some of these nuclei receive projections from those parts of the cerebral cortex, amygdala, and hippocampus (particularly ventral hippocampal regions) associated with overall regulation of stress responses. Consequently, one of their major functions is to integrate and channel processed telencephalic information directly to the PVH and other parts of the hypothalamus (Fig. 2A).

6. Cortex

Because the cerebral cortex is ultimately involved with formulating and regulating all voluntary behav-

iors, it must be considered a major integrative component of stress responses, particularly with respect to behavioral initiation, motor program selection, and prioritization. But as can be imagined, a detailed consideration of its function in this regard is beyond the scope of this article. Regarding cortical influences on neuroendocrine and autonomic motor output, these are generally indirect and are mediated through the LS, BST, amygdala, and SUBv or through other hypothalamic nuclei that have direct neuroendocrine connections (e.g., Fig. 2).

See Also the Following Articles

Amygdala; Brain Trauma; Cerebral Metabolism, Brain Imaging; Hippocampus, Overview; Paraventricular Nucleus

Bibliography

Blessing, W. (1997). "The Lower Brainstem in Bodily Homeostasis." Oxford Univ. Press, New York.

Herman, J. P., and Cullinan, W. (1997). Neurocircuitry of stress—Central control of the hypothalamo-pituitary-adrenocortical axis. *Trends Neurosci.* **20**, 78–84.

LeDoux, J. (1996). "The Emotional Brain." Simon & Schuster, New York.

Risold, P. Y., and Swanson, L. W. (1997). Connections of the rat lateral septal complex. *Brain Res. Rev.* **24**, 115–195.

Risold, P. Y., Thompson, R. H., and Swanson, L. W. (1997). The structural organization of connections between hypothalamus and cerebral cortex. *Brain Res. Rev.* **24**, 197–254.

Swanson, L. W. (1987). The hypothalamus. *In* "Handbook of Chemical Neuroanatomy" (A. Bjorklund, T. Hökfelt, and L. W. Swanson, Eds.), vol. 5, pp. 1–124. Elsevier, Amsterdam.

Swanson, L. W., and Petrovich, G. D. (1998). What is the amygdala? *Trends Neurosci.* **21**, 323–331.

Van de Kar, L. D, and Blair, M. L. (1999). Forebrain pathways mediating stress-induced hormone secretion. *Front. Neuroendocrinol.* **20**, 1–48.

Watts, A. G. (1996). The impact of physiological stimulation on the expression of corticotropin-releasing hormone and other neuropeptide genes. *Front. Neuroendocrinol* **17**, 281–326.

Brain Trauma

Brian Pentland

University of Edinburgh, Scotland

GLOSSARY

amnesia Loss or impairment of memory.
cognitive functions A term describing the mental processes related to thinking such as memory, orientation, attention, concentration, and perception.
metabolism The sum of the chemical processes in the body by which complex substances are made and broken down to maintain tissue and organ function.
posttraumatic amnesia (PTA) Amnesia relating to events that occurred after the trauma.
retrograde amnesia (RA) Amnesia relating to events that occurred before the trauma that caused it.

I. NATURE AND CONTEXT OF BRAIN TRAUMA

In Western countries in peacetime, 1 in 50 of the population will seek medical attention because of head injury each year and about 1 in 5 of these will be admitted to the hospital. Young men ages 15 to 25 years are particularly liable to suffer such trauma with the elderly as the next most common group. The human brain lies well protected inside the thick bone of the skull and it usually takes an external blow of considerable impact to transmit destructive forces to the underlying brain. The most common cause of such injuries is falls, followed by road traffic accidents, and, less commonly, work-related, assault, and sports injuries.

As many as half of those admitted to the hospital after brain trauma will have consumed alcohol shortly beforehand. This may cloud the individual's awareness of the otherwise alarming circumstances of the injury. Thus the young man who is intoxicated may not recall falling from a balcony or being struck by a passing car when the effects of the alcohol wear off. In addition, however, by its very nature brain trauma tends to result in a period of confusion associated with lack of memory, or amnesia. The period of lost memory is divided into that which preceded the trauma, retrograde amnesia (RA), and that which followed it, posttraumatic amnesia (PTA). After injury the person may not be able to recall events for minutes, hours, days, or months before impact. There is a tendency for the duration of this period of RA to shrink with the passage of time but, in most cases of severe brain trauma, the circumstances immediately preceding the injury are never remembered. Posttraumatic amnesia is defined as the period of loss of memory between injury and the time the person's confusion resolves and they regain continuous memory of day-to-day events. Indeed one of the most useful ways of classifying severity of brain damage is to measure the duration of PTA. Head injuries are classified as mild, moderate, or severe according to whether the PTA is less than an hour, less than a day, or more than a day respectively. In some people the PTA can extend for months.

It might be regarded as a blessing that some victims of serious road accidents, vicious assaults, or terrifying falls have no memory of the event or its early aftermath and so are spared painful and stressful recollections. Thus the process of the ambulance journey, emergency room admission, and surgical and intensive care management may all be forgotten. In contrast, if any or all of these events are experienced and remembered they may be perceived as stressful.

Even in a state of altered awareness or reduced consciousness after brain trauma the individual may be agitated and, for all intents and purposes, be anxious and stressed. It is not uncommon to see restless behavior with all the physical accompaniments of a stress reaction during the early postinjury period. Thus it would be incorrect to assume that the absence of memory of stress in the longer term meant that stress had not been experienced.

II. NONTRAUMATIC BRAIN INJURIES

Trauma is not the only form of sudden insult to the brain; similar acute damage can occur from a number of other causes such as stroke, lack of oxygen, and infection.

A. Stroke

The commonly used term "stroke" essentially implies an interruption of the blood supply to part of the brain. This may be because of a blockage of the blood flow, which results in an ischemic stroke, or leakage of blood (i.e., hemorrhage), which is described as a hemorrhagic stroke. Both come on quickly and usually without warning.

B. Anoxic and Metabolic Damage

A number of circumstances can result in the brain being denied oxygen and/or glucose, both of which are essential to normal functioning. The brain is probably the most sensitive organ in the body in terms of its need for oxygen and glucose. Lack of oxygen is referred to as hypoxia (or anoxia) and may result from cardiac or respiratory arrest, choking, strangulation, drowning, carbon monoxide poisoning, or drug overdose. The commonest cause of lack of glucose (hypoglycemia) is insulin overdose in people with diabetes. Metabolic disturbances other than lack of glucose would include sudden disruption to the body chemistry in association with serious disorders of the liver or kidneys. Finally, toxic chemicals may act by interfering with oxygen or glucose supply or may poison the brain by another mechanism. For convenience these uncommon cases are often grouped with hypoxic metabolic damage.

C. Infection

Infection of the brain (encephalitis or brain abscess) or its surrounding tissues (meningitis) may cause serious disruption to the functioning of the brain. While this may be short lived and temporary some individuals are left with significant residual problems and are regarded as having sustained permanent brain damage. People whose body defenses are impaired (e.g., those with AIDS or being treated with immunosuppressant drugs) are particularly liable to these conditions. While each of these forms of brain injury have characteristics peculiar to them and in common with trauma, all tend to occur suddenly. Thus the individual affected will usually have been functioning normally, going about their everyday lives, when they are struck down with a serious event. The subsequent events of hospital admission, intensive care, and monitoring are also similar to trauma cases. In contrast to trauma, these people may recall the onset of symptoms and remember more details of their early treatment.

Clearly, in cases of drug overdose, self-hanging, or drowning resulting in hypoxic brain injury, stress may have been a major factor preceding the brain injury and may persist afterward. Although the link is not firmly established, stress may contribute to high blood pressure, which is a major risk factor for both ischemic and hemorrhagic stroke.

III. CONSEQUENCES OF BRAIN INJURY

As the brain is essentially the organ which controls all that we think, feel, and do, when it is damaged the effects can be complex. Brain injury may result in impairments of movement (motor function); of sensation (sensory function); of vision, hearing and balance, smell, and taste (special senses); and of heart beat, respiration, and the control of bowel and bladder (autonomic function). In addition, how the person perceives the world and the abilities to remember, concentrate, reason, and judge (cognitive functions) may also be impaired. The person's emotional state may be disturbed and the attributes that constitute their individual personality, and so how others see them, are also frequently altered.

Often, especially in severe cases, those who survive brain injury present with a complex mixture of physical, cognitive, emotional, and behavioral disorders. Disentangling features of an individual's behavior which may relate to stress from those resulting from the damage itself is often difficult or impossible. However the phenomenon of frustration is commonly reported by people after brain damage—frustration at the loss or impairment of not only physical skills but also with having cognitive difficulties such as remembering things, finding the correct word, or being able to sustain concentration on a task. The process of rehabilitation involves relearning simple skills, which may be daunting for the individual, who feels so incapacitated.

The physical and psychological impairments limit the activities the person can do successfully and which range from basic aspects of self care and domestic chores to managing their own finances. The successful and resourceful husband and father may become a dependent member of the family, unable to fulfill his former roles. Even those who recover to a greater degree may be restricted in both work and leisure pursuits. Loss of employment after brain trauma is common, which in turn may result in financial hardship. Thus the person may be unable to pay the mortgage or rent, afford to keep their car, take a holiday, or go to a football game. These events and the change of personality that may occur after injury contribute to the high frequency of marital disharmony and breakdown which is well recognized after brain trauma. It is apparent, therefore, that the individual who survives significant brain injury may experience a number of consequences which are recognized in the general population as being major sources of stress. Loss of employment, change or loss of home, divorce, loss of friends, and loss of normal leisure activities are all common. Those who suffer more minor injuries and lesser degrees of loss may still experience considerable stress at their inability to fulfill tasks previously performed easily.

An additional major source of stress in some cases of brain trauma is the legal procedures related to claiming compensation. In general the process, reflecting the adversarial nature of most western legal systems, is protracted and involves repeated examinations.

IV. POSTTRAUMATIC STRESS DISORDER

Posttraumatic stress disorder (PTSD) is a specific psychiatric diagnosis the essential feature of which is the development of characteristic symptoms following an extreme traumatic experience associated with threat of death or serious injury. The individual reexperiences the event in various ways, avoids stimuli associated with the trauma, and shows increased arousal. The symptoms persist for at least a month and are associated with significant disruption of the individual's lifestyle.

Currently there is a degree of consensus that PTSD is uncommon after brain trauma but controversy continues as to its actual frequency. Some authorities have suggested that because brain injury results in loss of memory of injury PTSD cannot coexist. Others feel that it may be more common after milder injuries to the brain when the loss of memory, both RA and PTA, is shorter and posttraumatic stressful circumstances are recalled. Finally, it has been suggested that even if the person has no direct memory of the event they may develop PTSD as a reaction to the traumatic sequelae of the injury.

There have been a few reports of PTSD occurring after stroke and other forms of nontraumatic brain injury. Certainly people who recall periods in intensive care, from whatever cause, may view the experience as life threatening and suffer from disturbing recollections of the circumstances associated with increased arousal. Whether such people strictly fulfill the criteria for PTSD is probably not as important as recognizing the severe stress syndromes that do occur.

V. STRESS IN FAMILIES

No account of stress associated with traumatic and nontraumatic brain injury would be complete without at least the mention of the effect brain injury has on other family members. The individual who has suffered severe brain damage, besides perhaps not recalling the event and the early period in the hospital, may have little insight into how they have been altered by the experience. Their families, however, will often have spent agonizing days or weeks wondering if their loved one would survive, followed by anxious weeks or months wondering how much recovery would occur. With the passage of time they may then face the adjustments to their lives resulting from what is essentially the loss of a spouse, partner, parent, or supportive son or daughter. Contending with changes in roles within a family, coping with behavioral and personality changes, and the loss of the principal wage earner can impose huge burdens on other family members.

There is increased recognition of, although still inadequate provision for, the effects of stress on carers in these circumstances. Ill health, both physical and mental, is common in family members of those who survive severe brain injury. Clearly, the same major events such as loss of income, change of accommodation, loss of friends, and restrictions to social life can affect all family members. Divorce is common. The spouse or partner may have to give up their own job or career to become a caregiver or alternatively may have to seek employment to maintain an income. Children may also find themselves having to assume the responsibility of caring for a brain-injured parent, which may disrupt their education or career plans. The one spouse, in having to give attention to the other, or parents, focusing on an injured child, may be unable to provide support to other children in the family, whose mental health and scholastic performance may suffer.

As with other sources of stress, families vary in their ability to cope. There is no direct correlation between the severity of injury and its consequences and the level of stress experienced. Relatively minor brain damage in one individual in a family may produce changes in personality or behavior that other family members find very difficult to deal with. There is fortunately a growing awareness of this phenomenon, with professional help available to assist such families.

See Also the Following Articles

Amnesia; Brain and Brain Regions

Bibliography

American Psychiatric Association (1994). "Diagnostic and Statistical Manual of Mental Disorders" (4th ed.). American Psychiatric Association, Washington, DC.

Rosenthal, M., Griffith, E. R., Kreutzer, J. S., and Pentland, B. (1999) "Rehabilitation of the Adult and Child with Traumatic Brain Injury" (3rd ed.). Davis, Philadelphia.

Breast Cancer

Anne Moyer

Center for Health Care Evaluation, VA Palo Alto Health Care System and Stanford University Medical Center

GLOSSARY

BRCA1 and BRCA2 Two genes which when damaged or mutated greatly increase the risk of developing breast and/or ovarian cancer; individuals with such a mutation have a 50% chance of passing the mutated gene on to their children.

breast-conserving surgery Also called lumpectomy, the removal of a breast tumor and a small margin of normal tissue; radiation therapy is often used in conjunction with breast-conserving surgery.

breast self-exam Examining one's breast area visually and by touch for suspicious changes such as lumps or swelling, skin irritation or dimpling, or nipple pain or retraction; most breast cancers are identified by women themselves.

mammogram An x-ray of the breast that can identify abnormalities before they can be felt by a woman or her health care practitioner and before other physical symptoms develop.

metastasis The spread of cancer from the site of origin to other regions of the body via the lymph system or the bloodstream.

recurrence Cancer that has returned after treatment; breast cancer can recur locally (at the same site), regionally (in the nearby lymph nodes), and distantly (such as the lungs or bone).

Breast cancer is a malignant tumor that develops from the cells of the breast. Apart from skin cancer it is the most common cancer among women. Although the incidence of breast cancer has been steadily increasing among American women over the past 50 years, age-adjusted mortality from the disease has remained stable. Breast cancer can also occur in men, but is much more rare. Length of survival, in part, depends upon the extent of spread of the disease. If cancer is localized to the breast, the 5-year survival rate is 97%; if it has spread to surrounding regions, the rate is 77%; and if it has metastasized to distant sites, the rate is 22%. A majority of women diagnosed with breast cancer will survive 15 years.

I. STRESSES ASSOCIATED WITH BREAST CANCER RISK

All women are at risk for breast cancer. However, particular factors such as a family history of the disease, early menarche or late menopause, and not bearing children or having children after the age of 30 increase the likelihood of developing it. Concern about breast cancer has become salient for American women who, although heart disease is their leading killer, report it as the greatest threat to their health. Although more is being discovered about potential predictors, much uncertainty still remains. Established risk factors can explain only a small amount of the occurrence of breast cancer and approximately half of those diagnosed with the disease have none of these risk factors. Women concerned about their risk for breast cancer have few clear preventive options because factors such as one's family history cannot be altered and recommended modifications in diet, exercise, alcohol consumption, and body weight are no guarantee against contracting the disease.

Not surprisingly, women at higher risk for breast cancer tend to be more distressed. Women with a family history of the disease often overestimate their risk and their concern may be fairly resistant to cancer risk counseling. Anxiety about their own likelihood of developing breast cancer can be compounded by worry about the health of other affected and unaffected family members.

An important issue is how concern about cancer or being at increased risk affects health behaviors, especially those related to early detection and treatment. Screening procedures such as clinical and self breast examinations and mammograms can be anxiety provoking. Screening mammography has a significant false-positive rate, meaning that many women who have it are subject to unnecessary worry and the discomfort of diagnostic biopsies. Despite this, a recent review has determined that having a family history of breast cancer, being at higher risk, having a history of breast problems, and worrying more about breast cancer were associated with a greater rather than a lower likelihood of seeking a mammogram (McCaul *et al.*, 1996, *Health Psych.* **15**, 423–429). However, it has also been documented that anxiety can contribute to delay in seeking medical care once a women discovers a suspicious breast lump.

A small proportion of breast cancer cases, approximately 5–10%, can be attributed to an inherited susceptibility that greatly increases one's likelihood of getting the disease. A blood test to detect relevant inherited mutations in the genes BRCA1 and BRCA2 was recently developed and is becoming more widely available. However, the stresses associated with obtaining this risk information are complex. In order for results to be interpretable, the testing process often requires extensive documentation of the cancer history in one's family. This can be onerous within some families, particularly if there are rifts or a lack of contact. In addition, to identify the particular mutation potentially at work in a family, an affected family member is ideally the first individual tested. This is something that unaffected family members may be reluctant to ask them to do or the affected individual may resist.

Genetic information is especially potent because knowledge about one individual's status will reveal risk information about family members. Relatives may or may not be interested in learning their own risk. Genetic information can also be more complex than most health-related information. In the case of hereditary breast cancer, carrying an identified mutation means that one has only some increased *probability* of developing the disease. If one is found to carry a mutation, courses of action include more vigilant surveillance, taking the antiestrogen drug tamoxifen, or prophylactic surgical removal of healthy breasts. Prophylactic surgery is an option that can reduce the likelihood of getting breast cancer, but will not eliminate the possibility that it will develop. Thus, once one has knowledge of one's mutation status, decisions about one's options can also be a source of turmoil. Finally, concerns about employment or insurance discrimination based on the results of genetic tests remain legitimate.

Despite these challenges, for some women the advantages of having risk information outweigh the disadvantages and can assist them in making decisions about their health care. Early surveys of women at risk for cancer generated concern that those who were more psychologically vulnerable would be more likely to seek genetic testing. However, research with women actually offered test results have shown that those who opt to learn their status have more cancer-specific distress but no more global distress than those who opt not to. Investigation into the psychological and social impact of this testing is in its infancy. Thus far, learning test results appears to result in decreased distress, especially for noncarriers, but more negative psychological outcomes can occur if test results conflict with one's prior expectations.

Concern about developing breast cancer presents quandaries for women with respect to other health-related decisions. For instance, postmenopausal estrogen replacement therapy may have protective effects against heart disease and osteoporosis, both important threats to women's health, but it is also suspected to increase the risk for breast cancer. Women are encouraged, with the help of their health care provider, to determine their own preferred course of action. In general, women making such decisions about their health care have been assisted by increased reporting of health-related issues in the media. However, the fact that reports are often conflicting can cause confusion and worry.

II. STRESSES ASSOCIATED WITH BREAST CANCER DIAGNOSIS AND TREATMENT

Breast cancer involves a myriad of stressors. Diagnosis, treatment, recovery, and long-term survival present a series of challenges that can contribute to psychological morbidity. In fact, a small proportion of women who have been treated for breast cancer show symptoms consistent with posttraumatic stress disorder. An initial diagnosis of breast cancer can provoke worries about loss of physical functioning, social value, and financial resources and fears of death. The time between diagnosis and treatment is an extremely stressful period, exacerbated by trying to gather and understand new information.

Treatment for breast cancer usually involves surgical removal of part or all of the breast. Pain, numbness, and arm stiffness and swelling are common. The cultural connection of the breast to femininity and sexuality means that surgery for breast cancer can threaten a woman's sense of attractiveness and alter sexual relations. Adjuvant treatment such as radiation therapy, chemotherapy, and hormonal therapy represent considerable physical and psychosocial challenges. Side effects from radiation can include itching, swelling, skin changes, and especially fatigue. With chemotherapy, there is nausea, hair loss, weight changes, infections, mouth sores, and altered taste sensations. Such physical effects can lead to depression, low self-esteem, family disruptions, sexual difficulties, and fear of losing a partner. Ironically, even the end of treatment can be difficult as patients lose the attention from medical personnel and the support of family and friends may diminish. The long-term challenges of living with breast cancer include worry about recurrence and fears about the prospect of cancer striking family members.

Coping with breast cancer can be especially difficult for certain populations of women. Single women, for instance, can suffer from isolation, inadequate support, and fears about disclosing their disease to new partners. Women are particularly vulnerable to suffering economically when struck with a life-threatening illness. Low-income women who develop breast cancer or women whose financial situation deteriorates due to their illness have numerous practical difficulties that compound an already difficult experience.

Of course, breast cancer not only affects the individual dealing with the disease but affects those in her social network as well. Partners of breast cancer patients often show significant psychological distress as they deal with the demands of added duties and responsibilities in addition to worrying about their partner's health. Dealing with a life-threatening illness also has numerous ramifications for the family. Breast cancer can disrupt the social, financial, vocational, and educational goals of family members. A key stressor faced by families is dealing with the uncertainty that the illness can bring.

Fortunately, in recent years more attention has been devoted to issues of quality of life for women with breast cancer. Some of the stressors associated with breast cancer diagnosis and treatment have been alleviated by developments in medical practice and changes in social mores. These include the use of less mutilating surgical procedures such as breast-conserving surgery, more openness about the once taboo topic of cancer, the availability of more information about the treatment and experience of breast cancer, the opportunity to play a more active role in one's medical treatment, and increased availability of supportive resources. However, some of these developments can also be stressful. For instance, being involved in decisions about treatment can involve the burden of assimilating a considerable amount of new information during a stressful period and thus perhaps feeling more responsible for one's treatment outcome.

III. THE ROLE OF STRESS IN THE ONSET AND PROGRESSION OF BREAST CANCER

The notion that stress might play a role in the occurrence of cancer is not new. The suggestion that stress and grief could predispose women to breast cancer was ventured in the scientific literature in the late 1800s. This idea is also embraced by women in the general public; when queried about the possible causes of breast cancer, stress is a prominently mentioned factor. Some research has focused on the effect of stressful life events, in particular, on the onset of breast cancer. Methodological difficulties in this area, however, include relying on retrospective accounts of stressful life events in women already diagnosed with cancer or a breast abnormality who may have recall biases due to knowledge of their diagnosis. Some investigators have sought to remedy this problem by making assessments of stress after women have had a diagnostic biopsy for a breast abnormality but before they have learned their results. More methodologically rigorous prospective studies would necessitate following a large number of individuals over an extended period of time to assess the relationship between the occurrence of stressful life events and the subsequent onset of breast cancer. Other methodological problems of studies in this area include lack of comparability of cases and controls on meaningful variables such as age and the fact that the period during which the occurrence of stressful events is assessed is typically shorter than the several years in which tumors are suspected to develop. One investigation in this area found that the incidence and perceived severity of life events occurring in the past 2 years were more severe for women with a breast abnormality that was later diagnosed as cancerous than for those for whom it was benign (Cooper and Faragher, 1989, *Cancer* 19, 415–422). Despite such intriguing findings, overall there is still limited evidence for the connection between stress and cancer onset. Because this link is still speculative, although popular, it is particularly important that it not be overstated such that cancer patients feel responsible for their disease.

Can stress or the reduction of stress play a role in the course of cancer once it is diagnosed? The results of one intervention study have generated much interest and enthusiasm. Women with metastatic breast cancer were assigned either to a supportive group where they were encouraged to express their emotions about cancer and confront their feelings about the disease, which could help alleviate their stress, or to a control group. Although the investigators were only anticipating enhancing quality of life, the group that received the intervention survived an average of almost 18 months longer than the control group (Spiegel *et al.*, 1989, *Lancet* 2, 888–891). Other

studies, however, have found conflicting results, meaning more is yet to be learned before definitive conclusions about the role of stress in cancer's course can be drawn.

One way in which stress might influence the progression of cancer is through alterations in immune functioning. Such changes can result directly from the action of the central nervous system or of stress-elicited hormones or through changes in behavior such as eating, sleeping, smoking, or adhering to medical care. One study documented that women with breast cancer reporting higher levels of stress showed lowered cellular immune responses, including natural killer cell toxicity and T-cell responses, both thought to be relevant to cancer progression (Anderson *et al.*, 1998, *J. Am. Cancer Inst.* 90, 30–36). However, further work is required to determine if such changes are the type or the magnitude that could influence tumor growth and metastasis in clinically meaningful ways. In addition, it remains to be discovered if efforts to improve immune function with stress reduction strategies could have effects on breast cancer progression.

IV. STRESS-REDUCING INTERVENTIONS FOR WOMEN WITH BREAST CANCER

Regardless of whether stress-reduction strategies will increase the length of survival of women with breast cancer, interventions that help women deal with the challenges of the disease can improve quality of life. A number of supportive interventions for cancer now exist. These include cognitive behavioral interventions that focus on changing specific thoughts or behaviors or on learning specific coping skills, educational programs that provide information, psychotherapy and counseling by professionals, and mutual support provided by nonprofessionals such as groups of fellow patients. In addition, relaxation and attentional distraction have been used to deal with the nausea and vomiting associated with chemotherapy. Such interventions have proved to be beneficial. A recent meta-analysis of randomized, controlled-outcome studies concluded that psychosocial interventions for cancer (which have included primarily breast cancer patients) have positive effects on emotional adjustment, functional adjustment, and treatment- and disease-related symptoms (Meyer and Mark, 1995, *Health Psych.* **14**, 101–108).

With limited resources for supportive interventions and the fact that not all cancer patients wish or are able to make use of them, it is important to consider viable alternatives to counseling and support groups. This has brought a focus on means to enhance natural support from those already in an individual's social network and alternatives to face-to-face interactions such as computer-facilitated support systems. The recent proliferation of self-help books and information available on the Internet related to breast cancer also offer promise.

See Also the Following Articles

CANCER; CANCER TREATMENT; ESTROGEN; GENETIC FACTORS AND STRESS; METASTASIZATION

Bibliography

Anderson, B. L., Kiecolt-Glaser, J. K., and Glaser, R. (1994). A biobehavioral model of cancer stress and disease. *Am. Psych.* **49**, 389–404.

Baum, A., Friedman, A. L., and Zakowski, S. G. (1997). Stress and genetic testing for disease risk. *Health Psych.* **16**, 8–19.

Cooper, C. L. (Ed.) (1988). "Stress and Breast Cancer." Wiley, Chichester, UK.

Cox, T., and MacKay, C. (1982). Psychosocial factors and psychophysiological mechanisms in the aeteology and development of cancers. *Soc. Sci. Med.* **16**, 381–396.

McCaul, K. D., Branstetter, A. D., Schroeder, D. M., and Glasgow, R. E. (1996). What is the relationship between breast cancer risk and mammography screening? A meta-analytic review. *Health Psych.* **15**, 423–429.

McGee, R., Williams, S., and Elwood, M. (1996). Are life events related to the onset of breast cancer? *Psych. Med.* **26**, 441–448.

Meyer, T. J., and Mark, M. M. (1995). Effects of psychosocial interventions with adult cancer patients: A meta-analysis of randomized experiments. *Health Psych.* **14**, 101–108.

Moyer, A., and Salovey, P. (1996). Psychosocial sequelae of breast cancer and its treatment. *Ann. Behav. Med.* **18**, 110–125.

Spiegel, D. (1990). Facilitating emotional coping during treatment. *Cancer* **66**, 1422–1426.

Spiegel, D., and Kato, P. M. (1996). Psychosocial influences on cancer incidence and progression. *Harvard Rev. Psychiat.* **4**, 10–26.

Tedder, E. J. (1998). "Understanding and Assisting Low-Income Women with Cancer." Hayworth, Binghamton, NY.

Bulimia

see Eating Disorders and Stress

Burnout

Christina Maslach
University of California, Berkeley

Michael P. Leiter
Acadia University

I. Definition and Assessment
II. A Process Model of Burnout
III. Organizational Context of Burnout and Engagement

GLOSSARY

burnout A psychological syndrome of exhaustion, cynicism, and inefficacy which is experienced in response to chronic job stressors.

cynicism A negative, callous, or excessively detached response to various aspects of the job.

engagement with work An energetic state of involvement with personally fulfilling activities that enhance one's sense of professional efficacy.

exhaustion Feelings of being overextended and depleted of one's emotional and physical resources.

inefficacy Feelings of incompetence and lack of achievement in work.

Burnout is a prolonged response to chronic emotional and interpersonal stressors on the job. It is defined by the three dimensions of exhaustion, cynicism, and inefficacy. As a reliably identifiable job stress syndrome, burnout clearly places the individual stress experience within a larger organizational context of people's relation to their work. Interventions to alleviate burnout and to promote its opposite, engagement with work, can occur at both organizational and personal levels. The social focus of burnout, the solid research basis concerning the syndrome, and its specific ties to the work domain make a distinct and valuable contribution to people's health and well-being.

I. DEFINITION AND ASSESSMENT

Burnout is a psychological syndrome of exhaustion, cynicism, and inefficacy in the workplace. It is considered to be an individual stress experience embedded in a context of complex social relationships, and it involves the person's conception of both self and others on the job. Unlike unidimensional models of stress, this multidimensional model conceptualizes burnout in terms of its three core components.

A. Burnout Components

Exhaustion refers to feelings of being overextended and depleted of one's emotional and physical resources. Workers feel drained and used up, without any source of replenishment. They lack enough energy to face another day or another person in need. The exhaustion component represents the basic individual stress dimension of burnout.

Cynicism refers to a negative, hostile, or excessively detached response to the job, which often includes a loss of idealism. It usually develops in response to the overload of emotional exhaustion and is self-protective at first—an emotional buffer of "detached concern." But the risk is that the detachment can turn into dehumanization. The cynicism component represents the interpersonal dimension of burnout.

Inefficacy refers to a decline in feelings of competence and productivity at work. People experience a growing sense of inadequacy about their ability to do the job well, and this may result in a self-imposed verdict of failure. The inefficacy component represents the self-evaluation dimension of burnout.

What has been distinctive about burnout is the interpersonal framework of the phenomenon. The centrality of relationships at work—whether it be relationships with clients, colleagues, or supervisors—has always been at the heart of descriptions of burnout. These relationships are the source of both emotional strains and rewards, they can be a resource for coping with job stress, and they often bear the brunt of the negative effects of burnout. Thus, if one were to look at burnout out of context and simply focus on the individual exhaustion component, one would lose sight of the phenomenon entirely.

The principal measure of burnout is the Maslach Burnout Inventory (MBI), which provides distinct assessments of each of the three burnout components. Different forms of the MBI have been developed for different types of occupations: the human services survey (MBI-HSS), the educators survey (MBI-ES), and the general survey (MBI-GS). As a result of international interest in burnout research, the MBI has been translated into many languages.

B. Burnout Correlates

Unlike acute stress reactions, which develop in response to specific critical incidents, burnout is a cumulative stress reaction to ongoing occupational stressors. With burnout, the emphasis has been more on the process of psychological erosion and the psychological and social outcomes of this chronic exposure rather than just the physical ones. Because burnout is a prolonged response to chronic interpersonal stressors on the job, it tends to be fairly stable over time.

1. Health Symptoms

Of the three burnout components, exhaustion is the closest to an orthodox stress variable and therefore is more predictive of stress-related health outcomes than the other two components. Exhaustion is typically correlated with such stress symptoms as: headaches, chronic fatigue, gastrointestinal disorders, muscle tension, hypertension, cold/flu episodes, and sleep disturbances. These physiological correlates mirror those found with other indices of prolonged stress. Similarly parallel findings have been found for the link between burnout and various forms of substance abuse.

In terms of mental, as opposed to physical, health, the link with burnout is more complex. It has been assumed that burnout may result in subsequent mental disabilities, and there is some evidence to link burnout with greater anxiety, irritability, and depres-

sion. However, an alternative argument is that burnout is itself a form of mental illness rather than a cause of it. Much of this discussion has focused on depression and whether burnout is a different phenomenon. Research has demonstrated that the two constructs are indeed distinct: burnout is job related and situation specific as opposed to depression, which is general and context free.

2. Job Behaviors

Burnout has been associated with various forms of job withdrawal—absenteeism, intention to leave the job, and actual turnover. However, for people who stay on the job, burnout leads to lower productivity and effectiveness at work. To the extent that burnout diminishes opportunities for satisfying experiences at work, it is associated with decreased job satisfaction and a reduced commitment to the job or the organization.

People who are experiencing burnout can have a negative impact on their colleagues both by causing greater personal conflict and by disrupting job tasks. Thus, burnout can be "contagious" and perpetuate itself through informal interactions on the job. There is also some evidence that burnout has a negative "spillover" effect on people's home life.

C. Engagement: The Opposite of Burnout

The opposite of burnout is not a neutral state, but a definite state of mental health within the occupational domain. Engagement with work is a productive and fulfilling state and is defined in terms of the same three dimensions as burnout, but the positive end of those dimensions rather than the negative. Thus, engagement consists of a state of high energy (rather than exhaustion), strong involvement (rather than cynicism), and a sense of efficacy (rather than inefficacy). One important implication of the burnout–engagement continuum is that strategies to promote engagement may be just as important for burnout prevention as strategies to reduce the risk of burnout. A workplace that is designed to support the positive development of the three core qualities of energy, involvement, and effectiveness should be successful in promoting the well-being and produc-

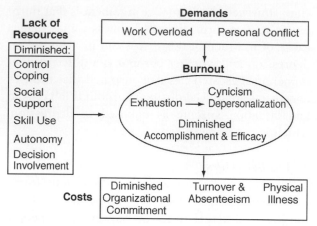

FIGURE 1 Process model of burnout. Modified and reproduced by special permission of the Publisher, Consulting Psychologists Press, Inc., Palo Alto, CA 94303 from **Maslach Burnout Inventory** by Christina Maslach, Susan E. Jackson, and Michael P. Leiter. Copyright 1996 by Consulting Psychologists Press, Inc. All rights reserved. Further reproduction is prohibited without the Publisher's written consent.

tivity of its employees and thus the health of the entire organization. From this perspective health is not limited to the physical or emotional well-being of individuals but is evident in enduring patterns of social interactions among people.

II. A PROCESS MODEL OF BURNOUT

There is an established body of evidence that burnout is related to the organizational environments in which people work. In general, the exhaustion and cynicism components of the syndrome arise from demands and conflicts confronting workers, while inefficacy is influenced by the lack of social support and opportunities to develop professionally. The complex relationships among various aspects of organizational environments with the three components of burnout have encouraged the development of structural models in much of burnout research. This approach permits researchers to examine the contribution of many potential influences and consequences simultaneously, separating unique contributors to the development of burnout from those that are redundant with one another. Figure 1 displays a

process model of burnout that summarizes major research findings.

In the center of Fig. 1 are the three components of burnout: exhaustion, cynicism (or depersonalization), and diminished efficacy (or accomplishment). The relationship from exhaustion to cynicism is the most reliable aspect of the process model. Exhaustion is not only strongly related to cynicism, but it mediates the relationship of organizational factors with cynicism. In contrast, the relationship of efficacy with the other two components of burnout does not necessarily signify direct causal paths between them. Various aspects of organizational environments can aggravate exhaustion or diminish effectiveness or do both simultaneously.

A. Contributing Factors to Burnout

1. Job Characteristics

The primary antecedents of the exhaustion component are work overload and personal conflict at work. Quantitative work overload demands that employees do too much work in too little time, while qualitative work overload is an issue when work demands require employees to accept responsibilities outside of their range of expertise (a problem particularly evident during major organizational transitions). Personal conflict has an impact on exhaustion both through its demands on the emotional energy of individuals as well as through its weakening of employees' confidence in the social environment of the organization.

A lack of resources to manage job demands also contributes to burnout. The most critical of these resources has been social support among colleagues. Support underscores shared values and a sense of community within the organization, which enhances employees' sense of efficacy. Another important resource is the opportunity for employees to participate in decisions that affect their work and to exercise control over their contributions.

2. Personal Characteristics

Although the research on burnout has focused primarily on the organizational context in which people work, it has also considered a range of personal qualities. Research on personality variables has found some consistent correlational patterns; basically, burnout scores are higher for people who have a less "hardy" personality, who have a more external locus of control, and who score as "neurotic" on the Five-Factor Model of personality. There is also some evidence that people who exhibit Type-A behavior (which tends to predict coronary heart disease) are more prone to the exhaustion dimension of burnout.

There are few consistent relationships of burnout with demographic characteristics. Although higher age seems to be associated with lower burnout, it is confounded with both years of experience and with survival bias (i.e., those who "survive" early job stressors and do not quit). Thus it is difficult to derive a clear explanation for this age pattern. The only consistent gender difference is a tendency for men to score slightly higher on cynicism. These weak demographic relationships are congruent with the view that the work environment is of greater significance than personal characteristics in the development of burnout.

III. ORGANIZATIONAL CONTEXT OF BURNOUT AND ENGAGEMENT

Inherent to the fundamental concept of stress is the problematic relationship between the individual and the situation. Within a work situation, burnout is an important mediator of the causal link between various job stressors and individual stress outcomes. Thus, the effects of both personal and job characteristics need to be considered jointly within the context of the organizational environment.

A. Job–Person Mismatch

A recent model proposes that the greater the gap, or mismatch, between the person and the job, the greater the likelihood of burnout. The model specifies not one but six areas in which this mismatch can take place. In each area, the nature of the job is not in harmony with the nature of the person, and the result is the increased exhaustion, cynicism, and inefficacy of burnout. On the other hand, when better fit exists in these six areas, then engagement with

work is the likely outcome. The six areas in which mismatches can occur are: workload, control, reward, community, fairness, and values. Each area of mismatch has a distinct relationship with burnout and engagement as reflected in the extant research literature.

B. Implications for Interventions

The personal and organizational costs of burnout provide have led to the development of various intervention strategies. Some try to treat burnout after it has occurred, while others focus on how to prevent burnout by promoting engagement. Intervention may occur on the level of the individual, workgroup, or an entire organization. At each level, the number of people affected by an intervention and the potential for enduring change increases.

The primary emphasis has been on individual strategies to prevent burnout rather than on social or organizational ones. This is particularly paradoxical given that research has found that situational and organizational factors play a bigger role in burnout than individual ones. Also, individual strategies are relatively ineffective in the workplace, where the person has much less control of stressors than in other domains of his or her life. There are both philosophical and pragmatic reasons underlying the predominant focus on the individual, including notions of individual causality and responsibility, and the assumption that it is easier and cheaper to change people instead of organizations. However, any progress in dealing with burnout will depend on the development of strategies that focus on the job context and its impact on the people who work within it.

See Also the Following Article

WORKPLACE STRESS

Bibliography

Cherniss, C. (1995). "Beyond Burnout." Routledge, New York.

Cordes, C. L., and Dougherty, T. W. (1993). A review and integration of research on job burnout. *Acad. Manag. Rev.* 18, 621–656.

Maslach, C., Jackson, S. E., and Leiter, M. P. (1996). "Maslach Burnout Inventory Manual," 3rd ed. Consulting Psychologists Press, Palo Alto, CA.

Maslach, C., and Leiter, M. P. (1997). "The Truth about Burnout." Jossey-Bass, San Francisco, CA.

Schaufeli, W., and Enzmann, D. (1998). "The Burnout Companion to Study and Practice." Taylor & Francis, Philadelphia, PA.

Schaufeli, W., Maslach, C., and Marek T. (Eds.) (1993). "Professional Burnout: Recent Developments in Theory and Research." Taylor & Francis, Washington, D.C.

Calbindin

Ferenc A. Antoni

MRC Brain Metabolism Unit, Edinburgh, Scotland

I. Role of Calbindin in Nerve Cells

GLOSSARY

EF-hand proteins A family of diverse proteins that bind Ca^{2+} with high affinity. The EF-hand motif refers to α-helical parts of these proteins that form the Ca^{2+} binding site(s).

C albindin is one of several EF-hand proteins found in the central nervous system with no clearly established physiological function.

I. ROLE OF CALBINDIN IN NERVE CELLS

The interest in this protein stems from the fact that it is selectively expressed in certain groups of hippocampal and cerebral cortical nerve cells, which appear to be relatively resistant to Ca^{2+}-mediated neurotoxicity. Furthermore, the levels of calbindin in the brain as well as other tissues are regulated by steroid hormones, including glucocorticoids and estrogens.

Ca^{2+}-mediated toxicity has been proposed to be important for the neurotoxic effects of glucocorticoids. According to the hypothesis put forward by R. M. Sapolsky, corticosteroids make nerve cells vulnerable to increases of intracellular free Ca^{2+} induced by excitatory amino acids. This is particularly evident in the CA1 area of the hippocampus. Sapolsky and co-workers have also postulated that this area of the hippocampus is important for the termination of the stress-induced increase of plasma cortisol. Thus if CA1 neurones are damaged by high levels of plasma corticosteroids, this may lead to a vicious positive feedback cycle progressively destroying the hippocampal target neurons of glucocorticoids thus leading to a decline in cognitive function due to chronic stress.

In addition to buffering of intracellular Ca^{2+}, overexpression of calbindin also reduced plasma membrane Ca^{2+} currents. Collectively, these actions would have beneficial effects in combating Ca^{2+}-mediated toxicity. Nonetheless, a lot more needs to be learned about the cellular functions of calbindin.

Bibliography

Baimbridge, K. G., Celio, M. R., and Rogers, J. H. (1992). Calcium-binding proteins in the nervous-system. *Trends Neurosci.* **15**, 303–308.

Krugers, H. J., Medema, R. M., Postema, F., and Korf, J. (1995). Region-specific alterations of calbindin-d28k immunoreactivity in the rat hippocampus following adrenalectomy and corticosterone treatment. *Brain Res.* **696**, 89–96.

Landfield, P. W., McEwen, B. S., Sapolsky, R. M., and Meaney, M. J. (1996). Hippocampal cell death. *Science* **272**, 1249–1251.

Lledo, P. M., Somasundaram, B., Morton, A. J., Emson, P. C., and Mason, W. T. (1992). Stable transfection of calbindin-D28k into the GH3 cell line alters calcium currents and intracellular calcium homeostasis. *Neuron* **9**, 943–954.

Mattson, M. P., Rychlik, B., Chu, C., and Christakos, S. (1991). Evidence for calcium-reducing and excito-protective roles for the calcium-binding protein calbindin-D(28k) in cultured hippocampal-neurons. *Neuron* 6, 41–51.

Meier, T. J., Ho, D. Y., Park, T. S., and Sapolsky, R. M. (1998). Gene transfer of calbindin D-28k cDNA via herpes simplex virus amplicon vector decreases cytoplasmic calcium ion response and enhances neuronal survival following glutamatergic challenge but not following cyanide. *J. Neurochem.* 71, 1013–1023.

Sapolsky, R. M. (1992). "Stress, the Aging Brain, and the Mechanisms of Neuron Death." MIT Press, Cambridge, MA.

Calcium-Dependent Neurotoxicity

John S. Kelly

University of Edinburgh, Scotland

I. Excitatory Aminoacid Neurotoxicity
II. Stress and Adrenal Corticoids
III. Therapeutics: Neuroprotectants

GLOSSARY

apoptosis or programmed cell death In contrast to necrosis, apoptotic cell death is an active and controlled process characterized morphologically by the maintenance of membrane integrity until very late in the death process. The cell membrane shows characteristic blebbing as the cell volume decreases. The nuclear proteins condense to form an easily recognized pattern, the intracellular organelles are well preserved, and the whole still-intact cell is engulfed by phagocytes. The packaging and removal process serves to minimize inflammation. However, under conditions where the phagocytic step is omitted, cells undergo secondary necrosis and rupture, spilling their contents into the surrounding tissue space.

free radicals When the blood supply or oxygen supply is compromised, toxic chemical species are formed which cause cell death either directly or by a process known as lipid peroxidation. The free radicals include a reduction of molecular oxygen to the superoxide anion (O_2^-), the formation of hydrogen peroxide (H_2O_2), hydroperoxyradicals (HOO*), hydroxyl radicals (OH*), and singlet oxygen ($^1O_2$) species.

ischemia and/or anoxia The brain is highly vulnerable to disturbances of the blood supply. Interruption of the blood supply (ischemia) or the delivery of blood containing an inadequate amount of oxygen (anoxia) leads to cell death as an area of the brain is deprived of oxygen, glucose, and other nutrients and the removal of carbon dioxide, lactic acid, free radicals, and other metabolites. Within a few minutes the most severely damaged cells die by necrosis and the area of damage is said to be infarcted. This is the process that underlies a stroke when the blood flow to the cerebral cortex and striatum is compromised by reduced blood flow in the middle cerebral artery.

lipid peroxidation Reactive metabolites and free radicals formed under anoxic or ischemic conditions set off a cascade of membrane destruction which also releases cytotoxic species known as lipid peroxyradicals (ROO*) and hyperoxides (ROOH). In normally perfused and oxygenated tissue, lipid peroxides and other reactive species are usually dealt with effectively by specific enzymes which require the presence of vitamin E and a variety of other compounds present in a normal diet known as antioxidants.

necrosis An explosive event caused by exposure to a catastrophic toxic event and characterized by almost instantaneous membrane lysis and the release of the intracellular contents into the extracellular space followed by an essentially inflammatory process. In ischemic tissue, glucose and glycogen are depleted within minutes and this leads to a fall in phosphocreatine levels and ATP with an inevitable failure of energy-dependent ion transporters and a loss of ion homeostasis. The passive entry of water into the energy-depleted cell causes intense swelling and osmolytic damage is sufficient to destroy the cytoplasmic organelles and the nuclear membranes.

For at least a decade, a rise in intracellular Ca^{2+} concentration ($[Ca^{2+}]_i$) has been considered as one of the most important factors in the a final common pathway that leads to cell death whether by necrosis or apoptosis. Direct activation of calcium-dependent lytic enzymes including proteases, lipases, nucleases; lipid peroxidation; damage to DNA; and rupture of mitochondria and cell membranes destroy cell structure. Accumulation of calcium phosphate within mitochondria disrupts these organelles, leading to impaired ATP production and indirectly to further disruption of Na^+ exchangers. Disruption of mitochondria may also trigger apoptotic programs which lead to the death of adjacent groups of cells. The area of damage may be enlarged by the activation of nitric oxide synthetase and free radical production.

I. EXCITATORY AMINO ACID NEUROTOXICITY

A common cause of calcium-mediated cell death is the excessive release of excitatory amino acids. During normal synaptic activity the local $[Ca^{2+}]_i$ is assumed to increase transiently following the episodic activation of excitatory amino acid receptors during synaptic activity. Although in the past this was thought to occur principally due to the Ca^{2+} entry through N-methyl-D-aspartate (NMDA) receptor/ion channels, Ca^{2+} entry is now known to occur through a number of the AMPA (α-amino-3-hydroxy-5-methyl-isoxazole) receptor subtypes and kainate receptors. Recently, relatively modest synaptic stimulation has been shown to lead to local increases in $[Ca^{2+}]_i$ following the activation of metabotropic receptors and the subsequent release of Ca^{2+} from the endoplasmic reticulum. Following the massive release of glutamate induced by ischemia and/or anoxia, the overactivation of these same excitatory amino acid receptor pathways leads to increase in $[Ca^{2+}]_i$ enhanced by the opening of voltage-activated Ca^{2+} channels. The substantial depolarization that accompanies the excessive activation of the excitatory amino acid receptors also leads to excessive levels of $[Na^+]_i$. In turn, high $[Na^+]_i$ impairs the sodium–calcium exchanger, leading to further increases in $[Ca^{2+}]_i$. Given the abundance of excitatory amino acids in the central nervous system it is easy to see how the release of glutamic acid from the cytosol of dead or degenerating neurones leads to the death of adjacent tissues. Additional factors may affect the ability of the neurons to resist the rise in $[Ca^{2+}]_i$, such as aging and the consequent impairment of DNA repair mechanisms, energetic impairment, environmental toxins, or viral infections.

II. STRESS AND ADRENAL CORTICOIDS

Prolonged physiological stress or the administration of corticosterone can also modify synaptic transmission and, in excess, enhance cell death. The same molecular machinery appears to be responsible for both the synaptic changes associated with learning and memory and cell death. Elevated $[Ca^{2+}]_i$, levels have been shown to accompany corticosterone-enhanced cell death. At least two mechanisms seemed to be involved; a reduction in glucose uptake, which results in an "energy crisis" and leads to a breakdown in Ca^{2+} homeostasis, and an inhibition of extracellular glutamate uptake into nerve terminals and glial cells. Interestingly, estradiol is protective.

III. THERAPEUTICS: NEUROPROTECTANTS

Therapeutic attempts to attenuate the damage caused by a rise in $[Ca^{2+}]_i$ have focused on excitatory amino acid receptor blockade. In the main, Ca^{2+} channel antagonists have proved disappointing. However, drugs such as riluzole, lamotrigine, and gabapentin are thought to limit glutamate release and or block Na^+ channels. In more chronic situations, antioxidants may prove useful. Other studies have suggested that neurotrophic factors such us glial-derived growth factor, neurotrphin-3, cardiotrophin, insulinlike growth factor, and immunophillin antagonists may all be neuroprotective. Clearly, the possibility that $[Ca^{2+}]_i$ can also trigger apoptosis may lead to the discovery of new treatments, given the large number of antiapoptopic drugs currently being tested *in vitro*.

See Also the Following Article

APOPTOSIS

Bibliography

Beal, M. F., Hyman, B. T., and Koroshetz, W. (1993). Do defects in mitochondrial energy metabolism underlie the pathology of neurodegenerative diseases? *Trends Neurosci.* **16**, 125–131.

Cassarino, D. S., and Bennett, J. P. Jr. (1993). An evaluation of the role of mitochondria in neurodegenerative diseases: Mitochondrial mutations and oxidative pathology, protective nuclear responses, and cell death in neurodegeneration. *Brain Res. Rev.* **29**, 1–25.

Kim, J. J., and Yoon, K. S. (1998). Stress: Metaplastic effects in the hippocampus. *Trends Neurosci.* **21**, 505–509.

Kinloch, R. A., Treherne, J. M., Furness, L. M., and Hajimohamadreza, I. H. (1999). The pharmacology of apoptosis. *Trends Pharmacol. Sci.* **20**, 35–42.

Kristián, T., Ouyang, Y., and Siesjö, B. K. (1996). Calcium-induced neuronal cell death in vivo and in vitro: Are the pathophysiologic mechanisms different? *In* B. K. Siesjö and T. Wieloch (Eds.), "Molecular Mechanisms of Ischemic Brain Damage" (B. K. Siesjö and T. Wieloch, Eds.), pp. 107–113. Lippincott-Raven, Philadelphia.

Lipton, S. A., and Rosenberg, P. A. (1994). Excitatory amino-acids as a final common pathway for neurologic disorders. *N. Engl. J. Med.* **330**, 613–622.

Louvel, E., Hugon, J., and Doble, A. (1997). Therapeutic advances in amyotrophic lateral sclerosis. *Trends Pharmacol. Sci.* **18**, 196–203.

Mattson, M. P., Guthrie, P. B., and Kater, S. B. (1989). A role for Na^+-dependent Ca^{2+}-extrusion in protection against neuronal excitotoxicity. *FASEB J.* **3**, 2519–2526.

Olney, J. W. (1978). Neurotoxicity of excitatory amino acids. *In* "Kainate Acid as a Tool in Neurobiology" (E. G. McGreer, J. W. Olney, & P. L. McGreer, Eds.), pp. 95–121. Raven, New York.

Rang, H. P., Dale, M. M., and Ritter, J. M. (1995). Chemical transmission and drug action in the central nervous system. *In* "Pharmacology" (H. P. Rang, M. M. Dale, and J. M. Ritter, Eds.), pp. 491–518. Churchill–Livingstone, Edinburgh.

Snyder, S. H., Sabatini, D. M., Lai, M. M., Steiner, J. P., Hamilton, G. S., and Suzdak, P. D. (1998). Neural actions of immunophilin ligands. *Trends Pharmacol. Sci.* **19**, 21–26.

Calcium, Role of

Ferenc A. Antoni

MRC Brain Metabolism Unit, Edinburgh, Scotland

I. Calcium in the Extracellular Fluid
II. Intracellular Calcium

GLOSSARY

heterotrimeric G proteins A group of proteins that consist of three subunits (α, β, γ) and that couple cell surface receptors to their effector enzymes. Upon activation of cell surface receptors by their ligands, heterotrimeric G proteins dissociate into the α-subunit and the $\beta\gamma$-complex, both of which regulate the activity of effector enzymes such as adenylyl cyclase in the cell membrane.

second messengers These are generated by extracellular stimuli arriving at the cell surface and they transduce the extracellular signal toward the interior of the cell.

C alcium ions are ubiquitous second messengers in biological systems.

I. CALCIUM IN THE EXTRACELLULAR FLUID

Calcium is found in several compartments of the body. Extracellular Ca^{2+} is in ionized form as well as in protein-complexed form. There are G-protein-coupled cell surface receptors in several cells of the body that detect and respond to ionized Ca^{2+} above 1.5 mM. These receptors activate the polyphospho-inositide cycle through the coupling protein G_q and may inhibit adenylyl cyclase through G_i or G_o. Apart from the parathyroid gland where these receptors control the secretion of parathyroid hormone, the role of the G-protein-coupled Ca^{2+} sensor remains to be explored. It is, however, clearly expressed in the brain as well as the adenohypophysis where corticotropes appear to express this receptor.

II. INTRACELLULAR CALCIUM

Inside cells, Ca^{2+} is found in several pools (e.g., smooth endoplasmic reticulum and mitochondria) maintained by various transporter proteins and intracellular ion channels. Intracellular free Ca^{2+} is fundamental for a multitude of regulatory processes including intracellular signal transduction.

The action of proteins induced by glucocorticoids in hippocampal neurons and anterior pituitary corticotrophs appears to require intracellular Ca^{2+}. Glucocorticoids augment Ca^{2+} influx through voltage-operated ion channels in CA1 hippocampal neurons and increase the level of L-type Ca^{2+} channel subunit mRNA in this system. In pituitary corticotroph cells, blockade of the Ca^{2+}-activated protein phosphatase calcineurin markedly reduces the efficiency of glucocorticoid feedback inhibition of adrenocorticotropin release.

Glucocorticoids enhance the vulnerability of hippocampal neurons to Ca^{2+}-induced neurotoxicity. Thus prolonged hypercortisolemia such as that seen in chronic stress, Cushing's disease, or depression may lead to neuronal loss in the hippocampus. Further, this mechanism may also contribute to the decline of mental function during aging as plasma cortisol levels are known to rise with age. This has led to the "glucocorticoid cascade" and to the "calcium" hypotheses of aging.

See Also the Following Article

Cushing's Syndrome

Bibliography

Antoni, F. A. (1996). Calcium checks cyclic AMP—Mechanism of corticosteroid feedback in adenohypophysial corticotrophs. *J. Neuroendocrinol.* 8, 659–672. 1996.

Berridge, M. J. (1998). Neuronal calcium signaling. *Neuron* 21, 13–26.

Brown, E. M., Chattopadhyay, N., Vassilev, P. M., and Hebert, S. C. (1998). The calcium-sensing receptor (CaR) permits Ca^{2+} to function as a versatile extracellular first messenger. *Recent Prog. Horm. Res.* 53, 257–280.

Kerr, D. S., Campbell, L. W., Thibault, O., and Landfield, P. W. (1992). Hippocampal glucocorticoid receptor activation enhances voltage-dependent Ca^{2+} conductances: Relevance to brain aging. *Proc. Natl. Acad. Sci. USA* 89, 8527–8531.

Landfield, P. W., McEwen, B. S., Sapolsky, R. M., and Meaney, M. J. (1996). Hippocampal cell death. *Science* 272, 1249–1251.

Landfield, P. W., Thibault, O., Mazzanti, M. L., Porter, N. M., and Kerr, D. S. (1992). Mechanisms of neuronal death in brain aging and Alzheimers-disease—Role of endocrine-mediated calcium dyshomeostasis. *J. Neurobiol.* 23, 1247–1260.

Nair, S. M., Werkman, T. R., Craig, J., Finnell, R., Jöels, M., and Eberwine, J. H. (1998). Corticosteroid regulation of ion channel conductances and mRNA levels in individual hippocampal CA1 neurons. *J. Neurosci.* 18, 2685–2696.

Sapolsky, R. M. (1994). The physiological relevance of glucocorticoid endangerment of the hippocampus. *Ann. N. Y. Acad. Sci.* 746, 294–307.

SmithSwintosky, V. L., Pettigrew, L. C., Sapolsky, R. M., Phares, C., Craddock, S. D., Brooke, S. M., and Mattson, M. P. (1996). Metyrapone, an inhibitor of glucocorticoid production, reduces brain injury induced by focal and global ischemia and seizures. *J. Cereb. Blood Flow Metab.* 16, 505–508.

EOS entries: "Adenylyl cyclases and stress response" and "Calbindin."

Cancer

David Spiegel

Stanford University School of Medicine

I. OVERVIEW: MIND/BODY INTERACTIONS AND CANCER

Cancer research has productively focused on the pathophysiology of the disease, emphasizing tumor biology as predictors of disease outcome at the expense of studying the role of the body's psychophysiological reactions to tumor invasion. These reactions are mediated by brain/body mechanisms, including the endocrine, neuroimmune, and autonomic nervous systems. While a large portion of the variance in any disease outcome is accounted for by the specific local pathophysiology of that disease, some variability must also be explained by "host resistance" factors, which include the manner of response to the stress of the illness.

Prior to 1981, a series of classic experiments in animals showed that crowded living conditions accelerated the rate of tumor growth and mortality in rats. In a recent authoritative review of human stress literature, McEwen (1998) documents the adverse health effects of cumulative stressors and the body's failure to adapt the stress response to them. Activa-

tion of the hypothalamic-pituitary-adrenal axis (HPA) is an adaptive response to acute stress, but over time in response to cumulative stress the system's signal-to-noise ratio can be degraded so that it is partially "on" all the time, leading to adverse physiological consequences, including abnormalities of glucose metabolism, hippocampal damage, accumulation of abdominal fat, and depression. Abnormalities of HPA function, including glucocorticoid receptor hypersensitivity, have also been found to be associated with posttraumatic stress disorder. Thus adverse events, ranging from traumatic stressors to cumulative minor ones, are associated with HPA dysregulation. Persistently elevated or relatively invariant levels of cortisol may, in turn, stimulate tumor proliferation. Possible mechanisms include differential gluconeogenesis response of normal and tumor tissue to glucocorticoid signals to secrete glucose into the blood, activation of hormone receptors in tumors, or immunosuppression. Indeed, glucocorticoids are potently immunosuppressive, so the effects of acute and chronic stress and hypercortisolemia may include functional immunosuppression as well, as has been shown extensively in animals. There is a growing body of evidence of stress-induced immunosuppression in humans as well. This in turn could influence the rate of cancer progression.

II. CUMULATIVE EFFECTS OF CHRONIC STRESS

Allostatic load has been defined as the price that the body has to pay for maintaining allostasis, or stability through physiologic change. Recently, it has been suggested that increased allostatic load, which may occur through cumulative build-up of stress over a lifespan, may significantly hinder the functioning of different physiologic systems. Cancer itself constitutes a series of stressors: the threat to life and health, the disruption of social activities, the rigors and side effects of treatment. A given individual's psychological and physiological response pattern to stress in general is likely to be exacerbated by the diagnosis and treatment of cancer, thereby intensifying mind/body connections mediated by the stress-response system.

Recurrence or metastasis of cancer can be considered a more severe chronic stressor. Both short-term and long-term alterations in psychological state (e.g., major depression) are known to be correlated with endocrine changes. Stress is associated with increased sympathetic nervous system (SNS) and HPA axis activity. Catecholamine hormones and cortisol (released during SNS and HPA activity) are elevated in cancer patients as well as in bereaved and depressed subjects.

Abnormalities in the circadian rhythm of cortisol have been observed in subjects undergoing psychological stress (e.g., depression, unemployment, post-traumatic stress disorder) and some types of physical stress (e.g., shift work and excessive workloads).

III. STRESS REACTIVITY AND DISEASE PROGRESSION

That the stress of cancer is felt psychologically is indicated by the fact that as many as 80% of breast cancer patients report significant distress during initial treatment. Estimates of the prevalence of psychiatric disorders among newly diagnosed cancer patients has ranged from 30 to 44% and 20 to 45% exhibit emotional morbidity 1–2 years later. Even though the majority of women diagnosed with breast cancer do not meet criteria for a psychiatric diagnosis, the vast majority experience the diagnosis of cancer as a major stressor, and 10% have severe maladjustment problems as long as 6 years later. Thus, breast cancer is a disease which causes considerable psychological stress.

Reactivity to stressors involves not only the initial response but the system's ability to reset itself after stress. Older organisms seem to reset themselves after a stressor less readily, leaving stress-responsive systems more tonically upregulated for longer periods of time after cessation of the stressor. Cancer particularly affects older people, and chronic disease-related stressors are likely to further decrease the flexibility of stress-response mechanisms. Dr. Robert Saplosky and colleagues (1985) found that stressed older animals not only had persistently elevated cortisol levels after the stress was over, but also much more rapid growth of implanted tumors. This finding was confirmed by Ben-Eliyahu *et al.,* who also identified suppressive effects of stress hormones on NK cells as one potential mediator of the effect. It may not be so much the magnitude of stress-induced elevation of corticosteriods that is important in cancer outcomes, but rather, the duration or persistence of the elevation.

IV. STRESS AND CANCER INCIDENCE AND PROGRESSION

The converse of social support is social stress. There is evidence that social stress such as divorce, loss of a job, or bereavement is associated with a greater likelihood of a relapse of cancer. Ramirez and colleagues (1989) matched women with breast cancer that had recurred to a sample that remained disease-free. The relapsed group had experienced significantly more major life stress, such as bereavement and loss of jobs. For example, the frequency of family deaths or job loss among the relapsed patients yielded a relative risk of 5.67 compared to nonrecurrent breast cancer patients. However, using a better prospective design, Barraclough et al. followed 204 newly diagnosed breast cancer patients for 42 months after diagnosis and initial treatment. No relationship was found between stressful life events and risk of disease progression. The authors note that this was a limited follow-up time, but observed higher rates of bereavement in the nonrelapsing group. However, other studies have supported Ramirez *et al.*'s observation. Geyer interviewed 92 women with undiagnosed breast lumps prior to diagnostic surgery regarding stressful life events during the previous 8 years. Those women later determined to have a malignancy ($N = 33$) had experienced more stressful events than did women with benign tumors. Threat and loss were related to the likelihood of a malignancy independent of but as strongly as age. These studies are both prospective to some degree, but differ in that the dependent variable for the Barraclough study (like that for the Ramirez study) was recurrence, while that for the Geyer study was incidence, which could account for the apparently contradictory findings. Similar results have been obtained among malignant melanoma patients. Havlik *et al.* recruited 56 stage I and stage II melanoma patients into a retrospective study of stressful life events prior to diagnosis. A control group of 56 general surgery patients was randomly selected from hospital records. The melanoma patients had experienced significantly more stressful life events (p <0.01). While the issue is not completely resolved, and more well-conducted prospective studies at both points in the natural history of the disease are needed, three of these four studies indicate a relationship between stress and cancer.

A recent meta-analysis which relies heavily on the European literature, however, concluded that there is no effect of stress on cancer incidence. They reported no effect of bereavement among 11 studies (OR 1.06, 95% CI 0.95–1.18, n.s.) but there was a twofold effect for other stressors (OR 2.63, 95% CI 2.34–2.96). However, they based their final null conclusion on six studies they deemed to be of "higher quality" because of the use of population controls, blinding of interviewers, and other methodological issues. In these studies there was no effect of stress on cancer incidence. While this review clearly raises important questions about the stress/cancer link, it does so only after dismissing findings of the majority of studies in the field. Furthermore, another more recent meta-analysis concludes that stress, loss, and depression are related to breast cancer incidence. Both reviews address cancer incidence, not progression. It may well be that factors which influence cancer progression are quite different from those affecting incidence. While this may seem counterintuitive, since the tumor burden is much greater as disease advances (by the time of death a typical cancer patient may have about a kilogram of tumor in his or her body), the setting of disease progression is one in which physiological resources are stretched to their limit due to the higher tumor burden and cumulative effects of dis-

ease-related distress and disability. Even minor variations in somatic response to stress may have an effect on disease course at this point.

V. COPING STYLE

A. Physiological Responses

While stress may weaken the body's capacity to resist progression of cancer, coping well with stress may counteract this effect. Work on psychological stress suggests that control or, more particularly, lack of control is a key factor of the magnitude of physiological stress responses. People who feel helpless in response to stress may exhibit more exaggerated physiological evidence of stress, while greater self-efficacy in coping may dampen stress effects. In breast cancer patients, the belief that one could control the course of disease was significantly associated with good adjustment. Indeed, several studies have shown that it is not so much the intensity of the stressor but its perceived controllability that determines its effects. Changes in coping styles have been associated with changes in immune function, even over periods of less than a month. For example, in a study of the effects of emotional disclosure, subjects who discontinued their avoidance and engaged more fully in discussion of a stressful or traumatic topic exhibited decreases in antibody titres to the Epstein–Barr virus, indicating more successful surveillance of the latent virus by lymphocytes.

Expression rather than suppression of emotion has been postulated to reduce stress by discharging physiological arousal. Stress-related immune fluctuations due to the threat or onset of illness has also been shown to be reduced in those with an increased ability to cope with changes in one's life through assertive communication. Active coping through openly expressing concerns and emotions is one factor which could influence endocrine and immune alterations which may be related to disease progression.

B. Disease Progression

Coping-style variables that have been associated with cancer incidence include anger suppression and "restrained aggression and introversion." Variables associated with slower progression include "fighting spirit," expressed distress, assertive uncooperativeness, and assertiveness (being non-"type C"). Being emotionally reserved has been found to increase substantially the risk of mortality (odds ratio of 3.9) among lung cancer patients as well. While the solidity of the evidence for these relationships varies, it is of interest that those putatively associated with cancer incidence and more rapid progression are similar—emotional suppression and nonassertiveness.

Antoni and Goodkin found that a passive coping style is related to the promotion of cervical neoplasia. Goldstein and Antoni also found that breast cancer patients were more likely to employ a repressive coping style as compared to noncancer patients. Measures of this construct (repression/sensitization as a defensive style) have been reported to account for as much as 44% of the variance in the progression of breast cancer.

VI. PSYCHOSOCIAL INTERVENTIONS AND ENDOCRINE FUNCTION

Psychosocial treatments appear to buffer the effects of stress on endocrine function. For example, one intervention study found that biofeedback and cognitive therapy were associated with reduced cortisol levels in newly diagnosed breast cancer patients. Social support provided by the intervention may ameliorate the effect of stress on endocrine function. Indeed, providing social support during stress can profoundly alter the endocrine consequences of the stressor. Levine modeled this effect in squirrel monkeys: Although animals produced large elevations in plasma cortisol if they were stressed when alone, stress-induced elevations were reduced by 50% when animals had one "friend" present and 100% when five "friends" were present. Thus, interventions which provide social support have potential to ameliorate endocrine stress responses.

VII. SOCIAL SUPPORT AS A STRESS BUFFER

Thus the social environment can have a buffering effect on stress. Being socially "embedded" is associated with less autonomic arousal than social isolation. Indeed, social connection has profound consequences for health. Being well integrated socially reduces all-cause age-adjusted mortality by a factor of 2, about as much as having low versus high serum cholesterol levels or being a nonsmoker. Furthermore, the nature of one's position in the social hierarchy has health consequences, including relatively higher status within the same social class. People are statistically more likely to die after rather than before their birthday and important holidays, which are usually important times for social bonding/companionship.

Thus the presence of adverse emotional events such as traumatic stressors seems to have negative potential health consequences, while good social relations seem to be associated with positive health outcomes. There is evidence from three of six published randomized trials that psychosocial support is associated with longer survival for patients with breast cancer, malignant melanoma, and lymphoma. One component of the effective interventions is dealing directly with emotional distress associated with fears regarding disease progression. There is evidence that resilience to stress, including disease-related distress, is associated with emotional style. Indeed, finding meaning in the midst of experiencing a distressing situation has been linked with a positive psychological state. Better adaptation does not involve being persistently upbeat or rigidly maintaining a positive attitude, but rather dealing directly with negative affect as well. Positive and negative emotion are not merely opposite sides of one dimension. Rather, suppression of negative emotion tends to reduce experience of all emotion, positive and negative. There is evidence that breast cancer patients who express more "negative" emotion, including anger and uncooperativeness, or realistic optimism, termed "fighting spirit," actually live longer.

VIII. PHYSIOLOGICAL MECHANISMS OF STRESS AND SUPPORT-RELATED EFFECTS ON CANCER PROGRESSION

Mechanisms by which emotional expression and social support may influence survival time in cancer is an intriguing problem. Possibilities range from body maintenance activities, such as diet, sleep, and exercise, to interaction with physicians, to stress and support-mediated effects on endocrine and immune function. These systems, which are part of routine somatic control and maintenance functions in the body, are influenced by psychological and social variables and are also involved in host resistance to tumor progression. For example, there is evidence that social support serves to buffer the effects of stress on the endocrine system, blocking stress-induced elevations in plasma cortisol. Cortisol may, in turn, stimulate tumor proliferation via differential gluconeogenesis in normal and tumor tissue, activation of hormone receptors in tumor, or immunosuppression.

IX. PSYCHOENDOCRINOLOGY OF CANCER

A. Disease Prognosis

High levels of stress hormones such as cortisol may be associated with worse disease prognosis. Since breast cancers are often hormone sensitive (hence the effectiveness of tamoxifen and other hormone-receptor blockers in delaying disease progression). In a study of patients operated on for breast and stomach carcinoma, the failure of morning cortisol levels to decrease within 2 weeks after admission was associated with shorter survival times. Direct evidence for effects of the HPA axis in the development of breast cancer comes from a study in which high serum levels of DHEA, a correlate of HPA axis activity, predicted the subsequent development of breast cancer 9 years later in normal postmenopausal women who had donated blood for a serum bank. Thus, correlational evidence suggests that physiological stress responses associated with poor adjustment to cancer may, indeed, speed disease progression.

B. Disease Progression

Mechanisms have been proposed whereby the neuroendocrine correlates of stress may promote neoplastic growth. Stress hormones may suppress immune resistance to tumors or act via differential effects on gluconeogenesis in healthy versus tumor cells. Tumor cells may become resistant to the catabolic action of cortisol, which inhibits the uptake of glucose in numerous cell types. In such cases, energy would be preferentially shunted to the tumor and away from normal cells by cortisol. Several studies have found an association between stress-related elevation of glucocorticoids and more rapid tumor growth in animals. Another hypothesis suggests that hormones of the HPA axis may actually promote the expression of breast cancer oncogenes. In addition, since stress-related increases in SNS and HPA activity are known to have generally suppressive effects on immune function, it is certainly plausible that immune functions important in resistance to breast tumor growth are thereby suppressed. Elevation of glucocorticoids is associated with clinically significant immunosuppression, and enhanced secretion of norepinephrine during stress has also been associated with suppression of lymphocyte function.

1. Cortisol

There are considerable data indicating that the HPA constitutes a likely connection between psychosocial factors and disease progression. Stress is processed through CNS neurotransmitter systems such as norepinephrine, dopamine, and endorphins, which regulate hypothalamic releasing factors such as CRF and pituitary hormones such as prolactin and ACTH and, through these, adrenocortical steroids and medullary hormones. Cortisol is the classic stress hormone, elevated in response to stress for prolonged periods, and is immunosuppressive.

The role of endogenous corticosteroids in breast cancer progression is worthy of further exploration, since (1) steroid hormone levels are responsive to psychosocial stressors through the HPA via CRF, ACTH, and the response of the adrenal in producing them and (2) because breast cancer is a hormone-sensitive tumor, as evidenced by the effectiveness of steroid-receptor blockers such as tamoxifen in delaying progression. The National Cancer Institute found in a large multicenter trial that tamoxifen is effective in reducing the incidence of breast cancer in high-risk women. While the specific receptors blocked involve estrogen and progesterone, cross-reactivity with androgenic steroids and the dedifferentiated state of tumor tissue make the range of corticosteroids of potential interest.

2. Prolactin

Other hormones which are elevated by stress, such as prolactin, growth hormone, and thyroid hormones, may also influence the course of disease. Prolactin is of special interest because of its role as both a tumor promoter and a stress hormone. There is evidence that a majority of breast carcinomas have prolactin receptors and that the presence of prolactin stimulates the growth of such tumors in tissue culture at physiological levels, perhaps by stimulating the development of estrogen receptors. Prolactin has been found to stimulate prostate carcinoma growth as well (Webber, 1986). Indeed strong positive correlations between prolactin and both estrogen and progesterone receptor levels in breast tumors have been noted. The surgical stress of radical mastectomy results in transiently elevated serum prolactin levels, perhaps through the removal of target tissue and a disruption in feedback mechanisms. Prolactin levels rise in response to other stressful stimuli as well. Since other pituitary hormones such as ACTH clearly reflect stress, it is possible that prolactin is secreted in response to stress and thereby promotes tumor growth. Thus, there is evidence for facilitative effects on tumor growth by stress hormones via several different mechanisms. Conversely, a treatment which reduces psychological stress might reduce prolactin secretion and therefore retard stimulation of tumor cells either directly or through enhanced estrogen and progesterone receptor induction.

C. Acute Medical Illness

Many of these stress hormones are immunosuppressive when elevated. Acute medical illness is associated with increased secretion of ACTH and cortisol, and surgical stress is associated with lower dehydroepiandrosterone (DHEA); cortisol ratios (i.e., a combination of relatively low DHEA and relatively high cortisol) and higher prolactin levels. In spousal bereavement, cortisol levels are elevated, while natural

killer (NK) cytotoxicity is decreased. Furthermore, there is no reason why disease-related stresses which include social isolation, death anxiety, pain, and sleep disturbance should not affect immune function at the clinically observable level; for example, defenses against the progression of viral infection. Yet little is known about these mechanisms and their effects on clinical infection. Recently, Cohen *et al.* showed that vulnerability to systemic infection by rhinovirus is significantly mediated by stress. This model might well apply as well to vulnerability to cancer progression, to the extent that immune function modulates it. As noted earlier, Levine has shown in squirrel monkeys that social support is a buffer against the endocrine response to stress (a shock paired with a light flash). The elevation in plasma cortisol seen when the animal is stressed alone is reduced by 50% when the animal has one "friend" with him, and there is no elevation in cortisol at all in response to the same stressor when the animal has five "friends" present. Thus a change in the social environment profoundly alters the physiological consequences of a stressor. This would plausibly apply to humans coping with stressors as well. The interrelationships among social and psychophysiological stress response factors is an important mediating system that bears examination in future research on cancer progression.

Thus there is good reason to believe that psychosocial stress caused by the diagnosis of medical illness, bereavement, social isolation, and suppression of emotional expression may adversely affect the immune and endocrine systems, with clinically relevant consequences for the body's ability to resist disease progression. Conversely, enhanced psychosocial support via group therapy or other means may plausibly improve medical outcome by buffering the consequences of such stress and thereby ameliorating immune and endocrine function.

X. PSYCHONEUROIMMUNOLOGY OF CANCER

There is a growing body of research which provides evidence of associations between psychological factors and immune function. Subjects experiencing such stressors as being a caregiver for an Alzheimer's patient, divorce or bereavement, or being in a poor relationship have been shown to have greater distress and lower helper/suppressor cell counts and ratios, lower total T-lymphocyte numbers, lower NK cell activity, and poorer response to Epstein–Barr virus. Cohen *et al.* showed that vulnerability to systemic infection by rhinovirus is significantly mediated by stress and, recently, that people with larger social networks are less susceptible to viral infection.

Further evidence comes from work showing that immune organs such as the spleen are heavily innervated and there are receptors for a variety of neurotransmitters on the cell membranes of lymphocytes. Stress hormones are known to influence cell adhesion molecules on lymphocytes, providing a possible mechanism by which stress could alter lymphocyte trafficking and therefore immune function. There is good evidence for this hypothesis in work by Dhabhar *et al.,* who demonstrated that stress and the circadian corticosterone rhythm induce significant changes in leukocyte distribution in animals. Moreover, they have shown that acute stress significantly enhances a cutaneous delayed-type hypersensitivity (DTH) response (an *in vivo* measure of cell-mediated immunity). In contrast, chronic stress significantly suppressed DTH responses, and stress-induced trafficking of leukocytes to the skin may mediate these changes of immune function. Most interestingly, the authors were able to mimic the effects of acute and chronic stress on DTH responses by administration of corticosterone at doses similar to physiological levels following either acute or chronic stress, suggesting that glucocorticoids may be an important mediator of DTH responses during stress.

Thus, there is growing evidence for links between psychological stress, glucocorticoid responses, and immunosuppression. In rats, for example, stress significantly decreased NK cytotoxicity, increased levels of cortisol and ACTH, and increased the metastatic spread of mammary tumor to lung tissue. In stage I and stage II breast cancer patients, higher perceived social support and active seeking of social support have been related to increased NK cell activity while lower NK cell activity has been shown to predict disease recurrence. Thus, psychological factors have

been associated with changes in immune measures, and these changes may influence the rate of cancer progression.

XI. PSYCHOSOCIAL INTERVENTIONS AND IMMUNE FUNCTION

Psychosocial treatments designed to improve coping and assist in stress reduction have been associated with improvements in both immune function and physical health in cancer patients. Supportive relationships seem to modulate stress-induced immunosuppression, for example, among medical students undergoing examination stress. Even disclosure of traumas in journals has been associated with better immune function. Stress-related immunosuppression may be mitigated by active coping styles or social support. After a 6-week psychiatric intervention for newly diagnosed malignant melanoma patients conducted by Fawzy, *et al.,* α-interferon-augmented cytotoxic activity of NK cells was elevated in the intervention subjects 6 months later and a survival benefit was observed, although there was no direct relationship between changes in NK cell activity and survival time. Natural killer cells are known to kill tumor cells of many different types when tested either *in vitro* or in animal studies and may be particularly prone to stress-induced suppression.

XII. IMMUNE FUNCTION AND DISEASE PROGRESSION

It is not always clear whether changes in serum immune or endocrine measures are a cause of or result from changes in disease status. Indeed, the immune surveillance theory of cancer development and progression has been questioned. Cancer is not, after all, an immunodeficiency disease, and immunosuppressed patients such as those with AIDS are at higher risk only for rare cancers such as Kaposi's sarcoma. However, research in animals as well as in humans suggests that immunosuppression may be a factor in the rate of disease progression, and *in vitro* measures of immune function which are salient to disease progression are affected positively by social support and adversely by stress.

There is evidence from nonclinical populations that social integration buffers against stress-induced suppression of NK cell activity. It thus makes sense that the addition of intensive social support in groups for women undergoing substantial medical and other stressors might have a similar buffering effect. Thus, although definitive clinical links have not been made, there is evidence that NK cell activity is associated with the rate of breast cancer progression. This immune parameter, which is affected by stress and social support, also varies with disease progression, making it a reasonable candidate for investigation into mediators of the effects of group support on the rate of breast cancer progression.

Thus, there is good reason to believe that psychosocial stress caused by the diagnosis of cancer may adversely affect endocrine and immune function, with clinically relevant consequences for the body's ability to resist disease progression. Conversely, enhanced psychosocial support via group therapy or other means may plausibly improve medical outcome by ameliorating the immune and endocrine consequences of such stress.

XIII. STRESS AND AUTONOMIC RESPONSES

Cacioppo and colleagues have examined the effects of psychological stress on autonomic responses including heart-rate reactivity and cardiac vagal reactivity (as indexed by respiratory sinus arrhythmia reactivity). They found that individuals who demonstrated greater autonomic responses to brief laboratory stress also showed higher stress-related increases in ACTH and cortisol. Thus, autonomic tone may be a good index of reactivity of the HPA axis to acute stress, and autonomic measures are less invasive than the repeated blood sampling that is often required to measure short-term changes in HPA axis activity. Results of psychoneuroimmunological studies have shown that heart rate reactivity after a stressor was also related to changes in NK cell activity, suggesting that measurement of

stress-induced changes in autonomic tone may be of value in defining possible mechanisms underlying psychosocial effects on immune function. Failures to mount a corticosteroid response to stress may place an undue burden on other stress-response mechanisms, such as the autonomic nervous system. Loss of vagal tone is often seen in poor stress responders, leading to cardiovascular burden and possibly to immune effects as well. Autonomic tone has not only been associated with stress, but also with emotion regulation. Indeed, baseline levels of cardiac vagal tone and vagal tone reactivity have also been associated with behavioral measures of reactivity and the expression of emotion. Thus cardiac vagal tone can also serve as an index of emotion and parasympathetic influences on heart rate may be related to emotional expression during participation in a psychotherapeutic support group.

XIV. CONCLUSION

The literature cited above provides evidence that an individual's manner of responding to disease-related stress may affect the rate of disease progression as well as their psychological adjustment. The stress-response system is most effective when it is on when needed and off when it is not. Variance in the rate of cancer progression may be accounted for by more or less adaptive stress-response systems. This effect of stress and stress response on cancer progression may be mediated by the endocrine, immune, or autonomic nervous systems or some combination of the three. There is evidence that stress is a uniform part of the experience of cancer and its treatment, that various coping styles affect stress-mediated physiological effects, and that these in turn may affect the somatic response to cancer progression. Furthermore, various psychosocial interventions have proven effective in enhancing coping with this stress, and some have demonstrated an effect on disease progression. This evidence suggests that assistance with stress management should become a standard component of cancer treatment.

See Also the Following Articles

Bibliography

Glaser, R. *et al.* (1998). The influence of psychological stress on the immune response to vaccines. *Ann. N.Y. Acad. Sci.* **840**, 649–655.

McEwen, B. S. (1998). Protective and damaging effects of stress mediators. N. Engl. J. Med. **338**(3), 171–179.

Ramirez, A. J. *et al.*, (1989). Stress and relapse of breast cancer. Br. Med. J. **6669**, 291–293.

Sapolsky, R. M., and Donnelly, T. M. (1985). Vulnerability to stress-induced tumor growth increases with age in rats: Role of glucocorticoids. *Endocrinology* **117**(2), 662–666.

Spiegel, D. (1999). Healing words: Emotional expression and disease outcome. J. Am. Med. Assoc. **281**, 1328–1329.

Cancer Treatment

Fawzy I. Fawzy and Andrea L. Canada
UCLA School of Medicine

Nancy W. Fawzy
John Wayne Cancer Institute, Saint John's Health Center, Santa Monica, California

I. The Cancer Problem
II. Psychosocial Interventions
III. Intervention Outcomes
IV. Conclusion

GLOSSARY

active-behavioral coping methods Those things an individual actually does that focus on dealing with problems and tend to make a person feel better in both the short and the long term.

active-cognitive coping methods Those mental thoughts and techniques that focus on dealing with problems and tend to make a person feel better in both the short and the long term.

avoidance methods Both the behavioral and mental techniques that a person uses to feel better in the short term but are not directed at solving problems and, therefore, fail to work in the long term.

T he stress associated with the diagnosis and treatment of cancer can result in significant reductions in patient quality of life. Fortunately, numerous psychosocial interventions for patients with cancer have been found quite effective in assisting with such stress. Interventions, including education, stress management, coping skills training, and support, have resulted in notable improvements in the psychological and physical health of the patient with cancer.

I. THE CANCER PROBLEM

Cancer remains a significant health problem in the United States with over 1 million new cases reported each year. Although many patients still die from their cancer, major advances in medical care have occurred. Over the past 30 years, many patients have been cured and long term survival for some types of cancer has increased significantly. Therefore, today's patient with cancer may be placed in one of three basic categories. The first category consists of those patients who are cured and yet need to deal with a chronic fear of recurrence. The second category of cancer patients includes those who are not cured but have a long term prognosis. These patients must face dealing with a chronic disease. The third category consists of those patients who, despite medical advances, are terminal and must deal with death and dying.

Regardless of the category in which a patient finds himself/herself, the adverse psychological effects associated with the diagnosis and treatment of cancer can be quite severe. Cancer is associated with high rates of emotional distress which may include major depression, dysthymia, or adjustment disorder with depressed mood. Other possible affective responses to cancer are anxiety, anger, guilt, helplessness, hopelessness, denial, disbelief, and grief. In addition to such psychological effects, the diagnosis and treatment of cancer are often accompanied by adverse physical symptoms. These can include pain, insomnia, fatigue, shortness of breath, nausea and vomiting, and changes in appetite and activity. In addition, the stress associated with diagnosis and treatment is believed to negatively effect immune parameters and other somatic variables in the patient with cancer.

II. PSYCHOSOCIAL INTERVENTIONS

Fortunately, various psychological interventions have been developed to assist the patient with cancer in dealing with diagnosis and treatment. A review of the literature over the past 20 years suggests that available interventions for the management of cancer-related stress include one or more of the following basic components: education, stress management (including behavioral training), coping skills training, and emotional support.

A. Education

The overall goal of education for the cancer patient is to replace the sense of helplessness and inadequacy due to uncertainty and lack of knowledge with a sense of mastery and control. Educational interventions not only offer diagnosis and treatment specific information to patients, but may also enhance adjust-

ment and improve coping skills. Those interventions currently in use provide the cancer patient with information about his/her particular diagnosis and treatment side-effects as well as how to manage the side-effects. Cancer prevention information and how to recognize the warning signs of new or recurrent cancers may also be taught. In addition, general education relevant to a healthy lifestyle is often provided. Such topics as good nutrition, exercise, immune functioning, and effective communication are but a few examples.

B. Stress Management

As stress is associated with physical disease and illnesses (e.g., headache, GI problems, heart disease, hypertension, susceptibility to infections), it is logical to assume that making and sustaining even minor lifestyle changes that reduce stress can improve the odds for better health and greater quality of life. Research has shown that a generalized decrease in stress allows the patient to cope more effectively with the overall emotional impact of cancer, enhance compliance with medical regimens, and assist in the management of treatment side-effects (e.g., pain, nausea and vomiting, and insomnia). In such an intervention, the patient learns how to recognize personal sources of stress and then how to eliminate or modify the source of stress through problem-solving or a change in cognitive appraisal or attitude. Patients are also taught how to change the physiological response to the stressor by replacing it with a relaxation response. Such responses are learned through behavioral training and include the techniques of progressive muscle relaxation (PMR), deep breathing, meditation, biofeedback, hypnosis, self-hypnosis, guided imagery, yoga, and Tai chi.

C. Coping Skills Training

The goal of coping skills training is to teach the cancer patient how to deal with diagnosis, treatment, and life in general using effective cognitive and behavioral methods. An example of such an intervention is one in which patients are introduced to three types of coping: active-behavioral and active-cognitive, both of which are usually effective coping methods, and avoidance, which is generally ineffective in the long term. Active–behavioral methods may include exercising, improving diet, using physical relaxation techniques, expressing feelings, going out more socially or "treating" oneself, and finding out more about the disease. Active-cognitive methods may include thinking about the illness 1 day at a time, praying and trusting one's belief in God or a higher power, accepting the reality of the diagnosis but not equating it with a poor prognosis, forming a mental plan of action, thinking more about the meaning of life and what is really important, using some kind of mental relaxation technique, and trying to maintain/use positive thinking. Avoidance techniques include self-blame; social isolation; procrastination; and tension reduction through eating, sleeping, drinking alcohol, smoking, or taking drugs more than usual. Following instruction, participants are often asked to apply these coping strategies to common theoretical problems/situations encountered (e.g., diagnosis, treatment issues, body image, communication, interpersonal relationships, anxiety/depression, and death). After discovering effective ways to deal with these theoretical problems through active-behavioral and active-cognitive means, patients are asked to apply the techniques to their own real-life situations.

D. Emotional Support

Interventions for patients with cancer can be delivered in individual, patient group, or family settings. Whatever the format, psychosocial interventions can be an invaluable source of support for the patient with cancer. A safe environment provides patients with the much-needed opportunity to express the feelings they have about their disease and its treatment.

In group therapy, patients also have the opportunity to learn healthier ways of dealing with their illness from others in similar situations. The sense of community experienced through group participation provides the patient with a new and important social network at a time when isolation is common and when more emotional support is needed.

Individual psychotherapy is a long-established method which is also used to ease the distress and disruption that accompanies the diagnosis of cancer. Support, compassion, and empathy from a therapist form the cornerstone of such interventions.

Psychotherapeutic interventions have also been used to enhance family support. Improved communication; role flexibility; and adjustment to changing medical, financial, social, and vocational realities are targeted. An atmosphere of openness and shared problem-solving in the family is associated with affective improvements in the patient with cancer.

E. Combination Therapies

Research has shown that education, behavioral training, coping skills training, and support have been generally helpful when used separately but are even more powerful and enduring when used in combination, especially in a group format. The explanation for this success may be that patients are given multiple tools with which to cope. It may also be that different individuals come to the cancer experience with different coping skills and resources already available. In this case, their existing coping skills are reinforced and supplemented in those areas in which they are lacking. In addition, the group format provides tremendous emotional support and is more cost effective than an individually delivered intervention. A summary of the types of interventions that have been proven helpful for patients with cancer is provided in Table I.

III. INTERVENTION OUTCOMES

Over the years, the outcomes of psychosocial interventions for the patient with cancer have yielded improvements in both psychological and biomedical functioning.

A. Psychological Outcomes

Educational interventions for patients with cancer have resulted in increases in knowledge about the disease and treatment compliance and decreases in anxiety and depression. Such interventions have also been shown to enhance coping skills. Behavioral training interventions have resulted in decreased

TABLE I
Effective Therapies for the Patient with Cancer

Education	Stress management	Coping skills training	Support
Diagnosis	Stress management	Coping mechanisms	Emotional support
Test results	Stress source	Active-behavioral (e.g.,	Expression
Symptoms	Stress reaction	problem-solving)	Validation
Treatment	Eliminate/modify stressor	Active-cognitive (e.g., cognitive	Group therapy
Options	Relaxation response	restructuring)	Disease specific
Side-effects	PMR	Avoidance (e.g., drinking,	Social network
Dealing with effects	Meditation	smoking more)	Individual therapy
Disease	Deep breathing		Patient specific
Recurrence	Biofeedback		Family
Prevention	Hypnosis		Communication
Health	Guided imagery		Role flexibility
Nutrition	Yoga		Adjustment
Exercise	Tai chi		

TABLE II
A Sampling of Intervention Outcomes

Category	Type of intervention	Results	Reference
Psychological outcomes	Education	Decreased depression	Pruitt *et al.* (1993) *Psycho-oncology* **2**, 55
	Behavior training	Decreased anxiety	Gruber *et al.* (1993), *Biofeedback Self Regul.* **18**, 1
	Education, support	Increased effectiveness in dealing with psychosocial problems	Gorden *et al.* (1980) *J. Consult. Clin. Psychol.* **48**, 743
Physical outcomes	Behavior training	Decreased anticipatory nausea	Arakawa (1997) *Cancer Nurs.* **20**, 342
	Education	Decreased pain intensity	de Wit *et al.* (1997) *Pain* **73**, 55
	Behavior training	Increased immune parameters	Lekander *et al.* (1997) *Psychother. Psychosom.* **66**, 185
Combined outcomes	Support	Decreased emotional distress, reduced pain, increased survival rates	Spiegel *et al.* (1981) *Arch. Gen. Psychiat.* **38**, 527 and Spiegel *et al.* (1989) *Lancet* **2**, 888
	Education, stress management, coping skills training, support	Decreased emotional distress, enhanced coping, increased immune parameters, increased recurrence-free intervals and survival rates	Fawzy *et al.* (1993) *Arch. Gen. Psychiatr.* **50**, 681

anxiety, while supportive interventions, delivered in individual, group, and family formats, have been shown to reduce emotional upset, confusion, social isolation, and anxiety and depression and to improve quality of life, communication, coping skills, sleep, adjustment, body image, and self-concept.

B. Physical Outcomes

Both educational and behavioral training interventions have been shown effective in assisting the patient with cancer-related pain. Behavioral training has also been found to be quite helpful in reducing the frequency, severity, and duration of side-effects from chemotherapy (i.e., anticipatory nausea and vomiting). In fact, some studies demonstrate an increase in food intake as a result of such lowered physiological arousal.

Finally, a growing body of literature suggests that psychosocial interventions for patients with cancer may result in improvements in immune functioning and increases in recurrence-free intervals and survival rates. Behavioral training has been associated with decreased cortisol levels, elevations in immune system functioning, and improvements in immune parameters (e.g., Natural Killer cell activity, lymphocyte numbers and responsiveness, etc.). Supportive interventions and combination therapies involving follow-up assessments over many years have also demonstrated reductions in cancer recurrence and death rates for patients participating in such interventions. A sampling of intervention outcomes in patients with cancer is provided in Table II.

IV. CONCLUSION

The emotional and physical stressors encountered by the cancer patient are numerous and unique. Based on a review of the literature, cancer patients may benefit both biomedically and psychologically from a variety of psychosocial intervention programs. A structured, psychosocial intervention consisting of education, stress management, coping skills training, and group support offers the greatest potential for positively effecting emotional and physical functioning in the patient with cancer. It should be noted that such psychosocial interventions need to be used as an integral part of competent, comprehensive medical care and not as an independent treatment modality for cancer.

See Also the Following Articles

AVOIDANCE; CANCER; COPING SKILLS; SOCIAL SUPPORT; STRESS MANAGEMENT, CAM APPROACH

Bibliography

Anderson, B. L. (1992). Psychosocial interventions for cancer patients to enhance quality of life. *J. Consult. Clin. Psychol.* **60**, 552–568.

Compass, B. E., Haaga, D. A., Keefe, F. J., Leitenberg, H., and Williams, D. A. (1998). Sampling of empirically supported psychological treatments from health psychology: Smoking, chronic pain, cancer, and bulimia nervosa. *J. Consult. Clin. Psychol.* **66**, 89–112.

Fawzy, F. I., Fawzy, N. W., Arndt, L. A., and Pasnau, R. O. (1995). Critical review of psychosocial interventions in cancer care. *Arch. Gen. Psychiat.* **52**, 100–113.

Iacovino, V., and Reesor, K. (1997). Literature on interventions to address cancer patients' psychosocial needs: What does it tell us? *J. Psychosoc. Oncol.* **15**, 47–71.

Trijsburg, R. W., van Knippenberg, F. C. E., and Rijpma, S. E. (1992). Effects of psychological treatment on cancer patients: A critical review. *Psychosom. Med.* **54**, 489–517.

Cannon, Walter

see Homeostasis

Captivity, Adaptation to

Richard H. Rahe

University of Nevada School of Medicine

S tress occurs in common as well as in unusual life situations. Few life experiences, however, are as stressful as being held hostage or political prisoner. From work in the field, plus a review of the relevant literature, six stages of adaptation to captivity have been conceptualized. Further, it became apparent that the time course over which these stages took place progressively lengthened from the first to the final stage. The initial stage appeared to occur over seconds to minutes, the next stage over minutes to hours, the third stage over hours to days, the fourth stage over days to weeks, the fifth stage over weeks to months, and the sixth stage over months to years. In the presentation of adaptation to captivity that follows, a general description of each stage is amplified by the mention of key captor and captive behaviors as well as useful coping techniques at each stage of adaptation to captivity.

I. STARTLE/PANIC

Full development of this stage is influenced greatly by the setting in which a captive is taken. Hostage takings are generally unanticipated and life-threatening. A common theme is an abrupt transition from life as usual to sudden, often forceful and brutal, subjugation. Such a transition is impossible to assimilate quickly. Panic, coupled with fears of imminent death, is a common reaction over these first seconds to minutes.

Captors at this stage are generally highly excitable and fervently driven by political and/or ideological causes. Captives may well be at a loss as how to deal with them. To challenge their actions, even by a scornful laugh, may lead to an impulsive retaliation, including execution.

Successful coping with capture is constrained by the extreme brevity of this stage. Emotional control should be gained as quickly as possible. Some captives cope with initial shock in a dissociated state, feeling more like observers than participants. Most are in a state of dazed shock, unable to take any integrated action. The ability to bring one's mind into focus on details of the surroundings, such as counting the number of captors or studying their features, may help to limit panic.

II. DISBELIEF

Captives from Western countries are accustomed to protections under the law with an emphasis on human rights. When suddenly thrust into a situation where all personal freedoms are forcibly withdrawn, victims may respond with utter disbelief. They may think: "This can't be happening" or "Surely the police will be here shortly." Such expectations can lead to severe disappointment and disillusion.

Captor behavior during this time can be tyrannical, with beratings and physical restraint. Dehumanization includes stripping away clothes and personal possessions, binding, blindfolding, and taking photographs of the subjugated captives for later propaganda use. Captives may even be tortured to achieve "confessions." Captors' plans for the captives may be unstable at this stage, with frequent moves of the group from one location to another. Captives typically have little chance to communicate with their fellows, and attempts to do so are likely to bring swift and painful retaliation.

Many prisoners cope with this stage by convincing themselves that conditions will improve shortly. Hopes for rescue may be sustaining, and sometimes rescue does, indeed, occur. However, captives are probably best off trying to "escape" their circumstances through turning their attentions inward. Some will engage in thoughts of retaliation whereas others will focus on images of loved ones, prayer, valued objects, or elements of home and freedom.

III. HYPERVIGILANCE

Although efforts by captives to orient themselves to their new environments may start at the very beginning of captivity, the emergence of a hypervigilant stage releases unexpected talents of observation. Assessing mileage while being driven blindfolded, remembering labrynthine pathways through city streets, and accurately keeping track of passing time are examples of such orientation skills that emerge.

Captor behavior is usually unpredictable over the first days of captivity, as leaders are often confused about their ultimate goals and objectives. Generally, some form of interrogation will begin, with an emphasis on intelligence gathering. Guards tend to be highly attentive to possible escape attempts during these early days of captivity.

Early in their incarceration, captives turn their hypervigilance to orienting tasks. Even when confined in a cell without daylight, nonvisual cues (changing of the guards, when meals are served, etc.) are gleaned to construct a 24-h cycle. Captives examine their surroundings in minute detail, including the behavior of their guards. They also structure their environment as much as possible—sandals placed here, the latrine bucket there, and so forth.

During this hypervigilance, captives frequently misinterpret bits of conversations overheard between their captors, particularly concerning "release of the captives." One American hostage held in Iran was convinced that he heard plans for the group's imminent release during his guard's telephone conversation. Disappointment, of course, is then inevitable.

IV. RESISTANCE/COMPLIANCE

This stage begins when the captors begin their coercion of captives into cooperating with them. De-

mands to sign "confessions" of "crimes" or enforced public appearances to help dramatize their captors' goals are examples of such coercion. Interrogations at this point change from intelligence gathering to exploitation. The degree to which a captive capitulates to these tactics depends on the severity of the torture applied combined with the captive's ability to resist. It is clear from the literature that anyone can be forced to cooperate with his captors if sufficient physical and psychological torture is brought to bear. Nonetheless, persons who have been trained to resist such demands do much better than those who have not had such training.

Captor behavior at this stage is so similar across prisoner of war and civilian hostage situations that it is as if they all read from the same manual. The original architects of many of these behaviors were the secret police in Czarist Russia, with modifications introduced by the state police in Nazi Germany. Asian refinements were added a decade later by North Korean military. These behaviors include intimidating arrest, imprisonment for indeterminate lengths, physical and nutritional deprivation, disturbances of body rhythms, physical and sensory isolation, deprivation, stressful (often brutal) interrogations, unpredictable responses from guards and inquisitors, frequent threats of death, and attempts to "reeducate" the captive.

Isolation appears to be an extraordinarily stressful captor tactic, dreaded by many more than physical torture. Settings used are generally cramped, filthy, and pest-ridden. They are usually uncomfortably hot or cold, with poor lighting and ventilation. Communication with fellow captives, and even with guards, is usually prohibited. Finally, extremely few allowances are provided for personal hygiene. Periods of isolation may be alternated with "friendly" interrogations, especially if the captive becomes eager for human contact. Interrogations are nearly always unpredictable as to their timing (day or night), duration, and approach of the interrogator. The overall aim is to "soften" captives resistance and make them susceptible to the will of their captors.

Captive behavior is highly variable. Some will attempt to resist all coercive attempts until they are thoroughly beaten and broken. Others will prove to be unable to withstand even moderate deprivations without making major confessions. Most captives, however, learn to resist torture, isolation, and other deprivations until severe physical and/or psychological damage become a likely result of their continued resistance. They then comply sufficiently for captors to suspend their tortures, giving the captive critical time to rest and recover. Clever "admissions" during interrogations, especially "information" that takes a long time to validate, can provide precious time for a captive to replenish physical and mental reserves.

One extremely important coping maneuver is physical fitness. Hours of physical training can be carried out in extremely confined settings. Flexibility exercises minimize the risk of joint dislocations or bone fractures during ensuing torture sessions. Running in place promotes endurance conditioning, with attendant feelings of well-being and the ability to sleep. Another very important coping activity is communication with fellow captives. The ingenuity of captives in passing voice, hand, tap, or other signals to their cohorts is truly remarkable. Using such methods, communication can be carried out even with persons who are confined to isolation. To feel part of a supportive network of fellow sufferers provides immeasurable sustenance to a captive. Religious faith, prayer, and thoughts of loved ones also exert major supportive influences.

V. DEPRESSION

When captives begin to confront their several recent losses, particularly if they dwell upon these, they frequently enter into depression. In reality, captives have lost not only their freedom and most everything that they valued in life, but they may have even lost their future. Further, they are deprived of information about the outside world and are often misled by captors as to the degree of interest in their welfare shown by their own government and countrymen. Perhaps most cruel is the indeterminate length of captivity. Prisoners of war sometimes reflect with envy on civil prisoners who have finite prison sentences to serve.

Captor behavior at this point is generally limited to custodial care. Unless there is a continuing need for propaganda statements, interrogations are greatly reduced in number. Guards may be changed as the routine generates little excitement for the original captors. Escape may become possible at this time due to laxity of the new guards. Captors may occasionally reassert their position of control by staging prisoner movements, issuance of new policies, and so forth.

Captives often develop classical signs and symptoms of depression. They may wish to spend most of their day in bed. Loss of appetite far exceeds the poor quality of food provided. Large weight losses ensue. Communication between captives may be avoided even though opportunities for such interaction present themselves. Guilt over performance during their interrogations may be felt. Thoughts of suicide may become widely prevalent, but actual suicide attempts are rare.

Coping with depression is aided enormously by a strong support group. Repeated documentation exists of virtually life-saving influences of support persons or groups in the lives of depressed captives. To use one's intellect constructively to combat potentially devastating boredom is an excellent coping skill. Even a single book can be read and reread with new meanings found on each reading. Creative work, such as writing, can be extremely helpful. Even without these tools, use of one's intelligence to elaborate future life plans can be achieved. One captive, deprived of paper and pencil, composed books of children stories in his mind and upon release wrote and published them.

Use of humor has an immense coping value. Getting the best of one's guards, on occasion, not only provides humorous remembrances that can be savored later, but gives captives a moment of control in what otherwise is a totally uncontrolled life situation.

VI. EVENTUAL ACCEPTANCE

Until this stage, captives have actively resisted the idea of a prolonged incarceration. Part of the reason for their depression was an awakening of awareness that a rapid release or rescue won't occur. Thus, this final stage of adaptation starts with the conviction that a more productive use of time must be made if the captive is to survive his ordeal.

Captive behavior remains custodial in the main. With the exception of "reeducational" sessions given in some prisoner of war settings, captors are primarily concerned with keeping their victims alive and presentable as "bargaining chips" for future negotiations.

Much as a sailor steers a disabled ship by simply concentrating from one wave to the next, captives find that it is best to live their lives 1 day at a time. Although they may dwell on the past, not much thought is given to a future more distant than tomorrow. Small things begin to take on huge importance. A frequent preoccupation is what will be served, generally with rice, for the next meal. Meal times, exercise periods, bedtime, and so on are carried out with compulsive regularity. Social niceties may disappear and personal appearance may slide. Swearing and crude language can become the norm. Interpersonal difficulties often arise more from an intolerance as to how a roommate chews his food than from philosophical or political differences.

The passage of time becomes distorted. As characterized in Thomas Mann's famous novel, "The Magic Mountain," although a single day may appear to progress very slowly, weeks and months seems to fly by. Captives have been amazed to find, upon release, that they greatly underestimated the time they spent on various activities. Involvement in creative tasks makes time pass swiftly. A German prisoner of war, held along with Americans in Vietnam, composed a German–English–French dictionary. He utilized cloth from his prison pajamas for a book cover, charcoal and water for his ink, paper obtained from his captors, and foil from fellow prisoners' cigarette packets insulated his book's cover. When he was fully absorbed in this project he found that "There just weren't enough hours in the day."

Development of new knowledge is assiduously pursued in long-term captivity situations. Some captives learn a second language from their cell mates. Others build homes in their imagination—board by board, nail by nail. One prisoner of war held in North Vietnam reviewed his entire schooling and found that he could recall the names of every classmate, where each one sat in class, the names of every one of his teachers, and even the subject matter they covered in class. Reading and writing are important coping activities. Even if they are never delivered, writing letters to family and loved ones is an enormous source of support.

Group activities lend vital cohesive forces to the captive group. These activities range from church services, group games, theater, to fitness activities. Even forced labor can become a sustaining activity, as is illustrated so aptly in Boulle's famous novel, "The Bridge Over the River Kwai."

VII. COMMENT

The emphasis in this article on adaptation to captivity stress is on the captive. Very little is mentioned about the stresses on the immediate family of the captive. Certainly, family members experience their own stages of adaptation, some of which are quite different from those of captives. They not only have to deal with loss of their relative, but with a near-constant intrusion of the public and press. Families also need a support group. This need was demonstrated for families of Vietnam POWs, as well as for families of Americans captured in Iran. These families developed their own association for purposes of enhanced communication, solidarity, and political influence. These associations proved to be extremely effective. An enormous amount of information remains to be learned of the experiences of such family members, both during the captivity period and following their captive's return.

See Also the Following Articles

Captivity, Recovery from; Depression Models; Prison; Prisoners of War; Torture

Bibliography

Boulle, P. 1954. "The Bridge Over the River Kwai." Vanguard Press, New York.
Diehl, B., personal communication.
Guarino, L. 1991. "A P. O. W.'s Story: 2801 Days in Hanoi." Ivy Books, New York.
Gunderson, E. K. E., and Rahe, R. H. 1974. "Life Stress and Illness." Charles C. Thomas, Springfield, Ill.
Hinkle, L. E., Jr., and Wolff, H. G. 1956. Communist interrogation and indoctrination of "enemies of the state." *Arch. Neurol. Psychiat.* 115–174.
Hubbell. J. G. 1976. P. O. W. The Reader's Digest Press.
Mann, T. 1924. "The Magic Mountain." S. Fischer Verlag, Berlin.

Rahe, R. H. 1990. Life change, stress responsivity, and captivity research. *Psychosom. Med.* **52**, 373–396.

Rahe, R. H. 1995. Stress and psychiatry. *In* "Comprehensive Textbook of Psychiatry" (H. I. Kaplan and B. J. Sadock, eds.), Vol. 6. William and Wilkins, Baltimore.

Rahe, R. H., and Arthur, R. J. 1978. Life change and illness studies: past history and future directions. *J. Hum. Stress* **4**, 3–15.

Rahe, R. H., Karson, S., Howard, N. S., Rubin, R. T., and Poland, R. E. 1990. Psychological and physiological assessments on American hostages freed from captivity in Iran. *Psychosom. Med.* **52**, 1–16.

Schwinn, M., and Diehl, B. 1973. "We Came to Help." Harcourt, Brace, and Jovanovich, New York.

Stockdale, R., and Stockdale, S. 1984. "In Love and War." Harper & Row, New York.

Wolf, S., and Ripley, H. S. 1954. Reactions among allied prisoners of war subjected to three years of imprisonment and torture by the Japanese. *Am. J. Psychiat.* **104**, 180–193.

Captivity, Recovery from

Richard H. Rahe

University of Nevada School of Medicine

I. Brief Euphoria
II. Hyperarousal
III. Compliance/Resistance
IV. Denial
V. Restitution
VI. Gradual Readjustment
VII. Comment

Recovery from prisoner of war and hostage captivity is presented in six stages of adaptation to this extremely challenging life stress. The time course over which these stages take place progressively lengthens from the first through the final stage. The initial stage appears to occur over seconds to minutes, the next stage lasts over minutes to hours, the third stage over hours to days, the fourth stage over days to weeks, the fifth stage over weeks to months, and the sixth stage over months to years. The literature, along with the author's experience, also suggests that recovery from captivity can be similarly summarized into six stages. Additionally, the duration of the stages of recovery appears to be similar to the duration of the complementary stages of adaptation to captivity. Helpful coping is presented for each of these six stages. This article also points out the enormous difficulties medical personnel face in attempting to carry out optimal treatment for returned captives.

I. BRIEF EUPHORIA

Despite preconceived notions of the general public about how jubilant a captive will be upon release, a true rejoicing rarely materializes. Captives initially feel euphoric, but this feeling is fleeting and celebrations planned for their return may fall flat. When excaptives are returned to the United States by plane, the air crew may have champagne aboard and decorations in place, only to find that the "celebration" consists of a brief cheer upon take-off followed in a few seconds to quiet conversations and individual contemplation.

Released captives' behavior is, in large part, guided by a deep mistrust that the return may amount to another false hope. Emotional restraint and careful evaluation of events are typical. Excaptives generally realize, however, that the public wishes a show of enthusiasm upon their return and they try not to disappoint their greeters. This display, however, tends to be rather hollow and fragile.

II. HYPERAROUSAL

Hyperarousal following release is appreciably different from the hypervigilance seen during adaptation to captivity. In the hypervigilant stage, captives' alertness is high, their observational powers keen, and they are aware of even subtle cues regarding the behavior and motivations of others. In the hyperaroused state, returnees are overstimulated and mentally slowed. The commotion around them, along with the great assortment of stimuli, can render them virtually "punch-drunk."

During this early phase of recovery, it is critical to protect them from overzealous politicians, well-wishers of all sorts, and particularly from the press. Sensitive politicians will make their presence brief and then depart, along with their entourage. Well-wishers can be a significant problem in terms of crowd control. Most difficult to manage are members of the press. If the period of captivity has been a long one, family members may have developed close friendships with representatives of the press. These family members may require repeated explanations as to the need to shield the excaptive from news media exploitation. In his or her vulnerable state, an excaptive may agree to probing interviews in which statements are made that they live to regret.

Thoughts and behaviors of releasees may be marked by confusion and exhaustion. Often, during their transition to freedom, former captives have been severely sleep deprived. Because returnees do not wish to offend any of their greeting party, they may talk at length with all who approach them.

A treatment imperative, therefore, is to protect returnees from further exhaustion. As physical examinations and psychological debriefings are often needed, the best place for these assessments may be a hospital with limited access to the public. In the case of the returned hostages from Iran, an Air Force hospital in Germany proved to be ideal for these purposes. The debriefings themselves had a positive effect on excaptives, through ventilation of strong emotions and the opportunity to obtain feedback on how they performed during captivity. The press and well-wishers were kept at the perimeter of the hospital. Although telephone contact was allowed between returnees and their family and friends, actual visits were discouraged. These restrictions allowed necessary examinations to be conducted in a restful and recuperative setting.

III. COMPLIANCE/RESISTANCE

Initially, returnees are likely to comply with most every request. They are, of course, accustomed to following orders from their guards and captors, without much thought given as to their own preferences. A danger, therefore, exists for health care personnel to request too much. For example, hours of psychological testing or other paramedical activity not related directly to their immediate care will often be completed without demurral. As the excaptives begin to regain feelings of individual power, they start to resist such activities, and they do have power. Who is going to reprimand a noncompliant man or woman who has just returned from months to years of severe mental and physical deprivation?

The transition from compliance to resistance became obvious to physicians caring for the exhostage group released from Iran around the third hospital day. Initially, the former captives were extremely candid and cooperative. Most were grateful for the clinical interactions. Two to 3 days later, many started to become somewhat cavalier about keeping their appointments, began to skip ward routines, and stayed out past bedtime hours. Some limit setting was needed. Korean War POW early rehabilitation programs, conducted as the men returned home aboard ship, were similarly disrupted when releasees' resistances to treatment continued unchecked.

Treatment plans should allow for this emerging independence. For example, some time from the hospital routine should be allowed for shopping, a meal out, and so forth. The hospital setting should not cause returnees to be treated as inpatients. Wearing of leisure clothing instead of hospital pajamas should be adopted. Doctors, nurses, and other health care providers must watch their own countertransference reactions. Offering too much, too soon, and/or attempts to personally "help" the former captive "make up" for past deprivations can lead to counterproductive and unprofessional activities.

Allowance for ample communications between returnees is very important. All returnees from Iran were placed in the same wing of the hospital. Between their physical, psychiatric, and dental examinations, returnees mingled in common areas, passed on information of importance to the group, and shared personal experiences. Many of the former hostages did not possess a representative knowledge of the experiences of other captives until these exchanges.

IV. DENIAL

After medical examinations and debriefings and a few days of rest and recuperation, released captives should begin to meet the press. This is a time to make personal statements regarding their captivity experiences. However, one question the press will ask repeatedly is "What kinds of problems are you now having due to the stresses of your captivity?" A returnee might answer this question quite candidly on his first day or two after release, but as he begins the denial stage his answer will be: "The doctors may think that something bad may happen, but I know that I will be perfectly okay." There is a readiness of the public to believe such answers, as they reinforce a hero image for the former captives. Such statements, however, frequently cover over significant physical and/or psychological difficulties and should not be taken at face value.

It is important for health care providers not to be taken in by denial, but also not to vigorously challenge it. Gentle reminders to continue with periodic follow-up should be given and lines of communication be kept open. Later, possible entry into treatment, if needed, can be proposed. Often working with family members is important at this point.

Denial also presents problems in the area of impulsive activities following release. A proneness to buy expensive cars or to invest savings accrued during captivity into poorly conceived financial schemes has been seen. Many entrepreneurs will try to utilize the excaptive's notoriety to support their own enterprises.

V. RESTITUTION

Efforts toward making restitution point to an interesting psychological phenomenon. The area of food is a good example. Due to generally severe and prolonged nutritional deprivation, most hostages return with a lean body habitus that, combined with the plentiful exercise they carried out in captivity, renders them extremely fit. Some weight gain over the first few months home would be expected. However, moderate to gross obesity was seen in some of the returned hostages from Iran in just a few months after their release. When questioned as to how they gained so much weight over such a short period of time, a characteristic answer was "I just felt I couldn't deny myself."

A second area of restitution occurs in readjustments among family members. Long-term captivity, especially with extended periods of social isolation, appears to have the greatest impact. Captives' emotional and intellectual functions may have become dulled from the monotony of prison life. Table manners and bathroom and sleeping habits acquired in captivity may be unacceptably crude in the home situation and disconcerting to family members. Further, spouses, children, and other family members may have become accustomed to managing daily events for themselves. The excaptive may try too hard to reestablish family structure and function that existed before his or her capture. In another vein, a former captive may try to provide, over a very short period of time, all of the love and attention they were prevented from giving their family members during captivity.

A third problem area is return to work. Employers are frequently tempted to offer a long vacation to returnees. Returnees themselves generally wish to resume work as soon as possible. This is frequently due to a need to reaffirm their previous skills and demonstrate their "worth" to their organizations. In some cases, particularly those involving long-term captivity, job refresher courses or even retraining are necessary for easing returnees back into job situations that have changed dramatically in their absence. In the instances of returned military exhostages held along with U.S. Embassy officials in Iran, most were given 3 months of vacation (in addition to their first 2 weeks of treatment and official receptions). This prolonged nonwork period led to problems for several men in terms of how to utilize this time profitably. The long time away from the military also contributed to decisions of some of the men to resign from the military and take jobs that had been offered to them during this interval.

Family and friends should be advised to expect to hear frequent recitals of excaptives' experiences. These family members and close friends often feel they should inhibit such recitations due to their fears that speaking about captivity will likely recreate sufferings. Just the opposite appears to be true. Giving lectures and speeches on their captivity experience can be very therapeutic for releasees. If an excaptive has a talent for writing, the preparation of an article or even a book about their experiences may help tremendously in working through their captivity experiences.

VI. GRADUAL READJUSTMENT

If criteria for readjustment from captivity stress simply included whether former captives returned to work or whether their marriages remained intact, the majority would be quickly declared as recovered. Markers for more complete recovery are more subtle than these. Illness following return is often an example of incomplete recovery. In follow-up studies of American POWs from Korea, as well as from Asian POW camps in World War II (where torture and nutritional deprivation were extremely severe), returned POWs showed significantly increased illness rates for infectious, cardiovascular, degenerative, and psychiatric disorders for over the next 25 to 30 years. Even accidental deaths were higher in the returned captive group than for controls over this time span. In contrast, when returned naval aviators from prisoner of war captivity in North Vietnam were similarly studied, elevated illness rates for physical and psychological illness were seen to persist for only 8 years following their return. Thus, even with the best outcome, these studies point to an enduring effect of severe and prolonged captivity experience on physical and psychological health.

If the criterion for recovery is freedom from the "psychological scars" of captivity, complete recovery may never occur. Lifelong anxieties and depression have been seen in victims of especially severe captivity stress, such as Nazi concentration camp survivors.

Hardly a day goes by that they do not suffer distressing psychiatric symptoms emanating from their Holocaust experiences.

Lesser captivity trauma should yield fewer long-term problems. During the first years following return from captivity, excaptives from Iran had an opportunity to put into effect many of the personal life revisions that they gave ample thought to during their incarceration. Changes in career pattern were frequently carried out. Divorce and later remarriage were not uncommon. New life changes, such as return to school, residential moves, and changes in friends and activities, were reported frequently. Such life changes in and of themselves take time for adjustment. Recovery from captivity, therefore, goes hand in hand with adaptation to new life decisions and directions taken following return.

VII. COMMENT

In comparing individuals' adaptation to captivity with their recovery from that experience, one is impressed with the reliance on self and/or other captives during captivity contrasted to the acceptance of aid from health care personnel. Many excaptives have difficulty with such a transition and continue to feel that because they took care of themselves in captivity they are fully qualified to care for themselves and their families after release. The author is aware of a few returnees who went through years of disabling psychiatric problems before they could admit to themselves that they needed medical help. Much remains to be learned regarding this final readjustment period. In reports and in books written by the returnees themselves, the long-term adjustments of many have been difficult.

See Also the Following Articles

Captivity, Adaptation to; Concentration Camp Survivors; Prisoners of War; Vietnam Veterans, Postwar Experiences of

Bibliography

Beebe, G. W. (1975). Follow-up study of World War II and Korean War prisoners. II. morbidity, disability, and maladjustment. *Am. J. Epidemiol.* **101**, 400–422.

Blakey, S. (1978). "Prisoner at War: The Survival of Commander Richard A. Stratton." Anchor Press/Doubleday, Garden City, NY.

Boulle, P. (1954). "The Bridge Over the River Kwai." The Vanguard Press, New York.

Brill, N. Q. (1946). Neuropsychiatric examination of military personnel recovered from Japanese prison camps. *Bull. US Army Med. Dept.* **5**, 429–438.

Clavell, J. (1962). "King Rat," Dell Publishers, New York.

Engdahl, B., Dikel, T. N., Eberly, R., and Blank, A. (1997). Poattraumatic stress disorder in a community group of former prisoners of war: A normative response to severe trauma. *Am. J. Psychiat.* **154**, 1576–1581.

Hall, R. C. W., and Malone, P. T. (1976). Psychiatric effects of prolonged Asian captivity: A two-year follow-up. *Am. J. Psychiat.* **133**, 786–790.

Hall, R. C. W., and Simmons, W. C. (1973). The POW wife. *Arch. Gen. Psychiat.* **29**, 690–694.

Howard, N. (1980). Personal communication regarding the plane ride from Algeria to Germany with the released American hostages from Iran.

Matusek, P. (1975). "Internment in Concentration Camps and Its Consequences." Springer-Verlag, New York.

Neizger, M. D. (1970). Follow-up study of World War II and Korean War prisoners. I. Morbidity, disability, and maladjustment. *Am. J. Epidemiol.* **91**, 123–138.

Rahe, R. H. (1980–1986). Personal experiences with the immediate care, and one year and five year follow-up evaluations, of the 52 Americans held hostage in Iran.

Richlin, M., Shale, J. H., and Rahe, R. H. (1980). Five-year medical follow-up of Navy POWs repatriated from Vietnam. *US Navy Med.* **71**, 1926.

Segal, H. A. (1954). Initial psychiatric findings of recently repatriated POWs. *Am. J. Psychiat.* **111**, 358–363.

Segal, J. (1973). Therapeutic considerations in planning the return of American POWs to continental United States. *Milit. Med.* **2**, 73–77.

Spaulding, R. C. (1977). The Pueblo incident: Medical problems reported during captivity and physical findings at the time of release. *Milit. Med.* **142**, 681–684.

Cardiovascular System and Stress

Paul Hjemdahl

Karolinska Hospital, Stockholm, Sweden

Mental stress elicits a cardiovascular response pattern typical of the "defense reaction," with increases in heart rate and cardiac output and redistribution of blood flow to different organs in both animals and humans. Blood pressure increases despite a net decrease in systemic vascular resistance, which is related to vasodilatation in large tissues, notably skeletal muscle and adipose tissue, whereas vasoconstriction occurs in the kidneys, splanchnic organs, and skin. The classic "stress hormone" epinephrine is a marker of perceived stress (arousal), but less important as a mediator of cardiovascular responses to stress than differentiated changes in sympathetic nerve activity and release of norepinephrine. Also other neurohormonal influences, release of nitric oxide from endothelial cells, and activation of platelets, with subsequent release of vasoactive constituents, may contribute to vascular responses. Stress is implicated in cardiovascular disease, both as an enhancing factor in the slow development of atherosclerosis and as a trigger of acute events, such as myocardial infarction and death. Possible mechanisms, such as atherosclerotic plaque rupture and prothrombotic effects of stress, are briefly discussed.

I. BACKGROUND

The cardiovascular system adapts to stress by changes which, from a teleological perspective, are meant to improve the chances of survival when the organism is threatened. The response pattern has been called the "defense reaction" and serves, in its simplest form, to prepare the organism for fight or flight. Animal experiments by Hilton, Folkow, and others have established a typical pattern of cardiovascular responses to stress, which may be elicited by electrical stimulation of certain regions of the brain as well as by environmental stimuli in awake animals. The defense reaction involves elevations of cardiac output and blood pressure and a redirection of blood flow from the kidneys and splanchnic organs to skeletal muscle. A similar response pattern is elicited by mental stress in humans. Short-term survival benefits of the changes associated with the defense reaction may not be parallelled by beneficial consequences in the long term when elicited repeatedly in individuals living in an urban society with everyday stresses.

Research on the importance of psychosocial factors and "stress" in cardiovascular disease has been rather intense. There is consensus that stress is of importance, but its exact role in cardiovascular pathophysiology has been somewhat illusive for many reasons—What is "stress"? How do "positive" and "negative" stress differ? How can stress be quantitated? Is laboratory stress testing relevant for the everyday situation? How do personality factors influence cardiovascular responses to "stress" and the consequences of these responses? Despite this complexity, it is clear that stress in terms of stimuli that influence the cardiovascular system in a certain direction is involved in cardiovascular disease and the consequences. This article focuses on the effects of mental stress on the cardiovascular system and the mechanisms probably involved, with a few comparisons with the effects of physical exercise and other stressors.

A. Historical Perspective

The development of current concepts of stress are discussed elsewhere in this encyclopedia. From a cardiovascular point of view it is pertinent to mention the work of Walter B. Cannon, who, in the first decades of this century, studied the responses of animals to stress. He described the "fight or flight" reaction and a homeostatic theory of how organisms adapt to threatening environmental influences. Cannon recognized the importance of the sympathetic system and proposed that the adrenal glands secreted "sympathin," which mediated the responses to stress. However, von Euler could later show that sympathetic nerves use the neurotransmitter norepinephrine, whereas the circulating hormone secreted by the adrenal glands was a related substance, epinephrine. Later, adrenocorticotropic hormone (ACTH) and glucocorticoids secreted from the adrenal cortex were added to the list of "stress hormones." Goldstein (1995a) reviewed the homeostatic mechanisms in relation to research on stress and distress (from Darwin and Bernard to present date). He noted the lack of a unifying concept of stress and that this reflects the complexity with which the organism may respond to stress, due to feedback regulation and the multiplicity of systems involved in the control of homeostasis.

II. METHODOLOGICAL COMMENTS

Methodological issues are discussed elsewhere in this encyclopedia. In cardiovascular stress research, the conditions for resting measurements are most important, since any expression of cardiovascular reactivity to stress depends on the basal value with which the stress value is compared. In fact, the basality of resting measurements (as reflected by, e.g., heart rate and plasma epinephrine levels) may be the most important determinant of study results. The stress test used should, of course, be standardized when comparing stress reactivity in individuals or between groups. Responses should be of sufficient amplitude to allow discrimination between different conditions and reasonably reproducible. Many factors, including personality factors, modulate the perception of stress and the degree of arousal caused by the stressor as well as cardiovascular responses elicited by it (Fig. 1).

A. What Is a Relevant Stressor?

For a cardiologist, "stress testing" means to evaluate if myocardial ischemia can be provoked by a

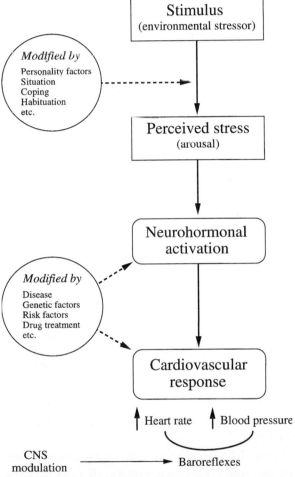

FIGURE 1 Stimulus–response scheme for cardiovascular responses to psychological stress. The perception of "stress" is modified by multiple factors, which reinforce or attenuate the arousal evoked by the stimulus. The cardiovascular response is mediated by neurohormonal activation. Several factors may modify the neurohormonal activation as well as responses to the mediating neurohormones. Finally, the cardiovascular responses may be buffered by baroreflexes aimed at maintaining blood pressure at prestimulus levels, but the efficiency of the baroreflex is attenuated during stress.

stimulus that increases myocardial oxygen demand, such as physical exercise. However, mental stress may also provoke ischemia. Any increase in mental activity—even quiet speaking and REM periods (dreaming) during sleep—will evoke cardiovascular changes. In fact, REM sleep may even precipitate myocardial infarction. Interviews on sensitive personal issues may be most relevant when studying the cardiovascular risks of stress, but cannot be standardized when comparing individuals or groups. The question is if laboratory stress tests mimic responses elicited by mental stimuli normally encountered. Herd (1991) used an operational definition of relevant stressors whereby "a psychological stressor is one that causes a predictable stress response in a predictable percentage of index subjects" and went on to define the cardiovascular stress response as changes seen in the defense reaction. Various standardized stress tests have been developed which fit this definition.

Among the most common mental stress tests for cardiovascular research are mental arithmetics (MA) and Stroop's color-word conflict test (CWT). Tests may also be based on auditory feedback or video games. Mental arithmetics is simple to administer, but test results are influenced by the speed of the test, and by (variable?) harassment of the subject; individuals may also have very different abilities to cope with mathematics. Mental arithmetics produces substantial responses in some studies (e.g., those of Brod and coworkers), but weak responses in other studies. The CWT is administered in different ways, and the magnitudes of responses depend on the version used (how color-words are presented, how responses are made, and if there is auditory interference as well). We have used MA (in various versions, with or without external pacing) and CWT in a modification with auditory interference developed by Frankenhaeuser in the 1960s and have found the latter to be particularly useful.

Adaptation to the same stressor occurs upon repeated administration, whereas responses to a novel stressor are either intact or enhanced. Such adaptation involves information processing (coping, etc.) rather than desensitization of the target organs. Animal experiments suggest that chronic stress can even result in enhanced responses to a novel stressor, due to increased synthesis, storage, and release of neurotransmitters.

In clinical research, it may be difficult to find newly diagnosed patients who have not received any treatment. When drug treatment is discontinued, one should minimize carryover effects or rebound phenomena by allowing sufficient time for treatment effects to disappear. For example, diuretics may have long-lasting effects on sodium and fluid balance, and withdrawal of a β-blocker may lead to rebound phenomena with increased β-adrenoceptor sensitivity. Such after-effects may persist longer than is appreciated by many authors and should be taken into account.

III. NEUROHORMONAL MECHANISMS

Before describing the cardiovascular responses to mental stress, neurohormonal systems that may be involved are briefly commented on and are discussed in relation to these responses. In general, neurogenic control is suited for fine-tuned influences on individual organs or cells, whereas hormonal influences are diffuse. (For detailed information on mechanisms governing blood flow in various organs see Bennet and Gardiner, 1996).

A. The Sympathoadrenal System

The sympathoadrenal system is involved in short-term (phasic) responses to stress. Epinephrine (adrenaline), which is often considered to be *the* "stress hormone," is secreted during stress, and epinephrine levels in plasma or urine reflect the degree of "arousal" experienced.

The sympathetic nerves may operate in a differentiated fashion, with varying levels of activity and varying responses to stress in different organs. Muscle sympathetic nerve activity during stress may even differ in different parts of the body (see below). Thus, the common term "sympathetic tone," which indicates synchronized activity throughout the body, is not appropriate. If possible, sympathetic activity should be studied locally, in the organ of interest.

Norepinephrine is the principal neurotransmitter of sympathetic nerves, although the cotransmitter neuropeptide Y may contribute to vasoconstrictor responses when sympathetic nerves fire at high frequencies. Norepinephrine stimulates α- and β_1-adrenoceptors. Catecholamines are rapidly cleared from plasma, with half-lives of 1–2 min, but the effect of a sympathetic nerve impulse is much shorter than that, due to local inactivating mechanisms, such as reuptake of norepinephrine into the nerve. Norepinephrine may also function as a circulating hormone, when the plasma levels of norepinephrine are markedly elevated, such as during physical exercise. Resting levels of norepinephrine in plasma are ≈ 1 nmol/liter, and threshold levels for hormonal effects are 3–4 nmol/liter. Sympathetic nerve activity may be monitored in humans by (1) direct recordings of impulse activity in nerves supplying skeletal muscle and skin, but not in organs of perhaps greater interest in the context of mental stress; (2) analyses of heart rate variability (for cardiac sympatho-vagal balance); and (3) measurements of norepinephrine levels in plasma and norepinephrine release from various organs. Measurements of norepinephrine release and spillover into plasma can be refined by the use of an isotope dilution method involving infusions of radiolabeled norepinephrine, which was developed by Esler and coworkers.

These different techniques all have their technical difficulties and limitations. They complement each other, since the release of norepinephrine from sympathetic nerves is influenced by prejunctional regulation (i.e., variable release per nerve impulse) and the sensitivity of the receptors involved may vary when measuring functional responses, such as heart rate.

Epinephrine may, as a circulating hormone, stimulate α- and β-adrenoceptors in all organs. Under certain circumstances epinephrine can be taken up into and rereleased from sympathetic nerves in such quantities that a role as a cotransmitter is possible, but this is normally not important. Thus, epinephrine is the classic hormonal link of the sympathoadrenal system.

There is functional differentiation of sympathetic neuroeffector mechanisms; β_1-adrenoceptors appear to be innervated and β_2-adrenoceptors noninnervated or "humoral" receptors. This leads to epinephrine being functionally β_2-selective at physiological concentrations in blood plasma (even though it is also an effective β_1-agonist in *in vitro* systems) and provides a possibility to study the importance of epinephrine for physiological responses to stress by examining the β-adrenoceptor subtype involved in the response. Similarly, α_1-adrenoceptors appear to be innervated, and α_2-adrenoceptors noninnervated in the cardiovascular system, which has therapeutic implications and allows separation of neurogenic and humoral influences.

B. Cholinergic Mechanisms

The heart is under dual autonomic control, with excitatory sympathetic nerves (stimulating β_1-adrenoceptors) and inhibitory vagal nerves (releasing acetylcholine and stimulating muscarinic receptors). Acetylcholine is very rapidly inactivated after its release, allowing beat-to-beat control of heart rate. The intrinsic rate of the sinus node is ≈ 90–100 beats/min. Thus, the resting heart rate is controlled to a large extent by vagal activity. Increased physical fitness reduces resting heart rate by increasing vagal activity. Stress may thus increase heart rate by activating sympathetic nerves and/or by inhibiting the parasympathetic vagus nerve.

Animal research on vasodilator responses in skeletal muscle has demonstrated sympathetic vasodilator nerves which release acetylcholine. Work by Hilton suggested that such vasodilator nerves did not exist in primates, but early studies in humans suggested that it indeed was possible to elicit cholinergic vasodilatation in the forearm with certain stressors. However, the literature on cholinergic vasodilatation in human skeletal muscle is divided, and it cannot be definitely stated that this mechanism is of importance or under which conditions it may contribute.

C. Other Mediators and Mechanisms

The renin–angiotensin system may be activated by stress. Renin release from the kidney is under the influence of several factors, one of which is sympathetic nerve activity and β_1-adrenoceptor stimulation. Salt deprivation increases renin secretion, and salt loading decreases it. Renin catalyzes the formation of angiotensin II, which is a potent vasoconstrictor peptide with several other biological actions, including the enhancement of aldosterone secretion. Thus, the system is salt conserving. The relative importance of angiotensin II and norepinephrine as mediators of vasoconstriction during stress may vary. High sodium intake tends to enhance cardiovascular responses to mental stress, but this is most likely independent of the renin–angiotensin system, which should be down-regulated under such conditions.

There are several neuropeptides (e.g., neuropeptide Y and calcitonin gene-related peptide) and other peptides (e.g., atrial natriuretic factor and endothelin) which may be involved in cardiovascular responses to stress. Their roles during stress have not been sufficiently elucidated, in part due to lack of good antagonists for human use, to be commented on briefly in this context.

Platelets store serotonin (5-hydroxytryptamine), which is released when the cells are activated, and activated platelets synthesize thromboxane A$_2$. Both of these substances may stimulate platelets (positive feedback) and cause vasoconstriction, especially when the vascular endothelium is not functioning normally. Stress may activate platelets.

Flow-mediated vasodilatation has been known for a long time. Furchgott showed the importance of endothelial cells for vasodilator responses and proposed the existence of an endothelium-derived relaxing factor (EDRF). Nitric oxide (NO) was shown by others to be an important component, if not the only EDRF. Nitric oxide released from the vascular endothelium serves both as a vasodilator and an inhibitor of platelet adhesion and aggregation, and inhibition of NO synthesis or defective NO production by the endothelial cells may increase vascular tone and the risk of thrombosis. Nitric oxide appears to be a rather ubiquitos substance in the body, which may be involved in neurogenic mechanisms and influence cardiac function as well. However, the importance of this for stress responses of the cardiovascular system is unknown. Flow-mediated vasodilatation (i.e., NO) is probably important for vasodilator responses to stress in some organs.

IV. BAROREFLEXES AND BLOOD PRESSURE REGULATION

The cardiovascular system is regulated in a complex manner, with compensatory adjustments when changes are elicited by various stimuli. Normally this fine-tuned system strives to maintain a certain blood pressure (which may be either normal or high, if the individual has hypertension) via arterial baroreflexes which serve to dampen the change. If blood pressure rises there is reflexogenic inhibition of the heart and reduced vasocontrictor nerve activity. Conversely, if the blood pressure decreases there is reflexogenic stimulation of the heart, with increases in heart rate and cardiac output and a compensatory increase in vasoconstrictor nerve activity. If cardiac output is lowered, by, e.g., drug treatment, peripheral blood flow will decrease to maintain the blood pressure. In the long term, baroreflexes are reset to the new blood pressure level if, e.g., a patient with hypertension is treated with a blood pressure-lowering drug.

There are also receptors which sense venous pressure and participate in volume regulation. If venous pressure decreases, reflexogenic and hormonal changes occur, which serve to conserve salt and water (i.e., renal responses) and to maintain blood pressure by increasing venous tone and reducing peripheral blood flow. The kidney is intimately involved in the regulation of blood pressure according to Guyton's classic theory of cardiovascular homeostasis. However, there are also indications that blood pressure is a regulated variable and that neurogenic mechanisms are important for both short- and long-term levels of blood pressure.

During stress, the influence of baroreflex regulation of the circulation diminishes, and centrally elicited pressor mechanisms may operate under less influence of reflexogenic modulation than if blood pressure is increased by other maneouvers (Fig. 1). As discussed by Julius, there seems to be some blood pressure-sensing mechanism which regulates blood pressure during stress, as interference with one pressor mechanism often leads to another one taking over and the pressor response to the stimulus remains intact.

V. HUMAN STUDIES OF CARDIOVASCULAR RESPONSES TO MENTAL STRESS

Figure 2 illustrates schematically how mental stress elevates blood pressure in humans, based on results from a number of studies. Pressor responses to mental stress generally depend on the increase in cardiac output, since systemic vascular resistance decreases. In an early series of investigations, Brod and coworkers studied the cardiovascular responses to mental stress, mainly forced MA (using procedures creating substantial hemodynamic responses), in normotensive and hypertensive subjects. An example is given in Fig. 3, which shows that arousal caused by the suggestion of exercise elicited qualitatively similar responses as mental arithmetics. A few examples of responses to CWT, from our work, are mentioned below.

A. Cardiac Responses

The increase in cardiac output is caused mainly by an increase in heart rate, but an increase in stroke volume also contributes (Fig. 2). Tachycardia may be elicited by both increased sympathetic nerve activity and vagal withdrawal. Increases in stroke volume are related to increased contractility (which can be demonstrated by, e.g., echocardiography) as well as an increase in venous return, which supports the filling of the heart in diastole. Thus, work by Brod and coworkers has demonstrated that stress causes venoconstriction, which results in centralization of the blood volume and supports cardiac filling. Studies with pacing alone have shown that an isolated increase in heart rate does not efficiently elevate cardiac output—an increase in contractility and an adequate distension of the heart in diastole contribute to the stress response.

The effects of β-blockade by metoprolol (β_1 selective) or propranolol (nonselective) on some invasive hemodynamic variables are illustrated in Fig. 4. Healthy volunteers were subjected to CWT (the Frankenhaeuser version), which was found to elicit clear-cut and rather reproducible (see control group) responses. The two β-blockers inhibited the heart

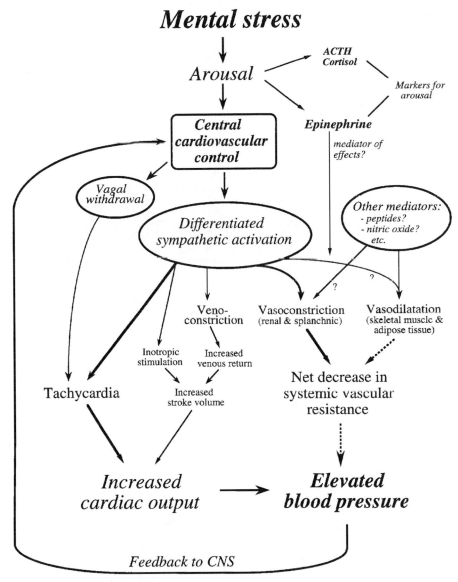

FIGURE 2 Schematic representation of the cardiovascular response pattern of the defense reaction. The pressor response is mainly cardiac output dependent, and the increase in cardiac output depends mainly on an increase in heart rate. The vascular response is a net reduction of systemic vascular resistance, but responses of individual organs vary considerably. Adrenocorticotropic hormone, cortisol, and epinephrine are markers of the arousal evoked by the stressor. Established and possible mediators of the cardiovascular responses are indicated in the figure. Modified from Hjemdahl (1993).

rate response similarly, indicating that the sympathetic component was β_1 mediated (neurogenic). The vagal component in the tachycardia elicited by mental stress is reflected in the persisting, although blunted, tachycardia seen after β-blockade in suffi-

cient doses to eliminate the increase in stroke volume during stress (Fig. 4). The stroke volume response was attenuated by metoprolol and abolished by propranolol, suggesting contributions of both neurogenic (norepinephrine) and hormonal (epinephrine)

O.G. Normal B.P.

effects. However, stroke volume is also sensitive to afterload, and the effects of β-blockade on systemic vascular resistance may have influenced the stroke volume response to stress.

The coronary circulation is to a large extent regulated by cardiac metabolism, and it is difficult to separate β-adrenoceptor mediated coronary vasodilatation from that induced by increased cardiac metabolism and flow-mediated vasodilatation. However, α-adrenergic coronary vasoconstriction may occur when the endothelium is dysfunctional or when cardiac metabolism is inhibited.

B. Peripheral Vascular Responses

The decrease in systemic vascular resistance during mental stress is related to vasodilatation in skeletal muscle and adipose tissue, whereas there is vasoconstriction in the kidneys, splanchnic organs, and skin (Fig. 2). The experiment of Brod and coworkers (Fig. 3) illustrates marked vasodilatation in the forearm, simultaneously with reduced renal clearance of paraaminohippurate (i.e., renal vasoconstriction) and a decrease in skin temperature (i.e., vasoconstriction in skin); other experiments have show splanchnic vasoconstriction.

1. Limb Blood Flow

The decrease in systemic vascular resistance in the experiments illustrated in Fig. 4 was attenuated by β_1-blockade and abolished by propranolol. These effects of β-blockade may reflect blockade of vascular β-adrenoceptors (which are of the β_2-subtype) and/ or peripheral vascular adaptation to the effects of β-blockade on the cardiac response to stress. The increase in blood pressure during mental stress was little influenced by β-blockade (data not shown), in agreement with the results of several other studies. If, as discussed by Julius, blood pressure is the primarily

regulated variable, attenutation of the increase in cardiac output would result in compensatory changes in vascular responses in order to achieve the same level of blood pressure during stress as would be obtained without such attenuation. Vasodilator responses would then be secondary to, and governed by, cardiac responses.

The above experiments included measurements of calf blood flow (by plethysmography) and adipose tissue and skeletal muscle blood flow (by isotope clearance methods). Figure 5 shows similar vasodilatation in adipose tissue, skeletal muscle (the gastrocnemius muscle), and the entire calf in reponse to CWT. β-Blockade inhibited these vasodilator responses similarly, as shown above for systemic vascular resistance. In other studies even greater vasodilator responses than those seen in the leg were found in the human forearm with the same stress test (Fig. 6). Of interest are findings by Rusch and coworkers that blood flow responses of the arm and leg to different stimuli (including MA) differed and that vasodilatation was more prominent in the arm than in the leg. Others have found differences in the baroreceptor-mediated control of limb blood flow in the leg and the forearm. Recordings of muscle sympathetic nerve activity by Anderson and coworkers showed that MA increased muscle sympathetic activity in the leg, but not in the arm, when simultaneously recorded (Fig. 7). Thus, the sympathetic response to mental stress is so differentiated that differences in muscle sympathetic nerve activity can even be seen between the upper and lower limbs. Increases in muscle sympathetic nerve activity may serve to buffer the vasodilator response to stress.

Nitric oxide release and flow-mediated vasodilatation may be involved in the blood flow response of skeletal muscle to mental stress. Other possible mediators are acetylcholine (although we found no neurogenic component in the sustained forearm va-

---

FIGURE 3 Comparison of general and regional hemodynamic responses to mental arithmetic stress and suggestion of heavy muscular exercise in a healthy subject from the studies of Brod and coworkers. Mental stress and the anticipation of physical stress elicited similar cardiovascular responses, both of which resemble the defense reaction. Illustrated are cardiac output (C.O.), systemic vascular resistance (T.P.R.), skin temperature, renal paraaminohippurate clearance (C_{PAH}), renal vascular resistance (RR), extrarenal vascular resistance (ERR), and forearm blood flow and vascular resistance. From Brod (1963), with permission from the BMJ Publishing Group.

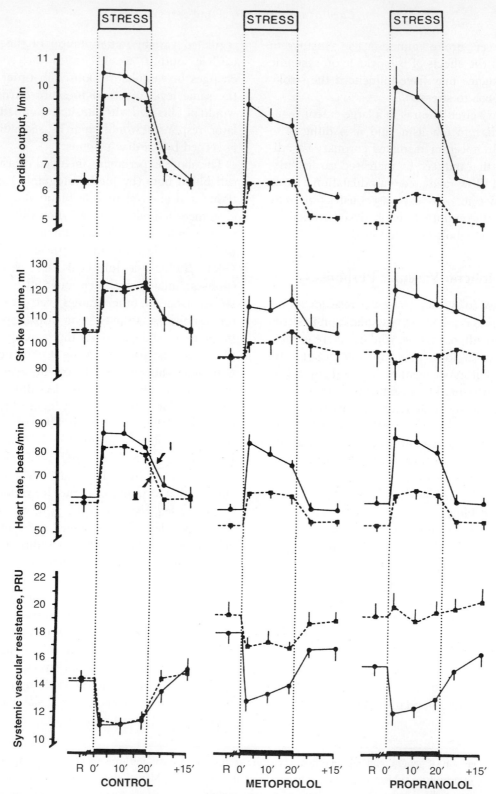

FIGURE 4 Cardiac and systemic vascular responses to mental stress induced by CWT (the Frankenhaeuser version of Stroop's color-word conflict test) in healthy male volunteers. Thirty subjects were divided into three groups in which CWT (STRESS) was repeated without treatment (CONTROL) or after intravenous injection of the β_1-blocker metoprolol or the nonselective β-

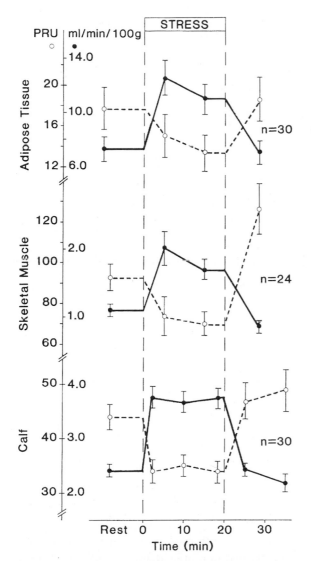

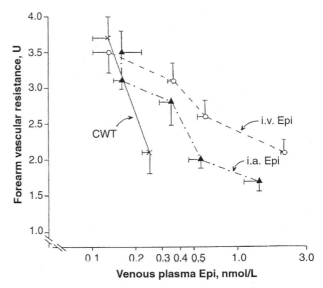

FIGURE 6   Forearm vascular responses to CWT and to intravenous (i.v.) and intraarterial (i.a.) infusions of epinephrine in relation to epinephrine concentrations before and during interventions. Mental stress elicited a marked forearm vasodilator response with a small increase in venous plasma epinephrine. Responses to i.a. epinephrine were greater than those to i.v. epinephrine, suggesting reflexogenic buffering of the forearm vasodilator response to systemic epinephrine. Intrapolation of vasodilator responses to the epinephrine concentration achieved by the same individual during CWT showed that epinephrine may have contributed 10–30% of the vasodilator response to stress. From Lindqvist and coworkers (*Am. J. Physiol.* 1996, **270**, E393–E399), with permission from the American Physiological Society.

FIGURE 5   Peripheral vascular responses to mental stress (CWT) in the experiments illustrated in Fig. 4. Mental stress elicited similar vasodilatation in adipose tissue of the abdomen (similar responses were found in adipose tissue on the thigh), skeletal muscle (gastrocnemius muscle), and the calf. Tissue blood flows were determined by the local clearance of ^{133}Xenon, and calf blood flow was measured by venous occlusion plethysmography. From Linde and coworkers (*Am. J. Physiol.* 1989, **256**, E12–E18), with permission from the American Physiological Society.

sodilator response to CWT), vasodilating peptides, and epinephrine, which is discussed below.

Thus, it is well established from work in several groups and with several different stress tests that limb blood flow increases due to vasodilatation in skeletal muscle and adipose tissue, whereas there is vasoconstriction in skin. Interestingly, skeletal muscle vasodilatation appears to differ in different regions of the body. The mechanisms involved are not entirely clear.

blocker propranolol. Illustrated are cardiac output (measured by thermodilution), stroke volume, heart rate, and systemic vascular resistance. The mean arterial pressure response to stress (≈ 20 mm Hg) was little affected by the treatments given. From Freyschuss and coworkers (*Am. J. Physiol.* 1988, **255**, H443–H451), with permission from the American Physiological Society.

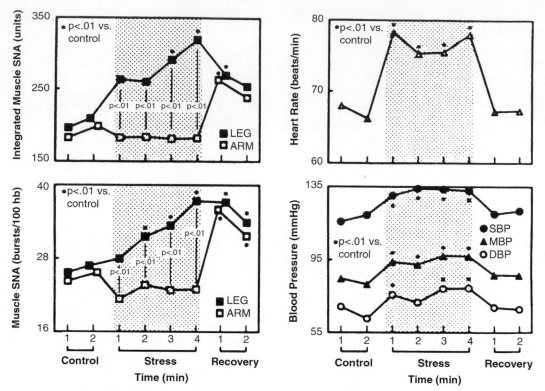

FIGURE 7 Simultaneously recorded muscle sympathetic nerve activity (MSNA) in the arm and leg as well as heart rate and blood pressures in healthy individuals during mental arithmetics. Muscle sympathetic nerve activity is expressed both as integrated nerve activity, and as bursts/100 heart beats. Muscle sympathetic nerve activity increased in the leg, but not in the arm in response to mental stress, indicating that skeletal muscle blood flow is under different neurogenic modulation in different regions of the body during stress. From Anderson, Wallin, and Mark (*Hypertension* 1987, 9(Suppl. 3), 114–119), with permission from the publisher (Lippincott, Williams & Wilkins).

2. Renal Blood Flow

The kidneys, which receive ≈20% of the cardiac output, are important in the regulation of blood pressure—both in the short and long term—and appear to be a target for stress effects. Several groups have shown renal vasoconstriction, renin release, and/or altered renal function in response to mental stress. Examples are shown in Fig. 3 for the work of Brod and coworkers, and in Table I for our work. Of particular interest is that renal vascular responses to mental stress may be enhanced in hypertension. Thus, Hollenberg and coworkers found that very mild stress induced by a nonverbal IQ test (which did not increase blood pressure) elicited clear-cut renal vasoconstriction among hypertensives, but not among normotensives without a family history of hypertension; those with a family history of hyper-

tension had an intermediate response. Renin release was similarly differentiated among individuals in the Hollenberg study.

Tidgren and coworkers performed a series of investigations of renal vascular responses to different stimuli, based on a renal venous thermodilution technique which allowed rapid measurements of renal blood flow. Table I illustrates some of these results. It may be seen that mental stress (CWT) increased renal vascular resistance by close to 50% and increased the renal overflows of renin and norepinephrine markedly. The isometric handgrip exercise was less efficient, especially regarding renin release, despite a similar increase in mean arterial pressure (approximately 20 mm Hg with both stimuli). The renal vasoconstrictor response to mental stress was similar to that elicited by dynamic exercise of moderate in-

TABLE I

A Comparison of Responses to Mental Stress (Induced by CWT, the Frankenhaueser Version), Isometric Handgrip Exercise (Maximum Effort), and Dynamic Exercise (Graded Supine Exercise, Levels 2 and 3 Are Shown) in Healthy Male Volunteers[a]

Condition	Renal vascular resistance (PRU)	Renal renin release (units/min)	Norepinephrine			Epinephrine arterial (nmol/liter)	Heart rate (beats/min)	Source of data[b]
			Arterial (nmol/liter)	Renal venous (nmol/liter)	Renal overflow (pmol/min)			
Rest	0.15 ± 0.01	75[c]	0.78 ± 0.06	1.09 ± 0.10	252 ± 29	0.26 ± 0.04	59 ± 2	1
Mental stress	0.22 ± 0.02***	247***	1.34 ± 0.11***	2.93 ± 0.54***	708 ± 79***	0.68 ± 0.11***	81 ± 5***	
Rest	0.16 ± 0.02	54 ± 17	0.98 ± 0.13	1.24 ± 0.14	228 ± 34	0.24 ± 0.03	56 ± 2	2
Isometric handgrip	0.20 ± 0.03*	≈60 (n.s.)[d]	1.49 ± 0.16***	2.36 ± 0.29***	508 + 73***	0.38 ± 0.04***	68 ± 3***	
Rest	0.14 ± 0.02	69 ± 28	0.87 ± 0.08	1.05 ± 0.11	201 ± 33	0.32 ± 0.07	67 ± 3	3
Exercise (60%)[d]	≈0.22**	≈200**	≈3**	≈5**	≈1000**	≈0.5**	≈140***	
(maximum effort)	0.33 ± 0.03***	825 ± 302***	11.4 ± 2.45***	19.8 ± 5.69***	3039 ± 806***	2.12 ± 0.54***	175 ± 6***	

[a] Renal blood flow was measured by a renal venous thermodilution technique (see reference 2), and renal vascular resistance was calculated on the basis of intraarterially determined blood pressures. PRU, peripheral resistance units. For transformation of catecholamine values, 1 nmol/liter = 169 pg/mliter (norepinephrine) or 183 pg/mliter (epinephrine). Mean values ± SEM (or median) for resting and peak values are shown ($n = 8$–12). Further details may be found in references cited in table.

[b] Sources of data: (1) Tidgren and Hjemdahl (1989), *Am. J. Physiol.* **257**, F682–F689; (2) Tidgren and Hjemdahl (1988), *Acta Physiol. Scand.* **134**, 23–34; (3) Tidgren and coworkers (1991), *J. Appl. Physiol.* **70**, 2279–2286.

[c] Median values reported, due to skewed distribution of renin release.

[d] Estimated from graphs; n.s., not significant.

* $p < 0.05$.

** $p < 0.01$.

*** $p < 0.001$.

tensity (60% of maximum effort). Heart rate and arterial plasma epinephrine increased more with CWT than with isometric handgrip, whereas dynamic exercise increased heart rate still more, with a smaller increase in epinephrine at a similar level of renal vasoconstriction. Thus, the patterns of responses differ between these three stimuli. The renal vasoconstrictor and renin responses to mental stress were correlated to the renal norepinephrine overflow response (i.e., sympathetic nerve activity). The possible importance of epinephrine is discussed below.

Animal studies by di Bona, Koepke, Thorén and others have shown that renal vasoconstriction as well as decreases in renal sodium excretion and increases in renin release elicited by mental stress are sympathetically mediated and that these responses are enhanced in spontaneously hypertensive animals. Thus, the sympathetic nerves are important for renal responses to stress. Work in humans is less extensive, but the results discussed above tend to support the conclusion that the kidney is a target organ for stress and that sympathetic nerve activity is involved.

3. Is Epinephrine an Important Stress Hormone?

When given intravenously, epinephrine increases cardiac output mainly by increasing stroke volume. This is perceived as tachycardia (or "the heart is pumping harder"), even though heart rate is relatively little influenced unless the dosage of epinephrine is high. The increase in stroke volume is related to an increase in cardiac contractility as well as a reduction of afterload due to the systemic vasodilatation elicited by epinephrine. During stress, however, the increase in cardiac output is mainly related to an increase in heart rate, due to increased cardiac sympathetic nerve activity and vagal withdrawal. Even though the human heart is endowed with β_2-adrenoceptors, which may be activated by epinephrine, the cardiac response to stress is thus mainly neurogenic.

Epinephrine is a potent vasodilator when infused intravenously or intraarterially. The vasodilator response is elicited by β_2-adrenoceptor stimulation, and the α-agonistic effects of epinephrine become apparent only after blockade of vascular β_2-adreno-ceptors or at supraphysiological concentrations of epinephrine. In the absence of β-blockade intrave-nously infused epinephrine does not change mean arterial pressure within the physiological range, but concentration-dependent decreases in diastolic blood pressure (reflecting systemic vasodilatation) and increases in systolic blood pressure (reflecting increased stroke volume) are elicited. The impor-tance of epinephrine for vascular responses to stress may be deduced from comparisons of plasma concen-trations achieved during stress and those required for physiological responses as well as by effects of β-blockade. Figure 6 illustrates intraindividual com-parisons of responses to CWT and infused epineph-rine with regard to the forearm circulation; similar comparisons were made in our kidney studies.

Intravenously infused epinephrine may elicit re-flexogenic increases in muscle sympathetic nerve ac-tivity. This is seen in Fig. 6, which illustrates that epinephrine is more efficient when infused locally (intraarterially) compared to intravenously. When vasodilator responses to CWT and epinephrine were compared, we found that epinephrine only contrib-uted to a small extent (10–30%, on average). Data on local infusions of propranolol support this con-tention. Thus, epinephrine does not explain the vaso-dilatation in human skeletal muscle during mental stress.

In the kidney study of mental stress (Table I), there was no vasoconstrictor (or vasodilator) response to intravenously infused epinephrine, even at plasma concentrations as high as 6 nmol/liter. Renal norepi-nephrine overflow was little influenced, but there was a concentration-dependent increase in renin release from the kidney. Epinephrine might thus contribute to renin release ($\approx$20% of the response), but not to renal vasoconstriction during mental stress.

In summary, the cardiovascular responses to men-tal stress in humans cannot be explained by epineph-rine, but this hormonal link of the sympathoadrenal system may contribute to certain responses. The con-ception that epinephrine is *the* stress hormone is not correct from a functional point of view. However, the epinephrine response to stress does reflect the stress perceived and the arousal of the individual

and is a good marker for the stimulus intensity of a stressor.

VI. PATHOPHYSIOLOGICAL ASPECTS

"Stress" is considered to be involved in the patho-genesis of several cardiovascular disease states, and stress may provoke acute cardiovascular complica-tions, such as myocardial infarction and sudden death in individuals with symptomatic or asymp-tomatic atherosclerosis. However, for reasons dis-cussed above, it is difficult to define the exact role of stress in cardiovascular disease. Animal studies have shown that repeated mild activation of the defense reaction (by stress or by electrical stimula-tion of certain brain regions) may contribute to the development of hypertension. In addition, animals and humans with a genetic predisposition for hyper-tension often show enhanced cardiovascular and neurogenic reactivity to stress. Animal studies have also shown that stress may accelerate the develop-ment of atherosclerosis, as illustrated by elegant experiments by Clarkson, Kaplan, and Manuck in cynomolgus monkeys, and by Henry in mice. In humans, it has been more difficult to link stress to atherosclerosis, but there are indications that stress, anxiety, and personality factors are involved. Fur-thermore, biobehavioral modifications may alter the course of coronary artery disease. Thus, stress may indeed be involved in the pathogenesis of atheroscle-rosis, in agreement with popular views on the subject.

Various everyday stresses may trigger serious car-diovascular events, such as myocardial infarction, stroke, and sudden death (due to arrhythmia or myo-cardial infarction). Work by Mittleman, Muller, Wil-lich, and others has shown diurnal variation in the incidence of myocardial infarction and that physical or mental stress preceeds myocardial infarction or sudden death more frequently than would be ex-pected by chance.

Acute myocardial infarction involves thrombosis in the coronary arteries, which may be triggered by many factors, including stress. The hemodynamic changes associated with mental or physical stress increase the risk of atherosclerotic plaque rupture, which is a potent stimulus for local thrombus formation. The mechanisms involved in thrombosis are complex and involve platelets and the coagulation system as well as factors that oppose coagulation and dissolve blood clots (fibrinolysis). Stress-induced platelet activation may lead to the release of vasoactive substances which promote ischemia and thrombus formation. Platelet activation may be enhanced by endothelial dysfunction (reduced release of NO and prostacyklin), increased shear stress in an atherosclerotic vessel, and other platelet-activating effects of stress which also operate in healthy individuals. Endothelial dysfunction also promotes vasoconstrictor responses to stress in the coronary arteries and may contribute to imbalances between blood flow and metabolic demands (i.e., myocardial ischemia). The ischemic myocardium is vulnerable to life-threatening arrhythmias, especially when sympathetic activity is increased and vagal activity is reduced, as is the case during stress. Thus, stress elicits cardiovascular and neurohormonal changes which are beneficial to the healthy subject, but detrimental to patients with coronary artery disease. In addition, stress produces prothrombotic alterations which may further increase the risk of myocardial infarction.

See Also the Following Articles

ADRENALINE; ARTERIAL BAROREFLEX; ATHEROSCLEROSIS; BETA-ADRENERGIC BLOCKERS; BLOOD PRESSURE; HEART DISEASE/ATTACK

Bibliography

Bennet, T., and Gardiner, S. M. (Eds.) (1996). "Nervous Control of Blood Vessels." Harwood, Amsterdam.

Brod, J. (1963). Haemodynamic basis of acute pressor reactions and hypertension. *Br. Heart J.* **25**, 227–245.

Byrne, D. G., and Rosenman, R. H. (Eds.) (1990). "Anxiety and the Heart." Hemisphere, New York.

Folkow, B. (1982). Physiological aspects of primary hypertension. *Physiol. Rev.* **62**, 347–504.

Fuster, V., Badimon, L., Badimon, J. J., and Cheseboro, J. H. (1992). The pathogenesis of coronary artery disease and the acute coronary syndromes. *N. Engl. J. Med.* **326**, 242–250/310–318.

Goldstein, D. S. (1995a). Stress as a scientific idea—A homeostatic theory of stress and distress. *Homeostasis* **36**, 177–215.

Goldstein, D. S. (1995b). Clinical assessment of sympathetic responses to stress. *Ann. N.Y. Acad. Sci.* **771**, 570–593.

Hemingway, H., and Marmot, M. (1998). Psychosocial factors in the primary and secondary prevention of coronary heart disease: a systematic review. *In* "Evidence Based Cardiology" (S. Yusuf, J. A. Cairns, A. J. Camm, E. L. Fallen, and B. J. Gersh, Eds.), pp. 269–285. BMJ Books, London.

Herd, J. A. (1991). Cardiovascular responses to stress. *Physiol. Rev.* **71**, 305–330.

Hjemdahl, P. (1993). Plasma catecholamines—Analytical challenges and physiological limitations. *Baillere's Clin. Endocrinol. Metab.* **7**, 307–353.

Hjemdahl, P., Larsson, P. T., and Wallén, H. (1991). Effects of stress and β-blockade on platelet function. *Circulation* **84**, VI44–VI61.

Julius, S. (1988). The blood pressure seeking properties of the central nervous system. *J. Hypertens.* **6**, 177–185.

McCarty, R., Horwatt, K., and Konarska, M. (1988). Chronic stress and sympathetic-adrenal medullary responsiveness. *Soc. Sci. Med.* **26**, 333–341.

Shepherd, J. T., and Weiss, S. M. (Eds.) (1987). Conference on Behavioral Medicine and Cardiovascular Disease. *Circulation* **76**(II), I-1–I-224.

Steptoe, A., and Vögele, C. (1991). Methodology of mental stress testing in cardiovascular research. *Circulation* **83**, II-14–II-24.

Vane, J. R., Änggård, E. E., and Botting, R. M. (1990). Regulatory functions of the vascular endothelium. *N. Engl. J. Med.* **323**, 27–36.

Verrier, R. L., and Mittleman, M. A. (1996). Life-threatening cardiovascular consequences of anger in patients with coronary heart disease. *Cardiol. Clin.* **14**, 289–307.

Willerson, J. T., Golino, P., Eidt, J., Campbell, W. B., and Buja, L. M. (1989). Specific platelet mediators and unstable coronary artery lesions: Experimental evidence and potential clinical implications. *Circulation* **80**, 198–205.

Willich, S. N., and Muller, J. E. (Eds.) (1996). "Triggering of Acute Coronary Syndromes—Implications for Prevention." Kluwer, Dordrecht.

Caregivers, Stress and

Steven H. Zarit and Joseph E. Gaugler

Pennsylvania State University

I. Who Are Caregivers?
II. Perceived Stress
III. Mental Health Consequences of Caregiving
IV. Physical Health Outcomes
V. Interventions for Caregivers

GLOSSARY

family caregiving Informal (i.e., unpaid) and intensive assistance provided to a disabled relative (e.g., an elderly relative with Alzheimer's disease or a child with cystic fibrosis).

objective stress The occurrence of care demands.

primary stress Stress that is directly related to the provision of care.

secondary stress Stress that occurs in life domains outside of the care situation (e.g., work) but is a direct or indirect result of caregiving.

subjective stress Caregivers' emotional appraisals of care demands.

C are of disabled individuals emerged in the last part of the 20th century as a major source of stress to the family. The convergence of several sociodemographic factors placed increasing responsibilities and strains on the family. The aging of the population has meant that more older people are living to advanced ages where they have increased risk of disabilities and require regular assistance. Individuals with special needs (mental retardation, chronic mental illness) are also living longer, with their aging parents or siblings often providing sustained assistance. The result of deinstitutionalization of people with chronic mental illnesses without adequate resources for community treatment often places primary responsibility for care on families. Children with a variety of problems (behavioral, mental retardation, chronic illness) are another source of strain on families. As the number of people needing care has increased, family re- sources for providing care have in all likelihood decreased. For an elder who needs assistance, the first line of defense is his/her spouse, but that person is also likely to be elderly and to have age-associated disabilities that limit the amount of help that can be given. The longer life of people with mental retardation often means ongoing responsibility for their aging parents. With women's increasing participation in the workplace, daughters have less time to help parents or for the special needs of their own children. A number of other factors (increased divorce rates, relative decline in income of lower SES groups in the 1980s and 1990s, the increased economic necessity of dual-earner families) have also diminished the resources families might depend on to care for a disabled relative. Under these circumstances of increased needs for assistance and diminished resources, it is not surprising that caregiving stress has become a prominent issue.

I. WHO ARE CAREGIVERS?

Caregiving is an ongoing process in family relationships, whether it is the mutual and often reciprocal assistance a husband and wife offer each other or the care provided to a dependent child. Although these normative care situations can be stressful under some circumstances (such as difficult family transitions, like divorce) we limit our focus to care of someone with special needs. For older people, the assumption of the primary caregiving role is governed by what Cantor (1975) calls the Hierarchical Compensatory Model. When a spouse is available, he/she almost always takes on primary care responsibility. Almost one-half of primary caregivers to disabled elders are spouses, 29% are daughters, 6% are sons, and 17% are related in other ways to the care recipient or are non-kin. Spouses feel greater obligation to care for one another, although some adult children may assist a severely disabled parent for many years. Other family members may help out in a secondary role. For example, children will help one parent care for the other or siblings may assist one another in caregiving duties. These secondary caregivers can be very supportive, but sometimes their involvement leads to misunderstandings and conflict when the primary caregiver has one set of (sometimes unspoken) expectations and the secondary caregiver has another or when caregivers at a distance try to control or direct what the primary caregiver is doing.

Adult children who care for a parent have sometimes been portrayed as "the sandwich generation," that is, caught between the needs of their parents and their own children. The proportion of adult children caregivers with young children of their own, however, is relatively small. It is more typical for children to be assisting their parents at a point in the life cycle when their own children are grown. Indeed, parents tend to provide more help and assistance to their children than they receive until fairly late in life. Parents also continue helping children with chronic physical or mental health problems, though siblings may also be involved in care, especially if parents are deceased or disabled.

II. PERCEIVED STRESS

Pearlin and colleagues identify primary stressors, those problems and challenges embedded in the caregiving situation, and secondary stressors, that is, the ramifications of providing care on other areas of the person's life. Stressors can also have objective and subjective dimensions. Among primary stressors are such things as assistance with tasks of daily living, supervision, and management of behavioral and emotional problems. Caregivers' emotional reactions to the occurrence of care demands represent primary subjective stressors. In general, caring for someone with behavioral and emotional disturbances is more difficult than assisting a physically disabled person. This has been found both in care of an older person and of children. Pearlin and colleagues have also

posited another stressor specific to degenerative illnesses: loss of the relationship.

Secondary stressors include such things as conflict between the caregiver and his/her spouse and with other family members and work-caregiving strain. A child with special needs can also affect the relationship of parents to their other children. Employed caregivers are sometimes viewed as experiencing overwhelming demands, but many caregivers experience benefits from working, including gaining a sense of competence and getting a break from care routines. Their involvement in care activities, however, can sometimes lead to higher absenteeism. Some caregivers also leave the work force soon after taking on those responsibilities. Having more flexibility in work schedules helps caregivers sustain both roles. Interestingly, employees caring for another adult (ages 18–64) report higher levels of caregiver strain than those employees assisting an elder.

III. MENTAL HEALTH CONSEQUENCES OF CAREGIVING

As stress "proliferates" or spreads to life domains beyond the care situation, caregivers' psychological well-being may be affected. Family caregivers are more likely to suffer from feelings of anger, anxiety, and depression than age-matched controls. Depressive symptoms have also been found to increase over time among caregivers when compared to matched controls. Studies have attempted to determine which caregivers may be especially vulnerable to psychological distress (particularly depression). For example, kin relationship and gender have been associated with caregiving depression (i.e., spouses and women are more likely to be depressed). Also, African-American caregivers are generally less depressed and report less burden than white caregivers.

Comprehensive models of the caregiving process have been developed that examine the interrelationships among different dimensions of caregiving stress. Analyses based on these models have found that behavior problems are consistently related to caregiver depression. How caregivers subjectively evaluate these problems, however, mediates the relation between behavior problems and depressive symptoms. Models of the stress process also highlight the protective qualities of psychosocial resources. Social support, such as emotional or instrumental assistance from family members and/or friends, can diminish the psychological distress associated with caregiving. Having a greater sense of personal mastery (that is, the ability to take charge of or influence the events in one's life) has also been shown to reduce the negative impact of stressors.

IV. PHYSICAL HEALTH OUTCOMES

In addition to negatively affecting psychological well-being, providing intensive assistance to a disabled family member can impact caregivers' physical health. Several deleterious health outcomes have been identified among family caregivers of elderly relatives suffering from dementia. Compared to controls, family caregivers of dementia patients experience declines in cellular immunity and suffer from infectious diseases for longer periods of time. In addition, spousal caregivers of demented elderly relatives are more likely to indicate declines in perceived health (i.e., "how would you rate your health at the present time?") than adult children or other caregivers. Parents of children with special needs also have higher rates of health symptoms.

While there is empirical evidence supporting the prevalence of negative physical health among family caregivers, the psychosocial mechanisms that impact health are less clear. Gallant and Connell found that caregivers experiencing higher levels of care demands or stressors or who were depressed reported a decline over time in positive health behaviors (i.e., exercise, sleep patterns, weight maintenance, smoking, and alcohol consumption). Higher self-efficacy (a type of belief similar to mastery) was associated with lower depression and, in turn, engaging in more positive health behaviors. Positive social support provided to caregivers by family and friends can also improve physical health outcomes, while low levels of social support are more likely to be associated with negative changes in immune system functioning. In sum, positive psychosocial resources, such as social support, self-efficacy, and mastery appear to alleviate

the negative psychological and health implications of family caregiving.

V. INTERVENTIONS FOR CAREGIVERS

Interventions for family caregivers have generally emphasized building competence and increasing social support as ways of lowering stress and improving well-being. Caregivers learn about their family member's special needs and develop coping strategies that help them manage stressful features of the situation more effectively. These strategies can include controlling problem behavior, managing competing demands, and learning to use stress-reduction techniques when stressful events in their lives build up.

Attention to the family as a system may be a particularly important part of treatment. Other family members are a readily available source of support as well as a potential source of increased stress and conflict. Bringing relevant family members together in a family meeting or family counseling program can be effective in building support for the primary caregiver and reducing misunderstandings.

Supportive services, such as temporary respite care, can be helpful in lowering stress on family caregivers. Sometimes, however, families find it more stressful to deal with bureaucratic procedures than to go without help. The cost of services can also be a barrier to greater use.

One of the most common sources of assistance for families caring for a relative with special needs is a support group. Support groups are widely available for many different kinds of situations, including parents of children with special needs and caregivers of the elderly. Groups are an effective mechanism for sharing information about resources which may be available in the community and learning how to get around bureaucratic barriers. They also provide a unique type of support, the understanding of people who are experiencing a similar situation. Support groups, however, are not as effective as individual and family counseling in lowering acute stress.

See Also the Following Articles

AGING AND PSYCHOLOGICAL STRESS; ALZHEIMER'S DISEASE

Bibliography

Aneshensel, C. S., Pearlin, L. I., Mullan, J. T., Zarit, S. H., and Whitlatch, C. J. (1995). "Profiles in Caregiving: The Unexpected Career." Academic Press, New York.

Anthony-Bergstone, C. R., Zarit, S. H., and Gatz, M. (1988). Symptoms of psychological distress among caregivers of dementia patients. *Psychol. Aging* 3, 245–248.

Blacher, J., Lopez, S., Shapiro, J., and Fusco, J. (1997). Contributions to depression in Latina mothers with and without children with retardation: Implications for caregiving. *Family Relat.* 46, 325–334.

Cantor, M. H. (1975). Life space and the social support system of the inner city elderly of New York. *Gerontologist* 15, 23–27.

Floyd, F. J., and Gallagher, E. M. (1997). Parental stress, care demands, and the use of support services for school-age children with disabilities and behavior problems. *Family Relat.* 46, 359–371.

Gallant, M. P., and Connel, C. M. (1998). The stress process among dementia spouse caregivers: Are caregivers at risk for negative health behavior change? *Res. Aging* 20, 267–297.

Haley, W. E., West, C. A. C., Wadley, V. G., Ford, G. R., White, F. A., Barrett, J. J., Harrell, L. E., and Roth, D. L. (1995). Psychological, social and health impact of caregiving: A comparison of Black and White dementia family caregivers and non-caregivers. *Psychol. Aging* 10, 540–552.

Kiecolt-Glaser, J. K., Dura, J. R., Speicher, C. E., Trask, J., and Glaser, R. (1991). Spousal caregivers of dementia victims: Longitudinal changes in immunity and health. *Psychosom. Med.* 53, 345–362.

Mittelman, M. S., Ferris, S. H., Shulman, E., Steinberg, G.,

Ambinder, A., Mackel, J., and Cohen, J. (1995). A comprehensive support program: Effect on depression in spouse-caregivers of AD patients. *Gerontologist* 35, 792–802.

Monahan, D. J., and Hooker, K. (1995). Health of spouse caregiver of dementia patients: The role of personality and social support. *Social Work* 40, 305–314.

Pruchno, R., Patrick, J. H., and Burant, C. J. (1997). African American and white mothers of adults with chronic disabilities: Caregiving burden and satisfaction *Family Relat.* 46, 335–346.

Satin, W., La Greca, A. M., Zigo, M. A., and Skyler, J. S. (1989). Diabetes in adolescence: Effects of multifamily group intervention and parent simulation of diabetes. *J. Pediatr. Psychol.* 14, 259–275.

Scharlach, A. E., and Fredriksen, K. I. (1994). Elder care versus adult care: Does care recipient age make a difference? *Res. Aging* 16, 43–68.

Schulz, R., and Williamson, G. W. (1991). A 2-year longitudinal study of depression among Alzheimer's caregivers. *Psychol. Aging* 6, 569–578.

Seltzer, M. M., Greenberg, J. S., Krauss, M. W., Gordon, R. M., and Judge, K. (1997). Siblings of adults with mental retardation or mental illness: Effects on lifestyle and psychological well-being. *Family Relat.* 46, 395–405.

Suárez, L. M., and Baker, B. L. (1997). Child externalizing behavior and parents' stress: The role of social support. *Family Relat.* 46, 373–381.

Wallander, J. L., Varni, J. W., Babani, L., Banis, H. T., DeHaan, C. B., and Wilcox, K. T. (1989). Disability parameters, chronic strain and adaptation of physically handicapped children and their mothers. *J. Pediatr. Psychol.* 14, 23–42.

Whitlatch, C. J., Zarit, S. H., and von Eye, A. (1991). Efficacy of interventions with caregivers: A reanalysis. *Gerontologist* 31, 9–14.

Catecholamines

Ulf Lundberg

Stockholm University, Sweden

I. Role of the Catecholamines
II. Summary and Conclusions

GLOSSARY

dopamine A transmitter in the central nervous system which stimulates β-1-receptors and, in high doses, α-1-receptors. Dopamine is also a precursor to the formation of epinephrine and norepineprine but is generally not considered a stress hormone.

epinephrine A stress hormone secreted from the adrenal medulla in response to stimulation from the sympathetic nervous system. It activates all adrenergic receptors and β-receptors in particular, with effects on heart rate and dilatation of blood vessels in the muscles and constriction of blood vessels in the skin.

lipolysis Refers to the release of lipids into the blood stream.

norepinephrine A stress hormone secreted from the adrenal medulla that also serves as a neuro transmitter in the sympathetic and central nervous system. Most of the circulating levels of norepinephrine are produced by sympathetic nerve endings. Norepinephrine mainly effects α-receptors, causing constriction of blood vessels and increased blood pressure.

SAM system The sympathetic adrenal medullary system, where the catecholamines epinephrine and norepinephrine are secreted.

The catecholamines have been of central interest and importance in stress research since the first demonstrations of the role of sympathetic arousal in response to stress exposure early in the 20th century. Numerous animal experiments have illustrated the active defense reaction and the "emergency function" of the adrenal medulla, which increases the organism's chances of survival by "fight-or-flight." During the past 3 decades, a considerable number of studies in humans, in laboratory as well as in natural settings, have confirmed and extended the conclusions from the animal studies. The aim of this article is to summarize research and conclusions relevant to the role of catecholamines in stress and health, including their assessment and methodological considerations as well as gender differences in catecholamine responses to stress.

I. ROLE OF THE CATECHOLAMINES

Secretion of the catecholamines is regulated by mental influence (from the cortex) on the hypothalamus in the central nervous system, which activates the sympathetic adrenal–medullary (SAM) system. Walter B. Cannon first demonstrated the important role of sympathetic activation in emotional responses to stress exposure. Norepinephrine was identified later by Ulf von Euler (1948). On the basis of animal experiments Cannon described the "fight-or-flight response," or the "emergency function" of the adrenal medulla. The SAM system is activated when the individual is challenged in its control of the environment and this defense reaction prepares the body for battle. The catecholamines do not pass the blood–brain barrier but exert their effects peripherally.

The cardiovascular and neuroendocrine functions activated by the catecholamines mobilize energy to the muscles, the heart, and the brain and, at the same time, reduce blood flow to the internal organs and the gastrointestinal system. In response to physical threat this is an efficient means for survival as it increases the organism's capacity for fight or flight. In modern society, however, elevated catecholamine levels are probably more often caused by threats of a social or mental rather than physical nature. In general, mental efficiency is also positively associated with elevated catecholamine levels. Mental stress is a very potent stimulator of epinephrine output, whereas norepinephrine, having an important role in blood pressure homeostasis, is more closely associated with physical activity and demands and body posture.

Numerous studies from laboratory experiments, as well as from natural settings, illustrate the sensitivity of the catecholamines to various physical, psychological, and psychosocial conditions in humans and animals. In experimental studies, catecholamine responses have been examined in response to physical stressors, such as noise, electric shocks, heat, cold, and so on, and to mental and cognitive stressors, such as performance tests, harassment, cognitive conflict, time pressure, monotony, fear, and anticipation of stress. The influence of various real-life conditions on the catecholamines have been investigated during daily stress at work, at home, at school, at day-care centers, at hospitals, on commuter trains or buses, and during intense stress induced by, for instance, parachute jumping and the defense of a doctoral thesis.

A. Health and Behavior

The catecholamines and their concomitant effects on other physiological functions, such as blood pressure, heart rate, and lipolysis, may serve as objective indicators of the stress that an individual is exposed to. However, these bodily effects are also assumed to create a link between psychosocial stress and increased health risks. Lasting elevated catecholamine levels are considered to contribute to the development of atherosclerosis and predispose to myocardial ischemia. The elevated catecholamine levels also make the blood more prone to clotting, thus reducing the risk of heavy bleeding in case of tissue damage but at the same time, increasing the risk of arterial obstruction and myocardial infarction. The role of the catecholamines in hypertension is also of great importance.

Elevated catecholamine secretion in response to challenge has been demonstrated for the stress-related and coronary-prone Type A behavior pattern. Additional support for a role of the catecholamines in the development of coronary heart disease is obtained from studies showing that high job strain (high demands and low control) and high catecholamine levels are related to elevated risk of coronary

heart disease (CHD). Catecholamine activation is also known to interact with the other major neuroendocrine stress system, namely the hypothalamic-pituitary-adrenocortical (HPA) axis and the secretion of cortisol, and form an integrated stress response which seems to potentiate several health risks including CHD. Negative emotional stimulation activates via higher brain centers both the secretion of catecholamines and cortisol. High epinephrine levels seem to enhance the HPA response and low levels to diminish it, and the corticotropin releasing factor (CRF), which activates the HPA-axis, also seems to stimulate sympathetic outflow.

The catecholamines also serve an important role in human performance and behavior. The secretion of the catecholamines is not only related to the individual's physical capacity, but also to factors such as mental effort and cognitive performance. Under normal levels of stress and arousal, a further increase in catecholamine output is associated with improved performance, whereas under conditions of very intense stress, additional increase in catecholamine output may cause deterioration in mental functioning and disorganized behavior. In summary, the level of performance and mental well-being can be described as an inverted-U function of the intensity of stress, which means positive correlations with catecholamine secretion at low and moderate levels of stress and negative correlations at very high levels. The optimal level of performance is located at higher stress levels for simple tasks compared with more complex ones and varies between individuals depending on personality characteristics, mental state, and so on.

B. Assessment

Blood levels of catecholamines change rapidly (within a minute) in response to stress exposure. A small but relatively constant fraction of the circulating levels of epinephrine and norepinephrine in the blood is excreted into the urine. Consequently, assessment can be made from blood (usually plasma) as well as from urine. In general, results from studies based on blood and urine samples are highly consistent, showing significant positive relationships between changes in urinary and plasma catecholamines in response to stress.

Plasma catecholamine levels readily reflect acute stress responses during exposure to short-term stress and have been used extensively in animal research. Urinary catecholamines also respond rapidly to stress exposure but, depending on the time between urine sampling, the urine in the bladder provides an integrated measurement representing the mean stress level for a more extended period of stress exposure. Using voluntary voiding, the normal period between urine sampling is 2–3 h, which means that urinary catecholamines are preferable for the study of longer periods of stress or chronic stress exposure. A normal procedure for studying long-term stress could involve taking urine samples at regular intervals over days or weeks.

Due to the rapid changes in plasma catecholamine levels, frequent blood sampling via an indwelling catheter is necessary in order to obtain representative measures of circulating levels for longer periods of time, which is usually not feasible in, for example, the study of work stress. Other problems associated with venipuncture are that norepinephrine concentrations vary between sampling sites due to differences in regional blood flow and reuptake by the nerve terminals and that blood sampling in itself may cause increased levels of epinephrine secretion.

For methodological reasons, human plasma catecholamines have been studied almost exclusively in the laboratory, whereas urinary catecholamines have been used extensively in the study of human stress in natural settings. The advantages of urinary measurements in the study of, for example, work stress are that they do not interfere with the subject's normal habits and environment and that they cause no harm or pain to the subject. In addition, integrated measurements are provided for longer periods of time—relevant for the study of the psychosocial stress associated with different conditions at work. The amount of urinary catecholamines excreted during a particular period of time can be determined by the concentration of the sample multiplied by the total urine volume. Thus, in the study of urinary catecholamines, the total volume of the sample has to be measured after voiding. In addition, the pH level of the urine should be adjusted to about 3.0 (using acid) to prevent the catecholamines from dete-

rioration. The acidified urine sample should then be kept frozen ($-18°$ C) until analyzed.

In cases where the time between voiding of urine is unknown or the total volume of the sample has not been properly measured, the catecholamine concentration can be related to a reference substance such as creatinine, which is considered to be secreted at a constant rate. Provided that reliable measurements are obtained and the subject is able to empty his or her bladder completely, the results from these two methods are highly correlated. The most common method for catecholamine assessment in blood or urine is high-performance liquid chromatography with electrochemical detection. This and other modern methods (e.g., enzymatic methods) have high sensitivity and specificity. An earlier method used extensively during the period from 1960 to 1980 is the flurophotometric method of Euler and Lishajko, which is reliable for the determination of urinary catecholamines but not sensitive enough for the analysis of plasma, where the concentration of the catecholamines is lower.

C. Methodological Considerations and Confounders

The catecholamines have a pronounced circadian pattern, which has to be taken into consideration in the study of responses to stress. Under normal night-sleep/day-wake conditions, the catecholamines peak in the middle of the day and reach their lowest levels during night sleep. The circadian rhythm of epinephrine remains relatively stable even during several nights of sleep deprivation, whereas norepinephrine is more influenced by physical activity. Consistent changes in the sleep/wake pattern, for example, in habitual night work or east-to-west traveling over 12-h time zones, completely reverse the circadian rhythm of the catecholamines in about a week. Variations in shift work and frequent east–west flights disturb the normal circadian rhythm and produce a "flattened" curve of catecholamine secretion as well as problems in staying alert and sleep disturbances. Other (nonpsychological) factors influencing catecholamine secretion are the intake of caffeine (coffee), alcohol, and nicotine (cigarette smoking); medication (β-blockers, diuretics etc.); and heavy physical exercise.

In the study of stress and catecholamines, the influence by confounders has to be controlled by requesting the participants to refrain from smoking, drinking coffee, and so on or by controlling the effects on the catecholamines by asking the participants to consume the same amount of cigarettes and coffee in the control condition as in the experimental situation.

Moderate or small seasonal variations in catecholamines have been reported as well as variations during the menstrual cycle. Norepinephrine levels have also been found to increase with old age. As related to weight, children have higher levels than adults, but as related to body surface area the excretion rates are relatively stable from the first years of life into adulthood.

Individual variations in baseline levels are pronounced but relatively stable over time. For instance, the highest epinephrine level may be 10 times greater than the lowest. This variation is likely to be related to individual differences in renal clearance and body weight, but psychological differences between individuals with high and low baseline catecholamine levels have also been reported. During mild stress, such as carrying out normal daily work, the epinephrine output increases by 50–100% above the resting level, whereas more severe mental stress and intense cognitive and emotional demands may cause epinephrine to rise from 8 to 10 times the resting level. There are no "normal" levels of catecholamine and no threshold limits, but clearly pathological levels can be found in association with, for example, adrenal tumors.

In order to reduce the influence of circadian rhythms and of individual differences in baseline levels, it is generally recommended that the individual's response to stressful conditions be compared with his or her corresponding baseline level. The two measurements have to be obtained at the same time of day, which means that they must be made on separate days. By studying the relative change from baseline rather than absolute levels, the variation between individuals is considerably reduced and the statistical power is increased without having to increase the sample size.

Reliable baseline levels can be obtained in situations where the individual is alone and able to relax completely. In an experimental study this can be achieved by inviting subjects to come to the laboratory after the experimental session and making sure that they are confident that they will not be exposed to any kind of stressor. In order to help the subject to relax, a quiet environment, light entertainment with music and/or suitable reading materials, as well as relaxation training can be used. In studying stress in natural settings, such as the work environment, baseline levels of catecholamines can be obtained by giving the worker a paid day off from work. He or she is then instructed to relax alone at home and avoid any activity that might contribute to stress, such as shopping, cleaning, taking care of children, heavy physical exercise, and so on.

Epinephrine secretion is particularly sensitive to novel stimulation and stress associated with anticipation. Exposure to the laboratory and the experimental equipment to be used may induce as high or higher epinephrine levels than the actual stress tests. This means that catecholamine levels before an experiment usually cannot be used as baselines. The anticipation and novelty effects can be reduced or eliminated by asking the subject to visit the laboratory before the experiment to become familiar with the methods of measurement and the equipment to be used. Similarly, at the workplace, the stress induced by the investigation per se can be avoided by performing measurements (urine sampling, etc.) one or several days before the actual data collection to make the participants familiar with all aspects of the study.

D. Gender Differences

In the early 1970s, men were consistently found to be more responsive to experimental stress by showing greater elevations in epinephrine than women. Although women performed as well or usually even better than the men on the various stress tests used in the experiments, their epinephrine secretion did not increase very much. During more intense stress (examination stress), women's epinephrine output was found to increase significantly but still to a lesser extent than that of men in the same situation.

A possible explanation for these gender differences is that the performance tests used to induce stress were less challenging to women than to men. In keeping with this, it was found that emotional stress associated with accompanying a child to the hospital had a more pronounced effect on the mothers' catecholamine levels. The importance of gender roles is also illustrated by the fact that women in male-dominated occupations and lines of education seem to respond to performance stress with epinephrine responses similar to their male colleagues. Recent studies comparing men and women matched for education and occupational level showed similar catecholamine responses to stress in women as in men.

Although, the possible influence of biological factors, such as steroid sex hormones, on catecholamine responses cannot be excluded, it seems as if psychological factors and gender role patterns, in general, are more important for the differences in catecholamine responses between men and women.

In men, a significant positive correlation is usually found between perceived stress and performance, on the one hand, and catecholamine responses at work, on the other. The more intense or frequent the stress exposure at work the higher the catecholamine output. In women, however, corresponding relationships are more inconsistent. Stress exposure and catecholamine levels at work seem to "spill over" into nonwork situations. Women with high catecholamine levels at work tend to have high catecholamine levels after work, and women exposed to elevated work stress (e.g., by working overtime) have elevated catecholamine in the evening or during the weekend at home. A likely explanation for this is that there is a greater interaction between the stress from paid employment and unpaid work at home for women than there is for men. This has to be taken into consideration in the study of women's stress and workload.

E. Positive and Negative Stress

As described by Henry, activation of the SAM system and high catecholamine output are associated with an active coping style and dominant behavior among animals, whereas passive coping and the "defeat reaction" are associated with activation of the HPA axis, high cortisol levels, and submissive behavior. A similar but less consistent pattern of findings has been reported in humans.

In human stress, epinephrine levels are significantly elevated by stress caused by over- as well as by understimulation compared with more optimal environmental conditions. This means that work overload, a very high work pace, too much responsibility, and role conflicts as well as simple, monotonous, and repetitive jobs or lack of meaningful activities (e.g., unemployment) may contribute to elevated epinephrine levels. However, as demonstrated by Levi, epinephrine output reflects the intensity of stress rather than its emotional valence. Intensive pleasant stimulation, such as watching a funny movie, may induce elevated epinephrine levels as well as does unpleasant stimulation.

II. SUMMARY AND CONCLUSIONS

The two catecholamines, epinephrine and norepinephrine, are very sensitive to behavioral, emotional, and cognitive stimulation and the magnitude of the response seems to be closely related to the intensity of perceived stress regardless of the emotional quality. Epinephrine mainly reflects mental stress, whereas norepinephrine is more sensitive to physical demands and body posture. Much less is known about the role of dopamine under stress.

The catecholamines may thus serve as objective indicators of the intensity of stress that an individual is exposed to. However, they also play an important role in the development of several health problems and thus create a link between stress and disease. In order to obtain valid and reliable measurements, strict control of possible confounders is necessary at all stages of the process—preparing the subjects; determining baselines; collecting, preparing, and storing the samples; performing the hormone assay; and so on.

Acknowledgment

Financial support has been obtained from the Swedish Council for Research in the Humanities and Social Sciences and the Bank of Sweden Tercentenary Foundation.

See Also the Following Articles

ADRENAL MEDULLA; FIGHT-OR-FLIGHT RESPONSE

Bibliography

Cannon, W. B. (1914). The emergency function of the adrenal medulla in pain and the major emotions. *Am J. Physiol.* 33, 356–372.

Frankenhaeuser, M. (1983). The sympathetic-adrenal and pituitary-adrenal response to: comparison between the sexes. *In* "Biobehavioral Bases of Coronary Heart Disease" (T. M. Dembroski, T. H. Schmidt, and G. Blümchen, Eds.), pp. 91–105. Basel, New York.

Henry, J. P. (1992). Biological basis of the stress response. *Integral Physiol Behav. Sci.* 66–83.

Henry, J. P., and Stephens, P. M. (1977). "Stress, Health, and the Social Environment: A Sociobiologic Approach to Medicine." Springer-Verlag, New York Heidelberg Berlin.

Hjemdahl, P., Larsson, P. T., Bradley, T., Åkerstedt, T.,

Anderzén, I., Sigurdsson, K., Gillberg, M., and Lundberg, U. (1989). Catecholamine measurements in urine with high-performance liquid chromatography with amperometric detection—Comparison with an autoanalyser fluorescence method. *J. Chromatogr.* 494, 53–66.

Levi, L. (1996). Stress and distress in reponse to psychosocial stimuli. *Acta Med. Scand. Suppl.* 528.

Lundberg, U. (1996). The influence of paid and unpaid work on psychophysiological stress responses of men and women. *J. Occ. Health Psychol.* 1, 117–130.

Lundberg, U., de Château, P., Winberg, J., and Frankenhaeuser, M. (1981). Catecholamine and cortisol excretion patterns in three year old children and their parents, *J. Hum. Stress.* 7, 3–11.

von Euler, U. S. (1948). Identification of the sympathomimetic ergone in adrenergic nerves of cattle (sympathin N) with laevo-noradrenaline. *Acta Physiol. Scand.* 16, 63–74.

von Euler, U. S., and Lishajko, F. (1961). Improved technique for the fluorimetric estimation of catecholamines. *Acta Physiol. Scand.* 51, 348–355.

CD4, CD8 Cells

see Lymphocytes

Cell Death

see Apoptosis

Central Nervous System

see Brain and Brain Regions

Central Stress Neurocircuits

Sara Kollack-Walker, Heidi E. W. Day, and Huda Akil

University of Michigan

I. Overview of Stress: Inputs, Outputs, and Evaluative Processes
II. Hypothalamo-Pituitary-Adrenocortical Axis
III. Initiation of the Stress Response
IV. Termination of the Stress Response
V. Concluding Remarks

GLOSSARY

homeostasis Maintaining constancy of the internal environment of the body.
stress Any stimulus that disturbs or interferes with the normal physiological or psychological equilibrium of an organism.
stressor Stimulus input that produces stress and initiates a stress response.
stress response The body's adaptations designed to reestablish equilibrium.

An understanding of central stress neurocircuits requires knowledge of neuroanatomical pathways that underlie detection of various stimuli leading to a stress state, perception of those inputs as stressful (when appropriate), and mediation of select response outputs. In this article the basic neurocircuitry involved in regulation of the hypothalamo-pituitary-adrenocortical (HPA) axis is reviewed. The HPA axis mediates secretion of glucocorticoids in response to a variety of stimuli ranging from immune responses to hemorrhaging to social defeat. Thus, it is important to understand how such diverse stimuli can lead to activation of the HPA axis. The stress-induced increases in glucocorticoids act to maintain homeostasis as well as to mobilize energy stores for "fight or flight" reactions. Although these actions can and do occur together, it is possible to isolate and study homeostatic regulation from the more global defense response. These phenomena can be distinct in terms

of arousal, emotional salience, conscious perception, and behavioral responsivity. As a consequence, it is also important to understand how the brain responds to different "types" of stressful events.

I. OVERVIEW OF STRESS: INPUTS, OUTPUTS, AND EVALUATIVE PROCESSES

Stress has been described as a multidimensional concept consisting of three major components: the stimulus input, an evaluative process, and the response output. The *stimulus input,* or stressor, simply refers to an event that produces stress and elicits a stress response (e.g., glucocorticoid secretion). In many cases, the link between stimulus inputs and response outputs requires perception of a given event as stressful. This *evaluative process* includes not only processing of stimulus-specific information and coding of the stressor's intensity and intermittency, but also comparison of the current situation to previous experiences. In addition, this evaluative process reflects the organism's ability to "cope" with the stressor (e.g., degree of controllability, real or perceived). The *response output,* or stress response, is the body's adaptations designed to reestablish physiological or psychological equilibrium. Depending on the particular stimulus input, a limited or broad range of responses will be initiated (Fig. 1).

This concept of stress has been modified to reflect the notion that some stimulus inputs can lead to a stress response without requiring evaluation per se. Consequently, various authors in the field have classified stressors in distinct ways: physical versus psychological or systemic versus neurogenic/processive. The key element associated with such distinctions is the need for a stimulus input to be perceived as stressful. For example, the experience of novelty as

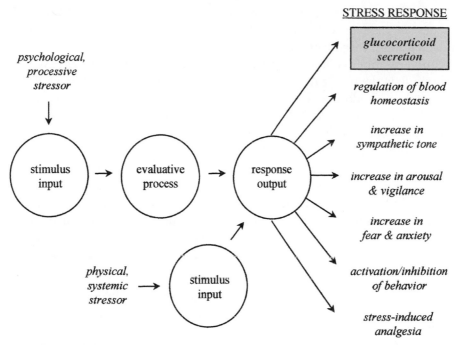

FIGURE 1 Schematic diagram illustrating the basic relationship between stimulus inputs and response outputs.

a mild stressor requires perception of a situation as different with the potential to encounter threatening stimuli. A novel environment would be classified as "processive," involving higher order processing within the central nervous system in order to identify the present situation as unique in comparison to previous experiences. In contrast, other stimulus inputs are thought to elicit a stress response without prior evaluation. For example, hemorrhaging activates various reflexes designed to return blood volume to normal values. In this case, it is not necessary to perceive blood loss as stressful—the reaction is automatic. Hemorrhaging would be considered "systemic" involving perturbations in homeostasis or a threat to an individual's internal environment.

Although stressors can be distinguished in terms of the "type" of stimulus input and the need for evaluative processing, a key component of the response output involves activation of the hypothalamo pituitary adrenocortical (HPA) axis. The HPA axis mediates release of glucocorticoids from the adrenal cortex, and glucocorticoids play an important role in energy metabolism and the maintenance of homeostasis. In this article the basic elements of the

HPA axis, including a description of specific brain pathways implicated in HPA axis regulation, are reviewed. In our discussion, how the brain responds to two distinct stressors—an immune challenge, as an example of a systemic stressor, and social defeat, as an example of a processive and psychological stressor, are considered. Lastly, we will consider how a stress response is terminated, a process linked to distinct neurocircuits and stress-induced increases in glucocorticoids.

II. HYPOTHALAMO-PITUITARY-ADRENOCORTICAL AXIS

The hypothalamo-pituitary-adrenocortical axis is involved in control of secretion of glucocorticoids from the adrenal cortex. Neurons within the medial parvocellular subdivision of the paraventricular nucleus of the hypothalamus (mpPVN) synthesize corticotropin-releasing hormone (CRH), and project to the median eminence, releasing CRH into hypophyseal portal blood vessels to reach specific cells within the anterior pituitary called corticotrophs. The binding of CRH to its receptor on the corticotroph's cell membrane stimulates a cascade of intracellular events leading to the release of adrenocorticotrophin hormone (ACTH) into general circulation. Corticotropin-releasing hormone is the major ACTH secretagog, although a number of additional molecules have been implicated in facilitating ACTH release (e.g., vasopressin). Adrenocorticotrophin hormone acts upon specific receptors in the adrenal cortex to stimulate the synthesis and release of glucocorticoids into general circulation. Depending upon the species, the major glucocorticoid secreted from the adrenal cortex will vary—cortisol (human), corticosterone (rat), or both (hamster).

III. INITIATION OF THE STRESS RESPONSE

A variety of approaches have been taken to identify brain regions involved in regulation of the HPA axis. Our current state of knowledge is based upon studies that have utilized *tract tracing* to identify afferent inputs into the mpPVN, *expression of immediate early genes* to identify "activated" brain regions, *lesions* to determine the importance of a given set of inputs for stress-induced glucocorticoid secretion, and *pharmacological* and *biochemical analyses* to determine the role of particular neurotransmitters and neuropeptides in HPA axis regulation. Several key

Brainstem Afferents:

Catecholamines play an important role in the regulation of mpPVN neurons. These afferents originate from the medulla and include adrenergic (C1-C3) and noradrenergic (A1,A2) inputs; C1 and A1 neurons exist within ventrolateral medulla (VLM), and C2 and A2 neurons reside within nucleus of the solitary tract (NTS); C3 neurons are present within the dorsomedial medulla. In addition, the parabrachial nucleus (PBN) receives input from NTS (as well as from other brain regions) and provides another source of afferent input into mpPVN. These brain nuclei are involved in processing and transmitting visceral sensory information.

Serotonergic input to the mpPVN originates from B7-B9 cell groups within the brainstem, and serotonergic terminals have been shown to contact CRH neurons at the ultrastructural level. This input has been linked to adrenocortical activity in response to photic stimuli and electrical stimulation of various brain regions, but appears less critical for HPA axis activation in response to ether stress or restraint.

A number of cell groups within the midbrain and pons also project directly to mpPVN. Auditory information may reach mpPVN via relays within the posterior intralaminar (PIL), peripeduncular (PP), pedunculopontine (PPN), and laterodorsal tegmental (LDTg) nuclei. Visual information is also processed by neurons within the PPN and LDTg nuclei as well as by neurons within the intergeniculate leaflet (IGL). Many of these brain regions as well as the periaqueductal gray (PAG) have been implicated in processing somatosensory and nociceptive information. Several of these cell groups utilize the neurotransmitter acetylcholine (ACh), and ACh has been shown to have stimulatory effects on CRH secretion.

Circumventricular Afferents:

Circumventricular organs lack a blood-brain-barrier allowing specific molecules within the bloodstream to gain access to the brain. The subfornical organ (SFO) and vascular organ of the lamina terminalis (OVLT) project directly, and indirectly via synaptic relay in the median preoptic nucleus, to mpPVN. The area postrema (AP) influences the HPA axis indirectly via projections to brainstem nuclei (NTS, VLM). There is some suggestion that these circumventricular organs can show selectivity to bloodborne signals with SFO and OVLT critical for responding to changes in blood composition (e.g., salt-loading), while the AP has been shown to be somewhat more responsive to increases in the levels of interleukin-1β.

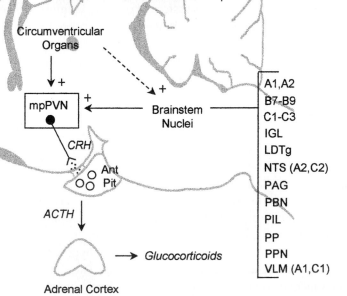

FIGURE 2 Schematic diagram summarizing the role of brainstem and circumventricular afferents in regulation of the functional activity of mpPVN neurons. This afferent input has been associated with activating the HPA axis in response to systemic and physical stressors.

findings obtained from these data are summarized in Figs. 2 and 3.

Is there a common set of pathways within the central nervous system critical for initiating a stress response or do different "classes" of stressors activate the HPA axis through distinct neurocircuits? The data collected, thus far, provide evidence in support of both arguments. Indeed, different classes of stressors appear to activate the HPA axis largely through distinct pathways, although this does not preclude the possibility that multiple pathways may be involved, especially for complex stressors that have both physical and psychological components. Furthermore, within a given class, it is possible to see activation patterns that are similar, presumably

reflecting, at least in part, the activation of brain pathways critical for glucocorticoid secretion.

A. Homeostatic Regulation: Systemic, Physical Stressors

Stressors that are systemic or physical in nature involve a reaction to a threatening stimulus in an individual's internal milieu leading to the activation of regulatory mechanisms that serve to restore homeostasis. A variety of stimulus inputs are under homeostatic control including body temperature, immune responses, and changes in blood volume and composition. For many of these stimuli, it is absolutely critical that the levels of these variables be

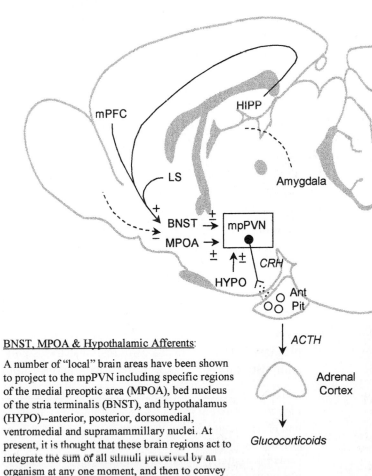

this integrated information to the mpPVN to effect a coordinated HPA axis response.

Many of these afferents utilize the inhibitory neurotransmitter GABA. GABA has been shown to inhibit the release of ACTH and corticosterone in vivo, GABAergic terminals contact parvocellular PVN neurons, and $GABA_A$ receptors have been identified on mpPVN neurons. This GABAergic input may reflect the presence of an inhibitory tone on the HPA axis.

In addition, mpPVN neurons receive additional inputs from hypothalamic nuclei that effect excitatory influences (dopamine, neuropeptide Y, substance P, glutamate) or inhibitory influences (ACTH, B-endorphin, substance P) on the HPA axis.

Limbic Afferents:

Several forebrain structures have been linked to regulation of the HPA axis including the prefrontal cortex (mPFC), hippocampus (HIPP), amygdala, and lateral septum (LS). These brain regions are believed to play a critical role in the perception of a stimulus input as stressful and in the activation of various effector mechanisms that reflect an emotional state including motoric and autonomic responses, vocalizations, and glucocorticoid secretion.

Neurons within mPFC, LS and HIPP have been linked to inhibitory regulation of the HPA axis. In contrast, various subdivisions of the amygdala mediate excitatory control. These limbic brain regions are thought to control glucocorticoid secretion via synaptic relays within the BNST, MPOA and HYPO.

BNST, MPOA & Hypothalamic Afferents:

A number of "local" brain areas have been shown to project to the mpPVN including specific regions of the medial preoptic area (MPOA), bed nucleus of the stria terminalis (BNST), and hypothalamus (HYPO)--anterior, posterior, dorsomedial, ventromedial and supramammillary nuclei. At present, it is thought that these brain regions act to integrate the sum of all stimuli perceived by an organism at any one moment, and then to convey

FIGURE 3 Schematic diagram summarizing the role of BNST, MPOA, and hypothalamic and limbic afferents in regulation of the functional activity of mpPVN neurons. The limbic system has been linked to activating the HPA axis in response to processive and psychological stressors.

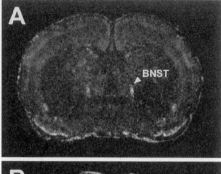

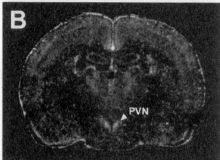

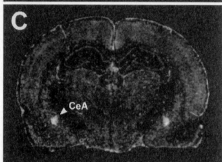

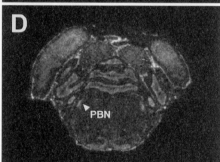

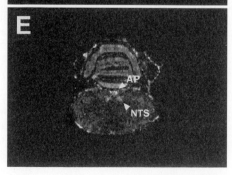

maintained within a certain range for survival. Because of this link to survival, systemic stressors are associated with activation of brainstem and circumventricular afferents that have direct projections to mpPVN neurons. In many cases, excitation of the HPA axis is dependent upon ascending catecholaminergic input.

For example, activation of an inflammatory or immune response increases the production and release of various cytokines (e.g., interleukin-1β), which leads to excitation of the HPA axis. This rise in glucocorticoids is an adaptive response that serves to inhibit the immune system, limiting its scope of attack and decreasing the likelihood that the immune system will attack "self." Figure 4 illustrates the general pattern of c-*fos* mRNA expression that occurs within the brain of a male rat 30 min following systemic administration of interleukin-1β (IL-1β). As evident from the photomicrographs shown, the pattern of neuronal activation is fairly localized with increased expression of c-*fos* mRNA observed within bed nucleus of the stria terminalis (BNST); central amygdaloid nucleus (CeA); mpPVN; parabrachial nucleus (PBN); nucleus of the solitary tract (NTS); circumventricular organs including area postrema (AP); and barrier-related structures including meninges, cerebral vasculature, and choroid plexus. Additional studies have reported activation of neurons within the medial preoptic area (MPOA), supraoptic nucleus of the hypothalamus (SON), magnocellular and autonomic subdivisions of PVN, thalamus, and catecholamine cell groups of the ventrolateral medulla (VLM; A1 and C1 cell groups) and NTS (A2 and C2 cell groups).

Increased expression of c-*fos* mRNA within the PVN presumably reflects excitatory control of the pituitary–adrenocortical axis in response to systemic administration of IL-1β. Catecholaminergic input

FIGURE 4 Series of photomicrographs illustrating the location of c-*fos* mRNA within the brain of a male rat following systemic administration of interleukin-1β. Note the selective pattern of neuronal activation with increases in c-*fos* mRNA present within the bed nucleus of the stria terminalis (BNST), paraventricular nucleus of the hypothalamus (PVN), central nucleus of the amygdala (CeA), nucleus of the solitary tract (NTS), and area postrema (AP).

from the NTS and ventrolateral medulla is critical for activating mpPVN neurons in response to IL-1β, as lesions that destroy these ascending pathways can drastically reduce c-*fos* expression within mpPVN neurons and other measures of HPA axis activity. In accordance, c-*fos* mRNA levels are increased within neurons of the adrenergic (C1, C2) and noradrenergic (A2) cell groups, and retrograde tract-tracing studies have shown that the majority of these "activated" neurons project to mpPVN. Systemic administration of IL-1β can activate these catecholaminergic cell groups via two main pathways. The NTS receives visceral sensory information carried by the vagus and glossopharyngeal nerves, and there is evidence that these sensory afferents can respond to IL-1β in the periphery. In addition, neurons within the area postrema can transduce IL-1β present in the bloodstream into a neural signal that is then transmitted to neurons within the NTS and VLM. In support of this second pathway, c-*fos* mRNA levels are elevated within the area postrema in response to IL-1β.

The lateral subdivision of the central nucleus of the amygdala (CeA) and the dorsolateral region ("oval nucleus") of the BNST also showed prominent activation following IL-1β administration. Although both of these brain regions have been implicated in stress-induced glucocorticoid secretion, it is unlikely that their activation following interleukin administration reflects HPA axis regulation. This conclusion is based on several findings. First, neurons within the lateral CeA do not project to the PVN, but rather to three main regions—medial CeA, restricted parts of the BNST (including the oval nucleus), and the parabrachial nucleus in the pons. Second, while tract-tracing studies show a significant proportion of cells within the NTS and VLM that project to mpPVN and contain Fos protein, a similar finding is not observed for neurons within CeA or BNST. Third, administration of indomethacin, a prostaglandin synthesis inhibitor, blocks the ability of neurons in area postrema to transduce IL-1β into a neural signal. This effect results in decreased activation of neurons within NTS and VLM, leading to decreased activation of mpPVN neurons and a reduction in ACTH release. However, indomethacin administration does not reduce c-*fos* expression within CeA, suggesting that the mechanisms associated with HPA axis regulation in response to IL-1β administration are distinct from those controlling activational processes within CeA. The role of CeA and BNST during an immune-mediated stress response is currently unknown, although it is suggested that activation of these brain regions may activate autonomic responses such as bradycardia or sympathetic excitation of select target organs.

B. "Fight or Flight" Response: Processive, Psychological Stressors

Stressors that are processive and psychological in nature involve a reaction to a threatening stimulus in an individual's external environment. Such reactions are associated with increased arousal and vigilance, often eliciting a state of fear (or increased anxiety) and, in many instances, leading to a global response output that has been termed "fight or flight." The image conveyed by "fight or flight" is one of an active state—secretion of glucocorticoids and other neurohormones, activation of the sympathetic division of the autonomic nervous system leading to increases in heart rate, blood pressure and respiration, and display of behavioral responses designed to effectively cope with the threatening event. A processive stressor requires the processing of exteroceptive signals from multiple sensory modalities that lead to perception of the stimulus input as stressful. This evaluative process may also reflect psychological variables including predictability and controllability of the stressor as well as "coping" strategies. Because of this need for higher level processing, processive stressors are thought to activate limbic afferents that control HPA axis activity via synaptic connections with BNST, MPOA, and hypothalamus (HYPO).

In our laboratory, we have studied the effects of social defeat in the male Syrian hamster as one model of a processive, psychological stressor. Using a resident-intruder paradigm, the pairing of two isolated male hamsters results in fighting, with one male ("dominant") behaving aggressively, attacking and chasing the other male ("subordinate") that reacts submissively, defending against attack and displaying flight. The subordinate male is stressed as evidenced by elevated levels of glucocorticoids, while the dominant male is not. Figure 5 illustrates the general pattern of c-*fos* mRNA expression that occurs

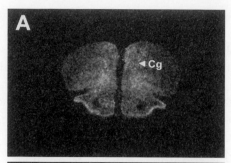
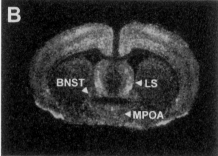
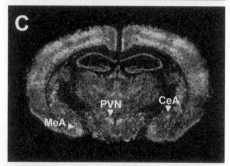
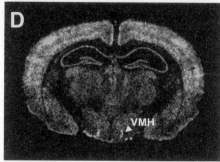
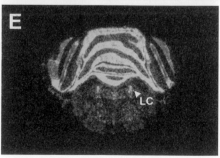

within the brain of a socially defeated male 30 min after the onset of fighting. This series of photomicrographs reveals a global pattern of activity encompassing vast regions of the neocortex, septum, amygdala, hypothalamus, and brainstem. By analyzing c-*fos* mRNA expression within different control groups and in dominant and subordinate males, it is possible to identify patterns of neuronal activity associated with handling, fighting, and the stress of defeat. Activation observed in numerous brain regions in handled control, dominant, and subordinate males presumably reflects the detection of exteroceptive signals leading to an increase in arousal and conscious awareness. In contrast, selective activation of brain regions in subordinate males most likely reflects processes associated with the perception of the stimulus input as threatening and stressful as well as mediation of various response outputs leading to the "fight or flight" response. In subordinate males, c-*fos* mRNA increased selectively within the cingulate cortex (medial prefrontal cortex), lateral septum, BNST, MPOA, several hypothalamic nuclei (paraventricular, anterior, ventromedial, arcuate, and supramammillary), CeA, amygdalohippocampal area, periaqueductal gray, dorsal raphe, cuneiform nucleus, and locus coeruleus.

The limbic system plays an important role in regulating HPA axis activity in response to processive and psychological stressors. Following defeat, significant increases in neuronal activation were observed within mPFC, lateral septum, and amygdala. The hippocampus also plays an important role in HPA axis activity, although c-*fos* mRNA levels were not selectively increased within this brain region. This negative finding has been reported following other stress paradigms. The majority of studies have linked

FIGURE 5 Series of photomicrographs illustrating the location of c-*fos* mRNA within the brain of a male hamster following social defeat. Note the global pattern of brain activity observed throughout the brain. A selective pattern of neuronal activation was observed in the cingulate cortex (Cg), lateral septum (LS), bed nucleus of the stria terminalis (BNST), medial preoptic area (MPOA), paraventricular (PVN) and ventromedial (VMH) nuclei of the hypothalamus (PVN), central nucleus of the amygdala (CeA), and locus coeruleus (LC).

mPFC, lateral septum, and hippocampus to inhibition of glucocorticoid secretion (see next section). In contrast, numerous studies have implicated the amygdala in excitatory regulation of the HPA axis. For example, electrical stimulation of neurons within the medial, cortical, and central nuclei have all been shown to stimulate glucocorticoid secretion. Furthermore, lesions of the medial and central nuclei can decrease ACTH and corticosterone secretion in response to stress. Following defeat, a significant increase in c-*fos* mRNA expression was observed within CeA consistent with a possible role of this amygdaloid nucleus in activating the HPA axis. Although activated neurons were also detected within the medial and cortical subdivisions, the levels present in subordinate males were not different from that observed in handled control or dominant males. It is at present unclear whether c-*fos* expression within the medial and cortical amygdaloid nuclei following social defeat reflects an increased propensity to stimulate glucocorticoid secretion that is differentially regulated at more central levels (e.g., enhanced in subordinate animals but inhibited in handled control and dominant males). Alternatively, activation within these brain regions may be associated with processes that are not specific to stress, such as coupling sensory cues with behavioral arousal.

While there is some evidence to suggest that the medial and central nuclei can project to the PVN, the input is limited and primarily focused toward autonomic subdivisions of this nucleus. The majority of anatomical studies suggest that the limbic system can influence the HPA axis via synaptic relays within the BNST, MPOA, and hypothalamus. Indeed, lesions of neurons within the BNST, MPOA, and hypothalamus have been shown to have either excitatory or inhibitory effects on HPA axis activity. Furthermore, tract-tracing studies reveal that many neurons within these three brain areas project directly to the mpPVN. Following defeat, significant increases in c-*fos* expression were observed throughout the BNST, MPOA, and hypothalamus. Additional work will be required to identify specific groups of neurons within these brain areas that are activated during defeat and that project to mpPVN.

The global pattern of brain activation seen following defeat is also observed in response to many other "processive" or psychological stressors including conditioned fear, audiogenic stress, footshock, restraint, immobilization, and swim stress. Following many of these stressors, significant increases in neuronal activation can be seen within various components of the limbic system. Of interest, activation of neurons within CeA is not always reported in studies involving this class of stressors. Thus, it is at present unclear if the activation observed within the CeA is related to glucocorticoid secretion. It is possible that brain activity following defeat reflects psychological and physical processes, with increased expression of c-*fos* mRNA within CeA (and dorsolateral BNST) synonymous with brain activity observed following systemic or physical stressors (e.g., processing of painful stimuli associated with biting attacks). Furthermore, the lack of a significant increase in neuronal activation observed within the hippocampus in response to defeat and observed following other stressors suggests that c-*fos* expression may not be a perfect "marker" for identifying all neurons activated during stress. Indeed, this latter point argues for the need to use multiple measures of neuronal activity as we attempt to understand how the brain responds to various stressors.

IV. TERMINATION OF THE STRESS RESPONSE

In addition to understanding how the HPA axis is activated during a stressful event, it is equally important to identify the mechanisms involved in terminating or limiting this response. Specific brain regions and stress-induced increases in glucocorticoids play an important role in terminating the stress response.

A. Neuronal Regulation

Local neurocircuits utilizing gamma-aminobutyric acid (GABA) as a neurotransmitter have been implicated in inhibitory regulation of the HPA axis. Lesions placed within the BNST, MPOA, or hypothalamus (including the arcuate, ventromedial, and suprachiasmatic nuclei) can increase the levels of ACTH and corticosterone secreted basally and in response to stress. All of these regions contain substantial populations of GABA-containing neurons, and, most recently, it has been shown that mRNA levels of the GABA biosynthetic enzyme glutamic acid decarboxylase increase within these brain areas in response to stress.

In addition, neurons within the lateral septum, mPFC, and hippocampus have also been linked to inhibitory regulation of the HPA axis. For example, lesions placed within any of these brain regions can prolong glucocorticoid secretion in response to stress. In addition, electrical stimulation of the hippocampus has been shown to inhibit glucocorticoid secretion. These data suggest that one function of these limbic brain regions may be to limit or terminate activity within the HPA axis. The major neurotransmitter utilized by neurons within the mPFC and hippocampus is the excitatory neurotransmitter glutamate. It is possible that afferents from the mPFC and hippocampus act to excite GABA neurons within the BNST, MPOA, and hypothalamus, leading to increased inhibition of the HPA axis.

B. Hormonal Regulation

Glucocorticoids act to inhibit the HPA axis at multiple levels—pituitary, PVN, and higher brain centers and in different time domains—fast, intermediate, and slow (genomic). The genomic, and, to some extent, the intermediate forms of inhibition appear to involve the classic mechanism of steroid–receptor-mediated regulation of gene transcription. Elevated levels of glucocorticoids bind to glucocorticoid receptor (GRs), activating the receptor and causing it to translocate to the nucleus where the steroid–receptor complex binds to DNA, leading to decreased transcription of CRH and AVP genes in the hypothalamus and decreased transcription of the POMC gene in the pituitary. The mechanisms that underlie fast feedback inhibition are not well understood. This form of inhibition occurs too rapidly to be explained by changes in gene transcription. It is possible that glucocorticoids act at GRs to mediate nongenomic effects or, alternatively, glucocorticoids may interact with a different class of glucocorticoid sensitive receptors (e.g., membrane receptors).

Glucocorticoids are also thought to act at higher brain centers to inhibit the HPA axis. For example, lesions of the hippocampus lead to an increase in the expression of CRH and AVP mRNA within mpPVN neurons, even though basal levels of glucocorticoids are elevated, suggesting that glucocorticoid negative feedback has been reduced following hippocampal damage. Lesions of the hippocampus have also been shown to attenuate the ability of exogenous glucocorticoids to inhibit secretion of stress hormones, although not all studies support this contention. Similarly, implants of glucocorticoids into the mPFC or MPOA have been shown to block restraint-induced secretion of stress hormones. These findings suggest that glucocorticoids interact with neuronal elements to increase inhibitory control over the HPA axis. How this effect is mediated at the level of neurons and neurocircuits is presently unknown.

V. CONCLUDING REMARKS

This article was designed to provide the reader with a general understanding of how the brain responds to an acute stress exposure highlighting important differences in brain activity in response to stressors that are systemic and physical in nature versus those that are processive and psychological. However, we are beginning to gather information indicating that the relationship between stress and brain activity is more complex than simply a reflection of the "class" of stressor involved. Indeed, how the brain responds to stress can be influenced by a number of associative factors including the intensity, intermittency, chronicity, and context of the stress exposure as well as the individual's ability to effectively "cope" with stress. The challenge will be to understand how these more subtle aspects of stress responsiveness are coded within central stress neurocircuits.

See Also the Following Articles

Amygdala; Brain and Brain Regions; Hippocampus, Overview

Bibliography

Akil, H., and Morano, M. I. (1996). The biology of stress: From periphery to brain. *In* "Biology of Schizophrenia and

Affective Disease" (S. J. Watson, Ed.), pp. 15–48. American Psychiatric Press, Washington, DC.

Campeau, S., Day, H. E. W., Helmreich, D. L., Kollack-Walker, S., and Watson, S. J. (1998). Principles of psychoneuroendocrinology. *Psychiatr. Clin. North Am.,* **21,** 259–276.

Cullinan, W. E., Herman, J. P., Helmreich, D. L., and Watson, S. J. (1995). A neuroanatomy of stress. *In* "Neurobiological and Clinical Consequences of Stress: From Normal Adaptation to PTSD" (M. J. Friedman, D. S. Charney, and A. Y. Deutch, Eds.), pp. 3–26. Raven, New York.

Day, H. E. W., and Akil, H. (1996). Differential pattern of c-*fos* mRNA in rat brain following central and systemic administration of interleukin-1-beta: Implications for mechanism of action. *Neuroendocrinology* **63,** 207–218.

Herman, J. P., and Cullinan, W. E. (1997). Neurocircuitry of stress: Central control of the hypothalamo-pituitary-adrenocortical axis. *Trends Neurosci.* **20,** 78–84.

Kollack-Walker, S, Watson, S. J., and Akil, H. (1997). Social stress in hamsters: Defeat activates specific neurocircuits within the brain. *J. Neurosci.* **17,** 8842–8855.

Levine, S., and Ursin, H. (1991). What is stress? *In* "Stress: Neurobiology and Neuroendocrinology" (M. R. Brown, G. F. Koob, and C. Rivier, Eds.), pp. 3–21. Marcel Dekker, New York.

Sawchenko, P. E., Brown, E. R., Chan, R. K. W., Ericsson, A., Li, H.-Y., Roland, B. L., and Kovacs, K. J. (1996). The paraventricular nucleus of the hypothalamus and the functional neuroanatomy of visceromotor responses to stress. *Prog. Brain Res.* **107,** 201–222.

Cerebral Metabolism, Brain Imaging

Klaus P. Ebmeier

University of Edinburgh and MRC Brain Metabolism Unit, Scotland, United Kingdom

I. Imaging Methods
II. Structural Brain Changes Associated with Stress
III. Functional Imaging after Stressful Challenge
IV. Pharmacological Imaging in Stress Disorders
V. Conclusions

GLOSSARY

cingulate cortex Evolutionary old limbic cortex overlying the corpus callosum, whose fibers connect the two brain hemispheres.

hippocampus Evolutionary old part of the temporal lobe, associated with memory and emotional functions, part of the limbic system.

ligand Substance binding to a receptor, e.g., for a neurotransmitter.

orbitofrontal cortex Part of the frontal cortex nearest to the eyes, connected with limbic structures.

radiotracer Radioactive substance injected in small (trace) amounts for diagnostic purposes.

tomography Three-dimensional reconstruction of brain maps from radiation given off by the brain (emission tomography) or from shadows of traversing rays (transmission scan).

The brain is one of the best-protected human organs, only accessible to scrutiny after injury or *post mortem.* For this reason, much of our knowledge of the brain stems from studies after brain injuries—so-called lesion-psychology. The randomness and the lack of selectivity of brain injuries limit these studies. Over the past decades, however, *in vivo* imaging methods have been developed that allow for the visualization of structure and function of the living brain. There is a variety of imaging modes available, based on different physical processes. In order to understand the potential and the limitations of these, some knowledge of the basic principles is necessary. Neuroimaging methods are generally divided into structural and functional imaging modes. Of the former, X-ray computerized tomography (CT) has been generally replaced by magnetic resonance imaging (MRI), which in addition to giving a higher spatial resolution provides a better contrast between different soft tissue types, such as gray and white matter. The functional emission tomographies are based on radioactive, gamma-ray-emitting substances that are injected or inhaled. These tracers distribute throughout the brain following the pattern of cerebral perfusion or the density distribution of certain brain receptors.

I. IMAGING METHODS

A. Positron Emission Tomography (PET)

Positron Emission Tomography is dependent on the ability of the scanner to detect two gamma photons traveling in opposite directions, which result from the annihilation of a single positron. The origin of these photons is, therefore, on a straight line between the two detectors registering a coincident signal. The energy from positron emission is relatively high, but the emitters have a short half-life (minutes), which keeps the administered dose of radiation low. However, a particle accelerator (cyclotron) and a radiochemist are required to generate the radio-emitting isotopes and to synthesize the required compounds *in situ*. Positron emitters in common use are ^{18}F-fluoro-deoxy-glucose (FDG), which is taken up into neurons just like the energy provider glucose, but then is not further metabolized so that it reflects the regional pattern of brain activity. Cerebral blood flow markers, such as ^{15}O-labeled water, give an almost identical distribution of activity to FDG. Carbon-11 and ^{18}F can be incorporated into many receptor ligands to provide radiolabels representing specific binding to these receptors. Examples are ^{11}C-raclopride, a dopamine $D_{2,3}$ receptor ligand; ^{11}C-methyl-spiperone, a $D_{2,3,4}$ ligand, or ^{18}F-fluoro-dopa, a marker of dopamine synthesis. The spatial resolution of PET is in the region of 5 mm.

B. Single Photon Emission CT (SPECT)

Radioisotopes emitting photons in the gamma-frequency range with a radioactive half-life in the hours range can be employed as SPECT ligands. In contrast to PET, where theoretically all coincident signals are exploited to localize the source of the radiation, SPECT needs to restrict the field of view of the detectors with collimators in order to localize the origin of the signal (Fig. 1). Collimators absorb much of the activity from the field of vision, so that SPECT is less sensitive than PET. Tracers used are ^{99m}Tc-labeled exametazime and bicisate and ^{123}I-labeled IMP for perfusion imaging and, e.g., ^{123}I-iomazenil for (benzodiazepine-)receptor binding. Modern SPECT cameras have a resolution of 7–12 mm.

C. Magnetic Resonance Imaging (MRI)

Different from X-ray and emission CT, which can be understood from the basic principles of optics, MRI is based on manipulating the resonance frequencies of nuclei, such as ^{1}H-protons or ^{31}P-phosphorous, by systematically changing the magnetic field strength across the volume of interest. Magnetic field strength is directly proportional to the magnetic resonance frequency of, e.g., hydrogen nuclei in water, so that their spatial position can be frequency encoded. The strength of signal in the frequency domain, in k-space, then, corresponds to the proton density at a particular spatial coordinate. Apart from proton density, relaxation times such as $T1$ and $T2^*$

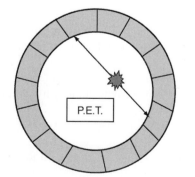

FIGURE 1 Principles of Action for positron emission tomography and single photon emission tomography (see text).

are extracted from such frequency domain data and provide important information in illness and during the normal functioning of the brain. The resolution for MRI is in the 1–2 mm range.

1. Functional MRI

T2* changes, for example, occur when oxygenated hemoglobin loses its oxygen. In active brain regions, regional blood flow increases beyond the consumption of oxygen, so that a local excess of oxygen-saturated hemoglobin results. This forms the basis of blood oxygen-level-dependent (BOLD) imaging, the most commonly used functional (f)MRI method. Functional MRI is likely to take over from emission CT as the method of choice for brain activity imaging. It does not involve any radiation exposure and can, therefore, be repeated many times. It also has a greater spatial (2–5 mm) and time resolution (about 100 ms) than PET or SPECT.

2. Magnetic Resonance Spectroscopy

Local magnetic field strengths vary relative to their molecular, i.e., chemical, context. This results in slight changes of resonance frequency that can be measured with magnetic resonance spectroscopy (MRS). Magnetic resonance spectroscopy thus allows for the chemical imaging of certain biologically important molecules. Nuclei commonly used in MRS are ^1H which, after suppression of the water signal, yields measures of compounds such as glutamate, lactate, N-acetyl-aspartate, choline and creatinine or ^{31}P, which gives estimates of the markers of energy metabolism ATP/ADP and of membrane metabolism, phosphomono-/diesters, and phosphocreatinine. The volumes studied with MRS lie in the range of several cubic centimeters.

II. STRUCTURAL BRAIN CHANGES ASSOCIATED WITH STRESS

Psychiatric tradition holds that so-called functional illness, that is, the functional psychoses and in particular the neuroses, are not associated with gross brain lesions or structural abnormalities. In schizophrenia and bipolar affective disorder this orthodoxy has been challenged almost from the begin-

ning of the century. More recently, it has been claimed that stress-related disorders, such as depression and anxiety, particularly if posttraumatic or chronic, are also associated with localized structural brain abnormalities. These changes typically affect the hippocampus. They have been reported in war veterans with posttraumatic stress disorder, in victims of sexual or physical abuse, and in chronically depressed patients (Fig. 2). This fits in with the increase in stress hormones, such as cortisone, often found in these patient groups. There is some evidence from animal data that high cortisone levels are toxic to hippocampal cells. These cells in turn are responsible for a negative feedback to the hypothalamo-pituitary-adrenocortical (HPA) axis. Once hippocampal damage occurs, the consequent loss of HPA inhibition may lead to an acceleration of cell damage that could also be responsible for the associated emotional and cognitive changes. So far, cross-sectional studies have shown associations of hippocampal atrophy with stress related disorders. In order to exclude the possibility that preexisting hippocampal damage makes subjects vulnerable to stress-related disorders, longitudinal studies in populations at risk are necessary.

III. FUNCTIONAL IMAGING AFTER STRESSFUL CHALLENGE

A. General Principles

Brain regions involved in the expression and experience of stressful feelings can be identified experimentally by comparing brain perfusion or metabolism after stressful stimuli and after neutral stimuli matched for physical features and cognitive demands. This modular approach assumes that subtracting brain activity maps of two task conditions reveals the brain structures responsible for the aspect contained in one task but not the other. For example, a video with snake or spider scenes is shown to patients with snake or spider phobia and healthy volunteers and compared with an alternative video of neutral park scenes matched for color, intensity of light, and movement. Brain regions only activated during the phobic stimuli in the phobic group are

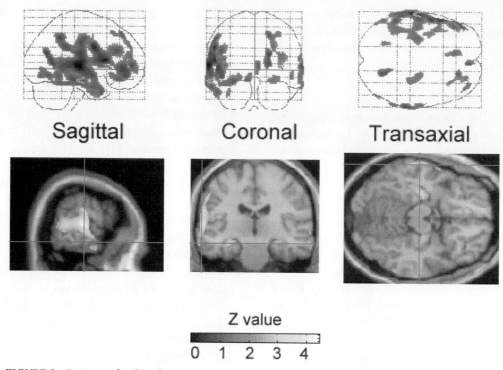

Sagittal   Coronal   Transaxial

Z value

0   1   2   3   4

FIGURE 2   Regions of reduced gray matter density in patients with chronic depression (reproduced with permission from Ebmeier *et al.* (1998). *Br. J. Psychiat.,* 172, p. 531).

thought to be related to phobic symptoms. In addition to this subtraction methodology, measures of psychopathology, such as anxiety scales, can be correlated with regional brain activity in order to confirm a relationship between symptom severity and regional brain activation. Figure 3 highlights the cingulate cortex, where activity changes as severity of depression fluctuates during the course of a day. Cingulate cortex is also involved in the expression of posttraumatic stress and induced mood changes.

If a mental task is required during the scan, it is important to ensure equal task performance between groups. For example, to make sure that inspection of photos and evocation of imagery is done equally thoroughly, subjects can be asked to remember and recall details of the images after the scan. Finally, the strength of association between different brain areas may be relevant in that during pathological states widespread brain activity may be driven by a primarily abnormal component of a circuit so that altered and possibly increased connectivity between various structures results.

B. Specific Findings

The sensory modality of stimulus presentation may play an important role in the brain responses observed. However, increased activity in visual association cortex, which is often found during anxiety states, may also represent increased vigilance associated with "fearful scanning" of the environment. A more general hypothesis to be tested by functional imaging studies is that a core anxiety system may comprise elements of the paralimbic belt, e.g., posterior medial orbitofrontal, anterior cingulate, insular, parahippocampal, and anterior temporal cortexes. In fact, studies of a variety of anxiety disorders, including posttraumatic stress disorder, have shown activation of this brain system, together with subcortical structures, such as basal ganglia, thalamus, and brain stem. Posterior cingulate cortex has been implicated with anxiety and specifically with episodic memory processes related to threatening stimuli. Anxiety affects peripheral as well as CNS metabolism and perfusion. Cervical sympathetic fibers, part of the auto-

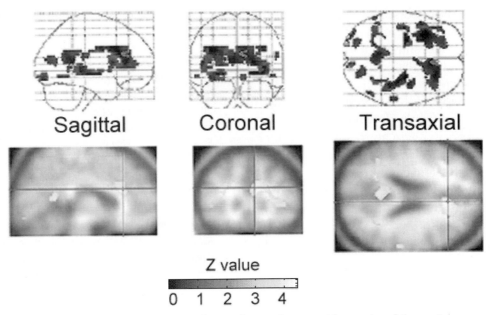

Sagittal   **Coronal**   **Transaxial**

Z value

0 1 2 3 4

FIGURE 3 Prefrontal and cingulate perfusion changes with severity of depression.

nomic nervous system, may be responsible for reduced brain perfusion during high anxiety. Finally, increased muscular activity in the temporalis muscle has been responsible for the misattribution of overactivity to anterior temporal lobe.

IV. PHARMACOLOGICAL IMAGING IN STRESS DISORDERS

Two methods are available to investigate the effects of drugs on brain function. The net effect of a drug on brain metabolism can be examined by infusing the drug during the uptake of a blood flow marker. Unfortunately, this method does not allow for the regional distinction between excitatory or inhibitory synaptic activity. The second method involves the use of receptor ligands. Ligand concentrations can give a measure of receptor numbers. There is, for example, some evidence that the number of benzodiazepine receptors is decreased in panic disorder. If the ligand has intermediate affinity to the receptor in question, it can be displaced by the natural neurotransmitter so that the activity of the endogenous transmitter system can be assessed.

V. CONCLUSIONS

The technical advances in the field of neuroimaging have made it possible to examine brain activity and brain structure in living subjects. It is possible to measure the concentration of biologically relevant molecules and the number of receptors in a particular neurotransmitter system. The usual way of employing these methods is by selecting a group of patients and a matched control group. Both groups are compared with regard to an objective measure derived from the image. There are two possible limitations to our ability to draw valid conclusions from such data. The first is that because of the cost of imaging studies a relatively small sample from the larger population of patients has to be selected. Whether the group actually studied is representative for the disorder depends on whether its selection has been subject to any bias. Many sources of bias can occur in the selection for an investigation that needs a significant amount of cooperation from subjects. The ideal, i.e., that subjects are randomly selected from the underlying population, is virtually never achieved, so conclusions always have to be tentative and need independent replication. The other limitation is inherent in the cross-sectional design of virtually all studies. An association study usually does not allow for any establishment of causality. Hippocampal atrophy may be the result of chronic stress or it may the predisposing factor that makes subjects vulnerable to developing the stress-related disorder. To circumvent this difficulty, longitudinal follow-up designs are necessary. These are costly and require an early identification of subjects at risk. They are also likely to require a longer time to come to fruition, so the jury on the relevance of the changes described to date is still out.

See Also the Following Articles

Brain and Brain Regions; Hippocampus

Bibliography

Bremner, J. D., Innis, R. B., Ng, C. K., Staib, L. H., Salomon, R. M., Bronen, R. A., Duncan, J., Southwick, S. M., Krystal, J. H., Rich, D., Zubal, G., Dey, H., Soufer, R., and Charney, D. S. (1997b). Positron emission tomography measurement of cerebral metabolic correlates of yohimbine administration in combat-related posttraumatic stress disorder. *Arch. Gen. Psychiat.* **54**, 246–254.

Bremner, J. D., Randall, P., Scott, T. M., Bronen, R. A., Seibyl, J. P., Southwick, S. M., Delaney, R. C., McCarthy, G., Charney, D. S., and Innis, R. B. (1995). MRI-based measurement of hippocampal volume in patients with combat-related posttraumatic stress disorder. *Am. J. Psychiat.* **152**, 973–981.

Bremner, J. D., Randall, P., Vermetten, E., Staib, L., Bronen, R. A., Mazure, C., Capelli, S., McCarthy, G., Innis, R. B., and Charney, D. S. (1997a). Magnetic resonance imaging-based measurement of hippocampal volume in posttraumatic stress disorder related to childhood physical and sexual abuse—A preliminary report. *Biol. Psychiat.* **41**, 23–32.

Benkelfat, C., Bradwejn, J., Meyer, E., Ellenbogen, M., Milot, S., Gjedde, A., and Evans, A. (1995). Functional neuroanatomy of CCK4-induced anxiety in normal healthy volunteers. *Am. J. Psychiat.* **152**, 1180–1184.

Ebmeier, K. P., Steele, J. D., MacKenzie, D., O'Carroll, R. E., Kydd, R. R., Glabus, M. F., Blackwood, D. H. R., Rugg.,

M. D., and Goodwin, G. M. (1995). Cognitive brain potentials and regional cerebral blood flow equivalents during two- and three-sound auditory "oddball" tasks. *Electroencephalogr. Clin. Neurophysiol.* **95**, 434–443.

Fredrikson, M., Fischer, H., and Wik, G. (1997). Cerebral blood flow during anxiety provocation. *J. Clin. Psychiat.* **58** (Suppl. 16), 16–21.

Freeman, T. W., Cardwell, D., Karson, C. N., and Komoroski, R. A. (1998). *In vivo* proton magnetic resonance spectroscopy of the medial temporal lobes of subjects with combat-related posttraumatic stress disorder. *Mag. Res. Med.* **40**, 66–71.

Gurvits, T. V., Shenton, M. E., Hokama, H., Ohta, H., Lasko, N. B., Gilbertson, M. W., Orr, S. P., Kikinis, R., Jolesz, F. A., McCarley, R. W., and Pitman, R. K. (1996). Magnetic resonance imaging study of hippocampal volume in chronic, combat-related posttraumatic stress disorder. *Biol. Psychiat.* **40**, 1091–1099.

Kaschka, W., Feistel, H., and Ebert, D. (1995). Reduced benzodiazepine receptor binding in panic disorders measured by iomazenil SPECT. *J. Psychiat. Res.* **29**, 427–434.

Maddock, R. J., and Buonocore, M. H. (1997). Activation of left posterior cingulate gyrus by the auditory presentation of threat-related words: An fMRI study. *Psychiat. Res.* **75**, 1–14.

Malizia, A. L., Cunningham, V. J., Bell, C. J., Liddle, P. F., Jones, T., and Nutt, D. J. (1998). Decreased brain GABA(A)-benzodiazepine receptor binding in panic disorder: preliminary results from a quantitative PET study. *Arch. Gen. Psychiat.* **55**, 715–720.

Mathew, R. J., Wilson, W. H., Humphreys, D., Lowe, J. V., and Wiethe, K. E. (1997). Cerebral vasodilation and vasoconstriction associated with acute anxiety. *Biol. Psychiat.* **41**, 782–795.

McEwen, B. S., and Magarinos, A. M. (1997). Stress effects on morphology and function of the hippocampus. *Ann. N. Y. Acad. Sci.* **821**, 271–284.

Ownby, R. L. (1998). Computational model of obsessive-compulsive disorder: Examination of etiologic hypothesis and treatment strategies. *Depression Anxiety* **8**, 91–103.

Rauch, S. L., Savage, C. R., Alpert, N. M., Fischman, A. J., and Jenike, M. A. (1997). The functional neuroanatomy of anxiety: A study of three disorders using positron emission tomography and symptom provocation. *Biol. Psy.* **42**, 446–452.

Rauch, S. L., Savage, C. R., Alpert, N. M., Miguel, E. C., Baer, L., Breiter, H. C., Fischman, A. J., Manzo, P. A., Moretti, C., and Jenike, M. A. (1995). A positron emission tomographic study of simple phobic symptom provocation. *Arch. Gen. Psy.* **52**, 20–28.

Shah, P. J., Ebmeier, K. P., Glabus, M. F., and Goodwin, G. M. (1998). Cortical grey matter reductions associated with treatment resistant chronic unipolar depression: a controlled MRI study. *Br. J. Psychiat.* **172**, 527–532.

Shin, L. M., Kosslyn, S. M., McNally, R. J., Alpert, N. M., Thompson, W. L., Rauch, S. L., Macklin, M. L., and Pitman, R. K. (1997). Visual imagery and perception in posttraumatic stress disorder. A positron emission tomographic investigation. *Arch. Gen. Psychiat.* **54**, 233–241.

Stein, M. B., Koverola, C., Hanna, C., Torchia, M. G., and McClarty, B. (1997). Hippocampal volume in women victimized by childhood sexual abuse. *Psychol. Med.* **27**, 951–959.

Chaperone Proteins

Alberto J. L. Macario and Everly Conway de Macario

New York State Department of Health and State of New York University at Albany

I. Definition
II. Classification
III. Biology
IV. Phylogenetic Domains
V. Physiology
VI. Pathology and Medicine
VII. Mechanism
VIII. To Fold, Refold, or Degrade

GLOSSARY

chaperone machine A functional chaperoning complex formed by the chaperone Hsp70(DnaK) and the co-chaperones Hsp40(DnaJ) and GrpE.

chaperonin A molecular chaperone belonging to the 60-kDa family.

chaperonin system type I A chaperoning complex formed by the 60-kDa chaperonin and a 10-kDa cochaperonin that is present in bacteria and in the eukaryotic cell organelles of bacterial origin.

chaperonin system type II A chaperoning complex formed by subunits of the 60-kDa family in archaea and by these subunits and others with various sizes in the eukaryotic cell cytosol.

molecular chaperone A molecule that assists polypeptides in the process of folding to achieve a final, functional configuration or to regain such configuration after reversible denaturation. The paradigm is the stress protein called Hsp70(Dnak).

phylogenetic domain The highest order of classification of all living cells (domain, kingdom, phylum, class, order, family, genus, species) that represents, the major evolutionary lines of descent, or phylogenetic lineages. Three domains have been identified: Bacteria (or eubacteria), Archaea (archaebacteria), and Eucarya (eukaryotes)—the former two are prokaryotes.

stress (heat-shock) proteins Products of the stress (heat-shock) genes, many of which are molecular chaperones, such as the components of the chaperone machine.

stress (heat-shock) response The series of intracellular events caused by cell stressors. The most prominent of these events is the induction of stress (heat-shock) genes with the production of stress (heat-shock) proteins.

A protein molecule is a chain whose links are amino acids. The number, type, and order of amino acids in the chain are determined by the gene that encodes the protein. These three attributes constitute the primary structure. To reach a functional status, a protein must acquire higher levels of complexity. It must fold onto itself to achieve secondary and tertiary structures. In addition, some proteins must associate with others to form a quaternary structure before they are capable of realizing their functional potential.

The functional configuration of a protein once acquired may be partially of completely lost in a process called protein denaturation. This happens when a cell is stressed. There are a number of cell stressors of physical (e.g., heat) or chemical (e.g., alcohol) nature that may cause protein denaturation.

While the information necessary to achieve a final, functional configuration is provided by the primary structure, many proteins need assistance to fold properly, or to refold in case of reversible denaturation. This assistance is provided by molecular chaperones.

I. DEFINITION

Chaperone proteins, or molecular chaperones, are proteins that assist others to fold properly during or after synthesis, refold after partial denaturation, and translocate to the locale of the cell where they reside and function. They are also involved in the regulation of their own genes and in the presentation of proteins destined for degradation by proteases. Some chaperones are proteases themselves.

Many chaperones are stress (heat-shock) proteins, namely they increase in quantity on cell stress (also termed heat shock, although heat is not the only stressor known) to counteract the protein-denaturing effects of stressors (e.g., heat, alcohol, ischemia–hypoxia, heavy metals, hypersalinity). This is the reason why stress proteins and molecular chaperones are usually treated together, as a single large group of heterogeneous components, and why they are named Hsp (for heat shock protein). Thus, there are many cell stressors that cause stress or heat shock, and many stress or heat-shock proteins, but not all of the latter are molecular chaperones. Likewise, not every molecular chaperone is a stress protein.

As it may be inferred from their multiplicity of function, molecular chaperones are promiscuous; they interact with a variety of molecules. They are also ubiquitous because they occur in all cells, tissues, and organs, with very few known exceptions. Furthermore, molecular chaperones are present in the various compartments of the eukaryotic cell—nucleus, cytosol, and organelles, such as mitochondria and choloroplasts—and in the prokaryotic cell cytoplasm and periplasm.

II. CLASSIFICATION

Stress proteins, including the chaperones, are grouped into families whose members have similar molecular masses, (Tables I and II). Genes encoding most of these proteins are stress inducible, whereas genes for the other proteins are expressed constitutively, i.e., they are transcribed in the absence of stress.

The most studied are the Hsp70 and Hsp60 families, although considerable progress has been made in the investigation of proteins belonging to other families, e.g., Hsp40 and Hsp90, high molecular weight proteases, and the small heat-shock proteins (sHsp).

III. BIOLOGY

A convenient way of learning about chaperones and stress proteins is to look at them from an evolutionary-phylogenetic standpoint, while keeping in mind that the separation between prokaryotes and eukaryotes is not absolute inasmuch as the eukaryotic cell contains prokaryotic components. For instance, mitochondria are the remnants of ancient α-proteobacteria that entered into a symbiotic association with a primitive eukaryotic cell. Similarly, chloroplasts are what has evolved from primitive symbiotic cyanobacteria. Even the eukaryotic nucleus contains in its DNA genes derived from bacteria. In this regard, genes encoding chaperones of the Hsp60 and Hsp70 families are of particular interest. These chaperones are present in the mitochondria, chloroplasts, endoplasmic reticulum (ER), and other organelles (see Table II), but their genes reside in the nucleus. These genes are transcribed in the nucleus, and the chaperones are synthesized in the cytosol and are finally translocated to the organelle of destination. In fact, it has been the comparative analyses of Hsp70 and Hsp60 amino acid sequences that have shown convincingly the origin of the genes

TABLE I
Stress (Heat-Shock) Proteins and Chaperones in Prokaryotes

Family		Examples[a]	
Name(s)	Weight (kDa)	Bacteria	Archaea
Heavy; high molecular weight; Hsp100	100 or higher		
Hsp90	81–99	HtpG	
Hsp70; DnaK; chaperones	65–80	DnaK; Hsc66	Hsp70(DnaK)
Hsp60; chaperonins	55–64	GroEl	TF55; chaperonin subunits
Hsp40; DnaJ	35–54	DnaJ	Hsp40(DnaJ)
Small Hsp; sHsp	34 or lower	GroES; Hsc20; GrpE; PPIase	GrpE; sHsp; PPIase; prefoldin

[a] Explanations and details may be found in the articles listed in the Bibliography.

that encode them and have provided strong support to the notion that the eukaryotic cell is an assemblage of parts, several of which are prokaryotic in origin.

IV. PHYLOGENETIC DOMAINS

Since the late 1970s the notion that all living cells can be sorted out into three main lines of evolutionary descent, or phylogenetic domains, has gained acceptance, although many points remain controversial and the limits between domains at the beginning are less well defined than it was thought when this division of all life was first proposed. Nevertheless, it is helpful to think of stress proteins and chaperones within the context of the three domains; Bacteria (eubacteria), Archaea (archaebacteria), and Eucarya (eukaryotes)—the former two being prokaryotes. Why is this helpful? Because archaea (i.e., members

TABLE II
Stress (Heat-Shock) Proteins and Chaperones in Eukaryotes

Family		Examples[a]			
Name(s)	Weight (kDa)	Cytosol	Mitochondria	Endoplasmic reticulum	Chloroplast
Heavy; high molecular weight; Hsp100	100 or higher	Hsp101(Hsp102); Hsp105; Hsp110		Hsp170(Grp170)	
Hsp90	81–99	Hsp90(Hsp83); Grp94		Hsp90(GRP94; Grp94)	
Hsp70; chaperones	65–80	Hsp70(Hsp72); Hsc70(Hsp73); SSA1-4; SSB1-2	mhsp70; SSC1	BiP(Grp78); SSi1p; Kar2; Lhs1	Hsp70(DnaK)
Hsp60; chaperonins	55–64	CCT (TRiC; TCP1) subunits	Hsp60(Cpn60)	RBP	Cpn60 (rubisco-binding protein)
Hsp40; DnaJ	35–54	Hsp40; Hdj1(MAS5); Sis1; Ydj1	Hsp40; Mdj1p; Mdj2p	Hsp40; Hsp47; Sec63p; Scj1p; JEM1	Hsp40(DnaJ); ANJ1; TLP40
Small Hsp; sHsp	34 or lower	Hsp10; PPIase; PDIase; prefoldin(Gim); α-crystallin family	GrpE (Yge1; Mye1p); PPIase	Cpn20; PPIase; PDIase; Hsp10(Cpn10)	GrpE; Cpn10

[a] Explanations and details may be found in the articles listed in the Bibliography.

of the domain Archaea) are indeed different from bacteria and eucarya (i.e., members of the domains Bacteria and Eucarya, respectively) in what concerns the Hsp70 and Hsp60 chaperones. For example, bacteria possess the Hsp70 (also named DnaK), Hsp40 (also termed DnaJ), and GrpE stress proteins that constitute the molecular chaperone machine and the Hsp60–Hsp10 molecules that constitute the GroEL/S or chaperonin type I system, whereas archaea and eucarya have different counterparts.

The structure and functions of the molecular chaperone machine and of the chaperonin system type I are relatively well characterized in the bacterium *Escherichia coli*. There is also considerable information on the eucaryal Hsp70 complex and on the chaperonin system, which is of type II, namely different from that found in bacteria. Intriguingly, different archaea either do not have an identifiable chaperone machine or have one of bacterial type with the Hsp70(DnaK), Hsp40(DnaJ), and GrpE components, but they all have a type II chaperonin system. The fact that archaea have an eukaryotic type chaperonin system is remarkable because archaea are prokaryotes like bacteria.

Also interestingly, eukaryotes have the bacterial type Hsp60 chaperonin system in their organelles, bearing witness to the bacterial origins of the latter. Thus, one of the most exciting fields of biology nowadays is the analysis of chaperonins and chaperones in organisms representing the three phylogenetic domains and their main branches, understanding their evolution, and elucidating the relationships between species and between organelles and their prokaryotic ancestors.

Another point of great interest from both evolutionary and physiological standpoints is that a number of archaeal species do not have Hsp70(Dnak) or the other components of the chaperone machine, Hsp40(DnaJ) and GrpE. This peculiarity is remarkable because it represents the only exception known to the rule that every organism has an Hsp70 system (in fact, Hsp70 is considered one of the most conserved proteins in nature). Absence of the gene triad that constitutes the chaperone machine is noteworthy also because it poses the question of how can these organisms achieve protein biogenesis and survive stress without this machine.

V. PHYSIOLOGY

With few exceptions, prokaryotes have only a single *hsp70(dnaK)* gene, which is active under normal physiological conditions and is activated further by stressors. In the latter case, an increase in Hsp70(DnaK) over the basal or constitutive levels is observed, which may be due to increased transcription, translation, decreased mRNA, and/or Hsp70(DnaK) degradation. In contrast, eukaryotes have more than one *hsp70(dnaK)* gene. Essentially, one gene is active physiologically and responds to physiological signals—it is said to be constitutively induced—whereas the other gene is induced by stressors. The former gene is designated cognate *hsp70*, abbreviated *hsc70*, whereas the protein is termed Hsc70. In fact, eukaryotic cells may have more than one representative of the two types of the *hsp70* gene, and both types may respond to physiological stimuli, e.g., those derived from cell cycle and cell differentiation events. Therefore, *hsp70(dnaK)* is also interesting from the point of view of cell physiology during development and histogenesis and is an important player in pathology and disease.

VI. PATHOLOGY AND MEDICINE

Molecular chaperone genes and proteins, as well as chaperonins and other stress genes and proteins, are being studied at the present time to determine their role in the maintenance of health and in the development of disease. It is conceivable that failure of the chaperoning processes would lead to the accumulation of misfolded proteins that will not work or to misplaced proteins that will not reach their destination in the cell to work properly. In both instances, the accumulation of nonfunctional proteins will encumber the cell and impede its normal life—this is why protein degradation is also an important cellular function, part of which depends on molecular chaperones.

Molecular chaperones are also potential tools for preventing protein denaturation or for restoring partially denatured proteins, during surgery, for example, when ischemia–hypoxia (a strong cell stressor) is unavoidable.

VII. MECHANISM

The mechanism of action of chaperones at the molecular level has not been fully elucidated for any organism or particular family, but there is considerable information on the Hsp70(DnaK) and Hsp60 (chaperonin) systems in *E. coli*. The question is how chaperones interact to help a polypeptide to acquire its final three-dimensional (native) configuration based on its primary structure. It is known that chaperones do not provide steric information or form part of the final product. It is believed that the Hsp70(DnaK) system in the cytosol binds nascent polypeptides to prevent their aggregation either within themselves or with other polypeptides in the immediate surroundings. In this manner, the Hsp70(DnaK) machine would maintain the newly made polypeptide in a foldable-competent status. In contrast, the Hsp60 (chaperonin) system GroEL/S acts posttranslationally and assists in the folding of polypeptides that range in size between 25 and 55 kDa. Hence, one might say that without chaperones most polypeptides would aggregate, and the few that would proceed in the right direction to achieve a physiologically active configuration would do so very slowly and inefficiently. Within this context, it is easy to realize that chaperones and chaperonins, and other stress proteins, such as the sHsp, play a critical role in cell survival during stress when the tendency to protein denaturation and aggregation is strong.

The binding of polypeptides to, and their release from, Hsp70(DnaK) is ATP dependent and involves the other members of the Hsp70(DnaK) machine, Hsp40(DnaJ) and GrpE. Hsp40 binds the polypeptide in need of assistance and presents it to the Hsp70–ATP complex. As this complex binds the Hsp40-tagged polypeptide, Hsp40 catalyzes ATP hydrolysis, which increases the strength of the binding between Hsp70-ATP and the polypeptide. GrpE then comes into action and catalyzes the exchange of ATP for ADP on Hsp70. When Hsp70 is again complexed with ATP, its affinity for the polypeptide diminishes and the latter is released because it has folded correctly or because it has to be processed further by the Hsp60 system GroEL/S.

The GroEL/S complex in *E. coli* is a cylindrical cage or barrel. GroEL (the Hsp60 component) forms two heptameric rings with a central cavity. GroES (the Hsp10 subunit) forms a single heptameric ring and serves as a lid for the two-ring GroEL barrel. The polypeptide-folding mechanism would be as follows: the unfolded polypeptide reaches the entrance to the GroEL barrel unassisted or ushered by the chaperone machine, enters into the cavity, and binds hydrophobic patches in the wall of the barrel. The GroES ring then binds, together with ATP, the GroEL cylinder, closing it. Thus, a hydrophilic folding cage or chamber is created and the polypeptide finds itself in an environment in which it becomes soluble and can fold correctly. ATP binding to the other GroEL ring releases GroES opening the barrel, which allows the folded polypeptide to escape into the cytosol. The cycle is repeated if the folding process was incomplete.

The details just described have been inferred from experiments *in vitro* with *E. coli*. It is not known to what extent the *in vitro* findings reproduce the *in vivo* mechanisms. Also, the mechanism of Hsp70–Hsp60 chaperoning in locales other than the cytosol, e.g., in the mitochondria, differs from those described earlier. Similarly, the mechanism of action of the other families of chaperones are also different in many details.

In conclusion, from studies pertaining to the *E. coli* cytoplasm it may be said that while the Hsp70(DnaK) chaperone machine intervenes early in protein synthesis, during translation, to prevent aggregation of the majority of the nascent polypeptides, the Hsp60 chaperonin system acts later. The GroEL/S complex intervenes posttranslationally and only to assist a minority of the new polypeptides that reach it either unassisted or ushered by the chaperone machine. The rest of the *E. coli* newly made polypeptides do not use the GroEL/S chaperonin system and probably fold in the cytosol assisted only by the chaperone machine.

VIII. TO FOLD, REFOLD, OR DEGRADE

The protein contents and quality of a cell vary according to the cell's needs imposed by physiological (e.g., cell cycle or differentiation stage) and environmental changes (e.g., nutrient limitation, fall in pH, temperature upshift, hyperosmolarity). The array of different proteins and the quantities of each of them must be adjusted precisely to the requirements of every moment during the cell's life. This delicate balance is achieved by various complementary, coordinated mechanisms that essentially either increase or decrease the concentration of any given protein in its native, functional configuration in any given cell locale. Also, when proteins are damaged by stressors, they must be restored to normality (native as opposed to denatured or unfolded—or misfolded—status) or eliminated if the damage is too pronounced beyond repair.

Stress proteins, particularly those that are molecular chaperones, play a key role not only in protein biogenesis and in restoring partially damaged proteins to a functional pool, as was described in the preceding sections, but they are also involved in eliminating molecules that cannot be recovered. For the latter purpose, stress proteins act in conjunction with proteases or exercise their own proteolytic power. Because of their dual role—assistance in the generation and recovery of polypeptides, as well as in their destruction—stress proteins are considered essential tools for the cell to maintain protein balance.

Proteins for degradation are normal or abnormal. On the normal sense, some proteins have a short life span; they are naturally unstable as required by their transient tasks inside the cell. Examples are transcription regulatory factors that need to be eliminated to downregulate the expression of certain genes. The same is true for some repressors; which have to be removed when the gene they regulate must be upregulated or induced. As mentioned earlier, many abnormal (denatured) proteins are generated by stress. In addition, abnormal proteins may appear in the cell in the absence of stress because of transcriptional, translational, and/or processing errors.

Whatever the case, unfit or unnecessary proteins must be eliminated or restored to a functional status; the cell must make a decision on whether to try to fold, refold, or degrade. In the latter alternative, the cell will be freed from junk and, at the same time, will be provided with building blocks to synthesize new molecules. Proteins destined to degradation must be recognized by proteases, and for this purpose they have tags that are "seen" by the proteolytic enzymes. Some molecular chaperones provide the tag and present the protein for degradation to the protease.

In conclusion, molecular chaperones not only assist in the generation of protein molecules, but also contribute to their elimination when they are potentially dangerous or no longer necessary to the cell.

See Also the Following Articles

Heat Shock Genes, Human; Heat Shock Proteins; Heat resistance; Heat Shock Response, Overview

Bibliography

Bukau, B., and Horwich, A. L. (1998). The hsp70 and hsp60 chaperone machines. *Cell* **92**, 351–366.

Caspers, G-J., Leunissen, J. A. M., and de Jong, W. W. (1995). The expanding small heat-shock protein family, and structure predictions of the conserved "α-crystallin domain." *J. Mol. Evol.* **40**, 238–248.

Craven, R. C., Tyson, J. R., and Stirling, C. L. (1997). A novel subfamily of Hsp70s in the endoplasmic reticulum. *Trends Cell Biol.* **7**, 277–282.

Cyr, D. M., Langer, T., and Douglas, M. G. (1994). DnaJ-like proteins: Molecular chaperones and specific regulators of Hsp70. *Trends Biochem. Sci.* **19**, 176–181.

Fisher, G., Tradler, T., and Zarnt, T. (1994). The mode of action of peptidyl prolyl *cis/trans* isomerases *in vivo*: Binding vs. catalysis. *FEBS Lett.* **426**, 17–20.

Hartl, F. U., and Martin, J. (1995). Molecular chaperones in cellular protein folding. *Curr. Opin. Struct. Biol.* **5**, 92–102.

Herman, C., and D'Ari, R. (1998). Proteolysis and chaperones: The destruction/reconstruction dilemma. *Curr. Opin. Microbiol.* **1**, 204–209.

Kelley, W. L. (1998). The J-domain family and the recruitment of chaperone power. *Trends Biochem. Sci.* **23**, 222–227.

Lee-Yoon, D., Easton, D., Murawski, M., Burd, R., and Subjeck, J. R. (1995). Identification of a major subfamily of large hsp70-like proteins through the cloning of the mammalian 110-kDa heat shock protein. *J. Biol. Chem.* **270**, 15725–15733.

Macario, A. J. L. (1995). Heat-shock proteins and molecular chaperones: Implications for pathogenesis, diagnostics, and therapeutics. *Int. J. Clin. Lab. Res.* **25**, 59–70.

Macario, A. J. L., Lange, M., Ahring, B. K., and Conway de Macario, E. (1999). Stress genes and proteins in archaea. *Microbiol. Mol. Biol. Rev.* **63**, 923–967.

Martin, J., and Hartl, F. U. (1997). Chaperone-assisted protein folding. *Curr. Opin. Struct. Biol.* **7**, 41–52.

Missiakas, D., Raina, S., and Georgopoulos, C. (1996). Heat shock regulation, *in* "Regulation of Gene expression in *Escherichia coli*" (E. C. C. Lin and A. S. Lynch, Eds.), pp. 481–501, Chapman and Hall, New York.

Morano, K. A., Liu, P. C. C., and Thiele, D. J. (1998). Protein chaperones and the heat shock response in *Saccharomyces cerevisiae*. *Curr. Opin. Microbiol.* **1**, 197–203.

Netzer, W. J., and Hartl, F. U. (1998). Protein folding in the cytosol: Chaperonin-dependent and -independent mechanisms. *Trends Biochem. Sci.* **23**, 68–73.

Obermann, W. M. J., Sondermann, H., Russo, A. A., Pavletich, N. P., and Hartl, F. U. (1998). In vivo function of Hsp90 is dependent on ATP binding and ATP hydrolysis. *J. Cell Biol.* **143**, 901–910.

Ranson, N. A., White, H. E., and Saibil, H. R. (1998). Chaperonins. *Biochem. J.* **333**, 233–242.

Richardson, A., Landry, S. J., and Georgopoulos, C. (1998). The ins and outs of a molecular chaperone machine. *Trends Biochem. Sci.* **23**, 138–143.

Ryan, M. T., Naylor, D. J., Hoj, P. B., Clark, M. S., and

Hoogenraad, N. J. (1997). The role of molecular chaperones in mitochondrial protein import and folding. *Int. Rev. Cytol.* **174**, 127–193.

Schlicher, T., and Soll, J. (1997). Chloroplastic isoforms of DnaJ and GrpE in pea. *Plant Mol. Biol.* **33**, 181–185.

Suzuki, C. K., Rep, M., van Dijl, J. M., Suda, K., Grivell, L. A., and Schatz, G. (1997). ATP-dependent proteases that also chaperone protein biogenesis. *Trends Biochem. Sci.* **22**, 118–123.

Van den Ussel, P., Norman, D. G., and Quinlan, R. A. (1999). Molecular chaperones: Small heat shock proteins in the limelight. *Curr. Biol.* **9**, R103–R105.

Waters, E. R., Lee, G. J., and Vierling, E. (1996). Evolution, structure and function of the small heat shock proteins in plants. *J. Exp. Bot.* **47**, 325–338.

Wimmer, B., Lottspeich, F., van der Klei, I., Veenhuis, M., and Gietl, C. (1997). The glyoxysomal and plastid molecular chaperones (70-kDa heat shock protein) of watermelon cotyledons are encoded by a single gene. *Proc. Natl. Acad. Sci. USA* **94**, 13624–13629.

Chernobyl, Stress Effects of

Lars Weisaeth

University of Oslo

I. The Chernobyl Accident: Somatic Health Consequences
II. Short-Term Stress Effects
III. Long-Term Stress Effects
IV. Short- and Long-Term Stress Effects in Far-Off Areas

GLOSSARY

etiology The study of the causes of disease.
pathogenesis Origination and development of a disease.
shock trauma Severe psychic experience, usually involving threat to life, for which the individual was totally unprepared.
thyroid gland An endocrine gland located in the base of the neck producing thyroxine.

I. THE CHERNOBYL ACCIDENT: SOMATIC HEALTH CONSEQUENCES

The nuclear reactor accident in Chernobyl, Ukraine, on April 26, 1986—the largest and most dangerous accident of its kind in the world until then—created acute, short-term, and long-term effects both locally and farther away. The officially reported death toll seems extremely low, 32 deaths during the initial fire-fighting period. Four years after the accident the increase in thyroid pathology started; a positive correlation was detected between the thyroid exposure dose of caesium-137, and the incidence of thyroid cancer in children and adolescents. Controversies are still going on regarding the number of deaths among the 600,000 "liquidators," with many heterogeneous subgroups including early involved firefighters and soldiers removing debris and building the sarcophagus over the wrecked reactor.

In Belarus, Ukraine, and Russia, five million people were exposed to low levels of ionizing radiation over an extended period of time. It has been important but difficult to make a clear distinction between the immediate and deferred direct effects arising from exposure to radiation and the possible indirect psychosomatic effects. Complex psychosomatic or somatopsychological processes may be at work. People in the affected areas naturally feared that they had been exposed to radiation that might cause future health damage.

The political strategy of the Soviet experts and authorities in the management of the postaccident situation involved "psychiatrization" ("blaming the victim") of the health consequences of the accident. For example, the term "radiophobia" was widely used already from 1986 to explain population reactions, despite evidence of objective reasons for a certain degree of fear.

II. SHORT-TERM STRESS EFFECTS

The explosion in the nuclear power plant contained the stressful stimuli typical of shock trauma. This is likely to produce acute stress reactions and later posttraumatic stress disorder (PTSD), a psychiatric disorder characterized by intrusive recollections and reliving of the trauma, and symptoms of avoidance and hyperarousal. Unlike the time-limited danger exposures carrying a high risk of PTSD, additional stressors inherent in the radioactive contamination were ongoing, future oriented, somatically based, and not confined to a single past event that could be processed by the senses.

The Chernobyl nuclear plant accident started a sequence of events that has continued to unfold over several years, thereby creating a situation of chronic stress. For the exposed, the Chernobyl nuclear accident had no clearly defined "low point" from which "things would gradually get better." Exposures to a high-risk environment, even when the feared consequence, such as cancer, may never materialize, elicit stress reactions that are influenced by individual per-

ceptions of the danger. The fear was aggravated by the lack of adequate information immediately after the accident.

Human contamination of the biosphere is a comparatively new type of crisis. Rather than merely an ecological and medical emergency, it was also a social and political crisis. In the affected regions covering thousands of square kilometers, a "culture of uncertainty" developed. The environmental contamination was not possible to see, hear, smell, taste, or touch. In a "silent disaster" it is impossible for humans to determine if and when they are being exposed, as they are totally dependent on experts for information. Because of the secretiveness of the Soviet authorities, news about the accident was released several days after the accident. Only then did the populations in nearby towns become aware of the radiation they had been exposed to and the entailing threat of long-term illness. These people were struck by fear and then by distrust in political authorities.

When people were evacuated from their homes, they suffered considerable stress because they were kept ignorant about what was going on. They underwent disruption in community infrastructure and social interaction and faced uncertainty about future housing and employment. Many evacuees who moved to new settlements were particularly depressed in their new homes because of financial difficulties, fear of isolation, and concern for the health of their children. The tense situation caused considerable stress, which, combined with the constant fear of health damage from the radioactive fallout, led to a rising number of health disorders being reported to local outpatient clinics.

People received late and reluctant information leading to widespread rumors. Until 30 months after the accident, Soviet authorities admitted contamination of only some villages. This obvious disinformation resulted in widespread indifference, denial of danger, and public distrust in government. People suffered from various symptoms frequently called "chronic radiation sickness," the exact definition of which remains to be described. Fatigue, loss of memory, loss of appetite, and psychosomatic symptoms were among the most frequently documented symptoms in the clinics. Similarly, in recent years, several authors have suggested that psychological factors may be involved in the etiology and pathogenesis of the health problems occuring after toxic exposure. A number of terms have been proposed to describe this syndrome: "chronic environmental stress syndrome," "informed of radioactive contamination syndrome," and "toxic stress syndrome."

III. LONG-TERM STRESS EFFECTS

The breakdown of the Soviet Union in 1989 increased the level of stress in affected populations dramatically. Added to the ecological crisis, chronic political, economic, military, social, and psychological crises introduced a cluster of stressors to ordinary men and women. Insecurity, unpredictability, and shortages in food and other life necessities caused severe hardships. Within this total situation of need, the relative importance of the Chernobyl problem was reduced. The numerous health problems reported by the local population of all ages are, however, attributed to the radioactivity. Even the fall of the Soviet Union has been attributed to the Chernobyl accident. However, problems in everyday life are so demanding that many people cannot muster the necessary energy to maintain adequate precautions concerning the radioactive contamination. Thus, attribution and indifference appear to be common stress reactions. Studies in the affected region have shown that the psychological impact of exposure to noxious agents has induced a wide range of health effects, including symptoms of anxiety, depression, nonspecific somatic complaints, especially fatigue and headaches, loss of concentration, subclinical physiological changes, increased illness awareness, lowered thresholds for illness roles, and increased help-seeking behaviors.

IV. SHORT- AND LONG-TERM STRESS EFFECTS IN FAR-OFF AREAS

Paradoxically, people in more remote areas—as far away as Norway and Sweden—were alarmed at a fairly early stage due to nuclear monitoring and Western news media. These countries received heavy fallout due to unfortunate wind direction and rain.

Reactions varied among public awareness, alarm, and shock. Studies have shown that an information crisis developed in the first weeks following the Chernobyl disaster. The information crisis resulted from a combination of factors: (1) the shortcoming of previous public education on the matter, (2) the shortage of reliable data on the location and concentration of the radioactive material, (3) the diffuse threat, ambiguous risk, and theoretical complexity of the subject, (4) the seeming contradiction between the health authorities assurance on the one hand that the radiation level was not dangerously high, whereas on the other hand some precautions had to be taken, (5) the experts' obvious difficulties in formulating simple information on complicated matters and statistical risks, and (6) the media focusing on conflicts, particularly between experts.

Although the majority of the population was psychologically affected by the crisis in that all but few had some reactions to it, only a small proportion (1–3%) seemed to have developed posttraumatic stress reactions of such a severity that they needed or sought help. Data analysis showed that the degree of exposure, sex, age, educational level, general threat perception, and previous mental health were associated both with information and with reaction variables. Women were significantly more alarmed than men.

From 1986 to 1993 there was a moderate trend toward better understanding of the media coverage, a better knowledge of how to protect oneself against radioactive fallout, and better preparedness and higher appreciation of the information providing guidance.

Immediate, simple, and reliable information to the public is of crucial importance in the management of silent disaster. It is therefore highly alarming that international comparative studies show striking discrepancies in the credibility of public information sources and various mass media. The poor rating of Russian information sources may pose severe problems in future Chernobyl-type accidents.

See Also the Following Articles

Nuclear Warfare, Threat of; Three Mile Island, Stress Effects of

Bibliography

Baum, A. 1986. Toxins, technology, disaster. *In* "Cataclysms, Crisis and Catastrophes: Psychology in Action" (G. R. Van den Bos and B. K. Bryant, eds.), pp. 9–53. American Psychological Association, Washington, DC.

Collins, D. L., and Carvalho, A. B. 1993. Chronic stress from the Goiania Cs radiation accident. *Behav. Med.* **18**, 149–157.

Davidson, L. M., Baum, A., and Collins, D. L. 1982. Stress and control related problems at Three Mile Island. *J. Appl. Soc. Psychol.* **12**, 349–359.

Dew, M. A., and Bromet, E. J. 1993. Predictors of temporal patterns of psychiatric distress during 10 years following the nuclear accident at Three Mile Island. *Soc. Psychiat. Epidemiol.* **28**, 49–55.

Girard, P., and Dubreuil, G. H. 1996. Stress in accident and post accident management at Chernobyl. *J. Radiol, Prot,* **16**, 167–180.

Green, B. L., Lindy, J. D., and Grace, M. C. 1994. Psychological effects of toxic contamination. *In* "Individual and Community Responses to Trauma and Disaster: The Structure of Human Chaos" (R. J. Ursano, B. G. McCaughey, and C. S. Fullerton, eds.) pp. 154–194. Cambridge Univ. Press, Cambridge.

Hansen, E., and Tønnessen, A. 1998. "Environment and Living Conditions on the Kola Peninsula." Fafo Institute for Applied Social Sciences and University of Oslo, Report 260.

Weisæth, L. 1991. Psychosocial reactions in Norway to nuclear fallout from the Chernobyl disaster. *In* "Communities at Risk. Collective Responses to Technological Hazards" (S. R. Couch and J. S. Kroll-Smith, eds.), pp. 53–80. Peter Lang, New York.

Weisæth, L., and Tønnessen, A. 1995. Public reactions in Norway to radioactive fallout. *Radiat. Prot. Dosimet.* **62**, 101–106.

World Health Organization. 1995. Health consequences of the Chernobyl accident. Results of the IPHECA pilot projects and related national programmes. Summary Report, WHO, Geneva.

Child Abuse

Cynthia Cupit Swenson and Cora E. Ezzell

Medical University of South Carolina

I. Child Physical Abuse
II. Child Sexual Abuse
III. Child Neglect

GLOSSARY

failure to thrive In infancy this is indicated by a growth delay with postural signs (poor muscle tone, persistence of infantile postures) and behavioral signs (unresponsive, minimal smiling, few vocalizations) and may be a result of child neglect.

posttraumatic stress disorder (*PTSD*) Occurs in up to half of children who have been sexually or physically abused. Adults who were abused as children may also experience PTSD. Key features of PTSD are reexperiencing intrusive memories about the abuse (e.g., having nightmares, think- ing about it when you don't want to), avoiding things that remind the individual of the abuse (e.g., the bedroom, smell of a certain cologne), and hyperarousal (e.g., being easily startled). Additional symptoms of PTSD may include extreme anxiety, repetitively reenacting the abuse (e.g., children sometimes reenact with dolls, stuffed animals), extreme anger, and isolation.

shaken baby syndrome Refers to an injury to the brain of an infant that results from vigorous shaking. Shaken baby syndrome is a form of physical abuse and often results in death to the child.

I. CHILD PHYSICAL ABUSE

Child physical abuse involves physical injury of a child under age 18 by an adult and includes signs such as bruises, welts, cuts, broken bones, burns, skull fractures, poisoning, internal injuries of soft tissue and organs and injuries to the bone or joint.

A. Epidemiology

Many parents in the United States use corporal punishment (slapping, hitting, or spanking) as a means of correcting their children. In some cases physical punishment crosses the line and becomes physical abuse. According to figures gathered by government agencies, annually over 1 million children experience physical abuse by an adult. National telephone surveys by researchers in the mental health field indicate that as many as 13% of children reported experiencing a physical assault by a family member and as many as 33% endorsed a physical assault by someone outside the family.

B. Etiology

A broad body of research indicates that whether a child is at risk of physical abuse is determined by multiple factors. These include parent factors, child factors, family factors, and social network factors. Parent factors related to the risk of physical abuse include health problems, substance abuse, depression, poor impulse control, deficits in knowledge of child development, authoritarian parenting, low involvement with the child, and having a history of family violence. It should be noted that experiencing physical abuse as a child does not cause later perpetration of abuse. Approximately one-third of parents who were physically abused as children later abuse their own child. Although children do not cause adults to abuse them, child factors such as aggression, noncompliance, and difficult temperament in infancy may increase a parent's stress level, thus increasing the risk for abusive management of the behavior. Family factors that increase the abuse risk include marital conflict, an unsatisfactory marital relationship, and domestic violence. A supportive marital or partner relationship may reduce the risk for physical abuse. Last, a number of social network factors may increase the risk of abuse. Physically abusive families are generally socially isolated. Parents have limited contact with friends and general dissatisfaction with their social network. The isolation extends beyond immediate friends in that physically abusive parents have low use of community resources and little involvement in community activities.

C. Medical and Mental Health Effects of Child Physical Abuse

Medically, child physical abuse injuries vary from mild trauma such as bruising or redness, to more severe trauma such as broken bones, brain injury, or death. Research has shown that 10% of injuries of children seen in an emergency department are due to child abuse. Mental health effects of child physical abuse include behavioral and emotional symptoms. Not every physically abused child will experience all of the effects, as they differ by child and by abuse experience. In fact, some physically abused children may not show mental health difficulties. Among the difficulties experienced, physical aggression toward peers, siblings, and adults is the most common. Some physically abused children show limited skills for problem-solving and for developing relationships with others. Trauma-related emotional symptoms may result and include difficulties such as fear, anxiety, low-self esteem, depression, and PTSD. The emotional and behavioral symptoms resulting from child physical abuse may endure into adulthood and leave individuals at risk of substance abuse, depression, and committing violent crimes.

D. Treatment Approaches

To reduce child symptoms related to abuse and the risk of reabuse, psychosocial treatment may be indicated. Although many existing treatments focus on helping the parent or the child, the child abuse field is moving toward more comprehensive treatments that include the parent, child, family, and other people (e.g., minister, teacher) who are important to helping reduce abuse risk. As noted earlier in Section I,B, child physical abuse is related to multiple factors. As such, it seems that addressing all those factors (i.e., parent, child, family, social network) is key to resolving the problem. For the parent, treatment may involve teaching appropriate expectations for the child's age, managing anger, stopping substance abuse, or working to relieve depression. For the child, treatment may involve reducing anxiety related to memories or fears of the abuse, managing anger, developing ways to make friends, problem-solving, improving school performance, and resolving conflicts with peers or adults. For the family, treatment may focus on improving family relations, developing nonphysical ways to manage anger in the household (e.g., calm down then talk it out), and getting involved with people in the community or other social networks.

II. CHILD SEXUAL ABUSE

Child sexual abuse can be physical, verbal, or visual and includes the following: sexual touching and fondling; exposing children to adult sexual activity or pornographic movies and photographs; having children pose, undress, or perform in a sexual fashion on film or in person; "peeping" into bathrooms or bedrooms to spy on a child; and/or sexual penetration or attempted penetration.

A. Epidemiology

The actual prevalence of sexual abuse is difficult to determine due to the low rates of reporting and the nature of child disclosure (i.e., initial denial is common). National surveys, that involve directly interviewing a random sample in the general population rather than statistics reported to agencies indicate that very young children as well as older teenagers can be victims of sexual abuse. Retrospective data from these surveys suggest that from 32 to 38% of females and 13 to 16% of males reported that they experienced sexual abuse prior to age 18.

B. Etiology

At present no particular profile predicts which individuals are likely to sexually abuse children. Sexual offenders may be adolescents or adults. As with other forms of maltreatment, sexual abuse appears related to more than characteristics of the individual offender. That is, sexual abuse relates to multiple interacting factors. The majority of research on etiology has focused on offender characteristics. Individuals who sexually abuse children are more likely to exhibit depression, a history of committing nonsexual crimes, reduced social skills, and interpersonal isolation than nonsexual offenders. Although clinical literature often presents sexual offenders as having a history of their own victimization, research indicates that the majority do not have this history. Other factors that relate to sexual abuse include relationship to the victim and family factors. Contrary to popular opinion, sexual abuse is least likely to be committed by a stranger to the child and most likely to be committed by a family member, neighbor, caregiver, other relative, friend, and/or acquaintance. Family factors may differ for adolescent and adult offenders. Families of adolescent sexual offenders evince relatively low warmth and cohesion and high rates of parental difficulties such as substance abuse and spousal violence. The reader must keep in mind that although these multiple factors relate to sexual abuse, whether they are causative is unknown at present.

C. Medical and Mental Health Effects of Child Sexual Abuse

No single sign or behavior definitively indicates that a child has been sexually abused. Although physical evidence (e.g., sexually transmitted disease) is often conclusive of abuse, this evidence occurs in only about 15% of child abuse cases. Moreover, one-fourth to one-half of sexually abused children display no immediate symptoms. Nonetheless, sexual abuse can clearly impact children's mental health in a wide variety of ways and behavioral or emotional symptoms depend on the child's age and development. Preschool-aged children are more likely to show anxiety, nightmares, PTSD, internalizing (e.g., depression) and externalizing (e.g., aggression) behaviors, and sexual acting-out. School-aged children are more likely to experience fears, aggression, and school problems. Adolescents are more prone to depression, withdrawal from others, suicidal attempts, somatic complaints, illegal acts, and substance abuse. Many of these symptoms persist into adulthood and may intensify with additional life stressors.

D. Treatment Approaches

Although limited treatment research exists for sexual abuse victims or offenders, current literature is pointing toward the importance of including the child, parent, and family in the treatment. To address the difficulties children may experience, treatment components deal directly with the specific symptom. Typical components of child treatment are (a) psychoeducation regarding who is responsible for the abuse (the offender), common mental health effects related to abuse, typical course of symptoms, and general knowledge regarding sexuality; (b) cognitive restructuring to correct any misconceptions they may have about the abuse (e.g., "I am ruined for life"); (c) relaxation strategies to manage anxiety; and (d) exposure techniques to break the link between anxiety and reminders of the abuse.

For nonoffending parents, treatment may include strategies such as psychoeducation and coping (i.e., similar to that conducted with the child), communication with the child about the sexual abuse, behavior management, and how to believe and support the child. For some nonoffending parents, psychosocial problems such as depression, their own abuse history, or substance abuse may need to be addressed.

For sexual offenders, treatment is often individual or group and commonly covers components such as masturbatory satiation and arousal conditioning, covert sensitization, cognitive restructuring, sex education, social skills training, biofeedback, and relapse prevention. Although research is limited, current studies indicate some promise for cognitive behavioral treatment with adult offenders. For adolescent offenders, community-and-family-based treatment programs show promise. Including the whole family in treatment is important to getting the abuse out in the open, discussing it, having the offender take responsibility, and having all family members participate in a plan for reducing risk and preventing relapse.

III. CHILD NEGLECT

Child neglect includes omissions in the care of a child that result in harm or risk of harm to the child. Neglectful parental behaviors include failure to provide medical or mental health care, failure to provide adequate food or clothing, neglect of the home, and allowing dirty clothing and poor personal hygiene.

A. Epidemiology

Child neglect is the most common form of maltreatment, accounting for 45 to 55% of reported cases and leading to one-third of all child deaths. Reported to affect over a million children annually, child neglect rates are likely underestimated because neglect leaves no visible injury and may be undetected.

B. Etiology

As with child physical abuse, neglect is determined by multiple factors. Substance abuse is a major parental factor involved in neglect. High rates of depression also characterize neglectful parents. Irritable temperament may make interacting with the infant unpleasant and stressful for a parent, increasing the risk of neglect. Neglectful families receive little support for managing stress as they tend to be socially isolated families headed by a single parent. In families with two parents, domestic violence increases the risk of neglect.

C. Medical and Mental Health Effects of Child Neglect

The medical effects of neglect will depend on the nature of the neglect. Children who are not provided adequate physical care may suffer injuries due to accidents or delays in growth and physical development, such as failure to thrive. Medical complications may occur when a child suffers medical neglect. Most commonly, medical neglect involves noncompliance with health care. In addition, neglected children have been found to exhibit delays in cognitive functioning such as language and academics. Last, delays in social and behavioral development of neglected children may start in infancy with an avoidant or resistant attachment to the caregiver. As these children grow they may show less affection than nonneglected children, isolative play, withdrawn behavior, and an increased risk for delinquency and criminal activity.

D. Treatment Approaches

Given that the occurrence of child neglect relates to multiple factors (i.e., parent, child, family, social network), treatment of the problem calls for a comprehensive approach to address all those factors. It is surprising that the form of child maltreatment that occurs the most often, neglect, has received little research attention. For infants, the emphasis will need to be on improving basic care and physical affection with the baby and understanding child development. For young children through adolescents, treatment may focus on increasing family interactions, monitoring of the child, and setting family rules and limits. Certainly, significant parent problems such as substance abuse and depression must be treated to enable parents to parent.

See Also the Following Articles

Childhood Stress; Domestic Violence; Sexual Assault

Bibliography

Briere, J., Berliner, L., Bulkley, J. A., Jenny, C., and Reid, T. (1996). "The APSAC Handbook on Child Maltreatment." Thousand Oaks, CA, Sage.

Crouch, J. L., and Milner, J. S. (1993). Effects of child neglect on children. *Crim. Justice Behav.* 20, 49–65.

Finkelhor, D., and Dziuba-Leatherman, J. (1994). Children as victims of violence: A national survey. *Pediatrics* 94, 413–420.

Kendall-Tackett, K. A., Williams, L. M., and Finkelhor, D. (1993). Impact of sexual abuse on children: A review and synthesis of recent empirical studies. *Psychol. Bull.* 113, 164–180.

Swenson, C. C., and Hanson, R. F. (1998). Sexual abuse of children: Assessment, research and treatment. *In* "Handbook of Child Abuse Research and Treatment" (J. R. Lutzer, Ed.), pp. 475–497. New York, Plenum.

Swenson, C. C., Henggeler, S. W., Kaufman, K. L., Schoenwald, S. K., and Randall, J. (1998). Changing the social ecologies of adolescent sexual offenders: Implications of the success of multisystemic therapy in treating serious antisocial behavior in adolescents. *Child Maltreatment* 3, 330–338.

Swenson, C. C., and Kolko, D. J. (in press). Long-term management of the developmental consequences of child physical abuse. *In* "The Treatment of Child Abuse" (R. Reece, Ed.).

Childhood Stress

Seija Sandberg

Helsinki University Hospital, Finland

I. Definitions of Stress
II. Measurement of Stress
III. Effects of Stress
IV. Specific Forms of Stress

GLOSSARY

contextual threat The level of threat caused or implied by the life event to an average child of the same age, sex, and biographical characteristics as the child in question. Thus, it is simultaneously an objective and personalized measure.

life event Any event or circumstance occurring in the life of a child that may have the potential of altering his or her present state of mental or physical health.

long-term psychosocial experiences Ongoing processes where delineation of a beginning and end stage is not always possible. They may be adverse (e.g., parental marital disharmony or financial hardship) or desirable hedonically positive, or socially required for normal development, or for protection against negative experiences (e.g., supportive relationship with a parent or having a close friend).

modifier A variable, aspect or characteristic that exerts modifier effects on risk. If the risk is intensified then the variable carries a vulnerability effect, if the risk is diminished then the variable carries a protective effect.

negative events Life events exerting a particular undesirable impact on a child.

positive events Life events that are hedonically positive, enhance self esteem, or have a beneficial effect on child's life circumstances.

stress, stressor, and stress reaction A form of stimulus, an inferred inner state, and an observable response reaction, respectively.

I. DEFINITIONS OF STRESS

A. Stress, Stressor, and Stress Reaction

The word stress, as originally applied in physics, refers to a constraining, deforming, or distorting force or pressure. The distortion in the stressed object is called strain. The relatively new word stressor is used to refer to causal stress. To encompass both meanings, stressor and strain, child stress can be defined as any intrusion into children's normal physical or psychosocial life experiences that acutely or chronically unbalances physiological or psychological equilibrium, threatens security or safety, or distorts physical or psychological growth/development and the psychophysiological consequences of such intrusion or distortion.

B. Harmful vs Beneficial Stress

The traditional view of stress as a significant discrepancy between the demands of a situation and the organism's capability to respond, resulting in detrimental consequences, implies that all stress is harmful. However, as far as children are concerned, the opposite is sometimes true. Mild stressors are often benign and sometimes even growth-promoting.

C. Additive and Synergistic Stress

Apart from their individual effects, stressors can also act additively and synergistically. For example, deprivation and malnutrition can each compound fetal alcohol effects. Even the same cause can stress the child through two or more different mechanisms. Thus, maternal alcoholism can stress the fetal brain chemically and then psychologically stress the newborn infant through maternal unavailability, neglect, or abuse. Poverty can stress the child through malnutrition, inadequate environmental stimulation, and poor parenting due to worry, preoccupation, and discouragement.

II. MEASUREMENT OF STRESS

A. Chronic Stress

There exists a variety of questionnaire and interview measures for the assessment of chronic stress in childhood, usually stemming from enduring adverse circumstances such as environmental deprivation, parental unemployment or illness, and family discord or criminality. Also, the two widely used diagnostic schedules, the DSM-IV and the ICD-10, contain a separate axis for systematic measurement of stressors of likely relevance for children's mental health.

B. Life Events

1. Questionnaires

The first generation of measures of stress in childhood were based on the questionnaire format to provide overall scores of degree of life change. The assumption was that change per se, not necessarily the unpleasant nature of the experiences, was stressful for children. In parallel with these overall approaches, numerous studies of specific life events such as family break-up, bereavement, and disasters such as floods, earthquakes, or hijacking were carried out.

2. Interview Measures

a. The Meaning of Life Experiences The realization that it was necessary to take into account the social context of life events in order to assess their meaning and hence their stressful quality constituted perhaps the most significant research advance. The clear implication of this was that interviews rather than questionnaire approaches were needed for adequate assessment of life events.

b. Undesirability, Cognitive Appraisal, and Independence   A major reappraisal of psychosocial stress research involved the emphasis on the need to differentiate between desirable and undesirable life changes and highlighting the role of cognitive appraisal of the events. Other major advances involve the focus on the distinction between events that could have been brought about by the person's own actions stemming from psychiatric disorder and those that are independent of disorder.

c. Contextual Threat   Ratings of contextual threat have by now become the standard measure of the "objective but personalized" impact of life events in research on adults and are increasingly also employed in child studies.

III. EFFECTS OF STRESS

A. Developmental Interferences

1. Physical Development

The ill effects of compromised prenatal, perinatal, and early postnatal care on the child's development and well-being have been recognized for at least half a century. For example, a complex relationship exists between prematurity, illness, and outcome in which environmental factors play a central role. Likewise, children who fail to thrive demonstrate an intricate interplay between caloric and protein intake, touch, and the release of growth hormone.

2. Neurodevelopment

a. Neuroanatomy   The brain develops sequentially from brain stem to cortex and operates in a hierarchical manner. It is also organized by use: to develop properly, undifferentiated neuronal systems are dependent on environmental cues such as neurochemical and hormonal factors. These factors in turn are dependent on the child's sensory experiences. A narrow window appears to exist during which specific experiences are required for the optimal development of a brain area. After birth no new neurons are formed and brain development consists of an ongoing process of wiring and rewiring. Early experiences can cause the final number of these synapses to decrease or increase. The brain also operates in a use-dependent fashion; only the frequently activated connections are retained. Infants who just sit in their cribs and have little opportunity to explore or experiment and who are rarely spoken to may fail to develop neural pathways that facilitate later learning.

Neurotransmitters and hormones play a major role in neuronal migration and differentiation and synaptic proliferation; massive increases in catecholamine activity caused by prolonged or severe stressors is expected to have a significant impact on brain development. The hippocampus is a likely target for the effects of early stress because neurogenesis in this area continues to postnatal life. The amygdaloid nuclei are critically involved in the formation of emotional memory and in stress-induced memory enhancement. They are also some of the most sensitive areas of the brain for the development of kindling, a process whereby repeated stimulus produces greater and greater alteration in neuron excitability. Repeated traumatization of a child may lead to limbic kindling. Experience can challenge the mature brain; during critical periods in early childhood it can organize brain systems—nurture becomes nature. This makes it more appropriate to speak of early childhood malleability than resilience.

b. Neurophysiology   When a child is exposed to a strong stressor a series of interactive, complicated neurophysiological reactions take place in the brain, the autonomic nervous system, the hypothalamus-pituitary-adrenocortical axis, and in the immunosystem, with a concomitant release of stress hormones. Neurophysiological activation during acute stress is usually rapid and reversible. When the stressor is more prolonged, however, these changes may no longer be reversible. Stress-induced sensitization occurs with the systems underlying the stress-response becoming more sensitive to future stressful events. Children growing up in a persistently threatening environment develop stress response systems in midbrain and brainstem areas that are overreactive and hypersensitive. This may be highly adaptive, but only as long as the child remains in a violent, chaotic environment. Profound cognitive disturbances can accompany this process.

Some young children, especially girls, however, react in the opposite way by freezing rather than by becoming visibly anxious or hyperactive. Flooding of adrenocortical hormones during periods of acute stress may also have negative consequences on memory and the anatomical substrates of memory.

3. Psychological Development

a. Cognitive Development Persistent environmental stress and deprivation can significantly impair the development of the child's cognitive abilities, including attention skills, memory, and language as well as intellectual capabilities. In addition, a child's level of cognitive development is an important determinant of how he or she will deal with trauma. Ability to label and express feelings, to receive reality-based feedback, and to incorporate the experience into a narrative are relevant developmental achievements.

b. Emotional Development Because a child's most pressing emotional needs change over time, a particular trauma may have more influence during one stage of development than during another, and the same trauma may be differently interpreted at different times.

B. Mental Health Effects

A range of research strategies have demonstrated beyond all reasonable doubt that psychosocial factors exercise a causal effect on children's psychosocial functioning and also that they contribute in a major way to the multifactorial causation of psychiatric disorders in childhood. In this respect, the main risk stems from chronic psychosocial adversity such as unhappy family life, parental psychopathology (including substance abuse and criminality), parental stress stemming from poverty or unemployment, or being the victim of bullying or other victimization. Acute stressful life events, especially those that carry long-term threat to the psychological security of the child add to the risk caused by chronic stressors or in some instances constitute sufficient risk in their

own right. Their main effect, however, appears to serve as determining the timing of a new episode of disorder in a child already at risk due to chronic stress or made vulnerable through lack of emotional support.

1. Individual Differences

There are large individual differences in children's response to life experiences. A major reason for this may lie in the crucial importance of the personal meaning of the particular experience involved. In addition, previous experiences are likely to color a person's reaction to a new experience. Stressful life events can be strengthening as well as weakening; they can "steel" as well as "sensitize." Other factors determining individual differences are the child's age, sex, temperament, locus of control, and family support.

2. Additivity of Stressful Experiences

There is no doubt that a single major life event such as bereavement or shipwreck can be quite sufficient on its own to lead to psychiatric disorder. However, it also appears that there is a cumulative, or even potentiating, effect when several major life events occur together during a short period of time. Furthermore, the potentiating effect of chronic adversities on the stressful impact of acute life events and the multiplicative effect of the cooccurrence of several chronic adversities has been demonstrated in children.

3. Potentiation of Stress

Chronic adverse circumstances such as unhappy family life, parental psychopathology, substance abuse or criminality, economic hardship or stressors in the school environment all increase the risk for child psychiatric disorder in themselves. Their presence also makes it much more likely that acute stressful events will occur, often directly stemming from the ongoing adversity. Discord leading to divorce or criminality resulting in a jail sentence, from the child's point of view, both involve separation from a parent. Apart from increasing the likelihood of stressful life events occurring, chronic adversity is also prone to potentiate their adverse effects.

4. Vulnerability and Protective Mechanisms

There also exist complex vulnerability and protective mechanisms, i.e., those that increase and those that decrease stress effects. These include interactions, not just main effects. Such mechanisms need to be considered in relation to the child's individual characteristics as well as to their experiential properties.

5. Beneficial Stress

There are both beneficial and harmful stress experiences. The distinction is likely to lie in the child's temperamental qualities and in how the particular past experience has been coped with. This has implications for the prevention of children's mental health problems. This is likely to lie only partly in the avoidance of stressors and very largely in helping children to overcome negative experiences. The overcoming of stress can be strengthening: ensuring that children encounter stressors at times and in ways that make it more likely that they will come out on top with a sense of accomplishment rather than with feelings of fear and humiliation.

6. Positive Experiences as Protectors

The evidence available so far fails to support the notion that hedonically positive events and life situations would have an ameliorating effect on psychiatric risk. However, a supportive confiding relationship with adults appears to be important in counteracting the harmful effect of children's stressors.

7. Mediating Mechanisms

There are a number of mechanisms through which psychosocial stressors lead to psychiatric disorder. Some acute life events bring about lasting adverse alterations in life circumstances. Examples include bereavement and parental divorce. Thus, for a child, the ill effects stemming from the loss of parent are highly dependent on whether the loss is associated with family discord or leads to serious impairment in parenting. Loss that does not have these adverse sequelae may be painful at the time, but usually remains of limited significance as a causal factor for persisting psychiatric disorder. Besides, discordant family relationships lead to psychiatric disorder in the absence of any identifiable life event. Stress may

be also associated with loss that is only in the person's mind. The mechanism of cognitive threat is a likely possibility. Young children, for example, appraise their situation and contemplate their life circumstances in ways that differ from those typical of adults.

Recurrent hospital admission is a known stressor in young children with the key mediating mechanisms being the disturbed parent–child relationship engendered by the child's behavior upon the return home. A similar situation concerns the birth of a sibling. Here the disturbance of the prior parent–child relationship is more important, suggesting that the main stress for the child may reside in the parental reaction rather than in the child's response to the event as such.

8. Chain Events

In relation to children, it is also important to consider mediating mechanisms in long-term consequences, i.e., how adverse early experiences influence later psychosocial functioning. Here the sequelae frequently depend on chain events that involve a number of different links reflecting separate psychological mechanisms such as learned maladaptive emotional responses, self-perpetuating behavior patterns or habits, lowered self-esteem influencing the ability to deal with future experiences, inadequate coping skills, internal working models of insecure relationships, or behavior that serves to shape later environments or increase the individual's exposure to stressful life events.

9. Turning Points

Turning points in development is another issue likely to affect long-term sequelae of childhood stress. The concept of a turning point refers to an experience either internal (as with puberty) or external (as with dropping off at school) that carries with it the potential for enduring change because the experience either closes doors or opens up opportunities or because it is associated with a lasting alteration in important life circumstances. Most turning points concern very ordinary life experiences, but, in each case, the particular individual circumstances are crucial. Therefore, life events need to be conceived not just in terms of their threat features, but also in terms of their effects on the person's social group and life opportunities.

C. Psychosomatic Responses

Psychosomatic symptom development represents the body's response to prolonged or frequent attempts to maintain homeostasis. Children's psychosomatic responses range from recurrent abdominal pain and headaches to failure to thrive. Also, stress-induced exacerbations in asthma, diabetes, colitis, and rheumatoid arthritis are well-known. The choice of the somatic manifestation is likely to be influenced by a combination of genetic predisposition and learned patterns of behavior.

IV. SPECIFIC FORMS OF STRESS

A. Prenatal Stress

Prenatal stress appears to be one environmental factor that can affect neurobiology of the neonate so that it responds to common events and stimuli differently than if it had remained unstressed. Chronic unpredictable psychological stress during pregnancy may have long-lasting effects on brain activity and behavior in the offspring. Prenatal effects on fetal neurobiological development are easily confused with genetic predisposition. Future research to determine how prenatal environmental effects contribute to persisting and trait-like organization of neurobiological systems will markedly further our understanding of how genetic and postnatal environmental factors play a role in the expression of developmental psychopathology.

Prenatal stress most likely has diffuse rather than specific effects on developing brain mechanisms. It may influence the way in which the neonate responds to his/her environment and to the caregiver. The neonate may, for example, be more fussy and difficult, affecting how the caregiver is able to cope. Thus, prenatal stress appears to set the infant's neurobiology into state in which vital attachments are hard to achieve and adverse experiences more likely. The adverse experiences can in turn result in further neurobiological deflection of development.

B. Trauma Response

Traumatic events impact structures in the central nervous system—though the exact mechanism of this remains unknown at present. Structures underlying cognitive, affective, sensory, integrative, regulatory, neuroendocrine, and motor functions are coordinated in the life-threat response. This may allow neuronal networks, excited during a life threatening event, to become identified for later potentiation, thus forming the basis for permanent registration in memory.

In younger children whose brains are maturing in use-dependent interaction with their environment, aspects of such memory states may become lifelong traits. Children using a dissociative adaptive defense in an acute response to trauma later demonstrate primarily dissociative or somatic symptoms. On the other hand, children who use primarily hyperarousal adaptation acutely have more chronic hyperarousal symptoms, such as startle response, anxiety, motor hyperactivity, sleep disturbance, or tachycardia.

C. Death of a Parent

Of all the life stresses a child might experience, the death of a parent seems most devastating, the loss least reparable, and the potential for harmful psychological consequences greatest. Parental death during childhood has been implicated in the development of immediate, delayed, and long-term psychiatric morbidity. However, results have been mixed in studies that retrospectively examine bereavement as a vulnerability factor for depressive disorders in adult life.

There is a good deal of consensus about several aspects of childhood bereavement. These include the high likelihood of mood disturbance, especially in the first few months. Symptoms of both depression and anxiety predominate. However, the symptom severity for the majority of bereaved children does not reach a clinical level, and in most there will be a natural decrement in overt symptoms even during the first year. In younger children regressive behaviors including tantrums, night fears, separation difficulties, and clinginess predominate. Older children frequently react with scholastic problems, while in adolescents there may be mixed symptoms of anger, depression, or delinquency. In all cases, the reaction of the surviving parent is crucial for how the child will cope.

D. Parental Divorce

Specific differences in young persons' responses to parental divorce have been identified based on developmental stages. Preschool children typically respond with regression in recently attained developmental accomplishments. Enuresis, disturbed sleep, and clinging behavior are examples of this. Still functioning at a preoperational level of cognitive development, they are prone to feelings of guilt for having caused the divorce. Young elementary-school children show deterioration in their school functioning. Because of cognitive limitations and/or denial, they may not view divorce as permanent and may hold on to elaborate reunion fantasies. Older children frequently display high levels of anger directed at one parent or the other as they struggle to understand the causes of the divorce and their need to focus blame on someone or something. Adolescents typically react with strong emotions such as intense anger or depression, even suicidal ideation. Some, however, channel their reactions and take on additional responsibility for the younger siblings, for example. Most children remain with their mother after divorce. In this situation, boys tend to fare less well and usually benefit from remarriage. Thus, a father figure's presence and influence seems necessary for optimum cognitive development, analytical thinking, and assertiveness in boys. A daughter's need for father, although not as immediately obvious, surfaces in adolescence and is apparently not easily satisfied by stepfathers, with whom stepdaughters often have conflicts.

E. Child Abuse

An act of violence by a parent or trusted caretaker that causes pain, potential disfigurement, and lack of confidence in the ability or motivation of that adult to provide protection is stressful to a dependent child, threatening their security and safety. Compared with physical abuse, emotional abuse and ne-glect are more difficult to define, with the instances of emotional abuse being the least likely to be recognized and reported. Also, neglect of a dependent child may be as dangerous as physical abuse. To be stressful, the insult does not even need to be aimed directly at the child. Passively witnessing home violence, verbal or physical, can also stress the child. The child who has been abused suffers from the acute consequences of the event, which in physical abuse are manifested externally as bruises, burns, or lacerations, and internally as hemorrhages, ruptures, and fractures. Chronic abuse leads to chronic stress from anticipation of future attacks, often leaving the child in a persistent state of anxiety for as long as the offending agent remains in the immediate environment. The typical runaway child is likely to come from an abusive family, indicating that stresses of the home environment may be more intense than the uncertainties and potential misfortunes of life on the street.

Posttraumatic Stress Disorder (PTSD) has been proposed as one model for the long-term manifestations of child sexual abuse. Children's initial reactions to abuse may not predict their future effects. The child who has handled the stress through denial may be unable to make the association if the abuse is discovered much later.

The most recently recognized form of child abuse is Munchausen's Syndrome by Proxy (MSBP), which results when the parent intentionally causes a condition in a child in order to deceive the physician. Lasting harm may result from both the actions of the abusing parent, more frequently the mother, and from the medical interventions aimed at diagnosis and treatment. The consequences of MSBP include dwarfing of psychological development at the very level of basic parental trust. Behavioral responses include feeding difficulties, withdrawal, hyperactivity, and various somatic complaints.

F. Poverty, Deprivation, and Discrimination

Children are also stressed by events in the world outside the family. Such stressors include, for example, poverty, environmental deprivation, and discrimination. Poverty, often stemming from parental unemployment or illness, reduces family resources such as diet, clothing, medical care, education, and recreation. The ensuing reduction in peer acceptance may be particularly stressful to children in those circumstances. Discrimination, whether it occurs in the form of racism, ethnic prejudice, or other forms of social exclusion, almost invariably has pernicious influence on a child. The amount of stress experience is, however, also determined by the child's personality, coping skills, and available support.

G. Community Violence and War

Like other traumatic stress, war and terrorism may comprise a number of stressors including separation, deprivation, fear, physical danger, and loss of control. The child is knocked out of his accustomed routine and in some cases is deliberately separated from his or her home or family. The child's reaction to the stressful event may also be heavily influenced by the reactions of adults around. When the experience has a strong personal connotation—in the form of direct contact with the war or terrorist or if the child has sustained a significant loss—the likelihood of psychiatric disorder is considerable. Feelings of guilt, psychic numbing, and an indelible image of the destructive event are common in children surviving disasters. Anxiety, sleep problems, emotional lability, forgetfulness, and disturbed orientation often linger for some time.

See Also the Following Articles

Adolescence; Child Abuse

Bibliography

Arnold, L. E. (1990). "Childhood Stress." Wiley, New York.

Author (1994). "American Psychiatric Association: Diagnostic and Statistical Manual of Mental Disorders," 4th Ed. (DSM-IV). American Psychiatric Association, Washington, D.C.

Coddington, R. D. (1972). The significance of life events as aetiological factors in the diseases of children. I. A study of professionals. *J. Psychosom. Res.* **16**, 7–18.

Garmezy, N., and Rutter, M. (1983). "Stress, Coping and Development in Children." McGraw–Hill, New York.

Goodyer, I. (1990). "Life Experiences, Development and Psychopathology." Wiley, Chichester, UK.

Perry, B. D. (1996). "Maltreated Children, Brain Development and the Next Generation." Norton, New York.

Rutter, M., and Sandberg, S. (1992). Psychosocial stressors: concepts, causes and effects. *Eur. Child Adol. Psychiatr.* **1**, 3–13.

Sandberg, S., Rutter, M., Giles, S., Owen, A., Champion, L., Nicholls, J., Prior, V., McGuinness, D., and Drinnan, D. (1993). Assessment of psychosocial experiences in childhood: Methodological issues and some illustrative findings. *J. Child Psychol. Psychiatr.* **34**, 879–897.

World Health Organization (1992). "International Classification of Diseases," 10th Revision. World Health Organization, Geneva.

Child Sexual Abuse

Judith A. Cohen

MCP-Hahnemann University School of Medicine

I. DEFINITION AND EPIDEMIOLOGY

Child sexual abuse is not a clinical disorder or diagnosis in itself. It is rather a variety of events or experiences to which there may be a wide range of behavioral and emotional responses. In this sense, sexual abuse is best conceptualized as a life stressor rather than as a distinct clinical entity. The legal definition of child sexual abuse varies from state to state and there is little consensus regarding what acts constitute sexual abuse among mental health care providers. A common operational definition of sexual abuse is sexual exploitation involving physical contact between a child and another person. Exploitation implies an inequality of power between the child and the abuser, on the basis of age, physical size, and/or the nature of the emotional relationship. Physical contact includes anal, genital, oral, or breast contact. This definition obviously encompasses a number of different behaviors; sexual abuse is therefore not a unitary phenomenon.

It is difficult to know the exact incidence and prevalence of sexual abuse in our society because most sexual abuse is not reported immediately, and sometimes it is never reported. The Third National Incidence Study on Child Abuse and Neglect estimated that more than 300,000 children were sexually abused in the United States in 1993. However, this study includes only reported cases of sexual abuse. This is probably an underestimation of the frequency of sexual abuse, as there is evidence that only about one-fifth of true abuse cases are actually reported.

Although sexual abuse occurs across religious, racial, and socioeconomic lines, several factors may put children at higher risk for sexual abuse. There is some controversy over the relationship between social class and child sexual abuse. Some researchers have found that reported cases of sexual abuse have come predominantly from families in the lower socioeconomic levels of society, but other studies have not supported this relationship. It is likely that this apparent relationship is due to a reporting bias because economically disadvantaged families are more likely to be scrutinized by social service agencies.

Other risk factors for child sexual abuse identified by Finkelhor and Barron include a poor relationship between the child and parent; having a stepfather (which in itself appeared to more than double a girl's vulnerability to sexual abuse); having a mother who worked outside the home or who was emotionally distant or often ill; and having a mother or father who did not live with the child for a period of time. As noted previously, gender is also a risk factor for child sexual abuse, with girls being at higher risk than boys. Finkelhor also identified several factors that did *not* appear to be correlated with sexual abuse. For example, physical abuse was not associated with sexual abuse. Religion, ethnic background, family size, crowding, and alcohol abuse by either parent were also *not* found to be risk factors for sexual abuse in this study.

II. SYMPTOMATOLOGY

There is also a great deal of variability in the behavioral, emotional, and social consequences of child sexual abuse. As a group, sexually abused children have been found to manifest significantly more behavioral and emotional difficulties than nonabused children. Some researchers have found significant levels of self-reported depression in these children while others have not. A significant number of these children and adolescents exhibit posttraumatic stress disorder and other anxiety symptoms.

Certain clinical issues appear to be common to most sexually abused children. These include feeling different or "damaged" compared to other children, feeling responsible for the abuse, feeling angry, fearful, or sad, taking on inappropriate behaviors and roles (including sexual ones), and losing trust in others. Briere's research on the Trauma Symptom Checklist for Children (TSC-C) provided empirical support for these difficulties. The factor analysis of the TSC-C demonstrated six discrete symptom fields: difficulties with sexual concerns, dissociation, anger, posttraumatic stress, depression, and anxiety symptoms.

Finkelhor discussed four *traumagenic dynamics* of sexual abuse, which included traumatic sexualization, stigmatization, powerlessness, and betrayal. The Children's Attributions and Perceptions Scale (CAPS) measures issues parallel to these traumagenic dynamics in addition to measuring attributions about the sexual abuse. This study demonstrated that feeling different from peers (stigmatization), personal attribution for negative events, impaired trust (betrayal), and decreased perceived credibility (one aspect of powerlessness) were significant issues for sexually abused children compared to a normal control group. Wolfe and colleagues developed The Children's Impact of Traumatic Events Scale (CITES) to measure "abuse-specific" thoughts and attributions. Factor analyses revealed distinct issues, including attributions, betrayal, guilt, helplessness, intrusive thoughts, sexualization, and stigmatization. Thus, strong empirical evidence shows that sexually abused children have clinical issues and difficulties specific to sexual abuse, which can be measured by newly developed standardized instruments.

Friedrich demonstrated that sexually abused children exhibit significantly higher rates of sexually inappropriate behavior than nonabused populations. These may arise as a result of learning inappropriate behaviors through the abusive experience or the fact that children with preexisting sexually inappropriate behavior are more likely to be targeted as victims of sexual abuse. However, there may be other, non-abuse-related reasons for children to exhibit sexually inappropriate behaviors. These behaviors are therefore not diagnostic of sexual abuse. It is also important to note that the majority of sexually abused children do *not* exhibit sexually inappropriate behaviors.

It should be clear from this discussion that there is no such entity as a "child sexual abuse syndrome." That is, there is no "characteristic" presentation that clinically distinguishes sexually abused children from nonsexually abused children. Rather, sexual abuse may result in a variety of clinical presentations. Sexual abuse therefore cannot be "diagnosed" by the clinical features present at evaluation. Such a determination depends on careful history taking and interviews with the child and significant others.

III. ASSESSMENT

Because child sexual abuse is an event (or events) rather than a clinical syndrome, and psychological responses to this experience differ considerably, one would expect psychiatric diagnoses in sexually abused children to also vary considerably. This has been documented in the literature. Psychiatric diagnoses have been evaluated by McLeer and colleagues in sexually abused and nonsexually abused children referred for outpatient pediatric assessment using the schedule for affective disorders and schizophrenia for school aged children (K-SADS). The only significant difference in diagnoses between the two groups was the higher prevalence of posttraumatic stress disorder (PTSD) in sexually abused (42.3%) vs nonsexually abused (8.7%) children. In other diagnostic categories, there were no significant differences. Of interest is the fact that attention deficit hyperactivity disorder was the most common diagnosis in both groups.

The process of determining accurate DSM-IV psychiatric diagnoses in sexually abused children is similar to that used in nonabused populations. The issue of determining whether a particular child has experienced sexual abuse is a complex medical, psychiatric, and legal process, which is beyond the scope of this article. In addition to determining DSM-IV diagnosis, there are several special areas of concern related to the sexual abuse experience that should also be addressed when assessing sexually abused children. These include possible legal involvement, child protective services interventions, medical issues related to the abuse, and other "abuse-related" issues of the child and family. Factors such as the type of sexual abuse experienced, how long it was going on, and the identity of the perpetrator may have direct effects on the child's and/or family's emotional reactions, attitudes, and concerns about the abuse. Some families may be most upset because the abuse involved actual intercourse, whereas to other families this may be less important than the fact that the abuse was perpetrated by a trusted family member. This information is helpful in determining appropriate therapeutic interventions.

The child's and family's perceptions of *why* the sexual abuse occurred are also important. Does the family blame the perpetrator, the child, the parents, or some combination? The child's symptoms may be more closely related to these attributions than to the specific details of the abuse itself. Specifically, children who blame themselves rather than the perpetrator may be more likely to experience guilt and poor self-esteem; children who blame the abuse on the unpredictability of the world may have more difficulty with fear and anxiety symptoms. Similarly, parents who blame the abuse in part on the child's behavior or appearance may be less likely to be supportive of the child, or even less likely to view the experience as abuse.

The parent's emotional reaction to their child's sexual abuse also has an effect on child symptomatology. Maternal depression and low levels of maternal support correlate with greater behavioral and emotional symptoms in sexually abused children. Higher levels of parental distress related to the child's sexual abuse have also been found to predict higher levels of behavioral problems in the child.

Because of the complex legal and child protective issues involved in cases of child sexual abuse, it is essential for the clinician to clearly define his or her role in the case. There are many differences between treatment and forensic roles and these should be kept separate and distinct as much as possible. It is regarded as a conflict of interest to evaluate a child for credibility of sexual abuse allegations, or to evaluate a child and parents for custody determination following sexual abuse, and then to provide ongoing treatment for that child or family.

IV. TREATMENT

Several randomized controlled treatment studies for sexually abused children have been published since 1990. Deblinger and colleagues evaluated the effectiveness of abuse-focused cognitive-behavioral therapy (CBT) in decreasing PTSD and other psychological difficulties in 100 sexually abused children. Graduated exposure and cognitive reframing were key elements in this CBT intervention. Subjects were randomly assigned to one of four treatment conditions: child treatment only, mother treatment only, mother and child treatment, or usual community care. Children who received the CBT treatment exhibited significantly fewer PTSD symptoms than children who did not receive this treatment. Children whose mothers received CBT exhibited fewer externalizing symptoms and depressive symptoms compared to children whose parents did not receive CBT.

Cohen and Mannarino compared abuse-focused CBT to nondirective supportive therapy (NST) provided during individual sessions to sexually abused preschoolers and their primary caretakers. Cognitive reframing of attributional errors related to the abuse was a key element of this CBT intervention. Children receiving CBT intervention showed more symptomatic improvement than those receiving NST. This differential treatment response was particularly strong with regard to children's sexually inappropriate behavior. Follow-up assessments indicated that these treatment group differences were sustained over the course of 12 months.

This study also evaluated the impact of several child and family factors on treatment outcome. The strongest predictor of outcome was the parent's emotional reaction to the sexual abuse. Specifically, higher levels of parental distress at pretreatment strongly predicted higher levels of the child's posttreatment symptomatology. On a parallel study for sexually abused children aged 8–14 years, CBT was superior to NST in improving depressive symptoms and social competency. In these older children, a higher level of parental support was a strong predictor of positive treatment outcome. Thus, there is growing evidence that abuse-focused CBT interventions are efficacious in decreasing symptomatology in sexually abused children. Both studies also lent support to the importance of including nonoffending parents in treatment. More research is needed to further assess the efficacy of CBT and other potentially effective interventions and to clarify what components of these treatments may be most effective for which subgroups of children. Detailed descriptions of the CBT interventions utilized in these studies have been published. Other books detailing CBT interventions specifically designed for sexually inappropriate behaviors and sexually abused boys are also available. Such CBT treatment interventions may be provided either individually or in a group setting.

Most abuse-focused CBT interventions include the following components:

1. Direct discussion of the sexual abuse experience (including desensitization through gradual exposure)
2. Discussion of thoughts and feelings about the sexual abuse
3. Correction of attributional errors and other cognitive distortions about the sexual abuse
4. Psychoeducation regarding sexual abuse
5. Relaxation and stress management techniques
6. Safety training
7. Enhancement of problem-solving skills
8. Education on behavioral management (contingency reinforcement programs, etc.)
9. Enhancement of parental support for the child

Other treatment approaches for sexually abused children (such as family therapy, use of psychotropic medication, psychodynamic therapy) have not been empirically demonstrated to be effective. However, this may be due to the complexities of designing research protocols for these interventions rather than their lack of utility for this population. There are probably many efficacious therapeutic techniques for sexually abused children. Follow-up studies have indicated that many sexually abused children recover fully from this stressful experience and do not suffer ongoing negative sequelae. It is hoped that future research will more clearly elucidate which treatment approaches are most likely to result in this positive outcome.

Bibliography

Briere, J. 1995. "The Trauma Symptom Checklist for Children." Psychological Assessment Resources, Odessa, FL.

Cohen, J. A., and Mannarino, A. P. 1993. A treatment model for sexually abused preschool children. *J. Interpers. Violence* **8**, 115–131.

Cohen, J. A., and Mannarino, A. P. 1996. A treatment outcome study for sexually abused preschool children: Initial findings. *J. Am. Acad. Child Adolesc. Psychiat.* **35**, 42–60.

Cohen, J. A., and Mannarino, A. P. 1998. Interventions for sexually abused children: Initial treatment outcome findings. *Child Maltreat.* **3**, 17–26.

Deblinger, E., and Heflin, A. H. 1996. "Treating Sexually Abused Children and Their Nonoffending Parents: A Cognitive Behavioral Approach." Sage, Newbury Park, CA.

Deblinger, E., Lippmann, J., and Steer, R. 1996. Sexually abused children suffering posttraumatic stress symptoms: Initial treatment outcome findings. *Child Maltreat.* **1**, 104–114.

Finkelhor, D. 1987. The trauma of child sexual abuse: Two models. *J. Interpers. Violence* **2**, 348–366.

Finkelhor, D., and Barron, L. 1986. Risk factors for sexual abuse. *J. Interpers. Violence* **1**, 43–71.

Friedrich, W. N. 1998. "The Child Sexual Behavior Inventory." Psychological Assessment Resources, Odessa, FL.

Mannarino, A. P., and Cohen, J. A. 1996. Family related variables and psychological symptom formation in sexually abused girls. *J. Child Sex. Abuse* **5**, 105–119.

McLeer, S. V., Callaghan, M., Henry, D., and Wallen, J. 1994. Psychiatric disorders in sexually abused children. *J. Am. Acad. Child Adolesc. Psychiat.* **33**, 313–319.

Wolfe, V. V., Gentile, C., and Wolfe, D. A. 1989. The impact of child sexual abuse on children: A PTSD formulation. *Behav. Ther.* **20**, 215–228.

Cholesterol and Lipoproteins

Catherine M. Stoney and Montenique Finney

Ohio State University

GLOSSARY

cholesterol A fat-soluble particle in the body used to form
   cholic acid in the liver and for the formation of cell membranes.
hemoconcentration The generally transient and reversible filtration of fluid from the intravascular space.
lipids Chemical compounds in the body that are miscible
   with each other and which provide energy and a variety
   of intracellar functions. They include triglycerides, phospholipids, and cholesterol.
lipoproteins Particles circulating in the blood that contain
   triglycerides, phospholipids, cholesterol, and protein.
reactivity Physiological responsivity to an external stimulus.

I. STRUCTURE AND FUNCTION OF CHOLESTEROL AND LIPOPROTEINS

Lipoproteins are particles circulating in the blood
that contain triglycerides, phospholipids, cholesterol, and protein (Fig. 1). Triglycerides are synthesized in the liver and adipose tissue and are utilized
as energy sources. Phospholipids are transported in
lipoproteins, are formed in all cells of the body, and
are particularly important in the formation of cellular
membranes. Cholesterol, both exogenous and endogenous forms, also circulates in the lipoproteins and
is used to form cholic acid in the liver. As with
phospholipids, the most important function of cho-

lesterol is the formation and permeability of cell
membranes. High circulating concentrations of low-
density lipoprotein–cholesterol (LDL-c) and low circulating concentrations of high-density lipoprotein–
cholesterol (HDL-c) are associated with an increased
risk of coronary heart disease (CHD).

II. VARIABILITY OF CHOLESTEROL AND LIPOPROTEINS

Not long ago there was a widely held belief that
blood cholesterol concentrations were relatively stable, showing only moderate elevations with age. Today, it is well demonstrated that there are large intraindividual variations in plasma cholesterol,
triglycerides, and LDL-c levels. The variability within
individuals is on the order of 10–20% over the course
of a day or a week, and this degree of variability
remains the case even under reasonably standardized conditions.

Investigations of the factors responsible for such
fluctuations are clinically relevant, because in order
to make reasonable clinical decisions regarding assessment and treatment of hypercholesterolemia, an
understanding of normal, biologically based variations in cholesterol concentrations will be informative. As importantly, however, is the understanding
of the causes of this variability in order to better
understand the process of cholesterol regulation.

A. Environmental Influences on Lipid Variability

A variety of stimuli alter the blood concentrations
of lipids. For example, numerous investigations have
demonstrated that psychological stress reliably influences blood concentrations of the cholesterol and
lipoproteins. A separate and smaller literature dem-

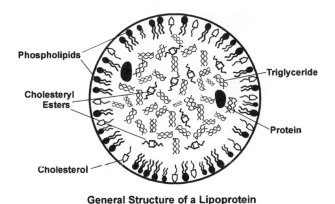

General Structure of a Lipoprotein

FIGURE 1   General structure of a lipoprotein.

onstrates that individuals differ in their lipid responses to dietary challenge. Importantly, an exaggerated lipid responsivity to diet is associated with an increased risk of CHD. To the extent that exaggerated lipid responses to environmental stimuli are atherogenic, investigation of the role of stress on lipid concentrations is warranted. The task among behavioral scientists dedicated to investigating the phenomenon of stress-associated lipid changes is to delineate the potential mechanisms responsible for the effects, which will ultimately lead to either a confirmation or refutation of the notion that stress-associated lipid changes are atherogenic.

B. Models Linking Stress with Lipid Variability

Several models have been proposed as potential pathways by which stress alters lipid concentrations in the blood; one such model is presented here (Fig. 2). Although the pathways are not mutually exclusive and are likely to be different under varying conditions of psychological stress, models such as these suggest ways of considering the current literature and point to obvious avenues for future endeavors.

III. CHRONIC STRESS MECHANISMS

During chronically or pervasively stressful situations, cholesterol concentrations are elevated. A number of naturalistic studies have demonstrated

that the stress associated with a major disaster or major stressor, such as the experience of earthquake, loss of job and income, and bereavement, can result in increases in total cholesterol, LDL-c, and triglycerides. Among better controlled, laboratory studies of chronic stress, generally similar associations are noted. Although there is not complete agreement, the preponderance of studies supports the notion that stress changes, or is in some way associated with, lipid concentrations in the blood. A meta-analysis of the bulk of the literature examining chronic or pervasive stressor effects on lipids demonstrates overall support for the notion that chronic stress is associated with elevated total cholesterol and LDL-c concentrations (Table I). Several prospective studies have further substantiated the notion that even when cholesterol concentrations are not elevated during periods of increased workload, there are still positive and significant associations between increased perceived stress and total cholesterol.

A. Behavioral Influences

Although it has been tempting to suggest that lipid changes are a result of stress-associated behavioral changes, such as diet and exercise modifications, which in turn increase lipid levels, data have not confirmed this as an adequate explanation. For example, a very early series of single case studies examined individuals while residing in a metabolic ward for periods of time ranging from 1 to 5 months. Diet, physical activity, exercise, and medication use were regulated closely among these individuals, and total cholesterol concentrations were established frequently. Simultaneously, diaries were maintained periodically by both patients and the nursing staff, reporting on mood and perceived stress experienced. Total cholesterol levels were quite variable over time, even under the tightly controlled conditions of a metabolic ward. Moreover, total cholesterol fluctuations were clearly more prominent during times of self-reported perceived stress.

More contemporary studies of much larger groups of men and women have similarly found that the chronic stress-associated lipid elevations are maintained even after rigidly controlling variations in diet, exercise, sleep, medication use, and physical activity.

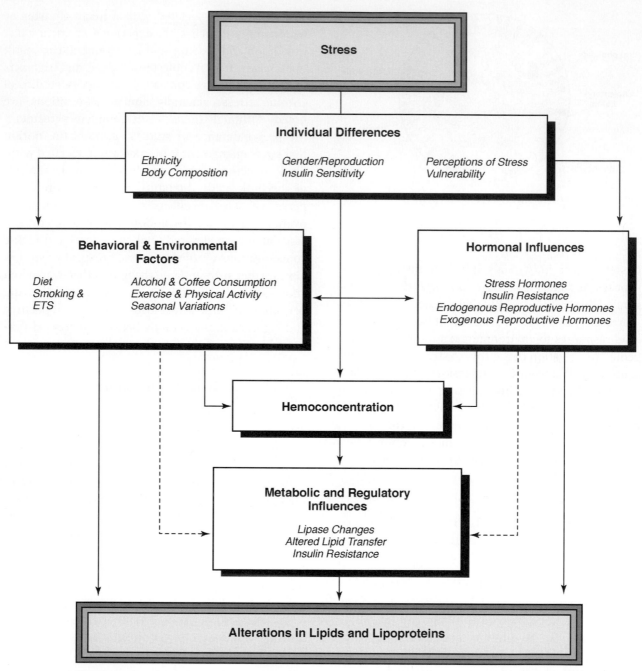

FIGURE 2 Potential pathways by which stress alters lipid concentrations in the blood. (Reprinted with permission of the American Psychological Association.)

For example, it has been shown that healthy men and women undergoing several weeks of predictable but potent work stress had elevated blood total cholesterol, LDL-c and triglycerides relative to lower work stress periods, independent of changes in diet, exercise, physical activity, medication use, and sleep patterns. Taken together, it is clear that lipid alterations during psychological stress are not operating as a function of indirect effects of stress-induced behavior changes.

TABLE I
Meta Analysis on the Effects
of Chronic Stressors on Lipids

Lipid variable	Number of studies	Unweighted effect size (d)	P
Total cholesterol	14	0.406	0.0001
LDL-c	9	0.358	0.0001
Triglycerides	3	−0.014	0.05
Free fatty acids	5	0.071	0.05

B. Hormonal Influences

One way that stress might influence lipid concentrations is through stress-induced hormonal changes that affect lipid metabolism. For example, stress-induced sympathetic nervous system activity leads to concomitant increases in catecholamines (epinephrine and norepinephrine), glucocorticoids (cortisol), and free fatty acids. These increases have resultant effects on metabolism of the lipoproteins. For example, catecholamines can directly stimulate adipose tissue to release free fatty acids into circulation through the process of lypolysis. Specifically, epinephrine induces the release of free fatty acids; studies suggest that during epinephrine infusion and mental stress, free fatty acid concentrations increase concomitantly. Epinephrine-induced increases in free fatty acids may be the result of increased blood flow through adipose tissue or stimulation of adipose β_2 receptors. In either case, the accumulation of circulating free fatty acids can trigger the production of triglyceride-rich, very low-density lipoprotein (VLDL) catabolism, which in turn will eventually result in increased concentrations of circulating LDL-c. Further, epinephrine will decrease VLDL secretion and increase LDL-c uptake by stimulating α_1 receptors.

Like epinephrine, norepinephrine influences lipoprotein metabolism. Increased norepinephrine activity stimulates adipose β receptors. This may result in diminished lipoprotein lipase activity, a subsequent decline in triglyceride clearance, lower levels of HDL, and increasing levels of VLDL, intermediate density lipoproteins (IDL), and LDL. Norepinephrine also decreases hepatic triglyceride lipase activity, which can increase plasma concentrations of both HDL-c and triglyceride-rich lipoproteins.

Cortisol may also influence the mobilization of lipids and lipid metabolism through activation of the hypothalamic–pituitary–adrenocortical system. Cortisol sensitizes adipose tissue to the lipolytic effects of catecholamines and increases concentrations of free fatty acids. Moreover, cortisol and free fatty acids stimulate the secretion of VLDL, increase the synthesis of hepatic triglycerides, and increase insulin insensitivity in the tissues. Insulin regulates triglyceride synthesis and hepatic production of VLDL. Thus, the decreased activity of insulin during stress inhibits the regulation of triglycerides and the production of VLDL. Further, insulin resistance and increased levels of cortisol suppress hepatic LDL receptors and catabolism, thereby delaying LDL clearance. Cortisol also stimulates apolipoprotein B (apo B) secretion from cultured rat hepatocytes.

This pathway of stress-associated, epinephrine-induced free fatty acid release from adipose tissue, enhanced hepatic cholesterol secretion, and increased circulating LDL-c concentrations has some empirical support. Chronic epinephrine infusions into cynomolgus monkeys produce significant total cholesterol concentration increases, and the same pattern has been noted among humans. Additional data regarding the effects of cortisol are also available. For example, several types of stressors have been shown to simultaneously elevate LDL-c, total cholesterol, and apo B and plasma cortisol; in some studies, the changes in cortisol positively predicted changes in lipids. Thus, the sympathetic–adrenal–medullary axis and the hypothalamic–pituitary–adrenocortical systems are likely to play a key role in modulating lipid and lipoprotein metabolism during times of pervasive, chronic psychological stress. There are currently significant and continuing efforts to delineate these pathways more definitively.

IV. ACUTE STRESS MECHANISMS

The hypothesis that chronic stress affects lipids due to stress-induced hormonal changes has considerable appeal, but it is unlikely to account for the abundant additional data demonstrating rapid and transient increases in plasma cholesterol concentrations during acute psychological stress. For example, many laboratory-based investigations have shown that very short-term stressors, such as those that might occur over a period of several minutes to an hour or two, can induce rapid and transient increases in blood concentrations of total cholesterol, LDL-c, apo B, and triglycerides. A meta-analysis of the most recent of these investigations has supported the notion that short-term stress reliably elevates total cholesterol, LDL-c, triglycerides, and free fatty acids (Table II). These elevations are clearly not a function of hormonally induced increased synthesis of lipids because the enhanced rate of lipoprotein entry into the circulation would simply take longer. Kinetic studies document that the manufacture of VLDL from fatty acids and subsequent conversion of LDL requires several hours to days to accomplish. Investigations of acute stress effects have also demonstrated little concordance between catecholamine and cortisol responses and acute changes in blood lipid concentrations. The effects of acute psychological stress on lipid concentrations are therefore likely to operate through a different set of mechanisms.

A. Hemoconcentration Influences

Psychological stress causes a generally transient and rapid decrease in the volume of blood plasma, with a resultant mild hemoconcentration of blood cells. This phenomenon is similar to the acute decreases in intravascular plasma volume that occur with postural changes, with a resultant posture-induced hemoconcentration of serum lipids. These plasma volume shifts can occur by increased red cell mass, alterations in kidney functioning, and/or through hemodynamically induced fluid shifts. Whatever the mechanism of the fluid volume shifts, it is clear that the resultant hemoconcentration leads to higher lipid concentrations in the blood. We know that increased lipid concentrations in the blood during stress are partially, but not fully, accounted for by hemoconcentration. Although there are some exceptions, generally speaking, during mild stressors that induce only modest changes in catecholamines and blood pressure, most of the lipid increases can be shown to be accounted for by plasma volume shifts. However, during more profound psychological stressors, increases in cholesterol and LDL-c are generally significant even after correction for transvascular plasma volume shifts.

B. Metabolic Influences

This state of affairs has led to the speculation that there may be a metabolic explanation for the acute stress-induced elevation in blood lipid concentrations. We have reasoned, for example, that if stress does have a direct influence on blood lipid levels, that individuals might clear a standard triglyceride load differently during a stress, relative to a nonstress period. In a test of this hypothesis, a standard intravenous load of intralipid was administered to a group of middle-aged men and women under a condition of psychological stress and then again during a condition of no psychological stress. In this test, which is similar to a glucose tolerance test, a triglyceride determination is made and then a standard bolus of intralipid is administered. Serial triglyceride determinations are then made over time, and the disappearance rate constant (K_2) is calculated. Thus, K_2 defines the clearance rate of the exogenous fat solution, with a higher K_2 value indicating a more efficient clearance of triglycerides from the circulation. When administering this test to a group of healthy individuals, we found that K_2 values declined significantly during stress, relative to a nonstress period, showing that the increases in lipids during acute stress are due to altered clearance rates. We have also found that individuals who are slow to clear a triglyceride load are more hostile than those who are more efficient

TABLE II

Meta Analysis on the Effects of Acute Stressors on Lipids

Lipid variable	Number of studies	Unweighted effect size (d)	P
Total cholesterol	25	0.306	0.0001
LDL-c	14	0.291	0.0002
Triglycerides	24	0.341	0.0001
Free fatty acids	37	0.717	0.0001

at clearing the triglyceride load imposed. These data are the most compelling to date to indicate that blood lipid concentrations are altered during psychological stress because of altered triglyceride metabolism and that this may be related to an increased risk of coronary heart disease.

V. CLINICAL IMPLICATIONS

There is little doubt about the presence of a direct relationship between blood cholesterol concentrations and the development and initiation of cardiovascular diseases. For example, chronically elevated LDL-c is associated with an elevated incidence of coronary artery disease, and lowering LDL-c concentrations produces a regression of coronary atherosclerosis and coronary artery events in some individuals. Elevations in triglycerides and low levels of HDL-c are also correlated positively with both coronary artery disease (CAD) and CHD, although it is not clear to what degree lowering triglyceride or raising HDL-c levels will result in a diminished risk for cardiovascular diseases.

Although there are no prospective investigations of the clinical relevance of stress-associated elevations in lipids, data from several cross-sectional investigations are informative. A number of investigations have demonstrated that healthy individuals at an elevated risk for the future development of cardiovascular diseases have more profound short-term elevations in blood lipid concentrations during stress, relative to a nonstress period. For example, men, postmenopausal women, and healthy young off-spring of parents with documented myocardial infarction all have greater elevations in total cholesterol and LDL-c during acute psychological stress, relative to women, age-matched premenopausal women, and healthy offspring of parents with no cardiovascular disease, respectively. Additionally, psychosocial factors that have been shown to be related independently to CHD risk, such as hostility and anxiety, are also associated with total cholesterol and LDL-c concentrations. Future cross-sectional and prospective investigations examining the extent to which stress-induced elevations in lipid concentrations are atherogenic are warranted.

See Also the Following Article

CARDIOVASCULAR SYSTEM AND STRESS

Bibliography

Brindley, D. N., McCann, B. S., Niaura, R. S., Stoney, C. M., and Suarez, E. C. 1993. Stress and lipoprotein metabolism: Modulators and mechanisms. *Metabolism* 42(Suppl. 1), 3–15.

Castelli, W. P., Garrison, R. J., and Wilson, P. W .F. 1986. Incidence of coronary heart disease and lipoprotein cholesterol levels: The Framingham Study. *J. Am. Med. Assoc.* 256, 2835–2838.

Stoney, C. M., and West, S. 1997. Lipids, personality, and stress: Mechanisms and modulators. *In* "Lipids and Human Behavior" (M. Hillbrand and R. T. Spitz, eds.). APA Books, Washington, DC.

Wolf, S., McCabe, W. R., Yamamoto, J., Adsett, C. A., and Schottstaedt, W. W. 1962. Changes in serum lipids in relation to emotional stress during rigid control of diet and exercise. *Circulation* 26, 379–387.

Chronic Fatigue Syndrome

Anthony J. Cleare and Simon Wessely

Guy's, King's, and St. Thomas' School of Medicine and the Institute of Psychiatry, London

GLOSSARY

myalgic encephalomyelitis (ME) This term was invented to describe an outbreak of unexplained illness that affected the staff of the Royal Free Hospital in 1955. It has become linked to CFS in the past 10 or more years. Because encephalomyelitis is a specific pathological process not found in these patients the term should not be used.

neurasthenia A term introduced to medicine in 1869 to describe an illness characterized by chronic physical and mental exhaustion, a precursor for modern CFS. Originally thought to be an organic disease of the central nervous system and caused by depletion of the energy supply to the brain resulting from such insults as overwork or infection, it was latterly seen as a psychological condition linked to depression and anxiety. Now an archaic term, although retained in the latest International Classification of Disease (ICD 10).

postviral fatigue syndrome (PVFS) A term used to describe chronic fatigue syndrome apparently triggered by a viral infection. Because of the frequency of viral infections and the relative lack of any evidence implicating viral infection in most cases of CFS the term is to be avoided unless there is clear-cut evidence of a relevant infective trigger.

somatization A condition where the patient presents with a physical symptom which is attributed to a physical disease, but is more likely to be associated with depression or anxiety.

C hronic Fatigue Syndrome (CFS) is an operationally defined syndrome characterized by a minimum of 6 months of severe physical and mental fatigue and fatigability made worse by minor exertion. Other symptoms such as muscle pain, sleep disorder, and mood disturbance are common (Table I). Other common causes of chronic fatigue must be considered before the diagnosis can be made.

I. HISTORICAL ASPECTS

The term chronic fatigue syndrome is a new arrival on the medical scene, but it is not a new illness. The condition known to the Victorians as neurasthenia is clearly its forerunner, not just in terms of symptoms, but presumed etiologies, treatments, and much else. As neurasthenia gradually shifted from a physical to a psychological etiology, its popularity declined, and the diagnosis had effectively vanished by the Second World War, except in parts of Asia. Chronic fatigue syndrome appeared in the 1980s in response to a variety of events, including renewed claims to have found a physical, infective cause for ill health, a series of well-publicized epidemic outbreaks, and the general change in doctor–patient relationships during this period. The term CFS and its variants are now widely used in the English-speaking and Scandinavian world, but not elsewhere.

II. SYMPTOMATOLOGY

The hallmark of CFS is severe fatigability of both mental and physical functions after minimal exertion. It is accompanied by other common symptoms, chiefly muscle pain, sleep disorder, and mood disturbance. Some sufferers complain of symptoms affecting most bodily functions. Chronic fatigue syndrome should not be diagnosed without some complaints of physical fatigue and fatigability (reduced functional

TABLE I
Consensus Operational Criteria for CFS[a]

Patients must have
1. Chronic fatigue
   New onset (not lifelong)
   At least 6 months duration
   Substantial functional impairment (occupational, social
       or personal activities)
   Not substantially alleviated by rest
2. At least 4 of the following for at least 6 months
   Memory or concentration impairment
   Sore throat
   Tender lymph nodes
   Muscle or multijoint pain
   Headaches
   Unrefreshing sleep
   Postexertional malaise lasting >24 h
3. No medical illness explaining the symptoms
4. No diagnosis of
   Psychosis (schizophrenia, mania or psychotic de-
       pression)
   Eating disorder (anorexia nervosa, bulimia nervosa)
   Dementia
   Alcohol or substance abuse
   Severe obesity (body mass index >45)

[a] From Fukuda *et al.* (1994) *Ann. Intern. Med.* **121**, 953–959.

capacity, symptoms after minor exertion, postexertional myalgia, and others) and mental fatigue and fatigability (poor concentration, symptoms made worse by mental effort, subjective memory disturbances, etc.). Because there are many causes of chronic fatigue and fatigability, it is essential that an appropriate physical examination, mental state examination, and simple investigations are always carried out before diagnosing CFS.

III. EPIDEMIOLOGY

Chronic fatigue is one of the commonest somatic symptoms—between 20 and 30% of most populations studied report symptoms such as exhaustion and feeling tired all the time. Some of these are short-term complaints, but around 10% of those attending general practice will complain of chronic fatigue suf-

ficient to interfere with their lifestyle and lasting at least 6 months. Operationally defined CFS is less common—the best estimates suggest around 1% of primary care attendees fulfill criteria. Even when all those with comorbid psychiatric disorders are excluded, a reasonable estimate of prevalence of "pure" CFS is around 0.5%. Few of these subjects will use a term such as CFS, ME, or its variants to describe the illness. Those seen in specialist clinics are more likely to be women, come from upper social classes, especially from the professions, and often have firmly held views on the physical nature of their illness. However, this may reflect more selection bias than any intrinsic aspect of CFS.

An operational definition should not be taken as endorsing the concept of CFS as a discrete disorder—in fact epidemiological research suggests that it is not, and it is best viewed as the extreme end of a normally distributed spectrum of fatigability, much in the same way that high blood pressure is not a discrete disorder distinguishable from moderate blood pressure.

Is it a single illness? Almost certainly not, although efforts to define valid subgroups have not yet been fruitful. Dividing those with an abrupt onset to symptoms from those with a more insidious origin seems to have some merit. Differences exist between the minority of cases with long illness histories, severe disability and multiple symptoms, who show overlap with the concept of somatization disorder, and the larger group with less disability, fewer symptoms, and shorter illness durations.

Another area of confusion is the relationship between CFS and other medically unexplained syndromes. Especially in specialist practice, there are considerable overlaps between CFS and the condition recognized by rheumatologists as fibromyalgia. It is likely that the boundaries between CFS and other unexplained and/or controversial syndromes such as irritable bowel syndrome and multiple chemical sensitivity are similarly fuzzy. Another area of overlap is between chronic fatigue and chronic pain. The analogies are many. The increased rates of affective and somatic symptoms, the role of avoidance behavior in sustaining symptoms, the role of physical factors as precipitants, the need for rehabilitation rather than cure, and the role of social and economic factors in perpetuating disability and causing conflict both with and between doctors.

IV. ETIOLOGY

A. Muscle

Although muscle pain and complaints of muscle fatigability are common, there is little objective evidence that symptoms have a primary neuromuscular origin. Most studies of neurophysiological function have been normal, particularly once the secondary effects of inactivity are taken into account. There may be a small group whose symptoms are related to primary muscle dysfunction, but given the importance of mental fatigue and fatigability, central rather than peripheral explanations are more likely to be relevant for most patients.

B. Viruses

While it is common for patients to date the onset of their symptoms to common viral infections, a controlled prospective study found that subjects who consulted their physician with viral symptoms showed the same rate of subsequent chronic fatigue as those consulting for other reasons. There is, however, consistent evidence that certain viral agents causing severe illness, such as the Epstein–Barr virus (EBV), viral hepatitis, Q fever, or viral meningitis are associated with prolonged fatigue reactions. Approximately 16% of subjects with documented EBV infection suffer fatigue of at least 6 months duration. Several factors increase the risk of developing prolonged fatigue after such infections. These include preexisting fatigue, previous psychiatric disorder and a prolonged convalescence from illness (bed rest and/or time off work). The response of the doctor may be important too: provision of a sick note and an unclear diagnosis have both been associated with the development of CFS.

C. Life Events

The literature regarding the effects of life events in CFS is still conflicting. It is clear that, as in other conditions, adverse life events in CFS are strongly associated with the development of psychological disorders. There is some evidence that negative life events may be related to the development of acute fatigue and to the subsequent chronicity of this fatigue. Positive life events may be protective. The biological aspects of stress, primarily the adrenal axis, are considered in Section IVF.

Two other specific stresses are worthy of mention. About one-third of patients suffer from significant fatigue following major surgical operations; preoperative fatigue and psychological morbidity act as risk factors. Second, the overtraining syndrome afflicts athletes who engage in periods of excessive exercise and bears many similarities with the symptoms of CFS. Once more both psychological and physiological factors interact to produce the final clinical picture.

D. Psychological Disorder

The relationship between psychiatric disorder and CFS remains controversial, but there is no doubt that such a relationship exists. Exact rates of psychiatric disorder vary from study to study, but overall between one-half and two-thirds of clinical samples fulfill criteria for psychiatric disorder as well as CFS. The greater the number of symptoms and the greater the disability, the greater the chance of psychiatric disorder. More important, a series of controlled studies have shown that these rates are too high to be explained simply as a reaction to physical disability (Table II). There is no single explanation for this overlap. Some is due to misdiagnosis. Some may reflect a common neurobiological origin to CFS and psychiatric disorder. Much is due to the overlap between the criteria used to diagnosis CFS and those for the common psychiatric disorders. No study has ever reported complete congruence between CFS and psychiatric disorder.

The commonest psychiatric disorder reported in studies of CFS is depression, almost certainly because of the considerable overlap between the operational criteria for both disorders. This has led to a relative neglect of anxiety disorders. However, in some respect CFS shares more similarities with anxiety than with depression—particularly in terms of neuroen-

TABLE II

Studies Comparing Prevalence of Psychiatric Disorder in CFS Compared to Medically Ill Controls

Control group	Proportion with psychiatric disorder (%)		Relative risk of psychiatric disorder in CFS
	CFS	Controls	
Neuromuscular diseases	72	36	2.0
Myopathies	45	6	7.5
Rheumatoid arthritis	41	13	3.3
Multiple sclerosis	23	8	2.9
Multiple sclerosis	45	16	2.8

docrine dysfunction, the role of fear and avoidance behavior, and treatment response.

E. Neuropsychological Function

Chronic fatigue syndrome patients frequently complain of considerable difficulties with memory, attention, and concentration. There have been at least 20 studies of cognitive functioning in CFS published to date. The results of neuropsychological testing are inconsistent. In general they do not reflect the severity of the subjective complaints encountered. Some may be explained by depression, anxiety, and/or sleep disturbance. There is evidence of deficits in higher and more complex cerebral function, such as selective attention.

F. Neurobiological Factors

1. Neurochemistry

Early studies in normal subjects showed that fatigue after exercise was associated with a rise in plasma levels of tryptophan and, theoretically, increased brain serotonin (5-HT) production. In CFS, increased cerebrospinal fluid levels of 5-HIAA relative to controls suggested increased turnover of 5-HT in the CNS (brain and spinal cord). Many studies have used direct challenges of brain serotonergic receptors, measuring neuroendocrine responses as in-

dices of the functional status of these receptors. These have generally revealed enhanced responses, suggesting increased serotonergic neurotransmission or enhanced postsynaptic 5-HT receptor function. These findings are important set in the context of similar studies in major depression which reveal the opposite change: reduced serotonergic function (Fig. 1). The importance of these changes is not yet understood. It is possible they are of physiological significance, since 5-HT is known to be important in the physiological control of sleep, appetite, and mood. In parallel with the opposite 5-HT changes, these features are disturbed in opposite directions in classic endogenous depression (insomnia, anorexia, agitation) and CFS (hypersomnia, hyperphagia, and retardation). Given what we know about brain physiology, it is also conceivable that these changes could be secondary to low cortisol levels or the effects of inactivity, sleep disturbance, or disruption of circadian rhythms.

Although there have been individual studies of other neurotransmitter dysfunction in CFS, further study is needed before drawing any conclusions.

2. Neuroendocrinology

Abnormal function of the hypothalamo-pituitary-adrenal (HPA) axis has been demonstrated in several centers. Common to most studies is the finding of reduced adrenal cortisol output, measured in urine, plasma, or saliva. Once more, this finding is of sig-

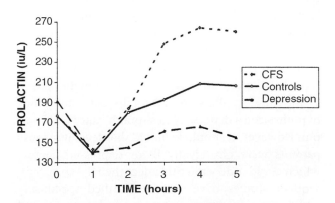

FIGURE 1 Prolactin response to D-fenfluramine (30 mg administered orally) used as an index of serotonergic function in patients with major depression, CFS (without comorbid depression), and healthy controls. Illustration adapted from Cleare *et al.* (1995). *J. Affective Disord.* **35**, 283–289.

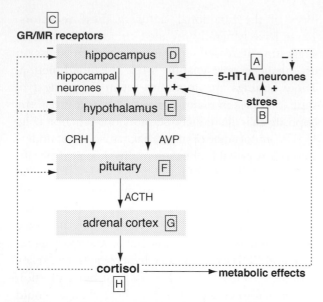

© GR/MR receptors

FIGURE 2 Figure showing components of HPA axis and directions of positive and negative feedback loops. Abbreviations are: CRH (corticotrophin releasing hormone); ACTH (corticotrophin); AVP (argenine vasopressin); MR (mineralocorticoid receptors); GR (glucocorticoid receptors). Abnormalities in axis are marked by letters A–H; details of these are given in Table III. Figure adapted from Cleare *et al.* (1995) *Br. J. Hospital Med.* **55**, 571–574.

TABLE III
Sites of Possible HPA Axis Abnormalities
in CFS Shown in Figure 2

(A)	Increased 5-HT$_{1A}$ neuronal function
(B)	Increased psychological or physical stress
(C)	Impaired hippocampal negative feedback
(D)	Previous hippocampal damage from depression- or chronic stress-induced hypercortisolaemia
(E)	Reduced central drive to HPA axis
(F)	Impaired pituitary response to CRH or stress
(G)	Abnormal adrenal cortex response to ACTH
(H)	Hypocortisolism

nificance in being the reverse of that seen in major depression. The underlying HPA axis disturbance which might cause this reduction in cortisol output remains unclear. In the original landmark study, Demitrack and colleagues found a blunted corticotrophin (ACTH) response to corticotrophin-releasing hormone (CRH), raised evening ACTH levels, and an adrenal cortex hyperresponsive to low-dose ACTH challenge but hyporesponsive at higher doses. While these results were not totally consistent, they hypothesized a deficiency in suprapituitary CRH output. However, it should be noted that several of these patients were chronically ill or depressed, factors which could independently affect the HPA axis. Subsequent studies have not yet clarified specifically which parts of the axis may be dysfunctional and at times are contradictory. The inconsistent results obtained in the different centers could be accounted for by the differing nature of the patient samples and the different test protocols used.

3. Neuroimaging

Studies using magnetic resonance imaging to assess brain structure have shown no excess of abnormalities when compared to appropriate controls, such as patients with depression. Again, while a number of studies using PET or SPET to obtain functional measures do show changes in blood flow or metabolism relative to healthy controls, results are highly variable and show considerable similarity to those seen in anxiety and depression.

G. Immunology

Initial views of CFS emphasized immunological changes as an inherent part of the syndrome (CFIDS—chronic fatigue and immune dysfunction syndrome). Over 40 studies have given conflicting results—normal, increased, or decreased cell-mediated and humoral immune markers. The most frequent finding is that of a mild immune activation, but it is unclear if this is secondary to the decreased cortisol tone (see above) or frequent mood disorder found in CFS. There has been little evidence of a relationship between immune dysfunction and clinical parameters or outcome and no evidence at all of any clinical immunological problems. Likewise, although abnormal cytokine release in response to antigen challenge is a tempting model for CFS, this would have to be centrally mediated and has not been proven.

H. Cognitive-Behavioral Factors

The cognitive behavioral model separates out factors which may have precipitated chronic fatigue from secondary factors thought to maintain fatigue and disability. These are listed below.

1. Effects of inactivity: prolonged rest is an effective strategy in the short term, but counterproductive in the medium and long term. With the passage of time, more symptoms and greater fatigue will continue to occur at progressively lower levels of exertion. Inactivity therefore sustains symptoms and increases sensitivity to them.

2. Inconsistent activity: many sufferers are not persistently inactive; instead, excessive or prolonged rest is followed by a burst of activity which is out of proportion to the preceding level of inactivity. This pattern may also be reinforced by the sense of frustration often encountered in sufferers and perhaps also by preexisting personality and lifestyle factors. Many patients have attempted sudden increases in activity and find that they culminate in exhaustion, for which the inevitable response is further rest. This "stop–start" pattern means that while extremes of disability are often avoided, sufferers are unable to build up a sustained level of recovery. This pattern often leads to the characteristic complaint of CFS sufferers, that of delayed fatigue and myalgia, well-recognized physiological phenomena that occur between 24 and 48 h after any exertion in excess of a person's current (and not previous) fitness.

3. Illness beliefs and fears about symptoms can influence disability, mood, and behavior in any illness. In CFS, unhelpful and inaccurate illness beliefs, reinforced by much ill-informed media coverage, include fear that any activity which causes an increase in fatigue is damaging or impossible, that "doing too much" causes permanent muscle damage, that CFS is due to a persistent virus or progressive immune disorder, that CFS is irreversible or untreatable, and that rest is the only remedy.

4. Symptom focusing: Many patients have come to rely on day-to-day monitoring of their own symptoms as the best method of determining activity levels hour by hour. Concern about the meaning and significance of symptoms, interpreted as "warning signals," is heightened by the unpredictable nature of CFS. Increased concern leads to heightened awareness, selective attention, and "body watching," which can then intensify both the experience and perceived

frequency of symptoms, thereby confirming illness beliefs and reinforcing disability.

I. Social Factors

The role of social support remains to be fully clarified. One recent study suggested that certain forms of support may be helpful, while others are detrimental.

V. TREATMENT

A. Pharmacotherapy

1. Antidepressants

Two placebo-controlled studies of fluoxetine in CFS showed divergent results, one indicating no benefit, even in depressed CFS patients, the other showing mild benefit to both fatigue and depression. Little other controlled evidence exists, though there are suggestions that phenelzine or low-dose tricyclics may be helpful, the latter particularly so if pain or insomnia predominate.

2. Low-Dose Hydrocortisone

Because of the finding of reduced cortisol levels, two studies investigated a replacement strategy. A full replacement dose (30 mg daily) produced mild benfit, but also endogenous adrenal suppression. Smaller doses (5–10 mg daily) produced large reductions in fatigue in about 28% compared to 9% in the placebo group, without adrenal suppression. Potential side-effects probably preclude such strategies as routine treatments, but suggest that low cortisol levels may be a significant perpetuating factor in fatigue chronicity.

3. Other

Claims have been made for several other treatments, including magnesium supplements, evening primrose oil, and immunotherapy. None have yet passed the tests of replication or safety.

B. Graded Exercise

Given the incontrovertible relationship between lack of exercise and chronic fatigue, graded exercise is an obvious treatment for CFS. Research has shown that providing account is taken of the level of deconditioning, CFS patients can perform graded exercise without adverse effects. Clinical trials have confirmed the considerable benefits. However, improvement is not related to measures of fitness, suggesting the benefits of exercise are more behavioral than physiological and may reflect increased confidence and decreased avoidance behavior. Nevertheless, many patients are reluctant to engage in such programs, usually because of fears of possible adverse consequences.

C. Cognitive Behavioral Therapy

Cognitive Behavioral Therapy is a promising line of treatment. First of all, it encourages a collaborative approach to treatment, emphasizes the importance of engagement, and should avoid the drop-out rates encountered in simple exercise programs. Treatment depends on challenging some of the unhelpful illness beliefs encountered in some specialist clinics; overcoming behavioral avoidance by encouraging consistent, modest activity followed by graded increases; and, finally, looking at cognitive factors associated with predisposition and relapse (see Section IVG above). Controlled trials confirm the benefits of treatment. In one study two-thirds of patients had a good outcome 6 months after the end of treatment, compared to one in five receiving relaxation as a control for nonspecific effects of treatment. One problem, however, is the shortage of skilled therapists. Good outcome is associated with altered beliefs about the relative merits of rest versus exercise.

VI. PROGNOSIS

The prognosis of patients attending specialist clinics and not receiving rehabilitation is poor. Poor prognosis is associated with holding very firm convictions of an exclusively physical origin to symptoms. This is not a problem *per se,* but is probably associated with continuing behavioral avoidance and firm beliefs about the adverse effects of activity. Given that most patients do not reach a specialist clinic until they have been ill for some years, it may

also simply be that chronicity predicts chronicity. There is insufficient knowledge about the prognosis of the larger problem of CFS in the community and in primary care, but it is likely to be more optimistic.

VII. SYNTHESIS

One theme that emerges from the literature of all the fatigue syndromes is the possibility of a general disorder of perception, perhaps of both symptoms and disability. At the heart of this misperception lies the sense of effort. Chronic fatigue syndrome patients clearly experience increased effort in everyday physical and mental tasks, reflected in a sense of painful muscle exertion and painful cognitive processing. This increased effort is the not the result of increased neuromuscular or metabolic demands (a Victorian concept), nor does it result in any substantial decline in actual muscle or cognitive performance. The result is a mismatch between patients' evaluation of their physical and mental functioning and the external evidence of any consistent deficits. The basis of this disorder of effort must remain speculative, particularly since the perception of effort is a complex topic. It is possible that it is because the sufferer needs to devote more attention, or even energy, to processes that the rest of us find automatic, be it muscular exertion or mental concentration. Why that should be remains unclear.

From this fundamental problem flow other problems identified in CFS, such as increased symptom monitoring, decreased tolerance, increased anxiety, and so on. These are not unique to CFS and have been described in fibromyalgia and irritable bowel syndrome. Thus some centrally mediated disorder of perception of information may underlie the experience of fatigue syndromes and explain the widespread discrepancies between the intensity of symptoms and disability and objective testing of a number of different parameters, both physiological and neuropsychological.

See Also the Following Articles

Cognitive Behavioral Therapy; Myopathy

Bibliography

"Chronic Fatigue Syndrome: Report of a Committee of the Royal Colleges of Physicians, Psychiatrists and General Practitioners." (1996). Royal Colleges of Physicians, London.

Demitrack, M. (1997). Neuroendocrine correlates of chronic fatigue syndrome: A brief review. *J. Psych. Res.* **31**, 69–82.

Komaroff, A., and Fagioli, L. (1996). Medical assessment of fatigue and chronic fatigue syndrome. *In* "Chronic Fatigue Syndrome: An Integrative Approach to Evaluation and Treatment," (M. Demitrack and S. Abbey, Eds.), pp. 154–184. Guildford, New York.

Lloyd, A. R., Wakefield, D., and Hickie, I. (1993). Immunity and the pathophysiology of chronic fatigue syndrome. *In* "Chronic Fatigue Syndrome" (A. Kleinman and S. Straus, Eds.), pp. 176–187. Wiley, Chichester.

McCully, K., Sisto, S., and Natelson B. (1996). Use of exercise for treatment of chronic fatigue syndrome. *Sports Med.* **21**, 35–48.

Moss-Morris, R., Petrie, K., Large, R., and Kydd, R. (1996). Neuropsychological deficits in chronic fatigue syndrome: Artefact or reality? *J. Neurol. Neurosurg. Psychiat.* **60**, 474–477.

Sharpe, M. (1996). Chronic Fatigue Syndrome. *Psychiatr. Clin. North Am.* **19**, 549–573.

Wessely, S. (1994). The history of chronic fatigue syndrome. *In* "Chronic Fatigue Syndrome" (S. Straus, Ed.), pp. 41–82. Dekker, New York.

Wessely, S., Hotopf, M., and Sharpe, M. (1998). "Chronic Fatigue and Its Syndromes." Oxford Univ. Press, Oxford, UK.

Wessely, S. (1995). The epidemiology of chronic fatigue syndrome. *Epidemiol. Rev.* **17**, 139–151.

White, P. (1997). The relationship between infection and fatigue. *J. Psychosom. Res.* **43**, 346–350.

Wilson, A., Hickie, I., Lloyd, A., and Wakefield, D. (1994). The treatment of chronic fatigue syndrome: Science and speculation. *Am. J. Med.* **96**, 544–549.

Wright, J., and Beverley, D. (1998). Chronic fatigue syndrome. *Arch. Dis. Child* **79**, 368–374.

Circadian Rhythms, Effects of Prenatal Stress in Rodents: An Animal Model for Human Depression

S. Maccari

Université de Lille, France

O. Van Reeth

Université Libre de Bruxelles, Belgium

GLOSSARY

circadian rhythms Biochemical, physiological, and behavioral processes that reoccur in a cyclic fashion with a period of about 24 h (*circa die*, "about a day").

free-running Term used to characterize the expression of circadian rhythms in the absence of any 24-h synchronizing information from the external environment.

prenatal stress procedure   Pregnant female rats were individually restrained three times a day (at 09:00, 12:00 and 17:00 h) for 45 min in transparent plastic cylinders (7 cm diameter, 19 cm long) and exposed to bright light (1500 lux). This manipulation was performed daily during the last week of pregnancy until delivery. Control pregnant females were left undisturbed in their home cages.

sleep–wake cycle   The various vigilance states are as follows. Wake (W): low-voltage fast electroencephalogram (EEG) activity, high electromyogram (EMG) activity, and numerous eye movements; Light slow wave sleep (SWS1): high-voltage slow cortical waves interrupted by low-voltage fast waves and reduced EMG activity; Deep slow wave sleep (SWS2): continuous high-amplitude slow wave activity in EEG, very low EMG activity, and no electrooculogram (EOG) activity; Paradoxical sleep (PS): low-voltage fast cortical waves with a regular θ-rhythm, absence of muscular tone, and presence of rapid eye movements.

Prenatal stress (PNS) can influence an individual's development and induce changes that persist into adulthood. Mechanisms underlying this phenomenon have been extensively examined by using an animal model of prenatal stress in rats. Among the behavioral attributes of adult prenatally-stressed rats, increased "emotionality," "anxiety", and changes in various neurobiological systems including the hypothalamo-pituitary-adrenal (HPA) axis have been shown. Given that the adaptive capabilities of an organism depend, through the circadian system, on its temporal organization and its synchronization with the external environment we thought to determine whether PNS could have long-term effects on circadian rhythms, including sleep–wake cycles. It has recently been shown that PNS induces a phase advance in the circadian rhythm of both corticosterone secretion and locomotor activity in adult rats. Furthermore, prenatally-stressed rats exhibit a significant increase in the amount of paradoxical sleep over the 24-h recording session, positively correlated to plasma corticosterone levels.

Taken together, results indicate that PNS induces an increased stress response and abnormal circadian and sleep function in adult rats, suggesting an underlying dysfunction of their circadian clock system.

Among the various biological traits exhibited by depressed patients there are changes in circadian rhythmicity and paradoxical sleep regulation, and our recent observation on the effects of PNS in rats raises the possibility that PNS could represent an interesting and original animal model of latent or potential depression in humans.

I. PRENATAL STRESS, AN EARLY ENVIRONMENTAL MANIPULATION DURING A CRITICAL PERIOD

The prenatal environment exerts profound influences on the development of an organism, inducing changes which extend from early to later life. Clinical studies have shown that offspring of mothers experiencing stress during pregnancy displayed long-term behavioral abnormalities. However, due to difficulties inherent to human research, this phenomenon has been examined most extensively using the prenatal stress (PNS) rat model. Adult prenatally-stressed rats exhibit behavioral abnormalities under stressful conditions, such as increased "anxiety," "emotionality," or depression-like behaviors. Among the biological substrates possibly mediating these behavioral disorders, the hypothalamo-pituitary-adrenal (HPA) axis, involved in an animal's ability to cope with stress, appears to be a good candidate. Indeed, PNS is responsible for an increase in stress-induced plasma adrenocorticotropin (ACTH) levels, a prolongation of stress-induced corticosterone secretion, and a decreased binding capacity of hippocampal corticosteroid receptors. These behavioral and physiological changes seem to depend upon the gender of the animals, with substantially more marked effects of PNS in females than in males. Among the neurotransmitters involved in those hormonal and behavioral responses, acetylcholine plays a critical role. Prenatal stress has long-term effects on the development of forebrain cholinergic systems and induces an increase in hippocampal acetylcholine release after acute stress or CRH microinjections. Those long-term neuroendocrinological effects are mediated, at least in part, by stress-induced maternal corticosterone increase during pregnancy.

Taken together, these studies support the idea that

PNS disrupts the organism's capabilities to cope with stress and that prenatally stressed rats have biological traits similar to those observed in depressed patients. Indeed, like depressed patients, prenatally stressed rats do escape from the feedback inhibition responsible for returning corticosterone secretion to basal levels after stress. Finally, like in depressed patients in which cholinergic hyperactivity is described, prenatally stressed rats exhibit cholinergic hypersensitivity after a CRH challenge.

II. CIRCADIAN RHYTHMS AND ADAPTATION TO EXTERNAL ENVIRONMENT

Most biochemical, physiological, or behavioral processes within the organism fluctuate on a regular basis throughout the 24-h day. These daily rhythms arise from an internal time-keeping system, the circadian clock, located in the hypothalamic suprachiasmatic nuclei (SCN). In the absence of any environmental input, these rhythms persist with a period of about 24 h and are therefore referred to as "circadian rhythms."

The circadian time-keeping system is essential for the optimal functioning and adaptation of the organism to the dramatic changes in the environment imposed by the Earth's rotation on its axis. Indeed, the circadian system maintains temporal synchronization not only between the organism and daily changes in the physical environment, but also between diverse internal physiological processes. For many years, the circadian system was thought to be only sensitive to changes in the light–dark cycle. However, it has been shown that circadian function and/or sleep patterns can also be reset by neurochemical or behavioral stimuli. Among those stimuli, steroids can have marked effects on the functioning of the circadian system and chronic stress in adult rats can induce changes in sleep patterns and circadian rhythms.

Perinatal events seem to have complex influences on the long term development of circadian function. For instance, it is known that abnormal development of the visual system in anophtalmic mice has clear effects on the integrity of the SCN and on the development of behavioral rhythms. Restricted access to the natural mother has been shown to shift endogenous corticosterone rhythm of rat pups. Despite the fact that postnatal events have complex influences on the long-term development of the circadian clock, very little attention has been given to the possible effects of prenatal stress on circadian clock function.

III. INFLUENCE OF PRENATAL STRESS ON CIRCADIAN RHYTHMICITY AND SLEEP

A phase advance in the timing of the rise of corticosterone in prenatally stressed rats compared to control rats has recently been shown. More precisely, PNS induced higher levels of total and free corticosterone secretion at the end of the light period in both males and females and hypercorticism over the entire diurnal cycle in females. The effects of prenatal stress on corticosterone secretion could be mediated, at least in part, by a reduction in hippocampal corticosteroid receptors at specific times of day. Our results also show that stress prepartum could alter the pattern of corticosterone secretion in pregnant females and that there is a significant phase advance in the circadian rhythm of locomotor activity relative to the entraining light–dark cycle in prenatally stressed rats. When subjected to an abrupt shift in the light–dark cycle, male and female prenatally stressed rats resynchronized their activity rhythm to the new light–dark cycle slower than control rats. In temporal isolation in constant darkness, the free-running period of locomotor activity was significantly shorter in prenatally stressed rats compared to control rats.

In view of those changes in circadian rhymicity, the effects of PNS on the sleep–wake cycle in adult rats have been investigated. Male prenatally stressed rats exhibited a significant increase in the amount of paradoxical sleep (PS) over the 24-h recording session, positively correlated to plasma corticosterone levels. Other changes include an increased sleep fragmentation and light slow wave sleep (SWS 1) time and a slight decrease in the percentage of deep slow wave sleep (SWS 2) relative to total sleep time. The present results demonstrate that exposure to PNS can produce long-term and selective changes in both the structure and the continuity of sleep. Although there are preliminary reports of abnormal "sleep-like behaviors" in prenatally stressed monkeys and prenatally stressed humans, the data provide the first polygraphic demonstration of long-term effects of PNS on the sleep–wake cycle when the animals reach adulthood.

Taken together, results indicate that PNS induces an increased stress response and abnormal circadian and sleep functions in adult rats, suggesting an underlying dysfunction of the circadian clock. These results parallel, to some extent, circadian and sleep changes found in depressed patients. Indeed, abnormalities in a variety of overt circadian rhythms, including the cortisol rhythm, have been documented in depressed patients. Furthermore, alteration in the sleep–wake cycle is an of hallmark of human depression, with changes including a shortened PS latency, an increase in the amount and frequency of PS during the first part of the night, increased sleep fragmentation, and a decrease in the amount of slow wave sleep.

Added to previous findings of higher "anxiety" and "emotionality" in prenatally stressed rats, dysfunction of their HPA axis and circadian timing system and the observation of long-term changes in their sleep structure supports the validity of the "prenatal stress" model as an animal model of depression. In contrast to other stress-related animal models of depression, the persistence of all induced abnormalities after stressor removal in PNS rats could be seen as particularly advantageous for the design and testing of new therapeutic strategies in mood and sleep disorders.

See Also the Following Article

CIRCADIAN RHYTHMS, GENETICS OF

Bibliography

Barbazanges, M., Piazza, P. V., Le Moal, M., and Maccari, S. (1996). Maternal glucocorticoid secretion mediates long-term effects of prenatal stress. *J. Neurosci.* **16**, 7783–7790.

Day, J. C., Koehl, M., Deroche, V., Le Moal, M., and Maccari, S. (1998). Prenatal stress enhances stress- and corticotropin-releasing factor-induced stimulation of hippocampal acetylcholine release in adult rats. *J. Neurosci.* **18**, 1886–1892.

Dugovic, C., Maccari, S., Weibel, L., Turek, F. W., and Van Reeth, O. (1999). High corticosterone levels in prenatally-stressed rats predict persistent paradoxical sleep alterations. *J. Neurosci.* **19**, 8656–8664.

Holsboer, F. (1989). Psychiatric implications of altered limbic-hypothalamic-pituitary-adrenocortical activity. *Eur. Arch. Psychiat. Neurol. Sci.* **238**, 302–322.

Kant, G. J., Pastel, R. H., Bauman, R. A., *et al.* (1995). Effects of chronic stress in sleep. *Physiol. Behav.* **57**(2), 359–365.

Koehl, M., Barbazanges, A., Le Moal, M., and Maccari, S. (1997). Prenatal stress induces a phase advance of circadian corticosterone rhythm in adult rats which is prevented by postnatal stress. *Brain Res.* **759**(2), 317–320.

Maccari, S., Piazza, P. V., Kabbaj, M., Barbazanges, A., Simon, H., and Le Moal, M. (1995). Adoption reverses the long-term impairment in glucocorticoid feedback induced by prenatal stress. *J. Neurosci.* **15**, 110–116.

McCormick, C. M., Smythe, J. W., Sharma, S., and Meaney, M. J. (1995). Sex-specific effects of prenatal stress on hypothalamic-pituitary-adrenal responses to stress and brain glucocorticoid receptor density in adult rats. *Dev. Brain Res.* **84**, 55–61.

Meijer, A. (1985). Child psychiatric sequelae of maternal war stress. *Acta Psychiatr. Scand.* **72**, 505–511.

Vallée, M., Mayo, W., Dellu, F., Le Moal, M., Simon, H., and Maccari, S. (1997). Prenatal stress induces high anxiety and postnatal handling induces low anxiety in adult offspring: correlation with stress-induced corticosterone secretion. *J. Neurosci.* **17**(7), 2626–2636.

Weinstock, M. (1997). Does prenatal stress impair coping and regulation of hypothalamic-pituitary-adrenal axis? *Neurosci. Biobehav. Rev.* **21**(1), 1–10.

Circadian Rhythms, Genetics of

Fred W. Turek and Martha Hotz Vitaterna

Northwestern University, Chicago

I. Different Genetic Approaches
II. Inbred Strains
III. Identification of Single Gene Mutations

GLOSSARY

circadian rhythms Biochemical, physiological, and behavioral events that reoccur in a cyclic fashion with a period of about 24 h.

circadian clock An internal timing mechanism which regulates the expression of circadian rhythms. In mammals, a master circadian clock is located in the hypothalamic suprachiasmatic nucleus (SCN).

entrainment Process by which an internal circadian clock is entrained or synchronized to the period of an external stimulus that usually has a period of about 24 h. In nature, the light–dark cycle is the primary external environmental signal that entrains the circadian clock to the 24-h period of the day that is due to the rotation of the earth on its axis.

free-running Term used to describe circadian rhythms persisting in the absence of any 24-h synchronizing information from the external environment. The expression of free-running circadian rhythms with a period close to (e.g., 23–25 h) but rarely exactly 24 h demonstrates the endogenous nature of the circadian clock underlying the expression of circadian rhythms.

inbred strain A set of animals that is produced by at least 20 consecutive generations of sister × brother or parent × offspring mating. Animals of an inbred strain are nearly fully homozygous, which thus provides a defined and consistent genotype for analysis.

S imilar to the stress response, the expression of circadian rhythms enables the organism to adapt to changes in the external environment. Of course, the changes in the environment that represent the substrate for the evolution of circadian rhythmicity occur on a relatively predictable basis that coincides with the 24-h rhythms in the external environment

due to the rotation of the earth on its axis. Interestingly, many of the metabolic and endocrine events associated with stress also show predictable circadian rhythmicity, indicating that these two adaptive systems are highly integrated with one another. Both systems are under tight genetic control and this article focuses on the evidence for the genetic control of circadian rhythms and the genes that have been discovered to underlie this control.

I. DIFFERENT GENETIC APPROACHES

Early studies in invertebrates demonstrated that the period of the circadian clock was clearly under genetic control since 24-h rhythms developed in organisms never experiencing any 24-h changes in the physical environment. Furthermore, rearing mice on non-24-h cycles as extreme as 20 or 28 h has only small (i.e., on the order of a few minutes) and transient effects on the free-running period of the circadian clock when animals are subsequently housed under conditions of constant darkness (i.e., the free-running period remains within a few minutes of 24 h). Until recently, evidence that genetic differences define the characteristics of the circadian clock system in mammals has been determined primarily by comparing properties of circadian rhythms between different inbred strains of the same species. As reviewed in the next section of this article, differences in various circadian rhythm parameters have been observed between different strains, indicating that the genetic makeup influences the expression of circadian rhythms in mammals. While interstrain differences in circadian parameters indicate genetic regulation of circadian properties, they provide little information on specific genes involved in circadian timing. Animals with single-gene mutations that lead to the abnormal expression of circadian rhythms have proved enormously useful in identifying the genetic mechanisms that underlie rhythmicity, and the findings from these mutant animals are described in section III below.

II. INBRED STRAINS

Studies of inbred strains offer a simple technique for separating genetic (i.e., between-strain) and environmental (i.e., within-strain) sources of variance in the physiological and behavioral parameters of interest. The use of inbred strains to study circadian properties has relied almost exclusively on strains of rats, mice, and hamsters that were inbred with no attempt being made to select for specific circadian characteristics. Nevertheless, a number of alterations in different properties of circadian rhythmicity have become fixed in the genomes of inbred strains of rodents including the length of the free-running period, the entrained phase relationship to the light–dark cycle, the response to various environmental manipulations, and changes in the amplitude and waveform of circadian rhythms. One example of differences in circadian characteristics for four different strains of the golden hamster is provided in Fig. 1. The four inbred strains are designated BIO 1.5, BIO 87.20, MHA/SsLak, and LSH/SsLak. Significant differences among the strains were found in the free-running period in constant light (LL) and constant dark (DD) as well as in the phase angle of entrainment (Fig. 1). A shorter free-running period in both LL and DD and an earlier onset of activity were characteristic of the BIO 1.5 strain, with the MHA/SsLak and LSH/SsLak strains being intermediate in these measures, while a longer period was associated with later activity onset in the BIO 87.20 strain. The correlated strain differences in period and phase angle of entrainment indicate that a common set of genetic differences influence these parameters. In contrast, strain differences in phase shifts in the free-running rhythm of activity to a 1-h white light pulse were not found. These results indicate that the free-running period can be affected by genetic factors which do not necessarily contrib-

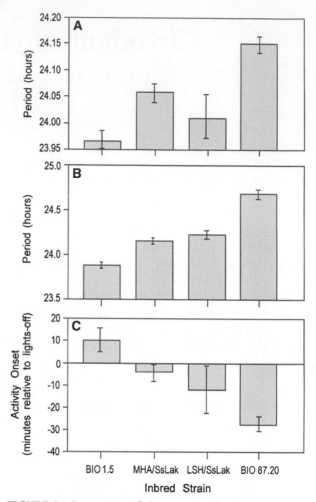

FIGURE 1   Parameters of the circadian locomotor activity rhythm of four inbred strains of golden hamsters exposed to different environmental light conditions. (A) The free-running period in constant darkness. Means and standard errors of 12 hamsters per strain are represented. (B) The free-running period in constant light. Means and standard errors of 10 hamsters per strain are represented. (C) The phase relationship between activity onset and time of lights off during entrainment to an LD 14:10 cycle (positive values indicate activity onset before lights off, and negative values indicate activity onset after lights off). There is a high correlation between all three measures with the BIO 1.5 strain having the shortest period and earliest activity onset, MHA/SsLak and LSH/SsLak being intermediate in all three measures, and BIO 87.20 having the longest period and latest activity onset. These results indicate that a common set of genetic differences between strains affects all three parameters.

ute to the response of the circadian clock to light. These genetic differences could be due to differences in the clock itself or at some input pathway to the clock.

While the use of inbred strains with different circadian characteristics has not been very useful in identifying genes regulating circadian behavior, the use of new techniques should enable researchers to find the genes responsible for quantitative differences in circadian behavior. With high-density genetic maps in the mouse, techniques are now available to map quantitative trait loci, making it possible to identify multiple genes involved in differences between inbred strains.

III. IDENTIFICATION OF SINGLE GENE MUTATIONS

Induced mutagenesis has uncovered single gene mutations in bacteria, plants, and invertebrates that alter such basic clock properties as the period of free-running rhythms, entrainment to light–dark cycles, and temperature compensation. Multiple alleles have been identified at the two most well-studied genetic loci in the fruit fly *Drosophila* (the *per* gene) and the bread mold *Neurospora* (the *frq* gene), with different alleles inducing a variety of circadian phenotypes. In addition to being useful in analyzing the formal properties and the physiological mechanisms that underlie rhythmicity, genetic analysis of these mutations has led to the cloning of these and other circadian clock genes and the ability to study their molecular structure, expression, and function.

In mammals, only two genes have been identified by mutations which influence the circadian clock. While other candidate circadian clock genes have been identified (such as by homology to other organisms), the disruption in the circadian phenotype in mutants provides convincing evidence that these genes actually function in the circadian clock. A spontaneous mutation has been found in the hamster, which defines a single gene called *tau* that affects the period of the clock as well as a number of other clock properties. Induced mutagenesis has uncovered a single-gene mutation in the mouse, called *Clock*, which affects both the period of free-running

rhythms as well as the ability to maintain rhythmicity in constant darkness.

A. The *tau* Mutation in Hamsters

The first evidence that the period of a circadian rhythm in mammals could be influenced in a major way by a single gene was reported for golden hamsters in 1988 by Ralph and Menaker. One male hamster from a commercial supplier was found to have a free-running period in constant darkness of 22 h. Since such a short period for a circadian rhythm had never been reported in the thousands of animals that had been studied in many different laboratories, this animal stood out as a candidate for having a spontaneous mutation that affected circadian period. Subsequent breeding experiments revealed that this serendipitously discovered short-period male was heterozygous for a single autosomal mutant gene which was called *tau*. Further crosses established that the mutant allele was semidominant and that the phenotype for the free-running period in the homozygous animal was about 20 h. *Tau* is expressed equally in males and females, and the ranges of the circadian periods between the three genotypes do not overlap.

In addition to affecting the period of the free-running rhythm of activity, the *tau* mutation has a number of other effects on the circadian clock system. Exposure of wild-type and homozygous mutant hamsters free-running in constant darkness to single 1-h pulses of light throughout the circadian cycle reveals much larger phase shifts in the mutant animals. Interestingly, while such large phase shifts are not observed in young wild-type hamsters, such phase shifts have been observed in very old nonmutant hamsters. A possibility is that both the *tau* mutation and advanced age may alter the circadian clock in a similar manner, either weakening the coupling between two or more circadian oscillators that are thought to comprise the circadian pacemaker or reducing the amplitude of the driving circadian oscillation.

The paucity of genetic information in the hamster has inhibited progress in using the *tau* mutation to understand the molecular nature of *tau* and its role in the circadian organization. In contrast, finding a similar mutation to *tau* in the mouse would enable researchers to clone murine genes by map position due to the extensive genetic maps that have been (and are continuing to be) made for the mouse. Fortunately, a mutation that has a major effect on the circadian organization in the mouse has recently been discovered.

B. The *Clock* Mutation in Mice

The finding that the majority of clock mutants that have been isolated in lower organisms as well as the *tau* mutation were semidominant suggested that it might be possible to screen for abnormal phenotype in heterozygous mice that were the offspring of males that had been exposed to the chemical mutagen *N*-ethyl-*N*-nitrosourea (ENU). Such an approach proved to be successful using male mice of the inbred strain C57BL/6J (B6) that were injected with ENU and, following recovery of fertility, were allowed to mate with untreated B6 females. The offspring of such matings were then tested for any circadian abnormalities by monitoring the rhythm of locomotor activity first under an LD 12:12 cycle and later during exposure to DD. The first-generation offspring (G1) of such matings would be heterozygous for any induced mutations. Normal B6 mice show robust entrainment to a light–dark cycle and have a circadian period of between 23.3 and 23.8 h under free-running conditions (Fig. 2A). During the testing of 304 G1 offspring, we found a single animal (G1-25) that had a free-running period of about 24.8 h (Fig. 2B), which was 6 standard deviations from the mean (Fig. 2).

The mating of the putative mutant animal to normal B6 females yielded 23 progeny, who were then tested for free-running period in DD. About half of the animals (10) had periods in the range of normal animals, while the other half (13) had periods that were closer to the founder animal (24.5–24.8 h). A 1:1 phenotypic ratio is what is expected among progeny for a fully penetrant autosomal mutation. Numerous other crosses with other inbred strains have been carried out, and all of the observed phenotypic ratios for the mutation are consistent with those predicted for a single-locus semidominant autosomal mutation.

The prediction from classic Mendelian genetics for a single-locus semidominant autosomal mutation is that when heterozygote animals are crossed, one-fourth of the offspring will have two wild-type alleles, one-half will have one wild-type and one mutant allele (heterozygous), and one-fourth will have two mutant alleles (homozygous). Thus, it would be expected that in a cross of two mutant mice with a circadian period of about 24.7 h, one-fourth of the offspring would have the wild-type period, one-half would have a period of about 24.7 h, while one-fourth of the animals would have an unpredictable phenotype. Indeed, from the intercrosses of heterozygous mutant animals with a long-period phenotype, three phenotypic classes were found in the F2 generation with the expected 1:2:1 ratio. The new phenotype observed was one in which the period of the rhythm was between 26 and 29 h in length under DD conditions. However, in essentially all of the animals showing the long-period phenotype, there was a complete loss of circadian rhythmicity within about 2 weeks (Fig. 3). It should be noted that circadian rhythms normally would persist indefinitely in mice kept in constant darkness. In view of the major effect of the mutation on circadian period, as well as on persistence of rhythmicity, the mutation was named *Clock*.

Because *Clock* segregates as a single gene, it was possible to map its chromosomal location by linkage analysis. Simple sequence length polymorphisms (SSLPs) were used as genetic markers to map the *Clock* gene locus to the midportion of mouse chromosome 5 in a region that is syntenic with human chromosome 4. Subsequently using a combination of mapping, sequencing, transcription unit identification, and transgenic rescue techniques, the *Clock* gene was cloned and found to encode a novel transcriptional regulatory protein having a basic helix-loop-helix DNA-binding domain, a PAS protein dimerization domain (named for *Per*, *AHR*, *ARNT*, and *Sim*, the first genes found to have this domain) and a Q-rich activation domain. The mutant form of the CLOCK protein is thought to lack a portion of the activation domain found in wild-type protein, and thus, while capable of protein dimerization, transcriptional activation would be diminished or lost.

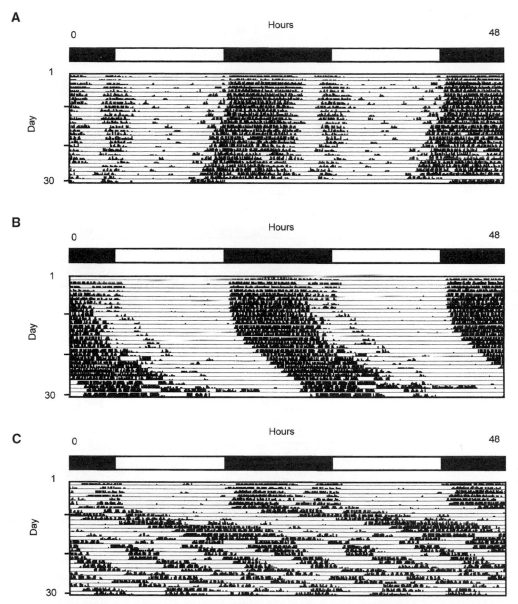

FIGURE 2 Activity records of mice with different *Clock* genotypes. The F2 or F3 progeny of an interstrain (BALB/cJ × C57BL/6J) intercross are shown. Activity records are double-plotted with the light–dark cycle indicated by a bar at the top. All animals were transferred to constant darkness (DD) on the 8th day shown. (**A**) A wild-type (+/+) mouse's activity record. This individual had a free-running period of 23.5 h. (**B**) A heterozygous (*Clock*/+) mouse's activity record. This individual expressed a free-running period which gradually lengthened to 24.7 h. (**C**) A homozygous (*Clock*/ *Clock*) mouse's activity record. This mouse expressed a free-running period of 28.7 h upon initial transfer to constant darkness but subsequently lost significant circadian rhythmicity.

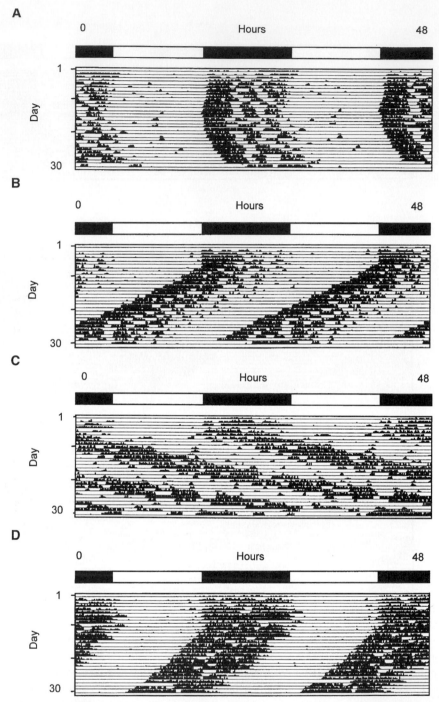

FIGURE 3 Transgenic rescue of the *Clock* mutation. Additional transgenic copies of *Clock* were introduced into the genome. By crossing transgenic animals with animals of different *Clock* genotypes, mice of different *Clock* genotypes, with or without transgenic wild-type copies of *Clock*, could be produced. (**A**) A heterozygous (*Clock/ +*) mouse's activity record. (**B**) Activity of a heterozygous (*Clock/+*) mouse with additional transgenic copies of the wild-type allele of *Clock*. (**C**) A homozygous (*Clock/ Clock*) mouse's activity record. (**D**) Activity of a homozygous (*Clock/Clock*) mouse with additional transgenic copies of the wild-type allele of *Clock*.

C. Circadian Clock Genes in Flies and Mice Come Together

At the time the *Clock* gene was discovered in mice, mammalian homologs to the fly (or any other species) circadian clock genes (*per* and a second one called *tim*) had not been identified. Subsequently, at least three mammalian homologs of *per* and one of *tim* have been identified based on DNA sequence homology. In addition, the presence of the PAS dimerization domain in CLOCK protein suggested that it may form a heterodimer similar to that of the PER–TIM complex in flies. A screen for potential partners for the CLOCK protein using the yeast two-hybrid system revealed that a protein of unknown function, BMAL1, was able to dimerize with the CLOCK protein. Furthermore, fly homologs of *Clock* and *Bmal1* have now been found and it appears that in both flies and mice the four circadian clock genes (*per, tim, Clock,* and *Bmal1*) interact through a series of positive and negative feedback loops and together represent a major portion of the 24-h molecular circadian clock. While other genes may also play a central role in the molecular machinery that comprises the cellular circadian clock, it is now clear that at least four of the circadian clock genes have been identified with remarkable similarities between the function of these genes in fruit flies and mice.

D. Circadian Clock Genes in Humans

While no specific gene has been clearly identified as a component of the molecular circadian clock in humans, the recent discovery of circadian clock genes in mice indicates it is only a matter of time before these or other genes are identified as components of the human circadian timepiece. A number of laboratories are at present attempting to use linkage analysis to identify such genes in small pedigrees of families with specific circadian disorders such as Advanced Sleep Phase Syndrome or Delayed Sleep Phase Syndrome. Such an approach is expected to uncover altered alleles for clock genes that have been identified in lower organisms and/or lead to the discovery of new genes that regulate circadian rhythmicity in humans. In addition, since human orthologs of the murine clock genes have been identified on a basis of sequence similarity, it is now possible to determine the allelic variability of these genes in the human population and to determine if this variability is associated with any specific circadian phenotype and or circadian abnormalities. It will also be of great interest, both from a scientific as well as a medical perspective, to determine if the expression of human clock genes is altered under various pathophysiological conditions as well as during stress.

See Also the Following Article

Circadian Rhythms, Effects of Prenatal Stress in Rodents

Bibliography

Allada, R., White, N. E., So, W. V., Hall, J. C., and Rosbash, M. (1998). A mutant Drosophila homolog of mammalian *Clock* disrupts circadian rhythms and transcription of *period* and *timeless*. *Cell* 93, 791–804.

Antoch, M. P., Song, E.-J., Chang, A.-M., Vitaterna, M. H., Zhao, Y., Wilsbacher, L. D., Sangoram, A. M., King, D. P., Pinto, L. H., and Takahashi, J. S. (1997). Functional identification of the mouse circadian *Clock* gene by transgenic BAC rescue. *Cell* 89, 655–667.

Darlington, T. K., Wager-Smith, K., Ceriani, M. F., Staknis, D., Gekakis, N., Steeves, T. D. L., Weitz, C. J., Takahashi, J. S., and Kay, S. A. (1998). Closing the circadian loop: CLOCK-induced transcription of its own inhibitors *per* and *tim*. *Science* 280, 1599–1603.

Dunlap, J. C. (1996). Genetics and molecular analysis of circadian rhythms. *Annu. Rev. Genet.* 30, 579–601.

Gekakis, N., Staknis, D., Nguyen, H. B., Davis, F. C., Wilsbacher, L. D., King, D. P., Takahashi, J. S., and Weitz, C. J. (1998). Role of the CLOCK protein in the mammalian circadian mechanism. *Science* 280, 1564–1569.

King, D. P., Zhao, Y., Sangoram, A. M., Wilsbacher, L. D., Tanaka, M., Antoch, M. P., Steeves, T. D. L., Vitaterna, M. H., Kornhauser, J. M., Lowery, P. L., Turek, F. W., and Takahashi, J. S. (1997). Positional cloning of the mouse circadian *Clock* gene. *Cell* 89, 641–653.

Kondo, T., Tsinoremas, N. F., Golden, S. S., Johnson, C. H., Kutsuna, S., and Ishiura, M. (1994). Circadian clock mutants of cyanobacteria. *Science* 266, 1233–1236.

Konopka, R. J., and Benzer, S. (1971). *Clock* mutants of Drosophila melanogaster. *Proc. Natl. Acad. Sci. USA* 68, 2112–2116.

Millar, A. J., Carre, I. A., Strayer, C. A., Chua, N. H., and Kay, S. A. (1995). Circadian clock mutants in *Arabidopsis* identified by luciferase imaging. *Science* **267**, 1161–1163.

Pinto, L., Vitaterna, M. H., and Turek, F. W. (1999). Genetic control of circadian rhythms. *In* "Chronobiology: Principles and Practice of Sleep Medicine" (F. W. Turek, Ed.), 3rd ed. Saunders, Philadelphia.

Ralph, M. R., and Menaker, M. (1988). A mutation of the circadian system in golden hamster. *Science* **241**, 1225–1227.

Sangoram, A. M., Saez, L., Antoch, M. P., Gekakis, N., Staknis, D., Whiteley, A., Fruechte, E. M., Vitaterna, M. H., Shimomura, K., King, D. P., Young, M. W., Weitz, C. J., and Takahashi, J. S. (1998). Mammalian circadian autoregulatory loop: a timeless ortholog and mPer1 interact negatively regulate CLOCK-BMAL1-induced transcription. *Neuron* **21**, 1101–1113.

Takahashi, J. S. (1995). Molecular neurobiology and genetics of circadian rhythms in mammals. *Annu. Rev. Neurosci.* **18**, 531–553.

Tei, H., Okamura, H., Shigeyoshi, Y., Fukuhara, C., Ozawa, R., Hirose, M., and Sakaki, Y. (1997). Circadian oscillation of a mammalian homologue of the *Drosophila period* gene. *Nature* **389**, 512–516.

Turek, F. W., and Van Reeth, O. (1996). Circadian rhythms. *In* "Handbook of Physiology: Environmental Physiology" (M. J. Fregly and C. M. Blatteis, Eds.), Ch. 58, pp. 1329–1360. Oxford Univ. Press, Oxford, UK.

Turek, F. W., Pinto, L., Vitaterna, M., Penev, P., Zee, P. C., and Takahashi, J. S. (1995). Pharmacological and genetic approaches for the study of circadian rhythms in mammals. *Frontiers Neuroendocrinol.* **16**, 191–223.

Vitaterna, M. H., King, D. P., Chang, A.-M., Kornhauser, J. M., Lowrey, P. L., McDonald, J. D., Dove, W. F., Pinto, L. H., Turek, F. W., and Takahashi, J. S. (1994). Mutagenesis and mapping of a mouse gene, *Clock*, essential for circadian behavior. *Science* **264**, 719–725.

Cocaine

see Drug Use and Abuse

Cognition and Stress

Mark N. O. Davies

Nottingham Trent University, England

Geoffrey Underwood

University of Nottingham, England

I. Cognitive Foundation of Stress
II. Coping Strategies for Stress
III. Detrimental Impact of Stress on Cognition

GLOSSARY

cognitive appraisal The process by which the response of a person to an emotionally laden environmental demand is dependent upon the individual's interpretation of the information available (including physiological changes). In relation to stress, cognitive appraisal underpins the person's perception of whether they can deal with the demand they face.

driving hazard An event (usually involving another road user) that causes the driver to take evasive action.

ecological model An umbrella term to cover models of stress that emphasize the dynamic relationship between the individual and the environment. Typical examples are the transactional and interactionist models of stress.

feedback An important concept with respect to the control of behavior. If feedback is present, a circuit or loop of information is formed. This loop generates information (output) that is fed back to the information source (input) to modulate the output.

Cognition involves a resource-limited mediating system that enables us to make adaptive responses to events. It results in sensations being transformed into perceptions, perceptions into memories, and comprehended events into general mental models. These general mental models allow us to organize information about the world so that we can formulate and execute plans to generate optimal performance (adaptive responses). Early models of cognition emphasized serial processing; however, it has become clear that the cognitive system is more interactive involving parallel and cascading processes. Stress can have influences throughout the cognitive system. Sub-optimal performance can result from changes at many levels from perception through problem solving. Furthermore, stress can be a product of the same processes. This reciprocity between stress and cognition is clearly a complex relationship. In what follows we shall discuss the role of cognition in the development of the stress response, the adaptive responses of cognitive processes, and the detrimental effects of stress upon a component of cognition (i.e., memory).

I. COGNITIVE FOUNDATION OF STRESS

We all have a common understanding of what is meant when someone comments that they are experiencing stress in their life. However, underlying this simple statement is a complex issue of definition. Although the term stress is often used freely to describe an everyday state, it may represent different concepts to different people. There are three main ways of viewing stress. First, stress can be taken as an external force, so a person can be described as being *under* stress at work. In this context stress is a causal agent. Alternatively, stress can be viewed as a perturbation of a system (i.e., the body) due to external forces that usually are referred to as stressors. In this case stress is seen as the product rather than the cause. This "effector definition" underpinned one of the most influential models of stress that arose out of medicine in the 1950s referred to as Selye's General Adaptation Syndrome. Selye specified stress as a nonspecific response to demand on the body. Thus the stress response was independent of the stressor. The response syndrome was expressed as a universal pattern of defense reactions composed of three stages: (1) alarm reaction, (2) resistance or adaptation, and (3) collapse. In this medical model Selye ignored the role of psychological factors.

In the 1970s and 1980s there was a move away from simple product models of stress toward more ecologically valid models. These ecological models attempted to embrace not only external stressors and the body's response, but to introduce as central to the understanding of stress the importance of a psychological dimension. Such models have gone under different names such as *transactional* or *interactionist* models. Common to the ecological models of stress is the central role that cognitive appraisal plays in the stress response of individuals.

The ecological models represent the relationship between the person and the environment as dynamic in nature. Thus the person is seen to enter a *transaction* or to *interact* with the environment. Consequently, stress arises out of a *perceived* lack of fit between the demands of the environment and the resources available to the individual to cope with the demand. Thus, the general scenario is that a demand (stressor) is placed on an individual, the person perceives the demand and assesses their ability to cope with the demand (perceived goodness of fit), and any resulting mismatch between demand and perceived capacity to deal with the demand results in stress. Stress leads to the employment of one or more coping strategies (coping), the outcome of which is monitored and fed back into the perception of fit (see Fig. 1 for summary).

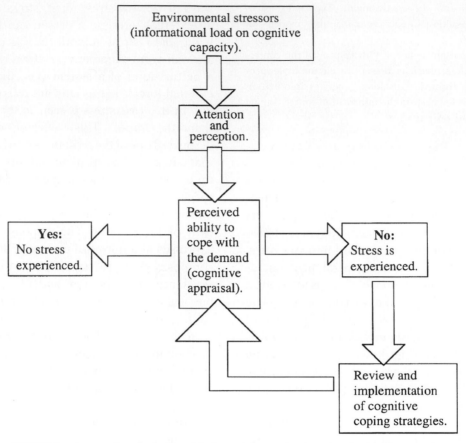

FIGURE 1   A general ecological model of cognitive mechanisms involved in the experience and management of stress.

II. COPING STRATEGIES FOR STRESS

Central to the formulation of stress as an ecological process is the role of cognitive appraisal as espoused by Lazarus and others. In the first instance, a person will appraise the relevance of an external event (e.g., increased workload) to their own situation. This is referred to as primary appraisal. Secondary appraisal incorporates the coping strategies available and an evaluation of their likely efficacy. The review of the success or otherwise of the coping strategies applied and the emergence of new information may impact upon the cognitive appraisal undertaken at the secondary level, leading to changes in the coping strategies used. This has been referred to as reappraisal. In Fig. 1 initial appraisal and reappraisal are incorporated within the feedback circuit. The goal is therefore to minimize the distress experienced and max-

imize any potential positive benefits. The most robust case at present argues for a three-factor model of coping that covers the management of emotional responses, problem solving, and avoidance.

The coverage of stress in textbooks usually emphasises the negative consequences of experiencing stress. It should be remembered that stress is a natural process that has evolved to offer adaptive benefits. It is only when coping strategies fail to accrue benefits that we should conceive stress as detrimental to an individual. A clear example of the beneficial, adaptive consequences of stress is illustrated by the allocation of cognitive resources during emergency situations. The handling of hazards while driving is a skill that places a series of demands on the cognitive system, from perception to the execution of automatic response processes. These demands can act as stressors even though most of us encounter them so frequently that we are accustomed to thinking of them as part of everyday life. Stress as an adaptive response, as with emotion generally, helps to draw a person's attention to an event in the environment that requires action.

When learning to drive we process a rapidly changing visual display and execute a carefully coordinated sequence of responses to ensure that the vehicle maintains its intended path. For most novice drivers the demands exceed their perceived ability to cope until the relationships between environmental input and the necessary responses have been learned. To develop the skill of driving, a person has to respond to the environment and incorporate feedback from actions taken and the advice from the driving instructor.

After months of driving experience the basic control of the vehicle is no longer a stressful activity—the organization of responses is now within the cognitive capacity of the driver. The driver perceives that the demands of driving can be met. Thus the processing of responses are described as automatic in that the driver, when changing gear, does not consciously think about how far to depress the clutch pedal or the timing of the gear stick movement. These coordinated actions can occur while the driver is studying the road ahead or is engaged in conversation. Under these circumstances the tasks are being performed without consideration of the feedback from the environment; that is, the person ignores the information available to confirm that the action has had the required effect. A valuable observation made in this connection is that when we rely upon open-loop control we are likely to make a range of performance errors that are distinct from those that we make when sensitive to feedback information. Under these circumstances well-established habits are likely to develop as an automatic response to stress.

When we fail to attend to our position in a plan of action we are vulnerable to error. The cognitive capacities of well-practiced drivers are very good at coping with the demands of vehicle control; nevertheless, a significant proportion of road traffic accidents can be attributed to performance error. These are stressful events; particularly for drivers who have an accident history and who may be reminded of the consequences of failing to take evasive action. The

cognitive decisions involved in responding to driving hazards are currently an active area of research for cognitive psychologists.

Underwood and colleagues have investigated how drivers gather information during a simulation of an unexpected driving hazard. The eye movements of drivers are recorded as they watch video recordings taken from the driver's position of a naturally moving vehicle. During the video a series of typical hazards are presented, such as other road users crossing the path of the video-vehicle with very abrupt time-to-contact trajectories. The research has shown that newly qualified drivers differ from experienced drivers in their fixation patterns. Experienced drivers inspect the hazardous object for a shorter duration. However, no difference has been detected in the pattern of focusing when the hazard appears. The short inspection time for experienced drivers is indicative of three possibilities. First, they require less time to recognize the hazard and its likely consequences (cf. word recognition by a skilled reader). Second, practiced drivers know that when a hazardous event occurs there is often a secondary hazard. The final option is that experienced drivers perceive they have the ability to cope with the ensuing problem and therefore allocate the optimum proportion of their cognitive resources to the task. In contrast, inexperienced drivers who are less sure concerning their ability to cope with the unexpected demand automatically apply a greater proportion of their cognitive resources to attending to the hazard. These interpretations of the data are not mutually exclusive.

A hazardous environment will require attention. The ability to focus quickly, estimate collision trajectory and time-to-contact are clearly adaptive skills that many species possess. However, driving has magnified the problem since the speed involved and the complexity of the environment go beyond the natural scale of our species. Whereby ducking a punch only involves stress after the event, the need to process information both consciously and unconsciously over a period measured in seconds rather than milliseconds when facing driving hazards involves its own type of stressors. Therefore the initial fixation is adaptive, but how inexperienced and experienced drivers cope with the information sampled depends on their perceived ability to cope with the situation and the availability of coping strategies (e.g., execution of an action plan to stop the car from skidding).

III. DETRIMENTAL IMPACT OF STRESS ON COGNITION

Traditionally the relationship between stress and performance has been represented by an inverted U function where arousal substitutes for stress. The argument being that too little or too much arousal (stress) leads to sub-optimal performance. However, the evidence available does not support such a simple description. Rather, the relationship between stress and performance should be viewed as multidimensional in nature. Researchers have largely failed to agree on how to generally represent the relationship as the impact of the stressor appears to vary dependent on its nature (e.g., noise) and the type of task involved (e.g., memory task). This fits with an ecological model of stress in that a person's response to a particular stressor is dependent on that individual's appraisal of the demand placed on them in a given context. The impact of a stressor is likely to have its greatest influence through the attentional system as previously highlighted with reference to driving hazards. As perceived demand on limited cognitive capacity increases, attentional resources dedicated to perceptuomotor processing will be preferentially diverted to support cognitive appraisal and coping strategies.

A. Work Stress

Occupational psychologists have modeled work stress as a behavioral response pattern to stress in relation to work demands. On the surface, a surprising result has consistently been obtained. An increase in work stress does not automatically result in a fall in work performance (primary task). Psychologists such as Hockey have proposed that the desire to maintain efficiency with regard to primary task performance does not mean that stress has had no impact on the individual. Rather, the behavioral route by which the impact of work stress can be measured is thought to vary. Hockey has identified three indi-

rect routes: compensatory costs, strategic adjustment, and fatigue after-effects. Thus, with an increase in work demand a person may experience an increase in negative emotions (compensatory costs) or rescheduling of task requirements which leaves the goal of the primary task untouched (strategic adjustment). A further possibility is to record a breakdown in cognitive performance after completion of the primary task (fatigue after-effects). This is not easily detected and requires sensitive tests that allow differential performance with respect to cognitive effort and level of risk associated with decisions. These indirect routes are seen as optional regulatory activities that help to maintain optimal performance on the primary task. Of course circumstances will arise whereby the coping strategies, whether focused on the primary task or involving indirect routes, fail. A situation commonly associated with chronic levels of stress.

B. Stress, Memory, and Dementia

One of the cognitive performance indicators investigated in terms of the impact of a number of stressors is memory. Nonprofessional shoplifters represent an everyday example of the impact of stress on memory. In a large percentage of cases the items stolen prove to be irrelevant to the shoplifter or worth little in monetary terms. A common response in these people is that their "mind was elsewhere." The agent for such absentmindedness has been identified as stressful life events (e.g., divorce). For an event to be perceived as stressful it does not have to be a negative experience. For example, having a child or reaching the final of a sporting championship may well be experienced as stressful. The key issue is how the individual appraises the demands they are likely to face and their ability to cope.

Anecdotal or opportunistic data is helpful in illuminating the cost of stress on cognitive function; however, additional, systematic investigation is required to dissect out the relationship between stress and cognition. One such study chose to focus on novice skydivers. The study looked at a range of cognitive performance tasks. The skydivers were asked to perform the tasks the day before they jumped for the first time. They were assessed a second time just before embarking on the plane prior to their jump. To measure stress levels both self-report and heart rate data was collected. Not surprisingly, the stress variables confirmed that there was an increase in the stress response from the first to the second test session. Parallel to this increase in stress, there was a drop in the memory performance of the subjects on a digit span test from the first to the second testing stage.

The effect of traumatic events on individuals with respect to a chronic stress response is now widely recognized under the heading of post-traumatic stress disorder (PTSD). In simple terms PTSD involves the generation of significant psychological distress relating to a particular traumatic event. The emphasis in the literature has been on the diagnosis of PTSD and the development of therapies to help afflicted individuals. However, there is a growing interest in the relationship between chronic levels of stress and in particular memory. Work in the neurosciences has begun to unravel the relationship between chronic stress and the biological foundations of memory. Both animal and human models have been used to look at the relationship between stress levels and the hippocampus. The hippocampus resides on both the left and right side of the brain. It is widely recognized that damage to the hippocampus in human beings as well as other mammals through injury, disease, or surgery can significantly impair memory function. The work recently completed by Lupien and colleagues has shown that in aged humans a raised level of cortisol (stress hormone) is associated with reduced hippocampal volume and deficits in allied memory tests compared to cortisol-normal controls. It is generally accepted that memory is a product of structural and biochemical changes at the cellular level. The evidence that exposure to a raised and chronic level of cortisol is associated with significant changes in anatomy and function of the hippocampus has led researchers to propose a link between exposure to chronic stress levels, memory impairment, and possibly dementia. For the future it would be valuable to investigate the possible links between PTSD and memory performance.

See Also the Following Articles

ALARM PHASE AND GENERAL ADAPTATION SYNDROME; COPING SKILLS; HIPPOCAMPUS, OVERVIEW; MEMORY AND STRESS; MEMORY IMPAIRMENT; SELYE, HANS; WORKPLACE STRESS

Bibliography

Fisher, S. (1986). *Stress and strategy*. London: LEA.

Idzikowski, C., and Baddeley, A. D. (1987). Fear and performance in novice parachutists. *Ergonomics* 30: 1463–1474.

Lazarus, R. S., and Folkman, S. (1984). *Stress, appraising and coping*. New York: Springer.

Lazarus, R. S., and Smith, C. A. (1988). Knowledge and appraisal in the cognition–emotion relationship. *Cognition and Emotion* 2: 281–300.

Lupien, S. J., de Leon, M., de Santi, S., Convit, A., Tarshish, C., Nair, N. P. V., Thakur, M., McEwen, B. S., Hauger, R. L., and Meaney, M. J. (1998). Cortisol levels during human aging predict hippocampal atrophy and memory deficits. *Nature Neuroscience* 1: 69–73.

Porter, N. M. and Landfield, P. W. (1998). Stress hormones and brain aging: Adding injury to insult? *Nature Neuroscience* 1: 3–4.

Underwood, G. (1998). *Eye guidance in reading and scene perception*. Oxford: Elsevier.

Cognitive Behavioral Therapy

Giovanni A. Fava

University of Bologna, Italy and State University of New York at Buffalo

I. Definition of Cognitive Behavioral Therapy
II. Specific Techniques
III. Applications of Cognitive Behavioral Therapy in the Stress Response

GLOSSARY

cognitive therapy A brief psychotherapeutic approach aimed to changing thinking.
exposure A brief psychotherapeutic approach based on exposure to feared situations or stimuli.
problem-solving training A brief psychotherapeutic approach for improving problematic situations and/or interpersonal conflicts.
rational-emotive behavior therapy A brief psychotherapeutic treatment that relies on persuasion and reason.
stress-management approaches A set of diverse techniques for reducing psychophysiological activation.

C ognitive behavioral therapy is a brief psychotherapeutic treatment that seeks to produce change in cognition and behavior. The term includes a number of diverse therapeutic procedures, such as cognitive therapy, rational-emotive psychotherapy, problem-solving intervention, and exposure. It may yield a reduction in the psychophysiological activation that is associated with the stress response, or an improvment in coping skills, or both.

I. DEFINITION OF COGNITIVE BEHAVIORAL THERAPY

The term cognitive behavioral therapy subsumes a number of diverse therapeutic procedures, such as cognitive therapy, rational-emotive psychotherapy, problem-solving interventions, and exposure. In a restrictive definition, it indicates psychotherapeutic approaches that explicitly seek to produce change in cognition as a means of influencing other phenomena of interest, such as affect or behavior. This definition excludes specific behavioral interventions, such as exposure, that may work through cognitive mediation, but are not primarily intended to produce change by influencing thinking. A broader definition stems from the growing awareness that most psychotherapeutic approaches combine cognitive and behavioral elements, even though in different ways and to different extents. As a result, both cognitive and behavioral approaches may legitimately belong to the broader rubric of cognitive behavioral therapy. The past 2 decades have witnessed an increasing awareness of the common ingredients that pertain to the psychotherapeutic process (Table I) and that cognitive behavioral approaches share (Table II).

In randomized controlled trials, behavior therapy (exposure) alone and cognitive therapy alone obtained similar improvements in obsessive-compulsive disorder, in agoraphobia with panic attacks, in posttraumatic stress disorder, and in hypochondriasis. This is leading to a weakening of classic paradigms and theories underlying each specific psychotherapeutic approach and to the necessity of paradigm shifts in our understanding of clinical changes [Marks, I. (1999). Is a paradigm shift occurring in brief psychological treatment? *Psychother. Psychosom.* **68**, 169–170]. According to an evidence-based viewpoint, the term cognitive behavioral therapy has a broad connotation and may indicate any brief psychological therapy which uses the ingredients that are listed in Table II. The relative weight of each (or additional) ingredient may vary from one technique to the other, as defined by treatment protocols. In clinical practice, it may even vary from one case to the other or according to the stages of application of psychotherapy. For instance, in cognitive behavioral management of drug-resistant major depression disorder, behavioral techniques may

TABLE I
Nonspecific Therapeutic Ingredients That Are Shared by
Most Forms of Psychotherapy

Ingredients	Characteristics
1. Attention	The therapist's full availability for specific times.
2. Disclosure	The patient's opportunity to ventilate thoughts and feelings
3. High arousal	An emotionally charged, confiding relationship with a helping person.
4. Interpretation	A plausible explanation of the disturbed symptoms.
5. Rituals	A ritual or procedure that requires the active participation of both patient and therapist and that is believed by both to be the means of restoring the patient's health.

characterize the initial phase of treatment, whereas cognitive restructuring is applied only at a later point in time [Fava, G. A., Savron, G., Grandi, S., and Rafanelli, C. (1997). Cognitive behavioral management of drug resistant major depressive disorder. *J. Clin. Psychia.* 58, 278–282].

II. SPECIFIC TECHNIQUES

The therapeutic techniques that are used in cognitive behavioral therapy may range from modification

TABLE II
**Main Common Characteristics of
Cognitive Behavioral Therapies**

The therapy tends to be short (less than 20 sessions)

The therapy is structured and follows a prearranged schema of development.

The attention is centered on current problems.

Patient and therapist agree on the goals of treatment, which are clearly defined.

The patient is encouraged to perform self-observation of thinking and/or behavior, which may lead to their characterization (functional analysis).

Homework assignments (whether consisting of self-observation or performing specific tasks) are given and reviewed by the therapist.

The therapy aims at developing the patient's control over his or her own problems or behaviors.

of emotional and relaxation responses (e.g., stress management techniques) to cognitive restructuring (e.g., cognitive therapy). The most important approaches (in terms of clinical acceptance and effectiveness or future implications) are listed in Table III. Exposure (mainly graded, planned, homework exposure to distressing stimuli) has emerged as the most effective behavioral technique in anxiety disorders. In the setting of disturbances such as obsessive-compulsive disorder exposure to avoided cues may be associated with response prevention (staying in contact with those cues during the ensuing discomfort). Exposure appears to be a key factor in therapeutic change and may be implemented by diverse protocol, whose effectiveness, however, depends on the degree of *in vivo* exposure by the patient as a homework assignment. Operant conditioning derives from Skinner's work on the importance of contingencies in behavior, that is, whether a given response is followed by a positive or negative reinforcer. More than a specific strategy, it is a technique which may be incorporated in more complex strategies, such as dietary programs. Techniques based on relaxation methods achieved wide popularity in the 1970s and have been documented to be effective when emphasis is placed on enhanced muscular control, as in many cases of functional medical disorders. Relaxation may be seen as part of stress-management approaches which are aimed at reducing arousal and combine various therapeutic ingredients, such as stress-inoculation training. This technique combines cognitive restructuring with behavioral self-management techniques. Patients are encouraged to apply these

TABLE III
Cognitive Behavioral Interventions

Exposure

Response prevention

Operant conditioning

Relaxation

Stress-inoculation training

Problem-solving training

Rational-emotive behavior therapy

Cognitive therapy

Well-being therapy

skills to a series of increasingly difficult tasks in order to cope with problematic life events. Problem-solving training emphasizes social problem-solving as the primary coping strategy. This transactional approach uses a set of sequential procedures for dealing with problematic situations and interpersonal conflicts. In Ellis' rational emotive behavior therapy, patients are taught to examine the rationality as the primary mechanism of change. Beck's cognitive therapy is today probably the most widely endorsed cognitive intervention. Patients are encouraged to identify their beliefs, to treat them as hypotheses to be tested and are taught alternative explanations. Both rational-emotive therapy and cognitive therapy incorporate behavioral components in their approach. Well-being therapy uses cognitive restructuring and behavioral interventions for enhancing psychological well-being. It is aimed at changing beliefs, attitudes, and behaviors that are detrimental to well-being [Fava, G.A., Rafanelli, C., Cazzaro, M., Grandi, S., and Conti, S. (1998). Well-being therapy. *Psychol. Med.* **28**, 475–480].

III. APPLICATIONS OF COGNITIVE BEHAVIORAL THERAPY IN THE STRESS RESPONSE

Cognitive behavioral intervention may have two distinct yet ostensibly related roles in the modulation of stress response. One is concerned with a reduction in the psychophysiological activation that is associated (e.g., stress-management approaches). The other is related to the transactional model of stress, which emphasizes cognitive appraisal (how an event is interpreted by the individual) and coping (e.g., cognitive therapy). There is substantial evidence, based on randomized controlled studies, that cognitive behavioral treatment may improve the outcome and quality of life of several psychiatric and medical disorders (Tables IV and V). Further, it may improve health-promoting behaviors, such as changing harmful lifestyle patterns and habits, and modify illness attitudes and behaviors. In view of the role of psychological well-being in human health and disease [Ryff, C. D., and Singer, B. (1998). The contours of positive

human health. *Psychol. Inquiry* **9**, 1–28] it is conceivable, but yet to be tested, that well-being therapy may offer another route to improve the stress response. The absence of wellness may in fact create conditions of vulnerability to life adversities and an increase in psychological well-being may increase an individual's coping skills.

TABLE IV

Evidence-Based Applications of Cognitive Behavioral Therapy in Psychiatric Disorders

Mood disorders
Panic disorders and agoraphobia
Social phobia
Generalized anxiety disorder
Simple phobia
Posttraumatic stress disorder
Hypochondriasis
Obsessive-compulsive disorder
Anorexia nervosa
Bulimia nervosa
Psychosis and schizophrenia
Personality disorders
Alcoholism and drug dependence

TABLE V

Evidence-Based Applications of Cognitive Behavioral Therapy in the Medical Setting

Chronic pain
Chronic fatigue syndrome
Coronary heart disease
Hypertension
Tension headache
Diabetes
Cancer
Asthma
Epilepsy
Obesity
Irritable bowel syndrome
Inflammatory bowel disease
HIV infection and AIDS
Arthritis
Preparation to medical procedures
Smoking

See Also the Following Articles

Behavior Therapy; Child Sexual Abuse; Coping Skills; Stress Management

Bibliography

Beck, A. T. (1976). "Cognitive Therapy and the Emotional Disorders." International Universities Press, New York.

Bergin, A. E., and Garfield, S. L. (Eds.) (1994). "Handbook of Psychotherapy and Behavior Change," 4th ed. Wiley, New York.

Ellis, A. T. (1962). "Reason and Emotion in Psychotherapy." Lyle Stuart, New York.

Emmelkamp, P. M. G., Bouman, T. K., and Scholing, A. (1992). "Anxiety Disorders." Wiley, Chichester.

Fava, G. A., and Freyberger, H. (Eds.) (1998). "Handbook of Psychosomatic Medicine." International Universities Press, Madison, CT.

Frank, J. D., and Frank, B. (1991). "Persuasion and Healing," 3rd ed. The John Hopkins Univ. Press, Baltimore, MD.

Marks, I. (1987). "Fears, Phobias, and Rituals." Oxford Univ. Press, New York.

Meichenbaum, D. (1985). "Stress Inoculation Training." Pergamon, New York.

Combat, Acute Reactions to

Richard H. Rahe

University of Nevada School of Medicine

Disabling psychological reactions to combat have been witnessed frequently, yet codified differently, by U.S. observers in each of the country's wars. Diagnoses coined for these conditions have varied from "nostalgia" in the Civil War, to "shell shock" in World War I, to "war neurosis" and "combat exhaustion" in World War II, to "battle fatigue" in the Korean and Vietnam conflicts. In most instances, what is described is either a precipitous, or a gradual, breakdown in a serviceman's ability to perform his combat functions, accompanied by a variety of distressing and disabling body symptoms. Modern-day interest in this disorder is perhaps highest in the Israeli armed forces because of their soldiers' intense exposures to combat over the past 3 decades.

A common assumption in psychiatry is that disabling psychological reactions to combat, despite their differing characteristics and their several descriptive titles, comprise a unitary condition. Variability in parameters such as onset, symptoms, and recovery is thought to be secondary to the afflicted individual's strengths and weaknesses. That is to say, a young, inexperienced, frightened soldier may develop a disabling psychological reaction his first week in combat compared with an older, battle-worn, sergeant who breaks down only after months of intense fighting. Treatment principles of immediacy, proximity, and expectancy are often thought to apply equally to both of these examples.

Drawing from the combat psychiatry literature as well as from studies of human stress encountered in a variety of settings one can make a case for distinguishing acute combat reactions from chronic ones. In so doing, clinical presentations, precipitating factors, treatment approaches, and expectations to return to duty become more specific. Furthermore, preventive measures for these two conditions differ. Finally, this classification is in accord with current thinking regarding posttraumatic stress disorder, which was recently classified into acute and chronic forms in the Diagnostic and Statistical Manual—IV of the American Psychiatric Association.

I. ACUTE COMBAT REACTION

The Israeli Defense Forces in the 1980s and 1990s have used the term "battle shock" to denote their experiences with disabling psychological reactions to combat that appear within hours after stress exposure. In civilian settings, one finds very similar conditions in acute stress reactions and panic states. In brief, an acute combat reaction is characterized by an abrupt onset of physiological hyperarousal following a brief exposure to an intensely stressful event(s). Signs and symptoms of this disorder, its treatment and prevention, follow below.

A. Signs and Symptoms

Early manifestations of this reaction are common to all soldiers facing battle. It is, therefore, the degree of response that leads to a diagnosis. A very early sign is a notable reluctance of a soldier to leave a secure setting. The vulnerable person will often be one of the last in line proceeding toward danger, casting frequent glances back toward safety. He may unnecessarily check and recheck his equipment—these adventitial body movements representing a displacement of his anxiety. The person may also show marked difficulty in understanding instructions and even carrying out simple tasks.

Widely opened eyes, dilated pupils, and rapid, shallow breathing signal strong sympathetic nervous system activation. The sympathetic nervous system involvement is the major physiological component of an acute combat reaction. If blood or urinary measures for catecholamines could be gathered from soldiers with this disorder, epinephrine and norepinephrine should both be significantly elevated. It is also likely that the soldier's serum cortisol would be elevated throughout this reaction.

As an acute combat reaction worsens, the affected soldier may not take cover during an assault or he may remain hidden in a bunker and unable to fire his weapon or to care for a buddy in trouble. In its most severe form, affected individuals may show an "overflow" of undirected motor activity, which may mimic tics or seizures. Conversely, hyperarousal can also lead to a "freezing" of motor function, which may resemble paralysis.

An acute combat reaction can develop, and resolve, within a matter of minutes. As recovery from this entity can be very rapid, the soldier may show a dramatic transition from gross panic one minute to rational thought and behavior a few minutes later. Therefore, a cardinal rule is not to move an afflicted soldier further than the battle aid station closest to the front lines and watch for a likely rapid recovery.

B. Precipitants

It should be emphasized that no single factor can totally account for the development of an acute combat reaction. Rather, it is the sum of separate forces acting in concert over a short period of time. Precipitating forces may emanate from the environment, they may be the result of interpersonal stresses, and they may stem from the individual himself.

Environmental stresses, such as fatigue, hunger, cold, heat, and so forth, are common experiences of men in battle. They take on additional significance when other precipitants of acute battle stress coexist. For example, when a battle is being waged in sustained heat (such as a desert war) and soldiers are dehydrated, an intense action with a high casualty rate becomes all the more stressful. Add to this situation abrupt disorientation, so that the soldier does not know in which direction it is safe to move, followed by a surprise attack from an unsuspected direction, these several environmental forces, acting together, are very likely to precipitate an acute combat reaction.

Interpersonal factors are, for the most part, a reflection of command. Having seasoned combat veterans in close proximity to inexperienced soldiers, where they can serve as role models, is enormously helpful. Reserve status, rather than a regular commission and membership in a support unit (usually armor), is a major interpersonal precipitant of this disorder. Soldiers who are members of elite units, where esprit and morale are generally quite high, tend to perform far better in combat than men in less cohesive units. A further interpersonal stress occurs when reserves are brought forward to replace the dead and injured. These reserves may be assigned to tanks still bloody from the previous campaign and find themselves communicating, by radio, with persons they've never met. In this situation reserves are seen to have extremely high rates of acute combat reaction.

Factors of age and inexperience are major personal precipitants of this disorder. An infantrymen in his late 20s or early 30s has a much higher probability of developing an acute combat reaction than one in his late teens or early 20s. Soldiers are especially vulnerable to acute combat reactions when they witness death for the first time. One of the major functions of military training is to prepare the soldier for the rigors of battle so that he can function almost reflexively in that environment. Yet it is impossible to train men for the experience of seeing their fellow soldiers killed. Finally, the length of time that men have been together appears to be a powerful force in combat and, accordingly, a predictor for low rates of acute combat reaction.

A particularly stressful personal factor is to be assigned as a "new guy" to an already established unit. The replacement is seen as "an intruder" by the group and a reminder that one of their buddies was killed or wounded. It may take weeks to months for a new soldier in a unit to lose this "new guy" label.

C. Treatment

Treatment of an acute combat reaction should be immediate. It is far easier to reverse this disorder in its early stages than when the condition lingers. This means that the location where treatment is provided is usually at, or very near, the front lines of battle. Importantly, the person who carries out treatment is usually not a doctor—more likely it is a fellow soldier or a medic/corpsman.

The most important first step in treatment is to help the affected individual to gain control over his hyperaroused physiology. Rapid, shallow breathing will quickly cause hypocapnia with resultant light-headedness and feelings of panic. Hypothermia, hyperthermia, and tachycardia can produce similar effects. The first rule in such a situation is to stop. Once the person begins to "cool down" (often literally), rational thinking can return. Counting slowly, and/or making respiratory expirations last longer than inspirations, are easy remedies to remember. When

rational thinking returns, reorientation can take place and military priorities can be reestablished.

An acutely stressed individual will often show a need to talk about his recent experiences. A buddy or medic should hear the story once, perhaps twice. Further recitations will have little further anxiety-reducing effects. Following one or two recitals, the man should be evaluated for being sent back to his unit (with a buddy) versus instituting rest and replenishment over the next 24 to 48 h. These men can be treated at a battle aid station or in a separate section of a field hospital. Medications, if required, are generally hypnotics and antianxiety preparations. Because of this condition's ready reversibility, return to duty rates can be as high as 95%.

It has become a rule not to mix soldiers with disabling psychological reactions to combat with others who are physically wounded. When that occurs, men with psychological reactions quickly identify with the wounded and their psychological disabilities increase. A special effort must be made to keep these two classes of patients apart; otherwise, in the normal logistical flow of patients' rearward those with acute combat reactions will be separated from their unit. A special problem arises when a soldier experiences both an acute combat reaction and a physical wound. He is usually treated for the wound and not for his psychological condition.

D. Prevention

Environmental, interpersonal, and personal aspects of prevention should be considered as much as the precipitation of this disorder in a multifactorial framework. It takes efforts in several areas to appreciably reduce the likelihood of acute combat reaction.

It is military doctrine to keep soldiers properly fed, warm, and rested whenever possible. When these conditions cannot be met, as is frequently the case in battle, command should realize that the chances for acute stress reactions are thereby increased. Although resupplies may not be under a commander's control, communications with his men regarding the progress of the campaign, the motivations and armament of the enemy, and so forth are certainly within his influence. Also, battle plans should be phrased in clear, concise, easy-to-remember language.

A most effective preventive force is realistic training. Seldom, however, is such training carried out. Perhaps the best example of currently performed preventive training is that of survival, evasion, resistance, and escape training conducted by the U.S. Navy and U.S. Air Force. These 1- to 2-week programs are designed for aviators—who, by the nature of their duties, are at high risk for capture and prisoner-of-war status. However, realistic training for combat troops could be provided. An important element of such training would be allowing soldiers to actually experience panic symptoms under controlled conditions. Treatment steps of stopping and controlling hyperphysiology (allowing return of rational thinking and action) could then be implemented. Also, mental rehearsal prior to stress training of the steps a soldier should follow in a panic situation should be part of this training.

Physical fitness, of an endurance nature, leads to increased parasympathetic tone. This parasympathetic tone may well act as a "brake" on the sympathetic nervous system's hyperarousal during panic-producing situations. Personal commitment to battle and attitude under stress are greatly shaped by the soldier's training. Ideally, he should incorporate many of the ideals and attitudes of his instructors. John Wooden, the eminently successful basketball coach at UCLA, encouraged his players to "Be quick, but don't hurry." Such an attitude imparts a perception of personal control over fast-moving events.

See Also the Following Articles

COMBAT REACTION, CHRONIC; WAR-RELATED POSTTRAUMATIC STRESS DISORDER

Bibliography

American Psychiatric Association (1994). "Diagnostic and Statistical Manual," 4th ed., Author, Washington, DC.

Bachrach, A. J. (1984). Stress physiology and behavior under water. *In* C. H., Shilling, C. B., Carlson, and R. A. Mathias, (Eds.), "The Physician's Guide to Diving Medicine." Plenum, New York.

Belenky, G. L., Noy, S., and Solomon, Z. (1985). Battle stress: the Israeli experience. *Military Rev.* 29–37.

Belenky, G. L., Tyner, C. F., and Sodetz, F. J. (1983). Israeli Battle Shock Casualties: 1973 and 1982. Report NP-83-4, Walter Reed Army Institute of Research, Division of Neuropsychiatry, Washington, DC.

Bourne, P. G. (1970). "Men, Stress and Vietnam." Little, Brown, Boston.

Brill, N. Q., and Beebe, G. W. (1955). A follow-up study of war neuroses. *VA Med. Monogr.*

Cantor, J. R., Zillman, D., and Day, K. D. (1978). Relationship between cardiovascular fitness and physiological response to films. *Percept. Mot. Skills* 46, 1123–1139.

Glass, A. J. (1954). Psychotherapy in the combat zone. *Am. J. Psychiat.* 110, 725–731.

Glass, A. J. (1958). Observations upon the epidemiology of mental illness in troops during warfare. *In* "Symposium on Preventive and Social Psychiatry, April 15–17, 1957." Walter Reed Army Institute of Research, U.S. Govt. Printing Office, Washington, DC.

Grinker, A. A., and Spiegel, J. P. (1945). "Men under Stress." Blakiston, Philadelphia.

Keller, S., and Seraganian, P. (1984). Physical fitness and autonomic reactivity to psychosocial stress. *J. Psychosom. Res.* 28, 279–287.

Kellett, A. (1980). Combat Motivation: Operational Research and Analysis Establishment. Report No. R-77, Ottawa, Department of National Defense.

Kentsmith, D. K. (1986). Principles of battlefield psychiatry. *Military Med.* 151, 89–96.

Kormos, H. R. (1978). The nature of combat stress. *In* C. R. Figley, (Ed.), "Stress Disorders Among Vietnam Veterans: Theory, Research and Treatment." Brunner/Mazel, New York.

Mason, J. W., Hartley, L. H., Kotchen, E. H. *et al.* (1973). Plasma cortisol and norepinephrine responses in anticipation of muscular exercise. *Psychosom. Med.* 35, 406–414.

Mason, J. W., Sachar, E. J., and Grinker, A. A. (1965). Corticosteroid responses to hospital admission. *Arch. Psychiat.* 13, 1–8.

(1870). "Medical and Surgical History of the War of the Rebellion," Vol. I, U.S. Government Printing Office, Washington, DC.

Missri, J. C., and Alexander, S. (1978). Hyperventilation syndrome: A brief review. *J. Am. Med. Assoc.* 240, 2093–2096.

Mullins, W. S. (Ed.) (1973). "Neuropsychiatry in World War II," Vol. II. Office of the Surgeon General (Army), Washington, DC.

Schifferle, P. J. (1985). The technology of teamwork. *Armor Mag.* Nov–Dec, pp 10–13.

West, L. J. (1958). Psychiatric aspects of training for honorable survival as a prisoner of war. *Am. J. Psychiat.* 115, 329–336.

Combat Reaction, Chronic

Richard H. Rahe

University of Nevada School of Medicine

O ften confused with acute combat reaction is the chronic form of this disorder. The subject often develops chronic combat disorder without experiencing the acute form. The signs and symptoms, precipitants, treatment, and prevention of chronic combat reaction are presented in this article. The history of this disorder in American military psychiatry is also mentioned. It is important to note that this disorder has many similarities to "burnout."

I. CHRONIC COMBAT REACTION

Chronic combat reaction is the "other side of the coin" from the acute reaction described in a separate article. An earlier term for this disorder, "combat fatigue," was literally ordered into use by General Omar N. Bradley in 1943. Colonel Long wrote: "Of the possible diagnostic terms discussed, this word [exhaustion] was chosen because it was thought to convey the least implication of neuropsychiatric disturbance."

As in acute combat reactions, causes of this condition are multiple. Men developing chronic combat reactions have typically been under stress for many weeks, months, or perhaps even years. Their physiological state appears to be characterized by hypoarousal. Instead of fight/flight physiology these men tend to show signs and symptoms of conservation/withdrawal. The affected soldier frequently isolates himself from his peers and shows signs and symptoms of depression. Once established, this combat reaction is extremely difficult to reverse. In animal studies of "defeat situations," a similar syndrome is seen. Signs and symptoms, precipitants, treatment, and prevention of chronic combat reaction are presented below.

A. Signs and Symptoms

Early signs include impairment of previously displayed skills, severely lowered frustration tolerance, excessive griping, and even mild to moderate paranoia. As these characteristics are frequently manifested in all combat troops, it can be a subtle distinction to determine when they exceed the normal range and signal concern. In a word, when these traits cause a man to significantly isolate himself from his peers, it is time to evaluate the individual. If excessive alcohol or drug use and/or signs and symptoms of depression are also found, the diagnosis should be strongly suspected.

If urine and blood samples could be collected in the field, catecholamines should be at normal or even low levels in men with chronic combat reactions. In contrast, cortisol should be significantly and persistently elevated throughout the circadian cycle. In a variety of chronic stress reactions, the baseline for cortisol secretion appears to be "reset" to a higher level. A further biochemical correlate of chronic stress is serum cholesterol. This high-density lipid is frequently seen in low serum concentrations during acute stress situations and in high concentrations over a prolonged stress period (weeks to months).

In its most severe form, the soldier with a chronic combat reaction is so slowed in his thinking and motor movements that he appears to resemble a robot. His vacant-eyed look seems to focus far into the distance and has been labeled the "1000-yard stare." At this point the man is totally unable to function.

B. Precipitants

Whereas intensity of battle is a major precipitant of an acute combat reaction, duration of battle is a major force shaping a chronic combat reaction. As in the acute disorder, high casualty rates add to the likelihood of a reaction. Frequently, a direct relationship has been seen between wounded-in-action rates and disabling psychological reactions to combat.

A critical environmental precipitant is lack of mobility and/or progress in battle. This condition was widely prevalent during World War I, when trench warfare resulted in men spending up to 2 to 3 years in the same labyrinth of tunnels. In *Goodbye to All That,* British author Robert Graves wrote about his years in the trenches, where battles seemed never to progress and the only way out was to be wounded or killed.

Interpersonal forces include preexisting life stresses. Home and personal problems may "follow" the man as he goes off to the front. Another interpersonal precipitant is loss of confidence in leadership. If a mistake in tactics is made, for example, a bombing strike hits friendly forces, the soldier may feel that his lack of confidence in command is justified.

On a personal level, when a soldier loses his sense of purpose, and especially when he perceives that there is "no end in sight" to his long-lasting stress, his risk for this condition increases markedly. Finally, preexisting neurosis or character pathology is a personal factor which increases the liability of a soldier to develop a chronic combat reaction.

C. Treatment

The first line of treatment for this disorder is buddy and/or group support. This is most effective in the early stages of the disorder. Even then, because the affected individual is constantly complaining and mistrustful, it takes a strong commitment on the part of the group to bring him back into the fold. Such a group commitment has been seen to function extremely well in prisoner-of-war settings. Here, if buddy or group efforts failed to halt the withdrawal of a fellow prisoner, that person often died. The cause of death appeared to be greatly influenced by the person's loss of hope and giving up.

When specialized care is required for this condition, it means more time (from a few days to 3 to 4 weeks), more professionals (psychiatrists, psychologists, and possibly exercise therapists), and more resources (medications, a site for prolonged and specialized care) than is the case for acute combat reactions. The treatment site should be located near the front lines of battle but should be secure enough that it does not have to be moved frequently. The Israeli Defense Forces experimented with such a camp just inside their northern border during the Lebanon incursion. Here the men received medications (chiefly hypnotics and anxiolytics), rest and replenishment, daily group therapy, and daily exercise sessions. This "walk 'em and talk 'em" approach resulted in return to duty rates between 40 and 70%.

Therapy may also include attempts to modify prebattle life stresses. If, for example, the individual is worried about the health of his wife or children, some communication (preferably by telephone) might be allowed. Personal visits, especially periods of home leave, are frequently counterproductive. This is because once the person becomes enmeshed in his family setting, his resolve to return to the front begins to weaken and his return to duty becomes increasingly unlikely.

In the long term, treatment of chronic combat reactions should include an appraisal of the person's need for renewal. Often job redefinition and/or retraining becomes appropriate. In animal studies of chronic stress, when conservation/withdrawal is seen, the animal becomes particularly motivated to learn new, and more adaptive, behaviors.

D. Prevention

Most line commanders will strive to control environmental stresses such as fatigue, heat, cold, hunger, and sleep deprivation in their men. However, the maintenance of communication and morale in a situation of long and deadly conflict is no easy task. A tremendously important support mechanism for American prisoners of war in Vietnam was maintenance of communication. Via the chain of command, each man was given an important role to carry out in their ongoing struggle to survive with dignity.

Another important preventive measure is having predictable intervals set aside for rest and recovery. This may not be possible in some long-term battle situations, but when it is, the effects are extremely salutary. Knowing that one would be rotated home one year to the day from arrival in Vietnam greatly assisted many soldiers in getting through their combat tours. It should be noted, however, that this policy also had undesirable effects, in that it inhibited group bonding and restricted identity with the man's unit.

One interpersonal preventive measure frequently underemployed for combat troops is to allow for closure after a period of prolonged stress. Closure was inadvertently done well in the days of troop ship transport for soldiers returning from Europe and Asia following World War II. Aboard ship the men had ample opportunities to discuss their war experiences, compare their reactions with others, and to "talk out" their various distressing thoughts and emotions. In a related manner, bringing men to and rotating them from combat as a unit markedly helps to prevent this disorder. Talking among trusted buddies is extremely supportive throughout a combat tour and on the return home.

In terms of personal preventive measures, one of the most disturbing early stresses reported by prisoners of war was their awareness of all the things they had "left undone" prior to being taken captive. One has enough to think about during the early stages of a long-term stress without additional concerns regarding the lack of a will, the lack of sufficient insurance, and other problems left for the family.

Almost all persons experiencing chronic stress find physical fitness of an endurance nature to be of tremendous help. Endurance exercises not only help to pass time during periods of lull but also aid in maintaining feelings of vigor and well-being. Of nearly equal importance is that exercise greatly facilitates sleep. Finally, a fitness program may counter the tendency toward hypoactivity seen in chronic combat reactions.

Perhaps the single most important personal preventive strategy for long-term stress is developing a sense of pace. Prisoners of war and hostages held for a year or more testify to the critical importance of the acquired skill of "taking one day at a time." Much like a mountain climber who slowly but relentlessly proceeds up the slope, a soldier must learn to pace himself so that sustained function is possible over many days, months, and even years. Also like the mountain climber, some energy should be held in reserve. Occasionally, one has to draw upon this reserve in order to meet setbacks and/or unexpected demands. Personal traits of acceptance, humility, and humor can substantially facilitate this pacing.

A word should be said about the incredible importance of humor in prolonged stress situations. The ability to laugh, not only with others, but at oneself, is vital. Former prisoners of war have claimed that single instances of a humorous circumstance made them feel better for weeks to months later.

Personal beliefs, such as conviction of cause, faith, and basic optimism, are tremendously sustaining. Even if these personal characteristics are not present in individuals at the beginning of a prolonged period of stress, they can be developed through supportive group interactions.

II. COMMENT

It is recognized that the responses of some individuals to stress may fall between acute and chronic reactions, and these persons may show features of both disorders. For example, U.S. Navy enlisted men involved in a collision of ships at sea were seen in a psychiatric outpatient clinic some months after the accident. These sailors apparently had not fully recovered from the acute stress and went on to develop signs and symptoms of depression. Treatment objectives in these cases were initially providing brief attention to the acute stress and to assess for unreasonable self-blame and guilt. Then, there was a shift in attention toward more long-term issues of professional and personal readjustment.

The role of the military psychiatrist in the prevention of posttraumatic disorders is a challenging one. For acute military stresses, such as in the example given above, the concept of a rapid psychiatric intervention team appears to be ideal. The clinical focus for these victims is short term, with triage of persons with extreme reactions and/or poor coping from the majority of men and women who will recover with only mild to moderate symptoms. The intervention team should provide general education and aid in the mobilization of community support, utilizing the resources and personnel of the local command whenever possible. Victims most disturbed should be treated immediately. Prompt treatment might well prevent, or at least moderate, a chronic posttraumatic stress disorder in this highly susceptible group. In addition, the entire group of victims might be monitored, by questionnaire, at regular intervals across the next decade.

For victims of chronic stress the medical officer's approach should be quite different. First, every person exposed should be thoroughly evaluated, both medically and psychologically. Following the provision of immediate physical and psychological care, efforts should be directed toward facilitating closure from the stress. Group therapy and general group meetings are extremely helpful to accomplish this objective. Then, the entire group should be monitored, with periodic medical follow-up visits, over the ensuing decade. The goal with victims of chronic stress is to find, and when found to moderate, a possible snowballing of readjustment difficulties across subsequent years. Work, home, and interpersonal problems, rather than dwelling on the initial stress situation, become the focal issues of treatment.

Bibliography

Belenky, G. L., Noy, S., and Solomon, Z. (1985). Battle stress: The Israeli experience. *Military Rev.,* 29–37.

Belenky, G. L., Tyner, C. F., and Sodetz, F. J. (1983). Israeli Battle Shock Casualties: 1973 and 1982. Report NP-83-4. Walter Reed Army Institute of Research, Division of Neuropsychiatry, Washington, DC.

Brill, N. Q., and Beebe, G. W. (1955). "A Follow-Up Study of War Neuroses." VA Medical Monograph, Washington, DC.

Figley, C. A. (1980). "Strangers at Home: The War, the Nation, and the Vietnam Veteran." Praeger, New York.

Glass, A. J. (1954). Psychotherapy in the combat zone. *Am. J. Psychiat.* 110, 725–731.

Grinker, A. A., and Spiegel, J. P. (1945). "Men under Stress." Blakiston, Philadelphia.

Henry, J., and Stephens, P. (1977). "Stress, Health, and the Social Environment: A Socio-Biologic Approach to Medicine." Springer-Verlag, New York.

Hubbell, J. G. (1976). "P.O.W." The Reader's Digest Press, New York.

Kormos, H. R. (1978). The nature of combat stress. *In* C. R. Figley (Ed.), "Stress Disorders among Vietnam Veterans: Theory, Research and Treatment." Brunner/Mazel, New York.

Kushner, F. H. (1973). Doctor's report from a V. C. prison. *Medical World News,* April.

McCaughey, B. G. (1986). The psychological symptomatology of a U.S. Naval disaster. *Military Med.* 151, 162–165.

McCaughey, B. G. (1987). U.S. Navy Special Psychiatric Rapid Intervention Team (SPRINT). *Military Med.* 152, 133–135.

Mullins, W. S. (Ed.) (1973). "Neuropsychiatry in World War II," Vol. II. Office of the Surgeon General (Army), Washington, DC.

Rahe, R. H., and Genender, E. (1983). Adaptation to and recovery from captivity. *Military Med.* 148, 577–585.

Rahe, R. H., Rubin, R. T., Arthur, R. J. *et al.* (1968). Underwater demolition team training: Serum uric acid and cholesterol variability. *J. Am. Med. Assoc.* 206, 2875–2880.

Rahe, R. H., Rubin, R. T., and Arthur, R. J. (1974). The three investigator study: Serum uric acid, cholesterol, and cortisol variability during the stresses of everyday life. *Psychosom. Med.* 36, 358–368.

Sachar, E. J. (1980). Hormonal changes in stress and mental illness. *In* D. T. Krieger, J. D. Hughes, and M. A. Sunderland (Eds.), "Neuroendocrinology." Sinquer, Boston.

Schwinn, M., and Diehl, B. (1973). "We Came to Help." Harcourt, Brace, and Jovanovich, New York.

Schurr, P. P., Spiro, A., Aldwin, C. M., and Stukel, T. A. (1998). Physical symptom trajectories following trauma exposure: Longitudinal findings from the normative aging study. *J. Nerv. Ment. Dis.* 186, 522–528.

Segal, J. (1973). Therapeutic considerations in planning the return of American POW's to the continental United States. *Military Med.* 138, 73–77.

Solomon. Z., Oppenheimer, B., and Noy, S. (1986). Subsequent military adjustment of combat stress reaction casualties—A nine-year follow-up study. *Military Med.* 151, 8–11.

Stockdale, J., and Stockdale, S. (1984). "In Love and War." Harper Row, New York.

Wolf, S., and Ripley, H. S. (1954). Reactions among allied prisoners of war subjected to three years of imprisonment and torture by the Japanese. *Am. J. Psychiat.* 104, 180–193.

Combat Stress Reaction

Matthew Dobson

New South Wales Health Department, Australia

GLOSSARY

combat stress reaction A term for the acute psychological breakdown experienced by combat soldiers as a result of their exposure to the stress of individual, unit, and battle factors in the war zone.

posttraumatic stress disorder (PTSD) A psychiatric diagnosis referring to a chronic pathological reaction following exposure to a traumatic event. This reaction is characterized by the intrusive reexperiencing of the traumatic event, the avoidance of stimuli associated with the traumatic event, a reduced responsiveness to the external world, and a range of autonomic and cognitive symptoms.

risk factor A term for a variable which epidemiological evidence suggests is associated with an increased probability of a specific health outcome. The nature of this association is not necessarily causal.

proximity A treatment principle which states that psychiatric casualties should be treated on or near the battlefield.

immediacy A treatment principle which states that psychiatric casualties should be treated as soon as possible after symptom onset.

expectation A treatment principle which states that psychiatric casualties should be treated with the expectation that the soldier will return to their unit.

Combat Stress Reaction (CSR) is an acute psychological breakdown experienced by combatants in a war zone. It is characterized by labile, polymorphic manifestations ranging from overwhelming anxiety, irritability, and restlessness to psychological withdrawal, confusion, and psychomotor retardation. Other characteristics include apathy, anxiety, depression, paranoia, conversion symptoms, signs of sympathetic arousal, and psychosomatic reactions such as diarrhea, abdominal pains, nausea, and vomiting. The defining criterion for CSR is that a soldier ceases to function effectively as part of their combat unit by acting in a manner which endangers their life and/or the lives of their fellow soldiers.

I. INTRODUCTION

Combat stress reaction is a significant concern for the military because of its potential impact on the fighting effectiveness of a combat unit. It has been estimated that the ratio of psychiatric casualties to the number of soldiers killed or wounded in action during a battle of average intensity is 1 : 1 : 4. Belenky reported that the ratio of psychiatric casualties to wounded was 30 : 100 in the 1973 Arab–Israeli War and 23 : 100 in the 1982 Lebanon War. By way of comparison, the ratio of psychiatric to wounded casualties for the American Army in the Second World War was 36 : 100. All of these estimates attest to the significant impact of psychiatric casualties on the fighting capacity of a military unit.

For a number of reasons the availability of scientific evidence on CSR is limited. In part this is due to the difficulty of conducting prospective epidemiological investigations on the acute stress responses of combat soldiers during wartime. It is also a reflection of the elusive nature of CSR. That is, the polymorphic and labile nature of CSR means that clear diagnostic criteria cannot be developed. Another reason is that the introduction of the Posttraumatic Stress Disorder (PTSD) diagnosis in DSM III marshaled an extensive research effort into examining the long-term effects of combat exposure, in particular, among U.S. veterans of the Vietnam War. While the political and social factors driving this research effort were understandable, the voluminous research literature available on PTSD only serves to highlight the absence of empirical data on CSR. The only exception to this is a series of controlled studies on Israeli CSR casualties by Zahava Solomon and her colleagues. The aim of this article is to provide an overview of CSR by reviewing the literature on (1) the relationship between CSR and combat-related PTSD, (2) the identification of risk factors for CSR, (3) the effectiveness of frontline treatment for CSR, and (4) the use of prevention programs to reduce CSR symptoms.

II. COMBAT STRESS REACTION AND COMBAT-RELATED POSTTRAUMATIC STRESS DISORDER

An adequate conceptualisation of CSR must define the relationship between this acute reaction and the range of other stress responses that may be experienced by combat soldiers. Combat exposure can elicit a range of stress responses which can be divided into three categories: (1) a transient, nonpathological stress response, (2) CSR, and (3) Posttraumatic Stress Disorder. This division recognizes the need to distinguish between a soldier's adaptive response to combat stress and an acute or chronic reaction. An adaptive response would be the manifestation of a transient stress response that is commensurate with the stress of daily life on or near the battlefield. Combat Stress Reaction differs from a transient stress response in that it is an acute stress reaction which incapacitates a soldier to the degree that s/he can no longer function in combat. In some cases, CSR can be transient, with the soldier able to return to military duty after a few days rest from combat. In other cases, it may be the precursor to the development of combat-related PTSD. This form of PTSD is a chronic psychopathological stress reaction which occurs in soldiers after they have been exposed to a combat-related trauma. It should be noted that CSR is not a necessary precursor to the onset of combat-related PTSD. However, it has been suggested that CSR creates a latent vulnerability that can lead to

the subsequent development of combat-related PTSD long after the war has ended.

Combat Stress Reaction and combat-related PTSD are similar in that they share a number of common symptoms such as increased physiological arousal, startle reactions, restlessness, and psychological withdrawal. However, CSR differs from PTSD in that it may not necessarily develop following exposure to a specific combat event. Combat Stress Reaction also differs in its symptoms of confusion, nausea, vomiting, and paranoid reactions. The critical pathological difference between these stress responses is that the symptoms associated with combat-related PTSD will endure. In PTSD symptom duration is expected to last for at least a month with the trauma being persistently reexperienced throughout the course of the disorder.

The relationship between CSR and combat-related PTSD has been extensively investigated in a series of studies examining the postwar adaptation of Israeli combat veterans. Solomon, Weisenberg, Schwarzwald, and Mikulincer assessed the prevalence and severity of combat-related PTSD in 382 Israeli CSR casualties 1 year after they had received treatment. Control group subjects were selected from those combat veterans who had fought in the same units as the CSR casualties but had not exhibited any symptoms or presented for treatment. Matching with CSR casualties also occurred on the following variables: age, education, military rank, and assignment. The results showed that 59% of the CSR group developed PTSD in comparison to 16% in the control group. There was also a significant difference in the number of PTSD symptoms reported. The CSR group reported a higher number of PTSD symptoms that their control group counterparts who also had PTSD. These findings suggest that those CSR casualties who develop PTSD experience a more intense form of the disorder than those combat veterans who develop PTSD without a history of CSR.

In a subsequent study, Solomon and Mikulincer found that 1, 2, and 3 years after the war, symptoms of combat-related PTSD were more prevalent among CSR casualties than among their matched controls. Similar trends were observed for social functioning, perceived self-efficacy in battle, and somatic complaints. The only reduction in symptom levels observed over the study occurred when the intensity of intrusion and avoidance symptoms dropped substantially in the 3rd year. However, the authors noted that this reduction in symptom levels should not be seen as evidence that CSR veterans were getting better. These findings suggest that CSR casualties are more vulnerable to the subsequent development of combat-related PTSD.

III. RISK FACTORS FOR COMBAT STRESS REACTION

The identification of risk factors for CSR is central to an understanding of the etiology of combat-related psychopathology. As discussed earlier, the epidemiological literature on Israeli combat veterans has shown that a higher percentage of CSR casualties subsequently developed PTSD in comparison to controls with no CSR history. This suggests that an understanding of the risk factors for CSR may provide further insight into the factors associated with the development of chronic combat-related stress reactions such as PTSD.

The intensity of combat exposure has been identified as a significant risk factor for CSR. Belenky reported the findings from an Israeli Defence Force study which correlated objective measures of combat stress such as battle type and availability of tactical and logistic support with the incidence of physical and psychiatric casualties. This study found that those battalions exposed to higher levels of combat stress had a higher casualty rate as well as a higher ratio of psychiatric to physical casualties.

In addition to the intensity of combat exposure, there are a variety of other factors in the combat environment which may affect CSR onset. In a review of the clinical presentation of 158 U.S. Army stress casualties during Operation Desert Storm, McDuff and Johnson identified a number of environmental stressors associated with stress reactions. While this study does not purport to be a systematic investigation of CSR risk factors, it demonstrated that a soldier's exposure to fatigue, cold, sleep deprivation, poor unit leadership, lowered morale, and threats to personal safety led to the onset or worsening of combat-related stress symptoms.

The identification of modifiable risk factors for CSR will play an important role in the development of effective prevention programs for combat soldiers. Despite this, there are few published studies which focus solely on CSR risk factors. A search of the recent research literature identified two controlled studies which investigated the association between a range of variables and CSR onset. Solomon, Noy, and Bar-On examined the association between demographic, military, and personality variables and CSR. One of the strengths of this study is that the researchers were allowed access to official military records in order to collect data on these variables. Age, education, combat suitability, military rank, and type of military service were identified as risk factors for CSR. These risk factors suggest that the onset of CSR can be accounted for by a combination of individual and situational factors.

The findings of this study showed that 80% of the sample of psychiatric casualties were reservists. The psychiatric casualty rate for reservists was in marked contrast to the rate for career soldiers, which was the lowest of any of the groups studied. It appeared that a soldier's reservist status was a marker for a number of interrelated risk factors, all of which increased vulnerability to combat stress. As the reservists were the oldest group of soldiers studied, the authors suggested that their age may have reduced their capacity to deal with the physical aspects of frontline service. Furthermore, reservists were more likely to have been exposed to combat in previous wars, which in turn may have reduced their capacity to cope with any subsequent exposure to combat stress. Being older, reservists were more likely to have established family and career commitments. These factors increased the stress on reservists when they had to adapt from civilian to military life. Also, in contrast to the career soldier, reservists had to make this change in a relatively short period of time. Solomon and Flum (1988) investigated the association between life events and CSR. It was hypothesized that a combatant's exposure to stressful life events before the war may have increased their vulnerability to CSR. However, the findings of this study did not provide support for this hypothesis. There was no relationship between the number, magnitude, or type of life event experienced by an individual prior to combat and CSR onset. However, prewar life events were implicated in the subsequent onset of PTSD.

IV. TREATMENT OF COMBAT STRESS REACTION

Frontline treatment interventions for psychiatric casualties are based on the principles of proximity, immediacy, and expectancy. These principles indicate that casualties should be treated in a setting close to the combat zone (proximity) as soon as possible after the onset of the CSR (immediacy) with the expectation that the soldier will return to the frontline following their recovery (expectation). In the frontline setting, the main aim of treatment is to restore a casualty's depleted physiological condition by satisfying his/her needs for sleep, food, and drink. This will usually last for a few days and take place in an area of relative "safety." During this time, the casualty is provided with the opportunity to discuss his/her traumatic experiences.

One of the advantages of providing treatment on or near the frontline is that it allows the casualty the opportunity to maintain their role as a soldier in a military unit. This enables access to his/her combat peers and opportunities for ventilation. This, in turn reinforces the soldier's sense of commitment to their combat unit. Another benefit of treatment in this setting is that it acts as a form of desensitization by exposing the soldier to conditions similar to those which precipitated the CSR. Also, the immediate provision of treatment in the frontline places the expectation on the soldier that they will be able to return to their combat duties.

Other principles of combat psychiatry which have been cited in the literature include simplicity and centrality. Simplicity refers to the use of uncomplicated treatments such as rest, food, and a hot shower to provide the CSR casualty with a respite from the stresses of combat. Centrality refers to the process of assessing all CSR casualties at a central screening area so that an experienced team of mental health professionals can minimize the likelihood of inappropriate evacuations to the rear.

While the principles of frontline treatment have been in use since the First World War, it is only recently that the question of their effectiveness has been subject to empirical investigation. Belenky highlighted the successful use of frontline treatment by the Israeli Army during the Lebanon War, with 60% of CSR casualties returning to combat duties within 72 h. This return rate confirms the earlier findings of Solomon and Benbenishty, who investigated the relative contribution of proximity, immediacy, and expectancy in CSR recovery. Their study followed-up 82% of the CSR casualties experienced by the Israeli Army during the Lebanon War to compare the effectiveness of frontline treatment versus treatment in a civilian setting at the rear (for security reasons, the precise number of subjects involved in this study could not be provided by the authors). Data on the immediacy and expectancy principles were collected through the use of self-report questionnaires. The outcome measures in this study were return to military unit and PTSD onset.

The results demonstrated a strong association between each of the frontline treatment principles and a CSR casualty's unit return rate. A high percentage of CSR casualties who were treated at the front (43%) or near the border with Lebanon (59%) returned to their unit. In contrast, a significantly lower percentage of CSR casualties returned to their unit after being airlifted to the rear (21%) or treated in a civilian facility at the rear (28%). A high percentage of those soldiers who received treatment immediately after the onset of a CSR returned to their unit (44%), while those who waited until after the war had ended before seeking treatment showed the lowest return rate (24%). Of the three treatment principles, expectancy displayed the strongest association with the unit return rate. Combat Stress Reaction casualties who perceived that their therapist expected them to return "at all costs" had a higher unit return rate (53%) than those casualties who were unclear about their therapist's expectations (26%).

The application of frontline treatment principles also had a significant impact on PTSD. While the relationship between proximity and PTSD did not reach statistical significance, there was a strong trend suggesting that treatment proximity was a factor in the subsequent development of PTSD. When treatment occurred at the front (52%) or near the border (48%), the percentages of CSR casualties who subsequently developed PTSD were 52 and 48% respectively. When treatment occurred outside the war zone, this percentage increased significantly (66%). There was also a significant relationship between treatment immediacy and PTSD onset. In this study, the highest rate of PTSD (74%) was observed among those CSR casualties who had waited until after the war to seek treatment. In a similar vein to the unit return rate findings, Solomon and Benbenishty reported a strong relationship between expectancy and PTSD. Those casualties who perceived that their therapist expected that they would return to their unit "at all costs" exhibited the lowest rate of PTSD (55%).

V. PREVENTION OF COMBAT STRESS REACTION

As combat is an unpredictable and chaotic experience, prevention programs for combat soldiers can only be formulated in general terms. The development of specific prevention programs targeting CSR must address the complex interaction between individual, unit, and battle factors which determine a soldier's vulnerability to combat stress. These programs need to recognize that the occupation of being a combat soldier routinely exposes the individual to multiple stressful and/or traumatic events and that over time, this will reduce a soldier's capacity to cope with combat stress. This is further complicated by a soldier's perception of combat and their role in the war zone. A soldier's subjective interpretation of a battlefield event as "stressful" or "traumatic" will be shaped by their acceptance of the violent nature of their occupation as well as their previous experience with such an event.

Prevention programs for CSR should also acknowledge that combat soldiers can be exposed to high levels of prolonged combat stress without ever being exposed to a specific traumatic event. This means that those prevention programs which target specific mental health outcomes such as PTSD should not be seen as providing a complete alternative to the complex task of preventing CSR. As military personnel, combat soldiers also have to deal with all of the normal occupational stresses that would be experienced on a daily basis in any large hierarchical organization in the civilian setting. It has generally been expected that in the combat setting, those individuals most likely to experience this form of prolonged occupational stress, such as combat soldiers or medical personnel, will by virtue of their selection, training, and background be able to cope with the effects of their exposure.

The U.S. Army's approach to the management of combat stress during Operation Desert Storm highlighted the importance of identifying and managing individual, unit, and battle factors in the onset of CSR. Examples of individual factors include combat experience, sleep, food, fitness, and stability of personal life. Also, a soldier's perception of their preparedness for combat, the loss of a family member at home, and/or a major threat to family during their service can affect their capacity to deal with combat stress. Unit factors include length of rest periods, the tactical situation, adequacy of supplies, communications, terrain, group cohesiveness, leadership, and morale. As noted previously, the intensity of combat exposure is a known risk factor for CSR. Specific examples of combat stressors include exposure to human suffering, risk of capture by the enemy, fear of torture, threat of personal injury, and death.

It is argued that prevention programs must target the range and type of combat stressors that soldiers are likely to encounter. Stress management techniques can be used to educate soldiers about the inevitability of experiencing fear during combat. The value of this experience should be emphasized and soldiers should be assisted to manage any anticipatory anxieties that they might have about maintaining control of their emotions in combat. Other stress management techniques such as problem solving, conflict resolution, and relaxation can also be used to strengthen a soldier's ability to cope with the stressors that they are likely to encounter in the course of fulfilling their military duties as a combat soldier. These techniques can also be used by those combatants who have the added responsibility of leadership to manage their own stress levels.

Military training provides an opportunity for the prevention of combat stress through the use of realistic training exercises. Using live ammunition, these exercises are designed to simulate the life-threatening challenges inherent in the combat experience.

The successful completion of such exercises should increase a soldier's confidence in their ability to deal with the future stress of combat. As Oei, Hennessy, and Lim noted in their review of the literature on military training, the use of well-rehearsed drills during training exercises should lead to the development of automatic reactions in soldiers. When these are activated in combat they reduce the level of cognitive demands upon the individual, which in turn minimizes the effect of combat stress.

For those military personnel who are in a support role, which may or may not involve active participation in combat, a general program of education about the likely occupational and interpersonal stresses that are frequently encountered in this setting would be beneficial. Based on the experiences of military personnel during the Vietnam War, this might include discussing (1) the problems associated with fighting an ambiguous enemy, (2) defining the individual's role in the war zone, (3) a realistic appraisal of their contribution to the war effort, and (4) reasonable expectations of leadership.

VI. SUMMARY

Combat Stress Reaction is an acute psychological breakdown which incapacitates a soldier to the degree that they are no longer able to function in combat. It is characterized by labile and polymorphic manifestations ranging from overwhelming anxiety and confusion to psychological withdrawal and psychomotor retardation. The variety of symptoms which are manifested during a CSR has meant that clear diagnostic criteria have not been developed. Risk factors for CSR include the intensity of combat exposure, age, education, combat suitability, military rank, and type of military service. Treatment for CSR is based on the principles of proximity, immediacy, and expectancy. These treatment principles emphasize the need to treat CSR casualties in a setting near the combat zone as soon as possible after symptom onset and with the expectation that the soldier will be able to return to combat after a brief period of rest and recuperation. The task of preventing CSR provides a complex challenge to military psychiatry. It requires an understanding of the interplay between a diverse range of individual, unit, and battle variables. Based on the evidence available to date, the use of realistic exercises during military training and the implementation of stress management techniques can play a role in minimizing the impact of combat stress.

See Also the Following Articles

Combat, Acute Reactions to; Korean Conflict, Stress Effects of; Persian Gulf War, Stress Effects of

Bibliography

American Psychiatric Association (1980). "Diagnostic and Statistical Manual of Mental Disorders," 3rd ed. Author: Washington, DC.

Belenky, G. (1987). Psychiatric casualties: The Israeli experience. *Psychiat. Ann.* 17(8), 528–531.

Camp, N. (1993). The Vietnam war and the ethics of combat psychiatry. *Am. J. Psychiat.* 150, 1000–1010.

Dobson, M., and Marshall, R. (1997). Surviving the war zone experience: Preventing psychiatric casualties. *Military Med.* 162, 283–287.

Grinker, R., and Spiegel, J. (1945). "Men under Stress." Blakiston, New York.

Jones, F., and Hales, R. (1987). Military combat psychiatry: A historical review. *Psychiat. Ann.* 17(8), 525–527.

Kormos, H. (1978). The nature of combat stress. *In* C. Figley (Ed.), "Stress Disorders among Vietnam Veterans," pp. 3–22. Brunner/Mazel, New York.

McDuff, D., and Johnson, J. (1992). Classification and characteristics of Army stress casualties during operation desert storm. *Hospital Commun. Psychiat.* 43(8), 812–815.

Marshall, R., and Dobson, M. (1995). The treatment of trauma reactions in war veterans: The seductive elegance of the PTSD diagnosis. *In* W. Vialle (Ed.), "Why Psychology?: Selected Papers from the 29th Annual Australian Psychological Society Conference."

Miller, L. (1995). Tough guys: Psychotherapeutic strategies with law enforcement and emergency services personnel. *Psychotherapy* 32, 592–600.

Oei, T., Lim, B., and Hennessy, B. (1990). Psychological dysfunction in battle: Combat stress reactions and posttraumatic stress disorder. *Clin. Psychol. Rev.* 10, 355–388.

Solomon, Z. (1993). "Combat Stress Reaction: The Enduring Toll of War." Plenum, New York.

Solomon, Z., and Benbenishty, R. (1986). The role of proximity, immediacy, and expectancy in frontline treatment of combat stress reaction among Israelis in the Lebanon war. *Am. J. Psychiat.* **143**(5), 613–617.

Solomon, Z., Noy, S. and Bar-On, R. (1986). Risk factors in combat stress reaction—A study of Israeli soldiers in the 1982 Lebanon War. *Israeli J. Psychiat. Relat. Sci.* **23**(1), 3–8.

Solomon, Z., and Mikulincer, M. (1987). Combat stress reactions, posttraumatic stress disorder, and social adjustment: A study of Israeli veterans. *J. Nerv. Ment. Dis.* **175**(5), 277–285.

Solomon, Z., Weisenberg, M., Schwarzwald, J. and Mikulincer, M. (1987). Posttraumatic stress disorder among frontline soldiers with combat stress reaction: The 1982 Israeli experience. *Am. J. Psychiat.* **144**(4), 448–454.

Solomon, Z., and Flum, H. (1988). Life events, combat stress reaction and post-traumatic stress disorder. *Soc. Sci. Med.* **26**(3), 319–325.

Solomon, Z., Laror, N. and McFarlane, A. (1996). Acute Post-traumatic reactions in soldiers and civilians. *In* B. Van der Kolk, A. McFarlane, and L. Weisaeth (Eds.) "Traumatic Stress: The Effects of Overwhelming Experience on Mind, Body and Society," pp. 102–114. The Guilford Press, New York.

Weisaeth, L. (1996). PTSD: The stressor-response relationship. *Bailliere's Clin. Psychiat.* **2**(2), 191–216.

Community Studies

Charles J. Holahan
University of Texas at Austin

Rudolf H. Moos
Department of Veterans Affairs and
Stanford University Medical Center

Jennifer D. Ragan
University of Texas at Austin

I. Life Stressors and Illness
II. Stress Moderators
III. Integrative Predictive Models

GLOSSARY

acute stressors Stressors that occur at a discrete point in time, such as a natural disaster or the death of a family member.

chronic stressors Stressors that endure over time, such as ongoing problems in a marriage and long-term difficulties with a troublesome supervisor at work.

coping strategies Cognitive and behavioral efforts to reduce or adapt to stressful conditions and associated emotional distress; most approaches distinguish between strategies oriented toward approaching versus avoiding the problem.

personal resources Relatively stable personality and cognitive characteristics that operate as stress moderators, such as dispositional optimism and self-efficacy.

social resources Social factors that operate as stress moderators, such as emotional support and assistance from family members and friends.

stress moderators Personal and social factors that can moderate the potential effects of stressors, functioning either as protective or vulnerability factors when stressors occur.

Community studies use naturalistic and observational strategies to examine the prevalence and effects of naturally occurring acute and chronic stressors within community samples. Early studies emphasized the potential detrimental effects of stressors, later studies considered protective factors that may moderate stressor effects, and the most recent studies have examined integrative predictive models of the stress and coping process.

I. LIFE STRESSORS AND ILLNESS

A. Stressors Examined in Community Studies

Community studies investigate (1) cumulative stressors (e.g., overall life change during a year) and

(2) specific stressors (e.g., a major earthquake; see Table 1). Most community studies have examined *cumulative* stressors. Early studies focused on *acute* life change events, stressors which occur at a discrete point in time. A common measurement instrument was Holmes and Rahe's (1967, *J. Psychosom. Res.* **11**, 213–218) *Social Readjustment Rating Scale,* which uses weighted life change units to index cumulative life change events, such as the death of a family member or a financial setback. Eventually, recognizing that many life stressors are ongoing, investigators began to examine *chronic* stressors that endure over time, such as social role strains and ongoing daily hassles. A typical measurement instrument has been the *Daily Hassles Scale* (see Lazarus and Folkman), which indexes cumulative hassles, such as troublesome neighbors and traffic problems.

Specific major life events and life crises constitute the second focus of community studies. Researchers have studied natural disasters, such as Hurricane Andrew in Florida, and technological disasters, such as the Three Mile Island nuclear accident in Pennsylvania. Medical illnesses, such as heart disease, cancer, and diabetes, also are specific major life events. Community studies are focusing increasingly on how people cope with illness as well as with the stress of caregiving for medically ill individuals. It should be noted that, although major life events and crises often have an acute onset, they tend to initiate chronic

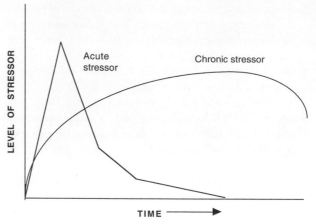

FIGURE 1 The time course of acute versus chronic stressors (adapted from Wheaton, 1994).

stressors, such as persisting economic and family problems. In fact, these enduring secondary stressors may account for many of the adverse effects of acute life events and crises.

B. Stress Reactions

Findings with diverse community samples have shown that life change events (particularly negative changes) are associated with psychological stress reactions that involve anxiety and depression. Among both minor stressors and severe events, interpersonal problems and losses are especially likely to be associated with depressive reactions. Chronic stressors appear to be more strongly linked to psychological distress than are acute events. Even though chronic stressors typically are less severe than acute life events, their effects may last longer and be more pervasive (see Fig. 1).

Life stressors may elicit physiological stress reactions (e.g., circulatory, digestive, and musculoskeletal problems) that are mediated through activation of the sympathetic nervous system. In addition, Cohen and Herbert explain that life stressors are associated with susceptibility to less serious infectious diseases (e.g., colds, influenza, and herpes) and possibly to the onset and exacerbation of autoimmune diseases, such as rheumatoid arthritis. Underlying these latter findings is an apparent correlation between life stressors and both cellular (e.g., reduced lymphocyte

---

TABLE I

Common Types of Life Stressors Assessed in Community Studies[a]

Cumulative stressors	Specific stressors
Negative life change events	Natural disasters
Chronic daily hassles	Technological disasters
Social role strains	Adjusting to professional school
	Job loss
	Divorce
	Bereavement
	Medical illness
	Caregiving
	Environmental stressors

[a] Stressors toward the top of each column tend to be more acute and those toward the bottom of each column tend to be more chronic.

proliferation) and humoral (e.g., decreased antibody production) indices of immune suppression.

Despite the consistency of these stressor effects, they typically accounted for less than 10% of individual differences in distress. Moreover, individuals showed highly variable reactions to stressors. By the early 1970s these findings engendered a new approach to conceptualizing the stress-and-coping process that has been described as "stress resistance." From an initial emphasis on people's deficits and vulnerabilities, contemporary community studies have evolved to place increasing emphasis on protective factors that can moderate the potential adverse effects of life stressors.

II. STRESS MODERATORS

A. Personal and Social Resources

A variety of relatively stable personality characteristics operate as protective factors that can help individuals to remain mentally and physically healthy when stressors occur. Especially important may be personality characteristics that relate broadly to personal control, such as dispositional optimism, self-efficacy, and an internal locus of control. For example, a constellation of personality dispositions Kobasa and her associates (1982, *J. Person. and Soc. Psychol.* **42**, 168–177) termed "hardiness" (comprised of control, commitment, and challenge) operates as a psychological protective factor when stressors occur. In contrast, negative personality characteristics, such as neuroticism and low self-esteem, can operate as vulnerability factors that increase health risk under high stressors.

Social resources also play a key role in protecting individuals from the potential adverse effects of life stressors. Social resources include emotional support as well as guidance and assistance from family members, friends, and one's broader social networks. Some aspects of social support, such as social companionship, may be related to better health and well-being regardless of the level of stressors experienced. Others, such as informational support, may function as "stress buffers," which have stronger positive effects on health when individuals are experiencing a

high level of stressors. Moreover, studies that consider both the positive and negative aspects of relationships show that negative aspects of relationships are as strongly related to poorer adjustment as positive aspects of relationships are related to better adjustment (see Box 1).

B. Coping Strategies

A large number of community studies have examined the role of coping strategies in stress resistance. Coping encompasses cognitive and behavioral efforts to reduce or adapt to stressful conditions and associated emotional distress. Most conceptualizations distinguish between coping strategies that are oriented toward *approaching* and confronting the problem and strategies that are oriented toward reducing tension by *avoiding* dealing directly with the problem (see Table II). People who rely more on approach coping strategies, such as problem solving and seeking information, tend to adapt better to life stressors. In contrast, avoidance coping strategies, such as denial and wishful thinking, generally are associated with psychological distress.

Although we can draw overall conclusions about the relative efficacy of approach and avoidance coping strategies, such generalizations necessarily oversimplify the process of adaptation. Individuals adapt best when their coping efforts match situational demands. Individuals who are flexible in their choice of coping should show better adaptation than persons who have a more restricted or rigid coping repertoire. For example, Suls and Fletcher point out that avoidance coping may be adaptive in the short-term with time-limited stressors, such as pain, blood donation, and uncomfortable medical diagnostic procedures. Moreover, approach coping processes are most effective in situations that are controllable.

C. Personal Agendas

An individual's personal agendas in the domain in which a stressor occurs shape the meaning and impact of the stressor. People function in multiple environments that often reflect different personal needs and commitments. Individuals appraise life stressors in the light of these personal agendas, and such ap-

BOX 1

Moos and Moos developed a *Life Stressors and Social Resources Inventory* (LISRES, 1994, Odessa, FL: Psychological Assessment Resources) to provide a comprehensive picture of the interrelated stressors and social resources in a person's life. The Inventory includes nine indices of life stressors and seven indices of social resources. For example, Fig. 2 shows an illustrative LISRES profile for a 66-year-old woman with rheumatoid arthritis (scores are standardized, with a mean of 50 and a standard deviation of 10). Although

she reported well-above-average physical health stressors, she had below-average stressors in six of the other seven domains. Moreover, she also had above-average social resources in her work setting and in her relationships with her spouse, extended family, and friends. At an 18-month follow-up, this favorable balance of moderate stressors and high resources enabled her to manage quite well; she reported high self-confidence and below-average depression.

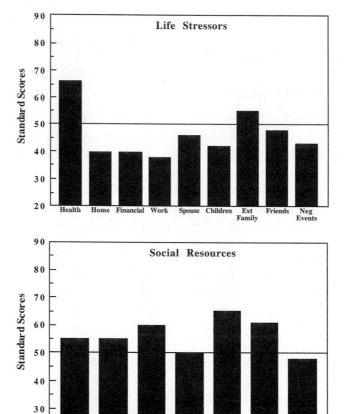

FIGURE 2   A Life Stressors and Social Resources profile for a woman with rheumatoid arthritis (adapted from Moos and Moos, 1994; Reproduced by special permission of the Publisher, Psychological Assessment Resources, Inc., 16204 North Florida Avenue, Lutz, Florida 33549, from the LISRES-A by Rudolf if Moos, Ph.D, Copyright 1994 by PAR, Inc. Further reproduction is prohibited without permission of PAR, Inc.

TABLE II
Four Basic Categories of Coping Strategies along with Eight Associated Coping Subtypes[a]

Basic coping categories	Coping subtypes
Cognitive approach	*Logical analysis* ("Did you think of different ways to deal with the problem?")
	Positive reappraisal ("Did you think about how you were much better off than other people with similar problems?")
Behavioral approach	*Seeking guidance and support* ("Did you talk with a friend about the problem?")
	Taking problem-solving action ("Did you make a plan of action and follow it?")
Cognitive avoidance	*Cognitive avoidance* ("Did you try to forget the whole thing?")
	Resigned acceptance ("Did you lose hope that things would ever be the same?")
Behavioral avoidance	*Seeking alternative rewards* ("Did you get involved in new activities?")
	Emotional discharge ("Did you yell or shout to let off steam?")

[a] Sample coping items are shown in parentheses (from the "Coping Responses Inventory," Moos, 1993, 3rd ed., Odessa, FL: Psychological Assessment Resources). Adapted and reproduced by special permission of the Publisher, Psychological Assessment Resources, Inc., 16204 North Florida Avenue, Lutz, Florida 33549, from the Coping Responses Inventory by Rudolf Moos, Ph.D., Copyright 1993 by PAR, Inc. Further reproduction is prohibited without permission from PAR, Inc.

praisals can either enhance or reduce the stressfulness of a situation. For example, because chronic stressors provide a context within which new acute events are interpreted, they may alter the threshold at which events have negative impacts on health. Job loss during a period of bereavement may adversely affect health in part because it amplifies a more pervasive sense of personal loss.

Similarly, when an event threatens or disrupts a domain in which a person has central commitments, that event is more likely to have an adverse outcome. For example, Brown and his colleagues (1987, *Br. J. Psychiat.* 150, 30–42) found that women who experienced a new severe event in a life domain in which they had marked difficulties or in a domain that matched an area of marked personal commitment were almost three times more likely to develop a depression than were women who experienced a new severe event in some other domain. At the same time, strong commitments can sustain coping efforts in the face of profound obstacles, such as coping with bereavement or a life-threatening illness.

III. INTEGRATIVE PREDICTIVE MODELS

A. Resource Depletion

One set of community studies has examined how life stressors can deplete psychosocial resources. Applying a "support deterioration" model, Kaniasky and Norris (1993, *J. Pers. Soc. Psychol.* 64, 395–408) demonstrated that both personal and community losses were related to declines in flood victims' perceptions of kin and nonkin support up to 6 months postdisaster. Research on combat stress and the stress of caregiving also has shown that stressors can deplete personal and social resources. In part, resource depletion may be tangible—stressful life events like loss of income or loss of loved ones entail real reductions in resources. However, resource depletion also may have a cognitive component, perceived support appears to be especially vulnerable to deterioration after crises.

Resource loss may operate as a mediator between

life stressors and a decline in psychological functioning. For example, Kaniasky and Norris showed that perceptions of reduced nonkin support among flood victims mediated between disaster distress and subsequent depressive symptomatology. Disaster-related stressors depleted nonkin support 6 months later; in turn, this loss in support mediated between initial stressors and later depression. Similarly, a depletion of personal and social resources has been shown to mediate the relationship between stressors and psychological distress in several studies of community samples.

B. Coping Mediation

More recently, community studies have begun to develop an integrated understanding of how life stressors, psychosocial resources, and coping are related to one another. One effort has examined how coping strategies provide a key mechanism through which psychosocial resources enhance functioning during stressful periods. Personal and social resources may be linked to health under high stressors primarily because they encourage more adaptive coping strategies. For example, persons with higher levels of self-efficacy tend to approach challenging situations in an active and persistent style, whereas those with lower levels of self-efficacy are less active or tend to avoid such situations. Social resources can enhance coping efforts by bolstering feelings of self-confidence as well as by providing informational guidance that aids in assessing threat and in planning coping strategies.

Based on these findings, Holahan and Moos proposed a "resources model of coping" that unified earlier work on predicting coping responses and predicting adjustment. In the model personal and social resources relate to adaptive functioning under high stressors by fostering more adaptive coping efforts. In a test of the model with a sample of community adults facing high stressors, Holahan and Moos (1991, *J. Abnorm. Psychol.* 100, 31–38) found that adaptive personality characteristics and family support operated prospectively as coping resources; in turn, coping mediated between initial resources and later health status 4 years later. Similarly, among women coping with breast cancer and students ad-

justing to law school, more adaptive coping efforts operated as a mediator through which optimism related to better psychological adjustment.

C. Personal Growth

Life crises can be "constructive confrontations" that challenge an individual and provide an opportunity for personal growth. Individuals may emerge from a crisis with greater self-confidence, new coping skills, closer relationships with family and friends, and a richer appreciation of life. For example, Holahan and Moos (1990, *J. Pers. Soc. Psychol.* 58, 909–917) found that about one-third of people who experienced a high level of life stressors showed improved psychological functioning over a 1-year follow-up. These individuals showed an increase in personal and social resources, perhaps due to positive feedback from effective coping with stressors. Growth occurred despite the fact that many stressors involved profound adaptive demands, such as serious financial setbacks and the deaths of friends or family members.

Of course, beneficial outcomes to life crises may emerge only after an initial stage of emotional distress and disorganization. Yet, many people are remarkably resilient in the face of adversity. About half of women who experience a marital break-up show long-term improvements in psychological functioning. These women may become more assertive, develop more realistic views of themselves, and experience increased self-esteem with successful new careers. Similarly, survivors of serious illness often show more concern for and sense of community with others, a change in focus from the constant pressure of work to family relationships, and heightened awareness of religious and humanitarian values.

See Also the Following Articles

DISASTERS, PUBLIC, EFFECTS OF; LIFE EVENTS SCALE

Bibliography

Cohen, S., and Herbert, T. B. (1996). Health psychology: Psychological factors and physical disease from the perspective of human psychoneuroimmunology. *Annu. Rev. Psychol.* **47**, 113–142.

Coyne, J. C., and Downey, G. (1991). Social factors and psychopathology: Stress, social support, and coping processes. *Annu. Rev. Psychol.* **42**, 401–425.

Holahan, C. J., and Moos, R. H. (1994). Life stressors and mental health: Advances in conceptualizing stress resistance. *In* W. R. Avison and I. H. Gotlib (Eds.), "Stress and Mental Health: Contemporary Issues and Prospects for the Future" (pp. 213–238). Plenum, New York.

Kessler, R. C. (1997). The effects of stressful life events on depression. *Annu. Rev. Psychol.* **48**, 191–214.

Lazarus, R. S., and Folkman, S. (1984). "Stress, Appraisal, and Coping." Springer-Verlag, New York.

Suls, J., and Fletcher, B. (1985). The relative efficacy of avoidant and nonavoidant coping strategies: A meta-analysis. *Health Psychology* **1985**, 249–288.

Wheaton, B. (1994). Sampling the stress universe. *In* W. R. Avison and I. H. Gotlib (Eds.), "Stress and Mental Health: Contemporary Issues and Prospects for the Future" (pp. 77–114). Plenum, New York.

Comparative Anatomy and Physiology

Alan G. Watts

University of Southern California

I. Stress Responses Defined
II. Stress Responses in Invertebrates
III. Stress Responses in Vertebrates

GLOSSARY

cyclostome A member of the order Cyclostomata (class Agnatha) hagfish and lampreys. These primitive vertebrates have relatively rudimentary endocrine and nervous systems that are thought to represent evolutionarily early examples of these functions.

cytokine A regulatory protein secreted by white blood cells and a variety of other cells in the body. Cytokines can regulate cells of the immune system and modulate immune responses, but act in a relatively local manner.

elasmobranch Cartilaginous fish, e.g., sharks, skates, and rays.

fenestrated capillary A specialized capillary that has transcellular circular openings in the endothelial walls allowing the passage of large molecules or cells in or out of the capillary. They are particularly prevalent in regions where secretory products are released into the vasculature.

mesoderm One of the three principal layers of the mammalian embryo from which vascular tissues are derived.

tetrapod A four-limbed vertebrate.

I. STRESS RESPONSES DEFINED

Using the simplest and most wide-ranging definition, a stressor can be thought of as any alteration in the animal's environment (internal or external) requiring a response that, if not invoked, could develop into a threat to survival. In some instances the disturbance may only require a simple avoidance reflex that moves the animal away from an external threat, whereas in others it may invoke an internally directed motor response nullifying a homeostatic disturbance. Considered in this rather all encompassing way, stress responses are fundamental characteristics displayed by all living organisms. Protozoans display an avoidance reaction to a detrimental change in the local environment, e.g., increased CO_2 concentrations in the water; more complex multicellular organisms, such as coelenterates and platyhelminths, can generate motor patterns that allow them to make the appropriate distinction between a threat and a meal. All animals utilize some sort of avoidance (generally reflexive) reaction that can be considered a stress response to an aversive presence in the environment. However, more complex invertebrates and all vertebrates also have evolved sets of physiological responses that provide the organism with the ability to adapt their metabolic and immune systems to deal with the consequences of stress. In these animals, physiological and neural systems involving learning and memory also provide organisms with anticipatory features, allowing them to generate conditioned or habituated responses, as well as the capability of dealing with the more extended consequences of stress.

II. STRESS RESPONSES IN INVERTEBRATES

Stress responses in invertebrates can be divided into two broad categories: (i) those concerned with abrogating the stressor and (ii) adaptive changes invoked to deal with the metabolic consequences of the stressor. In invertebrates, the nervous system generally deals with the first, whereas cellular interactions of a chemical nature (endocrine and immune) generally deal with the second.

A. Neural

For avoidance responses, sessile invertebrates generally confront a threat by retracting vulnerable body parts into a protective shell or environmental surroundings, whereas more mobile species have the ability to move away from the threat as fast as possible. In most metazoans, the effector of these responses is the nervous system. Simple invertebrates such as coelenterates have avoidance reactions that may involve little more than invoking the stimulus/response properties of their nerve nets. In more advanced invertebrates, these avoidance reactions are neurophysiologically quite complex and involve the regulation of specific neural networks by sensory inputs (e.g., air currents). These networks coordinate the very rapid muscle contraction required for fleeing (e.g., jumping, flying, turning, or running). These responses appear to involve populations of giant interneurons found in the abdominal ganglia that may, because of their fast conduction velocities, bring about the very rapid stimulus/response interactions required for

these behaviors. However, the detailed role of these neurons and the wider functioning of this circuitry remain unclear. Although all of these avoidance responses have the characteristics of a reflex, studies from species such as *Aplysia* have shown that contributions from learning and memory mechanisms cannot be overlooked.

B. Endocrine

Arthropods use hormones to regulate their metabolism in a way that is beneficial during periods of stress. In a manner somewhat analogous to the secretions of the vertebrate chromaffin cell/adrenal medulla system, some insects (e.g., locusts, cockroaches) produce adipokinetic hormones (AKH) in the gland cells of the corpora cardiaca. These hormones increase heart rate and carbohydrate and protein metabolism. They also produce hyperglycemia through the breakdown of glycogen to trehalose in the fat bodies and muscles and its facilitated transport into the hemolymph. Starvation, increased activity, and stress all elevate the secretion rate of these hormones.

Complex invertebrates such as annelids, insects, and mollusks possess quite sophisticated immune functions that utilize interleukin-like signaling molecules and cytotoxic activities derived from "natural killer" cells. These systems are activated by stressors. Some invertebrates also synthesize corticotropin-releasing hormone (CRH)-and proopiomelanocortin (POMC)-derived peptides that are related to their vertebrate homologues. In mollusks, CRH and adrenocorticotropin (ACTH) are capable of releasing biogenic amines from hemocytes (cells that appear to have both endocrine and immune functions), and at least some of the cells that are capable of phagocytosis also exhibit ACTH immunoreactivity. ACTH-like molecules have even been identified in some protozoans, suggesting their great phylogenetic antiquity. Indeed, the existence of those "endocrine" signals capable of regulating carbohydrate metabolism and immune responses— properties required to generate adaptive responses to stressors—appear to have developed very early in evolution.

III. STRESS RESPONSES IN VERTEBRATES

Not surprisingly, stress responses in vertebrates have more components, variety, and complexity than those found in invertebrates. Although some vertebrate stress responses are similar in principle to those exhibited by invertebrates (e.g., avoidance; endocrine secretions that increase energy substrate availability; adaptations that restrict reproduction) because of their more complex central nervous systems, vertebrates possess a greater flexibility and adaptive capability.

A. Comparative Anatomy

The general organization of those parts of the neural and endocrine systems involved with mediating stress responses are remarkably well conserved across all vertebrate classes.

1. Neurohypophysis

The neurohypophysis comprises the median eminence of the tuber cinereum, the infundibular stem, and the neural lobe of the pituitary gland. The median eminence and the neural lobe both contain terminals of neuroendocrine motor neurons. However, those neurons that regulate ACTH secretion terminate in the median eminence. With appropriate increases in firing rate they release releasing factors (CRH and, in some mammals, vasopressin) into hypophysial portal blood. Those neurons that release oxytocin and vasopressin/vasotocin into the general circulation terminate on fenestrated capillaries in the neural lobe. The neural lobe appears to be better developed in tetrapods than in fish, which may be related to the larger amount of stored hormone required for the increased hydrostatic stresses of terrestrial existence. With a few exceptions (e.g., in cyclostomes the neurohypophysis is quite poorly developed), the generalized organization of the neurohypophysis is retained across the vertebrate spectrum.

2. Corticotropes

The anterior pituitary of all vertebrates contains cells that synthesize adrenocorticotropin. In evolutionarily older species (e.g., reptiles and elasmobranchs), there is less intermingling of cell types within the anterior pituitary than is found in more recent species. Proopiomelanocortin is cleaved to produce ACTH in anterior pituitary corticotropes in all vertebrate classes where it acts to increase glucocorticoid secretion. Negative glucocorticoid feedback signals also appears to operate in all vertebrate classes examined.

3. Catecholaminergic and Corticosteroidogenic Tissues

The analogue of the adrenal gland is critical to the stress response of all vertebrates. In mammals it is called the adrenal—or in older literature, the suprarenal—gland because of its position close to the kidneys. In mammals the adrenal gland has a characteristic cortical and medullary structure: the medulla is neural in origin and synthesizes catecholamines for release into the bloodstream on sympathetic stimulation; the cortex is mesodermal in origin and is the site of glucocorticoid and mineralocorticoid synthesis. Although cells performing these functions are found in all vertebrates, the way they are arranged and their anatomical association vary from class to class. In amphibians, reptiles, and fish this tissue is found between renal tissue and is sometimes called the interrenal gland.

All vertebrates possess tissue that can secrete catecholamines into the bloodstream during stress. Catecholamines (usually adrenaline and noradrenaline) universally increase cardiovascular muscle tone, increase heart rate, and can rapidly mobilize fat and carbohydrate stores. There has been a trend during evolution toward a close relationship between catecholamine-synthesizing and steroidogenic tissue. Thus, in cyclostomes and some elasmobranchs, chromaffin cells are widely scattered along large veins and the dorsal body wall, but steroidogenic tissue has been more difficult to identify. In many vertebrate classes, catecholaminergic tissue is interspersed with steroidogenic tissue. In mammals, however, chromaffin cells are aggregated in the adrenal medulla and are separate from the steroid-synthesizing cells in the adrenal cortex, although a close functional relationship does exist.

4. Sympathetic Branch of the Autonomic Nervous System

Sympathetic motor activation plays an important role in the stress responses in virtually all vertebrates. However, it is poorly developed in cyclostomes where there are no sympathetic chains and relatively little sympathetic innervation of the viscera. In teleost fish, catecholamine secretion is regulated by preganglionic sympathetic activation. However, other regulators, such as glucocorticoids, can also play an important role. It is possible that the chromaffin cell system first evolved to function as the principal regulator of the cardiovascular and energy metabolism under all conditions, not just stress, but as the sympathetic innervation of the cardiovascular system became more sophisticated and was able to regulate visceral organ function under basal conditions, actions of the chromaffin system during stress became the more important function.

5. Juxtaglomerular Apparatus

Renin and the cells that contain juxtaglomular granules are found in all vertebrates other than cyclostomes. In more recently evolved vertebrates, these are aggregated in a specific juxtaglomerular apparatus (juxtaglomerular cells and the macula densa), whereas in others only juxtaglomerular cells are seen. In teleost and more primitive fish species these are often quite distal from the glomerular apparatus.

B. Comparative Physiology

Vertebrates invoke sets of stress responses that target three critical physiological systems: those involved by fluid balance, energy metabolism, and tissue damage and immune function. Each set has specific neural and endocrine components.

1. Impact of Stress on the Regulation of Fluid Balance

Protecting the fluid compartments of the body is a prime physiological concern, and those physiological systems that contribute to this function are usually activated during stress. Two sets of hormones have evolved to regulate fluid balance: the renin/angiotensin system protects the extracellular fluid compartment, whereas the posterior pituitary lobe hormone regulates the intracellular fluid compartment. Additionally, autonomic reflexes are available to regulate cardiovascular and hemodynamic function through the control of vascular tone. Both systems are stimulated by stress.

a. Renin/Angiotensin System
The renin/angiotensin system targets vascular smooth muscle, mineralocorticoid-synthesizing tissue in the adrenal cortex, and some circumventricular organs in the brain. Renin is present in all jawed vertebrates, but is absent in the cyclostomes. Its original function may have been to increase blood pressure through vasoconstriction, with its dipsogenic and other effects (e.g., increased release of mineralocorticoids) appearing later.

b. Vasotocin/Vasopressin
Maintaining body fluid composition between narrow limits is a requirement for survival for all organisms. This becomes absolute in animals that live in environments of varying temperature or water availability or in animals that move from one major environment to another. Any variation that challenges the fluid balance constitutes a stressor that needs to be regulated. The vertebrate brain has evolved a very simple reflex loop to help with this regulation, and such a function has remained reasonably unchanged for the 500 million years since the evolution of cyclostomes. It involves direct projections from osmoreceptors to the neuroendocrine neurons that synthesize vasopressin (in mammals) or vasotocin (in birds, reptiles, and most amphibians and fish, including cyclostomes). In this manner, one of the simplest and phylogenetically oldest vertebrate neuroendocrine stress response is probably the reflex release into the circulation of vasopressin/vasotocin that occurs as plasma osmolality increases. The original function of vasotocin (which is still its primary action in some amphibians) may have been a V_1 receptor-mediated vasoconstrictive effect that reduces blood flow to the kidney and thereby fluid loss. In this respect, vasotocin is a more potent vasoconstrictor than its evolutionary descendant, vasopressin. However, during evolution a V_2-mediated action on kidney tubules became the predominant action.

2. Impact of Stress on the Regulation of Energy Metabolism

a. Glucocorticoids The stress-induced release of glucocorticoids is found widely throughout vertebrate classes, where they act to promote gluconeogenesis. Stress-induced hyperglycemia reportedly occurs in all classes of vertebrates that have been investigated from cyclostomes to mammals, although the contribution of glucocorticoids to this effect is far from clear in more simple vertebrates. It is worth considering that in many respects, the hypothalamo-pituitary-andoenal axis (HPA) motor response to stress is a more proactive than a reactive event. Although ACTH and corticosterone secretion are obviously triggered by the stressor, they are not the motor responses that act to remove the *immediate* consequences of the stress, as occurs with, for example, the action of adrenaline on hypoglycemia. The actions of elevated plasma corticosterone levels (mediated in part by interactions with leptin, insulin, and the thyroid hormones) anticipate the *possibility* that the stressor will lead to a debilitating sequence of events, particularly the catabolic effects of negative energy balance. In those vertebrate classes that have been studied, the principal function of corticosteroids is on intermediate metabolism, particularly in stimulating proteolysis and then gluconeogenesis.

b. Catecholamines of Chromaffin Cell Origin Increased circulating catecholamines lead to hyperglycemia in all vertebrates examined, although noradrenaline and adrenaline show differences in efficacy across different classes. Also, the tissue that is targeted varies; in mammals both muscle and liver are responsive to adrenaline, whereas only liver glycogen is mobilized in cyclostomes. Stress will increase plasma catecholamines in teleost fish and elasmobranchs.

c. Inhibition of Reproduction A variety of stressors will inhibit reproductive function in most vertebrates. The simplest of these is the negative energy balance resulting from food restriction or starvation. Here a mechanism (possibly involving elevated neu-ropeptide Y synthesis in the hypothalamic arcuate nucleus) leads to the inhibition of reproductive function, so ensuring that limited energy supplies are not used to raise offspring in adverse conditions. Related stressors such as social crowding may also restrict reproductive capacity for the same reason, although the neural mechanism responsible for this effect is unclear.

3. Impact of Stress on the Regulation of Immune Function

Immune activation and the consequent increases in circulating interleukins that occur during some stressors provide a marked stimulus to the vertebrate HPA axis. In mammals this elevates CRH release into the portal vasculature, and hence ACTH release. An increased glucocorticoid release in response to cytokines has been noted in all the mammals, reptiles, birds, and amphibians that have been investigated. However, it should be noted that data are very scanty in nonmammalian classes. In turn, corticosteroids have a suppressive effect on immune function. During acute stress this operates as a dampening effect to restrain any adverse effect of immune stimulation, but in chronic stress this can have a deleterious effect, leading to increased infections and mortality. These types of effect have been seen in a wide variety of vertebrates.

Bibliography

Barrington, E. J. W. 1963. "An Introduction to General and Comparative Endocrinology." Clarendon Press, Oxford.

Bentley, P. J. 1998. "Comparative Vertebrate Endocrinology." Cambridge Univ. Press, Cambridge.

Burrows, M. 1996. "The Neurobiology of an Insect Brain." Oxford Univ. Press, Oxford.

Highnam, K. C. 1977. "Comparative Invertebrate Endocrinology." University Park Press, Baltimore.

Ottaviani, E., and Franceschi, C. 1996. "The neuroimmunology of stress from invertebrates to man." *Prog. Neurobiol.* 48, 421–440.

Turnbull, A., and Rivier, C. 1999. Regulation of the hypothalamo-pituitary-axis by cytokines: Actions and mechanisms of action. *Physiol. Rev.* 79, 1–71.

Wendelaar Bonga, S. E. 1997. The stress response in fish. *Physiol. Rev.* 77, 592–625.

Complementary Medicine
in North America

David Spiegel

Stanford University School of Medicine

I. Hypnosis
II. Mindfulness-Based Stress Reduction
III. Relaxation Training
IV. Acupuncture
V. Biofeedback
VI. Conclusion

GLOSSARY

complementary medicine Generally the use of therapies not traditionally a part of the Western health care system, but more often an element of Eastern medicine and philosophy.

While modern medical science has provided cures for many bacterial infections, life-extending treatments for viral infections such as HIV, symptom-reducing interventions for heart disease, and has converted many kinds of cancer from a terminal to a chronic disease, it is especially striking that large numbers of North Americans now turn to allied medical traditions and recently developed treatments for help with disease. In some ways, traditional medicine's success is also its weakness. The acute disease model emphasizes diagnosis, definitive treatment, and cure. In some situations this works, but in many it does not. The leading killers of North Americans, heart disease, stroke, and cancer, are by and large chronic and progressive rather than curable illnesses. The application of a curative model, in a setting in which disease management is often the most productive approach, leaves both doctors and patients frustrated. Rather than feeling satisfied when a disease is well managed, doctors and patients often feel disappointed that it has not been cured. The old adage of medicine is that our job is to "cure rarely, to relieve suffering often, and to comfort always." At the end

of the 20th century it is as though that adage had been rewritten; that our job is to "cure always, relieve suffering if one has the time, and leave the comforting to someone else." Patients do indeed turn elsewhere for comfort. Complementary and alternative medicine doctors are one such place. In addition, we seem to have a model of intervention which may pay lip service to the integration of mind and body, but in fact in Western medicine we are primarily "closet Cartesians." We act as though the only real problems are physical ones and thus the only real interventions are physical ones. By and large, doctors no longer conceive of talking, comforting, guiding, and educating patients as "real" interventions. Rather, it is something to do until the injection is ready. An illness can be a lonely journey and patients crave people who understand what the journey is like and can stay the course with them. Thus the apparent appetite for complementary and alternative medicine is stimulated by the vacuum of modern medical care. This vacuum, by the way, is being intensified by the business managers of modern North American medicine who pump even more time and energy out of the doctor/patient interaction by saddling doctors with more patients per hour, reducing their autonomy, and treating them like assembly line workers instead of professionals. This can only further desiccate the doctor/patient relationship and limit the opportunities for medical compassion to enhance medical care.

A recent study indicates that 42% of North Americans utilize some form of "alternative" treatment, a substantial increase from the already sizeable figure of one-third in 1990. However, more than two-thirds of them utilize standard medical treatment as well, suggesting that as far the patients are concerned, these interventions are *complementary* rather than *alternative*. A study in the Kaiser health care system indicates that the majority of complaints which lead to seeking alternative services are pain (52%) and anxiety (25%). Thus patients seek complementary care for sensible reasons, bringing problems that are not life-threatening and that are often ignored or minimized in mainstream medical treatment. However, the relationship between complementary and standard medical care is complicated by the fact that three-quarters of those individuals who use alternative services do not tell their primary care physicians that they are obtaining these alternative or complementary services, so their use of them has the potential to undermine or at least complicate their medical care.

The application of a curative model, in a setting in which disease management is the best that can be delivered, leaves both doctors and patients dissatisfied and disappointed because cure is not the only issue. Indeed, recent research shows that burnout is lowest among those oncologists with the best communication skills. Presumably these physicians, who often deal with inability to cure, find other ways to effectively understand and address their patients' needs and concerns. Indeed, palliative care physicians show relatively low levels of job stress, in part because the emphasis on care rather than cure is overt rather than a source of job strain. They have reduced stress in a difficult situation by changing goals.

I. HYPNOSIS

There are a variety of well established and thoroughly studied methods for teaching patients how to increase their control over mental distress and concomitant somatic discomfort. Hypnosis, for example, is a state of aroused, attentive focal concentration accompanied by a reduction in peripheral awareness. It has proven effectiveness in facilitating anxiety control and inducing analgesia. The techniques most often employed involve a combination of physical relaxation and imagery that provides a substitute focus of attention for the painful sensation. Hypnosis can be quickly induced in a matter of seconds, and patients can be taught self-hypnosis to provide ongoing anxiety and pain control. The ability of hypnotizable individuals to dissociate, or separate psychological from somatic response, can be used to maintain physical relaxation even in the face of emotional distress. This can also help patients to restructure their understanding of the situation that is making them anxious, in part because they are approaching it while in an unusually relaxed state. This is an important concept in many complementary treatments for anxiety such as meditation, massage, biofeedback, and hypnosis: you may not be able to alter the stressor itself, but you can enhance your control over your psychological and somatic response to the stressor. This can, in turn, enhance the array of options available to you for dealing with that stressor, since you are more in control of somatic symptoms and less preoccupied with the effect the stressor has on you.

Self-hypnosis, for example, has been shown to be quite useful in helping medical patients suffering from procedure anxiety. A recent randomized trial employing hypnosis during interventional radiology procedures demonstrated that patients offered training in hypnosis had less pain, fewer procedural interruptions, less cardiovascular instability, and less anxiety while utilizing only 12% as much analgesic medication from a PCA device.

II. MINDFULNESS-BASED STRESS REDUCTION

Similarly, other techniques involving breathing exercises, self-monitoring and -regulation, and meditation techniques have proven quite effective in stress management in the medical setting; several are based on adaptations of Buddhist meditation practices. Jon Kabat-Zinn has developed such a model which involves teaching patients with pain, anxiety, and other illness-related problems a mindfulness meditation practice: (1) control their attentional processes, (2) induce physical comfort/relaxation, and (3) maintain a present orientation. This method helps patients learn to experience more choice in the management of their perceived stress and to reduce anxiety about the future by more richly immersing themselves in the range of their present experiences, both positive and negative. This helps them accept but put into perspective worries about the future by maintaining enjoyment of the present.

Research with this technique has produced promising results. Kabat-Zinn and colleagues demonstrated in a randomized trial that psoriasis patients who listened to an audiotape teaching mindfulness-based stress reduction had significantly more rapid healing of their skin lesions than did control patients who listened to music. Thus mindfulness training may influence the course of disease as well as reduce stress-related anxiety and pain.

III. RELAXATION TRAINING

Other techniques based on meditative traditions have also been introduced for stress reduction. Benson and colleagues have popularized an approach that involves brief exercises designed to help patients manage daily stress and have termed the approach "the relaxation response." Simple brief relaxation exercises have been helpful in managing such problems as mild to moderate hypertension and are recommended in such situations prior to or in conjunction with antihypertensive medication treatment.

IV. ACUPUNCTURE

This ancient Chinese technique is primarily employed in this country for chronic pain and, to a lesser extent, for habit problems or substance abuse. Given the interaction between pain and stress in chronic illness, the pain relief obtained through this technique can also reduce secondary stress and anxiety. Needles are inserted into locations thought to mediate pain perception and healing, usually alone, but sometimes with either mild electrical stimulation (electroacupuncture) or in combination with an herbal preparation (moxibustion). Acupuncture analgesia has been found to be reversed by administration of naloxone, an opiate antagonist, so mediation via endogenous opiates is possible. Subjects who are more highly hypnotizable have been found to be more likely to respond to acupuncture analgesia than those who are not, suggesting a role for spontaneous trance induction as well. Many patients find that they achieve a sense of well-being after acupuncture treatment which provides them with a respite from the stress of chronic illness.

V. BIOFEEDBACK

Biofeedback involves the use of telemetry to record peripheral muscle tension, skin temperature, or skin conductance (reflecting sweating) to inform people about their physiological responses and their ability to modulate them. This approach has been effective in treating tension and migraine headaches, managing stress, and treating psychophysiological disorders such as Reynaud's disease, which involves vasoconstriction. Training with the equipment is utilized to teach patients how to enhance their ability to manage physiological responses to stress, tension, or other symptoms and thereby feel less secondary anxiety when a stressful situation arises.

VI. CONCLUSION

There is little doubt that North Americans are voting with their pocketbooks and their feet for complementary and alternative treatments. Research has shown that some of them produce specific therapeutic benefits, whereas others clearly do not. Even if relief of symptoms is a small but real effect, when the big picture is overwhelming, small amounts of mental and/or physical control can go a long way toward reassuring patients that they can more effectively manage disease. Stress is a normal part of life and a natural, if unwelcome, part of the course of disease. The extent to which stress produces distress can be modified by a variety of treatments which engage patients as participants in their own care. While results vary, these approaches should be viewed as an opportunity rather than as a threat, a potentially useful addition to health care.

See Also the Following Articles

ALTERNATIVE THERAPIES; HOMEOSTASIS; HYPNOSIS; RELAXATION TECHNIQUES

Bibliography

Benson, H. (1996). "Timeless Healing: The Power and Biology of Belief." Scribner, New York.

Eisenberg, D. M., Davis, R. B., *et al.* (1998). Trends in alternative medicine use in the United States, 1990–1997: Results of a follow-up national survey. *J. Am. Med. Assoc.* **280,** 1569–1575.

Kabat-Zinn, J., Wheeler, E., *et al.* (1998). Influence of a mindfulness meditation-based stress reduction intervention on rates of skin clearing in patients with moderate to severe psoriasis undergoing phototherapy (UVB) and photochemotherapy (PUVA). *Psychosom. Med.* **60,** 625–632.

Lang, E., Joyce, J., *et al.* (1996). Self-hypnotic relaxation during interventional radiological procedures: Effects on pain perception and intravenous drug use. *Int. J. Clin. Exp. Hyp.* **XLIV**(2), 106–119.

Spiegel, D., Stroud, P., *et al.* (1998). Complementary medicine. *West. J. Med.* **168,** 241–247.

Spiegel, H., and Spiegel, D., (1987). "Trance and Treatment: Clinical Uses of Hypnosis." American Psychiatric Press, Washington, DC.

Compulsive Behavior

see Obsessive-Compulsive Disorder

Concentration Camp Survivors

J. David Kinzie

Oregon Health Sciences University

I. History of Concentration Camp Syndrome
II. Nazi Concentration Camp Survivors
III. Prisoners of War Concentration Camp Survivors
IV. Cambodian Pol Pot Concentration Camp Survivors
V. Conclusions

GLOSSARY

concentration camp A camp where prisoners of war, enemies, aliens, or political prisoners are confined. The term implies that physical mistreatment, torture, indiscriminate murder, and genocide can occur.

depression A specific psychiatric disorder consisting of lowered mood and symptoms, such as decreased interest in most activity, loss of appetite and weight, poor sleep, fatigue, feelings of worthlessness, poor concentration, and recurrent thoughts of death.

holocaust The systematic destruction of over six million European Jews by the Nazis before and during World War II.

posttraumatic stress disorder A specific psychiatric disorder following psychological trauma with symptoms of reexperiencing, such as nightmares and flashback; avoidance behavior, such as attempts to avoid thoughts and memories of the events; and hyperarousal symptoms, such as irritability, startle response, and difficulty sleeping.

I. HISTORY OF CONCENTRATION CAMP SYNDROME

There is probably no more stressful environment than that of a concentration camp, where people are detained for their combatant or alien status, their political views, or even their ethnicity. The purpose of such camps are often to control, punish, or kill its occupants. Words cannot describe the worse conditions, but crowded living, forced labor, starvation diets, lack of medical treatment, torture, and random or systematic murder are usual. Understandably, the physical and mental effects on the survivors are severe. A constant and persistent group of symptoms were found among survivors of Nazi concentration camps, which then became known as the concentration camp syndrome. This consists of marked anxiety, motor restlessness, hyperapprehensiveness (startle reactions) sleep disturbance, nightmares, difficulty in concentrating, obsessive rumination about the traumatic events, depression, and survivor guilt. Some symptoms seem to represent a form of brain damage, and early researchers found that beatings, malnutrition, and disease were the cause of this disorder; however, it eventually became apparent that the severe psychological trauma itself was the cause of this disorder, and it could occur in previously emotionally healthy persons. Several psychiatrists describing the survivors reported that none have escaped the effects; although the effects may be a subtle personality change, such as apathy, seclusiveness, suspiciousness, hostility, and mistrust. The concentration camp syndrome never became a formal American Psychiatric Association diagnosis, but it had much similarity with diagnosis of posttraumatic stress disorder (PTSD), which was recognized in 1980.

II. NAZI CONCENTRATION CAMP SURVIVORS

A. Background Persons

Six million people (mostly Jews) were killed in Nazi concentration camps. Some camps (Auschwitz and Treblinka) were for exterminations. Others had less systematic murder, but were characterized by starvation, forced labor, torture, endemic disease, beatings, inadequate clothing, death marches, and a lack of proper medical facilities. While living with constant threats to their lives, camp prisoners were subjected to medical experimentation, gross humiliation, and separation from family and were forced to witness severe cruelty to others. They were defenseless without privacy or any means of protection. The experience lasted 4 years before liberation came at the end of World War II. Much information up to now has been accumulated on the effects of the survivors.

B. Physical Effects

In a study of physical sequelae of the Holocaust in Norway, survivors had a higher mortality rate, more frequent hospitalizations, and higher incidents of sick periods. Physical symptoms, such as headaches, persistent dizziness, and gastrointestinal complaints, which can persist 50 years later, were common. However, most survivors have reported symptoms with a psychogenic component. Few differences have been found for such diagnostic disorders as arthritis, cancer, and Parkinson's disease.

C. Psychiatric Effects

There have been many community-based, large-scale studies on the Holocaust survivors, some 40 years after the events. Unlike the previous studies on patients seeking clinical help, these have consistently shown more distress in symptoms and lower mood in survivors than in controls.

In one study, 43% of survivors had symptoms compared to 28% of controls. However, there was considerable overlap and some survivors had less symptoms than controls. In one study, 40 years after the Holocaust, 46.8% of survivors met the diagnosis of PTSD. Although the trauma experiences of the Holocaust victims were universally severe, some evidence that the more severe trauma, i.e., surviving a death camp setting or being incarcerated longer, had more symptoms. Greater psychological problems were seen in those who experienced the Holocaust as children and showed more PTSD symptoms. Female victims report more distress than males. The Nazi concentration camp victims tended to remain vulnerable to reactivation of symptoms during stress, whether this redevelopment of PTSD symptoms occurred in actual trauma, such as scud missile attacks during the Gulf

War, or a perceived threat, such as a sense of increased anti-Semitism. The Nazi concentration camps were so horrible and the evil committed was so beyond comprehension that clinical terms may not do justice to the existential and theological despair of mankinds inhumanity.

III. PRISONERS OF WAR CONCENTRATION CAMP SURVIVORS

A. Background

Wars and upheaval in this century have led to thousands experiencing captivity by the enemy often with malnutrition, overcrowding, torture, poor diet, inadequate shelter, and terrorizing executions. The long-term effects have been reported in survivors in the United States, Australia, Israel, Canada, Holland, Great Britain, and, more recently, Bosnia Herzegovina.

B. Physical Health

American prisoners of war (POWs) from Japan had excess mortality from accidents and tuberculosis. POWs from the Korean War had increased cognitive deficits that were related to the amount of captivity and weight loss.

C. Psychiatric Effects

Follow-up studies of the POWs demonstrated a uniformly high rate of persistent and debilitating psychiatric disorders. High rates of psychiatric hospitalizations for neurosis were found in WWII POWs of Germany and Japan. In another study, high rates of anxiety reaction, alcoholism, and even schizophrenia have been found with greater occurrence in the POWs held by Japan, which inflicted more cruelty on the prisoners. More than 40 or 50 years after WWII and the Korean War, over half had at sometime a diagnosis of PTSD and 30% had a current diagnosis of PTSD. The severely traumatized group of POWs held by Japan had a PTSD lifetime prevalence of 84% and a current diagnosis of 58%. PTSD

also greatly increases the risk of other disorders, including depression and alcoholism. From a series of studies, we know that the POW concentration camp experience has severe and persistent effects, with up to 50% having PTSD, depression, and alcohol abuse. Many studies found that few survivors actively sought medical treatment and were suffering quite privately.

IV. CAMBODIAN POL POT CONCENTRATION CAMP SURVIVORS

A. Background

One of the most recent and best studied concentration camp experiences was that afflicted on the Cambodian people by the radical Marxist Pol Pot regime between 1975 and 1979. During this brutal time, millions of people were rounded up and placed in isolated camps with forced labor, no medical facilities, starvation diets, indiscriminate beatings, and murders, often with family members watching helplessly. One-fourth to one-third of Cambodia's 7 million people died during this time. Many survivors went to Thailand as refugees and were later given asylum in Western countries.

B. Physical Health

Even after they have improved physically from acute effects, many Cambodian refugees continue to report somatic complaints; from 15 to 20% reported much health impairment. A high percentage (43% in one study) had documented hypertension, but it is difficult to know if this is an effect of the trauma, refugee status, or even dietary changes.

C. Psychiatric Disorders

The first studies on Cambodian concentration camp survivors found that the symptoms of nightmares, startle reaction, intrusive memories of events, a strong tendency to avoid thinking about this, and marked concentration problems persisted. In addition to these symptoms of PTSD, most have major depressive symptoms. In a community study (nonpatients), 50% of Cambodians were found to have PTSD and 50% also had depression. The depression symptoms increased over time, unlike the PTSD symptoms, which tend to wax and wane, but continue to affect about 50% of Cambodians even 12 years later. An important finding was the marked sensitivity to stress. Cambodians who witnessed accidents, underwent surgery, or even saw violence on television had acute PTSD symptoms involving the trauma in Cambodia. Interestingly, drug and alcohol abuse was a rare condition among Cambodians, unlike the POWs.

V. CONCLUSIONS

The concentration camp syndrome, as first described following the Nazi Holocaust, represented a catastrophic stress and resulted in a common symptom pattern present in most survivors. These symptoms included marked anxiety, restlessness, startle reaction, sleep disturbances, nightmares, poor concentration, and excessive rumination about the traumatic events. The concentration camp syndrome was never recognized as an official American Psychiatric Association diagnosis but its symptoms are the core of what is now called posttraumatic stress disorder. The symptoms have been found in other concentration camp survivors, such as POWs and the more recent Cambodian concentration camp survivors. The response is the result of extreme stress and indicates that such stress can produce a psychiatric disorder that is severe and persistent in many people.

An associated aspect of the disorder is the tendency to have reactivation of symptoms when further stress occurs. A real or symbolic threat can reproduce symptoms or behavior (such as extreme fear or nightmares) just as if the person were in the concentration camp. This speaks to the powerful memories that such extreme stress can cause, even though these memories may be repressed for a time.

Treatment of the concentration camp syndrome originally was not satisfactory, probably because the early methods used psychoanalysis (or similar techniques), which seemed too stressful for the patients. Current techniques using mediation to reduce nightmares, sleep disorders, hyperarousal, and supportive psychotherapy seem to help the patient integrate the experience and reconnect emotionally to others.

An emerging issue is that children of concentration camp victims also seem to suffer indirect effects and may be more vulnerable to PTSD than others. Even under the most extreme conditions, only about 50% of concentration camp victims suffer the full PTSD (concentration camp syndrome) or other physical or psychiatric disabilities. Reasons for this vulnerability of some and resiliency of others are unknown, but genetic factors are thought to play a part. The relationship between such massive psychological trauma and the development of psychiatric disorders is an important area of research.

See Also the Following Articles

HOLOCAUST, STRESS EFFECTS OF; KOREAN CONFLICT, STRESS EFFECTS OF; PRISONERS OF WAR; SURVIVOR GUILT

Bibliography

Danieli, Y. 1998, "International Handbook of Multigenerational Legacies of Trauma," Plenum Press, New York.

Eitinger, L. 1980. "The Concentration Camp Syndrome and Its Late Sequela," (J. Demsdale, ed.) Hemisphere, New York.

Hunter, E. J. 1988. "The Psychological Effects of Being Prisoners of War in Human Adaptation to Extreme Stress from the Holocaust to Vietnam," (J. P. Wilson, Z. Harel, and B. Kahana, eds.). Plenum Press, New York.

Kinzie, J. D. 1988. "The Psychiatric Effects of Massive Trauma on Cambodian Refugees in Human Adaptation to Extreme Stress" (J. P. Wilson, Z. Harel, and B. Kahuna, eds.). Plenum Press, New York.

Krystal, H., ed. 1968. "Massive Psychic Trauma" International Universities Press, New York.

Marsella, A., Bornemann, T., and Ekblad, S., eds. 1994. "Amidst Peril and Pain." American Psychiatric Association, Washington, DC.

Matussek, P. 1975. "Internment in Concentration Camps and Its Consequences." Springer-Verlag, New York.

Stenger, C. A. "American Prisoners of War in WWI, WWII, Korea, Vietnam, Persian Gulf, and Somalia." Department of Veterans Affairs Advisory Committee on Former Prisoners of War, Washington, DC.

Congenital Adrenal Hyperplasia (CAH)

see Adrenogenital Syndrome

Conservation of Resources Theory

Stevan E. Hobfoll and Jennifer S. Kay

Kent State University, Ohio

I. Conservation of Resources Theory
II. Resources
III. Resource Categories
IV. Principles of Conservation of Resources Theory
V. Corollaries of Conservation of Resources Theory
VI. Conclusion

GLOSSARY

Conservation of Resources (COR) Theory States that stress has central environmental, social, and cultural bases in terms of the demands on people to acquire and protect the circumstances that insure their well-being and distance themselves from threats to well-being.

resources Those objects, personal characteristics, conditions, or energies that are valued by the individual or that serve as the means for attainment of other objects, personal characteristics, conditions, or energies.

stress Occurs in circumstances that represent a threat of loss or actual loss of the resources required to sustain the individual-nested-in-family-nested-in-social-organization. Further, because people will invest what they value to gain further, stress occurs when individuals do not receive reasonable gain following resource investment, this itself being an instance of loss.

traumatic stressors Severe, typically infrequent and unexpected events that usually include serious threat to life and well-being.

High-risk situations such as war, natural disasters, and crime and victimization as well as the onset of a serious illness put people's coping resources to a test and can result in psychological stress and distress. Because these situations are widespread, it is important that we examine the effects that high-risk situations have on people and why some can go through them relatively unscathed, whereas others are almost completely debilitated. As many as 2 million American households experience injuries and physical damage each year from fire, floods, hurricanes, tornadoes, and earthquakes. Over the past 2 decades, natural disasters and other calamities have killed about 3 million people worldwide and adversely affected the lives of at least 800 million more people. Between 1974 and 1980, there were 37 major catastrophes in the United States alone. In addition, few families are spared the pain of having a family member who has a serious illness or one who passes away. Although in the United States we think of war as something that does not effect us directly, global conflict is widespread, and communications have forced us to share in the suffering many go through in wars elsewhere. This article explores Conservation of Resources Theory as applied to high risk situations as one theoretical backdrop for explaining the differences in people's coping successes and their subsequent psychological reactions.

I. CONSERVATION OF RESOURCES THEORY

Conservation of Resources (COR) Theory examines and describes the nature of psychological stress and its likely consequences. Traditionally, stress theories have concentrated on people's individual appraisals of stressful situations as the determining factor of how much distress they will experience. Conservation of Resources Theory states that stress is neither first nor foremost a product of individuals' appraisal of events, but that it has central environmental, social, and cultural bases in terms of the demands on people to acquire and protect the circumstances that insure their well-being and distance themselves from threats to well-being. The theory posits that stress emanates from difficulty achieving the common goals toward which members of a culture strive. In this regard, stress is largely culturally determined because most of the major demands placed on people have a shared social context and that culture is a social phenomenon. Through personal experience and learning, people come to recognize what they need in order to affirm the acquisition and ownership of what is important directly, indirectly, and symbolically for success within their culture and for sheer survival. These things that individuals value are called resources.

II. RESOURCES

Resources are those objects, personal characteristics, conditions, or energies that are valued by the individual or that serve as the means for attainment of other objects, personal characteristics, conditions, or energies. Conservation of Resources Theory's basic tenet is that people strive to retain, protect, and build resources and that what is threatening to them is the potential or actual loss of these valued resources. In addition, people also endeavor to foster that which they value. Therefore, people work to acquire resources that they do not have, preserve those resources they have, protect resources when they are threatened, and cultivate resources by positioning themselves so that their resources can be put to best use.

Stress occurs in circumstances that represent a threat of loss or actual loss of the resources required to sustain the individual-nested-in-family-nested-in-social-organization. Further, because people will invest what they value to gain further, stress is predicted to occur when individuals do not receive reasonable gain following resource investment, this itself being an instance of loss.

It follows, that psychological stress is a reaction to the environment in which there is (1) the threat of a net loss of resources, (2) the net loss of resources, or (3) a lack of resource gain following the investment of resources. Individual-nested-in-family-nested-in-social-organization implies that these levels are enmeshed because there is no organization or family without individuals and individuals must rely on social attachments for well-being, self-esteem, and survival.

III. RESOURCE CATEGORIES

The Conservation of Resources model identifies resources whose loss is likely to result in stress. Since there is a common basis of human survival, most of these resources are valued across cultures, whereas others are more culturally or familially determined. Three different methods have been considered to categorize these resources. The first method categorizes resources into internal and external types. Several researchers have used this distinction. Internal resources are those that are possessed by the self or are within the domain of the self. This includes resources such as optimism, self-esteem, and a sense of mastery. External resources are those resources that are not provided by the individual, but are external to it. These include resources like social support, employment, and economic status.

Another method of classification of resources is a structurally based system that divides resources that have meaningful differences. The resulting four resource categories are (1) object resources, (2) personal resources, (3) condition resources, and (4) energy resources. Object resources (e.g., shelter, transportation) are valued because of some aspect of their physical nature or because of their acquiring secondary status values based on their rarity and expense. Personal characteristics are resources to the extent that they generally aid stress resistance. These include both skills and personal traits. Some examples of these are social competence, self-esteem, and a sense of mastery. Conditions are resources to the extent that they aid in obtaining other valued conditions or are themselves goals that people value. Some examples of condition resources are marriage and tenure. These resources are important because they lay the structural groundwork for access to other resources. Energies include resources such as time, knowledge, and money. They acquire value from their ability to be exchanged for resources in the previous three categories. Because of the common basis for human survival, many resources are valued across cultures. However, the order of importance of resources will vary along with differing cultural values, and some resources may be present in some cultures and not others.

The third method of classification of resources is based on the proximity of the resource to survival. Primary resources are those that directly correlate to survival. These include ample food, shelter, safety, and clothing. Secondary resources are those that contribute indirectly to primary resources. These include social support, marriage, and optimism. Tertiary resources include those things that are symbolically related to primary or secondary resources. These include money as well as workplace and social conditions that allow availability or access to secondary resources and resources that signify social status.

IV. PRINCIPLES OF CONSERVATION OF RESOURCES THEORY

A. Principle 1

There are two major principles that follow from the basic proposition of Conservation of Resources Theory. The first principle is that *resource loss is disproportionately more salient than resource gain*. Therefore, given an equal amount of loss and gain, loss will have a much greater impact. According to COR theory, it is the loss and the threat of loss of resources that principally define stress. This principle has also been developed in work by Tversky and Kahneman in their Prospect theory. Their theory states that the gradient of loss is steeper than the gradient for gain, which results in a bias in favor of loss. In experiments they have shown that when problems are framed or worded in terms of loss, greater risk will be taken to try to preserve resources than if the same situation is framed in terms of potential gain. Studies that separate loss from gain events also confirm that only loss events are related to psychological distress and illness. Therefore, it appears that losing resources will be much more notable and will have a greater impact than the equivalent gain.

If loss is more salient than gain, resource loss should have a greater impact on psychological distress than gain. This was examined empirically. First, groups of students, community members, and psychologists nominated resources that they valued. Next, different groups of people added resources that they felt were important that did not already appear on the list and deleted resources they felt were not valued. This process was repeated with about 50 different groups until no new resources were added that had not been deleted by more than one group prior and until no new deletions were judged to be necessary, ending with a final list of 74 resources.

Next, 255 students and 74 community members indicated whether they had lost or gained each of the 74 resources recently as well as during the past year. They repeated this process twice, separated by 3 weeks. They were also administered well-known anxiety and depression scales. Results indicated that neither recent resource gain nor resource gain during the past year had any direct impact on psychological distress for either group. Recent resource loss and resource loss during the past year, in contrast, had major negative effects on psychological distress. People were deeply negatively effected when they lost resources, but were hardly impacted when they experienced resource gain.

Researchers have applied COR theory to study the impact of both Hurricane Hugo, which affected South Carolina in 1990, and the Sierra Madre earthquake that hit Los Angeles county in 1991. They examined how resource loss influenced the mobilization of resources and also how loss effected mental health. It was found that the greater the resource loss, the more coping individuals engaged in and the more psychologically distressed they became. They also found that the influence of resource loss was both of greater magnitude and independent of the influence of positive coping responses. Supporting COR Theory, resource loss was more important in predicting psychological distress than were personal characteristics and coping behavior.

The impact of resource loss on coping, physical health, and psychological well-being was examined further after Hurricane Andrew struck South Florida in 1992. Comparing the impact of resource loss to other factors, it was found that resource loss had the single most profound influence. The greater the resources people lost, the greater was their psychological distress and the worse their immune resistance. It was also found that individuals' sense of optimism counterbalanced much of the negative influence of resource loss. Therefore, those people who had resources, including optimism, were more likely to successfully cope with Hurricane Andrew than did those individuals who lacked resources.

Traumatic stress entails the rapid loss of resources and the resources lost are usually the ones held with highest value by individuals. The rapidness of resource loss is related to the fact that traumatic stressors (1) attack people's most basic resources, (2) typically occur unexpectedly, (3) make excessive demands on remaining resources, (4) are outside of the realm for which resource utilization strategies have been developed, and (5) leave a powerful mental image that is easily evoked by cues associated with the event. The excessive demands placed on an individual by a war or natural disaster are such that no amount of resources could prevent severe initial reaction to stress. At best, it is expected that a healthy individual could make a reasonably rapid recovery that could be a matter of weeks, months or years, depending on the trauma. For many traumatic events, it would be expected that negative sequelae be lifelong, but hopefully limited to certain life domains so that most normal functioning continues.

Chronic stressful conditions also have been found to chip away at resources and strong resource reservoirs. For example, social support has been found to diminish for mothers of chronically ill children and for women with breast cancer. In addition, under chronic stress conditions, resources that remain have been found to have increasingly limited effectiveness.

This may be the case because loss begets further loss and can lead to loss spirals. Under a chronic stressful condition, not only do people experience more and more loss, they also may deplete resources until they have few resource reserves to contribute to the stress resistance process.

Although loss is more salient than gain in COR Theory, resource gain is an important facet of stress, even if it is secondary. Resource gain is important because it is woven with loss. Loss can be prevented, counterbalanced, or forestalled through resource gain. If initial losses occur, previously stored resources can be applied to minimize the impact of loss. Resource gain also increases in meaning in the face of loss. This occurs because people take stock of their resources when loss occurs. People enact gain cycles in the wake of loss, in part to offset current resource loss, but also because they become more aware of future losses and look to prevent them. Consistent with the idea that resource gain is important in the face of loss, researchers examining workers who were laid off from their jobs found that those people with financial savings did not experience the harmful effects of unemployment. However, they found that prior to the worker's job loss, their savings had little positive impact, supporting the idea that resource gain or surpluses (in this case a savings account) increases in significance during a loss.

B. Principle 2

The second principle that follows from COR Theory is that *people must invest resources in order to protect against resource loss, recover from loss, and to gain resources.* Conservation of Resources Theory states that resources are central to the experience of stress. Stress occurs when resources are lost or threatened, and people use resources to prevent or offset loss and to make other resource gain. This investment of resources occurs by several mechanisms. The first mechanism of resource investment deals with the total investment of a resource. The second kind of resource investment involves risking the resource without total investment. Resource investment may also occur directly or through substitution. Resource investment may counterbalance loss, protect against threat of loss, or contribute toward resource gain.

When mastery, optimism, social support, finances, or status are put into place to offset a major stress event, the importance of Principle 2 is underscored. First, the resource must be ample enough to be used. Low self-esteem will have limited value, just as little money can do little good to offset financial losses. The second principle of COR Theory also suggests a more subtle point. Specifically, because people typically have little experience with major stressors, they may not know how to employ their resources in these special circumstances. Just as combat troops must learn to apply their skills under increasing pressure, people will learn and adjust to even catastrophic circumstances. However, the cost of resource investment will accelerate as people will at first misuse resources, hold back on resource use to preserve resource integrity, and will need to allow for a quick depletion of resources in some instances.

V. COROLLARIES OF CONSERVATION OF RESOURCES THEORY

A. Corollary 1

In addition to the two major principles presented previously, there are four corollaries of COR Theory that outline rules that allow for definitive predictions as to how resources function over time. The first corollary states that

> Those with greater resources are less vulnerable to resource loss and more capable of orchestrating resource gain. Conversely, those with fewer resources are more vulnerable to resource loss and less capable of achieving resource gain. Moreover, those who lack resources are more likely to experience extreme consequences, as without adequate resource reserves they are less likely to have resources to invest in the wake of initial losses.

Resources may be used either individually or in combination with other resources. In addition, stress often makes multiple demands on people that require different combinations of resources. However, those people with greater resources will be less negatively affected by initial resource loss and will be more likely to create gain cycles because they can invest resources that are not required for everyday functioning. Those people with fewer resources will be more deeply impacted by a major crisis or by chronic demands and will have few resource reserves to assemble. Therefore, initial setbacks will be devastating and result in immediate and rapid loss spirals.

B. Corollary 2

The second corollary of COR Theory states that *those who lack resources are not only more vulnerable to resource loss, but that initial loss begets future loss.* People rely on resources to apply to losses, and therefore with each loss there are fewer resources that can be utilized or invested in gains that might influence the occurrence of stress. With a depleted resources pool, future challenges are increasingly less likely to be met and a downward spiral increases in momentum. This results in depleted resource reserves that are less capable of mobilizing to defend against future challenges. This further suggests that loss cycles will have initially higher velocity for resource-poor individuals or groups, as they are from the outset in a resource-challenged state characterized by their resources being already stretched in protection of the self, family, or social system. Therefore, this corollary predicts that loss cycles will have progressing momentum and strength.

When exposed to very high-risk situations, people may lose not only their tertiary and secondary resources, such as transportation and a sense of mastery, but may lose primary resources, such as food and shelter that are necessary for survival. In this way, the psychological stress that people experience in a high-risk situation is not only taxing because of its severity, but is also taxing because of the vast array of resources that it may effect and deplete.

Where individuals are not equipped to gain resources, especially if they are in a loss spiral, they are also likely to be particularly vulnerable. For example, in many disasters such as war, the country may be in such turmoil that it is very difficult for people to gain resources such as employment or money. Individuals may also not be equipped to gain resources because they might have limited access to opportunities to protect themselves or to gain access to the resources available to others in society. Furthermore, resources are not distributed equally in society, and those people who lack resources are most vulnerable to additional losses. Those with weak resources have been found to have the least success under high stress. Loss spirals develop because people lack the resources to offset the cascading of loss. If resources are used to prevent loss of other resources, such loss would be predicted to lead to further decreases in the likelihood of possessing necessary resource reserves. In this manner, people who have weak or few resources prior to the onset of a high-risk situation, like a natural disaster, will psychologically do worse and will experience more loss spirals than those who had stronger or greater resources prior to the disaster.

Environmental circumstances, like high-risk situations such as war, natural disasters, chronic illness, and rape, often threaten or result in multiple depletions of people's resources. These losses are important because resources have instrumental value to people and they have symbolic value in that they help to define for people who they are. Hence, rapid resource loss impacts people's ability to mobilize resistance resources as challenges to the social fabric that binds communities and sustains people as a safety net. Further, ongoing major losses ebb away at people's sense of identity that may result in helplessness and other extreme behaviors evidenced in panic, mob action, and even barbarism.

C. Corollary 3

The third corollary of the Conservation of Resources Theory states that *those who possess resources are both more capable of gain and that initial resource gain begets further gain.* If initial resource gains are made, then greater resources become available for investment. When initial gains are achieved, additional resources become available for investment and individuals and social systems are less vulnerable to loss and loss spirals. In addition, individuals do not necessarily need to rely on these resource surpluses for reserves, so they can benefit further by employing them for gains' sake. However, because resource loss

is more potent than resource gain, gain cycles will have less momentum or speed and less impact than loss cycles and people will be motivated to sustain resistance reserves for future misfortune. Seen in this light, in the case of major and traumatic stress, gain cycles will often only occur well after the events' initial impact. Even then, gain cycles will often begin from a depleted base and might better be framed as rebuilding cycles.

D. Corollary 4

The fourth and final corollary affirms *that those who lack resources are likely to adopt a defensive posture to guard their resources.* For those with few resources, the cost of resource investment surpasses demands and makes the individual or organization vulnerable. A defensive posture keeps a maximum of resources in reserve in case the person needs to offset a future loss.

Those people who lack resources are predicted to take a defensive posture in order to guard their resources. Those with weak resources have been found to use their resources best when challenged by everyday stressors, but to have the least success under high-stress conditions. In studying victims of Hurricane Andrew, researchers found that resource loss resulted in a marked increase in use of denial coping. This, in turn, placed victims at increased risk for PTSD. To expend resources from a depleted system may be too risky a venture. Instead, a shutdown response may best preserve limited resource pools until the storm (literally in this case) blows over.

VI. CONCLUSION

In conclusion, loss is particularly salient because it is disproportionately weighted in the human experience and it is harder to prevent loss than to obtain resource gain. Therefore resource loss is more powerful and more potent than resource gain. Conservation of Resources Theory states that when loss occurs it is more depleting of resources than gain is resource generating. It is clear that high-risk situations deplete resources as well as resource reserves and can result in loss spirals. Conservation of Resources Theory defines psychological stress as a reaction to the environment in which there is the threat of a net loss of resources, the net loss of resources, or a lack of resource gain following the investment of resources. In high-risk situations such as war, natural disasters, or sudden illness, many if not all of these threats can occur. Therefore, COR Theory would explain people's distress following a high-risk situation, not as an individualized response based solely on characteristics of the individual, but as one that occurs because of the threats to resources as shared within a community.

Although loss is more salient than gain, this is not to imply that resource gain is not important. Resource gain is important because it can prevent, counterbalance, or forestall loss. However, in a high-risk situation, many factors may prevent resource gain and therefore limit the role of gain in forestalling loss cycles. Because of the long tail of resource loss that follows major stressful circumstances, follow-up to protect the individual and social system are needed on a long-term basis.

See Also the Following Article

DISASTERS, PUBLIC, EFFECTS OF

Bibliography

Bolger, N., Vinokur, A., Foster, M., and Ng, R. (1996). Close relationships and adjustment to a life crisis: The case of breast cancer. *J. Personal. Soc. Psychol.* 70, 283–294.

Carver, C. S. (1993). "Coping with Hurricane Andrew." Paper presented at the 15th International Conference of the Stress and Anxiety Research Society, Madrid, Spain.

Freedy, J. R., Saladin, M. E., Kilpatrick, D. G., Resnick, H. S., and Saunders, B. E. (1994). Understanding acute psychological distress following natural disaster. *J. Traum. Stress* 7, 257–273.

Freedy, J. R., Shaw, D. L., Jarrell, M. P., and Masters, C. R. (1992). Towards an understanding of the psychological impact of natural disasters—An application of the conservation resources stress model. *J. Traum. Stress* 5, 441–454.

Hobfoll, S. E. (1988). "The Ecology of Stress." Hemisphere, New York.

Hobfoll, S. E. (1998). "Stress, Community and Culture." Plenum, New York.

Kessler, R. C., Turner, J. B., Blake, J., and House, J. S. (1988). Effects of unemployment on health in a community survey: Main, modifying and mediating effects. *J. Soc. Issues* 44, 69–85.

Lazarus, R. S., and Folkman, S. (1984). "Stress, Appraisal, and Coping." Springer-Verlag, New York.

Schönpflug, W. (1985). Goal-directed behavior as a source of stress: Psychological origins and consequences of inefficiency. *In* "The Concept of Action in Psychology" (M. Frese and J. Sabini, Eds.), pp. 172–188. Erlbaum, Hillsdale, N.J.

Tversky, A., and Kahneman, D. (1974). Judgement under uncertainty: Heuristics and biases. *Science* 185, 1124–1131.

Control and Stress

Andrew Steptoe

St. George's Hospital Medical School, University of London, United Kingdom

GLOSSARY

behavioral control (instrumental or objective control) The situation when the organism has at its disposal a behavioral response that can prevent, reduce, or terminate stressful stimulation.

cognitive control A form of psychological coping related to perceived control over one's reactions to aversive events.

locus of control A set of generalized control beliefs concerning the extent to which individuals feel that aspects of their lives are determined by their own activities and abilities (internal locus of control) or are governed by external factors.

perceived control The belief that one can exert control over stressful events, based on the appraisal of the situation and appropriate perceptions of competence (self-efficacy expectancies) and expectations concerning the outcome of making a response.

S tressors come in many guises, from confrontation with a predator through death of a close relative to conflict at work or living in crowded noisy conditions. When we try to understand what aspects of situations make them more or less threatening, the concept of control emerges as a crucial feature. Stressors differ in the extent to which they can be controlled, and behavioral control is typically associated with a diminution of stress responses. Sometimes the perception of control is sufficient to reduce stress reactions, even though control itself is never actually exercised. For example, studies of people who are anxious about dentistry have shown that telling people they can give a signal that will stop the procedure reduces pain and anxiety, even though they never use the signal. Humans and other animals also seek out information about impeding threatening events and about ways of coping with the situation. This phenomenon is known as cognitive control and is an important weapon in the armory of psychological coping. Finally, there are control beliefs or the sense of control that people have in specific areas or over their lives and destiny more generally. A sense of control is generally adaptive for health, but the need for control may under some circumstances be maladaptive and lead to an inflexibility in coping with difficult problems. Since control has so many facets, there is a danger that the construct is misused and disguises careless reasoning. In this article, the different aspects of control and stress are described, along with evidence related to physiological responses, well-being, and health. The ways in which control can be enhanced to improve quality of life, ameliorate pain, and promote rehabilitation are also discussed.

I. BEHAVIORAL CONTROL AND PHYSIOLOGICAL STRESS RESPONSES

Behavioral control can be defined as having at one's disposal a behavioral response that can prevent, reduce, or terminate stressful stimulation. Natural stressors vary across the entire spectrum of controllability. Some events, such as the unexpected death of a family member, are outside personal control. But in many situations there is an element of behavioral control. People who regularly find themselves stuck in traffic jams on their morning journey to work may feel helpless, but actually have some control; they might choose to use some other form of transport; to start their journey at a different time; to select a different route, stop, and take a break until the traffic clears; and so on.

Study of the impact of behavioral control over stress is complicated by the fact that many of the most aversive life events are uncontrollable. Comparisons between controllable and uncontrollable events may therefore be confounded with the aversiveness of the experience. Experimental studies provide the best opportunity to examine the effects of behavioral control, since aversiveness can be held constant. The yoked design championed by Jay Weiss and later by Martin Seligman and others has served to illustrate the effects of behavioral control most clearly. In this paradigm, a pair of rodents is exposed to identical intermittent aversive stimuli (electric shocks or loud noise). One animal is able to make a behavioral response which either terminates the stimuli or delays their onset, while the second animal has no response available. The amount of aversive stimulation experienced by both depends on the effectiveness of the performance of the one in the behavioral control condition, and any differences in physiological responses or pathology will result from the availability of behavioral control.

Table I summarizes some of the many physiological and pathological advantages conferred by control in this design. It can be seen that behavioral control is associated with amelioration of physiological stress

TABLE I
Adverse Effects of Uncontrollable Stress in Comparison with Exposure to Matched Controllable Aversive Stimulation[a]

Decreased food/water consumption
Greater weight loss
Higher plasma corticosterone
Increased gastric lesions
Reduced production of specific antibodies
Reduced lymphocyte reactivity
Decreased cytotoxic activity of natural killer cells
Decreased tumor rejection
Increased susceptibility to malignancy

[a] For details, see Steptoe, A. (1990). Psychobiological stress responses. *In* M. Johnston and L. Wallace (Eds.), "Stress and Medical Procedures." Oxford Univ. Press, Oxford, UK.

responses and pathological outcomes. These range from reduced levels of neuroendocrine response to slower proliferation of experimentally implanted malignancies.

Not all the biological responses to uncontrollable stress are detrimental. For example, uncontrollable conditions tend to lead to greater stress-induced analgesia than matched controllable conditions, and this mechanism may permit organisms to endure stressful stimulation at a reduced level of physical discomfort.

Research in humans has gone some way to duplicating these effects, with differences in the magnitude of acute cardiovascular and endocrine responses. However, an important caveat concerns the effort or response cost associated with maintaining behavioral control.

A. Control and Effort

Effects of the type shown in Table I have generally emerged in studies in which behavioral control is easy to exert. For example, electric shock may be avoided by a lever press on a simple schedule of reinforcement. However, control may require great effort to maintain and can be associated with a degree of uncertainty as to whether it has been successful. Under these circumstances, physiological activation may be greater than that elicited in uncontrollable situations. This was illustrated in the classic human experimental studies carried by Paul Obrist. Obrist randomized human volunteers to three conditions in a shock avoidance reaction time study. All participants had to respond rapidly to aversive stimuli and were informed that successful performance would lead to avoidance of electric shock. Three criteria were employed: an "easy" condition in which even slow reaction times would be successful, a "hard" condition in which participants had to maintain or improve performance over time, and an "impossible" condition in which the reaction time criterion was too fast for most people. The impossible condition is comparable to uncontrollable stress, while the other two conditions represent easy and effortful behavioral control respectively. The number of shocks administered was held constant across conditions. It was found that the greatest physiological activation was present not in the impossible or uncontrollable condition, but in the hard condition. This physiological reaction pattern was sustained by selective activation of β-adrenergically mediated sympathetic nervous system responses. Later studies have established that the enhanced physiological reactions associated with control under these circumstances are related to the effort expended, with greater effort being correlated with heightened norepinephrine responses.

B. Control and Fear

Lack of control over aversive stimuli potentiates fear responses. One study in rats used the yoked control design described earlier over a single session. Twenty-four hours later, the animals were placed in a different environment and given two brief shocks so as to generate conditioned fear. The freezing response was much greater among rats that previously had no control over shock compared with those that had been able to exert behavioral control, and differences lasted several days. The response was blocked by benzodiazepines [Maier, S. F. (1990). Diazepam modulation of stress-induced analgesia depends on the type of analgesia. *Behv. Neurosci.* **104**, 337–345].

Evidence suggests that this behavioral response to uncontrollable stress is associated with release of serotonin in the dorsal raphe nucleus and amygdala. Experiments using *in vivo* microdialysis have shown that uncontrollable stress leads to increased levels of extracellular serotonin in both these sites, while animals exposed to controllable stress show no such elevation.

Research on human fear also suggests that control is relevant. Fear of pain during medical and dental procedures is strongly associated with perceptions of uncontrollability. Fear of social threats (for example, when the individual is threatened with physical or sexual assault) is also greater when people believe the situation is uncontrollable.

C. Control and Work

Control is important to understanding the physiological and health consequences of stressful events in human life. One area in which control has emerged as a key variable is in the study of work stress. Jobs vary on many dimensions of control. Some work is self-paced, while other tasks are externally paced by machines or other people. In some jobs, workers have choice about their posture, when they can take rest breaks, and how the work should be done. Flexibility in work hours, participation in decision making, and autonomy at work are all factors that vary across jobs. In psychophysiological studies, it has been found that cardiovascular and neuroendocrine activation is greater during externally paced than self-paced work, even when the actual pace of work is held constant. People working in low-control jobs show elevated blood pressure during the working day which may be sustained in the evening. Evidence is also accumulating which suggests that coronary heart disease risk is elevated in people engaged in low-control work. One recent study evaluated control of work pace (operationalized as to whether the work was externally paced and the worker could choose when to take breaks) and health during pregnancy in a large sample of Norwegian working women. It was found that after statistical adjustment for age, parity, education, smoking, and manual work, greater control was associated with less preeclampsia, less low back pain, and a reduced probability of low birth weight in comparison with low control over work [Wergland, E., and Strand, K. (1998). Work pace control and pregnancy health in a population-based sample of employed women in Norway. *Scand. J. Work Environ. Health* **24**, 206–212].

There is also a substantial literature which indicates greater autonomy and participation at work are associated with higher levels of self-reported job satisfaction, commitment to work, better performance, and reduced levels of emotional distress, staff turnover, and absenteeism. However, these studies illustrate a complication in human research in control, since it is clear that control cannot be seen solely as an objective characteristic of the environment, but depends on subjective perceptions.

II. PERCEIVED CONTROL

Perceived control is the sense that one has control over aversive events. Objective differences in behavioral control are presumably mediated by perceived control. Thus the benefits of having control over a particular aspect of work (such as being able to make a personal telephone call if necessary) will only be manifest if the worker realizes that this option is available. Perceived control is the result of a subjective judgement, based on the individual's appraisal of the situation. It has two elements. The first is a perception that the situation is potentially controllable, and the second is that the individual can take the correct action. There may be circumstances in which events are perceived as controllable, but no action is taken since people lack (or believe they lack) appropriate behavioral competence. Psychologists such as Albert Bandura have postulated a distinction between outcome expectations and self-efficacy expectations to characterize these two aspects.

It is generally found that distress is associated with a perception that events are uncontrollable, and this phenomenon may operate independent of objective behavioral control. Thus two individuals may experience the same event, such as the breakdown of an important personal relationship. One may perceive that the event was outside their control, due to the callousness of their partner, the circumstances in which they lived, or the predatory behavior of a third party. Another person may perceive themselves to have been responsible; if they had not been preoccupied with their own work or had responded to the needs of their partner, then the relationship might not have floundered. One student who has failed an academic examination may attribute this to their own lack of preparation and effective revision, while another may blame arbitrary examiners or bad luck in the selection of questions.

Human beings seek to understand their experiences in life by developing explanations for aversive events and often construe events retrospectively as having been controllable (for example, "if I had not stayed later than I planned at that party, and had not decided to walk down that street, I would not have been assaulted"). Such cognitive attributions may be maladaptive in leading to self-blame for occurrences over which one has little control, but also may help to impose sense and order on a world which may otherwise appear cruel and arbitrary.

A. Sense of Control

Perception of control is not restricted to individual aversive experiences, but also relates to domains of life or even to life in general. The term "locus of control" is used to describe these generalized control beliefs. This construct was first introduced by Rotter, who argued that people varied in the extent to which they believed that important outcomes were determined by their own internal abilities and activities or by external factors. Locus of control has since been elaborated in two important ways. First, locus of control may be domain specific, with different levels of belief in personal control over different aspects of life (health, work, personal relationships etc.) Second, it maybe useful to understand locus of control as consisting of three dimensions: belief in internal control, chance, and powerful others. For example in the domain of health, people can be categorized according to the extent to which they believe that their health is determined by their own actions (internal control), that whether they remain healthy is a matter of fate or luck (belief in chance), and that their health is influenced by the competence of doctors and other health professionals (belief in powerful others). A dimensional perspective implies that people may simultaneously hold strong beliefs about more than one set of influences. They may believe, for instance, that they have quite a lot of control over their health, while at the same time believing that doctors are also very influential.

Sense of control is an individual belief pattern that also has developmental and social determinants. Animal studies indicate that monkeys provided with experiences of controllable (contingent) events early in life are subsequently less reactive to stressful events in adulthood. The experience of a major uncontrollable event in childhood, such as the death of one's mother, is associated with increased likelihood of depression following negative life events in adult life. Differences in sense of control may also relate to social class, with economically more deprived people facing greater external obstacles and fewer opportunities to influence events than do the better off. One recent study assessed sense of mastery (e.g., agreement with the statement "whether I am able to get what I want is in my own hands") and perceptions of constraints (e.g., "there is little I can do to change many of the important things in my life") in three large population surveys. It was found that sense of mastery was greater in higher than lower income sectors of the sample, while perceived constraints were less. The financially better off also reported greater life satisfaction and less depression and rated their health as better. However, not all the lower income respondents had low mastery and high constraint ratings. It was found that individuals in the low-income sectors with high mastery ratings had life satisfaction, depression, and health ratings comparable with those of the high-income group. So sense of control can modulate social class differences in well-being [Lachman, M. E., and Weaver, S. L. (1998). The sense of control as a moderator of social class differences in health and well-being. *J. Person. Soc. Psychol.* 74, 763–773].

III. COGNITIVE CONTROL AND COPING

Another closely related phenomenon is cognitive control, which can be defined as the belief that one can control one's reactions to events. It is a common characteristic to seek out information about events even when they cannot be controlled behaviorally. The person who has an abnormal result on a medical test and is scheduled for further examination may try to find out about the test and its consequences from acquaintances, libraries, or other sources of information. The purpose of this information seeking is not to control the outcome, but to feel "in control" by reducing uncertainty and increasing the predictability of the situation and to manage reactions to the result by anticipatory coping. This type of control, sometimes known as secondary control, is closely allied with the repertoire of other coping responses that people mobilize in an effort to regulate their responses to aversive experiences. It has important uses in medical settings, where the procedures for psychological preparation for surgery and stressful medical procedures have the effect of increasing cognitive control by providing information and helping patients develop a range of coping responses.

People vary in the extent to which they exert effort

to establish control over the situations with which they are confronted. A high need for control may be maladaptive in some circumstances. Studies of work stress indicate that when high need for control is blocked by low extrinsic rewards (such as poor pay or promotion prospects), the individual may be placed at increased risk for coronary heart disease.

IV. CONTROL AND WELL-BEING

A. Control and Aging

Growing old is associated with a diminution of control. When people retire from work, their economic power is reduced, they have less authority than before, and their social networks shrink. Impaired physical health may increase the person's sense of vulnerability, while they are exposed more often to uncontrollable events such as the death of contemporaries. A number of studies have documented the links between aging and the loss of control, though there are exceptions. "Successful aging," or the maintenance of well-being and effective functioning despite chronological progression, is coupled with maintenance of beliefs in personal control. People may adapt by lowering their valuation of the importance of areas of life over which they lose control and by investing in social relationships more selectively than before. The impact of increasing sense of control and autonomy on the well-being of elderly population has also been investigated. Randomized trials of increased involvement in decision making in institutionalized elderly groups have demonstrated improvements in mood and activity levels associated with enhanced control.

B. Control and Pain

The effects on pain of having control over the source of painful stimulation have been studied extensively. These experiments suggest that having behavioral control leads to a reduction in the subjective and physiological impact of the painful stimulus and may also increase pain tolerance. However, the benefits of control depend on the confidence that people have in their response efficacy, so perceptions are again important. It is interesting that the favorable effects of control over acute pain are observed despite the fact that stress-induced analgesia is elicited when there is a lack of control. It is likely that control allows behavioral and cognitive coping methods to be deployed that in turn reduce distress.

Chronic clinical pain is associated with feelings of helplessness, lack of control, and depression. Some authorities have argued that there may be a progression from feelings of personal helplessness in the early phases of a chronic pain problem to general helplessness (the belief that no one is able to control the pain) in later stages. The impact of chronic pain on well-being is that of a uncontrollable stressor, since by definition a pain that becomes chronic has not been alleviated and so has not been controlled. The generalization of distress about pain to disability and depression mirrors the phenomenon of learned helplessness.

The links between control and pain can be harnessed for patient care. As noted earlier, providing patients with control over sources of potential pain (for example, during dental examinations) can increase tolerance. Patient-controlled analgesia is used in a variety of medical settings and has benefits both in terms of emotional well-being and analgesic use. Several studies have found that when patients can control the level of analgesia, they use less medication than if it is provided by the physician. Rehabilitation programs for patients with chronic pain have a strong element of increasing perceived control by providing patients with greater and more effective coping options.

C. Control and Illness

Most serious illnesses bring with them strong feelings of loss of control. When people have heart attacks or are diagnosed with cancer, they feel that they are no longer in control of their bodies, and their future plans are put in jeopardy so that they lose a sense of control over their destiny. Loss of control is often accompanied by other facets of helplessness, including hopelessness, distress, and passivity. Similar patterns occur in chronic health problems. For example, high levels of perceived control over asthma are associated with better self-manage-ment skills, reduced risk of hospitalization, and less restricted activity, independent of the severity of asthma itself. Some studies have found that recovery from serious illness such as stroke and major fractures is positively correlated with high internal control beliefs.

Many procedures for improving the emotional state of patients have the effect of enhancing perceived control. Thus the methods used to prepare women for childbirth increase perceived control by providing a repertoire of coping response. Stress management procedures during cardiac rehabilitation enhanced perceived control and patient self-efficacy by increasing confidence in the resumption of normal activities. A particular area in which the issue of control has been contentious surrounds patient choice. To what extent should patients be involved in medical decision making? A number of studies indicate that although patients desire information about issues surrounding medical decisions, they often prefer to delegate responsibility for the decision itself to the doctor. This should not be seen as too surprising since it is the typical pattern found in any society with specialist roles. While we might want to know all the facts, we would expect the car mechanic to decide how to fix an engine or the chef to use judgement and skill to prepare the complicated dish we have ordered. Patients often wish to be involved in decision making, particularly when there is a genuine choice of more than one effective alternative, but seldom wish to take authority completely away from the physician.

V. CONCLUSIONS

Control has emerged over recent years as a powerful explanatory variable in stress research. It is relevant to a wide variety of settings, from basic experimental research on neuroendocrinology and neurochemistry to the experience of people in different socioeconomic sectors of society. There is a danger such an attractive integrating notion will be misused and employed as a global explanation for completely unrelated phenomena. However, if care is taken not to confuse the different meanings of control, the construct has considerable value in understanding stress.

See Also the Following Articles

Behavior, Overview; Coping, Stress and; Life Events Scale; Surgery and Stress; Workplace Stress

Bibliography

Adler, N. E., Boyce, T., Chesney, M. A., Cohen, S., Folkman, S., Kahn, R., and Syme, L. (1994). Socio-economic status and health: The challenge of the gradient. *Am. Psychol.* **49**, 15–24.

Bandura, A. (1997). "Self-Efficacy: The Exercise of Control." Freeman, New York.

Guadagnoli, E., and Ward, P. (1998). Patient participation in decision-making. *Soc. Sci. Med.* **47**, 329–339.

Maier, S. F., and Watkins, L. R. (1998). Stressor controllability, anxiety and serotonin. *Cog. Ther. Res.* **22**, 595–613.

Rodin, J. (1986). Aging and health: Effects of the sense of control. *Science* **233**, 1271–1276.

Sauter, S. L., Hurrell, J. J., and Cooper, C. L. (Eds.) (1989). "Job Control and Worker Health." Wiley, Chichester.

Steptoe, A., and Appels, A. (Eds.) (1989). "Stress, Personal Control and Health." Wiley, Chichester.

Coping Skills

Anita DeLongis and Melady Preece

University of British Columbia

GLOSSARY

cognitive reappraisal A form of coping that focuses on changing one's attitude toward a stressful situation.

coping Cognitive and behavioral efforts to manage stress.

emotion-focused coping Attempts to manage one's emotions during stressful periods.

problem-focused coping Attempts to directly change a stressful situation.

relationship-focused coping Attempts to manage one's social relationships during stressful periods.

C oping describes cognitive and behavioral responses to a stressful situation. These responses are determined by the interaction between characteristics of the person and characteristics of the situation. When these responses are particularly effective in reducing strain, due to the expertise with which they are selected and employed, we could say these responses are particularly skillful. When an individual experiences a stressor that threatens to overwhelm current personal resources, an intervention that emphasizes coping skills training can be helpful. However, there is no one coping skill that, once learned, becomes a magic bullet, effective with all kinds of stress. An important part of being a skilled coper is being able to match a stressful situation with the most effective strategy that is appropriate for the given context.

I. STRESS, APPRAISALS, AND COPING

Everyone experiences stress at times during life. However, what is extremely stressful to one individual may not be at all stressful to another. According to Lazarus' model of stress and coping, how a situation is evaluated, or appraised, determines the degree of stress experienced by the individual. Lazarus described two main categories of cognitive appraisals of stressful situations, primary appraisals and secondary appraisals. Primary appraisals involve the individual's assessment of the situation as stressful or not stressful. Situations appraised as stressful can involve harm or loss or the threat of harm or loss or else be perceived as a challenge. Secondary appraisals involve the individual's consideration of what might or can be done. These two types of appraisals often occur in parallel processes that may be so automatic as to escape conscious awareness.

Coping is loosely defined as things we think and actions we take to ameliorate the negative aspects of a stressful situation. How we manage stress is critical because overwhelming stress can cause psychological distress as well as have both short- and long-term negative consequences for physical health. The ability to cope successfully with a stressful situation depends on a number of factors. Primary among these are the resources one brings to the stressful situation. These resources include one's personality, age, income, education, previous experiences, social support, and physical and mental health. Both resources and subjective appraisals are important determinants of the degree of stress experienced by the individual. If a situation is not appraised as taxing one's resources or ability to cope, it may not be experienced as stress at all. Features of the situation are also important in shaping coping responses. Certainly there are many types of stressors that would be a tremendous strain for almost any individual.

A. Goals of Coping

Cohen and Lazarus have identified five main goals of coping efforts as common to most stressful situations. We may seek to (1) reduce harmful environmental conditions and enhance the prospect of recovery. We may also attempt to (2) tolerate or adjust to the negative events or realities. Of course, we will also want to (3) maintain a positive self-image, (4) keep our emotional equilibrium, and (5) preserve satisfying relationships with others. Depending upon our most pressing goals, the constraints of the situation, and our available resources, we may attempt to cope with a stressful situation in a variety of ways. In describing different ways of coping, a distinction has historically been made between problem-focused coping, which involves attempts to change the situation; and emotion-focused coping, which is directed more toward tolerating or adjusting to a negative event and attempting to preserve or regain one's emotional equilibrium. More recently, researchers have also begun to study relationship-focused coping, which encompasses ways of coping that are designed to preserve the quality of important social relationships.

B. Ways of Coping

1. Problem-Focused Coping

Problem solving is a strategy that quickly comes to mind as an effective way of attempting to remedy a negative situation. Defining the problem, generating alternative solutions, comparing these alternatives in terms of their likely costs and benefits, selecting a likely solution, and then acting on it are steps that most of us take when we determine a situation to be one that we can do something about. However, these strategies involve *changing only the situation.* Other problem-focused coping strategies may be geared toward *changing ourselves,* such as finding alternative channels of gratification or developing new standards of behavior. Another problem-focused strategy that can have positive outcomes for the individual involves learning new skills and procedures, thereby increasing one's coping resources.

Many problem-focused coping strategies that can be enumerated for specific situations do not generalize broadly across all types of stressors. For example, problem-focused strategies used to cope with chronic pain may not be useful for coping with a pressing deadline at work. Even in situations where problem-focused strategies could be used to great effect, if the individual perceives the level of threat to be very high, it may be impossible for such strategies to be employed. A number of researchers have shown that excessive threat has negative effects on cognitive functioning and on the capacity for information processing. A common example of this often occurs in a physician's office, when patients must be given bad news about their health. At such times, patients may have difficulty comprehending any additional information about treatment and prognosis that the physician may wish to convey. This phenomenon is due to a reduction in cognitive functioning brought about by the patient's experience of feelings of threat.

Another important determinant of problem-focused coping is the individual's perception of the situation as one that is amenable to change. In a study of middle-aged men and women coping with stressful encounters, Folkman and Lazarus found that people placed more emphasis on problem-focused coping when the encounter was one the person felt could be acted on. However, if the encounter was judged as one requiring acceptance, more emphasis was put on emotion-focused coping.

2. Emotion-Focused Coping

Emotion-focused coping strategies are numerous and apply more generally across the majority of stressful situations. The primary goal of such strategies is to lessen emotional distress. Some of the ways that this may be achieved are through avoidance, distancing, self-blame, and wishful thinking. Another approach may be to minimize the threat of the situation via cognitive reappraisal. Cognitive reappraisals involve changing the meaning of the situation without changing it objectively. For example, a stressed person may focus on how much worse things could be, perhaps by comparing themselves to others less fortunate. Noting how much better one's situation is than some others is called "engaging in downward social comparisons." Such strategies are considered types of cognitive reappraisal. There are also emotion-focused strategies directed toward diverting attention from the problem, such as engaging in physical exercise, meditating, having a drink, expressing one's anger, or seeking emotional support.

3. Relationship-Focused Coping

Recently, attention has also been directed toward the ways that people attempt to maintain their important social relationships during periods of stress. People in enduring relationships cannot concern themselves only with the situation they are facing, but must also consider the implications for their partner and for the relationship. This focus on relationships during stressful episodes may be particularly important when a loved one has a chronic illness or disability. For example, O'Brien and DeLongis pointed out the usefulness of empathic coping by caregivers of Alzheimer's patients. Other types of relationship-focused coping involve providing support and attempting to compromise when there is a disagreement. Not all attempts to manage relationships during stressful periods have positive effects. Coyne has found that emotional overinvolvement can have serious negative consequences on the health of family members.

Although some people are more skilled at coping with stress than others, it is impossible to identify a set of coping strategies that can be called "good" ways of coping. The context in which the stressful situation occurs, the type of problem, the other people involved, and the personality characteristics of the individual, are only some of the factors that affect how to best deal with the situation. Further, two people might use identical strategies with different degrees of success, depending upon how skillfully the strategy is implemented. However, researchers have pinpointed some general ways of coping that appear to be either adaptive or maladaptive in particular types of situations. Some of the more common types of stressful situations and what we know about coping with them are discussed below.

II. COPING WITH TRAUMATIC EVENTS

Experiencing a traumatic event, such as robbery, rape, domestic violence, or a severe automobile accident can sometimes have far-reaching psychological effects that outweigh the physical harm suffered by the victim. Janoff-Bulman has suggested that we are able to function in the world because we believe the world to be a benevolent place where what happens to us is a result of our own actions. Experiencing a traumatic event shakes these core assumptions, so that victims must not only cope with the physical injury they may have suffered, but also deal with the shocking realization of their personal vulnerability.

A. Beliefs in a "Just" World

Coping with a traumatic event involves the process of rebuilding one's belief in a "just" world. Some of the cognitive strategies commonly used are comparing oneself to more unfortunate others, focusing on one's positive actions during the event, or reinterpreting the negative event as having a beneficial purpose. Many victims also engage in self-blame, even if they were victims of an unprovoked attack. Research has found that self-blame after a rape is generally associated with higher levels of distress and lower levels of self-esteem. But for some individuals, believing that an assault was related to something they did, such as walking alone at night on a deserted street, helps them to feel more in control of preventing a future victimization. Other victims attempt to regain their sense of control by implementing changes in their lives that give them a greater sense of security, such as installing an alarm system or being more cautious and vigilant when away from home. When taken to the extremes of avoiding all social contact and staying home whenever possible, however, such strategies may serve to prolong feelings of fear and vulnerability.

B. Role of Social Support

Another important source of help for victims of traumatic events is the support of family and friends. Being able to express negative emotions about the event to trusted companions can often promote successful coping. Close others can help to bolster feelings of self-worth in the victim as well as provide tangible assistance, such as accompanying victims to doctors and to court. However, sometimes social support can provide unique problems for victims. Too often, *other* people's beliefs in a "just" world are threatened by the victim's experience, and they may find themselves blaming the victim in order to preserve their own sense of security. Expressing such attitudes to a victim can result in further trauma.

Some victims of a traumatic event find formal support from trained professionals helpful. If there has been a criminal attack, victims who report it to the police will often be offered support and counseling from victims' services connected with the police and the courts. If the offender is caught and punished, the victim may feel some vindication, strengthening the sense of living in a "just" world. However, participation in the criminal justice system, with the lengthy interviews and court appearances, can also serve to enhance the stressfulness of already traumatic events.

III. COPING WITH CHRONIC PAIN

For clinical purposes, pain is often considered chronic if it has endured for 6 months or longer. Common types of chronic pain are lower back pain; joint pain as a result of rheumatoid arthritis or osteoarthritis; headaches; and various myofascial pain syndromes, usually associated with diffuse aching musculoskeletal pain. Most pain coping efforts are directed toward two main goals: (1) prevention or reduction of pain and (2) maximization of quality of life despite pain. Whether a particular coping strategy may be effective in an individual's efforts to manage their pain depends on the nature of the pain, the expectation of relief, the specific situation, and a host of other factors. However, there are consistent findings that point to a relationship between particular classes of coping strategies and the degree of impairment. Here we describe three classes of coping strategies that have been studied in depth: catastrophizing, avoidance, and relaxation/distraction.

A. Catastrophizing

Catastrophizing is a cognitive process that includes negative self-statements and excessively negative beliefs about the future. Pain patients may express such things to themselves or to others, saying; "This pain will never go away" or "I can't cope with this pain anymore." Such catastrophizing has been found to be associated with poor outcomes, such as increased pain and depression in patients with chronic pain.

B. Avoidance

Another generally maladaptive group of coping strategies is termed "avoidance" strategies. Avoidance behaviors include reducing physical movement and exercise to avoid an increase in pain, but often also include avoidance of other nonpainful activities, such as social activities or certain types of work. Avoidance is often adaptive in the early period after an injury, when pain is intense and healing is ongoing. However, once healing has occurred, such behaviors can become maladaptive. Because avoidance does not necessarily decrease pain severity, it serves to increase the experience of pain and disability in two ways. First, patients experience a reduction in their feelings of self-efficacy and an increase in feelings of helplessness. Second, as a reaction to the lack of pain relief provided by preliminary avoidance behaviors, patients tend to increase their level of avoidance. This creates a negative cycle with the patient continuing to experience pain and depression, which can be further exacerbated by isolation and a focus on pain sensations.

C. Relaxation/Distraction

Probably the most adaptive method of coping with chronic pain involves behaviors or cognitions that divert the patient's attention from the pain and toward some more positive experience. Activities such as socializing, reading, and painting reduce emphasis on the experience of pain and have beneficial effects on mood as well. Activities requiring a focus of attention tend to reduce activation of the sympathetic nervous system, leading to further reductions in pain intensity. Guided relaxation, or transformational imagery techniques, in addition to reducing pain, can also serve to increase feelings of self-efficacy.

There are many coping interventions designed to reduce the experience of pain, whether it is from chronic injuries or from medical treatments. Pain clinics teach techniques such as biofeedback, hypno-sis, and various forms of cognitive imaging. All of these coping skills have been found to be effective in helping patients to cope with pain.

D. Helping a Family Member Cope with Chronic Pain

How family members interact with a chronic pain patient also has an effect on the patient's coping. By encouraging the patient to increase adaptive coping responses and by not reinforcing such pain behaviors as rubbing, grimacing, and groaning with overly solicitous responses, chronic pain patients can be helped to cope more effectively with their pain. Family members can also be included in pain treatments so they can assist in relapse prevention once treatment is terminated. Most importantly, any efforts to help a family member cope with chronic pain must include an assessment of the multiple contexts involved and focus on attaining a balance between the risk of further pain and the negative impact of pain avoidance on the patient's quality of life.

IV. COPING WITH JOB STRESS

There are many different sources of stress in the workplace, and they vary from job to job. There may be stress inherent in the type of work being performed; workers may feel uncomfortable with their role in the organization; there may be interpersonal conflicts with coworkers. Stress can also arise from feelings of job insecurity or lack of advancement as well as poor communication between levels of management. Finally, stress can be caused by difficulties balancing career and home life and difficulties providing for one's family.

Although the sources of stress may vary across situations, the negative impact of stress in the workplace is quite similar. Table I outlines some of the potential negative outcomes of this kind of stress. Physical reactions can include symptoms such as rising blood pressure, increased heart rate, fatigue, headaches, and back pain. Psychological reactions may include mood swings, lowered self-esteem, irritability, anxiety, and depression. In terms of personal

TABLE I
Potential Reactions to Job Stress

Physical reactions	Psychological reactions
Fatigue	Apathy
Headaches	Anger
Back pain	Irritability
Hypertension	Depression
Heart disease	Anxiety
	Lowered self-esteem
Behavioral reactions	Organizational reactions
Sleep disorders	Accidents
Substance abuse	Lower productivity
Smoking	Increased absenteeism

Source. Neunan, J. C., and Hubbard, J. R. (1997). Stress in the workplace: An overview. *In* J. R. Hubbard and E. A. Workman (Eds.), "Handbook of Stress Medicine: An Organ System Approach." Boca CRC Press, Boca Raton, FL.

behavior, the experience of severe job stress can be implicated in the development of sleep disorders and substance abuse. At the organizational level, job stress may result in increased accidents, lower productivity, and higher levels of absenteeism.

It has generally been proposed that problem-focused strategies are more likely to be appropriate for work-related stressors. Indeed, problem-focused strategies are more often used in coping with work stress than in coping with many other types of stress, such as caring for an ill family member. However, problem-focused strategies can only be implemented when the worker has some degree of control over how the problem is handled. When the stressor at hand involves an organizational merger, with ensuing restructuring and widespread job loss, workers are faced with a highly stressful situation with which they have no experience and over which they have little control.

The responsibility for implementing problem-solving behavior in a stressful work situation lies both with the individual and the organization. Further, in order to be effective, the approach chosen must lead to satisfactory outcomes for both parties. Interventions to reduce stress in the workplace can target the individual, the organization, or the relationship between the individual and the organization.

A. Coping with Job Stress at the Individual Level

Coping skills training at the individual level can include relaxation programs and skill training in areas of time management and assertion. Coping strategies can be divided into four categories: (1) those aimed at psychological conditions, such as planning ahead, managing one's life, making realistic self-assessments; (2) those aimed at physical or physiological conditions, such as diet, exercise, and sleep; (3) those aimed at changing one's behavior, such as becoming less intense, relaxing, taking time out, and developing social support networks; and (4) those aimed at changing one's work environment, such as changing to a less demanding job or organization.

B. Coping with Job Stress at the Organizational Level

Any coping efforts undertaken by the individual are not likely to have a long-lasting effect if the organization remains a stressful place to work. Elkin and Rosch have suggested a range of possible organization-directed strategies to reduce stress in the workplace. These strategies include redesigning the work environment, establishing flexible work schedules, encouraging participative management, providing social support and feedback, establishing fair and family-friendly employment policies, and sharing the rewards of organizational success.

V. COPING WITH CHRONIC ILLNESS

Given the improvements in treatment of chronic illnesses, people who comply with medical advice and obtain proper amounts of exercise and nutrition can often live relatively normal lives for a long time after diagnosis. It is therefore important to understand how successful coping with illness can aid in adaptation. Moos and Schaeffer identified seven major adaptive tasks in coping with illness. These are broken down into general tasks and illness-related tasks and are listed in Table II.

TABLE II
Seven Major Adaptive Tasks in Coping with Illness

General tasks
  Maintaining emotional equilibrium
  Maintaining a sense of self, including competence and
    mastery
  Maintaining good relations with family and friends
  Preparing for future concerns

Illness-related tasks
  Dealing with the physiological consequences of the
    illness
  Dealing with the treatment and hospital environment
  Developing and maintaining good relations with health
    care workers

Source. Moos, R. H., and Schaeffer, J. A. (1984). The crisis of physical illness. *In* R. Moos (Ed.), "Coping with Physical Illness" (pp. 3–26). Plenum, New York.

A. How Care-Providers Can Help Patients Cope with Illness

Medical procedures and the pain that may accompany them can be tolerated more easily when medical practitioners are aware of the psychological needs of individual patients. Some patients cope better when they understand clearly all procedures and their associated risks and benefits. However, other patients may prefer to be provided with less information and cope better when they are not confronted with such details.

The timing of the information provided to the patient is also critical. For example, showing children a film describing an upcoming medical procedure can reduce their anxiety when shown the day before they are admitted to the hospital. However, the same film may have little effect when shown immediately before the procedure is to be conducted. Similarly, pregnant women who are taught stress-management techniques for pain during labor tend to report less pain, anger, and fatigue and tend to be more effective overall during childbirth. Attempts to teach these techniques during labor tend to be less effective. Techniques that allow patients to feel they have some control over their pain also tend to reduce the intensity of the pain experienced. For example, allowing patients to control the timing and dosage of pain medication has been found to reduce the perception of pain as well as the overall amount of pain medication used.

1. Coping with Cancer

Coping interventions that also provide support and information are often helpful in improving cancer patients' mood. A series of studies by Fawzy and colleagues provided support for the effectiveness of coping interventions with melanoma patients. The intervention consisted of a 6-week group treatment that included health education, training in problem-solving skills and stress management, and psychological support. Six months later, patients who attended the group intervention had better immune functioning and more positive mood than a group of patients who had not participated. After 5 years, only 10% of the patients who participated in the intervention had died, in comparison to nearly one-third of the patients who had not attended.

2. Coping with Chronic Heart Disease (CHD)

Research on coping with CHD has shown that during the first stage of recovery following a heart attack, strategies such as denial, that reduce anxiety and anger, are more beneficial than active coping strategies. However, after discharge from a coronary care unit, active coping strategies can be implemented. For example, interventions that focus on stress management, as well as educational interventions that emphasize lifestyle changes and compliance with medical advice, are important in increasing both health and well-being. However, these types of interventions should not be offered during the first stage of the disease, when supportive interventions are more useful.

VI. COPING AND MENTAL HEALTH

Biopsychosocial models of psychopathology suggest that a combination of biological, psychological, and social factors may best explain the development and maintenance of disorders. Some possible ways that stress may be implicated in mental disorders, as described by Coleman, Butcher, and Carson, are enumerated in Table III.

A. Coping and Depression

A form of emotion-focused coping that has been implicated in depression is ruminative coping. Rumination is defined as passively and repetitively focusing on symptoms of distress and the surrounding circumstances. Nolen-Hoeksema and colleagues have found that a tendency to engage in ruminative coping is consistently related to longer or recurrent periods of depressed mood.

Social support from close others can often be helpful in managing negative emotions. However, seeking social support can sometimes backfire in the case of depressed individuals. The behavior of someone who is depressed can sometimes become aversive to those people who are closest to him or her. Further, the depressed person may seek support in such a way that the possibility of rejection, whether intentional or accidental, is almost guaranteed. Such a response may serve to plunge the person further into the downward spiral of depression.

B. Coping and Anxiety

Prominent symptoms of anxiety are sometimes the results of maladaptive attempts to cope. Many of these behaviors take the form of avoidance. Avoidance of feared stimuli relieves anxiety in the short term, so it may become a strategy the individual uses repeatedly. However, by never confronting the feared object or situation, the apprehension associated with it increases and other more adaptive strategies tend to remain unlearned.

Anxious individuals tend to cognitively appraise fearful situations as ones where they have little or no control, either over the event or over their reactions to it. Such a lack of self-efficacy can lead to continuing avoidance and to increases in anxiety. Training in cognitive reappraisal and other coping skills can reduce the frequency and severity of the experience of fear.

VII. COPING EFFECTIVENESS TRAINING PROGRAM (CET)

For individuals to become more effective at coping, it is necessary for them to develop the ability to appraise stressful contexts more adaptively and then to cope more efficiently with the demands of these contexts. Folkman, Chesney, and colleagues developed a group-based coping intervention at the Center for AIDS Prevention Studies at the University of California at San Francisco. This intervention follows closely Lazarus' model of stress and coping. The intervention focuses on helping individuals to change their appraisals, improve their coping skills, and obtain beneficial social support when needed. Although this intervention has been tested with HIV-positive men, it is designed to apply to people coping in a broad range of stressful contexts. The CET is unique in that it teaches both problem- and emotion-focused skills and teaches methods for selecting coping behaviors that will have the maximum effectiveness in a given situation.

A. Appraisal Training

The first skill participants learn is to distinguish between global stressful conditions and specific stressful situations. It is much easier to cope effectively with a specific stressor than a vague, complex,

---

TABLE III

Ways That Stressful Conditions May Be Implicated in the Development of Mental Disorders

As a primary cause:	Conditions that must be present for the disorder to occur.
As a predisposing cause:	Conditions that occur prior to onset of the disorder.
As a precipitating cause:	Conditions that overwhelm the individual's resources to cope and trigger the disorder.
As a reinforcing cause:	Conditions that maintain the disorder once it has developed.

Source. Falsett, S. A., and Ballenger, J. C. (1997). Stress and anxiety disorders. *In* J. A. Hubbard and E. A. Workman (Eds.), "Handbook of Stress Medicine: An Organ System Approach." CRC Press, Boca Raton, FL.

global condition (e.g., coping with traveling to the medical clinic or coping with the fears associated with receiving lab results versus coping with AIDS more generally). Second, participants learn to distinguish between those aspects of specific stressors that are amenable to change (e.g., finding ways to spend time while waiting for lab results) and those aspects that are unchangeable (e.g., the lab results *per se*). They are then taught to rely on emotion-focused coping strategies to handle aspects of stressors that are unchangeable and to use problem-focused coping strategies for aspects of stressors that are changeable.

B. Coping Training

In group sessions, participants focus first on unchangeable situations and the emotion-focused strategies that can be used with these stressors. Strategies developed and practiced include cognitively reframing the situation as less stressful, selectively attending to positive aspects of the situation, making positive comparisons, distancing oneself from aspects of or thoughts about the stressful situation, and using humor to diminish the negative impact of the situation. They also consider maladaptive forms of emotion-focused coping, such as smoking, drug use, or overeating, and examine the consequences of these forms of coping. Next, participants consider problem-focused strategies that can be used with aspects of stressful situations that are changeable. Various decision-making strategies are taught, including ways to evaluate the probable outcomes of different approaches to a problem. Participants are also trained in communication skills, such as listening, communicating, and negotiating.

C. Social Support Training

The CET also has a component to help people to obtain the social support they need from others. Support is considered to be either informational, emotional, or tangible and participants are taught to identify those members of their social network whom are most able to provide the specific type of support required and how to best enlist their aid.

VIII. SUMMARY

There are a number of factors that determine whether an individual can cope effectively with a particular stressor. An important first step is to appraise the situation in a positive yet realistic manner. Further, breaking up a global stressor into those aspects that can be changed and those that must be accepted can facilitate the identification of potential coping strategies. Practicing new coping strategies, considering the possible consequences of several different approaches, and obtaining support from others are techniques that can facilitate a reduction in the negative consequences of stress. For those situations that threaten to overwhelm an individual's current resources, coping interventions that provide support, information, and skills training are often effective.

See Also the Following Articles

AVOIDANCE; CAREGIVERS, STRESS IN; CONTROL AND STRESS; COPING, STRESS AND; WORKPLACE STRESS

Bibliography

Aldwin, C. (1994). "Stress, coping, and development: An integrative perspective." Guilford, New York.

Cohen, F., and Lazarus, R. (1979). Coping with the stresses of illness. *In* G. C. Stone, F. Cohen, and N. E. Adler (Eds.), "Health Psychology: A Handbook" (pp. 217–254). Jossey–Bass, San Francisco.

Craig, K. D. (in press). Emotions and psychobiology. *In* P. D. Wall, and R. Melzack (Eds.), "Textbook of Pain" (4th ed.). Churchill Livingstone, Edinborough.

Fawzy, F. I., Cousins, N., Fawzy, N. W., Kemeny, M. E., Elashoff, R., and Morton, D. (1990). A structured psychiatric intervention for cancer patients. 1. Changes over time in methods of coping and affective disturbance. *Arch. Gen. Psychiat.* **47**, 720–725.

Fawzy, F. I., Fawzy, N. W., Hyun, C. S., Elashoff, R., Guthrie, D., Fahey, J. L., and Morton, D. (1993). Malignant melanoma: Effects of an early structured psychiatric intervention, coping, and affective state on recurrence and survival 6 years later. *Arch. Gen. Psychiat.* **50**, 681–689.

Fawzy, F. I., Kemeny, M. E., Fawzy, N. W., Elashoff, R., Morton, D., Cousins, N., and Fahey, J. L. (1990). A structured psychiatric intervention for cancer patients. 2. Changes over time in immunological measures. *Arch. Gen. Psychiat.* **47**, 729–735.

Folkman, S., Chesney, M., McKusick, L., Ironson, G., Johnson, D. S., and Coates, T. J. (1991). Translating coping theory into intervention. *In* J. Eckenrode (Ed.), "The Social Context of Coping" (pp. 239–259). Plenum, New York.

Hubbard, J. R., and Workman, E. A. (1997). "Handbook of Stress Medicine: An Organ System Approach" CRC Press, Boca Raton, FL.

Lazarus, R. S., and Folkman, S. (1984). "Stress, Appraisal, and Coping." Springer-Verlag, New York.

Leventhal, E. A., Leventhal, H., Shacham, S., and Easterling, D. V. (1989). Active coping reduces reports of pain from childbirth. *J. Consult. Clin. Psychol.* **57**, 365–371.

Lyons, R. F., Sullivan, M. J. L., Ritvo, P. G., and Coyne, J. C. (1995). "Relationships in Chronic Illness and Disability." Sage, Thousand Oaks, CA.

Maes, S., Leventhal, H., and DeRidder, D. T. D. (1990). Coping with chronic diseases. *In* M. Zeidner and N. S. Endler (Eds.), "Handbook of Coping." Wiley, New York.

Michenbaum, D. H., and Jaremko, M. E. (Eds.) (1983). "Stress Reduction and Prevention." Plenum, New York.

Moos, R. (Ed.) (1984). "Coping with Physical Illness." Plenum, New York.

Newman, J. D., and Beehr, T. (1979). Personal and organizational strategies for handling job stress: A review of research and opinion. *Person. Psychol.* **32**, 1–43.

O'Brien, T. B., and DeLongis, A. (1997). Coping with chronic stress: An interpersonal perspective. *In* B. H. Gottlieb (Ed.), "Coping with Chronic Stress" (pp. 161–190). Plenum, New York.

Rachman, S. J. (1990). "Fear and Courage," (2nd ed.), Freeman, New York.

Zeidner, M., and Endler, N. S. (1996). "Handbook of Coping: Theory, Research, and Applications." Wiley, New York.

Coping, Stress and

Richard H. Rahe

University of Nevada School of Medicine

I. The Life Stress and Illness Model
II. Discussion

GLOSSARY

defenses A variety of psychological defense mechanisms, such as denial, displacement, repression, and reaction formation.
illness behavior The recognition and assessment of body symptoms, along with the seeking and following of medical advice.

S tressful life events can include challenges of the first order. However, many life-change events occurring in a person's life are of low to moderate intensity and are part of their normal life experience. When do these events reach a level where they exert influences leading to illness? How is it that some individuals tolerate traumatic life events with only temporary discomfort while others, exposed to the same events, react with severe and long-lasting disability? To help answer these questions I developed the following photography-inspired lens-and-filter model.

Six stages of processing are presented. These are perception, defenses, psychophysiological response, coping, illness behavior, and illness. Most persons go through the first four stages and return to preexisting health. Only when defenses are excessive and/or coping is insufficient do stressed individuals go on to experiencing illness.

I. THE LIFE STRESS AND ILLNESS MODEL

The first activity that helped create this model was an experiment to determine the relative significances of 42 typical life-change events. This allowed for quantitative estimates to be made of a person's recent life stress. Recent life-change magnitudes for large samples of humans were seen to correlate positively and significantly for near-future (the following 6 months to 1 year) illness. The list of events was enlarged in 1975 and has been rescaled twice—once in 1978 and again in 1995. When comparing the average life-change magnitude values over 30 years (1965 to 1995), an increase of 45% was found. Thus, life changes appear to increase in their challenges to adaptation at a rate of 1.5% per year.

The next activity was to choose a graphic representation of how individuals process life-changes stress. I selected a series of photographic filters and lenses. From this model, a person's exposure to stressful life-change events, their psychological and physiological

reactions, and their coping and illness behaviors could all be illustrated in six steps (see Fig. 1). An explanation of these steps, and five relevant figures, follows below.

A. Step 1

Recent life-change severity is influenced greatly by a person's perception of the varying significances of these events. In Figs. 1 and 2, a person's recent life-change exposure is represented by a series of light rays. The thickness of these light rays indicates differing life-change unit (LCU) magnitudes. Thick dark lines represent highly significant events, such as marriage, divorce, and death of a parent. Thinner lines signify less meaningful events, such as a resi-

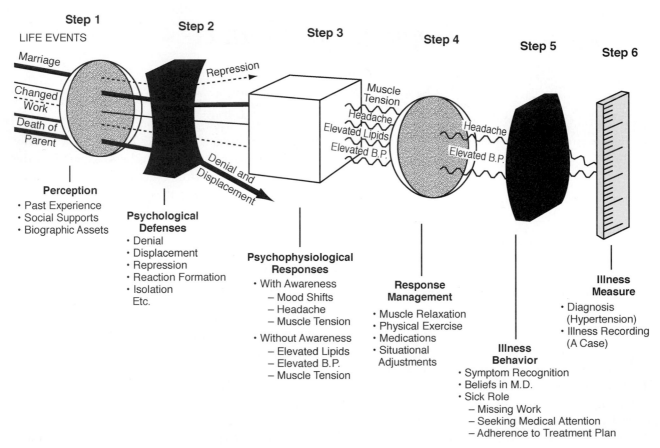

FIGURE 1

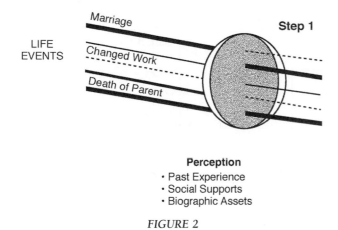

LIFE EVENTS

Marriage

Changed Work

Death of Parent

Step 1

Perception
- Past Experience
- Social Supports
- Biographic Assets

FIGURE 2

dential move or a purchase of an average-priced automobile.

The influence of perception on altering persons' particular evaluation of their recent life-change events is shown in Step 1 by a polarizing filter. Just as a polarizing filter will diminish the intensities of some light rays and augment others, perception of the significance of the recent events may be diminished or augmented according to persons' past experiences with similar events as well as by their current social supports. Early life influences (intelligence, educational level, social class, etc.) can also lead to alterations in perceptions of recent life-change events. For example, a poorly educated, financially destitute person may likely perceive losing his job as substantially more of a life change than would a highly educated, financially secure individual.

B. Step 2

Once challenged by significant recent life-change events, a person quickly employs a variety of psychological defense mechanisms, such as denial, displacement, repression, and reaction formation in an unconscious, almost reflexic, manner. As a result, these defenses tend to "diffract away" the potential impact of these life events on the person's psychophysiology. Hence, I chose a negative lens for this step in the model. Psychological defenses are quite literally a person's first line of defense against threats from the environment.

Some individuals employ their psychological de-

fenses so strongly, and so persistently, that they may show nearly complete insulation from expected psychophysiological responses (Step 3). For example, it has been reported that some patients with myocardial infarction, hospitalized in a coronary care unit, use denial to such a degree that they convince themselves they never had a heart attack in the first place. Such strongly defended persons have even been shown to develop fewer cardiac arrhythmias and to experience better survival rates than do more realistically oriented heart patients.

For most individuals, psychological defenses are extremely helpful in the short term but prove to be maladaptive over the long run. To use the coronary patient as an example once again, his use of one or more psychological defenses may help him survive his first few days in the coronary care unit, but unless he eventually learns to deal with the realities of his illness he may not stop smoking, or reduce his body weight, or begin a physical fitness program. Therefore, defenses alone are insufficient for long-term adaptation to life change trauma.

C. Step 3

Recent life-change stress that is not deflected by a person's psychological defenses quickly stimulates a wide variety of psychophysiological responses (Step 3). Those responses can be divided into two categories: responses of which the person is aware, such as sweating, pain, or muscle tension and those responses that occur outside of a person's awareness, such as elevated serum lipids and rises in blood pressure (see Fig. 3).

A second example is a patient with cancer. In a life situation in which recent life stress events are not deflected away by strong and persistent psychological defenses, the patient may react with feelings of helplessness, hopelessness, and depression. These psychological reactions may, in turn, suppress important brain communications related to immunological competence and thereby facilitate an exacerbation of the cancer.

D. Step 4

Once persons become aware of their psychophysiological responses to recent life stress, and especially

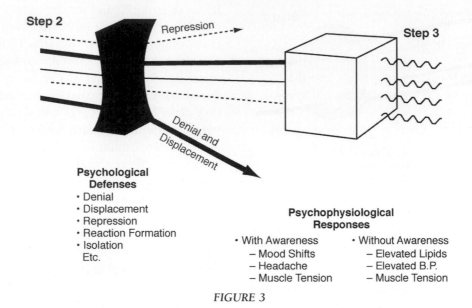

FIGURE 3

if these responses are interpreted as worrisome, these responses are labeled symptoms. The person may then decide to employ one or several response-management (coping) techniques in order to combat these symptoms. For example, he or she may try muscle relaxation, meditation, exercise, and/or various medications. A color filter is used in the model to indicate that successful coping can "absorb" some of the psychophysiological activation (symptoms) much in the same manner that a color filter absorbs light rays of particular frequencies (Fig. 4). The term coping is restricted to consciously regulated practices by a person, which are designed to reduce, and hopefully to eliminate, worrisome symptoms.

Response management is a potent area for coping with challenges from the environment. Since defenses are of short-term effectiveness, it is coping that achieves lasting results. To use the cancer patient once again as an example, after experiencing feelings of helplessness and hopelessness, he or she may institute behaviors such as seeking medical care, utilizing social support, and developing their spirituality. These traditional and nontraditional coping activities may help to reduce, or even eliminate, depressive symptoms. Additionally, this coping may also coun-

teract psychophysiological activations that promoted the expression of cancer in the first place.

E. Step 5

When persons' abilities to cope with their environmental challenges are insufficient, and their attendant psychophysiological arousal cannot be "absorbed," body symptoms are likely to be sustained, leading to tissue breakdown, organ system dysfunction, and disease. A positive lens is pictured in Fig. 4 to represent illness behavior. As symptoms of headache and elevated blood pressure continue in the figure, the person in this example may decide to seek medical care. It is clear from epidemiological studies that at least as many people with sustained symptoms secondary to poorly managed life stress fail to seek medical care as those who do come to medical attention. Therefore, doctors see only a portion of persons experiencing the effects of unresolved life stress leading to protracted bodily symptoms and disease.

F. Step 6

The final steps in the model (see Fig. 5) represent a person with long-lasting symptoms, progressing to

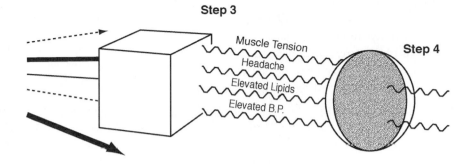

Step 3

Muscle Tension
Headache
Elevated Lipids
Elevated B.P.

Step 4

Psychophysiological Responses

· With Awareness	· Without Awareness
– Mood Shifts	– Elevated Lipids
– Headache	– Elevated B.P.
– Muscle Tension	– Muscle Tension

Response Management

· Muscle Relaxation
· Physical Exercise
· Medications
· Situational Adjustments

FIGURE 4

the point of disease, who sought medical consultation and received one or more diagnoses. The patient's illnesses, and their treatment, are documented in a medical record.

Many epidemiological studies utilize the medical record as a major criterion for definition of a "case." To illustrate the gross nature of such case studies, persons exposed to a significant recent life stress, such as surviving a flood or an earthquake, would only be part of such an epidemiological study of stress and illness if they followed the entire path displayed in Fig. 1 and became a case. All persons who defended well and/or coped successfully with the trauma, and all those who became symptomatic but did not report for medical care, would be missed.

II. DISCUSSION

Using the lens-and-filter model, persons who manage to remain healthy following severe recent stress appear to do so by successfully managing Steps 1 through 4. Conversely, those who do not manage these four steps well are frequently the ones who develop long-lasting symptomatology and likely precipitation of an illness.

Perception, psychological defenses, and coping skills seem to develop early in life. It appears to be extremely beneficial to be endowed with an abundance of biological (genetic) and biographical (acquired) assets. Returned prisoners of war and political captives who generally stayed healthy during and following captivity appeared to have been "born and bred" to do well with traumatic stress. That is, they

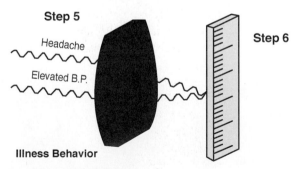

Step 5

Headache
Elevated B.P.

Step 6

Illness Behavior

· Symptom Recognition
· Beliefs in M.D.
· Sick Role
 – Missing Work
 – Seeking Medical Attention
 – Adherence to Treatment Plan

Illness Measure

· Diagnosis (Hypertension)
· Illness Recording (A Case)

FIGURE 5

had a high number of biological and biographical assets. Conversely, those who became clinically ill during and following captivity tended to display overly negative perceptions of the stress, exaggerated and/or prolonged defenses, and restricted coping behaviors—both early in their lives as well as during and following their capture.

See Also the Following Articles

Control and Stress; Coping Skills; Life Events Scale; Psychotic Disorders

Bibliography

Cassileth, B. R., Lusk, E. J., Hutter, R., (1984). Concordance of depression and anxiety in patients with cancer. *Psychol. Rep.* 54, 588–590.

Croog, S. H., Shapiro, D. S., and Levine, S. (1971). Denial among male heart patients. *Psychosom. Med.* 33, 385–397.

Fawzy, F. L., Kemeny, M. E., and Fawzy, N. W. (1990). A structured psychiatric intervention for cancer patients II: Changes over time in immunological measures. *Arch. Gen. Psychiat.* 47, 729–735.

Hackett, T. P. (1978). The use of groups in the rehabilitation of the post-coronary patient. *Adv. Cardiol.* 24, 127–135.

Holmes, T. H., and Rahe R. H. (1967). The social readjustment rating scale. *J. Psychosom. Res.* 11, 213–218.

Rahe, R. H. (1969). Life crisis and health change. *In* P. R. A. May and R. Wittenbom (Eds.), "*Psychotropic Drug Response: Advances in Prediction.* pp. 92– 125. Charles C. Thomas, Springfield, IL.

Rahe, R. H. (1988). Anxiety and physical illness. *J. Clin. Psychiat.* 49, (10, Suppl.), 26–29.

Rahe, R. H. (1990). Life change, stress responsivity, and captivity research. *Psychosom. Med.* 52, 373–396.

Rahe, R. H., and Arthur R. J. (1978). Life change and illness studies: Past history and future directions. *J. Hum. Stress,* 4, 3–13.

Rahe, R. H., Ward H. W., and Hayes V. (1979). Brief group therapy in myocardial infarction rehabilitation: Three to four-year follow-up of a controlled trial. *Psychosom. Med.* 41, 229–242.

Coronary Heart Disease

see Heart Disease/Attack

Corticosteroid-Binding Globulin (Transcortin)

Beverley E. Pearson Murphy

McGill University

GLOSSARY

affinity The degree of association between two entities. It is expressed as the ratio of complexed to free reactants at equilibrium—the affinity constant—which is the reciprocal of the dissociation constant.

binding capacity An expression of the number of binding sites available for a ligand.

corticosteroids Those steroids made by the adrenal cortex.

ligand An entity bound by noncovalent forces to another (usually larger, usually protein) entity.

steroids Molecules containing the perhydrocyclopentanophenanthrene nucleus, including sterols, bile acids, sex hormones, adrenocortical hormones, cardiac glycosides, and sapogenins.

I. DISCOVERY AND DEFINITION OF CORTICOSTEROID-BINDING GLOBULIN

The presence of a human plasma protein binding corticosteroids with high affinity (5–$8 \times 10^7 M^{-1}$) and low capacity (10^{-9}–$10^{-8} M$) was discovered in 1956 independently by I. E. Bush and by W. H. Daughaday. In 1958, A. A. Sandberg and W. R. Slaunwhite discovered a similar protein, which they called transcortin, which turned out to be identical with corticosteroid-binding globulin (CBG). Similar proteins have been found, many by U. S. Seal and R. P. Doe, in almost all species of vertebrates. A CBG-like protein has even been described in the eukaryotic fungus *Candida albicans*, with a K_a of $1.6 \times 10^8 M^{-1}$ at 0°C, which might represent a primitive form of either the mammalian glucocortocoid receptor or of CBG.

Corticosteroid-binding globulins differ from species to species in their relative affinities for various steroids. Most bind cortisol and corticosterone the most strongly; many bind progesterone very strongly; aldosterone is bound weakly. The guinea pig possesses a second corticosteroid-binding protein—progesterone-binding globulin (PBG)—in addition to CBG; PBG rises more than 100-fold in pregnancy. Although CBG binds testosterone and estradiol weakly, many species have, in addition to CBG, a sex hormone-binding globulin (SHBG) which binds these and related steroids more strongly.

Corticosteroid-binding globulin is very low or undetectable in the plasma of the spiny anteater, an egg-laying mammal, and in the plasma of the New World squirrel monkey.

II. BIOLOGICAL ROLE OF CORTICOSTEROID-BINDING GLOBULIN

Serum proteins such as albumin and CBG increase the solubility in biological fluids of steroids which are otherwise poorly soluble in aqueous solutions. However, the limited capacity and high affinity of CBG for glucocorticoids and progesterone has led to the accepted model of CBG action—that CBG provides a plasma store of tightly bound steroid which is less able to diffuse into cells, while "free" or unbound steroid passes freely across cell membranes to initiate hormone action. Since the binding to CBG is rapidly reversible, steroid may quickly be transferred from the bound to the free state. Thus CBG is a major determinant regulating the concentration of the hormones that it binds. On exposure to serine protease from inflammatory granulocytes, CBG is cleaved and releases all or most of its bound steroid; thus it seems likely that this process may permit enhanced delivery of cortisol to sites of inflammation (see below).

Changes of CBG in fetal life occur as a result of normal development, possibly promoting the delivery of glucocorticoids to sites of rapid growth and tissue remodeling.

In the human, the unbound fraction of cortisol is usually about 10% of total cortisol; in Cushing's syndrome, where CBG levels are decreased and total cortisol levels increase, this fraction rises to about 25% of the total, while in adrenal insufficiency it falls to about 6% of total cortisol.

III. PHYSICAL CHARACTERISTICS OF CORTICOSTEROID-BINDING GLOBULIN

A. Structure

The molecular weight of CBG is 50–60 kDa, and there is one cortisol-binding site per molecule. The degree of sequence similarity among species is 60–70%. Corticosteroid-binding globulin is a monomeric glycoprotein (with the possible exception of New World primate CBGs, which may circulate as dimers), consisting of about 380 amino acids with a molecular weight of about 42,000 (Fig. 1). Relatively large differences in the apparent molecular size among species is probably due to variations in carbohydrate composition. The human CBG sequence is thought to contain six consensus sites for N-glycosyl-

ation. Only two of these sites have been retained throughout evolution, and these are located in highly conserved regions and may therefore be functionally important. The gene for CBG is localized to chromosome 14. The deduced primary structure of CBG suggests a greater than 30% homology with the SERPIN (serine protease inhibitor) superfamily of proteins. This family includes α_1-proteinase inhibitor (A1-P1), α_1-antichymotrypsin (ACT), and thyroxine-binding globulin. Both A1-P1 and ACT are located close to the region containing the human CBG gene. The PBG of guinea pig has a molecular weight of about 80 kDa and has one binding site per molecule.

B. Temperature Dependence

Corticosteroid-binding globulin binding in all species is temperature dependent, being maximal at about 4°C. At temperatures above 60°C, it is rapidly destroyed—in about 20 min. Stability is increased at higher cortisol concentrations. Between 37° and 40°C there is a rapidly increasing rate of dissociation which may be important physiologically in febrile states, resulting in more rapid release of cortisol to the tissues. Similarly, local elevation of temperature as a consequence of inflammation may contribute to more available cortisol at these sites. Binding activity is usually retained after a single freezing but is lost with repeated thawing and freezing. Many CBGs in serum are stable for long periods at 4°C—human CBG is stable for months or years provided bacterial contamination is prevented, e.g., by addition of 0.1% sodium azide. Guinea pig PBG is more resistant to heating than most CBG's.

C. Affinity

The affinity constant for the binding of cortisol to human CBG is about $1 \times 10^9 M^{-1}$ at 4°C and $5 \times 10^7 M^{-1}$ at 37°C. The CBGs of most other species are in the range of 10^7–$10^9 M^{-1}$ at 4°C and are also lower at 37°C. A relatively high association constant ($0.9 \times 10^8 M^{-1}$) has been observed for ovine plasma.

D. pH

Binding activity is also dependent on pH; for human CBG, it is maximal at about pH 8, but irrevers-

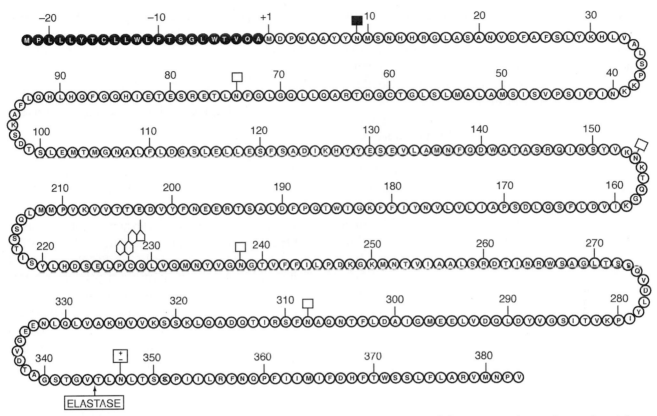

FIGURE 1 Primary structure of the human CBG precursor. The amino terminus of the mature polypeptide is inferred from published data and the proposed signal peptide comprises 22 amino acids shown in shaded circles. Potential sites for N-glycosylation are shown as squares, with a filled square indicating the site that is known to be utilized and ± representing partial utilization. The elastase cleavage site is marked by an arrow and the cysteine residue, which is conserved between species, is indicated. From G. L. Hammond (1990). *Endocr. Rev.* **11**, 65–79. © The Endocrine Society.

ible denaturation takes place below pH 5. In the guinea pig, PBG is more resistant to low pH than is CBG.

E. Electrophoresis

Electrophoretically, CBG behaves as an α^1-globulin.

F. Relationship to Albumin Binding

Steroids are also bound by albumin in all species. The free fraction is usually 6–14% of the total, with the CBG-bound fraction being 67–87% and the albumin-bound fraction at 7–19%. In the squirrel monkey, about one-half is free and half is bound to albumin; this is the only vertebrate species in which CBG appears to be virtually absent.

G. Effect of Reducing Agents

Binding of cortisol and progesterone to purified human CBG is reversibly decreased by adding strong reducing agents such as dithiothreitol and β-mercaptoethanol but not by the milder sodium ascorbate; only the affinity is decreased, while the number of binding sites remains the same.

H. Binding Specificity

1. Mammals

Although the specificity and affinity of the steroid-binding site vary among species, maximal binding usually coincides with the biologically more important glucocorticoid (either cortisol or corticosterone) in a given species. The ratio of cortisol to corticosterone varies widely among species, and the relative binding affinities for the two steroids also differ widely. Thus in human plasma, where cortisol predominates, CBG binds cortisol equally strongly as corticosterone, while in the rat, which produces only corticosterone, CBG binds the latter steroid more strongly. In the green iguana, there is high binding of cortisol (3056 nmol/liter) but no detectable binding of corticosterone, while in the porcupine fish the binding to corticosterone (1250 nmol/liter) is much higher than that of cortisol (67 nmol/liter). For human plasma, Dunn *et al.* have calculated the binding distribution of endogenous steroids in normal men and in nonpregnant and pregnant women (Table I). In many species, progesterone, 11-desoxycortisol, and other steroids are also bound to CBG (see Table II). Alterations in ring A of strongly binding steroids cause a drastic drop in binding affinity; this is less marked in the CBG of avian species and in PBG.

2. Progesterone-Binding Globulin of Guinea Pig (PBG)

While human and many other species of CBG bind progesterone strongly, the guinea pig is the only species known to possess a separate CBG-like protein—PBG—which binds progesterone almost exclusively.

3. Marsupials

The affinity of CBG in marsupials is similar to that of mammals, but the binding site concentrations are generally lower.

4. Synthetic Steroids

Some synthetic steroids, such as prednisolone, which is a glucocorticoid, and danazol (WII 131), which is not, also bind to CBG and compete with cortisol for binding sites. Dexamethasone, another synthetic glucocorticoid, is not bound to human CBG but does bind to chicken and dog CBG. Bovine serum is unusual in that, in addition to a CBG, which binds cortisol strongly, it contains a protein which binds triamcinolone acetonide, a synthetic glucocorticoid, very strongly. Taken as 100%, triamcinolone–acetonide-binding exceeded that of betamethasone (47%), triamcinolone (33%), dexamethasone 2%, cortisol 2%, and progesterone 2%.

IV. PHYSIOLOGICAL VARIATION

In the human, CBG binding capacity of men and women is similar (600–700 n*M*) and changes little

TABLE I
CBG-Bound Endogenous Steroids in Human Plasma[a]

Steroid	Men nmol/liter[1]	Men %[2]	Late pregnancy nmol/liter	Late pregnancy %	Follicular nmol/liter	Follicular %	Luteal nmol/liter	Luteal %
Cortisol	400	90	740	95	400	90	400	90
Cortisone	72	38	110	59	54	39	54	38
Corticosterone	12	78	48	90	7.0	78	13	78
4-Androstene-3,17-dione	4.1	1.4	13	2.3	5.4	1.4	5.4	1.3
5-Pregnen-3β-ol-20-one	2.2	0.4	15	0.4	2.2	0.2	4.4	0.2
17-Hydroxyprogesterone	1.8	41	14	66	1.8	42	5.9	41
Androsterone	1.5	0.5	1.5	1.4	1.5	0.5	1.5	0.5
Testosterone	1.3	3.4	4.7	4.7	1.3	2.3	1.3	2.2
Etiocholanolone	1.2	0.4	1.2	1.3	1.2	0.5	1.2	0.4
Aldosterone	0.4	21	5.8	41	0.2	22	0.5	21

[a] Data from Dunn *et al.* (1981). J. Clin. Endocrinol. Metab. 53, 58–68. © The Endocrine Society.
[1] Total concentration.
[2] % bound to CBG.

TABLE II

Steroid Competition for Sites on CBG in Various Species and on PBG of Pregnant Guinea Pig

Species	Plasma conc'n (%)	Steroid added[a]							
		F	B	S	P	H	E	T	A
Human	2.5	100	83	89	20	74	16	4	3
Rhesus monkey	0.5	20	100	17	43	7	4	6	2
Dog	1.25	100	54	85	9	44	44	5	5
Cat	1.25	100	80	104	20	50	80	<1	<1
Beef	12.5	100	57	60	29	27	68	15	3
Rabbit	1.25	100	40	56	16	19	64	14	2
Rat	0.5	30	100	17	27	2	9	9	7
Mouse	0.5	12	100	<0.5	15	6	15	0	0
Chicken	2.5	100	83	125	89	37	270	10	9
Horse	1.0	100	30	28	2	22	2	0.5	<1
Guinea pig PBG[b]	0.025	<0.5	<0.5	0.9	100	0.6	<0.5	8	<0.5

Note. The tracer used was ^{3}H-corticosterone for all but pregnant guinea pig serum, where ^{3}H-progesterone was used. The relative binding activity of the steroid added was determined at 50% displacement of the steroid indicated at 100%. Data are from Murphy and others, reviewed by Westphal (1986).

Abbreviations: F = cortisol; B = corticosterone; S = 11-desoxycortisol; P = progesterone; H = 17-hydroxyprogesterone; E = cortisone; T = testosterone; A = aldosterone.

[a] Determined at 4–10°C, using Florisil as adsorbent (which gives slightly different values from equilibrium dialysis).

[b] Serum from guinea pig in late pregnancy was used.

from ages 1–60. Plasma levels of CBG vary from 10 to 500 nM in most vertebrate species—it is exceptionally high in the green iguana (3000 nM) and squirrel (2500 nM). They are low in New World monkeys—only 1–10% of those in Old World primates and humans; the affinity is also lower, resulting in a much higher fraction of unbound plasma cortisol, possibly to compensate for the target organ resistance to glucocorticoids which characterizes this group. In the squirrel monkey, the only mammal known which appears to lack CBG, half the cortisol is albumin bound and half is free. In rat and guinea pig, female CBG levels are about twice those of males, a difference which is abolished by neonatal gonadectomy. The concentration of CBG in lymph is slightly lower than that in blood, while concentrations in synovial fluid and in pleural effusion are higher and those in spinal fluid and in amniotic fluid are very low. Corticosteroid-binding globulin passes into milk, in human milk the concentration has been reported to be 1–15% that of plasma and in rat milk about 25% that of plasma. A CBG-like protein which binds progesterone strongly has been reported in human breast cyst fluids. Because there is little or no CBG or albumin in saliva, salivary cortisol is often used as an index of free cortisol.

A. Pregnancy

In human pregnancy, CBG levels rise to levels more than twice those of nonpregnant women. The affinity is unchanged. The increase is due to the increased levels of estrogens in pregnancy. Progesterone–binding, both free and total, increases steadily until the end of pregnancy; the free fraction rises from 6% of total at week 24 to 13% at week 40.

Elevated levels of CBG up to 30-fold have been observed by Seal and Doe to occur during pregnancy in mammals with a hemochorial type of placentation (rodents, cats, dogs, moles, shrews, manatees, and most primates), but not in those with other types such as endotheliochorial, choriovitelline, epitheliochorial, or syndesmochorial, the biological significance of this difference is not known. The increase in CBG is minimal in the rat (see Fig. 2). Corticosteroid-binding steroid rises 3- to 4-fold in the guinea pig, where PBG is also present and rises more than 100-

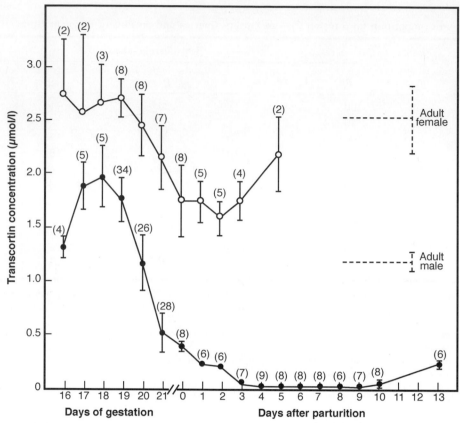

FIGURE 2 Serum CBG concentrations in fetal and neonatal rats (●) and in pregnant and lactating rats (○). The concentrations are expressed as means ± SD and the number of animals or pools (days 16–18 for the fetuses) is given in parentheses. The normal serum concentration of four female and four male rats on day 154 of life is indicated on the right. From van Baelen *et al.* (1977), reproduced by permission of the Society for Endocrinology.

fold. Progesterone-binding globulin differs from CBG in that it is not stimulated by estrogen.

In the pregnant baboon, CBG capacity rises from a nonpregnant value of about 330 ng/ml to about 590 ng/ml at gestational age 60–120 days and falls by term to about 420 ng/ml; the cortisol levels remain unchanged at about 440 ng/ml. Contrasting with the human, baboon, and rat, maternal CBG in rhesus monkeys is lower than that of the nonpregnant female and does not increase with estrogen administration.

B. Fetus and Neonate

While fetal corticosteroid levels rise in many species during pregnancy, CBG levels vary considerably

with species, but in many fall rapidly postpartum. In most species, early postpartum fetal CBG levels are lower than adult values.

Compared to the adult (700 nmol/liter), CBG levels are lower in the human fetus and neonate—about 250 nmol/liter in late gestation and immediately postpartum—rise to about 500 nmol/liter by 30 days postpartum and to adult levels by several months of age.

The level of CBG in the fetal rat rises from about 1.3 μmol/liter at 16 days gestation to a maximum of about 2 μmol/liter at 28 days after which it falls rapidly to 0.4 μmol/liter at birth and to less than 0.1 μmol/liter at 3 days following birth (Fig. 2). It remains at this low level—less than 3% of adult values—until day 9, after which it rises slowly, being about 25% that of the adult by 15 days and reaching adult values by 6 weeks. Dexamethasone treatment accelerates the decrease in CBG concentration. Early in the last third of gestation, CBG mRNA levels in the fetal rat and rabbit are as high or higher than in their mothers but then decline, although levels in their mothers continue to increase; these observations support the concept that CBG production is independently regulated in mother and fetus. The decline in fetal rat CBG before birth may promote an increase in free corticosterone levels necessary for lung maturation. Corticosteroid-binding globulin levels in the neonatal rat are increased by thyroxine which increases hepatic biosynthesis. Although the CBG mRNA levels of rats reach adult levels by 3 weeks, serum CBG concentrations do not reach adult levels until 6 weeks of age, probably due to a higher clearance rate of CBG in infant rats. However the level of free cortisol appears to be unaffected. Despite the low neonatal values of CBG in rats, hippocampal glucocorticoid receptor occupancy/translocation (i.e., hormone-bound receptor) was noted by Viau *et al.* to be similar at all ages, both under basal conditions and following stress.

The sheep differs from this pattern—fetal CBG levels increase markedly over the last 2 weeks before term—from 50 nmol/liter cortisol bound to 250 nmol/liter at term, while unbound and albumin-bound cortisol increase from 3 to 58 nmol/liter and the total cortisol rises 13- to 15-fold. During this time, no changes occur in the maternal plasma. After birth the CBG binding capacity of the neonate falls rapidly to about 90 nmol/liter by 4 days and to 17 nmol/liter by 14 days; total and free corticoids also decrease, but more slowly. The increase of CBG in fetal sheep plasma before term has been shown to depend on an intact fetal pituitary and does not involve thyroid function; the affinity of fetal CBG is similar to that of adult CBG. Possibly the rise in CBG contributes to the onset of parturition since administration of glucocorticoids will induce parturition in this species.

In the baboon, fetal serum CBG capacity at 100–132 days gestation is similar to that of the mother and decreases at term by half. Fetal serum cortisol is low (about 100 nmol/liter) before 168 days gestation and reaches about 1400 nmol/liter after term delivery. Affinity constants are the same throughout.

C. Hereditary Deficiency

This has been shown in a few human families, where the concentration was reduced to about one-half the normal, but familial low levels of CBG are rare and no convincing case of completely absent CBG in the human has been documented, suggesting that absence of CBG may be a lethal mutation, although cases with low CBG have no clinical apparent abnormalities. Corticosteroid-binding globulin appears to be identical in all human races. A variant of CBG, containing slightly altered carbohydrate, occurs in pregnant women and accounts for 4–14% of total plasma CBG at term; its function is not yet clear.

D. Changes with Diet

Slight changes occur with diet—a high-carbohydrate diet may result in a 20% fall in CBG.

E. Possible Fatal Drop in CBG

A remarkable change in CBG occurs in the male *Antechinus stuartii*, a shrew-like marsupial. In this species, all the males die within 3 weeks of the beginning of their first and only mating period in late winter. Over this period there is a precipitous fall in CBG levels, while the plasma corticosteroid concentrations remain high. No such changes occur in the females. Since these changes in the males result in a large increase in free cortisol, it is possible that the males die of hypercorticism.

F. Response of CBG to Stress

Acute severe stress to rats (e.g., immobilization for 1 h or tail shocks over 2 h) causes a fall in CBG which is apparent by 6 h, maximal at 24 h, and persists for 24–48 h; in one study this decrease was prevented by adrenalectomy but not receptor blockade using RU-486. In another study, adrenalectomy did not prevent the decrease in rats that received basal corticosterone replacement or were pretreated with RU-486.

Despite the low values of CBG in the neonatal rat, in response to stress (restraint for 1 h or separation from the mother) the ACTH and the free corticosterone levels increase and this increase persists for

48 h. Such increases are associated with an increased glucocorticoid receptor occupancy/translocation similar to that of stressed adults.

In rats in which an inflammatory process was induced by a subcutaneous injection of turpentine, CBG levels had decreased by two-thirds, while the corticosteroid levels were very high. While the high corticosteroid levels might be expected to decrease CBG levels, the effect was still present after adrenalectomy, suggesting that changes in glucocorticoid concentration are not necessary for this change. At the same time as the CBG levels were low, levels of haptoglobin, an "acute phase serum protein" rose 6- to 10-fold. Corticosteroid-binding globulin levels in pregnant rats treated similarly showed a 3-fold decrease of CBG, while their 19-day-old embryos were not affected.

Alexander and Irvine found that social stress in horses caused a decrease in CBG binding capacity (horses new to a herd were confined in a small yard with dominant resident horses for 3–4 h daily for 3 to 14 days). This decrease in CBG, seen after 3–4 days and increasing over the 2-week period, was accompanied by an increase in free cortisol so that the total cortisol concentrations remained unaltered.

In comparing the homology of CBG cDNA, it was found that there is no sequence homology with any steroid hormone receptor. However, the homology with the SERPIN (serine protease inhibitor) superfamily of proteins exceeds 30%. The proteins in the SERPIN superfamily share a typical tertiary structure responsible for the marked inhibition of serine proteases. In contact with neutrophil elastase, released by neutrophils in large amounts at sites of inflammation, CBG is cleaved, resulting in a 10-fold fall in its affinity for cortisol and thereby releasing its cortisol. Such a mechanism may permit the free cortisol to remain in high concentration at sites of inflammation, while maintaining basal free cortisol concentrations at other sites.

G. Response of CBG to Other Pathological Factors in Humans

Increases in CBG also occur with the administration of oral contraceptive agents or other estrogen-containing preparations. They are due to increased synthesis rather than to reduced turnover. Tamoxifen and clomiphene also raise CBG levels. On the other hand, androgens such as testosterone decrease them; other anabolic steroids such as methandrostenolone and oxymetholone increase them slightly. Corticosteroid-binding globulin levels are reduced in patients with liver cirrhosis, nephrotic syndrome, and in some cases of hypertension and hyperthyroidism, while elevated levels have been reported in some cases of acute leukemia, lymphoma, chronic active hepatitis, lung cancer, untreated adrenal insufficiency, adrenocortical hyperplasia, and disorders of male and female puberty. A slightly enhanced CBG capacity has been observed in juvenile-onset diabetics. A decreased CBG concentration, corrected by vitamin B12 administration, has been observed in some cases of pernicious anemia.

Glucocorticoids decrease CBG levels so that increased CBG levels are found after adrenalectomy, while decreased levels are found in Cushing's syndrome (whether endogenously or exogenously produced). A rapid fall in CBG occurs in septic shock (see above), reaching a nadir at about 24 h due to a marked increase in rate of removal, since the half-life of CBG is about 5 days; this may occur by proteolysis at sites of inflammation. In cases of shock due to severe acute infection by *Candida albicans*, the CBG activity may be virtually absent.

V. BINDING OF CBG TO CELL MEMBRANES

A number of reports suggest that CBG binds to various cell membranes, including prostate, epididymis, testis, mammary carcinoma cells, uterus, pituitary, kidney, spleen, muscle, lung, and placenta. While many of these await confirmation, it appears that CBG does bind to some cell membranes with a K_d of about 0.9 μM at physiological temperatures; this binding requires calcium and/or magnesium ions and is negligible at 4° or 23°C. The physiological significance of this binding is still unknown.

A. Biosynthesis

The liver is the main site of CBG synthesis and CBG is synthesized by hepatocytes in culture. Corticosteroid-binding globulin mRNA has been detected in extrahepatic tissues—spleen, ovary, testis, and lung—of various species, but only in low amounts, and their significance is uncertain. Corticosteroid-binding globulin production is regulated independently in mother and fetus. Guinea pig PBG is made in only very small amounts by the liver, and the large rise in pregnancy is due mainly to synthesis by the placenta.

B. Degradation of CBG

The half-life of human CBG is about 5 days under usual circumstances but is decreased with severe stress.

The serum clearance in early postnatal life in the rat is about twice as rapid (50% in about 7 h) as in the adult animal (about 14 h). Such rapid clearance might promote the delivery of glucocorticoids to sites of rapid growth and tissue remodeling.

VI. MEASUREMENT OF CORTICOSTEROID-BINDING GLOBULIN

Corticosteroid-binding globulin is measured either by its binding capacity for glucocorticoids or by radioimmunoassay. Since the forces binding steroids to CBG are relatively weak and readily dissociable—about an order of magnitude lower than covalent linkages—the binding methods must not disturb the thermodynamic equilibrium existing between the bound and unbound fractions.

Most of these binding methods have been described by Westphal; they include equilibrium dialysis, ultrafiltration, gel electrophoresis, radioimmunodiffusion, isoelectric focusing, gel filtration, Millipore filtration (pore size 0.45 μm), centrifugal ultrafiltration, and fluorescence quenching.

Perhaps the most widely used method has been equilibrium dialysis in which the concentration of steroid is measured on two sides of a dialysis membrane separating two solutions, one containing CBG and the other not. The distribution of the ligand on the two sides of the membrane are measured after equilibrium has been achieved. More recently, CBG is also often measured using radioimmunoassay techniques.

VII. USE OF CORTICOSTEROID-BINDING GLOBULINS TO MEASURE STEROIDS BY COMPETITIVE PROTEIN-BINDING

Human CBG was the first protein used for the determination of glucocorticoids (by B. E. P. Murphy *et al.* in 1963) using the principle of competitive protein-binding (displacement analysis, radiotransinassay), which is identical to that of radioimmunoassay. In this type of analysis, the specificity of the assay depends on the binding properties of the binding protein and the conditions under which the assay is carried out. The endogenous steroid or ligand is quantitated according to its competition with a tracer ligand, usually a radioisotopic form of the endogenous ligand, for binding sites on the protein, and the displacement of the tracer steroid is estimated against a series of standards of the ligand being measured. Thus, for example, the binding of radiolabeled cortisol will be gradually lowered by increasing amounts of endogenous cortisol, giving a standard curve.

Such a method involves two major steps: (1) preparation of the sample by removal of the binding protein in the sample to be measured and separation from competing analogs if required and (2) quantitation of the steroid being measured by equilibration of the tracer, a series of standards of the ligand to be measured, and the unknown sample with the binding-protein and separation of protein-bound and unbound steroid and the measurement of tracer in one of them. Since the equilibration is carried out at high dilutions of the protein, the addition of gelatin (0.5 g/liter) enhances the apparent binding and considerably improves the sensitivity of most assays.

Although no CBG is entirely specific for cortisol alone, the amounts of competing steroids in human plasma are usually small. Although human CBG was the first to be used in this way, dog and horse CBG or indeed many others, can be similarly employed. In human pregnancy, progesterone is an important competitor but can be easily removed by extraction into hexane, which does not extract cortisol; the extracted progesterone can then itself be measured using CBG and a series of progesterone standards. Even better, progesterone may be measured using PBG of pregnant guinea pig serum, which has high specificity for progesterone and very little for cortisol or corticosterone. Since no protein is ever specific for a single ligand (and monoclonal antibodies are no exception), care must be taken to ensure that specificity is achieved under the conditions used. Because of the high affinity of CBG for cortisol, the sensitivity of such a method is very great, so that picogram amounts are readily measured. If chromatographic techniques are employed, other competing steroids can also be measured, as in the case of progesterone above. Since different species of CBG's provide proteins with varying specificity and affinity, they can be used for the assay of many different steroids (Table II). Maximum sensitivity is achieved by using a high dilution of the protein and a low volume for equilibration (usually 0.1 ml). Either the bound or unbound tracer is measured; this can be done using many different techniques, such as gel filtration; adsorption to charcoal, Fuller's earth, or Florisil; equilibrium dialysis, and so on. Precision and accuracy are similar to those of radioimmunoassay.

See Also the Following Articles

CORTICOSTEROID RECEPTORS; CORTICOSTEROIDS AND STRESS

Bibliography

Alexander, S. L., and Irvine, C. H. G. (1998). The effect of social stress on adrenal axis activity in horses: The importance of monitoring corticosteroid-binding globulin capacity. *J. Endocrinol.* **157**, 425–432.

Ballard, P. L., Kitterman, J. A., Bland, R. D., Clyman, R. I., Gluckman, P. D., Platzker, A. C. G., Kaplan, S. L., and Grumbach, M. M. (1982). Ontogeny and regulation of corticosteroid-binding globulin capacity in plasma of fetal and newborn lambs. *Endocrinology* **110**, 359–366.

Dunn, J. F., Nisula, B. C., and Rodbard, D. (1981). Transport of steroid hormones: Binding of 21 endogenous steroids to both testosterone-binding globulin and corticosteroid-binding globulin in human plasma. *J. Clin. Endocrinol. Metab.* **53**, 58–68.

Hammond, G. L. (1990). Molecular properties of corticosteroid binding globulin and the sex-steroid binding proteins. *Endocr. Rev.* **11**, 65–79.

Murphy, B. E. P. (1967). Some studies of the protein-binding of steroids and their application to the routine micro and ultramicro measurement of various steroids in body fluids by competitive protein-binding radioassay. *J. Clin. Endocrinol. Metab.* **27**, 973–990.

Rosner, W. (1991). Plasma steroid-binding proteins. *Endocrinol. Metab. Clin. North Am.* **20**, 697–720.

Seal, U. S., and Doe, R. P. (1967). The role of corticosteroid-binding globulin in mammalian pregnancy: Proceedings of the 2nd International Congress on Hormonal Steroids. *Excerpta Med Intern Congr Series* **132**, 697.

Van Baelen, H., Vandoren, G., DeMoor, P. (1977). Concentration of transcortin in the pregnant rat and its foetuses. *J. Endocr.* **75**, 427–431.

Viau, V., Sharma, S., Meaney, M. J. (1996). Changes in plasma adrenocorticotropin, corticosterone, corticosteroid-binding globulin, and hippocampal glucocorticoid receptor occupancy/translocation in rat pups in response to stress. *J. Neuroendocrinol.* **8**, 1–8.

Westphal, U. (1971). "Steroid–Protein Interaction." Springer-Verlag, New York.

Westphal, U. (1986). "Steroid–Protein Interaction II." Springer-Verlag, New York.

Corticosteroid Receptors

O. C. Meijer and E. R. de Kloet

Leiden University, The Netherlands

B. S. McEwen

Rockefeller University

GLOSSARY

adrenalectomy Surgical removal of the adrenal glands from the body.

corticosteroid hormones Hormones synthesized and secreted from the adrenal gland in response to stress and also during the diurnal rhythm. The main endogenous glucocorticoids are corticosterone in rodents and cortisol in humans.

corticosteroid receptors Intracellular receptor molecules for corticosteroid hormones. On hormone binding they function as transcription factors in the nucleus of the cell to change mRNA and protein synthesis of target genes. There are two types: mineralocorticoid receptors and glucocorticoid receptors.

hypothalamo–pituitary–adrenal axis The brain-controlled activation pathway for the secretion of corticosteroid hormones after stress through a hormonal cascade, involving release of corticotrophin-releasing hormone from the paraventricular nucleus of the hypothalamus in the brain and ACTH from the pituitary gland.

hippocampus A cortical brain structure involved in declarative and spatial memory and the cognitive aspects of emotions, with high expression of both types of corticosteroid receptors.

stress A state caused by a real or perceived challenge to homeostasis, which is accompanied by a hormonal stress response.

The effects of cortisol and corticosterone (CORT), the main glucocorticoid hormones in primates and rodents, respectively, are mediated by two types of intracellular receptor molecules: glucocorticoid receptors (GRs or " type II receptors") and mineralocorticoid receptors (MRs or "type I"). In periph-eral tissues, CORT acts almost exclusively via GRs to affect energy stores, bone metabolism, and inflammatory and immune responses. MRs in epithelial cell types, as present in kidney and colon, are protected from endogenous CORT by the enzyme 11β-OH-steroid dehydrogenase (11β-HSD) so that aldosterone may bind to regulate sodium balance in the body. In nonepithelial targets, such as the brain, both MRs and GRs function as receptors for CORT to act in either synergy or antagonism. GRs and MRs are members of the steroid hormone receptor superfamily and, accordingly, act as transcription factors to change the expression levels of target genes. These genomic effects have a relatively slow onset and long duration. Very high doses of CORT may also acutely affect the activity of neuronal cells, presumably via membrane receptors. However, no such receptors have been identified in mammals to date. MRs and GRs have different pharmacological properties and distribution in brain. Corticosteroid receptors in the brain and pituitary play a crucial role in the regulation of the stress response and in mediating the effects of CORT on mood and cognition.

I. CORTICOSTEROID RECEPTOR PROPERTIES

A. Activation of Corticosteroid Receptors

The lipophilic CORT diffuses readily through the plasma membrane of cells to bind to its receptors. Corticosteroid receptors are part of a cytoplasmic multiprotein complex that consists of one receptor molecule and several heat shock proteins (hsp). Binding of CORT leads to a rapid chain of events that consists of dissociation of the hsp, multiple phosphorylation steps, and increased affinity of the ligand-activated receptor for nuclear domains: the ligand–receptor complex translocates to the cell nucleus to exert its action on gene expression and protein synthesis.

An important determinant of corticosteroid receptor activation is access of the ligand to the receptor, which depends on several factors besides the total plasma concentration of CORT. First, circulating hormone is bound to CBG/transcortin and with a much lower affinity to serum albumin. Of the average corticosterone concentration circulating over a 24-h period in the rat, less than 5% is not bound to CBG, i.e., is free and biologically available.

Second, the enzyme 11β-HSD type 2 converts cortisol and corticosterone to their inactive 11-dehydro metabolites in mineralocorticoid target tissues. Conversely, the 11β-HSD type 1 isoform, which is often colocalized with GRs, can catalyze the reverse reaction and generate cortisol from cortisone within a target cell. This reaction takes place in the liver and may also be relevant for certain areas in the brain.

A third determinant of access, which particularly pertains to synthetic glucocorticoids, is the mdr1a P-glycoprotein. This protein is expressed in the apical membranes of endothelial cells of the blood–brain barrier. mdr1a P-glycoprotein functions as an energy-dependent pump, which limits access to the brain of xenobiotic agents, including synthetic steroids. Accordingly, the brain (but not the pituitary) is resistant to the penetration of moderate amounts of dexamethasone.

B. Corticosteroid Receptor Diversity in Pituitary and Brain

Although GRs and MRs both act as high-affinity receptors for CORT in the brain, these receptor types differ significantly with respect to their pharmacology, distribution, and physiological effects.

1. Structure

The human GR gene is localized on chromosome 5 whereas the MR gene is localized on chromosome 4, indicating an early duplication of their common ancestor during evolution. Despite this early divergence, their genomic organization is very similar, notwithstanding differences at the 5' and 3' ends. The overall structure of GR and MR protein follows that of the other members of the steroid hormone receptor family. The molecules are generally viewed as consisting of three domains: a highly conserved DNA-binding domain (95% homology between MR and GR), flanked by the C-terminal ligand-binding domain (60%), and a large N-terminal domain that contains a transactivation function and is highly variable between MR and GR (15%) and between species.

2. Pharmacology

Although GR and MR are both high affinity receptors for CORT, they differ in their affinities for several ligands. In the case of cortisol and corticosterone, MR has an approximately 10-fold higher affinity than GR. The important consequence of this is that GRs and MRs are occupied differentially during the day and during stress responses. MRs are already occupied extensively under basal trough conditions, whereas the saturation of GRs requires hormone levels that occur after stress or after the circadian peak. Because of its high, almost tonic occupation, it has been hypothesized that the amount of bioactive receptor protein is an important level of regulation for MRs, whereas the GR signal depends primarily on ligand concentration. Synthetic glucocorticoids have higher affinity for GR than for MR, but their access to brain GR is hampered by the mdr1a gene-encoded P-glycoprotein (see Section I,A).

3. Distribution

GR is expressed ubiquitously in many different tissues and cell types. In tissues such as liver, lung, and adrenal medulla, GRs are crucial for appropriate development. MRs have a much more limited distribution, and as receptors for CORT (as opposed to mineralocorticoids), they have been characterized in brain and some lymphoid tissues. The pituitary, outside the blood–brain barrier, contains GRs as well as MRs, although no specific function for MRs has been described for any of its cell types.

Throughout the brain immunocytochemical and *in situ* hybridization procedures have shown a widespread distribution of GR in neurons and glial cells. Particularly high GR concentrations are found in the limbic system (hippocampus—with relatively low concentrations in the CA3 region—septum, and amygdala), in the parvocellular neurons of the paraventricular nucleus of the hypothalamus (PVN), and in the supraoptic nucleus. In the PVN, the biosynthesis and release of parvocellular vasopressine, corticotrophin-releasing hormone (CRH), and other neuropeptides are under glucocorticoid control. GRs are also present in relatively high concentrations in the ascending monoaminergic neurons of the brain stem. Moderate GR levels are also found in many thalamic nuclei and in patch-like distribution in the striatal areas, as well as throughout the cortical hemispheres (see Fig. 1).

In the brain, MRs have a more restricted topography than GRs. High MR densities have been found in the neurons of the hippocampal formation, lateral

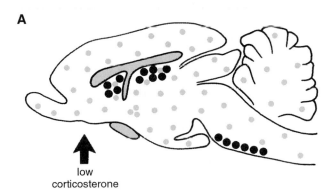

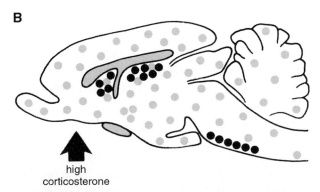

FIGURE 1 Distribution of MR and GR in the rat brain. Schematic distribution of MRs (black circles) and GRs (grey circles) in the rat brain. MR expression is more restricted and especially high in the hippocampus. MRs are substantially occupied by CORT under basal conditions, i.e., at the circadian trough under nonstressed conditions (A). GRs show a widespread distribution, are only partially occupied under basal conditions (A) and become more fully activated at the circadian peak of CORT secretion or after stress (B). Reprinted from Joëls and de Kloet (1992) with permission.

septum, medial and central amygdala, olfactory nucleus, layer II of the cortex, and in brain stem sensory and motor neurons. This distribution of MRs is essentially the same as discovered in 1968 by McEwen with the cell nuclear retention of radioligand after the administration of tracer doses of $[^3H]$-corticosterone to adrenalectomized rats. Aldosteron-preferring MRs involved in salt homeostasis are localized in the anterior hypothalamus and circumventricular organs, such as the chorioid plexus.

The subcellular localization of MRs and GRs was studied in hippocampal neurons by dual labeling immunocytochemistry and confocal microscopy. It was observed that MRs and GRs are distributed non-homogeneously over the nucleus. Both receptors are concentrated in about 1000 clusters scattered throughout the nucleoplasm. Many clusters contain exclusively either MRs or GRs, although a significant number of domains were found to contain both receptor types. The latter clusters are candidate sites where the two receptors could interact to establish a coordinated regulation of gene expression. This would imply that GR and MR homodimers, as well as the possible MR/GR heterodimers, are associated with distinct nuclear domains.

4. Corticosteroid Receptor Variants

Alternative splicing of the 3′ end of the human GR pre-mRNA creates a hGRβ variant in addition to the common hGRα. However, it should be noted that rodent GR pre-mRNA lacks this splice site, and GRβ could not be detected in rodent tissue. Translation of GRα and GRβ mRNA produces two proteins, which are almost identical, but differ in their carboxy-terminals, which implies that GRα binds cortisol whereas GRβ does not. However, *in vitro* experiments suggest that GRβ is capable of binding to glucocorticoid-responsive elements (GREs) and can form homodimers as well as heterodimers with GRα. Accordingly, GRβ has been shown to block GR-mediated transactivation *in vitro*, whereas it does not seem to interfere with transrepression. In the human brain, GRβ mRNA is found in the hypothalamus and the hippocampus, but the relative abundance is subject to debate and may be only 1% relative to GRα. Thus, validation of the possible role of GRβ as a dominant-negative factor awaits further studies.

Expression of the human MR gene may result in the formation of at least four transcripts, which are derived from two different promoters. The two main transcripts, MRα and MRβ differ only in the 5′ untranslated exon 1 and thus are translated into the same 985 amino acid MR protein. In rat, an MR transcript derived from exon 1 is detectable in very low amounts. Another intriguing splice variant has been described. The use of an alternative splice site between exon 3 and 4 creates a 12-bp insertion, which, after translation, corresponds to 4 additional amino acids in the amino acid sequence bridging the two zinc finger domains of the DNA-binding domain. The functional analysis and relevance of these MR variants await further studies.

Receptor variants may play an important role in disease states. Thus, individuals with familial glucocorticoid resistance may express a GR variant and, as a consequence, have deficient GR function and impaired glucocorticoid feedback resulting in hypercorticism. However, they lack symptoms of Cushing's syndrome as ACTH and cortisol levels are also at a higher set point, and GRs are, in general, less sensitive to glucocorticoid activation. The symptomatology of familial glucocorticoid resistance is usually related to the overproduction of adrenal mineralocorticoids and androgens in response to ACTH. Although these severe inherited deficits in GRs, resulting in asymptomatic hypercorticoidism, are rare disorders in humans, there are also pronounced species differences in guinea pigs, prairie voles, and New World monkeys. These animals display a normal circadian rhythm in hypothalamo–pituitary-adrenal axis HPA activity, but ACTH and cortisol are circulating at a much higher level. Apparently, the elevated set point in hypothalamo–pituitary-adrenal axis (HPA) regulation is an adequate adaptation.

C. Regulation of Transcription through Corticosteroid Receptors

As members of the steroid hormone receptor superfamily, ligand-activated GR and MR exert their effects by acting as transcription factors to up- or downregulate protein and peptide levels in the cell. MRs and GRs may stimulate or repress transcription by several mechanisms (see Fig. 2).

1. Transactivation via GREs

GR and MR contain a nearly identical DNA-binding domain that recognizes specific DNA elements in the regulatory regions of genes: glucocorticoid response elements (consensus sequence: GGTACAnnnTGTt/cCT). The steroid receptors bind as homodimers and perhaps also as heterodimers to GREs to stimulate transcription. In general, GRs are more potent activators of transcription than MRs, at least in *in vitro* conditions. Heterodimers of MR and GR have been shown in cell systems to have at times characteristics that are different from either type of homodimer. The strong synergizing effect of GR-activated transcription on multiple GREs is not observed with MR activation, probably due to the limited homology of the N-terminal sequences. Tyrosine amino transferase (TAT) and phenylethanolamine-N-methyltransferase (PNMT) are examples of genes that are regulated via GREs.

2. Repression via Negative GREs

GRs (and possibly MRs) can also repress gene transcription by binding to DNA. DNA elements that are involved are known as "negative GREs" (nGREs). The sequence of nGREs can be highly variable and differs from the consensus sequence for positively acting GREs. The mechanism by which transcription is repressed also differs between cases. One mechanism involves the binding of GRs to the nGRE to occlude adjacent or overlapping binding sites on the DNA for positively acting transcription factors. An nGRE has been described for the human POMC gene.

3. Repression via Protein–Protein Interactions

The mode of action generally referred to as transrepression involves repression by GRs of gene transcription activated by other transcription factors, such as Activating Protein-1 (AP-1), Nuclear Factor-κB (NF-κB), and cAMP Response Element Binding Protein (CREB). GRs interfere with these other factors via protein-protein interactions. This may happen independently of binding of GRs to the DNA, and dimerization of GRs is not required. The target genes involved lack GREs.

Corticosteroid receptors may also activate genes in synergy with other, nonreceptor transcription factors. On elements known as composite GREs, GRs

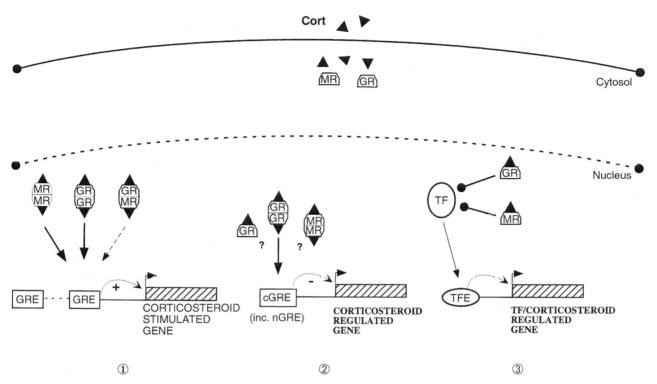

FIGURE 2 Three molecular mechanisms of regulation of gene expression. (1) GRs and MRs bind as homo- and heterodimers to GRE sequences to stimulate transcription. (2) GRs (and possibly MRs) bind to "negative GRE" sequences that diverge from consensus GRE. Through mechanisms such as occlusion of adjacent sites they repress transcription. (3) GRs and MRs interfere through protein–protein interactions with other transcription factors (TF) at times independent of binding of the steroid receptors to the DNA. This results in antagonism of the effects of the TF (e.g., AP-1 or NF-κB).

bind to the DNA in close proximity to another transcription factor and may either repress or enhance the effect of this other factor. In the case of the proliferin "cGRE", the GR enhances the effect of the adjacently bound transcription factor AP-1 greatly if the latter consists of c-*jun*/c-*jun* homodimers. In contrast, GR binding leads to repression of the action of c-*jun*/c-*fos* heterodimers. Interactions with other transcription factors depend by definition on the presence of these factors, which can be regulated by extracellular signals other than steroid hormones. This demonstrates that the effects of CORT vary widely and are context-dependent.

Dissociation between MR- and GR-mediated events may arise through these "cross-talk" mechanisms, as it has been shown that GRs suppresses AP-1 activity under conditions where MR is ineffective. It is probable that the unique N-terminal regions of the GR and the MR account for the different properties with respect to transrepression.

II. CELLULAR EFFECTS OF CORTICOSTEROID HORMONE ACTIVATION

Activation of intracellular corticosteroid receptors in many cell types may induce a variety of cellular responses, influencing diverse processes such as cellular structure, energy metabolism, or signal transduction. Changes in cellular structure usually develop over the course of several days, whereas effects on energy metabolism or signal transduction may already become apparent within an hour. In peripheral tissues, activation of GRs leads to pronounced cellular effects, e.g., apoptosis of thymocytes (via antagonism of NF-κB activity) and induction of gluconeogenesis in hepatocytes (through induction of critical enzymes). Here, focus lies on the effects of MRs and GRs in the brain, as these are important factors in regulation of the HPA axis and of adaptation to stress in general. Although the delayed onset

TABLE I

Characteristics of the Two Corticosteroid Receptor Types

1. Mineralocorticoid receptor (MR; type 1)

    High affinity for cortisol and corticosterone ($K_d \approx 0.5$ nM)

    Agonist: Aldosteron (epithelial cell types as in kidney), cortisol (brain)

    Antagonists: Spironolactone, RU 28328

    Limited distribution in periphery (kidney, colon, lymphocytes) and brain (limbic brain)

2. Glucocorticoid receptor (GR; type 2)

    Lower affinity for cortisol and corticosterone ($K_d \approx 5.0$ nM)

    Agonists: Cortisol, dexamethasone, RU 28362

    Antagonists: RU 38486

    Ubiquitous expression in periphery and brain

of the observed effects—as opposed to the rapidly induced effects by neurosteroids—favors gene-mediated effects via MRs and GRs, the molecular mechanism has, in many cases, not been resolved.

A. Differential Effects at the Level of a Single Structure: MR and GR in the Hippocampus

The principal cell types in the hippocampus, a brain structure involved in declarative memory processes and (possibly) mood, express both MRs and GRs. Effects of differential occupation on firing characteristics have been particularly well studied for CA1 pyramidal cells. A conspicuous feature of CORT actions on cellular activity in the hippocampus is the apparent lack of effect when neurons are studied under basal conditions. Only when neurons are shifted from their basal condition, e.g., by the action of neurotransmitters, do CORT effects become visible. The general picture emerging is that conditions of predominant MR activation, i.e., at the circadian trough at rest, are associated with the maintenance of neuronal excitability so that excitatory inputs to the hippocampal CA1 area result in considerable excitatory hippocampal output. In contrast, additional GR activation, e.g., following acute stress, generally depresses the transiently activated CA1 hippocampal output. A similar effect is seen after ADX, indicating

a U-shaped dose-response dependency of these cellular responses to corticosteroids. Most of the CORT effects described in this article have been shown to depend on *de novo* protein synthesis, indicating that effects on transcription of as yet unidentified target genes are responsible for the observed phenomena.

The U shape of CORT on neuronal excitability that is determined by differential MR and GR activation is reflected in a number of parameters. An intrinsic cellular property is the voltage-gated Ca current; this current is small under conditions of predominant MR occupation and is elevated when GRs become activated in addition. Basal and stimulus-induced intracellular Ca levels were also found to be increased by substantial GR activation, which may be explained by steroid effects on Ca-buffering or extrusion mechanisms. In accordance with these steroid effects, the Ca-dependent accommodation and AHP amplitude were found to be small with predominant MR activation.

MR and GR activation also modulate the responses to several neurotransmitters. With respect to amino acid-mediated synaptic transmission in the hippocampus, responses to both excitatory (glutamatergic) and inhibitory (GABAergic) inputs are maintained at a stable level when MRs are predominantly activated, i.e., with low CORT levels. When GRs become occupied additionally as a consequence of rising CORT levels, excitatory transmission (and thus CA1 hippocampal output) is reduced. At very high steroid levels inhibitory networks are also impaired. These GR-mediated effects may involve the impairment of energy metabolism. The high efficiency of amino acid transmission with predominant MR activation is also reflected in long-term plastic changes involving this hippocampal network. Plasticity-related phenomena are most pronounced with moderate CORT levels so that most of the MRs and only part of the GRs are activated; when CORT levels are either reduced or enhanced, synaptic potentiation/depression is far less effective. Thus, varying concentrations of CORT as a consequence of stress will have consequences for the efficacy of synaptic potentiation in the hippocampus.

In addition to amino acid input, hippocampal neurons also receive considerable input mediated by biogenic amines such as acetylcholine, norepinephrine, and serotonin. Norepinephrine acts via a β-adrenergic receptor to increase excitability of the CA1 hippocampal area. High CORT levels, occupying GRs, reduce the norepinephrine effect, again leading to a reduction in responsiveness of the hippocampal neurons.

Serotonin (5-hydroxytryptamine, 5HT) evokes many different effects in CA1 hippocampal neurons, of which 5HT1A receptor-mediated hyperpolarization of the membrane is most prominent. This hyperpolarization is small in amplitude with predominant MR occupation; additional GR activation increased 5HT responses. This is seen both when CORT is applied exogenously and after acute stress. Although CORT through MR activation also down regulates 5HT1A receptor mRNA expression and binding capacity, acute functional impairment is not likely brought about through reduced binding capacity.

B. Effects on Neurotransmitter Systems

CORT influences many cell types in the brain, and it is worthwhile to analyze its effects at the level of neurotransmitter systems, as opposed to a single cell type or nucleus. Major targets for coordinate regulation through corticosteroid receptors are the norepinephrine, dopamine, and serotonin systems. Modulation may take place at the level of both the presynaptic, and the postsynaptic cell. As for most aspects of CORT action, the effects are permissive in nature: the genomic effects of steroid receptor activation are revealed in the context of activated systems.

1. Serotonin: Coordinate Regulation via MRs and GRs

A concept of coordinate regulation via MRs and GRs has emerged for the serotonin system, particularly in relation to its projection on the hippocampus. Under basal conditions, when corticosteroid levels are low, there is predominant activation of MRs. As described earlier, the response of hippocampal 5HT1A receptors under these conditions is low. In addition, MRs in certain hippocampal areas suppress expression of the 5HT1A receptor. Thus, a situation of predominant MR occupation is associated with low responses to serotonin in the hippocampus. Serotonin release in the hippocampus is increased during and after stress conditions that are associated with increased levels of CORT, i.e., increased activation of GR in serotonergic and hippocampal neurons. When the stress-induced GR occupation is prevented, no increased release of serotonin is observed in animals. CORT acts via GR, presumably on the activity of the rate-limiting enzyme for serotonin synthesis (tryptophan hydroxylase), and via attenuation of negative feedback inhibition by serotonin in the serotonergic neurons in the midbrain. At the postsynaptic level in the hippocampus, acute GR activation leads to increased responses to 5HT1A receptor activation. Thus, while MR-mediated actions of CORT inhibit hippocampal responses, GR occupation is required for the stress-induced increased activity of serotonin cells and for the increased responsiveness of 5HT1A receptor-mediated responses.

When CORT is chronically elevated to levels in the GR-occupying range, *hypo*responses to serotonin are observed in hippocampal neurons and endocrine challenge tests. It is unclear which molecular changes underlie the transition from stimulatory to inhibitory effects of high levels of CORT on serotonergic transmission.

2. Catecholamines

Dopaminergic and catecholaminergic cells also depend on GR occupation for development and function. As in the case of stress-induced serotonin activity, increased activity of the mesolimbic dopamine system in the adult rat depends on GR activation. Dopamine release in the nucleus accumbens and neuronal and behavioral responses to dopamine agonists such as apomorphine, are stimulated by CORT via GR. Sensitization to repeated treatment with drugs that increase dopaminergic transmission, such as cocaine, depend on GR activation. GR-mediated activation and sensitization of DA systems are important for understanding the relationship between stress and drug addiction in the context of individual response characteristics and have implications for psychopathology. Increased DA is involved in the symptoms of psychosis and depression, which

TABLE II

Milestones in Brain Corticosteroid Receptor Research

Year	Milestone
1968	First report on selective retention of [³H]corticosterone in hippocampus
1975	Low retention of [³H]dexamethasone in hippocampus; high in pituitary
1980	Selective MR agonists discriminate between MR and GR
1982	*In vitro* hippocampus and kidney cytosol contain MR and GR
1983	GR acts as transcription factor through DNA binding
1985	MR and not GR retains [³H]corticosterone in hippocampus
1985	Cloning of GR
1985	First brain map of immunoreactive GR neurons
1987	Cloning of MR
1988	11β-HSD confers aldosteron specificity to MR
1990	Transrepression of AP-1-induced transcription via GR
1991	First brain map of immunoreactive MR neurons
1993	Differential effects of MR and GR on transrepression
1994	*In vitro* demonstration of MR/GR heterodimers
1994	Mechanistic differentiation between transactivation and transrepression GR
1995	mdrla Pgp in blood–brain barrier hampers brain entry of dexamethasone
1995	GR knockout mice
1996	Colocalized immunoreactive MR/GR clusters in hippocampal neuronal nuclei
1998	"Knock in" mice that express a dimerization-deficient mutant of GR

are often associated with elevated basal levels of circulating CORT and escape from dexamethasone suppression.

In the periphery, there are clear effects of CORT on epinephrine: the expression of the PNMT gene, and in fact the development of the adrenal medulla, depend on GR activation. CORT also potentiates epinephrine responses at the target level. In the central nervous system, GRs are abundantly present in the majority of the neurons in midbrain norepinephrine cell groups. Although studies with adrenalectomized rats show a permissive function of corticosteroids

for norepinephrine cells during ontogeny and stress (e.g., in relation to memory formation), the effect of GR activation in these cells and their postsynaptic targets are not as clear as for other transmitters.

Postsynaptically, CORT region-dependently regulates adrenergic receptor expression, e.g., induces the inhibitory α_2 receptor in the hypothalamic paraventricular nucleus. In the hippocampus, the electrophysiological effects of norepinephrine are attenuated via a GR-dependent mechanism. Stress levels of CORT reduce the cyclic AMP generation induced by norepinephrine acting via β-adrenergic receptors in the hippocampus.

3. Neuropeptide Systems

In addition to the classical neurotransmitter systems, many peptidergic systems are controlled via corticosteroid receptors, both at the level of peptide synthesis and at the level of postsynaptic receptors. These peptides are involved in many aspects of brain function, including hypothalamic control of the HPA axis and regulation of metabolism and feeding. The best-studied examples are POMC-derived peptides, CRH and AVP, because of their critical role in activation of the HPA axis. Both CRH and AVP mRNA levels are suppressed by CORT in the parvocellular division of the PVN, presumably via GR activation. However, this type of regulation is cell type-dependent, as in the amygdala CRH mRNA is upregulated by corticosteroids. In the hippocampus, corticosteroid receptors mediate regulation by CORT of neuropeptide Y and dynorphin mRNA levels; in the caudate-putamen and nucleus accumbens, corticosteroid receptors mediate regulation by CORT of preproenkephalin, neurokinin A, and preprodynorphin mRNA levels.

C. Cellular Viability

Structural changes of hippocampal neurons were observed both with chronic absence and chronic overexposure to CORT, indicating that the steroid-dependent expression of genes is of crucial importance for hippocampal integrity.

1. Chronic Absence of Corticosteroids

Removal of the adrenal glands results within 3 days in apoptotic-like degeneration of mature granule cells in the rat dentatus gyrus, but not in other hippocampal fields. The degeneration and associated loss of synaptic function can be prevented by treatment with MR ligands. In contrast to most brain regions, the dentate gyrus shows neurogenesis even during adulthood, which can be blocked by chronic stress and adrenal steroids. Lack of MR activation as a consequence of ADX results in increased cell birth and cell death. It has been argued that MR activation maintains the balance between cell birth and cell death in the dentate gyrus by enhancing the excitatory input to this region. However, newborn neurons in the dentate gyrus do not express corticosteroid receptors, suggesting that the steroid effects on neurogenesis are indirect and possibly involve the modulation of excitatory transmission and neurotrophins.

2. Chronic Exposure to High Corticosteroid Levels

Ample evidence now shows that chronic elevation of CORT levels leads to atrophy in parts of the hippocampus, as well as to increased vulnerability to excitotoxic insults. CA3 pyramidal neurons seem to be particularly vulnerable, although effects in the CA1 and dentate subfield have also been reported. Three weeks of restraint stress in rats causes the regression of apical dendrites of hippocampal CA3 pyramidal neurons. This effect is mimicked by 3 weeks of treatment with a high dose of corticosterone and does not occur when corticosterone secretion is blocked by cyanoketone treatment. The regression occurring after 3 weeks of high levels of CORT is reversible, and available data support the view that an imbalance of excitatory over inhibitory signals, leading indirectly to an enhanced Ca influx in the CA3 pyramidal neurons, contributes to the observed degeneration. Lack of neurotrophic capacity may also contribute to enhanced neuronal vulnerability. Indeed, chronic stress or administration of CORT affects Brain-Derived Neurotrophic Factor (BDNF), Nerve Growth Factor (NGF), and basic Fibroblast Growth Factor (FGF) and TGF expression in the hippocampus.

A critical duration of overexposure to steroids is essential for the atrophy of CA3 neurons to develop: temporary high levels of the hormone decrease responsiveness to excitatory amino acids and reduce excitability. It is only in conditions of chronically enhanced corticosteroid exposure that local depolarization is sustained and breakdown of inhibitory networks occurs. Hippocampal neurons will subsequently be subjected to a substantial GR-dependent rise in intracellular Ca levels. Following this line of reasoning beneficial effects exerted by phasic activation of GRs are turned into damaging actions when GRs are activated chronically.

III. BEHAVIOR AND THE STRESS RESPONSE

The differential effects on neuronal functioning that CORT exerts via MRs and GR, and the differential occupation of these receptors as a function of the behavioral state of the animal suggest fundamentally different roles for CORT via MR- and GR-mediated processes. MRs are occupied by basal levels of CORT, and thus mediate tonic hormonal influences. This might function to prepare the animal for upcoming challenges and determine the magnitude and/or nature of initial responses. This so-called *proactive* mode of control includes effects on the processing of sensory information, interpretation of environmental stimuli, and selection of the appropriate behavioral strategy. GRs, however, are occupied after plasma CORT levels have become elevated after challenges/ stress. Their role may be to generally mediate *reactive* processes that serve to restore homeostasis, to facilitate behavioral adaptation of the animal, and to prepare the animal for a next exposure to a stressor.

A. Corticosteroid Receptors and HPA Axis Control

Both MRs and GRs are involved in the feedback control of the HPA axis activity, but the temporal and neuroanatomical aspects of feedback differ substantially for each receptor type. Apart from primary feedback sites, the hippocampus has received a lot of attention, particularly because it contains the highest concentrations of both MRs and GRs in the brain.

Pituitary corticotrophs and PVN (being part of the HPA axis) contain the primary feedback sites for stress levels of CORT. The effects of CORT on pituitary, PVN, and brain stem catecholaminergic nuclei involve the activation of GRs. Limbic inputs impinging on the PVN (via hypothalamic GABAergic neurons) express high levels of MR in addition to GR, suggesting dual regulation of these inputs by CORT. Moreover, the effect of these inputs can be either inhibitory on HPA activity (from hippocampus) or excitatory (e.g., from amygdala).

Pharmacological experiments in rats have shown that MR occupation suppresses HPA axis activity under basal conditions around the circadian trough: in adrenalectomized animals, hormone levels can be normalized with an IC_{50} of about 0.5 nM in terms of circulating free corticosterone, which is in the range of the MR K_d value. In intact animals, MR antagonists lead to an increase in corticosterone levels at the time of the circadian trough. Accordingly, MR activation serves to control HPA axis activity in a proactive manner.

At the circadian peak, much higher levels of exogenous corticosteroids are required to normalize ADX-induced increases in HPA axis activity, and half-maximal suppression is achieved by a free concentration of about 5 nM, close to the K_d of GRs. However, exclusive activation of GRs is insufficient to suppress the circadian peak, and MR activation appears to be indispensable. One episodic rise in CORT levels by injection or ingestion via the normal evening drink is sufficient to occupy both receptor types and to maintain ACTH levels with small amplitude changes over the 24-h period. These GR-mediated effects observed after exogenous glucocorticoids thus are also involved in maintenance of HPA activity.

Elevated CORT facilitates the termination of the HPA response to stress, and various temporal (fast and slow feedback) domains have been distinguished. These GR-mediated effects triggered in response to stress represent the reactive mode of feedback operation.

1. Hippocampal MR and GR

Lesioning and electrical stimulation studies suggest an overall inhibitory influence of the hippocampus on HPA activity. The effects of intracerebroventricular MR antagonists in rats (see earlier discussion:

elevation of basal trough levels of corticosterone and enhanced adrenocortical responses to novelty) are likely mediated by hippocampal MRs. Consistent with the MR specificity of the response, a corticosterone implant in the dorsal hippocampus has been shown to suppress ADX-induced elevations in ACTH levels, whereas dexamethasone implants were ineffective. Finally, the systemic administration of spironolactone can increase basal HPA activity in humans, although this response has not been noted in all studies. Thus, hippocampal MRs appear to mediate the effect of CORT in maintaining the tone of basal HPA activity.

GR activation in the hippocampus, however, may not be involved in negative feedback, but rather serves to suppress hippocampal output, leading to a disinhibition of the HPA axis. In fact, there is some experimental evidence that intrahippocampal (in contrast to intracerebroventricular) administration of GR agonists does lead to an activation of the HPA axis. The nature of HPA regulation via hippocampal MRs and GRs is also consistent with the cellular actions they evoke in the hippocampus: predominant MR activation (comparable with local antiglucocorticoid application) maintains hippocampal excitability, and through transsynaptic inhibitory projections to PVN basal HPA activity. Conversely, with rising CORT concentration, GR activation suppresses the hippocampal output, resulting in a disinhibition of PVN neurons. The functions mediated by both receptor types are linked. A deficiency in MR is predicted to allow a corticosterone response more readily, thus leading to more pronounced GR-mediated effects. This illustrates the importance of balance in MR- and GR-mediated effects involved in HPA regulation.

2. Indirect Effects

Observations on HPA regulation have often been made without consideration of the steroid effects on higher brain functions involved in arousal and processing of information. Brain areas projecting to the PVN have profound and long-lasting consequences for feedback regulation. Many systems with inputs to the PVN generally express GRs and contain numerous colocalized neuropeptides, which also regulate PVN activity in their own right.

The activation of a particular afferent neuronal

network innervating the PVN area is stressor-specific and depends on the nature of the stimulus. If it constitutes a direct threat to survival through physical stressors (e.g., respiratory distress, hemorrhage, inflammation, infection, and trauma), the ascending aminergic pathways promptly activate the autonomic and neuroendocrine centers in the hypothalamus. If sensory stimuli are subject to appraisal and interpretation, processing in higher brain regions is required, which may subsequently lead to the modulation of GABAergic tone and a change in synthesis of CRH, VP, and other neuropeptides of the PVN secretagogue cocktail. Activation of brain stem and limbic circuitry is not separated, but is in fact mutually interactive, as stress-induced CORT enters the brain readily and feeds back on all components of the neural stress circuitry, but in a context-dependent manner.

B. Control over Learning and Memory via MR and GR

Activation of central corticosteroid receptors does not necessarily cause a behavioral change, but rather influences information processing, thereby affecting the likelihood that a particular stimulus elicits an appropriate behavioral response. For example, the GR-mediated effects on the dopaminergic reward system may render animals more susceptible to addiction, but by themselves cause no such state. Through coordinate MR- and GR-mediated actions in higher brain areas, e.g., neocortical regions, and limbic areas such as hippocampus, septum, and amygdala, CORT affects learning and memory processes. Therefore, when studying the modulation of behavioral responses by CORT, the time and duration of the hormone action, as well as its context, need to be considered.

The hippocampal formation plays a key role in animals' reactivity to novelty and provides an essential contribution to learning and memory. Stress hormones, including CORT, are secreted during learning and are necessary for establishment of an enduring memory. In this context the role of CORT on acquisition, consolidation, and retrieval of information has been studied for more than four decades. Many different tests revealed that administration of exogenous

corticosterone in the appropriate temporal context, i.e., in close relation to training, potentiated memory in a dose-related fashion. From studies involving the use of specific corticosteroid receptor antagonists, antisense oligonucleotides, and transgenic animals, it is clear that these effects of corticosteroids require GR activation. These effects via GR in the context of stress-induced elevated hormone levels represent a reactive mode of action.

Studies with specific antagonists have shown that MRs modulate ongoing behavioral activity, as demonstrated by effects of MR blockade during, but not after the training session. These effects mediated by MR regulate sensory integration underlying the evaluation of environmental information and response selection and thus have the capacity to subsequently affect memory storage for spatial and avoidance behavior. MR-mediated effects on behavioral response selection and reactivity may again be interpreted as a proactive mode of action, aimed to maintain homeostasis.

Thus, hippocampal MRs mediate effects of CORT on the appraisal of information and response selection, whereas GR function does not so much modify these aspects of sensory integration but rather promotes processes underlying the consolidation of acquired information. However, exposure to high CORT levels in a different context (e.g., as a consequence of an additional stressor) may interfere with consolidation processes, as it may signal different, and more relevant, stimuli to the animal. The MR- and GR-mediated effects on information processing facilitate behavioral adaptation. This also promotes the inhibitory control exerted by higher brain circuits over HPA activity.

IV. CORTICOSTEROID RECEPTORS IN PATHOLOGY

Inappropriate activation of corticosteroid receptors through aberrant levels of hormone leads to well-known pathologies: Cushing's disease, immunosuppressed states (glucocorticoid excess), Addison's disease (glucocorticoid deficiency), and (pseudo)mineralocorticoid excess states that are associated with high blood pressure. In the brain, the situation is much more complex. Depending on the region, both MR and GR can mediate the effects of CORT, and the balance in activation of these two receptor types may be critical in determining the effects of CORT on neuronal systems. For example, animal studies show that the balance of MR- and GR-mediated activities in hippocampal circuits determines excitability, stress responsiveness, and behavioral reactivity. Also, the effects of corticosteroid receptor activation often depend on the cellular context, as a result of "cross-talk" with other signaling cascades. Genetically determined differences in any of the signaling pathways involved can lead to a predisposition of adverse effects of CORT.

Significant changes in CORT signaling in the brain can result from chronic stress exposure and inefficient operation of the HPA axis, resulting in over- or underexposure to circulating CORT and from genetically determined or acquired changes in relative abundance of MR and GR (and associated factors). All these changes may lead to disturbances in mood and affect, and neurodegenerative phenomena, via direct actions on relevant brain structures, as well as via modulation of the HPA axis activity. However, the specific contribution of brain MR and GR to these cognitive and affective deficits has not been established.

Disturbed CORT signaling in brain appears to be causally involved in enhancing vulnerability to depression. In this context, it is extremely interesting that the tricyclic antidepressants not only restore 5HT and noradrenergic transmission in brain, but also increase the expression of brain corticosteroid receptors, in parallel with normalization of HPA tone. In contrast to depression, posttraumatic stress disorder, chronic fatigue syndrome, and fibromyalgia are associated with a *hypo*activity of the HPA axis.

Evidence from animal experiments and in humans shows that a disregulated HPA axis, corticosteroid receptor deficits, and elevated CORT levels during stress are associated with age and may lead to an enhanced vulnerability to neurodegenerative disorders, particularly in the hippocampus. GR-mediated impairment in the energy metabolism of hippocampal pyramidal cells is thought to play a role here. The "glucocorticoid cascade hypothesis" has received much attention over the last years: hypercorticism would, over time, lead to damage to the hippocampus, which in turn would lead to disinhibition of the HPA axis and further elevation of CORT levels. A central assumption of this hypothesis is that hippocampal GRs were thought to promote escape from negative feedback via downregulation. However, there is little evidence for a direct negative feedback function of hippocampal GRs: the role of the hippocampus appears to be indirect and involved more with the shutoff of the neural activity that drives HPA output, operating in concert with output from the amygdala and pathways via the bed nucleus of the stria terminalis. Thus, the mechanisms that lead to the progressive hyperactivity and disregulation of the HPA axis in some individuals, as they age, are evidently more complex than envisioned in the "glucocorticoid cascade hypothesis" and their elucidation will require a more extensive understanding of the role of other brain structures besides the hippocampus and the hypothalamus in HPA regulation.

See Also the Following Articles

Catecholamines; Corticosteroids and Stress; HPA Axis

Bibliography

Ahima, R., Krozowski, Z., and Harlan, R. (1991). Type I corticosteroid receptor-like immunoreactivity in the rat CNS: Distribution and regulation by corticosteroids. *J. Comp. Neurol.* **313**, 522–538.

Arriza, J. L., Weinberger, C., Cerelli, G., Glaser, T. M., Handelin, B. L., Housmann, D. E., and Evans, R. M. (1987). Cloning of human mineralocorticoid receptor cDNA: Structural and functional kinship with the glucocorticoid receptor. *Science* **237**, 268–275.

Chandler, V. L., Maler, B. A., and Yamamoto, K. R. (1983). DNA sequences bound specifically by glucocorticoid receptor in vitro render a heterologous promoter hormone responsive in vivo. *Cell* **33**, 489–499.

Cole, T. J., Blendy, J. A., Monaghan, A. P., Krieglstein, K., Schmid, W., Aguzzi, A., Fantuzzi, G., Hummler, E., Unsicker, K., and Schütz, G. (1995). Targeted disruption of the glucocorticoid receptor gene blocks adrenergic chromaffin cell development and severely retards lung maturation. *Genes. Dev.* **9**, 1608–1621.

De Kloet, E. R., Vreugdenhil, E., Oitzl, M. S., and Joëls, M. (1998). Brain corticosteroid receptor balance in health and disease. *Endocr. Rev.* **19**, 269–301.

De Kloet, E. R., Wallach, G., and McEwen, B. S. (1975). Differences in corticosterone and dexamethasone binding to rat brain and pituitary. *Endocrinology* **96**, 598–609.

Edwards, C. R. W., Stewart, P. M., Burt, D., Brett, L., McIntyre, M. A., Sutanto, W., De Kloet, E. R., and Monder, C. (1988). Localization of 11β-hydroxysteroid dehydrogenase: Tissue specific protector of the mineralocorticoid receptor. *Lancet* **2**, 986–989.

Funder, J. W., Pearce, P. T., Smith, R., and Smith, A. I. (1988). Mineralocorticoid action: Target tissue specificity is enzyme, not receptor, mediated. *Science* **242**, 583–586.

Fuxe, K., Wikström, A. C., Okret, S., Agnati, L. F., Härfstrand, A., Yu, Z. Y., Granholm, L., Zoli, M., Vale, W., and Gustafsson, J. Å. (1985). Mapping of the glucocorticoid receptor immunoreactive neurons in the rat tel- and diencephalon using a monoclonal antibody against rat liver glucocorticoid receptors. *Endocrinology* **117**, 1803–1812.

Heck, S., Kullmann, M., Gast, A., Ponta, H., Rahmsdorf, H. J., Herrlich, P., and Cato, A. C. B. (1994). A distinct modulating domain in glucocorticoid receptor monomers in the repression of activity of the transcription factor AP-1. *EMBO J.* **13**, 4087–4095.

Herman, J. P., and Cullinan, W. E. (1997). Neurocircuitry of stress: Central control of the hypothalamo-pituitary-adrenocortical axis. *Trends. Neurosci.* **20**, 78–84.

Hollenberg, S. M., Weinberger, C., Ong, E. S., Cerelli, G., Oro, A., Lebo, R., Thompson, E. B., Rosenfeld, M. G., and Evans, R. M. (1985). Primary structure and expression of a functional glucocorticoid receptor cDNA. *Nature* **318**, 635–641.

Joëls, M., and De Kloet, E. R. (1992). Control of neuronal excitability by corticosteroid hormones. *TINS* **15**, 25–30.

Jonat, C., Rahmsdorf, H. J., Park, K. K., Cato, A. C. B., Gebel, S., Ponta, H., and Herrlich, P. (1990). Antitumor promotion and antiinflammation: Down-modulation of AP-1 (fos/jun) activity by glucocorticoid hormone. *Cell* **62**, 1189–1204.

Krozowski, Z. S., and Funder, J. W. (1983). Renal mineralocorticoid receptors and hippocampal corticosterone-binding species have identical intrinsic steroid specificity. *Proc. Natl. Acad. Sci. USA* **80**, 6056–6060.

Liu, W., Wang, J., Sauter, N. K., and Pearce, D. (1995). Steroid receptor heterodimerization demonstrated in vitro and in vivo. *Proc. Natl. Acad. Sci. USA* **92**, 12480–12484.

McEwen, B. S. (1999). Stress and hippocampal plasticity. *Annu. Rev. Neurosci.* **22**, 105-122.

McEwen, B. S., Weiss, J. M., and Schwartz, L. S. (1968). Selective retention of corticosterone by limbic structures in rat brain. *Nature* **220**, 911–912.

Moguilewsky, M., and Raynaud, J. P. (1980). Evidence for a specific mineralocorticoid receptor in rat pituitary and brain. *J. Steroid. Biochem.* **12**, 309–314.

Pearce, D., and Yamamoto, K. R. (1993). Mineralocorticoid and glucocorticoid receptor activities distinguished by non-receptor factors at a composite response element. *Science* **259**, (1993) 1161–1165.

Reichardt, H. M., Kaestner, K. H., Tuckermann, J., Kretz, O., Wessely, O., Bock, R., Gass, P., Schmid, W., Herrlich, P., Angel, P., and Schütz, G. (1998). DNA binding of the glucocorticoid receptor is not essential for survival. *Cell* **93**, 531–541.

Reul, J. M. H. M., and De Kloet, E. R. (1985). Two receptor systems for corticosterone in rat brain: Microdistribution and differential occupation. *Endocrinology* **117**, 2505–2511.

Schinkel, A. H., Wagenaar, E., Van Deemter, L., Mol, C. A. A. M., and Borst, P. (1996). Absence of the mdr1a P-Glycoprotein in mice affects tissue distribution and pharmacokinetics of dexamethasone, digoxin, and cyclosporin A. *J. Clin. Invest.* **96**, 1698–1705.

Trapp, T., and Holsboer, F. (1996). Heterodimerization between mineralocorticoid and glucocorticoid receptors increases the functional diversity of corticosteroid action. *Trends. Pharmacol.* **17**, 145–149.

Van Steensel, B., Van Binnendijk, E. P., Hornsby, C. D., Van der Voort, H. T. M., Krozowski, Z. S., De Kloet, E. R., and Van Driel, R. (1996). Partial colocalization of glucocorticoid and mineralocorticoid receptors in compartments in nuclei of rat hippocampal neurons. *J. Cell Sci.* **109**, 787–792.

Veldhuis, H. D., Van Koppen, C., Van Ittersum, M., and De Kloet, E. R. (1982). Specificity of adrenal steroid receptor system in the rat hippocampus. *Endocrinology* **110**, 2044–2051.

Corticosteroids and Stress

Allan Munck

Dartmouth Medical School

GLOSSARY

cytokines Peptide hormones, produced particularly by activated cells of the immune system but by other cells as well, that transmit signals between cells and organs via specific cell membrane receptors.

glucocorticoid receptor (*GR*) Protein molecule with a relatively low-affinity specific binding site for glucocorticoids, present in the cytoplasm and nucleus of almost all nucleated cells, where it regulates expression of particular genes when activated by binding of a glucocorticoid. Glucocorticoid receptors are members of the "nuclear receptor" family.

glucocorticoids (*GCs*) Cortisol and corticosterone, the steroid "stress hormones" produced by the adrenal cortex under control of adrenocorticotropic hormone (ACTH) that act on almost all nucleated cells in the body. The term is also used for synthetic analogs like dexamethasone.

11β-hydroxysteroid dehydrogenase type 2 (*11β-HSD2*) Enzyme in mineralocorticoid target cells (e.g., kidney and some brain cells) that inactivates GCs, thus allowing access to MRs by aldosterone. May also regulate GC concentrations in some GC target cells.

hypothalamic-pituitary-adrenal (*HPA*) *axis* Physiological link between the central nervous system and adrenocortical production of GCs. In response to signals including stress and negative feedback from GCs, the hypothalamus pro-duces the peptides, corticotrophic releasing hormone (CRH), and vasopressin (VP) that regulate pituitary output of the adrenocorticotropic hormone. Adrenocorticotropic hormone, also a peptide, in turn controls synthesis and secretion of GCs from the adrenal cortex.

mineralocorticoid Aldosterone, the steroid hormone produced in the adrenal cortex under control of angiotensin II that stimulates mainly cells in the kidney to reabsorb sodium and water. The term is also used for the much weaker natural steroid deoxycorticosterone and for synthetic analogs.

mineralocorticoid receptor (*MR*) Protein molecule with a high-affinity specific binding site for mineralocorticoids and glucocorticoids, present in the cytoplasm and nucleus of kidney, brain, and some other cells where it regulates expression of particular genes when activated by binding of either a mineralocorticoid or a glucocorticoid. Mineralocorticoid receptors are members of the "nuclear receptor" family.

I. GLUCOCORTICOIDS, MINERALOCORTICOIDS, AND STRESS

Although Thomas Addison's discovery of the essential role of the adrenal gland for survival dates back to the mid-19th century, not until the 1930s did Hans Selye promulgate the physiological concept of "stress" and implicate hormones of the adrenal cortex in protecting the organism against stress. By then Walter Cannon had established the role of the adrenal medulla and the sympathetic system in so-called "fight-or-flight" responses, but the adrenal medulla, in contrast to the cortex, is not essential for life. An intimate relation between the adrenal cortex and stress became evident from observations that stress from all kinds of challenges to homeostasis—

cold, infection, inflammation, trauma, hypoglycemia, psychological shock, emotional distress, pain, heavy exercise, hemorrhage, and others—stimulates secretion of adrenocortical hormones and causes hyperplasia of the adrenal cortex. Furthermore, addisonian patients, adrenalectomized animals, and other adrenally insufficient organisms were the least capable of resisting the sometimes fatal onslaught of stress, and administration of adrenocortical extracts protected against stress.

At first the adrenal cortex was thought to regulate a multitude of effects on metabolism and salt and water balance, along with stress, through a single hormone. Eventually two principal steroid hormones were identified, the glucocorticoids (GCs) and the mineralocorticoids. Each was found to be essential for survival, the mineralocorticoids by controlling electrolyte balance, mainly via actions on the kidney, and the GCs by protecting against stress, through mechanisms that were to remain obscure for decades. The purpose of this article is to discuss from a modern perspective the mechanisms by which GCs protect against stress.

II. BASAL AND STRESS-INDUCED GLUCOCORTICOID LEVELS: FUNCTIONS IN STRESS?

As shown schematically in Fig. 1, basal levels of cortisol in humans and primates (and of corticoste-

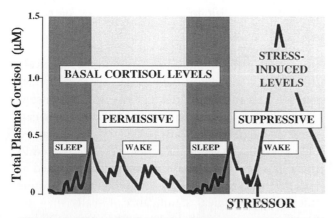

FIGURE 1 Schematic depiction of diurnal variation of basal cortisol levels in humans and a stress-induced surge. "Permissive" and "suppressive" refer to the roles proposed for each of these glucocorticoid regimens in protecting against stress.

rone in rats and mice) vary in a characteristic circadian pattern, rising during sleep to a maximum at the start of the waking period and then subsiding during the active period. Superimposed on this periodicity are erratic spikes in cortisol levels caused by brief episodes of secretion. Stress at any time causes a rapid increase in GC secretion to give peak GC levels that may be several times higher than those attained under basal conditions.

The questions that are discussed here are: What role do basal GC levels play in protecting the organism against stress? Is there some significance to the pattern of circadian variation? What role do stress-induced GC levels play? Anticipating the conclusions, tentative answers to these questions, already intimated in Fig. 1, are briefly as follows. Basal levels of GCs exert mainly permissive actions that prepare or "prime" some of the organism's homeostatic defense mechanisms for action, reaching a peak of preparedness as the diurnal activities begin. Stress-induced levels, which for many years were assumed by physiologists to enhance stress-activated defense mechanisms, in fact probably function to suppress such defense mechanisms in order to prevent them from overshooting and damaging the organism. In order to deal with the questions posed it is necessary first to survey some of the basic mechanisms and physiological consequences of GC actions.

III. CORTICOSTEROID RECEPTORS

Intracellular receptors for GCs and mineralocorticoids, GRs and MRs respectively, were identified during the 1960s and cloned in the 1980s. Glucocorticoid receptors were first characterized by their presence in GC target cells and their ability to specifically bind radioactively labeled cortisol and related GCs. MRs were characterized in mineralocorticoid target tissues by their ability to bind aldosterone. Cortisol and corticosterone, the natural GCs, bind to GRs with dissociation constants in the range of normal GC concentrations in blood. Similarly, aldosterone binds to MRs with a dissociation constant in the range of normal aldosterone concentrations in blood, 100–1000 times lower than GC concentrations.

In the late 1980s it was discovered that cortisol and corticosterone bind to MRs with almost the same dissociation constant as aldosterone (i.e., with much higher affinity than to GRs). The paradox of how aldosterone in the intact organism can bind to MRs in the face of overwhelming concentrations of GCs was eventually resolved with the identification in mineralocorticoid target cells of the enzyme 11β-hydroxysteroid dehydrogenase type 2 (11β-HSD2), which "protects" the MRs by rapidly inactivating GCs so that in those target cells only aldosterone has access to MRs. Mineralocorticoid receptors that are unprotected, however, can respond to GCs at concentrations much lower than those required to activate GRs.

The role of MRs as mediators of GC actions has so far been studied most extensively in the central nervous system. Both GRs and MRs are found in the brain and spinal cord, MRs being particularly abundant in the dentate gyrus and pyramidal cells of the hippocampus as well as other regions of the limbic system. There appears to be no 11β-HSD2 in the hippocampus, so hippocampal MRs are bound and activated mainly by GCs. Only MRs in the anterior hypothalamus and circumventricular organs are protected by 11β-HSD2 and are therefore controlled by aldosterone. Glucocorticoid receptors are more widely dispersed in the central nervous system than MRs and are present in both neurons and glial cells.

Glucocorticoid receptors and MRs, when activated by hormone binding, initiate hormone actions by translocating to the nucleus and activating or repressing particular genes in each cell. Most GC and mineralocorticoid actions are thought to be produced through such "genomic" mechanisms, which are relatively slow, usually taking hours to become manifest. There is mounting evidence, however, that certain rapid effects of these and other steroid hormones may be mediated by nongenomic effects transmitted through membrane receptors.

IV. PERMISSIVE AND SUPPRESSIVE GLUCOCORTICOID ACTIONS

In the 1950s Dwight Ingle found that adrenalectomized animals can respond normally to moderate stress if administered GCs at basal levels and concluded that although stress-induced levels are required to protect against severe stress, they may not be necessary for moderate stress. He proposed that basal GC levels have "permissive" effects that are necessary for some homeostatic functions to respond to stress, distinguishing those effects from the regulatory effects of high GC levels espoused by Selye. Selye had introduced a unified theory of stress and had proposed the controversial hypothesis that by increasing levels of adrenocortical hormones stress causes "diseases of adaptation," among them rheumatoid arthritis and allergy.

Permissive actions of GCs on a variety of defense mechanisms have since been found. Their common though not invariable characteristics are that they enhance actions of mediators of stress-induced responses, including those of catecholamines and other hormones, and that they are produced by basal levels of GCs. Permissive actions would thus occur during the unstressed periods indicated in Fig. 1 and can be regarded as preparing for or anticipating a stressful episode. They can account for the substantially improved resistance to moderate stress of organisms lacking adrenocortical function, including addisonian patients, when given maintenance levels of GCs. Among several mechanisms for permissive actions, one that will be discussed later is the induction by GCs of receptors for mediators of stress responses. Some other ways GCs are known to increase sensitivity of signaling pathways are by strengthening coupling of a receptor to G proteins or by increasing cAMP synthesis.

Suppressive actions of GCs are better known than permissive actions and have been more extensively investigated because of their close link to the widespread clinical applications of GCs as immunosuppressants, anti-inflammatory agents, and for treatment of lymphoproliferative diseases. As explained below, for many years after they were discovered in the 1940s, the suppressive actions were regarded as pharmacological effects of great therapeutic value but no physiological significance. Usually they are manifested at relatively high, stress induced GC levels. They are exerted through many mechanisms, but one that is fairly general is by suppression of mediators of stress-responses.

V. CARBOHYDRATE METABOLISM

The early observations that GCs raise and maintain blood glucose gave the hormones their name. They also stimulated hepatic glycogen deposition. Long, Katzin, and Fry, in a classic 1940 paper, showed that GCs stimulate gluconeogenesis from amino acids derived from protein catabolism and decrease glucose oxidation. Ingle later found that GCs decrease glucose utilization and cause insulin resistance. Much work since that time has elucidated some of the molecular mechanisms of these and other actions. In the case of glucoconeogenesis there is increased activity of phosphoenolpyruvate carboxykinase and other rate-limiting enzymes. Inhibition of glucose transport and insulin resistance are due to decreased translocation of glucose transporters to the cell membrane and decreased synthesis of insulin receptor substrate-1 (IRS-1). Liver glycogen is increased partly in response to activation of glycogen synthase. Among ideas advanced to explain how GCs protect against stress was that of Selye, who suggested that GCs provide for an increased demand for glucose. This idea did not survive experimental tests, which showed that glucose alone cannot substitute for GCs.

Glucocorticoids are permissive for gluconeogenesis and glycogenolysis stimulated by catecholamines and glucagon. These reactions are components of responses to the stress of a fight-or-flight situation as well as to insulin-induced hypoglycemia. Glucocorticoid stimulation of glycogen synthesis can be regarded as preparing the organism for a future stressful episode.

How GC actions on carbohydrate metabolism protect the organism may be viewed in two distinct ways. The ethological view, which considers how evolutionary pressures have molded GC actions for survival of, for example, a confrontation between predator and prey, emphasizes the permissive role of GCs in acutely raising blood glucose to fuel muscular activity. The metabolic view, on the other hand, sees GCs, through their anti-insulin and permissive actions, as protecting the organism from insulin-induced hypoglycemia, such as can occur after a meal. Glucocorticoids share this role with other so-called counterregulatory hormones, catecholamines, and glucagon.

VI. CARDIOVASCULAR ACTIONS

It has long been known that addisonian patients, adrenalectomized animals, and other organisms deficient in GCs or GC activity are relatively insensitive to the actions of vasoactive agents like norepinephrine, vasopressin, and angiotensin II. Glucocorticoids at basal levels permissively enhance that sensitivity in both vascular and cardiac tissues. These actions may be due partly to enhancement of α1B- and β_2-catecholamine receptors and angiotensin II type 1 receptors in smooth muscle cells as well as to increased sensitivity of receptor-G protein coupling and adenylyl cyclase. Glucocorticoids also increase cardiac output, which may be related to induction in cardiocytes of Na,K-ATPase.

Although there is evidence that GCs suppress catecholamine release, which would counter the permissive actions, permissive enhancement clearly predominates in the cardiovascular stress response.

VII. ELECTROLYTE AND FLUID VOLUME BALANCE

Glucocorticoid deficiency is associated with decreased ability to excrete water, which at one time was used as a test for GC insufficiency. It appears to be due to a decreased rate in glomerular filtration and to increased synthesis of vasopressin (VP), both of which are reversed by administered GCs. Underlying mechanisms are not known, but may be related to increased synthesis and secretion of atrial natriuretic factor (ANF) and increased levels of ANF receptors on endothelial cells. Inhibition of VP synthesis is part of the negative feedback mechanism by which GCs regulate their own concentration and appears to be due to decreased synthesis of VP.

Some of these actions are central to the role of glucocorticoids in stress. In rats the stress of hemorrhage has been found to elicit a powerful vasoconstrictor response from VP, catecholamines, and renin. Without GCs the VP response can overshoot, leading to ischemia and death in adrenalectomized animals. Stress-induced GCs protect the organism by limiting the increase in VP levels and hence the ischemia.

VIII. ANTI-INFLAMMATORY AND IMMUNOSUPPRESSIVE ACTIONS

High levels of GCs suppress many functions. The inflammatory and immune systems are among those in which suppressive actions are most pronounced. Thymus enlargement in the absence of the adrenal cortex was recognized before the turn of the century. Selye showed that stress causes thymus atrophy, a GC action now known to be due to induction of programmed cell death or apoptosis in lymphocytes.

The anti-inflammatory actions of GCs, which account for most of the clinical applications of these hormones, were reported in 1949 by Hench, Kendall, Slocumb, and Polley, who found that treatment with GCs dramatically improved the symptoms of patients with rheumatoid arthritis. These observations had two unexpected consequences. One was that they contradicted Selye's hypothesis of diseases of adaptation, which rapidly lost support. The other was that GC physiologists were unable to reconcile the finding that GCs suppressed a defense mechanism, in this case inflammation, with their long-standing belief that stress-induced GC levels helped resist stress by enhancing activity of defense mechanisms. Despite an alternative view proposed by Marius Tausk in a 1951 review that unfortunately had very limited circulation, physiologists categorized the anti-inflammatory actions as pharmacological consequences of high, unphysiological levels of GCs. The closely related immunosuppressive actions suffered the same fate. As a result, the spectacular development of new applications and synthetic analogs for GCs, the miracle drugs of the 1950s, proceeded with little or no involvement by GC physiologists. The view advanced in germinal form by Marius Tausk in the context of GC therapy was revived independently in 1984 in the context of GC physiology. It held that anti-inflammatory and immunosuppressive actions of GCs, far from being pharmacological, are prototypes for the physiological role of stress-induced GCs in stress. That role is to prevent stress-induced defense reactions from overshooting and harming the organism.

A great deal of evidence now supports the view that anti-inflammatory and immunosuppressive actions are physiological, and are exerted by endogenous GCs. For example, in rats adrenalectomy or administration of the glucocorticoid antagonist RU486 increase inflammatory responses, showing that endogenous GCs can control inflammation. Autoimmune reactions are also under control of endogenous GCs. Striking experiments have shown that Lewis rats, which are extremely sensitive to arthritis after injection with streptococcal cell wall polysaccharide (SCW) and to experimental allergic encephalomyelitis (EAE) after injection with myelin basic protein, have a defect in biosynthesis of corticotropin releasing hormone (CRH, the hypothalamic hormone that along with VP stimulates ACTH release from the pituitary). That defect reduces the ACTH, and hence the GC, response to an antigenic challenge. As expected, treatment with GCs protects Lewis rats from SCW.

Glucocorticoids may also influence immune responses through permissive actions. For example, mitogenic responses of rat peripheral or splenic T cells in culture are reduced if the rats have been adrenalectomized. The responses can be restored by treating the rats with low physiological doses of corticosterone, as well as by brief exposure of the cells to low concentrations of corticosterone or aldosterone. These observations led to the suggestion that the permissive effects in this case were mediated by MRs and possibly involved induction of IL-2 (interleukin-2) receptors. The acute phase response is a case in which GCs both potentiate induction of acute phase proteins by cytokines like IL-1 and IL-6 and suppress production of the cytokines.

Permissive actions of GCs at stress-induced levels appear to have been revealed by experiments in which normal humans were given endotoxin to stimulate increases in plasma TNFα (tumor necrosis factor-α) and IL-6. Cortisol was infused at rates that gave stress-induced levels at various times before or after the endotoxin. When given within 6 h of endotoxin, cortisol suppressed the cytokine response. But when given 12, 32, 72, or 144 h before endotoxin, cortisol markedly enhanced the response.

IX. ACTIONS ON THE CENTRAL NERVOUS SYSTEM

Electrophysiological experiments have been conducted with hippocampal tissue isolated from adrenalectomized rats and treated with GCs at various concentrations. Low concentrations of corticosterone, which mainly activate MRs, were found to decrease afterhyperpolarization of neuronal membranes and enhance neuronal excitability, whereas high concentrations of corticosterone or specific glucocorticoid agonists that activate GRs but not MRs suppressed excitability. Thus GCs at low concentrations, corresponding to basal levels, permissively maintain neuronal excitability via MRs, whereas GCs at high concentrations, corresponding to stress-induced levels, suppress stimulated neuronal activity via GRs.

X. EFFECTS VIA CYTOKINES AND OTHER MEDIATORS

As already indicated, suppressive actions of GCs are in many cases mediated by inhibition of production or activity of cytokines, the "hormones of the immune system," as well as of other mediators. Mediators like the cytokines constitute a communications network between cells of defense mechanisms that respond to stress-induced challenges. Stress-induced mediators known to be suppressed by GCs are listed in Table I under various categories. Neurotransmitters like the catecholamines, for example, respond to sudden "fight or flight" challenges; inflammatory

agents respond to tissue damage; cytokines and chemokines respond to infection and inflammation; and so on. Mediators are essential for propagating stress responses. By blocking them GCs can dampen the stress responses, preventing them from overshooting and damaging the organism. At the same time GCs also protect the organism from toxic effects that most of these mediators produce when in excess.

Many well-known GC effects on cell traffic may be initiated through inhibition of chemokines (also known as chemotactic cytokines), which regulate traffic and homing of leukocytes by binding to cell-surface receptors and are actively secreted during inflammation. Some mediators are suppressed by GCs under some conditions and stimulated under others. They are marked in Table I with ($\pm$). Other mediators, like transforming growth factor β (TGF-β), may only be stimulated. There are mediators, like macrophage colony stimulating factor (M-CSF), that appear not to be affected by GCs at all.

The asterisks in Table I mark several mediators that have receptors that are induced by GCs. The possibility that induction of mediator receptors accounts for some permissive actions has already been noted. Some cytokines, like IL-1 and IL-6, not only communicate between cells of the immune and inflammatory systems but also, as first proposed by Besedovsky and Sorkin, may signal the HPA system that the immune system is activated, thereby constituting a negative feedback loop through which GCs are summoned to control activated immune reactions.

TABLE I

Mediators Suppressed by Glucocorticoids and Mediator Receptors Induced by Glucocorticoids

Cytokines	Chemokines	Inflammatory agents	Hormones and neurotransmitters
IL-1*	LIX	Eicosanoids	CRH*
IL-2*	MCP-1	Bradykinin	VP*
IFN-γ*	RANTES	5-HT*	Oxytocin
TNF-α	MIP-1α	Histamine	ACTH
GM-CSF*	CINC/gro	Collagenase	β-endorphin
IL-3		Elastase	LH
IL-4*($\pm$)		Plasminogen	Insulin*
IL-5		activator	Norepinephrine*
IL-6*			Epinephrine ($\pm$)
IL-10($\pm$)			Nitric oxide
IL-12			Substance P

* Receptors induced by glucocorticoids.

XI. UNIFIED VIEW OF THE PROTECTIVE ROLES OF GLUCOCORTICOIDS IN STRESS

As described above, on the cardiovascular system GCs exert actions that are predominantly permissive, on others, like inflammation, the actions are mainly suppressive, and on some, like the neural and immune systems, they may be both. How are these opposing influences reconciled when both are present, with one enhancing and the other suppressing the defense response? The question can be analyzed with a simple but not wholly unrealistic model in which suppressive actions are assumed to be due to reduction in concentration of a mediator and permissive actions to induction of the mediator's receptors.

Figure 2 illustrates such an analysis. A lymphokine receptor, R, is permissively induced by cortisol over a concentration range corresponding roughly to that in Fig. 1 (keeping in mind that at low cortisol concentrations less than 10% of total cortisol is free), following a dose–response curve chosen to parallel binding of cortisol to GRs. The lymphokine, L, is suppressed according to an identical dose–response curve of opposite sign. Through these actions cortisol regulates the concentration of the lymphokine–receptor complex, LR, as determined by the equations in the inset. The bell-shaped curve for LR and LR activity is then a composite dose–response curve that represents schematically the outcome of the dual permissive and suppressive GC actions on the hypothetical defense mechanism that the lymphokine regulates (the simple curves for R and L represent, respectively, the outcome for defense mechanisms subject to pure

permissive and suppressive actions). This model assumes that both permissive and suppressive actions are mediated by GRs. If permissive actions were mediated by MRs, the dose–response curve for induction of R and the ascending limb of the bell-shaped curve would be shifted to the left, as would the peak of the bell-shaped curve. Qualitatively similar conclusions would apply, however.

It should be evident that any permissive and suppressive actions with roughly comparable dose–response curves, whether transmitted via a lymphokine or other mechanism, will yield a somewhat similar bell-shaped curve. The curve corresponds well with the physiological roles of glucocorticoids we have sketched earlier. Basal GC concentrations fluctuate during normal diurnal variation from the left end of the cortisol scale to about where the bell-shaped curve peaks and can be viewed as permissively "priming" some of the organism's defense mechanisms in preparation for a period of activity. Suppressive actions are present at all cortisol concentrations, but predominate only at high, stress-induced levels toward the right end of the cortisol scale, where they are required to prevent defense mechanisms from overshooting. In the absence of GCs, depending on the nature of the stressor an organism may succumb to stress either because its defense mechanisms are not adequately primed (perhaps what happens in addisonian crisis if the cardiovascular system cannot respond) or because the defense mechanisms overshoot (as occurred in the examples cited earlier after hemorrhage or an inflammatory challenge).

Thus, in summary, GCs can be thought of as protecting the organism from stress through two separate but related mechanisms. On the one hand they are essential before a stressful episode to permissively prime certain defense mechanisms, a task generally accomplished by basal GC levels. On the other, they are essential after a stressful episode to prevent some defense mechanisms from overshooting, a task generally requiring stress-induced GC levels.

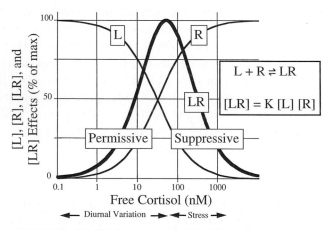

FIGURE 2 Model of a cortisol-regulated lymphokine system. Cortisol is assumed to permissively increase the concentration of lymphokine receptors R and to suppress the concentration of the lymphokine L, according to dose–response curves that correspond to binding of cortisol to GRs with a dissociation constant of 30 n*M*. The concentration and activity of the lymphokine–receptor complex LR is determined by the equations in the inset, yielding the bell-shaped curve with a rising permissive branch at basal cortisol concentrations and a falling suppressive branch at stress-induced concentrations. Brackets denote concentrations. Below the cortisol concentration scale are indicated roughly the ranges covered during basal diurnal variation and stress. See text for further details.

See Also the Following Article

GLUCOCORTICOIDS, OVERVIEW

Bibliography

Besedovsky, H. O., and del Rey, A. (1996). Immuno-neuro-endocrine interactions: Facts and hypotheses. *Endocr. Rev.* 17, 64–102.

De Kloet, E. R., Vreugdenhil, E., Oitzl, M. S., and Joëls, M. (1998). Brain corticosteroid receptor balance in health and disease. *Endocr. Rev.* 19, 269–301.

Ingle, D. J. (1954). Permissibility of hormone action: A review. *Acta Endocrinol.* 17, 172–186.

Munck, A., Guyre, P. M., and Holbrook, N. J. (1984). Physiological functions of glucocorticoids in stress and their relation to pharmacological actions. *Endocr. Rev.* 5, 25–44.

Munck, A., and Náray-Fejes-Tóth, A. (1994). Glucocorticoids and stress: Permissive and suppressive actions. *Ann. N. Y. Acad. Sci.* 746, 115–130.

Selye, H. (1946). The general adaptation syndrome and the diseases of adaptation. *J. Clin. Endocrinol. Metab.* 6, 117–230.

Sternberg, E. M., Young, S. W., III, Bernardini. R., Calogero, A. E., Chrousos, G. P., Gold, P. W., and Wilder, R. L. (1989). A central nervous system defect in biosynthesis of corticotropin-releasing hormone is associated with susceptibility to streptococcal cell wall-induced arthritis in Lewis rats. *Proc. Natl. Acad. Sci. USA* 86, 4771–4775.

Tausk, M. (1951). Hat die Nebenniere tatsächlich eine Verteidigungsfunktion? *Das Hormon (Organon, Holland)* 3, 1–24.

Wiegers, G. J., Labeur, M. S., Stec, I. E. M., Klinkert, W. E. F., Holsboer. F., and Reul, J. M. H. M. Glucocorticoids accelerate anti-T cell receptor-induced T cell growth. *J. Immunol.* 155, 1893–1902.

Corticosterone

see Corticosteroids and Stress

Corticotropin

see Adrenocorticotropic Hormone

Corticotropin Releasing Factor (CRF)

Alan Teik Lim

Mental Health Research Institute of Victoria, Australia

GLOSSARY

adenylyl cyclase–cyclic AMP system An important component of a common signal transduction system that generates cAMP from ATP following the activation of the membrane-bound enzymes adenylyl cyclases. The latter is triggered by subunits of G-proteins that are activated by receptors belonging to the superfamily of seven membrane-spanning receptors. The augmented level of intracellular cAMP in turn activates protein kinase A that phosphorylates proteins to accomplish important cell functions.

G proteins A superfamily of proteins that acts as intermediates between seven membrane-spanning receptors and membrane bound enzymes to generate biochemical signals. Following activation by the receptors, the subunits of G proteins augment or suppress the activity of adenylyl cyclases, phosphlipase C, and ion channels through direct bindings to these proteins to modulate their functions.

hypophysiotropic hormones Small proteins or peptides produced in cell bodies of hypothalamic neurons and transported along axons to the external layer of median eminence. The peptides are considered neurohormones as they are released into portal blood to modulate the functions of various types of pituitary cells. These neurohormones include corticotropin releasing factor, growth hormone releasing hormone, luteinizing hormone releasing hormone, thyrotropin releasing hormone, somatostatin, and others.

in situ hybridization A method commonly used to identify sites of protein or peptide productions at cellular level by demonstrating the presence of corresponding mRNA signals. Specific mRNA signals on fixed tissue sections or cultured cells are detected by crossbinding with short sequence of radioactive or labeled nucleotides complimentary to the equivalent part on the mRNA of interest.

portal blood The pool of blood that flows from the median eminence of the hypothalamus toward the pituitary gland. It carries hypophysiotropic neurohormones released from the median eminence to act upon respective receptors in various cell types of the anterior pituitary.

radioimmunoassay A sensitive technique particularly useful for measuring small quantities of peptides in the concentration of picograms. It is performed by first raising antibodies against peptides or antigens of interest. Displacement of the bound radioactive antigens or peptides from the antibodies by standard amounts of unlabeled antigens or synthetic peptides are established. By comparison to the standard displacement chart, the unknown quantity of the peptide is estimated by calculating the extent of its displacement of the labeled peptide from the antibodies.

The term corticotropin releasing factor (CRF) was first coined about 40 years ago to describe a hypothalamic derivative that explicitly induces the release of pituitary adrenocorticotropin hormone (ACTH). In 1981, the 41-amino-acid sequence of CRF was characterized by Vale and his colleagues at The Salk Institute. The neuropeptide has satisfied all the requirements as a hypophysiotropic hormone that specifically activates pituitary corticotrophs to augment the production of proopiomelanocortin (POMC), the precursor of ACTH, and the release of ACTH.

I. STRUCTURE AND GENE

Corticotropin Releasing Factor (CRF: Human, Rat) Ser - Glu - Glu - Pro - Pro - Ile - Ser - Leu - Asp - Leu - Thr - Phe - His - Leu - Leu - Arg - Glu - Val - Leu - Glu - Met - Ala - Arg - Ala - Glu - Gln - Leu - Ala - Gln - Gln - Ala - His - Ser - Asn - Arg - Lys - Leu - Met - Glu - Ile - Ile - NH$_2$ [M.W. 4758.1]

The sequence of CRF is highly preserved across species. In the case of human and rats, they are identical and share greater than 90% homology when compared to that of monkey and sheep. The carboxyl terminus of CRF-41 is critical for biological activity and the minimal sequence that retains full CRF activity in the rat species is 15-41. The shorter peptide has a much higher ED50 than CRF-41 because of its lower affinity to the receptors. Whereas C-terminal truncated peptide CRF9-41 in α-helix conformation acts as an antagonist to type I CRF receptors, human CRF6-33 and CRF9-33 do not possess biological activities but bind strongly to CRF-binding proteins. The amino acid sequence of CRF shares structure similarity in greater than 40% to that of urocortin, amphibian sauvagine, and fish urotensin I, all of which are biologically active in releasing ACTH from pituitary corticotrophs.

The human and rat CRF genes share great similarity, as they both contain two exons separated by an intervening sequence. The first exon contains approximately 10 bp of the 5'-untranslated region of the mRNA. Exon II contains 15 bp of the 5' untranslated region of the mRNA, the protein coding region, and the complete 3'-untranslated region of the mRNA. The two genes are very homologous, suggesting that it has been highly conserved through evolution. The DNA sequence encoding the CRF protein shows 94% homology and the homology decreases to 80% for the rest of the CRH precursor. Similarly, greater than 90% homology between the human and rat is also found in 5'-flanking DNA sequences representing DNA regulatory elements for CRF gene regulation. In this region, there are consensus sequences putative for interactions with transcription proteins mediating the biochemical effects of glucocorticoids and derivatives from protein kinase A and protein kinase C activities.

II. SITES OF PRODUCTION AND PATHWAYS

In the brain, CRF is produced predominantly in the parvocellular subdivision of paraventricular nuclei (PVN) of the hypothalamus. These CRF-producing cells are hypophsiotrophic and involved in the regulation of pituitary corticotrophs, as approximately 90% of the cells send their axons to the external layer of the median eminence (ME). From this pathway, CRF-41 is released into the portal blood to act on pituitary corticotorphs. Another CRF-41 pathway reaches the ME from magnocellular neurons of the PVN and the supraoptic and the accessory magnocellular nuclei of the hypothalamus. This pathway contains low levels of CRF-41, perhaps 10% of the amount found in the parvocellular pathway and the neuropeptide comes predominantly from oxytocinergic magnocellular neurons and the neurites project mainly to the neural lobe of the pituitary.

A substantial proportion of CRF-producing neurons in the PVN are capable of expressing vasopressin (AVP). Prominent expression of the AVP mRNA signal, as determined by *in situ* hybridization or of AVP peptides by immunohistochemistry, has been demonstrated in CRF neurons after the removal of circulating glucocorticoids by adrenalectomy. In adrenalectomized rats, there is a concurrent increase in the production of the two neurohormones in CRF neurons and in their release into portal blood as confirmed by radioimmunoassay. Corticotropin releasing factor and vasopressin act synergistically and induce a marked augmentation of pituitary POMC synthesis and ACTH release from pituitary corticotrophs. Although the physiological significance of this biological process remains unclear, it may act as a safety measure to enable pituitary ACTH to rapidly increase circulating glucocorticoids when the adrenal steroids reach a low level.

Corticotropin releasing factor-containing neurons are also present in hippocampus, amydala, and in cortex. Whereas CRF axons from these sites do not project to the median eminence, they show synaptic formations in regions that are rich in CRF type I receptors and may involve in modulating anxiety, cognition, and memory. This is in contrast to the distribution of CRF type II receptors as the latter correlates better with that of the axonal terminals of urocortin-producing neurons. Unlike CRF, hypothalamic or central urocortin neurons do not take part in the regulation of pituitary corticotrophs.

Corticotropin releasing factor-41 and its receptors are also found in cells intrinsic to spinal cord, peripheral lymphoid organs, gonads, placental endometrium, and adrenal glands. In these tissues, the peptides are likely to play a paracrine role by modulating the functions of adjacent cells or blood vessels in the same tissues. In some of these organs, CRF is known to induce vascular relaxation and involves in inflammatory responses. It is of interest to note that, whereas the CRF mRNA species of the rat hypothalamus is approximately 1400 bases, those found in the adrenal and gonads of the same species are larger by approximately 200 and 500 bases. These additional lengths of basepairs are found mainly at the nontranslated sites of the mRNA.

III. BIOCHEMICAL ACTIONS AND PHYSIOLOGICAL FUNCTIONS

Hypothalamic CRF is the principle hypophysiotropic activator of pituitary corticotrophs for the release of ACTH. Circulating ACTH in turn augments the synthesis and the release of corticosteroids from adrenal glands. Besides exerting biochemical actions on the brain and peripheral tissues involved in stress response, one of the important roles of corticosteroids is to produce a negative feedback to dampen the activity of hypothalamic CRF neurons and pituitary corticotrophs. These hieratical levels of interactions and the negative feedback loop of circulating adrenoglucocorticoids form the basis of the stress circuit commonly known as the hypothalamus-pituitary-adrenal axis.

The biochemical effect of CRF on corticotrophs is mediated through the activation of type I CRF receptors (CRF-RI) in corticotrophs of anterior pituitary and of the intermediate lobe. The receptor is a 415-amino-acid protein comprising seven membrane-spanning domains. It belongs to the superfamily of G-protein-coupled receptors and is also activated by urocotin, urotensin, and sauvagine.

Corticotropin releasing factor binds to the receptors with high specificity and affinity with a K_d in the nanomolar range. Following its activation, the receptor couples GTP-binding proteins to effector enzymes, adenylyl cyclases that produce intracellular cAMP. The latter acts on protein kinase A to augment POMC mRNA expression and the release of ACTH. Consequently, derivatives of cAMP as well as agents that increase the intracellular levels of this second messenger, for example, forskolin, mimic the effects of CRF-41 in all respects while the inhibitor of cAMP-dependent kinase blocks the stimulating effects of CRF-41.

Besides acting on the adenylyl cyclase-cAMP system, CRF-41 also increases the level of cytosolic free calcium through facilitating influx of calcium from the extracellular medium. In addition, CRF-41 also activates pathways related to arachidonic acid metabolism and produces metabolites that may stimulate or inhibit ACTH secretion.

A. Interaction with Vasopressin

Whereas vasopressin also stimulates the release of ACTH, the action of vasopressin is mediated through V3 receptors in pituitary corticotrophs. The V3 receptors belong to the G-protein coupling receptor superfamily but the receptor acts by triggering membrane-bound phopholipase C to increase the turnover of inositol phosphate and diacylglycerol. This biological process is markedly different from that of CRF-41, as it results in enhancing protein kinase C activity. Hence, the stimulating effect of vasopressin synergizes with the action of CRF-41 in amplifying ACTH release by two- to three fold through the interaction of protein kinase A- and protein kinase C-dependent pathways.

Besides vasopressin, there are other peptides and neurotransmitters that are also capable of stimulating the release of ACTH in a less efficient manner than CRF. The effects of these compounds on ACTH release in general are additive to CRF-41. These include oxytocin, angiotensin II and cholecystokinin, noradrenalin, and adrenalin. On the other hand, a truncated form of atrial natriuretic factor (ANF5-28) of hypothalamic origin, which is released into the portal blood, inhibits the baseline, CRF-stimulated expression of POMC mRNA, and release of ACTH.

B. Effects of CRF in the Brain

Besides modulating pituitary corticotrophs, CRF-41 also acts on the central nervous system through two receptors, CRF-RI and CRF-RII. The CRF-RII has 431 amino acids, and shares 68% similarity to its counterpart. The CRF-RI is found in forebrain with a widespread signal throughout all areas of the neo-, olfactory, and hippocampal cortices. It is also present in subcortical limbic structures, in the septal region, and amygdala while low levels are seen in ventral thalamic and medial hypothalamic nuclei. In brain stem, high levels of receptors are found including in the cerebellar and deep nuclei and pre-cerebellar nuclei. The CRF-RI has been implicated in mediating behavioral changes associated with anxiety and the development of a functional HPA axis. Corticotropin releasing factor-41 has also been implicated to play an important role in augmenting the central sympathetic system that involves in the modulation of the central cardiovascular system. On the other hand, CRF-41 suppresses growth and the reproductive system by inhibiting the release of growth hormone releasing hormone and luteinizing hormone releasing hormone at the hypothalamic level.

See Also the Following Articles

Adrenocorticotropic Hormone (ACTH); Corticotropin Releasing Factor-Binding Protein; Corticotropin-Releasing Factor Receptors; Vasopressin

Bibliography

Antoni, F. A. (1986). Hypothalamic control of adrenocorticotropin secretion: Advances since the discovery of 41-residue corticotropin-releasing factor. *Endocr. Rev.* 7, 351–378.

Chen, R., Lewis, K. A., Perrin, M. H., and Vale, W. W. (1993). Expression cloning of a human corticotropin-releasing factor receptor. *Proc. Natl. Acad. Sci. USA* 90(19), 8967–8971.

Potter, E., Sutton, S., Donaldson, C., Chen, R., Perrin, M., Lewis, K., Sawchenko, P. E., and Vale, W. (1994). Distribution of corticotropin-releasing factor receptor mRNA expression in the rat brain and pituitary. *Proc. Natl. Acad. Sci. USA* 91(19), 8777–8781.

Smith, G. W., Aubry, J. M., Dellu, F., Contarino, A., Bilezikjian, L. M., Gold, L. H., Chen, R., Marchuk, Y., Hauser, C., Bentley, C. A., Sawchenko, P. E., Koob, G. F., Vale, W., and Lee, K. F. (1998). Corticotropin releasing factor receptor 1-deficient mice display decreased anxiety, impaired stress response, and aberrant neuroendocrine development. *Neuron* 20(6), 1093–1102.

Swanson, L., Sawchenko, P. E., Lind, R. W., and Rho, J. H. (1987). The CRH motoneuron: Differential peptide regulation in neurons with possible synaptic, paracrine and endocrine outputs. *In* "The Annals of the New York Academy of Sciences: The Hypothalamic-Pituitary-Adrenal Axis Revisited" (W. F. Ganong, M. F. Dallman, and J. L. Roberts Eds.) Vol. 512, pp. 12–23.

Tan, T., Yang, Z., Huang, W., and Lim, A. T. (1994). ANF(1-28) is a potent suppressor of Pro-opiomelanocortin (POMC) mRNA but a weak inhibitor of EP-LI release from AtT-20 cells. *J. Endocrinol.* 143, R1–R4.

Turnbull, A. V., and Rivier, C. (1997). Corticotropin-releasing factor (CRF) and endocrine responses to stress: CRF receptors, binding protein, and related peptides. *Proc. Soc. Exp. Biol. Med.* 215(1), 1–10.

Vale, W., Spiess, J., Rivier, C., and Rivier, J. (1981). Characterization of a 41-residue ovine hypothalamic peptide that stimulates secretion of corticotropin and beta-endorphin. *Science* 213, 1394–1397.

Corticotrophin Releasing Factor-Binding Protein

Philip J. Lowry, C. F. Kemp, and Russell J. Woods

University of Reading, United Kingdom

GLOSSARY

corticotrophin releasing factor (CRF) A hypothalamic peptide comprising 41 amino acid residues, secreted in response to stressful stimuli into the hypothalamopituitary portal system causing release of corticotrophin (ACTH) from the anterior pituitary gland.

corticotrophin releasing factor-binding protein (CRF-BP) A 37-kDa protein which binds CRF and is found in the circulation of higher primates as well as in both membrane bound and free forms in the brain of all vertebrates hitherto examined.

I. INTRODUCTION

Under experimental conditions, the corticotrophin releasing factor-binding protein (CRF-BP) is able to bind CRF and render it biologically inactive. As CRF-BP expression overlaps with CRF receptor expression in several areas of the brain, including the pituitary gland, it has been postulated that its function is to modulate the neuroendocrine and transmitter activities of CRF. The presence of CRF-BP in the periphery of higher primates as well indicates that this protein is involved in modulating the action of CRF in the periphery, where CRF has known proinflammatory effects (this is in contrast to the centrally derived anti-inflammatory action of CRF via the release of cortisol). Thus the CRF-BP may play a pivotal role

in the crossover of endocrine, immune and higher functions in both acute and chronic stress responses.

II. DISTRIBUTION

A. Central CRF-BP

From histochemistry and *in-situ* hybridization membrane-bound CRF-BP is observed to be expressed in rat brain predominantly in the cerebral cortex including archipaleo- and neocortical fields (see Fig. 1). It is present also in subcorticotrical limbic structures (amygdala, bed of the stria terminalis) and sensory relays of the auditory, olfactory, vestibular and trigeminal systems, several Raphe nuclei, and some cell groups of the brain stem reticular core. Hypothalamic expression occurs only in the ventral premammillary and dorsomedial nuclei. It is expressed in both neurones and glial astrocytes as well as in pituitary corticotrophs. Its wide distribution does not consistently match the more limited distribution of CRF and expression of CRF1 and CRF2a receptors in the brain does not coincide completely with either CRF or CRF-BP mRNA.

B. Peripheral CRF-BP

It is suspected that in addition to the brain form, only higher primates have circulating CRF-BP. Humans express CRF-BP in the liver and it circulates in the plasma of both sexes at concentrations, measured by immunoradiometric assay, of between 50 and 100 μg per liter. The liver is the probable source of CRF-BP in plasma as concentrations are much reduced in patients with chronic liver disease. By contrast, kidney failure is associated with elevated

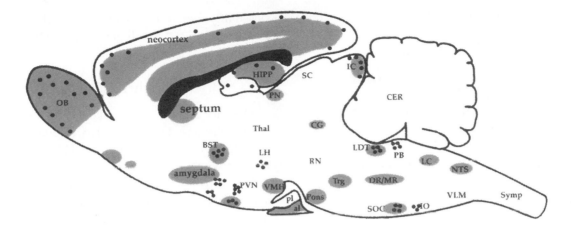

OB:	olfactory bulb	AD:	auditory bulb
BST:	bed nucleus of the stria terminalis	PVN:	paraventricular nucleus
SO:	supraoptic nucleus	Sch:	suprachlasmatic nucleus
VMH:	ventromedial hypothalamic nucleus	LH:	lateral hypothalamus
Thal:	thalamus	PN:	perfect nucleus
CG:	central grey	SC:	superior colliculus
IC:	inferior colliculus	HIPP:	hippocampus
CER:	cerebellum	RN:	red nucleus
Pons:	pontine nuclei	Trg:	trigeminal
LDT:	lateral dorsal tegmental nucleus	DR/MR:	dorsal/medial raphe nucleus
PB:	parabrachial nucleus	LC:	locus coreolus
NTS:	nucleus of the solitary tract	SOC:	superior olivary complex
IO:	inferior olive	VLM:	ventro-lateral medulla
Symp:	sympathetic related areas		

FIGURE 1 The distribution of the corticotrophin releasing factor-binding protein in the rat brain.

plasma levels indicating that CRF-BP (not bound to ligand) is normally cleared by the renal route. Plasma levels are remarkably constant from day to day. In molar terms plasma CRF-BP vastly exceeds CRF and therefore never approaches saturation by ligand except in the last few weeks of pregnancy. The placenta of primates also expresses CRF and it has been suggested that the binding protein serves in late pregnancy to help prevent stimulation of the maternal pituitary by the large amounts of placental CRF released into the circulation. Not only is hormonal activity abolished after binding to CRF-BP but it is in the bound form that most CRF may be removed from the maternal circulation. The CRF-BP is also measurable in fetal blood and amniotic fluid and may have a further role in the modulation of CRF activity associated with the onset of labor. Corticotrophin releasing factor stimulates the release of prostaglan-

dins from fetal membranes and potentiates their induction of myometrial contractility. These activities are presumed to be modulated by CRF-BP in the fetal and maternal circulation.

In contrast to late pregnancy, when plasma levels of CRF-BP are lower than normal, in both rheumatoid arthritis and septacemia the concentrations are significantly elevated (by up to 50%). Whereas the lowering of CRF-BP levels in pregnancy seems to be triggered by secretion of placental CRF, the raised levels in these active immune states appears to be caused by increased secretion by the liver. Presumably this is due to the activation of the acute phase response elements found in the 5'-flanking region of the CRF-BP gene (see Section IV). It is likely that the bioactivity of circulating CRF is always attended by some degree of modification imposed by the presence of its binding protein.

III. PROPERTIES

A. Ligand Binding

The affinity of human CRF-BP for human CRF is high (k_D = 0.1 nM). That for ovine CRF, which differs at 7 of the 41 amino acid residues, is 200-fold lower; however, CRF from both species have equal affinities for the pituitary CRF1 receptor. Sheep CRF-BP has 86% homology in its amino acid sequence with human and rat CRF-BP yet it binds human CRF with a 10-fold higher affinity than ovine (CRF k_D = 0.15 nM as opposed to 1.75 nM). Furthermore, a truncated version of human CRF, CRF 6-33, binds CRF-BP with reduced affinity but does not bind to CRF1 or CRF2 receptors. These considerations indicate that the structural determinants required for ligand binding by the binding proteins and the CRF1 receptors are very different. The recent discovery of urocortin, a new member of the CRF family of peptides, has shown that CRF receptor/binding protein interactions may be further complicated by the participations of additional ligands. Discrepancies in the central distribution of "CRF" receptors, CRF-BP, and CRF terminals is evidence that novel ligands for CRF-BP remain to be discovered. The relative affinities for CRF and CRF-like ligands are shown in Table I.

With the exception of the synthetic peptide antagonist α-helical CRF 9-41, CRF-like ligands interacting with CRF-BP *in vitro* induce dimerization. Formation of dimers has not been demonstrated to occur *in vivo* but CRF administered to humans intravenously is cleared rapidly from the circulation. The possibility therefore exists that CRF-BP not only inactivates CRF but, by dimerizing, targets the ligand for elimination.

B. Physicochemical Properties

The CRF-BP has a molecular mass of 37 kDa and the mature polypeptide consists of 298 amino acid residues. Its structure is composed predominantly of β-sheet with little evidence of α-helical folding.

Corticotrophin releasing factor-binding protein is subject to two posttranslational modifications. These have been investigated using human recombinant CRF-BP. It has a consensus sequence for N-glycosylation of asparagine residue 204. Enzymic removal of the glycosyl moiety does not affect binding of CRF. A potential phosphorylation site exists at serine residue 233 although phosphorylation has been found by experiment to occur instead at serine 206. Upon storage, affinity-purified, recombinant CRF-BP also undergoes cleavage between amino acid residues 234 and 235 even in the presence of protease inhibitors, yielding fragments of 28 and 9.6 kDa molecular mass. Some degree of protein unfolding has been observed, by tryptophan excitation fluorescence, to occur prior to this *in vitro* cleavage. It is not known whether it is accompanied by dephosphorylation. Protein fragments of similar size have been observed in the synovial fluid of patients suffering from rheumatoid arthritis, although it is not clear whether this is a consequence of the inflammation or if it is involved in the pathogenesis of this condition. Under nonpathological conditions IGF-binding proteins also undergo dephosphorylation and cleavage, both of which are regulated by and affect ligand binding. In the case of IGF-binding protein-3 cleavage is regulated by IGF-1. Unlike CRF-BP, cleavage of IGF-binding proteins reduces their affinity for ligand, whereas after cleavage of CRF-BP, binding of human CRF to the 28 kDa N-terminal fragment is unimpaired.

IV. REGULATION OF GENE EXPRESSION

Characterization of the upstream region of the CRF-BP gene has revealed acute phase response ele-

---

TABLE I
Order of Ligand Affinities for CRF-BP and the
CRF Receptors

CRF-BP : Urotensin > Urocortin ≥ hCRF > Sauvagine > oCRF

CRFR1 Receptor : Urocortin > hCRF = oCRF = Urotensin = Sauvagine

CRFR2a Receptor : Urocortin > Sauvagine > Urotensin > hCRF > oCRF

CRFR2b Receptor : Urocortin > Sauvagine = Urotensin > hCRF = oCRF

---

ments, one of which (located at −305) is known to bind the transcription factor NF-$\kappa\beta$. This factor, which regulates immunoglobulin and interleukin expression, is thought to be important in activating liver-specific genes, such as angiotensin, in response to acute stress, inflammation and injury. Another element (located at −676) binds INF-1, which is known to regulate the interferon gene.

More recent evidence has revealed multiple potential transcription factor binding sites in the 5′ flanking region of both the rat and human CRF-BP gene. These include a CREB/ATF site, a LF-A1 site, an OTX site, an AP-2 site, two Sp1 sites, and two AP-1 sites, as well as those mentioned previously. The CREB/ATF and AP-2 sites suggest that cAMP may be important for the regulation of the CRF-BP gene, and this is corroborated by the fact that primary rat neuronal or astrocyte cultures, stimulated with forskolin or isobutylmethylxanthine, have been shown to increase levels of CRF-BP mRNA. It has also been demonstrated using the G_s protein-coupled CRF receptor in the AtT-20 pituitary cell line that CRF-BP gene expression is positively regulated by CRF, suggesting a mechanism for refining the action of CRF on the stress axis at the level of gene expression.

V. ROLE OF CRF-BP IN THE STRESS RESPONSE

The stress axis and the immune system are interrelated and stress influences the course and pathology of the immune response to infectious disease and to autoimmune stimuli. Intravenous administration of CRF, a key component of the stress axis, elicits visceral and neuroendocrine changes that mimic the body's reaction to stress. Peripheral CRF receptors have been identified on cells of the testes, ovaries, adrenal medulla, heart, uterus, skeletal muscle, lung, kidney, and vasculature. Furthermore, CRF receptors have been reported to exist on circulating lymphocytes and macrophages as well as on mast cells. There is evidence for the hypothesis that peripheral

proinflammatory effects of CRF in humans may be modulated by circulating CRF-BP, whereas the central anti-inflammatory response to stress may be modulated by membrane-bound CRF-BP in the brain. It has been shown that CRF is displaced from CRF-BP when human brain tissue is treated with an analog of CRF that displaces bound CRF. *In vivo*, displacement of CRF from CRF-BP by central administration of a truncated form of CRF (CRF 6-33) to rats had an anxiolytic effect. It improved learning and memory presumably by making more free CRF available to interact with CRF receptors. These observations demonstrate that CRF-BP is certainly capable of modulating the actions of CRF.

See Also the Following Articles

CORTICOTROPIN RELEASING FACTOR; CORTICOTROPIN RELEASING FACTOR RECEPTORS

Bibliography

Behan, D. P., De Souza, E. B., Lowry, P. J., Potter, E., Sawchenko, P., and Vale, W. (1995). Corticotrophin releasing factor (CRF) binding protein: A novel regulator of CRF and related peptides. *Front. Neuroendocrinol.* 16, 362–382.

Behan, D. P., Maciejewski, D., Chalmers, D., and De Souza, E. B. (1995). Corticotropin-releasing factor binding protein (CRF-BP) is expressed in neuronal and astrocytic cells. *Brain Res.* 689, 259–264.

Chalmers, D. T., Lovenberg, T. W., Grigoriadis, D. E., Behan, D. P., and DeSouza, E. B. Corticotrophin-releasing factor receptors: from molecular biology to drug design. TiPS. 17:166–172; 1996.

Kemp, C. F., Woods, R. J., and Lowry, P. J. (1998). The corticotrophin releasing factor-binding protein: An act of several parts. *Peptides* 19 (6), 1119–1128.

Linton, E. A., Wolfe, C. D. A., Behan, D. P., and Lowry, P. J. (1988). A specific carrier substance for human corticotrophin releasing factor in late gestational maternal plasma that could mask its ACTH releasing activity. *Clin. Endocrinol.* 28, 315–324.

Turnbull A. V., and Rivier C. (1997). Corticotrophin-releasing factor (CRF) and endocrine responses to stress: CRF receptors, binding protein and related peptides. *P.S.E.B.M.* 215, 1–10.

Corticotropin-Releasing Factor Receptors

Dimitri E. Grigoriadis

Neurocrine Biosciences, Inc., California

GLOSSARY

adenylate cyclase One of the signaling molecules for G-protein-coupled receptors. Upon activation by a specific G-protein, this transmembrane protein will either increase or decrease the rate of conversion of ATP to cAMP.

corticotropin-releasing factor (*CRF*) A 41 amino acid peptide secreted primarily by the hypothalamus into the hypophyseal portal vasculature to act on the pituitary and cause the release of adrenocorticotropic hormone (ACTH).

g-protein A heterotrimeric protein that has high affinity for GTP and interacts with the cytoplasmic domains of a receptor transducing the signal from the activated (ligand bound) receptor to the second messenger-signaling protein inside the cell.

g-protein-coupled receptor A protein that typically spans a cell membrane seven times with extracellular and intracellular loops coordinating the binding of a ligand outside the membrane with a signal transduction mechanism inside the membrane.

hypothalamic–pituitary–adrenal axis The hormonal pathway thought to mediate the primary stress response. CRF secreted from the hypothalamus acts on the pituitary to release ACTH, which in turn acts on the adrenals to produce and release glucocorticoids. Glucocorticoids feedback to the pituitary to decrease ACTH release and also act on the hypothalamus to decrease CRF release in a negative feedback loop.

The corticotropin-releasing factor (CRF) has been widely implicated as having a major role in the modulation of endocrine, autonomic, behavioral, and immune responses to stress. CRF receptors are part of the superfamily of seven transmembrane domain G-protein-coupled receptors (GPCRs) and mediate the effects of CRF and its related peptides on pituitary–adrenal function, behavior, and cognition.

I. INTRODUCTION

Half a century ago, Geoffrey Harris first proposed the concept that the hypothalamus plays a primary role in the regulation of the pituitary–adrenocortical axis. Subsequently, during the 1950s, Guillemin and Rosenberg and Saffran and Schally independently observed the presence of a factor in extracts of the hypothalamus that could stimulate the release of adrenocorticotropic hormone (ACTH, corticotropin) from anterior pituitary cells *in vitro*. This extract was termed corticotropin-releasing factor. Although CRF was the first hypothalamic hypophysiotropic factor to be recognized, its chemical identity remained unknown largely due to the presence in hypothalamic extracts of other weaker secretagogues of ACTH secretion such as vasopressin, catecholamines, and angiotensin II. These agents, along with their synergistic effects with CRF on ACTH secretion and in combination with the relative lack of specificity of *in vitro* bioassays, hindered the purification of this peptide. The development of radioimmunoassays for ACTH and quantitative *in vitro* methods for assaying hypophysiotropic substances, along with the utilization of ion exchange and high-performance liquid chromatographic techniques, led to successful purification of CRF from sheep hypothalamic extracts in 1981 by Vale and colleagues at the Salk Institute. They were the first to report the isolation, characterization, synthesis, and *in vitro* and *in vivo* biological activities of a 41 amino acid hypothalamic CRF peptide that fulfilled all of the criteria for a hypothalamic corticotropin-releasing factor. Over a decade of research subsequent to the discovery of the peptide clearly demonstrated that in addition to its role in regulating an organism's response to physical, emotional, and environmental stress, CRF is widely distributed in the central nervous system (CNS) where it produces a wide spectrum of autonomic, electrophysiological, and behavioral effects consistent with a neurotransmitter or neuromodulator role in the brain.

The recent cloning of multiple CRF receptor subtypes and the identification of a specific binding protein for the peptide have precipitated a new era in CRF research. In addition, the identification of urocortin, a novel member of the CRF family of peptides, has expanded the notion that this system is under multiple regulatory factors and plays a much more complex role in the central nervous system than previously thought. This article focuses primarily on studies that elucidate the molecular biological, pharmacological, anatomical, and functional characteristics of mammalian CRF receptors.

II. CORTICOTROPIN-RELEASING FACTOR (CRF) RECEPTOR FAMILY

A. Molecular Biology/ Receptor Structure

The CRF receptors belong to the superfamily of GPCRs and, as such, have been shown to contain seven putative transmembrane domains and function through the coupling of a stimulatory guanine nucleotide-binding protein. These receptors also fall within the recently described, and still-growing, family of "gut-brain" neuropeptide receptors, which includes receptors for calcitonin, vasoactive intestinal peptide, parathyroid hormone, secretin, pituitary adenylate cyclase-activating peptide, glucagon, and growth hormone-releasing factor. These receptors all share considerable sequence homology and all stimulate adenylate cyclase in response to their respective agonist activation.

B. CRF$_1$ Receptors

Vale and colleagues first cloned the CRF$_1$ receptor in 1993 from a human Cushing's anterior pituitary corticotropic adenoma using the technique of expression cloning. The protein was characterized as a 415 amino acid protein with seven putative transmembrane domains and five potential extracellular N-linked glycosylation sites. In addition, the protein contained putative sites for protein kinase C phosphorylation in the first and second intracellular loops and in the C-terminal tail, as well as casein kinase II and protein kinase A phosphorylation sites in the third intracellular loop. The human gene has been localized on chromosome 17 at position 17q12-22. Shortly after the elucidation of this human form, several groups identified the CRF$_1$ form of the receptor from a variety of other species. All species of CRF$_1$ receptor mRNAs thus far identified encode proteins of 415 amino acids that are 98% identical to one another. The human CRF$_1$ receptor gene contains at least two introns and is found in a number of alternative splice forms, none of which to date have been found to have any physiological significance. This is in contrast to the mouse where the gene has been identified to contain at least 12 introns. The various kinase and phosphorylation sites predicted on these proteins, although not fully characterized, may serve as regulatory elements in the control of receptor expression and/or function. The potential N-linked glycosylation sites on the N-terminal extracellular domain are characteristic of most GPCRs and confirm the glycosylation profiles determined by earlier chemical affinity cross-linking studies. Indeed, the molecular weight predicted from the deglycosylated forms of the CRF$_1$ receptor in earlier biochemical studies was virtually identical to that obtained from the cloned amino acid sequence.

C. CRF$_2$ Receptors

Shortly after the cloning and characterization of the CRF$_1$ receptor, another subtype of this family for this hormone was identified. This receptor constituted the CRF$_2$ subtype of the family and initially represented two splice forms termed CRF$_{2\alpha}$ and CRF$_{2\beta}$ receptors. The CRF$_{2\alpha}$ receptor, originally described by Lovenberg and colleagues, is a 411 amino acid protein with approximately 71% identity to the CRF$_1$ receptor. The CRF$_{2\beta}$ receptor, which has been cloned from rat, mouse, and human, contains 431 amino acids and differs from the $CRF_{2\alpha}$ isoform in that the first 34 amino acids in the N-terminal extracellular domain are replaced by a unique sequence 54 amino acids in length. The $CRF_{2\gamma}$ receptor has most recently been identified only in human brain. This splice variant uses yet a different 5' alternative exon for its amino terminus and replaces the first 34 amino acid sequence of the $CRF_{2\alpha}$ receptor with a unique 20 amino acid sequence. Thus, although the CRF_2 receptor exists as three isoforms, $CRF_{2\alpha}$, $CRF_{2\beta}$, and $CRF_{2\gamma}$, there are at present no known functional splice variants for the CRF_1 receptor. Between the CRF_1 and the CRF_2 receptors, very large regions of amino acid identity exist, particularly between transmembrane domain five and transmembrane domain six. This similarity argues strongly for the conservation of biochemical function as it is this region that is thought to be the primary site of G-protein coupling and signal transduction. All three CRF_2 receptor subtypes contain five potential N-glycosylation sites that are analogous to those found on the CRF_1 receptor subtype. The genomic structure of the human CRF_2 receptor gene is similar to that of the mouse CRF_1 receptor described earlier and has 12 introns, the last 10 of which interrupt the coding region in identical positions. These gene sequences, however, diverge significantly at the 5' end. The chromosomal mapping of the human CRF_2 gene has been localized to chromosome 7 p21-p15.

III. PHARMACOLOGICAL CHARACTERISTICS

The rat and human forms of the CRF receptor family have been transfected into a variety of mammalian cell lines that do not normally express these receptors, including COS-7 (monkey kidney), Chinese hamster ovary (CHO) and Ltk⁻ (mouse fibroblast) cells. Although rat tissue was commonly available for the study of the CRF_1 receptor, the expression in stable mammalian cell lines of the human CRF_2 receptor proteins enabled, for the first time, direct biochemical and pharmacological study of these subtypes without the requirement for scarce human brain tissue.

As will be discussed in the subsequent sections of this article, CRF receptor subtypes exhibit a clear and distinct pharmacological profile with respect to the endogenous and related peptides known to activate this system. In addition, $CRF_{2\alpha}$ and $CRF_{2\beta}$ receptors display very subtle differences in the pharmacological profiles with respect to one another, which suggests that some specific conformation of the protein can be attributed to the N-terminal extracellular domains and is critical for the high-affinity binding of CRF. In fact, as a result of the distinct pharmacological difference between the two receptor subtypes, it became necessary to radiolabel a nonmammalian CRF-like ligand ([^{125}I]sauvagine) in order to completely characterize the CRF_2 receptor subtype. Previous studies examining the detailed binding characteristics of CRF peptides with respect to the peptide structure have revealed that all of the CRF peptides must be amidated at their carboxy terminus for potent activity. It is very interesting to note that deamidation of any of the CRF-like peptides results in a complete loss of activity at either receptor subtype, again suggesting that at least some similarity between the two subtypes must exist.

A. Ligand-Binding Profile of CRF_1 Receptors

CRF_1 receptors expressed in mammalian cell lines described earlier demonstrate reversible, saturable, high-affinity binding to CRF and its related peptides with the pharmacological and functional characteristics comparable to those found in the variety of animal or human tissues described previously in the literature. Human and rat CRF_1 receptors in stably transfected Ltk⁻ cells demonstrate binding to a single homogeneous population of receptors with apparent affinities (K_D) of 130 and 168 pM and receptor densities (B_{max}) of 97 and 588 fmol/mg protein, respectively. The pharmacological rank orders of potency in stably transfected cell lines with either human or rat CRF_1 receptors were identical to the established profile for the CRF receptor in the rat frontal cortex where urocortin = urotensin I = sauvagine > ovine CRF (oCRF) = rat/human CRF (r/h CRF) = bovine CRF > D-Phe r/hCRF(12-41) > α-helical ovine CRF(9-41) ≫ r/hCRF(6-33), r/hCRF(9-33), r/hCRF

(1-41)OH, VIP and arginine vasopressin (AVP). These data demonstrate that although there are subtle differences between rat and human forms of the receptor in terms of amino acid sequence, the differences are not significant enough to alter the ability of these peptides to bind or interact with this subtype.

B. Ligand-Binding Profile of CRF$_2$ Receptors

The CRF$_2$ receptor isoforms have also been expressed in stable mammalian cell lines and have been demonstrated to bind CRF-related peptides and function through stimulation of cAMP production. In general, although some minor differences exist in the rank order profile of the CRF$_2$ splice variants to each other (mainly related to fragments of CRF peptides), as a subtype they are quite distinct from either the CRF$_1$ receptor subtype or the CRF-binding protein. When expressed in stable cell lines, these receptors exhibit the following pharmacological rank order profile: urocortin = sauvagine = urotensin I > astressin > r/hCRF > D-Phe CRF(12-41) = α-helical CRF(9-41) $\gg$ oCRF $\gg$ r/hCRF(6-33), oCRF(6-33), r/hCRF(1-41)OH, GHRH, AVP, and VIP. Data thus far on the CRF$_{2\gamma}$ receptor suggest a rank order of potencies similar to the other two splice variants with urocortin = sauvagine > urotensin I > r/hCRF. Without exception, it is clear that the mammalian CRF peptides oCRF and r/hCRF have weaker affinity for the CRF$_2$ receptor, whereas urocortin has equal affinity for both CRF$_1$ and CRF$_2$ receptor subtypes.

C. Guanine Nucleotide Characteristics of CRF Receptors

Characteristic of receptor systems that are coupled to adenylate cyclase as a second messenger system is the exclusive link to a guanine nucleotide-binding protein. These transducing proteins mediate the ligand-binding event at the receptor to an activation of an intracellular pathway, in this case beginning with the conversion of ATP to cAMP. In vitro, guanine nucleotides have been shown to decrease the specific binding of agonists for a great number of seven transmembrane neurohormone or neurotrans-

mitter receptors coupled to G-proteins, presumably by uncoupling the G-protein from the receptor and changing its conformation such that it now has low affinity for its agonist. Both CRF receptor subtypes transfected in stable mammalian cell lines were used to determine the guanine nucleotide sensitivity of the cloned receptors. The effects of guanine nucleotides on the binding of [^{125}I]oCRF (for CRF$_1$ receptors) or [^{125}I]sauvagine (for either CRF$_1$ or CRF$_2$ receptors) inhibited radioligand binding by 50–70% (where 100% inhibition was defined by 1 μM unlabeled r/hCRF). The nonhydrolyzable forms of guanine nucleotides [Gpp(NH)p and GTP-γ-S] were more potent than GTP itself. The order of potencies were GTP-γ-S > Gpp(NH)p > GTP with ED$_{50}$ values of ~ 20–45, 200–800, and 2500–3000 nM, respectively. These effects on binding in both human and rat CRF$_1$ or CRF$_2$ receptor stable cell lines were specific for the guanine nucleotides because the adenosine nucleotide ATP was ineffective in altering the binding at equimolar concentrations (ED$_{50}$ > 10,000 nM). These data confirmed that the heterologous expression of the human or rat receptors in mammalian cell lines functioned in the same manner as has been characterized in native tissues.

D. Second Messenger Characteristics of CRF Receptors

In addition to the adenylate cyclase system, other signal transduction mechanisms have been postulated to be involved in the actions of CRF. For example, CRF has been shown to increase protein carboxylmethylation and phospholipid methylation in AtT-20 cells. Preliminary evidence suggests that CRF may regulate cellular responses through products of arachidonic acid metabolism. Furthermore, although evidence in anterior pituitary cells suggests that CRF does not regulate phosphotidylinositol turnover or protein kinase C activity directly, stimulation of protein kinase C either directly or by specific ligands (vasopressin or angiotensin II) enhances CRF-stimulated adenylate cyclase activity and ACTH release and inhibits phosphodiesterase activity. Thus, the effects of CRF in native tissues such as anterior pituitary cells, neurons, and other cell types expressing CRF receptors are likely to involve complex interactions among several intracellular second messenger systems. All of this evidence has thus far been gathered from native tissues that exhibit binding profiles consistent with the CRF receptor. As will be elucidated later, these studies have most probably been examining second messenger profiles of the CRF_1 receptor in various tissues primarily due to the ubiquitous nature of this subtype compared to the CRF_2 receptor in the rat. Clearly, the most common and well-studied second messenger system for the CRF receptor is the coupling to the adenylate cyclase system. In fact, there is no evidence to date that the heterologous expression of human CRF receptors transfected into mammalian cells functions in any manner other than through the stimulation of the production of cAMP.

In the pituitary gland, CRF initiates a cascade of enzymatic reactions beginning with the receptor-mediated stimulation of adenylate cyclase, which ultimately regulates pro-opiomelanocortin (POMC) peptide secretion and possibly synthesis. POMC-derived peptide secretion mediated by the activation of adenylate cyclase is dose related and exhibits appropriate pharmacology consistent with activation of the CRF_1 receptor. Similarly, in the brain and spleen, the pharmacological rank order profile of CRF-related peptides for the stimulation of adenylate cyclase is analogous to the profile seen in pituitary and in keeping with the affinities of these compounds for receptor binding. In addition, the putative CRF receptor antagonist α-helical ovine CRF(9-41) inhibits the CRF-stimulated adenylate cyclase observed in brain and spleen homogenates.

To further characterize the stable CRF receptor transfectants, the ability of CRF-related and unrelated peptides to stimulate CRF_1 or CRF_2 receptor-mediated cAMP production from the cells has been examined. The rank order of the peptides in stimulating cAMP production in these cells was in keeping with their rank order in inhibiting [^{125}I]oCRF or [^{125}I]sauvagine binding to the CRF_1 or CRF_2 receptor, respectively, and at least for the CRF_1 receptor, this rank order was virtually identical to the second messenger pharmacological profile reported previously in brain, pituitary, or spleen.

In addition to stimulation studies, CRF-stimulated cAMP production could be inhibited competitively by the putative peptide antagonists D-Phe CRF(12-41) and α-helical CRF(9-41) in both CRF_1- and CRF_2-expressing cell lines, demonstrating that the expressed CRF receptors in these cell lines were indeed functional. Interestingly, both D-Phe CRF(12-41) and α-helical CRF(9-41) inhibited the stimulated cAMP response with the same EC_{50} in both receptor subtype preparations. This suggests that although there is some fundamental difference in the pharmacological specificity of these two receptor subtypes when examining agonists, they must still possess some similarities in their structure of the binding site, at least as far as peptide antagonists are concerned. These results clearly suggest that not only subtype-specific and subtype-selective compounds can be identified for these two receptor subtypes, but that mixed antagonists are possible and could bring to light possible subtle functions of the two receptor subtypes.

IV. DISTRIBUTION OF CRF RECEPTOR SUBTYPES

Receptor autoradiographic studies and more recent *in situ* hybridization studies have localized CRF-binding sites and CRF receptor mRNA, respectively, in slide-mounted sections of many tissues from a variety of species identifying these proteins in anatomically and physiologically relevant areas. For example, in the pituitary gland, CRF_1 expression is detectable in both anterior and intermediate lobes with particularly high expression in clusters within the anterior lobe. In fact, a good correlation exists between the actions of CRF on corticotropes of the anterior pituitary and the distribution of [^{125}I]oCRF- or [^{125}I]sauvagine-binding sites and CRF_1 mRNA. Within the anterior lobe, CRF_2 receptor expression is detectable in only a few scattered cells. Thus, in terms of hypothalamic–pituitary–adrenal (HPA) axis activity, CRF_2 receptors may mediate CRF effects at the level of the hypothalamus (see later), whereas CRF_1 receptors are responsible for CRF-induced changes in ACTH release in pituitary corticotropes.

Although there is a general correspondence of the distribution of [^{125}I]oCRF- or [^{125}I]sauvagine-binding sites and CRF_1 or CRF_2 mRNA in brain with the functional actions of CRF, there are several brain areas with some apparent discrepancies. For example, CRF has potent electrophysiological and behavioral effects in the locus coeruleus, whereas the distribution of binding sites and CRF_1 or CRF_2 mRNA is not noteworthy in this brain stem nucleus. Physiologically, it is also tempting to speculate that other subtypes as yet unidentified may be responsible for the actions of the neurotransmitter in those regions where CRF seems to have profound actions but no appreciable labeling of the receptor is observed. The localization and distribution of CRF_2 receptors in mammalian brain coupled with the discovery of urocortin, a novel mammalian analog of CRF, have accounted for some of these discrepancies. However, species differences in the localization of receptor subtypes and peptides among rodent, nonhuman primate, and human tissues have made it somewhat difficult to extrapolate behavioral studies in rodent models to human effects. It is important to note that since most of the autoradiographic studies in the literature thus far in rodents have utilized $[^{125}I]oCRF$ or various forms of $[^{125}I]rat/human CRF$, the primary labeling, localization, and distribution would be almost exclusively attributable to the CRF_1 receptor subtype.

Within the rat brain, CRF_1 receptor expression was very high in neocortical, cerebellar, and sensory relay structures, whereas CRF_2 receptor expression was generally confined to subcortical structures, including the lateral septal region, the bed nucleus of the stria terminalis, the amygdaloid area, and the olfactory bulb. The contrast in expression patterns between CRF receptor subtypes was particularly evident within the septal region: CRF_2 mRNA expression was very high in lateral septal nuclei but very low in the medial septum, the septal nucleus where CRF_1 mRNA abundance was most evident. The lateral septum, by virtue of widespread reciprocal connections throughout the brain, is implicated in a variety of physiological processes. These range from higher cognitive functions such as learning and memory to autonomic regulation, including food and water intake. In addition, the septum plays a central role in classical limbic circuitry and is thus important in a variety of emotional conditions, including fear and aggression. The lateral septum thus acts as both an integrator of limbic circuitry and an interface between telencephalic and diencephalic areas. The high level of CRF_2 receptor expression in this area suggests a role for CRF_2 receptors in modulating limbic circuitry at the level of the lateral septum.

The heterogeneous distribution of CRF_1 and CRF_2 receptor mRNA suggests distinctive functional roles for each receptor in CRF-related systems. The selective expression of CRF_2 receptor mRNA within hypothalamic nuclei such as the ventromedial nucleus and the paraventricular nucleus indicates that the anorexic actions of CRF in these nuclei are likely to be CRF_2 receptor mediated. CRF_2 receptor mRNA was evident throughout the rostrocaudal extent of the hypothalamus, particularly within the paraventricular nucleus whereas CRF_1 receptor expression was limited. The distribution of cells expressing CRF_2 receptor mRNA within the PVN coincides with the cellular distribution of CRF mRNA, suggesting a possible autoreceptor role for CRF_2 receptors in this nucleus. Because the CRF neurons of the PVN play a classic hypophysiotropic role in controlling ACTH release from the anterior pituitary, it is tempting to speculate that CRF_2 receptors may act to selectively regulate hypophysiotropic and/or autonomic-related CRF neurons. As such, this receptor subtype may be central to the control of the mammalian hypothalamo–pituitary–adrenal stress system. More detailed studies using double labeling of the peptides and their receptors will be required to dissect out the discrete role of this subtype. Whatever the case may be, the high level of CRF_2 receptor expression within the hypothalamic structures is certainly suggestive of a role for CRF_2 receptors in modulating autonomic-related CRF projection neurons. With regard to HPA axis activity, we speculate that the paraventricular nuclear CRF_2 receptors could also act to modulate CRF neurosecretory neurons in response to stress. In essence, providing a short-loop feedback role. Ono and colleagues have proposed such a role of CRF in a positive ultrashort loop feedback effect on stress-induced ACTH release. In this regard, the comparatively lower affinity of CRF for the CRF_2 receptor subtype may be of physiological design to allow the activation of CRF_2 receptors only under conditions of chronic stress or prolonged CRF release.

A more detailed examination of the precise localization of CRF_2 receptor splice variants, $CRF_{2\alpha}$ and $CRF_{2\beta}$, indicates discrete anatomical distributions in the rat. The $CRF_{2\alpha}$ form is expressed primarily within the brain whereas the $CRF_{2\beta}$ variant is localized in both the CNS and the periphery. Within the brain, it appears that the $CRF_{2\alpha}$ form represents the predominant neuronal CRF_2 variant whereas the $CRF_{2\beta}$ splice form is localized on nonneuronal elements, such as the choroid plexus of the ventricular system and cerebral arterioles. In the periphery, $CRF_{2\beta}$ mRNA is expressed at high levels in both cardiac and skeletal muscle with lower levels evident in both lung and intestine. The $CRF_{2\gamma}$ isoform has yet to be identified in the rodent; however, reverse transcription-polymerase chain reaction (RT-PCR) analysis of human brain mRNA demonstrated expression in septum, amygdala, hippocampus, and frontal cortex. The full characterization of the $CRF_{2\gamma}$ subtype has not yet been elucidated in terms of native characteristics and function largely due to its nonexistence in rodent tissues. This type of species selectivity will make it difficult to completely examine the role of the CRF_2 receptor subtype unless suitable animal models can be found.

V. SUMMARY AND CONCLUSIONS

The corticotropin-releasing factor is the primary regulator of the endocrine, autonomic, and behavioral response to stress via mechanisms in both the brain and the periphery. The endocrine stress response begins with activation of the hypothalamic–pituitary adrenal axis, resulting in the release of the corticotropin-releasing factor into the hypophyseal portal vasculature. CRF then mediates its actions through cell surface receptors coupled to the activation of adenylyl cyclase. Centrally, CRF is found throughout the brain and its role in mediating emotional or behavioral stress is less well defined. As described in this review, CRF receptors can be classified into four functionally distinct subtypes: CRF_1, $CRF_{2\alpha}$, $CRF_{2\beta}$, and $CRF_{2\gamma}$ which encode 411, 415, 431, and 397 amino acid proteins, respectively. These receptors differ with respect to their structure, tissue distribution, and pharmacological specificity for CRF-related ligands. Urocortin, a mammalian CRF-related peptide with close sequence homology to fish urotensin, interacts with high affinity with all three CRF receptors and may represent the naturally occurring ligand for $CRF_{2\alpha}$ receptors. The areas of distribution of these CRF receptors in brain are correlated well with the immunocytochemical distribution of CRF and urocortin pathways and pharmacological sites of action of CRF and urocortin. Although species differences currently apparent in the number and subtype of at least the CRF_2 receptor preclude our complete correlation of animal studies with humans, identification of the multiple subtypes has led to an enhanced understanding of this increasingly complex system. It is becoming increasingly clear that the multiple receptor subtypes must mediate different functional and pathophysiological actions of this family of neuropeptides, and future studies aimed at identifying additional subtypes or peptides with high affinity will only serve to fully elucidate the role of this key neurohormone in the pathophysiology of stress.

Acknowledgments

The work described has resulted from the collaborative efforts of many individuals. Special thanks to Drs. Errol De Souza, Derek Chalmers, Timothy Lovenberg, Stephen Heinrichs, Chen Liaw, and Nicholas Ling for their scientific contributions.

See Also the Following Articles

Adrenocorticotropic Hormone (ACTH); Corticotropin Releasing Factor (CRF); HPA Axis; Paraventricular Nucleus

Bibliography

Almeida, O. F. X., Hassan, A. H. S., and Holsboer, F. (1993). Intrahypothalamic neuroendocrine actions of corticotropin-releasing factor. *In* "Corticotropin-Releasing Factor" (D. J., Chadwick, J., Marsh, and K., Ackrill, Eds.), p. 151. Wiley, Chichester.

Behan, D. P., Grigoriadis, D. E., Lovenberg, T., Chalmers, D., Heinrichs, S., Liaw, C., and De Souza, E. B. (1996). Neurobiology of corticotropin releasing factor (CRF) receptors and CRF-binding protein: Implications for the treatment of CNS disorders. *Mol. Psychiat.* **1**, 265–277.

Chalmers, D. T., Lovenberg, T. W., Grigoriadis, D. E., Behan,

D. P., and De Souza, E. B. (1996). Corticotropin-releasing factor receptors: From molecular biology to drug design. *Trends Pharmacolog. Sci.* **17**, 166–172.

Chen, R., Lewis, K. A., Perrin, M. H., and Vale, W. W. (1993). Expression cloning of a human corticotropin-releasing-factor receptor. *Proc. Natl. Acad. Sci. USA* **90**, 8967–8971.

De Souza, E. B. (1987). Corticotropin-releasing factor receptors in the rat central nervous system: Characterization and regional distribution. *J. Neurosci.* **7**, 88–100.

De Souza, E. B. (1992). Corticotropin-releasing hormone receptors. *In* "Handbook of Chemical Neuroanatomy: Neuropeptide Receptors in the CNS" (A. Bjorklund, T. Hokfelt, and M. J., Kuhar, Eds.), pp. 145–185. Elsevier, Amsterdam.

Donaldson, C. J., Sutton, S. W., Perrin, M. H., Corrigan, A. Z., Lewis, K. A., Rivier, J. E., Vaughan, J. M., and Vale, W. W. (1996). Cloning and characterization of human urocortin. *Endocrinology* **137**, 2167–2170.

Dunn, A. J., and Berridge, C. W. (1990). Physiological and behavioral responses to corticotropin-releasing factor administration: Is CRF a mediator of anxiety of stress responses? *Brain Res. Rev.* **15**, 71–100.

Grigoriadis, D. E., Lovenberg, T. W., Chalmers, D. T., Liaw, C., and De Souza, E. B. (1996). Characterization of corticotropin-releasing factor receptor subtypes. *In* "Neuropeptides: Basic and Clinical Advances" (J. N. Crawley, and S. McLean, Eds.), pp. 60–80. N.Y. Academy of Sciences, New York.

Kostich, W. A., Chen, A., Sperle, K., and Largent, B. L. (1998). Molecular identification and analysis of a novel human corticotropin-releasing factor (CRF) receptor: The CRF$_{2\gamma}$ receptor. *Mol. Endocrinol.* **12**, 1077–1085.

Liaw, C. W., Lovenberg, T. W., Barry, G., Oltersdorf, T., Grigoriadis, D. E., and De Souza, E. B. (1996). Cloning and characterization of the human CRF$_2$ receptor gene and cDNA. *Endocrinology* **137**, 72–77.

Lovenberg, T. W., Chalmers, D. T., Liu, C., and De Souza, E. B. (1995). CRF$_{2\alpha}$ and CRF$_{2\beta}$ receptor mRNAs are differentially distributed between the rat central nervous system and peripheral tissues. *Endocrinology* **136**, 4139–4142.

Lovenberg, T. W., Liaw, C. W., Grigoriadis, D. E., Clevenger, W., Chalmers, D. T., De Souza, E. B., and Oltersdorf, T. (1995). Cloning and characterization of a functionally distinct corticotropin-releasing factor receptor subtype from rat brain. *Proc. Natl. Acad. Sci. USA* **92**, 836–840.

Menzaghi, F., Heinrichs, S. C., Merlo Pich, E., Weiss, F., and Koob, G. F. (1993). The role of limbic and hypothalamic corticotropin-releasing factor in behavioral responses to stress. *In* "Corticotropin-Releasing Factor and Cytokines:

Role in the Stress Response" (Y. Tache, and C. Rivier, Eds.), pp. 142–154. Annals of the New York Academy of Sciences.

Ono, N., De Castro, J. C. B., and McCann, S. M. (1985). Ultrashort loop positive feedback of corticotropin (ACTH)-releasing factor to enhance ACTH release in stress. *Proc. Natl. Acad. Sci. USA* **82**, 3528–3531.

Owens, M. J., and Nemeroff, C. B. (1991). Physiology and pharmacology of corticotropin-releasing factor. *Pharmacolog. Rev.* **43**, 425–473.

Petrusz, P., and Merchenthaler, I. (1992). The corticotropin-releasing factor system. *In* "Neuroendocrinology" (C. B. Nemeroff, Ed.), pp. 129–184. CRC Press, Boca Raton, FL.

Rivier, J., Rivier, C., and Vale, W. (1984). Synthetic competitive antagonist of corticotropin-releasing factor: Effect on ACTH secretion in the rat. *Science* **224**, 889–891.

Sanchez, M. M., Young, L. J., Plotsky, P. M., and Insel, T. R. (1999). Autoradiographic and in situ hybridization localization of corticotropin-releasing factor 1 and 2 receptors in nonhuman primate brain. *J. Comp. Neurol.* **408**, 365–377.

Sawchenko, P. E., and Swanson, L. W. (1990). Organization of CRF immunoreactive cells and fibers in the rat brain: Immunohistochemical studies. *In* "Corticotropin-Releasing factor: Basic and clinical studies of a neuropeptide" (E. B. De Souza, and C. B. Nemeroff, Eds.), pp. 29–52. CRC Press, Boca Raton, FL.

Swanson, L. W., Sawchenko, P. E., Rivier, J., and Vale, W. W. (1983). The organization of ovine corticotropin-releasing factor immunoreactive cells and fibers in the rat brain: An immunohistochemical study. *Neuroendocrinology* **36**, 165–186.

Tache, Y., Gunion, M. M., and Stephens, R. (1990). CRF: Central nervous system action to influence gastrointestinal function and role in the gastrointestinal response to stress. *In* "Corticotropin-Releasing Factor: Basic and Clinical Studies of a Neuropeptide" (E. B. De Souza, and C. B. Nemeroff, Eds.), pp. 299–308. CRC Press, Boca Raton, FL.

Vale, W., Spiess, J., Rivier, C., and Rivier, J. (1981). Characterization of a 41-residue ovine hypothalamic peptide that stimulates secretion of corticotropin and β-endorphin. *Science* **213**, 1394–1397.

Vaughan, J., Donaldson, C., Bittencourt, J., Perrin, M. H., Lewis, K., Sutton, S., Chan, R., Turnbull, A. V., Lovejoy, D., Rivier, C., Rivier, J., Sawchenko, P. E., and Vale, W. (1995). Urocortin, a mammalian neuropeptide related to fish urotensin I and to corticotropin-releasing factor. *Nature* **378**, 287–292.

Cortisol

see Corticosteroids and Stress

Crime Victims

Ian Robbins

St. George's Hospital, London, England

I. Victimization
II. Psychological and Physical Health Consequences
III. Responses to Specific Crimes
IV. Support and Treatment Services

GLOSSARY

acute stress disorder (*ASD*) A disorder which may occur in the immediate aftermath of severe trauma. The diagnostic features include dissociation in the form of numbing, reduction in awareness, derealization, depersonalization, and dissociative amnesia. There is anxiety and increased arousal, which often accompanies reexperiencing of the trauma. As a consequence there is avoidance of reminders of the trauma and impairment in social or occupational functioning. The diagnosis of ASD requires three dissociative symptoms but only one symptom from the intrusion, avoidance, and arousal categories.

posttraumatic stress disorder (*PTSD*) Occurs following exposure to a traumatic event in which the person witnessed or was confronted with an event that involved actual or threatened death or serious injury to themselves or others and where their response involved intense fear, helplessness, or horror. It is characterized by persistent reexperiencing in the form of recurrent, intrusive thoughts or images and/or distressing dreams or flashbacks. There may be intense distress or arousal when confronted with reminders of the event. As a consequence there may be persistent avoidance of things associated with the trauma and numbing of general responsiveness. There may also be sleep disturbance, irritability or outbursts of anger, diffi-

culty in concentration, hypervigilance, and exaggerated startle response. The symptoms result in significant impairment of social, occupational, or other important areas of functioning and need to last longer than 1 month for a diagnosis to be made.

I. VICTIMIZATION

It is difficult to estimate the extent of criminal victimization in part because most victims of crime do not report the event to the police, resulting in an underrepresentation within the criminal statistics compiled from police data. Most crime differentially targets and damages victims who are poor, marginalized, and disempowered within society; individuals are usually targeted because of what they represent rather than because of who they are. Examples of this can include racially motivated attacks or sexual assaults. Within the United Kingdom the recent British Crime Survey of 1998 points to an 83% increase in crime since 1981, with the largest increase being in violent crime. Women are more likely to be at risk for sexual or domestic violence, whereas men are more likely to report physical violence from strangers.

Being the target of a crime may result in the individual feeling that he or she is a victim. Ochberg reported that victims feel "diminished," "pushed down," "exploited," and "invaded." There is a feeling of stigmatization and of being isolated by the experience, with a shattering of basic assumptions about the predictable orderly nature of the world where bad things are perceived as only happening to people who deserve it. Individuals lose their sense of autonomy and their belief in being able to control their own lives is shattered, with a consequent increase in feelings of vulnerability. This is often associated with a belief that others do not understand unless they have experienced being a victim themselves. This feeling may be reinforced by the critical response they experience from friends or family when their recovery is not sufficiently rapid.

There may also be a considerable amount of self-blame, which may take two forms: behavioral or characterological. Behavioral self-blame is concerned with aspects of behavior which, if changed, could reduce the possibility of reoccurrence, whereas characterological self-blame implies that the victimization is attributable to the sort of person that they are. Clearly, behavioral self-blame, since it implies the possibility of increased control over events, is more "healthy" than characterological blame.

II. PSYCHOLOGICAL AND PHYSICAL HEALTH CONSEQUENCES

Victims of violence may experience a sense of detachment or depersonalization at the time of the attack. While this may be a protective mechanism in the immediate aftermath of an attack, it may well hinder subsequent recovery and recent evidence suggests that it may predict the subsequent development of Posttraumatic stress disorder (PTSD). While dissociation is not a feature of PTSD it is one of the major features of the diagnosis of acute stress disorder (ASD). Recent research has found that a diagnosis of ASD 1 month after experiencing a violent crime predicted the development of PTSD in 83% of cases at 6-month follow-up.

Many of the psychological consequences fit within the PTSD framework, with as many as 27% of all female crime victims meeting the criteria for diagnosis. Assaultive violence is more damaging than other types of crime, with higher rates of PTSD relating to increased perception of threat to life and extent of physical injury. In addition to PTSD, depression, anxiety, and substance abuse are common consequences of criminal victimization.

As well as the direct effects of the crime in terms of physical damage, victims are more likely to have poorer physical health and report increased drug and cigarette and alcohol consumption, health care neglect, risky sexual behavior, and eating disorders.

III. RESPONSES TO SPECIFIC CRIMES

A. Rape and Sexual Assault

Definitions as to what constitutes rape vary across countries. Within the United Kingdom the definition has recently been extended to include nonconsensual anal intercourse as well as vaginal intercourse. This change allows sexual attacks on men to be treated for the first time in law as rape, although it has to be acknowledged that the majority of victims of rape are women. Most sexual offences are unreported and the rate of successful prosecution is low. Rape trauma syndrome was described by Burgess and Holstrom in 1974, but is now regarded as a variant of PTSD. Being the victim of a completed rape, being injured, and the extent of the perception of threat to life are predictive of increased rates of subsequent mental health problems in the longer term as are prior victimization, previous psychological problems, and the lack of available social support. A third of women who report rape develop long-term psychological and social problems. A similar pattern is described in male victims of sexual assault by Mezey and King.

B. Stalking

Stalking has as yet been relatively poorly researched. Pathe and Mullen describe severe social disruption and psychological distress with high levels of anxiety, persistent intrusive recollections and flashbacks, and suicidal thoughts. There are profound economic and social consequences of stalking, as victims often feel compelled to leave their employment or change their address. Over a third of victims in the Pathe and Mullen study met the criteria for PTSD.

C. Domestic Violence

Domestic violence, like sexual violence, is primarily but not exclusively directed against women. It is defined as an act carried out with intent to physically injure another person, usually an intimate partner. Recent surveys in the United Kingdom have suggested a lifetime prevalence of domestic violence of 1 of 4 women and an annual prevalence of 1 of 9 women. Battered woman syndrome, first described in the 1970s, contains within it many of the features of PTSD and describes the emotional, cognitive, and behavioral consequences. It is associated with apparent "learned helplessness," whereby the victims of domestic violence appear to be unable to extricate themselves from abusive relationships. Rather than being helplessness this unwillingness to leave an abusive partner may in fact be a rational appraisal of the danger involved in freeing themselves from an abusive partner. The degree of risk is seen in terms of the possibility that the domestic violence may end up causing severe physical injury and can progress to homicide. The consequences of domestic violence include depression, anxiety, suicidal behavior, substance abuse, and somatization. It is a frequent cause of divorce and homelessness and may be associated with child abuse.

D. Workplace Violence

Workplace assaults have increased in frequency and severity in recent years and are associated with increased job stress, reduced job satisfaction, and the likelihood of carrying weapons to work. Males are most likely to be involved in fatal workplace assaults, while women are more likely to be involved in nonfatal assaults. Health care workers are particularly affected, with the rates for health and social care workers being 10 times those in nonhealth care industries. Around a quarter of nurses and doctors report physical assaults in the course of their work.

E. Murder

Murder, unlike death by natural causes, disproportionately affects the young, leaving relatives, particu-

larly parents, feeling as if their future has been taken from them. Relatives of murder victims often feel stigmatized and isolated, with a sense of shame and betrayal, which results in their being unable to communicate their distress or make emotional contact with others. The impact of traumatic bereavement may include physical symptoms, cognitive impairment, depression, and phobic avoidance as well as impaired work and social functioning. There is often a feeling of being let down by the criminal justice system, which compounds the sense of loss.

F. Robbery and Burglary

The effects of burglary may include PTSD but are generally less severe and long lasting. They may, however, include depression and anxiety and a sense of violation, which may the most distressing and difficult aspect to resolve. Robbery, unlike burglary, involves direct contact with the perpetrator as well as a degree of threat to life and is therefore more likely to result in PTSD. Predictors of good recovery include a lower perception of threat to life, having had a preexisting view of the world as meaningful and orderly, and a rapid reduction of symptoms within the first month, whereas a depressive and avoidant coping style, fear of future violence, and increased somatic symptoms over time are associated with a poorer outcome.

G. Mass Shootings and Terrorist Crimes

While terrorist crimes are relatively infrequent, their social impact is much more widespread, inducing a climate of fear and uncertainty. For individuals caught up in terrorist attacks the degree of threat to life and the extent of physical injury sustained during the attack are the best predictors of psychological problems, particularly PTSD, both in the immediate and longer term. In the context of Northern Ireland a number of studies have found significant numbers of those with direct experience of terrorist incidents to be suffering from PTSD. This is in contrast to research on the impact of terrorist violence on the general population, which has been unable to detect a relationship between terrorist violence and resultant mental health problems in the population at large.

Studies which have looked at the impact of shootings tend by their very nature to be small scale but have found significant levels of distress and high rates of PTSD and other psychiatric disorders, with 33% or more being diagnosed as suffering from ASD in the immediate aftermath and this diagnosis being predictive of PTSD symptoms at follow-up several months later. Similarly, being held hostage has been related to high levels of subsequent distress both in victims and in their families. Victims of hostage taking may experience strong attachment and paradoxical gratitude toward the captors, with positive emotions including compassion and romantic love occurring. This may be expressed as profound gratitude for being allowed to live and has become referred to as Stockholm Syndrome.

IV. SUPPORT AND TREATMENT SERVICES

There are few culturally accepted rituals used to support victims of crime. This means that a major strategy in treatment and support services involves normalizing the process. In the first instance this may be best achieved by victim support schemes, which offer practical assistance such as in accompanying people to court hearings, guiding them through the process of applying for compensation, and dealing with the complexities of the criminal justice system. They also offer emotional support and the opportunity to ventilate emotions following a crime. Referrals to schemes are often automatically made by the police but may also be made from mental health professionals or may be requested by victims themselves. Despite the high prevalence of PTSD in victims of crime who participate in the criminal justice system there is still ample evidence that they do not have adequate access to mental health services. This occurs despite awareness that victims of serious crimes and the families of murder victims may develop psychiatric illnesses which require referral to mental health services for specialist treatment.

There has been an assumption that early intervention is more successful. There are few controlled studies of the impact of early intervention. Those which do exist seem to be evenly divided between three categories, i.e., bringing about improvement, having no impact, and resulting in deterioration, so as yet it is not possible to assume that early intervention is either effective or at least harmless. Research on victims of serious crimes such as rape suggests that in the immediate aftermath the majority of victims would meet the diagnostic criteria for PTSD but that by 4–5 months this decreases substantially to less than half. If recovery does not occur during this time then subsequent improvements may be slow, resulting in chronic problems. The fact that the majority of victims may recover spontaneously should not diminish the need for provision of adequate services for the significant minority who do not improve.

The effects of criminal victimization may be severe and incapacitating and may have long-term economic and social consequences. Victims of crime are rarely vocal on their own behalf and as a consequence their needs may be unrecognized, both in the population at large and by health professionals in particular.

See Also the Following Articles

SEXUAL ASSAULT; TERRORISM; VIOLENCE

Bibliography

Brewin, C. J., Andrews, B., Rose, S., and Kirk, M. (1999). Acute stress disorder and posttraumatic stress disorder in victims of violent crime. *Am. J. Psychiat.* **156**, 360–366.

Burgess, A. W., and Holmstrom, L. L. (1974). Rape trauma syndrome. *Am. J. Psychiat.* **131**, 981–986.

Davis, R. C., Taylor, B., and Lurigio, A. J. (1996). Adjusting to criminal victimisation: The correlates of post crime distress. *Violence & Victims* **11**(1), 21–38.

Eisele, G. R., Watkins, J. P., and Mathews, K. O. (1998). Workplace violence at government sites. *Am. J. Indust. Med.* **33**(5), 485–492.

Figley, C. R. (1985). "Trauma & Its Wake," (Vol. 1). Brunner Mazel, New York.

Hilberman, E. (1976). "The Rape Victim." Basic Books, New York.

Kilpatrick, D. G., Saunders, B. E., Amick-McMullan, A., Best,

C. L., Veronen, L. J., and Resnick, H. (1989). Victim & crime factors associated with the development of crime-related post traumatic stress disorder. *Behav. Ther.* **20**, 199–214.

Kilpatrick, D. G., Saunders, B. E., Veronen, L. J., Best C. L., and Von, J. M. (1987). Criminal victimisation: Lifetime prevalence, reporting to police and psychological impact. *Crime Delinq.* **33**(4), 479–489.

Lees, S. (1996). "Carnal Knowledge: Rape on Trial." Hamish Hamilton, London.

Maguire, M. (1982). "Burglary in a Dwelling." Heinemann, London.

Mezey, G. C., and King, M. B., (1989). The effects of sexual assault on men: A survey of 22 victims. *Psychol. Med.* **19**, 205–209.

Mirlees-Black, C., Budd, T., Partridge, S., and Mayhew, P.

(1998). "The 1998 British Crime Survey." HMSO, England and Wales.

Ochberg, F. M. (1988). "Post Traumatic Therapy and Victims of Violence." Brunner Mazel, New York.

Pathe, M., and Mullen, P. (1997). The impact of stalkers on their victims. *Br. J. Psychiat.* **170**, 12–17.

Resnick, H. S., Kilpatrick, D. G., Dansky, B. S., Saunders, B. E., and Best, C. L. (1993). Prevalence of civilian trauma and post traumatic stress in a representative national sample of women. *J. Consult. Clin. Psychol.* **61**(6), 984–991.

Van der Kolk, B. A., McFarlane, A. C., and Veisaeth, L. (Eds.) (1996). "Traumatic Stress: The Effects of Overwhelming Experience of Mind, Body and Society." The Guildford Press, London.

Walker, L. E. (1979). "The Battered Woman." Harper and Row, New York.

Critical Thermal Limits

Joachim Roth

University of Marburg Medical School, Germany

I. Critical Thermal Limits of Ambient Temperature
II. Critical Thermal Limits of Body Temperature

GLOSSARY

homeotherm The pattern of temperature regulation in a species in which the cyclic variation in core temperature is maintained within arbitrarily defined limits ($\pm 2°C$) despite much larger variations in ambient temperature.

thermal balance Equality between heat gain and heat loss to maintain body temperature at a constant level.

thermoeffector An organ and its function, respectively, which affects heat balance in a controlled manner as part of the process of temperature regulation.

Critical thermal limits can be defined for homeotherms (1) as the highest and lowest ambient temperatures at which the rate of evaporative heat loss or the rate of metabolic heat production must be increased to maintain thermal balance, or (2) as the highest and lowest ambient temperatures at which the capacity for temperature regulation is exceeded and core temperature changes (development of hyper- or hypothermia), or (3) as the lethal highest and lowest body core temperatures.

I. CRITICAL THERMAL LIMITS OF AMBIENT TEMPERATURE

A. Critical Thermal Limits for Activation of Thermoeffectors

Within a certain range of ambient temperature heat production is at its minimum. This temperature range is called "thermoneutral zone" or "metabolically indifferent zone." Within the thermoneutral zone there are no regulatory changes in metabolic heat production or evaporative heat loss. The absolute highest and lowest limits as well as the width of the thermoneutral zone depend on body size, heat insulation, the heat transfer coefficient of the surrounding medium, (water, wind) and the status of acclimation. For example, the metabolism of the arctic white fox does not start to rise until the ambient temperature decreases below −40°C, while a nude human starts to increase heat production at external air temperatures of 27°C and lower. The zones of thermal neutrality for a number of representative homeothermic species are shown in Fig. 1.

B. Critical Thermal Limits for the Thermoregulatory Capacity

The so-defined highest critical thermal limit depends on the capacity of the thermoeffector, i.e., the capacity to dissipate heat by evaporation of water, and on body size. At a low relative humidity of about 15%, the average external heat tolerance limits are 60°C for humans, 56°C for dogs and cats, 42°C for rabbits, 39°C for rats, and 37°C for mice. As long as a sufficient amount of water is supplied these species can tolerate the listed ambient temperatures for longer periods. The limit of cold tolerance primarily

TABLE I
Highest Lethal Body Temperatures in Some Representative Homeothermic Species

Species	Lethal temperature (°C)	Remarks
Mouse	43.3	
Rat	42.5	50% lethal
Guinea pig	42.8	50% lethal
Rabbit	43.4	50% lethal
Cat	43.4	50% lethal
Dog	41.7	50% lethal
Human	45.0	Short-term survival
Human	43.0	Usually fatal

[a] Data compiled from Precht *et al.* (1973); copyright notice of Springer-Verlag.

depends on the effectiveness of the heat insulation which covers the body. Thus, it is not surprising that naked humans, without an insulating hair coat, possess only moderate cold resistance. Unclothed humans can maintain a constant body core temperature for about 1 h at an ambient air temperature of −1°C, while rats can withstand an external temperature of −25°C and the arctic white fox a temperature of −80°C for 1 h without any decrease in core temperature. In contrast to the quality of insulation, the extent of possible changes in the metabolic rate is a less important factor for the external limit of cold tolerance. In homeothermic animals whose insulation is poorer, the cold-induced increase of metabolic heat production is stronger than in well-insulated animals and starts at higher ambient temperatures.

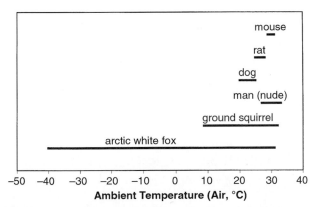

FIGURE 1 Thermoneutral zones (metabolically indifferent zones) of some homeothermic species. The left end of each bar indicates the ambient temperature at which the minimal resting metabolic heat production starts to increase. The right end of each bar indicates the ambient temperature at which mechanisms of heat dissipation (sweating, panting) are activated (modified from Precht *et al.*, 1973; copyright notice of Springer-Verlag).

II. CRITICAL THERMAL LIMITS OF BODY TEMPERATURE

This kind of thermal range refers only to the highest and lowest body core temperatures that a given species can survive. With regard to the lethal body temperature limits, the time factor, i.e., the duration of extreme body temperatures, is critically important.

TABLE II
Lowest Lethal Body Temperatures in Some Representative Homeothermic Species

Species	Lethal temperature (°C)	Remarks
Rat	13	Cardiac arrest
Rat	−3	Supercooled, artificial hypo- thermia, revival
Guinea pig	17–21	
Cat	14–16	
Dog	15–18	
Dog	0–2	Extracorporal circulation revival
Human	24–26	Average accidental hypo- thermia
Human	18	Lowest accidental hypo- thermia, revival
Human	9	Artificial hypothermia, 45 min cardiac arrest, revival

[a] Some cases of revival after artificial hypothermis and rewarming are included. Data compiled from Precht *et al.* (1973); copyright notice of Springer-Verlag.

A. Upper Limit of Body Temperature

The highest lethal body temperatures of homeotherms fall within quite a narrow range, which is only a few degrees above the normal body core temperature. The upper lethal body temperatures of some species are summarized in Table I. It should be noted that a number of organs or even parts of the body can be warmed to temperatures higher than the general lethal body temperature. Due to this fact, experimentally induced local hyperthermia is used in oncotherapy with the aim of destroying tumor cells.

B. Lower Limit of Body Temperature

The lowest lethal body temperatures for homeotherms are usually between 15 and 20°C. By use of special techniques for cooling and rewarming it is possible to lower body temperature of a subject or an animal far below the usually lethal levels and to revive them unharmed. The lower lethal body temperatures of some species including a few cases of revival under extreme conditions are summarized in Table II.

See Also the Following Articles

Heat Resistance; Hyperthermia; Hypothermia; Pressures, Effects of Extreme High and Low

Bibliography

Cossins, A. R., and Bowler, K. (1987). "Temperature Biology of Animals." Chapman and Hall, London.

Fregly, M. J., and Blatteis, C. M. (1996). "Handbook of Physiology: Environmental Physiology," Vol. 1, Section 4. Oxford Univ. Press, New York.

Precht, H., Christophersen, J., Hensel, H., and Larcher, W. (1973). "Temperature and Life." Springer-Verlag, Berlin.

Sharma, H. S., and Westman, J. (1998). "Progress in Brain Research: Brain Function in Hot Environments," Vol. 115. Elsevier, Amsterdam.

Crowding Stress

Peter Csermely

Semmelweis University, Budapest, Hungary

GLOSSARY

amyloidosis A severe pathological change of various organs and tissues where aggregated amyloid fibers develop and induce the destruction of affected cells.

channeling Interaction of enzymes catalyzing consecutive enzyme reactions where the product of the "first" reaction becomes the substrate of the "second" enzyme by a directed molecular transfer largely avoiding free diffusion.

hypothalamic-pituitary-adrenal (HPA) stimulation/axis A major peripheral mechanism of the stress response, involving three major constituents: the corticotrophin releasing hormone (CRH), corticotrophin (ACTH), and glucocorticoids.

molecular crowding A term to denote a dense population of molecules (usually macromolecules) where aggregation, diffusion, hydration, and other properties of the individual molecules are significantly altered.

C rowding stress is a type of psychosocial stress induced by an increased density of population. Population density may be raised either by increasing the number of species living in the same area and/or by reducing their living space. Crowding stress induces complex changes at the behavioral, physiological, and molecular levels, which differ, depending if crowding stress is acute or chronic. Crowding stress can also be interpreted at the molecular level: molecular crowding promotes aggregation of various macromolecules and causes profound changes in numerous physicochemical parameters of their solution.

I. INTRODUCTION

As outlined above, studies on crowding stress consider an exceptionally high number of variables. Several consequences of crowding stress may differ greatly, depending if population density is raised by increasing the number of species living in the same area or by reducing living space. If crowding is increased to such an extent that it leads to confinement, malnutrition, or an increased incidence of infections, other complications develop. Crowding stress may be "acute" (transient), i.e., the effects manifest after a few days, or "chronic," i.e., changes occur after prolonged overcrowding lasting for weeks, months, or even years. While mice or rats are the most commonly used species in crowding stress experiments, studies have been performed with almost all types of domesticated animals, various fishes, and even humans. Though the conclusions of these studies can be directly compared only within the same species, some general trends can be observed. This article focuses on these general aspects of crowding stress.

II. CROWDING STRESS: PSYCHOSOCIAL EFFECTS

Crowding as a chronic source of stress constitutes a major threat to psychological well-being. Dense populations are characterized by considerably increased aggressive behavior. Crowded monkeys (even well fed), including females and young, have brutal fights and wound and kill each other. Crowding stress adversely affects gonadal functions and if it occurs during pregnancy may inhibit reproductive activity of the second generation through masculinization of female pups. Chronic crowding leads to deficits in learning tasks and has been used in animal models to induce depression. In human populations crowding stress is proposed to be an important factor in the development of increased urban insanity/schizophrenia.

III. PHYSIOLOGICAL CHANGES IN CROWDING STRESS

Crowding stress (especially if chronic) suppresses immune functions. Disturbed immune regulation leads to increased autoantibody levels and may be one of the factors behind the increased occurrence of childhood asthma. Various infections and increased susceptibility to poisoning are more likely to occur under crowded conditions. A widely established example indicates that household overcrowding is related to an increased prevalence of ulcer-inducing *Heliobacter pylori* infections. *Heliobacter pylori* infections and stress-induced gastric lesions significantly contribute to the development of ulcers and stomach cancer. Due to digestive problems and occasional appetite loss chronic stress induces weight loss. In several organs, such as in kidneys and adrenals, chronic crowding stress induces intensive amyloidosis. Chronic overcrowding in many cases leads to hypertension in the resting state or to "relative hypertension" after exercise.

IV. POSSIBLE MOLECULAR MECHANISMS OF CROWDING STRESS

Crowding stress considerably impairs central histamine, noradrenaline, and vasopressin production but does not change the corticotrophin releasing hormone (CRH) system, which is involved in hypothalamic-pituitary-adrenocortical (HPA) stimulation. This is possibly the cause of decrease in appetite and consequent weight loss. Hypothalamic-pituitary-adrenocortical stimulation leads to compromised immune function and suppression of gonadal functions. Chronic HPA stimulation may lead to osteoporosis, chronic gastrointestinal pain, and retarded growth. Thus prolonged activation of the hypothalamic-pituitary-adrenocortical axis may explain many of the psychological/physiological symptoms resulting from chronic overcrowding, such as gastrointestinal problems, weight loss, sensitivity to infections, and decreased reproductive activity.

Crowding stress may impair cellular signaling mechanisms, such as changes in intracellular calcium levels, especially in elderly subjects. Impaired signaling may significantly contribute to immune suppression and decreased adaptive mechanisms.

V. CROWDING OF WORMS

The signaling mechanisms can be studied more easily in simple organisms. The fruit fly *Drosophila melanogaster* ceases to develop in overcrowded cultures. Food limitation and overcrowding also induce arrested development of the worm *Caenorhabditis elegans*, leading to the formation of the so-called "dauer larva". Daf-7, a homolog of the human transforming growth factor-β (TGF-β), prevents dauer larva commitment. Several other members of the dauer larva regulating Daf family are receptor serine-threonine kinases similar to the human TGF-β receptor. Mutations of another signaling pathway of *C. elegans* may quadruple the adult lifetime of the worm besides disturbing its dauer larva development. Thus, disturbances in signaling due to crowding stress may have profound consequences in the longevity of (simpler) organisms.

VI. MOLECULAR CROWDING

Crowding induces changes in the "behavior" of macromolecules as well. If the total volume of a macromolecular species occupies a significant fraction of the total volume of the solution we refer to such a medium as "crowded." Under experimental conditions molecular crowding is induced by polyethylene glycol or by dextrane. An intracellular environment where the total amount of macromolecules usually occupies more than one-third of the total volume is a typical example of molecular crowding.

Positively, molecular crowding induces an increased association of macromolecules, enhancing channeling between enzymes catalyzing consecutive enzyme reactions or improving signaling efficiency in organized signaling cascades.

Yet at such a high density macromolecules begin to compete for water molecules, their hydration becomes compromised, and, consequently, osmotic stress occurs. The large amount of macromolecules and their immobilized hydrate shell constitute a large "excluded volume" which requires significant adjustments in physicochemical kinetics and equilibrium of various intracellular processes.

See Also the Following Article

INDUSTRIALIZED SOCIETIES, STRESS AND

Bibliography

Barker, D. J., Coggon, D., Osmond, C., and Wickham, C. (1990). Poor housing and high rates of stomach cancer in England and Wales. *Br. J. Cancer* **61**, 575–578.

Bugajski, J., Borycz, J., Glod, R., and Bugajski, A. J. (1995). Crowding stress impairs the pituitary-adrenocortical responsiveness to the vasopressin but not corticotrophin-releasing hormone stimulation. *Brain Res.* **681**, 223–228.

Csermely, P. (Ed.) (1998). Stress of life from molecules to Man. *Ann. N.Y. Acad. Sci.* **851**.

Csermely, P., Pénzes, I., and Tóth, S. (1995). Chronic overcrowding decreases cytoplasmic free calcium levels in the T lymphocytes of aged CBA/CA mice. *Experientia* **51**, 976–979.

Galpin, O. P., Whitaker, C. J., and Dubiel, A. J. (1992). *Heliobacter pylori* infection and overcrowding in childhood. *Lancet* **339**, 619.

Goeckner, D. J., Greenough, W. T., and Mead, W. R. (1973). Deficits in learning tasks following chronic overcrowding in rats. *J. Pers. Soc. Psychol.* **28**, 256–261.

Kaplan, B. A., and Mascie-Taylor, C. G. (1985). Biosocial factors in the epidemiology of childhood asthma in a British national sample. *J. Epidemol. Community Health* **39**, 152–156.

Larsen, P. L., Albert, P. S., and Riddle, D. L. (1995). Genes that regulate both development and longevity in *Caenorhabditis elegans*. *Genetics* **139**, 1567–1583.

Marchlewska-Koj, A. (1997). Sociogenic stress and rodent reproduction. *Neurosci. Biobehav. Rev.* **21**, 699–703.

Naitoh, H., Nomura, S., Kunimi, Y., and Yamaoka, K. (1992). "Swimming-induced head twitching" in rats in the forced swimming test induced by overcrowding stress: A new marker in the animal model of depression? *Keio J. Med.* **41**, 221–224.

Ren, P., Lim, C. S., Johnsen, R., Albert, P. S., Pilgrim, D., and Riddle, D. L. (1996). Control of *C. elegans* larval development by neuronal expression of a TGF-beta homologue. *Science* **274**, 1389–1391.

Rohwer, J. M., Postma, P. W., Kholodenko, B. N., and Westerhoff, H. V. (1998). Implications of macromolecular crowding for signal transduction and metabolite channeling. *Proc. Natl. Acad. Sci. USA* **95**, 10547–10552.

Zimmerman, S. B., and Minton, A. P. (1993). Macromolecular crowding: Biochemical, biophysical and physiological consequences. *Annu. Rev. Biophys. Biomol. Struct.* **22**, 27–65.

Cultural Factors

John W. Berry and Bilge Ataca

Queen's University, Kingston, Ontario, Canada

GLOSSARY

acculturation A process of cultural and psychological change that results from contact between two cultural groups.

adaptation A process of change that seeks to improve the fit between cultural groups and/or individuals and their habitat; it may result in outcomes that range from well to maladapted.

culture A shared way of life of a group of people, including their symbolic, social, and material products; cultures are transmitted to new members over generations.

ecology The study of relationships between human organisms and their physical habitats, including their biological, cultural, and psychological adaptations to these habitats.

strategies Various ways employed by cultures and individuals to adapt to their habitats, including adjustment, reaction, and withdrawal (e.g., coping strategies and acculturation strategies).

stress The cultural and psychological consequences that occur when changes exceed the capacity of groups and individuals to adapt.

H uman behavior is influenced by factors external to the individual. Among these factors, the most fundamental are those that are broadly cultural; these contexts, and experiences within them, demonstrably shape human development and action. Stress and coping are among those behaviors so shaped. According to Aldwin, culture can influence stress and coping in four ways: the types of stressors experienced, the appraisal of these stressors, the choice of coping strategies, and the institutional supports for coping with stressors.

I. CULTURE AS ADAPTATION

Among the many approaches to understanding *culture* is the view that human groups develop a way of dealing with recurrent problems in their ecosystems; these solutions are widely shared among members of a society and transmitted to their offspring. That is, cultures are *adaptive* to context, and, to the extent that these adaptations are successful, their *fit* is enhanced and *stress* is reduced: "Culture is man's most important instrument of adaptation" (Cohen, 1968, p. 1). The empirical foundations for this conception of culture were laid by Forde and Kroeber, who demonstrated that in Africa and North America, culture areas generally mapped onto ecological areas; in both continents, broadly shared features of culture were associated with ecological features in a particular group's habitat. This conception of culture has permitted work in both anthropology and cross-cultural psychology to align with stress, coping, and adaptation frameworks that are widely used in psychology.

When ecological conditions are relatively stable and there is sufficient carrying capacity (i.e., support from the habitat), cultural adaptations are also stable. However, when there is ecosystem disturbance due to internal or external forces (such as natural disaster, invasion, etc.) or when there is a chronic shortfall in the ability of the habitat to sustain the cultural group, then new adaptations are required if the group is to survive. In these terms, ecosystem changes constitute stressors, attempts to find innovative ways to manage day-to-day existence constitute coping, and the solutions achieved (successful or not) constitute adaptation.

Concern with these two sources of influence (internal and external) has given rise to an ecocultural model that attempts to understand cultural and psychological phenomena as the result of adaptation to ecological factors and to those that arise from contact with other cultures (the process of acculturation). Both during the process and when there is limited adaptive success, two kinds of stress may result: *cultural stress* and *acculturative stress.*

For both kinds of stress, it is useful to consider some fundamental strategies of coping with these internal and external stressors. There are at least three ways to achieve adaptation: *adjustment, reaction,* and *withdrawal.* In the case of adjustment, behavioral changes are in a direction that reduces the conflict (that is, increases the congruence) between the environment and the behavior by changing the behavior to bring it into harmony with the environment. In general, this variety is the one most often intended by the term adaptation and may indeed be the most common form of adaptation. In the case of reaction, behavioral changes are in a direction which retaliates against the environment; these may lead to environmental changes which, in effect, increases the congruence between the two, but not by way of cultural or behavioral adjustment. In the case of withdrawal, behavior is in a direction which reduces the pressures from the environment; in a sense, it is a removal from the adaptive arena. These three varieties of adaptation are similar to the distinctions in the psychological literature made between moving *with or toward,* moving *against,* and moving *away from* a stimulus.

II. CULTURAL STRESS

As noted above, cultural stress occurs when extant or novel situations *within* the culture place demands on the group and its individual members that exceed their capacity to respond. Rather than maintaining or improving their "fit," the responses of the group and individuals fail, and adaptation is unsuccessful. From the point of view of ecological anthropology, examples of successful adaptations are the most common; this is because those that are not successful fail to survive and are unavailable for contemporary observation. However, archaeology provides numerous examples of cultures that disappeared as a result of failure to adapt. Despite this imbalance in cases, there are examples of societies and individuals under cultural stress due to the extreme circumstances that

they face at present. Two of these are described: the Ik of northern Uganda and the Mossi and Fulani of Burkina Faso.

The classic portrayal of the Ik was presented by Turnbull. This cultural group had lived for centuries as hunting and gathering nomads in a semidesert region at the intersection of Uganda, Sudan, and Kenya. Their main territory was a valley that had been taken over by the government to create a National Park, from which they were excluded. With their old economic subsistence base taken away and agriculture impossible, they attempted to survive by raiding the cattle herds of neighboring groups. As the carrying capacity of their territory was reduced (exacerbated by failure of the rains), the social fabric of the Ik deteriorated. According to Turnbull, they "abandoned useless appendages . . . those basic qualities such as family, cooperative sociality, belief, love, hope and so forth, for the very good reason that in their context, these militated against survival" (1972, p. 289).

This portrait is one of extreme ecological change, one that was rather quickly followed by social, cultural, and psychological change, all of them maladaptive. In this extreme case, the stressors were so severe that the cultural resources were incapable of providing any coping strategies other than intense striving for individual survival. Severe hunger generated "loss of any community of interest, familial or economic, social or spiritual" (p. 157) and eventually resulted in a maladaptive "everyone for himself" strategy that in the end failed.

A second example of cultural stress, one that also resulted from ecological change, is that of two groups in the Sahel region of West Africa. Ongoing environmental degradation (deterioration of the soil, loss of nutrients, reduction in wildlife) has led to loss of food resources and income and constituted a major set of stressors in the lives of two societies in this region. The Fulani (pastoralists) and the Mossi (agriculturalists) had differentially adapted to this semiarid ecosystem, one grazing their cattle over a large territory, the other enclosing small land areas for cultivation. In this study, coping with environmental change was directly assessed (by questionnaire) as was their locus of control and two psychological outcomes (feelings of marginality and of personal stress). With respect to coping, two factors emerged, the first representing a combination of problem-solving and support-seeking and the second mainly avoidance strategies; this split resembles the Lazarus and Folkman distinction between problem-focused and emotion-focused coping. For the locus-of-control measure, three factors were obtained: the first represented individual effort, the second nonpersonal control, and the third was uninterpretable. Both the Marginality and Stress scales produced single factors.

Structural analyses of the impact of ecological and cultural factors on the two psychological outcomes were carried out. The carrying capacity of the ecosystem was introduced as the latent variable, with four variables (environmental degradation, land use, cattle, and modernity) used as independent variables. The ecosystem provided a higher carrying capacity for the pastoralists than for the agriculturalists and consequently the former were less marginalized and stressed. According to Van Haaften and Van de Vijver (1996, p. 426), "this finding is in agreement with the common observation that nomadic people (the pastoralists) are less susceptible to environmental stressors than are sedentary people (the agriculturalists). Unlike the latter, the former can move away from environmental stressors."

With these two examples, it is possible to identify links between ecological, cultural, and psychological changes in human populations. Evidence from these anthropological and psychological sources show clearly that when cultural groups experience stressors, collective and individual coping can sometimes lead to successful adaptation and sometimes not, resulting in stress.

III. ACCULTURATIVE STRESS

When ecosystem and cultural changes are introduced from outside, the process of acculturation is initiated. In essence, acculturation refers to both the cultural and psychological changes that follow from contact between two or more cultural groups. At the cultural group level, these changes can occur in the physical, political, economic, or social domains (e.g., urbanization, loss of autonomy and livelihood, and the reorganization or even the destruction of social relationships). At the individual level, changes in the psychology of the individual take place.

It had been previously thought that acculturation inevitably brings social and psychological problems. However, such a negative and broad generalization no longer appears to be valid. Variability in psychological acculturation exists and is associated with three differing views about the degree of difficulty that is thought to exist during acculturation: behavioral shifts, acculturative stress, and psychopathology. The first is one that considers psychological changes to be rather easy to accomplish. Here, psychological adaptations to acculturation are considered to be a matter of learning a new behavioral repertoire that is appropriate for the new cultural context. This also requires some "culture shedding" to occur (the _un_learning of aspects of one's previous repertoire that are no longer appropriate); and it may be accompanied by some moderate "culture conflict" (where incompatible behaviors create difficulties for the individual).

In cases where serious conflict exists, then individuals may experience _acculturative stress_ if they cannot easily change their repertoire. Drawing on the broader stress and adaptation paradigms, this approach advocates the study of the process of how individuals deal with acculturative problems on first encountering them and over time. In this sense, acculturative stress is a stress reaction in response to life events that are rooted in intercultural contact. Within this orientation, depression (due to cultural loss) and anxiety (due to uncertainty about how to live) are the problems most frequently found in a series of recent studies in Canada.

When major difficulties are experienced, then the _psychopathology_ perspective is most appropriate. Here, changes in the cultural context exceed the individual's capacity to cope because of the magnitude, speed, or some other aspect of the change, leading to serious psychological disturbances, such as clinical depression and incapacitating anxiety.

Long-term adaptation to acculturation is variable, ranging from well adapted to maladapted, varying from a situation where individuals can manage their new lives very well to one where they are unable to carry on in the new society. Short-term changes during acculturation are sometimes negative and often disruptive in character. However, for most acculturating individuals, after a period of time, some long-term positive adaptation to the new cultural context usually takes place.

In part, variations in adaptation result from the *acculturation* strategy adopted by individuals. These strategies derive from individuals orienting themselves to two fundamental issues faced during acculturation: (1) To what extent do individuals seek to maintain their heritage culture and identity? and (2) To what extent do they seek to have contact with and participate in the larger society? These two issues can be responded to along two attitudinal dimensions, with generally positive or negative ("yes" or "no") responses at opposite ends. Orientations to these two intersect to define four acculturation strategies. From the point of view of nondominant groups, when individuals do not wish to maintain their cultural identity and seek daily interaction with other cultures, the *assimilation* strategy is defined. In contrast, when individuals place a value on holding on to their original culture and at the same time wish to avoid interaction with others, then the *separation* alternative is defined. When there is an interest in both maintaining one's original culture, while in daily interactions with other groups, *integration* is the option; here, there is some degree of cultural integrity maintained, while at the same time seeking, as a member of a cultural group, to participate as an integral part of the larger social network. Finally, when there is little possibility or interest in cultural maintenance (often for reasons of enforced cultural loss) and little interest in having relations with others (often for reasons of exclusion or discrimination), then *marginalization* is defined. Acculturation strategies have been shown to have substantial relationships with positive adaptation: integration is usually the most successful, marginalization is the least, and assimilation and separation strategies are intermediate.

Adaptation is also multifaceted; psychological, sociocultural, marital, and economic adaptation have recently been distinguished in the acculturation literature. *Psychological adaptation* refers to a set of internal psychological outcomes including a clear sense of personal and cultural identity, good mental health,

and the achievement of personal satisfaction in the new cultural context. *Sociocultural adaptation* involves the mastery of day-to-day relationships in the new and changing social environment (including friends, school, and bureaucratic relationships). *Marital adaptation* relates to the accommodation of spouses in the process of acculturation when each is faced with the new culture and forms of behavior and different ways of acculturating. And finally, *economic adaptation* refers to the process by which individuals cope with and reestablish sustainable work relationships in the new economic system (including problems of status loss, under-/unemployment, and status mobility).

Each of these four domains of adaptation to acculturation may entail acculturative stress. In all four, the source of the stressors lies in the contact between groups and the resulting process of cultural change. It is important to note that acculturative stress is not a unique *form* of stress, but has unique *antecedents* (residing in the process of acculturation). Moreover, many of the *outcomes* are closely linked to the unique features of the acculturation process (such as experiencing cultural identity problems, acquiring culturally appropriate social skills, rearranging marital relations to take new cultural expectations into account, and experiencing difficulties due to employment discrimination in the new society). Thus, acculturative stress can be said to be a special kind of stress because of both its special set of stressors and its special set of outcomes. Following are examples of these four facets of acculturative stress.

Psychological and sociocultural adaptation were initially distinguished by Ward and colleagues in the sojourner acculturation literature. As noted above, psychological adaptation mostly involves one's psychological well-being and satisfaction in a new cultural context, whereas sociocultural adaptation refers to one's ability to acquire culturally appropriate knowledge and skills and to interact with the new culture and manage daily life. These two forms of adaptation are interrelated; dealing successfully with problems and positive interactions with members of the dominant culture are likely to improve one's feelings of well-being and satisfaction; similarly it is easier to accomplish tasks and develop positive interpersonal relations if one is feeling good and accepted.

Although related, these two forms of adaptation are conceptually and empirically distinct. Conceptually, they reflect two distinct theoretical approaches to acculturation. Psychological adaptation is better interpreted in terms of a stress and coping model; sociocultural adaptation is better viewed from a social learning perspective. Stress and coping models are based on the notion that both positive and negative life changes are intrinsically stressful in that they require adaptive reactions. Acculturation has been viewed as entailing such stress-inducing life changes, which increase susceptibility to physical and mental illness. The second approach draws on a combination of social skills and culture learning models. Individuals experiencing culture change are socially unskilled in the new cultural setting. Social learning models emphasize the importance of the acquisition of social skills and knowledge appropriate to the new culture.

Psychological and sociocultural adaptation are also empirically distinct, in that they usually have different experiential antecedents. Research has shown that psychological adaptation, defined in terms of well-being or mood states (e.g., depression, anxiety, stress), was predicted by personality, life changes, and social support variables. Searle and Ward found that extroversion, life events, and satisfaction with host national relations predicted psychological adaptation in Malaysian and Singaporean students in New Zealand. Locus of control, life changes, and personal relationship satisfaction accounted for a substantial portion of variance in psychological well-being in student and adult sojourners. In contrast, assessed in terms of social difficulty, sociocultural adaptation was predicted by variables which are related more strongly to cognitive factors and social skills acquisition, such as cultural knowledge, cultural distance, cultural identity, language ability, length of residence in the new culture, and amount of contact with hosts. Extending this framework to immigrant couples, Ataca also found that these two dimensions of adaptation were associated with different variables. Psychological adaptation of married Turkish immigrant couples in Canada was associated with the personality variable of hardiness, social support, accultura-tion attitudes, and perceived discrimination, while sociocultural adaptation was mostly related to variables that are instrumental in acquiring social skills in the new culture, namely, English language proficiency and contact with Euro-Canadians.

Ataca introduced the concept of marital adaptation as the third dimension of the overall adaptation of Turkish immigrant couples and examined marital variables in relation to the different dimensions of adaptation. Findings supported the distinctiveness of marital adaptation from psychological and sociocultural adaptation. Better marital adaptation was mostly associated with variables specific to marital life, namely, fewer marital stressors and greater marital support. Marital variables also displayed close relations with psychological adaptation. Marital stressors and support explained a significant amount of variance in psychological adaptation. This is in line with the literature on the relationship between marital variables and psychological distress among immigrants. Marital stressors were found to have an impact on both the marital distress and the depressive and psychosomatic symptoms of Indo-Canadian women. Naidoo found that South Asian women in Canada who had supportive husbands were less stressed. While the marital life of Turkish immigrants was related to psychological well-being, it was unrelated to sociocultural adaptation. The social skill learning necessary to function in the new cultural context was neither impeded nor facilitated by the conjugal relationship.

Immigrants typically suffer high rates of un-/underemployment. Lack of knowledge of language, of training, and discrimination force many immigrants into low-skill jobs. Conversely, high levels of education, occupational skills, and professional training received in the home country are often not recognized by authorities in the new country, resulting in underemployment. For example, it was reported that the majority of well-educated and qualified Turkish immigrants in Montreal experienced barriers to successful integration into the labor force, followed by a decline in income and overall status in the first 6 months of arrival. This was mainly due to lack of competence in both official languages, recognition of credentials, and Canadian work experience. A full recovery in income, but not in occupational status, was made over time.

Under-/unemployment, low incomes, and the concomitant loss in one's socioeconomic status constitute sources of stress and are related to psychological symptoms, including depression. Satisfactory employment in the country of settlement, on the other hand, is related to life satisfaction and emotional well-being. Aycan and Berry found that a greater decline in "present status" in Canada compared to the "departure status" from Turkey was associated with high psychological stress among Turkish immigrants. Those who experienced greater status loss were also less satisfied and less likely to describe themselves as accomplished in economic life. Duration of unemployment and current employment status had critical implications for Turkish immigrants' psychological well-being and adaptation. The longer the immigrants were unemployed, the more likely they suffered from psychological stress, negative self-concept, alienation from the society, and adaptation difficulties.

Studying the adaptation of both professional and nonprofessional Turkish immigrants in Toronto, Ataca found that those of low socioeconomic status were more stressed, yet more satisfied with their lives than those of high socioeconomic status. This finding again points out to the consequence of the loss of status professional immigrants experience. Immigrants of lower status make comparisons with what their economic condition used to be like and feel satisfied, while those of higher status make comparisons with their cohorts in Turkey and feel deprived. In this context, it was reported that low socioeconomic status and family income were also highly associated with high feelings of disturbance among South Asian women in Canada. Socioeconomic status is again an important predictor of stress in the studies with African- and Mexican-American females and Korean-American women.

In conclusion, stress does not take place in a vacuum: contextual factors, especially cultural ones that have been outlined here, clearly play a role. The importance of ecological and acculturative factors have been emphasized in order to provide a macrolevel view of how stress and coping are shaped.

Within these, micro-level experiences have been identified to illustrate the close links between culture and stress.

See Also the Following Articles

CULTURAL TRANSITION; ECONOMIC FACTORS AND STRESS; HEALTH AND SOCIOECONOMIC STATUS; INDIGENOUS SOCIETIES, STRESS AND; SOCIAL STATUS AND STRESS

Bibliography

Aldwin, C. M. (1994). "Stress, Coping, and Development." Guilford, New York.

Argyle, M. (1980). Interaction skills and social competence. *In* "Psychological Problems: The Social Context" (P. Feldman and J. Orford, Eds.), pp. 123–150. Wiley, Chichester.

Ataca, B. (1998). "Psychological, Sociocultural, and Marital Adaptation of Turkish Immigrants in Canada." Unpublished doctoral thesis, Queen's University, Kingston, Ontario, Canada.

Aycan, Z., and Berry, J. W. (1996). Impact of employment-related experiences on immigrants' psychological well-being and adaptation to Canada. *Can. J. Behav. Sci.* **28**, 240–251.

Beiser, M., Barwick, C., Berry, J. W., daCosta, G., Fantino, A. M., Ganesan, S., Lee, C., Milne, W., Naidoo, J., Prince, R., Tousignant, M., and Vela, E. (1988). "After the Door Has Been Opened: Mental Health Issues Affecting Immigrants and Refugees in Canada." A report of the Canadian Task Force on Mental Health Issues affecting Immigrants and Refugees. Ministry of Multiculturalism and Citizenship and Health and Welfare Canada, Ottawa, Ontario.

Berry, J. W. (1970). Marginality, stress and ethnic identification in an acculturated Aboriginal community. *J. Cross-Cult. Psychol.* **1**, 239–252.

Berry, J. W. (1976). "Human Ecology and Cognitive Style: Comparative Studies in Cultural and Psychological Adaptation." Wiley, New York.

Berry, J. W. (1990). Psychology of acculturation. *In* "Cross-Cultural Perspectives" (J. Berman, Ed.), Vol. 37, pp. 201–234. Univ. of Nebraska Press, Lincoln.

Berry, J. W. (1992). Acculturation and adaptation in a new society. *Int. Migration* **30**, 69–86.

Berry, J. W. (1997a). Cultural and ethnic factors in health. *In* "Cambridge Handbook of Psychology, Health and Medicine" (A. Baum, S. Newman, J. Weinman, R. West, and

C. McManus, Eds.), pp. 98–103. Cambridge Univ. Press, Cambridge, UK.

Berry, J. W. (1997b). Immigration, acculturation, and adaptation. *Appl. Psychol. Int. Rev.* **46**, 5–68.

Berry, J. W., and Kim, U. (1988). Acculturation and mental health. *In* "Health and Cross-Cultural Psychology: Towards Applications" (P. R. Dasen, J. W. Berry, and N. Sartorius, Eds.), pp. 207–238. Sage, Newbury Park, CA.

Berry, J. W., Kim, U., Minde, T., and Mok, D. (1987). Comparative studies of acculturative stress. *Int. Migration Rev.* **21**, 491–511.

Berry, J. W., Poortinga, Y. H., Pandey, J., Dasen, P. R., Saraswathi, T. S., Segall, M. H., and Kagitcibasi, C. (Eds.) (1997). "Handbook of Cross-Cultural Psychology" (2nd ed.). Allyn & Bacon, Boston, MA.

Brown, D. E. (1981). General stress in anthropological field work. *Am. Anthropol.* **83**, 74–92.

Cohen, Y. (1968). Culture as adaptation. *In* "Man in Adaptation" (Y. Cohen, Ed.), pp. 40–60. Aldine, Chicago.

Dona, G., and Berry, J. W. (1994). Acculturation attitudes and acculturative stress of Central American refugees in Canada. *Int. J. Psychol.* **29**, 57–70.

Dyal, J. A., Rybensky, L., and Somers, M. (1988). Marital and acculturative strain among Indo-Canadian and Euro-Canadian women. *In* "Ethnic Psychology: Research and Practice with Immigrants, Refugees, Native Peoples, Ethnic Groups, and Sojourners" (J. W. Berry and R. C. Annis, Eds.), pp. 80–95. Swets and Zeitlinger, Lisse, The Netherlands.

Forde, D. (1934). "Habitat, Economy and Society." Methuen, London.

Furnham, A., and Bochner, S. (1982). Social difficulty in a foreign culture: An empirical analysis of culture shock. *In* Cultures in Contact: Studies in Cross-Cultural Interaction (S. Bochner, Ed.), pp. 161–198. Pergamon, Oxford.

Horney, K. (1955). *In* "Schools of Psychoanalytic Thought" (R. Munroe, Ed.), Holt, New York.

Jayasuriya, L., Sang, D., and Fielding, A. (1992). "Ethnicity, Immigration and Mental Illness: A Critical Review of Australian Research." Bureau of Immigration Research, Canberra.

Kim, U., and Berry, J. W. (1986). Predictors of acculturative stress: Korean immigrants in Toronto, Canada. *In* "Ethnic Minorities and Immigrants in a Cross-Cultural Perspective" (L. Ekstrand, Ed.), pp. 159–170. Swets & Zeitlinger, Lisse, Netherlands.

Kroeber, A. (1939). "Cultural and Natural Areas of North America." Univ. of California Press, Berkeley.

Lazarus, R. S., and Folkman, S. (1984). "Stress, Appraisal and Coping." Springer-Verlag, New York.

Malzberg, B., and Lee, E. (1956). "Migration and Mental Disease." Social Science Research Council, New York.

Murphy, H. B. M. (1965). Migration and the major mental disorders. *In* "Mobility and Mental Health" (M. Kantor, Ed.), pp. 221–249. Thomas, Springfield.

Mishra, R. C., Sinha, D., and Berry, J. W. (1996). *"Ecology, Acculturation and Psychological Adaptation: A Study of Advasis in Bihar."* Sage, New Delhi.

Naidoo, J. C. (1985). A cultural perspective on the adjustment of South Asian women in Canada. *In* "From a Different Perspective: Studies of Behavior across Cultures" (I. R. Lagunes and Y. H. Poortinga, Eds.), pp. 76–92. Swets and Zeitlinger, Lisse, The Netherlands.

Quesada, G. M., Spears, W., and Ramos, P. (1978). Interracial depressive epidemiology in the southwest. *J. Health Social Behav.* **19**, 77–85.

Sands, E., and Berry, J. W. (1993). Acculturation and mental health among Greek-Canadians in Toronto. *Can. J. Community Mental Health* **12**, 117–124.

Searle, W., and Ward, C. (1990). The prediction of psychological and socio-cultural adjustment during cross-cultural transitions. *Int. J. Intercult. Relat.* **14**, 449–464.

Shin, K. R. (1994). Psychosocial predictors of depressive symptoms in Korean-American women in New York City. *Women & Health* **21**, 73–82.

Slavin, L., Rainer, K., McCreary, M., and Gowda, K. (1991). Toward a multicultural model of the stress process. *J. Counsel. Dev.* **70**, 156–163.

Spradley, J. P., and Phillips, M. (1972). Culture and stress: A quantitative analysis. *Am. Anthropol.* **74**, 518–529.

Turnbull, C. (1972). "The Mountain People." Simon and Schuster, New York.

Van Haaften, E. H., and Van de Vijver, F. J. R. (1996). Psychological consequences of environmental degradation. *J. Health Psychol.* **1**, 411–429.

Vega, W. A., Kolody, B., Valle, R., and Weir, J. (1991). Social networks, social support, and their relationship to depression among immigrant Mexican women. *Hum. Organizat.* **50**, 154–162.

Ward, C., and Kennedy, A. (1992). Locus of control, mood disturbance and social difficulty during cross-cultural transitions. *Int. J. Intercult. Relat.* **16**, 175–194.

Ward, C., and Kennedy, A. (1993a). Psychological and sociocultural adjustment during cross-cultural transitions: A comparison of secondary school students overseas and at home. *Int. J. Psychol.* **28**, 129–147.

Ward, C., and Kennedy, A. (1993b). Where's the culture in cross-cultural transition? Comparative studies of sojourner adjustment. *J. Cross-Cult. Psychol.* **24**, 221–249.

Ward, C. (1996). Acculturation. *In* "Handbook of Intercultural Training" (D. Landis and R. Bhagat, Eds.), pp. 124–147. Sage, Thousand Oaks, CA.

Westermeyer, J. (1986). Migration and psychopathology. *In* "Refugee Mental Health in Resettlement Countries (C. L. Williams and J. Westermeyer, Eds.), Washington: Hemisphere, Washington, D.C.

World Health Organization (1991). "The Mental Health Problems of Migrants: Report from Six European Countries." WHO, Geneva.

Zheng, X., and Berry, J. W. (1991). Psychological adaptation of Chinese sojourners in Canada. *Int. J. Psychol.* **26,** 451–470.

Cultural Transition

Maria S. Kopp

Semmelweis University of Medicine, Budapest, Hungary

I. Cultural Transition in the Central-Eastern-European (CEE) Countries as "Field Experience"
II. Changing of Attitudes and Values and Cultural Transition

GLOSSARY

cognitive appraisal The interpretation of an event or situation with respect to one's attitudes, values, and well-being.

coping Constantly changing cognitive and behavioral efforts to manage specific external and/or internal demands that are appraised as taxing or exceeding the resources of the person.

depressive symptomatology Symptoms of mood disturbances characterized by negative thoughts (for example, feelings of helplessness, inadequacy, loss of control, and low self-esteem), decreased motivation and interest in life, and such physical symptoms as sleep disturbances and fatigue. In civilized countries the prevalence of depressive symptomatology is around 20%.

learned helplessness A condition of loss of control created by subjecting to unavoidable trauma (such as shock, relative deprivation, etc.). Being unable to avoid or escape (flight or fight) an aversive situation produces a feeling of helplessness that generalizes to subsequent situations. Learned helplessness is the best animal model of human depressive symptomatology.

social status The social status of an individual has come to mean his worth relative to other group members. This eval-

uation of worth must be at least tacitly understood and agreed upon by interacting individuals.

sociocultural identification Introjecion of socially meaningful behavioral patterns (usually social roles) through significant persons, via nonverbal communication and contextual and situational cues, thereby also acquiring motivation to actualize the given behavior patterns in fantasy and in action. Learning by model, model following behavior, model learning, and imitation are behavioral descriptions of the same phenomenon. Identification is a psychoanalytic term, meaningful from a developmental and intrapsychic point of view.

I. CULTURAL TRANSITION IN THE CENTRAL-EASTERN-EUROPEAN (CEE) COUNTRIES AS "FIELD EXPERIENCE"

A. Cultural Transition and Health in CEE Countries

A unique "field experience" of cultural and socioeconomic transition has taken place in the CEE countries in the past several decades. Until the end of the 1970s, the mortality rates in the Central-Eastern-European (CEE) countries, including Hungary, were better than those of Britain and Austria. Subsequently, whereas in Western Europe the life expectancy rose continuously, in the CEE countries, such as in Poland, the Czech and Slovac Republics, and Romania, this tendency reversed. By 1990 the Hungarian mortality rate was the highest in Europe. This deterioration cannot be ascribed to deficiencies in health care because during these years there was a significant decrease in infant mortality rate and were improvements along other dimensions of health care. Until 1990 it was not due to a declining standard of living: between 1970 and 1988 the GDP rose by more than 200% in Hungary, and in 1988 the economic status of the lowest socioeconomic strata was even better than in 1970.

The changes in Hungary and other CEE countries since 1970 have been due to a gradually intensifying social and economic polarization. Whereas a large part of the population lived at nearly the same low level in 1970, by the end of the 1980s a large fraction of society had achieved a higher socioeconomic level, having obtained one or more cars, their own property, and substantially higher income. Gaps within society had consequently widened.

Multivariate analysis showed that it was not the relatively worsening socioeconomic situation itself that resulted in the higher morbidity rates, but a depressive symptomatology. If someone does not have a car and therefore feels that s/he is disadvantaged, that s/he cannot properly provide for her/his family, then this is the state of mind which intensifies deterioration of both mental and physical health.

B. Self-Destructive Cycles between Cultural and Socioeconomic Transition, Depressive Symptomatology, and Health

A self-destructive cycle can be envisaged between the relatively worsening socioeconomic situation and depressive symptomatology, which together have a major causal role underlying higher morbidity and mortality rates. It is not a bad socioeconomic situation itself, but rather the subjective evaluation, cognitive appraisal of the relative disadvantage, which seems to be the most significant risk factor, since at equal living standards, Hungarian and other CEE health statistics were significantly better than those of other European countries until the 1970s.

Amidst rapid socioeconomic and cultural changes, those left behind continually blame themselves or their environment, see their future as hopeless, and experience feelings of permanent loss of control and helplessness. Judging one's own situation negatively and feelings of powerlessness and loss of control are the main factors in the development of depressive symptomatology. This view of life at a time when society is rapidly polarizing, especially when most of society sees individual advancement as their only goal, becomes very common. Parallel with the increase in socioeconomic gaps within society was an enormous decrease in perceived social support and increase in sense of loss of control not only in individuals, but in masses of people who felt rejected.

The sudden transition of the society continuously created situations in which the psychological and physiological balance could only be maintained with great difficulty; there was a need for a change in attitudes and ways of coping. Only people with flexible coping resources adapted successfully.

C. Health Consequences of Depressive Symptomatology

There are many possible explanations for depressive symptomatology having an important role in higher morbidity and mortality rates during cultural and socioeconomic transition. The depressive condition affects the perceived state of health and can lead to disability even without organic illness. Depression has a very close relationship with self-destructive behaviors, such as smoking and alcohol consumption, and suicidal behavior is especially common among depressive people. Those suffering from permanent mood disorder and depression are more vulnerable to various diseases and are less able to improve their social situation, so that they easily fall into a sustained vicious circle. In recent decades, depression, "vital exhaustion," and hopelessness have been identified as important independent risk factors of coronary disease. Learned helplessness or learned hopelessness, which can be regarded as the most appropriate model for depression, is associated with decreased immunological activity and affects tumor growth and vulnerability to various infections.

D. Mediating Role of Social Cohesion and Social Capital

In recent years, foregoing studies suggest that cultural and social identity, sociocultural identification, social capital, and social cohesion are among the most important health protection factors in modern societies. Where they exist, wealthier people are prepared to make sacrifices for the community, and the disadvantaged do not feel that they have been completely left to themselves in a hostile world. Trust in each other, esteem for shared values, the acceptance and interiorization of cultural and social identity results in a high level of social cohesion in the society, which is the foundation not only of health but of economic wealth and prosperity.

Wilkinson, who through a study of statistics of developed countries drew attention to the fundamental risk of social disadvantage, also considers the phenomenon of social cohesion to be the most important factor behind differences between countries. For a lower-level British civil servant, it is not his relative poverty itself which is the cause of his bad health because during the German bomb raids the death rates of the London population greatly decreased despite difficult living circumstances. The weakening of social cohesion is a significant factor in the emergence of large social differences and the associated deterioration in health—not only in CEE countries, but in developed countries as well.

II. CHANGING OF ATTITUDES AND VALUES AND CULTURAL TRANSITION

A. Psychological Definition of Freedom and Democracy

The question is whether the crisis experienced in human communities nowadays is a necessary part of civilization. The latest results of behavioral science studies point out that, beyond the concomitant phenomenon of lifestyle, we can see the root cause of crisis in the fact that in modern society new possibilities for arousing anxiety have taken place.

During previous centuries the basic optimization principles were survival, subsistence, and maintaining the family, which dominated the behavior of the mass of people. As the result of technological development this is no longer fundamentally necessary in civilized countries. At the same time, the previously fixed order and communal forms of passing on values has ceased. A young person's "self" was formed on the basis of feedback from the family, the extended family, and contemporaries in the community of the village or small town. Nowadays this process takes place within a nuclear or broken family and through mass communication, which seemingly provide feelings of community, but in reality the person rarely receives the continuity of patterns and values with which they can identify themselves. While there are undeniable benefits in the move away from more tight-knit rule-bound traditional societies, under the conditions of continous cultural and socioeconomic transition the loss of balance in human–environment system became more apparent. A solitary, anxious human being, deprived of relationships, values, goals, and self-esteem can be used for the necessary functions of society and can be arbitrarily changed and manipulated. So we must recognize that technological developments have established the preliminary conditions for creating such anxiety.

The most effective tactic employed by a dictator is to create anxiety. In order to maintain or increase their power the person or group who possesses the most information can afford to either deprive others of information or give it as a reward, thereby creating anxiety in their environment. Arousing anxiety is not only a means, but the essence of a dictatorship. A dictator wants to assure total decisional freedom for him- or herself at all times, and therefore does not pledge him-/herself even to those things which would serve its own interests. This is characteristic of all dependent relationships, where the least dependent has the right to deprive the other of information and thus keep the other in a situation in which they have no control. This occurs not only in totalitarian societies, but can also happen in families, schools, or jobs. Thus, we encounter the abuse of power and the different ways of arousing anxiety every day, but we still do not give it enough attention; we do not recognize it in its embryonic forms and we do not understand how this slow-action poison kills.

We can also arrive at the psychological definition of freedom and democracy through understanding the essence of anxiety. In a psychological sense freedom means that possessing the necessary, essential information needed to evaluate, solve, and control our situation and being able to contribute actively to shaping our situation. Democracy means these rights—both the right and the responsibility of information and action.

B. Misuse of Anxiety in Cultural Transition

How does this apparently purely psychological and medical phenomenon, anxiety, become a basic concept which can shape society? We can ask whether anxiety has an adaptive function: is there any need for anxiety? If we imagine a completely anxiety-free person, he or she does not recognize prospective danger and hence does not avoid dangerous situations and cannot be controlled by social sanctions. Some criminals and some people with antisocial personality disorder belong to this type. In such cases, those in the environment suffer while themselves follow their momentary drives.

Social coexistence requires a certain degree of anxiety—one learns as a child in which situations to expect punishment—a mother's frowning look or a bad mark in school. The avoidance of anxiety is a very important driving force from the first moments of life. If the rules of punishment are foreseeable and are commensurate with the mistakes made, then anxiety can have an adaptive function. But if the rules are opaque or do not exist, then powerlessness and defenselessness can become a weapon in the hands of those who have power. If parents punish on a whim rather than for a reason, then the child will not understand; he cannot understand when he is threatened by danger. If a teacher or university lecturer asks questions from material which the student could not learn, he hammers insufficiency and failure into the student. If the leaders, the managers, the politicians, those who possess more information do not make the rules clear, then they assure their arbitrary authority by causing anxiety in the deprived masses. The 20th century has created the possibility of causing such total anxiety, spread by the mass

communication media as Hitler's or Stalin's radio speeches were transmitted by the loudspeakers of a whole empire.

It is obvious from the above that, since creating anxiety can involve issues of money, benefit, and power, there are enormous advantages in knowing how to deal with these powers effectively. Films, newspapers, magazines, and books infiltrate the community and human relationships and can belittle or deny values and mold people into a mass which can be lead. This type of mass manipulation can occur even if the manipulators' aim differ from what is intended.

The ideology of the consumer society, to control human behavior through the liberation of instincts and search for pleasure, degrades human beings to the level of animal behavior since an animal's decisions are influenced by its instincts to preserve its physiological balance. To achieve dominance by any means is a natural need in such a system.

On every level of society there is, day by day, a life-and-death struggle between the following two types of behaviors: either accepting and respecting other people establishing agreement and a community of free people, and bringing the value of democracy into being or arousing anxiety by withholding information from others. Not the slogans but the behavior classifies the participants.

The question is whether humans will be able to adapt themselves to the circumstances formed by history or whether a lack of adaptive ability leads the whole human race into extreme peril. This adaptation has to be realized both on level of the individual and on that of society.

See Also the Following Articles

Cultural Factors; Industrialized Societies, Stress and; Self-Esteem; Social Status and Stress

Bibliography

Fukuyama (1995). "Trust, the Social Virtues and the Creation of Prosperity." The Free Press, New York.
Kaplan, G. A. (1995). Where do shared pathways lead? *Psychosom. Med.* 57, 208–212.

Kawachi, I., and Kennedy, B. P. (1997). Health and social cohesion: Why care about income inequality, *Br. Med. J.* **314**, 1037–1040.

Kopp, M. S., Szedmák, S., and Skrabski, Á. (1998). Socioeconomic differences and psychosocial aspects of stress in a changing society. *Ann. N. Y. Acad. Sci.* **851** (3), 538–545.

Marmot, M. G., and Syme, S. L. (1976). Acculturation and coronary heart disease in Japanese-Americans. *Am. J. Epidemiol.* **104**, 225–247.

Wilkinson, R. G. (1994). The epidemiological transition: From material scarcity to social disadvantage? *Daedalus* **123** (4), 61–77.

Cushing's Syndrome, Medical Aspects

Stefan R. Bornstein, Constantine A. Stratakis, and George P. Chrousos

National Institute of Child and Health Development, National Institutes of Health

Cushing's syndrome can be divided into two groups: adrenocorticotropic hormone (ACTH)-dependent and ACTH-independent. The term "Cushing's disease" is associated with only the central form of ACTH excess, caused by a corticotrophic micro- or macroadenoma of the pituitary.

GLOSSARY

adrenocorticotropic hormone (ACTH) Pituitary hormone stimulating release of adrenal glucocorticoids.
corticotropin-releasing hormone The main regulator of the endocrine stress access. Stimulates pituitary ACTH.
Cushing's syndrome Caused by state of hypercortisolemia.
transsphenoidal surgery (TSS) Surgical procedure of choice to remove pituitary tumors. This procedure utilizes the nasal approach, avoiding the necessity of opening the skull.

C ushing's syndrome (CS) results from chronic hypercortisolemia. It is a symptom complex that reflects excessive tissue exposure to exogenous or endogenous glucocorticoids, characterized by growth deceleration or complete arrest, gonadal and thyroid dysfunction, progressive adiposity, dermopathy (atrophy, purple stretch marks, bruises, hirsutism), muscle tenderness, hypertension, insulin resistance, increased cholesterol level, and osteoporosis.

I. EPIDEMIOLOGY

The overall incidence of spontaneous Cushing's syndrome is approximately two to four new cases per million of population per year, with a female to male preponderance. Approximately 10% of these cases occur in children and adolescents. Adrenocorticotropin hormone-dependent Cushing's syndrome accounts for about 85% of endogenous cases in adults, adolescents, and children older than 7 years of age (Table I). Cushing's disease is responsible for 80% of these cases; the remaining 20% is caused by ectopic ACTH or, very rarely, ectopic corticotropin-releasing hormone secretion. Benign cortisol-secreting adenomas or adrenocortical carcinomas are rare and account for 10–15% of endogenous cases in children older than 5. In children younger than 5, adrenocortical carcinomas and primary pigmented nodular adrenal disease (PPNAD) are the more frequent causes of endogenous CS. Primary pigmented nodular adrenal disease is a form of adrenal tumors

TABLE I

Classification of Endogenous Cushing's Syndrome and Rate of Occurrence in Children Older than 7 Years[a]

Classification	Percentage
ACTH-dependent	**85**
Pituitary (Cushing's disease)	80
(includes MEN-I)	
Ectopic ACTH	20
(includes MEN-I)	
Ectopic CRH	Rare
ACTH-independent	**15**
Adrenal adenoma	30
(includes MEN-I)	
Adrenal carcinoma	70
Primary pigmented adrenocortical disease	0.5–1
(PPNAD)	
McCune-Albright's syndrome	Rare
"Transitional states"	Rare

[a] Modified from Magiakou and Chrousos (1994).

that occurs frequently in association with Carney complex, a multiple endocrine neoplasia and lentiginosis syndrome. With the increasing utilization of glucocorticoids for a wide range of nonendocrine diseases, the exogenous, iatrogenic CS has become more frequent and is more prevalent than the endogenous forms.

II. ETIOLOGY

Endogenous CS results from increased secretion of cortisol by the adrenal cortex and is due to ACTH hypersection (ACTH-dependent CS) or the autonomous hyperfunction of the adrenocortical cells (ACTH-independent CS). Some forms of ACTH-independent CS have recently been discovered to be due to aberrant expression of neuroendocrine or cytokine receptors (such as GIP, vasopressin, β-receptor, or interleukin-1), putting the adrenal tissue under a trophic stimulus, which is not under the control of the regular negative feedback. *Cushing's disease,*

the ACTH-dependent form of endogenous CS, is due to an ACTH-secreting, benign corticotroph tumor of the anterior pituitary gland. *Ectopic ACTH-secreting tumors* occur mostly in patients with bronchial carcinoma. In addition, other tumors may present with ectopic ACTH production (thymus, liver, renal carcinoma, etc.).

Exogenous CS results from chronic administration of glucocorticoids (for treatment of neoplastic, autoimmune, and other diseases) or ACTH (for the treatment of certain seizure disorders).

III. PATHOPHYSIOLOGY

The main stimulus for the release of cortisol from the adrenal cortex is ACTH, which is produced by the corticotrophs of the anterior pituitary, which, in turn, are under the regulatory influence of hypothalamic CRH and vasopressin (Fig. 1). The ambient plasma free cortisol levels regulate ACTH secretion in a negative feedback fashion. Normally, less than 10% of plasma cortisol is in the free form, with the majority being bound to cortisol-binding globulin (or "transcortin").

In the physiologic state, ACTH and cortisol have a circadian pattern of secretion, established early in infancy and in accordance with other human circadian biologic activities. The peak of ACTH and cortisol secretion occurs in the morning (between 7:00 and 8:00 A.M.), and is lowest is in the late evening hours (around midnight). This physiological circadian rhythm is blunted in Cushing's syndrome.

The adrenals have an amazing ability to adapt to states of hyper- or hypofunction. They use more than 10 times the cardiac output and blood volume that would correspond to their organ weight. Therefore, they are unique in demonstrating signs of hormonal excess and stress. Chronic stimulation of adrenal tissue with ACTH in Cushing's disease or ectopic ACTH-secreting tumors will cause hypertrophy of the adrenals, leading in particular to an increase in size of the *zona fasciculata*. The adrenal cortex under-

---

FIGURE 1 Diagnostic algorithm for Cushing's syndrome (modified from Bornstein, Stratakis, and Chrousos, *Ann. Intern. Med.,* 1999).

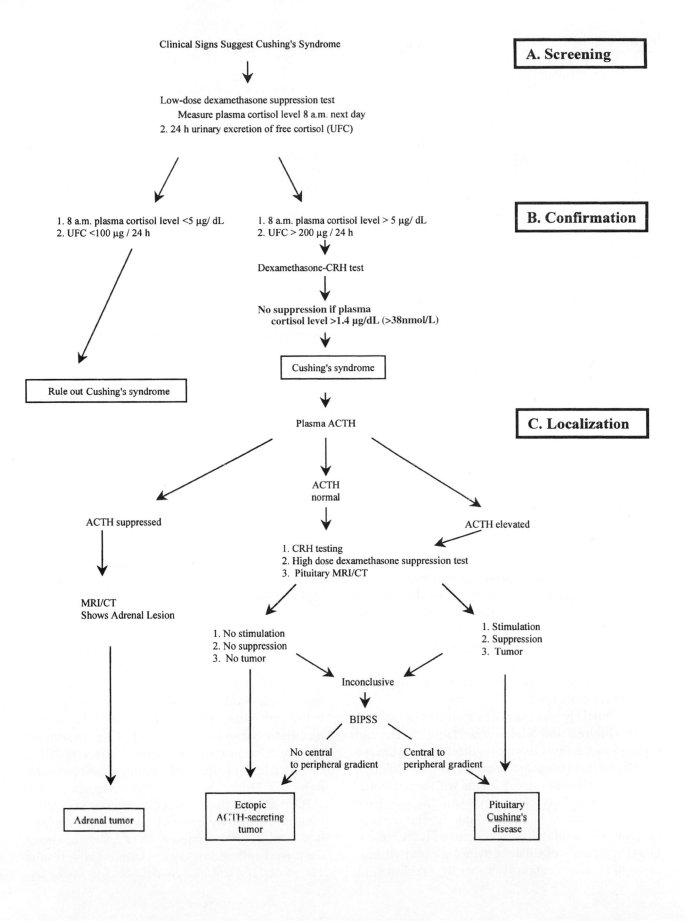

A. Screening

Clinical Signs Suggest Cushing's Syndrome

Low-dose dexamethasone suppression test
    Measure plasma cortisol level 8 a.m. next day
2. 24 h urinary excretion of free cortisol (UFC)

B. Confirmation

1. 8 a.m. plasma cortisol level <5 µg/ dL
2. UFC <100 µg / 24 h

1. 8 a.m. plasma cortisol level > 5 µg/ dL
2. UFC > 200 µg / 24 h

Dexamethasone-CRH test

No suppression if plasma
    cortisol level >1.4 µg/dL (>38nmol/L)

Cushing's syndrome

Rule out Cushing's syndrome

Plasma ACTH

C. Localization

ACTH suppressed

ACTH
normal

ACTH elevated

MRI/CT
Shows Adrenal Lesion

1. CRH testing
2. High dose dexamethasone suppression test
3. Pituitary MRI/CT

1. No stimulation
2. No suppression
3. No tumor

1. Stimulation
2. Suppression
3. Tumor

Inconclusive

BIPSS

No central
to peripheral gradient

Central to
peripheral gradient

Adrenal tumor

Ectopic
ACTH-secreting
tumor

Pituitary
Cushing's
disease

goes hypervascularization and the cells increase in mitochondria, smooth endoplasmic reticulum, and filopodia, indicating increased activation of steroido-synthesis.

Glucocorticoids are vital for survival because they participate greatly in the stress response of humans. Glucocorticoids affect all tissues and organ systems, and the glucocorticoid receptor is ubiquitously present. Glucocorticoids have profound catabolic activities: they inhibit growth and reproduction, promote proteinolysis, and suppress the immune and inflammatory reaction. These effects are behind some of the cardinal clinical manifestations of CS: delayed growth and bone maturation, hypogonadism, dermopathy, loss of muscular tissue, and frequent fungal or saprophytic infections.

IV. CLINICAL PICTURE

Table II summarizes the clinical features of CS in children and adolescents. An early and common sign in almost all patients is obesity, which is generalized or truncal, and is characterized by moon facies (facial rounding) and plethora. Growth retardation or complete arrest is present in 90% of the children. Other clinical manifestations include sleep disturbances, muscle weakness and fatigue, hirsutism, and typical purple skin striae. Hypertension, carbohydrate intolerance or diabetes, amenorrhea, advancement or arrest of pubertal development, and easy bruising or spontaneous fractures of ribs and vertebrae may also be encountered. Although all patients may exhibit some of these features at the time of diagnosis, few, if any, will have all of them. Photographs of the patient, taken over a period of years, are helpful in the clinical evaluation.

The clinical presentation can identify the cause of CS in children and adolescents. Thus, severe and rapidly progressing Cushing syndrome points toward an adrenal neoplasm or, although rare in children, ectopic ACTH syndrome. Patients with adrenocortical carcinomas may be asymptomatic or may have abdominal pain or fullness, symptoms and signs of Cushing syndrome (30%), virilization (20%), combined symptoms of Cushing syndrome and virilization (30%), feminization (10%), or hyperaldosteron-

TABLE II
Clinical Presentation of CS in Pediatric Patients[a]

Symptoms/signs	Frequency (percentage)
Weight gain	90
Growth retardation	83
Menstrual irregularities	81
Hirsutism	81
Obesity (Body Mass Index >85 percentile)	73
Violaceous skin striae	63
Acne	52
Hypertension	51
Fatigue-weakness	45
Precocious puberty	41
Bruising	27
Mental changes	18
"Delayed" bone age	14
Hyperpigmentation	13
Muscle weakness	13
Acanthosis nigricans	10
Accelerated bone age	10
Sleep disturbances	7
Pubertal delay	7
Hypercalcemia	6
Alkalosis	6
Hypokalemia	2
Slipped femoral capital epiphysis	2

[a] Modified from Magiakou *et al.* (1994).

ism (5–10%). Cushing's syndrome is periodic or intermittent in a significant percentage (~10%) of children and adolescents.

V. LABORATORY FINDINGS

The first step in diagnosing noniatrogenic CS is the biochemical documentation of endogenous hypercortisolism, which can usually be accomplished by outpatient tests. The first test is *measurement of 24-h urinary free cortisol excretion* (UFC) corrected for body surface area and/or the determination of 24-h urinary 17-hydroxycorticosteroid (17OHCS) excretion (corrected per gram of excreted creatinine). Urinary free cortisol excretion is a good first-line test for documentation of CS, with, assuming correct collection, very few false-negative results. The second test is the *single-dose dexamethasone sup-*

pression test. The overnight 1-mg (in young children 15 μg/kg body weight) dexamethasone suppression test is a useful screening procedure for hypercortisolism. It is simple, with a low incidence of false-normal suppression (less than 3%). The same test, however, has a high incidence of false-positive results (approximately 20 to 30%). A plasma cortisol level $> 5 \mu$g/dl suggests endogenous hypercortisolism and needs to be followed by a 24-h urine collection for determination of UFC or 17-OHCS levels.

Cushing's syndrome is generally excluded if the aforementioned tests are normal, although one should remember that periodic and intermittent cortisol hypersecretion, which may occur in patients with Cushing's syndrome of any etiology, may confuse the picture.

Once CS has been diagnosed, the differential diagnosis is investigated via dynamic testing of the function of the hyopthalamic-pituitary-adrenal (HPA) axis as well as imaging studies. It is essential that dynamic endocrine testing is performed while the patient is hypercorticortisolemic and that, in order to avoid mistakes, this state should always be documented at the time of testing. All adrenal blocking agents should be discontinued for at least 6 weeks prior to testing.

The major tests in differential diagnosis of CS and their interpretations include the following: (see also Fig. 1)

1. *Liddle dexamethesone suppression test*. The standard high-dose, low-dose dexamethesone suppression test (2 mg @ 6 hours over 2 days) is a reliable procedure for differentiating Cushing's disease from ectopic ACTH syndrome.

2. *Overnight 8-mg dexamethesone suppression test*.

3. *Corticotropin-releasing hormone stimulation test*. The ovine (o) CRH test is of equal or greater value than the standard dexamethasone suppression test in differentiating Cushing's disease and ectopic ACTH syndrome.

4. *Petrosal-sinus sampling with CRH test*.

VI. RADIOGRAPHIC FINDINGS

Imaging techniques can help clarify the etiology of hypercortisolism. These include computed tomographic (CT) scanning and magnetic resonance imaging (MRI) of the pituitary gland and CT scan, MRI, and ultrasound imaging of the adrenal glands. Computed tomographic and MRI scans of the chest and abdomen are also used when tumors secreting ectopic ACTH are suspected.

VII. TREATMENT

The preferred treatment for CS depends upon the specific cause of the hypercortisolism, which must be firmly and unequivocally established. The optimal treatment is correction of hypercortisolism without permanent dependence on hormone replacement.

A. Cushing's Disease

1. Transsphenoidal Surgery (TSS)

Transsphenoidal surgery is the treatment of choice for most cases of CS caused by pituitary microadenomas. It is indicated if the presence of a pituitary microadenoma can be demonstrated preoperatively by imaging techniques or bilateral inferior petrosal-sinus blood sampling (BIPSS). In most specialized centers, the success rate of first TSS exceeds 90%. If BIPSS has lateralized the microadenoma and the surgeon cannot identify it at surgery, 75–80% of patients can be cured by ipsilateral hemihypophysectomy.

Usually, successful TSS leads to the cure of hypercortisolism without using permanent glucocorticoid replacement. Approximately 5% of patients suffer recurrences; this is most common in patients with pituitary macroadenomas. The success rate of repeat TSS is considerably lower (approximately 50–60%).

Complications include transient or permanent, partial or complete anterior pituitary insufficiency, including in order of frequency, hypothyroidism, growth hormone deficiency, hypogonadism, and adrenal insufficiency. Transient diabetes insipidus or inappropriate antidiuretic secretion syndrome are also common. Success after TSS is defined as a decrease in serum cortisol or UFC to an undetectable level in the immediate postoperative period. After a successful TSS, a period of adrenal insufficiency occurs in most of patients cured, during which glucocorticoids must be replaced at a dose of 12–15 mg/m²/day. This abnormality of the HPA axis can last as long as a year or longer. It is rare, though possible, that it is permanent. The replacement dose of hydrocortisone is maintained for 3 months, and adrenocortical function is evaluated at that time with a rapid Cortrosyn test (250 mg ACTH 1–24 iv bolus, with plasma cortisol measured at 0, 30, and 60 min). If the test is normal (cortisol >18 and >20 μg/dl at 30 and 60 min, respectively), glucocorticoid replacement is discontinued. If the response is subnormal, the patient is reevaluated at 3-month intervals. About 70–80% of the patients will have an normal test at 6 months postoperation. Patients should be given extra glucocorticoids during stress (two times replacement dose for minor stress such as febrile illness or dental surgery, and 8–10 times replacement dose for major stress, such as major trauma or surgery).

2. Pituitary X-radiation with or without Mitotane

This is an alternative treatment which may be used after failure of TSS, when there is presence of cavernous sinus wall invasion by the tumor, or in patients judged unsuitably for surgery. The total recommended dosage of pituitary irradiation is 4500 to 5000 rad. High-voltage, conventional X-radiation is administered in 180- to 200-rad fractions over a period of 6 weeks. Success rate is ~40–50%, without mitotane, and ~80% with mitotane (see below).

3. Pharmacotherapy

Drug therapy alone is rarely used to treat Cushing's disease, except temporarily, prior to definitive treatment. *Mitotane* (Lysodren) is the only available pharmacologic agent that both inhibits biosynthesis of corticosteroids and destroys adrenocortical cells secreting cortisol, thus producing a long-lasting effect. Therapy with mitotane (up to 3 gr/day) is usually combined with radiotherapy. *Aminoglutethimide*, up to 1 g a day orally in four divided doses, or *metyrapone*, up to 1 g a day in four divided doses, may also be used alone or in combination with mitotane. During treatment, UFC excretion should be monitored and the regimen should be titrated to maintain this parameter in the normal range. If adrenal insuf-

ficiency is suspected, oral hydrocortisone should be added.

Ketoconazole (up to 1400 mg/day or 20 mg/kg/day) or *trilostane* have also been used alone or in combination with mitotane to control some of the symptoms and metabolic abnormalities associated with Cushing's disease. Combinations are recommended because they usually prevent "breakthroughs" that occur when the drugs are used alone. In addition, one can use moderate doses with less side effects from each agent.

4. Bilateral Adrenalectomy

The indications for this procedure have been dramatically changed by the success and low morbidity of TSS. Bilateral adrenalectomy is a possible treatment for patients who have failed selective pituitary adenomectomy or hemihypophysectomy. The major disadvantages of this surgery are that the individual is committed to lifelong daily gluco- and mineralocorticoid replacements, that it does not eliminate the cause underlying the hypersecretion of ACTH, and that relapses, though rare, may occur as a result of growth of adrenal rest tissue or an adrenal remnant. Furthermore, perioperative mortality is approximately 3 times higher than that of TSS, although it can be minimized by careful perioperative preparation. Also, Nelson syndrome (i.e., large pituitary macroadenomas secreting great amounts of ACTH and lipotropin resulting in skin hyperpigmentation) may occur in approximately 10–15% of patients with Cushing's disease treated with bilateral adrenalectomy. These tumors can impair vision and should be treated surgically and by radiotherapy.

B. Ectopic ACTH-dependent CS

The preferred treatment for ectopic ACTH secretion is surgery aimed at completely excising the tumor, if resectable and of known location. If there is evidence of adjacent lymph node invasion, local radiation can be recommended after surgery for some tumors, such as carcinoids. If surgical resection is impossible or if the tumor is hidden, blockade of steroidogenesis is indicated; if necessary, bilateral adrenelactomy is considered.

C. Primary Adrenal Disease

The therapeutic approach to ACTH-independent Cushing's syndrome is also surgical. Unilateral or bilateral adrenalectomy is the recommended therapy, depending on whether one or both adrenals are affected. For cases of PPNAD, bilateral adrenalectomy is recommended, even if abnormalities are undetected by imaging studies in both adrenal glands. The cure rate of benign adenomas and PPNAD should be 100%. Aggressive surgical therapy is suggested for adrenocortical carcinomas, as it is the only approach that has been known to increase survival rate.

See Also the Following Articles

ADRENAL CORTEX; ADRENOCORTICOTROPIC HORMONE (ACTH); CUSHING'S SYNDROME, NEUROPSYCHIATRIC ASPECTS; GLUCOCORTICOIDS, OVERVIEW

Bibliography

Bornstein, S. R., Stratakis, C. A., and Chrousos, G. P. (1999). Adrenocortical tumors: Recent advances in basic concepts and clinical management. *Ann. Intern. Med.* **130**, 759–771.

Chrousos, G. P., Schulte, H. M., Oldfield, E. H., Gold, P. W., Cutler, G. B., Jr., and Loriaux, D. L. (1984). The corticotropin-releasing factor stimulation test: An aid in the evaluation of patients with Cushing syndrome. *N. Engl. J. Med.* **310**, 622–626.

Oldfield, E. H., Doppman, J. L., Nieman, L. K., *et al.* (1991). Petrosal sinus sampling with and without corticotropin-releasing hormone for the differential diagnosis of Cushing's syndrome. *N. Engl. J. Med.* **325**, 897–905.

Magiakou, M. A., and Chrousos, G. P. (1994). *In* "The Pituitary Gland" (H. Immura, Ed.), 2nd ed., pp. 491–508. Raven, New York.

Magiakou, M. A., Mastorakos, G., Oldfield, E. H., *et al.* (1994). Cushing's syndrome in children and adolescents: Presentation, diagnosis and therapy. *N. Engl. J. Med.* **331**, 629–636.

Tsigos, C., and Chrousos, G. P. (1996). Differential diagnosis and management of Cushing's syndrome. *Ann. Rev. Med.* **47**, 443–461.

Cushing's Syndrome, Neuropsychiatric Aspects

Monica Starkman

University of Michigan Medical School

I. Neuropsychiatric Symptoms in Patients with Spontaneous Untreated Cushing's Syndrome
II. Improvement in Neuropsychiatric Symptoms after Treatment
III. Brain-Imaging Studies in Cushing's Syndrome
IV. Mechanisms for the Behavioral Effects of Cortisol

GLOSSARY

hippocampus A brain structure which is part of the limbic system and key to learning and memory.
libido Desire for sexual activity.
mental status evaluation Standard bedside clinical tests used to examine mental functions.

neuropsychological studies Tests of various aspects of cognition, including verbal functions, visuospatial functions, learning, and memory.
sleep EEG An electroencephalogram taken during sleep to measure brain electrical activity and study the structure of sleep.

Cushing's disease, the major type of spontaneous Cushing's syndrome, is the classic endocrine disease characterized by hypersecretion of cortisol. Intriguingly, "emotional disturbances" were already recognized as a feature of the disease in Harvey Cushing's original description in 1932. This association was then confirmed by retrospective chart reviews. More recently, studies of patients with spontaneous Cushing's Syndrome examined prior to treatment have characterized the disturbance and shown that the majority manifest clinical features seen in patients with a primary psychiatric major depressive disorder (MDD). Patients with Cushing's disease and syndrome exhibit a consistent constellation of symptoms including abnormalities in mood (irritability and depression), vegetative functions (decreased libido and increased insomnia), and cognitive functions (decreased concentration and memory).

I. NEUROPSYCHIATRIC SYMPTOMS IN PATIENTS WITH SPONTANEOUS UNTREATED CUSHING'S SYNDROME

A. Mood and Affect

Irritability, a very frequent symptom seen in close to 90% of patients, is usually the earliest behavioral symptom to appear. It begins close to the onset of the earliest physical symptom (weight gain) and prior to the appearance of other physical manifestations of Cushing's syndrome. Patients describe themselves as being overly sensitive, unable to ignore minor irritations, and feeling impatient with or pressured by others. In addition, overreactivity and easy development of anger occur. Patients feel they are often on the verge of an emotional explosion and that the intensity of anger experienced is also increased.

Depressed mood is reported by 60–80% of patients. There is a range in the intensity of depressed mood. Some patients describe short spells of sadness; others experience feelings of hopelessness and giving up. Suicide attempts are infrequent but may occur. Hypersensitivity and oversentimentality lead to crying spells. For some, crying also occurs as the behavioral response to anger and frustration and feeling unable to respond effectively. Patients also experience spontaneous onset of depressed mood or crying in the absence of any proceeding upsetting thought or event.

The time course of the mood disturbances is noteworthy. Most patients report that their mood disturbances are intermittent rather than sustained. Sometimes they wake up depressed and remain depressed throughout the day or the next day as well. Alternatively, the onset of depressed mood and/or crying might occur during the day, often suddenly. The duration of each depressive episode is usually 1 to 2 days and rarely longer than 3 days at a time. A frequent weekly total is 3 days per week. There is no regular cyclicity, however, so patients cannot predict when a depressive day will occur. Although there are intervals when they might not experience pleasure, these patients do not experience the unrelenting, unremitting inability to experience pleasure that is characteristic of patients with severe psychiatric depressive illness. There are intervals when they retain the capacity for pleasure, finding enjoyment in hobbies and interpersonal relationships. At times, patients may find it difficult to initiate such activities, although once others mobilize them, they enjoy them. Some patients do experience decreased interest in their environment.

Social withdrawal is less common, but can occur. Sporadic withdrawal might occur because of the patient's need to remove himself or herself from a situation of overstimulation that elicits the fear of impending emotional dyscontrol. Guilt is infrequent; if present, it is not excessive, self-accusatory, or irrational, but related to remorse about angry outbursts and inability to function well at work and in the family. Hopelessness is infrequent, but if present, is attributed to the increasing physical and emotional disability that has puzzled their physicians and been resistant to treatment interventions until the diagnosis of Cushing's syndrome is finally made.

A minority of patients experience episodes of elation-hyperactivity early in the course of the illness. These episodes of elation are described as a "high." Patients are more ambitious than usual and might attempt to do more than their ability and training make reasonable. Increased motor activity is present, with restlessness and rapidly performed activities. Patients report embarrassment that their speech is both loud and rapid. As the illness progresses and new physical signs of Cushing's syndrome begin to appear, this type of episode becomes rare or disappears entirely.

A percentage of patients report generalized anxiety. New-onset panic disorder has also been observed in patients with Cushing's syndrome. In addition, even patients who do not experience psychic anxiety describe episodic symptoms of autonomic activation such as shaking, palpitations, and sweating.

B. Biologic Drives

Abnormalities in four areas of basic biological vegetative drives are present.

1. *Fatigue.* This is reported by 100% of patients.
2. *Libido.* A decrease in libido is very frequent and reported by close to 70% of patients. In fact, this is one of the earliest manifestations of Cushing's disease, beginning when the patient is experiencing the first onset of weight gain.
3. *Appetite and eating behavior.* More than 50% of patients have an alteration in their appetite; in 34% appetite is increased; in 20% it is decreased.
4. *Sleep and dreams.* Difficulty with sleep, particularly middle insomnia and late insomnia (early morning awakening) is found in more than 80% of the patients. Difficulty with early insomnia (not falling asleep at bedtime) is not as frequent. One-third of the patients report an alteration in the frequency or quality of their dreams which are increased in their frequency and intensity and become bizarre and very vivid. Some patients report they have lost the ability to wake themselves out of a nightmare. Sleep EEG studies indicate that there are many similarities between Cushing's disease patients and patients with MDD. For example, both groups show significantly less total sleep time, lower sleep efficiency, and shortened rapid eye movement (REM) latency compared to normal subjects.

C. Cognition

Cognitive symptoms are a prominent part of the clinical picture. Most patients report difficulty with concentration, inattention, distractibility, and shortened attention span. Some patients report episodes of scattered thinking, while others note slow thinking. Thought blocking may occur in more severe instances. Patients may find themselves using incorrect words while speaking or misspelling simple words. Perceptual distortions are very rare.

Impairment of memory is one of the most frequent symptoms, reported by 80% of patients. Patients report problems with registration of new information. They commonly repeat themselves in ongoing conversations. They easily forget items such as appointments made, names of people, and location of objects.

Most patients have no disorientation or overt clouding of consciousness, and the waking electroencephalographs (EEGs) are not characteristic of delirium. On mental status bedside clinical evaluation, difficulties with tests such as mental subtraction and recall of recent United States presidents are seen in close to 50% of the patients. Detailed neuropsychological studies reveal that individuals vary in the severity of degree of cognitive dysfunction, ranging from minimal or moderate to the severe deficits in a variety of subtests seen in close to one-third of patients. Verbal functions and learning are particularly impaired.

D. Specific Features of the Neuropsychiatric Symptoms

The psychiatric symptoms that develop in Cushing's syndrome are not simply a nonspecific response to severe physical illness. Irritability and decreased libido occur early, often before patients are aware that they have any physical problems other than weight gain. Later, when depressed mood appears, it is not simply the demoralization seen in the medically ill, but episodic sadness and crying, sometimes occurring in the absence of depressive thought content. The incidence of depressive disorders is greater than in comparison groups with other types of pituitary tumors or hyperthyroidism. Although they have difficulty with concentration and memory, patients with Cushing's syndrome are not delirious.

The overwhelming majority of patients with spontaneous Cushing's syndrome do not have very severe neuropsychiatric disturbances of a psychotic or confusional nature, as patients receiving corticosteroids for treatment of certain physical disorders sometimes may. This can be understood by considering that patients with spontaneous Cushing's syndrome differ from those receiving high-dose steroids in several respects. The level of circulating cortisol in the former is not as high as the equivalent amount of steroid administered to the latter. Patients with Cushing's syndrome also differ from those receiving exogenous steroids in that they are exposed to sustained elevated cortisol levels for months to years and are less subject to sudden acute shifts and rapid rates of change of steroid levels that occur during short-term treatment with high-dose corticosteroids.

Although similar in many respects to the major depressive disorders, the depression seen in Cushing's syndrome does have certain distinguishing clinical characteristics. Summarizing these, irritability is a prominent and consistent feature, as are symptoms of autonomic activation such as shaking, palpitations, and sweating. Depressed affect is often intermittent, with episodes lasting 1 to 3 days, recurring very frequently at irregular intervals. Patients usually feel their best, not their worst, in the morning. Psychomotor retardation, although present in many patients, is usually not so pronounced as to be clinically obvious and is usually apparent only in retrospect after improvement with treatment. The majority of these patients are not withdrawn, monosyllabic, unspontaneous, or hopeless. Their guilt, when present, is not irrational or self-accusatory and is primarily related to their realistic inability to function effectively. Significant cognitive impairment, including disorders of concentration, learning, and memory, is a consistent and prominent clinical feature.

II. IMPROVEMENT IN NEUROPSYCHIATRIC SYMPTOMS AFTER TREATMENT

Significant improvements in depression rating scores occur after treatment produces decreases in cortisol. In treated patients, improvements in depressed mood begin with a decrease in the frequency of days when the patient felt depressed. In addition, each episode lasts a shorter period of time, perhaps only a few hours instead of 1 to 2 days. The patients also describe a change in quality of the depressive mood, so that they no longer experience it being as deep. They no longer feel depressed without some external precipitating reason. A mood change comes on gradually and abates gradually, rather than appearing suddenly as before. Crying becomes less frequent, is less easily elicited by environmental upsets, occurs only with some identifiable external precipitant, and is of shorter duration.

The time course of improvement in depressed mood compared to improvement in other neurovegetative symptoms is of interest. In patients with Cushing's disease who manifest depressed mood at initial evaluation and are subsequently studied during the first 12 months after treatment, improvement in symptoms other than depressed mood occur prior to improvement in depressed mood. Depressed mood is less likely than irritability and sleep, for example, to be among the first cluster of symptoms to improve. Interestingly, this lag is similar to that seen in psychiatric patients with depressive episodes treated with antidepressants, in whom improvements in sleep and psychomotor activity often occur prior to improvement in depressed mood. Cognitive testing indicates improvement in many, but not all, cognitive functions after treatment.

Antidepressant medication, the tricyclics in particular, produces little or no improvement in the depressive syndrome when administered to patients with active, untreated Cushing's syndrome. There is less experience with the newer selective serotonin reuptake inhibitors, but patients report only partial effectiveness with these drugs. After treatment, antidepressants may prove helpful when depressed mood lingers after treatment has lowered cortisol levels or is exacerbated because steroid levels have declined rapidly and sharply.

III. BRAIN-IMAGING STUDIES IN CUSHING'S SYNDROME

Brain-imaging technology has provided further information about the effects of cortisol on brain structure and function. Preliminary studies indicate that patients with Cushing's disease show a reduction in the metabolism of glucose in several brain regions. The hippocampus is a brain structure key to learning and memory. In Cushing's syndrome, greater elevations in cortisol are associated with smaller hippocampal formation volume. Reduced hippocampal formation volume is associated with lower scores for verbal learning and recall. After treatment reduces cortisol levels, the hippocampal formation increases in volume more consistently and to a greater degree than the caudate head, a brain structure examined for comparison. Greater decreases in cortisol are associated with greater increases in hippocampal formation volume.

IV. MECHANISMS FOR THE BEHAVIORAL EFFECTS OF CORTISOL

The neuropsychiatric abnormalities seen in untreated Cushing's syndrome are related, at least in part, to the effect of elevated levels of cortisol. Possible mechanisms for the effect of cortisol on mood, cognition, and vegetative functions include a direct effect of the steroid on receptors of central nervous system cells; the synthesis or function of neurotransmitters; effects on glucose metabolism and electrolytes; and increasing the sensitivity of the brain to neuroactive substances such as excitatory amino acids.

While this article has focused on a single adrenal steroid, cortisol, levels of other adrenal glucocorticoids as well as sex steroids produced by the adrenal, such as testosterone, are also altered in patients with Cushing's syndrome. These substances likely modify the effect of cortisol on psychopathology, and their role remains to be elucidated.

See Also the Following Articles

CUSHING'S SYNDROME, MEDICAL ASPECTS

Bibliography

Brunetti, A., Fulham, M. J., Aloj, L., DeSouza. B., Nieman. L., Oldfield. E. H., DiChiro, G. (1998). Decreased brain glucose utilization in patients with Cushing's disease. *J. Nucl. Med.* **39**,786–790.

Cohen, S. I. (1980). Cushing's syndrome: A psychiatric study of 29 patients. *Br. J. Psychiat.* **136**, 120–124.

Jeffcoate, W. J., Silverstone, J. T., Edwards C. R., and Besser, G. M. (1979). Psychiatric manifestations of Cushing's syndrome: Response to lowering of plasma cortisol. *Q. J. Med.* **48**, 465–472.

Kelly, W. F., Checkley, S. A., Bender, D. A., and Mashiter, K. (1983). Cushing's syndrome and depression—A prospective study of 26 patients. *Br. J. Psychiat.* **142**, 16–19.

Loosen, P. T., Chambliss, B., DeBold, C. R., Shelton, R., and Orth, D. N. (1992). Psychiatric phenomenology in Cushing's Disease. *Pharmacopsychiatry* **25**, 192–198.

Mauri, M., Sinforiani, E., Bono, G., Vignati, F., Berselli. M. E., Attanasio, R., and Nappi, G. (1993) Memory impairment in Cushing' s disease. *Acta Neurol. Scand.* **87**, 52–55.

Sonino, N., Fava, G. A., Belluardo, P., Girelli, M. E., and Boscaro, M. (1993). Course of depression in Cushing's syndrome: Response to treatment and comparison with Grave's disease. *Horm. Res.* **39**, 202–206.

Starkman, M. N., and Schteingart, D. E. (1981). Neuropsychiatric manifestations of patients with Cushing's syndrome: Relationship to cortisol and adrenocorticotropic hormone levels. *Arch. Intern. Med.* **141**, 215–219.

Shipley, J. E., Schteingart, D. E., Tandon, R., and Starkman, M. N. (1992). Sleep architecture and sleep apnea in patients with Cushing's disease. *Sleep* **15**, 514–518.

Starkman, M. N., Schteingart, D. E., and Schork, M. A. (1981). Depressed mood and other psychiatric manifestations of Cushing's syndrome: Relationship to hormone levels. *Psychosom. Med.* **43**, 3–18.

Starkman, M. N., Schteingart, D. E., and Schork, M. A. (1986). Cushing's syndrome after treatment: Changes in cortisol and ACTH levels, and amelioration of the depressive syndrome. *Psychiat. Res.* **17**, 177–188.

Starkman, M. N. (1987). Commentary on M. Majewska: Actions of steroids on neuron: Role in personality, mood, stress and disease. *Integr. Psychiat.* **5**, 258–273.

Starkman. M. N., Gebarski, S. S., Berent, S., and Schteingart, D. E. (1992). Hippocampal formation volume, memory dysfunction, and cortisol levels in patients with Cushing's syndrome. *Biol. Psychiat.* **32**, 756–765.

Starkman, M. N., Giordani, B., Gebarski, S., Berent S., Schork, M. A., and Schteingart, D. E. (1999). Decrease in cortisol reverses human hippocampal atrophy following treatment of Cushing's Disease. *Biol. Psychiatr.* (in press).

Trethowan, W. H., and Cobb, S. (1952). Neuropsychiatric aspects of Cushing's Syndrome. *Arch. Neurol. Psychiat.* **67**, 283–309.

Tucker, R. P., Weinstein, H. E., Schteingart, D. E., and Starkman, M. N. (1978). EEG changes and serum cortisol levels in Cushing's syndrome. *Clin. Electroencephalogr.* **9**, 32–37.

Whelan, T. B., Schteingart, D. E., Starkman, M. N., and Smith, A. (1980). Neuropsychological deficits in Cushing's syndrome. *J. Nerv. Ment. Dis.* **168**, 753–757.

Cytokines

Gailen D. Marshall, Jr.

University of Texas—Houston Medical School

Jeffrey L. Rossio

National Cancer Institute, Frederick Cancer Research and Development Center

GLOSSARY

cytokine Small-molecular-weight glycopeptides produced by a variety of cell types that serve to modulate immune and inflammatory responses.

psychoneuroimmunology The study of the relationships between neurocognitive behaviors, neuroendocrine response, and immune changes occurring in response to stress.

stress Perturbation of homeostatic state by environmental factors demanding an adaptive response from the host.

T helper cell Lymphocyte that plays a central role in immune modulation by selectively activating various immune and nonimmune cells through the production of specific cytokine combinations.

I mmunoendocrinology is the study of the impact of soluble products of the immune system on endocrine and neuroendocrine networks as part of the bidirectional communication between the immune and endocrine systems.

I. RELATIONSHIPS BETWEEN STRESS AND IMMUNITY

A. Stress Defined

Stress is best thought of as a psychophysiological process, usually experienced as a negative emotional state. Stressors, defined as events posing threat, harm, or challenge, are judged in the context of personal and environmental factors and, if appraised as threatening or challenging, initiate specific physiologic responses directed at reducing or eliminating the stress (fight or flight). The field of psychoneuroimmunology seeks to establish the link between behavior, neuroendocrine functions, and immune responses.

B. Impact of Stress on Health

A common clinical observation is the often adverse relationship between stress and human disease. Various sources have estimated that up to 75% of all visits to physicians' offices are stress related. This appears to be particularly true in relationship to immune-based dysfunction such as increased susceptibility to infections, autoimmune, allergic, and asthmatic diseases. Stress is also suspected to play a role in morbidity and mortality in other immune-based diseases such as cancer, HIV disease, inflammatory bowel diseases, and even aging. Stress may also cause persistent increases in sympathetic nervous system activity, including increased blood pressure, heart rate, and catecholamine secretion as well as platelet aggregation, which may explain, at least in part, the known association between stress, immune alterations, and cardiovascular disease. Emerging evidence suggests that sleep alterations can modulate the stress–health relationship. Acute stressors and adverse naturalistic events are associated with sleep disruptions as measured by self-report and polysomnography. Poor sleep, in turn, is associated with subsequent decrements in mental health including symptom reporting, incident cases of mood and anxiety disorders, and immune function. Sleep disruptions have also been associated with adverse physical health outcomes, including increased morbidity and mortality compared to populations with adequate patterns and duration of sleep.

C. Role of Cytokines in the Normal Immune Response

In the normal host, presentation of antigen for a specific protective immune response elicits a complex series of events that results in a mixed cellular and humoral protective response, the intensity and nature of which depends upon the specific inciting antigen. Generally speaking, extracellular parasites (i.e., bacteria) incite primarily a humoral response while intracellular parasites (i.e., viruses, fungi, mycobacteria, etc.) elicit a cell-mediated response. Antiviral immunity is particularly complex because both arms are necessary for host resistance–cellular immunity to eliminate the virus-infected host cells and humoral immunity that produces antiviral neutralizing antibodies to prevent reinfection. The host immune response has a variety of mechanisms to direct the immune response into the humoral vs cellular direction—nature of antigen-presenting cells, major histocompatibility complex (MHC) restriction, and availability of specific T- and B-cell components. However, the central control of the cellular vs humoral response to an antigenic challenge appears to be via production of a specific cytokine milieu.

All cytokines have certain properties in common. They are all small-molecular-weight peptides or glycopeptides. Many are produced by multiple cell types such as lymphocytes, monocytes/macrophages, mast cells, eosinophils, and even endothelial cells lining blood vessels. Each individual cytokine can have multiple functions depending upon the cell that produces it and the target cell(s) upon which it acts (called pleiotropism). Also, several different cytokines can have the same biologic function (called redundancy). Physiologically it appears that most cytokines exert their most important effects in a paracrine and/or autocrine rather than endocrine fashion. Their major functions appear to involve host defense or maintenance and repair of the blood elements.

Cytokines are categorized by their major specific function(s). There are five major categories of cytokines. Interferons are so named because they interfere with virus replication. There are three major types based upon the source of the interferon. Interferon-α (IFNα) is produced by the buffy coat layer from white blood cells, interferon-β (IFNβ) by fi-broblasts, and interferon-γ (IFNγ) by activated T cells and natural killer (NK) cells. Interferon-γ is an important immunoregulatory molecule in determining intra- vs extracellular host defense responses.

The colony-stimulating factors are so named because they support the growth and differentiation of various elements of the bone marrow. Many are named by the specific element they support such as granulocyte colony-stimulating factor (G-CSF), macrophage colony-stimulating factor (M-CSF), and granulocyte-macrophage colony-stimulating factor (GM-CSF). Other CSFs include interleukin (IL)-3, which can stimulate a variety of hematopoietic precursors and is being evaluated as a therapy in aplastic anemia and bone marrow transplantation, and c-Kit ligand (stem cell factor), which has recently been demonstrated as a cytokine necessary to cause the differentiation of bone marrow stem cells into their various precursor elements for eventual differentiation into RBC, WBC, and megakaryocytes (platelets).

The tumor necrosis factors (TNF) are so called because injecting them into animals causes a hemorrhagic necrosis of their tumors. Tumor necrosis factor-α is produced by activated macrophages and TNFβ is produced by activated T cells (both T_H and CTL). These molecules appear to be involved in the pathogenesis of septic shock and much research is aimed at trying to inhibit their activity in septic patients.

The newest group described is the chemokines that are so named because of their common ability to induce chemotaxis of a variety of cell types to areas of inflammation. It appears that they are intimately involved in selective types of inflammatory cell infiltrates both because of the specific chemokine milieu produced as well as selective expression of particular chemokine receptors on specific inflammatory cell subpopulations. They are categorized based upon their chemical composition of cystenyl receptors. Examples include RANTES, macrophage inflammatory peptides (MIPs), and eotaxin.

The largest group is the interleukins, so named because their fundamental function appears to be communication between (inter-) various populations of white blood cells (leukocytes, -leukin). They are produced by a variety of cell types such as monocytes/macrophages, T cells, B cells, and even nonleukocytes such as epithelial cells.

A central source of these cytokines comes from CD4+ helper T-cell subpopulations, often referred to as TH1 and TH2 cells. Human TH1 cells secrete a specific cytokine profile including IFNγ and TNFβ. These cytokines are important helper factors in the generation of cellular immune responses including antigen-specific cytotoxic T lymphocytes (CTL) and NK cells. Additionally, IFNγ in particular has an antagonistic activity against TH2 cytokines. Interleukin-12 (IL-12) produced primarily by activated macrophages and other antigen-presenting cells (APC) plays a central role in inducing IFNγ production. In contrast, TH2 cells secrete IL-4, IL-5, IL-9, IL-10, and IL-13, which are involved in isotype switching of B cells as well as proliferation and differentiation into antibody-secreting plasma cells. In particular, IL-4 and IL-13 are involved in the isotype switch from IgM to IgE, the antibody responsible for classic allergic disease. Both IL-4 and IL-10 are also regulatory cytokines, antagonizing the activities of TH1 cytokines. In humans, helper T cells can have a third cytokine secretory pattern. For example, TH0 cells are capable of secreting all of the above-mentioned cytokines and are often thought of as precursors that differentiate into the TH1 or TH2 pathway with antigen challenge. Thus it can be said that the nature, intensity, and duration of a specific immune response depends upon the delicate balance between TH1 and TH2 numbers and/or activities. Since it is now appreciated that many other cell types besides TH cells produce IFNγ, IL-4, IL-5, IL-9, and IL-10, many scientists now refer to these as type-1 and type-2 cytokines, supporting cellular and humoral immune responses respectively.

D. Impact of Stress on Neuroendocrine and Immune Function

Extensive research efforts have also examined various psychosocial variables in order to predict patterns of adjustment to stressful situations. These variables include optimism, social support, and coping responses, all of which have been found to buffer the psychological, cardiovascular, endocrine, and immune effects of stress and predict overall adjustment

to stressful life events. Further, social support and coping strategies can moderate these effects. There is also research indicating that coping style mediates the effects of social support on distress, such that patients who receive social support may use fewer avoidance coping strategies and therefore have lower overall distress. Similarly, in addition to the direct effects optimism has on adjustment to stressful situations, some researchers have found that the benefits of an optimistic disposition are mediated through its effects on both social support and coping responses. These data lend support to the notion that many of these immune imbalances can be reversed with various forms of stress management.

II. IMPACT OF STRESS AND BEHAVIOR ON CYTOKINE EXPRESSION

It has been suggested that acute vs chronic stress may exert distinct effects on host immunity. Acute stress may produce an adaptive immune response that is actually protective of the normal host. Natural killer cell activity as well as certain potentially antiviral cytokines increase in normal individuals who undergo acute laboratory stressors. Interestingly, chronic stress exposure appears to result in the opposite effect with decreases in NK function and antiviral cytokines. It has also been reported that acute psychological and/or physiological stresses can be associated with adverse clinical outcomes. It is plausible that chronic stress disrupts the ability of some individuals to generate a protective homeostatic immune response when faced with acute stressful events.

A. Inflammatory Cytokines

When the host is subjected to infection, trauma, or injury, a series of cellular and molecular events occur to defend against potential invading organisms and initiate tissue repair. Collectively, these events are called *inflammation* and are of central importance in the maintenance of homeostasis. The normal components of inflammation involve the production of a variety of cytokines that function to recruit and activate the cellular components of inflammation and tissue repair, which include neutrophils, mast cells, macrophages, and fibroblasts. This cellular cascade can be initiated by local microbial invasion through production of substances such as endotoxin (lipopolysaccharide, LPS) or the host neuroendocrine system with production of molecules such as substance P (sP). Acute inflammation is characterized by the recruitment of PMN, basophils/mast cells, and the production of fibrinogen to aid in hemostasis. If the inflammatory response continues and becomes chronic, the PMN are replaced by mononuclear cells such as lymphocytes and monocytes/macrophages.

Stimulation of neurons can cause localized release of sP, which results in tissue edema from peripheral vasodilatation. Substance P can also stimulate tissue mast cells to become activated and release preformed histamine and other chemical mediators of inflammation including cytokines such as IL-4 and GM-CSF. Augmenting the response, histamine (H) can bind to H1 and H2 receptors located on sensory nerve bodies and axons, further stimulating the release of sP and thus potentiating the inflammatory reaction.

The major inflammatory cytokines are often considered to be TNFα, IL-1β, and IL-6. This is accompanied by the production of hepatic proteins collectively known as acute phase reactants that function to limit the activity and spread of invading microorganisms. Studies have shown the increase in serum inflammatory cytokine levels with certain types of acute stress is likely due to mononuclear phagocyte activation. Epinephrine has a similar effect on increasing inflammatory cytokine production *in vitro* and is known to be increased *in situ* during acute stressful events. Acute stress also causes the increased production of sP, which appears to promote upregulation of many cytokines, including the primary inflammatory TNFα and IL-1β. The mechanism may be direct through stimulation of lymphocytes or indirect through the induction of increased adrenal catecholamine secretion with stress.

Chronic stress is usually associated with diminished inflammatory response and poor wound healing. The inflammatory cytokine–APR networks can be inhibited by corticosteroids. Chronic stress, through the activation of the HPA axis, can increase systemic cortisol levels, thus acting as an inhibitor of inflammation. The increase in inhibitory cytokines, especially IL-10, that accompanies chronic stress may also contribute to the anti-inflammatory activity of stress.

Finally, in certain inflammatory diseases, there appears to be a paradoxical response to chronic stress that results in exacerbation of inflammatory pathways. While the mechanisms have not been established, it appears to involve more the systemic balance between pro- and anti-inflammatory cytokines rather than the absolute levels of any specific cytokine. Further, therapeutic interventions for stress reduction have demonstrated a salutary effect in subpopulations of patients identified as having high stress levels.

B. Immunoregulatory Cytokines

Recent work has demonstrated that the examination of only a single component of an immune response can lead to inaccurate conclusions regarding immunosuppression vs dysregulation. The reporting of a TH1/TH2 cytokine network subsequently expanded to include other cytokine-producing cells helps to explain the observations that an inappropriate humoral response to an antigen that requires a cellular response (and vice versa) is as harmful to the host as is generalized immunosuppression. Cytokines can function in an immunoregulatory fashion, both by up- and downregulating the overall immune response as well as directing it toward a cellular, humoral, or mixed response. This is in response to the antigen-presenting cell directing a host response against intra- vs extracellular parasite invasion.

Stress has been reported to have distinct effects on immunoregulatory cytokine production. A fundamental cytokine for expansion of an ongoing immune response is IL-2. Corticosteroids decrease IL-2 production by T cells. Investigations using rodent models have shown that IL-2 levels and production capability is decreased with various forms of stress. The continuance of diminished IL-2 is observed in adrenalectomized animals and indicates the complex nature of this phenomenon. Similar observations have been made for IFNγ. In rodents, IL-2 and IFNγ are produced by TH1 cells while IL-4, -5, and -10 are produced by TH2 cells. Several studies in animal and humans have shown the decrease in TH1 (type 1) cytokines with a concomitant rise in TH2 (type 2) cytokines in stress models such as chronic restraint, medical student exams, major depressive disorders, and chronic pain.

In contrast, acute stress in normal animals and humans has been reported to cause at least a transient increase in NK cell activity accompanied by increased IFNγ and decreased IL-10 production. This may represent an innate host immune response against intracellular parasites similar to the demargination of granulocytes for extracellular parasite defense in the peripheral blood observed with acute stress. Some studies report that the changes in type-1/type-2 cytokine production are different with acute stress superimposed on a chronically stressed host. This could, at least in part, explain the observation of increased susceptibility to infections, particularly viral, observed in chronically stressed individuals.

C. Effector Cytokine Networks

Aside from inflammatory and immunoregulatory activities, cytokines also have direct effector functions. These functions include thermal, antiviral, cytotoxic, and cell trafficking activities. Interleukins-1 and -6 and TNFα have all been described as endogenous pyrogens and function to alter the core temperature as a host defense against invading microorganisms. Antipyretic drugs decrease the sensitivity of the hypothalamus to the effects of these cytokines. Interferon-γ can have a direct antiviral interferon effect. It also activates macrophages to increase antigen processing of viral particles and cytotoxic T lymphocytes (CTL) and NK cells to kill virally infected target cells. Cytotoxic T lymphocytes make TNFβ (lymphotoxin) in response to specific antigen challenge that can directly kill the target cell. In order for a host immune response to be protective, the elements of the response must reach and remain at the site of the antigen challenge. This occurs primarily through the production of chemokines and adhesion molecules. Specific combinations are critical to insure the proper type, sequence, and duration of inflammatory cell influx.

The effects of stress on these effector networks

have not been extensively investigated. Body temperature in situations of acute stress has been reported to increase in both humans and animal models. No significant changes have been reported with chronic stress. As IFNγ levels decrease with chronic stress, it is not surprising that increased incidence, duration, and susceptibility to viral infections occur in these affected populations. This may be the result of the decreased CTL and NK cell activity seen with chronic stress. Adhesion molecule expression on lymphocytes and target tissue cells as well as chemokine secretion are both inhibited by glucocorticoids and thus could be expected to diminish in stress environments where HPA axis activity is high.

III. IMPACT OF CYTOKINES ON STRESS AND BEHAVIOR

It has been appreciated for some time that cytokines can have a direct effect on the CNS and thus psychological components of the host. This can occur directly through effects on certain parts of the brain that control behavior directly (i.e., hippocampus) or indirectly through the neuroendocrine network involving the hypothalamic–pituitary axis. The end result is that cytokine production can affect behavior in both positive and negative ways for host homeostasis.

A. Effects of Cytokines on the Central Nervous System

This area is only recently emerging as a field of study. Much impetus for study has been through the increased use of recombinant cytokines for the treatment of a variety of diseases. Central nervous system side effects of these agents lead to speculation as to the components of the CNS most affected. Although there is evidence to suggest that recombinant cytokines do not directly cross the blood brain barrier (BBB), the relationships are nonetheless clear. The patterns with the cytokines are remarkably similar: an acute "flu-like" illness followed by chronic phase (neurasthenia) with continued cytokine administration. The nature and severity of the chronic symptoms appear dose related but occur virtually with all regimens given for more than 2 months. More severe symptoms such as psychomotor and cognitive disorders as well as delirium and coma may develop at any point in the therapeutic regimen and appear to be related to underlying CNS dysfunction (aging, history of brain injury, and concomitant CNS disease).

The IFNs (α, β, γ), T-cell growth factors (IL-2, -4, -12), proinflammatory cytokines (IL-1, -6, TNFα), and hematopoietins (GM-CSF, IL-3, stem cell factor) have all been given to patients with a variety of illnesses. Their biochemistry and receptor bindings are largely unique yet all share similar CNS toxicities, suggesting mechanisms based upon common albeit as yet undescribed physiologic activities.

Another area of research that suggests a direct effect of cytokines on CNS activity is pain perception. Pain is a protective host response generated in answer to tissue injury. It is mediated by afferent sensory nerves in the midst of tissue injury producing enhanced sensitivity to further noxious (hyperesthesia) as well as innocuous (allodynia) stimuli. The peripheral sensory nerve releases sP into the injured area which in turn can modulate the production and secretion of inflammatory cytokines (such as TNFα and IL-1) from resident inflammatory cells which promote the pain response. The effect appears to be indirect through production of nerve growth factor, prostaglandins, and the like, since no cytokine receptors have been demonstrated in peripheral nerve tissue.

Pain control in peripheral as well as in central nervous tissue can involve endogenous opiate receptors. Corticotropin releasing factor (CRF) is part of the HPA axis upregulated in stress responses. It also upregulates the secretion of endogenous opiate precursors in both peripheral and central nervous tissues. Interleukin-1 can potentiate the CRF response. Of note, both IL-1 and CRF receptors are present on lymphocytes and are upregulated during inflammation. Binding of either IL-1 or CRF causes these lymphocytes to secrete β-endorphins. Although IL-1 can mediate hyperesthesia in normal tissue, it appears that IL-1, through upregulation of CRF re-

ceptors, can mediate analgesia through the local production of β-endorphin.

B. Effects of Cytokines on Neuroendocrine Networks

The effect of HPA as well as sympathetic adrenal medullary hormones on immune function has been extensively studied. Much work has been done to characterize the effects of various cytokines on neuroendocrine networks to further define the bidirectional communication between neuroendocrine and immune systems. Research to date strongly suggests that the mechanism for this bidirectional "cross talk" involves shared ligands and receptors. While stress is known to affect immunity primarily through its effect on neuroendocrine networks, stimulation of the immune system by invading microorganisms produces a cytokine milieu that can have a direct effect on the neuroendocrine network through CNS receptor binding.

There are multiple neuroendocrine hormones produced in the immune system including adrenocorticotropic hormone (ACTH), CRF, thyroid stimulating hormone (TSH), leutinizing hormone, follicle stimulating hormone, prolactin, growth hormone, and somatostatin. This explains the observation of various immune activations (including cytokine production) noted *in vitro* after incubation of immune cells with these hormones. The exact physiologic role of these immune cell-derived neuropeptides is still not established.

However, when a microorganism invades the host, immune activation leads to cytokine production that finds its way to the BBB. There it does not pass but binds to neuronal cells in the hypothalamus via specific cytokine receptors. Although there are many different possible cytokine combinations that may bind CNS tissue, common neuroendocrine effects include upregulation of ACTH and downregulation of TSH release. Interleukins-1, -2, and -6 and TNFα all activate the adrenal axis through the stimulation CRF and/or ACTH directly. Both IL-1 and TNFα inhibit the gonadal axis through downregulation of leutinizing hormone release hormone; TNFα and

IFNγ can inhibit the thyroid axis through downregulating thyrotropin releasing factor.

C. Effects of Cytokines on Behavior

Turning again to the studies using recombinant cytokine therapy, neurocognitive defects with various cytokines have been described. Further, somnolence, psychoses, depression, and personality changes have all been reported during cytokine therapy. Yet it is the so-called sickness behavior (malaise, social withdrawal, somnolence, hyperesthesia) associated with cytokine release after infection, trauma, or even stress that best demonstrates the effects of cytokines on behavior.

Another condition implicating the relationship between cytokines and behavior is depression. Major depressive disorders commonly occur after stressful episodes and are associated with increased HPA hormone levels. Interestingly, cardinal clinical symptoms of depression (somnolence, anorexia, diminished libido) all can be induced by select cytokines. Interleukin-1, TNFα, and IFNγ are all soporific when administered systemically. Anorexia is a major clinical sign in both depression and infections. Tumor necrosis factor-α, IL-1, and IL-6 have all been reported to suppress appetite in both animal models and humans receiving recombinant cytokine therapies. Libido requires an intact hypophyseal–pituitary activity to stimulate production of sex hormones. These can also be regulated by the inflammatory cytokines noted above. Of note, several studies report increased IL-1 and IL-6 levels with decreased IL-2 and IFNγ in plasmas from depressed patients.

IV. SUMMARY

The relationships between stress, distress, immunity, and health are now generally accepted but still not fully defined. Cytokines play a central role in immune responses and are quite sensitive to the effects of both acute and chronic stress through the neuroendocrine network. This can be both a physiological protective system as well as pathologically imbalanced or suppressed. Many factors influence the balance between cytokine and neuroendocrine networks and impact host defense mechanisms against infection, hypersensitivity diseases, and cancer. The stressors that influence host dense can be psychological, physiological, or a combination. Cytokines can, in turn, influence neuroendocrine networks, CNS function, and even behavior directly. A better understanding of the cytokine–neuroendocrine cross talk and the influence of various stressors on that cross talk offer opportunity for future interventional strategies for stress-related illnesses.

See Also the Following Articles

Corticotropin-Releasing Factor; Cytokines, Stress and Depression; Cytotoxic Lymphocytes; Immune Response; Immune Suppression; Natural Killer (NK) Cells

Bibliography

Agarwal, S. K., and Marshall, G. D. (1998). Glucocorticoid-induced type 1/type 2 cytokine alterations in humans: A model for stress-related immune dysfunction. *Interferon Cytokine Res.* **18**, 1059–1068.

Glaser, R., Kiecolt-Glaser, J. K., Marucha, P. T., MacCallum, R. C., Laskowski, B. F., and Malarkey, W. B. (1999). Stress-related changes in proinflammatory cytokine production in wounds. *Arch. Gen. Psychiat.* **56**, 450–456.

Herz, A. (1995). Role of immune processes in peripheral opioid analgesia. *Adv. Exp. Med. Biol.* **373**, 193–199.

Hori, T., Katafuchi, T., Take, S., Shimizu, N., and Niijima, A. (1995). The autonomic nervous system as a communication channel between the brain and the immune system. *Neuroimmunomodulation* **2**, 203–215.

Kiecolt-Glaser, J. K., Glaser, R., Gravenstein, S., Malarkey, W. B., and Sheridan, J. (1996). Chronic stress alters the immune response to influenza virus vaccine in older adults. *Proc. Natl. Acad. Sci. USA* **93**, 3043–3047.

Marshall, G. D., Jr., Agarwal, S. K., Lloyd, C., Cohen, L., Henninger, E. M., and Morris, G. J. (1998). Cytokine dysregulation associated with exam stress in healthy medical students. *Brain Behav. Immun.* **12**, 297–307.

Marx, C., Ehrhart-Bornstein, M., Scherbaum, W. A., and Bornstein, S. R. (1998). Regulation of adrenocortical function by cytokines—Relevance for immune-endocrine interaction. *Horm. Metab. Res.* **30**, 416–420.

Miller, A. H. (1998). Neuroendocrine and immune system interactions in stress and depression. *Psychiatr. Clin. North Am.* **21**, 443-463.

Moynihan, J. A., Kruszewska, B., Brenner, G. J., and Cohen, N. (1998). Neural, endocrine, and immune system interactions. Relevance for health and disease. *Adv. Exp. Med. Biol.* **438**, 541–549.

Muller, N., and Ackenheil, M. (1998). Psychoneuroimmunology and the cytokine action in the CNS: Implications for psychiatric disorders. *Prog. Neuropsychopharmacol. Biol. Psychiat.* **22**, 1–33.

Plotnikoff, N. P., Faith, R. E., Murgo, A. J., and Good, R. A. (1999). "Cytokines, Stress and Immunity." CRC Press, Washington, DC.

Selye, H. (1935). A syndrome produced by diverse noxious agents. *Nature* **138**, 32–44.

Cytokines, Stress, and Depression: A Mechanism Involving Corticotrophin-Releasing Factor

Cai Song

University of British Columbia

I. Introduction
II. Cytokine and Immune Changes in Stress and Depression
III. Changes in Concentrations of Corticotrophin-Releasing Factor and Receptors during Stress and Depression
IV. Interaction between Cytokines and Corticotrophin-Releasing Factor
V. Conclusion

GLOSSARY

corticotrophin-releasing factor (CRF) Produced by CRF-like neurons in the many brain regions in response to stress and immune challenge.

cytokine Soluble substances secreted by different leukocytes that have a variety of effects on other immune, neuron, and endocrine cells.

inflammatory response A complex process, comprising many events, initiated by tissue damage caused by endogenous factors and immunological activation.

in vivo microdialysis A probe is inserted into any nucleus of the brain in a free-moving animal and the release of neurotransmitters can be measured by collecting microdiates at any time and in condition.

macrophage A large phagocytic cell of the mononuclear series that can produce proinflammatory cytokines, such as interleukin-1, interleukin-6, interferon, and tumor necrosis factor.

olfactory bulbectomized rats An animal model of depression. In these animals, changes in behavior, neurochemistry, and endocrine functioning are similar to those that occur in depressed patients.

Overproduction of proinflammatory cytokines may be one of the causes of depression. Many effects of cytokines on the central nervous system, endocrine system and behavior during stress or depression are mediated by corticotrophin-releasing factor.

I. INTRODUCTION

Cytokines are a heterogenous group of polypeptides produced by different leukocytes in response to a wide range of physiological and pathological stimuli. Cytokines and their receptors have been located in many tissues including those in the peripheral and central nervous system (CNS). Cytokines can pass through the blood–brain barrier into the CNS. Some neurone, astrocyte, and microglia cells also produce cytokines in the brain. In recent years, the interaction between the CNS and cytokines has been extensively studied. These investigations have revealed that changes in neurotransmitter synthesis, release, and metabolism in stress, depression, and other CNS disorders significantly alter the activities of immune cells and cytokine production. Conversely, central or peripheral administration of some proinflammatory cytokines markedly change neurotransmission, induce the secretion of corticotrophin-releasing factor (CRF) and cortisol, and cause anxious and stressful behavior in both humans and experimental animals.

Stress causes many behavioral, neurophysiological, endocrine, and immunological changes in which CRF plays a critical role. Corticotrophin-releasing factor is a 41-amino-acid peptide which is the major physiological regulator of the secretion of adrenocorticotropic hormone (ACTH) from the pituitary gland. In the central nervous system, CRF-containing neurons are highly concentrated in the cortex, limbic system, and brain stem nuclei. The functions of these brain regions are involved in cognitive, emotion, and autonomic regulation. The highest density of CRF neurons are found in the paraventricular nuclea (PVN) of the hypothalamus, amygdala, certain thalamic nuclei, substantia nigra, and locus coeruleus (LC). Corticotrophin-releasing factor receptors are localized in the highest densities in the septum, hippocampus, hypothalamus, brain stem, olfactory bulbs, cerebral cortex, amygdala, spinal cord, and cerebellum. In these brain regions, proinflammatory cytokine interleukin (IL)-1 and its receptors also widely exist. However, the receptor distribution of many other proinflammatory cytokines in the brain are still unclear. In the periphery, CRF-like immunoreactivity and receptors have been found in the pituitary, adrenal gland, thymus, and spleen. Corticotrophin-releasing factor like immunoreactivity is also present in lymphocytes and other leukocytes. Thus CRF distribution indicates that CRF integrates not only endocrine but also

neurophysiologic and immunological responses to stress.

II. CYTOKINE AND IMMUNE CHANGES IN STRESS AND DEPRESSION

Some stressor-caused immune changes are similar to those observed in depression. Cellular immune functions are suppressed, but humoral immune responses seem increased. Stress from physical exercise significantly suppresses natural killer cell (NK) activity, neutrophil phagocytosis, and lymphocyte proliferation, but elevates blood IL-1 and IL-6 concentrations. Psychological stress also significantly suppresses most cellular immune functions and increases the concentrations of IL-1, IL-6, IL-6 signal transfer protein GP130, and IL-1 receptor antagonist (IL-1RA). In animal studies it has been shown that novel environmental stress such as exposure to the "open field" also increases IL-6 release from macrophages, while restraint and foot-shock stress largely stimulates IL-1 and IL-6 production in the rat. In depressed patients significant decreases in these cellular activities and increases in acute phase proteins, some antibodies, and complements have been consistently reported. Peripheral mononuclear released IL-1β, tumor necrosis factor (TNF)-α, and IL-6 are increased and a decrease or nonchange in the IL-2 concentration has been found. Similarly, IL-1RA and IL-6R are also increased in these patients.

These changes indicate that an inflammatory response occurs in depressed patients. In animal models, pretreatment of antidepressants before stress exposure can prevent most immune changes. In depressed patients, antidepresant treatment attenuates reduced cellular functions and decreases IL-1, IL-6, and TNF-α production. *In vitro* studies have found that incubating selective serotonin reuptake inhibitors at clinical treatment concentration with human whole blood significantly inhibits the release of proinflammatory cytokines, but increases natural immune inhibitor cytokines (IL-1RA and IL-10). Conversely, the release of proinflammatory cytokines in the immune response may modulate neurotransmission, activate the hypothalamic-pituitary-adrenal (PHA) axis, and change mood and behavior. It has been reported, for instance, that macrophage produced IL-1β, IL-6, and TNF-α stimulate the hypothalamus to release CRF, which elevates the ACTH and cortisol concentrations in the blood. This effect can be blocked by pretreatment of IL-1RA. Central administration of IL-1β or TNF-α to rats increases anxious behavior in the elevated plus maze, suppresses exploration and sex behavior, and causes anorexia. Central administration of IL-1 has also been shown to impair spatial memory in rodents. In clinical investigation, it has been found that patients showed most symptoms of depression after receiving TNF-α or interferon (IFN) for treatment of cancer.

The brain, response to an immune challenge is similar to its response to a stressor. Thus the injection of endotoxin or Newcastle disease virus markedly increases the utilization of hypothalamic noradrenaline (NA) and serotonin (5-HT). A similar study has found that administration of sheep red blood cells to rats also significantly increases the NA concentration and turnover in the PVN of the hypothalamus and locus coeruleus (LC). Such changes are similar to those that occur following a stressful challenge.

A series of studies using *in vivo* microdialysis have shown that systemic administration of IL-1β and IL-6 caused a significant elevation in the concentrations of MHPG, 5-hydroxyindoleacetic acid (5-HIAA), dihydroxyphenylacetic acid (DOPAC), and homovanillic acid (HVA) and a decrease in NA in the nucleus accumbens of the rat. Application of a mild stressor to these cytokine-treated rats synergistically enhanced the extracellular concentrations of MHPG, 5-HIAA, and HVA. Lymphocyte-produced IL-2 produced opposite effects. When applying a mild or severe stressor to olfactory bulbectomized rats, an experimental model of depression, the neurotransmitter changes are the same as those observed after IL-1 administration.

III. CHANGES IN CONCENTRATIONS OF CRF AND RECEPTORS DURING STRESS AND DEPRESSION

The stressful effects of CRF have been widely studied. Corticotrophin-releasing factor content is significantly increased and CRF receptors are down- or upregulated by different kinds of stressors. Experimental or laboratory stress, such as restraint for 3 h, results in an increase in CRF release from the LC, but a decrease in CRF concentration in the dorsal vagal complex. Corticotrophin-releasing factor receptors in the anterior pituitary are significantly reduced. A significant loss of CRF-binding sites in the hypothalamus occurs after severe chronic immobilization stress. Moreover, it has been reported that the downregulation of CRF receptors in the amygdala resulted from an increase in the intercerebral CRF level. Physical stressors, such as pain, heat, cold, or noise, and immune stress, such as inflammation or infection, markedly increase CRF production and CRF mRNA expression in the CNS and periphery and change CRF receptor density. In contrast psychosocial stress, such as chronic psychosocial conflict in male tree shrews, significantly reduced the number of CRF-binding sites in the anterior of the pituitary, the dentate gyrus, and the CA1–CA3 area of the hippocampus.

During stress, CRF is also involved in neurotransmitter changes. Physiological and immunohistochemical studies have suggested that CRF may serve as a neurotransmitter to activate the CNS. Corticotrophin-releasing factor directly acts on catecholamine-containing dendrites in the LC and the forebrain. The coexistence of dopamine (DA) , 5-HT, acetylcholine (ACh), or NA with CRF in the PVN of the hypothalamus was also found. Therefore, CRF modulates neurotransmitter metabolism in those brain regions. Acute and subchronic icv administration of CRF dose-dependently increased the concentrations of NA, DA, and their metabolites in the hypothalamus and prefrontal cortex of the rat. The level of the 5-HT metabolite 5-HIAA was also significantly increased after CRF administration. The central nucleus of the amygdala mediates cardiovascular and autonomic changes associated with emotional and stress responses. Corticotrophin-releasing factor microinjection into the amygdala significantly increase heart rate, blood pressure, and plasma catecholamine concentrations. Corticotrophin-releasing factor is an important link between stress and affective disorders. In depressed patients, the concentration of CRF is elevated in the CSF compared to the normal controls. The number of CRF receptor is decreased in the frontal cortex of suicide victims. Patients showed a blunted ACTH response after iv administration of CRF. These changes could be reversed by antidepressants or ECT treatment. Similar to depression, anxiety or panic attacks are associated with increase CRF release and a hyperactive HPA system. Animal studies have shown that CRF infusion into the LC causes only anxiety, while CRF administration into the LC and parabrachial nucleus causes both anxiety and depression.

IV. INTERACTION BETWEEN CYTOKINES AND CRF

Corticotrophin-releasing factor in the periphery has paracrine effects which are similar to those of hypothalamic CRF; that is CRF action counterbalances local stressful events, such as pain and inflammation. In inflammatory and arthritis models, a significant increase in CRF immunoreactivity or CRF mRNA expression are found. Moreover, CRF receptors are present in the inflamed synovia of the arthritis model of rats. In animal modes of pain, CRF and its receptors are also upregulated. Corticotrophin-releasing factor could inhibit swelling, edema, and dye leakage in the paw produced by hot, cold, and chemical injures. These CRF proinflammatory actions suggest that the peptide may be involved in autoimmune diseases.

Central CRF administration causes a wide impairment of immune functions resembling those observed in stress and depression. During stress exposure, CRF release is largely increased. It has been reported that foot-shock, restraint, or anesthesia markedly suppress NK cell cytotoxicity and lymphocyte proliferation. This suppression is prevented by central pretreatment of CRF antagonist or antibody. Intracerebroventricular administration of CRF for 5 days significantly suppressed lymphocyte proliferation and neutrophil phagocytosis and increased the number of neutrophils and leukocyte aggregation. Central CRF administration also largely reduces NK cell number and activity. Similar immune changes have also been reported in depressed patients.

In infection or inflammation, proinflammatory cytokines, IL-1, IL-6, TNF-α, and CRF coordinate and

integrate the brain-endocrine-immune response. Cytokines stimulate the hypothalamus, amygdala, and pituitary to release CRF and CRF acts on the CNS, endocrine, and immune systems. As mentioned earlier, CRF receptors have been located on immune cells such as monocyte- macrophages and T-helper lymphocytes, but not on T-suppressor cells. Corticotrophin-releasing factor mRNA has been found in rat's spleen and thymus. These immune organs can synthesize and secrete CRF. When splenocytes are *in vitro* cultured with IL-2, the proliferation is significantly increased. The addition of CRF (10^{-9} mol) results in the suppression of, IL-2-stimulated effects on splenocytes in a dose-dependent manner, an effect which may be related to the increase in intracellular cAMP induced by CRF. When CRF and α-helical CRF were added together into the culture, IL-2 stimulatory function was restored. *In vitro* CRF at a concentration of 10^{-14} mol also stimulated the migration of human monocytes. Stress or CRF-induced changes in endocrine, immune functioning and behavior can be prevented by IL-1RA pretreatment; conversely IL-1 and TNF cause most stress-like changes in behavior, endocrine, and CNS and can be blocked by CRF antagonist or antibody.

V. CONCLUSION

The macrophage theory of depression postulates that overproduced proinflammatory cytokines may be one of the causes of depression. Immune-induced increases in CRF and receptors may be the key factor that integrates ACTH and neurotransmitter functions during stress or depression (Fig. 1). Autoimmune disorders, heart disease, tissue damage, allergy, influenza, cancer, infection, and inflammation can all activate macrophage cells to overproduce proinflammatory cytokines. There are several ways that cytokines and CRF may interact during stress and depression. First, these cytokines may directly stimulate CRF release from the brain or indirectly increase CRF release by combining with cytokine receptors in the brain, which change the release of NA, DA, 5-HT, and ACh and activate the catecholamine innervation of the PVN. This innervation appears to

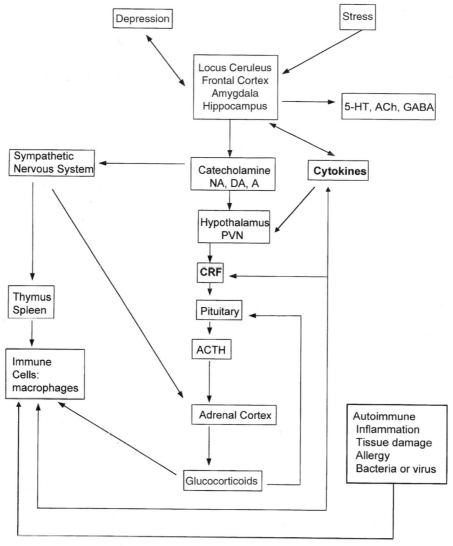

FIGURE 1　Schematization of the relationship among cytokines, CRF, neurotransmitters, glucocorticoids, and immunity in depression or stress.

play a critical role in the control of the rhythmic patterns of baseline HPA secretions and in HPA stress responses. Depletion of PVN catecholaminergic innervation was shown to inhibit the secretion of CRF and other peripheral hormones. Corticotrophin-releasing factor secreted from the hypothalamus stimulates the pituitary to released ACTH, which regulates the adrenal cortex to produce glucocorticoids. Cortisol or corticosterone released into the blood combine with their receptors in immune cells and mostly suppress immune functions. Second, CRF modulation of the immune system is not only by means of gluco-

corticoids. Corticotrophin-releasing factor released from the CNS into the blood can directly combine with its receptors on immune cells and in endocrine organs. Third, NA and CRF produced from PVN may influence the activity of the sympathetic nervous system (SNS) and increase NA and neuropeptide Y release. It has been well established that sympathetic nerves innnervate lymphoid organs. Noradrenaline and neuropeptide Y released from the SNS can also combine with their receptors present on lymphocytes and NK cells and exert a regulatory effect on immune and endocrine functions. It has been demonstrated that increased sympathetic tone during aging, stress, and depression is associated with a decline in immune functioning, whereas *in vivo* chemical sympathectomy suppresses cell-mediated responses and enhances antibody responses. Therefore, in stress and depression these complex interactions between cytokines and CRF may have a causal relationship to the changes in behavior and in the central nervous system.

See Also the Following Articles

Corticotropin Releasing Factor (CRF); Corticotropin Releasing Factor Receptors; Immune Cell Distribution, Effects of Stress on; Natural Killer (NK) Cells

Bibliography

Audhya, T., Jain, R., and Hollander, C. (1991). Receptor-mediated immunomodulation by corticotropin-release factor. *Cell. Immunol.* 134, 77–84.

Brown, M. R., and Gray, T. S. (1988). Peptide injections into the amygdala of conscious rats: Effects on blood pressure, heart rate and plasma catecholamines. *Regul. Pept.* 21, 95–106.

Calogero, A. E. (1995). Neurotransmitter regulation of the hypothalamic corticotropin-releasing hormone neuron. *Ann. N.Y. Acad. Sci.* 771, 31–40.

Connor, T. J., and Song, C. (1999). Neurogenic and metabolic stressors provoke differential effects on accumbal serotonergic neurotransmission in the olfactory bulbectomized rat: An *in vivo* microdialysis study. *Neurorep.* 10, 523–528.

De Souza, E. B. (1995). Corticotropin-releasing factor receptors: Physiology, pharmacology, biochemistry and role in central nervous system and immune disorders. *Psychoneuroendocrinology* 20, 789–819.

Felten, D. L. (1993). Direct innervation of lymphoid organs: Substrate for neurotransmitter signaling of cells of the immune system. *Neuropsychobiology* 28, 110–112.

Friedman, E. M., and Irwin, M. (1995). A role for CRH and the sympathetic nervous system in stress-induced immunosuppression. *Ann. N.Y. Acad. Sci.* 771, 396–418.

Holsboer, F., Spenglen, D., and Heuser, I. (1992). The role of corticotropin-release hormone in the pathogenesis of Cushing's disease, anorexia nervosa, alcoholism, affective disorders and dementia. *Prog. Brain. Res.* 93, 385–417.

Leake, A., Perry, E. K., Perry, R. H., Fairbairn, A. F., and Ferrier, I. N. (1990). Cortical concentrations of corticotropin-release hormone and its receptor in Alzheimer type dementia and major depression. *Biol. Psychiat.* 28, 603–608.

Madden, K. S., Sanders, V. M., and Felten, D. L. (1995). Catecholamine influences and sympathetic neural modulation of immune responsiveness. *Ann. Rev. Pharmacol. Toxicol.* 35, 417–448.

Nemeroff, C. B. (1988). The role of corticotropin-releasing factor in the pathogenesis of major depression. *Pharmacopsychiatry* 21, 76–82.

Song, C., Earley, B., and Leonard, B. E. (1995). Behavioral, neurochemical, and immunological responses to CRF administration: Is CRF a mediator of stress? *Ann. N.Y. Acad. Sci.* 771, 55–72.

Song, C., Merali, Z., and Anisman, H. (1999). Interaction of stress and cytokines interleukine-1, -2 and -6 at the nucleus accumbens: An *in vivo* microdialysis. *Neuroscience* 88, 823–836.

Cytotoxic Lymphocytes

Mary Ann Fletcher, Nancy G. Klimas, and Roberto Patarca

University of Miami

GLOSSARY

cytokines (lymphokines) Peptides or glycopeptides which act in a manner analogous to hormones to regulate the immune system.

cytolytic (cytotoxic) lymphocytes White blood cells which have the capacity, by means of direct cell-to-cell contact, to cause the lysis and subsequent death of target cells.

T lymphocytes White blood cells which have on their surface membranes an antigen recognition structure, the T-cell receptor. T lymphocytes include both helper cells (CD4 T cells) and cytotoxic cells (CD8 T cells)

large granular lymphocytes (lgl) As their name implies, these cells are larger and contain more intracellular granules than most lymphocytes. These lymphocytes, called natural killer (NK) cells, can form conjugates with and lyse target cells, such as tumor cells or virus-infected cells, without the mediation of antigen recognition. Association of an antibody against the target cell with such LGL through Fc receptor interaction with the Fc portion of the antibody can result in a type of cytotoxicity called antibody-dependent cellular cytotoxicity (ADCC). Exposure of the LGL to activating cytokines, such as interleukin-2, results in a more potent cytotoxic cell called the lymphokine-activated killer (LAK) lymphocyte.

I. TYPES OF CYTOTOXIC EFFECTOR CELLS

Lymphocyte-mediated cytotoxicity is a form of cellular immunity whose existence was first documented in experiments on transplant rejection. In 1960, Andre Govaerts showed that lymphocytes from dogs which had received and rejected a kidney transplant destroyed cultured kidney cells from the donor dog *in vitro*. Govaerts' experiments provided the first proof for the existence of cellular immunity. In 1967, K. Theodor Brunner, Albert A. Nordin, and Jean-Charles Cerottini developed the radioactive chromium (^{51}Cr)-release assay as a quantitative tool to assess lymphocyte-associated cytolysis. Radioactive chromium, a radioactive metal that binds intracellular proteins, is used to label target cells. Release of intracellular proteins occurs relatively quickly upon lysis of target cells, and the amount of released metal is proportional to the amount of lysed cells. Use of this assay proved the existence of cytotoxic T lymphocytes (CTLs) that, without antibodies or complement, specifically kill the target cells toward which they have been sensitized through immunization or transplantation. Moreover, the cytolytic activity measured with this assay reflected changes in the frequency rather than in the lytic capacity of individual effector CTLs.

The ^{51}Cr-release assay also allowed the discovery of other types of lymphocyte-mediated cytolytic activities. The second model of cytolysis defined by Peter Perlmann and Goran Holm in 1968 required that the target cell first react with antibodies to activate the cytolytic mechanism. This antibody-dependent cellular cytotoxicity (ADCC) was nonspecific, present in nonimmunized individuals, and lacked memory, i.e., the cytolytic activity did not increase with immunization. Cells that mediate ADCC were termed killer (K) cells and were shown to inhibit tumor growth upon activation with cytokines or biological response modifiers (lymphokine-activated killer cells, LAK).

A third type of lymphocyte-mediated cytolysis was discovered by several immunologists, among whom were Ronald B. Herberman, Rolf Kiessling, and George Klein. The latter researchers were looking for tumor-specific cellular immunity but found that lymphocytes from both cancer patients and normal controls could lyse tumor cells. These lymphocytes were called natural killer (NK) cells since their activity against tumor-transformed and virus-infected cells occurred naturally without immunization. Most NK cells are large granular lymphocytes (LGL) and constitutively cytocidal.

Cytolytic mechanisms involving nonlymphocytic cells, such as monocytes through their expression of tumor necrosis factor (TNF)-α or nitric oxide, are not discussed in this article but can be assessed using the same approaches.

II. MECHANISMS OF TARGET CELL KILLING

Lymphocyte-mediated cytolysis can be conceptually divided into three distinct stages: conjugate formation (binding of effector to target), triggering (signal transduction), and lethal hit (granule exocytosis). Studies of lytic (killers), nonlytic conjugate-forming (binders), and nonconjugate-forming (free) cells suggest that the ability to perform the different stages of cytotoxicity may be acquired at different points in cell maturation with lytic function preceding responsiveness to target cell-specific triggering. Once triggered, the cytolytic process may propagate as effector cells detach from lysed targets and recycle to initiate new lytic interactions.

Direct membrane-to-membrane contact between cytolytic and target cells (conjugate formation) is a prerequisite for lysis to occur. Cell membrane receptors and adhesion molecules mediate conjugation, and transmission electron microscopy reveals extensive cellular membrane interdigitation at the contact region. Cytotoxic T lymphocyte–target cell adhesion is principally mediated by T cell receptor–MHC–peptide interactions and adhesion strengthening steps, although several other molecules mediate binding of the different types of lymphocytolytic effectors to target cells. Early metabolic events that usually follow CTL–ligand interaction include membrane phospholipid methylation, phosphatidylinositol (PI) metabolism, and transient increase in intracellular calcium. Phosphatidylinositol breakdown leads to the formation of inositol triphosphate (IP3) and diacylglycerol (DAG). Inositol triphosphate

(IP3) raises the levels of intracellular calcium, and DAG activates protein kinase C (PKC). Interleukin (IL)-2, which increases NK cell activity, activates PKC; and cAMP which inhibits NK cell-mediated lysis, inhibits PI breakdown.

Two proposed mechanisms of lymphotoxicity currently seem valid: (1) a membranolytic one initiated by the formation of pores in target cell membranes by secreted molecules of lymphocyte origin, such as perforin (pore-forming protein, PFP, cytolysin, C9-related protein) and granzymes (fragmentins); and (2) a nonsecretory one initiated by receptor-mediated triggering of apoptosis, including target cell surface molecules, but not involving the secretion of pore-forming agents and granzymes. The latter two mechanisms are not mutually exclusive.

Upon recognition of their targets, CTL and LGL exocytose cytoplasmic granules, thereby releasing lytic and immunoregulatory molecules. The cytoskeletal microtubule system plays a pivotal role in the delivery of the lytic substances. For instance, IL-2 induces polarization of tubulin in NK cells, laminin is involved in the killing phase, and cholera toxin inhibits granzyme release. Granule exocytosis also requires extracellular calcium for the regulated secretion of lytic granule components, binding of the secreted perforin to the membrane of the target cell, and the polymerization of perforin to polyperforin. Although perforin lyses a variety of target cells nonspecifically, cytolytic cells are generally more resistant to the lytic effect of perforin. The protective mechanism is insufficiently characterized at present.

Some cytolytic lymphocytes express little or no lytic granules and perforin or they lyse target cells under conditions in which perforin and granzymes are neither secreted nor lytic, as is also evident in perforin-deficient mice. In the latter cases, cytolytic cell-mediated lysis and release of intracellular (^{51}Cr-labeled) components are preceded by fragmentation of target cell DNA while lysis induced by perforin typically occurs without DNA fragmentation.

III. EFFECTS OF STRESS HORMONES ON CYTOTOXIC LYMPHOCYTES

Elevations in cortisol, norepinephrine (NE), and epinephrine (E) may be accompanied by decrements in immune function. Adrenal cortical hormones may directly impair or modify several components of cellular immunity including the cytolytic activity of T-lymphocytes and NK cells. Corticosteroids inhibit cellular responses to antigens and impair NK cell activity. Corticosteroids may communicate with lymphocytes via transcriptional cytoplasmic receptors. Hence, the literature supports the concept that elevated levels of cortisol are associated with impaired immune system functioning with accompanying depression of cytokine production. Sympathetic noradrenergic fibers innervate both the vasculature and parenchymal regions of several lymphoid organs. Elevations in peripheral catecholamine may depress immune functioning. This interaction is likely mediated through β-adrenergic receptors on lymphocytes. In addition to catecholamine and corticosteroids, pituitary and adrenal peptide stress hormones such as met-enkephalin, β-endorphin, and substance P stimulate T-cell and NK cell responses. Lymphocytes also have receptors for many neurotransmitter/neurohormones including serotonin, cholinergic agonists, and β-adrenergic agonists.

IV. EFFECTS OF STRESS ON CYTOLYTIC LYMPHOCYTES

Those biological, psychological, and social factors that are involved in physiological stress responses and capable of immunomodulatory effects are listed below.

A. Biophysical Stimuli

Several biophysical stimuli are associated with immunomodulation including tobacco, ethanol, and recreational drug usage. Smoking tobacco is reported to be associated with significant decreases in cytotoxic T cells. Ethanol use is correlated with depressed cell-mediated immunity and to diminished NK cytotoxicity. Intravenous drug usage is associated with depressed cellular immune functioning. The specific mechanisms by which these substances affect immune functioning are not fully elucidated but some of these substances are associated with alterations in those physiological stress response systems noted previously. For instance, nicotine in cigarette smoke

is associated with catecholamine discharge and ethanol consumption is also linked with catecholamine elevations due to blockage of reuptake.

B. Psychological Factors

The *in vivo* exposure of the cells of the immune system to neuropeptides, hormones, and cytokines is related to psychosocial factors such as life stressor burden, social support availability, coping style, and psychological mood state. Several psychological variables are associated with altered immune functioning. These include mental depression and suppression/repression of affectivity, perceived helplessness, intrusive thoughts associated with an adverse event, and coping styles. Clinical depression or depressed affect is linked with impaired cellular immune functioning, although the literature regarding this relationship is controversial. Depression is associated with neuroendocrine abnormalities, particularly hypercortisolemia. The impact of depression on immunity may be stronger in older subjects and in those with more severe depression. Severity of depressive symptomatology was associated with decreased NK activity. Depressive symptoms were predictive of decrements in NK activity among women when measured before and after the death of their husbands. Sleep deprivation, a condition often associated with depression, leads to reduced NK cytotoxicity.

Intrusive thoughts to an adverse situation or event are related to changes in immunological parameters. In the months following Hurricane Andrew, there was a lower level of NK cytotoxicity in those individuals of a community sample who had intrusive cognitions regarding the storm. Elevated antibody titers to Epstein–Barr virus (EBV) were associated with an avoidant style of cognitive processing in college students (suggesting indirectly a decrement in cellular immune function and poorer control of latent herpes viruses).

C. Social Variables

Social stressors are associated with elevations in stress hormone levels and impaired immune functioning in the animal and human literatures. Social stressors most commonly associated with immunomodulation of cytotoxic activity in studies of humans include loneliness, marital disruption and distress, being an Alzheimer's caregiver, and bereavement. Urinary excretions of NE and E are elevated in bereaved subjects and in subjects threatened with a loss as compared to normals. Animals subjected to uncontrollable stressors had immune system decrements such as decreased NK cell cytotoxicity. The experience of sustained stressful periods (e.g., studying for medical school examinations) by normal individuals is associated with poorer control of latent viral infections, impaired lymphocyte production of cytokine, diminished T-cell killing of virus-infected cells, and decreases in NK cell number and lytic activity. In a series of behavioral immunology studies in which social support, mood, and NK activity were evaluated among breast cancer patients, a lack of social support predicted poorer NK activity. A longitudinal study of homosexual men noted that NK cytotoxicity was decreased in men who have lost friends and/or partners to AIDS.

V. STRESS, CYTOTOXIC LYMPHOCYTES, AND HUMAN DISEASES

A strong correlation exists between levels of psychological stress and the development of colds in rhinovirus-inoculated volunteers as well as between stress and upper respiratory infections, necrotizing ulcerative gingivitis infections, and acute EBV infection (mononucleosis). Because the cellular immune system has a major role in the prevention of viral infections and in the suppression of the activation of latent viral infections, any factor which changes the function of the immune system may alter disease progression.

Antibody titers to EBV are consistently elevated in stressed subjects. Reactivation of latent herpesvirus infections, including EBV, cytomegalovirus, human herpes viruses type 6, herpes simplex types 1 and 2, is an important consequence of the loss of cellular immune function. In HIV infection, some individuals survive for longer periods than others and are called "long-term survivors" and a subset of these remain asymptomatic for extended periods and are denoted "long-term nonprogressors." Among many factors that may contribute to disease progression, the stress/endocrine/immune connection should not be neglected. In a pilot study of long-term nonprogressors it was noted that men who had very low CD4 counts had normal NK cytotoxicity. This suggests that natural cell immunity may act as a compensatory protective mechanism in the face of the virtual absence of T helper cells.

See Also the Following Articles

Cytokines; Immunity; Natural Killer (NK) Cells

Bibliography

Antoni, M., August, S., LaPerriere, A., Baggett, L., Klimas, N. G., Ironson, G., Schneiderman, N., and Fletcher, M. A. (1991). Psychological and neuroendocrine measures related to functional immune changes in anticipation of HIV-1 serostatus notification. *Psychosom. Med.* **52**, 496–510.

Esterling B., Antoni, M., Fletcher, M. A., Marguilles, S., and Schneiderman, N. (1994). Emotional disclosure through writing or speaking modulates latent Epstein-Barr virus reactivation. *J. Consult. Clin. Psych.* **62**, 130–140.

Fletcher, M. A., Ironson, G., Goodkin, K., Antoni, M., Schneiderman, N., and Klimas, M. A. (1998). "*Stress and Immune Function in HIV-1 Disease*" (E. Workman and J. Hubbard, Eds.), pp. 229–242. CRC Press, Boca Raton, FL.

Ironson, G., Wyings, C., Schneiderman, N., Baum, A., Rodriquez, M., Greenwood, D., Benight, C., Antoni, M., LaPerriere, A., Huang, H-S., Klimas, N. G., and Fletcher, M. A. (1997) Posttraumatic stress symptoms, intrusive thoughts, loss and immune function after Hurricane Andrew. *Psychosom. Med.* **59**, 128–141.

Kemeny, M., Zegans, L., and Cohen, F. (1987). Stress, mood, immunity, and recurrence of genital herpes. *Ann. N. Y. Acad. Sci.* **496**, 735–736.

Kiecolt-Glaser, J., Glaser, R., Strain, E., Stout, J. C., Tarr, K. L., Holliday, J. E., and Speicher, C. E. (1986). Modulation of cellular immunity in medical students. *J. Behav. Med.* **9**, 311–320.

Herberman, R. and Holden, H. (1978). Natural cell-mediated immunity. *Adv. Can. Res.* **27**, 305.

Klimas, N. G., Morgan, R., Salvato, F., Flavia, Van Reil, Millon, C., and Fletcher, M. A. (1992). "*Chronic Fatigue Syndrome and Psychoneuroimmunology*: Stress and Disease Progression: Perspectives in Behavioral Medicine" (N. Schneiderman, P. McCabe, and A. Baum, Eds.), pp. 121–137. Erlbaum, Hillsdale, NJ.

Patarca, R., Fletcher, M. A., and Podack, E. (1997). "*Cytolytic Cell Functions*" (N. Rose, E. deMacario, J. Folds, H. C. Lane, and R. Nakamura, Eds.), pp. 296–303. M Press, Washington, D.C.

Solomon, G. F., Benton, D., Harker, J. O, Bonivida, B., and Fletcher, M. A. (1994). Prolonged asymptomatic states in HIV-seropositive persons with fewer than 50 CD4+ cells per mm^3. *Ann. N.Y. Acad. Sci.* **741**, 185–190.

Starr, K. R., Antoni, M., Hurwitz, B. E., Rodriquez, M. R., Ironson, G., Fletcher, M. A., Kumar, M., Patarca, R., Lutgendorf, S., Quillian, R. E., Klimas, N., and Schneiderman, N. (1996). Patterns of immune, neuroendocrine and cardiovascular stress responses in asymtomatic human immundeficiency virus seropositive and seronegative men. *Int. J. Behav. Med.* **3**, 135–162.

Death Anxiety

Robert Kastenbaum

Arizona State University

GLOSSARY

existentialism A philosophical position that emphasizes the individual as alone in the world and responsible for his or her own life and values.

hospice A programmatic approach to providing comfort to terminally ill people and their families (see also palliative care).

near-death experience An altered state of consciousness usually occurring after traumatic injury and is often recalled as a comforting and revelatory episode.

ontological confrontation An experience that forces one to acknowledge the reality and salience of death.

palliative care Medical and nursing procedures designed to relieve pain and suffering rather than extend life by all possible means.

thanatophobia Fear of death and of whatever has become associated with death.

Death anxiety refers to stress that is occasioned by heightened awareness of personal mortality. The term usually encompasses concern about the rigors of the dying process as well as the loss of life. The concept sometimes is expanded to include anxiety about the death of others or the ways in which others might be affected by one's own death. The core concept, however, is centered around the *ontological confrontation:* awareness that one's own life must end.

The article begins with a review of basic findings from empirical studies of death anxiety as a charac-teristic of the individual and then moves to situational influences and to theories that attempt to explain these phenomena.

I. EMPIRICAL AND CLINICAL STUDIES OF DEATH ANXIETY

The experience of anxiety is much the same whatever its source: a sense of danger and foreboding accompanied by physical manifestations such as changes in heart rate and respiration. Precisely how death anxiety differs from other forms of anxiety—if at all—is a question that has received little attention. Instead, most academic studies have relied on self-report questionnaires. Respondents usually respond by agreeing or disagreeing with direct questions such as "I fear dying a painful death," although other approaches are sometimes used as well.

A. Self-Reported Death Anxiety in Everyday Life

Healthy adults have most often been the participants in death anxiety studies, with attention given to their level of anxiety and possible gender, age, and other demographic differences.

1. The General Population: How Anxious about Death?

Most adults in the United States report themselves as having moderately low levels of death anxiety. This finding often has been interpreted to mean that we labor to keep our anxieties hidden both from ourself and others. Some studies have shown that when exposed to death-related messages we may undergo physical signs of stress at the same time that we report feeling no anxiety at all. It is therefore argued that we are all anxious about death on a deeper level of experience, although reluctant to admit to it. The alternative interpretation is that our self-reports should not be overanalyzed, rather, the simple truth is that our daily lives are seldom disturbed by anxious thoughts about death. This issue is revisited in the section on theoretical approaches to death anxiety.

2. Is There a Gender Difference in Death Anxiety?

Women in the United States usually report higher levels of death anxiety. The few studies conducted in other nations find the same pattern. We can choose among several interpretations:

1. Women are too anxious about death
2. Men are not anxious enough
3. There is no actual difference in level of death anxiety between the sexes, but women are more willing to acknowledge and express their concerns
4. There *is* a substantive difference in attitudes toward death, but this difference is not well characterized as death anxiety.

In weighing these alternative interpretations it is useful to recognize the exceptional contribution made by women in providing care and comfort to dying people and their families. Much of the leadership and "manpower" in the international hospice movement have come from women, who also are far more likely than men to enroll in death education courses. Such observations, along with a few studies that penetrate into the dynamics behind death anxiety scores, suggest that women are more responsive to the needs of people with life-threatening conditions and are more cognizant and accepting of their own feelings about death. In general, men seem more guarded and uncomfortable with their feelings of death-related vulnerability. These gender differences have been related to childhood socialization patterns in which the expression of feelings, especially those

of vulnerability, are encouraged in girls but discouraged in boys.

"Death anxiety" is too broad a term to characterize the complex feelings experienced by both men and women. A relatively stronger response to death-related situations can represent a keener awareness of mortality and/or a stronger inclination to recognize mortal danger and comfort those in need. In general, women may be "too anxious" about death if the criterion is subjective comfort, but men may be "not anxious enough" if the criterion is the readiness to respond to the mortal jeopardy of self and others.

3. Is There an Age Difference in Death Anxiety?

Do we become more anxious as we grow older because of the decreasing distance from death? Or do we become less anxious because we develop a more mature outlook on life and death?

Available data indicate that older people in general do not report higher levels of death anxiety. Overall, age shows only a weak relationship with death anxiety. Age differences, when found, indicate less fear of death among elderly people. Interview and observational studies further support the conclusion that most people do not become more anxious about death as they move through the later years of life. Concerns are more likely to center around the challenges and stresses of daily life such as protecting relationships and self-esteem. There are methodological problems, however, that should be kept in mind. Today's elders have experienced a passage through unique historical circumstances. When the baby boomers and younger generations reach their later adult years they, too, will have experienced unique personal and sociocultural life histories. The fact that most elders have been reporting low or moderate levels of death anxiety could represent their distinctive life experiences rather than a process inherent in life span development. Qualitative studies have identified specific concerns that are most salient for people at different points in their life spans. Young people seem most apprehensive about the possible loss of loved ones, death as punishment, and the finality of death. Midlife adults express most concern about premature death and fear of pain in dying. Older adults do not fear death as much as the prospect of becoming helpless and dependent on others during their final phase of life.

On the basis of available data, then, we can reject the hypothesis that, in general, we become more anxious about death with advanced age because of the decreased distance from death. It is tempting to conclude that death anxiety is tempered by increasing maturity with age. Self-actualization and existential theories propose that acceptance of death is a mark of maturity. It has not been established, however, that there is only one form of maturity: philosophical acceptance. This is an attractive proposition rather than an established fact. Furthermore, other explanations might account for the relatively low death anxiety found among elderly adults. For example, some people experiencing social isolation, financial concern, and age-related physical problems express a readiness to have their lives come to an end—an attitude that is also reflected in the high completed suicide rates for elderly white men. Low death anxiety might then be related to dissatisfaction with a life that is no longer considered worth living.

4. What Are the Demographics of Death Anxiety?

People in favorable socioeconomic circumstances tend to report lower levels of death anxiety. Education and affluence seem to be buffers against death anxiety but not very powerful or dependable buffers. Growing up in an intact family and having a secure interpersonal environment also offer some protection against high death anxiety. Married people generally live longer and are less likely to commit suicide. We might therefore expect that married people would experience less anxiety than those single or divorced, but, surprisingly, this proposition has not been examined systematically.

Religious belief might be expected to bear strongly on death anxiety. One might speculate that believers will have less fear of death because they expect to have a meaningful afterlife. One might also take the opposite view that fear of punishment for sin might intensify death anxiety among believers. In general, however, no clear pattern of association has been discovered between religious belief and death anxiety. Religion enters into our death orientations in a complex manner that interacts with particular reli-

gious affiliation, cultural history, individual history, and situational context. Studies of terminally ill people suggest that anxiety about suffering and dependency during the dying process is usually more salient than fear of death or nonbeing. Religious faith and belief in an afterlife seem to help many people face the prospect of death, but they are still vulnerable to concerns about the terminal experience and the effects of their death on others. Religion does bear on death anxiety, but in ways that must be learned by attention to individual situations. Unfortunately, even less has been learned about possible ethnic and racial differences in death anxiety because studies have focused mostly on Anglo's. It has become clear, however, that many people feel more secure during their final illnesses when they know that they will be given full benefit of the religious and social customs that are meaningful within their group.

5. What Are the Personality and Lifestyle Correlates of Death Anxiety?

Several findings have emerged on the relationship between death anxiety and personality or lifestyle. People whose lives are disturbed and inhibited by a variety of other fears are also likely to have relatively high death anxiety as well. People with "humorless authoritarian personalities" are the least likely to sign the organ donation forms attached to their drivers' licenses, suggesting a higher level of death-related anxiety. A dominating need to control situations and to win at all costs has been related to a feeling of vulnerability: catastrophic anxiety and death must be warded off by exercising power over the course of events. Similarly, some people who seem to live outside of themselves through causes and cults do so to achieve a sense of participatory immortality and thereby escape the sting of death anxiety. In contrast, people with deep interpersonal attachments who have a strong sense of purpose in life tend to have a lower level of death anxiety.

B. Death Anxiety in Particular Situations

Our focus now shifts from characteristics of the individual to the type of situation in which individuals may find themselves. We draw now upon a wide range of observations beyond self-report questionnaires.

1. *Transitional Situations*

We often experience heightened death anxiety in transitional situations. Starting or losing a job and moving to a new community are common examples of transitions that have no evident relationship with death, but which can engage feelings of uncertainty and threat. Separation, divorce, and other significant changes in relationships can also arouse a sense of vulnerability, which, on the emotional map, is not far from fear of mortality. Even detection of the first gray hair can trigger recognition that one is no longer young, thereby arousing fears of aging and death that had been previously kept under control. Determined attempts to look young often express a convergence of fears: "I will be less attractive, less valued, less useful, and I will become the sort of person who is most likely to die—the oldtimer."

Societal conditions can also generate a stressful sense of transition and uncertainty throughout the community. Apprehension about unemployment, inflation, inadequate health care benefits, and difficulties in coping with bureaucracy and technology can all contribute to a sense of helplessness which, in turn, increases permeability to awareness of mortality. A society that has lost confidence in its purpose and competence may contribute to heightened death anxiety throughout all ages, ranks, and echelons.

2. *Touched by Death*

Exposure to death does not always make us anxious. Sometimes we shed or seal off such episodes quickly before they can penetrate our awareness. At the extreme, we may deny the reality or significance of the event, as when the victim of a heart attack insists that he is just fine and does not need medical attention. More often though we use less extreme and more subtle defensive strategies to avoid the impact of an exposure to death. For example, at his funeral we may not permit ourselves to acknowledge a possible resonance between the neighbor who died of pulmonary disease and our own habit of smoking. It's too bad about the neighbor, but I don't smoke the same brand of cigarettes. Many of us are gifted in the ability to shed exposures to death in order to preserve the comforting routines of everyday life.

Nevertheless, some exposures to death do get through to us. Usually these exposures take one of two forms: a personal brush with death or the death of another person.

It is not uncommon for the stress reaction to develop a little *after* a life-threatening emergency. A competent driver or pilot, for example, is likely to respond to an emergency with quick and skillful actions. Only some time later when the danger has passed will the emotional reaction seize its opportunity, perhaps taking the form of a psychophysiological or other nonvoluntary reaction. Anxiety aroused in consequence of a "close call" with death generally dissipates quickly, although the person may then be more sensitive to future situations that have some resemblance. What has become known as a near-death experience (NDE) is a different case. These episodes almost invariably involve risk to life that the individual could not deal with through personal initiative and action (e.g., the passenger in a car hit in a broadside collision). The NDE is an episode split-off from the person's usual life and is marked by unusual, dream-like events. Instead of intense anxiety, however, many reports depict a remarkable feeling of serenity and liberation. Some people believe they have not only been touched by death but were actually "in death" for a short period of time. There are varying interpretations of the actual state of being during a NDE, but a great many reports that anxiety about death completely dissipated after the experience.

In contrast, the death of another person is often mentioned as the "wake up call" that leads to anxious realization of one's own mortality. Most often it is the death of a parent that produces an increased sense of personal vulnerability. "Death is coming after *me,* now!" as a fiftyish woman exclaimed after the death of her mother. The death of a long-lived cultural icon can also lead to feelings of vulnerability and abandonment. We also are likely to experience an upsurge of death-related anxiety when a person seen as much like ourselves passes away. Our behavior toward others when they are terminally ill, during the funeral process, and for sometime afterward can be influenced markedly by anxieties aroused by our feeling that "this could be happening to me."

3. Facing Death: Life-Threatening Illness

The prospect of our own death may flash before us in a fast-developing episode as already noted. It is a different matter, however, when the threat is enduring and relentless, as in the case of life-threatening illness. Individuals differ markedly in the ways they cope with a persistent threat to life, and the specific nature of their conditions also has its effect (e.g., a cardiac disorder that might end one's life at any time or advanced pulmonary disease in which every breath is a struggle as the disease continually progresses). Nevertheless, there are also some issues that arise in the course of the illness that often intensify anxiety. These include (a) uncertainty about diagnosis and prognosis; (b) learning that one has a life-threatening condition; (c) progression of symptoms and dysfunctions that suggest that treatment efforts are failing; (d) interpersonal cues that others also recognize the end is approaching, along with concern about losing one's most valued relationships; (e) concern about practical end-of-life matters; (f) concern about the overall meaning of one's life; and (g) anxiety about experiencing helplessness and pain in the end phase of the dying process.

Anxiety peaks most often arise at two points: upon learning (or believing) that one is terminally ill or in the last days or weeks of life when death may appear to be a welcome release. Experiencing both panic and depression, some people develop suicidal ideas when they first come up against the imminent prospect of their death. Trustworthy and sensitive communication on the part of medical personnel can reduce the risk of a plunge into despair or an anxious leap into self-destruction. Other professional caregivers, friends, and family can also allay the fear that one is being abandoned to pain and death. The second anxiety peak, again accompanied by depression, arises as a result of continued physical deterioration, fatigue, and apprehension regarding total loss of function. "I'm just so tired of dying" is how more than one person has expressed it. Here the issue is not death anxiety in the usual sense, but anxiety about being forced to go through further suffering for no good reason that the person can see. Euthanasia is not sought by all people in the end phase of their terminal illnesses, however. Many continue to experience life as meaningful and to be protected from disabling anxiety by positive belief systems and loving support from the people most important to them.

The anxiety and depression often associated with terminal illness have often been alleviated by competent palliative care, such as practiced by hospice organizations. The medical establishment has shown signs of agreeing with the hospice premise that pain should be regarded as one of the vital signs to be assessed and effectively treated in all physician–patient interactions. Team approaches to the comfort of terminally ill people and their families with priorities given to the dying person's own lifestyle and values have also contributed to reducing anxiety throughout the final phase of life.

4. Major Mental Health Problems

People who feel that their worlds are exploding or collapsing often express intense anxiety about death. Some of the most striking expressions of death anxiety are found during psychotic episodes, whether functional or triggered by a drug-altered state of mind. Whatever the specific cause, it is usually the sense of losing total control over one's life that has precipitated the episode, with dying and death serving as metaphorical expressions of this panic. When depression dominates, afflicted individuals may even present themselves as dead, thereby having passed beyond the reach of death anxiety. Helpful interventions include providing a higher degree of stability and simplicity in the sociophysical environment and creating situations in which the individual can again begin to experience again a sense of competence and control. Approaches as different as expressive and drug therapies can also be useful.

II. THEORIES OF DEATH ANXIETY

General theories of stress and anxiety have potential for contributing to the understanding of death-related concerns. This section focuses on theories that were intended specifically for the comprehension of death anxiety.

A. Freud and Becker: Rival Theories

Two theories may be considered classic for their bold positions and widespread influence. These views could not be more opposed in their fundamental propositions, although there are commonalities as well.

Sigmund Freud held that we cannot truly have a fear of death because we cannot believe in our own death. Personal death is not comprehended by the foundational logic of our unconscious processes, while on the conscious level, we have not actually experienced death. When people express a fear of death (thanatophobia) then, it should be regarded as a phobic symptom that must be probed to discover the actual, deeper source of anxiety lodged in childhood experiences and stimulated by current life developments. This influential view relegated death anxiety to a derived, secondary status and thereby not of much interest in its own right. Later in his own pained and stressful life Freud came to see dying and death as issues very much deserving of attention, but it was his earlier formulation that continued to prevail. Ernest Becker challenged Freud's interpretation from an existential standpoint. For Becker, *all* anxiety is an expression of death anxiety. It is our fundamental fear of nonbeing that attaches itself to an almost infinite variety of situations and symbols. Furthermore, society exists largely to protect us from being consumed by death anxiety. Becker charges that our language and customs are designed to disconnect us from ontological encounters with mortality. Despite all of its technological innovations, our postmodern civilization is basically a theatrical performance piece to which we all contribute our talents and suspension of disbelief. We agree not to notice that we all happen to be mortal. The person who really believes in death, and is therefore really anxious about it, is often the person we call schizophrenic. Being "normal" means being fairly successful in protecting ourselves against facing up to reality.

Both the Freudian/psychoanalytic and the Becker/existential theories have served as useful guides to observation and reflection. Different as they are, however, both share the premise of universal application and the flaw of unverifiability. We can discover expressions of death anxiety that are attributable to a variety of other circumstances (e.g., transitional situations), but not necessarily those identified by Freud. We can also discover continuing examples of death denial or taboo in our society, but there are also many exceptions that should not be overlooked. Neither theory lends itself to clear-cut and systematic evaluation from an evidential standpoint.

B. Emerging Theories

Several new theories have emerged, each offering a distinctive perspective on death anxiety and each drawing upon a distinctive realm of empirical research. Terror management theory is an empirically oriented offshoot of Becker's position. The core proposition is that self-esteem and a positive worldview serve as effective barriers to death anxiety. When we feel ourselves imperiled, we can call upon our sense of self-worth and confidence as well as our belief that our society is basically sound and that the universe a good place in which to dwell. Whatever contributes to the growth of self-esteem and confidence and whatever contributes to the moral character and resilience of society can stand between ourselves and mortal terror.

Developmental learning theory places death anxiety within the mainstream of sociobehavioral research. We learn to fear, avoid, or cope with death-related phenomena just as we learn to deal with all other life challenges: through a long process of maturation and social interaction. It is not necessary to assert either that all anxiety or no anxiety is related to death or that we all have some kind of fixed response to death-linked situations and symbols. As a society and as individuals the shape and intensity of our anxieties and coping strategies are pretty much in our own hands and are likely to vary from generation to generation. *Edge theory* shifts the emphasis from fear of death to the readiness to respond to threats to life. Two frequently held assumptions are set aside. The question of whether we can truly comprehend death is not as important as it once seemed. The point is that we *do* recognize threats to survival, whether of ourself or of others. A vigilance function is with us from birth. Like other living creatures, we are equipped with the ability to detect serious threats and go "on alert." The second assumption set aside is the belief that the relatively low death anxiety scores reported by most people represent a concealment of the true state of things. In the traditional view, we invest much psychic energy into trying to hide our intense anxieties about death from ourselves and others. According to edge theory, we do not carry about a burden of repressed death anxiety. Instead, our moderate everyday approach to life is occasionally challenged by a potentially dangerous situation. We have a momentary sense of being on the edge of nonbeing. In such situations we go on alert and try to identify the source of the danger. If we can then either dismiss or take action to overcome the threat we experience only a sense of heightened activation. It is when we feel on the edge and cannot respond to the threat that we are likely to be flooded by death anxiety.

Points of difference aside, current research and theory suggest that the understanding of stress management throughout life requires attention to the ways in which we come to terms with our mortality.

See Also the Following Articles

ANXIETY; CONTROL AND STRESS; FEAR; FREUD, SIGMUND; SELF-ESTEEM

Bibliography

Becker, E. 1973. "The Denial of Death." Free Press, New York.

Breznitz, S., ed. 1983. "The Denial of Stress." International University Press, New York.

Freud, S. 1951 (original work 1913). Thoughts for the times on war and death. *In* "Collected Works," Vol. IV, pp. 288–317. Hogarth Press, London.

Kastenbaum, R. 1998. "Death, Society, and Human Experience," 6th ed. Allyn & Bacon, Boston.

Kastenbaum, R. 1999. "The Psychology of Death," 3rd ed. Springer, New York.

Kaufmann, W. 1976. "Existentialism, Religion and Death" New American Library, New York.

Lonetto, R., and Templer, D. 1986. "Death Anxiety." Hemisphere, New York.

Death Guilt

see Survivor Guilt

Defensive Behaviors

D. Caroline Blanchard, Mark Hebert, and Robert J. Blanchard

University of Hawaii

GLOSSARY

chronic mild stress (CMS) A pattern of anhedonia involving reduced positive response toward normally rewarding items such as a sweetened liquid or intracranial stimulation in reward sites following intermittent exposure to a variety of mildly stressing stimuli or events. These behavioral outcomes, like those of both LH and subordination, have been shown to be responsive to antidepressant drugs.

defensive behavior an array of evolved behavioral responses (e.g., flight, freezing, etc.) to threat stimuli such as predators or attacking conspecifics. Individual defensive behaviors are modulated by features of both the threat stimulus and of the situation in which they are encountered. Many defensive behaviors are relatively consistent across mammalian species and may be a component of stress- or defense-related psychopathologies.

defensive threat/attack Display of weapons (e.g., teeth and claws) and strength (e.g., through loud vocalization) in response to close contact by an attacker followed by bites or blows to particularly vulnerable sites on the attacker's body (typically face and eyes).

dominance/subordination A pattern of relationships between a consistent winner (dominant) and a consistent loser (subordinate) in agonistic encounters. Both dominant and subordinate often show behavioral and physiological signs of stress, but these may be modulated by compensatory mechanisms in the dominant that are not available to the subordinate. Subordination has been used as a model of chronic social stress.

learned helplessness (LH) A pattern of impaired learning, particularly in active avoidance situations, and of reduced activity in a threat context following exposure to uncontrollable aversive events. This, like the chronic mild stress paradigm, has been proposed as a model of depression.

offensive attack Attack, typically but not always toward conspecifics, in the context of a dispute over important resources such as territory, access to mates, or food. Offensive attack is aimed toward species-typical sites on the opponent, often areas in which bites or blows do little serious damage. In contrast to defensive threat/attack, fear reduces offensive attack.

risk assessment a pattern of orientation, attention, and exploration with regard to potential threat stimuli, enabling an animal to gather information as to their location, identity, and threat status. This information facilitates an optimally adaptive response to genuine threat or promotes a return to nondefensive behavior if no threat is present.

Defensive behaviors are those activities that occur in response to the host of life-threatening dangers encountered in every natural environment from predators, from conspecific attack, and from threatening features of the environment. They constitute the behavioral component of the stress response and have evolved on the basis that, to particular types of threat stimuli and in particular situations, each such behavior has proved to be optimally adaptive in terms of enhancing the extended reproductive success of the individual. These behaviors range from active investigation of threat stimuli through actions facilitating escape from or termination of a threat. As the extended reproductive success of females may importantly reflect survival of offspring in their care, the optimal defensive behaviors for males and females may differ: The magnitude and mechanisms of gender difference in defense are poorly understood, but there is speculation that these may be related to the substantial and consistent differences in vulnerability to particular psychiatric disorders for men and women.

I. DEFENSIVE BEHAVIORS AND THE STIMULI THAT ELICIT THEM

Much recent work on defensive behaviors has focused on response to predators or attacking conspecifics, threat stimuli that (especially the former) elicit a number of defensive behaviors in rodents without the necessity of pain or prior experience. While the defensive behaviors of higher primates are undoubtedly more complex than those of rodents and may involve some specific learning components, there appears to be an essential continuity of defense patterns across mammals such that research on the behavioral, neural, and neurochemical aspects of the defense systems may be very relevant to analysis of defense-related behaviors, including psychopathologies, in people.

Defensive behaviors are modulated by features of both the threat stimulus and the situation in which it is presented. The major (self-) defensive behaviors are listed below.

1. Flight from the threatening stimulus and avoidance of that stimulus if it is at a distance. These behaviors are facilitated by the presence of an escape route or a place of concealment and are dominant responses to high-level threat when such features are available.

2. Freezing, when no escape route or place of concealment is available. Freezing involves orientation toward the threat source and immobility in a species-typical posture. Like flight, it increases in intensity as the threat approaches, up to a level of proximity that elicits defensive threat/attack.

3. Defensive threat occurs as the threat stimulus nears the subject. It consists of a weapons display (teeth bared, claws unsheathed) and loud, sonic vocalizations such as screams.

4. Defensive attack occurs at even shorter threat–subject distances. This attack is often oriented toward particularly vulnerable sites such as the predator/attacker's face and eyes.

5. Risk assessment: if the threat is potential rather than present (e.g., predator odor or novel situation) or of low intensity, defense may involve active risk assessment, including sensory sampling (visual/auditory scanning, sniffing) and approach and investi-

gation of the threat source alternating with rapid retreat. Risk assessment is associated with "low-profile" postures and rapid movement interspersed with periods of immobility; these reduce the likelihood of detection as the animal approaches and investigates the threat stimulus. These activities enable the gathering of information, facilitating identification and localization of the threat source. If it proves to be a real danger, defenses such as flight or defensive threat/attack ensue. Alternatively, if risk assessment permits a determination that the situation is safe, then the animal can resume its normal activities (food gathering, self- or offspring care, etc.).

6. Alarm vocalizations occur in many (most?) mammalian species with a colonial lifestyle. Such cries warn other group members of an approaching predator. In some primate species, different types of predator (e.g., terrestrial vs aerial) elicit different alarm cries, permitting the listener to take defensive action appropriate to that predator.

These defensive behaviors all occur in the context of physical threat. Threat to resources elicits a very different behavior (offensive attack or aggression), which has a much weaker association with fearfulness or psychological stress. Both offensive and defensive (i.e., self-defensive) attack toward conspecifics in mammals tend to be oriented toward specific areas on the body of the opponent, and these target sites may provide an additional means of differentiating offensive and defensive attack modes. The former tends to be aimed at sites where bites or blows will produce pain without a high risk of damage to vital organs, while the latter is typically targeted toward the face of the threatener. This, for both conspecific and predator attackers, is both the site of particularly vulnerable and important organs such as the eyes and of the major offensive weapons of many animals (teeth). Because conspecific attack is so precisely targeted, an additional group of defenses against conspecific threat involves concealment of these especially likely targets of attack. These "target-protection" defenses, in combination with attacker behaviors that seek to thwart the defender (target concealment) strategy and reach the preferred attack target, may give fighting among conspecific mammals a "dance-like" quality in which the actions of one animal are immediately countered by appropriate actions of the other.

All of these defensive behaviors involve a strong component of orientation toward (or in the case of flight, away from) the threat stimulus. In contrast, analyses of chronic internal pain (a stressful event not involving an external stimulus) suggest that the behavioral defense to this may be quiescence, involving reduced activity, and inattention to external stimuli.

II. DEFENSIVE BEHAVIORS: CROSS-SPECIES GENERALITY

These defensive behaviors, and their specific associations with particular elements of the threat stimulus and the environment in which it is encountered, show a high degree of cross-species generality in mammals. The generality is probably not limited to mammals, but mammals do appear to rely more strongly on this range of behavioral defenses than do other animals. Structural defenses (e.g., armor, venom, poisonous tissues) and cryptic coloration are emphasized in lower vertebrates and invertebrates, while birds show an obvious specialization toward flight.

The behavioral repertory, including defensive behavior, of higher primates is more varied and sophisticated than that of more primitive mammals (e.g., rodents). However, the same defensive behaviors noted for rodents also occur in primates, albeit with greater elaboration of cognitive and communicatory elements. As examples, primates, as compared to rodents, show greater differentiation of alarm cries and may be capable of communicating danger from terrestrial vs aerial vs burrowing predators; they can easily learn to be defensive to particular stimuli based on observations of the fear responses of other group members to those stimuli; they display "reconciliation" behaviors following stressful conspecific encounters that may reduce the chance of future stress between these individuals.

III. DEFENSIVE BEHAVIORS AS INDEPENDENT BIOBEHAVIORAL SYSTEMS

Individual defensive behaviors are so precisely controlled by relevant features of the threat stimulus and situation that they can be independently elicited and manipulated in experimental tests. Research on the brain mechanisms involved in these behaviors indicates that they represent the differentiated output of forebrain emotional processing systems, serving as a number of parallel links between elements of these forebrain systems such as the amygdala, the hindbrain, and peripheral motor and sympathetic pathways for defense. The periaqueductal gray (PAG) region contains a number of longitudinally coursing columns in which electrical and excitatory amino acid stimulation can produce defensive threat/attack, flight, and freezing or quiescence: some controversy surrounds interpretation of stimulation of the ventral PAG column in terms of the last pair of alternatives. It is particularly interesting that the PAG has been "mapped" in both cats and rats and that the specific areas where particular behaviors are elicited by stimulation appear to be very consistent. The PAG is not, however, the only system in which defensive behaviors are differentially represented. Defensive vocalizations and other elements of defensive threat/attack can be elicited by stimulation of the hypothalamus and other forebrain sites, while risk assessment is believed to be associated with the activity of components of the septohippocampal system, the output of which may or may not be routed through the PAG. In addition to anatomical differences, there appear to be differences in the neurochemistry of the biobehavioral defensive systems, providing a basis for findings (described below) of differential response of these systems to psychoactive drugs.

IV. ACUTE VERSUS CHRONIC BEHAVIORAL DEFENSES

In addition to acute exposure paradigms, a number of models of chronic social or predator threat have been devised and used to evaluate behavioral and physiological effects of longer term stress. In a particularly desirable habitat, with females and a burrow system, male rodents quickly create a strong dominance hierarchy based on victory and defeat. Defeated subordinate male rats spend most of their time within a particular chamber or tunnel from which they attempt to exclude the victorious male (dominant): defensive threat/attack is a particularly effective defense in a tunnel. From these sites, subordinates also consistently monitor the dominant's location, avoiding the "surface" area when it is present and fleeing when they are in the open area and the dominant appears. Subordinates spend most of their waking time in defensive behavior and lose weight even when food and water are freely available.

Much of the defensive behavior of a subordinate rat to a dominant is very similar to that seen on initial exposure to a threat stimulus, except that it is more protracted. However, prolonged exposure to threat/stress may produce deleterious behavioral changes such as reduced activity and a shift away from active defense toward more passive defenses and possibly to a "quiescent" state in which the animal becomes less, or less effectively, attentive to possible environmental dangers. In learning situations, particularly those involving an active avoidance response, deficits in responding by animals chronically exposed to an uncontrollable stressor are characterized as indicating "learned helplessness (LH)." A potentially similar phenomenon in subordinate rats involves greatly prolonged risk assessment without transition to nondefensive behavior. This may also reflect a learning deficit and it, like the active avoidance deficit of "LH" rats, may be quite maladaptive: the prolonged (and often inadequately cautious) risk assessment behavior exposes the animal to danger if a threat is present, while the failure to resume normal behavior patterns is maladaptive if there is no threat present.

Another behavior associated with chronic stress (in a chronic mild stress (CMS) model) is "anhedonia," typically indexed by reduced consumption of sweetened liquids. In fact, the CMS animals may actually show heightened preference for more intensely sweetened liquids.

V. DEFENSIVE BEHAVIORS, STRESS, AND PSYCHOPATHOLOGY

Defensive behaviors—both those that are seen in response to acute threat and the altered patterns expressed after chronic threat/stress—have many parallels to the behavioral components of a range of human psychopathologies. In particular, risk assessment behaviors appear to be very similar to the increased "vigilance and scanning" characteristic of generalized anxiety disorder, while reduced activity, anhedonia, and deficits in active avoidance learning have parallels in depression.

An additional parallel between the chronic stress models and depression is through alterations of the hypothalamic-pituitary-adrenal (HPA) axis functioning and changes in brain neurotransmitter systems. Different physiological systems have often been emphasized in investigations of the various chronic stress models (LH, CMS, Subordination) such that a consensus on their commonality of effects is difficult to obtain. The HPA axis changes appear to be most severe for subordinates, many of whom show greatly decreased levels of corticosterone binding globulin, reduced corticosterone (CORT) response to acute stress, and reduced corticotropic releasing factor (CRF) in the paraventricular nuclei of the hypothalamus, indicating involvement of brain mechanisms in this deficit. Subordinates also show sharply reduced levels of testosterone, reflecting both peripheral and central effects of stress, with the former appearing prior to the latter. For the most part, learned helplessness is not associated with these hormonal effects, particularly when the criterion of experience of "uncontrollable" vs "controllable" shock is applied. This very stringent criterion, using chronic but controllable shock as a control condition, may be obscuring some important changes in stress-linked physiological systems. As befits the label of "chronic mild stress" the CMS model also fails to produce notable hormonal changes. However, all three models have been associated with brain neurochemical changes, particularly involving biogenic amines, and a number of these brain changes as well as the behaviors with which the models are associated have been shown to be reversible after treatment with antidepressants. These hormonal and brain effects, in addition to the changes in defense and other behaviors after chronic stress, suggest that animal models of chronic stress may provide some very relevant analogs to depression and further emphasize the potential value of use of these behaviors as preclinical models for research on the pharmacology of emotion-linked disorders.

This approach has produced many interesting results. Risk assessment behaviors show a selective response to anxiolytic drugs such as classic benzodiazepines and the newer 5-HT1A agonists such as buspirone and gepirone. Antipanic drugs (e.g., alprazolam, imipramine, fluoxetine, and phenelzine) decrease flight behaviors, while the panicogenic agent yohimbine increases flight. As with clinical findings, effects of these antipanic drugs on flight require chronic administration, while initial injection of imipramine and fluoxetine may actually exacerbate defense. Both CMS and LH models have proved to be responsive to a variety of antidepressant drugs. However, the various behavioral effects of the latter, such as reduced activity and disrupted learning of an active avoidance response, may show differential patterns of response to antidepressant and anxiolytic drugs. Both acute and chronic social defeat produce behavior changes that are normalized by fluoxetine, a selective serotonin reuptake inhibitor that has antidepressant as well as antipanic effects. These findings suggest that while acute and chronic stress may produce a wide pattern of changes in defensive and other behaviors it is the behavioral response itself rather than the stress paradigm that may provide the clearest and most direct relationship to particular stress-linked psychopathologies. Each type of psychopathology is defined in terms of a group or pattern of focal symptoms, and these may, in some cases, be viewed as representing dysfunctions in the brain systems underlying particular defensive behaviors; for example, panic–flight; anxiety–risk assessment. Although these concepts are still at an early stage of development, they suggest a novel direction for animal models of psychopathology and provide clear behavioral criteria for analysis of brain and peripheral systems involved in the complex biobehavioral response to threat and stress.

See Also the Following Articles

AGGRESSIVE BEHAVIOR; FIGHT-OR-FLIGHT REACTION

Bibliography

Blanchard, R. J., Griebel, G., Henrie, J. A., and Blanchard, D. C. (1997). Differentiation of anxiolytic and panicolytic drugs by effects on rat and mouse defense test batteries. *Neurosci. Biobehav. Rev.* 21, 783–789.

Bandler, R., and Keay, K. A. (1996). Columnar organization in the midbrain periaqueductal gray and the integration of emotional expression. *Prog. Brain Res.* 107, 285–300.

Blanchard, D. C., Spencer, R., Weiss, S. M., Blanchard, R. J., McEwen, B. S., and Sakai, R. R. (1995). The visible burrow system as a model of chronic social stress: Behavioral and neuroendocrine correlates. *Psychoendocrinology* 20, 117–134.

Davis, M. (1997). Neurobiology of fear responses: The role of the amygdala. *J. Neuropsychiatr. Clin. Neurosci.* 9, 382–402.

Gray J. A., and McNaughton N. (in press). "The Neuropsychology of Anxiety: An Enquiry into the Functions of the Septo-hippocampal System," 2nd ed. Oxford Univ. Press: Oxford, UK.

Maier, S. F., Ryan, S. M., Barksdale, C. M., and Kalin, N. H. (1986). Stressor controllability and the pituitary–adrenal system. *Behav. Neurosci.* 100, 669–674.

Willner, P., Muscat, R., and Papp, M. (1992). Chronic mild stress-induced anhedonia: A realistic animal model of depression. *Neurosci. Biobehav. Rev.* 16, 525–534.

Denial

see Emotional Inhibition

Dental Stress

Tibor Károly Fábián and Gábor Fábián

Semmelweis Medical University, Budapest, Hungary

GLOSSARY

denture intolerance Appearance of *all kinds* of (psychogenic) symptoms reported by the *patient* in interaction with the *fixed or removable dentures* or with the *prosthodontic treatment;* with the absence of detectable pathological conditions of the related tissues and the absence of detectable insufficiency of the denture.

depth, psychological Related to unconscious psychological processes.

odontophobia All kinds of phobic reactions related to the dental treatment, to the dentist, or to the dental surgery office.

orofacial Localized in, or related to, the hard or soft tissues of the mouth, the tongue, the teeth, or the face.

palliative dental treatment Alleviating or relieving without surgical treatment.

panic disorder Disorder with a symptom of recurrent intensive alarm attacks linked with various body reactions and fear of death.

phonetic Relating to speech sound.

photoacoustic stimulation Flash light stimuli through closed eye and rhythmic noise stimuli through the ear at the same time.

prosthodontic treatment Diagnosing, planing, making, and inserting fixed or removable artificial devices to replace one or more teeth and associated tissues.

psychosymbolic function Conscious and unconscious psychological function of an organ.

Dental stress is a collective noun of all psychological stress effects in the field of dentistry. The most common and widely known phenomenon is the patient's stress in the dental chair. In addition to this simple anxiety from dental treatment, the various phobic reactions related to dentistry and some cases of panic disorder form the group of acute dental stress. Chronic stress effects related to dentistry represent another group of dental stress, including several orofacial manifestations of different conditions caused by chronic stress effects. As a third group, mistakes of the patient–dentist relationship caused by acute or chronic stress effects should be mentioned.

I. SOME CHARACTERISTICS OF ACUTE STRESS IN DENTISTRY

Problems related to acute stress effects are markedly different from those of chronic stress effects. In addition to differences in the characteristics of symptoms, the onset of acute stress problems occurs mostly before age 20, and most of the patients have at least partial remission at times, and a high proportion of the patients were aware of having been exposed to anxiety-provoking life situations related to dental treatments. In the case of simple or increased anxiety patients and other odontophobic patients (with the exception of needle phobia), it is characteristic that they accept the need of psychotherapic techniques to solve their problem and are much more cooperative to these treatments than patients suffering from needle phobia or panic disorder. As a common cause of this behavioral difference, needle phobic and panic disorder patients usually recognize their indisposition (usually simple collapse, or panic attack if any) as a "result" of a "life dangerous allergic reaction" to injected anesthetics, which develops as rigid, not-compromising behavior. The differential diagnosis of a real allergy of local anesthetics, panic disorder, and needle phobia is extremely important.

A real allergy can cause life dangerous anaphylactic shock and the use of local anesthetics should be strictly avoided. In the case of panic disorder, some data from the literature suggest that the immune reaction regulated by IgE can be increased, which means a higher risk of anaphylactic shock. Because of this the use of local anesthetics are relatively contraindicated and great care should be exercised if using local anesthetics. For needle phobic patients the contraindication of the use of local anesthetics (if any) is only psychological.

II. CHRONIC STRESS-INDUCED OROFACIAL MANIFESTATIONS

Chronic stress as a psychopathologic condition of the nervous system can result in several orofacial manifestations, such as temporomandibular dysfunction, chronic facial pain, psychogenic taste disorders, some salivation problems, certain recurrent oral ulcerations or inflammations, some oral allergic reactions, "burning mouth" syndrome, facial tic, and bruxism. In this group of symptoms, the chronic stress effect usually originates from unconscious psychological problems. These manifestations usually appear in the second half of life, when the physiologic and, above all, the psychosymbolic function of the teeth is disturbed by tooth destruction or tooth loss (although in some cases psychogenic manifestations can be found in childhood or in youth as well). This psychosymbolic function of the teeth and mouth is rooted in the fact that the shape of the mouth and teeth is one of the most important sexual characteristics and has strong symbolic meaning related to sexuality and aggressiveness. However, tooth loss, especially edentulousness, results of losing sexual characteristics, the facial aesthetics, and retail symbolic meaning of losing the living force, growing old, evanescence, and death. Because of these multiple psychological meanings and importance of the mouth and the teeth, many of the psychopathological mechanisms related to sexuality, aggressivity, autoaggressivity, or death anxiety can lead to orofacial manifestations, especially if these important psychosymbolic functions are damaged by tooth or mouth disorders. Because these mechanisms are subcon-

scious for the patients, patients refuse psychotherapy and are attached to the dentist and dental treatment, producing special problems and the need of dental professionals competent in psychotherapy.

III. STRESS-RELATED MISTAKES OF THE PATIENT–DENTIST RELATIONSHIP AND DENTURE INTOLERANCE

The relationship of the patient and the dentist is based on and is modified by four basic factors (if the dentist is supposed as a person with optimal behavior and thinking):

Factor A. Conscious wishes of the patient related to the result of dental treatment (i.e., to have a nice smile, be able to chew, to have attractive dentures with proportional teeth).

Factor B. Unconscious wishes of the patient related to the result of dental treatment (i.e., be younger, stop from getting older, feel like a woman/man again).

Factor C. Conscious wishes of the patient related to the dentist (i.e., works perfectly, works inexpensively, works without pain, is kind).

Factor D. Unconscious wishes of the patient related to the dentist (i.e., loves me like my mother/ father did, punishes/does not punish me as my father did, accepts me as a "member of the family," lets me nearer, saves me).

From the viewpoint of the different types of dental treatment in the case of factors A and B, prosthodontic treatment can be rather problematic because of the great impact of prosthodontic treatment on missing aesthetic, sexual, nutritional, or phonetic functions of the teeth (factor A) and, consequently, on the psychosymbolic functions of the teeth (factor B). Similarly, prosthodontic treatment subserves psychological manifestations because the treatment can be rather uncomfortable for the patient and it can be extremely expensive, producing pressure and aggression (factor C). Moreover, prosthodontic treatment usually lasts longer and provides enough time for the patient to develop emotional binding to the dentist (factor D). For a successful dental treatment, especially prosthodontic treatment, the dentist should be able to detect, recognize, and deal with all four factors. Usually, this is not impossible and may even not be too difficult, but in the case of patients being under acute psychological stress conditions (i.e., existential trauma, workplace problems, relationship problems with the sexual partner) or under chronic psychological stress conditions (i.e., depression, neuroses, chronic anxiety, death anxiety, schizophrenic or paranoid reactions), unconscious factors (factors B and D) can produce strong difficulties. When curing patients suffering from psychological stress, significant errors of the patient–dentist relationship may develop, and denture intolerance appears regularly as a symptom and psychological indicator of these mistakes. In these cases, special treatment of the patient by a dentist specialized and competent in psychotherapy may be essential.

IV. METHODS TO ELIMINATE STRESS EFFECTS IN DENTISTRY

In acute dental stress, numerous methods are available to solve the problem: clinical rehearsal, video training, eye movement desensitization and reprocessing, behavior therapy, cognitive therapy, hypnotherapy, and different drugs containing midazolam, ketamine, β blockers, MAO blockers, and nitrous oxide. In denture intolerance (acute or chronic stress induced) or chronic psychological stress manifestations in the orofacial region, the treatment possibilities are quite different because the patient usually does not accept the need of psychotherapic help. Special techniques should be used to lead the patient from the field of dental treatment to the field of psychotherapy. A gradual increasing amount of psycotherapic discussions should be used during palliative dental treatment until definitive psychotherapy can be started. Relaxation and relaxing hyp-

notic techniques in this phase can be useful as well. The combination of relaxing hypnotherapy with photoacoustic stimulation seems to be a very powerful method, as it is an interesting personal experience (it motivates the patient to take part of this kind of therapy) and it provides a significant antidepressive effect. Whenever "real" psychotherapy can be started, depth-psychological hypnotherapic interventions (or all kind of techniques suitable in depth-psychological treatment) can be effective.

See Also the Following Article

Surgery and Stress

Bibliography

Berggren, U. (1984). Dental fear and avoidance: A study of aetiology, consequences and treatment. Public Dental Service City of Göteborg, University of Göteborg Faculty of Odontology, Göteborg, Sweden.

Fábián, T. K., and Fábián, G. (1998). Stress of life, stress of death: Anxiety in dentistry from the viewpoint of hypnotherapy. *In* "Stress of Life from Molecules to Man" (P. Csermely, ed.), Vol. 851, pp. 495–500. The New York Academy of Sciences, New York.

Hakeberg, M. (1992). Dental anxiety and health: A prevalence study and assessment of treatment outcomes. Public Dental Service City of Göteborg, University of Göteborg Faculty of Odontology, Göteborg, Sweden.

Kent, G. G., and Blinkhorn, A. S. (1991). "The Psychology of Dental Care" 2nd ed. Wright-Butterworth-Heinemann, Oxford.

Mehrstedt, M., and Wikström, P.-O. Eds. (1997). "Hypnosis in Dentistry." Milton Erickson Society, Munich, Germany.

Pilling, L. F. 1983. Psychiatric aspects of diagnosis and treatment. *In* "Diagnosis and Treatment in Prosthodontics" (W. R. Laney and J. A. Gibilisco, eds.), pp. 129–141. Lea & Febiger, Philadelphia.

Schmierer, A. 1997. "Einführung in der zahnärztliche Hypnose," 2nd ed. Quintessenz Verlags, Berlin, Germany.

Staats, J., and Krause, W.-R. 1995. "Hypnotherapie in der zahnärztlichen Praxis." Hüthig Ltd., Heidelberg, Germany.

Depersonalization

Marlene Steinberg

University of Massachusetts Medical Center and Yale University School of Medicine

GLOSSARY

amnesia A specific and significant block of past time that cannot be accounted for by memory.

depersonalization Detachment from one's self, e.g., a sense of looking at one's self as if one were an outsider.

derealization A feeling that one's surroundings are strange or unreal. Often involves previously familiar people.

dissociation Disruption in the usually integrated functions of conscious memory, identity, or perception of the environment. The disturbance may be sudden or gradual, transient or chronic.

identity alteration Objective behavior indicating the assumption of different identities, much more distinct than different roles.

identity confusion Subjective feelings of uncertainty, puzzlement, or conflict about one's identity.

Depersonalization is characterized by a sense of detachment from the self. The symptom itself may manifest in a variety of Axis I or Axis II psychiatric disorders. The DSM-IV prefers to define depersonalization, not in functional or nosologic terms, but phenomenologically as in an alteration in the perception or experience of the self. The sense of detachment itself may be experienced in various ways. Commonly it appears as out-of-body experiences giving a sense of division into a participating and an observing self, resulting in the sense of going through life as though one were a machine or robot. In some cases, there exists a feeling that one's limbs are changing in size or are separated from the body. As is made clear later in this article, it is important to distinguish between recurrent severe depersonalization characteristic of the dissociative disorders, including depersonalization disorder, mild or moderate episodic depersonalization sometimes observed in patients with other nondissociative Axis I or II disorders, and the isolated episode experienced by persons in the healthy population (normal controls).

I. DEFINITION AND CHARACTERISTICS

Although depersonalization was first described in 1872, it was not named until 1898, when Dugas contrasted the feeling of loss of the ego with a real loss. In 1954, Ackner remedied the lack of clear-defined boundaries of the symptom by describing the four salient features: (1) feeling of unreality or strangeness regarding the self, (2) retention of insight and lack of delusional elaboration, (3) affective disturbance resulting in loss of all affective response except discomfort over the depersonalization, (4) an unpleasant quality which varies in intensity inversely with the patient's familiarity with the symptom. The author has defined depersonalization as one of the five core symptoms of dissociation (see above), the other four consisting of amnesia, derealization, identity confusion, and identity alteration. Each of the five dissociative disorders have characteristic symptom profiles of these core dissociative symptoms.

Episodes of depersonalization accompany or even may precipitate panic attacks and/or agoraphobia; they may also be associated with dysphoria. Chronic depersonalization frequently results in the patient's acceptance of the symptoms in a manner of resignation. Patients experience difficulty putting their experience into words, but often compare their feelings to such states as being high on drugs, having the ability to fly out of their bodies for short periods, seeing themselves from the outside, or floating in space and watching themselves. Other descriptions encountered in case studies include feelings of being unreal, of being dead, of having various body parts disconnected, or feeling like an automaton or a character in a film. Depersonalization is frequently accompanied by a lack of all feeling, a numbness which may be attributed to and/or misdiagnosed as depression.

Depersonalization has been reported to be the third most common complaint among psychiatric patients, after depression and anxiety. Incidence of actual depersonalization has been difficult to determine because of (a) the relative strangeness of the symptoms, (b) the difficulty patients experience in communicating them, and (c) the lack, until recently, of diagnostic tools for the systematic assessment of depersonalization. Detection is further complicated by the fact that depersonalization is not accompanied by altered external or social behavior, but by an altered state of perception on the part of the patient.

II. ETIOLOGY

Few systematic investigations have been made of the incidence of depersonalization and of the disorders with which it coexists. Various biological and psychodynamic theories have been advanced for the etiology of depersonalization: (1) physiologic or anatomical disturbance, with feelings of depersonalization produced by temporal lobe function and various metabolic and toxic states; (2) the result of a preformed functional response of the brain to overwhelming traumata; (3) a defense against painful and conflictual affects such as guilt, phobic anxiety, anger, rage, paranoia, primitive fusion fantasies, and exhibitionism; (4) a split between the observing and the participating self, allowing the patient to become a detached observer of the self; and (5) the result of a child's being raised in an environment which systematically fails to know some part of the child, who then experiences that part as tentative and as a result is unable to accurately assess the self.

Depersonalization has been reported to be a normal reaction to life-threatening events, such as accidents, serious illnesses, near-death experiences, anaphylactic reactions, and complications of surgery. Depersonalization is frequent among victims of sexual abuse, political imprisonment, torture, and cult indoctrination. Symptoms of depersonalization are often associated with hypnosis, hypnogogic and hypnopompic states, sleep deprivation, sensory deprivation, hyperventilation, and drug or alcohol abuse.

Depersonalization itself is a nonspecific symptom and not necessarily pathognomic of any clinical disorder. It is the persistence and nature of depersonalization that differentiates depersonalization in normal subjects versus subjects with dissociative and nondissociative disorders. Figure 1 presents a table useful for distinguishing between normal and pathological depersonalization. Figure 2 summarizes the spectrum of depersonalization.

The "Differential Diagnosis Tree of Depersonalization" (Fig. 3) illustrates procedures for distinguishing between depersonalization disorder and other disorders which may resemble it. The differential diagnosis of patients experiencing recurrent or persistent depersonalization should include the dissociative disorders, various other psychiatric disorders, and possible organic etiology.

III. ASSESSMENT WITH THE SCID-D

The Structured Clinical Interview for DSM-IV Dissociative Disorders (*SCID-D*), the first diagnostic tool for assessing dissociative symptoms and disorders, has been utilized to systematically investigate depersonalization symptoms. Developed in 1985 and extensively field tested, it is the only diagnostic instrument enabling a clinician to detect and assess the presence and severity of five core dissociative symptoms and the five dissociative disorders (dissociative amnesia, dissociative fugue, depersonalization disorder, dissociative identity disorder, and dissociate disorder not otherwise identified) as defined by DSM-IV criteria. The *SCID-D* is a semistructured diagnostic interview with good-to-excellent interrater and test–retest reliability and discriminant validity. Guidelines for the administration, scoring, and interpretation of the *SCID-D* are reviewed in the *Interviewer's Guide to the SCID-D*. Severity rating definitions were

Common Mild Depersonalization	Transient Depersonalization	Pathological Depersonalization
Context Occurs as an isolated symptom	Occurs as an isolated symptom	Occurs within a constellation of other dissociative or nondissociative symptoms or with ongoing interactive dialogue
Frequency One or few episodes	One episode that is transient	Persistent or recurrent depersonalization
Duration Depersonalization episode is brief; lasts seconds to minutes	Depersonalization of limited duration (minutes to weeks)	Chronic and habitual depersonalization lasting up to months or years
Precipitating Factors • Extreme fatigue • Sensory deprivation • Hypnagagic and hypnopompic states • Drug or alcohol intoxication • Sleep deprivation • Medical illness / toxic states • Severe psychosocial stress	• Life-threatening danger. This is a syndrome noted to occur in 33% of individuals immediately following exposure to life-threatening danger, such as near-death experiences and auto accidents (Noyes, et al., 1977) • Single, severe psychological trauma	• Not associated with precipitating factors in column 1. • May be precipitated by a traumatic memory. • May be precipitated by a stressful event, but occurs even when there is no identifiable stress. • Occurs in the absence of a single immediate severe psychosocial trauma.

FIGURE 1 Distinguishing between normal and pathological depersonalization. Reprinted with permission from Steinberg M: Handbook for the Assessment of Dissociation: A Clinical Guide. Washington, DC, American Psychiatric Press, Inc., 1995.

developed to allow clinician's to rate the severity of symptoms in a systematic manner and are included in the *Guide*.

The *SCID-D* can be used for symptom documentation and for psychological and forensic reports. Early detection of dissociative disorders, including depersonalization disorder, benefits from the use of this specialized instrument, the format of which includes open-ended questions designed to elicit spontaneous descriptions of endorsed dissociative symptoms. The *SCID-D* has been demonstrated to be a valuable tool in differential diagnosis with patients of different ages (it can be used in adolescents as well as adults), backgrounds, previous psychiatric histories, and

presenting complaints. It also plays a useful role in treatment planning, patient follow-up, and symptom monitoring.

Correct diagnosis is vital to proper treatment of the disorder. If the depersonalization is secondary to an underlying primary disorder, the symptom may be alleviated by treatment of the underlying illness. In instances where patients experience only occasional episodes of depersonalization in the context of other nondissociative symptoms, the clinician may consider a diagnosis of nondissociative psychiatric disorder. The presence of depersonalization disorder itself will be characterized by recurrent depersonalization.

DID and DDNOS	Non-Dissociative and Personality Disorders	No Psychiatric Disorder
Depersonalization questions elicit descriptions of identity confusion and alteration	No spontaneous elaboration	No spontaneous elaboration
Includes interactive dialogues between individual and depersonalized self	No interactive dialogues	No interactive dialogues
Recurrent - persistens	None - few episodes	None - few episodes

Note:
DID = Dissociative Identity Disorder, DDNOS = Dissociative Disorder, Not Otherwise Specified

FIGURE 2 The spectrum of depersonalization on the SCID-D-R. Reprinted with permission from: Steinberg M: Interviewer's Guide to The Structured Clinical Interview for DSM-IV Dissociative Disorders-Revised. Washington, D.C. American Psychiatric Press, Second Edition, 1994.

IV. CASE STUDY

The process of differential diagnosis of depersonalization may best be illustrated by presenting a case study. The study demonstrates the utility of the *SCID-D* in diagnostic assessment, patient education, and treatment planning. For space reasons, conventional formatting and content have been abbreviated.

Sample SCID-D Psychological Evaluation

Demographic information and chief complaint: S.W. is a 31-year-old administrative assistant at a community college who presented with the complaint of feeling detached from herself since adolescence.

Past psychiatric history: Although the patient had no history of hospitalization for psychiatric disturbance, she began treatment for an episode of depression which interfered with her employment and social relationships. Although admitting to past casual use of marijuana, she had never been in treatment for substance abuse disorder.

Family history: S. had a younger sibling; both children grew up in an intact but emotionally unsupportive family. Patient reported that both parents suffered mood swings and unpredictable temper outbursts.

Mental status exam: S. answered questions with relevant replies; although she seemed slightly depressed, her affect appeared full range. She denied hallucinations, both auditory and visual, and evidenced no psychotic thinking. She denied acute suicidal or homicidal ideas.

SCID-D evaluation: The *SCID-D* was administered to systematically evaluate the patient's dissociative symptoms and was scored according to prescribed guidelines. Significant findings from the *SCID-D* interview follow. S. denied experiencing severe episodes of amnesia, but endorsed a persistent sense of depersonalization, resulting in distress and interference with occupational and personal functioning. This feeling of depersonalization had been chronic and occurred all the time rather than episodically. Although the feeling varied in intensity with her overall stress level, the experience of depersonalization was always characterized by a general sense of detachment from life rather than by disturbances in body image or a split between participating and observing parts of the self. Only a single isolated out-of-body experience had occurred. S. experienced feelings of derealization which varied in intensity with the depersonalization, but she reported the depersonalization as the most distressing symptom. She described recurrent anxiety and panic episodes triggered by the depersonalization; it was the combination of depersonalization and panic attacks which led to the depression that brought her into therapy. S. reported that the depersonalization has eroded her sense of control over her occupational functioning and other significant areas of her life, but she did not attribute feelings of loss of control to identity confusion or alteration. She denied having internal dialogues, visual images of parts of her personality, feelings of possession, or acquiring unexplained possessions or skills. Her descriptions of internal struggle were focused on her feelings of unreality, not on conflicts between different aspects of her personality or different personalities within herself.

Assessment: S.'s symptoms are consistent with a primary diagnosis of a dissociative disorder based on DSM-IV criteria

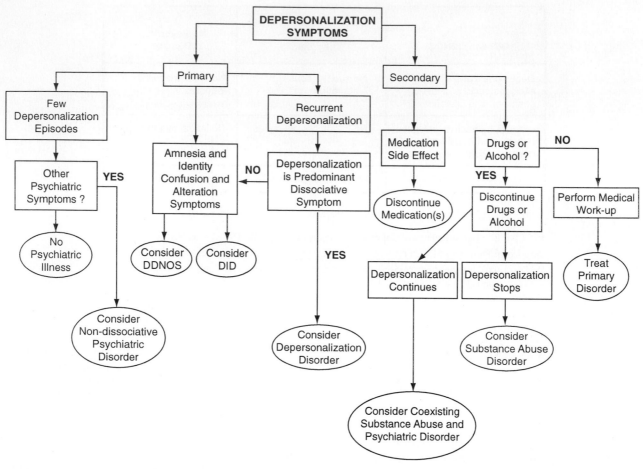

FIGURE 3 Differential diagnosis decision tree of depersonalization. Reprinted with permission from: Steinberg M: Interviewer's Guide to The Structured Clinical Interview for DSM-IV Dissociative Disorders-Revised. Washington, D.C. American Psychiatric Press, 1994.

and ICD-10 criteria. Specifically, in the absence of substance abuse disorder or other organic etiology, her severe chronic feelings of unreality toward herself, and the accompanying dysfunction (in the absence of other dissociative symptoms such as identity confusion and alteration), are consistent with a diagnosis of depersonalization disorder.

Recommendations: Although detailed discussion of treatment for depersonalization disorder is beyond the scope of this assessment, it would be standard practice to conduct a follow-up interview to review the findings of the *SCID-D* evaluation, to educate the patient regarding her symptoms, and to begin the process of individual psychotherapy.

V. CONCLUSIONS

Recent advances in accurate diagnostic tools allow for early detection and accurate differential diagnosis

of depersonalization. Research based on the *Structured Clinical Interview for DSM-IV Dissociative Disorders(SCID-D-R)* indicates that depersonalization occurs in individuals without psychiatric illness who experience none to few brief episodes as well as in individuals with dissociative disorders who experience recurrent to ongoing episodes. In addition to the frequency of the depersonalization, the nature, severity, and context also distinguishes cases of dissociative disorder from other nondissociative disorders. Further research is necessary in the form of controlled double-blind studies comparing the efficacy of pharmacotherapeutic agents. As the *SCID-D-R* allows for the assessment of the severity of depersonalization based on operationalized criteria, pharmacotherapy trials can now be systematically performed and can evaluate baseline and postmedication severity levels of depersonalization. Given the frequency of misdiagnosis in patients suffering from depersonalization and other dissociative symptoms, earlier detection of dissociative disorders using the *SCID-D-R* can allow for rapid implementation of effective treatment.

See Also the Following Articles

AMNESIA; DISSOCIATION

Bibliography

Ackner, B. (1954). Depersonalization I: Aetiology and phenomenology. *J. Ment. Sci.* **100**, 838–853.

American Psychiatric Association. (1994). "Diagnostic and Statistical Manual of Mental Disorders," 4th ed. (DSM-IV). American Psychiatric Association, Washington, DC.

Bowman, E. S., and Markand, O. (1996). Psychodynamics and psychiatric diagnoses of pseudoseizure subjects. *Am. J. Psychiat.* **153**(1), 57–63.

Dugas, L. (1898). Un cas de depersonalization (A case of depersonalization). *Revue Philosophique 1898* **45**, 500–507.

Noyes, R. Jr., and Kletti, R. (1977). Depersonalization in response to life-threatening danger. *Compr. Psychiat.* **18**, 375–384.

Steinberg, M. (1994a). "The Structured Clinical Interview for DSM-IV Dissociative Disorders—Revised (SCID-D)," 2nd ed. American Psychiatric Press, Washington, DC.

Steinberg, M. (1994b). "The Interviewers' Guide to the Structured Clinical Interview for DSM-IV Dissociative Disorders—Revised," 2nd ed. American Psychiatric Press, Washington, DC.

Steinberg, M. (1995). "Handbook for the Assessment of Dissociation: A Clinical Guide." American Psychiatric Press, Washington, DC.

Steinberg, M. (1996a). "A Clinician's Guide to Diagnosing Dissociative Symptoms and Disorders: The SCID-D." Multi-Health Systems (Cassette Recording and Audiotape Manual), Toronto, Ontario, Canada.

Steinberg, M. (1996b). "Tips and Techniques for Assessing and Planning Treatment with Dissociative Disorder Patients: A Practical Guide to the SCID-D." Multi-Health Systems, (Cassette Recording and Audiotape Manual), Toronto, Ontario, Canada.

Steinberg, M. (1996). Assessment of dissociation in trauma survivors and PTSD. *In* J. Wilson and T. Keane (Eds.), "Assessing Psychological Trauma and PTSD: A Handbook for Practitioners." Guilford Press, New York.

Steinberg, M., and Steinberg, A. (1995). Systematic assessment of Dissociative Identity Disorder in adolescents using the SCID-D: Three case studies. *Bull. Menninger Clin.* **59**(2), 221–251.

Steinberg, M., and Hall, P. (1997). The SCID-D diagnostic interview and treatment planning in dissociative disorders. *Bull. Menninger Clin.* **61**(1), 108–120.

Steinberg, M., Rounsaville, B., and Cicchetti, D. (1990). The Structured Clinical Interview for DSM-III-R-Dissociative Disorders: Preliminary report on a new diagnostic instrument. *Am. J. Psychiat.* **147**, 76–82.

Steinberg, M., Rounsaville, B., Buchanan, J., Raakfeldt, J., and Cicchetti, D. (1994). Distinguishing between Multiple Personality and Schizophrenia using the Structured Clinical Interview for DSM-IV Dissociative Disorders. *J. Nerv. Ment. Disord.* 495–502.

Depression and Manic-Depressive Illness

Robert T. Rubin

Center for Neurosciences Research, Allegheny General Hospital, Pittsburgh

GLOSSARY

affect The objective (observable) component of emotions (appearing depressed, angry, elated, etc.) in contrast to mood.

antidepressants Drugs that influence neurotransmitter function and that are used in the treatment of depression.

bipolar illness (disorder) Synonym for manic-depressive illness (disorder).

cerebral cortex The outer layer of the brain, composed mainly of nerve cells (neurons).

cerebral ventricles Cerebrospinal fluid-filled spaces within the brain.

electroconvulsive therapy (ECT) Passing a brief electric current through the brain to induce a grand-mal convulsive seizure as treatment for severe depression or bipolar disorder.

mood The subjective (experienced) component of emotions (feeling sad, happy, angry, etc.) in contrast to affect.

neurotransmitters Chemicals that carry messages from one nerve cell to another.

The terms "depression" and "manic-depression" cover a spectrum of disorders that range from tempo-rarily feeling "down" to melancholic major depression and severe bipolar illness (episodes of both mania and depression), both of which are thought to have a genetic and biological basis and are incapacitating in their severity and duration. The depressive phase of these disorders may be so severe that the person contemplates suicide and may even attempt it. Supportive psychotherapy is usually sufficient for the treatment of mild, time-limited depressions. More severe and incapacitating depressive illness, as well as bipolar illness, most often requires treatment with antidepressant medications and other mood-stabilizing drugs combined with behavioral therapies to help improve the person's outlook on and control over his or her life circumstances.

I. INTRODUCTION

The term "depression" covers a spectrum of disorders. These range from temporarily feeling "down" about something that has gone wrong in one's life to long and severe depressions that have a genetic and biological basis and that often are incapacitating to the afflicted person in his or her occupational and social life. The terms "manic-depression" or "bipolar illness" designate an often serious disorder in which there are inappropriate mood swings in both directions—excessive elation as well as significant depression. Depression and manic-depression are psychiatric disorders that currently are considered "functional" in that there is no clearly understood central nervous system (CNS) pathophysiology underlying them. This is a dynamic nomenclature, however—as knowledge about the pathology of the brain in these and other psychiatric illnesses increases, the adjective "functional" conveys less and less meaning. Furthermore, when these mood disorders are so severe that they impair the daily functioning of the individual, somatic (physical) treatments are almost always required, including antidepressants, mood-stabilizing drugs such as lithium, and, when drug therapy fails, electroconvulsive therapy (ECT).

This article focuses on the more severe disorders of mood, in particular major depression (unipolar depression) and bipolar disorder. The CNS substrates of these illnesses are being examined in several ways, and their genetic underpinnings are slowly being defined. Structural and functional imaging studies of the brain are providing some anatomical localization, limited by the resolution of the imaging techniques and the particular imaging method used.

Several classes of antidepressant drugs are useful for treating major depression, but the balance among chemical systems (neurotransmitters) in the brain makes it difficult to predict which antidepressant will work best for a particular patient. Lithium is the most broadly effective treatment for bipolar illness, but a number of anticonvulsant and antipsychotic drugs, as well as antidepressants, also may be helpful. Stress can play a major role in the severity and duration of both major depression and bipolar disorder, and the illnesses themselves, given the incapacitating nature of their symptoms, can be very stressful to afflicted persons. In both disorders, one's psychological pain and despair can be so severe that suicide may be contemplated and even attempted.

II. CLINICAL CHARACTERISTICS OF MAJOR DEPRESSION AND MANIC-DEPRESSION

Major depression and manic-depression are classified among the mood disorders. Major depression (unipolar depression) consists of one or more depressive episodes, defined as 2 weeks or more of depressed mood or loss of interest or pleasure in nearly all activities, with at least four additional symptoms: increased or decreased appetite and/or weight; increased or decreased sleep; change in psychomotor activity (retardation or agitation); decreased energy; feelings of worthlessness or guilt; difficulty thinking, concentrating, or making decisions; or repeated thoughts of death, including suicidal thoughts, plans, or attempts. The symptoms

must be severe enough to cause significant distress or to interfere with the person's occupational or social functioning. Finally, the major depressive episode must not be a direct result of a drug or an underlying medical condition.

Based on the above criteria for the diagnosis of major depression, it can be seen that it is a very broad category of mental illness. Patients may or may not have many of the more physiological symptoms, such as changes in appetite or weight, sleep disturbance, or psychomotor retardation or agitation. To address this, subtypes of major depressive disorder have been defined that require a more restricted list of symptoms. In particular, melancholic major depression focuses more on physiological symptoms. Its diagnosis includes having the criteria for major depression plus either loss of pleasure in all or almost all activities or lack of reactivity to usually pleasurable stimuli, along with at least three additional symptoms: a distinct quality to the depressed mood (different from a feeling of grief); the depressive symptoms being regularly worse in the morning; early morning awakening (at least 2 h earlier than usual); marked psychomotor retardation or agitation; significant loss of appetite and/or weight; and excessive or inappropriate guilt. Melancholic major depression often requires antidepressant medication, and sometimes ECT, for effective treatment.

Another feature of major depression may be the presence of a thought disorder (psychotic features), which may require treatment with antipsychotic as well as antidepressant drugs. The timing of major depressive episodes also may be linked to the season of the year, particularly to the light–dark cycle— seasonal affective disorder, as this condition is known, usually occurs in the winter when the days are short. Exposure to very bright light for several hours each morning may be useful as an adjunct to antidepressant drugs in the treatment of seasonal affective disorder.

A manic episode consists of a period of abnormally and persistently elevated, expansive, or irritable mood lasting for at least 1 week (less if the person is hospitalized), with at least three additional symptoms: inflated self-esteem or grandiosity; decreased need for sleep; pressure of speech; flight of ideas or subjective feeling that his or her thoughts are racing;

being easily distracted; increased activities (work, social, sexual) or psychomotor agitation; and excessive involvement in pleasurable activities that are potentially harmful (e.g., excessive alcohol intake, buying sprees, sexual indiscretions, or foolish business decisions). As with major depression, the symptoms must be severe enough to cause significant distress or to interfere with the person's occupational or social functioning, and the manic episode must not be a direct result of a drug or an underlying medical condition. As with major depression, a thought disorder (psychotic features) also may be part of the clinical picture.

Bipolar I disorder is defined as a clinical course of one or more manic episodes or mixed episodes, the latter being defined as criteria for both manic episode and major depression having been met nearly every day for at least 1 week. The most common form of bipolar illness is manic episodes alternating with major depessive episodes, which may or may not be separated by intervals of normal mood. Mixed episodes are less common, and the rarest is manic episodes only, with no depressive features. Occasionally several major depressive episodes may occur before the first manic episode becomes evident. Bipolar II disorder is defined as recurrent major depressive episodes with hypomanic episodes. Hypomanic episodes must meet the criteria for manic episodes, except they can be of shorter duration and lesser severity.

The lifetime prevalence of major depression is about 10–25% for women and about half that for men; thus, it is one of the commonest psychiatric disorders. About twice as many adolescent and adult females are affected as males. In children, the prevalence of major depression is about equal between boys and girls. Thus, the hormonal changes of puberty may play a role in its greater incidence in adolescent and adult females. In contrast to widespread clinical belief a few decades ago, there is no increase in major depression in women at the time of menopause. About a third of major depressions improve with treatment and do not recur; about a third show remission with treatment but do recur a number of times throughout the life of the individual, and about a third may improve with treatment, but there remains a chronic, underlying depression of lesser se-

verity. This chronic depression may meet the criteria for dysthymic disorder, which requires, among other criteria, depressed mood for more days than not for at least 2 years. Major depressive episodes occurring against a background of dysthymia has been called "double depression."

Major depression can cooccur with many other psychiatric illnesses such as anxiety disorders, eating disorders, drug abuse and alcoholism, dementias, and psychotic disorders as well as in the context of many medical illnesses. In these instances, it is referred to as secondary major depression, in contrast to primary major depression, in which the depressive illness itself predominates. Primary major depression also may have some of the above-listed illness as secondary diagnoses; the determining factor is which came first. For example, anxiety symptoms sufficient to meet a diagnosis of generalized anxiety disorder occur with some frequency in major depression and are considered secondary because the depressive illness preceded them. In particular, depressive pseudodementia should be considered in elderly depressed patients who have significant impairment of cognitive function and who might otherwise be diagnosed as having a dementia such as Alzheimer's disease. The distinction between depressive pseudodementia and true dementia is extremely important because pseudodementia resolves with successful treatment of the underlying depression, whereas true dementia generally does not respond to current treatments.

Not only is major depression an important illness today, within 25 years it is predicted to be the second most incapacitating illness throughout the world, just a small percentage behind cardiovascular disease. Thus, major depression is fast becoming a significant public health problem.

The lifetime prevalence for bipolar I illness is about 1% and for bipolar II illness is about 0.5%. These illnesses usually begin in adolescence or young adulthood and are equally prevalent in males and females. As mentioned, recurrent, alternating manic and depressive episodes represent the most common form; if four or more manic or depressive episodes occur within a year, the illness is considered rapidly cycling and may require frequent hospitalizations and certain medication combinations for its control.

As with the other severe psychiatric disorders, both major depression and manic-depression can be made worse by stressful life situations. Major depression not uncommonly is preceded, if not precipitated, by a significant loss in a person's life, be it death of a significant other, job loss, or financial reversal. As mentioned, the psychological pain and turmoil of a severe depression, coupled with additional physical factors such as insomnia, can in turn be extremely stressful to the sufferer, and, on occasion, suicide may be considered the only way out. Fortunately, almost every major depression is treatable, and suicidal thoughts that are present in the depths of the depressive episode almost always disappear with treatment.

Bipolar disorder is more internally driven (less affected by external stressors), but the illness itself can have extremely stressful consequences for the individual. During a manic episode the person may run afoul of the law and be arrested; he or she may spend their life savings foolishly and be reduced to poverty; or he or she may behave recklessly and suffer physical injury, for example by reckless or drunken driving with involvement in an auto accident or sexual promiscuity with the contraction of a disease such as AIDS. Bipolar disorder, being a recurrent disorder, can result in many psychiatric hospitalizations over an individual's lifetime.

III. BIOLOGICAL CHARACTERISTICS OF MAJOR DEPRESSION AND MANIC-DEPRESSION

There appears to be a genetic contribution to both major depression and bipolar disorder. Both illnesses more frequently coexist in monozygotic (single-egg) than in dizygotic twins, but the difference is much more pronounced for bipolar disorder. Similarly, there is a higher incidence of these disorders in the first-degree relatives of patients with both major depression and bipolar disorder; again, the relationship is stronger for bipolar disorder. For both of these illnesses, however, as for all the major psychiatric disorders, the modes of inheritance have not been established. Except for a few bipolar disorder fami-

lies, the modes of inheritance do not appear to fit either an autosomal or an X-linked pattern, but most likely are multifactorial, involving several genes of varying influence. Nongenetic contributing factors, as well as different genetic loadings in different families, may interact to produce the same phenotypic outcome.

There are several neurochemical theories of the etiology of depression and bipolar disorder, all of which involve abnormal function of CNS neurotransmitters and/or the chemical changes they activate in nerve cells (neurons). Neurotransmitters (for example serotonin, norepinephrine, and dopamine) are chemicals in the brain that are released by neurons and carry chemical messages across a short space (synapse) to neighboring neurons that have receptors for that neurotransmitter. Deficiencies of norepinephrine and serotonin neurotransmission, and excessive acetylcholine neurotransmission, are among the oldest theories and best supported by research studies.

In both unipolar major depression and the depressive phase of bipolar disorder, reductions in the metabolic products of norepinephrine and serotonin have been found in blood, urine, and cerebrospinal fluid, suggesting that both these neurotransmitter systems may be underactive, but the reductions in metabolites have been relatively small. In manic patients, administration of physostigmine, a drug that inhibits the breakdown of acetylcholine, immediately stops the mania and produces a depressionlike state. Physostigmine also produces a depressionlike state in normal subjects. These findings suggest an overactivity of cholinergic neurotransmission in depression, and other studies have shown depressed patients to be supersensitive to cholinergic drugs in their sleep patterns, constriction of the pupils of their eyes, and so on.

The most compelling evidence for the neurotransmitter theories of depression comes from the effects of drugs used to treat major depression and bipolar disorder (see Section VII below). There are several classes of antidepressant drugs, and many of them block the cell membrane transporters for norepinephrine and/or serotonin, which recycle the neurotransmitters from the synapse back into the nerve cells that released them. By blocking transporter uptake, antidepressants increase synaptic neurotransmitter concentrations. Studies have shown that in the intact human being, even very specific neurotransmitter uptake inhibitors eventually influence multiple neurotransmitter systems because of the physiological interactions among them. If one neurotransmitter system is perturbed by a drug acting on it specifically, the other systems tend to change to come back into balance with it.

The time course for full clinical response to all antidepressant drugs is 3–6 weeks, even though their specific pharmacological effects occur within 12–24 h. What is common to almost all antidepressants is that downregulation of postsynaptic noradrenergic receptors in the CNS occurs over the same number of weeks as required for the clinical response. Noradrenergic receptor downregulation may be an ultimate result of the increased availability of norepinephrine as a synaptic neurotransmitter, signaling that noradrenergic neurotransmission has increased to such an extent that the number and sensitivity of postsynaptic receptors need to be reduced in compensation. This finding suggests that a common neurochemical pathology in depressed patients may be a relative underactivity of noradrenergic neurotransmission, which is rectified by drug treatment.

There are disturbances in several physiological systems that occur as part of depression and the depressive phase of bipolar disorder. Sleep disturbance has been mentioned as part of the diagnostic criteria. Electrophysiological studies of sleep (polysomnography) have revealed typical changes, including less total sleep time, fragmentation of the orderly cycling of sleep stages with more frequent awakenings throughout the night, and early occurrence of rapid eye movement sleep (REM or dreaming sleep). In normal persons, the first REM episode occurs about 60–90 minutes after sleep is established (REM latency). This interval may be severely shortened in major depression, so much so that the person may go directly into REM sleep when sleep is first established (sleep-onset REM). The occurrence of REM sleep is influenced by CNS cholinergic neurotransmission; as mentioned, administration of cholinergic neurotransmission-stimulating drugs to depressed persons and control subjects while asleep produces a significantly shorter REM latency in the depressives than

in the controls. This is one of the findings supporting the cholinergic overdrive hypothesis of major depression.

Another important physiological disturbance in major depression and bipolar disorder is increased activity of the hypothalamic-pituitary-adrenal cortical (HPA) axis. This endocrine axis consists of cells in the hypothalamus of the brain that secrete corticotropin-releasing hormone (CRH) and vasopressin (AVP), which are carried to the anterior pituitary gland and stimulate the secretion of corticotropin (ACTH) from the anterior pituitary into the blood stream. In turn, ACTH stimulates the adrenal cortex to secrete glucocorticoids, mineralocorticoids, and adrenal androgens into the blood stream. Glucocorticoid hormones increase glucose production in the liver, inhibit glucose metabolism by body tissues, and promote lipid breakdown in fat tissue; the principal glucocorticoid in humans is cortisol (hydrocortisone). Mineralocorticoid hormones reduce the excretion of sodium and enhance the excretion of potassium and hydrogen ions by the kidney; the principal mineralocorticoid in humans is aldosterone. Adrenal androgenic hormones have weak male sex hormonelike effects.

The HPA axis is very responsive to both physical and psychological stressors. The secretion of CRH is regulated by several of the CNS neurotransmitters considered important in depressive illness, including norepinephrine, serotonin, and acetylcholine. The increased activity of this endocrine axis that occurs in 30–50% of patients with major depression and in the depressive phase of bipolar disorder is likely caused by an underlying neurotransmitter dysfunction in the brain. Increased HPA axis activity can be documented by the finding of increased ACTH and cortisol in blood, urine, and cerebrospinal fluid and by ACTH and cortisol resistance to suppression with the potent, synthetic adrenal glucocorticoid dexamethasone. Dexamethasone acts primarily at the pituitary gland to suppress the secretion of ACTH, which, in turn, suppresses the secretion of hormones from the adrenal cortex. Under normal conditions, this suppression is complete and relatively long lasting. When there is abnormal driving of the HPA axis by the brain or pathology within the HPA axis itself, however, the suppressive effect of dexamethasone is weaker and of shorter duration. When stimulated for a period of time, endocrine glands often hypertrophy (grow in size), and both increased pituitary size and increased adrenal gland size have been reported in major depression. Adrenal size reverted to control values following successful antidepressant treatment.

IV. NEUROIMAGING STUDIES IN MAJOR DEPRESSION AND MANIC-DEPRESSION

With the advent of neuroimaging techniques, it now is possible to probe the structure and function of the living human brain. Brain structure can be viewed with X-ray computed tomography (CT) and magnetic resonance imaging (MRI). Magnetic resonance spectroscopy (MRS) can determine the concentrations of certain chemical substances in the CNS. Nuclear medicine techniques such as single-photon and positron-emission computed tomography (SPECT and PET) allow the visualization and quantitation of regional cerebral blood flow, glucose metabolic rate, and neurotransmitter receptor occupancy, which are indirect probes of regional neuronal function. Both SPECT and PET use radiolabeled compounds as tracers; as these compounds decay, high-energy photons are emitted which are counted by external detectors. The distribution of the tracer molecules is computed, and cross-sectional images of the brain are created in which image brightness is proportional to the underlying physiological process being measured.

Studies of brain structure with CT and MRI in patients with major depression and bipolar disorder have demonstrated a number of abnormalities, but it is not clear how specific these changes are. Enlarged cerebral ventricles in relation to overall brain size have been reported in a number of studies, but similar findings have been reported in patients with other psychiatric illnesses, such as schizophrenia. Different groups of patients (unipolar and bipolar), different ways of measuring and reporting ventricular volume, and different control groups have been used, but meta-analysis of many studies has pointed toward a significant enlargement of the ventricles in unipolar and bipolar patients compared to controls. The differ-

ence is more marked in elderly subjects. There appears to be no consistent relationship between structural changes in the brain and severity of the illness.

An interesting MRI finding in elderly persons is subcortical hyperintensities. These are areas within the white matter (neuron fiber tracts) and the subcortical gray-matter nuclei (neuron cell bodies) that are bright on T_2-weighted MRI scans. They are associated with risk factors for cerebrovascular disease and may be areas of local brain swelling and of small, old strokes. Elderly patients with major depression and bipolar patients of both middle age and late-life consistently have been found to have more extensive (in total area) subcortical white-matter hyperintensities than do age-matched healthy controls. Whether an increased burden of these hyperintensities contributes to, or at least precedes, the onset of the depression and whether there is greater cognitive (intellectual) impairment in patients with more hyperintensities remain unknown. It is known, however, that the presence of subcortical hyperintensities in elderly depressed patients correlates with a greater sensitivity to antidepressant medications, a greater risk of developing tardive dyskinesia (a movement disorder) from neuroleptic (antipsychotic) medication, and a longer recovery time from ECT.

Magnetic resonance spectroscopy has been used to study several compounds in the brain in major depression and bipolar disorder. Phosphomonoesters, a component of cell membranes, have been found to be both elevated and decreased. Phosphocreatine, a high-energy phosphate, has been more consistently decreased. Magnetic resonance spectroscopy of fluorine-containing drugs, such as some antidepressants, and of lithium provides brain concentrations of these compounds in patients under treatment and may eventually be helpful in guiding dosage adjustments to achieve maximum therapeutic response.

The SPECT and PET functional neuroimaging studies of major depression and bipolar disorder have shown decreased prefrontal cortical and anterior cingulate gyrus blood flow and glucose metabolism, although these findings have not been consistent. In addition, there have been inconsistent reversals of these abnormalities in treated patients, but it does appear that successful antidepressant pharmacotherapy is associated with increased blood flow and/or metabolism in the prefrontal cortex, cingulate cortex, and/or the basal ganglia (caudate nucleus globus pallidus and putamen).

V. BRAIN CIRCUIT THEORIES OF MAJOR DEPRESSION AND MANIC-DEPRESSION

Brain circuit theories of major depression and bipolar disorder all represent variations on the postulated involvement of certain areas of the frontal parts of the brain (frontal lobes) and their functional interconnections with deeper parts of the brain—the cingulate gyrus, basal ganglia, thalamus, and other structures, including hippocampus and amygdala. Several of these structures comprise the limbic system, a phylogenetically older part of the brain that influence emotional coloration and behavioral reactivity. In a general sense, the frontal lobes of the brain mediate executive functions; that is, an individual's decision-making and behavioral actions based on detailed evaluation of environmental demands, along with an appreciation of their historical context and a coordinated affective/emotional component. Particular areas of the frontal cortex mediate executive behavior, social behavior, and motivation. The underlying theme of the brain circuit theories of major depression and the depressive phase of bipolar disorder is that the prefrontal cortex cannot effectively modulate the limbic system component of emotions, so that what in a normal individual would be an expression of sadness becomes magnified and prolonged into a major depression when the interactive circuitry is not functioning properly. The aforementioned reductions in prefrontal cortical blood flow and glucose metabolism, as determined by functional neuroimaging with SPECT and PET, support this brain circuit theory.

VI. PSYCHOLOGICAL TESTING IN MAJOR DEPRESSION AND MANIC-DEPRESSION

Many general psychological tests contain questions pertaining to mood, and these tests usually give a score that indicates the degree of depression. Since depression and manic-depression are often recognizable clinically, however, psychological testing is usually not done unless there are ancillary questions, such the possibility of associated dementia or psychosis. Psychological testing also may be helpful in differentiating depressive pseudodementia from primary dementia. In a patient presenting with dementia, an indication of depressive features on psychological testing, which may not have been apparent clinically, usually signals the need for antidepressant treatment. In such cases, following successful treatment of the depression, the dementia also should have improved, which can be determined by repeat psychological testing.

There also are some rating scales designed specifically to quantitate depression. The Hamilton Rating Scale for Depression, which is scored by the person examining the patient, and the Beck Depression Inventory, which is scored by the patient himself or herself, are two of the most commonly used scales. The Hamilton Scale tends to emphasize the physiological aspects of depression, such as sleep and appetite disturbance and physical symptoms of anxiety. The Beck Inventory emphasizes the cognitive component of depression; that is, how the person thinks about himself or herself when depressed.

VII. TREATMENT OF MAJOR DEPRESSION AND MANIC-DEPRESSION

The first issue in the treatment of major depressive and bipolar disorder patients is to assess their immediate personal safety in light of the severity of their illness. For depressed patients this always includes an assessment of their suicide potential. For manic patients, it includes not only an assessment of their suicide potential, especially in mixed bipolar disorder, but also whether their behavior is harmful; e.g., excessive alcohol intake, buying sprees, sexual indiscretions, or foolish business decisions, as mentioned earlier. The most certain way to interrupt behavioral indiscretions and protect the individual from suicide attempts is hospitalization in a specialized psychiatric unit whose staff is trained in the care of such patients. If the patient resists hospitalization, an involuntary "hold" may be medically and legally justified. A locked psychiatric unit, which prevents the patient from leaving, may be necessary until the illness is sufficiently under control that the patient's better judgement returns.

Treatment of major depression and bipolar disorder almost always requires drug therapy with antidepressants and/or mood-stabilizing drugs. There are several chemical classes of antidepressant drugs, and they have specific pharmacological activities in the CNS. As mentioned above, many of them block the transporters for norepinephrine and/or serotonin, which recycle the neurotransmitters from the synapse back into the nerve cells that released them. By blocking transporter uptake, antidepressants increase synaptic neurotransmitter concentrations.

The time course for a full clinical response to antidepressant drugs is 3–6 weeks, even though their pharmacological effects occur within 12–24 h. Often, improved sleep may be an early sign of response to medication, especially with antidepressants that have sedative side effects. Objective signs of improvement usually precede the patient's feeling better; e.g., the person may be sleeping and eating better, may have more energy and a higher level of activities, and may be speaking more cheerfully, but he or she still may be complaining about feeling as depressed as before. The subjective depressed mood is often the last aspect of the illness to improve. Because the subjective experience of depression is so psychologically painful and stressful, it is very important that a patient with suicide potential not be released from the hospital until he or she is in sufficient behavioral control to no longer be a suicide risk after discharge.

As mentioned, some antidepressants are specific uptake inhibitors of norepinephrine and others of serotonin, but it is not possible to predict which depressed patient will respond to which antidepressant. This is most likely on the basis of the physiological interactions of neurotransmitter systems, and, as indicated above, the fact that almost all antidepressants result in downregulation of postsynaptic noradrenergic receptors over the same time course as clinical improvement occurs. Antidepressants therefore are usually chosen on the basis of side-effects and

cost, those under patent being more expensive than those available in generic form. Many of the older antidepressants have prominent side-effects, such as causing dry mouth, blurred vision, and especially changes in the electrical conduction system of the heart. This last side-effect can be particularly dangerous in accidental or deliberate drug overdose. The class of antidepressant drugs in greatest use currently are the selective serotonin uptake inhibitors, which have about the same efficacy as the other antidepressants but have fewer side-effects, especially cardiac. This makes them generally safer drugs to use, but they have other side-effects that must be considered, including weight gain and decreased sexual drive.

The other major class of drugs, used especially in bipolar disorder, are the mood stabilizers. For manic patients, lithium is the most effective. Lithium is a metal ion, in the same class in the periodic table of elements as sodium and potassium. Lithium has a number of effects on neurotransmission in the CNS. It has a relatively narrow therapeutic index; that is, the blood concentrations at which lithium exerts toxicity are not very far above the concentrations required for its therapeutic effect. Therefore, patients taking lithium require frequent measurement of their circulating lithium concentrations, especially at the outset of treatment, to determine the daily dose necessary to achieve a therapeutic blood level. Lithium takes several weeks to achieve its full antimanic effect. It is a mood stabilizer rather than a pure antimanic compound, so that bipolar patients who switch from mania into depression are usually continued on their lithium if an antidepressant is added.

For major depressive and bipolar patients, additional dimensions of their illnesses may suggest the need for other medications in addition to antidepressants and lithium. For example, prominent psychotic features in either illness may call for an antipsychotic medication to be used concomitantly. For treatment of depression, hormone supplements such as estrogens in women and thyroid hormone may be helpful. For treatment of bipolar disorder, a number of anticonvulsant medications have been shown to be effective, often as augmentation of lithium treatment.

To prevent relapse, successful pharmacologic treatment of major depression is usually continued for 9–12 months at a maintenance drug dose, before slow reduction of medication is attempted. Bipolar patients need to have medication adjustments made according to the frequency of their manic and depressive mood swings; it may take years for the timing of these cycles to be clearly understood. Both disorders should be viewed as chronic illnesses, often relapsing over a person's lifetime.

If strenuous attempts at drug treatment of either disorder fail, ECT often will provide definitive relief of symptoms. Usually, 10 treatments are given, 3 per week. The patient may suffer some memory loss during and following the treatments, but this is short lived, whereas the therapeutic effect can be remarkable, especially in patients resistant to drug therapy. Maintenance ECT, often one treatment every month or so, can be useful to keep the person in remission from his or her illness.

In addition to pharmacotherapy and ECT, psychotherapies of different types, such as cognitive-behavioral therapy, often are useful to help the person change his or her lifestyle and manner of thinking about adversity. Improvement in self-esteem often results, which may protect against future episodes of depression or at least may reduce their severity.

VIII. CONCLUSIONS

Major depression and manic-depression (bipolar disorder) represent serious psychiatric illnesses. In addition to interfering with occupational and social functioning, these illnesses put the sufferer at personal risk—a potential for suicide attempts in the case of depression and impulsive behaviors such as excessive alcohol intake, buying sprees, sexual indiscretions, and foolish business decisions in the case of a manic episode. Severe life stressors often precede a depressive episode, and both illnesses create their own stresses in the sufferer, including the psychological pain of depression and the untoward consequences of unrestrained manic behavior. Fortunately, there are effective pharmacological treatments that can produce remission in the majority of patients, and for those who do not respond to drug treatment, ECT is an excellent therapeutic modality.

See Also the Following Articles

ANTIDEPRESSANT ACTIONS ON GLUCOCORTICOID RECEPTORS; CYTOKINES, STRESS, AND DEPRESSION; DEPRESSION MODELS; DISTRESS

Bibliography

Akiskal, H. S. (1995a). Mood disorders: Introduction and overview. *In* "Comprehensive Textbook of Psychiatry" (H. I. Kaplan and B. J. Sadock, Eds.), Vol. VI, 6th ed., pp. 1067–1079. Williams & Wilkins, Baltimore.

Akiskal, H. S. (1995b). Mood disorders: Clinical features. *In* "Comprehensive Textbook of Psychiatry" (H. I. Kaplan and B. J. Sadock, Eds.), Vol. VI, 6th ed., pp. 1123–1152. Williams & Wilkins, Baltimore.

American Psychiatric Association (1994). "Diagnostic and Statistical Manual of Mental Disorders (DSM-IV), 4th ed., pp. 317–391. American Psychiatric Association, Washington, DC.

Baldessarini, R. J. (1996). Drugs and the treatment of psychiatric disorders: Depression and mania. *In* "Goodman & Gilman's The Pharmacological Basis of Therapeutics" (J. G. Hardman and L. E. Limbird, Eds.), 9th ed., pp. 431–459. McGraw-Hill, New York.

Blazer, D. (1995). Mood disorders: Epidemiology. *In* "Comprehensive Textbook of Psychiatry" (H. I. Kaplan and B. J. Sadock, Eds.), Vol. VI, 6th ed., pp. 1079–1089. Williams & Wilkins, Baltimore.

Bloom, F. E. (1996). Neurotransmission and the central nervous system. *In* "Goodman & Gilman's The Pharmacological Basis of Therapeutics" (J. G. Hardman and L. E. Limbird, Eds.), 9th ed., pp. 267–293, McGraw-Hill, New York.

Bloom, F. E., and Kupfer, D. J. (Eds.) (1995). "Psychopharmacology: The Fourth Generation of Progress." Raven, New York.

Cummings, J. L. (1995). Anatomic and behavioral aspects of frontal-subcortical circuits. *Ann. N. Y. Acad. Sci.* 769, 1–13.

Gabbard, G. O. (1995). Mood disorders: Psychodynamic etiology. *In* "Comprehensive Textbook of Psychiatry" (H. I. Kaplan and B. J. Sadock, Eds.), Vol. VI, 6th ed., pp. 1116–1123. Williams & Wilkins, Baltimore.

Green, A. I., Mooney, J. J., Posener, J. A., and Schildkraut, J. J. (1995). Mood disorders: Biochemical aspects. *In* "Comprehensive Textbook of Psychiatry" (H. I. Kaplan and B. J. Sadock, Eds.), Vol. VI, 6th ed., pp. 1089–1102. Williams & Wilkins, Baltimore.

Hirschfeld, R. M. A., and Shea, M. T. (1995). Mood disorders:

Psychosocial treatments. *In* "Comprehensive Textbook of Psychiatry" (H. I. Kaplan and B. J. Sadock, Eds.), Vol. VI, 6th ed., pp. 1178–1189. Williams & Wilkins, Baltimore.

Krishnan, K. R. R., and Doraiswamy, P. M. (Eds.) (1997). "Brain Imaging in Clinical Psychiatry." Marcel Dekker, New York.

Merikangas, K. R., and Kupfer, D. J. (1995). Mood disorders:

Genetic aspects. *In* "Comprehensive Textbook of Psychiatry" (H. I. Kaplan and B. J. Sadock, Eds.), Vol. VI, 6th, ed., pp. 1102–1116. Williams & Wilkins, Baltimore.

Post, R. M. (1995). Mood disorders: Somatic treatment. *In* "Comprehensive Textbook of Psychiatry" (H. I. Kaplan and B. J. Sadock, Eds.), Vol. VI, 6th ed., pp. 1152–1178. Williams & Wilkins, Baltimore.

Depression Models

Keith Matthews

University of Dundee, Scotland

GLOSSARY

anhedonia The loss of the capacity to experience pleasure, a core symptom of depression.

intracranial electrical self-stimulation An experimental technique whereby a small electrical charge can be delivered directly into the substance of the brain of an awake, freely moving subject via an implanted electrode.

limbic system An arrangement of anatomically related brain structures that are hypothesized to play a critical role in the production and regulation of emotion.

mesolimbic dopamine projection A grouping of dopamine-secreting neurones that arise in the midbrain to innervate a range of higher brain structures that includes the nucleus accumbens in the ventral striatum.

validity The authenticity of a presumed relationship between two separate events or observations.

I. DEPRESSION MODELS

The brain pathologies that mediate the cognitive, motivational and motor abnormalities of depressive disorders remain elusive. Similarly, the brain mechanisms that confer individual vulnerability to stress and those that precipitate and sustain clinical depression are poorly understood. One approach to these problems has been to try to model the complex neurobiological and behavioral alterations associated with human depression in laboratory animals. Thus, the term depression model refers to any experimental preparation that facilitates the study of human depression-related phenomena by comparing target behaviors or biological functions across species. Usually this involves the generation of behavioral or physiological changes in laboratory animals following an explicit intervention; for example, the application of stress. It should be emphasized that such models of a complex disease state need not actually produce the disease in the laboratory animal. It is sufficient that a depression model strive to reproduce one critical aspect of the disease process. Similarly, it is not essential that the phenomenon under study demonstrate a response to antidepressant drug administration, although this is often sought. This overview of depression models first addresses general theoretical considerations concerning the validity of the approach followed by a review of candidate neural mechanisms through which stress might influence behavioral responses to reward. This is followed by a brief review of stress-based animal models of depression.

II. VALIDITY AND UTILITY OF DEPRESSION MODELS

Depression models serve many different purposes and the inherent value of each is determined by the specific aims and utility of the individual model. When considering the validity and utility of a model it is therefore critical to establish the explicit purpose intended for that preparation. There are several scholarly and comprehensive reviews of procedural details and the relative merits of different animal models of depression that achieve this purpose (see Bibliography). Although depression models can be categorized and evaluated according to almost any aspect of their construction, there is general agreement on the utility of addressing different aspects of validity separately. The validity spectrum includes construct validity and the related concepts of discriminant and convergent validity, predictive validity, face validity and etiological validity.

The construct validity of a model refers to the accuracy with which the model replicates the key abnormalities or phenomena under study within the clinical condition. For example, if a model somehow encapsulated a blunting of the capacity to experience pleasure, it could be considered to demonstrate substantial construct validity with respect to anhedonia, one of the defining features of clinical depression. Of course, to comment on construct validity, there is an implicit requirement that the target phenomenon be well defined, either behaviorally or neurobiologically, within the clinical state. For many aspects of depressive disorders, this remains problematic. Nevertheless, judgements can be made as to whether observations in a model appear to bear a meaningful relationship to those of the clinical disorder. Models with strong construct validity represent attempts to replicate core clinical phenomena in a laboratory context and are driven by specific hypotheses concerning the etiology, clinical features, and pathophysiology of depression. Such models are frequently labeled "theoretical" models. All models that recruit the application of stress for the generation of behavioral and neurobiological change can be considered "theoretical" models.

A closely related concept to construct validity is that of etiological validity, whereby the circum-stances or events that lead to development of the target phenomenon in the model are substantially similar to those generating the same phenomenon in the clinical disorder. Etiological validity can usefully be considered a refinement of the more general concept of construct validity. For many depression models, the experimenter-initiated intervention is considered to mimic an environmental event of causal significance. However, such assumed relationships are problematic since the causal antecedents of depressive disorders, including those best studied, genetic vulnerability and stress, remain poorly defined.

The predictive validity of a model refers to its ability to correctly discriminate between interventions that are known to have effective antidepressant properties. Typically, these interventions are drug treatments. Depression models with strong predictive validity are widely used within the pharmaceutical industry to screen new molecules for potential antidepressant activity, hence the term "assay" models. The most potent models within this category are capable of discriminating pharmacologically diverse chemical antidepressant treatments with few false positive or negative results. For a strong assay model, there is no requirement that aspects of the preparation bear meaningful relationship with features of the clinical disorder.

The face validity of a model refers to whether specific features of the model bear resemblance to discrete aspects of the clinical disorder, i.e., whether a phenomenological similarity exists, irrespective of whether there is a plausible or established theoretical relationship between the two observations. In this respect, face validity can be differentiated from construct validity. Where two or more depression models are being compared with each other, regardless of whether of "theoretical" or "assay" nature, it is possible to comment on the degree to which observations from each appear to reflect aspects of the same construct. Hence, two or more different models may demonstrate convergent or discriminant validity. Whereas convergent validity refers to the degree to which the same aspect of a single phenomenon or construct can be accessed and quantified by different models, discriminant validity reflects the capacity of a model to measure different aspects of a single target phenomenon from those measured by related models. All models can be judged on the degree to which the target phenomena can be reproduced within and between studies—the reliability of the model. In the absence of reliability, no model can be considered to have utility. Hence, both validity and reliability are essential for any animal model of depression.

III. RELATIONSHIP BETWEEN STRESS AND DEPRESSION

An enduring clinical literature suggests that individual vulnerability to stress and subsequent predisposition to develop certain disease states, notably depression, is related, at least in part, to a history of early environmental adversity. Similarly, the onset and recurrence of adult depression can reliably be predicted by the presence of environmental stressors, often labeled "life events" (Paykel, E. S. and Hollyman, J. A., 1984, *Trends Neurosci.* **12**, 478–481). Furthermore, clinical studies have consistently implicated abnormalities in the regulation of key neuroendocrine responses to stress in patients with depression, with a hyperactivity of the hypothalamic-pituitary-adrenal (HPA) axis that is probably driven by hypersecretion of the hypothalamic peptide corticotrophin-releasing factor (CRF) (Heim, C., Owens, M. J., Plotsky, P. M., and Nemeroff, C. B., 1997, *Psychopharmacol. Bull.* **33**, 185–192). In humans and other animals, HPA axis activation leads to stimulation of the release of glucocorticoid hormone (in humans cortisol and in other species corticosterone) from the cortex of the adrenal glands. Glucocorticoid hormones are released in response to a wide variety of psychological and physical stressors and represent a core component of adaptive responsivity to environmental change and threat. Given the strong epidemiological associations between stress, HPA axis dysregulation, and human depression, animal models frequently employ the application of stress as the core manipulation to bring about behavioral or physiological change.

Much emphasis has been placed on the capacity for stress to reduce or impair the performance of behaviors that serve to bring animals into contact with key stimuli or appetitive reinforcers within their environment. Engagement with such stimuli is inferred to convey pleasant or pleasurable hedonic consequences. Reduced engagement is generally interpreted as evidence that the stimuli no longer confer such consequences, at least to the same degree. Hence, stress attenuates engagement with pleasurable stimuli in laboratory animals (see Bibliography). This phenomenon of reduced engagement with previously pleasurable or reinforcing events and stimuli is observed in humans with depression and is incorporated in current psychiatric diagnostic and classification systems as a core feature of depression. What remains unclear, however, is how stress brings about such effects, although actions on the limbic system are plausible candidates.

IV. ANATOMY OF REWARD

A. Limbic System

To consider mechanisms by which stress might interact with neural function and, ultimately, interfere with behavioral responses to reward, a review of the neuroanatomy of reward is pertinent. The concept of specific brain structures mediating emotional function and the capacity to experience "pleasure" originated with the description of the "Papez circuit" (Papez, J. W., 1937, *Arch. Neurol. Psychiatr.* **38**, 725–743), at least in a form that bears resemblance to current thinking. Observations of close anatomical associations between structures such as the hypothalamus, the cingulate cortex, the thalamus, and the hippocampus prompted speculation that they might act together to integrate emotional expression with visceral and endocrine responses. Subsequently, this notion was developed further into the concept of the "limbic system" (Maclean, P. D., 1949, *Psychosom. Med.* **11**, 338–353), adding the amygdala and septum to those structures implicated by Papez. Support for the notion of a specific neural basis for emotion and motivation has accrued steadily from subsequent experimental, accidental and therapeutic lesion studies in animals and humans. Thus, the "limbic system" concept has evolved over the years and its anatomical constitution has been refined with increasing complexity and sophistication to accommodate advances in neuro-anatomy and observations from animal behavioral studies.

B. Mesolimbic Dopamine System

The demonstration of an area in the hypothalamus which, when electrically stimulated, led to a powerful augmentation of approach behavior and vigorous self-administration of electrical current deep within the brain (Olds, J., and Milner, P., 1954, *J. Comp. Physiol. Psychol.* **47**, 419–427) imparted great impetus to the search for specific reward or "pleasure" circuits. Subsequently, research during the 1970s and 1980s identified the mesolimbic dopamine projection as a key component of the neural circuitry mediating the psychological construct of "reward" (see, for example, Fibiger, H. C., and Phillips, A. G., 1988, *Ann. N.Y. Acad. Sci.* **537**, 206–215). Although the exact relationship between the mesolimbic dopamine system and "reward" still remains to be determined, it is involved in the control of motivational arousal and the ability to flexibly and adaptively execute behavioral responses to motivationally salient stimuli, both pleasurable and aversive (stressful). Hence, interference with normal function in this structure would be expected to adversely affect engagement with reinforcing stimuli in the environment. Recent evidence suggests that parallel projections from dopaminergic neurones in the midbrain to the prefrontal cortex may also play a critical, complementary role in the control of such behavior.

C. Anatomy and Function of the Mesolimbic Dopamine System

The mesolimbic dopamine projection arises from cell bodies located in the ventral tegmentum in the midbrain, projecting upward and forward to the amygdala, the lateral septum, the bed nucleus of the stria terminalis, the hippocampus, and to the nucleus accumbens (a component of the ventral striatum). On its journey forward, the mesolimbic dopamine projection passes through the lateral hypothalamus via a thick cable of fibers known as the medial forebrain bundle. Appetitive reinforcers (a term to describe stimuli that are inferred to convey pleasant or

pleasurable hedonic consequences), including biologically meaningful stimuli such as food, sex and drugs of abuse (e.g., heroin and cocaine), are dependent upon the functional integrity of the mesolimbic dopamine projection for their behavioral effects (Robbins, T. W., and Everitt, B. J., 1992, *Semin. Neurosci.* **4**, 119–127). Such appetitive reinforcers elicit approach behavior and contact. Thus, the nucleus accumbens, a structurally defined subregion of the ventral striatum where ascending dopaminergic neurones synapse with intrinsic striatal neurones and descending glutamatergic projections from limbic cortical structures (such as the hippocampus, amygdala, and prefrontal cortex) represents a critical locus for the processing and execution of goal-directed behavior. Interference with dopaminergic transmission, either by lesioning the cell bodies in the midbrain, the terminal fields in the nucleus accumbens, or by the local administration of dopamine receptor antagonist drugs, leads to a profound disruption of a range of "rewarded" behaviors, including intracranial electrical self-stimulation, the self-administration of psychostimulant drugs of abuse (e.g., cocaine and amphetamine), and responding for primary and conditioned appetitive reinforcers. In addition, the local infusion of dopamine receptor agonist drugs into the nucleus accumbens leads to augmentation of responding for a range of appetitive reinforcers, including psychostimulant drugs of abuse. Indeed, the nucleus accumbens and the mesolimbic dopamine system are widely believed to represent the critical sites through which drugs of abuse exert their reinforcing and "addictive" effects (Koob, G. F., Sanna, P. P., and Bloom, F. E., 1998, *Neuron* **21**, 467–476).

D. Stress and the Mesolimbic Dopamine Projection

The mesolimbic dopamine projection is also critically involved in the integrated neural response to stress. The application of a wide range of stressors, both acute and chronic, provokes behavioral and neurochemical consequences that involve the mesolimbic dopamine system (Cabib, S., and Puglisi-Allegra, S., 1996, *Psychopharmacology* **128**, 331–342). The nature of the responses depends on the detail of the stressor(s) applied, with stressor severity, controllability, predictability, and prior stress history determining the effect on dopamine transmission in the nucleus accumbens and in the prefrontal cortex. In parallel, Katz (1982, *Pharmacol. Biochem. Behav.* **16**, 965–968) and Zacharko and Anisman (1991, *Neurosci. Biobehav. Rev.* **15**, 391–405) demonstrated that the application of stress attenuated behavioral responses to reward (consumption of saccharin solution and responding for intracranial electrical self-stimulation respectively); again with different aspects of the stress experience determining the magnitude, duration, and reliability of the behavioral response. Correspondingly, there are compelling reasons to consider the mesolimbic dopamine projection and its principal target structure, the nucleus accumbens, as a critical locus for the mediation of the effects of stress on rewarded behavior, probably in concert with other circuitry such as the mesocortical dopamine projection and limbic cortical afferent structures, particularly the hippocampus and the prefrontal cortex.

V. STRESS MODELS OF DEPRESSION

Perhaps the best-known stress model of depression is that of learned helplessness. This model is not considered in this article, but is covered in detail elsewhere. There are many experimental demonstrations of the capacity for stress to disrupt, or at least modify, behavior directed toward positively reinforcing stimuli. For the purposes of this article, I focus on those procedures that have held greatest promise as valid animal models of depressive disorder.

A. Stress and Intracranial Electrical Self-Stimulation

Following work on the electrical stimulation of discrete brain areas in the conscious, behaving rat (intracranial self-stimulation, ICSS—see above), a specific hypothesis was formulated linking human depressive behaviors with dysfunction of brain reward pathways (Akiskal, H., and McKinney, W. T., 1972, *Science* **182**, 20–29). This hypothesis has been extensively tested in a series of experiments evaluat-

ing the interactions between responding for rewarding electrical brain stimulation, stress, and antidepressant drug administration (Zacharko, R. M., and Anisman, H., 1991, *Neurosci. Biobehav. Rev.* **15**, 391–405). Using this approach in the laboratory rat, these authors demonstrated regional specificity within the brain for stress-induced decrements in responding for ICSS, most notably within the terminal fields of the mesolimbic and mesocortical dopamine projection. Exposure to unpredictable electrical footshock induced a profound and enduring reduction in responding when ICSS electrodes were sited in the ventral tegmentum, the nucleus accumbens and medial prefrontal cortex, but not in the adjacent dorsal striatum. This regional specificity exhibited a close anatomical concordance with those structures known to respond to stress with alterations in dopamine function. Furthermore, chronic administration of the prototypical chemical antidepressant drug desmethylimipramine (DMI) prior to stress exposure significantly minimized the subsequent ICSS performance deficits. These data have been interpreted as demonstrating beneficial, or protective, effects of antidepressant drugs on the neural responses to stress, specifically in areas that are critically involved in the integration of behavioral responses to reward. However, additional studies employing different drug treatments, different electrode placements, and different strains of rat and mice have generated somewhat variable results.

B. Chronic Mild Unpredictable Stress

In an attempt to design models with greater face and etiological validity, several different procedures have been devised that employ the sequential presentation of relatively mild stressors to rats or mice. In these models, the effects of stress are quantified by the degree to which they alter the intake of drinking solutions that are preferred over standard drinking water under normal circumstances. For example, (Katz 1982, *Pharmacol. Biochem. Behav.* **16**, 965–968) observed that rats exposed to a chronic mild stress regime failed to increase fluid intake when saccharin was added to their drinking water. Extending this work, Willner and colleagues (Willner, P., Muscat, R., and Papp, M., 1992, *Neurosci. Biobe-*

hav. Rev. 16(4), 525–534) reported a series of studies that showed the rapid loss of preference for, or reductions in the absolute intake of, sucrose, saccharin, and saline solutions. The stressors included periods of strobe lighting, food and water deprivation, cage tilting, and group housing. As with the brain stimulation studies described earlier, the behavioral deficits seen with chronic mild stress are reputed to respond to chronic administration of chemical antidepressant drugs. However, like some other animal models of depression, there have been significant problems establishing these procedures reliably in different laboratories. The behavioral effects of chronic mild stress are, at best, modest and large numbers of subjects are required. Also, many studies have failed to include appropriate control measures.

C. Behavioral Despair

Also known as the Forced Swim Test, this model involves forcing rats (or mice) to swim in a tall water-filled cylinder from which there is no escape (Porsolt, R. D., LePichon, M., and Jalfre, M., 1977, *Nature* 266, 730–732). The water is sufficiently deep to preclude the animal from resting its limbs or tail on the bottom. When placed in this apparatus for the first time, the animal swims vigorously to maintain its head above water. With appreciation of the inescapable nature of its predicament, attempts to escape from the cylinder rapidly cease. Thereafter, the animal adopts an immobile posture that has been interpreted as an altered affective state reflecting "hopelessness" with respect to the possibility for escape. With repeated testing, the time to the onset of immobility decreases in control animals and this has been interpreted as a theoretical analog of "learned helplessness." While there are obvious problems with respect to the construct validity of this model, behavioral despair enjoys one of the most impressive records of all depression models with respect to pharmacological sensitivity and specificity. Hence, this model enjoys impressive predictive validity. The question of what exactly this model measures remains unanswered. Whereas other stress-based models demonstrate altered responding toward rewarding stimuli, this test reflects

something quite different. While an operational definition of the phenomenon is simple, a description of the underlying psychological processes and their relationship to human affective disorder is not.

D. Social Stress Models

This group of models rely on a different approach, that of disturbing social environment, usually during early life. These manipulations are potent, but naturalistic, stressors.

The disruption of mother–infant bonding or of peer bonding in young social animals generates a constellation of acute and chronic behavioral changes that resemble human depression and vulnerability to depression, respectively. Across a broad range of species, responses to separation follow a predictable course with definable phases. Initially, the infant displays so-called "protest" behaviors that include increased locomotor activity and vocalization. This subsides in time and is generally replaced by a second phase that is characterized by locomotor inactivity and an apparent disinterest in motivationally salient external environmental stimuli, so-called "despair." Depending on the species studied, there may also follow a third phase of "detachment," during which the infant displays indifference to being reunited with its mother and/or peers. Social behaviors in adulthood are often profoundly abnormal in such animals. There is considerable cross-species generality of this bi- or triphasic response to social separation, suggesting that it may be "hardwired" in the brain of many social mammals.

1. Nonhuman Primates

In the light of their phylogenetic proximity to humans, their advanced cognitive capacity, and their complex social structures, studies in monkeys have provided the bulk of the behavioral and neurobiological data in support of social separation models of depression. After numerous studies demonstrated the pathological effects of prolonged separation (weeks or months) of infant monkeys from their mothers, Hinde and colleagues reported enduring effects of brief separation (6 days) during infancy on subsequent behavioral development when tested at 12 and 24 months (Hinde, R. A., Spencer-Booth, Y., and Bruce, M., 1966, *Nature* **210**, 1021–1033). Alterations were observed with respect to the separated monkeys' responses to novelty and their independent exploration of the immediate environment. Thus, even brief periods of maternal separation appeared capable of inducing enduring alterations in behavior. However, there is no convincing evidence that either the acute or the chronic effects of early separation in monkeys bear meaningful relationships with human depression. In naturally occurring adverse social circumstances, such as falling in rank, monkeys can exhibit a prolonged withdrawal from social interaction and a suppression of aggression (Everitt, B. J., and Keverne, E. B., 1979; in E. S. Paykel and A. Coppen (Eds.) "Psychopharmacology of Affective Disorders," Oxford Univ. Press, Oxford). Thus, some nonhuman primate analogs of the common precipitants of human depressive episodes can induce "despair-like" reactions and behavioral changes reminiscent of human depression, thus conferring a degree of face validity. In turn, these responses are strongly influenced by genes (species differences), early social experience, social "support" networks, and other physical aspects of environment. Also, these "despair" responses are associated with physiological changes such as alterations in sleep architecture, phenomena that frequently accompany depressive episodes in humans. Mindful of the value of predictive validity in an animal model of depression, the effects of psychotropic drugs have also been tested in separated monkeys. Several groups have reported an attenuation of behavioral disruption following maternal and peer separation with chronic chemical antidepressant drug treatments (e.g., Suomi, S. J., Seaman, S. F., Lewis, J. K., DeLizio, R. B., and McKinney, W. T., 1978, *Arch. Gen. Psychiat.* **34**, 321–325). However, the pharmacological specificity of these effects is questionable, since chlorpromazine (an antipsychotic drug with very weak, if any, clinical antidepressant activity), alcohol, and diazepam have each been reported to have similar effects, depending on dose administered and actual measures recorded

(reviewed by Kraemer, G. W., 1992; *Behav. Brain Sci.* **15**, 493–541). However, repeated electroconvulsive stimulation, an analog of the highly effective antidepressant treatment electroconvulsive therapy (ECT), has also been shown to have an "antidespair" profile of effects.

2. Nonprimate Models

Recent work suggests that manipulation of the early social environment of the rat, and other rodents, may represent useful depression models. Repeated neonatal maternal separation in the rat leads to a robust impairment of the control of behavior by primary and conditioned reward in adulthood, with reduced responses to environmental novelty, to psychostimulant drugs, and to changes in reward magnitude (Matthews, K., Wilkinson, L. S., and Robbins, T. W., 1996, *Physiol. Behav.* **59**, 99–107). Some of these early experience-induced behavioral changes may model the hedonic changes found in human depression. To date, studies of the effects of antidepressant drugs have not been reported.

VI. CONCLUSIONS

Depression models fulfill many different purposes and can be evaluated according to different criteria. They have contributed to our understanding of the neural bases of reward and how stress affects brain function. Hypotheses generated in the clinic have stimulated model design and information from models has informed clinical practice. The inherent difficulties in attempting to construct valid animal models of human depression are largely offset by the potential utility of the approach. Depression models offer the opportunity to control and manipulate variables that epidemiological and clinical research suggests may be influential, for example, genotype, early social experience and magnitude, type and duration of environmental stressors. Cautious interpretation of model data can advance our understanding of a complex and devastating mental disorder.

See Also the Following Articles

Bibliography

Katz, R. J. (1981). Animal models and human depressive
disorders. *Neurosci. Biobehav. Rev.* 5, 231–246.

McKinney, W. T., and Bunney, W. E. (1969). Animal model
of depression: review of evidence and implications for research. *Arch. Gen. Psychiat.* 21, 240–248.

McKinney, W. T., Suomi, S. J., and Harlow, H. F.
(1971). Depression in primates. *Am. J. Psychiat.* 127,
49–56.

Willner, P. (1984). The validity of animal models of depression. *Psychopharmacology* 83, 1–16.

Depth, Effects of

see Pressures, Effects of Extreme High and Low

Desensitization

Ferenc A. Antoni

MRC Brain Metabolism Unit, Edinburgh, Scotland

I. Desensitization of the Stress Response
II. Cellular Mechanisms of Desensitization

GLOSSARY

heterotrimeric G proteins A group of proteins that consist of
three subunits (α, β, γ) and couple cell surface receptors
to their effector enzymes. Upon activation of cell surface
receptors by their ligands, heterotrimeric G proteins dissociate into the α-subunit and the $\beta\gamma$-complex, both of which
regulate the activity of effector enzymes in the cell membrane.

neuroendocrine motoneurons Hypothalamic nerve cells that
produce and secrete neurohormones into the hypophysial
portal circulation and thus regulate the synthesis and release of anterior pituitary hormones.

protein kinases Enzymes that tag proteins with phosphoryl
residues derived from ATP and GTP. The activity of protein
kinases may be regulated by a variety of intracellular messengers, protein–protein interactions, or phosphorylation
by other protein kinases.

Desensitization is a widespread phenomenon
in biological systems whereby the response to persistent or invariant stimuli is reduced.

I. DESENSITIZATION OF THE STRESS RESPONSE

As if to react selectively to new or stronger stimuli,
biological systems diminish their responses to persistent or stable stimuli in a process termed desensitiza-

tion, adaptation, or habituation. The stress response is no exception to this rule. A reduction of the activation of the hypothalamic-pituitary-adrenocortical (HPA) axis and behavioral arousal elicited by the same and repeatedly applied stressor occurs in most cases. This is called homotypic desensitization. The degree and speed of desensitization may depend on the frequency and the length of exposure to the stressor as well as on the genetic make-up of the experimental subjects. Heterotypic desensitization, a blunting of the response to several types of stress induced by repeated exposure to a single stressor is less common, but has been observed. More frequently, application of a heterotypic stressor in subjects that have undergone homotypic desensitization elicits an exaggerated HPA response to the heterotypic stimulus when compared with nondesensitized controls. This indicates that homotypic desensitization affects the stressor-specific mechanisms of the HPA response as well as the final common pathways of neuroendocrine regulation. Indeed, chronic stressors are known to increase dramatically the expression of vasopressin in the neuroendocrine motoneurons of the hypothalamic paraventricular nucleus while the expression of corticotropin-releasing factor remains essentially unchanged. This is likely to augment the pituitary response to stimuli that impinge on the neuroendocrine motoneurons and may well explain the enhanced pituitary adrenocorticotropin response to heterotypic stressors in subjects with homotypic desensitization. A general atenuation of the HPA response to several stressors occurs in lactating animals. This has been attributed to the suppression of the HPA axis at the level of the paraventricular nucleus by oxytocin. By contrast, stressor-specific habituation does not take place at the level of the paraventricular neuroendocrine motoneurons.

II. CELLULAR MECHANISMS OF DESENSITIZATION

At the cellular level, desensitization manifests itself in biological processes as diverse as bacterial chemotaxis and mammalian neurotransmission. Desensitization affects signal-transduction pathways by which cells detect and decode changes in the extracellular millieu. The molecular and cellular details of desensitization are particularly well explored with respect to hormone and neurotransmitter receptors coupled to heterotrimeric G-proteins (GPCR). Significantly, plasma membrane receptors for CRF, vasopressin, and catecholamines are in this category.

Upon binding their respective agonist ligands receptors activate heterotrimeric G-proteins, which leads to the stimulation of various intracellular effector enzymes that generate intracellular second-messenger molecules. Within a few seconds cells can diminish or virtually eliminate their agonist-evoked responses through a process that involves phosphorylation of the GPCRs on one or more intracellular domains. The cellular response to a given agonist may be desensitized by cellular exposure to that agonist itself in a process called *homologous* desensitization. Alternatively, desensitization of the response to a given agonist may be caused by agonists for distinct receptor signaling systems, in a process termed *heterologous* desensitization. Potentially affecting multiple receptor systems, heterologous desensitization involves phosphorylation of GPCRs by second-messenger-dependent kinases, such as cyclic AMP (cAMP)–dependent protein kinase and protein kinase C. In most cells a further elaborate system exists to "trap" activated GPCRs—the G protein-coupled receptor kinases and arrestins. These are distinct and independent of second-messenger-stimulated kinases; further, they are specific for activated GPCRs and are involved in homologous desensitization.

The common feature of all of these mechanisms is the phosphorylation of GPCRs and their consequent uncoupling from G proteins. Further, the receptors tagged by phosphorylation may be endocytosed and recycled upon dephosphorylation or eventually degraded, depending on the requirements of the cell. In some cases phosphorylation has been shown to switch the coupling of receptors to downstream signaling pathways. Thus, while one aspect of receptor action, e.g., the generation of cyclic AMP may be desensitized, signaling through another pathway, e.g., stimulation of microtubule-activated protein kinase, may be turned on.

Even longer term control of signal transduction pathways may involve the alteration of the transcription of receptor genes or their effector systems, potentially entirely reprofiling the cellular response as a result of prolonged exposure to receptor ligands.

See Also the Following Articles

ADRENOCORTICOTROPIC HORMONE (ACTH); CATECHOLAMINES; CORTICOTROPIN RELEASING FACTOR (CRF); HPA AXIS; VASOPRESSIN

Bibliography

Aguilera, G. (1994). Regulation of pituitary ACTH-secretion during chronic stress. *Front. Neuroendocrinol* 15, 321–350.

Antoni, F. A. (1993). Vasopressinergic control of anterior pituitary adrenocorticotropin secretion comes of age. *Front. Neuroendocrinol.* 14, 76–122.

Dhabhar, F. S., McEwen, B. S., and Spencer, R. L. (1997). Adaptation to prolonged or repeated stress—Comparison between rat strains showing intrinsic differences in reactivity to acute stress. *Neuroendocrinology* 65, 360–368.

Flugge, G. (1995). Dynamics of central nervous 5-HT$_{1A}$-receptors under psychosocial stress. *J. Neurosci.* 15, 7132–7140.

Ma, X. M., and Lightman, S. L. (1998). The arginine vasopressin and corticotrophin-releasing hormone gene transcription responses to varied frequencies of repeated stress in rats. *J. Physiol.-Lond.* 510, 605–614.

Pitcher, J. A., Freedman, N. J., and Lefkowitz, R. J. (1998). G protein-coupled receptor kinases. *Ann. Rev. Biochem.* 67, 653–692.

Dexamethasone Suppression Test (DST)

Robert T. Rubin

Center for Neurosciences Research, Allegheny General Hospital, Pittsburgh

I. Introduction
II. Increased Central Nervous System Driving of the Hypothalamic-Pituitary-Adrenal Cortical Axis
III. Cushing's Syndrome

GLOSSARY

adrenal androgens Hormones produced by the adrenal cortex that have weak male sex hormonelike effects.

adrenal cortex The outer layer of the adrenal glands, which secretes several steroid hormones, including glucocorticoids, mineralocorticoids, and adrenal androgens. The adrenals lie just above the kidneys.

aldosterone The principal mineralocorticoid produced by the adrenal cortex in humans.

amygdala Group of nerve cells in the temporal lobes of the brain that stimulates the secretion of corticotropin-releasing hormone and, in turn, the rest of the hypothalamic-pituitary-adrenal cortical axis.

corticotropin (adrenocorticotropic hormone; ACTH) A hormone produced by cells in the anterior pituitary gland that is carried by the blood stream to the adrenal cortex, where it stimulates the secretion of glucocorticoids, mineralocorticoids, and adrenal androgens.

corticotropin-releasing hormone (CRH) A hormone produced by neuroendocrine cells of the hypothalamus that is transported down the pituitary stalk to the anterior pituitary gland, where it stimulates the secretion of corticotropin.

cortisol (hydrocortisone) The principal glucocorticoid produced by the adrenal cortex in humans. Under normal circumstances, cortisol feeds back to the pituitary gland, hypothalamus, and other brain areas to reduce the secretion of CRH and ACTH, thereby reducing the secretion of cortisol and other adrenal cortical hormones.

dexamethasone A synthetic glucocorticoid having 25 times the potency of cortisol.

glucocorticoids Hormones produced by the adrenal cortex that increase glucose production in the liver, inhibit glucose metabolism by body tissues, and promote lipid breakdown in fat tissue. The principal glucocorticoid in humans is cortisol (hydrocortisone). When administered in high, therapeutic doses, glucocorticoids suppress immunological function, reduce inflammation, and decrease connective tissue and new bone formation.

hippocampus Group of nerve cells in the temporal lobes of the brain that inhibit the secretion of corticotropin-releasing hormone and, in turn, the rest of the hypothalamic-pituitary-adrenal cortical axis.

hypothalamic-pituitary-adrenal cortical (HPA) axis A hormone axis consisting of cells in the hypothalamus of the brain that secrete corticotropin-releasing hormone (CRH) and vasopressin (AVP), which stimulate the secretion of corticotropin (ACTH) from the anterior pituitary gland into the blood stream. In turn, ACTH stimulates the adrenal cortex to secrete glucocorticoids, mineralocorticoids, and adrenal androgens into the blood stream.

hypothalamus Area at the base of the brain that controls vital body processes including the production of hormones that stimulate and inhibit the secretion of anterior pituitary hormones.

mineralocorticoids Hormones produced by the adrenal cortex that reduce the excretion of sodium and enhance the excretion of potassium and hydrogen ions by the kidney. The principal mineralocorticoid in humans is aldosterone.

pituitary A gland, connected to the base of the brain by the pituitary stalk, that secretes several hormones into the blood stream that stimulate the adrenal cortex, the thyroid gland, the gonads (testes and ovaries), and other tissues of the body.

vasopressin (AVP; antidiuretic hormone; ADH) A hormone produced by cells in the hypothalamus that is transported down the pituitary stalk to (1) the anterior pituitary gland where, along with CRH, it stimulates the secretion of corticotropin and (2) the posterior pituitary gland, whence it is carried by the blood stream to the kidneys, where it reduces the excretion of water.

In the dexamethasone suppression test (DST), the potent, synthetic adrenal steroid hormone dexamethasone is used to test the "drive" of the hypothalamic-pituitary-adrenal cortical (HPA) axis. Dexamethasone acts primarily at the pituitary gland to suppress the secretion of ACTH, which, in turn, suppresses the secretion of hormones from the adrenal cortex. Under normal conditions, this suppression is complete and relatively long lasting. When there is abnormal driving of the HPA axis by the brain or pathology within the HPA axis itself, however, the suppressive effect of dexamethasone is weaker and of shorter duration. Depending on the degree of nonsuppression, certain abnormal processes may be suspected and/or confirmed.

I. INTRODUCTION

The HPA axis is regulated by two processes. One is "closed-loop" negative feedback of cortisol to hormone receptors in the hippocampus, hypothalamus, and pituitary gland. This suppresses the secretion of CRH, ACTH, and cortisol itself. This process is analogous to control of heat by a thermostat; at a certain temperature, the heat signals the thermostat to shut down the heater until the temperature drops; then the heater goes on again, and the cycle repeats itself. The second process is "open-loop" driving of the HPA axis by the central nervous system (CNS). Areas of the brain, including the amygdala, hippocampus, and hypothalamus, stimulate and inhibit the HPA axis to different degrees depending on the time of day, season of the year, and physical and environmental stressors. The HPA axis has a normal circadian (24-hr) rhythm: The secretion of CRH, ACTH, and adrenal hormones is greatest at 7–8 A.M., an hour or so after awakening, and at its lowest about 2–3 A.M. The difference in blood concentrations of ACTH and adrenal glucocorticoids such as cortisol is about fourfold between the nadir (low point) and the peak several hours later. If a person shifts his or her sleep–wake cycle, it takes about 2 weeks for the HPA axis to resynchronize its circadian rhythm.

The HPA axis is very stress responsive. Both physical and psychological stressors can cause increased activity of this hormone axis. In particular, novel stressors (stressors that are new experiences) cause HPA axis activation; with a person's repeated encountering of the stressor, there is less and less HPA axis response. This is particularly true of demanding tasks, which initially provoke an HPA axis response, but not after the person achieves mastery of the task through training and experience.

Pathological (abnormal) function of the HPA axis can occur from several causes. These include repeated, uncontrollable environmental stressors, functional psychiatric illnesses such as major depression and schizophrenia, and disorders of the HPA axis itself, such as hormone-secreting tumors of the pituitary gland and adrenal cortex. The DST is one of several endocrine tests that can help diagnose the particular pathological process resulting in abnormal HPA axis activity.

II. INCREASED CENTRAL NERVOUS SYSTEM DRIVING OF THE HYPOTHALAMIC-PITUITARY-ADRENAL CORTICAL AXIS

As mentioned, repeated, uncontrollable environmental stressors, functional psychiatric illnesses such as major depression and schizophrenia, and other conditions can increase CNS stimulation of the HPA axis to such a degree that it is relatively insensitive to dexamethasone suppression. Major depression is the best-studied psychiatric illness in this regard: 30–50% of major depressives have mildly to moderately increased HPA axis activity, consisting of increased blood concentrations of ACTH and cortisol at all times of the day and night, with preservation of the circadian rhythm of these hormones. Correlated with this increase is nonsuppression of ACTH and cortisol on the low-dose DST. In the low-dose DST, 1–2 mg of dexamethasone is given orally at 11–12 P.M., and blood samples are taken at 8, 16, and 24 h thereafter for measurement of circulating cortisol concentrations. Normally, cortisol is suppressed to very low levels (less than 50 ng/ml) for a full 24 h. Depressed patients with increased HPA axis activity often show early cortisol (and ACTH) "escape" from dexamethasone suppression. That is, there may be early suppression of these hormones the morning (8h) following dexamethasone administration, but hormone concentrations are prematurely increased in the 16- and/or 24-h blood samples.

The rapidity and degree of cortisol escape in the DST is an indication of the strength of CNS driving of the HPA axis. It alos may be a good indication of recovery form major depression. Depressed patients who have an initially abnormal DST, who are treated with antidepressant medication, and who have both a good clinical response and a reversion of their DST to normal are more likely to remain in remission when their medication is discontinued. On the other hand, patients who have an apparently good clinical response but who persist with an abnormal DST are more likely to require long-term antidepressant medication or even electroconvulsive treatment to remain in remission. In some patients with recurrent depressive episodes, the DST may become abnormal again before clinical symptoms emerge, signaling that a relapse may be imminent and allowing the physician to reinstitute treatment at the earliest possible time.

More problematic is the use of the DST to help diagnose major depression, especially the more severe, melancholic subtype. The DST has a sensitivity (true positive rate in major depressives) of about 50% and a specificity (true negative rate in other individuals) of about 90%. The predictive value of a positive DST thus is high when there is strong suspicion of major depressive illness in a given patient, as determined by clinical examination and other tests, but the predictive value is no better than chance when the DST is incorrectly used as a screening test for major depression (that is, when there is a low base rate of the illness in a given population). Because the metabolism of dexamethasone itself varies widely among individuals, measurement of circulating dexamethasone concentrations, along with cortisol concentrations, may help detect false-positive DSTs based on inadequate dexamethasone availability at the pituitary gland.

It also should be mentioned that underactivity of the HPA axis, along with enhanced suppression of ACTH and cortisol by dexamethasone, has been noted in patients with posttraumatic stress disorder (PTSD), such as in holocaust survivors and combat veterans and resulting from childhood sexual abuse. The reason for reduced, rather than increased, HPA axis activity in the face of repeated psychological reexperiencing of traumatic incident(s), as occurs in PTSD, has been hypothesized to be related to enhanced CNS glucocorticoid receptor feedback sensitivity.

III. CUSHING'S SYNDROME

Cushing's syndrome is the group of clinical signs and symptoms resulting from increased circulating glucocorticoids of long duration. There are many clinical changes in Cushing's patients, including obesity of the face and trunk, weakness and atrophy of limb muscles, increased blood pressure, imbalance of glucose metabolism, and psychological changes. There are two main types of Cushing's syndrome, ACTH dependent and ACTH independent.

Adrenocorticotropic hormone-dependent Cushing's syndrome results from increased pituitary secretion of ACTH, usually from a pituitary tumor (Cushing's disease); inappropriate ACTH secretion by nonpituitary tumors, often in the lungs; and inappropriate CRH secretion by nonhypothalamic tumors, in turn stimulating excessive pituitary ACTH secretion. These conditions, all involving excess ACTH production, cause enlargement of the adrenal glands and excessive cortisol secretion.

Adrenocorticotropic hormone-independent Cushing's syndrome is caused by primary tumors or abnormalities of the adrenal cortex itself, resulting in excessive cortisol secretion and suppression of ACTH production by the pituitary. Prolonged administration of glucocorticoids for the treatment of certain illnesses also may cause ACTH-independent Cushing's syndrome.

The DST is but one of several endocrine tests used to diagnose the different causes of Cushing's syndrome. Dexamethasone is administered in different dosage strengths and for different periods of time in a series of low- and high-dose tests. The relative resistance of ACTH and cortisol to dexamethasone suppression is noted, along with baseline circulating ACTH and cortisol concentrations and their response to stimulation by administered CRH. The excessive pituitary production of ACTH and adrenal production of cortisol in Cushing's disease are only partially suppressible by low-dose dexamethasone, but more suppressible by higher doses. In contrast, patients with nonpituitary sources of ACTH production will rarely show suppression of ACTH and cortisol by dexamethasone. Similarly, patients with ACTH-independent Cushing's syndrome will not show suppression of cortisol, even with high doses of dexamethasone, because their ACTH already is suppressed by the independently high circulating cortisol concentrations.

It should be emphasized that, in diagnosing the causes of Cushing's syndrome, the DST must be interpreted in the light of other endocrine findings. For example, one important distinction between the increased ACTH and cortisol production in some patients with major depression vs patients with Cushing's disease is that the former have preservation of their circadian rhythms of ACTH and cortisol,

whereas the latter often have high circulating hormone concentrations throughout the entire 24 h. Major depressives also do not have the clinical changes seen in Cushing's syndrome, because their body tissues are not exposed to continuously high circulating cortisol concentrations. The DST therefore must be considered as just one in a series of clinical examinations and laboratory studies used to determine the causes of increased HPA axis activity.

See Also the Following Articles

ADRENAL CORTEX; ADRENOCORTICOTROPIC HORMONE (ACTH); CORTICOTROPIN RELEASING FACTOR (CRF); CUSHING'S SYNDROME; HPA AXIS

Bibliography

Carroll, B. J., Feinberg, M., Greden, J. F., Tarika., J, Albala, A. A., Haskett, R. F., James, N. M. I., Kronfol, Z., Lohr, N., Steiner, M., de Vigne, J. P., and Young, E. (1981). A specific laboratory test for the diagnosis of melancholia: Standardization, validation, and clinical utility. *Arch. Gen. Psychiatr.* **38**, 15–22.

De Kloet, E. R. (1997). Why dexamethasone poorly penetrates in brain. *Stress* **2**, 13–20.

Orth, D. N., Kovacs, W. J., and DeBold, C. R. (1992). The adrenal cortex. *In* "Williams Textbook of Endocrinology" (J. D. Wilson and D. W. Foster, Eds.), 8th ed., pp. 489–619. W. B. Saunders, Philadelphia.

O'Sullivan, B. T., Cutler, D. J., Hunt, G. E., Walters, C., Johnson, G. F., and Caterson, I. D. (1997). Pharmacokinetics of dexamethasone and its relationship to dexamethasone suppression test outcome in depressed patients and healthy control subjects. *Biol. Psychiatr.* **41**, 574–584.

Rubin, R. T., and Poland, R. E. (1984). The dexamethasone suppression test in depression: Advantages and limitations. *In* "Biological Psychiatry: Recent Studies" (G. D. Burrows, T. R. Norman, K. P. Maguire, Eds.), pp. 76–83. John Libbey, London.

Rubin, R. T. (1994). Neuroendocrine aspects of stress in major depression. *In* "Stress in Psychiatric Disorders" (R. P. Liberman and J. Yager, Eds.), New York. Springer-Verlag, pp. 37–52.

Rush, A. J., Giles, D. E., Schlesser, M. A., Orsulak, P. J., Parker, C. R., Jr., Weissenburger, J. E., Crowley, G. T., Khatami, M., and Vasavada, N. (1996). The dexamethasone suppression test in patients with mood disorders. *J. Clin. Psychiatr.* **57,** 470–484.

Schimmer, B. P., and Parker, K. L. (1996). Adrenocortico-tropic hormone; adrenocortical steroids and their synthetic analogs; Inhibitors of the synthesis and actions of steroid hormones. *In* "Goodman & Gilman's The Pharmacological Basis of Therapeutics" (J. G. Hardman and L. E. Limbird, Eds.), 9th ed., pp. 1459–1485. McGraw–Hill, New York.

Stein, M. B., Yehuda, R., Koverola, C., and Hanna, C. (1997). Enhanced dexamethasone suppression of plasma cortisol in adult women traumatized by childhood sexual abuse. *Biol. Psychiatr.* **42,** 680–686.

Diabetes, Type 1

Afsane Riazi

University of Exeter, United Kingdom

Clare Bradley

Royal Holloway, University of London, United Kingdom

I. Stress and Type 1 Diabetes Onset
II. Stress and Type 1 Diabetes Control
III. Stress Management Training and Type 1 Diabetes Control

GLOSSARY

β-cells The cells in the islets of Langerhans in the pancreas that produce insulin.

diabetes mellitus A heterogeneous group of disorders, characterized by hyperglycemia and disturbances of carbohydrate, fat, and protein metabolism which are associated with absolute or relative deficiencies of insulin secretion and/or insulin action.

glycosuria Glucose in the urine.

hyperglycemia Excessive levels of glucose in the blood. This is a feature of untreated or undertreated diabetes mellitus.

hypoglycemia Abnormally low levels of glucose in the blood. Symptoms are idiosyncratic but may include trembling, faintness, sweating, palpitations, mental confusion, slurred speech, headache, loss of memory, and double vision. Severe, untreated hypoglycemia may lead to fits or coma and, on rare occasions, death. It can be caused by an overdose of insulin.

islet cell antibodies (ICAs) One type of autoantibody present in the blood when the body develops an autoimmune reaction to the pancreatic islet cells. The presence of ICAs is associated with an increased risk for developing Type 1 diabetes and has a predictive value several years before diabetes is clinically manifested.

insulin A peptide hormone produced in the β-cells of the islets of Langerhans in the pancreas. Insulin facilitates and accelerates the movement of glucose and amino acids across cell membranes. It also controls the activity of certain enzymes within the cells concerned with carbohydrate, fat, and protein metabolism.

Type 1 diabetes mellitus, also known as insulin-dependent diabetes mellitus (IDDM), juvenile-onset diabetes, or ketosis-prone diabetes, is the commonest form of diabetes to occur in children and young adults of European origin. Age at clinical onset of the condition is usually under the age of 40 years and often under 30 years. People who have Type 1 diabetes lose the ability to produce insulin. Exogenous insulin, usually delivered by injection, is needed continuously throughout the lifetime of a person with Type 1 diabetes with the possible exception of a brief honeymoon period, which may occur within a year of clinical onset when endogenous insulin production is temporarily restarted. The onset of Type 1 diabetes is abrupt, with severe thirst, excessive urination, and dramatic weight loss. Individuals usually present to the doctor with one or more of these symptoms and an elevated blood glucose level. Once developed, Type 1 diabetes can be managed by balancing a combination of insulin injections, intake of carbohydrates in the diet, and energy expenditure. The goal of treatment is to maintain blood glucose levels as close to the normal range as possible in order to reduce the risk of chronic complications while also avoiding the dangers of blood glucose falling to hypoglycemic levels.

I. STRESS AND TYPE 1 DIABETES ONSET

Although it has not been possible to determine the exact pathogenesis involved in the expression of Type 1 diabetes, it is clear that genetics play an important role. The genetic component of the condition is indicated by the increased prevalence of Type 1 diabetes in first-degree relatives of 5% compared with less than 1% in the general population. However, genetic susceptibility is not sufficient to cause diabetes since a majority of people with disease-associated alleles do not develop Type 1 diabetes. Environmental factors also play an important role in the overt expression of Type 1 diabetes, although the mechanisms are still unclear. Psychological stress may also have a role in increasing vulnerability to viral infection or impairing defence mechanisms against infection, thereby facilitating the progression of the hidden pathological process. For example, stress-related changes in immune function may increase the likelihood of viral or bacterial disease, which may provide the initial insult to the β-cells. A second mechanism whereby stress may be implicated in diabetes onset may occur around the time when diabetes becomes symptomatic. Stress-related counter regulatory hormone activity may aggravate the metabolic disturbance that has already developed. In fact, if the already-elevated blood glucose level increases to beyond the renal threshold, glycosuria will cause dehydration, which may then produce the first symptoms of overt diabetes. Many anecdotal accounts and descriptive reports of life stresses occurring synonymously with symptomatic Type 1 diabetes onset may reflect this second mechanism, where stress triggers overt manifestation of symptoms.

A. Animal Studies

It has been shown that stress may be associated with the onset of Type 1 diabetes in the genetic model for this type of diabetes. In the diabetes-prone BB Wistar rat, 30% to 70% of these animals have impaired glucose tolerance with hypoinsulinemia and hyperglycaemia by 150 days of age. It has been shown that these rats developed diabetes earlier, when exposed to restraint and crowding. It has also been found in the BB rat that chronic stress significantly increases the incidence of phenotypic expression of the gene for Type 1 diabetes. Eighty percent of the stressed males and 70% of the stressed female animals developed diabetes compared with 50% in both control groups. However, because of the range of additional immune and endocrinological abnormalities evident in the BB rats, generalizability of these findings to humans are limited.

B. Human Studies

Research has shown that people who go on to develop Type 1 diabetes are more likely to suffer a major family loss or an increase in other stressful life events before diagnosis. Some of these studies have been poorly controlled and were also prone to recall bias, where the pattern of life events reported may reflect an attempt to find an explanation for diabetes onset rather than a difference in the events actually encountered. However, a more carefully controlled study of life events by Robinson and Fuller, which avoided problems of recall bias, has also shown that people with diabetes had significantly more severe life events within the 3 years before diagnosis than either nondiabetic siblings or matched controls. It is possible that life events experienced over longer time periods may play a role in the etiology of Type 1 diabetes. It is clear from prospective studies of ICAs that many years may elapse between the actions of the possible stress-related causal agents to initiate cell damage and the symptomatic diabetes to appear.

Clear evidence of the effect of stress on diabetes onset is difficult to establish. It has not been thoroughly investigated in recent years, probably due to the methodological problems and interpretation of the findings which would involve expensive large prospective studies or reliance on retrospective methods to identify the relationship between stressful periods and the onset of the disease. On the other hand, researchers have given increased attention to the relationship between stress and diabetes control.

II. STRESS AND TYPE 1 DIABETES CONTROL

It is widely recognized among people with diabetes and their clinicians that psychological stress can impair glycemic control. Theoretically, stress-related hyperglycemia should be greater in Type 1 patients (compared to Type 2 patients) because Type 1 patients have little or no endogenous insulin to offset increased blood glucose levels. Stress may affect diabetes control in at least two ways. (1) A direct psychophysiological effect via sympathetic and pituitary activity resulting in the elevation of catabolic hormone levels and the suppression of anabolic hormones. In people with diabetes, this may result in increased blood glucose levels, although, for a small minority, less readily understood decreases in blood glucose levels result. (2) A behavioral mechanism whereby stress leads to behavioral changes capable of disrupting self-care behavior. For example, the occurrence of unexpected, frustrating events may disrupt diabetes self-care routines.

A. Acute Stress and Blood Glucose Control

Pioneering work examining the relationship between stress and diabetes was most often conducted in the laboratory, and the stresses induced were normally acute. Early research by Hinkle and others in the early 1950s induced stress in some of their patients by a psychiatric interview and found changes in their blood ketone levels that remitted when the stress was removed. These researchers carried out a series of studies which showed that both individuals without diabetes and individuals with diabetes (both Type 1 and Type 2 patients were studied) have a metabolic response to psychological stress which included changes in urine glucose, blood glucose, and blood ketones, but the response of those with diabetes was greater. Research in the 1960s included inves-

tigations of stress under hypnosis and examination stress, which resulted in a decrease in blood glucose levels. However, the early studies have been criticized on methodological and conceptual grounds. There was concern that the stressors used were not sufficiently potent or reproducible. Furthermore, the grouping together of heterogeneous patients with Types 1 and 2 diabetes and those with different degrees of blood glucose control in studies or very small groups were also a focus of criticism.

Several seemingly well-controlled acute stress studies conducted in the 1980s reported no significant changes in blood glucose control in response to potential stressors such as mental arithmetic and public speaking. However, in an attempt to meet the criticisms leveled at the earlier studies, these later studies have overlooked the possibility that individual differences in response to stress might be real and interesting and not a reflection of methodological inadequacies. More recent studies of experimental stress have examined physiological mechanisms hypothesized to mediate the relationship between stress and blood glucose control. There is evidence that reduced blood flow to the insulin injection site and insulin resistance over several hours may cause increased blood glucose levels in individuals with Type 1 diabetes in response to acute laboratory stressors. There is also evidence that the level of blood glucose rises in some patients and falls in others in response to a laboratory stressor (Stroop test) and that these changes can be largely explicable in terms of changes in injection-site blood flow. Vasodilation at the subcutaneous insulin injection site may in some cases lead to a paradoxical hypoglycemic effect during acute stress via an increased rate of absorption of insulin, an effect which is counterbalanced to a greater or lesser degree by increases in counterregulatory hormones. More commonly, absorption of insulin may fall during stress as a result of vasoconstriction and reduced skin blood flow and contribute to hyperglycemia.

Idiosyncratic blood glucose responses which were reliable across a 12-week time period within individuals with Type 1 diabetes have been reported in response to caffeine and to the competitive playing of a video game. Researchers have therefore begun to consider individual differences in response to stress to be real and interesting and not a reflection of methodological inadequacies. The inconsistent findings of previous research may have arisen at least in part because of differences in the stress-responsiveness of the individual patients recruited.

B. Life Stress and Diabetes Control

1. Major Life Events

Studies of major life events and diabetes control have produced fairly consistent results which have suggested that increased life events (over past several months to a year) are associated with raised blood glucose levels, usually measured by glycosylated hemoglobin (GHb) or the related measure of hemoglobin A1 (IIbA1) and hemoglobin A1c (HbA1c). These measures reflect average blood glucose levels over the previous 8 weeks (approximately). In some studies, more life events were reported by groups showing a stronger association between life events and HbA1c levels. This could be due to a perceptual bias which may have led people who experienced greater disturbance in association with life events to be more likely to recall the occurrence of life events. It could be that the subgroups did not actually differ in the number of life events reported, but only in their recollection of the events. However, Bradley in 1988 suggested a two-way causal link in which life events cause disruptions in diabetes control, which in turn cause increased life events. There is evidence that glycemic fluctuations themselves can contribute to behavioral changes. It is now well established that both hypo- and hyperglycemia can impair cognitive functioning. Cognitive impairment may in turn cause inadvertent behavioral changes (e.g., in poor self-care responses to feedback from blood glucose monitoring) which can affect blood glucose control. Poorly controlled diabetes may also result in mood changes causing interpersonal conflict and thereby increasing stress levels and associated physiological reactivity. Physical symptoms are also caused by extreme blood glucose levels, e.g., fatigue, and is often associated with high blood glucose levels. Hypoglycemic comas may have many consequences including accidents, job loss, and relationship problems. These relationships are described in the stress–blood glucose model shown in Fig. 1.

The practice of aggregating life stresses and blood glucose levels across time, incorporated by the major-

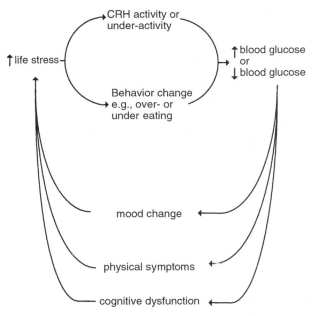

FIGURE 1 An elaborated two-way causal model of relationships between life stress and diabetes control. CRH = counter-regulatory hormone. (Reproduced from Bradley (1988) with permission from the publishers, John Wiley & Sons.)

ity of the life event studies, assumes minimal within-individual variation in stress and in blood glucose response. Such assumptions are not supported by common experience or by the literature, which suggests that stress experienced varies within individuals from day to day. Information about the variability of blood glucose levels is lost when measures of GHb are used which give only an average of blood glucose control. Hypoglycemia is not reflected in GHb measures because of its transient nature. Multiple observations of stress are required together with serial blood glucose measurement. Recent research has focused on the relationship between minor daily events and diabetes control (using serial blood glucose measurements) in order to overcome these methodological limitations.

2. Minor Daily Events

Investigations of minor events have provided more interpretable results with studies reflecting individual differences to stress that were also seen in some of the laboratory-based acute stress studies. Although the overall picture suggests that increased daily stress correlates with increased blood glucose levels in people with Type 1 diabetes, examination of individual differences in response to stress indicates that some people display blood glucose reactivity to stress and some people do not. In one study by Halford and colleagues, approximately half the sample of 15 participants with Type 1 diabetes had significant associations between stress and blood glucose levels, and this association was independent of the effects of diet and exercise self-management. Within those people who display stress-reactivity, most show an increase in blood glucose but there is also evidence to suggest that a smaller proportion of people show a decrease in blood glucose. Therefore, in order for people with Type 1 diabetes to take appropriate action to prevent or correct stress-related disruptions in diabetes control, they need to discover empirically how their own blood glucose levels respond to different kinds of stress.

C. Investigation of Correlates of Stress-Reactivity

There is some evidence to suggest that people with poor control of their diabetes may be more stress reactive (this was found both in studies where the stress being measured is laboratory based or that of life events). This supports the model in Fig. 1. There is also evidence from Stabler and colleagues that children with Type 1 diabetes who are classified as having Type A personality characteristics show elevated blood glucose levels after playing a stressful video game, whereas Type B children with Type 1 diabetes showed a decrease in blood glucose levels. However, there is also evidence from Aikens and colleagues that internality and self-esteem did not relate to stress-reactivity in the group of women with Type 1 diabetes studied. It is likely that individual differences in stress response are mediated by both physiological and psychological processes; however, further research is necessary to identify the variables associated with stress-reactivity.

III. STRESS MANAGEMENT TRAINING AND TYPE 1 DIABETES CONTROL

The overly simple model of life stress causing raised blood glucose levels has inspired the use of stress management training, particularly relaxation training, as an aid to diabetes control. Relaxation is thought to decrease the levels of both cortisol and catecholamines and hence is expected to prevent stress-induced increases in blood glucose levels.

The research to date supports the view that stress management techniques may be valuable to aid diabetes management for some people but not for others. It has been suggested that relaxation techniques are unlikely to do harm except when blood glucose is already tightly controlled and the insulin dosage is not appropriately reduced to balance the effects of relaxation on insulin requirements (which may well be reduced) and/or when used at a time when blood glucose is already low (<4 mmol/liter) and there is a risk of hypoglycemia. It is important to take the precaution of measuring blood glucose immediately before all relaxation training or practice sessions. Twenty minutes of relaxation can lead to a drop in blood glucose by as much as 3 mmol/liter. Such a substantial fall is only likely if blood glucose is well above the normal range of 4–6 mmol/liter to start with and probably results from a suppression of catecholamine secretion. It is recommended that relaxation training should not be conducted at blood glucose levels below 4 mmol/liter because of the risk of hypoglycemia. Relaxation training might be continued if the anticipated reduction in blood glucose were counteracted with pretraining intake of slow-release carbohydrate (e.g., an apple). A further precaution of measuring the blood glucose after a relaxation session, before leaving the therapist's office, is also recommended to avoid the risk of hypoglycemia while traveling home.

Several studies have reported some success with improvements in diabetes control following relaxation training (sometimes involving EMG biofeedback) in people with Type 1 diabetes. There is evidence to suggest that relaxation training is least useful for those people whose glycemic control is good to start with and most useful when used by people who not only have poor control of their diabetes but who feel that stress disrupts their diabetes control and who are currently experiencing stressful events. Although some studies have found no significant differences between relaxation and control groups in HbA1c levels or insulin requirements after relaxation training, information about the variability of the individual patients was rarely reported. In addition, lack of selection of patients likely to benefit from relaxation training may be responsible for the nonsignificant findings of some studies.

What is emerging from the studies of relaxation training in people with Type 1 diabetes is that it is most demonstrably useful for those who are showing stress-related disturbance of blood glucose control at the time. Assessment of patients' stress-reactivity before embarking on relaxation training in future studies will help in the identification of patients most likely to show benefit from relaxation training. To date, most studies have incorporated biofeedback into the relaxation training. Relaxation instructions alone would be more practical and less costly. Evaluation of low-technology forms of relaxation training with patients shown to be stress reactive would be a useful contribution to the state of present research. Such evaluation needs to take account of the fact that the benefits of relaxation training for blood glucose control will only be apparent during periods of stress when stress-reactive relaxation-trained individuals would be expected to have more stable blood glucose control than stress-reactive individuals who have not been trained. Improvements in blood glucose control will be more apparent if recruitment to such a study is restricted to individuals who show increased blood glucose under stress.

See Also the Following Articles

AUTOIMMUNITY; HYPOGLYCEMIA; INSULIN RESISTANCE AND STRESS; RELAXATION TECHNIQUES

Bibliography

Aikens, J. E., Wallander, J. L., Bell, D. S. H., and McNorton, A. (1994). A nomothetic–idiographic study of daily psychological stress and blood glucose in women with Type 1 diabetes mellitus. *J. Behav. Med.* 17, 535–548.

Bradley, C. (1988). Stress and diabetes. *In* "Handbook of Life Stress, Cognition and Health" (S. Fisher and J. Reason, Eds.), Wiley, Chichester.

Bradley, C. (1994). "Handbook of Psychology and Diabetes: A Guide to Psychological Measurement in Diabetes Research and Practice." Harwood, Chur, Switzerland.

Bradley, C., and Gamsu, D. S. (1994). Guidelines for encouraging psychological well-being: Report of a working group of the World Health Organization Regional Office for Europe and International Diabetes Federation European Region St. Vincent Declaration Action Programme for Diabetes. *Diab. Med.* 11, 510–516.

Bradley, C., Pierce, M., Hendrieckx, C., Riazi, A., and Barendse, S. (1998). Diabetes Mellitus. *In* "Health Psychology" (M. Johnston and D. Johnston, eds.), Vol. 8, *In* "Comprehensive Clinical Psychology" (A. S. Bellack and M. Hersen, Eds.), 277–304. Pergamon, Oxford.

Feinglos, M. N., Hastedt, P., and Surwit, R. S. (1987). Effects of relaxation therapy on patients with Type 1 Diabetes Mellitus. *Diab. Care* 10(1) 72–75.

Halford, W. K., Cuddihy, S., and Mortimer, R. M. (1990). Psychological stress and blood glucose regulation in Type 1 diabetic patients. *Health Psychol.* 9, 516–528.

Robinson, N., and Fuller, J. H. (1985). Role of life events and difficulties in the onset of diabetes mellitus. *J. Psychosom. Res.* 29, 583–591.

Shillitoe, R. (1994). "Counselling People with Diabetes." British Psychological Society, Leicester.

Stabler, B., Morris, M. A., Litton, J., Feinglos, M. N., and Surwit, R. S. (1986). Differential glycemic response to stress in Type A and Type B individuals with IDDM. *Diab. Care* 9, 550–551.

Diet and Stress, Non-Psychiatric

Jane Wardle

University College London

GLOSSARY

dieting Deliberate modification of food intake in order to lose weight.

disinhibition Acute loss of cognitive control over food intake.

emotional eating Eating in response to emotional cues.

hyperphagia Eating more than usual.

hypophagia Eating less than usual.

restrained eating The chronic tendency to try to exert control over food intake. It was first measured with the Restraint Scale, which included loss of control over eating and weight fluctuation as well as items reflecting attempts to diet. More recent measures of restraint have placed greater emphasis on the dieting component, conceptualizing the episodes of loss of control as forms of disinhibition of restraint, rather than part of the core concept.

I. INTRODUCTION

There is a widespread belief that stress influences eating behavior but considerable uncertainty about the direction of the effect; i.e., whether stress increases or decreases food intake. An analysis of the physiology of stress would lead us to expect decreased eating because stress slows gastric emptying and increases blood sugar levels, which should reduce appetite. Stress also promotes behaviors designed to cope with or escape from the source of stress, and under these circumstances eating might be accorded a lower priority. In contrast, the literature on human reactions to stress suggests that it can be associated with increased food intake or a shift toward a higher-fat diet.

Our knowledge of stress and eating comes from diverse areas of research, including clinical studies on the etiology of obesity and eating disorders, laboratory studies on dieting and the regulation of food intake, surveys of stress and health-related behaviors, and animal work on stress responses. The diversity of this literature means that there is great variation in the sources and intensity of the stressors that have been examined, the circumstances in which food is consumed, the quality of dietary information that can be gathered, and the populations that have been studied. On this basis, it may not be surprising to find that the links between stress and eating appear to be complex.

II. ANIMAL RESEARCH INTO STRESS AND EATING BEHAVIOR

Animal research appears to offer the ideal opportunity to examine the general, physiologically mediated effect of stress on food intake. Animals can be exposed to stress or a control condition; stressors can vary in quality, intensity, or duration; the animal's deprivation state can be manipulated; and the type of food supplied can be varied. However, to date the animal research has revealed an extraordinarily inconsistent set of results. Much of the early work used rats as the experimental subjects and tail-pinch as the stressor and typically found that food intake was increased by this procedure. However, tail pinch is now thought to represent an atypical stressor, if it is even stressful at all, and increased eating may be part of a general increase in oral behaviors, rather than a specific behavioral response. Other stressors have included electric shock, noise, immobilization, isolation, cold water swims and, defeat in fights, with varied effects on food intake from study to study, ranging from substantial increases in food intake in some studies to substantial decreases in other studies. Attempts to relate the direction of the effect on eating to the characteristics of the stressor have so far been unsuccessful, partly because many of the stressors have been used only very few times, while electric shock, which has been used a lot, shows inexplicable variation. To date, the only possible consistencies are that chronic stressors appear to have a more hyperphagic effect and social stressors may be more hyperphagic than physical stressors.

This confusing set of results means that the relationship between stress and eating has not yet been illuminated by studies of animal reactions to stress, despite the long history of this line of work.

III. HUMAN RESEARCH INTO STRESS AND FOOD INTAKE

Human research on stress and food intake has come from several research traditions. Naturalistic studies usually investigate community samples and attempt to gather information on food intake at high and low stress periods of life. The focus in these studies, as in most of the animal research, has been on the short- or medium-term general effect of stress on eating. Laboratory studies usually administer a stressful procedure in parallel with an eating task, then covertly assess food intake. The emphasis therefore is on the acute effects of stress. Most of the laboratory studies have taken an individual difference perspective, examining stress-related eating in relation either to weight or dietary restraint.

A. Naturalistic Studies

There are a variety of naturally occurring, but predictable, stressful circumstances that can provide an experimental context in which to study stress-related variations in diet. School or university examinations have been used as the stressor in several studies, and periods of high work stress in others. Food intake is recorded either in a diary record kept by the study participants, or with a 24-hour recall procedure. The food records are then analyzed to obtain estimates of intake of energy and nutrients. Biological measures such as weight or blood lipids have been included in some studies to provide another indicator of dietary change.

In around a dozen published studies there is one element of consistency, namely that none of them have found lower food intake, on average, at the higher stress time. Likewise there is little evidence for lower weight or lower serum cholesterol under stress. Otherwise the results have been divided. In some of the studies, both overall energy intake and intake of fat, are higher at the high stress time. In other studies, there is enormous individual variability, but no average difference in energy intake between low and high stress periods. The balance of evidence from this small group of studies has to be that stress in everyday life does not appear to have a hypophagic effect and it may, in some people and some circumstances, have a hyperphagic effect.

One explanation for the variability in results is the poor validity and reliability of measures of food intake. Keeping a food diary is an onerous task, so compliance is poor, and even among those who return a diary there are likely to be many errors; people forget foods, they are not able to assess the quantity accurately, and they complete the diary well after the eating event. Diary keeping is also reactive; i.e, it is likely to influence the behavior being monitored, either because of the increased attention, or the wish to present a "good" record to the experimenter. Unscheduled 24-hour recalls avoid the problem of reactivity but are still susceptible to forgetting and misreporting. They also provide a much more restricted snapshot of food intake. Methodological problems also arise from translating typical information on food intake (e.g., "I had a medium-sized cheese sandwich, but I am not sure if the bread was spread with butter or margarine, or what type of cheese it was") into any meaningful value for energy and nutrient intake. Even expert dietitians are reduced to estimating and guessing a good deal of the time. The poor quality of the data means that any results must be evaluated cautiously, and data from small samples could easily give a misleading impression.

A second explanation for variability in the results is the different kinds of stressor. The animal literature suggests that physical stressors might be more likely to elicit hypophagia and social stressors, hyperphagia. In human experiences, the stress of surgery for a hernia, which was used in one study, is qualitatively and quantitatively different from the stress of an examination or a period of long working hours used in other studies, and they could well have a different effect on food intake. However, at present there are too few human studies to make any systematic analyses of the differential effects of different types of stressor.

The third explanation is that individuals might vary in their response to stress, and the admixture of response types could differ from study to study. Few naturalistic studies have taken an individual difference perspective, but those that do indicate that there are important individual differences that need to be considered in examining the effects of stress. In one study, middle-aged men and women kept daily stress diaries over several weeks and at the same time recorded whether, on that day, they had eaten more, the same, or less than usual. The pattern of results showed that most individuals were consistent in their reactions to stress, with some consistently eating more on higher-stress days, and others consistently eating less. Over the sample as a whole, the hypophagic response predominated. Similarly, in surveys which ask respondents about how stress affects their eating, the majority report some effect of stress, with approximately equal proportions saying that they eat more and eat less under stress.

B. Laboratory Studies

Most laboratory studies have been based on the idea that the "biologically natural" response to stress is hypophagia, but that individuals who are either overweight or highly restrained eaters, are unresponsive to their internal signals. Participants are therefore characterized according to these features and hypothesized to respond differently to stress.

Laboratory stress studies have used a range of stressors, including unpleasant films, false heart rate feedback, and threat of public speaking. In the typical design, participants are exposed either to the stressor or to a control procedure, and food intake is assessed covertly, often disguised as a "taste-test" in which participants are asked to taste and rate some flavors

of a palatable food such as ice cream. The amount that is eaten is recorded accurately by preweighing then reweighing the food containers.

1. Obesity and Stress-Induced Eating

The clinical interest in stress-related eating stemmed from the psychosomatic theory of obesity, which suggested that for the obese, eating met emotional rather than nutritional needs, and that the tendency toward emotional eating explained why they had become obese in the first place. Eating was hypothesized to provide reassurance, and hence stress was predicted to trigger higher than usual food intake—so-called emotional eating. There is no doubt that many obese people report that they eat more under stress, but these clinical reports need to be examined in controlled studies, both to establish their validity and to see if stress-related eating is specific to obesity.

Laboratory studies on stress-related eating in the obese have produced mixed results, with some studies finding higher intake under stress in the obese and others not. There has also been variability in naturalistic studies, but on balance there is probably enough evidence to suggest that obesity is an indicator of a higher risk of stress-induced hyperphagia, or at least a lower likelihood of stress-hypophagia.

The other side of the psychosomatic theory was that eating would have an anxiolytic effect, and this has received less support. Clinically, many obese people admit that any solace they derive from eating is transient and rapidly followed by shame and regret at not having shown more self-control. In laboratory studies there has been no evidence that eating successfully reduces emotional arousal. These observations have largely discredited the basic idea of the psychosomatic theory, namely the idea that obesity represents a disorder of emotional reactions. However, there is still interest in the idea that the obese have a reduced sensitivity to internal satiety cues, and the fact that they do not show stress-hypophagia may be a consequence of this lack of internal responsiveness.

2. Restraint and Stress-Induced Eating

In 1972, a radical alternative to the psychosomatic theory of obesity was proposed, namely that any abnormalities of eating observed in the obese were not pre-existing tendencies, but a consequence of the steps that they were taking to reduce their weight. At first the emphasis was on the effects of maintaining a body-size below the hypothesised set-point. This was superseded by Restraint Theory which proposed that one of the important determinants of food intake regulation was the tendency to restrained eating—the combination of concern about eating and weight fluctuation. Most obese people and a significant proportion of normal-weight adults, particularly women, are constantly trying to restrict their food intake in order to reduce their weight. The habit of trying to restrict food intake could have the effect of changing the individual's relationship with food, such that the usual cues to hunger and fullness become less effective in regulating eating behavior. Restrained eaters were found to limit their food intake at times when external or emotional pressures were low, but at other times, restraint would be abandoned and the individual would then eat to capacity—so-called disinhibition.

One of the early observations on restrained eating was that among individuals who experienced anxiety in response to a stressor, food intake was increased among the restrained eaters and decreased among unrestrained eaters. This general pattern, involving an interaction between stress and restraint in predicting food intake has proved extremely robust. Across many different studies, with a wide range of stressors, restrained eaters almost always eat more in the stressed than the unstressed condition. In contrast, unrestrained eaters show more variation, sometimes eating the same, and sometimes less under stress. The results of these laboratory studies have been strikingly consistent in an area where most of the work is notable for its inconsistency.

There is now a growing interest in examining the role of restraint in predicting individual differences in responses to stress in real-life studies. At this stage there are only self-report studies, but so far the results are consistent with the laboratory studies in showing that restrained eaters are more likely to report stress-hyperphagia and unrestrained eaters are more likely to report hypophagia. These subjective results are supported by results from quantitative studies using psychometric measures of restraint and emotional eating, which find that higher restraint is associated with higher levels of emotional eating.

C. Human Studies on Stress and Meal Patterns/Food Choice

Studies of stress and eating usually focus on the amount of food consumed, but stress might also affect food choices or meal patterns. In the naturalistic studies which showed increased energy intake there was also an increase in the proportion of energy from fat. This could reflect an increased preference for fatty foods, or alternatively a different meal pattern. In most Western countries the proportion of fat in "meal-type" foods tends to be lower than in "snack-type" foods. If stress induced a shift from meals to snacks, then this would be reflected in a higher fat intake, and might also increase the total energy intake, since higher fat foods have a higher energy density.

In most naturalistic studies, it is not possible to distinguish meal pattern changes from food choice changes, since the data are presented in terms of daily intake of nutrients, without any information either on foods eaten or timing of consumption. Laboratory studies have also failed to address the food choice issue, because most of them use only a single type of food. However, there is some evidence that sweet, high-fat foods are the ones most likely to show an increase.

IV. MECHANISMS RELATING STRESS TO EATING

Theoretical considerations and empirical results indicate that the mechanisms linking stress to changes in food intake are far from straightforward. Figure 1 illustrates the three principal pathways that have been implicated in the work in this area. In the center is the simple biological pathway whereby the physiological effects of stress inhibit the physiological features of hunger (or perhaps mimic the effects of satiety) and hence modify appetite and food intake. Animal research has generally been used to test this pathway since it is assumed that animals' food intake is more directly controlled by the basic drives of

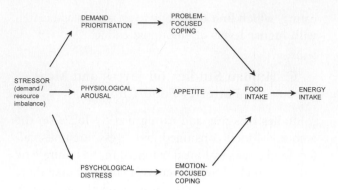

FIGURE 1   A psychobiological model of stress and diet.

hunger and satiety. On present evidence it would seem that some stressors probably induce hypophagia and others hyperphagia, implicating a more complex pathway from stress to food intake, even in animals. Humans have the advantage as research subjects in that they can tell us about their subjective experience, yet few studies have incorporated measures of hunger or satiety to address this issue. At present, therefore, there is little direct evidence for the hypothesized physiological depression of hunger. The best evidence available from human studies comes from the studies of food intake among normal-weight, nonrestrained eaters. In the laboratory, unrestrained eaters are either unaffected by stress or eat slightly less, which is somewhat supportive of a reduction in appetite, at least in some situations, and for some foods.

A second pathway (shown at the top of Fig. 1) results from consideration of the broader effects that stressors have across a range of aspects of life. In real life, stress motivates people to deploy resources toward dealing with the source of stress (so-called problem-focused coping). This may mean that longer term goals like dieting or healthy eating are temporarily set aside, with the consequent effects on food choices. Food intake should increase most in those who were normally restrictive, so women, healthy eaters, and dieters should show the strongest hyperphagic response to stress. This idea is given some support from the higher food intake in stressed restrained eaters, the higher fat and energy intake under stress among women in some of the naturalistic studies, and the observation that energy intakes in-

crease most among those who normally have a low energy intake.

The third pathway, shown at the bottom of Fig. 1, relates to the fact that stress also comes with an emotional coloring, so coping efforts are deployed not only to deal with the source of stress but also with the emotional state (emotion-focused coping). For some people, especially those who are usually self-denying over food, food may have a significant reward value and be used to provide emotional comfort. Women in particular often describe food in terms of treats and rewards, and the potential comfort to be derived from sweet foods is deeply enshrined in contemporary culture. Clearly this idea has echoes of the discredited psychosomatic theory of obesity, but it should be remembered that it was rejected not because of the absence of emotional eating, but because eating did not appear to be a successful anxiolytic. Other emotional coping strategies are also unsuccessful in the longer term (e.g., alcohol, smoking), but that doesn't prevent the smokers, drinkers and stress eaters from feeling that their habits serve a comforting role. In the field of eating disorders, excessive eating has been hypothesized to provide "escape from self-awareness," which is especially valued in response to ego-threatening stressors, so the idea that eating has a role, functional or dysfunctional, as an emotional coping strategy may have been rejected prematurely. If emotional eating was part of a stress-coping repertoire, it should be more common in restrained eaters, for whom food has a higher emotional value, and that, of course, is observed in all of the laboratory studies.

Finally, in real life, stresses are not usually single, transient and novel as they are in the laboratory. They are prolonged or repeated, they wax and wane, and they become a familiar part of the landscape. This means that stress reactions are likely to be modified over time. Adaptational processes should be triggered to protect body fat stores; if stress induces hypophagia in the short term, then in the longer term, the loss of body fat should up-regulate appetite and restore food intake to normal levels. Few human studies have looked at the effect of repeated stress exposures, but animal studies show that stress-hypophagia diminishes with repeated stress exposures. The inclusion of this dynamic perspective adds yet another dimension to an already complex process.

In summary, the relationship between stress and eating is a complex one, moderated in humans not only by the type of person, the type of stress and the types of foods which are available, but also by the dynamic relationship between the internal milieu and behavior over time. It is likely to challenge clinicians and researchers for some time to come, but it also provides one of the richest areas for demonstrating the importance of integrating biology and psychology to understand human behavior.

See Also the Following Articles

EATING DISORDERS AND STRESS; NUTRITION; OBESITY, STRESS AND

Bibliography

Greeno, C. G., and Wing, R. R. (1994). Stress-induced eating. *Psychological Bulletin* 115, 444–464.

Heatherton, T. F., and Baumeister, R. F. (1991). Binge-eating as escape from self-awareness. *Psychological Bulletin* 110, 86–108.

Herman, C. P., and Polivy, J. (1984). A boundary model for the regulation of eating. In A. J. Stunkard and E. Stellar (Eds.) *Eating and its disorders.* New York: Raven Press.

Robbins, T. W., and Fray, P. J. (1980). Stress-induced eating: Fact, fiction or misunderstanding. *Appetite* 1, 103–133.

Slochower, J. A. (1983) *Excessive eating: The role of emotions and environment.* New York: Human Sciences Press.

Stone, A. R., and Brownell, K. D. (1994). The stress-eating paradox: Multiple daily measurements in adult males and females. *Psychology and Health* 9, 425–436.

Disasters, Public, Effects of

Beverley Raphael and Matthew Dobson

Centre for Mental Health, New South Wales, Australia

I. Disaster Stressors
II. Stressor Elements
III. A Background of Disadvantage and Vulnerability
IV. Who is Affected?
V. Recovery Environment

GLOSSARY

disasters A class of events that can overwhelm individuals and their communities. Disasters elicit biological, psychological, and social stress reactions in individuals as well as affect the functioning of a community's social systems.

disaster stressors A range of events experienced by individuals in the course of their exposure to a disastrous situation. Disaster stressors may occur prior to, during, and in the aftermath of the disaster. The impact of these stressors is mediated by factors such as: an individual's perception of their role in the disaster and the community's awareness of its scope.

Disasters, by definition, are overwhelming events both for the communities they affect and for the individuals involved. The stress of disaster affects the functioning of social systems as well as creates biological, psychological, and social reactions in the persons affected. As an event, a disaster may be brief or long lasting, anticipated or unexpected, man-made or the result of natural forces, or an interaction of these. Such elements, as well as background strengths and vulnerabilities, may contribute to how the events are resolved and to the outcomes: positive or adverse.

A range of models have been considered in describing disaster response. These include the longitudinal systemwide reactive processes, namely warning, threat, impact, inventory, rescue, and recovery. This is one relatively simple model for a single-incident disaster (Raphael, 1986). Both individual and social system reactions may be relevant in each phase. Then there are a range of models for understanding the responses of individuals or groups, such as that of a person–environment interaction in response and processing.

More recently, the World Health Organization has suggested a classification that helps to provide a basis for conceptualizing, understanding, and planning a response to disasters: Natural and Human Disasters and Complex Emergencies (Mocellin, 1998). This classification reflects the complex and multiple disasters of famine, conflict, social disintegration, destruction of communities, and degradation of environment that may occur in some developing countries and cannot be easily conceptualized in the usual frameworks.

I. DISASTER STRESSORS

The stresses experienced by individuals depend on the nature of the disastrous event. For instance, a hurricane or flood may have been anticipated through recent warnings; from past experience there may be an effective response system in place. Alternatively, it may be that these natural occurrences are totally unexpected, affecting particularly vulnerable human habitats with few counterdisaster systems in place. Each of these, and multiple other circumstances, may mean that those involved experience effects ranging from the destruction of their homes, families, or communities to involvement in an exciting and unique challenge that has been successfully overcome. Another type of disaster is that associated with human failure, negligence, or even human malevolence. Driver failure in a transport accident or negligence of transport organizations may be examples of the former. A violent act such as the Oklahoma city bombing is an example of the latter. Although multiple classifications of disasters have been attempted they do not provide an easy guide to their consequences, or to the appropriate actions to deal with the stress or mental health effects they may generate. In addition, there are types of disaster associated with chronic and often hidden threats such as nuclear radiation and toxic waste. These generate a different pattern of reaction, for their threat is subtle and includes the possibility of damage to health, children, or to the likelihood of otherwise unknown effects.

II. STRESSOR ELEMENTS

A. Life Threat

This can be either personal life threat or threat to the lives of loved ones. This may be through natural forces, accident, technology, violence. It may also encompass the gruesome and mutilating deaths of others. For an individual, life threat, especially if associated with shock and helplessness, or even dissociation, may lead to reactive processes of reexperiencing, numbing of emotions, avoidance behavior, and heightened arousal. If arousal and distress are intense and perhaps triggering psychophysiological vulnerabilities, the reaction may develop into a pattern of psychiatric morbidity such as posttraumatic stress disorder (PTSD) or indeed other illnesses. However normally for the majority of individuals exposed, these reactive phenomena diminish over time.

Studies in disasters such as the Mount St. Helen volcanic eruption have shown the specificity of such life threat as stressor effects with relation to the development of PTSD, as have Pynoos *et al.* with children affected by a sniper shooting at school.

When deaths are massive and gruesome, levels of PTSD-type morbidity may be considerably higher, particularly for those who may have been more vulnerable following their initial dissociation. Lifton has spoken of a "death immersion," when levels of death are massive and horrific, as in Hiroshima. Unfortunately, genocides in modern conflict and war and mass killings can also provoke such an effect.

Some stress effects may also impact on physical health possibly through effects on immune factors, neuroendocrine response, altered health behaviors, the development of depression, and so forth. Indeed severe stressors of this kind may lead to sudden death, as has been demonstrated in a number of different studies of earthquakes.

For some individuals it is also possible to psychologically develop through dealing effectively with psychological trauma. This is well exemplified in the contributions of Victor Frankl and other Holocaust survivors. At a lesser level it has been systematically measured using the posttraumatic growth inventory.

For communities, massive deaths, or deaths of key figures, may threaten the functioning of the community and its survival. This was exemplified in the disaster where a slagheap destroyed the school at Abarfan but where the community did indeed survive and renew itself. Death-counts may provide an indicator of the degree to which a community may be affected by a disaster—but they are not the only stressor effect.

B. Losses

1. *Personal Losses*

These may range from the intense and personal loss of a primary attachment figure, a partner, child, or parent, to the loss of other family; members friends, neighbors, community members, work roles, or community leaders. These personal losses relate to the deaths of others. The normal reactive psychological processes for those dealing with these disaster stressors are bereavement, with grief and mourning for those to whom one was attached or for whom one cared or valued. There is usually an initial period of disbelief and perhaps even more so when the death is unexpected and untimely. This is especially the case in the midst of the chaos and threat frequently observed in a major disaster. This shock and denial, the sense of unreality and disbelief, can affect not only individuals, but communities.

The grief may be complicated by the life threat and traumatic stress-reactive processes that can occur in a traumatic bereavement. This type of situation (for instance in a massacre, in a plane crash, or, even more personally, in a motor vehicle accident) may mean that the processes of resolution of both trauma and grief are more complex and the risk of an adverse outcome much greater. Clinicians working with populations so affected recognize the need to deal separately and specifically with the effects of both sets of stressors reactions to facilitate resolution. They comment that the traumatic stress effects (i.e., those related to life threat) must often be dealt with first before it is possible to grieve. As with trauma effects, however, the majority of those bereaved in disaster

do resolve their personal loss, although some deaths, such as those of children or partners, create a greater risk of chronic and unresolved grief. It is of interest to note that in the epidemiological studies of the Mount St. Helen volcano effects, while threat experience tended to lead to a PTSD-type pattern of morbidity, loss was more likely to lead to depressive syndromes

2. *Other Losses*

These include loss of home, personal and treasured possessions (e.g., family photographs), work, workplace, neighborhood, and community. These effects have been studied by sociologists such as Erickson, who described a flood ravaging a mining valley and showed how there were not only the types of stressful experiences listed above, but also the disruption of neighborhoods and social networks when people were displaced into places of safety and shelter.

Thus, in the context of a public disaster, there are multiple losses of property, income, work, neighborhood, and social framework. These may not only produce grief, but also lead to ongoing deficits and disruptions, so their effects may be cumulative and profound. These may include not only loss of family and social structure, but also loss of opportunities for income and meaningful work. Furthermore, there is clear evidence of the value of social networks as protective and facilitating the resolution of experiences of loss, trauma, and disaster. The loss of these systems can create an additional and prolonged sense of despair in the postdisaster community.

C. Separation and Dislocation

As noted above there are many factors about disasters which by their nature separate family members and dislocate people from their homes and communities. There may be intense distress and searching behaviors as disaster-affected persons look for their loved ones, even placing their own lives at further risk. Information as to their whereabouts and opportunities for reunion may be the only influences that will lessen these behaviors. It may be, of course, that loved ones have died and grief will supervene. Being able to see the body of the loved one may be a very important factor in resolution of the loss. However, some disasters are such that bodies will never be found or are destroyed to the degree that only forensic identification is possible. Mutual support of those so affected may be important for resolution, as may be the support of the community in recognition and commemoration, perhaps of the site or in ceremony or memorial. These represent the coming together of individuals and the community and can provide a supportive framework for resolution and moving forward.

Dislocation, however, is more often related to the loss of homes, the move to shelter, and perhaps repeated moves to new places of safety or places to live until a new home is found. This is the sort of stressor that affects communities destroyed by natural disasters such as hurricanes, floods, and earthquakes, but also those tragically devastated by bombing and warfare. This is also one of the powerful stressors affecting refugees.

Dislocation stressors appear to affect mental health and well-being at a later stage and in more chronic ways. This was first observed in studies of the effects of a cyclone which devastated the northern Australian city of Darwin. Parker found that an initial rise of distress measured in a population of evacuees reflected a "mortality" or life-threat stress as noted above, while a subsequent rise months later reflected dislocation/relocation stressor effects. Other studies of those affected by this disaster have shown similar longer term stress effects related to dislocation.

D. Chronic Stressors

There have been anecdotal reports which suggest that people often feel that they and their communities overcame the horror of an acute incident such as a natural disaster, tragic and painful as it may have been, but that it is the ongoing chronic stresses afterwards that had the greater effect. These may be a direct consequence of the disaster—for instance, in the destruction of community facilities and resources, the inadequacy of temporary accommodation, or the disruption of social networks.

Disaster responses in communities are often described in terms of the initial "honeymoon phase," where there is enormous positive and often altruistic response in surrounding communities, nationally and even internationally. This is driven by a wish to undo, to make right, what has happened. Social boundaries fall and there are powerful affiliative tendencies at a local level. However, this lasts only for the first few days or weeks. Then the reality of what has happened, what it will take to recover, who will pay, and how long it will take, create a very different environment. Anger and scapegoating, chronic distress and frustration, and confrontation with bureaucracies that have returned to their predisaster levels of functioning all mean that there is an environment of "disillusionment." This may contribute further to the distress of the individual or may adversely influence the functioning of the community, leading to cynicism and disappointment. Fortunately, however, the majority of communities, like individuals, build on their resources and resilience, and recover. The experience of the catastrophe becomes part of a history of mastery and moving on. Tragically, however, for some communities the stigma of the catastrophe remains and the community is identified with the disaster and the disaster with the community, often in the most negative ways—for instance with the Chernobyl nuclear incident, or the Port Arthur Massacre.

Other disaster stresses are by their very nature chronic and ongoing or become that way. Degradation of the environment through industrial accidents or toxic waste disposal can produce such chronic effects. Others include drought and deforestation. And there is ongoing disaster stress in environments of chronic ethnic or other conflict including guerilla warfare or the years spent in refugee camps. The stress of chronic exposure to toxic environments is now recognized as having major psychological effects as well as potentially detrimental physical outcomes. Such stresses may be more subtle and profound and in time have ongoing effects on health.

III. A BACKGROUND OF DISADVANTAGE AND VULNERABILITY

Some communities affected by disaster, as well as some individuals, may confront these stressor experiences from a background of significant disadvantage.

These may be educational, social, economic disadvantages, all of which have been shown to contribute to more adverse outcomes for affected individuals and populations.

A. Previous Exposure

In addition, there is the issue of previous exposures to the stressors or to the disaster. In some people this will have built the individual's strength, will have added to the capacity to overcome the new threat, will have "innoculated" against the stress effects. For others it will have created the vulnerability of unresolved traumatization or unresolved grief that may surface again. While there may be opportunities to rework those earlier experiences, they are often not recognized. Earlier traumatization such as childhood sexual abuse or wartime suffering are examples that may not clearly link to the present context yet may still constitute sensitive wounds.

Communities that have been exposed in the past may develop a "disaster subculture." This may influence how they respond to warnings and to the disaster itself. This subculture reflects a belief system about what will happen, what can be done, what the outcomes may be. This may influence responses in either positive or negative ways, depending on the adaptability of the beliefs and their fit with the particular incident.

B. Displaced Persons

Other vulnerable populations may be those who are already dislocated from familiar settings, for instance, refugees or new immigrants or minority groups. They may lose papers, documents of identification. They may have as yet fragile links to their new community. They may not have the language, knowledge, or understanding needed to respond to the incident. Alternatively, they may have integrated these events in terms of earlier experiences of threat. They may experience intense fears for safety because the chaos of the disaster is similar to the chaos they have known. They have been identified as vulnerable groups in many disaster responses and may need special attention to facilitate their recovery.

Indigenous peoples may also face particular difficulties, with backgrounds that may have already involved life-threat through premature mortality and racist violence; losses through family disruptions, and deaths, loss of land, culture, identity, and meaning; and dislocation from place, tribe, or community. Socioeconomic, educational, and other disadvantages may all contribute further to the background of traumatization upon which a disaster, acute or chronic, natural or man-made, superimposes further and additional stresses, increasing the likelihood of adverse outcomes for individuals or communities.

C. Children

Children and young people may be vulnerable through separation, or by seeing effects on parents. Stresses of life-threat, loss, separation, and dislocation, can impact not only on present well-being but also on psychological and social development. This has been well demonstrated by Terr's in-depth studies showing that effects may appear in repetitive traumatic play and behavioral disruptions that are both aggressive and withdrawing. Pynoos *et al.* studied the effects of a school-based sniper attack and were able to show that mental health effects reflected the nature of the stressor experiences each child faced. For instance, those who experienced life-threat showed posttraumatic stress disorder phenomena, those who experienced a bereavement showed phenomena of grief and later depression, while those who experienced separation from their siblings showed separation-type adjustment phenomena. Effects may be delayed to the longer term, as McFarlane's study reported, where disaster-affected children's pattern of morbidity at first appeared less than that of the broader community, and was particularly "good," perhaps cushioning for the children the effect of what had happened. Their distress appeared later in the first year after a forest fire disaster, and was also linked to ongoing symptomatology in their parents. Other studies of children support these findings and emphasize the need to recognize both behavioral responses and development impact, as well as the centrality for the child of the family, and needs for affection and security if these stressors are to be dealt with. The school is also a very important environment of care and development. The effects on children may not be identified by teachers who have themselves been stressed. Behavioral reactions may only appear in the school setting, disrupting learning through effects on cognition and emotion. School-based interventions using a "work book" to facilitate working through a traumatic experience related to a forest fire disaster, for example, have been shown to lessen the risk of adverse outcomes.

D. The Elderly

Older people have been frequently described as vulnerable to disaster stresses. As with other studies in the mental health field no specific increase in psychosocial morbidity has been found among the elderly, and perhaps there is even a decrease in later years. There is no good evidence that they run a greater risk of mental health morbidity, although the patterns may be different, with higher arousal and lower intrusive (reexperiencing) symptoms than young adults similarly exposed. However, there is evidence that they may be more likely to die in a disaster, and perhaps this relates to the difficulties in response to warning, the physical attributes necessary for escape, or to a greater acceptance of death. There is, however, still a need to ensure that those individuals who may be vulnerable are encompassed in postdisaster response.

IV. WHO IS AFFECTED?

Determining those affected by a disaster may be difficult. Registration of victims provides a formal mechanism and this is often the role of organizations such as the Red Cross or Red Crescent or of formal institutions such as police services. But this only really describes the direct victims. A number of workers have developed classifications of the different levels of "victimhood" in disasters. In broad terms these include those directly experiencing the incident, who are often described as primary victims, to those who were not there but are profoundly affected, such as bereaved family members, to those involved in rescue and helping efforts, who may be seen as secondary or indirectly affected victims.

The distinction between "victim" and "helper" and the roles inherent in these words have been seen as potentially difficult: "victim" implying weak and helpless; "helper" implying strong and powerful. As those directly involved in the Hyatt Regency Hotel disaster in the U.S. were likely to be both victims and helpers in the early stages, this distinction may not be useful. There is ample evidence that both informal and formal helpers may be profoundly affected and that they may themselves need psychological assistance to recover.

It is of importance scientifically that a dose–response effect may be demonstrated for the levels of stressor experience, such as intensity of exposure or closeness to the epicenter of the disaster incident. Shore *et al.*'s excellent epidemiological study of the Mount St. Helen's eruption strongly supports this as well as the specificity of morbidity to stressors. This study also showed that relative risk of disaster-specific morbidity was heightened 2 years afterward and that higher levels occurred for women on a constellation of disorders such as PTSD, depression, and generalized anxiety disorder.

Weisæth also showed this clearly in his studies of a workforce affected by a paint factory explosion and fire. The highest levels of morbidity were found in those closest to the explosion, with lesser levels in those further away, and lesser still in those workers not on shift, but who would have been affected had they been. This latter vicarious traumatization was also shown in a ferry disaster.

Those affected may be affected by many things, both as individuals or as communities. They may be affected by any combination of the stressors identified above and perhaps many others; they may be affected by ongoing life difficulties or recent life events, although they may attribute their distress to the disaster experience. They may be affected, or even secondarily "injured," by the failure of others to acknowledge their suffering, their experience, what they have been through; by the convergence of helpers; by the inadequacy of disaster response; by a failure of the "emergency organization" of the community's initial response or the "recovery organization" of the subsequent period. They may have been positively supported and assisted by any or all of these factors. For instance, natural resilience or hardiness and social supports may interact to modulate the effects of exposure.

V. RECOVERY ENVIRONMENT

The recovery environment consists of those natural and introduced forces that may influence the recovery of individuals and communities from their experience. These include the natural processes of resilience that are vital for survival and the various adaptations that may support these such as coping strategies, personal resources, and social interaction. The more positive recovery environments are those in which the experience is acknowledged and help is offered, but the strengths of individuals and communities to overcome the disaster stresses are recognized, valued, and supported.

The response to disaster-affected persons and communities is often intense, and there may be a convergence of those wishing to help, including those offering both practical assistance, medical aid, debriefing and counseling, and subsequently welfare assistance. The altruism driving this wish to help represents the best of human values. Unfortunately, in this convergence there may be an excess of offers by the unskilled or those who may in turn become victims themselves. Debriefing may be part of such a response but there is no evidence that it is beneficial to the wider population. Psychological first aid is an important helping response— now recognized internationally. Focused counseling for traumatization or grief may be of value, but this needs to be based on evidence of effective interventions and delivered by skilled and knowledgeable personnel. The aim of any intervention may be "first to do no harm." Unfortunately there is a shortage of systematic investigations of the effectiveness of interventions postdisaster, perhaps because of the chaos of the event and aftermath, but also because of the methodological and ethical constraints of intervention and research at such times. The aim should *always* be "first to do no harm." Some beneficial effects have been found for systematic intervention in environments such as schools or in postdisaster of outreach and support as part of a disaster mental health response. There is a need for much further research to ensure that the human resources and others mobilized contribute to the common goals, are effective in enhancing social and health outcomes, and will be powerful and positive forces of normal recovery.

See Also the Following Articles

Bibliography

Erikson, K. (1994). "A New Species of Trouble: Explorations in Disaster, Trauma and Community." Norton, New York.

Foss, O. T. (1994) Mental first aid. *Soc. Sci. Med.* **38,** 479–482.

Frankel, V. (1962). "Man's Search for Meaning." Simon and Schuster, New York.

Lifton, R. (1979). "The Broken Connection: On Death and the Continuity of Life." Simon and Schuster, New York.

McFarlane, A. C. (1987). Post traumatic phenomena in a longitudinal study of children following a natural disaster. *J. Am. Acad. Child and Adol. Psychiat.* **26,** 764–769.

Parker, G. (1975). Psychological disturbance in Darwin evacuees following cyclone Tracy. *Med. J. Australia* **21,** 650–652.

Pynoos, R., Frederick, C., Nader, K., Arroyo, W., Steinberg, A., Eth, S., Nunez, F., and Fairbanks, L. (1987). Life threat and post-traumatic stress in school age children. *Arch. Gen. Psychiat.* **44,** 1057–1063.

Raphael, B. (1977). Preventive intervention with the recently bereaved. *Arch. Gen. Psychiat.* **34,** 1450–1454.

Raphael, B. (1986). "When Disaster Strikes: How Individuals and Communities Cope with Catastrophe." Basic Books, New York.

Raphael, B., Meldrum, L., and McFarlane, A. (1995). Does debriefing after psychological trauma work? *Br. Med. J.* **310,** 1479–1480.

Shore, J., Tatum, E., and Vollmer, W. (1986). Psychiatric reactions to disaster: The Mount St. Helen's experience. *Am. J. Psychiat.* **143**, 590–595.

Singh, B., and Raphael, B. (1981). Postdisaster morbidity of the bereaved: A possible role for preventive psychiatry? *J. Nerv. Ment. Dis.* **169**, 203–212.

Tedeschi, R. G., and Calhoun, G. (1996). The posttraumatic growth inventory: Measuring the positive legacy of trauma. *J. Traum. Stress* **9**, 455–471.

Terr, L. (1991). Childhood traumas: An outline and overview. *Am. J. Psychiat.* **148**, 1–20.

Weisæth, L. (1989). A study of behavioural responses to an industrial disaster. *Acta Psychiat. Scand.* **80** (Suppl. 355), 13–24.

Disaster Syndrome

Paul Valent

Melbourne, Australia

I. Features of the Disaster Syndrome
II. The Place of Disaster Syndrome in Disasters and among Similar Syndromes
III. Sense and Purpose of Disaster and Associated Syndromes
IV. Unfolding of Disaster Phases and of Disaster Syndromes
V. Treatment

GLOSSARY

disaster Usually refers to natural calamities such as floods, earthquakes, and fires. However, the term is also used more generically to include man-made calamities and other traumatic situations.

disaster phase Refers to time periods around disasters. Preimpact is the period before the disaster, impact is when it occurs, recoil is immediately after, postimpact is for days to weeks after, and recovery and reconstruction may go on for months or years.

survival strategies Biopsychosocial templates which evolved to enhance survival in specific circumstances. Examples are fight, flight, adaptation, and attachment.

trauma An experience in which one's life has been grossly threatened and from which a variety of biological, psychological, and social wounds and scars result.

traumatic situation Refers to external situations in which trauma occurs.

The term "disaster syndrome" was first used by Wallace in 1957 to describe a stunned, shocked state common in the impact phase of disasters. This is what the term has come to connote in disaster literature, and most of this article concentrates on this meaning of the term. Disaster syndrome overlaps with similar syndromes and they are drawn together into a coherent whole. Wallace described subsequent stages of disaster syndrome, which are now seen as part of subsequent disaster phases. Such disaster phases are briefly summarized here.

I. FEATURES OF THE DISASTER SYNDROME

Wallace described responses in Petun warriors who in 1649 returned to their village to find their kin had all been slain or captured. They sat down in the snow, mute, and no one stirred or spoke for half a day. Wallace noted that such responses are ubiquitously found in disasters and are variably described as "shock," "stupor," being "dazed," "stunned," and "numbed." He added that as well as sitting, victims may stand motionless or wander aimlessly. Emotions such as pain, grief, fear, and anger are missing, and people are docile. The state may last up to hours or even days, injured people remaining dazed longer.

II. THE PLACE OF DISASTER SYNDROME IN DISASTERS AND AMONG SIMILAR SYNDROMES

The behavioral features of the disaster syndrome are still valid in descriptions today and are called by the original name. However, various psychological, behavioral, and physiological lines of research have emphasized different aspects of what is behaviorally disaster syndrome and called them by different names. The psychological equivalent has been called psychic shock, the physiological equivalent general adaptation syndrome, while conservation-withdrawal syndrome spans all biopsychosocial aspects.

A. Psychic Shock

Psychic shock is the subjective view of being stunned. It has been studied most in bereavement and dying, seen there as the first stage of the grieving process. Subjective feelings of psychic shock as a response to being told news of death utilize physical metaphors such as an "assault," a "blow" to the face, head, or the guts, and as being "knocked out" or "winded." Psychological terms include being "overwhelmed," "not being able to take it," "the world shattering around one," and "sinking into a black hole." Defenses against such sensations include denial voiced as disbelief, and dissociation, described variably as feeling numb, experiencing a sense of unreality of the world or of oneself. A common description is looking at oneself and the events as if they were a film.

B. General Adaptation Syndrome

Selye described the general adaptation syndrome as a ubiquitous triad of physiological stress responses which were associated with psychic shock. The stress responses were enlargement of the adrenal cortex and increased levels of cortisone, shrinking of the thymus gland, spleen, and lymphatic structures (along with compromises of immunocompetence), and deep ulcers in the stomach. Selye noted that these responses helped organisms to adapt to overwhelming situations.

C. Conservation-Withdrawal Syndrome

Conservation-withdrawal syndrome, described by Engel and Schmale, expands on the definition of disaster syndrome by emphasizing immobility, quiescence, and unresponsiveness, accompanied by sagging muscles, feelings of extreme fatigue, constricted attention, and detachment.

Adding to the general adaptation syndrome, conservation-withdrawal is associated with parasympathetic, trophotropic activity, which may manifest in diminished heart rate to the point of arrhythmias and possibly asystoles and even death. Gastric secretions were noted to diminish, possibly because food intake does not occur in this state. The syndrome has been observed at all ages, ranging from neonates to adults, and in various situations where no definite course of action was possible.

III. SENSE AND PURPOSE OF DISASTER AND ASSOCIATED SYNDROMES

Initially it may be difficult to see responses to being overwhelmed as adaptive. However, just like physical shock helps survival, so may psychosocial shock. For instance, Darwin noted that immobility made animals less likely to be seen and be attacked, and the death-like state could stimulate predators to release their grip. Immobility could also help to scoop the unresisting person to safety and help members of the group to find its previously abandoned members. Further, the associated psychosocial limpness or docility may facilitate cooperation with helpers and their directions. Last, psychological encystment and conservation of energy could provide a buffer space for replenishment of reserves.

Selye and Engel and Schmale also saw their respective syndromes as primary regulatory organismic templates which enhanced survival of the species. They were at the opposite spectrum to fight and flight, and they occurred in situations where fight and resistance could be fatal, but "rolling with the punches," and surrendering old goals and finding new ones was advisable.

Valent integrated the biopsychosocial features and purposes of the above syndromes in a survival strategy which he called Adaptation. It adapted the organism to situations requiring initial surrender, but through processes such as grieving it facilitated turning to new hopeful situations and bonds. If this did not occur, physiological symptoms, depression, and other illnesses could occur (see below).

IV. UNFOLDING OF DISASTER PHASES AND OF DISASTER SYNDROMES

Features of later disaster phases and unfolding of disaster syndromes (or of the survival strategy Adaptation) follow.

A. Ensuing Disaster Phases

In the postimpact phases (Wallace's stages II and III) of disasters, survivors emerge from their cocoons. They are grateful to be alive, help others, and reconnect with family and friends. Survivors drop usual reserves to become a cohesive altruistic community. The accompanying optimism has been called the postdisaster euphoria. At the same time anger is often directed at outsiders whose help is seen as unempathic. In addition to Wallace's stages, recovery and reconstruction phases are the hard prolonged times of rebuilding the physical environment and internal lives. The names, timing, and contents of the phases are flexible, indicating fluctuating progression.

Similar phases occur in other traumatic situations, though different contents are emphasized in the literature. For instance, in bereavement psychological features are emphasized. After shock come phases of searching, then anger, guilt, and working

through followed by acceptance and turning to new bonds.

B. Unfolding of Disaster Syndrome

Physiological stress response derivatives of disaster syndrome (or the adaptation survival strategy) may manifest clinically as hypotension, dizziness, tiredness, fatigue, and the sense of being "ill". Prolonged compromised immunocompetence may help to account for the increased rates of infections, autoimmune diseases, and cancers following disasters, bereavements, and other traumas. Thus this specific response may be importantly involved in the frequent stress-induced maladies. Maladaptive psychological unfolding includes hopelessness, despair, giving in, unresolved and chronic grief, and clinical depression.

V. TREATMENT

The treatment of psychic shock, like physical shock, includes physical and psychological warmth, comfort, and support. Physical contact with another human, reassuring voice, explanations of what is happening, hope, and connection with loved ones are helpful. Later treatment depends on the nature of evolving symptoms and illnesses. The best treatment is prevention or mitigation of circumstances where people are overwhelmed.

See Also the Following Articles

ALARM PHASE AND GENERAL ADAPTATION SYNDROME; BEREAVEMENT; DISASTERS, PUBLIC, EFFECTS OF

Bibliography

Engel, G. L., and Schmale, A. H. (1972). Conservation-withdrawal: A primary regulatory process for organismic homeostasis. *In* "Ciba Foundation Symposium: Physiology of Emotion and Psychosomatic Illness." Elsevier, New York.

Selye, H. (1946). The general adaptation syndrome and the diseases of adaptation. *J. Clin. Endocrinol.* **6**, 117–196.

Raphael, B. (1984). "The Anatomy of Bereavement." Hutchinson, London.

Raphael, B. (1986). "When Disaster Strikes." Hutchinson, London.

Valent, P. (1998). "From Survival to Fulfillment: A Framework for the Life-Trauma Dialectic. " Taylor and Francis, Philadelphia, PA.

Wallace, A. F. C. (1957). Mazeway disintegration: The individual's perception of sociocultural disorganization. *Hum. Org.,* **16**, 23–27.

Disease, Stress-Induced, Overview

H. S. Willenberg, S. R. Bornstein, and G. P. Chrousos

National Institute for Child and Health Development, National Institutes of Health

I. Anatomy and Physiology of the Stress System
II. Stress and Disease
III. Disease and Stress

GLOSSARY

adaptive response Complex set of an organism's reactions to reestablish homeostasis.

adrenocorticotropic hormone (ACTH) Known under its scientific term "corticotropin." Regulates adrenal control release.

apoptosis Cell death initiated by several mechanisms in a regulated process. It is also termed "programmed cell death." Cells with this fate undergo a sequence of changes typical for this process.

arginine-vasopressin peptide hormone.

corticotropin-releasing hormone *Formerly also termed* corticotropin-releasing factor. Main regulator of ACTH.

homeostasis State of dynamic equilibrium.

LC/NE system locus ceruleus norepinephrine system.

proopiomelanocortin Polypeptide secreted by pituitary cells which is the basis for several hormones of the pituitary that are yielded by alternative processing, including corticotropin, melanocyte-stimulating hormones, and endorphins.

sympathetic-adrenomedullary system Part of the autonomic neural system.

stress State of threatened homeostasis.

stressor Forces that threaten to destroy the state of homeostasis.

Continuation of life depends on the ability of an organism to maintain a state of dynamic equilibrium or homeostasis. Homeostasis is constantly disturbed by entropic forces, the stressors. The state of threatened homeostasis is defined as stress. A complex set of behavioral and physical reactions, the adaptive response, is employed by the organism to reestablish balanced physiologic conditions. At the beginning of the 20th century, Walter Cannon and Hans Selye developed these modern concepts of stress and discussed the relation between stress and disease. In antiquity, Hippocrates had regarded health as the harmonious balance of the four key elements of life, water, fire, air, and earth, and had defined states of imbalance between these elements as disease. He had also described the adaptive response as the "healing power of nature."

The actual term "stress" was originally adapted from physics by Walter Cannon. In physics, it described the resistance of a body to applied pressure, following Hook's law of elasticity. An acting force may distort body elastically in a linear fashion or, if applied excessively in quality, quantity, or time, may produce nonlinear deformations. Similarly, stress may be a transient and time-limited state, well balanced by the adaptive responses of the organism, while excessive and prolonged stress may alter the physiologic and behavioral defense mechanisms, rendering them inefficient or deleterious.

I. ANATOMY AND PHYSIOLOGY OF THE STRESS SYSTEM

Structures that include components of a network of neural and endocrine responses that are activated adaptively during stress have been collectively called the stress system. On the cellular level, molecules such as the highly conserved heat—shock proteins (hsp) are primitive key elements of the cellular stress response. They comprise several families of proteins that are found across species and are classified depending on their molecular size (in kilodaltons) into hsp16-30, hsp60, hsp70, and hsp90. They have been shown to regulate cell and tissue homeostasis and to be protective when this is threatened by stressors.

The central components of the stress system are located in the hypothalamus and the brain stem, the phylogenetically oldest parts of the brain. These centers receive information input of internal and external origin and compute appropriate responses, which are effected by two main pathways, the endocrine hypothalamic-pituitary-adrenal (HPA) axis and the neural systemic sympathetic-adrenomedullary (SA) and parasympathetic systems. Their central regulators and peripheral end-products, corticotropin-releasing hormone (CRH), glucocorticoids, and catecholamines, are key hormones in the reestablishment and maintenance of cardiovascular, metabolic, immune, and behavioral homeostasis.

A. Hypothalamic-Pituitary-Adrenal Axis and Stress

Corticotropin-releasing hormone, the principal central regulator of the HPA axis, is mainly produced by parvocellular neurons of the hypothalamus, in the paragigantocellular and parabranchial nuclei of the medulla, and in the central nucleus of the amygdala. Its action on the pituitary gland is supported by arginine-vasopressin (AVP), also secreted by parvocellular neurons of the paraventricular hypothalamic nuclei (PVN). Corticotropin-releasing hormone induces production and secretion of corticotropin

(ACTH) from the pituitary, a hormone whose main target is the cortex of the adrenal gland. Intracerebroventricular administration of CRH causes activation of the stress system and behavioral patterns similar to those observed during stress.

The adrenal gland as the end-organ of the HPA axis is subject to functional changes of the stress system. It responds quite rapidly to sustained stimulation with hypertrophy and hyperplasia that can be monitored at the macroscopic, microscopic, ultrastructural, and molecular levels. In chronic stress, high levels of glucocorticoids and relatively low levels of ACTH are frequently observed. This dissociation between central activation of the HPA axis and adrenal cortex function represents an adaptation of the stress system, whereby medullary input and hypertrophy and hyperplasia of the *zona fasciculata* of the adrenal cortex sustain elevated glucocorticoid secretion in the presence of low normal ACTH concentrations.

Glucocorticoids exert their pleiotropic effects through ubiquitously distributed intracellular receptors in almost all tissues of the body. In addition, they participate in their own regulation of secretion through a classic negative feedback mechanism by binding to high-affinity mineralocorticoid and low-affinity glucocorticoid receptors in the frontal cortex, amygdala, hippocampus, hypothalamus, and pituitary. Exposure to pathologically elevated levels of glucocorticoids causes neurons to slow down their metabolism, while these neurons may undergo death by apoptosis. Therefore, this loop of HPA axis regulation serves to terminate or suppress an excessive response of the stress system.

B. Systemic Sympathetic-Adrenomedullary and Parasympathetic Systems

This axis originates from mostly norepinephrine cell groups of the locus ceruleus, medulla, and pons (LC/NE). Efferent projections of these neurons terminate throughout the brain and spinal cord as well as in the peripheral ganglia of the autonomic nervous system. Through a complex neural network, a wide spectrum of physiologic functions can be controlled. These include cardiovascular tone, respiration, skeletal muscle and adipose tissue metabolic activity, and gastrointestinal function. The adrenal medulla is an effector organ of this system, supplying the systemic circulation with epinephrine and norepinephrine. These catecholamines also potentiate ACTH-stimulated cortisol production by adrenocortical cells.

C. Coordination and Communication of HPA Axis and LC/NE System

Organization and implementation of a qualitatively and quantitatively appropriate stress response depends on fine-tuning of both the regulatory centers of the stress system and the response of target organs. Indeed, a complex network of neurons, neuronal and hormonal factors, and other cell mediators is at interplay at each level of interactions. Secretion of CRH and central catecholamines are controlled by neurons of the frontal cortex, mesocortical/mesolimbic system, and the amygdala–hippocampus complex. Neuronal pathways which produce γ-aminobutyric acid (GABA), substance P, and β-endorphin inhibit CRH-producing neurons. Corticotropin-releasing hormone is not only responsible for activation of the HPA axis but also for stimulation of LC/NE neurons in the brain stem.

The adrenal gland unites HPA and SA axes under a common capsule. A great degree of intermingling of cortical and medullary cells increases the area of contact between these systems. Besides the stimulation through corticotropin, ACTH-independent mechanisms seem to be involved in the adaptation to chronic stress. Stimulation of chromaffin cells leads to potentiation of glucocorticoid secretion, while glucocorticoids enhance catecholamine production by medullary cells.

D. Interplay of the Stress System with Major Endocrine, Immune, and Other Systems

Activation of the stress system helps the organism to overcome the influence of stressors and, therefore, postpones all functions that may interfere with the chance of the individual to survive. The stress system stimulates the mesocorticolimbic system, influencing motivation and reward phenomena. The stress sys-

tem also stimulates the amygdala and hippocampus. The former generates fear and anxiety, while the latter participates in the negative feedback control of the HPA axis; both recall implicit, emotion-laden memories. Neurons of the arcuate nucleus of the hypothalamus produce proopiomelanocortin (POMC)-derived peptides. Two of these, α-MSH and β-endorphin, inhibit the activity of the stress system. Projections to the brain stem and spinal cord elevate the gain threshold, producing the so-called stress-induced analgesia.

Activation of the stress system leads to inhibition of a number of endocrine axes. These include the gonadal, growth, and thyroid axes. Direct inhibition of central neural circuits is supported by the peripheral suppressive actions of glucocorticoids.

Other profound consequences of stress system activation are observed in the immune system. Important participants in the immunologic homeostasis are cytokine signals from cells of the immune tissue. All three major inflammatory cytokines, tumor necrosis factor-α, interleukin-1, and interleukin-6, produced at sites of inflammation in a cascadelike fashion, exert stimulatory effects on the HPA axis. Their actions are directed to all three levels of the HPA axis. The most potent mediator among them is interleukin-6; it causes elevation of CRH, AVP, ACTH, and glucocorticoids. Indirect actions of the inflammatory cytokines on the HPA axis are also attained through stimulation of noradrenergic centers in the brain stem. In chronic hypoactivation of the HPA axis, increased serum levels of interleukin-6 can be observed.

The stress system utilizes additional mechanisms to affect immune homeostasis. Besides the suppressive effect of glucocorticoids on the production of tumor necrosis factor-α, interleukin-1, and interleukin-6, glucocorticoids also inhibit the target tissue responses to cytokines through suppression of nuclear transcription factor-kB and AP-1. Glucocorticoids also cause a switch from T-helper type I cytokine profile to T-helper type II cytokine profile by inhibiting interleukin-12 and by stimulating interleukin-10. In this way, a shift from a cellular to a humoral immune response is promoted. In addition, glucocorticoids initiate apoptosis in eosinophils and in some T cells.

II. STRESS AND DISEASE

Stress plays an important role in self- and species survival, but also participates in the development and aging of every individual. The quality, intensity, and duration of stress are important in determining positive or negative effects on the organism.

There are two main conditions of the stress system that lead to pathology: An excessive and prolonged or a defective adaptive response to a stressor. In both cases, the dose–response relation between the potency of a stressor and the adaptive response of the organism is shifted to the left or right, respectively. Excessive or defective reactions to stressors that are associated with pathologic or physiologic states are summarized in Table I. More than half of the variance determining the stress response is due to inherited factors, while the remaining is due to early life constitutional factors and concurrent environmental input.

In the syndrome of major melancholic depression, a disproportionate activation of the generalized stress response is chronically manifested. Central activation with consequent elevation of CRH is followed by a blunted ACTH response of the pituitary to exog-enous CRH, probably due to downregulation of CRH receptors and/or increased glucocorticoid feedback. At autopsy, these patients have an increased number of CRH and AVP neurons in the parvoventricular nucleus of the hypothalamus and hippocampal atrophy. In addition, imaging and morphometric studies have shown that the pituitary and adrenals are enlarged. Sequelae of hypercortisolism include pseudo-Cushing syndrome manifestation, osteoporosis, and opportunistic infections. Similar observations were made in chronic active alcoholism, anorexia nervosa, in individuals that were sexually abused in their youth, and in obsessive-compulsive disorders.

Another example of hyperactivation of the stress system is critical illness. When entering a chronic state, interleukin-6 and possibly other cytokines synergize with corticotropin to maintain increased stimulation of the adrenal cortex. In this condition, a dissociation between ACTH and cortisol levels occurs. Similar to melancholic depression, these patients escape full HPA axis suppression following dexamethasone.

In the autoimmune/inflammatory syndrome of rheumatoid arthritis, a hypoactive HPA axis has been

TABLE I

Pathologic Conditions Associated with Altered Activity of the HPA Axis

States associated with altered regulation of the HPA axis		
Increased HPA activity	*Decreased HPA activity*	*Disrupted HPA activity*
Severe chronic disease	Atypical depression	Cushing's syndrome
Melancholic depression	Seasonal depression	Glucocorticoid deficiency
Anorexia nervosa	Chronic fatigue syndrome	Glucocorticoid resistance
Obsessive-compulsive disorder	Hypothyroidism	
Panic disorder	Adrenal suppression	
Chronic excessive exercise	Obesity	
Malnutrition	(hyposerotinergic forms)	
Diabetes mellitus	Nicotine withdrawal	
Hyperthyroidism	Vulnerability to inflammatory	
	disease (Lewis rat)	
Central obesity	Rheumatoid arthritis	
Childhood sexual abuse	Premenstrual tension	
	syndrome	
Pregnancy	Postpartum mood and	
	inflammatory disorders	
	Vulnerability to alcoholism	

reported. It appears that a defective glucocorticoid response to inflammation is an important factor in the pathogenesis of this disease.

III. DISEASE AND STRESS

There are pathologic conditions of the stress system leading to disease and, vice versa, diseases that alter the activity of the stress system in a pathologic fashion.

A. Stress System Disorders

The adaptive response to stress has three components. First, stress has to be sensed. Sensory neural and hormonal pathways have developed to connect the outside world and the rest of the body to the central nervous system. Hypersensitivity or hyposensitivity to stressors may cause disproportionate responses resulting in pathology. Therefore, disorders characterized by altered perception of signals to the stress system cause inefficient responses to natural challenges with consequent development of secondary diseases.

The second step covers the calculation and integration of the information input and the third step the response. Disorders of the central nervous system that influence these responses interfere with the stress system and develop pathology related to this interference.

Activation of the stress system is necessary to overcome homeostasis-threatening events, but excessive and prolonged activation may be self-destructive. Transient hypercortisolemia is necessary during surgery, sepsis, and other severe conditions. But hypercortisolemia also leads to hyperglycemia, hyperlipidemia-increased catabolism, and immune supression, all states that, if chronically present, have major adverse effects upon the body.

B. Diseases That Directly Influence the Stress System

Diseases generally disturb homeostasis and should be regarded as stressors. Conversely, every stressful influence that alters homeostasis of the organism in a long-term fashion could be regarded as a process that may cause disease.

Cushing's syndrome or Addison's disease lead to disintegration of the stress system, which fails to mount an adaptive response. Patients with these conditions develop multisystem disorders that result from excessive or defective cortisol effects on systems, whose proper function depends on an optimum of glucocorticoid activity.

See Also the Following Articles

Adrenal Insufficiency; Cushing's Syndrome; Endocrinology, Overview; Health Behavior and Stress; Homeostasis; Immunity

Bibliography

Bornstein, S. R., and Chrousos, G. P. (1999). Clinical review 104: Adrenocorticotropin (ACTH)- and non-ACTH-mediated regulation of the adrenal cortex—Neural and immune inputs. *J. Clin. Endocrinol. Metab.* 84(5), 1729–1736.

Bornstein, S. R., and Ehrhart-Bornstein, M. (1999). Interactions of the stress system in the adrenal: Basic and clinical aspects. *In* "Stress and Adaption: From Selye's Concept to Application of Modern Formulations" (C. L. Bolis and J. Licinio, Eds.), pp. 89–108. World Health Organization, Geneva.

Chrousos, G. P. (1998). Stressors, stress, and neuroendocrine integration of the adaptive response: The 1997 Hans Selye Memorial Lecture. *Ann. N.Y. Acad. Sci.* 851, 311–335.

Dissociation

Jose R. Maldonado

Stanford University

I. Models of Dissociation
II. Dissociative Disorders
III. Treatment
IV. Hypnosis as a Treatment Tool in the Psychotherapy of Dissociative Disorders
V. Legal Ramifications of Memory Work

GLOSSARY

dissociation Term used to describe the separation of whole segments of the personality (as in multiple personality) or of discrete mental processes (as in the schizophrenias) from the mainstream of consciousness or of behavior.

dissociative identity disorder (DID) A new term in the Diagnostic and Statistical Manual of Mental Disorder, Fourth Edition (DSM-IV) which replaces the term Multiple Personality Disorder (MPD). It is defined by the presence of two or more distinct identities or personality states that recurrently take control of the subject's behavior. Memory gaps in personal history with asymmetric selective amnesia are common. The basic problem in DID is a failure to integrate various aspects of identity, memory, and consciousness, usually due to intense trauma.

electroconvulsive therapy (ECT) The application of electricity to induce repetitive firings of brain neurons which produce seizures to treat psychiatric illnesses. Electroconvulsive therapy is a poorly understood technique by the lay population, but an extremely valuable and sometimes live-saving technique for patients suffering from a number of psychiatric disorders, particularly mood disorders [i.e., psychotic depression, catatonic states, some forms of bipolar (manic-depressive) disorders]. The technique was initially developed in the late 1930s and, after many changes and advances, is a safe and effective treatment modality.

eye movement desensitization and reprocessing (EMDR) A relatively new psychotherapeutic technique which utilizes artificially induced saccadic eye movements, concentration, and cognitive therapy in an attempt to deal with memories of trauma. The goals are to recover or reorganize memories then to reprocess or resturcture them in the context of therapy. It appears to be particularly useful in some cases of post traumatic stress disorder (PTSD).

narcosynthesis Use of pharmacological agents with the intention of altering mind states. In this article the term is used to describe the use of psychoactive pharmacological agents to elicit or facilitate the recovery of forgotten memories (i.e., truth serum). The most common medications used are sedative agents such as amobarbital (a barbiturate) or lorazepam (a benzodiazepine) in order to produce a semistuporous state, sometimes followed by the addition of a stimulant drug (such as amphetamines) in order to encourage the patient to uncover or discuss areas of psychological conflict. The theory behind this technique is that it lowers the patient's defenses and allows them to discuss psychologically charged and conflictual material by bypassing the patient's defenses. There is no proof that the information obtained by the use of this technique is in any way more truthful that that obtained in the course of interrogation or normal questioning.

suggestibility The ability to influence memory and/or behavior by suggestion.

trauma Bodily injury caused by violence; emotional shock (psychic trauma) with a lasting effect; a disordered psychic or behavioral state resulting from mental or emotional stress or physical injury.

D issociation can be understood as the mechanism by which we are able to separate mental processes and contents. Normally, the (nonpathological) mechanism of dissociation allows us to carry on more than one complex task or action simultaneously by keeping out of consciousness routine experiences or tasks. For example, it allows a person to watch a television program while knitting or cooking. Similarly, it allows individuals to successfully drive their car while listening and learning from a book on tape.

The mechanism of dissociation can also be elicited as an attempt to preserve some sense of control, safety, and identity in the face of overwhelming stress. Dissociation is usually elicited as a response to trauma, which threatens personal physical integrity, the safety of a loved one, or as a response of extreme isolation and abandonment. Unfortunately, dissociative defenses give victims a false sense of control while immediately providing temporary relief from the full impact of the traumatic experience. Because the use of dissociation allows people to separate themselves from the awareness of danger, some trauma victims act as if the event is not happening. Still others act as if it has never happened.

Pathological dissociation is usually the result of trauma. The form of trauma may vary widely from abandonment to overt physical trauma. Trauma may involve natural disasters (i.e., earthquakes, tornadoes, floods); man-made accidental disasters (i.e., war, nuclear plant explosions); large-scale man-made intentional disasters (i.e., Oklahoma city bombing, school shootings, terrorism); and more personal traumas, such as rape, car accidents, and even a traumatic medical procedure (i.e., surgery, chemotherapy). Probably the most publicized of all forms of trauma include the victims of childhood physical and sexual abuse.

The traumatic experience invariably objectifies its victim. The sense of helplessness engendered by such situations creates sudden challenges to normal ways of processing perception, cognition, affect, and relationships. Trauma in the form of both natural disaster and human assault causes disruption to normal cognitive and affective functions and forces its victims to reorganize mental, psychological, and physiological processes in an attempt to prevent the immediate impact of the trauma. This reorganization may take the form of various forms of dissociative processes, fostering separation from painful surroundings and realities (derealization) or from the victim's own body (depersonalization). Even though such defenses may initially be adaptive, directed at maintaining control at times of overwhelming stress, some trauma victims develop persistent dissociative, amnestic and anxietylike symptoms. The ultimate sequelae of trauma for a substantial minority of victims may be the development of traumatic stress disorders or dissociative disorders.

I. MODELS OF DISSOCIATION

There are several proposed models of dissociation. One such model suggests that some underlying neurological process (neurologic model), such as hemispheric disconnection or epilepsy, causes the manifested clinical symptoms of dissociation. The second model is the role enactment model. This model, also known as the social role demand theory, suggests that the symptoms associated to dissociative identity disorder (DID) represent an artificial construct rather than a true psychiatric disorder. The proponents of this model suggest that dissociation is a clinical artifact created out of conscious or unconscious needs on the part of patient to capture the attention of their doctors. Some have even suggest a direct iatrogenic etiology in which, according to them, therapists suggest the existence of symptoms. Finally, the Autohypnotic Model recognizes the connection between trauma, dissociation, and hypnotizability.

The autohypnotic model suggests that trauma victims dissociate or "forget" traumatic memories using self-hypnotic mechanisms in order to keep them out of consciousness because the reality is too painful to be faced. Memories may be stored at a conscious and/or unconscious level. The degree of amnesia varies, with some patients remembering all of the trauma and some only parts of it. Yet in some cases some memories are transformed and others interspersed with fantasy (i.e., some cases of ritual abuse or alien abduction). Later on, some memories slowly leak into the conscious mind. Because full memories are not available, it is difficult for patients to make sense of them. Some victims experience some of the "leaked" memories in the form of flashbacks or dreams. Other trauma victims isolate themselves due to the shame they feel in relation to the suspected trauma.

Even though dissociated memories may be temporarily unavailable to consciousness, they may continue to influence conscious (or unconscious) experiences and behavior. Clinical experience suggests that dissociated information continues to affect patients' moods, behavior, and cognitive processes. It is common for patients suffering from dissociative disorders to "feel" that something is wrong but to be unable to identify what. Many patients will experience a sense of discomfort or sometimes even panic when in specific situations. In fact, many of the symptoms experienced by trauma victims (i.e., flashbacks, psychosomatic symptoms) can be explained by the influence exerted by dissociated ("forgotten"or "inaccessible") memories.

Nevertheless, it is important to remember that not everyone exposed to trauma will develop dissociative symptoms. Studies conducted with war veterans suggest that less than 25% of soldiers exposed to trauma during combat go on to develop severe dissociation or posttraumatic syndrome. This suggests that other factors may be involved in the production of dissociative and anxiety symptoms. A leading factor may involve the developmental stage during which the trauma occurs. Available data suggests that, as a rule, the earlier in life the trauma occurs, the greater the psychological sequelae caused. This is probably due, in part, to the defense mechanisms and coping styles that the victim has had an opportunity to develop prior to the occurrence of the trauma, which in turn will modulate the way in which the victim perceives the experience and adapts to its impact and consequences.

II. DISSOCIATIVE DISORDERS

The Diagnostic and Statistical Manual (DSM-IV) recognizes four different dissociative disorders. These include **depersonalization disorder**, in which patients feel detached from their own mental processes or body and in which patients suffering from it describe a robotlike or out-of-body experience. **Dissociative amnesia** is a disorder in which patients exhibit an inability to recall important personal information. The memory loss (amnesia) may be for a part of the trauma (localized) or all (selective) of the traumatic experience. In extreme cases the amnesia may include personal information regarding their entire life (generalized amnesia). Patients suffering from **dissociative fugue** suddenly "go away," usually traveling far from home and developing a "new identity" while remaining amnesic to their past personal history. Patients suffering from **dissociative identity disorder** exhibit two or more "identities or personality states" accompanied by frequent memory gaps (i.e., amnesia).

A. Dissociative Amnesia (Psychogenic Amnesia)

The hallmark of this disorder is the inability to recall important personal information, usually of a traumatic or stressful nature, that is too extensive to be explained by ordinary forgetfulness. This is probably the most common of all dissociative disorders. In fact, amnesia is not only a psychiatric disorder by itself, but also a symptom, commonly found in a number of other dissociative and anxiety disorders. The highest incidence of dissociative amnesia has been described in the context of war and other natural and man-made disasters. Data suggests a direct relationship between the severity of the exposure to trauma and the incidence of amnesia.

In cases of dissociative amnesia patients are usually aware of their memory loss. Cases of dissociative amnesia can also be distinguished from amnesia of neurological origin because of their intact cognition and capacity to learn new information. The primary problem in amnesia patients is a difficulty in retrieval rather than encoding or storage; thus memory deficits are usually reversible. In fact, once the amnesia has cleared, normal memory function is resumed.

The epidemiology of this disorder is unknown. Nevertheless, dissociative amnesia is considered to be the most common of all dissociative disorders. The etiology of amnestic disorders is presumed to be posttraumatic, since they generally occur within the context of severe psychosocial stress. The duration of the disorder varies from a few days to a few years.

Even though it is possible to experience a single episode of amnesia, many patients have experienced several episodes during their lifetime. This is more common if the stresses that caused the initial episode are not resolved. The spontaneous resolution of the symptoms is rather common. In fact, many patients experience spontaneous recovery without more treatment than a protective environment. Sometimes more systematic treatment may be necessary.

The differential diagnosis of dissociative amnesia includes epilepsy, brain malignancy, head trauma, medication side effect (e.g., benzodiazepine use), chronic drug abuse and acute intoxication, cardiovascular and metabolic abnormalities, other dissociative disorders, organic brain syndrome, factitious disorder, and malingering.

B. Dissociative Fugue
(Psychogenic Fugue)

Dissociative fugue is characterized by the sudden, unexpected travel away from home or one's customary place of daily activities, with inability to recall some or all of one's past. As in the previous disorder, amnesia is present, causing a sense of confusion about personal identity. On occasion, patients assume a new identity.

Different from dissociative amnesia cases, patients suffering from fugue states appear "normal" to the lay observer. Patients usually exhibit no signs of psychopathology or cognitive deficit. Fugue patients differ from those with dissociative amnesia in that the former are usually unaware of their amnesia. Only upon resumption of their former identities do they recall past memories, at which time they usually become amnestic for experiences during the fugue episode. Often, patients suffering from fugue states take on an entirely new (and often unrelated) identity and occupation. In contrast to patients suffering from dissociative identity disorder, in fugue states the old and new identity do not alternate.

Not much is known regarding the etiology of this disorder. Nevertheless, the underlying motivating factor appears to be a desire to withdraw from emotionally painful experiences. Clinical data suggest that predisposing factors include extreme psychosocial stress such as war or natural and man-made disasters, personal and/or financial pressures or losses, heavy alcohol use, or intense and overwhelming acute stress such as assault or rape. The onset of some fugue episodes may occur during sleep or be associated with sleep deprivation.

As in cases of acute dissociative amnesia, the onset of the disorder is usually associated with a traumatic or overwhelming event accompanied by strong emotions such as depression, grief, suicidal or aggressive impulses, or shame. Dissociative fugue is the least understood dissociative disorder. This may be due to the fact that most of these patients do not present for treatment. Usually they do not come to the attention of medical personnel until they have recovered their identity and memory and return home. Typically, patients seek psychiatric attention once the fugue is over and are seeking to recover their original identity or retrieve their memory for events that occurred during the fugue.

C. Dissociative Identity Disorder
(Multiple Personality Disorder)

Dissociative identity disorder is defined by the presence of two or more distinct identities or personality states that recurrently take control of behavior. This disorder represents the failure to integrate various aspects of identity, memory, and consciousness. Characteristics of this disorder are memory disturbances and amnesia. The degree of amnesia is usually asymmetrical. That is, it selectively involves different areas of autobiographical information [i.e., "alters" (personality states or identities) differ in the degree of amnesia for the experiences of other alters].

Usually there is a primary or "host" personality that carries the patient's given name. Often the host is not completely aware of the presence of alters. Because of the presence of amnestic barriers, different personalities may have varying levels of awareness with respect to the existence of other personalities. On an average there are 2 to 4 personalities present at the time of diagnosis and usually up to 13 to 15 personalities are discovered during the course of treatment.

The symptoms that usually prompt patients or their families to seek treatment include memory deficits, moodiness, erratic and unpredictable behavior, depression, self-mutilation, suicidal ideation or attempts, or the overt manifestation of an alternate personality. Transition from one personality to another is usually sudden and is commonly triggered by environmental/interpersonal factors.

"Alter" identities may have different names, sexes, ages, and personal characteristics and often reflect various attempts to cope with difficult issues and problems. Personalities can either have a name and well-formed personalities, such as Rose, an 8-year-old girl, or be named after their function or description, such as "the Angry One."

The factors that can lead to the development of dissociative identity disorder are quite varied, but most authors seem to agree that physical and sexual abuse during childhood is the most common etiological factor in these patients. A history of sexual and/or physical abuse has been reported in 70–97% of patients suffering from dissociative identity disorder, with incest being the most common form of sexual trauma (68%). Other forms of childhood trauma that are associated with later development of DID include physical abuse other than sexual abuse (75%), neglect, confinement, severe intimidation with physical harm; witnessing physical or sexual abuse of a sibling; witnessing the violent death of a relative or close friend; traumatic physical illness to oneself, and near death experiences.

The actual incidence and prevalence of this disorder is unclear. The estimated prevalences of DID in the general population have been reported to range from 0.01 to 1%. The average time from the appearance of symptoms to an accurate diagnosis is 6 years. The average age at diagnosis is 29 to 35 years. It has been described to be more common in women than in men at a ratio of 3–9 : 1. Female patients are also reported to present more personalities (average of 15) than men (average of 8).

There is a high incidence of comorbid psychiatric and medical syndromes. Among the psychiatric symptoms, depression is the most common (85–88%), followed by insomnia, suicide attempts or gestures, self-destructive behaviors, phobias, anxiety, panic attacks, substance abuse, auditory and visual hallucinations, somatization, and psychoticlike behavior.

D. Depersonalization Disorder

Depersonalization is characterized by persistent or recurrent episodes of feelings of detachment or estrangement from oneself. Commonly individuals report feeling like a robot or as if they are living in a dream or a movie. Patients suffering from this condition describe their experience as if they were an outside observer of their own mental processes and actions. As opposed to delusional disorders and other psychotic processes, reality testing is intact. The phenomena associated with depersonalization are not uncommon. In fact, depersonalization is seen in a number of psychiatric and neurological disorders including agoraphobia and panic disorder, acute and posttraumatic stress disorder, schizophrenia, other dissociative disorders, personality disorders, acute drug intoxication or withdrawal, psychotic mood disorders, epilepsy, Meniere's disease, sensory and sleep deprivation, hyperventilation, and migraine headaches. In fact, people with no psychiatric condition can transiently experience symptoms of depersonalization. Because of this it is important that the diagnosis be applied only when the presence of symptoms cause severe impairment in functioning or marked distress.

The incidence and prevalence of this condition is unknown. The *symptom* of depersonalization has been described as being the third most common psychiatric symptom after depression and anxiety. It is believed that under severe stress up to 50% of all adults have experienced at least one single brief episode of depersonalization. On the other hand, up to 12–46% of average college students, nearly 30% of individuals exposed to life-threatening danger, and up to 40% of hospitalized psychiatric patients have experienced transient episodes of depersonalization. The sex distribution is unknown.

Theories for the etiology of this disorder range from the completely physiological, such as anatomical defects similar to epilepsy, to the purely psychological, such as a defense against painful and conflictual affects or the split between observing and participating ego/self, to combinations of all of the above as the result of a preformed functional response of the brain as an adaptation to overwhelming trauma. In any event, exposure to traumatic experiences seems to be the common etiological factor in this disorder. The course of the illness is usually chronic, with episodes of exacerbation usually following exposure to real or perceived stress.

III. TREATMENT

To date there are no controlled studies addressing the treatment of any of the dissociative disorders. All the information available reflects the experience and case reports of clinicians and specialized treatment centers. No single treatment modality has been systematically studied in this patient population.

Similarly, there are no established pharmacological treatments except for the use of benzodiazepines or barbiturates for drug-assisted interviews.

A. Dissociative Amnesia (Psychogenic Amnesia)

Before treatment is started it is necessary to establish that the amnesia or fugue state is of dissociative origin, ruling out the possibility of a neurological disorder such as temporal lobe epilepsy. Usually the initial step in the treatment is to provide a safe environment. Simply removing the person from the threatening situation and providing security and protection has allowed for spontaneous recovery. At times additional help may be needed to obtain the necessary biographical information or to facilitate the patient's recall. Among the adjuvants commonly used, hypnosis- and barbiturate- or benzodiazepine-facilitated recall are the most popular and better described.

No studies have addressed the efficacy of hypnosis in the treatment of dissociative amnesia. Nevertheless, most researchers in this area agree that hypnosis is a very useful tool for the recovery of repressed and dissociated memories. Once the amnesia has been reversed, treatment should be directed at restructuring the events and defining the factors that led to the development of the amnesia. This is followed by the establishment of appropriate defenses and mechanisms to prevent further need for dissociation. This is best done within the context of more extensive therapeutic work.

B. Dissociative Fugue (Psychogenic Fugue)

The treatment should involve provision of rest and assurances of safety, development of a trusting therapeutic relationship, recovery of personal identity, review of triggers or factors associated to the onset of the fugue, reprocessing of traumatic material, reintegration of traumatic memories into personal history, and returning the patient to his or her previous life.

Hypnosis and drug facilitated interviews have commonly been used during the stages of recovery of personal identity and memories associated with the onset of the fugue. Except for the facilitation of memory retrieval (narcosynthesis) or diminution of anxiety related to the therapeutic process, no pharmacotherapeutic agents have been systematically studied in the treatment of this condition. The treatments for acute dissociative amnesia and fugue states have been generally similar. Traditionally, hypnosis and Amytal narcosynthesis were the treatments of choice for memory recovery in amnesia and fugue. In fugue cases, treatment should be undertaken as quickly as possible while the repressed material is more readily accessible, before the memories have consolidated into a nucleus, thereby increasing the possibility of future flight episodes. Patients may also experience spontaneous memory recovery upon removal from the stressful situation, when exposed to cues from their past, or when they feel psychologically safe. Psychodynamic psychotherapy may help address the conflicts that precipitated the amnesia or fugue, thereby reducing subsequent dissociation under stress.

C. Dissociative Identity Disorder (Multiple Personality Disorder)

Treatment for DID generally involves (1) development of a therapeutic relationship based on safety and trust; (2) negotiation with the patient about cooperation with treatment; (3) development of a contract against harm to self or others; (4) history taking and understanding personality structure; (5) controlled abreaction and working through of traumatic experiences and frequently, repressed or dissociated material; (6) negotiating and modulating "conflicts" among aspects of identity and personality states; (7) development of mature and more appropriate, nondissociative defenses; and (8) working toward integration of alters.

Techniques such as hypnosis can facilitate control over dissociative episodes and integration of traumatic memories. Efforts at development of a social network and support system are helpful. Once integration has been achieved, further work is needed to deal with residual or renewed dissociative responses to external stress or internal conflicts and to further integration with society.

The treatment of DID is usually arduous, painful, and prolonged. Even though the ultimate goal is the achievement of integration, in some cases a reasonable degree of conflict-free collaboration among the personalities is all that can be achieved. Among clinicians, the most common treatment modality used is individual psychotherapy facilitated by the use of hypnosis. The average DID patient is seen twice a week for a period of about 4 years before integration is achieved. Multiple psychoactive drugs have been described for the treatment of associated symptoms. Clinical experience seems to suggest that patients suffering from DID do not experience spontaneous remission of their illness if left untreated.

Almost every psychotherapeutic and psychopharmacological treatment modality has been applied to patients suffering from DID, from group psychotherapy to family therapy, from antidepressants to antipsychotics to anticonvulsants to beta-blockers, from hypnosis to EMDR to ECT. All of them have been shown to have various degrees of success.

D. Depersonalization Disorder

Treatment modalities employed in the treatment of depersonalization disorder include paradoxical intention, record keeping and positive reward, flooding, psychodynamic psychotherapy, psychoeducation, psychostimulants, antidepressants, antipsychotics, anticonvulsants, benzodiazepines, electroconvulsive therapy, and hypnosis. In considering somatic treatments for depersonalization, it is important to determine whether the complaint represents the primary condition or whether it is secondary to another disorder. When an additional psychiatric diagnosis (i.e., anxiety or depression) is present and successfully treated, the symptoms of depersonalization usually improve or resolve. Thus, the most important aspect of the treatment of depersonalization disorder is careful assessment of possible psychiatric comorbidity and treatment of those conditions.

IV. HYPNOSIS AS A TREATMENT TOOL IN THE PSYCHOTHERAPY OF DISSOCIATIVE DISORDERS

Traumatic memories may be elicited or spontaneously emerge during the course of psychotherapy without the utilization of any technique for memory enhancement. Nevertheless, there may be instances when the judicious use of hypnosis as adjuvant to psychotherapy is recommended. For instance, hypnosis may facilitate access to repressed memories which have not emerged using other methods. Clinical experience suggests that many trauma victims respond to the traumatic event by using dissociative-like defenses during or after the trauma. In cases of repeated trauma, some victims "learn" how to trigger these dissociative responses (self-hypnosis-like defenses) in order to avoid further suffering.

Studies show that patients suffering from dissociative disorders are highly hypnotizable. Thus, if hypnotic-like states are elicited during traumatic experiences and some patients unknowingly used them in order to dissociate from their surroundings, it makes sense that the very entry into this same state could lead to the retrieval of memories and affects associated with the original trauma, as would be predicted by the theory of state-dependent memory. Hypnosis then can be useful both as a diagnostic tool and as a powerful therapeutic technique. Properly done, hypnotic techniques effectively facilitate symbolic restructuring of the traumatic experience.

The **Condensed Hypnotic Approach** uses hypnosis as a facilitator and has two major treatment goals: *to make conscious* previously repressed traumatic memories and to *develop a sense of congruence* between memories associated with the traumatic experience and patients' current realities and self-images. These goals can be achieved by the use of six consecutive and interdependent steps or stages. Each of them is designed to help patient's work through previously repressed memories while enhancing control over their dissociative mental processes. The six stages are confrontation, condensation, confession, consolation, concentration, and control.

During the first stage, *confrontation* of the trauma, patients come to terms with the factors and events associated to the trauma. The therapist's role at this time is that of a supportive nonjudgmental listener who avoids suggesting or implanting facts.

During the second stage, hypnosis is used to facilitate a *condensation* of the traumatic memories. There is little need to force patients to recount all the details of every traumatic episode. Thus, therapists can use hypnosis to define segments or episodes that summarize the traumatic experience without allowing patients to compulsively relive the entire trauma.

This is followed by the stage of *confession* of feelings and experiences that the patient is profoundly ashamed of and may have never told anyone before. During this stage the therapist should convey a sense of "being present" for the patient, while remaining neutral.

The recovery and confession of traumatic memories is often accompanied by an immense sense of shame and sorrow. Thus during the next stage, *consolation,* the therapist is more active and emotionally available to patients. It is appropriate to make empathic comments about the impact the experience must have had on them. Because of the frequent incidence of boundary violations during the episodes of abuse, therapists are warned to be extra careful regarding the ways in which care and empathy are expressed. At this point, therapists are reminded of the possibility of the development of a "traumatic transference" relationship. That is, patients may interpret the therapist's interest in their past as a pretext for making them suffer again. Because of the mobilization of painful emotions, therapists are experienced as being hurtful rather than helpful.

The intense *concentration* characteristic of hypnosis facilitates therapeutic work on selective traumatic memories. The structure of the hypnotic trance allows patients to "turn on" memories in the secure environment of the therapy session, while allowing patients to "shut them off" once the intended work has been completed at the end of the session. Hypnosis also provides the flexibility to work on one aspect of the memory without requiring patients to recall the entire trauma. Therefore, the hypnotic process promotes concentration on the desired goal while helping patients remain in control. Using the structured experience of the therapeutic trance, patients learn how think about the trauma in a constructive fashion.

Finally, patients should be helped to achieve an enhanced level of *control* while restoring a sense of mastery and order in their lives. In order to achieve that goal, therapists guide the therapeutic interaction in such a way that patients' sense of control over their memories is enhanced. Patients are allowed to "remember as much as can safely be remembered now" rather than been pushed to remember the entire

event at the therapists will or in a compulsive fashion. The therapeutic use of self-hypnosis teaches patients that they are in charge of the experience, thus they can regain control of their memories. It allows patients to learn to trust their own feelings, perceptions, and judgements. An important aspect in enhancing patients' sense of mastery is for them to learn not only how to control memories and symptoms, but, equally important, when to ask for help.

V. LEGAL RAMIFICATIONS OF MEMORY WORK

Every treatment involving potential repressed memories or childhood abuse must be preceded by a thorough explanation of the therapeutic and legal ramifications and a complete informed consent. Because of these potential problems some courts have restricted the admissibility of the testimony of hypnotized witnesses. Patients need to be warned about the fallibility surrounding hypnotically (or indeed, even nonhypnotically) recovered memories, including the possibilities of confabulation, concreting, and the difficulty of differentiating between fantasized or remembered memories. It is difficult to avoid potential contamination using any memory enhancement (i.e., imagery, hypnosis, EMDR, psychotherapy); thus one must use a neutral tone throughout the entire treatment. If hypnosis is to be used, therapists may guide patients through the experience, but at all times must avoid using leading or suggestive questions. The goal is to avoid contamination by introducing or suggesting information during the course of treatment. Indeed, hypnosis and any other non-hypnotic method of memory enhancement, including police interrogation, can distort memory by any of three ways: **confabulation**, the creation of pseudo-memories which are then reported as real; **concreting**, an unwarranted increased sense of confidence with which interrogated or hypnotized individuals report their memories, whether these are true or false; or as the result of an **additional recall trial**, that is, repeating it so many times that eventually it "sounds correct." More recently, there has been concern about the creation of "false memories." Nevertheless, we must remember that our mind is not an accurate tape recorder that registers every experience we have. Because of the way we register, encode, and recover filed memories, false memories are by no means rare. In fact, most people probably are in doubt about certain aspects of their past. At times it may be difficult to differentiate things that we have seen, said, done, dreamed, or just imagined. It is very likely that the most frequent source of false memory is the accounts we give to others of our experiences. Usually, such accounts are almost always made both more simple and interesting than the truth. In fact, memory can be understood as a capacity for the organization and reconstruction of past experiences and impressions in the service of present needs, fears, and interests. Thus, therapists must be aware that not every memory recovered with the use of hypnosis (or any other method of memory enhancement) is necessarily true. Hypnosis can facilitate improved recall of both true and confabulated material.

If memories of abuse are recovered, we do not encourage our patients to take legal action. There is no scientific evidence indicating that confrontation with alleged perpetrators of childhood abuse provides any therapeutic benefit to patients. The same is true for the pursuit of legal action or retribution toward perpetrators. It is impossible for therapists or the courts to be certain of the veracity of the memories recovered by either conventional therapy or hypnosis. Without objective external confirmation, therapists cannot distinguish memories that are real, those which are the result of confabulation, and the ones resulting from a combination of both. Furthermore, clinical experience in abuse cases suggests that not only would it be difficult to substantiate many of the allegations, but also little can be done in order to protect patients from the embarrassment, humiliation, and further "trauma" that would be imposed on them by virtue of the legal proceedings.

See Also the Following Articles

Amnesia; Disasters, Public, Effects of; Learned Helplessness; Multiple Personality Disorder; Trauma and Memory

Bibliography

American Psychiatric Association (1994). "Diagnostic and Statistical Manual of Mental Disorders, Fourth Edition." American Psychiatric Press, Washington, DC.

Braun, B. G., and Sachs, R. G. (1985). The development of multiple personality disorder: Predisposing, precipitating, and perpetuating factors *In* "Childhood Antecedents of Multiple Personality" (R. P Kluft, Ed.). American Psychiatric Press, Washington DC.

Chu, D. A., and Dill, D. L. (1990). Dissociative symptoms in relation to childhood physical and sexual abuse. *Am. J. Psychiat* 147, 887–892.

Coons, P. M., Bowman, E. S., and Pellow, T. A. (1989). Post-traumatic aspects of the treatment of victims of sexual abuse and incest. *Psychiat. Clin. North Am.* 12, 325–337.

Frischholz, E. J., Lipman, L. S., Braun, B. G., and Sachs, R. G. (1992). Psychopathology, hypnotizability, and dissociation. *Am. J. Psychiat.* 149, 1521–1525.

Hilgard, E. R. (1984). The hidden observer and multiple personality. *Int. J. Clin. Exp. Hyp.* 32, 248–253.

Kilhstrom, J. F. (1990). Repression, dissociation and hypnosis. *In* "Repression and Dissociation" (J. L. Singer, Ed.), pp. 180–208). Univ. of Chicago Press, Chicago.

Kluft, R. P. (Ed.) (1985). Childhood antecedents of multiple personality. *In* "Clinical Insights." American Psychiatric Press, Washington DC.

Kluft, R. P. (1993). Multiple Personality Disorder. *In* "Dissociative Disorders. A Clinical Review" (D. Spiegel, Ed.), pp 17–40. Sidran, Lutherville, MD.

Maldonado, J. R., and Spiegel, D. (1994). Treatment of post traumatic stress disorder. *In* "Dissociation: Clinical, Theoretical and Research Perspectives" (S. J. Lynn and J. Rhue, Eds.), pp. 215–241. Guilford, New York.

Maldonado, J. R., and Spiegel, D. (1998). Trauma, dissociation and hypnotizability. *In* "Trauma, Memory and Dissociation" (R. Marmar and D. Bremmer, (Eds.), pp. 57–106). American Psychiatric Press, Washington, DC.

Maldonado, J. R. Butler, L., and Spiegel, D. (1997). Treatment of dissociative disorders. *In* "A Guide to Treatments That Work." (P. E. Nathan and J. M. Gorman, Eds.), pp. 423–446. Oxford Univ. Press, Oxford, UK.

Nemiah, J. C. (1985). Dissociative disorders. *In* "Comprehensive Textbook of Psychiatry" (H. Kaplan and B. Sadock, Eds.), 4th ed., pp. 942–957. Williams & Wilkins, Baltimore, MD.

Putman, F. W. (1993). Dissociative phenomena. *In* "Dissociative Disorders: A Clinical Review" (D. Spiegel, Ed.), pp 1–14. Sidran Press, Lutherville, MD.

Ross, C. A., Norton, G. R., and Wozney, K. (1989). Multiple personality disorder: An analysis of 236 cases. *Can. J. Psychiat.* 34, 413–418.

Spiegel, D. (1984). Multiple personality as a post-traumatic stress disorder. *Psychiat. Clin. North Am.* 7, 101–110.

Spiegel, D. (1990). Hypnosis, dissociation and trauma: Hidden and overt observers. *In* "Repression and Dissociation" (J. L. Singer, Ed.), pp. 121–142. Univ. of Chicago Press, Chicago.

Spiegel, D., and Cardena, E. (1991). Disintegrated experience: The dissociative disorders revisited. *J. Abnorm. Psychol.* **100**(3), 366–378.

Spiegel, D., and Maldonado, J. R. (1999). Dissociative disorders. *In* "Textbook of Psychiatry" (R. Hales, S. C. Yudofsky, and J. A. Talbott, Eds.), 3rd ed., pp. 711–738. American Psychiatric Press, Washington, DC.

Spiegel, D., and Vermutten, E. (1994). Physiological correlates of hypnosis and dissociation. *In* "Dissociation: Culture, Mind and Body" (D. Spiegel, Ed.), pp 185–209. American Psychiatric Press, Washington, DC.

van der Kolk, B. A., Perry, J. C., and Herman, J. L. (1991). Childhood origins of self-destructive behavior. *Am. J. Psychiat.* **148**, 1665–1671.

van der Kolk, B. A., McFarlane, A. C., and Weisaeth, L. (Eds.) (1996). "Traumatic Stress: The Effects of Overwhelming Experience on Mind, Body and Society." Guilford, New York.

Distress

Gerald Matthews

University of Cincinnati

I. Introduction
II. Assessment of Distress
III. Influences on Distress
IV. Personality and Distress
V. Psychological Concomitants of Distress

GLOSSARY

affect A general term for emotional or feeling states, including specific emotions such as anxiety and depression.

neuroticism A personality trait associated with a predisposition to experience negative affect.

self-regulation The motivational and cognitive processes controlling goal-directed personal adaptation to the external environment.

stress A general term for the processes and responses associated with adaptation to demanding or challenging environments.

trait A personal disposition or characteristic showing long-term stability and influencing behavior in a range of situations.

I. INTRODUCTION

"Distress" is an imprecise term that typically refers to unpleasant subjective stress responses such as anxiety and depression. It is also sometimes used to describe behaviors and medical symptoms ("somatic distress"). The concept of distress derives from H. Selye's General Adaptation Syndrome (GAS): the generalized and developing physiological and psychological stress responses that may be elicited by noxious or threatening life events. Often, stress responses are characterized by difficulties in adapting to the external stressor, i.e., distress, although stress may sometimes have a stimulating, energizing effect ("eustress"). Distress may thus be conceptualized as the internal "strain" provoked by an external "stressor." However, this simple metaphor has been largely superceded by the view of R. Lazarus that stress responses reflect dynamic person–environment relationships. From this perspective, distress signals that adaptation to environmental demands is taxing or unsuccessful.

This article reviews the assessment of distress, the roles of situational factors and personality in generating distress, and its psychological significance, including clinical implications. Contemporary research on distress is dominated by two themes. The first is the extent to which a global distress concept is to be preferred to more specific stress responses such as anxiety and depression. The second theme is that distress must be understood within a wider framework of the person's active attempts to adapt to the physical and social environment.

II. ASSESSMENT OF DISTRESS

Distress is a broad label for a variety of stress responses, and so there is no single, generally accepted means of assessment. Typically, measurement of distress is questionnaire based, although, especially in animal and child research, distress may be operationalized as behaviors such as vocalizations. Approaches to assessment vary in two respects: (1) the timescale over which distress is measured and (2) the breadth of distress symptoms encompassed. Distress is typically assessed over the following timescales: (1) A transient state lasting for a few minutes; i.e., the person's immediate state of mind. (2) An episodic condition lasting for weeks or months; e.g., the distress provoked by a life event or a short-lived clinical disorder. (3) A personality trait, such as trait anxiety, which may show stability over decades.

The narrowest operationalizations of distress focus on negative affects such as anxiety and depression. C. D. Spielberger has developed questionnaires that assess these constructs at state and trait levels. Depending on the context, other indices of distress may be used in tandem with scales for negative affect. Distress may also describe cognitive responses, such as worry, lowered self-esteem, and lack of perceived control. In life-event research, indices of distress may include difficulties in social functioning and health problems. Specialized measures are used in specific contexts, such as scales for marital distress, trauma symptoms, and health concerns. Somatic distress measures have been developed on the basis that self-reported medical symptoms tend to intercorrelate. Hence, different measures of "distress" probably relate to different underlying constructs.

Distress may be defined more precisely through multivariate psychometric research. Studies of mood have identified orthogonal dimensions of negative affect and positive affect such that negative affect is a superordinate category relating to tension, unhappiness, irritability, and other negative affects, whereas positive affect covers states such as happiness and energy. For example, clinical anxiety and depression measures show considerable overlap (Clark, L. A. and Watson, D. (1991) *J. Abnorm. Psychol.* 100, 316–336). As a transient state, "distress" might then be identified with negative affect. Studies of episodic distress reactions and of personality traits have also supported the distinction between positive and negative affect. Other psychometric studies suggest that distress might also be seen as a cognitive-affective syndrome, in which negative affect is meshed with negative self-referent cognitions such as lack of perceived control.

III. INFLUENCES ON DISTRESS

Distress reflects both situational influences such as life events and intrapersonal influences such as personality traits. This section reviews situational influences, investigated either through controlled experiments or through correlational studies of real-life stressors. Events that threaten or damage an individual's well-being often provoke distress. Environmental factors promoting distress include (1) physical factors such as loud noise, (2) social factors such as criticism by others, and (3) ill health. Adverse affects of agents of these kinds are well documented, although there is considerable variation in their effects across individuals and across different occasions. However, there are competing psychological, cognitive, and social accounts of the mechanisms that link these external stressors to phychological stress responses.

A. Physiological Influences

Physiological studies of distress focus primarily on the brain mechanisms that may output and regulate negative affect. Evidence for a biological basis for distress is provided most directly by studies of brain damage in humans and animals. For example, damage to the amygdala may provoke extreme emotional responsivity. Learning studies link the central nucleus of this structure to fear conditioning such that it may function as the brain's "emotional computer" (LeDoux, J. 1994, *Sci. Am.* 270, 32–39). In humans, damage to the frontal lobes seems to provoke disinhibition syndromes in which disruption of emotional response is accompanied by loss of control of behavior. Pharmacological studies allow negative affects to be linked to the neurotransmitters sensitive to the drug concerned. Different negative emotions may be controlled by different brain systems: anxiolytic drugs operate through benzodiazepine receptors and antidepressants such as fluoxetine (Prozac) through serotonergic pathways. Another line of evidence is provided by psychophysiological studies that link anxiety states to the "fight–flight" reaction and the sympathetic branch of the autonomic nervous system. More generally, it has been suggested that both low and high levels of physiological arousal are accompanied by negative emotion.

Historically, the distress concept has been important to physiological research, for example, as a concomitant of Selye's GAS. Contemporary studies focus more on specific negative emotions, which appear to be influenced by different neural systems. The aim of contemporary work is not just to establish correspondences between subjective affect and brain processes, but to establish that affective responses are embedded within a functional system which controls the organism's adaptation to a particular type of stimulus or event. J. A. Gray has developed a detailed animal model within which anxiety is an output of a system supported by circuits in the septum, hippocampus, and frontal lobes. The septohippocampal system is activated by signals of punishment, nonreward, novelty, and fear. It operates to inhibit ongoing behavior and to focus attention on the threat. Hence, subjective distress is a concomitant of these adaptive processes. There is extensive evidence on the effects of anxiolytic drugs in animals which supports the model, but its application to human emotional distress and anxiety remains contentious.

B. Cognitive Influences

Cognitive models of stress are supported by experimental studies demonstrating that both the psychological and physiological impacts of stressors are moderated by the person's beliefs and expectancies. For example, negative moods may be induced by suggestive techniques such as reflecting on negative events or making statements that one is unhappy. Distress in the workplace reflects not just work demand, but also perceived control and decision latitude. Appraisal theories of emotion seek to link affect to the person's evaluation of external stimuli and their personal significance. Anxiety may then relate to appraisals of personal threat and uncertainty and depression to uncontrollable personal harm. Appraisal is not necessarily accessible to consciousness, and there may be several distinct appraisal processes operating in tandem.

The transactional stress theory of R. S. Lazarus embeds appraisal within a wider matrix of person–environment interaction within which negative emotions are tied to core themes describing the person–environment relationship. Core relational themes also relate to action tendencies. Transactional theory emphasizes the person's active attempts to cope with threatening or damaging events. In general, distress is likely to develop when the people appraise themselves as failing to cope adequately and as lacking in control over significant events. Contemporary theory also emphasizes the differing relational themes associated with different negative emotions. The dynamic nature of the stress process is supported by evidence for reciprocal relationships between distress and life events (Kaplan, A. B., and Damphousse, K. R. 1997, *Stress Med.* 13, 75–90), and between distress and health perceptions (Farmer, M. M., and Ferraro, K. F. 1997, *J. Health Soc. Behav.* 38, 298–311).

C. Social Influences

Disruption of social relationships associated with bereavement, marital discord, and unemployment are among the most potent factors eliciting distress. Conversely, availability of social support often functions to alleviate stress responses. Social psychologists characterize as inadequate attempts to locate distress solely within the individual. Instead, distress may reflect people's discourses about their problems and interpersonal interactions within a social and cultural context. For example, K. Oatley has attributed depression to loss of socially defined roles. Social psychologists also emphasize the importance of the expression and display of emotion, which reflects social motivations and norms.

IV. PERSONALITY AND DISTRESS

A. Neuroticism and Negative Affect

Some individuals appear to be generally more distress prone than others. Psychometric and experimental studies identify stable personality traits that relate to the person's predisposition to experience negative emotion. H. J. Eysenck identified a dimension of neuroticism associated with a low threshold for emotional arousal. A similar dimension comprises one of the factors described by the Five Factor Model of personality. In controlled studies neuroticism predicts negative moods such as depression and anxiety, although the strength of the relationship varies with situational stressors. Neuroticism is also elevated in patients suffering from emotional disorders. Longitudinal studies suggest that neuroticism is a factor predisposing clinical disorder, although there is some reciprocity between the personality trait and disorder. Neuroticism also relates to self-reported somatic distress. It remains controversial whether more neurotic individuals are genuinely more prone to illness or whether they are just prone to complain about physical symptoms (Stone, S. V., and Costa, P. T. Jr., 1990, in H. S. Friedman (Ed.), "Personality and Disease", Wiley). In addition, both the Eysenck and Five Factor models include an extraversion–introversion factor. Extraversion relates primarily to happiness and positive affect, but also correlates negatively with distress measures to some extent. One influential view is that neuroticism is essentially a dimension of negative affectivity, whereas extraversion may be identified with positive affect, although this perspective may be oversimplified. Current personality models generally adopt an interactionist perspective such that responses such as distress depend on the interaction of person and situation factors. Hence, although more neurotic individuals are more vulnerable to distress, the extent to which they experience greater distress than less neurotic persons on a given occasion varies with situational factors. A more subtle view of neuroticism is also suggested by life-event research. Consistent with the negative affectivity hypothesis, more neurotic individuals seem to experience life events as more distressing. However, neurotic persons also seem to experience a higher frequency of life events, which may reflect

behavioral difficulties in adapting to life circumstances (Magnus, K. *et al.*, 1993, *J. Personal. Soc. Psychol.* 65, 1046–1053).

B. Other Traits

Various more narrowly defined traits are associated with vulnerability to distress. Spielberger's anxiety and depression measures are among the best known. According to Spielberger, trait anxiety represents a predisposition to experience transient state anxiety in threatening environments, but, consistent with interactionism, the trait-anxious individual does not experience state anxiety on all occasions. Experimental studies suggest that trait anxiety correlates with state anxiety under conditions of ego threat, such as personal criticism. Negative affect is central to the definition of the Spielberger traits. Other traits such as optimism–pessimism, self-focus of attention, and attributional style are cognitively defined, but nevertheless correlate with distress indices.

Distress-related traits tend to intercorrelate with each other and also with broader measures of neuroticism and negative affectivity. One view is that the various traits predict distress because they overlap with neuroticism, and the narrower trait constructs may add little to the broad trait. It is plausible that neglect of neuroticism as a confound of other traits has added unduly to the complexity of the field. Nevertheless, there is evidence for discriminative validity for traits such as optimism–pessimism and self-focus of attention: distress is best predicted from multiple traits.

C. Contextualized Traits

Neuroticism and other traits appear to act as generalized factors predisposing distress across a variety of contexts. However, in many cases people possess traits linked to specific contexts, which predict distress over and above more generalized traits. A paradigmatic case is that of test anxiety. I. G. Sarason has developed scales that ask respondents specifically about their thoughts and feelings when required to take tests and examinations. People show stable individual differences in vulnerability to test anxiety, which predict how they feel and perform in examination settings. Researchers have focused on anxiety in various other settings, using measures of social anxiety, dental anxiety, computer anxiety and so forth. Such measures typically correlate with neuroticism but have better predictive validity in the appropriate context. The contexualized trait may reflect both neuroticism and the person's more specific stable cognitions of the context concerned. Much of this work has focused on anxiety as a distress symptom, but it is likely that contextualized traits predict other distress symptoms in a similar way. For example, individuals vulnerable to driver stress are prone to experience both anxiety and unhappiness during vehicle operation.

D. Psychological Explanations for Distress Vulnerability

There are competing explanations for individual differences in vulnerability to distress. Biological and cognitive models have been most fully articulated. Social psychological explanations are also relevant, although progress has been retarded by the reluctance of social psychologists to accept the validity of traits. Biological explanations are bolstered by demonstrations from kinship and adoption studies that distress-related traits are partially inherited. The tendency for distress vulnerability to run in families relates more to genetic predisposition than to the influence of the common family environment (Loehlin, J. C. 1992, "Genes and Environment in Personality Development," Sage). There is also an extensive literature on psychophysiological and biochemical correlates of neuroticism and other traits, although results are often weak or inconsistent. Hence, the pathways connecting genes for distress-prone personality to specific brain mechanisms are poorly understood, although various theories have been advanced. Eysenck claimed that neuroticism related to the sensitivity of the limbic system to emotional arousal. Gray has proposed a more fine-grained theory, which links trait anxiety to sensitivity of the septohippocampal system.

Cognitive explanations are supported by evidence that traits relate to the constructs of the transactional model of stress, especially appraisal and coping. Many studies have shown that neuroticism, trait anxiety and trait depression relate to a distinctive style

of cognition of environmental demands. Individuals with these characteristics are prone to a variety of negative self-appraisals; they appraise the world as demanding and threatening and themselves as ineffective in dealing with external demands. More neurotic individuals are prone to cope with potentially stressful events through emotion-focused strategies such as ruminating on their problems or criticizing themselves. Such strategies are frequently maladaptive and may sometimes even exacerbate the problem and contribute to clinical disorder. To a lesser degree, neuroticism also relates to avoidance of the problem and to reduced task-focused coping (Endler, N. S., and Parker, J. 1990, *J. Personal. Soc. Psychol.* 58, 844–854).

V. PSYCHOLOGICAL CONCOMITANTS OF DISTRESS

Distress has various behavioral correlates including impairment of objective performance, bias in selective attention, and overt clinical symptoms. These findings are explained by theories of self-regulation pioneered by C. S. Carver and M. F. Scheier and elaborated as a general theory of distress by A. Wells and G. Matthews. In these models, self-regulation operates homeostatically to reduce the discrepancies between actual and preferred status. Distress signals self-discrepancy and the need for coping efforts to reduce self-discrepancy and maintain adaptation to the external environment. The regulatory system may have physiological as well as psychological expressions. It also operates within a social context in that interactions with others provide strong cues towards actual status and ideal status reflects in part societal and cultural norms. Experimental studies of attention and performance identify biases in the cognitions supporting self-regulation, which may be the source of clinical disorders associated with distress.

A. Performance Impairment

Trait and state distress measures are associated with slower and/or less accurate performance on a variety of tasks. Both anxiety and depression tend to be associated with performance impairment. Contextualized distress measures are also typically associated with performance impairments within the context concerned: for example, test anxiety predicts poorer examination performance. Anxiety studies show that it is the cognitive rather than the emotional aspects of the anxiety state which interfere with performance. Self-referent worries appear to be especially damaging because attention and/or working memory may be diverted from the task at hand onto personal preoccupations. Detrimental effects of depression have been similarly ascribed to worry and rumination. Loss of performance may reflect loss of attentional resources, controlled processing, or working memory.

The impact of distress on performance depends on motivational factors. Performance may be maintained or even enhanced when good performance is appraised as instrumental in relieving distress through compensatory effort. Conversely, decrements are more likely when motivation and effort are low. Maintenance of performance effectiveness through effort is more likely in anxiety than in depressed states. It appears that impairment is not a fixed "cost" of distress, but a consequence of a style of self-regulation which promotes worry, self-focus of attention, and emotion-focused coping at the expense of performance goals.

B. Cognitive Bias

Distress is often associated with enhanced processing of negative stimuli. Such effects have been demonstrated in studies of experimentally induced moods, in studies comparing the performance of distressed patients with controls, and in studies comparing nonclinical groups selected for high and low distress. Some of the most reliable effects are found in studies of anxiety and selective attention. Anxious individuals are slow to name the color in which threat-related words are printed (the emotional Stroop effect) and also appear to attend preferentially to threat stimuli in other paradigms. Other distressed groups are similarly biased toward negative stimuli congruent with their source of distress. These effects may reflect either an automatic bias toward in-threat stimuli in vulnerable individuals or a consequence

of deliberately chosen strategies. Biases in memory are most reliable in studies of depression and negative mood, although comparable anxiety effects are also documented. Depressed individuals tend to show enhanced recall for negative events or stimuli at the expense of positive events. These effects seem most reliable when the test of memory is explicit rather than implicit and when some active processing of the memorized material is required. Various other tasks, including judgement and decision-making, also show cognitive bias. From the self-regulative perspective, distress may relate to the extent to which the person balances the goal of maintaining awareness of threat against focus on the immediate task at hand.

C. Clinical Disorder

Distress is a central symptom of both mood and anxiety disorders. A simple view of clinical distress is that it represents the upper extreme of a continuum of vulnerability to negative emotion. However, clinical disorder involves qualitative abnormalities of behavior in addition to distress such as avoidance of challenging situations, self-harm, and difficulties in social interaction. Distress in clinical depression and anxiety is bound up with problems in behavioral adaptation to everyday life. Self-regulative approaches to understanding distress contribute to understanding the maladaptive nature of these disorders. Central to both anxiety and depression are stable but false-negative beliefs about the self, which may be represented as "schemas" (Beck, A. T. 1967, "Depression: Causes and Treatment," Univ. of Philadelphia Press). Anxious persons believe themselves to be especially vulnerable to threats of certain kinds, whereas the depressed patient experiences cognitions of lack of self-worth and hopelessness. Cognitions and behaviors differ across clinical conditions, but, in general, unrealistic negative self-beliefs feed into faulty appraisal of the person's place in the external world, choice of ineffective coping strategies such as worry, and consequent distress.

The view of distress as a sign of maladaptive self-regulation has implications for therapy. In mild, subclinical distress conditions, it may be sufficient for the person to learn specific coping skills that permit them to manage the specific situations that provoke distress. For example, individuals with mild social anxiety may be helped by explicit instruction in social skills. Distress is alleviated both through the person's increased confidence and positive self-appraisal and through the likelihood that the person's greater skill will lead to more positive outcomes in the problematic situation. In more severe cases, stress management techniques such as skills training fail to address the underlying cognitive distortions which drive both distress and behavioral problems. Cognitive-behavior therapy seeks to uncover and modify faulty cognitions through a variety of techniques. Empirical studies show that clinical improvement in behavior and affect is accompanied by a decline in cognitive bias.

See Also the Following Articles

ALARM PHASE AND GENERAL ADAPTATION SYNDROME; ANXIETY; DEPRESSION AND MANIC-DEPRESSIVE ILLNESS; NEGATIVE AFFECT

Bibliography

Carver, C. S., and Scheier, M. F. (1981). "Attention and Self-Regulation: A Control Theory Approach to Human Behavior." Springer-Verlag, Berlin.

Eyenck, H. J., and Eysenck, M. W. (1985). "Personality and Individual Differences: A Natural Science Approach." Plenum, New York.

Gray, J. A. (1987). "The Psychology of Fear and Stress," 2nd ed. Cambridge Univ. Press, Cambridge, UK.

Lazarus, R. S. (1991). "Emotion and Adaption." Oxford Univ. Press, Oxford.

Matthews, G., and Deary, I. J. (1998). "Personality Traits." Cambridge Univ. Press, Cambridge, UK.

Oatley, K. (1992). "Best-Laid Schemes: The Psychology of Emotions." Cambridge Univ. Press, Cambridge, UK.

Sarason, I. G. (1984). Stress, anxiety and cognitive interference: Reactions to tests. *J. Personal. Soc. Psychol.* 46, 929–938.

Selye, H. (1976). "The Stress of Life." McGraw–Hill, New York.

Spielberger, C. D. (1972). Anxiety as an emotional state. *In* "Anxiety: Current Trends in Theory and Research" (C. D. Spielberger, Ed.), Vol. 1. Academic Press, London.

Thayer, R. E. (1996). "The Origin of Everyday Moods." Oxford Univ. Press, Oxford, UK.

Wells, A., and Matthews, G. (1994). "Attention and Emotion: A Clinical Perspective." Erlbaum, Hove, Sussex.

Diurnal-Nocturnal Effects

see Circadian Rhythms

Divorce, Children of

Kathleen N. Hipke, Irwin N. Sandler, and Sharlene A. Wolchik

Arizona State University

GLOSSARY

effect size A statistical indicator, expressed in standard deviation units, of the magnitude of the relation between two variables.

externalizing A constellation of psychological symptoms indicative of acting-out behavior, such as aggression and conduct problems.

internalizing A constellation of psychological symptoms experienced internally, such as depression and anxiety.

meta-analysis A quantitiative method of literature review in which measures of central tendency and variation are obtained for outcomes examined across multiple studies.

moderator A variable which affects the direction and/or strength of the relation between an independent or predictor variable (e.g., divorce) and a dependent or criterion variable (e.g., a child's mental health).

A large proportion of American children must cope with the stress of parental divorce every year, raising national concern over its consequences for their adjustment. Understanding the effects of parental divorce on children requires an understanding of the stress associated with divorce, the relation between divorce and children's mental health, and the factors which may serve to increase or decrease the stressfulness of this family transition for children.

I. DIVORCE-RELATED STRESS

Parental divorce has become a common experience for children. On the whole, the rate of divorce in the United States has increased over the course of the 20th century, with a particularly rapid rise beginning in the decades of the 1960s and 1970s. Currently, close to half of all marriages end in divorce, affecting over one-and-a-half million children a year. Although divorce rates vary among families of different demographic profiles, demographers estimate that 40% of all children born in the 1990s will live in a divorced, single-parent home at some point before they reach the age of 16.

Parental divorce is not a singular event. Rather, it marks a multitude of stressful changes and disruptions in children's social and physical environments which occur before, during, and after parental separation. For example, interparental conflict often begins many months and/or years prior to separation, can escalate around separation and/or divorce, and often continues well after separation as parents negotiate new parenting-related issues such as child custody, visitation arrangements, and child support.

As in the case of interparental conflict, many of the stressful changes and experiences faced by children of divorce occur in the family domain, involve interpersonal loss and/or conflict, and are not easily controllable by children. Several of these changes occur in children's relationships with parents. Despite an increasing emphasis on joint custody in many states, over 80% of all children of divorce still reside primarily with their mothers. Consequently, parental separation often means loss of daily contact with fathers. Moreover, father contact with children becomes increasingly infrequent over time. Relationships with mothers also change. Custodial mothers report high levels of stress as they negotiate the dual task of adjusting to the dissolution of marriage as well as to a new lifestyle. Juggling single parenthood, work demands, legal matters, and the renegotiation of social relationships places custodial mothers at increased risk for psychological distress and physical illness. Maternal stress and distress, in turn, have been linked to disruptions in parenting behavior.

Following divorce, custodial mothers are often less supportive, affectionate, and consistent in their discipline practices and engage in more conflict with children. In addition to erratic maternal behavior, children with continued father involvement may also face the challenge of residing in two households, where rules and discipline practices vary.

Many newly divorced families also face financial stress. Although both mothers and fathers may experience a decline in standard of living following divorce, women have traditionally experienced greater loss. Income loss can result in potentially stressful changes for children including moving residence, changing neighborhoods, and changing schools. While these transitions involve the loss of material possessions, children also face the loss of friends, teachers, and other important members of their social support networks.

When asked about the various changes that arise following divorce, children, parents, and clinicians who work with children of divorce agree that the most stressful experiences children face occur in the nuclear family domain. These include being blamed for the divorce, verbal and/or physical interparental conflict, and derogation of one parent by another. Other experiences perceived as highly stressful by children include derogation of parents by relatives or neighbors, having to give up possessions, and maternal psychological distress.

In addition to divorce-specific stress, 40% of divorced couples remarry before their youngest child reaches age 18. While remarriage can improve the financial and emotional support provided to parents, it requires complex family reconfiguration. For children, this includes the addition of a stepparent as well as other step-kin relations such as step-siblings, grandparents, and other extended family members. When additional children are born into the family following remarriage, half-sibling relationships are created. The incorporation of new members into the household alters family dynamics, including relationships with biological parents. In addition, children may face physical transitions such as an additional residential move or sharing of a room with other children. Remarriages are also more likely than first marriages to end in divorce. Thus, many children of divorce face multiple family transitions over the course of their childhood, each of which brings a new set of stressful changes to which children must adapt.

II. MENTAL HEALTH CONSEQUENCES

Divorce increases children's risk for developing mental health problems. Amato and Keith (1991a, *Psychol. Bull.* **110**, 26–46) used meta-analysis to synthesize findings from 92 studies conducted between 1957 and 1990 comparing children in divorced and intact families on several indicators of adjustment. The largest group difference, favoring children in intact families, was for conduct problems. Children from divorced homes engaged in more misbehavior, were more aggressive, and/or had higher rates of delinquency. Children from divorced homes also showed greater maladjustment in the areas of psychological adjustment (i.e., depression, anxiety, happiness), social adjustment, self-concept, and school achievement.

The importance of differences in children's adjustment across divorced and intact family configurations has been debated. Effect sizes are small to moderate. Amato and Keith's synthesis revealed evidence to suggest that more methodologically rigorous studies find smaller effects and that as divorce has become more common with time, the magnitude of the effects on children's mental health have declined. Moreover, findings from prospective longitudinal studies suggest that the effects are further reduced, albeit still statistically significant, when children's mental health prior to divorce is controlled. Unhealthy family processes and poor child mental health may exist several years prior to divorce, suggesting that it is not the divorce per se that causes maladjustment. These findings are consistent with the above view that divorce serves as a marker for a series of stressful family interactions and changes that take place before, during, and after divorce. Clinically, children of divorce do seem to represent a more seriously distressed group. They show higher levels of clinically significant psychological disorder. Moreover, adolescents from divorced homes engage in more high-risk behavior with potentially long-term consequences. For example, adolescents from divorced homes are more likely than those from intact homes to drop out of school, become sexually active or pregnant at an earlier age, and use drugs or alcohol.

Although some researchers have emphasized the transitory nature of divorce-related adjustment problems for children of divorce, recent longitudinal studies indicate that children are at elevated risk for difficulties several years after parental separation (e.g., Hetherington *et al.* 1992, *Monogr. Soc. Res. Child Dev.* **57**, 1–206). Evidence for negative consequences persisting into adolescence and adulthood is also accumulating. Chase-Lansdale and colleagues (1995, *Child Dev.* **66**, 1614–1634) recently found that children from divorced homes are at increased risk for emotional disorders at age 23, after controlling for their predivorce cognitive characteristics, emotional problems, and socioeconomic status at age 7. In a meta-analysis of 37 studies which compared adult children of from divorced and intact homes, Amato and Keith (1991b, *J. Marriage Fam.* **53**, 43–58) found adult children of divorce to be functioning more poorly on a range of indicators including depression, life satisfaction, marital quality and stability, educational attainment, income, occupational prestige, and physical health. Researchers have speculated that these long-term consequences are the result of disruptions in normal development during adolescence.

III. VARIABILITY IN RESPONSE

Undisputed is the fact that while children of divorce are at elevated risk for adjustment problems, there is tremendous variability in response. The majority show no adverse effects relative to children raised in intact families. Thus, research on children of divorce has shifted over the past few decades from examining the mental health consequences of divorce toward understanding why some children are adversely affected by divorce while others are not. Researchers have examined exposure to stress, parent–child relationships, and child characteristics as moderators of the relation between divorce and children's mental health.

A. Exposure to Stress

Greater exposure to stressful divorce-related changes is associated with increased mental health

problems among children. The overall frequency of divorce-related changes faced by children and families, as assessed by divorce events checklists, relates positively to difficulties in the domains of internalizing and externalizing symptoms, self-concept, and social and academic competence. Children exposed to more divorce-related changes also show maladaptive cognitions, including a reduced sense of perceived control over their environments. Recent research indicates that both the valence and stability of divorce-related experiences are important determinants of their relation to children's adjustment (Sandler *et al.* 1991, *Am. J. Commun. Psychol.* **19**, 501–520). Negative changes in children's environments are more harmful than positive changes. The maintenance of stable, positive experiences within the family, however, appears to help preserve a sense of stability and is related to fewer adjustment problems.

Studies have also examined the relations between specific types of divorce stress and children's mental health. For example, more limited economic resources postdivorce is related to increased maladjustment. There is increasing consensus that exposure to interparental conflict may be one of the most potent determinants of children's divorce adjustment. In studies with intact families, interparental conflict has consistently been shown to have a negative impact on children's adjustment. Similarly, in divorced families, children exposed to higher amounts of conflict evidence more adjustment problems. Researchers have suggested that postdivorce conflict, which often centers around childrearing issues, may be particularly harmful as it is more likely to create loyalty conflicts and foster a sense of self-blame among children.

B. Parent–Child Relationships

The degree to which the quality of children's relationships' with their parents is disrupted following divorce is predictive of adjustment. Children whose custodial mothers provide high levels of warmth, affection, and effective, consistent discipline following divorce exhibit fewer behavior problems, higher self-esteem, and better academic performance than children with low-quality mother–child relationships. Moreover, several studies show that high quality mother–child relationships mitigate the negative effects of divorce-related stress on children's adjustment. Less is known about how the role of noncustodial father–child relationships may serve to impact children's adjustment to divorce. Studies which examine whether the amount of postdivorce father–child contact is associated with children's adjustment are inconclusive. Recent studies, however, indicate that it is the quality and not quantity of father–child contact that is important to divorce adaptation. High quality father–child relationships are related to better child postdivorce adjustment than low quality relationships.

C. Child Characteristics

Research examining the association between child demographics, such as gender and age, and children's postdivorce adjustment have revealed few consistent differences. Although early research on children of divorce seemed to indicate less advantageous outcomes for boys relative to girls, Amato and Keith's aforementioned meta-analysis demonstrated that consistent sex differences are not evident when a large number of studies are considered. They did find that children in middle childhood and adolescence appear to be more negatively impacted by divorce than children of preschool or college age. However, far fewer studies examine divorce adjustment in these latter two age groups, making it difficult to draw firm conclusions regarding the effect of age on children's adaptation to divorce.

Recently, a body of literature has begun to emerge which shows that the manner in which children interpret and cope with divorce-related stress has implications for their adjustment. Children who lack an internal sense of control over their environment or who have a tendency to interpret stressful divorce-related changes in a characteristically negative style or as threatening to their well-being are more likely to experience postdivorce adjustment problems. Children who use positive cognitive or behavioral coping strategies, such as active problem solving or positive cognitive restructuring, are more likely to experience fewer psychological adjustment problems than children who employ avoidant coping strategies. Theoretically, researchers agree that the adaptive value of any specific coping strategy depends on context. Children may benefit most, for example, by cognitively reframing a situation that is largely outside of their control, while problem solving may be an adaptive strategy for more controllable situations.

Children's temperament, which theoretically modulates the expression of activity, emotionality, reactivity, and behavior, has also been implicated as important to children's postdivorce adjustment, although research in this area is in its infancy. Theoretically, children who have particularly negative or intense reactions to events and/or are unable to modulate their emotions and behavior are expected to be particularly vulnerable to stressful divorce experiences. In support, preliminary findings with children of divorce indicate that negative emotionality and impulsivity relate to higher symptom levels, while positive emotionality and the ability to focus attention relate to lower levels of symptoms.

IV. IMPLICATIONS FOR PREVENTION

It is unlikely that the presence of any single stressful experience resulting from divorce can fully explain whether children will exhibit psychological maladjustment. Rather, stressful contextual experiences, disturbances in family relationships, and children's own resources for coping with divorce-related stress combine to determine any individual child's response. Efforts to facilitate adaptation to divorce and prevent maladjustment have focused upon altering modifiable contextual, family, and/or child variables known to affect children's divorce adjustment.

Two types of preventive interventions have been developed to promote children's adaptation to divorce. The first, which targets custodial parents, focuses on teaching effective parenting skills after divorce to enhance the quality of the parent–child relationship and help parents shield children from stressful experiences such as interparental conflict. The second category of intervention involves children directly to enhance their abilities to adapt to divorce-related stress. Child-focused interventions generally seek to increase children's accurate understanding of divorce and teach new skills for coping with divorce-related changes. Although parent- and child-focused interventions for children of divorce are widespread, less than a dozen have been evaluated in an experimental or quasiexperimental fashion to date. Of those that have been evaluated, results have generally been positive, indicating that both parenting and child coping programs promote improved mental health among participating children.

See Also the Following Articles

ADOLESCENCE; CHILDHOOD STRESS; MARITAL CONFLICT; MARITAL STATUS AND HEALTH PROBLEMS

Bibliography

Amato, P. R., and Keith, B. (1991a). Consequences of parental divorce for the well-being of children: A meta-analysis. *Psychol. Bull.* 110, 26–46.

Amato, P. R., and Keith, B. (1991b). Parental divorce and adult well-being: A meta-analysis. *J. Marr. Fam.* 53, 43–58.

Grych, J. H., and Fincham, F. D. (1997). Children's adaptation to divorce: From description to explanation. *In* "Handbook of Children's Coping: Linking Theory and Intervention" (S. A. Wolchik and I. N. Sandler, Eds.) Plenum, New York.

Hetherington, E. M., Bridges, M., and Insabella, G. M. (1998). What matters? What does not? Five perspectives on the association between marital transitions and children's adjustment. *Am. Psychol.* 53, 167–184.

Wolchik, S. A., and Karoly, P. (1988). "Children of Divorce: Empirical Perspectives on Adjustment." Gardner, New York.

Domestic Violence

Tammy Maier-Paarlberg and Brad Donohue

University of Nevada at Las Vegas

I. Description
II. Consequences
III. Remediation Strategies
IV. Historical Perspectives

GLOSSARY

domestic violence Any act of maltreatment occurring in the home environment of the victim and perpetrated by a person who assumes the role of a caregiver or who is involved in an established relationship with the victim.

neglect The omission of appropriate caretaking functions which lead to a lack of self-preservation and growth in the dependent individual.

physical abuse A harmful act carried out on an individual with the intention of causing physical pain or injury.

sexual abuse Illegal, nonconsensual, or socially inappropriate contact or exposure of genitalia.

verbal/emotional/mental abuse The use of derogatory statements which cause the victim psychological pain or feelings of devaluation.

I. DESCRIPTION

Domestic violence includes all aspects of abuse and neglect which are perpetrated within the victim's home environment by a person who assumes the role of a caregiver or who is involved in an established relationship with the victim. Abuse and neglect have been around since the beginning of civilization; however, various forms of abuse have only recently been defined and studied extensively. Although definitions of abuse vary considerably, neglect and three types of abuse (physical abuse, sexual abuse, and psychological/mental/emotional/verbal abuse) have consistently been recognized in the domestic violence literature. This article provides an overview of domestic violence, including its risk factors, prevalence, and delineation of neglect and abuse.

A. Neglect

In general, neglect refers to the omission of appropriate caretaking functions which results in harm to the dependent individual. Victims of neglect are therefore dependent on a guardian or caregiver for self-preservation and growth. Most often, victims of neglect include children, adults who evidence severe mental or physical disabilities (e.g., mental retardation, Parkinson's disease), and elderly persons with medical complications or other problems associated with old age. Prevalence studies consistently indicate that neglect is the most frequently occurring form of maltreatment. For instance, the National Committee for the Prevention of Child Abuse reported 993,000 claims of child abuse in 1995, and of those claims, 54% were neglected, with male and female victims evidencing similar prevalence rates. Although risk factors are varied, they most often include substance abuse, physical disabilities, social isolation, psychiatric illness, social isolation, stress, poor parenting skills, and unrealistic expectations of the child's development. Persons of lower economic status appear to be overrepresented in abuse samples, perhaps because abuse is more common for these individuals, but also because they may be reported and charged with abuse more often due to reasons associated with poverty (e.g., relatively inadequate representation of legal counsel). Incidents of neglect include interfering with (or delaying) medical protocol, leaving small children unattended for extended periods of time in potentially dangerous situations (e.g., being left in an automobile while the caregiver drinks alcohol inside a bar), restricting or failing to provide sufficient nutrients or shelter, failure to repair home hazards (e.g., exposed electrical wires, broken steps), exposing victim to toxins or bacteria (e.g., failing to clean dog feces on kitchen floor where infant crawls), and restricting children from attending school. Indicators of neglect include dirty and unkempt bodies, rotten teeth, clothes that are too small or are in need of repair, and untidy and disheveled home environments.

B. Psychological Abuse

Psychological abuse, also known as verbal, mental, or emotional abuse, typically refers to derogatory statements which cause harm or interfere with the psychological adjustment of the victim. These statements are most often attacks on the victim's competence ("You can't do anything right, you're just a big dummy") or character (e.g., "You're a lazy, unpopular, good for nothing"). Psychological abuse is usually associated with obscenities, negative voice tones, excessive teasing, harmful threats, ridicule, or derogatory statements about the victim or persons who are liked by the victim. There does not appear to be significant gender differences regarding the prevalence of psychological abuse, as studies have consistently indicated that the vast majority of the population has experienced some level of psychological abuse from an adult family member in their lifetime. Interestingly, persons often underestimate the severity of psychological abuse relative to other forms of maltreatment because its consequences are subtle and there are few, if any, legal sanctions which mitigate against its use. Nevertheless, severe consequences of verbal abuse have been found, including depression, health problems, shyness, problem-solving deficits, anxiety, and difficulties with conflict resolution and other social skills. Moreover, psychological abuse is often a precursor of physical abuse by the perpetrator, and retaliatory aggression by the victim.

C. Physical Abuse

Physical abuse is usually defined as any harmful act carried out on an individual with the intention of causing pain or injury (e.g., kicking, bruises consequent a severe spanking, whipped with an extension cord, punching, biting, threatening with a knife or a gun). Victims are usually persons who are emotionally or financially dependent on the perpetrator (e.g., spouses, lovers, children, elderly). Although neglect is estimated to be the most frequently occurring form of maltreatment, physical abuse has probably received greater attention in the scientific literature. The National Coalition Against Domestic Violence in 1995 reported that 50% of all women will be battered in their lifetime by their intimate companions, sometimes resulting in fatalities. For instance, studies have consistently indicated that about a third of all murdered females are killed by their husbands or boyfriends, and at least 10% of maltreated women have been threatened or injured with a weapon. About half of the adult victims of physical abuse retaliate with physical violence of their own due to self-defense or escalation of violence, lending support to the notion that physical abuse in adults is often reciprocal. Indeed, males in dependent relationships also suffer from physical abuse; however, it is relatively less often reported to authorities and the maltreatment is usually not as severe. Interestingly, prevalence rates of physical abuse among homosexual adult relationships approximate those of heterosexual adult relationships.

Children are prime targets to be physically abused. Indeed, estimates of physical abuse victimization in children are usually around 30%. Perpetrators of child physical abuse are often of lower economic status, substance abusers, single parents, socially isolated, evince inadequate coping skills, and report a history of being maltreated as a child. Other risk factors include low birth weight, physical and mental disabilities, immaturity, child noncompliance and misconduct, impulsiveness, familiarity with developmental norms of children, stress, lack of empathy, and antisocial personality.

The number of studies conducted with elderly victims of physical abuse and other forms of maltreatment has recently increased, more so than in other age groups. Although this increased attention is due to multiple factors, several are fairly obvious. The human life span has increased, resulting in more elderly individuals who are living with age-associated medical problems and physical limitations. Changes in health care, among other factors, have forced older adults to reside with family who are often ill equipped to tolerate the added stress associated with their care, which often results in frustration for both the victim and perpetrator. A recent study of nursing home residents revealed that aggression from residents toward staff was the strongest predictor of elder abuse.

Investigations of the risk factors of elderly abuse are consonant with those of other age groups.

D. Sexual Abuse

Sexual abuse is generally defined as any illegal, nonconsensual, or inappropriate contact or exposure of genitalia, including sexual humiliation. However, legal definitions of sexual abuse vary considerably. For instance, some agencies (i.e., Federal Bureau of Investigation) have defined rape as attempted or completed vaginal intercourse with a female by force and against her will. Whereas states have adopted unique qualifiers to this term, such as gender neutrality; anal or oral penetration; insertion of objects; and being unable to give sexual consent because of mental illness, mental retardation, or intoxication. Other common patterns of sexual abuse include, but are not limited to, being forced to observe or perform pornography and fondling or kissing genitalia of a child or nonconsenting adult. About 10% of marriages have involved rape without physical violence, and the National Committee for the Protection of Child Abuse estimated that 11% of 993,000 reported abuse cases in the United States involved inappropriate sexual contact or exposure. Sexual abuse victimization may occur as early as infancy, and it is characteristically progressive, as approximately half of sexually abused children will continue to be abused until they leave the abusive home. Perpetrators of domestic sexual abuse are very often in-laws, foster parents, nonrelatives, older siblings, or cousins, but may also include other relatives living in the homes of the victim. A large percentage of rapes in college populations are committed by someone the victim knows. Factors that have been found to influence sexual abuse include neurological disorders, particularly frontal lobe abnormalities; sexually abuse or repeated witnessing of pornography of the perpetrator during childhood; mental illness; substance abuse; and dysfunctional family systems.

II. CONSEQUENCES

The consequences of abuse and neglect are, as might be inferred, extremely debilitating for the victim, and these negative consequences inevitably affect close relatives and friends of the victim. Consequences which have been identified include low self-worth, anxiety and mood disorders, problems maintaining pleasant functional relationships, problems in toileting, antisocial conduct and maltreatment of others, suicide, poor social and coping skills, problems in school or employment, substance abuse, and personality disorders. Malnutrition is a hallmark of neglect. Sexual abuse victims may demonstrate inappropriate or promiscuous sexual activity, including prostitution and other illegal sexual undertakings. A particular concern is the recapitulation of abuse, as more often than not the victim becomes a perpetrator with the passage of time.

III. REMEDIATION STRATEGIES

Professionals (i.e., teachers, police officers, ministers, health care workers) are mandated in most states to report suspected incidents of domestic violence. Familiarity with risk factors and consequences of domestic violence is of great assistance in the identification of abuse. However, professionals are often not trained, or able, to recognize abuse, particularly since victims are motivated to deny or minimize assaultive behaviors because their perpetrators are usually persons whom they often love, fear, or respect. Moreover, once identified, domestic violence is difficult to remediate. Initial strategies focus on assessing the victim's environment to determine if it is (1) safe for the victim to remain in the home with the perpetrator, (2) necessary to remove the victim from the home (live with other relative, foster care home, shelter), or (3) mandate that the perpetrator leave the home. Separation of the victim from the perpetrator is certainly the safest strategy regarding the termination of abuse. However, this approach is often not possible as relatives are frequently unavailable and shelters and foster care homes usually operate with inadequate funding causing them to sometimes be full, dangerous, or overcrowded. Moreover, familial separation is marked with changes that bring about stress (new school placements, feelings of abandonment and rejection, financial losses). There-

fore, separation is typically sought only when cases of maltreatment are severe (e.g., sexual abuse, repeated instances of physical abuse). Adult victims and perpetrators of domestic violence are usually forced to fund their own therapy. However, state child protective service agencies will provide psychologically based intervention for child victims and relevant family members at no cost, whenever indicated. Interventions may be focused on reunifying and improving the function of the existing family system or facilitating a comfortable and healthy transition for the victim without the perpetrator. Therapy is ordinarily mandated by the legal system for child victims and their perpetrators when the goal is family reunification. Of the interventions which have been evaluated, the cognitive-behavioral and stress-reduction strategies appear to be most promising. Cognitive-behavioral interventions most often include recognition of the early signs of abuse, learning strategies to improve safety and prevent escalation of abuse, restructuring faulty cognitions and beliefs about the abuse (e.g., victims may blame themselves for abuse, perpetrators might think the role of a woman is to serve her spouse), learning to improve appropriate social/assertion skills, anger-management skills training, contingency contracting (obtaining rewards which are contingent on behavioral improvement, e.g., good grades in school, compliance to directives of parent, making statements of affection), learning to eliminate home hazards, behavioral substance-abuse counseling (controlling urges to use substances, restructuring the environment so that drug use is less likely), vocational skills training, learning positive parenting techniques (e.g., reinforcing child for desired behaviors, positive practice, learning about child development and nutrition), multisystemic family therapy, and communication skills training. Stress-management strategies include bringing children to day cares or babysitters to enable the caregiver to acquire a relaxing break at home, learning problem-solving and coping skills, attending Parents Anonymous groups (an organization established to support victims and perpetrators of abuse), planning pleasant activities with the family, and encouraging/facilitating participation in community groups (e.g., church, boys' and girls' clubs).

IV. HISTORICAL PERSPECTIVES

Perceptions of domestic violence have changed markedly throughout history and across cultures. Indeed, it was not until the past century that laws were initiated to protect children and wives from being beaten by their parents and husbands, respectively. For instance, as recently as 1968 many states did not mandate professionals to report their knowledge of abusive treatment to abuse registries. Nevertheless, however, there have been radical improvements in public sentiment and the legal system regarding the eradication of domestic violence. In ancient times, individuals with mental and physical disabilities were scorned or killed to rid the state and parents of economic burden. Although treatment of children and women improved somewhat in most societies during the Middle Ages, neglect, ridicule, slavery, and harsh physical punishment continued. It is also interesting to note that children in 19th-century industrialized nations were forced to work up to 14 hours a day in hazardous conditions.

Improved rights of children and women were partially a result of humanitarians who wrote books about the injustice of domestic violence. For instance, during the Renaissance, Thomas Phaire wrote a book addressing the problems of children called *The Book of Chyldren,* and Locke and Rousseau wrote books in the late 1600s and early 1700s that mentioned issues pertaining to the development of children. Erin Pizzey's 1974 book *Scream Quietly or the Neighbors Will Hear* was one of the first manuscripts in the literature that specifically addressed remediation procedures for spousal abuse. National organizations, governmental meetings, and activists also influenced the passing of domestic violence protection laws. The Society for the Prevention of Cruelty to Children in the late 1800s was formed to protect rights and welfare of children. In 1909, President Roosevelt organized the first meeting in the White House on children welfare, which supported the Children's Bureau in 1912 to protect the welfare and rights of children. Pizzey was responsible for developing the first refuge home for female victims of spousal abuse in England in 1971, and the first refuge home for women and their children in the United States was initiated by the Women's Advocates in 1972. Although domestic violence continues today at relatively high rates, research and public opinion and protection laws against domestic violence are at their highest level of sophistication. Indeed, all 50 states currently require professionals to mandate suspected instances of domestic violence, and most states have explicitly allocated significant funding to the prevention and treatment of domestic violence programs.

See Also the Following Articles

CAREGIVERS, STRESS AND; CHILD ABUSE; MALE PARTNER VIOLENCE; MARITAL CONFLICT; SEXUAL ASSAULT

Bibliography

Bergen, R. (Eds.) (1998). "Issues in Intimate Violence." Sage, Thousand Oaks, CA.

Donohue, B., Ammerman, R. T., and Zelis, K. (1998). Child physical abuse and neglect. *In* "Handbook of Child Behavioral Therapy" (pp. 183–202). Plenum, New York.

Johnson, M., and Elliott, B. (1997). Domestic violence among family practice patients in midsized and rural communities. *J. Family Pract.* 44(4), 391–400.

Dopamine, Central

Gregg D. Stanwood and Michael J. Zigmond

University of Pittsburgh

GLOSSARY

agonist A drug that mimics the actions of a neurotransmitter at its receptor.

antagonist A drug that blocks the actions of a neurotransmitter at its receptor.

catecholamine A chemical containing a catechol nucleus (a benzene ring with two adjacent hydroxyl groups) and an amine group.

central nervous system (CNS) A general term referring to the entire brain and spinal cord.

dopamine (DA) A catecholamine used as a neurotransmitter in the central nervous system; also known as dihydroxyphenylethylamine.

hypothalamic-pituitary-adrenal (HPA) axis A principal component of the stress response that regulates the secretion of glucocorticoid hormones from the adrenal gland.

mesencephalon The midbrain; many DA cells have their soma, or cell bodies, located in two regions of the mesencephalon, the substantia nigra (SN) and the ventral tegmental area (VTA).

neuron/nerve The fundamental cellular unit of the nervous system.

neurotransmitter A chemical released by a neuron at a synapse to provide a signal to another neuron.

nucleus accumbens (NAS) A subcortical brain region thought to be an important interface for motivation and motor outputs; it consists of two subregions, the core and the shell.

prefrontal cortex A cortical region located toward the front of the brain involved in planning and other cognitive functions; it receives a dopaminergic input from the VTA and projects to the striatum and NAS.

striatum (or neostriatum) A region of the basal ganglia which is important for movement; the striatum receives a dopaminergic projection from the SN.

synapse A specialized contact zone which is the site of chemical communication between neurons.

tyrosine hydroxylase (TH) The rate-limiting enzyme in the synthesis of DA; it converts the amino acid tyrosine to dihydroxyphenylalanine (DOPA).

Dopamine is a chemical transmitter in the central nervous system that acts to modulate the actions of other transmitters. Physical or psychological stress results in an activation of nearly all neurons that use dopamine as their transmitter, causing an increase in dopamine release. Those dopamine neurons projecting from the mesencephalon to the prefrontal cortex are particularly sensitive to such stress. The mechanisms by which dopamine release is increased in response to stress appear to include (1) an increase in the firing rate of the dopamine neurons, (2) changes in the inputs to the dopamine terminals from adjacent cells, and (3) an increase in the activity of tyrosine hydroxylase, the rate-limiting enzyme in dopamine synthesis. The precise roles that these changes in dopamine neurotransmission play in the generation of stress and/or coping responses are not yet clear. However, the study of these mechanisms in animal models may lead to a more complete understanding of the biological bases of a number of psychiatric disorders.

I. INTRODUCTION TO NERVE CELLS AND SYNAPTIC TRANSMISSION

Nerve cells, or neurons, are the elementary signaling units within the nervous system. The highly complex behaviors of humans and other animals result from the specific interconnections of a vast number of these neurons. Neurons have four main regions: (1) the dendrites, which receive most of the information coming into the neuron; (2) the cell body, or soma, which processes that information and also contains the mechanisms of protein synthesis; (3) the axon, which carries an electrical signal called an action potential from the cell body to the nerve terminal; and (4) the terminal, which can respond to signals received from the axon and from adjacent neurons by releasing a chemical transmitter. Neurons communicate with one another through minute gaps between them known as synapses. The chemical transmitters released by the presynaptic terminal of a neuron diffuse across this synaptic space to act on specialized receptors on the dendrites and/or cell body of a neighboring postsynaptic neuron (Fig. 1).

II. OVERVIEW OF DOPAMINERGIC PATHWAYS IN THE CENTRAL NERVOUS SYSTEM

The nervous system uses many different transmitters, each with different functional characteristics. However, they can be broadly placed into two groups. The first are the rapidly acting transmitters that provide primary information. Many of the neurons that use acetylcholine or the amino acids glutamate and GABA fall into this category. The second group are the more slowly acting transmitters that have a modulatory influence on the actions of the first group. Dopamine (DA) is an important member of this second, modulatory group of transmitters. Dopamine has been implicated in a variety of functions including motor control, cognition, endocrine regulation, emotion, and cardiovascular regulation. Abnormali-

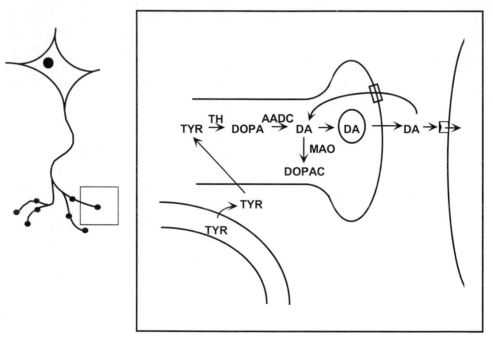

FIGURE 1 Schematic representation of the life cycle of dopamine. Upon accumulation of tyrosine (Tyr) by the neuron, tyrosine is sequentially metabolized by tyrosine hydroxylase (TH) and aromatic amino acid decarboxylase (AADC) to dopamine (DA). Dopamine is then accumulated into vesicles by the vesicular transporter, where it is poised for release and protected from degradation. Once DA is released, it can interact with postsynaptic dopaminergic receptors or different types of presynaptic autoreceptors that regulate transmitter release, synthesis, or firing rate. The accumulation of DA by the high-affinity membrane DA transporter (DAT) terminates the extracellular actions of DA. Once accumulated by the neuron, DA can be metabolized to inactive species by key degradative enzymes such as monoamine oxidase (MAO) or taken back up by the vesicular transporter.

ties in DA systems can lead to major neurological and psychiatric dysfunction.

Dopamine is a catecholamine, a term that refers to its biochemical structure. (Other catecholamines include norepinephrine (NE) and epinephrine, also known as adrenaline.) Dopamine is synthesized from tyrosine through the actions of two enzymes. First, tyrosine hydroxylase (TH), the rate-limiting enzyme in the process, converts L-tyrosine to dihydroxy-L-phenylalanine, or L-DOPA. Then aromatic amino acid decarboxylase (also known as DOPA decarboxylase) immediately converts L-DOPA to DA (Fig. 1). In some cells, DA is further converted to the neurotransmitter NE or even further to epinephrine, but in many neurons DA itself serves as an active neurotransmitter.

The rate at which DA is synthesized can be controlled in many ways. Dopamine can inhibit TH, a process termed end-product inhibition. Additional influences can be exerted by changes in the number or structure of the TH molecules or by changes in the availability of necessary cofactors for tyrosine hydroxylation. Because of these regulatory processes, neurons are usually able to match the rate of DA synthesis to the rate of DA utilization, thereby avoiding either the build-up or the depletion of the transmitter.

Dopamine release occurs in response to an influx of calcium into the nerve terminal which is triggered by the arrival of an action potential. Like DA synthesis, DA release is regulated by several processes. For example, DA can act back on the terminal from which it was released to inhibit subsequent release. Such influences represent negative feedback loops and act to keep the rate of DA utilization within relatively narrow limits.

Dopamine induces a wide range of cellular and biochemical effects in neurons by way of its actions on its specific postsynaptic receptor proteins. These effects include relatively rapid (seconds) modulation of biochemical events in the target cell resulting in changes in the responsiveness of the cell to other neuronal inputs as well as more gradual (minutes–hours) alterations in gene expression. The sensitivity of a target cell to DA is regulated: a period during which DA release is reduced causes an increase in the number of postsynaptic receptors and thus a supersensitivity of the neuron to DA, whereas an excess of DA leads to a decrease in receptors and in the sensitivity of the target.

The neurotransmitter actions of released DA are terminated by diffusion from the receptor site. It can then be transported into presynaptic terminals by high-affinity uptake sites. Once taken up, DA can be metabolized in the nerve terminal by monoamine oxidase (MAO) to dihydroxyphenylacetic acid (DOPAC) or further sequestered into storage vesicles for later reuse. Released DA can also be metabolized extraneuronally by catechol-*O*-methyltransferase (COMT) to 3-methoxytyramine. The product of MAO plus COMT is homovanillic acid.

There are several major dopaminergic pathways (Fig. 2). The two main mesencephalic regions containing DA cell bodies are the substantia nigra (SN) and ventral tegmental area (VTA). Axons of the DA cells in the SN form the nigrostriatal projection and provide the dopaminergic innervation of the caudate and putamen, or striatum. This region is part of the basal ganglia, a group of nuclei involved in motor and cognitive functions. Degeneration of the nigrostriatal DA neurons is the principal cause of Parkinson's disease.

Medial to the SN lies the VTA, from which the mesolimbic and mesocortical DA systems arise. The mesolimbic DA system innervates subcortical regions such as the nucleus accumbens (NAS), olfactory tubercle, and amygdala. The mesocortical system provides dopaminergic afferents to prefrontal, cingulate, and entorhinal cortex. Disruption of dopaminergic neurotransmission in these areas has been associated with neuropsychiatric illnesses such as schizophrenia. The tuberoinfundibular DA system is another important dopaminergic pathway; it connects the hypothalamus and pituitary gland. These DA neurons are important in the regulation of the hormone prolactin from the anterior pituitary.

III. RESPONSES OF DOPAMINERGIC SYSTEMS TO ACUTE STRESSFUL STIMULI

Most antidepressant drugs have direct pharmacological effects on catecholamine neurotransmission.

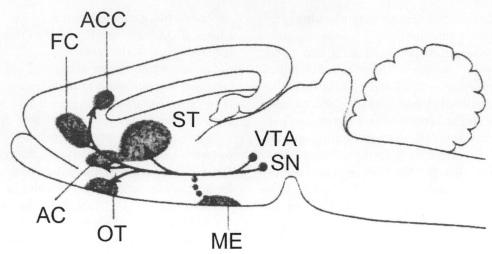

FIGURE 2 Schematic illustrating some of the major dopaminergic neurons and their projection areas. Abbreviations: AC, nucleus accumbens; ACC, anterior cingulate cortex; FC, frontal cortex; ME, median eminence; OT, olfactory tubercle; SN, substantia nigra; ST, striatum; VTA, ventral tegmental area. Figure adapted from *Basic Neurochemistry 5th ed.*, Raven Press, ©1994, editor-in-chief G. Siegel.

Many tricyclic antidepressants, for example, block the uptake of DA and other catecholamines, thus increasing the biochemical effects of these neurotransmitters. Based on the rationale that people suffering from anxiety and depressive disorders may have dysfunctions of brain catecholamine systems, changes in dopaminergic activity in response to stressful stimuli have been studied in a number of animal models. Some interesting effects have been observed as will be described below. However, it must also be noted that antidepressant drugs also have very prominent effects on NE and serotonin (5-hydroxytryptamine, 5-HT) systems, and it is likely that multiple neurotransmitter systems are involved in the pathophysiology of stress disorders and depression.

Rodent models of environmental stress include tail pinch and/or shock, immobilization, forced-swim, exposure to cold, and foot-shock. These stress-inducing procedures produce heterogeneous effects on the various dopaminergic projection systems. For example, the activity of tuberoinfundibular DA neurons is decreased by stressful stimuli, which results in an increase in plasma prolactin levels. This increase in prolactin likely plays a role in stress-induced activation of the immune system.

In contrast to the tuberoinfundibular DA neurons, the dopaminergic neurons that ascend from the midbrain are activated by stress. Mesocortical DA neurons projecting from the VTA to the prefrontal cortex appear to be particularly sensitive to acute stress so that relatively mild stressors lead to pronounced activation of DA neurotransmission in the prefrontal cortex. Stress-induced activation of DA neurotransmission also occurs in the mesolimbic and nigrostriatal pathways, but to lesser extents than in the prefrontal cortex (Fig. 3). Further heterogeneity is observed within the mesolimbic projections to the NAS. Stressors appear to activate dopaminergic activity to a greater extent in the NAS$_{shell}$ (the "limbic" NAS) subregion than in the NAS$_{core}$ (the "motor" NAS) and in the striatum.

Consistent with these differences in activation of DA terminal regions, it has been observed that VTA neurons increase their rate of firing during stress, but SN neurons respond only briefly if it all. Moreover, acute exposure to stress has been shown to increase TH activity in DA terminal regions and the rank-order of this effect is identical to that of the neurochemical measurements (prefrontal cortex > nucleus accumbens > striatum).

Collectively, these data demonstrate that in-

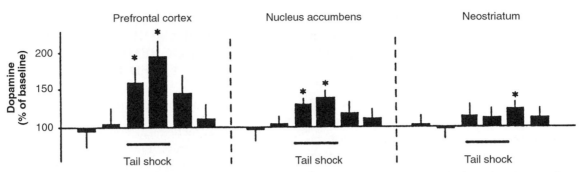

FIGURE 3 Effects of stress (30 min of tail shock) on extracellular dopamine in the prefrontal cortex, nucleus accumbens, and striatum. Asterisk indicates values significantly greater than baseline ($p < 0.05$). Figure adapted from Abercrombie *et al.* (1989).

creases in DA neurotransmission occur during exposure to acute stress. But what functional significance do these changes in DA activity represent? There are several lines of evidence suggesting that DA systems play critical roles in stress responses. First, antianxiety drugs such as benzodiazepines can reduce stress-induced increases in DA release, suggesting that the therapeutic actions of these compounds may be due at least in part to reversing increased dopaminergic activation. Second, lesions of midbrain DA neurons lead to a partial suppression of endocrine stress responses (see "Dopamine and the HPA Axis" below for a more complete discussion). Third, enhancement of DA signaling in the amygdala attenuates stress-induced ulcer formation and stress-induced increases in dopaminergic activity in the prefrontal cortex have been shown to be associated with behavioral coping responses. These and other data have been interpreted by some as indicating that stress-induced increases in dopaminergic activity are important components of coping responses to environmental stressors rather than being a reflection of anxiety.

Yet, in trying to understand the functional significance of the activation of brain DA systems, it must be kept in mind that DA neurotransmission can be increased by a variety of environmental and behavioral challenges that are not aversive. Such challenges include feeding, sexual activity, and exposure to drugs of abuse. Indeed, the dopaminergic pathway from the VTA to the NAS is critical for the reinforcing effects of many addictive drugs, including cocaine,

morphine, and nicotine, as well as direct brain stimulation. These two seemingly contradictory observations—DA release is increased by stress *and* by positively reinforcing stimuli—can be reconciled if one assumes that any stimulus that causes behavioral arousal leads to an increase in DA neurotransmission. Dopaminergic activation is probably essential for attention and survival. However, at some point the amount of activation becomes detrimental. For example, a rat trained to lever-press in order to receive injections of cocaine will respond at a very steady rate. Such an animal will exhibit elevated rates of DA release in the NAS and other brain regions. If the dose of cocaine per injection is suddenly increased, however, the animal will reduce its rate of lever pressing such that only enough cocaine is present to maintain the previous level of DA release. In other words, if given the choice, the animal will not allow the extent of DA activation to exceed some optimal level. It is likely that this optimum varies both from individual to individual and from physiological state to state.

IV. RESPONSES OF DOPAMINERGIC SYSTEMS TO CHRONIC STRESS

Animals are often confronted with repeated or prolonged exposure to stressors and this can lead to additional neurobiological and behavioral changes. Under certain conditions, habituation can result—the animal ceases responding to the stimulus. Under other conditions, however, sensitization can occur.

In this case, the animal's biological and/or behavioral responses increase—either to the next presentation of the same stimulus or to a different stimulus (Fig. 4). Whether a given paradigm leads to habituation or sensitization is likely determined by the exact nature and duration of the stressors used, the species, and/or the brain region examined.

Chronic stress can also lead to "cross-sensitization" to drugs of abuse such as cocaine, amphetamines, and opiates. It is possible that sensitization plays a role in the development of posttraumatic stress disorder, panic attacks, and psychosis. Furthermore, as DA can oxidize to form potentially toxic metabolites, it has been hypothesized that the prolonged elevations in DA observed with repeated stress may lead to impairments of cellular functioning, although this possibility has not yet been rigorously examined.

Many cellular and molecular changes have been described in the development of neurochemical and behavioral sensitization following chronic stress. For example, chronic intermittent or sustained stress has also been shown to induce changes in the number of DA receptors in several brain regions, including the prefrontal cortex and NAS. Chronic stress also leads to changes in TH expression in the VTA and in the activity of several components of DA receptor signaling in the NAS.

V. INTERACTIONS BETWEEN DOPAMINE AND OTHER NEUROCHEMICAL SYSTEMS ALTERED BY STRESS

A. Dopamine and the HPA Axis

Many neurochemical and hormonal systems are activated by stress. One of the best-characterized physiological responses to stress is the activation of the hypothalamic-pituitary-adrenal (HPA) axis. The HPA system controls secretion of glucocorticoids by the adrenal gland. Interestingly, several dopaminergic regions in the brain express glucocorticoid receptors and the density of the receptors in these regions parallels the ability of stress to increase the activity of DA neurons: receptor density is higher in VTA than SN. There is reason to believe that the correlation between glucocorticoid receptors and stress-induced changes in DA release has some functional significance. Administration of glucocorticoids can increase extracellular DA. Moreover, the suppression of stress-induced corticosterone secretion causes a reduction in the dopaminergic response to stress.

Glucocorticoid regulation of midbrain DA neurons also appears to be a biological substrate of the effects of stress on the propensity to develop drug abuse. Conversely, midbrain DA neurons also seem capable of regulating the HPA axis since loss of DA decreases the basal and stress-induced secretion of corticosterone.

B. Dopamine and Excitatory Amino Acids

Stress has been shown to increase the release of glutamate and other excitatory amino acids in many brain regions, including the prefrontal cortex, striatum, NAS, VTA, and hippocampus. The presence of glucocorticoids appears to be necessary for this response as adrenalectomy abolishes the stress-induced increase of extracellular glutamate, and corticosterone replacement restores this response. Glutamatergic neurons in the cortex project to the striatum and NAS as well as to the SN and VTA. Furthermore, glutamate agonists appear to increase the synthesis and release of DA in each of these regions, and it

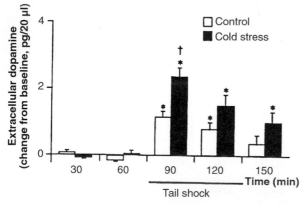

FIGURE 4 Effects of acute tail shock on extracellular dopamine in the prefrontal cortex of naive control rats and rats previously exposed to chronic cold (50°C) for 3–4 weeks. Asterisk indicates values significantly greater than baseline ($p < 0.05$). Figure adapted from Gresch *et al.* (1994).

has been hypothesized that stress-induced activation of glutamate may contribute to stress-induced increases in DA. The local administration of glutamate antagonists into the region of the midbrain containing DA cell bodies can block stress-induced increases in extracellular DA in the striatum. Additionally, stress-induced increases in DA synthesis can be blocked by local administration of a glutamate antagonist directly into the striatum itself. Glutamate antagonists can also block stress-induced increases in extracellular DA in the prefrontal cortex.

C. Dopamine and Norepinephrine

Norepinephrine is formed from DA and shares many of its basic characteristics. Acute exposure to stress causes an activation of NE neurons in the locus coeruleus and an increase in both the synthesis and release of NE. However, the relationship between these events and stress-induced changes in DA are unclear. Norepinephrine terminals in the prefrontal cortex can modulate the dopaminergic responses to stress. The NAS and striatum, on the other hand, exhibit increases in dopaminergic activity with stress, but are NE-poor regions; presumably NE–DA interactions have little significance in these regions.

D. Dopamine and Serotonin

The involvement of 5-HT in animal models of stress and depression has received great attention due to the antidepressant effects of selective 5-HT reuptake inhibitors (SSRIs) such as fluoxetine (Prozac). Acute exposure to stress leads to dramatic increases in 5-HT release in the striatum and other brain regions. Local administration of 5-HT agonists into the striatum can increase DA release, suggesting it is possible that stress-induced increases in DA release are at least partially mediated by increases in 5-HT. There is also a multitude of anatomical and electrophysiological evidence suggesting prominent interactions between 5-HT and DA in both cell body and terminal regions. However, the ability of 5-HT antagonists to influence stress-induced activation of DA release is only beginning to be examined.

E. Dopamine and Dopamine

In developing an understanding of the role of DA neurotransmission in stress, one must take into consideration the functional differences among different DA systems. In particular, it must be remembered that mesocortical DA neurons inhibit glutamatergic cortical pyramidal neurons which in turn can stimulate dopaminergic activity in nigrostriatal and mesoaccumbens neurons (see "Dopamine and Glutamate" above). Therefore, the less pronounced effects of acute stress on subcortical DA systems may be due in part to the suppression of subcortical DA systems by activated mesocortical DA neurons. Consistent with this hypothesis, depletion of DA in the prefrontal cortex enhances the stress-induced increase in dopaminergic transmission in the NAS$_{shell}$. Furthermore, injection of a DA receptor antagonist into the prefrontal cortex has been shown to block the DA stress response in the NAS. Last, under certain conditions chronic stress produces neurochemical tolerance in the prefrontal cortex but sensitization in subcortical areas.

Interactions between cortical and subcortical DA systems have also been proposed in the pathophysiology of schizophrenia. It has been suggested that a dysfunction of dopaminergic signaling in the prefrontal cortex can produce secondary disruptions in subcortical DA systems. In fact, decreases in the expression of TH and DA receptors in the prefrontal cortex have recently been described. The effects of cortical DA depletion on subcortical DA stress responses may thus be of particular clinical importance given that stress is known to exacerbate psychotic symptoms in schizophrenic patients.

See Also the Following Articles

Catecholamines; Dopamine, Adrenocortical; GABA

Bibliography

Abercrombie, E. D., Keefe, K. A., DiFrischia, D., and Zigmond, M. (1989). Differential effect of stress on *in vivo* dopamine release in striatum, nucleus accumbens and medial frontal cortex. *J. Neurochem.* 52, 1655–1658.

Anisman, H., Kokkinidis, L., and Sklar, L. (1985). Neurochemical consequences of stress: contributions of adaptive

processes. *In* "Stress: Psychological and Physiological Interactions" (S. R. Burchfield, Ed.), pp. 67–98. Hemisphere,
Washington DC.

Deutch, A. Y., and Roth, R. H. (1999). Neurotransmitters.
In "Fundamental Neuroscience" (Zigmond, M. J., Bloom,
F. E., Landis, S. C., Roberts, J. L., and Squire, L. R., Eds.),
pp. 193–234. Academic Press, San Diego, CA.

Finlay, J. M., and Zigmond, M. J. (1997). The effects of stress
on central dopaminergic neurons: Possible clinical implications. *Neurochem. Res.* 22, 1387–1394.

Goldstein, D. S. (1995). "Stress, Catecholamines, and Cardiovascular Disease." Oxford Univ. Press, New York.

Goldstein, L. E., Rasmusson, A. M., Bunney, B. S., and Roth,
R. H. (1996). Role of the amygdala in the coordination of
behavioral, neuroendocrine, and prefrontal cortical

monamine responses to psychological stress in the rat. *J.
Neurosci.* 16, 4787–4798.

Horger, B. A., and Roth, R. H. (1996). The role of mesopre-
frontal dopamine neurons in stress. *Crit. Rev. Neurobiol.*
10, 395–418.

Kalivas, P. W., and Stewart, J. (1991). Dopamine transmission in the initiation and expression of drug- and stress-
induced sensitization of motor activity. *Brain Res. Rev.*
16, 223–244.

Moghaddam, B. (1993). Stress preferentially increases extra-
neuronal levels of excitatory amino acids in the prefrontal
cortex: Comparison to hippocampus and basal ganglia.
J. Neurochem. 60, 1650–1657.

Piazza, P. V., and LeMoal, M. (1998). The role of stress in
drug self-administration. *Trends Pharmacol. Sci.* 19, 67–74.

Drosophila Genes and Anoxia

Gabriel G. Haddad

Yale University School of Medicine

I. Introduction
II. Genetic Approach: Mutagenesis Screen
III. Reverse Genetic Approach: Differential Display
IV. Known Genes: Genetic Networks
V. Conclusions

GLOSSARY

anoxia-inducible genes Genes that are activated by low
   oxygen.
anoxia tolerant Resistant to injury from anoxia.
hif1 Hypoxia-inducible factor.
mutagenesis screen Screen for a phenotype after mutagenesis
   of genome.
differential display Technique to screen for differentially expressed mRNA.

This article addresses the environmental
stresses of oxygen and glucose deprivation and their
consequences, especially in the central nervous system and in sensitive organs in early life. Such stresses
can be rather mild or moderate and can activate
mechanisms that allow the organism or a specific
tissue to adapt and survive the stress. More severe
stresses may be injurious to the organism and may
lead to cell death, tissue death, and ultimately death
of the whole organism.

I. INTRODUCTION

It is clear from a large body of literature that organisms vary greatly in their response to lack of oxygen.
Some, like mammals, are generally susceptible to
this stress, although mammalian newborns are more
resistant to such a stress than adults, more differentiated organs and tissues. In addition, tissues within
an organism, cells within an organ, and even cell
types within a region of an organ can be differentially
sensitive to the lack of oxygen and substrates. Con-

sider and compare, for example, the tolerance to a lack of oxygen in muscle to brain, hippocampal neurons to glial cells, and the CA1 layer to the dentate gyrus.

Since the turtle is an organism extremely tolerant to oxygen deprivation, it has been used extensively and is an excellent animal model for the study of tolerance to oxygen deprivation. However, several problems inherent to this model have prevented major progress in understanding the basis of the turtle tolerance. For example, a genetic approach is precluded. Since the late 1980s, we have searched for a model in which multiple approaches can be used, including molecular and genetic techniques. In this search, we have found that *Drosophila melanogaster* is extremely tolerant to oxygen deprivation. It can resist, without apparent injury, several hours of complete oxygen deprivation or anoxia. Clearly the advantages of using *Drosophila* are multiple: (1) genetic approaches can be easily adapted and used, (2) there are hundreds of markers and mutations on the *Drosophila* chromosomes that would facilitate mapping of mutations, (3) there are only three chromosomal pairs (the fourth is extremely small) in the *Drosophila* genome, (4) physiologic, molecular biologic, and genetic approaches are feasible in the fruit fly, and (5) whole-fly studies including transgenic fly work is rather easily performed. We have therefore developed this model further and performed a considerable number of investigations using the fruit fly. We have used three different approaches to address the genetic basis of the response of the fruit fly to low or absent environmental oxygen. In this article we summarize to date our findings using these different approaches.

II. GENETIC APPROACH: MUTAGENESIS SCREEN

In order to be able to perform a mutagenesis screen, we characterized the wild-type response to hypoxia using a number of behavioral and physiologic assays. We first subjected flies to extremely low oxygen concentrations (0.01%) and studied their physiologic and behavioral responses during anoxia and after the start of reoxygenation. Flies were first exposed to anoxia (complete lack of oxygen) for periods of 5–240 min. After 1–2 min in anoxia, *Drosophila* lost coordination, fell down, and became motionless. However, they tolerated a complete nitrogen atmosphere for up to 4 h following which they recovered. In addition, a nonlinear relation existed between time spent in anoxia and time to recovery. Extracellular recordings from flight muscles in response to giant fiber stimulation revealed complete recovery of muscle-evoked response, a response that was totally absent during anoxia (Fig. 1). Mean oxygen consumption per gram of tissue was substantially reduced in low oxygen concentrations (20% of control). We concluded from these studies that (1) *Drosophila melanogaster* is very resistant to anoxia and can be useful in the study of mechanisms of anoxia tolerance and (2) the profound decline in metabolic rate during periods of low environmental oxygen levels contributes to the survival of *Drosophila*.

A. Genetic Screen for Anoxia-Sensitive Mutants

We focused our screen for mutations on the X chromosome because the mutant phenotype can be observed in the immediate next generation without the need for single-pair matings. Mutagenized (X-ray, 4000 rad) C-S males, which were crossed to attached-X females [*c(1)ywf*], transmitted their X chromosome to the male offspring. More than 20,000 flies, carrying mutagenized chromosomes, were screened. A threshold, which is close to the 96th percentile of the wild-type distribution, was used to identify and isolate mutants. Eight mutations were identified and found to alter profoundly the distribution of recovery times (Fig. 2). The marked delay in recovery after anoxia displayed by these mutant flies suggested that they were much more sensitive to a lack of oxygen. We have therefore termed these mutants *hypnos* to describe (1) sensitivity to oxygen deprivation (*hy*poxia, a*no*xia, *s*ensitive) and (2) the phenotype of delayed recovery and "sleepiness."

B. Genetic Mapping

Mapping of the induced mutations was performed with X-chromosomal markers and complementation

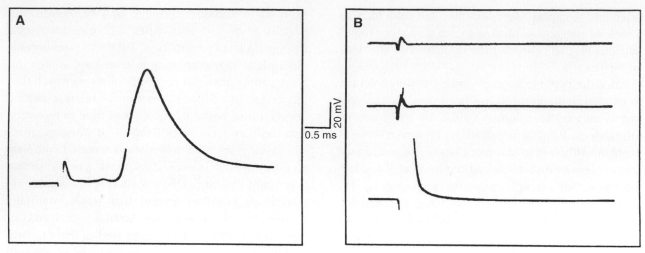

FIGURE 1 Effect of anoxia on evoked muscle response. Response of DLM in A. (B) Note the lack of response during anoxia, even afer a 10-fold increase in duration and intensity of stimulus.

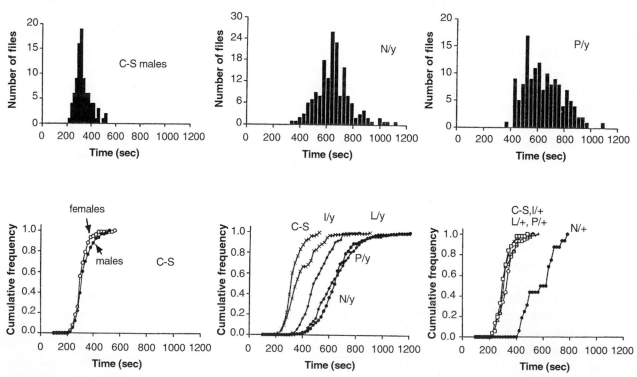

FIGURE 2 Distribution of cumulative frequency of recovery time in wild type (C-S) and mutant flies. See text for abbreviations for mutants.

tests. Several markers were used, including *y, cv, v, f, car,* and *su(f).* Complementation testing was done on several X-linked recessive mutations obtained. A number of these mutations were mapped and they seem to be spread in a number of locations on the X chromosome. For example, one of them is on the right side of *f* or *forked,* another is between *y* and *cv.* And yet another is between *cv* and *f.* One of the mutations has been refined in terms of the mapping and we have localized it to a rather narrow region, between *y* and *cv,* using deficiencies.

C. Hypnos Mutations Affect Central Nervous System Recovery from Anoxia

The behavioral testing, which showed delayed recovery from anoxia, led us to believe that the *hypnos* mutations affected the central nervous system. To further our understanding of the mutations we obtained, we directly examined the effect of these mutations on central nervous system function. Identified neurons that can be studied electrophysiologically in *Drosophila* are those of the Giant Fiber system. Stimulation of eye neurons, using low voltages, evoked spikes in the dorsal longitudinal muscle (DLM) with a long latency (4 ms). Experiments were carried out in three of the eight mutations (*hypnos-2*[P, L], *Hypnos-1*[N]) and on wild-type flies. In one mutant (*hypnos-2*[P]), which had a severe phenotype, long-latency evoked potentials could not be obtained, irrespective of the voltage and duration used. Flies having an allele of this locus (*hypnos-2*[L]) or with the other severe mutation (*Hypnos-1*[N]) had a baseline long latency recording that was similar to that of C-S flies. However, during recovery, whereas the DLM of wild-type flies started to respond after 2 min into recovery, flies with these two mutations had a much longer time to first evoked potential, with some mutant flies requiring up to 25–30 min for the first evoked response to occur.

The current genetic screen is not saturated and is restricted to the X chromosome. However, we had to screen more than 20,000 mutagenized flies to obtain hits in the same locus (two loci hit twice). This suggests that a limited number of genes can be mutated in *Drosophila* to produce similar phenotypes. Because these mutations profoundly disrupt the re-

covery from anoxia, we believe that this approach can be used effectively to dissect the genetic basis of responses to low oxygen.

III. REVERSE GENETIC APPROACH: DIFFERENTIAL DISPLAY

The idea behind this approach is to identify those genes that are differentially expressed during a condition or a stress. In our case, we use very low levels of oxygen and assess whether there are up- or downregulated mRNA during the period of hypoxia in comparison to naive or nonexposed flies. Ribonucleic acid differential display was performed as described by Liang and Pardee, with minor modifications. The DNAse-treated total RNA was used for reverse transcription. The cDNAs generated from PCR were blotted, the bands of interest located, cut out, and reamplified and cloned into the PCRII vector. To determine the relative size of selected candidate transcripts, Northern analysis was performed. To obtain full-length cDNA, we screened the fly head λgt11 library using the cDNA fragments which were isolated from the differential display. In addition, 5′ and 3′ RACE PCR were also performed.

In addition to the cloning of this particular gene, we have localized it on the X chromosome using *in situ* hybridization. This is usually helpful for developing mutants with P-elements and therefore examines the role of that particular gene in the context of the whole organism or cell (Fig. 3). Furthermore, we have also localized the mRNA of *fau* in the CNS of the fly as seen in Fig. 3. This figure shows that the *fau* mRNA is localized in certain areas such as the cortex.

A. Gene Expression Following Anoxia

The data from our differential display and Northern analysis clearly showed that certain genes were upregulated while others were downregulated during anoxia. From the PCR reactions, we found that the expression level of several transcripts was visibly affected by anoxia. We have selected one transcript, which was markedly upregulated to focus on and study. We termed this transcript *fau (fly, anoxia, up-*

A

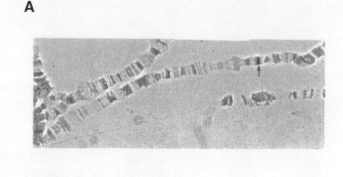

B₁   **B₂**

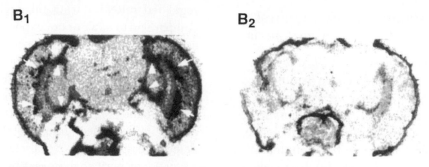

FIGURE 3   *In situ* hybridization of polytene chromosomes of gene fau (A). *In situ* hybridization of fau in the CNS of *Drosophila* (B1, antisense; B2, sense).

regulated). The *fau* cDNA and its deduced protein sequence have several interesting and potentially important characteristics. Seven ATTT motifs, for example, were found in its 3′-UTR. The AUUUA motifs reportedly play a role in stability and translocation of transient mRNAs. Therefore, the ATTT motifs found in *fau* cDNA may play a similar role in hypoxia-induced mRNAs and could regulate their expression. In addition, there are two (TA)$_{9-10}$ stretches in the 3′-UTR of this cDNA. Although their function is not clear, taken together, these unique sequences in the 3′-UTR with high GC content in the *fau* cDNA open reading frame may define a functional anatomy of transient or stress-induced mRNAs. The deduced protein sequence of *fau* cDNA also has a high number of phosphorylation sites, which makes it an appropriate substrate for phosphorylation. It is possible then that the *fau* protein can participate in metabolic pathways. Since our computerized search did not reveal significant homology with published sequences, the deduced *fau* protein is most likely a novel phosphorylated one.

B. Role of *fau* Protein

In spite of the fact that we have no direct evidence that this gene is involved in anoxic survival in *D. melanogaster*, we believe that *fau* plays an important role during anoxic stress based on the following reasons. (1) The expression of this gene was upregulated when the overall reduction of protein synthesis in general occurs during the lack of oxygen. (2) Overexpression of *fau* in transgenic flies prolonged their recovery from anoxia. (3) The putative protein encoded by this gene is probably highly regulated by phosphorylation, suggesting that it is active during O_2 deprivation. (4) The richness of the AUUU motif in 3′-UTR of this mRNA could make it a transient one, with a relevant function during O_2 deprivation.

It has been debated in the literature as to whether cells, particularly nerve cells, die from anoxia via mechanisms that induce active processes or via others that shut off pathways and protein synthesis. It is clear from a number of studies that survival and adaptation during anoxia or cell death resulting from anoxia involves the synthesis of proteins, although the overall net balance is a marked reduction in protein synthesis. Numerous studies, for example, have shown that there are genes that are selectively turned on or upregulated by oxygen deprivation. Our previous data have demonstrated that anoxia remarkably upregulated the expression of a heat-shock protein (HSP70) gene while it suppressed the expression of ubiquitin 4 in the fruit fly. A hypoxia-inducible factor 1 (HIF-1) was found to enhance the activation of transcription of the Epo gene as well as other genes by binding to DNA. Hence, we believe that during anoxic stress, tolerant cells such as those in *Drosophila* depress their oxygen consumption and requirements by lowering metabolic rate and reducing protein synthesis. However, a protein "hierarchy" within these cells exists for survival, i.e., there are certain proteins that are either newly induced or protected from proteolysis while the majority of proteins have a decreased or negligible synthetic rate and are down-regulated. It is possible then that proteins such as HIF are overly expressed in order to render cells better adapted to lack of oxygen. However, why would an increase Fau protein occur during hypoxia if an increase in this protein increases by itself the sensitivity to anoxia? At present we cannot be certain since we do not have a comprehensive picture of the various genes and gene products that are important during such stress. For example, we do not know the relation between Fau and other proteins.

IV. KNOWN GENES: GENETIC NETWORKS

This approach relies on genes known to be important in mammal's response to oxygen deprivation. This approach then aims at cloning and studying fruit flies in order to better delineate the genetic pathways and molecular mechanisms underlying the resistance of fruit flies to lack of oxygen. It is assumed that this challenge is better met in organisms such as *Drosophila* rather than in mammals because of the flexibility and feasibility of molecular approaches in this organism.

A. Expression of Known Genes

We analyzed mRNA expression of heat-shock proteins (HSP26 and HSP70), ubiquitins (UB, UB3 and UB4), cytochrome oxidase I (COX1), and superoxide dismutase (SOD) using slot-blot analysis. The expression of HSP genes, especially HSP70, was remarkably upregulated (up to a thousandfold), while those of UB4 and COXI were downregulated (10–60%) in response to the anoxic stress. The expression of UB3 gene was upregulated by 1.5X and the expression of the SOD gene was not significantly affected. In response to heat-shock stress, the expression of HSP genes increased by up to several thousandfold, the expression of UB genes increased modestly (23–91%), but the expression of SOD and COXI genes was reduced by about 25%. Furthermore, the expression patterns of HSP genes under anoxia and heat shock were clearly different. The expression of HSP genes peaked by 15 min into anoxia and then declined but stayed above baseline. In contrast, their expression increased as a function of time during heat exposure.

B. Known Pathways

One of the transcription factors that have been shown to be crucial for sensing the lack of oxygen is HIF1. This transcription factor has two subunits and, when they dimerize, they induce the expression of a number of genes including *Nitric oxide synthase* and *Vascular endothelial growth factor*. We and other investigators have cloned HIF1 ∃-subunit from *Drosophila*. The ∀-subunit has been cloned and both the ∀- and the ∃-subunits have relatively high homology to those of mammals. At present, we are examining the role of these genes in *Drosophila*. In addition, the approach here aims at examining the pathways that these genes are involved in.

V. CONCLUSIONS

Stress, as defined in this article involves the lack of oxygen. Generally, this type of stress has been equated with a pathophysiologic signal, i.e., with a condition that can lead to cell injury or cell death. However, it is apparent that, although this can certainly be true, especially in moderate or severe stress, it may not be so in milder stresses. In addition, the timing of the stress is exceedingly important. Even though it can be severe, hypoxic conditions in development or during organ formation can be tantamount to signals that are important in the induction of certain genes such as *VEGF*, which is crucial for organ development and embryogenesis. A failure of response to hypoxia, in such knockouts as in the HIF knockout, can lead to failure of embryogenesis and demise of the embryo. Indeed, fetal demise is observed in knockouts of both subunits of HIF and in that of *VEGF*.

See Also the Following Article

DROSOPHILA STUDIES

Bibliography

Akashi, M., Shaw, G., Hachiya, M., Elstner, E., Suzuki, G., and Koeffler, P. (1994). Number and location of AUUUA motifs: Role in regulating transiently expressed RNAs. *Blood* 83, 3182–3187.

Clegg, J. S., Jackson, S. A., and Warner, A. H. (1994). Extensive intracellular translocations of a major protein accompany anoxia in embryos of artemia franciscana. *Exp. Cell Res.* 212, 77–83. 1994.

Clegg, J. S., Jackson, S. A., Liand, P., and MacRae, T. H. (1995). Nuclear–cytoplasmic translocations of protein p26 during aerobic–anoxic transition in embryos of artemia franciscana. *Exp. Cell Res.* 219, 1–7.

Haddad, G. G., Sun, Y. A., Wyman, R. J., and Xu, T. (1997). Genetic basis of tolerance to O_2 deprivation in *Drosophila melanogaster*. *Proc. Natl. Acad. Sci. USA* 94, 10809–10812.

Haddad, G. G. and Jiang, C. (1993). O_2 deprivation in the central nervous system: On mechanisms of neuronal response, differential sensitivity and injury. *Prog. Neurobiol.* 40, 277–318.

Krishnan, S. N., Sun, Y. A., Mohsenin, A., Wyman, R. J. and Haddad, G. G. (1997). Behavioral and electrophysiologic responses of *Drosophila melanogaster* to prolonged periods of anoxia. *J. Insect Physiol.* 43(3), 203–210.

Liang, P., and Pardee, A. B. (1992). Differential display of eukaryotic messager RNA by means of the polymerase chain reaction. *Science* 257, 967–971.

Ma, E. and Haddad, G. G. (1997). Anoxia regulates gene expression in the central nervous system of *Drosophila melanogaster*. *Mol. Brain Res.* 46, 325–328.

Ma, E., Xu, T., and Haddad, G. G. (1999). Gene regulation by O_2 deprivation: An anoxia-regulated novel gene in *Drosophila melanogaster*. *Mol. Brain Res.* 63, 217–224.

Wang, G. L., and Semenza, G. L. (1993). Characterization of hypoxia-inducible factor 1 and regeneration of DNA binding activity by hypoxia. *J. Biol. Chem.* 268, 21513–21518.

Wang, G. L., and Semenza, G. L. (1995). Purification and characterization of hypoxia-inducible factor 1. *J. Biol. Chem.* 270, 1230–1237.

Drosophila Studies

Michael Allikian and John Tower

University of Southern California

GLOSSARY

chromosome puff An expansion or decomposition of a polytene chromosome band indicative of altered chromatin structure and high-level transcriptional activity.

P element The class II DNA transposable element which was engineered to carry modified or foreign genes into the *Drosophila* genome and allow germ-line transformation.

polytene chromosome Lengthwise alignment and coherance of the multiple copies of the chromosome in specialized polyploid cells which allows for light microscope visualization of banding patterns.

Powerful genetic and molecular tools combined with ease of culture have made *Drosophila* a leading model organism for studies of stress. For example, stress response gene induction was first discovered in the early 1960s in *Drosophila* as a characteristic pattern of polytene chromosome puffs in cells subjected to heat or oxidative stress. In the late 1970s *Drosophila* hsp genes were among the first eukaryotic genes cloned. The development of P element-mediated germ-line transformation in 1982 made *Drosophila* one of the first transgenic multicellular organisms. These and other discoveries led to pioneering and ongoing functional studies of stress responses and stress tolerance. A subset of the vast literature on *Drosophila* stress studies is discussed.

I. STRESS RESPONSE GENES INCLUDING THE HSPS ARE INDUCED IN RESPONSE TO HEAT AND OTHER STRESSES AND CAN CONFER STRESS TOLERANCE

In *Drosophila* six major hsps are induced in response to heat stress, hsp83, -70, -27, -26, -23, and -22, and several additional proteins exhibit smaller inductions. Hsp83 is constitutively expressed and upregulated severalfold during heat stress. Hsp83 is a member of the *hsp90* gene family which is highly conserved through evolution. Hsp83 functions include regulating the activity of proteins in signal transduction pathways whose functions in turn involve conformational changes. Hsp70 is the most highly conserved through evolution, and in *Drosophila* is induced over 1000-fold during heat stress. Based on studies of hsp70 family members in *Drosophila* and other organisms, hsp70 is thought to decrease protein denaturation and aggregation, facilitate refolding of partly denatured proteins, facilitate entry of damaged proteins into proteolytic pathways, and protect the organism from additional stress: experimental induction of hsp70 transgenes can confer thermotolerance to cultured *Drosophila* cells, and *Drosophila* transgenic for extra copies of hsp70 exhibit increased thermotolerance at certain stages of development. The *Drosophila* small hsps (-22, -23, -26, and -27) are related to each other and to small hsps from other organisms by a conserved α-crystallin protein domain and also appear to be molecular chaperones involved in stress resistance. The *hsr-omega* gene is also induced by heat stress, but produces no detectable protein product and may function in stress tolerance by an unusual mechanism.

The mechanism of *Drosophila* heat shock gene transcriptional induction by heat stress has been studied in detail, particularly for the *hsp70* gene. Binding sites for the "GAGA" and TBP (TATA-binding protein) transcription factors and other promoter sequences generate a "primed" promoter chromatin structure in unstressed cells. This structure includes a transcriptionally engaged RNA polymerase paused ~25 nucleotides downstream of the start site for transcription. This arrangement is thought to facilitate rapid induction upon stress. Heat stress causes trimerization and activation of the constitutively expressed heat-shock transcription factor (HSF), which is required for heat-shock gene induction. Heat-shock transcription factor binds to the heat shock response elements (HSEs) which are evolutionarily conserved promoter elements essential for transcriptional induction during heat stress. Heat-shock transcription factor binding to the HSEs results in release of paused polymerase and high-level transcription of the heat-shock gene.

Induction of the hsps also involves posttranscriptional regulation, as heat-shock gene RNAs are preferentially translated in heat-stressed cells and are more stable during heat stress.

II. DIFFERENT ENVIRONMENTAL STRESSES OR LABORATORY SELECTION FOR ALTERED STRESS RESISTANCE CAN AFFECT GENE ALLELE FREQUENCIES INCLUDING STRESS RESPONSE GENES

Drosophila isolated from different natural stress environments often exhibit correlated stress response phenotypes. For example, *Drosophila* isolated from hotter environments are generally more resistant to thermal stress. Similarly, laboratory populations of *Drosophila* selected over many generations for survival of a particular stress can exhibit increased resistance to that stress and exhibit correlated changes in allele frequencies in specific stress-response genes. Studies of this type provide a model for the relationship between environmental stress and evolution.

III. *DROSOPHILA* MOUNTS AN IMMUNE RESPONSE TO BIOTIC STRESS

The response to septic injury includes rapid induction of antibacterial and antifungal peptides. Induction is mediated in part by the evolutionarily conserved Toll/Dorsal signal transduction pathway, which is homologous to the Interleukin-1 Receptor/NF-κ B immune response pathway in mammals.

IV. LIFE SPAN AND AGING PHENOTYPES CORRELATE WITH STRESS RESISTANCE AND A CHARACTERISTIC PATTERN OF HSP EXPRESSION

Drosophila populations can be genetically selected for increased life span, and these populations exhibit increased resistance to various stresses, including dessication, starvation, and oxidative damage. Conversely, selection for increased resistance to specific stresses can result in increased life span. A subset of hsps are induced during aging, primarily hsp22 and hsp70. Mild heat stress which induces hsps can cause small increases in the life span of *Drosophila*. Slightly larger heat-induced increases in life span were achieved in *Drosophila* transgenic for extra copies of the *hsp70* gene. Finally, oxidative stress resistance and aging phenotypes have been altered in Drosophila transgenic for additional (or modified) oxygen radical defense genes, such as *catalase* and *superoxide dismutase*.

See Also the Following Articles

Bibliography

Belvin, M. P., and Anderson, K. V. (1996). A conserved signalling pathway: The *Drosophila* toll-dorsal pathway. *Annu. Rev. Cell Dev. Biol.* **12**, 393–416.

Bijlsma, R., and Loeschcke, V. (1997). "Environmental Stress, Adaptation and Evolution." Birkhauser-Verlag, Basel.

Hoffmann, A. A., and Parsons, P. A. (1991). "Evolutionary

Genetics and Environmental Stress." Oxford Univ. Press, Oxford.

Meister, M., Lemaitre, B., and Hoffman, J. A. (1997). Antimicrobial peptide defense in *Drosophila*. *Bioessays* **19**, 1019–1026.

Morimoto, R. I., Tissieres, A., and Georgopoulos, C. (1990). "Stress Proteins in Biology and Medicine." Cold Spring Harbor Laboratory Press, Cold Spring Harbor, NY.

Morimoto, R. I., Tissieres, A., and Georgopoulos, C. (1994). "The Biology of Heat Shock Proteins and Molecular Chaper-

ones." Cold Spring Harbor Laboratory Press, Cold Spring Harbor, NY.

Parsell, D. A., and Lindquist, S. (1993). The function of heat-shock proteins in stress tolerance: degradation and reactivation of damaged proteins. *Annu. Rev. Gen.* **27**, 437–456.

Tatar, M. (1999). Transgenes in the analysis of lifespan and fitness. *Am. Nat.* **154**, S67–S81.

Tower, J. (1996). Aging mechanisms in fruit flies. *Bioessays* **18**, 799–807.

Drug Use and Abuse

Alan I. Leshner

National Institute on Drug Abuse, National Institutes of Health

GLOSSARY

addiction A chronic, relapsing disease characterized by compulsive drug seeking and use and by neurochemical and molecular changes in the brain.

craving A powerful, often uncontrollable desire for drugs.

dopamine A neurotransmitter present in regions of the brain that regulate movement, emotion, motivation, and the feeling of pleasure.

receptors Locations at which neurotransmitters or drugs bind.

relapse A return to drug use despite an individual's attempt to remain abstinent.

withdrawal A variety of symptoms that occur after use of an addictive drug is reduced or stopped.

I. STRESS AND DRUG USE

Tremendous progress has been made in understanding drug abuse and addiction. We now know that addiction is a treatable brain disease and that the addicted brain is different from the nonaddicted brain. We also have gained greater insight into why people first begin to take drugs. Some people take drugs simply to have a novel or sensational experience. They are taking drugs for the experience of modifying their mood, their perceptions, or their emotional state. But there is also another group of people who take drugs for a different reason. Although they may take drugs to modify their mood or their emotional state, they seem to be using drugs to help them cope with their problems. These individuals are, in effect, self-medicating. They are trying to use drugs to help them cope in the same way that depressed people take antidepressants or anxious people take anxiolytic drugs. Of course, over time, drugs of abuse actually make the situation worse, not better.

Whatever their initial motivation, however, people take drugs because drugs make them feel good or better immediately, and this occurs because drugs essentially change the way the brain functions. We say that people take drugs because they like what they do to their brains. The problem is that, over time, prolonged drug use causes pervasive changes in brain function that last after the individual stops taking the drug, and these brain changes can have dramatic consequences for the individual and those with whom he or she interacts.

Recent data suggest that some of these neural changes may be contributing to what is one of the most puzzling aspects of addiction—relapse to drug use after periods of abstinence. Addiction is typically—though not always—a chronic illness characterized by occasional relapses, and it is that propensity to relapse that causes many of the problems that accompany addiction. Moreover, just as genetic factors have been found to play a role in individual vulnerability to drug use, addiction, and the likelihood of relapse once addicted, environmental factors also have been found to be important. These factors include the people, places, and paraphernalia associated with an addict's drug use. Simple exposure to these drug-related stimuli can cause tremendous feelings of craving and can precipitate relapses.

New findings from the laboratory are showing that stress is a major cause of relapse. It has long been known from anecdotal evidence that stress is associated with relapse to smoking and other drug use in humans. Historically, much attention has also focused on life stress as a cause of *initial* drug use, but we now are learning that it may be a factor in the relapse to drug use after long periods of abstinence. Moreover, we are beginning to understand some of the neurobiological underpinnings that are involved in relapse in humans.

II. ANIMAL MODELS OF ADDICTION AND RELAPSE: STRESS-INDUCED REINSTATEMENT

Many of the advances in our knowledge of the neurobiological basis of relapse have come from the use of animal research models systems, since it is so difficult, and often unethical, to do certain types of critical studies with human subjects. With the exception of LSD and some other hallucinogens, lab-

oratory animals will voluntarily take all of the drugs that are abused by humans. Animals take drugs in patterns similar to those used by humans, and they develop many of the characteristics of addiction, including what appears to be compulsive use. Also like humans, some animals are more vulnerable to the effects of drugs than others. For these reasons and because of the ethical and methodological difficulties in examining the role that stress plays in human drug-taking behavior, much of the work in the drug abuse and stress area has been done in animal models.

Thanks in large part to what behavioral scientists have come to understand about learning processes and motivation of human behavior, researchers have developed several animal models of drug abuse. The most commonly used model involves training an animal to voluntarily and repeatedly take, or self-administer, small amounts of drugs such as cocaine or heroin. This procedure is based on the operant learning principle that behavior is maintained by its consequences, or reinforcers. In this model, the laboratory animal performs some action, such as depressing a lever or poking his nose in a hole, to trigger the delivery of a drug either systemically or intravenously.

Forms of this self-administration model are used typically to study a number of aspects of drug abuse, including the initiation or acquisition of drug use behaviors, the maintenance or continuation of drug use, and relapse to drug use after abstinence. Importantly, exposure to stress has been found to increase the propensity of an individual to self-administer drugs of abuse under all three of these paradigms. This parallels what has been observed in the clinical environment where stress is thought to play a role in initial drug use, in the continuation of drug use, and in relapse. Animal models of relapse is our primary focus here.

The phenomenon of relapse or reinstatement to drug use is interesting and provocative because drug-seeking behavior does frequently reoccur even after relatively long periods of abstinence and for no clear, readily apparent reason. In the reinstatement model, animals are trained to self-administer drugs. Once this skill is well acquired, responding for the drug is extinguished by replacing the drug with a neutral or inactive solution. The animal's behavior is then studied after it has stopped performing the response associated with drug infusion. Once the animal's drug-taking behavior is extinguished, responding can be reinstated by a number of stimuli including sights or sounds recognizable from a previous drug-taking experience, a taste or priming dose of the drug itself, or exposure to stressors. Animal models are helping to examine the nature of these stimuli that reinstate responding for drug infusion.

To study cue- or environmental stimulus-induced relapse, the animal is presented with stimuli that had previously been associated with drug taking. This stimulus is presented after a prolonged period where the drug is no longer available to the animal. Such a stimulus might be a visual or auditory cue that the animal learned as a signal to predict drug availability. Drug priming or drug-induced relapse is studied by treating the animal with a small, priming dose of a drug, after which the animal quickly begins working again at the task to get more drugs. Stress-induced relapse or reinstatement is studied by presenting a brief laboratory stressor like mild intermittent foot shock that prompts the animal to take the drug again.

Interestingly, stress prompts a robust or powerful reinstatement of drug use, which may be more effective than any other stimuli. That is, stress may be the most powerful priming stimulus in these models, followed by exposure to small quantities of drugs, followed by environmental cues initially associated with drug use.

It is not known precisely how, or why stress reactivates drug seeking or causes relapse. Obvious explanations at the behavioral or psychological level suggest that, just as in cases of initial drug use, individuals may return to drug use during stress to reduce the impact of the stress, or to self-medicate.

However, recent attempts to understand the mechanisms that might mediate stress-induced relapse have suggested some interesting hypotheses. Specifically, some investigators have suggested that stress may reinstate drug seeking by activating brain systems common both to the biological adaptations to stress and to drug abuse. One proposed intermediary mechanism is the brain's regional release of the peptide corticotropin releasing factor (CRF).

III. THE ROLE OF CORTICOTROPIN RELEASING FACTOR (CRF) IN DRUG USE RELAPSE

As discussed elsewhere in this book, CRF initiates the biological stress response in both humans and animals. During all negative experiences studied to date, certain regions of the brain show increased levels of CRF. The increased CRF levels then trigger a biological cascade typical of all responses to stress. Corticotropin releasing factor stimulates the release of adrenocorticotropic hormone (ACTH) and endorphins from the pituitary into the general circulation. In turn, ACTH release causes the release of steroids, corticosterone, and/or cortisol from the adrenal cortex, which, in turn, feed back and help regulate CRF levels in the hypothalamus and other regions in the brain, including the amygdala and certain brainstem nuclei.

Corticotropin releasing factor interacts with at least two distinct receptor subtypes in the brain (CRF1 and CRF2), which are critical to CRF's actions. For example, genetically engineered "knockout" mice lacking the CRF1 receptor show impaired stress responses. These mice fail to show the expected increases in blood levels of ACTH and corticosterone after exposure to stressful stimuli. They also express less anxiety-related behavior under normal conditions and following withdrawal from ethanol. Although science is beginning to better understand these two receptors, the role for the CRF2 receptor in stress-mediated events has not been clearly delineated to date.

IV. DISRUPTION OF BEHAVIORAL INHIBITIONS

Stress also inhibits an inhibitory neural system located primarily in the medial prefrontal cortex. Activation of this system stops ongoing behavior in the presence of punishment or reward, a phenomenon long known to be related to those controlling drug use. Since numerous studies suggest that stressors have the capability to disinhibit a variety of behaviors that are usually under inhibitory control (i.e. aggression, sexual behavior), it is possible that stress induces relapse to drug seeking by disrupting behavioral inhibitions. Thus, brain systems and neurotransmitters involved in the inhibition of ongoing behavior may be involved in the reinstatement of drug seeking by stressors.

In short, stress appears to be a major trigger for relapse to drug seeking and use in both animals and humans. Also, importantly, there are brain mechanisms and systems that interact and are involved in both stress and drug use control systems.

V. HUMAN APPLICATION

What is the application to the human situation? Is the research in animals at all relevant to the human experience? As suggested earlier, human studies have also associated the body's stress systems with drug use and addiction. Many different studies of heroin addicts have shown that cortisol is suppressed during heroin addiction, elevated during withdrawal, and normalized during methadone maintenance. Moreover, the heroin addicts' responses to stress are atypical, and this has led Kreek and her colleagues to suggest that stress may both directly and indirectly contribute to the repeated incidences of relapse to heroin self-administration.

Importantly, other research suggests that altered responses to stress are elicited not only by opiates, but may also occur in users or former users of cocaine, alcohol, and possibly nicotine. Corticotropin releasing factor levels have been found to increase in limbic structures, such as the amygdala, during psychostimulant, opiate, ethanol, cannabinoids, and benzodiazepine withdrawal. Abstinence from virtually all addictive substances results in an elevation of CRF in the amygdala.

Elevated CRF levels are also found in other conditions that are particularly relevant to addiction, depression, and anxiety. The endocrine system responsive to stress is functionally dysregulated in individuals suffering from severe depression, meaning that CRF, typically responsible for regulating this system, is elevated in cerebrospinal fluid.

Given the high comorbidity between depression and drug addiction in humans and the recent evidence that CRF is elevated in both disorders, there is reason to think that the two may share certain neurobiological substrates. Of direct relevance, there is evidence that elevations in CRF levels may not only reflect depressed states, but may also contribute to the anxiety that sometimes accompanies depression. Recent studies have suggested that CRF can actually produce anxietylike responses in animals and that these effects are independent of CRF's effects on the rest of the pituitary–adrenal axis.

In states of addiction and particularly, in drug withdrawal, it may be that the elevated CRF levels during withdrawal that accompany abstinence from addicting drugs contribute to the anxiety and depression abstinent addicts experience rather than simply being a response to withdrawal. This increased negative affect then may be a trigger to relapse.

Another line of evidence that links depressive disorders with addiction, in addition to the increased CRF levels, is the fact that depressed opioid, cocaine, and alcohol users treated with antidepressants may reduce their drug use significantly more than nondepressed drug users. This finding suggests that antidepressants may alter the need for consumption of drugs of abuse in depressed individuals. This may be a factor in the success of the nicotine treatment Zyban, which is also marketed as Welbutrin, an antidepressant.

This leads to the development of the hypothesis that drug abuse causes people to take drugs to reverse some of the abnormalities associated with depression or to relieve the anxiety they have from drug withdrawal. The fact that CRF has been found to produce anxietylike behaviors in animals also supports the self-medication hypothesis and could represent a common mechanism linking abstinence or withdrawal from drug use, anxiety, and relapse. It also suggests that the antagonists of the CRF receptor may be a reasonable therapeutic target for antiaddiction medications.

VI. SUMMATION

Experimental studies in animals and anecdotal reports in humans suggest that stress can increase the likelihood that an addicted individual will relapse to drug use. One possible explanation for this effect is

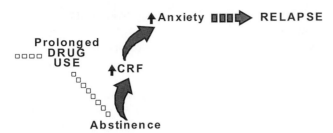

FIGURE 1 This diagram illustrates what many scientists believe happens when a recovering drug addict is exposed to stress after prolonged abstinence from drugs. Withdrawal from drugs is thought to elevate CRF levels, thus increasing anxiety in the individual. The addict may relapse to drug use to escape from the stressful situation and/or to alleviate the anxiety they have from not taking drugs.

that stress may actually modify the motivational and/ or reinforcing properties of abused drugs. One of the effects of stress is to modulate some of the neurobiological systems involved in motivation and rewards. By changing the activity of these systems, stressors could indirectly enhance an individual's responsiveness to drugs of abuse.

A second possibility is that stress increases the probability of relapse through increasing CRF levels and concomitant anxiety. The addict, then, would return to drug use not only to counteract the experiential effects of the stressor directly, but also to medicate or reduce the anxiety component of the stress experience. This kind of hypothesis is still suggested by converging evidence from research on the role of stress and stress mechanisms in drug seeking in animals using the reinstatement paradigm and from studies of stress responses and responsiveness of human subjects addicted to heroin, cocaine, alcohol, nicotine, cannabinoids, and so on (Fig. 1).

VII. FUTURE RESEARCH DIRECTIONS

The exact role that stress and its neurobiological mechanisms play in initial drug use and the transition to abuse and addiction as well as their role in relapse are not completely elucidated, though tremendous progress has already been made.

A culmination of research, particularly in animal reinstatement models, points to the fact that stressful experiences increase the vulnerability of an individual to relapse after extinction or abstinence. The availability of new animal models of stimulus-induced relapse, coupled with recent advances in understanding the neurobiology of emotional memory at the circuit, cellular, and molecular levels provide unprecedented opportunities to better understand the phenomenon of drug relapse. In particular, some of the future research directions that need to be pursued in this important area are listed below.

• The increased understanding of the biological mechanisms of stress could be helpful as we work to develop new therapeutic strategies to treat drug abuse and dependence. Corticotropin releasing factor systems could constitute the substrate for the development of new therapies for addiction.
• It may be possible one day to identify individuals who are particularly vulnerable to addiction and stress and thereby target them with specific psychosocial interventions.
• Training clinical staff to more accurately recognize their patients' stressors that lead to drug use, to identify individuals at risk for relapse.
• Stress reduction through stress management techniques as another possible treatment for relapse.
• New, nonpeptide CRF antagonists need to be developed and tested as potential therapies for drug addiction.

See Also the Following Articles

Alcohol, Alcoholism, and Stress; Corticotropin Releasing Factor; Interactions between Stress and Drugs of Abuse and Stress; Opioids

Bibliography

Breiter, H. *et al.* (1997). Acute effects of cocaine on human brain activity and emotion. *Neuron,* **19,** 591–611.

Hamamura, T., and Fibiger, H. (1993). Enhanced stress-induced dopamine release in the prefrontal cortex of amphetamine-sensitized rats. *Eur. J. Pharmacol.* **237,** 65–71.

Kreek, M. J., and Koob, G. (1998). Drug dependence: Stress and dysregulation of brain reward pathways. *Drug Alcohol Depend.* **51**, 23–47.

Lovallo, W. (1997). "Stress and Human Health." Sage, Thousands Oaks, CA.

Markou, A., Kosten, T., and Koob, G. (1998). *Neuropsychopharmacology* **18**(3), 135–174. Neurobiological similarities in depression and drug dependence: A self-medication hypothesis.

Piazzo, P., and Le Moal, M. (1998). Stress and drug self-administration. *Trends Pharmacol. Sci.*

Shaham, Y., Funk, D. *et al.* (1997). Corticotropin-releasing factor, but not corticosterone, is involved in stress-induced relapse to heroin-seeking in rats. *J. Neurosci.* **17**(7), 2605–2614.

Shaham, Y. (1996). Effect of stress on opioid-seeking behavior: Evidence from studies with rats. *Ann. Behav. Med.* **18**(4), 255–263.

Smith, G., Aubry, J. *et al.* (1998). Corticotropin releasing factor receptor 1-deficient mice display decreased anxiety, impairted stress response, and aberrant neuroscience development. *Neuron* **20**, 1093–1102.

Timp, P., Spanagel, R. *et al.* (1998). Impaired stress response and reduced anxiety in mice lacking a functional corticotropin-releasing hormone receptor 1. *Nat. Genet.* **19**(2) 162–166.

ISBN 0-12-226736-2

90038